T0135396

Lecture Notes in Computer Science　　13043

More information about this subseries at http://www.springer.com/series/7410

Kobbi Nissim · Brent Waters (Eds.)

Theory of Cryptography

19th International Conference, TCC 2021
Raleigh, NC, USA, November 8–11, 2021
Proceedings, Part II

 Springer

Editors
Kobbi Nissim
Georgetown University
Washington, WA, USA

Brent Waters
The University of Texas at Austin
Austin, TX, USA

NTT Research
Sunnyvale, CA, USA

ISSN 0302-9743   ISSN 1611-3349   (electronic)
Lecture Notes in Computer Science
ISBN 978-3-030-90452-4   ISBN 978-3-030-90453-1   (eBook)
https://doi.org/10.1007/978-3-030-90453-1

LNCS Sublibrary: SL4 – Security and Cryptology

This Springer imprint is published by the registered company Springer Nature Switzerland AG
The registered company address is: Gewerbestrasse 11, 6330 Cham, Switzerland

Preface

The 19th Theory of Cryptography Conference (TCC 2021) was held during November 8–11, 2021 at North Carolina State University in Raleigh, USA. It was sponsored by the International Association for Cryptologic Research (IACR). The general chair of the conference was Alessandra Scafuro.

The conference received 161 submissions, of which the Program Committee (PC) selected 66 for presentation giving an acceptance rate of 41%. Each submission was reviewed by at least four PC members. The 43 PC members (including PC chairs), all top researchers in our field, were helped by 197 external reviewers, who were consulted when appropriate. These proceedings consist of the revised version of the 66 accepted papers. The revisions were not reviewed, and the authors bear full responsibility for the content of their papers.

As in previous years, we used Shai Halevi's excellent Web Submission and Review software, and are extremely grateful to him for writing it, and for providing fast and reliable technical support whenever we had any questions.

This was the seventh year that TCC presented the Test of Time Award to an outstanding paper that was published at TCC at least eight years ago, making a significant contribution to the theory of cryptography, preferably with influence also in other areas of cryptography, theory, and beyond. This year the Test of Time Award Committee selected the following paper, published at TCC 2005: "Keyword Search and Oblivious Pseudorandom Functions" by Michael Freedman, Yuval Ishai, Benny Pinkas, and Omer Reingold. The award committee recognized this paper for "introducing and formalizing the notion of Oblivious Pseudorandom Functions, and identifying connections to other primitives such as keyword search, inspiring a vast amount of theoretical and practical work".

We are greatly indebted to many people who were involved in making TCC 2021 a success. A big thanks to the authors who submitted their papers and to the PC members and external reviewers for their hard work, dedication, and diligence in reviewing the papers, verifying the correctness, and in-depth discussions. A special thanks goes to the general chair Alessandra Scafuro, Kevin McCurley, Kay McKelly, and the TCC Steering Committee.

October 2021

Kobbi Nissim
Brent Waters

Organization

General Chair

Alessandra Scafuro   North Carolina State University, USA

Program Chairs

Kobbi Nissim   Georgetown University, USA
Brent Waters   NTT Research and University of Texas at Austin, USA

Program Committee

Masayuki Abe	NTT, Japan
Ittai Abraham	VMware, Israel
Benny Applebaum	Tel Aviv University, Israel
Gilad Asharov	Bar-Ilan University, Israel
Amos Beimel	Ben-Gurion University, Israel
Andrej Bogdanov	Chinese University of Hong Kong, Hong Kong
Elette Boyle	IDC Herzliya, Israel
Chris Brzuska	Aalto University, Finland
Mark Bun	Boston University, USA
Yilei Chen	Tsinghua University, China
Itai Dinur	Ben-Gurion University, Israel
Pooya Farshim	University of York, UK
Sanjam Garg	NTT Research and UC Berkeley, USA
Rishab Goyal	MIT, USA
Siyao Guo	NYU Shanghai, China
Iftach Haitner	Tel Aviv University, Israel
Mohammad Hajiabadi	University of Waterloo, Canada
Carmit Hazay	Bar-Ilan University, Israel
Yuval Ishai	Technion, Israel
Abhishek Jain	Johns Hopkins University, USA
Stacey Jeffery	CWI, The Netherlands
Lisa Kohl	CWI, The Netherlands
Ilan Komargodski	NTT Research and Hebrew University, Israel
Benoit Libert	CNRS and ENS de Lyon, France
Huijia Lin	University of Washington, USA
Alex Lombardi	MIT, USA
Vadim Lyubashevsky	IBM Research - Zurich, Switzerland
Jesper Buus Nielsen	Aarhus University, Denmark
Ryo Nishimaki	NTT, USA
Omkant Pandey	Stony Brook University, USA

Omer Paneth	Tel Aviv University, Israel	
Manoj Prabhakaran	ITT Bombay, India	
Leo Reyzin	Boston University, USA	
Alon Rosen	Bocconi University, Italy, and IDC Herzliya, Israel	
Guy Rothblum	Weizmann Institute of Science, Israel	
Christian Schaffner	QuSoft and University of Amsterdam, The Netherlands	
Peter Scholl	Aarhus University, Denmark	
Gil Segev	Hebrew University, Israel	
Justin Thaler	Georgetown University, USA	
Muthu Venkitasubramaniam	Georgetown University, USA	
Mark Zhandry	NTT Research and Princeton University, USA	

External Reviewers

Christian Badertscher	Leo De Castro	Jiaxin Guan
Mingyuan Wang	Suvradip Chakraborty	Divya Gupta
Damiano Abram	Sun Chao	Shai Halevi
Anasuya Acharya	Nai-Hui Chia	Mathias Hall-Andersen
Shweta Agrawal	Arka Rai Choudhuri	Hamidreza Khoshakhlagh
Adi Akavia	Ashish Choudhury	Patrick Harasser
Gorjan Alagic	Hao Chung	Dominik Hartmann
Bar Alon	Kai-Min Chung	Brett Hemenway
Pedro Alves	Michele Ciampi	Justin Holmgren
Miguel Ambrona	Geoffroy Couteau	Thibaut Horel
Prabhanjan Ananth	Jan Czajkowski	Pavel Hubacek
Ananya Appan	Amit Deo	Aayush Jain
Anirudh C.	Jelle Don	Dingding Jia
Gal Arnon	Xiaoqi Duan	Zhengzhong Jin
Thomas Attema	Leo Ducas	Eliran Kachlon
Benedikt Bünz	Yfke Dulek	Gabriel Kaptchuk
Laasya Bangalore	Christoph Egger	Pihla Karanko
James Bartusek	Jaiden Keith Fairoze	Akinori Kawachi
Balthazar Bauer	Islam Faisal	Jiseung Kim
Sina Shiehian	Luca de Feo	Fuyuki Kitagawa
Ward Beullens	Cody Freitag	Susumu Kiyoshima
Rishabh Bhadauria	Georg Fuchsbauer	Anders Konrig
Kaartik Bhushan	Chaya Ganesh	Venkata Koppula
Nir Bitansky	Juan Garay	Ben Kuykendall
Olivier Blazy	Rachit Garg	Changmin Lee
Alex Block	Romain Gay	Baiyu Li
Estuardo Alpirez Bock	Nicholas Genise	Xiao Liang
Jonathan Bootle	Ashrujit Ghoshal	Wei-Kai Lin
Lennart Braun	Niv Gilboa	Jiahui Liu
Konstantinos Brazitikos	Aarushi Goel	Qipeng Liu
Ignacio Cascudo	Junqing Gong	Tianren Liu

Sébastien Lord
Julian Loss
George Lu
Ji Luo
Fermi Ma
Bernardo Magri
Mohammad Mahmoody
Sven Maier
Monosij Maitra
Christian Majenz
Nikolaos Makriyannis
Giulio Malavolta
Noam Mazor
Audra McMillan
Jeremias Mechler
Pierre Meyer
Peihan Miao
Brice Minaud
Pratyush Mishra
Tarik Moataz
Tamer Mour
Varun Narayanan
Ngoc Khanh Nguyen
Oded Nir
Ariel Nof
Adam O'Neill
Sabine Oechsner
Eran Omri
Jiaxing Pan
Anat Paskin-Cherniavsky
Alain Passelègue
Naty Peter
Thomas Peters
Rolando La Placa
Bertram Poettering
Antigoni Polychroniadou

Alexander Poremba
Kirthivaasan Puniamurthy
Willy Quach
Yuan Quan
Rajeev Raghunath
Divya Ravi
João Ribeiro
Peter Rindal
Felix Rohrbach
Lior Rotem
Ron Rothblum
Mike Rosulek
Rahul B. S.
Benjamin Schlosser
André Schrottenloher
Gili Schul-Ganz
Nikolaj Schwartzbach
Sruthi Sekar
Srinath Setty
Sina Shiehian
Manasi Shingane
Omri Shmueli
Jad Silbak
Mark Simkin
Jaspal Singh
Luisa Siniscalchi
Adam Smith
Pratik Soni
Jana Sotáková
Akshayaram Srinivasan
Noah
    Stephens-Davidowitz
Gilad Stern
Patrick Struck
Hyung Tae
Mehrdad Tahmasbi

Atsushi Takayasu
Aishwarya
    Thiruvengadam
Søren Eller Thomsen
Pratyush Ranjan Tiwari
Alin Tomescu
Junichi Tomida
Ni Trieu
Eliad Tsfadia
Rohit Chatterjee
Xiao Liang
Neekon Vafa
Mayank Varia
Prashant Vasudevan
Satyanarayana Vusirikala
Alexandre Wallet
Mingyuan Wang
Mor Weiss
Douglas Wickstorm
David Wu
Keita Xagawa
Zhuolun Xiang
Shota Yamada
Takashi Yamakawa
Avishay Yanai
Kevin Yeo
Wang Yuyu
Shang Zehua
Chen-Da Liu Zhang
Cong Zhang
Jiapeng Zhang
Yiding Zhang
Yinuo Zhang
Yupeng Zhang
Giorgos Zirdelis
Sebastian Zur

Contents – Part II

Dory: Efficient, Transparent Arguments for Generalised Inner Products and Polynomial Commitments

Jonathan Lee[✉]

Microsoft Research, Nanotronics Imaging, Cuyahoga Falls, USA
jlee@nanotronics.co

Abstract. This paper presents Dory, a transparent setup, public-coin interactive argument for inner-pairing products between committed vectors of elements of two source groups. For a product of vectors of length n, proofs are $6 \log n$ target group elements and $O(1)$ additional elements. Verifier work is dominated by an $O(\log n)$ multi-exponentiation in the target group and $O(1)$ pairings. Security is reduced to the standard SXDH assumption in the standard model.

We apply Dory to build a multivariate polynomial commitment scheme via the Fiat-Shamir transform. For a dense polynomial with n coefficients, Prover work to compute a commitment is dominated by a multi-exponentiation in one source group of size n. Prover work to show that a commitment to an evaluation is correct is $O(n^{\log 8/ \log 25})$ in general ($O(n^{1/2})$ for univariate or multilinear polynomials); communication complexity and Verifier work are both $O(\log n)$. These asymptotics previously required trusted setup or concretely inefficient groups of unknown order. Critically for applications, these arguments can be batched, saving large factors on the Prover and improving Verifier asymptotics: to validate ℓ polynomial evaluations for polynomials of size at most n requires $O(\ell + \log n)$ exponentiations and $O(\ell \log n)$ field operations.

Dory is also concretely efficient: Using one core and setting $n = 2^{20}$, commitments are 192 bytes. Evaluation proofs are $\sim$18 kB, requiring $\sim$3 s to generate and $\sim$25 ms to verify. For batches at $n = 2^{20}$, the marginal cost per evaluation is <1 kB communication, $\sim$300 ms for the Prover and $\sim$1 ms for the Verifier.

1 Introduction

Zero-knowledge succinct arguments of knowledge (zkSNARKs) for the satisfiability of Rank-1 Constraint Systems (R1CS) are the subject of ongoing research. A general strategy to construct zkSNARKS for R1CS is to partition the proof into two phases. First, an information-theoretic argument reduces proving the existence of a satisfying assignment to a consistency check on commitments to evaluations of (possibly multi-variate) polynomials. Some computationally

---

Current Affiliation: Nanotronics Imaging; work done primarily at Microsoft Research.

© International Association for Cryptologic Research 2021
K. Nissim and B. Waters (Eds.): TCC 2021, LNCS 13043, pp. 1–34, 2021.
https://doi.org/10.1007/978-3-030-90453-1_1

sound argument with sub-linear verification time is used to show these commitments to evaluations are correct. These auxiliary arguments are variously inner-product arguments, or the more restricted *polynomial commitments*, introduced by Kate [27] and generalised to multivariate polynomials in [30].

Spartan [31] makes the independence of the information-theoretic argument and these auxiliary arguments explicit, provides an extensive overview of the history and details of prior works, and details key practical considerations relating to the uniformity of the computation to verify. There are multiple approaches in the literature to constructing these auxiliary arguments, and for each many concrete constructions. Non-exhaustively, Bulletproofs [15] use inner-product arguments and Hyrax [34] utilise polynomial commitments, both based on the logarithmic communication complexity discrete log-based work (LCC-DLOG) of Bootle et al. [13], which in turn uses ideas from [22]. Spartan [31] optimises this approach further, and Halo [14] applies these on cycles of pairing friendly curves to achieve recursive composition.

Ligero [3], Aurora [8], Virgo [35] and Fractal [18] use Interactive Oracle Proofs based on Reed-Solomon codes (RS-IOP) to prove that a polynomial is of bounded degree [6]. Supersonic and its follow on works [11,16] makes use of groups of unknown order to construct Diophantine ARguments of Knowledge (DARK-GUO) proofs for polynomial evaluations over fields. Other works rely on some trusted setup, which allows the use of other commitment schemes. For example PLONK [20] makes use of KZG [27] commitments directly, whilst [17] uses sublinear-sized KZG commitments as a component in their GIPP argument and polynomial commitment. In all cases these interactive arguments are then compiled to non-interactive arguments in the random-oracle model.

This paper introduces a new transparent setup argument for generalised inner products, inspired by Bootle et al. [13] but applying new techniques to achieve a logarithmic $\mathcal{V}$ complexity. This argument can be applied to give polynomial commitments for arbitrary numbers of variables, using two-tiered homomorphic commitments of Groth [23] applied to matrix commitment strategy of [34], as in Bünz et al. [17] for univariate and bivariate polynomials.

For transparent polynomial commitment schemes, there are four key operations: (1) $\mathcal{P}$ and $\mathcal{V}$ must generate public parameters; (2) $\mathcal{P}$ must commit to a polynomial and transmit that commitment to $\mathcal{V}$; (3, 4) $\mathcal{P}$ and $\mathcal{V}$ must compute, transmit and verify a proof of evaluation of the polynomial. We give the best achieved asymptotics of previous transparent polynomial commitment schemes, grouped by overall approach, in Fig. 1.

Unfortunately, implementations generally bundle their polynomial commitment with differing polynomial IOPs for some language, so concrete comparisons of the *polynomial commitments* in isolation are challenging. To allow for a somewhat concrete discussion, we first note typical object sizes and operation times for fast implementations of the required primitives at the 128-bit security level in Fig. 2. We note that blstrs is enhanced to apply torus-based pairing compression [29] of $\mathbb{G}_T$ for serialisation.

	Transparent Setup?	Communication Complexity		Time Complexity			
		Commit	Eval	Gen	Commit	Eval ($\mathcal{P}$)	Eval ($\mathcal{V}$)
LCC-DLOG	✓	$n^{1/2}$ |G|	$\log n$ |G|	$n^{1/2}$H	n G	$n^{1/2}$ G	$n^{1/2}$ G
RS-IOP	✓	1 |H|	$\log^2 n$ |H|	1	$n \log n$ H	$n \log n$ H	$\log^2 n$ H
DARK-GUO	✓	1 |G_U|	$\log n$ |G_U|	$n \log n$ G_U	n G_U	$n \log n$ G_U	$\log n$ G_U
KZG [27,30]	✗	1 |G_T|	$\log n$ |G_T|	n G_1	n G_1	n G_1	r P
GIPP [17]	✗	1 |G_T|	$\log n$ |G_T|	$n^{1/2}$ G_1	n G_1	$n^{1/2}$ P	$\log n$ G_T
This work	✓	1 |G_T|	$\log n$ |G_T|	$n^{1/2}P$	n G_1	$n^{1/2}P$	$\log n$ G_T

Fig. 1. Asymptotic comparisons for dense polynomials of degree n, neglecting Pippenger-type savings. We report the most expensive dominant operations for the most efficient instantiations of each class. H denotes a hash function. G denotes a group. G_1, G_2, G_T denote the two source groups and the target group of a pairing P. G_U is a group of unknown order. These schemes all generalise to multivariate polynomials of degree $(d_1, \ldots, d_r)$, setting $n = \prod_i (d_i + 1)$

Setting	Implementation		Size (bytes)	Time (μs)
Group of Unknown Order	ANTIC-QFB	|G_U|	832	27000
Hashing	rust-crypto	|H|	32	0.072
Group	curve25519-dalek	|G|	32	42
Group with Pairing	blstrs	|G_1|	48	110
		|G_2|	96	270
		|G_T|	192	470
		P	–	600

Fig. 2. Micro-benchmarks on a single core (AMD Ryzen 5 3600). For groups we give the serialised size in bytes of a group element, and the time taken to multiply a random point by a 256-bit scalar. P denotes a pairing computation, and \|H\| denotes hashing of a 512-bit message to a 256-bit digest.

1.1 Limitations of Prior Approaches

Unfortunately, each prior approach to transparent polynomial commitments have substantial problems in practice. Concretely, only LCC-DLOG based-schemes provide a linear-time Prover, which is key for large applications where $n \sim 2^{20\text{-}30}$. Unfortunately, these schemes require $\Omega(n^{1/2})$ computation by $\mathcal{V}$ to Eval a committed polynomial, and have similarly sized commitments. This is because they commit to a matrix with $O(n)$ entries by committing to the rows and later opening a commitment to some linear combination of the rows. Hyrax [34] and its successors saturate this bound with small concrete constants. However for large n these commitments remain quite large ($\gg$10 kB), and can be challenging in applications applications where the polynomial commitment is used as a routine and so many commitments must be sent.

RS-IOP-based schemes are built on Reed-Solomon based IOPPs, and would have attractive concrete costs, even with their asymptotic slowness, if the concrete constants were commensurate with the cost of hashing. Unfortunately the sound-ness error of the underlying IOPP is quite large and the *proven* bounds are worse still, requiring a number of repetitions linear in the security level. For example, libiop [7] runs the underlying proof in Fractal [18] ∼500 times to achieve provable 128-bit security. This large additional multiplicative constant largely closes the micro-benchmark gap with curve arithmetic, especially as multi-exponentiations in groups permit log savings using Pippenger's algorithm.

DARK-GUO-based schemes [11, 16] are built around groups of unknown order, which can be constructed transparently as class groups of quadratic number fields, or analogously as Jacobians of higher genus curves [19]. They have a long history of crpytographic use [12, 26, 28]. Unfortunately, general sub-exponential attacks on the order are known [10]; fast attacks on a low-density sets of weak groups are problematic for applications with transparent setup [19], which forces the group operation to be materially slower than operations on curves, as is seen in Fig. 2. In the particular case of Supersonic [11, 16], even with Pippenger-type accelera-tion $\mathcal{P}$ must perform $O(n\lambda)$ group operations, and generating parameters takes $O(n\lambda \log n)$ group operations, which is unlikely to be efficient in practice.

Finally, if transparent setup is given up then Kate commitments [27] and their multivariate generalisation [30] are available, generally requiring $O(n)$ operations in $\mathbb{G}_1$ for $\mathcal{P}$, $O(1)$ commitment sizes and a $\mathcal{V}$ time linear in the number of variables. This is combined with ideas from LCC-DLOG in [17] to achieve sublinear Prover computation for evaluation. Whilst performant, these systems have unprovable knowledge-of-exponent type assumptions for their security, which is undesirable.

1.2   Review of LCC-DLOG Techniques

Dory builds on the LCC-DLOG tradition, which construct inner-product argu-ments [13, 15, 17] or reductions of Hadamard products to inner products [22] with efficient Provers and sublinear communication from homomorphic commitments.

Explicitly for the inner product as a bilinear form, these provide arguments for inner products between vectors of scalars and group elements or generalised prod-ucts between the source groups of a pairing, where either input may be committed. Let these vectors have length n', WLOG a power of two (in most cases for polyno-mial commitments $n' = O(n^{1/2})$). The key idea, which is inherited in Dory, is to observe that for any vectors $\vec{u_L}, \vec{u_R}, \vec{v_L}, \vec{v_R}$, and any non-zero scalar a:

$$\langle \vec{u_L} || \vec{u_R}, \vec{v_L} || \vec{v_R} \rangle = \langle a\vec{u_L} + \vec{u_R}, a^{-1}\vec{v_L} + \vec{v_R} \rangle - a\langle \vec{u_L}, \vec{v_R} \rangle - a^{-1}\langle \vec{u_R}, \vec{v_L} \rangle.$$

So a claim about the inner product $\langle \vec{u}, \vec{v} \rangle$ of length n' can be reduced to some claims about the inner products of vectors of length $n'/2$. The Verifier uses the homomor-phic properties of the commitment scheme (WLOG of $\vec{u}$) and some Prover assis-tance to find commitments to these shorter vectors $\vec{u'} = a\vec{u_L} + \vec{u_R}$, $a^{-1}\vec{v_L} + \vec{v_R}$, and to a claim for a commitment to the product $\langle \vec{u'}, \vec{v'} \rangle$, for some Verifier challenge a. This procedure is applied recursively to obtain a claim about vectors of length 1, for which some sigma protocol are used. Computational soundness comes from rewinding the Prover, since $\vec{u}$ can be recovered from a few samples of $\vec{u'}$ considered as a function of a.

The key problem is that when the commitment key used for $\vec{u}$ is unstructured, the commitment to $\vec{u'}$ is made with some *challenge-dependent* commitment key. This point is typically implicit, since the entire iterated reduction and final proof is presented as a single protocol. In this case, what one sees is that the Verifier has some final $O(n')$ computation that must be performed, using the challenges to convert the initial commitment key to a single curve point.

In [22], similar techniques are applied to a sequence of vectors with common commitment keys, which allows the Verifier computation to be avoided, at the cost of being only able to combine inner-products rather than compute them. In [13,15], inner-product arguments are given, but with linear Verifier computation. These are generalised to pairing groups in [17], where the key point (following [14]) is that this Verifier computation can be expressed as the evaluation of a polynomial whose coefficients are entries in the original commitment key. In this case they structure the commitment key to allow this to be done by opening a Kate commitment. To construct polynomial commitments, these works use the matrix commitment idea of [22] in an essentially similar fashion as [17,34]. In its simplest form, this represents a polynomial $f(x)$ of degree $n = n'^2$ by a matrix M s.t.:

$$f(x) = (1, x, x^2, \ldots, x^{n'-1}) M (1, x^{n'}, x^{2n'}, \ldots, x^{n-n'})^T,$$

which is possible as each entry of M is multiplied by a distinct power x^i for $i \in \{0, \ldots, n-1\}$. In [34], the Verifier keeps a homomorphic commitment to each row of M, combines them by hand, and then engages in a $\sqrt{n}$-sized inner product argument. In this case the $\sqrt{n}$ lower bound is sharp, as either the initial linear combination or the inner-product argument must be this large. In [17], this outer combination is done with a multivariate Kate opening, using the structure-preserving commitment scheme of Abe et al. [2].

1.3   Core Techniques Enabling a Logarithmic Verifier in Dory

Symmetry of Messages and Commitment Keys: The structure-preserving commitment scheme of [2] has a symmetry between the messages and the commitment key; for some pairing group $(\mathbb{G}_1, \mathbb{G}_2, \mathbb{G}_T)$ if the message is a vector in $\mathbb{G}_1$ then the commitment key is a vector in $\mathbb{G}_2$ (and vice versa), with the commitment itself in $\mathbb{G}_T$. So the Verifier is free to treat parts of a commitment key as messages, and compute a commitment to them with a second commitment key. Additionally, the commitment key and all Verifier challenges are public, so we can hope to outsource computations on the commitment key to the Prover. This is not possible in the no-pairing setting of [13,15,34], and is not exploited in [17].

Structured Verifier Computation: The computations that the Verifier has to perform on the commitment key are highly structured; as observed in [14,17] that this inner product can be thought of as a multivariate polynomial evaluation. Equivalently, it is an inner product with a vector of scalars, which is a Kronecker products of $\log n'$ vectors of length 2 (each built from one of the Verifier's challenges); this kind of vector occurs throughout Dory, and we say that a vector with such a cauterisation has *multiplicative structure*. Given the first challenge a, the Verifier must turn the commitment key $\vec{\Gamma} = (\vec{\Gamma_L}\|\vec{\Gamma_R})$ into $\Gamma' = (f(a)\vec{\Gamma_L} + g(a)\vec{\Gamma_R})$, where f, g are cheap to compute; after this a can be discarded. Plainly if the verified holds structure-preserving commitments to $\vec{\Gamma_L}, \vec{\Gamma_R}$ they can quickly compute a commitment to Γ'. Once the remaining challenges are known, the Verifier's remaining computation with Γ' is a length $n'/2$ inner product. So we can hope to outsource this to the Prover. The key point is that given structure-preserving commitments to the commitment key, the Verifier can apply one (or a few) challenges to shrink the commitment key and have the Prover do the linear work of computing the actual inner product.

Naively, this let us to use a $\log n'$-round protocol along the lines of [13,15,17] as a black box to reduce computing a length n' inner product of committed vectors to computing a length $n'/2$ inner product on committed vectors derived from the commitment keys of the commitments used in the length n' inner product. If we recursively use this idea, we obtain an $O(\log^2 n')$-round protocol for length n' inner products.

Alternately, we can start to run these inner product arguments in parallel, so that the inner product arguments in parallel, so that after k rounds we would have $k + 1$ claims about inner products of $n'2^{-k}$-length vectors. This allows us to combine claims about vectors in the same group along the lines of the 'collapsing' observed in [14]. This makes each round somewhat more complex, but the number of claims remains $O(1)$, and so a logarithmic Verifier is feasible.

Structured Public Scalars: Finally, Dory must handle public vectors of scalars, or for a polynomial commitment the point of evaluation. For general inner products this seems hopeless, as even reading a full vector would be a linear lower bound. However, for polynomial commitments the polynomial size vector of scalars has multiplicative structure, as it is the evaluation of monomials for fixed values of variables. Conveniently, inner products of vectors of this form can be computed in only logarithmically many operations. For a small concrete example, $(1, x, y, xy, z, xz, yz, xyz) \cdot (1, a, b, ab, c, ac, bc, abc) = (1+ax)(1+by)(1+cz)$. So any final inner product of public vectors with a challenge-derived vector can, in the context of polynomial commitments, be computed in logarithmic time.

Public Parameters: We note that for Dory, the public parameters contain commitment keys for of every power-of-2 length less than n' in both $\mathbb{G}_1$ and $\mathbb{G}_2$, and commitments to the left and right halves of each commitment key (using the a commitment key of half the length). This use of public parameters with structure but without trusted setup can be seen as analogous to the *computational commitments* used in Spartan [31], as we perform some linear-size computation *once* during setup to accelerate the online proof generation and verification.

Batching: Throughout, ideas similar of those of Bowe et al. [14] allow these arguments to be batched for reduced verification time further (see Sect. 3.4, Sect. 4.4, Sect. 5.1, Sect. 6.2). Ultimately the cost of evaluating each additional polynomial commitment is reduced to $O(1)$ group operations and $O(\log n)$ additional operations in $\mathbb{F}$.

Application to Polynomial Commitments: In Sect. 6, similarly to Hyrax [34, Sect. 6] and Bünz et al. [17], we construct a polynomial commitment from a two-tiered homomorphic commitment to matrices. Prior approaches here break knowledge soundness (c.f. Definition 10). Ultimately, evaluation of a dense univariate or multilinear polynomial with n coefficients is reduced to to two inner products of size $O(n^{1/2})$ (see Sect. 5), between public vectors of scalars with multiplicative structure and vectors in $\mathbb{G}_1, \mathbb{G}_2$ respectively (see Sect. 4). Unlike prior works, these two inner products are proved together, saving a further $2\times$.

2 Preliminaries

2.1 Notation

Vector, matrix and tensor indices will begin at 1. For any two vectors v_1, v_2 we denote their concatenation by $(v_1\|v_2)$. We use $\otimes$ to denote the Kronecker product, sending an $m \times n$ matrix A and $p \times q$ matrix B to an $mp \times nq$ matrix built up of appended copies of B multiplied by scalars in A. For any vector v of even length we will denote the left and right halves of v by v_L and v_R; more formally: $v_L = ((1,0) \otimes I_{n/2})v$ and $v_R = ((0,1) \otimes I_{n/2})v$.

We write $\leftarrow_\$ S$ for a uniformly random sample of S, with the understanding that this encodes no additional structure; for example for groups $\mathbb{G}$ we assume that samples $g_i \leftarrow_\$ \mathbb{G}$ have unrelated logarithms, and $\mathcal{V}$ challenges are independent of the transcript. Techniques to sample from curves are known [9,25,32,33].

We write all groups *additively*, and assume we are given some method to sample Type III pairings [21] at a given security level. Then we are furnished with a prime field $\mathbb{F} = \mathbb{F}_p$, three groups $\mathbb{G}_1, \mathbb{G}_2, \mathbb{G}_T$ of order p, a bilinear map $e : \mathbb{G}_1 \times \mathbb{G}_2 \to \mathbb{G}_T$, and generators $G_1 \in \mathbb{G}_1$, $G_2 \in \mathbb{G}_2$ such that $e(G_1, G_2)$ generates $\mathbb{G}_T$. Concretely, classes of *pairing-friendly* curves (e.g. Barreto-Lynn-Scott [4] or Barreto-Naehrig [5] curves) are believed to satisfy these properties.

We generally suppress the distinction between e and multiplication of $\mathbb{F}, \mathbb{G}_1, \mathbb{G}_2$ or $\mathbb{G}_T$ by elements of $\mathbb{F}$, writing all of these bilinear maps as multiplication; we will also use $\langle, \rangle$ to denote the generalised inner products given by $\langle \vec{a}, \vec{b} \rangle = \sum_{i=1}^{n} \vec{a}_i \vec{b}_i$, with signatures: $\mathbb{F}^n \times \mathbb{F}^n \to \mathbb{F}$, $\mathbb{F}^n \times \mathbb{G}_{\{1,2,T\}}^n \to \mathbb{G}_{\{1,2,T\}}$ or $\mathbb{G}_1^n \times \mathbb{G}_2^n \to \mathbb{G}_T$.

2.2 Computationally Hard Problems in Type III Pairings

For Type III pairings there are no efficiently computable morphisms between $\mathbb{G}_1, \mathbb{G}_2$, so the standard security assumption is Symmetric eXternal Diffie-Hellman:

Definition 1 (SXDH [2]). *For* $(\mathbb{F}_p, \mathbb{G}_1, \mathbb{G}_2, \mathbb{G}_T, e, G_1, G_2)$ *as above, the Decisional Diffie-Hellman (DDH) assumption holds for* $(\mathbb{F}_p, \mathbb{G}_1, G_1)$ *and* $(\mathbb{F}_p, \mathbb{G}_2, G_2)$

A DDH instance in $\mathbb{G}_1$ can be mapped to one in $\mathbb{G}_T$ by $g \to e(g, G_2)$, so SXDH implies that DDH holds in $\mathbb{G}_T$. In any group, DDH implies DLOG, and so:

Lemma 1. *For* $(\mathbb{F}_p, \mathbb{G}_1, \mathbb{G}_2, \mathbb{G}_T, e, G_1, G_2)$ *satisfying SXDH,* $n = \texttt{poly}(\lambda)$ *and* $\mathbb{G} \in \{\mathbb{G}_1, \mathbb{G}_2, \mathbb{G}_T\}$, *given* $\vec{B} \xleftarrow{\$} \mathbb{G}^n$ *no non-uniform polynomial-time adversary can compute a non-trivial* $\vec{A} \in \mathbb{F}^n$ *such that* $\langle \vec{A}, \vec{B} \rangle = 0$.

SXDH also implies the Double Pairing and reverse Double Pairing assumptions:

Lemma 2. *For* $(\mathbb{F}_p, \mathbb{G}_1, \mathbb{G}_2, \mathbb{G}_T, e, G_1, G_2)$ *as above, given* $A_1, A_2 \leftarrow_\$ \mathbb{G}_1$ *no non-uniform polynomial-time adversary can compute non-trivial* $B_1, B_2 \in \mathbb{G}_2$ *such that:* $A_1 B_1 + A_2 B_2 = 0$. *Similarly, given* $A_1, A_2 \leftarrow_\$ \mathbb{G}_2$ *no adversary can compute non-trivial* $B_1, B_2 \in \mathbb{G}_1$ *such that* $B_1 A_1 + B_2 A_2 = 0$.

Lemma 3. *For* $(\mathbb{F}_p, \mathbb{G}_1, \mathbb{G}_2, \mathbb{G}_T, e, G_1, G_2)$ *as above and* $n = \texttt{poly}(\lambda)$, *given* $\vec{A} \xleftarrow{\$} \mathbb{G}_1^n$ *no non-uniform polynomial-time adversary can compute a non-trivial* $\vec{B} \in \mathbb{G}_2^n$ *such that:* $\langle \vec{A}, \vec{B} \rangle = 0$. *Similarly, given* $\vec{A} \leftarrow_\$ \mathbb{G}_2^n$, *no adversary can compute non-trivial* $\vec{B} \in \mathbb{G}_1^n$ *such that* $\langle \vec{B}, \vec{A} \rangle = 0$.

2.3   Succinct Interactive Arguments of Knowledge

We follow the presentation in [31]. Let $\mathcal{P}, \mathcal{V}$ be a pair of interactive PPT algorithms. Fix an algorithm Gen and public parameters $pp = \texttt{Gen}(\lambda)$, where λ a security parameter such that $O(2^{-\lambda}) = \texttt{negl}(\lambda)$ is negligible. For a NP language $\mathcal{L}$ there is a deterministic polynomial time $\texttt{Sat}_\mathcal{L}$ s.t. $\{\exists w : \texttt{Sat}_\mathcal{L}(\mathbb{x}, w) = 1\} \Leftrightarrow \mathbb{x} \in \mathcal{L}$. We denote the *transcript* of the interaction of two PPTs $\mathcal{P}, \mathcal{V}$ with random tapes $z_\mathcal{P}, z_\mathcal{V} \in \{0,1\}^*$ on $\mathbb{x}$ by $tr\langle \mathcal{P}(z_\mathcal{P}), \mathcal{V}(z_\mathcal{V}) \rangle(\mathbb{x})$.

Definition 2. *A public-coin succinct interactive argument of knowledge for an NP language $\mathcal{L}$ is a protocol between $\mathcal{P}, \mathcal{V}$ satisfying: properties:*

- **Completeness:** *If* $\mathbb{x} \in \mathcal{L}$, *for any* witness w, $\mathbb{x} \in \mathcal{L}$ *and* $r \in \{0,1\}^*$, $\mathbb{P}[\langle \mathcal{P}(pp, w), \mathcal{V}(pp, r) \rangle(\mathbb{x}) = 1 | \texttt{Sat}_\mathcal{L}(\mathbb{x}, w) = 1] \geq 1 - \texttt{negl}(\lambda)$.
- **Soundness:** *For* $\mathbb{x} \notin \mathcal{L}$, *any PPT Prover* $\mathcal{P}^*$, *and for all* $r \in \{0,1\}^*$, $\mathbb{P}[\langle \mathcal{P}^*(pp), \mathcal{V}(pp, r) \rangle(\mathbb{x}) = 1] \leq \texttt{negl}(\lambda)$.
- **Knowledge soundness:** *For any PPT adversary* $\mathcal{A}$, *there exists a PPT extractor* $\mathcal{E}$ *such that* $\forall \mathbb{x} \in \mathcal{L}, \forall r \in \{0,1\}^*$, *if* $\mathbb{P}[\langle \mathcal{A}(pp), \mathcal{V}(pp, r) \rangle(\mathbb{x}) = 1] \geq \texttt{negl}(\lambda)$, *then* $\mathbb{P}[\texttt{Sat}_\mathcal{L}(\mathbb{x}, \mathcal{E}^\mathcal{A}(pp, \mathbb{x})) = 1] \geq \texttt{negl}(\lambda)$.
- **Succinctness:** *Communication between* $\mathcal{P}$ *and* $\mathcal{V}$ *is sublinear in* $|w|$.
- **Public coin:** *Each* $\mathcal{V}$ *message* $\mathcal{M} \xleftarrow{\$} \mathcal{C}$, *for* $\mathcal{C}$ *some fixed set.*

Definition 3. *An interactive argument* $(\texttt{Gen}, \mathcal{P}, \mathcal{V})$ *for* $\mathcal{L}$ *is Honest-Verifier Statistical Zero-Knowledge (HVSZK) if there exists a PPT algorithm* $S(\mathbb{x}, z)$ *called the simulator, running in time polynomial in* $|\mathbb{x}|$, *such that for every* $\mathbb{x} \in \mathcal{L}$, $w \in \mathcal{R}_\mathbb{x}$, *and* $z \in \{0,1\}^*$, *the statistical distance between the distributions* $tr\langle \mathcal{P}(w), \mathcal{V}(z) \rangle(\mathbb{x})$ *and* $S(\mathbb{x}, z)$ *is* $\texttt{negl}(\lambda)$.

If we have a family of languages $\mathcal{L}_{\texttt{params}}$, we will often name a pair of interactive PPT algorithms $\texttt{Func} = (\mathcal{P}, \mathcal{V})$, and suppress reference to the tapes and prover witness, i.e. write that $\mathcal{P}, \mathcal{V}$ run $\texttt{Func}_{\texttt{params}}(\mathbb{x})$ successfully to mean that $\mathcal{P}$ possesses some witness w for $\mathbb{x} \in \mathcal{L}_{\texttt{params}}$ and $\langle \mathcal{P}(pp, w), \mathcal{V}(pp, r) \rangle(\texttt{params}, \mathbb{x}) = 1$.

Definition 4 (Witness-extended emulation [24,34]). *An public coin interactive argument* $(\mathsf{Gen}, \mathcal{P}, \mathcal{V})$ *for* $\mathcal{L}$ *has witness-extended emulation if for all deterministic polynomial time programs* $\mathcal{P}^*$ *there exists an expected polynomial time emulator* E *such that for all non-uniform polynomial time adversaries* A *and all* $z_\mathcal{V} \in \{0,1\}^*$, *the following probabilities differ by at most* $\mathtt{negl}(\lambda)$:
$\mathbb{P}[\mathcal{A}(t, \mathbf{x}) = 1 | pp \leftarrow \mathsf{Gen}(1^\lambda) \wedge (\mathbf{x}, z_\mathcal{P}) \leftarrow A(pp) \wedge t \leftarrow tr\langle \mathcal{P}^*(z_\mathcal{P}), \mathcal{V}(z_\mathcal{V})\rangle(\mathbf{x})]$ *and*
$\mathbb{P}[\mathcal{A}(t, \mathbf{x}) = 1 \wedge (\mathsf{Accept}(t) = 1 \Rightarrow \mathsf{Sat}_\mathcal{L}(\mathbf{x}, w) = 1) | pp \leftarrow \mathsf{Gen}(1^\lambda) \wedge (\mathbf{x}, z_\mathcal{P}) \leftarrow A(pp) \wedge (t, w) \leftarrow E^{\mathcal{P}^*(z_\mathcal{P})}(\mathbf{x})]$.

Witness-extended emulation implies *soundness* and *knowledge soundness*. For a $(2\mu + 1)$-move interactive protocol, a $(w_1, \ldots, w_\mu)$-*tree of accepting transcripts* is a tree of depth μ in which: (1) the root is labelled with $\mathbf{x}$ and the initial $\mathcal{P}$ message; (2) each node at depth i has w_i children, labelled with distinct $\mathcal{V}$ challenges and subsequent $\mathcal{P}$ message; (3) the concatenation of the labels on any path from the root to a leaf of the tree is an accepting transcript for the protocol.

Definition 5 (Tree extractability (arguments)). *A* $(2\mu + 1)$-*move interactive protocol* $(\mathcal{P}, \mathcal{V})$ *with Verifier message space* $\mathcal{C}$ *is* (W, ϵ)-*tree extractable if there exists a PPT algorithm extracting a witness from* $(w_1, \ldots, w_\mu)$-*tree of accepting transcripts with failure probability* $\leq \epsilon$, $\prod_i w_i \leq W$ *and* $\max_i(w_i) \leq \epsilon|\mathcal{C}|$.

Definition 6 (Tree extractability (reductions)). *We say an interactive protocol reducing* $\mathbf{x} \in \mathcal{L}$ *to* $\mathbf{x}' \in \mathcal{L}'$ *is* (W, ϵ)-*tree extractable if the composition of this argument with a final* $\mathcal{P}$ *message revealing a witness* w' *for* $\mathbf{x}' \in \mathcal{L}'$ *is a* (W, ϵ)-*tree extractable argument for* $\mathcal{L}$.

Lemma 4. *Let* $(\mathcal{P}, \mathcal{V})$ *be a* (W, ϵ)-*tree extractable reduction from* $\mathcal{L}$ *to* $\mathcal{L}'$, *and* $(\mathcal{P}', \mathcal{V}')$ *be a* (W', ϵ')-*tree extractable argument for* $\mathcal{L}'$. *Then the composition of* $(\mathcal{P}, \mathcal{V})$ *and* $(\mathcal{P}', \mathcal{V}')$ *is a* $(WW', \epsilon + W\epsilon')$-*tree extractable argument for* $\mathcal{L}$.

Proof. Let the first protocol be extractable from a $(w_1, \ldots, w_\mu)$-tree of accepting transcripts and the second from a $(w'_1, \ldots, w'_{\mu'})$-tree of accepting transcripts. We ask for a $(w_1, \ldots, w_\mu, w'_1, \ldots, w'_{\mu'})$-tree of accepting transcripts, which has size bounded by WW'. We run the PPT extractor for $(\mathcal{P}, \mathcal{V})$ on the depth w_μ subtree rooted at the origin, and for each new witness w' for $\mathbf{x}' \in \mathcal{L}'$ that it asks for we run the PPT extractor for $(\mathcal{P}', \mathcal{V}')$ on the depth $w_{\mu'}$ subtree rooted at this depth μ point. We run the inner extractor at most W times, so taking a union bound our overall failure probability is bounded by $\epsilon + W\epsilon'$.

Lemma 5 ([13, Lemma 1][34, Lemma 13]). *If* $W = \mathtt{poly}(\lambda)$ *and* $\epsilon = \mathtt{negl}(\lambda)$, *then any* (W, ϵ)-*tree extractable* $(\mathcal{P}, \mathcal{V})$ *has witness-extended emulation.*

We now state a lemma whose object is to obtain results similar to those provided by the Schwartz-Zippel lemma without requiring random evaluation points.

Lemma 6. *For* V *a finite vector space over* $\mathbb{F}$, *if* $g \in V[X, X^{-1}]$ *is a formal Laurent polynomial of degree* d *and order* e, *and* $g(x) = [0]_V$ *for* $d + e + 1$ *values of* $x \in \mathbb{F}$ *then* $g \equiv [0]_V$.

Proof. V is finite so has a basis $\{v_1, \ldots, v_k\}$. Each coefficient of g can be uniquely represented by a linear combination of the v_i, so there exist Laurent polynomials $f_i \in \mathbb{F}[X, X^{-1}]$ of degree at most d and order at most e such that: $g \equiv \sum_i v_i \cdot f_i$. At each of the given $d + e + 1$ values each of these f_i vanish. So $f_i(X) . X^e$ is a polynomial of degree $\leq d + e$, vanishing at $> d + e$ points. So each $f_i \equiv 0$ by the factor theorem and hence $g \equiv [0]_V$

Remark 1. Suitable vector spaces V for the above lemma include any $\mathbb{G}$ a group of order p, or any finite vector $\mathbb{G}^k$ of such a group, or Laurent polynomials in another variable Y of bounded degree and order (as a finite dimensional subspace of the vector space $\mathbb{G}^k[Y, Y^{-1}]$).

2.4   Commitments

As in [31], we work with the definitions of polynomial commitments from Bünz et al. [16], which allows interactive proofs for evaluations, rather than those of Kate et al. [27]. A *commitment scheme* for some space of messages $\mathcal{X}$ is a tuple of three protocols (Gen, Commit, Open):

- $pp \leftarrow \mathsf{Gen}(1^\lambda)$: produces public parameters pp.
- $(\mathcal{C}, \mathcal{S}) \leftarrow \mathsf{Commit}(pp; x)$: takes as input some $x \in \mathcal{X}$; produces a public commitment $\mathcal{C}$ and a secret opening hint $\mathcal{S}$.
- $b \leftarrow \mathsf{Open}(pp; \mathcal{C}, x, \mathcal{S})$: verifies the opening of commitment $\mathcal{C}$ to $x \in \mathcal{X}$ with the opening hint $\mathcal{S}$; outputs $b \in \{0, 1\}$.

Our commitment schemes sample $\mathcal{S}$ uniformly from some space, so we can pass it as a parameter, which gives a modified signature $\mathcal{C} \leftarrow \mathsf{Commit}(pp ; \mathcal{S})$.

Definition 7. *A tuple of three protocols (Gen, Commit, Open) is a commitment scheme for $\mathcal{X}$ if for any PPT adversary $\mathcal{A}$:*

$$\mathbb{P}\left[\begin{array}{c|c} b_0 = b_1 = 1 & pp \leftarrow \mathsf{Gen}(1^\lambda) \wedge (\mathcal{C}, x_0, x_1, \mathcal{S}_0, \mathcal{S}_1) = A(pp) \wedge \\ \wedge x_0 \neq x_1 & b_0 \leftarrow \mathsf{Open}(pp; \mathcal{C}, x_0, \mathcal{S}_0) \wedge b_1 \leftarrow \mathsf{Open}(pp; \mathcal{C}, x_1, \mathcal{S}_1) \end{array} \right] \leq \mathtt{negl}(\lambda).$$

Definition 8. *A commitment scheme (Gen, Commit, Open) provides hiding commitments if for all PPT adversaries $\mathcal{A} = (\mathcal{A}_0, \mathcal{A}_1)$:*

$$\left| 1 - 2 \cdot \mathbb{P}\left[b = \bar{b} \,\middle|\, \begin{array}{c} pp \leftarrow \mathsf{Gen}(1^\lambda) \wedge \\ (x_0, x_1, st) = \mathcal{A}_0(pp) \wedge b \xleftarrow{\$} \{0, 1\} \wedge \\ (\mathcal{C}, \mathcal{S}) \leftarrow \mathsf{Commit}(pp; x_b) \wedge \bar{b} \leftarrow \mathcal{A}_1(st, \mathcal{C}) \end{array} \right] \right| \leq \mathtt{negl}(\lambda)$$

If this holds for all algorithms, then the commitment is statistically hiding.

Pedersen and AFGHO Commitments: For messages $\mathcal{X} = \mathbb{F}^n$ and any $i \in \{1, 2, T\}$, the Pedersen commitment scheme is defined by:

$$pp \leftarrow \mathsf{Gen}(1^\lambda) = (g \xleftarrow{\$} G_i^n, h \xleftarrow{\$} G_i)$$

$$(\mathcal{C}, \mathcal{S}) \leftarrow \mathsf{Commit}(pp; x) = \{r \xleftarrow{\$} \mathbb{F} ; (\langle x, g \rangle + rh, r)\}$$

$$\mathsf{Open}(pp; \mathcal{C}, x, \mathcal{S}) = (\langle x, g \rangle + r(h) \overset{?}{=} \mathcal{C})$$

If DLOG in $\mathbb{G}_i$ is hard, then this is a hiding commitment scheme. Similarly, Abe et al. [2] define a structure preserving commitment to group elements. In this case we have $\mathcal{X} = \mathbb{G}_i^n$ for $i \in \{1, 2\}$ and:

$$pp \leftarrow \mathsf{Gen}(1^\lambda) = (g \xleftarrow{\$} \mathbb{G}_{3-i}^n, H_1 \xleftarrow{\$} \mathbb{G}_1, H_2 \xleftarrow{\$} \mathbb{G}_2)$$
$$(\mathcal{C}, \mathcal{S}) \leftarrow \mathsf{Commit}(pp \; ; \; x) = \{r \xleftarrow{\$} \mathbb{F} \; ; \; (\langle x, g \rangle + r \cdot e(H_1, H_2), r)\}$$
$$\mathsf{Open}(pp, \mathcal{C}, x, \mathcal{S}) = (\langle x, g \rangle + \mathcal{S} \cdot e(H_1, H_2) \stackrel{?}{=} \mathcal{C})$$

This is hiding as $r \cdot e(H_1, H_2)$ is uniformly random in $\mathbb{G}_T$. It is a commitment conditional on SXDH; providing two distinct openings violates Lemma 3). This commitment reduces to that of [2], since in that work an opening for a commitment to a vector $x \in \mathbb{G}_1^n$ would supply some $R \in G_1$ such that $\mathcal{C} = \langle x, g \rangle + e(R, H_2)$. Here, an opening provides $r \in \mathbb{F}$ such that $R = rH_1$, which is strictly stronger. Both the Pedersen and AFGHO commitments are additively homomorphic. **Commitments to matrices** Composing the Pedersen and AFGHO commitments yields a two-tiered homomorphic commitment [23] to matrices. Formally, we take $\mathcal{X} = \mathbb{F}^{n \times m}$, and for $M_{ij} \in \mathcal{X}$ we have:

$$pp \leftarrow \mathsf{Gen}(1^\lambda) = (\Gamma_1 \xleftarrow{\$} \mathbb{G}_1^m, H_1 \xleftarrow{\$} \mathbb{G}_1, \Gamma_2 \xleftarrow{\$} \mathbb{G}_2^n, H_2 \xleftarrow{\$} \mathbb{G}_2)$$

$$(\mathcal{C}, \mathcal{S}) \leftarrow \mathsf{Commit}(pp; M_{ij}) = \left\{ \begin{array}{c} r_{rows} \xleftarrow{\$} \mathbb{F}^n \; ; \; r_{fin} \xleftarrow{\$} \mathbb{F} \; ; \; H_T \leftarrow e(H_1, H_2) \; ; \\ V_i \leftarrow \mathsf{Commit}_{Pedersen}((\Gamma_1, H_1) \; ; \; M_{ij}, r_{rows,i}) \; ; \\ \mathcal{C} \leftarrow \mathsf{Commit}_{AFGHO}((\Gamma_2, H_T) \; ; \; \vec{V}, r_{fin} \; ; \\ (\mathcal{C}, (r_{rows}, r_{fin}, \vec{V})) \end{array} \right\}$$

$$\mathsf{Open}(pp; \mathcal{C}, M, \mathcal{S}) = \left(\begin{array}{c} \mathcal{C} \stackrel{?}{=} \sum_i \Gamma_{2i} \left(\sum_j M_{ij} \Gamma_{1j} + r_{rows,i} H_1 \right) \\ + r_{fin} \cdot e(H_1, H_2) \end{array} \right)$$

2.5 Polynomial Commitments and Evaluation from Vector-Matrix-Vector Products

Let $(\mathsf{Gen}_\mathbb{F}, \mathsf{Commit}_\mathbb{F}, \mathsf{Open}_\mathbb{F})$ be a commitment scheme for $\mathcal{X} = \mathbb{F}$ with public parameters $pp_\mathbb{F}$. We define polynomial commitments for multilinear polynomials, following [16,31], which (contra Kate [27]) allow interactive evaluation proofs.

Definition 9. *A tuple of protocols* $(\mathsf{Gen}, \mathsf{Commit}, \mathsf{Open}, \mathsf{Eval})$ *is an honest-verifier, zero-knowledge, extractable polynomial commitment scheme for ℓ-variable multilinear polynomials over $\mathbb{F}$ if* $(\mathsf{Gen}, \mathsf{Commit}, \mathsf{Open})$ *is a commitment scheme for ℓ-variable multilinear polynomials over $\mathbb{F}$, and Eval is an HVSZK interactive argument of knowledge for:*

$$\mathcal{R}_{\mathsf{Eval}}(pp, pp_\mathbb{F}) = \left\{ \langle (\mathcal{C}_G, \vec{x}, \mathcal{C}_v), (G, \mathcal{S}_G, v, \mathcal{S}_v) \rangle \;\middle|\; \begin{array}{l} G \in \mathbb{F}[X_1, \dots, X_\ell] \\ \wedge G \text{ is multilinear} \\ \wedge v \in \mathbb{F} \wedge G(\vec{x}) = v \\ \wedge \mathsf{Open}(pp; \mathcal{C}_G, G, \mathcal{S}_G) = 1 \\ \wedge \mathsf{Open}_\mathbb{F}(pp_\mathbb{F}; \mathcal{C}_v, v, \mathcal{S}_v) = 1 \end{array} \right\}.$$

Note that we have modified the definition from [16] by requiring evaluations $G(\vec{x})$ are committed, which is required for zkSNARK applications. We also define a weaker knowledge soundness property useful for R1CS SNARKs as in [13,31]:

Definition 10. *Random Evaluation Knowledge Soundness.*
For $pp \leftarrow \mathsf{Gen}(1^\lambda)$, $pp_\mathbb{F} \leftarrow \mathsf{Gen}_\mathbb{F}(1^\lambda)$, and commitment $\mathcal{C}_G$, the protocol:

$\mathcal{V} \rightarrow \mathcal{P}$: $\vec{x} \xleftarrow{\$} \mathbb{F}^\ell$
$\mathcal{P}$: $(\mathcal{C}_e, \mathcal{S}_e) \leftarrow \mathsf{Commit}_\mathbb{F}(pp_\mathbb{F}; G(\vec{x}))$
$\mathcal{P} \rightarrow \mathcal{V}$: $\mathcal{C}_\mathbb{F}$
$\mathcal{P}, \mathcal{V}$: *Accept if* $\mathsf{Eval}(pp, pp_\mathbb{F}; \mathcal{C}_G, \vec{x}, \mathcal{C}_v) = 1$.

---

is an argument of knowledge with witness-extended emulation for:

$$\mathcal{R}(pp, pp_\mathbb{F}) = \left\{ \langle \mathcal{C}_G, (G, \mathcal{S}_G) \rangle \; \middle| \; \begin{array}{c} \exists \vec{x}, v, \mathcal{C}_v, \mathcal{S}_v \; s.t. \\ \langle (\mathcal{C}_G, \vec{x}, \mathcal{C}_v), (G, \mathcal{S}_G, v, \mathcal{S}_v) \rangle \in \mathcal{R}_{\mathsf{Eval}}(pp, pp_\mathbb{F}) \end{array} \right\}.$$

We say a scheme providing this property in place of knowledge soundness is *random evaluation extractable*. We also note that prior polynomial commitment schemes in [13,17] satisfy only this weaker property. In these works, the commitment to a polynomial is a $n^{1/2}$ length list of commitments to lists of scalars of length $n^{1/2}$ (resp. a structure-preserving commitment to a list of Kate commitments to polynomials). However, for any particular point of evaluation $\vec{x}$, $\mathcal{P}$ only shows that know an opening of some $\vec{x}$-dependent linear combination of these commitments. So a Knowledge Soundness adversary may pick $\vec{x}$, then produce $\mathcal{C}_G$, without knowledge of openings of all rows (and hence without knowledge of a $G, \mathcal{S}_G$ opening of $\mathcal{C}_G$). In the R1CS SNARK context of [13], this is mitigated as the surrounding protocol enforces that $\vec{x} \leftarrow \mathbb{F}^\ell$ after $\mathcal{C}_G$ is made public.

Any polynomial f in variables $X_1, \ldots, X_\ell$ of degree $d_1, \ldots, d_\ell$ can be reformulated as a multilinear polynomial in $\{X_i, X_i^2, \ldots X_i^{2^{\lceil \log(d_i+1) \rceil - 1}} : i \in [\ell]\}$. For example, the bivariate polynomial $f(X_1, X_2) := 1 + X_1^2 X_2 + X_1^7$ can be written as a 4-variable multilinear polynomial $g(Y_1, Y_2, Y_3, Y_4) = 1 + Y_2 Y_4 + Y_1 Y_2 Y_3$, with $f(x_1, x_2) \equiv g(x_1, x_1^2, x_1^4, x_2)$. Any multilinear polynomial g in r variables can be written as a sum of monomials, so:

$$g(x_1, \ldots, x_r) = \sum_{(i_1, \ldots, i_r) \in \{1,2\}^r} T_{i_1, \ldots, i_r} \prod_{j \in \{1, \ldots, r\}} x_j^{i_j - 1},$$

where T is an order r tensor. In the given concrete example, T would be an $2 \times 2 \times 2 \times 2$ tensor T_{ijkl}, with $T_{1111} = T_{1212} = T_{2221} = 1$ and $T_{ijkl} = 0$ otherwise. Note that this sum is the contraction of T with the r vectors $(1, \vec{x}_i)$. In general, for any $n_1 \times \ldots \times n_r$ tensor T and $0 \leq k \leq r$ we can rearrange T into a $(\prod_{i<k} n_i) \times (\prod_{i \geq k} n_i)$ matrix M, such that:

$$\sum_{i_1=1}^{n_1} \cdots \sum_{i_r=1}^{n_r} T_{i_1 \ldots i_r} (\vec{v}_j)_{i_j} = (\otimes_{i<k} \vec{v}_i)^T M (\otimes_{i \geq k} \vec{v}_i)$$

for all vectors $\vec{v}_i \in \mathbb{F}^{n_i}$. Explicitly this is given by setting $M_{ij} := T_{i_1,\ldots,i_r}$ where:

$$i - 1 = (i_{k-1} - 1) + n_{k-1}((i_{k-2} - 1) + n_{k-2}(\cdots((i_2 - 1) + n_2(i_1 - 1)))),$$
$$j - 1 = (i_r - 1) + n_r((i_{r-1} - 1) + n_{r-1}(\cdots((i_{k+1} - 1) + n_{k+1}(i_k - 1))))$$

We select k to make the matrix M approximately square. In our concrete example $k = 2$ and M_{ij} is a 4×4 matrix with $M_{11} = M_{22} = M_{43} = 1$ and $M_{ij} = 0$ otherwise.

So the evaluation of f at some point x can be replaced with the evaluation of a multilinear polynomial in $r = \sum_i \lceil \log(d_i + 1) \rceil$, variables, which can in turn be replaced by a vector-matrix-vector product with vectors of length at most $2^m = 2^{\lceil r/2 \rceil} = O((\prod_i d_i)^{1/2} 2^{\ell/2})$. The vectors in this product have multiplicative structure, being formed as Kronecker products of vectors $(1, x_i^{2^j})$ for $i \in \{1, \ldots, r\}$, $j \in \{0, \ldots, \lceil \log(d_i + 1) \rceil - 1\}$. For univariate polynomials of degree d, $m \le (3 + \log d)/2$, and for multilinear polynomials in ℓ variables $m \le (\ell + 1)/2$. In the concrete example, we have:

$$f(x_1, x_2) \equiv g(x_1, x_1^2, x_1^4, x_2) = (1, x_1^2, x_1, x_1^3)^T M (1, x_2, x_1^4, x_1^4 x_2),$$

where the two vectors $(1, x_1^2, x_1, x_1^3) = (1, x_1) \otimes (1, x_1^2)$ and $(1, x_2, x_1^4, x_1^4 x_2) = (1, x_1^4) \otimes (1, x_2)$ have multiplicative structure.

3 An Inner-Product Argument with a Logarithmic Verifier

We begin by showing the simplest form of Dory: an argument for inner products between two vectors in $\vec{v}_1 \in \mathbb{G}_1^n$, $\vec{v}_2 \in \mathbb{G}_2^n$, committed with AFGHO commitments with generators $(\Gamma_2, e(H_1, H_2)) \in \mathbb{G}_2^n \times \mathbb{G}_T$ and $(\Gamma_1, e(H_1, H_2)) \in \mathbb{G}_1^n \times \mathbb{G}_T$.

We highlight the parts of protocols and calculations needed only for zero-knowledge in blue. Formally, we define a language:

$$(C, D_1, D_2) \in \mathcal{L}_{n, \Gamma_1, \Gamma_2, H_1, H_2} \subset \mathbb{G}_T^3$$
$$\Leftrightarrow \exists(\vec{v}_1 \in \mathbb{G}_1^n, \vec{v}_2 \in \mathbb{G}_2^n, r_C \in \mathbb{F}, r_{D_1} \in \mathbb{F}, r_{D_2} \in \mathbb{F}):$$
$$D_1 = \langle \vec{v}_1, \Gamma_2 \rangle + r_{D_1} \cdot e(H_1, H_2), \quad D_2 = \langle \Gamma_1, \vec{v}_2 \rangle + r_{D_2} \cdot e(H_1, H_2),$$
$$C = \langle \vec{v}_1, \vec{v}_2 \rangle + r_C \cdot e(H_1, H_2)$$

For n even, and $\Gamma'_{\{1,2\}} \in \mathbb{G}_{\{1,2\}}^{2^{n/2}}$, we will show (Sect. 3.2) an reduction from membership in $\mathcal{L}_{n, \Gamma_1, \Gamma_2, H_1, H_2}$ to membership in $\mathcal{L}_{n/2, \Gamma'_1, \Gamma'_2, H_1, H_2}$. In Sect. 3.1, we give an argument of knowledge for $\mathcal{L}_{1, \Gamma_1, \Gamma_2, H_1, H_2}$. In Sect. 3.4 we give an argument reducing two claims of membership of $\mathcal{L}_{n, \Gamma_1, \Gamma_2, H_1, H_2}$ to one. In Sect. 3.3 we discuss concrete efficiency and optimisations for $\mathcal{V}$.

3.1 Scalar-Product

We give a interactive argument of knowledge for $\mathcal{L}_{1, \Gamma_1, \Gamma_2, H_1, H_2}$. This requires showing the product of two elements $v_1 \in \mathbb{G}_1$ and $v_2 \in \mathbb{G}_2$ under AFGHO commitments; the analogous argument for Pedersen commitments is folklore. Since pairings are more expensive than multiplications in $\mathbb{G}_1$ or $\mathbb{G}_2$, we combine the usual final three checks into a single pairing with a Verifier challenge.

Scalar-Product$_{\Gamma_1,\Gamma_2,H_1,H_2}(C, D_1, D_2)$

Precompute: $H_T = e(H_1, H_2)$, $\chi = e(\Gamma_1, \Gamma_2)$

$\quad \mathcal{P}$ **witness:** $(v_1, v_2, r_C, r_{D_1}, r_{D_2})$ for $(C, D_1, D_2) \in \mathcal{L}_{1, \Gamma_1, \Gamma_2, H_1, H_2}$

$\mathcal{P}$: $r_{P_1}, r_{P_2}, r_Q, r_R \leftarrow_\$ \mathbb{F}$, $d_1 \leftarrow_\$ \mathbb{G}_1$, $d_2 \leftarrow_\$ \mathbb{G}_2$

$\mathcal{P} \to \mathcal{V}$: $\quad P_1 = e(d_1, \Gamma_2) + r_{P_1} H_T$, $\qquad\qquad P_2 = e(\Gamma_1, d_2) + r_{P_2} H_T$,

$\qquad\qquad Q = e(d_1, v_2) + e(v_1, d_2) + r_Q H_T$, $\quad R = e(d_1, d_2) + r_R H_T$,

$\mathcal{V} \to \mathcal{P}$: $c \leftarrow_\$ \mathbb{F}$

$\mathcal{P} \to \mathcal{V}$: $\quad E_1 \leftarrow d_1 + cv_1$, $\qquad E_2 \leftarrow d_2 + cv_2$,

$\qquad\qquad r_1 \leftarrow r_{P_1} + cr_{D_1}$, $\quad r_2 \leftarrow r_{P_2} + cr_{D_2}$, $\quad r_3 \leftarrow r_R + cr_Q + c^2 r_C$

$\mathcal{V}$: $d \leftarrow_\$ \mathbb{F}$, accept if:

$$e(E_1 + d\Gamma_1, E_2 + d^{-1}\Gamma_2) = \chi + R + cQ + c^2 C$$
$$+ dP_2 + dcD_2 + d^{-1}P_1 + d^{-1}cD_1$$
$$- (r_3 + dr_2 + d^{-1}r_1)H_T$$

Theorem 1. *For $\Gamma_1, H_1 \overset{\$}{\leftarrow} \mathbb{G}_1$, $\Gamma_2, H_2 \overset{\$}{\leftarrow} \mathbb{G}_2$, Scalar-Product is an HVSZK, public-coin, succinct interactive argument of knowledge for $\mathcal{L}_{1, \Gamma_1, \Gamma_2, H_1, H_2}$ with $(9, 9/|\mathbb{F}|)$-tree extractability under SXDH.*

Proof. Succinctness and the Public Coin property are immediate. The argument is complete as for an honest $\mathcal{P}$, $\mathcal{V}$ accepts:

$$e(E_1 + d\Gamma_1, E_2 + d^{-1}\Gamma_2) = e(d_1 + cv_1, d_2 + cv_2)$$
$$+ d \cdot e(\Gamma_1, d_2 + cv_2) + d^{-1} \cdot e(d_1 + cv_1, \Gamma_2) + e(\Gamma_1, \Gamma_2)$$
$$= \chi + c^2 \cdot e(v_1, v_2) + c[e(d_1, v_2) + e(v_1, d_2)] + e(d_1, d_2)$$
$$+ d \cdot e(\Gamma_1, d_2) + dc \cdot e(\Gamma_1, v_2) + d^{-1} \cdot e(d_1, \Gamma_2) + d^{-1}c \cdot e(v_1, \Gamma_2)$$
$$= \chi + R + cQ + c^2 C$$
$$+ dP_2 + dcD_2 + d^{-1}P_1 + d^{-1}cD_1 - (r_3 + dr_2 + d^{-1}r_1)H_T$$

HVSZK: Note that for an honest $\mathcal{P}$, E_1, E_2, Q are uniformly random in $\mathbb{G}_T$ and $r_1, r_2, r_3 \overset{\$}{\leftarrow} \mathbb{F}$. We split the final check into terms that are proportional to $d^{-1}, d, 1$:

$$P_1 = e(E_1, \Gamma_2) + r_1 H_T - cD_1, \qquad\qquad P_2 = e(\Gamma_1, E_2) + r_2 H_T - cD_2,$$
$$R = e(E_1, E_2) + r_3 H_T - cQ - c^2 C$$

To construct a simulator: Sample $Q, E_1, E_2 \overset{\$}{\leftarrow} \mathbb{G}_T^3$ and compute the challenge c from $\mathcal{V}$'s coins. Then sample $r_1, r_2, r_3 \overset{\$}{\leftarrow} \mathbb{F}$ and compute P_1, P_2, R as above.

Tree Extractability: We have $\mu = 2$ with an empty final $\mathcal{P}$ message, and set $w_1 = w_2 = 3$. So we have a tree of accepting transcripts for 3 values c, and for each c there are 3 accepting values of d. We fail if any of these 9 d are 0, which occurs with probability $\leq 9/|\mathbb{F}|$. Across all transcripts, $P_1, P_2, Q, R, C, D_1, D_2$ are constant, and E_1, E_2, r_1, r_2, r_3 can be interpolated as quadratics in c.

For each c, the final check contains terms in d only of form $d, 1, d^{-1}$, so is a check of equality of Laurent polynomials of degree and order 1. This difference vanishes for three distinct choices of d, so Lemma 6 implies the coefficients for each degree must be separately equal. So for each of the three challenge c:

$$e(E_1(c), E_2(c)) + r_3(c)H_T = R + cQ + c^2\, C \tag{1}$$
$$e(E_1(c), \Gamma_2) + r_1(c) \cdot e(H_1, H_2) = P_1 + cD_1 \tag{2}$$
$$e(\Gamma_1, E_2(c)) + r_2(c) \cdot e(H_1, H_2) = P_2 + cD_2 \tag{3}$$

For $i = 1, 2$, we interpolate $E_i(c) = d_i + cv_i + c^2 U_i$ and $r_i = r_{P_i} + cr_{D_i} + c^2 r_{U_i}$. Our first task is to show that $U_i = [0]_{G_i}$ and $r_{U_i} = 0$, i.e. that $\mathcal{P}$ is constrained to send E_1, E_2, r_1, r_2 that depend only *affinely* on c. Equation 2 is an equality of polynomials in $\mathbb{G}_T[c]$ of degree 2 which holds at 3 points. Applying Lemma 6, the coefficients are equal. Writing out the quadratic and linear coefficients gives:

$$e(U_1, \Gamma_2) + e(r_{U_1} H_1, H_2) = 0, \qquad e(v_1, \Gamma_2) + r_{D_1} H_T = D_1.$$

Since $\Gamma_2, H_2 \overset{\$}{\leftarrow} \mathbb{G}_2$, Lemma 3 forces the first equation to be satisfied by $U_1 = r_{U_1}H_1 = [0]_{G_1}$. We also have v_1, r_{D_1} satisfying our constraint on D_1. Similar considerations applied to Eq. 3 imply that $U_2 = [0]_{G_2}$, $r_{U_2} = 0$, and provide a v_2, r_{D_2} satisfying the constraint on D_2.

It remains to extract r_C to satisfy the constraint on C. We interpolate $r_3(c) = r_R + cr_Q + c^2 r_C$, and substitute our linear expressions for E_1, E_2 into Eq. 1:

$$R + cQ + c^2\, C = e(d_1, d_2) + r_R H_T + c(e(d_1, v_2) + e(v_1, d_2) + r_Q H_T)$$
$$+ c^2(e(v_1, v_2) + r_C H_T)$$

This is an equality of quadratics in $\mathbb{G}_T[c]$ holding at 3 distinct values, so from Lemma 6 the c^2 coefficients are equal. So $C = e(v_1, v_2) + r_C H_T$. Hence $(v_1, v_2, r_{D_1}, r_{D_2}, r_C)$ is a witness for $(C, D_1, D_2) \in \mathcal{L}_{1, \Gamma_1, \Gamma_2, H_1, H_2}$.

3.2 Dory-Reduce

We now show an interactive argument reducing membership of $\mathcal{L}_{2^m, \Gamma_1, \Gamma_2, H_1, H_2}$ to membership of $\mathcal{L}_{2^{m-1}, \Gamma_1', \Gamma_2', H_1, H_2}$. Informally, the simplest approach to this (neglecting zero-knowledge) would be to start with the 3 claims:

$$D_1 = \langle \vec{v_1}, \Gamma_2 \rangle, \qquad D_2 = \langle \Gamma_1, \vec{v_2} \rangle, \qquad C = \langle \vec{v_1}, \vec{v_2} \rangle,$$

and fold each in some LCC-DLOG-like [13,15,17] fashion with a $\mathcal{V}$ challenge α into claims about 2^{m-1} length vectors $\vec{v_{i\alpha}}, \Gamma_{i\alpha}$:

$$D_1' = \langle \vec{v_{1\alpha}}, \Gamma_{2\alpha} \rangle, \qquad D_2' = \langle \Gamma_{1\alpha}, \vec{v_{2\alpha}} \rangle, \qquad C' = \langle \vec{v_{1\alpha}}, \vec{v_{2\alpha}} \rangle,$$

$\mathcal{P}, \mathcal{V}$ would separately compute commitments $\Delta_1 = \langle \vec{v_{1\alpha}}, \Gamma_2' \rangle$ and $\Delta_{2\alpha} = \langle \Gamma_1', \vec{v_{2\alpha}} \rangle$ from α and precomputed data. We would then combine $v_{i\alpha}$ and $\Gamma_{i\alpha}$ for each i in accordance with additional Verifier challenges. This produces a final C'' from C', D_1', D_2', a final D_1'' from D_1' and Δ_1, and a final D_2'' from D_2' and Δ_2, with the Prover sending additional cross-terms to support these combinations. However, this approach requires sending at least 8 elements of $\mathbb{G}_T$ (two for each claim to fold and two for the final combining stage). Instead, in Dory-Reduce we effectively swap the order of these two stages, which allows sending only 6 elements of $\mathbb{G}_T$.

Dory-Reduce$_{m,\Gamma_1,\Gamma_2,\Gamma_1',\Gamma_2',H_1,H_2}(C, D_1, D_2)$

Precompute: $H_T = e(H_1, H_2)$, $\Delta_{1L} = \langle \Gamma_{1L}, \Gamma_2' \rangle$, $\Delta_{1R} = \langle \Gamma_{1R}, \Gamma_2' \rangle$,

   $\Delta_{2L} = \langle \Gamma_1', \Gamma_{2L} \rangle$, $\Delta_{2R} = \langle \Gamma_1', \Gamma_{2R} \rangle$, and $\chi = \langle \Gamma_1, \Gamma_2 \rangle$

   $\mathcal{P}$ **witness:** $(\vec{v_1}, \vec{v_2}, r_c, r_{D_1}, r_{D_2})$ for $(C, D_1, D_2) \in \mathcal{L}_{2^m, \Gamma_1, \Gamma_2, H_1, H_2}$

$\mathcal{P}$: $r_{D_{1L}}, r_{D_{1R}}, r_{D_{2L}}, r_{D_{2R}} \leftarrow_{\$} \mathbb{F}$

$\mathcal{P} \to \mathcal{V}$: $D_{1L} = \langle \vec{v_{1L}}, \Gamma_2' \rangle + r_{D_{1L}} H_T, \quad D_{1R} = \langle \vec{v_{1R}}, \Gamma_2' \rangle + r_{D_{1R}} H_T$

   $D_{2L} = \langle \Gamma_1', \vec{v_{2L}} \rangle + r_{D_{2L}} H_T, \quad D_{2R} = \langle \Gamma_1', \vec{v_{2R}} \rangle + r_{D_{2R}} H_T$

$\mathcal{V} \to \mathcal{P}$: $\beta \leftarrow_{\$} \mathbb{F}$

$\mathcal{P}(*)$: $\vec{v_1} \leftarrow \vec{v_1} + \beta \Gamma_1, \quad \vec{v_2} \leftarrow \vec{v_2} + \beta^{-1} \Gamma_2, \quad r_C \leftarrow r_C + \beta r_{D_2} + \beta^{-1} r_{D_1}$

$\mathcal{P}$: $r_{C_+}, r_{C_-} \leftarrow_{\$} \mathbb{F}$

$\mathcal{P} \to \mathcal{V}$: $C_+ = \langle \vec{v_{1L}}, \vec{v_{2R}} \rangle + r_{C_+} H_T, \quad C_- = \langle \vec{v_{1R}}, \vec{v_{2L}} \rangle + r_{C_-} H_T$

$\mathcal{V} \to \mathcal{P}$: $\alpha \leftarrow_{\$} \mathbb{F}$

$\mathcal{P}(**)$: $\vec{v_1}' \leftarrow \alpha \vec{v_{1L}} + \vec{v_{1R}}, \qquad\qquad \vec{v_2}' \leftarrow \alpha^{-1} \vec{v_{2L}} + \vec{v_{2R}}$

   $r_{D_1}' \leftarrow \alpha r_{D_{1L}} + r_{D_{1R}}, \qquad\qquad r_{D_2}' \leftarrow \alpha^{-1} r_{D_{2L}} + r_{D_{2R}},$

   $r_C' \leftarrow r_C + \alpha r_{C_+} + \alpha^{-1} r_{C_-}$

$\mathcal{V}(**)$: $C' \leftarrow C + \chi + \beta D_2 + \beta^{-1} D_1 + \alpha C_+ + \alpha^{-1} C_-$

   $D_1' \leftarrow \alpha D_{1L} + D_{1R} + \alpha\beta \Delta_{1L} + \beta \Delta_{1R}$

   $D_2' \leftarrow \alpha^{-1} D_{2L} + D_{2R} + \alpha^{-1}\beta^{-1} \Delta_{2L} + \beta^{-1} \Delta_{2R}$

$\mathcal{V}$: Accept if $(C', D_1', D_2') \in \mathcal{L}_{2^{m-1}, \Gamma_1', \Gamma_2', H_1, H_2}$

   $\mathcal{P}$ **witness:** $(\vec{v_1}', \vec{v_2}', r_C', r_{D_1}', r_{D_2}')$

Theorem 2. *For $\Gamma_1' \xleftarrow{\$} \mathbb{G}_1^{2^{m-1}}$, $H_1 \xleftarrow{\$} \mathbb{G}_1$, $\Gamma_2' \xleftarrow{\$} \mathbb{G}_2^{2^{m-1}}$, $H_2 \xleftarrow{\$} \mathbb{G}_2$, Dory-Reduce is an an HVSZK, public-coin, succinct interactive argument of knowledge for $\mathcal{L}_{2^m, \Gamma_1, \Gamma_2, H_1, H_2}$ with $(9, 12/|\mathbb{F}|)$-tree extractability under SXDH.*

To informally see why tree-extractability holds, we observe that the $\mathcal{P}$ witness for $(C, D_1', D_2') \in \mathcal{L}_{2^{m-1}, \Gamma_1', \Gamma_2', H_1, H_2}$ opens D_1', D_2' as binding commitments. $\mathcal{V}$ computes these commitments with bivariate Laurent polynomials, and across a tree of accepting transcripts $\mathcal{P}$ opens at enough points to allow an extractor to open each coefficient of each polynomial.

Since these commitments are binding, coefficients equal to 0 must be opened by $\vec{0}$, and coefficients $\Delta_{\{1,2\}\{L,R\}}$ must be opened by $\Gamma_{\{1,2\}\{L,R\}}$. So $\mathcal{P}$ is substantially constrained in their witness $\vec{v_1}', \vec{v_2}', \ldots$. The extractor also finds vectors opening $D_{\{1,2\}\{L,R\}}$ (which will end up being $v_{\{1,2\}\vec{\}\{L,R\}}}$).

Substituting these into the product constraint on C' (as a function of α, β), we again get an equality of bivariate Laurent polynomials at enough places to force equality of coefficients. Each of C, D_1, D_2 can be computed from coefficients of C', and these will turn out to be exactly the conditions on C, D_1, D_2 required to have found a witness $(v_1, v_2, \dots)$ for $(C, D_1, D_2) \in \mathcal{L}_{2^m, \Gamma_1, \Gamma_2, H_1, H_2}$. Essentially similar arguments are used throughout for tree-extractability.

Proof (Theorem 2). Succinctness and the Public Coin properties are immediate. HVSZK holds as all messages from $\mathcal{P}$ to $\mathcal{V}$ are uniformly random elements of $\mathbb{G}_T$, so are trivially simulated. Completeness holds from substituting the definition of $\mathcal{P}$'s witness into the constraints of $\mathcal{L}_{2^{m-1}, \Gamma'_1, \Gamma'_2, H_1, H_2}$, and cancelling terms to obtain the constraints of $\mathcal{L}_{2^m, \Gamma_1, \Gamma_2, H_1, H_2}$.

Tree Extractability: We have $\mu = 2$, and set $w_1 = w_2 = 3$. So we have a tree of accepting transcripts for 3 values β, and for each β 3 values of α. We fail if any of these challenges are 0, which occurs with probability $\leq 12/|\mathbb{F}|$. For each leaf, the Prover reveals the witness $(\vec{v_1}', \vec{v_2}', r'_C, r'_{D_1}, r'_{D_2})$. Our witness extraction is analogous to witness extraction of GIPA in [17] or of the improved inner product argument in [15, Appendix B].

D_{1L}, D_{1R} are constant for all transcripts in the tree. We interpolate C_+, C_- as a Laurent polynomials in $\mathbb{G}_T[\beta, \beta^{-1}]$ of degree 1 and order -1, and interpolate $\vec{v_1}', \vec{v_2}', r'_{D_1}, r'_{D_2}, r'_C$ can as bivariate Laurent polynomials of degree 1 and order -1 in variables α, β, with computable coefficients in $\mathbb{G}_1^{n/2}, \mathbb{G}_2^{n/2}, \mathbb{F}, \mathbb{F}$ and $\mathbb{F}$ respectively. Since $(C', D'_1, D'_2)(\alpha, \beta) \in \mathcal{L}_{2^{m-1}, \Gamma'_1, \Gamma'_2, H_1, H_2}$ for each leaf:

$$D'_1 = \alpha D_{1L} + D_{1R} + \alpha\beta\langle\Gamma_{1L}, \Gamma'_2\rangle + \beta\langle\Gamma_{1R}, \Gamma'_2\rangle$$
$$= \langle\vec{v_1}'(\alpha, \beta), \Gamma'_2\rangle + r'_{D_1}(\alpha, \beta) \cdot e(H_1, H_2),$$

holds for all 9 (β, α) pairs. For each challenge value of β, we have two Laurent polynomials in α of degree and order 1, equal at 3 values. So by Lemma 6 at each of these three β we have an equality of Laurent polynomials. So overall, we have a pair of Laurent polynomials in β of degree and order 1, whose coefficients are in a finite dimensional subspace of $\mathbb{G}[\alpha, \alpha^{-1}]$, with equality holding at 3 values of β. So applying Lemma 6 again, we have an equality of bivariate Laurent polynomials, and so each coefficient must match.

So monomials with α^{-1} or β^{-1} factors have vanishing coefficients. $\Gamma'_2 \xleftarrow{\$}$ $\mathbb{G}_2^{2^{m-1}}$ and $H_2 \xleftarrow{\$} \mathbb{G}_2$, so Lemma 3 implies that if we can compute $\vec{v}, r$ such that $\langle\vec{v}, \Gamma'_2\rangle + r \cdot e(H_1, H_2) = 0$, then $\vec{v} = \vec{0}$ and $r = 0$. So $\vec{v_1}', r'_{D_1}$ must be multilinear in α, β. Similarly the $\alpha\beta$ and β coefficients of $\vec{v_1}'(\alpha, \beta)$ must be vectors with inner products with Γ'_2 of $\langle\Gamma_{1L}, \Gamma'_2\rangle$ and $\langle\Gamma_{1R}, \Gamma'_2\rangle$ respectively, and so must be Γ_{1L} and Γ_{1R} respectively (or else we violate Lemma 3).

We apply symmetric arguments to $\vec{v_2}', r'_{D_2}$. So the interpolation of $\vec{v_1}'(\alpha, \beta)$ and $\vec{v_2}'(\alpha, \beta)$ provides vectors $\vec{v_{1L}}, \vec{v_{1R}}, \vec{v_{2L}}, \vec{v_{2R}}$ such that:

$$\vec{v_1}'(\alpha, \beta) = \alpha\vec{v_{1L}} + \vec{v_{1R}} + \beta(\alpha\Gamma_{1L} + \Gamma_{1R})$$
$$\vec{v_2}'(\alpha, \beta) = \alpha^{-1}\vec{v_{2L}} + \vec{v_{2R}} + \beta^{-1}(\alpha^{-1}\Gamma_{2L} + \Gamma_{2R})$$

We interpolate $r'_C(\alpha, \beta) = r_C + \beta r_{D_2} + \beta^{-1} r_{D_1} + \alpha f_\alpha(\beta) + \alpha^{-1} f_{\alpha^{-1}}(\beta)$, for $f_\alpha, f_{\alpha^{-1}}$ two Laurent polynomials of degree 1 and order -1. Then substituting into the constraint of $\mathcal{L}_{2^{m-1}, \Gamma'_1, \Gamma'_2, H_1, H_2}$ on C':

$$
\begin{aligned}
C' &= C + \chi + \beta D_2 + \beta^{-1} D_1 + \alpha C_+(\beta) + \alpha^{-1} C_-(\beta) \\
&= \langle \vec{v_1}'(\alpha, \beta), \vec{v_2}'(\alpha, \beta) \rangle + r'_C(\alpha, \beta) H_T \\
&= (\langle \vec{v_{1L}}, \vec{v_{2L}} \rangle + \langle \vec{v_{1R}}, \vec{v_{2R}} \rangle + r_C H_T) + \chi \\
&\quad + \beta(\langle \Gamma_{1L}, \vec{v_{2L}} \rangle + \langle \Gamma_{1R}, \vec{v_{2R}} \rangle + r_{D_2} H_T) + \beta^{-1}(\langle \vec{v_{1L}}, \Gamma_{2L} \rangle + \langle \vec{v_{1L}}, \Gamma_{2L} \rangle + r_{D_1} H_T) \\
&\quad + \alpha(\langle \vec{v_{1L}}, \vec{v_{2R}} \rangle + \langle \Gamma_{1L}, \Gamma_{2R} \rangle + \beta \langle \Gamma_{1L}, \vec{v_{2R}} \rangle + \beta^{-1} \langle \vec{v_{1L}}, \Gamma_{2R} \rangle + f_\alpha(\beta) H_T) \\
&\quad + \alpha^{-1}(\langle \vec{v_{1R}}, \vec{v_{2L}} \rangle + \langle \Gamma_{1R}, \Gamma_{2L} \rangle + \beta \langle \Gamma_{1R}, \vec{v_{2L}} \rangle + \beta^{-1} \langle \vec{v_{1R}}, \Gamma_{2L} \rangle + f_{\alpha^{-1}}(\beta) H_T)
\end{aligned}
$$

These are two bivariate Laurent series of degree 1 and order -1, equal at 3 values of α, for each of 3 values of β, and so applying Lemma 6 in two rounds we conclude they are equal coefficient by coefficient. In particular comparing the $1, \beta, \beta^{-1}$ coefficients:

$$
\begin{aligned}
C &= \langle \vec{v_{1L}}, \vec{v_{2L}} \rangle + \langle \vec{v_{1R}}, \vec{v_{2R}} \rangle + r_C H_T \\
D_1 &= \langle \vec{v_{1L}}, \Gamma_{2L} \rangle + \langle \vec{v_{1R}}, \Gamma_{2R} \rangle + r_{D_1} H_T \\
D_2 &= \langle \Gamma_{1L}, \vec{v_{2L}} \rangle + \langle \Gamma_{1R}, \vec{v_{2R}} \rangle + r_{D_2} H_T
\end{aligned}
$$

and so $((\vec{v_{1L}} || \vec{v_{2L}}), (\vec{v_{2L}} || \vec{v_{2R}}), r_C, r_{D_1}, r_{D_2})$ is the desired witness.

Remark 2. No property of Dory-Reduce depends on the construction of Γ_1, Γ_2. Instead we require only that the smaller commitment keys $(\Gamma'_1 || H_1), (\Gamma'_2 || H_2)$ are sampled randomly. In particular Γ_1, Γ_2 can depend on Γ'_1, Γ'_2 without affecting the tree-extractability of Dory-Reduce.

3.3   Dory-Innerproduct

The full inner product argument applies Dory-Reduce iteratively to shrink an inner-product to a product, and then applies Scalar-Product.

Dory-Innerproduct$_{\Gamma_{1,0}, \Gamma_{2,0}, H_1, H_2}(C, D_1, D_2)$
Precompute: $H_T = e(H_1, H_2)$, for all $j \in 0 \ldots m-1$ compute
$\Gamma_{1,j+1} = (\Gamma_{1,j})_L$, $\Gamma_{2,j+1} = (\Gamma_{2,j})_L$, for all $i \in 0 \ldots m$ compute
$\chi_i = \langle \Gamma_{1,i}, \Gamma_{2,i} \rangle$, and for all $i \in 0 \ldots m-1$ compute:

$$
\begin{aligned}
\Delta_{1L,i} &= \langle (\Gamma_{1,i})_L, \Gamma_{2,i+1} \rangle & = \Delta_{2L,i} &= \langle \Gamma_{1,i+1}, (\Gamma_{2,i})_L \rangle, \\
\Delta_{1R,i} &= \langle (\Gamma_{1,i})_R, \Gamma_{2,i+1} \rangle, & \Delta_{2R,i} &= \langle \Gamma_{1,i+1}, (\Gamma_{2,i})_R \rangle,
\end{aligned}
$$

$\mathcal{P}$ **witness:** $(\vec{v_1}, \vec{v_2}, r_C, r_{D_1}, r_{D_2})$ for $(C, D_1, D_2) \in \mathcal{L}_{2^m, \Gamma_{1,0}, \Gamma_{2,0}, H_1, H_2}$
For $j = 0 \ldots m-1$:
  $\mathcal{P}, \mathcal{V}$: $(C, D_1, D_2) \leftarrow$ Dory-Reduce$_{m-j, \Gamma_{1,j} \Gamma_{2,j}, \Gamma_{1,j+1}, \Gamma_{2,j+1}, H_1, H_2}(C, D_1, D_2)$
$\mathcal{P}, \mathcal{V}$: Scalar-Product$_{\Gamma_{1,m}, \Gamma_{2,m}, H_1, H_2}(C, D_1, D_2)$

Theorem 3. *If $\Gamma_{i,0} \xleftarrow{\$} \mathbb{G}_i^{2^m}$ and $H_i \xleftarrow{\$} \mathbb{G}_i$, then Dory-Innerproduct is an HVSZK, public-coin, succinct interactive argument of knowledge for $\mathcal{L}_{2^m,\Gamma_1,\Gamma_2,H_1,H_2}$ with $(9^{m+1}, 10.5 \cdot 9^m/|\mathbb{F}|)$-tree extractability under SXDH. If $n = 2^m = \mathtt{poly}(\lambda)$ then Dory-Innerproduct has witness extended emulation.*

Proof. Since $\Gamma_{i,0} \xleftarrow{\$} \mathbb{G}_i^{2^m}$, for any $j \geq 0$ we have $\Gamma_{i,j} \xleftarrow{\$} \mathbb{G}_i^{2^{m-j}}$ as it is the first 2^{m-j} elements of $\Gamma_{i,0}$. So for each round the requirements of Theorems 2 and 1 are satisfied. Succinctness, the Public Coin property, Completeness and HVSZK follow from the same properties of the two sub-arguments.

Tree-extractability follows from Lemma 4 applied round by round. We have $m + 1$ rounds each with $W = 9$, and the error bound ϵ is given by $(9^{m+1} + 12(9^m + 9^{m-1} + \ldots))/|\mathbb{F}| = 10.5 \cdot 9^m/|\mathbb{F}|$. When $n = 2^m = \mathtt{poly}(\lambda)$, then $W = \mathcal{O}(n^{\log 9}) = \mathtt{poly}(\lambda)$ and $\epsilon = \mathcal{O}(n^{\log 9}/|\mathbb{F}|) = \mathtt{negl}(\lambda)$. Witness extended emulation follows from Lemma 5.

Concrete costs of Dory-Innerproduct $\mathcal{P}$: In each call to Dory-Reduce, $\mathcal{P}$ sends 6 elements of $\mathbb{G}_T$ to $\mathcal{V}$. For the j-th call $\mathcal{P}$ performs 6 multi-pairings of size 2^{m-j-1}, $O(2^{m-j})$ operations in $\mathbb{F}$, and $O(1)$ operations in $\mathbb{G}_T$. For the call to Scalar-Product, $\mathcal{P}$ computes $O(1)$ pairings and exponentiations in $\mathbb{G}_T$. So the overall cost to $\mathcal{P}$ is dominated by multi-pairings of total size 6×2^m, $O(m)$ group operations, and $O(2^m)$ field arithmetic.

$\mathcal{V}$: Naively, in each invocation of Dory-Reduce $\mathcal{V}$ computes 10 exponentiations in $\mathbb{G}_T$, 2 inversions and 2 multiplications in $\mathbb{F}$, and $O(1)$ additional operations in $\mathbb{G}_T$ and additions in $\mathbb{F}$. In the invocation of Scalar-Product $\mathcal{V}$ computes 1 pairing, 7 exponentiations in $\mathbb{G}_T$, 1 inversion and 5 multiplications in $\mathbb{F}$, and $O(1)$ additional operations in $\mathbb{G}_T$ and additions in $\mathbb{F}$.

Deferring $\mathcal{V}$ Computation: $\mathcal{V}$'s computation depends only on the messages from $\mathcal{P}$ and the $4m+1$ precomputed values. For each call to Dory-Reduce, $\mathcal{V}$ uses the values $\Delta_{1L} = \Delta_{2L}, \Delta_{1R}, \Delta_{2R}, \chi$, and in the final check $\mathcal{V}$ uses $e(\Gamma_{1m}, \Gamma_{2m})$. We will use superscripts on group elements and subscripts on the challenge scalars to denote which call they came from. We assume that we precompute $\Delta^j_{\{1,2\}\{L,R\}}$ as before, but instead of computing χ_i for $i \in 0 \ldots m$, we compute: $\chi = \sum_{j=0}^{m-1} \langle \Gamma_{1j}, \Gamma_{2j} \rangle$ and $\chi_{fin} = \langle \Gamma_{1m}, \Gamma_{2m} \rangle$. Collapsing the Dory-Reduce rounds, we obtain the arguments for Scalar-Product:

$$C \leftarrow C + \chi + \beta_0 D_2^0 + \beta_0^{-1} D_1^0 + \sum_{j=0}^{m-1} (\alpha_j C_+^j + \alpha_j^{-1} C_-^j)$$

$$+ \sum_{j=1}^{m-1} \beta_j (\alpha_{j-1}^{-1} D_{2L}^{j-1} + D_{2R}^{j-1} + \alpha_{j-1}^{-1}\beta_{j-1}^{-1}\Delta_{2L}^{j-1} + \beta_{j-1}^{-1}\Delta_{2R}^{j-1})$$

$$+ \sum_{j=1}^{m-1} \beta_j^{-1} (\alpha_{j-1} D_{1L}^{j-1} + D_{1R}^{j-1} + \alpha_{j-1}\beta_{j-1}\Delta_{1L}^{j-1} + \beta_{j-1}\Delta_{1R}^{j-1})$$

$$D_1 \leftarrow \alpha_{j-1} D_{1L}^{m-1} + D_{1R}^{m-1} + \alpha_{m-1}\beta_{m-1}\Delta_{1L}^{m-1} + \beta_{m-1}\Delta_{1R}^{m-1}$$

$$D_2 \leftarrow \alpha_{j-1}^{-1} D_{2L}^{m-1} + D_{2R}^{m-1} + \alpha_{m-1}^{-1}\beta_{m-1}^{-1}\Delta_{2L}^{m-1} + \beta_{m-1}^{-1}\Delta_{2R}^{m-1}$$

which are substituted into the check in Scalar-Product. This reduces $\mathcal{V}$'s group operations to a multi-exponentiation in $\mathbb{G}_T$ of size $9m+9$, two exponentiations in $\mathbb{G}_T$, and one pairing. Using Montgomery's trick for batch inversions, we compute the coefficients with one inversion and $O(m)$ multiplications and additions in $\mathbb{F}$.

3.4   Batching Inner Products

Suppose we have $(C, D_1, D_2), (C', D_1', D_2') \in \mathcal{L}_{n,\Gamma_1,\Gamma_2,H_1,H_2}$, and $\mathcal{P}$ possesses witnesses $(\vec{v_1}, \vec{v_2}, r_C, r_{D_1}, r_{D_2})$ and $(\vec{v_1}', \vec{v_2}', r_C', r_{D_1}', r_{D_2}')$ respectively. Then we have the following two-to-one interactive argument:

Batch-Innerproduct$_{\Gamma_1, \Gamma_2}(C, D_1, D_2, C', D_1', D_2')$
Precompute: $H_T = e(H_1, H_2) \in G_T$
  $\mathcal{P}$ **witness:**$(\vec{v_1}, \vec{v_2}, r_C, r_{D_1}, r_{D_2})$ for $(C, D_1, D_2) \in \mathcal{L}_{n,\Gamma_1,\Gamma_2,H_1,H_2}$, and
  $(\vec{v_1}', \vec{v_2}', r_C', r_{D_1}', r_{D_2}')$ for $(C', D_1', D_2') \in \mathcal{L}_{n,\Gamma_1,\Gamma_2,H_1,H_2}$
$\mathcal{P}$: $r_X \leftarrow_\$ \mathbb{F}$
$\mathcal{P} \to \mathcal{V}$: $X = \langle \vec{v_1}, \vec{v_2}' \rangle + \langle \vec{v_1}', \vec{v_2} \rangle + r_X H_T$
$\mathcal{V} \to \mathcal{P}$: $\gamma \leftarrow_\$ \mathbb{F}$
$\mathcal{P}$: $\vec{v_1}'' \leftarrow \gamma \vec{v_1} + \vec{v_1}'$, $\vec{v_2}'' \leftarrow \gamma \vec{v_2} + \vec{v_2}'$,
  $r_{D_1}'' \leftarrow \gamma r_{D_1} + r_{D_1}'$, $r_{D_2}'' \leftarrow \gamma r_{D_2} + r_{D_2}'$, $r_C'' \leftarrow \gamma^2 r_C + \gamma r_X + r_C'$
$\mathcal{V}$: $D_1'' \leftarrow \gamma D_1 + D_1'$, $D_2'' \leftarrow \gamma D_2 + D_2'$, $C'' \leftarrow \gamma^2 C + \gamma X + C'$,
$\mathcal{V}$: Accept if $(C'', D_1'', D_2'') \in \mathcal{L}_{n,\Gamma_1,\Gamma_2,H_1,H_2}$
  $\mathcal{P}$ **witness:** $(\vec{v_1}'', \vec{v_2}'', r_C'', r_{D_1}'', r_{D_2}'')$

Theorem 4. *If $\Gamma_i \overset{\$}{\leftarrow} \mathbb{G}_i^n$, $H_i \overset{\$}{\leftarrow} G_i$, Batch-Innerproduct is an HVSZK, public-coin, succinct interactive argument of knowledge for $(\mathcal{L}_{n,\Gamma_1,\Gamma_2,H_1,H_2})^2$ with $(3, 3/|\mathbb{F}|)$-tree extractability under SXDH.*

Proof. Succinctness, the Public Coin property, Completeness, Soundness and HVSZK of this protocol are immediate.

To show tree extractability, we have $\mu = 1$ and set $w_1 = 3$. We are given witnesses for 3 distinct challenges γ. For $i \in \{1, 2\}$, we interpolate $\vec{v_i}''$ and r_{D_i}'' as quadratics in γ. Then from Lemma 6, the contribution of the quadratic terms to $D_i'' = \gamma D_i + D_i'$ is identically zero, and so from Lemma 3 there are no quadratic terms. Hence $\vec{v_i}''(\gamma) = \gamma \vec{v_i} + \vec{v_i}'$ for some $\vec{v_i}$ and $\vec{v_i}'$, and $r_{D_i}''(\gamma) = \gamma r + D_i + r_{D_i}'$, compatible with the commitments D_i, D_i'. Interpolating $r_C''(\gamma) = r_C' + \gamma r_X + \gamma^2 r_C$ and substituting in our affine $\vec{v_i}$:

$$\gamma^2 C + \gamma X + C' = C''(\gamma) = \langle \vec{v_1}''(\gamma), \vec{v_2}''(\gamma) \rangle + r_C''(\gamma) H_T$$
$$= \gamma^2(\langle \vec{v_1}, \vec{v_2}\rangle + r_C H_T) + \gamma(\langle \vec{v_1}, \vec{v_2}'\rangle + \langle \vec{v_1}', \vec{v_2}\rangle + r_X H_T) + (\langle \vec{v_1}', \vec{v_2}'\rangle + r_C' H_T).$$

Since this holds for 3 values of γ, Lemma 6 implies that the two polynomials have identical coefficients, so $C = \langle \vec{v_1}, \vec{v_2}\rangle + r_C H_T$ and $C' = \langle \vec{v_1}', \vec{v_2}'\rangle + r_C' H_T$ and we have extracted the required witnesses.

Concretely, in Batch-Innerproduct messages from $\mathcal{P}$ to $\mathcal{V}$ have size $|G_T|$; $\mathcal{P}$'s computation is clearly dominated by an $2n$-sized multi-pairing and $\mathcal{V}$'s computation is clearly $O(1)$ exponentiations in $\mathbb{G}_T$.

4   Inner Products with Public Vectors of Scalars

In the previous section, we constructed Dory-Innerproduct, a succinct argument of knowledge for generalised inner products between committed vectors in $\mathbb{G}_1^n$ and $\mathbb{G}_2^n$. For a polynomial commitment scheme we also require the ability to prove products of committed vectors with vectors of scalars with multiplicative structure. However, this structure is not preserved when instances are batched, so we will extend our arguments to allow for general vectors in $\mathbb{F}^n$. We define a family of languages, parameterised by a pair of vectors $\vec{s_1}, \vec{s_2} \in \mathbb{F}^n$:

$$(C, D_1, D_2, E_1, E_2) \in \mathcal{L}_{n,\Gamma_1,\Gamma_2,H_1,H_2}(\vec{s_1}, \vec{s_2}) \subset \mathbb{G}_T^3 \times \mathbb{G}_1 \times \mathbb{G}_2$$
$$\Leftrightarrow \exists(\vec{v_1} \in \mathbb{G}_1^n, \vec{v_2} \in \mathbb{G}_2^n, r_C, r_{D_1}, r_{D_2}, r_{E_1}, r_{E_2} \in \mathbb{F}):$$
$$D_1 = \langle \vec{v_1}, \Gamma_2 \rangle + r_{D_1} \cdot e(H_1, H_2), \quad D_2 = \langle \Gamma_1, \vec{v_2} \rangle + r_{D_2} \cdot e(H_1, H_2),$$
$$E_1 = \langle \vec{v_1}, \vec{s_2} \rangle + r_{E_1} H_1, \qquad E_2 = \langle \vec{s_1}, \vec{v_2} \rangle + r_{E_2} H_2,$$
$$C = \langle \vec{v_1}, \vec{v_2} \rangle + r_C \cdot e(H_1, H_2),$$

We extend the arguments of the previous section to these languages. Note that $(C, D_1, D_2, E_1, E_2) \in \mathcal{L}_{n,\Gamma_1,\Gamma_2,H_1,H_2}(\vec{s_1}, \vec{s_2})$ implies $(C, D_1, D_2) \in \mathcal{L}_{n,\Gamma_1,\Gamma_2,H_1,H_2}$.

4.1   General Reduction with $O(n)$ cost

There is a reduction from $\mathcal{L}_{n,\Gamma_1,\Gamma_2,H_1,H_2}(\vec{s_1}, \vec{s_2})$ to $\mathcal{L}_{n,\Gamma_1,\Gamma_2,H_1,H_2}$, with $O(n)$ cost to $\mathcal{P}, \mathcal{V}$, where the $\vec{s_i}$ are essentially multiplied by some $\mathcal{V}$-selected challenge in $\mathbb{G}_i$ and added to the witness vectors.

Fold-Scalars$_{n, \Gamma_1, \Gamma_2, H_1, H_2}(C, D_1, D_2, E_1, E_2, \vec{s_1}, \vec{s_2})$

Precompute: $H_T = e(H_1, H_2)$

   $\mathcal{P}$ **witness:** $(\vec{v_1}, \vec{v_2}, r_C, r_{D_1} r_{D_2}, r_{E_1}, r_{E_2})$ for

   $(C, D_1, D_2, E_1, E_2) \in \mathcal{L}_{n, \Gamma_1, \Gamma_2, H_1, H_2}(\vec{s_1}, \vec{s_2})$

$\mathcal{V} \to \mathcal{P}$: $\gamma \xleftarrow{\$} \mathbb{F}$

$\mathcal{P}(**)$: $\vec{v_1}' \leftarrow \vec{v_1} + \gamma \vec{s_1} H_1,$ $\vec{v_2}' \leftarrow \vec{v_2} + \gamma^{-1} \vec{s_2} H_2,$

        $r_C' \leftarrow r_C + \gamma r_{E_2} + \gamma^{-1} r_{E_1}$

$\mathcal{V}(**)$: $C' \leftarrow C + \langle \vec{s_1}, \vec{s_2} \rangle H_T + \gamma \cdot e(H_1, E_2) + \gamma^{-1} \cdot e(E_1, H_2),$

        $D_1' \leftarrow D_1 + e(H_1, \langle \vec{s_1}, \gamma \Gamma_2 \rangle),$ $D_2' \leftarrow D_2 + e(\gamma^{-1} \langle \Gamma_1, \vec{s_2} \rangle, H_2)$

$\mathcal{V}$: Accept if $(C', D_1', D_2') \in \mathcal{L}_{n, \Gamma_1, \Gamma_2, H_1, H_2}$

   $\mathcal{P}$ **witness:** $(\vec{v_1}', \vec{v_2}', r_C', r_{D_1}, r_{D_2})$

Theorem 5. *For $\Gamma_i \xleftarrow{\$} \mathbb{G}_i^n$, $H_i \xleftarrow{\$} G_i$, Fold-Scalars is an HVSZK, public-coin, succinct interactive argument of knowledge for $\mathcal{L}_{n, \Gamma_1, \Gamma_2, H_1, H_2}(\vec{s_1}, \vec{s_2})$ with $(3, 3/|\mathbb{F}|)$-tree extractability under SXDH.*

Proof. Completeness, Succinctness and Public-Coin are immediate. $\mathcal{P}$ messages are independent and uniformly random, so zero-knowledge is straightforward.

To show tree-extractability, we have $\mu = 1$ and $w_1 = 3$. We have 3 challenges of γ, and fail if any are 0, which occurs with probability at most $3/|\mathbb{F}|$. For $i \in \{1, 2\}$, we interpolate v_i' and r_i' as degree 1 order 1 Laurent polynomials in γ. Then from Lemma 6, the contribution of the γ^{-1} terms of v_1' and r_1' to D_1' are identically zero, and so from Lemma 3 there are no γ^{-1} terms. Similarly the γ term of $\vec{v_1}'$ must be $H_1 \vec{s_1}$. Similarly there are no γ terms in $\vec{v_2}'$ and r_2', and the γ^{-1} term of v_2' must be $H_2 \vec{s_2}$. So we find some $\vec{v_1}, \vec{v_2}$ such that: $\vec{v_1}'(\gamma) = \vec{v_1} + \gamma \vec{s_1} H_1,$ $\vec{v_2}'(\gamma) = \vec{v_2} + \gamma^{-1} \vec{s_2} H_2$. We interpolate $r_C'(\gamma) = r_C + \gamma r_{E_2} + \gamma^{-1} r_{E_1}$, and get:

$$C'(\gamma) = C + \langle \vec{s_1}, \vec{s_2} \rangle H_T + \gamma \cdot e(H_1, E_2) + \gamma^{-1} \cdot e(E_1, H_2)$$
$$= \langle \vec{v_1}'(\gamma), \vec{v_2}'(\gamma) \rangle + r_C'(\gamma) H_T$$
$$= \langle \vec{v_1}, \vec{v_2} \rangle + (r_C' + \langle \vec{s_1}, \vec{s_2} \rangle) H_T$$
$$+ \gamma \cdot e(H_1, \langle \vec{s_1}, \vec{v_2} \rangle + r_{E_2} H_2) + \gamma^{-1} \cdot e(\langle \vec{v_1}, \vec{s_2} \rangle + r_{E_1} H_1, H_2).$$

Since this holds for 3 values of γ, the $1, \gamma, \gamma^{-1}$ Lemma 6 implies that the coefficients must be equal, which immediately implies we have extracted the required witness.

4.2 Extending Dory-Reduce

We add $E_{1\beta} = \langle \Gamma_1, \vec{s_2} \rangle$, $E_{2\beta} = \langle \vec{s_1}, \Gamma_2 \rangle$ to $\mathcal{P}$'s first message. Prior to their second message, $\mathcal{P}$ samples $r_{E_{\{1,2\}}\{+,-\}} \xleftarrow{\$} \mathbb{F}$ and adds

$$\mathcal{P} \to \mathcal{V}: \quad E_{1+} = \langle \vec{v_{1L}}, \vec{s_{2R}} \rangle + r_{E_{1+}} H_1, \quad E_{1-} = \langle \vec{v_{1R}}, \vec{s_{2L}} \rangle + r_{E_{1-}} H_1,$$
$$E_{2+} = \langle \vec{s_{1L}}, \vec{v_{2R}} \rangle + r_{E_{2+}} H_2, \quad E_{2-} = \langle \vec{s_{1R}}, \vec{v_{2L}} \rangle + r_{E_{2-}} H_2$$

to their second message. After $\mathcal{P}$'s second message, $\mathcal{P}$ and $\mathcal{V}$ compute:

$$\mathcal{P}: \quad r'_{E_1} \leftarrow r_{E_1} + \alpha r_{E_{1+}} + \alpha^{-1} r_{E_{2-}}, \quad r'_{E_2} \leftarrow r_{E_2} + \alpha r_{E_{2+}} + \alpha^{-1} r_{E_{2-}}.$$
$$\mathcal{V}: \quad E'_1 \leftarrow E_1 + \beta E_{1\beta} + \alpha E_{1+} + \alpha^{-1} E_{2-},$$
$$E'_2 \leftarrow E_2 + \beta^{-1} E_{2\beta} + \alpha E_{2+} + \alpha^{-1} E_{2-},$$
$$\mathcal{P}, \mathcal{V}: \quad \vec{s_1}' \leftarrow \alpha \vec{s_{1L}} + \vec{s_{1R}}, \quad \vec{s_2}' \leftarrow \alpha^{-1} \vec{s_{2L}} + \vec{s_{2R}}$$

Theorem 6. *For $\Gamma'_2 \overset{\$}{\leftarrow} \mathbb{G}_2^{m-1}, H_2 \overset{\$}{\leftarrow} \mathbb{G}_2, \Gamma_1 \overset{\$}{\leftarrow} \mathbb{G}_2^{m-1}, H_1 \overset{\$}{\leftarrow} \mathbb{G}_1$, the extended Dory-Reduce is an HVSZK, public-coin, succinct interactive argument of knowledge for $\mathcal{L}_{2^m, \Gamma_1, \Gamma_2, H_1, H_2}(\vec{s_1}, \vec{s_2})$ with $(9, 12/|\mathbb{F}|)$-tree extractability under SXDH.*

Proof. Succinctness and the Public Coin properties are immediate. Completeness and HVSZK hold as in the proof of Theorem 2. $(9, 12/|\mathbb{F}|)$-tree extractability is implied by Theorem 2 as a witness for $(C, D_1, D_2) \in \mathcal{L}_{n, \Gamma_1, \Gamma_2, H_1, H_2}$ suffices.

4.3 Extending Dory-Innerproduct

We use the extended Dory-Reduce, and apply Fold-Scalars at $n = 1$:

Dory-Innerproduct$_{\Gamma_{1,0}, \Gamma_{2,0}, H_1, H_2}(C, D_1, D_2, E_1, E_2, \vec{s_1}, \vec{s_2})$
Precompute: $H_T = e(H_1, H_2)$, for all $i \in 0 \ldots m - 1$ compute:

$$\Gamma_{1,i+1} = (\Gamma_{1,i})_L, \qquad \Gamma_{2,i+1} = (\Gamma_{2,i})_L,$$
$$\Delta_{1L,i} = \langle (\Gamma_{1,i})_L, \Gamma_{2,i+1} \rangle, \quad \Delta_{1R,i} = \langle (\Gamma_{1,i})_R, \Gamma_{2,i+1} \rangle,$$
$$\Delta_{2L,i} = \langle \Gamma_{1,i+1}, (\Gamma_{2,i})_L \rangle, \quad \Delta_{2R,i} = \langle \Gamma_{1,i+1}, (\Gamma_{2,i})_R \rangle,$$

and for all $i \in 0 \ldots m$ compute $\chi_i = \langle \Gamma_{1i}, \Gamma_{2i} \rangle$.
$\mathcal{P}$ **witness:** $(\vec{v_1}, \vec{v_2}, r_C, r_{D_1}, r_{D_2}, r_{E_1}, r_{E_2})$ for
$(C, D_1, D_2, E_1, E_2) \in \mathcal{L}_{2^m, \Gamma_{1,0}, \Gamma_{2,0}, H_1, H_2}(\vec{s_1}, \vec{s_2})$
For $j = 0 \ldots m - 1$
$\quad \mathcal{P}, \mathcal{V}: (C, D_1, D_2, E_1, E_2, \vec{s_1}, \vec{s_2}) \leftarrow$
$\qquad$ Dory-Reduce$_{m-j, \Gamma_{1,j}, \Gamma_{2,j}, \Gamma_{1,j+1}, \Gamma_{2,j+1}, H_1, H_2}(C, D_1, D_2, E_1, E_2, \vec{s_1}, \vec{s_2})$
$\quad \mathcal{P}, \mathcal{V}: (C, D_1, D_2) \leftarrow$ Fold-Scalars$_{\Gamma_{1,m}, \Gamma_{2,m}, H_1, H_2}(C, D_1, D_2, E_1, E_2, \vec{s_1}, \vec{s_2})$
$\quad \mathcal{P}, \mathcal{V}:$ Scalar-Product$_{\Gamma_{1,m}, \Gamma_{2,m}, H_1, H_2}(C, D_1, D_2)$

Theorem 7. *If $\Gamma_{1,0} \overset{\$}{\leftarrow} \mathbb{G}_1^{2^m}, \Gamma_{2,0} \overset{\$}{\leftarrow} \mathbb{G}_2^{2^m}, H_1 \overset{\$}{\leftarrow} \mathbb{G}_1$ and $H_2 \overset{\$}{\leftarrow} \mathbb{G}_2$, then the extended Dory-Innerproduct is an HVSZK, public-coin, succinct interactive argument of knowledge for $\mathcal{L}_{2^m, \Gamma_1, \Gamma_2, H_1, H_2}(\vec{s_1}, \vec{s_2})$ with $(9^{m+1}, 10.5 \cdot 9^m/|\mathbb{F}|)$-tree extractability under SXDH. If $n = 2^m = \text{poly}(\lambda)$ then the extended Dory-Innerproduct has witness extended emulation.*

Proof. Succinctness and the Public Coin properties are immediate. Completeness and HVSZK hold as in the proof of Theorem 3. Tree-extractability and witness extended emulation when $n = \texttt{poly}(\lambda)$ is implied by Theorem 3 as a witness for $(C, D_1, D_2) \in \mathcal{L}_{n, \Gamma_1, \Gamma_2, H_1, H_2}$ suffices.

Concrete Costs of the Extended Dory-Innerproduct $\mathcal{P}$ sends 3 additional elements of $\mathbb{G}_1$ and $\mathbb{G}_2$ in each invocation of Dory-Reduce. $\mathcal{P}$ also computes exponentiations of total size $2 \times 2^{m-j}$ exponentiations in $\mathbb{G}_1$ and $\mathbb{G}_2$, and $O(2^{m-j})$ additional field arithmetic. So in total, $\mathcal{P}$'s work is: $(6P + 4\mathbb{G}_2 + 4\mathbb{G}_1 + O(1)\mathbb{F}) \times n + o(n)$ which is dominated by the $6n$ pairings, especially as multi-exponentiations in $\mathbb{G}_1, \mathbb{G}_2$ can be accelerated with variants of Pippenger's algorithm. The total size of $\mathcal{P}$'s messages is: $(6|G_T| + 3|G_2| + 3|G_1|) \log n + 4|G_T| + |G_2| + |G_1| + 5|\mathbb{F}|$. As before, $\mathcal{V}$ defers computation to reduce their costs. To compute the C, E_1, E_2 passed to Fold-Scalars requires, respectively, a multi-exponentiation in $\mathbb{G}_T$ of size $9m + 9$, a multi-exponentiation in $\mathbb{G}_1$ of size 4 m and a multi-exponentiation in $\mathbb{G}_2$ of size 4 m. The computation of the final D_1, D_2 and verification of Fold-Scalars and Scalar-Product require 3 additional pairings and $O(1)$ exponentiations. Whilst naively there are 5 pairings, 2 of them are pairings with H_1 and 2 are pairings with H_2, which can be combined in the final check of Scalar-Product.

$\mathcal{V}$ must also compute the final $\vec{s_1}, \vec{s_2}$ used as arguments to Fold-Scalars. In particular, these are the scalars: $\langle \vec{s_1}, \otimes_{i=0}^{m-1}(\alpha_i, 1) \rangle$, $\langle \vec{s_2}, \otimes_{i=0}^{m-1}(\alpha_i^{-1}, 1) \rangle$. For general vectors $\vec{s_1}, \vec{s_2}$, these require $O(n)$ operations in $\mathbb{F}$. However, when the vectors $\vec{s_i}$ themselves have multiplicative structure, we have the identity:

$$\langle \otimes_{i=0}^{m-1}(\ell_i, r_i), \otimes_{i=0}^{m-1}(a_i, 1) \rangle = \prod_{i=0}^{m-1} (\ell_i a_i + r_i),$$

which allows the computation of the product in $O(m)$ operations in $\mathbb{F}$. Similarly, a vector that can be written as a sum of ℓ vectors with multiplicative structure can have this inner product computed in $O(\ell m)$ operations in $\mathbb{F}$ (as in Sect. 4.4).

4.4 Extending Batch-Innerproduct

$\mathcal{P}$ samples $r_{Y_1}, r_{Y_2} \xleftarrow{\$} \mathbb{F}$, and we add:

$$\mathcal{P} \rightarrow \mathcal{V}: \quad Y_1 = \langle \vec{v_1}, \vec{s_2}' \rangle + \langle \vec{v_1}', \vec{s_2} \rangle + r_{Y_1} H_1, \quad Y_2 = \langle \vec{s_1}', \vec{v_2} \rangle + \langle \vec{s_1}, \vec{v_2}' \rangle + r_{Y_2} H_2$$

to $\mathcal{P}$'s first message. After receiving γ, $\mathcal{P}$ and $\mathcal{V}$ compute:

$$
\begin{aligned}
&\mathcal{P}: \quad r_{E_1}'' \leftarrow \gamma^2 r_{E_1} + \gamma r_{Y_1} + r_{E_1}', \quad r_{E_2}'' \leftarrow \gamma^2 r_{E_2} + \gamma r_{Y_2} + r_{E_2}' \\
&\mathcal{V}: \quad E_1'' \leftarrow \gamma^2 E_1 + \gamma Y_1 + E_1', \quad E_2'' \leftarrow \gamma^2 E_2 + \gamma Y_2 + E_2' \\
&\mathcal{P}, \mathcal{V}: \quad \vec{s_1}'' \leftarrow \gamma \vec{s_2} + \vec{s_2}', \quad \vec{s_2}'' \leftarrow \gamma \vec{s_1} + \vec{s_1}'
\end{aligned}
$$

Theorem 8. *If $\Gamma_1 \xleftarrow{\$} \mathbb{G}_1^n$, $\Gamma_2 \xleftarrow{\$} \mathbb{G}_2^n$, $H_1 \xleftarrow{\$} \mathbb{G}_1$ and $H_2 \xleftarrow{\$} \mathbb{G}_2$, the extended Batch-Innerproduct is an HVSZK, public-coin, succinct interactive argument of knowledge for $\mathcal{L}_{n,\Gamma_1,\Gamma_2,H_1,H_2}(\vec{s_1},\vec{s_2}) \times \mathcal{L}_{n,\Gamma_1,\Gamma_2,H_1,H_2}(\vec{s_1}',\vec{s_2}')$ with witness extended emulation under SXDH.*

Proof. Succinctness and the Public Coin properties are immediate. Completeness and HVSZK hold following the proof of Theorem 4. Witness extended emulation is implied by Theorem 4, as a witness for membership of $(\mathcal{L}_{n,\Gamma_1,\Gamma_2,H_1,H_2})^2$ suffices.

$\mathcal{P}$'s messages to $\mathcal{V}$ have size $|\mathbb{G}_T| + |\mathbb{G}_2| + |\mathbb{G}_1|$. As before, $\mathcal{P}$'s computation is dominated by a $2n$-size multi-pairing and $\mathcal{V}$'s group operations are $O(1)$ exponentiations. For general vectors $\vec{s_1}, \vec{s_2}$, $\mathcal{V}$ must perform $O(n)$ operations in $\mathbb{F}$. However, if $\vec{s_i}, \vec{s_i}'$ are some linear combination of ℓ, ℓ' vectors with multiplicative structure, then s_i'' is a linear combination of $\ell + \ell'$ vectors with multiplicative structure; this representation can be computed in $O(m)$ operations in $\mathbb{F}$.

5   Vector-Matrix-Vector Products

Let $n = 2^m$. Fix some commitment scheme for $\mathbb{F}$ and $\mathbb{F}^{n\times n}$ with public parameters $pp_{\mathbb{F}}$, $pp_{\mathbb{F}^{n\times n}}$ respectively, and define:

$$(\mathcal{C}_M, \mathcal{C}_y, \vec{L}, \vec{R}) \in \mathcal{L}_{VMV,n,pp_{\mathbb{F}^{n\times n}},pp_{\mathbb{F}}} \subset \mathbb{G}_T \times \mathbb{G}_1 \times \mathbb{F}^n \times \mathbb{F}^n$$
$$\Leftrightarrow \exists (M \in \mathbb{F}^{n\times n}, y \in \mathbb{F}, \mathcal{S}_M, \mathcal{S}_y) : y = \vec{L}^T M \vec{R},$$
$$Open(pp_{\mathbb{F}^{n\times n}}, \mathcal{C}_M, M, \mathcal{S}_M) = 1, \ Open(pp_{\mathbb{F}}, \mathcal{C}_y, y, \mathcal{S}_y) = 1.$$

This is a stepping stone to polynomial commitments, in which $\vec{L}, \vec{R}$ will have multiplicative structure. For a batch of ℓ evaluations these vectors will be linear combinations of ℓ vectors with multiplicative structure. We require public parameters pp_{VMV}, generated by the public coin Gen_{VMV}:

$$\Gamma_{1,0}, \Gamma_{1,fin}, H_1 \xleftarrow{\$} \mathbb{G}_1^{2^m} \times \mathbb{G}_1 \times \mathbb{G}_1, \quad \Gamma_{2,0}, \Gamma_{2,fin}, H_2 \xleftarrow{\$} \mathbb{G}_2^{2^m} \times \mathbb{G}_2 \times \mathbb{G}_2,$$

$$\forall i \in 1, \ldots, m: \qquad \Gamma_{1,i} = (\Gamma_{1,i})_L, \qquad\qquad \Gamma_{2,i} = (\Gamma_{2,i})_L,$$
$$\forall i \in 0, \ldots, m-1: \quad \Delta_{1L,i} = \langle \Gamma_{1,i+1}, \Gamma_{2,i+1} \rangle, \qquad \Delta_{2L,i} = \langle \Gamma_{1,i+1}, \Gamma_{2,i+1} \rangle,$$
$$\forall i \in 0, \ldots, m-1: \quad \Delta_{1R,i} = \langle (\Gamma_{1,i})_R, \Gamma_{2,i+1} \rangle, \qquad \Delta_{2R,i} = \langle \Gamma_{1,i+1}, (\Gamma_{2,i})_R \rangle,$$

$$\chi = \sum_{j=0}^{m-1} \langle \Gamma_{1,j}, \Gamma_{2,j} \rangle, \qquad \chi_{fin} = \langle \Gamma_{1m}, \Gamma_{2m} \rangle$$

$$H_T = e(H_1, H_2) \qquad\qquad \Upsilon = e(H_1, \Gamma_{2,fin})$$

We fix Pedersen commitment parameters $pp_{\mathbb{F}} = (\Gamma_{1,fin}, H_1)$, and parameters $pp_{\mathbb{F}^{n\times n}} = \{\Gamma_{1,0}, H_1, \Gamma_{2,0}, H_2\}$ for the matrix commitment from Sect. 2.4. Recall that if $\mathsf{Commit}(pp, M) = (T, (\vec{r_{\text{rows}}}, r_{\text{fin}}, \vec{T}'))$, then $\vec{T}' \in \mathbb{G}_1^n$ is a vector of Pedersen commitments to the rows of M with generators $(\Gamma_{1,0}; H_1)$, and T is a AFGHO commitment to $\vec{T}'$ with generators $(\Gamma_{2,0}; H_2)$. So T is a hiding commitment to M. The alert reader may note that $\vec{T}'$ depends only on M and $\vec{r_{\text{rows}}}$; it is retained in the opening hint by $\mathcal{P}$ to accelerate the evaluation proof.

The general strategy for an argument of knowledge for $\mathcal{L}_{VMV, n, pp_{\mathbb{F}^{n \times n}}, pp_{\mathbb{F}}}$ is as follows. The commitment to $y = \vec{L}^T M \vec{R}$ is $y_{com} = y\Gamma_{1,fin} + r_y H_1$. $\mathcal{P}$ can compute the vector $\vec{v} = \vec{L}^T M$, and by construction $y = \vec{L}^T M \vec{R} = \langle \vec{v}, \vec{R} \rangle$. Since the commitment is linearly homomorphic: $v_{com} := \langle \vec{L}, C' \rangle = \mathsf{Commit}_{\Gamma_{1,0}; H_1}(\vec{v}; \langle \vec{L}, \vec{r_{\text{rows}}} \rangle)$ is a hiding commitment to $\vec{v}$ with blind $r_v = \langle \vec{L}, \vec{r_{\text{rows}}} \rangle$. Recall also that T is a hiding commitment to $\vec{T}' \in \mathbb{G}_1^n$. So to prove $(T, y_{com}, \vec{L}, \vec{R}) \in \mathcal{L}_{VMV, n, pp_{\mathbb{F}^{n \times n}}, pp_{\mathbb{F}}}$, it suffices to prove knowledge of $\vec{T}' \in \mathbb{G}_1^n, \vec{v} \in \mathbb{F}^n, r_v, r_{\text{fin}}, r_y \in \mathbb{F}$ such that: $T = \langle \vec{T}', \Gamma_2 \rangle + r_{\text{fin}} H_T$, $\langle \vec{L}, \vec{T}' \rangle = \langle \vec{v}, \Gamma_1 \rangle + r_v H_1$, and $y_{com} = \langle \vec{v}, \vec{R} \rangle \Gamma_{1,fin} + r_y H_1$

$\mathsf{Eval\text{-}VMV\text{-}RE}_{pp_{VMV}}(T, y_{com}, \vec{L}, \vec{R})$

  $\mathcal{P}$ **witness:** $M, (\vec{T}', \vec{r_{\text{rows}}}, r_{\text{fin}}), r_y$

  $\mathcal{P}$: $\vec{v} = \vec{L}^T M$, $r_v = \langle \vec{L}, \vec{r_{\text{rows}}} \rangle$, $y = \langle \vec{v}, \vec{R} \rangle$, $r_C, r_{D_2}, r_{E_1}, r_{E_2} \xleftarrow{\$} \mathbb{F}$

  $\mathcal{P} \to \mathcal{V}$: $\quad C = e(\langle \vec{v}, \vec{T}' \rangle, \Gamma_{2,fin}) + r_C H_T$, $\quad D_2 = e(\langle \Gamma_1, \vec{v} \rangle, \Gamma_{2,fin}) + r_{D_2} H_T$,

  $\qquad\qquad E_1 = \langle \vec{L}, C' \rangle + r_{E_1} H_1$, $\qquad\qquad E_2 = y\Gamma_{2,fin} + r_{E_2} H_2$,

  $\mathcal{P}, \mathcal{V}$: Σ-protocol showing $\mathcal{P}$ knows $s \in \mathbb{F}^3$:

   $E_2 = s_1 \Gamma_{2,fin} + s_2 H_2 \wedge y_C = s_1 \Gamma_{1,fin} + s_3 H_1$

   $\mathcal{P}$ **witness:** $s = (y, r_{E_2}, r_y)$

  $\mathcal{P}, \mathcal{V}$: Σ-protocol showing $\mathcal{P}$ knows $t \in \mathbb{F}^2$:

   $e(E_1, \Gamma_{2,fin}) - D_2 = e(H_1, t_1 \Gamma_{2,fin} + t_2 H_2)$

   $\mathcal{P}$ **witness:** $t = (r_{E_1} + r_v, -r_{D_2})$

  $\mathcal{P}, \mathcal{V}$: $\mathsf{Dory\text{-}Innerproduct}_{\Gamma_{1,0}, \Gamma_{2,0}, H_1, H_2}(C, T, D_2, E_1, E_2, L, \vec{R})$.

   $\mathcal{P}$ **witness:** $(\vec{T}', \vec{v}\Gamma_{2,fin}, r_C, r_{\text{fin}}, r_{D_2}, r_{E_1}, r_{E_2})$

Theorem 9. *For pp_{VMV} sampled as above, $\mathsf{Eval\text{-}VMV\text{-}RE}$ is an HVSZK, public-coin, complete, succinct interactive argument of knowledge for $\mathcal{L}_{VMV}$. Assuming SXDH: If for fixed T and tuples $(\vec{L}^i, \vec{R}^i, y_{com}^i) \in \mathbb{F}^n \times \mathbb{F}^n \times \mathbb{G}_1$, $\vec{R}^i (\vec{L}^i)^T$ span $\mathbb{F}^{n \times n}$ and $\mathcal{P}$ can pass $\mathsf{Eval\text{-}VMV\text{-}RE}(T, y_{com}^i, \vec{L}^i, \vec{R}^i)$ with non-negligible probability for each i, then $M, \vec{T}', \vec{r_{\text{rows}}}, r_{\text{fin}}$ and the set $\{r_y^i\}_i$ can be extracted.*

Remark 3. Note that we do not claim that $\mathsf{Eval\text{-}VMV\text{-}RE}$ with $\vec{L}, \vec{R}$ sampled is $(O(n^2), O(n^2)/|\mathbb{F}|)$-tree extractable, as without the spanning condition on $\vec{L}, \vec{R}$ the transcript can be independent of at least one entry of M.

Proof. Completeness is straightforward from the definition of $\mathcal{P}$'s witnesses. Succinctness, the Public Coin property and HVSZK of $\mathsf{Eval\text{-}VMV\text{-}RE}$ follow straightforwardly from the same properties for the two auxiliary Σ-protocols and $\mathsf{Dory\text{-}Innerproduct}$.

Recall that in Gen_{VMV}, $\Gamma_{1,0}, \Gamma_{2,0}, \Gamma_{1,fin}, \Gamma_{2,fin}, H_1, H_2$ are all sampled, so on SXDH finding a non-trivial linear relationship between them contradicts Lemma 3. Given tuples $(\vec{L}^i, \vec{R}^i, y^i_{com})$ such that $\mathcal{P}$ passes Eval-VMV-RE for some fixed T with non-negligible probability, witness extract Dory-Innerproduct and the two sigma proofs in Eval-VMV-RE. For each i, we have (suppressing i superscripts):

$$\vec{v_1} \in \mathbb{G}_1^n, \vec{v_2} \in \mathbb{G}_2^n, S, y_C \in \mathbb{G}_1, D_2 \in \mathbb{G}_2, E_1, E_2 \in \mathbb{G}_T, y \in \mathbb{F}.$$

$$s_2, r_y, t_1, t_2, r_C, r_{D_1}, r_{D_2}, r_{E_1}, r_{E_2} \in \mathbb{F}:$$

$$e(E_1, \Gamma_{2,fin}) = D_2 + e(H_1, t_1\Gamma_{2,fin} - t_2 H_2) \quad (4),$$

$$E_2 = y\Gamma_{2,fin} + s_2 H_2 \quad (5), \qquad y_C = y\Gamma_{1,fin} + r_y H_1 \quad (6),$$

$$T = \langle \vec{v_1}, \Gamma_{2,0} \rangle + r_{D_1} \cdot e(H_1, H_2) \,(7), \qquad D_2 = \langle \Gamma_{1,0}, \vec{v_2} \rangle + r_{D_2} \cdot e(H_1, H_2) \,(8),$$

$$E_1 = \langle \vec{L}, \vec{v_1} \rangle + r_{E_1} H_1 \quad (9), \qquad E_2 = \langle \vec{R}, \vec{v_2} \rangle + r_{E_2} H_2 \quad (10)$$

Since T is a constant in (7), $\vec{v_1}^i, r^i_{D_1}$ must also be fixed for all i, as otherwise the difference of some pair gives a non-trivial relationship between Γ_2, H_2, contradicting Lemma 3. Then substituting (8, 9) into (4) we have for each i (suppressing i superscripts):

$$e(\langle \vec{L}, \vec{v_1} \rangle, \Gamma_{2,fin}) = \langle \Gamma_{1,0}, \vec{v_2} \rangle + e(H_1, (t_1 - r_{E_1})\Gamma_{2,fin} - (t_2 - r_{D_2})H_2) \quad (11)$$

Then if $\vec{v_2}^i$ is not a linear function of $\vec{L}^i$, there exists a linear combination of these relationships eliminating $\vec{L}^i$ from the left hand side (since $\vec{v_1}$ is a constant) without eliminating $\vec{v_2}$ on the right. So we would obtain a non-trivial relationship between $\Gamma_{1,0}, , H_1$, contradicting Lemma 3. From (5, 10) we have (suppressing i superscripts): $\langle \vec{R}, \vec{v_2} \rangle = y\Gamma_{2,fin} + (s_2 - r_{E_2})H_2$, and so if y^i and $(s^i_2 - r^i_{E_2})$ are not bilinear in $\vec{L}^i, \vec{R}^i$ we obtain a non-trivial relationship between $\Gamma_{2,fin}, H_2$, contradicting Lemma 3. In particular since $\vec{R}^i(\vec{L}^i)^T$ span $\mathbb{F}^{n \times n}$ we extract fixed matrices $M, B \in \mathbb{F}^{n \times n}$ such that $y^i = (\vec{L}^i)^T M \vec{R}^i$ and $s^i_2 - r^i_{E_2} = (\vec{L}^i)^T B \vec{R}^i$ for all i. So $\vec{v_2}^i = (\vec{L}^i)^T M \Gamma_{2,fin} + (\vec{L}^i)^T B H_2$. Substituting into (11), we have for each i (suppressing i superscripts):

$$e(\langle \vec{L}, \vec{v_1} - M\Gamma_{1,0} \rangle + (r_{E_1} - t_1)H_1, \Gamma_{2,fin}) = e(\langle \vec{L}^T B, \Gamma_{1,0} \rangle + (r_{D_2} - t_2)H_1, H_2)$$

and so either we find a non-trivial pairing relationship between $\Gamma_{2,fin}, H_2$, contradicting Lemma 3, or for all i and suppressing superscripts:

$$0 = \langle \vec{L}, \vec{v_1} - M\Gamma_{1,0} \rangle + (r_{E_1} - t_1)H_1 \,(12), \quad 0 = \langle \vec{L}^T B, \Gamma_{1,0} \rangle + (r_{D_2} - t_2)H_1 \,(13).$$

Similarly a non-trivial relationship between $\Gamma_{1,0}, H_1$ would violate Lemma 1. So Equation 13 implies that $(\vec{L}^i)^T B = 0$ and $r^i_{D_2} = t^i_2$ for all i, so $B = 0$. From

Equation 12 the first we deduce that $r^i_{E_1} - t^i_1$ must be a linear function of $\vec{L}^i$ and independent of $\vec{R}$, so we have some $r_{\text{rows}} \in \mathbb{F}^n$ such that $r^i_{E_1} - t^i_1 = (\vec{L}^i)^T r_{\text{rows}}$, which implies that $\vec{v}_1 = M\Gamma_{1,0} + r_{\text{rows}} H_1$. Substituting into (7) we find T equals $\langle M\Gamma_{1,0}, \Gamma_{2,0} \rangle + e(H_1, r_{D_2} H_2 + \langle r_{\text{rows}}, \Gamma_{2,0} \rangle)$, i.e. that T is a commitment to M with opening hint $(r_{\text{rows}}, r_{\text{fin}} = r_{D_2}, \vec{T}' = \vec{v}_1)$. Substituting $y = (\vec{L}^i)^T M \vec{R}^i$ into (6), y^i_C is a commitment to the evaluation. So we have extracted a matrix M, evaluations y^i and opening hints $\vec{T}', r_{\text{rows}}, r_{\text{fin}}$ and r^i_y consistent with the commitments.

We show a modified protocol for which tree extractability is achieved in isolation, where $\mathcal{P}$ shows that T can be opened at a random point:

Eval-VMV$_{pp_{VMV}}(T, y_{com}, \vec{L}, \vec{R})$

   $\mathcal{P}$ **witness:** $M, (\vec{T}', r_{\text{rows}}, r_{\text{fin}}), r_y$

$\mathcal{V} \to \mathcal{P}$: $u \leftarrow_\$ \mathbb{F}$

$\mathcal{P}, \mathcal{V}$: $\vec{L}' = (1, u, u^2, \ldots u^{n-1})$, $\vec{R}' = (1, u^n, u^{2n}, \ldots, u^{(n-1)n})$

$\mathcal{P}$: $r_{y'} \leftarrow_\$ \mathbb{F}$.

$\mathcal{P} \to \mathcal{V}$: $y'_{com} = \vec{L}' M R' \Gamma_{1,fin} + r_{y'} H_1$

$\mathcal{P}, \mathcal{V}$:

   Eval-VMV-RE$_{pp_{VMV}}(T, y_{com}, \vec{L}, \vec{R}) \wedge$ Eval-VMV-RE$_{pp_{VMV}}(T, y'_{com}, \vec{L}', \vec{R}')$

   $\mathcal{P}$ **witnesses:** $(M, (\vec{T}', r_{\text{rows}}, r_{\text{fin}}), r_y)$ and $(M, (\vec{T}', r_{\text{rows}}, r_{\text{fin}}), r_{y'})$

Theorem 10. *Eval-VMV is a HVSZK succinct interactive argument of knowledge for $\mathcal{L}_{VMV}$ with $(\mathcal{O}(n^{2+\log 9}), \mathcal{O}(n^{2+\log 9})/|\mathbb{F}|)$-tree extractability under SXDH.*

Proof. All properties except tree extractability are immediate.

We take $\mu = 1$ and set $w_1 = n^2$. Internal to each of the $2n^2$ calls to Eval-VMV-RE, the two sigma proofs are each $(2, 2/|F|)$-tree extractable, and Dory-Innerproduct is $(\mathcal{O}(n^{\log 9}), \mathcal{O}(n^{\log 9})/|F|)$-tree extractable.

So it suffices to show that this $\mathcal{O}(n^{2+\log 9})$-sized tree of accepting transcripts requires $\mathcal{P}$ to pass Eval-VMV-RE for T fixed and some collection of $\vec{L}^i, \vec{R}^i$ containing $\vec{L}, \vec{R}$ such that $\vec{R}^i(\vec{L}^i)^T$ span $\mathbb{F}^{n \times n}$. Reading off the entries in $\vec{R}'(\vec{L}')^T$ row-wise gives $1, u, u^2, \ldots, u^{n^2-1}$. Any linear dependence between these n^2 vectors would imply the existence of a non-zero polynomial of degree n^2-1 vanishing at n^2 distinct u, which is impossible. Hence they span $\mathbb{F}^{n \times n}$ as required.

5.1 Batching

From Sect. 4.4, we can batch multiple invocations of Dory-Innerproduct and so we similarly have an argument for a batches of Eval-VMV-RE or Eval-VMV. We can further optimise these batch argument by observing that the Sigma proofs in Eval-VMV-RE show knowledge of logarithms with respect to fixed bases $\Gamma_{2,fin}, H_2, \Gamma_{1,fin}, H_1$. So as is standard we linearly combine these claims with random challenges supplied by $\mathcal{V}$ and prove the combination, with negligible alteration to soundness and extractability.

5.2   Concrete Costs

For an $n \times n$ matrix M, the size of the public parameters is $(n+2)|\mathbb{G}_1| + (n+2)|\mathbb{G}_2| + (3\log n + 4)|\mathbb{G}_T|$, and running Gen requires sampling $n+2$ elements of $\mathbb{G}_1$, $n+2$ elements of $\mathbb{G}_2$, $3n$ pairings and $\log n$ additions in $\mathbb{G}_T$.

To Commit a matrix M, $\mathcal{P}$ samples $n+1$ elements of $\mathbb{F}$, and performs n multi-exponentiations of size $n+1$ in $\mathbb{G}_1$, a multi-pairing of size n, and an exponentiation and addition in $\mathbb{G}_T$. The n multi-exponentiations in $\mathbb{G}_1$ are over fixed generators $(\Gamma_{1,0}||H_1)$, so Pippenger-type optimisations save an asymptotic factor $2\log n$. Proving Eval-VMV-RE requires proving Dory-Innerproduct, three multi-exponentiations in $\mathbb{G}_1$ of size n and $O(1)$ additional exponentiations in $\mathbb{G}_1, \mathbb{G}_2, \mathbb{G}_T$. The messages from $\mathcal{P}$ to $\mathcal{V}$ have size $5|\mathbb{F}| + 2|\mathbb{G}_1| + 2|\mathbb{G}_2| + 3|G_T|$; $\mathcal{V}$'s computation is 5 exponentiations in $|\mathbb{G}_2|$, 3 exponentiations in $|\mathbb{G}_1|$, an exponentiation in $\mathbb{G}_T$ and 2 pairings. Beyond proving a batch of two instances of Eval-VMV-RE, proving Eval-VMV requires $\mathcal{P}$ perform $O(1)$ exponentiations in $\mathbb{G}_1$. The messages from $\mathcal{P}$ to $\mathcal{V}$ have size $|\mathbb{G}_1|$. $\vec{L}', \vec{R}'$ have multiplicative structure, so $\mathcal{V}$'s computation with them is $O(\log n)$ multiplications in $\mathbb{F}$.

6   Dory-PC

We recall the discussion in Sect. 2.5. Concretely, the evaluation of any multivariate polynomial in $X_1 \ldots X_\ell$ of degrees $d_1, \ldots, d_\ell$ at $\vec{x} \in \mathbb{F}^\ell$ can be replaced by the evaluation of a multilinear polynomial in $r = \sum_i \lceil \log(d_i + 1) \rceil$ variables, where the coefficients of the two polynomials are equal. Let $m = \lceil r/2 \rceil$. Following Sect. 2.5, we extract a $2^m \times 2^m$ or $2^{m-1} \times 2^m$ matrix M. If m is odd we replace M with $(1, 0) \otimes M$, which is square. Then $f(\vec{x}) = (1 - z)\vec{L}^T M \vec{R}$ where $\vec{L} = \otimes_{i=1}^m (1, \vec{x}_i)$ and $z = 0$ for r even, $\vec{L} = (1, z) \otimes (\otimes_{i=1}^{m-1}(1, \vec{x}_i))$ and $z \xleftarrow{\$} \mathbb{F}$ for r odd, and $\vec{R} = \otimes_{i=r-m+1}^r (1, \vec{x}_i)$. Note that the implicit extension to a polynomial in $2m$ variables has no impact, as the additional variable is unconditionally set to 0. So we have reduced polynomial evaluation to a vector-matrix-vector product, where the vectors $\vec{L}, \vec{R}$ have multiplicative structure. Dory-PC-RE uses the commitment scheme of Sect. 2.4, and uses Eval-VMV-RE as Eval. Similarly Dory-PC uses Eval-VMV as Eval.

Theorem 11. *Dory-PC-RE is an honest-verifier, statistical zero-knowledge, random evaluation extractable polynomial commitment scheme for r-variable multilinear polynomials. Dory-PC is an honest-verifier, statistical zero-knowledge, extractable polynomial commitment scheme for r-variable multilinear polynomials.*

Proof. All properties except extractability are immediate for both schemes. For Dory-PC, Theorem 10 proves extractability. For Dory-PC-RE: Suppose some $2^{r+1} = 2n^2$ distinct $\vec{x} \in \mathbb{F}^r$ are sampled. If the outer products $\vec{R}\vec{L}^T$ do not span $\mathbb{F}^{n \times n}$, there is some non-zero element of the dual whose inner product with these is 0; this gives a some non-zero multilinear polynomial vanishing for all $\vec{x}$. By the Schwartz-Zippel lemma and a union bound, this has probability at most $|\mathbb{F}|^2 . (r/|\mathbb{F}|)^{-2^{r+1}} = (r^2/|F|)^{2^r} = \mathtt{negl}(\lambda)$. Theorem 9 then completes the proof.

Since the vectors $\vec{L}, \vec{R}$ (and $\vec{L}', \vec{R}'$ in Dory-PC) have multiplicative structure, the remarks made in Sect. 4.3 apply; $\mathcal{V}$'s use of these vectors are restricted to computing inner products with vectors $\otimes_{i=0}^{m-1}(\alpha_i, 1)$, $\otimes_{i=0}^{m-1}(\alpha_i^{-1}, 1)$ which can be computed in $O(m)$ operations in $\mathbb{F}$ given $x, \alpha_i, \alpha_i^{-1}$.

6.1   Concrete Costs of Dory-PC-RE

Let $n = \prod_i(d_i + 1)$, and let $|M| = O(n)$ be the number of non-zero entries in the matrix M. In the worst case $d_i = 4$ and $m = \frac{3}{2 \log 5} \log n + O(1)$. For multilinear or univariate polynomials $m = \frac{1}{2} \log n + O(1)$.

Using the fact that the $2^m \times 2^m$ matrix has at most $|M|$ non-zero entries, $\mathcal{P}$'s time to run Commit is dominated by $|M| + 2^m$ exponentiations in $\mathbb{G}_1$ and 2^m pairings. From Sect. 5.2, $\mathcal{P}$'s time to run Eval is dominated by $O(2^m)$ pairings.

The size of $\mathcal{P} \to \mathcal{V}$ messages is $(6m+7)|\mathbb{G}_T| + (3m+3)(|\mathbb{G}_2| + |\mathbb{G}_1|) + 8|\mathbb{F}|$, and $\mathcal{V} \to \mathcal{P}$ messages are $O(m)$ sampled elements of $\mathbb{F}$. $\mathcal{V}$ computes a $9m + O(1)$ sized multi-exponentiation in $\mathbb{G}_T$ and $O(1)$ additional exponentiations and pairings.

6.2   Batching

Given a batch of ℓ polynomials with individual $m_i \leq m$, we can use the results of Sect. 5.1 to batch. The $\mathcal{P} \to \mathcal{V}$ messages then have size $(6m+3\ell+5)|\mathbb{G}_T| + (3m + 2\ell + 2)(|\mathbb{G}_2| + |\mathbb{G}_1|) + 8|\mathbb{F}|$. $\mathcal{P}$'s main computation remains $O(\ell \times 2^m)$ pairings, though the implied constant is reduced $3\times$. Deferring $\mathcal{V}$'s computations as before, $\mathcal{V}$'s performs an exponentiation in $\mathbb{G}_T$ of size $9m + 3\ell + 6$, exponentiations in $\mathbb{G}_1$ and $\mathbb{G}_2$ of size $3m + 2\ell + 2$, and a multi-pairing of size 4. Unfortunately, the computations with vectors $\vec{L}, \vec{R}$ cannot be efficiently batched, and so $\mathcal{V}$ performs an additional $2\ell m$ multiplications and additions in $\mathbb{F}$.

As a corollary, the concrete costs of a batch of ℓ instances of Dory-PC is given by the cost of a batch of 2ℓ instances of Dory-PC-RE, with an additional ℓ elements of $\mathbb{G}_1$ added to the $\mathcal{P}$ to $\mathcal{V}$ messages.

7   Implementation

We implemented Dory to provide polynomial commitments for dense multilinear polynomials, building on framework for non-interactive arguments and dense multilinear polynomials in the Spartan library [31]. This took $\sim$3400 LOC. Our implementation used the BLS12-381 curve as implemented in blstrs [1]. We implemented fast algorithms for computing (multiple) multi-exponentiations and torus based compression for serialisation of elements of $\mathbb{G}_T$ in $\sim$1650 LOC.

The implementation was evaluated on a machine with an AMD Ryzen 5 3600 CPU at 3.6 GHz and 16 GB RAM. All measurements were taken for a single core. We compare with Spartan-PC, a discrete-log based random evaluation extractable polynomial commitment scheme implemented in the Spartan library [31], which is a highly optimised derivative of the commitment scheme in [34] using Curve25519 as implemented by curve25519-dalek for its curve arithmetic. Throughout, we compare dense multilinear polynomials in m variables, i.e. with $n = 2^m$ random coefficients. We report results for a variety of polynomial sizes in Fig. 3.

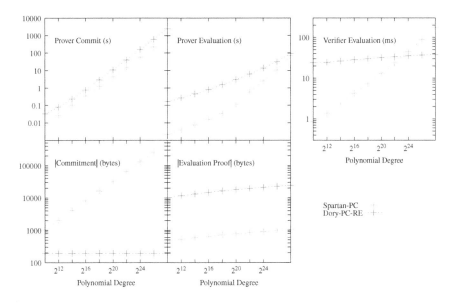

Fig. 3. Measured performance of Dory-PC-RE for varying polynomial degree.

As can be seen, Dory is slower than the baseline for $\mathcal{P}$ in Commit by a consistent factor ~ 2.7, matching the relative speed of $\mathbb{G}_1$ arithmetic on the implementations of Curve25519 and BLS12-381 as seen in Fig. 2.

The time taken for $\mathcal{P}$ to prove an evaluation is similarly somewhat slower than Spartan-PC. Naively scaling from microbenchmarks in Fig. 2 would suggest that Dory might be $\sim 45\times$ slower asymptotically. As can be seen, this is essentially true on small instances, but for $n \sim 2^{20}$ the linear $\mathbb{F}$ arithmetic to evaluating the polynomial becomes dominant for Spartan-PC; for $n = 2^{28}$ Dory is $\sim 30\%$ slower than Spartan-PC. Dory's $\mathcal{V}$ clearly shows $O(\log n)$ complexity to verify an evaluation, concretely taking $\sim (15 + 0.85 \log n)$ ms. The $\mathcal{V}$ of Spartan-PC scales like $n^{1/2}$, and is concretely slower than Dory for $n \gtrsim 2^{24}$.

In terms of communication complexity, Dory clearly shows a fixed 192-byte commitment size, whilst Dory' proofs are consistently larger than those of Spartan-PC by a factor ~ 24. This is this is the ratio between $6|\mathbb{G}_T|+3(|\mathbb{G}_2|+|\mathbb{G}_1|)$ in the BLS12-381 curve and $2|\mathbb{G}_1|$ in Curve25519, and so is the ratio between the $\log n$ contributions to the proof size in the two systems. In applications, one might expect to have ≈ 1 evaluation proof of each freshly committed polynomial; in this context the point where a Dory evaluation proof becomes smaller than a Spartan-PC commitment is $n = 2^{18}$.

Batching: Recall that Dory-PC effectively batches two evaluations of Dory-PC-PE. We use the batched Dory-PC-RE argument to open multiple committed polynomial evaluations. This naturally impacts the time taken for $\mathcal{P}$ to run Eval, the resulting proof size, and $\mathcal{V}$'s time taken to run Eval on the batch. We report results for a variety of batch sizes in Fig. 4.

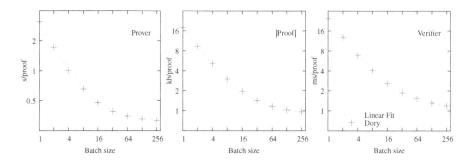

Fig. 4. Performance of Eval for batched Dory-PC-RE evaluations, $n = 2^{20}$.

As can be seen, the marginal costs to increase the batch size by one are small; the marginal $\mathcal{P}$ time is $\sim$305 s, the marginal contribution to the proof size is 912 bytes, and the marginal $\mathcal{V}$ time is $\sim$1.1 ms. For large batches, this provides $\mathcal{P}$ a constant $\sim$11.5$\times$ saving over proving each evaluation separately; for proof sizes and $\mathcal{V}$ large batches save a factor $\sim$2 log n.

References

1. blstrs (2020). https://github.com/filecoin-project/blstrs/
2. Abe, M., Fuchsbauer, G., Groth, J., Haralambiev, K., Ohkubo, M.: Structure-preserving signatures and commitments to group elements. In: Rabin, T. (ed.) CRYPTO 2010. LNCS, vol. 6223, pp. 209–236. Springer, Heidelberg (2010). https://doi.org/10.1007/978-3-642-14623-7_12
3. Ames, S., Hazay, C., Ishai, Y., Venkitasubramaniam, M.: Ligero: Lightweight sublinear arguments without a trusted setup. In: CCS (2017)
4. Barreto, P.S.L.M., Lynn, B., Scott, M.: Constructing elliptic curves with prescribed embedding degrees. In: Cimato, S., Persiano, G., Galdi, C. (eds.) SCN 2002. LNCS, vol. 2576, pp. 257–267. Springer, Heidelberg (2003). https://doi.org/10.1007/3-540-36413-7_19
5. Barreto, P.S.L.M., Naehrig, M.: Pairing-friendly elliptic curves of prime order. In: Preneel, B., Tavares, S. (eds.) SAC 2005. LNCS, vol. 3897, pp. 319–331. Springer, Heidelberg (2006). https://doi.org/10.1007/11693383_22
6. Ben-Sasson, E., Bentov, I., Horesh, Y., Riabzev, M.: Fast reed-solomon interactive oracle proofs of proximity. In: ICALP (2018)
7. Ben-Sasson, E., et al.: libiop: a C++ library for IOP-based zkSNARKs. https://github.com/relic-toolkit/relic

8. Ben-Sasson, E., Chiesa, A., Riabzev, M., Spooner, N., Virza, M., Ward, N.P.: Aurora: transparent succinct arguments for R1CS. In: Ishai, Y., Rijmen, V. (eds.) EUROCRYPT 2019, Part I. LNCS, vol. 11476, pp. 103–128. Springer, Cham (2019). https://doi.org/10.1007/978-3-030-17653-2_4

9. Bernstein, D.J., Hamburg, M., Krasnova, A., Lange, T.: Elligator: elliptic-curve points indistinguishable from uniform random strings. In: CCS (2013)

10. Biasse, J.-F., Jacobson, M.J., Silvester, A.K.: Security estimates for quadratic field based cryptosystems. In: Steinfeld, R., Hawkes, P. (eds.) ACISP 2010. LNCS, vol. 6168, pp. 233–247. Springer, Heidelberg (2010). https://doi.org/10.1007/978-3-642-14081-5_15

11. Block, A.R., Holmgren, J., Rosen, A., Rothblum, R.D., Soni, P.: Time- and space-efficient arguments from groups of unknown order. In: Malkin, T., Peikert, C. (eds.) CRYPTO 2021, Part IV. LNCS, vol. 12828, pp. 123–152. Springer, Cham (2021). https://doi.org/10.1007/978-3-030-84259-8_5

12. Boneh, D., Bünz, B., Fisch, B.: A survey of two verifiable delay functions. Cryptology ePrint Archive, Report 2018/712 (2018)

13. Bootle, J., Cerulli, A., Chaidos, P., Groth, J., Petit, C.: Efficient zero-knowledge arguments for arithmetic circuits in the discrete log setting. In: Fischlin, M., Coron, J.-S. (eds.) EUROCRYPT 2016, Part II. LNCS, vol. 9666, pp. 327–357. Springer, Heidelberg (2016). https://doi.org/10.1007/978-3-662-49896-5_12

14. Bowe, S., Grigg, J., Hopwood, D.: Recursive proof composition without a trusted setup. Cryptology ePrint Archive, Report 2019/1021 (2019)

15. Bünz, B., Bootle, J., Boneh, D., Poelstra, A., Wuille, P., Maxwell, G.: Bulletproofs: Short proofs for confidential transactions and more. In: S&P (2018)

16. Bünz, B., Fisch, B., Szepieniec, A.: Transparent snarks from dark compilers. Cryptology ePrint Archive, Report 2019/1229 (2019)

17. Bünz, B., Maller, M., Mishra, P., Tyagi, N., Vesely, N.: Proofs for inner pairing products and applications. Cryptology ePrint Archive, Report 2019/1177 (2019)

18. Chiesa, A., Ojha, D., Spooner, N.: Fractal: Post-quantum and transparent recursive proofs from holography. Cryptology ePrint Archive, Report 2019/1076 (2019)

19. Dobson, S., Galbraith, S.D., Smith, B.: Trustless groups of unknown order with hyperelliptic curves. Cryptology ePrint Archive, Report 2020/196 (2020)

20. Gabizon, A., Williamson, Z.J., Ciobotaru, O.: Plonk: Permutations over Lagrange-bases for oecumenical noninteractive arguments of knowledge (2019)

21. Galbraith, S.D., Paterson, K.G., Smart, N.P.: Pairings for cryptographers. Discrete Appl. Math. **156**(16), 3113–3121 (2008)

22. Groth, J.: Linear algebra with sub-linear zero-knowledge arguments. In: Halevi, S. (ed.) CRYPTO 2009. LNCS, vol. 5677, pp. 192–208. Springer, Heidelberg (2009). https://doi.org/10.1007/978-3-642-03356-8_12

23. Groth, J.: Efficient zero-knowledge arguments from two-tiered homomorphic commitments. In: Lee, D.H., Wang, X. (eds.) ASIACRYPT 2011. LNCS, vol. 7073, pp. 431–448. Springer, Heidelberg (2011). https://doi.org/10.1007/978-3-642-25385-0_23

24. Groth, J., Ishai, Y.: Sub-linear zero-knowledge argument for correctness of a shuffle. In: Smart, N. (ed.) EUROCRYPT 2008. LNCS, vol. 4965, pp. 379–396. Springer, Heidelberg (2008). https://doi.org/10.1007/978-3-540-78967-3_22

25. Icart, T.: How to hash into elliptic curves. In: Halevi, S. (ed.) CRYPTO 2009. LNCS, vol. 5677, pp. 303–316. Springer, Heidelberg (2009). https://doi.org/10.1007/978-3-642-03356-8_18

26. Jacobson, M.J., van der Poorten, A.J.: Computational aspects of NUCOMP. In: Fieker, C., Kohel, D.R. (eds.) ANTS 2002. LNCS, vol. 2369, pp. 120–133. Springer, Heidelberg (2002). https://doi.org/10.1007/3-540-45455-1_10

27. Kate, A., Zaverucha, G.M., Goldberg, I.: Constant-size commitments to polynomials and their applications. In: Abe, M. (ed.) ASIACRYPT 2010. LNCS, vol. 6477, pp. 177–194. Springer, Heidelberg (2010). https://doi.org/10.1007/978-3-642-17373-8_11

28. Lipmaa, H.: On diophantine complexity and statistical zero-knowledge arguments. In: Laih, C.-S. (ed.) ASIACRYPT 2003. LNCS, vol. 2894, pp. 398–415. Springer, Heidelberg (2003). https://doi.org/10.1007/978-3-540-40061-5_26

29. Naehrig, M., Barreto, P.S.L.M., Schwabe, P.: On compressible pairings and their computation. In: Vaudenay, S. (ed.) AFRICACRYPT 2008. LNCS, vol. 5023, pp. 371–388. Springer, Heidelberg (2008). https://doi.org/10.1007/978-3-540-68164-9_25

30. Papamanthou, C., Shi, E., Tamassia, R.: Signatures of correct computation. In: Sahai, A. (ed.) TCC 2013. LNCS, vol. 7785, pp. 222–242. Springer, Heidelberg (2013). https://doi.org/10.1007/978-3-642-36594-2_13

31. Setty, S.: Spartan: efficient and general-purpose zkSNARKs without trusted setup. In: Micciancio, D., Ristenpart, T. (eds.) CRYPTO 2020, Part III. LNCS, vol. 12172, pp. 704–737. Springer, Cham (2020). https://doi.org/10.1007/978-3-030-56877-1_25

32. Shallue, A., van de Woestijne, C.E.: Construction of rational points on elliptic curves over finite fields. In: Hess, F., Pauli, S., Pohst, M. (eds.) ANTS 2006. LNCS, vol. 4076, pp. 510–524. Springer, Heidelberg (2006). https://doi.org/10.1007/11792086_36

33. Tibouchi, M.: Elligator squared: uniform points on elliptic curves of prime order as uniform random strings. In: Christin, N., Safavi-Naini, R. (eds.) FC 2014. LNCS, vol. 8437, pp. 139–156. Springer, Heidelberg (2014). https://doi.org/10.1007/978-3-662-45472-5_10

34. Wahby, R.S., Tzialla, I., Shelat, A., Thaler, J., Walfish, M.: Doubly-efficient zkSNARKs without trusted setup. In: S&P (2018)

35. Zhang, J., Xie, T., Zhang, Y., Song, D.: Transparent polynomial delegation and its applications to zero knowledge proof. In: S&P (2020)

On Communication-Efficient Asynchronous MPC with Adaptive Security

Annick Chopard[1], Martin Hirt[1], and Chen-Da Liu-Zhang[2(✉)]

[1] ETH Zurich, Zürich, Switzerland
{achopard,hirt}@ethz.ch
[2] Carnegie Mellon University, Pittsburgh, USA
cliuzhan@andrew.cmu.edu

Abstract. Secure multi-party computation (MPC) allows a set of n parties to jointly compute an arbitrary computation over their private inputs. Two main variants have been considered in the literature according to the underlying communication model. Synchronous MPC protocols proceed in rounds, and rely on the fact that the communication network provides strong delivery guarantees within each round. Asynchronous MPC protocols achieve security guarantees even when the network delay is arbitrary.

While the problem of MPC has largely been studied in both variants with respect to both feasibility and efficiency results, there is still a substantial gap when it comes to communication complexity of adaptively secure protocols. Concretely, while adaptively secure synchronous MPC protocols with linear communication are known for a long time, the best asynchronous protocol communicates $\mathcal{O}(n^4\kappa)$ bits per multiplication.

In this paper, we make progress towards closing this gap by providing two protocols. First, we present an adaptively secure asynchronous protocol with optimal resilience $t < n/3$ and $\mathcal{O}(n^2\kappa)$ bits of communication per multiplication, improving over the state of the art protocols in this setting by a quadratic factor in the number of parties. The protocol has cryptographic security and follows the CDN approach [Eurocrypt'01], based on additive threshold homomorphic encryption.

Second, we show an optimization of the above protocol that tolerates up to $t < (1 - \epsilon)n/3$ corruptions and communicates $\mathcal{O}(n \cdot \mathsf{poly}(\kappa))$ bits per multiplication under stronger assumptions.

1 Introduction

Secure multi-party computation (MPC) allows a set of parties to compute a function of their private inputs, in such a way that the parties' inputs remain secret, and the computed output is correct. This must hold even when an adversary corrupts a subset of the parties.

This work was partially carried out while the author was at ETH Zurich.

K. Nissim and B. Waters (Eds.): TCC 2021, LNCS 13043, pp. 35–65, 2021.
https://doi.org/10.1007/978-3-030-90453-1_2

The problem of MPC [Yao82, GMW87, BGW88, CCD88, RB89] has been studied mostly in the so-called synchronous network model, where parties have access to synchronized clocks and there is an upper bound on the network communication delay. Although this model is theoretically interesting and may be justified in some settings, they fail to model real-world networks such as the Internet, which is inherently asynchronous. This gave rise to the asynchronous network model, where protocols do not rely on any timing assumptions, and messages sent can be arbitrarily delayed.

Asynchronous MPC protocols have received much less attention than their synchronous counterpart, partly because of their inherent difficulty and the weaker achievable security guarantees. In particular, one cannot distinguish between a dishonest party not sending a message, or an honest party that sent a message that was delayed by the adversary. As a result, parties have to make progress in the protocol after seeing messages from $n - t$ parties. This also implies that in this setting it is impossible to consider the inputs of all honest parties, i.e., the inputs of up to t (potentially honest) parties may be ignored. Moreover, one can show that the optimal achievable corruption tolerance in the asynchronous setting is $t < n/3$, even with setup, in both the cryptographic and information-theoretic setting; and perfect security is possible if and only if $t < n/4$.

1.1 Communication Complexity of Asynchronous MPC Protocols

The communication complexity in MPC has been the subject of a huge line of works. While the most communication-efficient synchronous MPC solutions without the usage of multiplicative-homomorphic encryption primitives achieve $\mathcal{O}(n\kappa)$ bits per multiplication gate (see e.g. [HN06, DI06, BH08, BFO12, GLS19, GSZ20]), asynchronous MPC protocols still feature higher communication complexities, most notably when it comes to protocols with adaptive security.

In the adaptive security setting, all protocols are information-theoretic. The first protocol was provided by Ben-Or et al. [BKR94], and later improved by Patra et al. [PCR10, PCR08] to $\mathcal{O}(n^5\kappa)$ per multiplication, and by Choudhury [Cho20] to $\mathcal{O}(n^4\kappa)$ per multiplication.

When considering static security, the most efficient protocols with optimal resilience $t < n/3$ provide cryptographic security. The works by Hirt et al. [HNP05, HNP08] make use of an additive homomorphic encryption, with the protocol in [HNP08] being slightly more efficient and communicating $\mathcal{O}(n^2\kappa)$ per multiplication. The work by Choudhury and Patra [CP15] achieves $\mathcal{O}(n\kappa)$ per multiplication at the cost of using somewhat-homomorphic encryption, and the work by Cohen [Coh16] achieves a communication independent of the circuit size using fully-homomorphic encryption.

Other efficient solutions have been provided for the $t < n/4$ setting. Notable works include the protocols in [SR00, PSR02, CHP13, PCR15], achieving information-theoretic security.

1.2 Contributions

In this paper, we consider the problem of MPC over an asynchronous network with adaptive security. Our contributions can be summarized as follows.

First, we present an adaptively secure protocol with optimal resilience $t < n/3$ and $\mathcal{O}(n^2\kappa)$ bits of communication per multiplication, improving over the state of the art adaptively-secure protocols by a quadratic factor in the number of parties. Note, however, that in contrast to the protocol in [Cho20] which is information-theoretic, our protocol has cryptographic security. The protocol follows the CDN approach [CDN01, DN03] and makes use of an additive threshold homomorphic encryption.

Second, we show a protocol that tolerates up to $t < (1 - \epsilon)n/3$ corruptions and communicates a $\mathcal{O}(n \cdot \mathsf{poly}(\kappa))$ number of bits per multiplication, assuming secure erasures, non-interactive zero-knowledge proofs, and access to a network providing *atomic send*[1] (see e.g. [BKLL20]), which guarantees that parties are able to atomically send messages to all other parties, and also guarantees that messages sent by honest parties cannot be retrieved back, even if the sender becomes corrupted. Note that a linear protocol with optimal resilience, and without the usage of any type of multiplicative-homomorphic encryption is not known even for the case of static security.

2 Preliminaries

We consider protocols among a set of n parties $P_1, \ldots, P_n$. We denote the security parameter by κ and use the abbreviation ewnp for "except with negligible probability". Our protocols are proven in the model by Canetti [Can00a]. A summary can be found in the full version [CHL21].

2.1 Communication and Adversary Model

Parties have access to a network of point-to-point asynchronous and secure channels (for details of the asynchronous network model, we refer the reader to [CR98]). Asynchronous channels guarantee *eventual* delivery, meaning that messages sent are eventually delivered, and the scheduling of the messages is done by the adversary. In particular, the adversary can arbitrarily (but only finitely) delay all messages sent and deliver them out of order.

We consider a computationally bounded adversary that can actively corrupt up to t parties in an adaptive manner. That is, as long as the adversary has corrupted strictly less than t parties, it can corrupt any party at any point in time based on the information during the protocol execution.

---

[1] This model has also been referred to as *weakly-adaptive* corruption, or simply adaptive corruption model in the literature.

2.2   Zero-Knowledge Proofs of Knowledge

In this subsection, we introduce the notion of patchable zero-knowledge proof of knowledge. For more details, see [DN03].

Definition 1. *A 2-party patchable zero-knowledge proof of knowledge for a predicate Q is a protocol between a prover P and a verifier V where P has as public input an instance z and as secret input a witness x and V has public input the instance z and output in $\{accept, reject\}$. The protocol needs to satisfy the following properties.*

- Completeness: *On common input z, if P's secret input x satisfies $Q(x, z) = true$, then V accepts.*
- Soundness: *There exists an efficient program K (the knowledge extractor) that can interact with any prover P' such that if P' succeeds to make V accept with non-negligible probability, then K can extract a witness x' from its interaction with P' such that $Q(x', z) = true$.*
- Zero-Knowledge: *For any efficient verifier V', there exists an efficient simulator S such that for any common input z, S can simulate a run of the protocol with V' in a computationally indistinguishable way.*
- Patchability: *Let z be an arbitrary instance and let $\tilde{t}$ be any step of the protocol. Let $T_{\tilde{t}}^{V'}(z)$ be the communication of the simulator (which might not know a witness to z) with a verifier V' in the simulated run of the protocol until step $\tilde{t}$. We require that there exists an efficient algorithm Pat that takes as input z, $\tilde{t}$, $T_{\tilde{t}}^{V'}(z)$ and a witness x such that $Q(x, z) = true$ and outputs randomness ν which satisfies the following: If an honest prover P executes the protocol with V' up to step $\tilde{t}$ on instance z and witness x using randomness ν, then the communication is identical to $T_{\tilde{t}}^{V'}(z)$. Furthermore, the randomness ν looks uniformly random to V'.*

All zero-knowledge proofs used in our protocol will be 2-party patchable zero-knowledge proofs of knowledge with constant communication complexity.

2.3   Universally Composable Commitments

In this section, we briefly introduce universally composable (UC) commitment schemes. A detailed exposition is given in the full version [CHL21].

A commitment scheme allows a party P to commit to a value v towards other parties without revealing information about v. If at any point in time, P wants to reveal v, then it can open the given commitment to v.

A universally composable (UC) commitment scheme is a commitment scheme in the UC framework [Can00b]. Like usual commitment schemes, a UC commitment scheme is hiding and binding. Additionally, it is extractable (that is, the simulator can extract the value a corrupted party committed to from its commitment) and equivocable (that is, the simulator can simulate a commitment on behalf of an honest party towards a corrupted party without knowing the committed value and later open the given commitment to any value it wants).

Since in our model we consider an adaptive adversary, we require that when the adversary corrupts a party, the simulator can patch the internal state of that party.

In our MPC protocol, we need the following additional property of our commitment scheme. A detailed discussion about the selective decommitment problem can be found in [DNRS03].

Selective Decommitment Security: Consider the following security game with an integer $t \in \{1, \ldots, n\}$ (representing the corruption threshold) and a message distribution M over R_{pk}^n as parameters.

– The challenger samples a uniform random bit $b \in_R \{0, 1\}$.
– The adversary sends a set of indices $I \subset \{1, \ldots, n\}$ of size $t' \in \{0, \ldots, t\}$ to the challenger.
– The challenger samples n messages according to the distribution M, enumerates them in the natural way and gives the messages with indices in I to the adversary. Next, for each message with index not in I, the challenger commits to it and gives the computed $n - t'$ commitments to the adversary.
– The adversary can adaptively choose up to $t - t'$ of the given commitments and the challenger gives the underlying messages and the randomness used to obtain the commitments in question to the adversary. As soon as the adversary does not want to choose any more commitments, it sends "End-Corruption" to the challenger.
– Upon receipt of the "EndCorruption"-message or if the adversary has already chosen $t - t'$ commitments, the challenger does the following. Let $I' \subseteq \{1, \ldots, n\}$ be the set of indices that are not in I and such that the adversary did not choose the commitments with indices in I'.
   • If $b = 0$, the challenger gives the messages underlying the commitments with indices in I' to the adversary.
   • Let $M_{I'}$ be the distribution M conditioned on the components with indices not in I' being equal to the messages already given to the adversary. If $b = 1$, the challenger samples $|I'|$ messages according to the distribution $M_{I'}$ and gives them to the adversary.
– The adversary outputs a guess b' for the value of the bit b.

The idea in the above game is that every party commits to one value and the adversary can corrupt up to t parties. In doing that, the adversary should not learn anything about the messages underlying the commitments of honest parties. This game can be generalized in a natural way to the case where each party P_i commits to a fixed number ℓ_i of values (and this number can be different for each party). For the sake of simplicity, we do not give the formal description of the more general game. We define the advantage of the adversary in the generalized game by

$$\mathrm{Advtg}^{M,t}_{\{\ell_1,\ldots,\ell_n\}} := |\Pr[b' = b] - \frac{1}{2}|.$$

We require from our commitment scheme that for all n-tuples $\{\ell_1, \ldots, \ell_n\}$ of integers, all message distributions M and all $t < n/3$, there does not exist any adversary that has non-negligible advantage $\text{Advtg}_{\{\ell_1, \ldots, \ell_n\}}^{M,t}$.

For all the commitments in our protocols, we will use a UC adaptively secure (equivocable and extractable) commitment scheme that satisfies the "Selective decommitment security" property above and has constant communication complexity.

2.4 Threshold Homomorphic Encryption

We briefly discuss threshold homomorphic encryption schemes. For a detailed exposition, see the full version [CHL21].

A threshold homomorphic encryption scheme is a tuple (KeyGen, Enc, Dec-Share, Comb) of four algorithms, where

- KeyGen is a probabilistic algorithm that takes a security parameter κ, the number of parties n and the threshold parameter t as input and outputs a uniformly distributed tuple $(pk, sk_1, \ldots, sk_n)$ where the public key pk is given to all parties and the secret key sk_i is given to P_i for all $i \in \{1, \ldots, n\}$.
- Enc is an efficient probabilistic non-interactive algorithm that takes as input a public key pk and a message m from the message ring R_{pk} and outputs an encryption $\text{Enc}_{pk}(m)$ of m. If we want to specify the randomness r used in the execution of the algorithm, we write $\text{Enc}_{pk}(m, r)$.
  The Enc algorithm is a homomorphism in the sense that there exists an efficient algorithm that takes as input the public key pk and two encryptions $\text{Enc}_{pk}(m_1, r_1)$ and $\text{Enc}_{pk}(m_2, r_2)$ of m_1 and m_2 and that outputs an encryption $\text{Enc}_{pk}(m_1, r_1) \oplus_{pk} \text{Enc}_{pk}(m_2, r_2) := \text{Enc}_{pk}(m_1 +_{pk} m_2, r_1 \boxplus_{pk} r_2)$ of $m_1 +_{pk} m_2$, where $+_{pk}$ and $\boxplus_{pk}$ are the group laws in the message space and the randomness space. Similarly, there exists an efficient algorithm that takes as input the public key pk, an encryption $\text{Enc}_{pk}(m, r)$ and a message $c \in R_{pk}$ and outputs a uniquely determined encryption $c \odot_{pk} \text{Enc}_{pk}(m, r)$ of $c \cdot_{pk} m$.
- DecShare is an efficient algorithm that takes as input an index $i \in \{1, \ldots, n\}$, the public key pk, the secret key sk_i and a ciphertext c and outputs a decryption share c_i and a proof that c_i is correctly computed using i, pk, c and sk_i.
- Comb is an efficient algorithm that takes as input the public key pk, a ciphertext c and pairs (c_i, p_i) where each pair has a different index. The algorithm outputs a message m or fails.

The scheme is correct (that is, if at least $t + 1$ distinct decryption shares with valid proofs for the same ciphertext c are given as input to the Comb algorithm, then it outputs the message underlying c) and threshold semantically secure (that is, without the help of at least one honest party, an adversary corrupting at most t parties cannot extract information about the plaintext underlying a given ciphertext). Furthermore, there exists a patchable zero-knowledge proof of plaintext knowledge and a patchable zero-knowledge proof of correct multiplication with constant communication complexity.

From the definition of threshold homomorphic encryption scheme, it follows that there is an algorithm Blind that takes an encryption of a message m and the public key pk as input and outputs a uniformly random encryption of m (without knowing m). For details, see the full version [CHL21].

For convenience, we introduce the following functions which we will often use. For an encryption M in the ciphertext space, we define

$$\mathsf{Enc}_{pk}^{M} : (x, r) \rightarrow \mathsf{Enc}_{pk}^{M}(x, r) = (x \odot_{pk} M) \oplus_{pk} \mathsf{Enc}_{pk}(0_{pk}, r).$$

We call a preimage with respect to the function Enc_{pk}^{M} of an encryption y a "preimage of y under (pk, M)". If we do not specify the second argument r of the function, then we implicitly mean that r is uniformly random in the randomness space. So (by the homomorphic property of the encryption scheme and because the randomness space is a group) $\mathsf{Enc}_{pk}^{M}(x)$ is a uniformly random encryption of $x \cdot_{pk} m$, where m is the value encrypted by M.

In our MPC protocol, we need the following additional properties of our encryption scheme.

- *Proof of compatible commitment:* Let $Q_{pk}^{M}((m', r_1, r_2), (y, B))$ be the binary predicate that is 1 if and only if $y = \mathsf{Enc}_{pk}^{M}(m', r_1)$ and (m', r_2) is the opening information for the commitment B. We require that there exist efficient patchable zero-knowledge proofs of knowledge for Q_{pk}^{M} with constant communication complexity for all public keys pk and all encryptions M under pk.
- *Lagrange arguments:* There exists an n-tuple $\{\alpha_1, \ldots, \alpha_n\} \in (R_{pk} \backslash \{0_{pk}\})^n$ of distinct elements such that for all $(i, j) \in \{1, \ldots, n\}^2$ we have that $\alpha_i - \alpha_j$ is invertible in R_{pk}. For these elements, the usual Lagrange polynomials and Lagrange coefficients are well-defined.
- *Patch:* Given a public key pk, two encryptions $E = \mathsf{Enc}_{pk}(0_{pk}, r_0)$ and $K = \mathsf{Enc}_{pk}(0_{pk}, r_K)$ of 0_{pk} under key pk and the randomness r_0 and r_K used, there exists an efficient probabilistic algorithm that given any constant x computes randomness r_E such that $E = (x \odot_{pk} K) \oplus_{pk} \mathsf{Enc}_{pk}(0_{pk}, r_E) = \mathsf{Enc}_{pk}^{K}(x, r_E)$.
- *Selective decryption security:* This property is similar to the "Selective decommitment security" property of our commitment scheme. For a detailed discussion, we again refer the reader to [DNRS03].

  Consider the following security game with a message distribution M over R_{pk}^n and a randomness distribution Rd over the n product of the randomness space as parameters.
  - The challenger samples a uniform random bit $b \in_R \{0, 1\}$.
  - The adversary sends a set of indices $I \subset \{1, \ldots, n\}$ of size $t' \in \{0, \ldots, t\}$ to the challenger.
  - The challenger samples n messages according to the distribution M and n randomness elements according to the distribution Rd, enumerates them in the natural way and gives the messages and randomness elements with

indices in I to the adversary. Next, for each message with index not in I, the challenger encrypts it using the corresponding randomness element (i.e. the randomness element with the same index) and gives the computed $n - t'$ ciphertexts to the adversary.

- The adversary can adaptively choose up to $t - t'$ of the given ciphertexts and the challenger gives the underlying messages and the randomness used to obtain the ciphertexts in question to the adversary. As soon as the adversary does not want to choose any more ciphertexts, it sends "EndCorruption" to the challenger.
- Upon receipt of the "EndCorruption"-message or if the adversary has already chosen $t - t'$ ciphertexts, the challenger does the following. Let $I' \subseteq \{1, \ldots, n\}$ be the set of indices that are not in I and such that the adversary did not choose the ciphertexts with indices in I'.
  * If $b = 0$, the challenger gives the messages underlying the ciphertexts with indices in I' to the adversary.
  * Let $M_{I'}$ be the distribution M conditioned on the components with indices not in I' being equal to the messages already given to the adversary. If $b = 1$, the challenger samples $|I'|$ messages according to the distribution $M_{I'}$ and gives them to the adversary.
- The adversary outputs a guess b' for the value of the bit b.

The idea in the above game is that every party encrypts one value and the adversary can corrupt up to t parties. In doing that, the adversary should not learn anything about the messages underlying the encryptions of honest parties. This game can be generalized in a natural way to the case where each party P_i encrypts a fixed number ℓ_i of values (and this number can be different for each party). For the sake of simplicity, we do not give the formal description of the more general game. We define the advantage of the adversary in the generalized game by

$$\text{Advant}_{\{\ell_1, \ldots, \ell_n\}}^{M, Rd} := |\Pr[b' = b] - \frac{1}{2}|.$$

We require from our encryption scheme that for all n-tuples of integers $\{\ell_1, \ldots, \ell_n\}$, all message distributions M and all randomness distributions Rd, there does not exist any adversary that has non-negligible advantage $\text{Advant}_{\{\ell_1, \ldots, \ell_n\}}^{M, Rd}$, even if it has access to a simulator for zero-knowledge proofs and the Pat algorithm.

Remark 1. By the homomorphic property of the encryption scheme, in the Patch property we have that $x \odot_{pk} K = \text{Enc}_{pk}(0_{pk}, r_0 \boxminus_{pk} r_E)$. Since multiplication by a constant is a deterministic algorithm and since the randomness space is a group, this implies that if r_0 is uniformly random from the randomness space, then r_E is also uniformly random from the randomness space.

In the full version [CHL21], we present the Paillier threshold encryption scheme which is an instantiation of the definition above.

3   Subprotocols

This section is devoted to the exposition of the subprotocols that will be used in the MPC protocol.

3.1   Agreement Protocols

Often, parties need to have agreement on certain values or objects. To achieve this, we use the following primitives in our protocol.

1. *Reliable consensus:* Reliable consensus is a weaker version of asynchronous consensus. It allows the parties to agree on one of the honest parties' input values without requiring termination if there is no pre-agreement. More precisely, every party has a (private) input and the primitive guarantees that if all honest parties have the same input, then all honest parties output their inputs. Furthermore, if an honest parties outputs a value, then all other honest parties output the same value. In the full version [CHL21], we discuss the definition of reliable consensus in more details and we present a reliable consensus protocol RC for $t < n/3$. Our protocol is based on Bracha's A-Cast protocol [Bra84] and has communication complexity $\mathcal{O}(n^2\kappa)$, where κ is the size any party's secret input.

2. *A-Cast:* A-Cast is an asynchronous broadcast protocol. It allows the parties to agree on the value of a sender without requiring termination if the sender is corrupted. More precisely, the sender has a private input and the primitive guarantees that if the sender is honest, then all parties output the senders message. Furthermore, if an honest party outputs a value, then all other honest parties output the same value. In the full version [CHL21], we discuss the definition of reliable broadcast in more details and we present Bracha's reliable broadcast protocol RBC for $t < n/3$ [Bra84]. The protocol has communication complexity $\mathcal{O}(n^2\kappa)$, where κ is the size of the sender's input. Moreover, we show that if the sender has computationally indistinguishably distributed input, then the RBC protocol maintains computational indistinguishability.

   In some situations, we use Patra's Multi-Valued-Acast protocol [Pat11] which is a reliable broadcast protocol that achieves linear communication complexity for messages of size $\Omega(n^3 \log(n))$. This allows us to improve the efficiency of our MPC protocol.

3. *Byzantine agreement:* Byzantine agreement allows the parties to agree on one of the honest parties' input values. It guarantees that all honest parties terminate and that they output the same value. For $t < n/3$, Byzantine agreement can be achieved with expected communication complexity $\mathcal{O}(n^2)$. For a more detailed definition of Byzantine agreement, see the full version [CHL21].

4. *ACS:* The agreement on a common subset (ACS) primitive allows the parties to agree on a set of at least $n - t$ parties that satisfy a certain property (a so-called ACS property). In the full version [CHL21], we discuss the definitions of ACS property and ACS protocol in more details and we present an ACS protocol ACS with communication complexity $\mathcal{O}(n^3)$.

3.2   Decryption Protocols

To decrypt ciphertexts of our threshold homomorphic encryption scheme, we use two decryption protocols. The PrivDec protocol is a straightforward private decryption protocol which takes as input the public key pk, the private keys $sk_1, \ldots, sk_n$, a ciphertext c and a party P and correctly decrypts c towards P even in the presence of an active adaptive adversary corrupting $t < n/3$ parties. The PubDec protocol is a public decryption protocol which takes as input $pk, sk_1, \ldots, sk_n$, $n - 2t$ ciphertexts $c_1, \ldots, c_T$ and uses the PrivDec protocol to correctly publicly decrypt $c_1, \ldots, c_T$ even in the presence of an active adaptive adversary corrupting $t < n/3$ parties. The PubDec protocol has communication complexity $\mathcal{O}(n^2\kappa)$ and thus achieves linear communication complexity per decrypted ciphertext. For details about these two protocols and their guarantees, see Appendix A.1.

Remark 2. Additionally to the properties in the definition of threshold homomorphic encryption scheme, we require the following from our encryption scheme. Let P be any party and let c_1 and c_2 be two computationally indistinguishably distributed ciphertexts with computationally indistinguishably distributed underlying plaintexts. An instance of the PrivDec protocol with (pk, c_1, P) as public input (and $sk_1, \ldots, sk_n$ as private inputs) is computationally indistinguishably distributed to an instance of the PrivDec protocol with (pk, c_2, P) as public input (and $sk_1, \ldots, sk_n$ as private inputs) even in the presence of an active adaptive adversary corrupting up to $t < n/3$ parties.

Remark 3. By inspection of the PubDec protocol in Appendix A.1, it is clear that the "computational indistinguishable decryption" property also holds for the PubDec protocol.

3.3   Multiplication

In this section, we briefly discuss the multiplication protocol. A detailed description is given in Appendix A.2.

The main idea for the multiplication protocol is to use circuit randomization [Bea92]. To make it more efficient, we apply the ideas of [DN07] and [BH08], namely we use the PubDec protocol to process up to $T = \lfloor \frac{n-2t}{2} \rfloor$ independent multiplication gates simultaneously. Hence, the multiplication protocol takes as input T independent multiplication gates, their encrypted inputs and their associated multiplication triples and outputs the encrypted outputs of the given gates. The protocol guarantees that if the inputs to the processed multiplication gates are computationally indistinguishably distributed, then the executions of the multiplication protocol are as well (see Proposition 1). Furthermore, it communicates $\mathcal{O}(n^2\kappa)$ bits.

3.4   Triple Generation

This subsection is devoted to the introduction of the Triples protocol which takes as input an integer ℓ and outputs ℓ encrypted multiplication triples. The protocol is based on the multiplication protocol in [DN03], the KFD-TRIPLES protocol in [HN06] and on [CP15]. We first adapted their protocols to the asynchronous setting using the ACS primitive and then improved efficiency by amortizing the cost of the ACS instances over the number of generated triples and using the communication efficient Multi-Valued-Acast protocol.

Protocol Triples

1: Every party P_j independently chooses uniformly random elements a_j^i in the message space R_{pk} and r_j^i in the randomness space for all $i \in \{1, \dots, \ell\}$. Then, P_j computes $A_j^i = \mathsf{Enc}_{pk}(a_j^i, r_j^i)$ and uses the Multi-Valued-Acast protocol to broadcast A_j^i for all $i \in \{1, \dots, \ell\}$. Finally, P_j proves to P_k in zero-knowledge that it knows the plaintext underlying A_j^i using the "proof of plaintext knowledge" property of the encryption scheme with instance A_j^i and witness (a_j^i, r_j^i) for all $i \in \{1, \dots, \ell\}$ and all $k \in \{1, \dots, n\}$.

2: Let Q be the property such that a party P_k satisfies Q towards another party P_j if and only if the broadcasts of all A_k^i with $i \in \{1, \dots, \ell\}$ terminated for P_j and P_j accepted all proofs of plaintext knowledge for A_k^i with $i \in \{1, \dots, \ell\}$. The parties run the ACS protocol with Q and obtain a set S of parties.

3: The parties wait until the broadcasts of all parties in S terminated and set $A^i = \bigoplus_{P_k \in S} A_k^i$ for all $i \in \{1, \dots, \ell\}$.

4: Every party P_j independently chooses uniformly random elements b_j^i in the message space R_{pk} and $r_j'^i$ in the randomness space for all $i \in \{1, \dots, \ell\}$. Then, P_j computes $B_j^i = \mathsf{Enc}_{pk}(b_j^i, r_j'^i)$ and $(C_j^i, r_j''^i) = \mathsf{Blind}(b_j^i \odot_{pk} A^i)$ and uses the Multi-Valued-Acast protocol to broadcast B_j^i and C_j^i for all $i \in \{1, \dots, \ell\}$. Finally, P_j proves to P_k in zero-knowledge that C_j^i was computed correctly using the "proof of correct multiplication" property of the encryption scheme with instance (B_j^i, A^i, C_j^i) and witness $(b_j^i, r_j'^i, r_j''^i)$ for all $i \in \{1, \dots, \ell\}$ and all $k \in \{1, \dots, n\}$.

5: Let Q' be the property such that a party P_k satisfies Q' towards another party P_j if and only if the broadcast of all (B_k^i, C_k^i) with $i \in \{1, \dots, \ell\}$ terminated for P_j and P_j accepted all proofs of correct multiplication for (B_k^i, A^i, C_k^i) with $i \in \{1, \dots, \ell\}$. The parties run the ACS protocol with Q' and obtain a set S' of parties.

6: The parties wait until the broadcasts of all parties in S' terminated and set $B^i = \bigoplus_{P_k \in S'} B_k^i$ and $C^i = \bigoplus_{P_k \in S'} C_k^i$ for all $i \in \{1, \dots, \ell\}$.

7: Each party outputs (A^i, B^i, C^i) for all $i \in \{1, \dots, \ell\}$.

To prove security of the above Triples protocol, we give the simulator $\mathcal{S}_{\mathsf{Triples}}$ who does not have access to the secret keys of honest parties.

Simulator $\mathcal{S}_{\mathsf{Triples}}$

The simulator $\mathcal{S}_{\mathsf{Triples}}$ executes the protocol acting honestly on behalf of the honest parties. If the adversary decides to corrupt a party P_i at any point of the protocol, $\mathcal{S}_{\mathsf{Triples}}$ gives all the information it holds on behalf of P_i about the execution of the Triples protocol to the adversary.

Lemma 1. *The* Triples *protocol above satisfies the following:*

- Termination: *All honest parties terminate the protocol and output ℓ triples.*
- Consistency: *All honest parties output the same triples.*
- Correctness: *The output triples are correct.*
- Secrecy: *The plaintexts underlying the output triples are unknown to the adversary. In other words, the adversary has no more information about these plaintexts than that the plaintexts underlying the third components are the product of the plaintexts underlying the corresponding first and second components.*
- Computational Uniform Randomness: *The distribution of the plaintexts underlying any output triple is computationally indistinguishable from the uniform distribution over the set of all triples $(a, b, a \cdot_{pk} b)$ for $a, b \in R_{pk}$.*
- Independence: *The plaintexts underlying any output triple are computationally independent of the plaintexts underlying all other output triples.*
- Privacy: *The adversary's views in the simulation and the protocol are perfectly indistinguishably distributed, i.e. the adversary does not learn anything.*
- Communication complexity: *The protocol communicates $\mathcal{O}(n^2 \ell \kappa + n^5 \log(n))$ bits.*

The proof is given in the full version [CHL21].

Remark 4. If we choose $\ell\kappa = \Omega(n^3 \log(n))$, we obtain that the Triples protocol communicates $\mathcal{O}(n^2\kappa)$ bits per triple.

4   Asynchronous Adaptively Secure MPC Protocol

In this section, we present an asynchronous MPC protocol based on the protocols in [CDN01, DN03, BH08]. Then we informally prove that our protocol is secure against an active adaptive adversary corrupting up to t parties.

4.1   Ideal Functionality

In this subsection, we define the specification that our protocol achieves. The following exposition is based on [BKR94, CDN00].
Let $f: \mathbb{N} \times \{0,1\}^* \times (\{0,1\}^*)^n \to (\{0,1\}^*)^n$ be an efficiently computable function.

Functionality

1: The trusted party receives the security parameter $\kappa \in \{0,1\}^*$ and the number of parties $n \in \mathbb{N}$ as input.
2: Every party P_i gives its input x_i to the trusted party. Corrupted parties are allowed to give wrong input, no input at all or — as long as the adversary has not specified the core set S in step 3 — change their inputs (for example after corruption of any party). If the adversary corrupts a party P_j at any point in time during or after this step, then the trusted party gives x_j to the adversary.

3: The adversary chooses a set of parties $S \subseteq \mathcal{P}$ of size at least $n - t$ and gives it to the trusted party.

4: The trusted party evaluates the function f on the given inputs of parties in S and using a default input d for parties not in S. From this, it obtains output y.

5: The trusted party sends y to all parties.

6: All honest parties output y. Corrupted parties can output whatever they like.

Recall that since we are in the asynchronous setting with at least $n - t$ honest parties, the size of the set S of parties whose inputs are considered for the evaluation of f is between $n - t$ and n. Note that it is not guaranteed that all parties in S are honest. However, we require from the adversary that it only includes corrupted parties in S for whom it gave input to the ideal functionality in step 2.

4.2   Informal Explanation of the Protocol

To achieve adaptive security in the asynchronous setting, we proceeded as follows. We started with the statically secure synchronous MPC protocol introduced by Cramer, Damgård and Nielsen [CDN01]. Next, we used circuit randomization [Bea92] to split the protocol into a preparation phase and a computation phase. After that, we adapted the protocol to the asynchronous setting using asynchronous broadcast and agreement on a common subset (ACS). Finally, we made the protocol adaptively secure by applying the techniques from Damgård and Nielsen [DN03], namely redefining the way values are encrypted and randomizing the output ciphertext in a specific way before decrypting it. Concretely, the new rule of encryption is: Given an encryption M and a value v to be encrypted, the encryption is set to $\mathsf{Enc}_{pk}^{M}(v)$. Recall that if we denote the value that M encrypts by m, then by the homomorphic property of the encryption scheme and by definition of the function Enc_{pk}^{M}, $\mathsf{Enc}_{pk}^{M}(v)$ is a uniformly random encryption of $v \cdot_{pk} m$. In the protocol, we will mostly choose $m = 1_{pk}$ to have an encryption of v while in the simulation we will often choose $m = 0_{pk}$ which helps the simulator to provide computationally indistinguishably distributed information. In detail, the idea of the protocol is the following.

Preparation Phase

– *Setup phase (steps 1–4)*: The keys for all the keyed primitives used in our protocol (namely the encryption scheme, the commitment scheme and the zero-knowledge proofs) are set up. Each party receives the keys it is entitled to along with public Lagrange arguments $\{\alpha_i\}_{i \in \{1,\ldots,n\}}$. Additionally, two public encryptions K and R are set up and given to all parties. The encryption K is a uniformly random encryption of 1_{pk} and the encryption R is a uniformly random encryption of 0_{pk}. In the simulation, the simulator will cheat by choosing K to be a uniformly random encryption of 0_{pk} and R to be a uniformly random encryption of 1_{pk}. By semantic security of the encryption scheme, this is computationally indistinguishable to the adversary.

Finally, the parties compute the circuit corresponding to the function to be evaluated and generate multiplication triples that will be used in the Evaluation phase to evaluate the multiplication gates of the circuit.

Computation Phase

– *Input phase (steps 1 and 2):* The parties receive their inputs x_i needed for the execution and want to give them to an agreed function f. To do so, every party reliably broadcasts an encryption of its input applying the new rule of encryption with $M = K$. While $\mathsf{Enc}_{pk}^K(x_i)$ is indeed an encryption of x_i in the real world (recall that in the protocol K is an encryption of 1_{pk}), it is an encryption of 0_{pk} in the simulation as there, K is an encryption of 0_{pk}. Hence, in the simulation all encryptions of inputs will be encryptions of 0_{pk} independently of the inputs of the parties. However, the simulator needs to be able to extract the inputs of corrupted parties because it has to provide those inputs to the ideal functionality on behalf of the corrupted parties. This is why every party commits to its input towards every other party using a UC commitment scheme. The extraction property of UC commitments allows the simulator to extract the correct inputs of corrupted parties (ewnp) and give them to the ideal functionality. To ensure correctness and prevent the adversary in the real world from having more power than an adversary in the ideal world, the parties need to prove in zero-knowledge (using the "proof of compatible commitment" property) that they know a preimage of the reliably broadcasted encryption $\mathsf{Enc}_{pk}^K(x_i)$ under (pk, K) and that the first component of this preimage is the same as the value that they committed to. This is important because without these proofs a corrupted party could just wait for the reliable broadcast of another party P_j to terminate and then set its input to the same as the one from P_j without knowing it. This is not possible in the ideal world and therefore, we want to prevent it in the protocol execution. Furthermore, the simulator extracts the inputs of the corrupted parties from the commitments whereas for the computation in the protocol we will use the encryptions. Thus, the simulator needs to ensure that the value underlying the commitment and the first component of the preimage under (pk, K) of the encryption are the same so that it does not give wrong inputs to the ideal functionality on behalf of the corrupted parties. Finally, the parties run the ACS protocol and obtain a set S of size at least $n - t$ of parties that successfully broadcasted an encryption of their input which they committed to. The inputs of the parties in S are the ones that will be taken into account in the evaluation of f. Thus, the ACS protocol needs to ensure that S only contains parties that successfully completed the reliable broadcast of their inputs and all their zero-knowledge proofs towards at least one honest party (so that everything is correct and the simulator can extract the correct inputs ewnp as it received at least one valid commitment to every input of the corrupted parties in S). All inputs of parties that are not in S are set to a default value. Each party then waits until the reliable broadcast for every party in S terminated. It is okay for the parties to wait until the reliable broadcast of the parties in S terminate because we saw that for all parties P_k in S, there exists an honest party for which the reliable broadcast of P_k terminated. By the properties of reliable broadcast this implies that the reliable broadcast of P_k eventually terminates for all honest parties.

The computation of the encryptions of the inputs, their reliable broadcast, the zero-knowledge proofs and the run of the ACS protocol are summed up in the BrACS protocol in Appendix B.

- *Evaluation phase (step 3)*: The parties evaluate the circuit on the encrypted inputs of the parties using the "$+_{pk}$-homomorphic" property, the "Multiplication by constant" property and the multiplication protocol from Appendix A.2. In the end, the parties get a ciphertext c (called $\mathsf{Enc}_{pk}(s)$ in the protocol and $\mathsf{Enc}_{pk}(\hat{s})$ in the simulation).

- *Randomization phase (steps 4–7)*: Before the parties jointly decrypt c, they randomize it. This is done so that the simulator can cheat. In fact, as we saw above, all inputs to the circuit in the simulation are encryptions of 0_{pk}. By the correctness of the gates, this implies that all ciphertexts in the circuit are encryptions of 0_{pk} (not counting the intermediate ciphertexts in the multiplication protocol). Hence, c is also an encryption of 0_{pk} and therefore, we cannot simply honestly decrypt c as otherwise the simulator would fail to provide a computationally indistinguishable simulation with overwhelming probability. Furthermore, our encryption scheme is not adaptively secure which is why we cannot decrypt c to anything but 0_{pk} either. Thus, the parties randomize the ciphertext before decrypting it honestly.

To randomize the ciphertext c, the parties do the following. Each party chooses a random r_i and reliably broadcasts the encryption $\mathsf{Enc}_{pk}^R(r_i)$. Then the parties agree on a set $\hat{S}$ of parties of size at least $t+1$ of successful broadcasts using the ACS protocol. Denote the indices of the parties in the set $\hat{S}$ by I. Next, the parties consider the unique polynomial p of degree $|I| - 1$ that goes through $\mathsf{Enc}_{pk}^R(r_i)$ at position α_i for all $i \in I$. They interpolate this polynomial at 0_{pk} and add this to c using the "$+_{pk}$-homomorphic" and the "Multiplication by constant" properties of the encryption scheme. This gives the new ciphertext c' (denoted by $\mathsf{Enc}_{pk}(s)'$ in the protocol and the simulation). In the real execution, R is an encryption of 0_{pk} under pk and therefore, all $\mathsf{Enc}_{pk}^R(r_i)$ are encryptions of 0_{pk} under pk. Since interpolation is a linear operation and the encryption scheme is homomorphic, the value of p at 0_{pk} will also be an encryption of 0_{pk} and thus c' will encrypt the same message as c. In the simulation however, R is an encryption of 1_{pk}. This will help the simulator to cheat. Concretely, the simulator will adjust the r_i's of honest parties so that at position 0_{pk}, p will have a uniformly random encryption of the output s (received from the ideal functionality) of the function f evaluated on the inputs of the parties. This is possible since $|I| \geqslant t + 1$ and hence, there is at least one honest party whose r_i is taken into account in the randomization and can be chosen by the simulator in the simulation. Since c is an encryption of 0_{pk} in the simulation, we get that c' encrypts s as wanted. But we need to integrate a mechanism that allows the simulator to choose the r_i's of honest parties according to those of corrupted parties. This is done in the following way.

Before reliably broadcasting $\mathsf{Enc}_{pk}^{R}(r_i)$ and agreeing on a set of successful broadcasts, the parties commit to their r_i and use the BrACS protocol to reliably broadcast $\mathsf{Enc}_{pk}^{K}(r_i)$ and agree on a set S' of successful broadcasts (including a successful proof of compatible commitment). By the ACS property we will use and by the guarantees of the ACS protocol, we have that the simulator received at least one valid commitment to r_k for every corrupted party $P_k \in S'$. Thus, it can extract all r_k from corrupted parties in S' ewnp (by the extraction property of UC commitment schemes). Now the simulator can adjust the r_i's of the honest parties as described above. Then the parties execute the BrACS for $\mathsf{Enc}_{pk}^{R}(r_i)$ (see above) but using the same commitments in the zero-knowledge proof as in the previous BrACS (with $\mathsf{Enc}_{pk}^{K}(r_i)$). We obtain a set S'' and encryptions $\mathsf{Enc}_{pk}^{R}(r_i)$ for all $P_i \in S''$. The ACS property the parties use in the second BrACS is slightly modified to ensure that the value used to compute the broadcasted encryption in the first BrACS (the one with $\mathsf{Enc}_{pk}^{K}(r_i)$) and the value used to compute the broadcasted encryption in the second BrACS (the one with $\mathsf{Enc}_{pk}^{R}(r_i)$) is the same except with negligible probability. Concretely, the property ensures that for all $P_i \in S''$ at least one honest party likes P_i for both BrACS executions. Since those BrACS protocols were run with the same commitments, we can be sure that the values used to compute the broadcasted encryptions are the same in both runs of the BrACS protocol. Then we set $\hat{S} = S' \cap S''$ and observe that $\hat{S}$ is of size at least $n - 2t \geqslant t + 1$ as wanted.

Note that the simulator has to know the r_k's of corrupted parties in $\hat{S} \subseteq S'$ before the broadcasting of $\mathsf{Enc}_{pk}^{R}(r_i)$ because while it can patch the encryptions and proofs of the first BrACS (with $\mathsf{Enc}_{pk}^{K}(r_i)$) due to K being an encryption of 0_{pk}, it can *not* do the same for the second BrACS (with $\mathsf{Enc}_{pk}^{R}(r_i)$) because R is an encryption of 1_{pk}.

- *Output phase (steps 8 and 9):* The parties decrypt c' and obtain s. Then they run the reliable consensus protocol on secret input s as termination procedure. The persistency property of reliable consensus ensures that everyone terminates on the same correct output s.

A detailed description of the protocol can be found in Appendix B.

4.3   Main Theorem

Our protocol achieves the following.

Theorem 1. *The MPC protocol in Appendix B t-securely realizes the ideal functionality in Subsect. 4.1 in the KG-hybrid model for $t < n/3$. The protocol communicates $\mathcal{O}(c_M n^2 \kappa + D n^2 \kappa + n^3 \kappa + n^5 \log(n))$ bits, where c_M is the number of multiplication gates in the circuit and D is the multiplicative depth of the circuit.*

The simulator and an informal proof of the theorem are given in the full version [CHL21].

Remark 5. It is straightforward to generalize the above protocol to the case where the function f takes c_I inputs and provides c_O outputs. If a party P_i has multiple inputs, it commits to each one of them, reliably broadcasts a random encryption of each one of them and proves compatible commitment for each one of them (in the BrACS). Furthermore, with multiple outputs, the parties execute steps 4–7 of the protocol for each encrypted output of the circuit and then reconstruct the randomized outputs towards the entitled parties. This results in an increase of the communication complexity by a quadratic factor per input and by a cubic factor per output, which leads to the following theorem.

Theorem 2. *There exists an MPC protocol that t-securely realizes the ideal functionality in Subsect. 4.1 in the KG-hybrid model for $t < n/3$. The protocol communicates $\mathcal{O}(c_M n^2 \kappa + D n^2 \kappa + c_I n^2 \kappa + c_O n^3 \kappa + n^3 \kappa + n^5 \log(n))$ bits, where D is the multiplicative depth of the circuit, c_M is the number of multiplication gates, c_I is the number of input gates and c_O is the number of (public and private) output gates in the circuit.*

Remark 6. This paper does not focus on round complexity. For information about round-efficient MPC, we refer the reader to [CGHZ16]. Our protocol has a round complexity that depends on the circuit depth.

5 Near-Linear MPC in the Atomic Send Model

In this section, we show how to improve the efficiency of our MPC protocol at the cost of stronger assumptions on the model and a slightly lower corruption threshold.

Taking a closer look at the communication complexity of the protocol in Appendix B reveals that the complexity is dominated by the communication in the Triples protocol. While the number of messages sent between the parties per produced triple (and hence per multiplication gate of the circuit) in the Triples protocol is quadratic in the number of parties, the computation phase of the protocol only needs near-linear communication per evaluated gate assuming a shallow circuit (except for the input phase which has quadratic communication complexity per input gate) . By considering slightly stronger assumptions on the model, we can reduce the communication complexity of the triple generation and obtain a near-linear MPC protocol.

5.1 Model

In this subsection, we present the model which will be used to achieve better efficiency in the generation of multiplication triples. The subsection is based on [BKLL20].

As before (see Subsect. 2.1), we consider multiparty computation among a set of n parties $P_1, \ldots, P_n$, where every pair of parties is connected by a secure asynchronous communication channel. A protocol in our setting comprises a number of atomic steps.

The adversary in the new setting is computationally bounded and can actively corrupt up to t parties in an atomic send adaptive manner. That is, as long as the adversary has corrupted strictly less than t parties, it can corrupt any party at any point in time considering all the information it has seen so far and make this party behave as it wishes for the remaining steps of the protocol. However, if in some step a party needs to send several messages simultaneously, then the adversary is only allowed to corrupt this party before or after it sent all the messages (that is, the adversary cannot corrupt the party in the midst of the sending). Furthermore, messages sent by any honest party P_i are guaranteed to arrive eventually, even if P_i is later corrupted. Once a party is corrupted, the adversary learns its internal state and the party remains corrupted until the end of the protocol.

We assume the existence of non-interactive zero-knowledge (NIZK) proofs and secure erasure. Moreover, we assume the existence of a trusted party that provides the parties with public and private setup information before the execution of a protocol, more details below. The size of the setup is defined to be the sum of the size of the total private setup information and the size of the public setup information (hence, we count the private information of each party separately, but the public information only once for all parties).

5.2   VACS

This subsection is devoted to the introduction of the VACS primitive. We follow the exposition in [BKLL20].

In the efficient WeakTriples protocol, we need a primitive that allows the parties to agree on a sufficiently large subset of their inputs satisfying a specific predicate. This can be achieved by the VACS primitive.

Definition 2. *Consider a predicate Q and an n-party protocol π, where every party P_i has a secret input m_i and outputs a multiset S of size at most n. Every honest party's input satisfies Q and every party terminates upon generating output. We say that π is a t-secure Q-validated ACS protocol (VACS) with q-output quality if for all adversaries corrupting up to t parties and for all inputs the following is satisfied:*

- *Q-Validity: Let S be the output of an honest party. Then for every $m \in S$, we have $Q(m) = 1$.*
- *Consistency: All honest parties agree on S.*
- *q -Output Quality: The output multiset S of every honest party is of size at least q and contains the inputs of at least $q - t$ parties that were honest at the beginning of the protocol.*

Theorem 3. *Let $0 < \epsilon < 1/3$, $t \leqslant (1 - 2\epsilon) \cdot n/3$ and $q \leqslant (1 + \epsilon/2) \cdot 2n/3$. There exists a t-secure Q-validated ACS protocol $\Pi_{VACS}^{q,Q}$ with q-output quality, expected setup size $\mathcal{O}(q\kappa^4)$ and expected communication complexity $\mathcal{O}((\mathcal{I} + \kappa^3) \cdot q\kappa n)$, where $\mathcal{I}$ is the size of any party's secret input. In addition to the properties of t-secure Q-validated ACS protocols, the $\Pi_{VACS}^{q,Q}$ protocol guarantees that the* output multiset S contains the inputs of at least $\frac{q}{2}$ parties that were honest at the beginning of the protocol except with probability smaller than $e^{\frac{-q\epsilon^2}{(2-3\epsilon)(2+\epsilon)}}$.

The construction of $\Pi_{\mathsf{VACS}}^{q,Q}$ and the proof of the first part of the theorem can be found in [BKLL20]. The second part of the theorem can be proven using Lemma 24 of [BKLL20].

5.3   Triple Generation

To obtain an efficient protocol for the triple generation in the atomic send model, we start with our Triples protocol from Subsect. 3.4 and make it more efficient using the VACS primitive, NIZK proofs and erasures. The following protocol is inspired by the protocols in [BKLL20]. It takes as input an integer ℓ and outputs ℓ encrypted multiplication triples.

Protocol WeakTriples

Let ℓ be the number of triples we want to generate . We assume that the parties have access to the setup for two runs of the VACS protocol with output quality κ.

1: Each party P_j independently chooses uniformly random messages $a_j^k \in R_{pk}$ and uniformly random elements r_j^k in the randomness space for all $k \in \{1, \ldots, \ell\}$. Then, P_j computes $A_j^k = \mathsf{Enc}_{pk}(a_j^k, r_j^k)$ and an NIZK proof $p_{1,j}^k$ of plaintext knowledge with instance A_j^k and witness (a_j^k, r_j^k) for all $k \in \{1, \ldots, \ell\}$. Finally, P_j erases (a_j^k, r_j^k) for all $k \in \{1, \ldots, \ell\}$.

2: The parties run an instance of the $\Pi_{\mathsf{VACS}}^{\kappa,Q}$ protocol with output quality κ, where every party P_j has input $\{(A_j^k, p_{1,j}^k)\}_{k \in \{1,\ldots,\ell\}}$ and $Q(\{(A_j^k, p_{1,j}^k)\}_{k \in \{1,\ldots,\ell\}}) = 1$ if and only if $p_{1,j}^k$ is a correct NIZK proof of plaintext knowledge with instance A_j^k for all $k \in \{1, \ldots, \ell\}$. The parties obtain a multiset S of size at least κ and define $A^i = \bigoplus_{j \,:\, \{(A_j^k, p_{1,j}^k)\}_{k \in \{1,\ldots,\ell\}} \in S} A_j^i$ for all $i \in \{1, \ldots, \ell\}$.

3: Each party P_j independently chooses uniformly random messages $b_j^k \in R_{pk}$ and uniformly random elements $\hat{r}_j^k$ in the randomness space for all $k \in \{1, \ldots, \ell\}$. Then, P_j computes $B_j^k = \mathsf{Enc}_{pk}(b_j^k, \hat{r}_j^k)$ and $(C_j^k, \tilde{r}_j^k) = \mathsf{Blind}(b_j^k \odot_{pk} A^k)$, where Blind is the blinding algorithm of the encryption scheme. Furthermore, P_j computes an NIZK proof $p_{2,j}^k$ of correct multiplication with instance (B_j^k, A^k, C_j^k) and witness $(b_j^k, \hat{r}_j^k, \tilde{r}_j^k)$ for all $k \in \{1, \ldots, \ell\}$. Finally, P_j erases $(b_j^k, \hat{r}_j^k)$, $\tilde{r}_j^k$ and the information used in the blinding algorithm for all $k \in \{1, \ldots, \ell\}$.

4: The parties run an instance of the VACS protocol $\Pi_{\mathsf{VACS}}^{\kappa,Q'}$ with output quality κ, where every party P_j has input $\{(B_j^k, C_j^k, p_{2,j}^k)\}_{k \in \{1,\ldots,\ell\}}$ and Q' is defined such that $Q'(\{(B_j^k, C_j^k, p_{2,j}^k)\}_{k \in \{1,\ldots,\ell\}}) = 1$ if and only if $p_{2,j}^k$ is a correct NIZK proof of correct multiplication with instance (B_j^k, A^k, C_j^k) for all $k \in \{1, \ldots, \ell\}$. The parties obtain a multiset S' of size at least κ and define $B^i = \bigoplus_{j \,:\, \{(B_j^k, C_j^k, p_{2,j}^k)\}_{k \in \{1,\ldots,\ell\}} \in S'} B_j^i$ and $C^i = \bigoplus_{j \,:\, \{(B_j^k, C_j^k, p_{2,j}^k)\}_{k \in \{1,\ldots,\ell\}} \in S'} C_j^i$ for all $i \in \{1, \ldots, \ell\}$.

5: Every party outputs (A^i, B^i, C^i) for all $i \in \{1, \ldots, \ell\}$.

Remark 7. Because we want to ensure that all parties who contribute to the triples know the plaintexts underlying their contributions and because the VACS protocol requires Q and Q' (defined in steps 2 and 4) to be predicates on the inputs of the parties to the VACS protocol, we need to use NIZK proofs.

To prove security of the above WeakTriples protocol, we give the simulator $\mathcal{S}_{\mathsf{WeakTriples}}$ who does not have access to the secret keys of honest parties.

Simulator $\mathcal{S}_{\mathsf{WeakTriples}}$

The simulator $\mathcal{S}_{\mathsf{WeakTriples}}$ executes the protocol acting honestly on behalf of the honest parties. If the adversary decides to corrupt a party P_i at any point of the protocol, $\mathcal{S}_{\mathsf{WeakTriples}}$ gives all the information it holds on behalf of P_i about the execution of the WeakTriples protocol to the adversary.

Lemma 2. *For $0 < \epsilon < 1/3$ and $t \leqslant (1 - 2\epsilon) \cdot n/3$, the WeakTriples protocol above satisfies the following:*

- Termination: *All honest parties terminate the protocol and output ℓ triples.*
- Consistency: *All honest parties output the same triples.*
- Correctness: *The output triples are correct.*
- Secrecy: *The plaintexts underlying the output triples are unknown to the adversary. In other words, the adversary has no more information about these plaintexts than that the plaintexts underlying the third components are the product of the plaintexts underlying the corresponding first and second components.*
- Computational Uniform Randomness: *The distribution of the plaintexts underlying any output triple is computationally indistinguishable from the uniform distribution over the set of all triples $(a, b, a \cdot_{pk} b)$ for $a, b \in R_{pk}$.*
- Independence: *The plaintexts underlying any output triple are computationally independent of the plaintexts underlying all other output triples.*
- Privacy: *The adversary's views in the simulation and the protocol are perfectly indistinguishably distributed, i.e. the adversary does not learn anything.*
- Communication complexity: *The protocol has expected communication complexity $\mathcal{O}(\ell\kappa^3 n + \kappa^5 n)$.*

The proof is given in the full version [CHL21].

5.4 Main Theorem for the Atomic Send Model

By replacing the instance of the Triples protocol in step 4 of the Preparation Phase of the MPC protocol in Appendix B by the WeakTriples protocol above, we can improve the communication complexity of our MPC protocol and achieve $\mathcal{O}(n \cdot \mathsf{poly}(\kappa))$ bits per multiplication. Furthermore, using the reliable broadcast protocol presented in [BKLL20] in our BrACS protocol, we can reduce the communication complexity per input and obtain the following theorem.

Theorem 4. *Let $0 < \epsilon < 1/3$ and $t \leqslant (1 - 2\epsilon) \cdot n/3$. There exists an MPC protocol that t-securely realizes the ideal functionality in Subsect. 4.1 in the KG-hybrid atomic send model and that has expected communication complexity $\mathcal{O}(c_M n \kappa^3 + D n^2 \kappa + c_I n \kappa^2 + c_O n^3 \kappa + n^3 \kappa + n \kappa^5)$, where D is the multiplicative depth of the circuit, c_M is the number of multiplication gates, c_I is the number of input gates and c_O is the number of (public and private) output gates in the circuit.*

A   Details of the Subprotocols

A.1   Decryption protocols

Private Decryption. The private decryption protocol PrivDec takes the public key pk, a ciphertext c and a party P as public input and the secret keys $sk_1, \ldots, sk_n$ as private inputs. The protocol has no public nor private output for all parties except for P, who privately outputs the plaintext underlying c. This section is along the lines of [BH08, CHP12, CP15].

Protocol PrivDec

1: Every party P_i computes $(c_i, p_i^c) = \mathsf{DecShare}(i, pk, sk_i, c)$, sends (c_i, p_i^c) to P and terminates.
2: As soon as P has received at least $t + 1$ pairs (c_k, p_k^c) from distinct parties P_k such that p_k^c is a valid proof for c_k from P_k, P uses the Comb algorithm to compute $m = \mathsf{Comb}(pk, c, \{(c_k, p_k^c)\}_{k \in \{1, \ldots, n\}})$, where P sets all the values that is has not received to $\bot$. Then P outputs m.

Lemma 3. *Every party that remains uncorrupted until the end of the execution terminates the PrivDec protocol. Furthermore, if P is honest at the end of the protocol, then its output m is the correct decryption of c even in the presence of an adaptive adversary actively corrupting up to $t < n/3$ parties. The protocol has communication complexity $\mathcal{O}(n\kappa)$.*

Proof. In this whole proof, an honest party is a party that is never corrupted by the adversary and remains honest during the whole execution of the protocol.
Termination: Clearly all honest parties apart from P terminate as they only need to compute a decryption share and send it to P. Furthermore, if P is honest, then it terminates since all honest parties send correct decryption shares. Hence, P eventually receives at least $n - t \geqslant t + 1$ correct decryption shares from distinct parties, runs Comb and obtains and outputs a message m.
Correctness: As we saw above, P eventually receives at least $t + 1$ correct decryption shares from distinct parties. Hence, thanks to correctness of the threshold homomorphic encryption scheme, we can deduce that P can compute the correct decryption m of c. If P is honest, then it computes and outputs m.
It is easy to see that the communication complexity is indeed $\mathcal{O}(n\kappa)$.
The proof works for an adaptive adversary corrupting at most t parties because

the reasoning above is independent of which parties the adversary corrupts at what point in time (we only talk about parties that remain honest during the whole execution of the protocol).

Amortized Public Decryption. The public reconstruction protocol PubDec takes the public key pk and $T = n - 2t$ ciphertexts $c_1, \ldots, c_T$ as public inputs and the secret keys $sk_1, \ldots, sk_n$ as private inputs. The protocol publicly outputs the plaintexts $m_1, \ldots, m_T$ underlying the ciphertexts $c_1, \ldots, c_T$. This section is along the lines of [DN07, CHP12, BH08, CP15].

Protocol PubDec

1: Every party defines the polynomial $g(x) = \sum_{j=1}^{T} x^{j-1} \odot_{pk} c_j$ and computes $v_i = g(\alpha_i)$ for all $i \in \{1, \ldots, n\}$.
2: The parties use their secret keys to run $\mathsf{PrivDec}(P_i, v_i)$ for all $i \in \{1, \ldots, n\}$. Let u_i be P_i's private output from $\mathsf{PrivDec}(P_i, v_i)$ for all $i \in \{1, \ldots, n\}$.
3: Every party $P_i \in \mathcal{P}$ sends u_i to all other parties.
4: Every party $P_i \in \mathcal{P}$ locally defines a set $\mathcal{P}'_i$ of parties and adds party P_k to $\mathcal{P}'_i$ as soon as it receives u'_k from P_k.
   For $j = 0, 1, \ldots t$, as soon as $|\mathcal{P}'_i| \geqslant T + t + j$, P_i applies an efficient algorithm PolyFind (for example the Berlekamp-Welch decoder) on the points $\{(\alpha_k, u'_k)\}_{P_k \in \mathcal{P}'_i}$ to check whether there exists a polynomial p of degree at most $T - 1$ such that at least $T + t$ of the input points lie on p. If this is the case, then PolyFind outputs this polynomial and P_i outputs $m_1 = p_1, \ldots, m_T = p_T$, where $p(x) = \sum_{j=1}^{T} x^{j-1} \cdot_{pk} p_j$, and terminates. Otherwise, P_i proceeds with iteration $j + 1$.

Lemma 4. *Every party that remains uncorrupted until the end of the execution terminates the PubDec protocol and outputs the correct decryptions of $c_1, \ldots, c_T$ even in the presence of an adaptive adversary actively corrupting up to $t < n/3$ parties. The protocol has communication complexity $\mathcal{O}(n^2 \kappa)$.*

Proof. In this whole proof, an honest party is a party that is never corrupted by the adversary and remains honest during the whole execution of the protocol.
Termination: (taken from [CHP12]) Since all honest parties participate in the $\mathsf{PrivDec}(P_i, v_i)$ protocols for all $i \in \{1, \ldots, n\}$, termination of the PrivDec protocol implies that all honest parties terminate steps 1–3. Next, define the polynomial $g'(x) = \sum_{j=1}^{T} x^{j-1} \cdot_{pk} m_j$. Since c_j is an encryption of m_j under pk for all $j \in \{1, \ldots, T\}$, the homomorphic property of the encryption scheme implies that $g(x)$ is an encryption of $g'(x)$ under pk for all $x \in R_{pk}$. In particular, this holds for $x = \alpha_k$ for all $k \in \{1, \ldots, n\}$. Hence, by the correctness of the PrivDec protocol and by definition of u_k, we have $u_k = g'(\alpha_k)$ for all honest parties P_k. Now, let P_i be an arbitrary honest party and let $\widehat{j}$ be the first iteration when all honest parties are in $\mathcal{P}'_i$ (note that every honest party eventually includes all honest parties in $\mathcal{P}'_i$ and since there are at most $n = T + 2t$ parties, we have $\widehat{j} \leqslant t$). Then, either PolyFind already found a polynomial in iteration j for $j < \widehat{j}$

and P_i terminated before iteration $\widehat{j}$ or in iteration $\widehat{j}$, $\mathcal{P}'_i$ is of size $T + t + \widehat{j}$ and contains $n - t = T + t$ honest parties. Hence, since g' is a polynomial of degree at most $T - 1$ and at least $T + t$ input points (namely the points from honest parties) lie on g', we can be sure that the PolyFind algorithm finds a polynomial and P_i terminates in step $\widehat{j}$. Hence, after at most $\widehat{j} \leqslant t$ iterations, P_i terminates. Note that if in an iteration j the PolyFind algorithm fails to find a polynomial that passes the checks, then P_i has not received all the $u'_k = u_k$'s from honest parties as otherwise the PolyFind algorithm would have succeeded (see above). Hence, if in an iteration the PolyFind algorithm fails to compute a suitable polynomial, then it is ok for P_i to proceed with the next iteration because it is guaranteed that P_i can eventually add at least one party to $\mathcal{P}'_i$ and as soon as P_i has all the u_k's from honest parties (i.e. all honest parties are in $\mathcal{P}'_i$), it can terminate (and this will happen before the tth iteration ended).

Correctness: Let P_i be any honest party. As P_i terminates, it found a polynomial p of degree at most $T - 1$ and a set of parties $\mathcal{P}''_i$ of size at least $T + t$ such that P_i received a message u'_k from all $P_k \in \mathcal{P}''_i$ and $u'_k = p(\alpha_k)$ for all $P_k \in \mathcal{P}''_i$. Since there are at most t corrupted parties, at least T of the parties in $\mathcal{P}''_i$ are honest. In the proof for termination, we saw that for honest parties, $u'_k = u_k = g'(\alpha_k)$. Therefore, there exist T distinct elements α_k with $p(\alpha_k) = g'(\alpha_k)$. Since T points uniquely define a polynomial of degree at most $T - 1$ and both p and g' are polynomials of degree at most $T - 1$, we can conclude that $p = g'$ and P_i can correctly compute and output the messages $m_1, \ldots, m_T$ underlying the ciphertexts $c_1, \ldots, c_T$.

The claim about the communication complexity follows directly from the communication complexity of the PrivDec protocol.

Again, the proof works for an adaptive adversary corrupting at most t parties because the reasoning above is independent of which parties the adversary corrupts at what point in time (we only talk about parties that remain honest during the whole execution of the protocol).

Remark 8. In every instance of the PubDec protocol, each party executes the PolyFind algorithm up to $t + 1$ times. By using local player elimination, we can reduce the number of runs of the PolyFind algorithm in m instances of the PubDec protocol to $t + m$ per party (instead of $m(t + 1)$). More precisely, if in iteration j the run of the PolyFind algorithm of an honest party fails to output a polynomial that passes the checks, then at least $j + 1$ of the inputs must be wrong (otherwise the PolyFind algorithm would have succeeded). Since every party outputs a polynomial satisfying all the checks at latest in round t, each party can then detect which inputs were wrong and can locally eliminate the parties that sent those wrong values. In any future run of the PolyFind algorithm in the PubDec protocol, the party ignores the values sent from parties it locally eliminated (respectively, it does not include parties it locally eliminated in $\mathcal{P}'_i$).

Remark 9. By reduction and by Remark 2, we can deduce that for $c_1^1, \ldots, c_T^1$ and $c_1^2, \ldots, c_T^2$ two computationally indistinguishably distributed sets of T ciphertexts with computationally indistinguishably distributed sets of underlying plaintexts, an instance of the PubDec protocol with $(pk, c_1^1, \ldots, c_T^1)$ as public input (and $sk_1, \ldots, sk_n$ as private inputs) is computationally indistinguishably distributed to an instance of the PubDec protocol with $(pk, c_1^2, \ldots, c_T^2)$ as public input (and $sk_1, \ldots, sk_n$ as private inputs) even in the presence of an active adaptive adversary corrupting up to $t < n/3$ parties.

A.2   Multiplication

This subsection presents the multiplication protocol which is based on [DN07] and the MULTIPLICATION GATE in the Computation Phase protocol of [BH08]. The protocol uses circuit randomization which was originally introduced in [Bea92].

Let $T = \lfloor \frac{n-2t}{2} \rfloor$. Our multiplication protocol processes up to T independent multiplication gates at the same time. To ensure independence of the gates, every run of the multiplication protocol only considers multiplication gates with a specific multiplicative depth.

The multiplication protocol takes as input T multiplication gates $m_1, \ldots, m_T$ with the same multiplicative depth, the $2T$ inputs $\{(X_i, Y_i)\}_{i \in \{1, \ldots, T\}}$ (encrypting the values $\{(x_i, y_i)\}_{i \in \{1, \ldots, T\}}$) to the given multiplication gates and the T encrypted multiplication triples $\{(A_i, B_i, C_i)\}_{i \in \{1, \ldots, T\}}$ (encrypting the values $\{(a_i, b_i, a_i \cdot_{pk} b_i)\}_{i \in \{1, \ldots, T\}}$) associated with the given multiplication gates $m_1, \ldots, m_T$. We require that the multiplication triples underlying the encrypted triples $\{(A_i, B_i, C_i)\}_{i \in \{1, \ldots, T\}}$ are unknown to the adversary and computationally uniformly and independently distributed over the space of all multiplication triples (the latter is equivalent to the plaintexts underlying the first and second components of the triples being computationally uniformly and independently distributed and the third component being the product of the first two). The protocol publicly outputs T encryptions $\{Z_i\}_{i \in \{1, \ldots, T\}}$, where the underlying plaintexts z_i are equal to $x_i \cdot_{pk} y_i$ for all $i \in \{1, \ldots, T\}$.

Protocol Multiplication

1: Every party locally computes $X_i \ominus_{pk} A_i$ encrypting $x_i -_{pk} a_i$ and $Y_i \ominus_{pk} B_i$ encrypting $y_i -_{pk} b_i$ for all $i \in \{1, \ldots, T\}$ using the "$+_{pk}$-homomorphic" property of the encryption scheme.
2: The parties use their secret keys to run PubDec($\{X_i \ominus_{pk} A_i\}_{i \in \{1, \ldots, T\}}, \{Y_i \ominus_{pk} B_i\}_{i \in \{1, \ldots, T\}}$) and obtain $x_i -_{pk} a_i$ and $y_i -_{pk} b_i$ for all $i \in \{1, \ldots, T\}$.
3: Each party locally computes $E_i = \mathsf{Enc}_{pk}((x_i -_{pk} a_i) \cdot_{pk} (y_i -_{pk} b_i), e)$ for all $i \in \{1, \ldots, T\}$, where e is the neutral element of the randomness space. Then, it computes $Z_i = E_i \oplus_{pk} [(x_i -_{pk} a_i) \odot_{pk} B_i] \oplus_{pk} [(y_i -_{pk} b_i) \odot_{pk} A_i] \oplus_{pk} C_i$ for all $i \in \{1, \ldots, T\}$.
4: Every party outputs $\{Z_i\}_{i \in \{1, \ldots, T\}}$.

Remark 10. 1. If $n - 2t$ is odd, then the parties only input $n - 2t - 1$ ciphertexts to the PubDec protocol in step 2. In that case, the parties additionally give

$\mathsf{Enc}_{pk}(0_{pk}, e)$ as input to the PubDec protocol, where e is again the neutral element of the randomness space, obtain the plaintext 0_{pk} as one of the outputs of PubDec and simply disregard it in all further steps.

2. If only $T' < T$ multiplication gates are input to the multiplication protocol (for example when there are less than T multiplication gates with the same multiplicative depth in a given circuit), then the parties execute the protocol normally doing all the computations for indices in $\{1, \ldots, T'\}$ instead of in $\{1, \ldots, T\}$ and adding the encryption $\mathsf{Enc}_{pk}(0_{pk}, e)$ to the inputs of the PubDec protocol $n - 2t - 2T'$ times (where e is again the neutral element of the randomness space).

The multiplication protocol achieves the following.

Proposition 1. *Let $m_1, \ldots, m_T$ be T multiplication gates with the same multiplicative depth and let $\{(A_i, B_i, C_i)\}_{i \in \{1, \ldots, T\}}$ be the encrypted multiplication triples associated with the given gates. Furthermore, let $\{(X_i^1, Y_i^1)\}_{i \in \{1, \ldots, T\}}$ and $\{(X_i^2, Y_i^2)\}_{i \in \{1, \ldots, T\}}$ be two computationally indistinguishably distributed sets of $2T$ ciphertexts. Then, even in the presence of an active adaptive adversary corrupting up to $t < n/3$ parties, an execution of the multiplication protocol with $\{(X_i^1, Y_i^1)\}_{i \in \{1, \ldots, T\}}$ as inputs to the given gates is computationally indistinguishably distributed from an execution of the multiplication protocol with $\{(X_i^2, Y_i^2)\}_{i \in \{1, \ldots, T\}}$ as inputs to the given gates.*

Proof. Using reduction it is easy to see that step 1 is computationally indistinguishably distributed in both executions (even if the adversary corrupts a party during step 1).

For step 2, we know by reduction that the ciphertexts $(\{X_i^1 \ominus_{pk} A_i\}_{i \in \{1, \ldots, T\}}, \{Y_i^1 \ominus_{pk} B_i\}_{i \in \{1, \ldots, T\}})$ and $(\{X_i^2 \ominus_{pk} A_i\}_{i \in \{1, \ldots, T\}}, \{Y_i^2 \ominus_{pk} B_i\}_{i \in \{1, \ldots, T\}})$ are computationally indistinguishably distributed. Furthermore, we know that the plaintexts underlying $\{A_i\}_{i \in \{1, \ldots, T\}}$ and the plaintexts underlying $\{B_i\}_{i \in \{1, \ldots, T\}}$ are unknown to the adversary and computationally uniformly and independently distributed. Therefore, the plaintexts underlying $\{X_i^1 \ominus_{pk} A_i\}_{i \in \{1, \ldots, T\}}, \{Y_i^1 \ominus_{pk} B_i\}_{i \in \{1, \ldots, T\}}), \{X_i^2 \ominus_{pk} A_i\}_{i \in \{1, \ldots, T\}}$ and $\{Y_i^2 \ominus_{pk} B_i\}_{i \in \{1, \ldots, T\}})$ are all unknown to the adversary and computationally uniformly and independently distributed and thus, they are computationally indistinguishably distributed. By Remark 9, we can conclude that step 2 of the multiplication protocol is computationally indistinguishably distributed in both executions, even if the adversary corrupts a party.

As for step 1, a reduction argument shows that steps 3 and 4 maintain computational indistinguishability (even if the adversary corrupts a party during these steps).

Proposition 2. *The multiplication protocol communicates $\mathcal{O}(n^2 \kappa)$ bits.*

B   Protocol

The protocol we present uses a key generation oracle (KG) which sets up all the public and private keys used in our protocol, gives the keys to the entitled parties and provides public Lagrange arguments for all parties. We assume that the simulator has access to an efficient key generation algorithm (KGA) that computes a computationally indistinguishably distributed set of public and private keys and Lagrange arguments. Furthermore, we assume that the parties have access to an encoder and a decoder algorithm that transform values from the message space of the encryption scheme to $\{0,1\}^*$ and vice versa. We do not explicitly mention when the parties use the encoder and decoder algorithms. They are implicitly used whenever a transformation is necessary.

The description of the protocol follows the structure of the FuncEval$_f$ Algorithm in [CDN00].

Protocol

Preparation Phase:

1: Every party P_i receives a security parameter κ, the number of parties n, a secret input $x_i \in \{0,1\}^*$ and a random string $b_i \in \{0,1\}^*$ as input. The adversary is given the inputs κ, n, a random string $b \in \{0,1\}^*$ and an auxiliary string $a \in \{0,1\}^*$.

2: The parties call the key generation oracle KG. Each party P_i gets the common inputs $pk, K, R, \{K_\nu\}_\nu, \{\alpha_i\}_{i \in \{1,\ldots,n\}}$ and the secret inputs $sk_i, \{K_\chi^i\}_\chi$, where $(pk, sk_1, \ldots, sk_n)$ is a uniformly random threshold encryption key, K is a uniformly random encryption of 1_{pk} under pk, R is a uniformly random encryption of 0_{pk} under pk, $\{K_\nu\}_\nu$ are the public keys used for the zero-knowledge proofs and the commitment scheme, $\{K_\chi^i\}_\chi$ are the private keys of P_i used for the zero-knowledge proofs and the commitment scheme and $\{\alpha_i\}_{i \in \{1,\ldots,n\}}$ are Lagrange arguments.

3: On input pk, every party computes the arithmetic circuit over R_{pk} corresponding to the function f evaluated on n inputs. We denote the gates in the circuit by $H_{pk}^1, \ldots, H_{pk}^l$.

4: Let c_M be the number of multiplication gates in the circuit. The parties execute the **Triples** protocol with input c_M and obtain a set of triples $\{(A_i, B_i, C_i)\}_{i \in \mathcal{I}}$, where $\mathcal{I}$ is the set of all indices of multiplication gates in the circuit.

Computation Phase:

1: Each party P_i commits to its secret input x_i towards every party P_j for all $j \in \{1,\ldots,n\}$ under the corresponding commitment key. For all $(i,j) \in \{1,\ldots,n\}$, let $C_{i \to j}$ be the commitment to x_i from P_i towards P_j and let (x_i, c_{ij}) be the opening information for $C_{i \to j}$.

2: Each party P_i chooses a uniformly random value r_{x_i} from the randomness space. The parties run the BrACS protocol from Appendix B with public input (pk, K) and secret input $(x_i, r_{x_i}, \{c_{ij}\}_{j \in \{1,\ldots,n\}}, \{C_{i \to j}\}_{j \in \{1,\ldots,n\}}, \{C_{j \to i}\}_{j \in \{1,\ldots,n\}})$ for every party P_i and obtain as output a set S and encryptions $\{\mathsf{Enc}_{pk}^K(x_i)\}_{i:\ P_i \in S}$.

3: Evaluate the circuit as in [CDN00]: While there are gates that have not been evaluated yet, let $J \subseteq \{1,\ldots,l\}$ be the set of non-evaluated gates that are ready to be evaluated. Evaluate all gates in J in parallel by doing for every $j \in J$:

a) If H_{pk}^j is an input gate for a party $P_i \in S$, then every party sets $\mathsf{Enc}_{pk}(h_j) = \mathsf{Enc}_{pk}^K(x_i)$. If H_{pk}^j is an input gate for a party $P_i \notin S$, then every party computes $d \odot_{pk} K$ using the "Multiplication by constant" property of the encryption scheme and sets $\mathsf{Enc}_{pk}(h_j) = d \odot_{pk} K$, where d is a default value.

b) If H_{pk}^j is a constant input gate for a constant c, then every party sets $\mathsf{Enc}_{pk}(h_j) = c \odot_{pk} K$ by using the "Multiplication by constant" property of the encryption scheme.

c) If H_{pk}^j is an addition gate for $\mathsf{Enc}_{pk}(h_{j_1})$ and $\mathsf{Enc}_{pk}(h_{j_2})$, every party sets $\mathsf{Enc}_{pk}(h_j) = \mathsf{Enc}_{pk}(h_{j_1}) \oplus_{pk} \mathsf{Enc}_{pk}(h_{j_2})$ using the "$+_{pk}$-homomorphic" property of the encryption scheme.

d) If H_{pk}^j is a multiplication by a constant gate for values c and $\mathsf{Enc}_{pk}(h_{j_1})$, every party sets $\mathsf{Enc}_{pk}(h_j) = c \odot_{pk} \mathsf{Enc}_{pk}(h_{j_1})$ using the "Multiplication by constant" property of the encryption scheme.

e) If H_{pk}^j is a multiplication gate , the parties wait until all the multiplication gates with the same multiplicative depth as H_{pk}^j are ready to be evaluated. As soon as this is the case , the parties split these multiplication gates into blocks of $\lfloor \frac{n-2t}{2} \rfloor$ gates. For each block, the parties use the multiplication protocol from Appendix A.2 with the following input: the gates in the block, their input ciphertexts and the encrypted multiplication triples associated with the gates in the considered block. From this, the parties obtain the encrypted outputs of all the multiplication gates with the same multiplicative depth as H_{pk}^j.

Let $\mathsf{Enc}_{pk}(s)$ be the output of the evaluated circuit.

4: Every party P_i generates a uniformly random r_i from the message space R_{pk}. Each P_i commits to r_i towards every party P_j for all $j \in \{1, \ldots, n\}$ under the corresponding commitment key. For all $(i, j) \in \{1, \ldots, n\}$, let $B_{i \to j}$ be the commitment to r_i from P_i towards P_j and let (r_i, b_{ij}) be the opening information for $B_{i \to j}$.

5: Every party P_i chooses a uniformly random value $r_{r_i}^K$ from the randomness space. Parties run the BrACS protocol (see Appendix B) with public input (pk, K) and secret input $(r_i, r_{r_i}^K, \{b_{ij}\}_{j \in \{1,\ldots,n\}}, \{B_{i \to j}\}_{j \in \{1,\ldots,n\}}, \{B_{j \to i}\}_{j \in \{1,\ldots,n\}})$ for every party P_i. The parties get as output a set S' and encryptions $\{\mathsf{Enc}_{pk}^K(r_i)\}_{i:\ P_i \in S'}$.

6: Every party P_i chooses a uniformly random value $r_{r_i}^R$ from the randomness space. Then, the parties run the BrACS protocol with public input (pk, R) and secret input $(r_i, r_{r_i}^R, \{b_{ij}\}_{j \in \{1,\ldots,n\}}, \{B_{i \to j}\}_{j \in \{1,\ldots,n\}}, \{B_{j \to i}\}_{j \in \{1,\ldots,n\}})$ for every party P_i. In this execution of the BrACS, we take a slightly modified ACS property Q, namely to all the conditions described in the BrACS protocol, we add that a party P_j only likes another party P_i if P_j likes P_i for the ACS property of the BrACS execution in step 5 (it is okay if P_j only likes P_i after the BrACS from step 5 terminated and input 0 to BA_i in the ACS of step 5). The parties obtain as output a set S'' and encryptions $\{\mathsf{Enc}_{pk}^R(r_i)\}_{i:\ P_i \in S''}$.

7: Let $\hat{S} = S' \cap S''$. Let I be the set of indices of the parties in $\hat{S}$ and let $\{\lambda_i\}_{i \in I}$ be the Lagrange coefficients of degree $|I| - 1$ over R_{pk} such that for any polynomial g of degree at most $|I| - 1$ we have $g(0_{pk}) = \sum_{i \in I} \lambda_i \cdot_{pk} g(\alpha_i)$ (precisely $\lambda_i = \prod_{\substack{j \in I \\ j \neq i}} (0_{pk} - \alpha_j) \cdot_{pk} (\alpha_i - \alpha_j)^{-1}$ for all $i \in I$). Every party P_i locally computes $\mathsf{Enc}_{pk}(s)' = \mathsf{Enc}_{pk}(s) \bigoplus_{pk}{}_{i \in I} (\lambda_i \odot_{pk} \mathsf{Enc}_{pk}^R(r_i))$.

8: The parties use their secret keys to run $\mathsf{PrivDec}(P_i, \mathsf{Enc}_{pk}(s)')$ for all $i \in \{1, \ldots, n\}$ and all parties obtain s.

9: The parties run the reliable consensus protocol RC taking as secret input the value s decrypted in the previous step (as soon as they obtain it).

BrACS. In this subsection, we discuss the BrACS protocol used in our MPC protocol. The subprotocol takes as public input the public key pk of the encryption scheme and an encryption M (in our protocol and simulation this is sometimes an encryption of 1_{pk} and other times an encryption of 0_{pk}). The message encrypted by M is denoted by m. For each party P_i the protocol takes as secret input a message a_i, a randomness r_{a_i}, n values c_{ij} and $2n$ commitments $C_{j \to i}$ and $C_{i \to j}$ for $j \in \{1 \ldots, n\}$. The $C_{j \to i}$'s represent commitments from P_j towards P_i. If P_i and P_j are both honest, (a_i, c_{ij}) is the opening information for the commitment $C_{i \to j}$ that P_j holds. The protocol publicly outputs a set S of parties and for each party $P_i \in S$ it publicly outputs an encryption of $a_i \cdot_{pk} m$.

Protocol BrACS

1: Every party P_i generates an encryption of $a_i \cdot_{pk} m$ by computing $\mathsf{Enc}_{pk}^M(a_i, r_{a_i})$ and reliably broadcasts $\mathsf{Enc}_{pk}^M(a_i, r_{a_i})$ using the RBC protocol.
2: Every P_i uses the "proof of compatible commitment" property in Subsect. 2.4 and proves to all P_j for $j \in \{1, \ldots, n\}$ with instance $(\mathsf{Enc}_{pk}^M(a_i, r_{a_i}), C_{i \to j})$ and witness (a_i, r_{a_i}, c_{ij}).
3: Let Q be the property such that a party P_k satisfies Q towards another party P_j if and only if the reliable broadcast of P_k in step 1 terminated for P_j and the proof in step 2 was accepted by P_j. The parties run the ACS protocol with property Q and obtain a set $S \subseteq \mathcal{P}$. Every P_i waits until the reliable broadcast of all parties $P_k \in S$ terminated. Then each party outputs S and for each $P_k \in S$ the value received from the terminated reliable broadcast.

Proposition 3. *The BrACS protocol achieves the following properties.*

a) The protocol terminates for all honest parties.
b) All parties agree on the set S and the encryptions of parties in S.
c) The set S is of size at least $n - t$.
d) Every honest party P_i in S succeeds to reliably broadcast a correct encryption $\mathsf{Enc}_{pk}^M(a_i)$ of $a_i \cdot_{pk} m$. This means that the reliable broadcast of $\mathsf{Enc}_{pk}^M(a_i)$ terminates for all honest parties and that at least one honest party P_j accepts the proof given by P_i in step 2, namely that P_i knows a preimage of $\mathsf{Enc}_{pk}^M(a_i)$ under (pk, M) and that the first component of this preimage is equal to the value P_i committed to with $C_{i \to j}$.
Furthermore, for every corrupted party P_i in S, the reliable broadcast of y of P_i in step 1 terminates for all honest parties and at least one honest party P_j accepts the proof (see above) given by P_i in step 2. Hence, with high probability, P_i knows values (a_i', c_{ij}') such that $y = \mathsf{Enc}_{pk}^M(a_i')$ and (a_i', c_{ij}') is the opening information to $C_{i \to j}$.

The proof is straightforward and therefore omitted.

References

[Bea92] Beaver, D.: Efficient multiparty protocols using circuit randomization. In: Feigenbaum, J. (ed.) CRYPTO 1991. LNCS, vol. 576, pp. 420–432. Springer, Heidelberg (1992). https://doi.org/10.1007/3-540-46766-1_34

[BFO12] Ben-Sasson, E., Fehr, S., Ostrovsky, R.: Near-linear unconditionally-secure multiparty computation with a dishonest minority. In: Safavi-Naini, R., Canetti, R. (eds.) CRYPTO 2012. LNCS, vol. 7417, pp. 663–680. Springer, Heidelberg (2012). https://doi.org/10.1007/978-3-642-32009-5_39

[BGW88] Ben-Or, M., Goldwasser, S., Wigderson, A.: Completeness theorems for non-cryptographic fault-tolerant distributed computation (extended abstract). In: 20th ACM STOC, pp. 1–10. ACM Press, May 1988. https://doi.org/10.1145/62212.62213

[BH08] Beerliová-Trubíniová, Z., Hirt, M.: Perfectly-secure MPC with linear communication complexity. In: Canetti, R. (ed.) TCC 2008. LNCS, vol. 4948, pp. 213–230. Springer, Heidelberg (2008). https://doi.org/10.1007/978-3-540-78524-8_13

[BKLL20] Lum, E., Katz, J., Liu-Zhang, C.D., Loss, J.: Asynchronous Byzantine agreement with subquadratic communication. Cryptology ePrint Archive, Report 2020/851 (2020). https://eprint.iacr.org/2020/851

[BKR94] Ben-Or, M., Kelmer, B., Rabin, T.: Asynchronous secure computations with optimal resilience (extended abstract). In: Anderson, J., Toueg, S., (eds.) 13th ACM PODC, pp. 183–192. ACM, August 1994. https://doi.org/10.1145/197917.198088

[Bra84] Bracha, G.: An asynchronous [(n − 1)/3]-resilient consensus protocol. In: Proceedings of the third annual ACM symposium on Principles of distributed computing, PODC 1984, pp. 154–162, New York, NY, USA. Association for Computing Machinery (1984). https://doi.org/10.1145/800222.806743

[Can00a] Canetti, R.: Security and composition of multiparty cryptographic protocols. J. Cryptol. **13**, 143–202 (2000). https://doi.org/10.1007/s001459910006

[Can00b] Canetti, R.: Universally composable security: A new paradigm for cryptographic protocols. Cryptology ePrint Archive, Report 2000/067 (2000). https://eprint.iacr.org/2000/067

[CCD88] Chaum, D., Crépeau, C., Damgård, I.: Multiparty unconditionally secure protocols (extended abstract). In: 20th ACM STOC, pp. 11–19. ACM Press, May 1988. https://doi.org/10.1145/62212.62214

[CDN00] Cramer, R., Damgård, I., Nielsen, J.B.: Multiparty computation from threshold homomorphic encryption. Cryptology ePrint Archive, Report 2000/055, October 2000. https://eprint.iacr.org/2000/055

[CDN01] Cramer, R., Damgård, I., Nielsen, J.B.: Multiparty computation from threshold homomorphic encryption. In: Pfitzmann, B. (ed.) EUROCRYPT 2001. LNCS, vol. 2045, pp. 280–300. Springer, Heidelberg (2001). https://doi.org/10.1007/3-540-44987-6_18

[CGHZ16] Coretti, S., Garay, J., Hirt, M., Zikas, V.: Constant-round asynchronous multi-party computation based on one-way functions. In: Cheon, J.H., Takagi, T. (eds.) ASIACRYPT 2016, Part II. LNCS, vol. 10032, pp. 998–1021. Springer, Heidelberg (2016). https://doi.org/10.1007/978-3-662-53890-6_33

[CHL21] Chopard, A., Hirt, M., Liu-Zhang, C.D.: On communication-efficient asynchronous MPC with adaptive security. Cryptology ePrint Archive, Report 2021/1174 (2021). https://ia.cr/2021/1174

[Cho20] Choudhury, A.: Optimally-resilient unconditionally-secure asynchronous multi-party computation revisited. Cryptology ePrint Archive, Report 2020/906 (2020). https://eprint.iacr.org/2020/906

[CHP12] Choudhury, A., Hirt, M., Patra, A.: Unconditionally secure asynchronous multiparty computation with linear communication complexity. Cryptology ePrint Archive, Report 2012/517 (2012). https://eprint.iacr.org/2012/517

[CHP13] Choudhury, A., Hirt, M., Patra, A.: Asynchronous multiparty computation with linear communication complexity. In: Afek, Y. (ed.) DISC 2013. LNCS, vol. 8205, pp. 388–402. Springer, Heidelberg (2013). https://doi.org/10.1007/978-3-642-41527-2_27

[Coh16] Cohen, R.: Asynchronous secure multiparty computation in constant time. In: Cheng, C.-M., Chung, K.-M., Persiano, G., Yang, B.-Y. (eds.) PKC 2016, Part II. LNCS, vol. 9615, pp. 183–207. Springer, Heidelberg (2016). https://doi.org/10.1007/978-3-662-49387-8_8

[CP15] Choudhury, A., Patra, A.: Optimally resilient asynchronous MPC with linear communication complexity. In: Proceedings of the International Conference on Distributed Computing and Networking (ICDCN), pp. 1–10 (2015)

[CR98] Canetti, R., Rabin, T.: Fast asynchronous Byzantine agreement with optimal resilience (1998). http://citeseerx.ist.psu.edu/viewdoc/summary?doi=10.1.1.8.8120

[DI06] Damgård, I., Ishai, Y.: Scalable secure multiparty computation. In: Dwork, C. (ed.) CRYPTO 2006. LNCS, vol. 4117, pp. 501–520. Springer, Heidelberg (2006). https://doi.org/10.1007/11818175_30

[DN03] Damgård, I., Nielsen, J.B.: Universally composable efficient multiparty computation from threshold homomorphic encryption. In: Boneh, D. (ed.) CRYPTO 2003. LNCS, vol. 2729, pp. 247–264. Springer, Heidelberg (2003). https://doi.org/10.1007/978-3-540-45146-4_15

[DN07] Damgård, I., Nielsen, J.B.: Scalable and unconditionally secure multiparty computation. In: Menezes, A. (ed.) CRYPTO 2007. LNCS, vol. 4622, pp. 572–590. Springer, Heidelberg (2007). https://doi.org/10.1007/978-3-540-74143-5_32 https://iacr.org/archive/crypto2007/46220565/46220565.pdf

[DNRS03] Dwork, C., Naor, M., Reingold, O., Stockmeyer, L.: Magic functions: In memoriam: Bernard m. dwork 1923–1998. J. ACM **50**(6), 852–921 (2003). https://doi.org/10.1145/950620.950623

[GLS19] Goyal, V., Liu, Y., Song, Y.: Communication-efficient unconditional MPC with guaranteed output delivery. In: Boldyreva, A., Micciancio, D. (eds.) CRYPTO 2019, Part II. LNCS, vol. 11693, pp. 85–114. Springer, Cham (2019). https://doi.org/10.1007/978-3-030-26951-7_4

[GMW87] Goldreich, O., Micali, S., Wigderson, A.: How to play any mental game or a completeness theorem for protocols with honest majority. In: Aho, A., (ed.) 19th ACM STOC, pp. 218–229. ACM Press, May 1987. https://doi.org/10.1145/28395.28420

[GSZ20] Goyal, V., Song, Y., Zhu, C.: Guaranteed output delivery comes free in honest majority MPC. In: Micciancio, D., Ristenpart, T. (eds.) CRYPTO 2020, Part II. LNCS, vol. 12171, pp. 618–646. Springer, Cham (2020). https://doi.org/10.1007/978-3-030-56880-1_22

[HN06]   Hirt, M., Nielsen, J.B.: Robust multiparty computation with linear communication complexity. In: Dwork, C. (ed.) CRYPTO 2006. LNCS, vol. 4117, pp. 463–482. Springer, Heidelberg (2006). https://doi.org/10.1007/11818175_28

[HNP05] Hirt, M., Nielsen, J.B., Przydatek, B.: Cryptographic asynchronous multiparty computation with optimal resilience. In: Cramer, R. (ed.) EUROCRYPT 2005. LNCS, vol. 3494, pp. 322–340. Springer, Heidelberg (2005). https://doi.org/10.1007/11426639_19

[HNP08] Hirt, M., Nielsen, J.B., Przydatek, B.: Asynchronous multi-party computation with quadratic communication. In: Aceto, L., Damgård, I., Goldberg, L.A., Halldórsson, M.M., Ingólfsdóttir, A., Walukiewicz, I. (eds.) ICALP 2008, Part II. LNCS, vol. 5126, pp. 473–485. Springer, Heidelberg (2008). https://doi.org/10.1007/978-3-540-70583-3_39

[Pat11] Patra, A.: Error-free multi-valued broadcast and byzantine agreement with optimal communication complexity. In: Fernàndez Anta, A., Lipari, G., Roy, M. (eds.) OPODIS 2011. LNCS, vol. 7109, pp. 34–49. Springer, Heidelberg (2011). https://doi.org/10.1007/978-3-642-25873-2_4

[PCR08] Patra, A., Choudhury, A., Pandu Rangan, C.: Efficient asynchronous multiparty computation with optimal resilience. Cryptology ePrint Archive, Report 2008/425 (2008). https://eprint.iacr.org/2008/425

[PCR10] Patra, A., Choudhary, A., Rangan, C.P.: Efficient statistical asynchronous verifiable secret sharing with optimal resilience. In: Kurosawa, K. (ed.) ICITS 2009. LNCS, vol. 5973, pp. 74–92. Springer, Heidelberg (2010). https://doi.org/10.1007/978-3-642-14496-7_7

[PCR15] Patra, A., Choudhury, A., Pandu Rangan, C.: Efficient asynchronous verifiable secret sharing and multiparty computation. J. Cryptol. **28**(1), 49–109 (2015). https://doi.org/10.1007/s00145-013-9172-7

[PSR02] Prabhu, B., Srinathan, K., Rangan, C.P.: Asynchronous unconditionally secure computation: an efficiency improvement. In: Menezes, A., Sarkar, P. (eds.) INDOCRYPT 2002. LNCS, vol. 2551, pp. 93–107. Springer, Heidelberg (2002). https://doi.org/10.1007/3-540-36231-2_9

[RB89]   Rabin, T., Ben-Or,M.: Verifiable secret sharing and multiparty protocols with honest majority (extended abstract). In: 21st ACM STOC, pp. 73–85. ACM Press, May 1989. https://doi.org/10.1145/73007.73014

[SR00]   Srinathan, K., Pandu Rangan, C.: Efficient asynchronous secure multiparty distributed computation. In: Roy, B., Okamoto, E. (eds.) INDOCRYPT 2000. LNCS, vol. 1977, pp. 117–129. Springer, Heidelberg (2000). https://doi.org/10.1007/3-540-44495-5_11

[Yao82] Yao, A.C.: Theory and applications of trapdoor functions (extended abstract). In: 23rd FOCS, pp. 80–91. IEEE Computer Society Press, November 1982. https://doi.org/10.1109/SFCS.1982.45

Efficient Perfectly Secure Computation with Optimal Resilience

Ittai Abraham[1], Gilad Asharov[2(✉)], and Avishay Yanai[1]

[1] VMWare Research, Herzliya, Israel
{iabraham,yanaia}@vmware.com
[2] Department of Computer Science, Bar-Ilan University, Ramat Gan, Israel
Gilad.Asharov@biu.ac.il

Abstract. Secure computation enables n mutually distrustful parties to compute a function over their private inputs jointly. In 1988 Ben-Or, Goldwasser, and Wigderson (BGW) demonstrated that any function can be computed with perfect security in the presence of a malicious adversary corrupting at most $t < n/3$ parties. After more than 30 years, protocols with perfect malicious security, with round complexity proportional to the circuit's depth, still require sharing a total of $O(n^2)$ values per multiplication. In contrast, only $O(n)$ values need to be shared per multiplication to achieve semi-honest security. Indeed sharing $\Omega(n)$ values for a single multiplication seems to be the natural barrier for polynomial secret sharing-based multiplication.

In this paper, we close this gap by constructing a new secure computation protocol with perfect, optimal resilience and malicious security that incurs sharing of only $O(n)$ values per multiplication, thus, matching the semi-honest setting for protocols with round complexity that is proportional to the circuit depth. Our protocol requires a constant number of rounds per multiplication. Like BGW, it has an overall round complexity that is proportional only to the multiplicative depth of the circuit. Our improvement is obtained by a novel construction for *weak VSS for polynomials of degree-2t*, which incurs the same communication and round complexities as the state-of-the-art constructions for *VSS for polynomials of degree-t*.

Our second contribution is a method for reducing the communication complexity for any depth-1 sub-circuit to be proportional only to the size of the input and output (rather than the size of the circuit). This implies protocols with *sublinear communication complexity* (in the size of the circuit) for perfectly secure computation for important functions like matrix multiplication.

Gilad Asharov is sponsored by the Israel Science Foundation (grant No. 2439/20), by the BIU Center for Research in Applied Cryptography and Cyber Security in conjunction with the Israel National Cyber Bureau in the Prime Minister's Office, and by the European Union's Horizon 2020 research and innovation programme under the Marie Skłodowska-Curie grant agreement No. 891234.

K. Nissim and B. Waters (Eds.): TCC 2021, LNCS 13043, pp. 66–96, 2021.
https://doi.org/10.1007/978-3-030-90453-1_3

1   Introduction

Secure multiparty computation is a major pillar of modern cryptography. Break-through results on secure multiparty computation in the late 80' prove feasibility with optimal resilience: perfect, statistical and computational security can be achieved as long as $t < n/3$ [7], $t < n/2$ (assuming broadcast) [36] and $t < n$ [27,40], respectively, where n is the number of computing parties such that at most t of them are controlled by a malicious adversary.

   In this paper we focus on secure computation with perfect security, which is the strongest possible guarantee: it provides unconditional, everlasting security. Such protocols come with desirable properties. They often guarantee adaptive security [12,32] and remain secure under universal composition [11]. A central foundational result in this context is the Completeness Theorem of Ben-or, Gold-wasser, and Wigderson [7] from 1988:

Theorem 1.1 (BGW with improvements [3,7,18,25]- informal). *Let f be an n-ary functionality and C its arithmetic circuit representation. Given a synchronous network with pairwise private channels and a broadcast channel, there exists a protocol for computing f with perfect security in the presence of a static malicious adversary controlling up to $t < n/3$ parties, with round complexity $O(\mathsf{depth}(C))$ and communication complexity of $O(n^4 \cdot |C|)$ words in point-to-point channels and no broadcast in the optimistic case, and additional $\Omega(n^4 \cdot |C|)$ words of broadcast in the pessimistic case.*[1]

   The communication complexity in the above statement (and throughout the paper) is measured in words (i.e., field elements), and we assume a word of size $O(\log n)$ bits.

   In the past three decades there has been great efforts to improve the communication complexity of the BGW protocol [3,25]. Theorem 1.1 states the round and communication complexity of the protocols after these improvements. Most recently, Goyal, Liu and Song. [28], building upon Beaver [5], and Beerliová and Hirt [6], achieved $O(n|C| + n^3)$ communication words (including all broadcast costs) at the expense of increasing the round complexity to $O(n + \mathsf{depth}(C))$.

   In some natural setting, e.g., secure computation of shallow circuits in high latency networks, this additive $O(n)$ term in the round complexity might render the protocol inapplicable. This state of affairs leads to the fundamental question of whether the communication complexity of perfectly secure computation can be improved *without* sacrificing the round complexity. Moreover, from theoretical perspective, the tradeoff between round complexity and communication complexity is an interesting one.

---

[1] In the optimistic case the adversary does not deviate from the prescribed protocol. Thus, in the pessimistic case (when it does deviate from the protocol) the adversary might only make the execution more expensive.

1.1   Our Results

We show an improvement of the communication complexity of perfectly secure protocols, without incurring any cost in round complexity. Notably, our improvement applies both to the optimistic case and to the pessimistic case:

Theorem 1.2 (Main technical result - informal). *Let f be an n-ary functionality and C its arithmetic circuit representation. Given a synchronous network with pairwise private channels and a broadcast channel, there exists a protocol for computing f with perfect security in the presence of a static malicious adversary controlling up to $t < n/3$ parties, with round complexity $O(\mathsf{depth}(C))$ and communication complexity of $O(n^3 \cdot |C|)$ words on point-to-point channels and no broadcast in the optimistic case, and additional $O(n^3 \cdot |C|)$ words of broadcast in the pessimistic case.*

Our result strictly improves the state of the art and is formally incomparable to the result of Goyal et al. [28]. Our protocol will perform better in high-latency networks (e.g., the internet) on shallow circuits when $\mathsf{depth}(C) \ll n$. Whereas the protocol of [28] performs better in low-latency networks (e.g., LAN), or when $\mathsf{depth}(C) \approx \Omega(n)$.

Sub-linear perfect MPC for sub-circuits of depth-1. As our second main result, we show for the first time that for a non-trivial class of functions, there is in fact a *sub-linear* communication perfectly secure MPC (in the circuit size). Specifically, we design a perfectly secure MPC that supports all functionalities that can be computed by depth 1 circuits. The communication complexity of our protocol depends only on the input and output sizes of the function, but not on the circuit size, i.e., the number of multiplications. We prove the following:

Theorem 1.3. *Let $n > 3t$, and let $\mathbb{F}$ be a finite field with $|\mathbb{F}| > n$. For every arithmetic circuit $G : \mathbb{F}^L \to \mathbb{F}^M$ of multiplication depth 1 (i.e., degree-2 polynomial), there exists a perfect t-secure protocol that computes $(y_1, \ldots, y_M) = G(x_1, \ldots, x_L)$ in $O(1)$ rounds and $O((M + L) \cdot n^3)$ words over the point-to-point channels in the optimistic case, and additional $O((M + L) \cdot n^3)$ broadcast messages in the pessimistic case. Specifically, the communication complexity is independent of $|G|$.*

The above theorem can also be applied to compute circuits with higher depth, while paying only communication complexity that is proportional to the number of wires between the layers, and independent of the number of multiplications in each layer. Similar techniques were shown in the statistical case [14], but no protocol is known for perfect security.

Application: Secure Matrix Multiplication. As a leading example of the usefulness of our depth 1 circuit protocol, consider matrix multiplication of two $T \times T$ matrices. This operation has inputs and outputs of size $O(T^2)$, but implementing it requires $O(T^3)$ multiplications (at least when implemented naïvely). The starting point (Theorem 1.1) is $\Omega(T^3 \cdot n^4)$ point-to-point in the optimistic case (and additional $\Omega(T^3 \cdot n^4)$ words of broadcast in the pessimistic case. Theorem 1.3 improves the communication complexity to $O(T^2 \cdot n^3)$ in the point-to-point channels with no additional broadcast in the optimistic case (and additional $O(T^2 \cdot n^3)$ words on broadcast in the pessimistic case). Our protocol also achieves $O(1)$ rounds in both the optimistic and pessimistic cases.

Secure matrix multiplication is a key building block for a variety of appealing applications. For example, anonymous communication [1] and secure collaborative learning. The latter involves multiplication of many large matrices (see [4,13,33–35,39], to name a few). For instance, the deep convolutional neural network (CNN) ResNet50 [38] requires roughly 2000 matrix multiplications, which, when computed securely, results in more than 4 billion multiplication gates. Using our protofocol of matrix multiplication, computing this task reduces by order of magnitudes, the communication to be proportional to computing only millions multiplications.

Secure Multiplication: A Natural Barrier of $\Omega(n)$ Secret Sharings
We give a very high level overview of our technical controbution, pointing to the core of our improvements. When viewed from afar, all secret-sharing based MPC protocols have a very similar flow. The starting point property is that polynomial secret sharing is additively homomorphic. This allows computing any linear combination (additional and multiplication by public constants) of secrets locally and with no interaction. The challenge is with multiplication gates: while multiplication can also be applied homomorphically (and non-interactively), it increases the degree of the underlying polynomial that hides the secret. Secure multiplication uses the fact that polynomial interpolation is just a linear combination of points on the polynomial, and hence a central part of the computation can be applied locally.

Given shares of the two inputs, every party shares a new secret which is its locally computed multiplication of its two shares. Then, all these new shares are locally combined using the linear combination of the publicly known Lagrange coefficients. This results in the desired new sharing of the multiplication of the two inputs.

This elegant framework for secure multiplication embeds a natural communication complexity barrier: each multiplication requires $\Omega(n)$ secret sharing (each party needs to secret share its local multiplication). In the malicious case, the secret sharing protocol is Verifiable Secret Sharing (VSS), hence, the total communication complexity in this framework is at least $\Omega(n \cdot \mathsf{comm}(VSS))$.

State of the art MPC for almost all settings matches this natural barrier, obtaining constant round protocols with optimal resilience using $O(n \cdot \mathsf{comm}(VSS))$ communication per multiplication complexity, where VSS is the best secret sharing for that setting.

The only exception we are aware of is the family pf BGW protocols for a malicious adversary, where all known improvements until now [3,7,25] require $\Omega(n^2 \cdot \mathsf{comm}(VSS))$ communication. This is because each party needs to share n invocations of VSSs of degree-t polynomials in order to prove that the secret it shared for the product is indeed equal to multiplication of the already shared multiplicands.

Weak VSS and the complexity of perfect MPC. The main technical contribution of this work is a multiplication protocol that meets the natural barrier and achieves communication complexity of $O(n \cdot \mathsf{comm}(VSS))$. Since $\mathsf{comm}(VSS)$ is $O(n^2)$ words in the optimistic case (and no broadcast) and $O(n^2)$ over the point-to-point channels and additional $O(n^2)$ words of broadcast in the pessimistic case, Theorem 1.2 is obtained. The improvement can thus be described as follows:

- Semi-honest BGW requires $O(n \cdot \mathsf{comm}(SS))$ communication per multiplication.
- Malicious BGW requires $O(n^2 \cdot \mathsf{comm}(VSS))$ communication per multiplication.
- Our malicious protocol requires $O(n \cdot \mathsf{comm}(VSS))$ communication per multiplication.

Our improved efficiency is obtained by replacing n invocations of degree-t VSSs with just one invocation of a *weak* VSS for degree-$2t$, which we denote by WSS. By weak VSS, we refer to the setting in which the parties' shares define a single secret at the end of the sharing phase, and during the reconstruction phase, the parties can either recover that secret or $\perp$. We show that a single weak VSS for a degree-$2t$ polynomial (along with a constant number of strong VSS) is sufficient to prove that the secret shared for the product is equal the multiplication of its two already shared multiplicands.

Lemma 1.4 (informal). *Given $n > 3t$, there is a protocol for implementing Weak Verifiable Secret Sharing with optimal resilience, for a polynomial of degree-$2t$ with communication complexity of $O(n^2)$ words on point-to-point channels in the optimistic case, and additional $O(n^2)$ words of broadcast in the pessimistic case, and $O(1)$ rounds.*

Our new weak verifiable secret sharing of degree-$2t$ has the same asymptotic complexity as verifiable secret sharing of degree-t. In addition to improving the efficiency of the core building block in secure computation (i.e. the multiplication), we believe it also makes it simpler, which is a pedagogical benefit.

Adaptive Security and UC. Protocols that achieve perfect security have substantial advantage over protocols that are only computationally secure: It was shown [32] that perfectly secure protocols in the stand-alone setting with a black-box straight-line simulator are also secure under universal composition [11]. Moreover, it was shown [12] that perfectly secure protocols in presence of a static malicious adversary (under the security definition in [22]) enjoy also perfect security in the presence of an adaptive malicious adversary, albeit with the weaker guarantee provided by inefficient simulation. We prove security in the classic setting of a static adversary and stand-alone computation. This implies UC security. The additional requirements under the definition of [22] hold in our protocols, and thus we derive also security in the presence of adaptive adversary (with inefficient simulation).

The Broadcast Channel Model. We analyze our protocol in the broadcast model and count messages sent over private channels and over the broadcast channel separately. In our setting $(t < n/3)$ the broadcast channel can also be simulated over the point-to-point channels. However, this comes with some additional cost. There are two alternatives: replace each broadcast use in the protocol requires $O(n^2)$ communication and $O(n)$ rounds [8,16], or $O(n^4 \log n)$ communication and expected constant round (even with bounded parallel composition [17,24,31]).

1.2   Related Work

Constant-Round per Multiplication. In this paper we focus on perfect security in the presence of a malicious adversary, optimal resilience and constant round per multiplication. Our protocol improves the state of the art in this line of work. As mentioned in Asharov, Lindell and Rabin [3], an additional verification protocol is needed for completing the specification of the multiplication step of BGW. In Theorem 1.1, we ignore the cost associated with those verification steps and just count the number of verifiable secret sharing needed, which is $\Omega(n^2)$ VSSs per multiplication gate. The protocol presented by Asharov, Lindell and Rabin [3] also requires $O(n^2)$ VSSs per multiplication gate. Cramer, Damgård and Maurer [18] presented a protocol that works in a different way to the BGW protocol, which also achieves constant round per multiplication. It has worst-case communication complexity of $O(n^5)$ field elements over point-to-point channels and $O(n^5)$ field elements over a broadcast channel. The optimistic cost is $O(n^4)$ field elements over point-to-point channels and $O(n^3)$ field elements over the broadcast channel.

Protocols that are Based on the Player Elimination Technique. There is a large body of work [6,19,28–30] that improves the communication complexity of information-theoretic protocols using the player elimination technique. All of these protocols have a round complexity that is linear in the number of parties. This is inherent in the player elimination technique since every time cheating is detected, two players are eliminated and some computations are repeated. In many cases player elimination would give a more efficient protocol than our approach. However, there are some cases, specifically for a low-depth circuit where n is large and over high-latency networks, in which our protocol is more efficient. Moreover, our protocol can achieve communication complexity which is sub-linear in the number of multiplication gates, depends on the circuits to be evaluated. We do not know how to achieve similar results on protocols that are based on Beaver multiplication triplets [5], such as the protocol of Goyal et al. [28]. These lines of work are therefore incomparable.

Lower Bounds. Recently, Damgård and Schwartzbach [21] showed that for any n and all large enough g, there exists a circuit C with g gates such that any perfectly secure protocol implementing C must communicate $\Omega(ng)$ bits. Note that Theorem 1.3 is sub-linear (in the circuit size) only for particular kind of circuits in which the circuit is much larger than the size of the inputs or its outputs. It is easy to find a circuit C with g gates in which our protocol must communication $O(n^4 g)$ in the pessimistic case. A lower bound by Damgård et al. [20] shows that any perfectly-secure protocol that works in the "gate-by-gate" framework must communicate $\Omega(n)$ bits for every multiplication gate. Our protocol deviates from this framework when computing an entire multiplication layer as an atomic unit.

1.3 Open Problems

Our protocol improves the communication complexity of constant round multiplication with optimal malicious resilience from $O(n^2 \cdot \mathsf{comm}(VSS))$ to $O(n \cdot \mathsf{comm}(VSS))$, matching the number of secret-shares in the semi-honest protocol. The immediate open problem is exploring the optimal communication complexity of verifiable secret sharing protocol. To the best of our knowledge, we are not aware of any non-trivial lower bound for perfect VSS (also see survey by C, Choudhury and Patra [9]). The VSS protocol requires $O(n^2)$ words in the optimistic case over the point-to-point channel, and additional $O(n^2)$ words over the broadcast channel in the pessimistic case.

Another possible direction to generalize our work is to mitigate between the two approaches for perfect security: Design a "hybrid" protocol that computes some sub-circuits using the linear communication complexity approach, and some sub-circuits using the constant-round per multiplication approach and achieving the best of both worlds. Another interesting direction is to make sublinear communication complexity improvement compatible with the protocols that are based on multiplication triplets.

2   Technical Overview

In this section we provide a technical overview of our results. We start with an overview of the BGW protocol in Sect. 2.1 and then overview our protocol in Sect. 2.2.

2.1 Overview of the BGW Protocol

In the following, we give a high level overview of the BGW protocol while incorporating several optimization that were given throughout the years [3,25].

Let f be the function that the parties wish to compute, mapping n inputs to n outputs. The input of party P_i is x_i and its output is y_i, where $(y_1, \ldots, y_n) = f(x_1, \ldots, x_n)$. On a high level, the BGW protocol works by emulating the computation of an arithmetic circuit C that computes f and has three phases. In the first phase, the input sharing phase, each party secret shares its input with all other parties. At the end of this stage, the value of each input wire of the circuit C is secret shared among the parties, such that no subset of t parties can reconstruct the actual values on the wires. In the second phase, the circuit emulation phase, the parties emulate a computation of the circuit gate-by-gate, computing shares on the output wire of each gate using the shares on the input wires. At the end of this stage, the output wires' values are secret shared among all parties. Finally, in the output reconstruction phase, P_i receives all the shares associated with its output wire and reconstructs its output, y_i.

The invariant maintained in the original BGW protocol is that each wire in the circuit, carrying some value a, is secret-shared among the parties using some random polynomial $A(x)$ of degree-t with a as its constant term. We follow the invariant of [3], and in our protocol, the parties hold bivariate sharing and not univariate sharing. That is, the secret is hidden using a bivariate polynomial $A(x, y)$ of degree-t in both variables in which the share of each party P_i is defined as $A(x, \alpha_i), A(\alpha_i, y)$, where α_i is the evaluation point associated with P_i. Maintaining bivariate sharing instead of univariate sharing removes one of the building blocks in the original BGW protocol, where parties sub-share their shares to verify that all the shares lie on a polynomial of degree-t. Obtaining bivariate sharing essentially comes for free. In particular, when parties share a value, they use a verifiable secret sharing protocol (VSS, see Sect. 2.2) [15,23,24], which uses bivariate sharing to verify that all the shares are consistent. However, in BGW, the parties then disregard this bivariate sharing and project it to univariate sharing. We just keep the shares in the bivariate form.

The Multiplication Protocol. In the input sharing phase, each party simply shares its input using the BGW's VSS protocol. Emulating the computation of addition gates is easy using linearity of the secret sharing scheme. The goal in the multiplication protocol is to obtain bivariate sharing of the value of the output wire of the multiplication gate using the shares on the input wires. Let a, b be the two values on the input wires, hidden with polynomials $A(x, y), B(x, y)$, respectively. The protocol proceeds as follows:

1. Each party P_i holds shares $f_i^a(x) = A(x, \alpha_i)$ and $f_i^b(x) = B(x, \alpha_i)$, each are univariate polynomials of degree-t. Each party P_i shares a bivariate polynomial $C_i(x, y)$ of degree-t such that $C_i(0, 0) = f_i^a(0) \cdot f_i^b(0)$.
2. Using a *verification protocol*, each party P_i proves in perfect zero knowledge that $C_i(0, 0) = f_i^a(0) \cdot f_i^b(0)$. We elaborate on this step below.
3. Given the shares on all (degree-t) polynomials $C_1(x, y), \ldots, C_n(x, y)$, the parties compute shares of the polynomial $C(x, y) \stackrel{\text{def}}{=} \sum_{i=1}^{n} \lambda_i \cdot C_i(x, y)$, where $\lambda_1, \ldots, \lambda_n$ are the Lagrange coefficients, by simply locally computing a linear combination of the shares they obtained in the previous step.

To see why this protocol is correct, observe that since each one of the polynomials $C_1(x, y), \ldots, C_n(x, y)$ is a polynomial of degree-t, then the resulting polynomial $C(x, y)$ is also a polynomial of degree-t. Moreover, define $h(y) \stackrel{\text{def}}{=} A(0, y) \cdot B(0, y)$ and observe that $h(y)$ is a polynomial of degree-$2t$ satisfying $h(0) = A(0, 0) \cdot B(0, 0) = ab$. It holds that $ab = \lambda_1 \cdot h(\alpha_1) + \ldots + \lambda_n \cdot h(\alpha_n)$. Thus,

$$C(0, 0) \stackrel{\text{def}}{=} \sum_{i=1}^{n} \lambda_i \cdot C_i(0, 0) = \sum_{i=1}^{n} \lambda_i \cdot f_i^a(0) \cdot f_i^b(0) = \sum_{i=1}^{n} \lambda_i \cdot h(\alpha_i) = ab \ ,$$

as required. Crucially, each $C_i(x, y)$ must hide $h(\alpha_i) = f_i^a(0) \cdot f_i^b(0)$ as otherwise the above linear combination would not result with the correct constant term. This explains the importance of the verification protocol.

BGW's verification protocol. In the verification protocol, the dealer holds the univariate polynomials $f_i^a(x), f_i^b(x)$ and a polynomial $C_i(x, y)$, and each party P_j holds a share on those polynomials, that is, points $f_i^a(\alpha_j), f_i^b(\alpha_j)$ and degree-t univariate polynomials $C_i(x, \alpha_j), C_i(\alpha_j, y)$. The parties wish to verify that $C_i(0, 0) = f_i^a(0) \cdot f_i^b(0)$.

Towards that end, the dealer defines random degree-t polynomials $D_1, \ldots, D_t$ under the constraint that

$$C_i(x, 0) = f_i^a(x) \cdot f_i^b(x) - \sum_{\ell=1}^{t} x^\ell \cdot D_\ell(x, 0) . \tag{1}$$

As shown in [3, 7], the dealer can choose the polynomials $D_1, \ldots, D_t$ in a special way so as to cancel all the coefficients of degree higher than t of $f_i^a(x) \cdot f_i^b(x)$ and to ensure that $C_i(x, y)$ is of degree t. The dealer verifiably shares the polynomials $D_1, \ldots, D_t$ with all parties, and then each party P_k verifies that the shares it received satisfy Eq. (1). If not, it complaints against the dealer. Note that at this point, since all polynomials $C_i, D_1, \ldots, D_t$ are bivariate polynomial of degree-t, and $f_i^a(x), f_i^b(x)$ are univariate polynomials of degree-t, it is possible to reconstruct the shares of any party P_k without the help of the dealer. The parties can then unequivocally verify the complaint. If a complaint was resolved to be a true complaint, the dealer is dishonest, we can reconstruct its points and exclude it from the protocol. If the complaint is false, we can also eliminate the complaining party.

An honest dealer always distributes polynomials that satisfy Eq. (1). For the case of a corrupted dealer, the term $f_i^a(x) \cdot f_i^b(x) - \sum_{\ell=1}^{t} x^\ell \cdot D_\ell(x, 0)$ defines a univariate polynomial of degree at most $2t$ for every choice of degree-t bivariate polynomials $D_1, \ldots, D_t$. If this polynomial agrees with the polynomial $C_i(x, 0)$ for all honest parties, i.e., on $2t + 1$ points, then those two polynomials are identical, and thus it must hold that $C_i(0, 0) = f_i^a(0) \cdot f_i^b(0)$, as required.

2.2   Our Protocol

Simplifying the Verification Protocol. In the above verification protocol, the dealer distributes t polynomials $D_1, \ldots, D_t$ using VSS. We show how to use a more efficient technique for accomplishing the verification task. Namely, we introduce a weak secret sharing protocol, for sharing a polynomial $D(x, y)$ of degree-$2t$ in x and degree-t in y. The dealer then chooses a *single* random polynomial $D(x, y)$ under the constraint that:

$$C_i(x, 0) = f_i^a(x) \cdot f_i^b(x) - D(x, 0) \tag{2}$$

The dealer distributes $D(x, y)$ and the parties jointly verify that (a) Eq. (2) holds and (b) that $D(0, 0) = 0$.

Our weak secret sharing protocol for distributing such $D(x,y)$ has *the same complexity as verifiable secret sharing of a degree-t polynomial*, and therefore we improve by a factor of $t = O(n)$. The secret sharing is weak in the sense that the parties cannot necessarily reconstruct the secret from the shares without the help of the dealer during the reconstruction. However, the verifiability part guarantees that there is a well-defined polynomial that can be reconstructed (or, if the dealer does not cooperate, then no polynomial would be reconstructed). Since the role of the polynomial $D(x,y)$ is just in the verification phase and requires the involvement of the dealer, to begin with, this weak verifiability suffices. If the dealer does not cooperate during the verification phase, then the parties can reconstruct its inputs and resume the computation on its behalf.

Our Weak Secret Sharing. Our weak verifiable secret sharing protocol is similar to the BGW verifiable secret sharing protocol. Introducing modifications to the protocol enables sharing of a polynomial of a higher degree, but in that case – satisfies only weak verifiability. We start with an overview of the verifiable secret sharing protocol and then describe our weak secret sharing protocol.

The Verifiable Secret Sharing Protocol. In a nutshell, the verifiable secret sharing protocol of BGW (with the simplifications of [23]) works as follows:

1. **Sharing:** The dealer wishes to distribute shares of a polynomial $D(x,y)$ of degree t in both variables. The dealer sends to each party P_i the degree-t univariate polynomials $f_i(x) = D(x, \alpha_i)$ and $g_i(y) = D(\alpha_i, y)$.
2. **Exchange sub-shares:**
   Each party P_i sends to party P_j the pair $(f_i(\alpha_j), g_i(\alpha_j))$. Note that if indeed the dealer sent correct shares, then $f_i(\alpha_j) = D(\alpha_j, \alpha_i) = g_j(\alpha_i)$ and $g_i(\alpha_j) = D(\alpha_i, \alpha_j) = f_j(\alpha_i)$. If a party does not receive from P_j the shares it expects to receive, then it broadcasts a complaint. The complaint has the form of complaint$(i, j, f_i(\alpha_j), g_i(\alpha_j))$, i.e., P_i complaints that it receives from P_j wrong points, and publishes the two points that it expected to receive, corresponding to the information it had received from the dealer.
3. **Complaint resolution – the dealer:** The dealer publicly reveals all the shares of all parties that broadcast false complaints – i.e., if party P_i complaints with points different than those given in the first round, then the dealer makes the share $(f_i(x), g_i(y))$ public.
4. **Vote:** The parties vote that whatever they saw is consistent. A party is happy with its share and broadcasts **good** if: (a) Its share was not publicly revealed. (b) The dealer resolved all conflicts the party saw in the exchange sub-shares phase, i.e., all its complaints were resolved by the dealer by publicly opening the other parties' shares. (c) All shares that the dealer broadcasts are consistent with its shares. (d) There are no parties (j, k) that complain of each other, and the dealer did not resolve at least one of those complaints. If $2t+1$ parties broadcast **good** then the parties accept the shares. A party that its share was publicly revealed updates its share to be the publicly revealed one.

Note that if more than $2t+1$ parties broadcast good then more than $t+1$ honest parties are happy with their shares. Those shares determine a unique bivariate polynomial of degree-t. Moreover, any polynomial that is publicly revealed must be consistent with this bivariate polynomial, as agreeing with the points of $t+1$ honest parties uniquely determine a polynomial of degree-t.

Weak Secret Sharing. Consider this protocol when the dealer shares a polynomial $D(x,y)$ that is of degree-$2t$ in x and degree-t in y, i.e., $D(x,y) = \sum_{i=0}^{2t} \sum_{j=0}^{t} d_{i,j} x^i y^j$ for some set of coefficients $\{d_{i,j}\}_{i,j}$. Here, if $t+1$ honest parties are happy with their shares and broadcast good, their polynomials also define a unique polynomial $D(x,y)$ of degree-$2t$ in x and degree-t in y. However, if there is a complaint and the dealer opens some party's share, since $f_i(x)$ is of degree-$2t$ it is not sufficient that these $t+1$ honest parties agree with that polynomial $f_i(x)$, and $f_i(x)$ might still be "wrong". This implies that the honest parties cannot identify whether their shares are compatible with the shares of the other honest parties (that their shares were publicly revealed), and further verification is needed, which seems to trigger more rounds of complaints. Guaranteeing all honest parties obtain consistent shares is a more challenging task.

To keep the protocol constant round, we therefore take a different route and do not require the dealer to publicly open any of the $f_i(x)$ polynomials! Still, it has to publicly open only the $g_i(y)$ polynomials, as those are of degree-t. Each honest party broadcasts good only if the same conditions as in VSS are met. At the end of this protocol, some honest parties might not hold $f_i(x)$ shares on the polynomial $D(x,y)$. Those parties will not participate in the reconstruction protocol. In the reconstruction phase, since the corrupted parties might provide incorrect shares and since some honest parties do not have shares, we cannot guarantee reconstruction of the polynomial $D(x,y)$ without the help of the dealer. However, we can guarantee that only the polynomial $D(x,y)$ can be reconstructed, or no polynomial at all.

Concluding the Multiplication Protocol. Recall that in our protocol, the parties also have to jointly verify that (a) Eq. 2 holds, and that (b) that $D(0,0) = 0$. We now elaborate on those two steps.

To verify that the polynomial $D(x,y)$ satisfies $D(x,0) = f_i^a(x) \cdot f_i^b(x) - C_i(x,0)$, each party P_j simply checks that its own shares satisfy this condition, i.e., whether $D(\alpha_j, 0) = f_i^a(\alpha_j) \cdot f_i^b(\alpha_j) - C_i(\alpha_j, 0)$. Note that if this holds for $2t+1$ parties, then the two polynomials are identical. Each party P_j checks its own shares, and if the condition does not hold then it broadcasts complaint(j). With each complaint the dealer has to publicly reveal the shares of P_j. Since all those polynomials were shared using (weak or strong) verifiable secret sharing, the parties can easily verify whether the shares that the dealer opens are correct or not.

To check that $D(0,0) = 0$, the parties simply reconstruct the polynomial $D(0,y)$. This is a polynomial of degree-t and it can be reconstructed (with the help of the dealer, as D is shared using a weak secret sharing scheme). Moreover, it does not reveal any information on the polynomials $f_i^a(x), f_i^b(x), C_i(x,0)$: In case of an honest dealer, the adversary already holds t shares on the polynomial $D(0,y)$ and it always holds that $D(0,0) = 0$, since the dealer is honest.

2.3   Extensions

Our zero knowledge verification protocol allows the dealer to prove that its shares of a, b, c satisfy the relation $c = ab$. The cost of the protocol is proportional to a constant number of VSSs. We show an extension of the protocol allowing a dealer that its shares of $(x_1, \ldots, x_L), (y_1, \ldots, y_M)$ satisfy $(y_1, \ldots, y_M) = G(x_1, \ldots, x_L)$, where G is any circuit of multiplication depth 1 (i.e., a degree-2 polynomial). The communication complexity of the protocol is $O(L+M)$ VSSs and not $O(|G|)$ VSSs (where —G— is the number of multiplication gates in the circuit G). This allows computing the circuit in a layer-by-layer fashion and not gate-by-gate and leads to sub-linear communication complexity for circuits where $|G| \in \omega(L+M)$.

2.4   Organization

The rest of the paper is organized as follows. In Sect. 3 we provide preliminaries and definitions. In Sect. 4 we cover our weak verifiable secret sharing, strong verifiable secret sharing and some extensions. Our multiplication protocol (with a dealer) is provided in Sect. 5 and its generalization to arbitrary gates with multiplicative gate 1 is given in Sect. 6. In the full version of the paper we provide the missing proofs, as well as an overview of how the dealer is removed and how to compute a general function, following the BGW approach.

3   Preliminaries

Notations. We denote $\{1, \ldots, n\}$ by $[n]$. We denote the number of parties by n and a bound on the number of corrupted parties by t. Two random variables X and Y are identically distributed, denoted as $X \equiv Y$, if for every z it holds that $\Pr[X = z] = \Pr[Y = z]$. Two parametrized distributions $\mathcal{D}_1 = \{\mathcal{D}_1(a)\}_a$ and $\mathcal{D}_2 = \{\mathcal{D}_2(a)\}_a$ are said to be identically distributed, if for every a the two random variables $(a, \mathcal{D}_1(a)), (a, \mathcal{D}_2(a))$ are identically distributed.

3.1   Definitions of Perfect Security in the Presence of Malicious Adversaries

We follow the standard, standalone simulation-based security of multiparty computation in the perfect settings [2,10,26]. Let $f : (\{0,1\}^*)^n \to (\{0,1\}^*)^n$ be an n-party functionality and let π be an n-party protocol over ideal (i.e., authenticated and private) point-to-point channels and a broadcast channel. Let the adversary, $\mathcal{A}$, be an arbitrary machine with auxiliary input z, and let $I \subset [n]$ be the set of corrupted parties controlled by $\mathcal{A}$. We define the real and ideal executions:

– **The real execution:** In the real model, the parties run the protocol π where the adversary $\mathcal{A}$ controls the parties in I. The adversary cannot modify messages sent over the point-to-point channel. The adversary is assumed to be rushing, meaning that in every round it can see the messages sent by the honest parties before it determines the message sent by the corrupted parties. We denote by $\text{REAL}_{\pi,\mathcal{A}(z),I}(\vec{x})$ the random variable consisting of the view of the adversary $\mathcal{A}$ in the execution (consisting of all the initial inputs of the corrupted parties, their randomness and all messages they received), together with the output of all honest parties.

– **The ideal execution:** The ideal model consists of all honest parties, a trusted party and an ideal adversary $\mathcal{SIM}$, controlling the same set of corrupted parties I. The honest parties send their inputs to the trusted party. The ideal adversary $\mathcal{SIM}$ receives the auxiliary input z and sees the inputs of the corrupted parties. $\mathcal{SIM}$ can substitute any x_i with any x_i' of its choice (for the corrupted parties) under the condition that $|x_i'| = |x_i|$. Once the trusted party receives (possibly modified) inputs $(x_1', \ldots, x_n')$ from all parties, it computes $(y_1, \ldots, y_n) = f(x_1', \ldots, x_n')$ and sends y_i to P_i. The output of the ideal execution, denoted as $\text{IDEAL}_{f,\mathcal{SIM}(z),I}(\vec{x})$ is the output of all honest parties and the output of the ideal adversary $\mathcal{SIM}$.

Definition 3.1. *Let f and π be as above. We say that π is t-secure for f if for every adversary $\mathcal{A}$ in the real world there exists an adversary $\mathcal{SIM}$ with comparable complexity to $\mathcal{A}$ in the ideal model, such that for every $I \subset [n]$ of cardinality at most t it holds that*

$$\left\{ \text{IDEAL}_{f,\mathcal{SIM}(z),I}(\vec{x}) \right\}_{z,\vec{x}} \equiv \left\{ \text{REAL}_{\pi,\mathcal{A}(z),I}(\vec{x}) \right\}_{z,\vec{x}}$$

where $\vec{x}$ is chosen from $(\{0,1\}^*)^n$ such that $|x_1| = \ldots = |x_n|$.

Corruption-aware Functionalities. The functionalities that we consider are *corruption-aware*, namely, the functionality receives the set I of corrupted parties. We refer the reader to [2, Section 6.2] for further discussion and the necessity of this when proving security.

Reactive Functionalities, Composition and Fybrid-world. We also consider more general functionalities where the computation takes place in stages, where the trusted party can communicate with the ideal adversary (and sometimes also with the honest parties) in several stages, to obtain new inputs and send outputs in phases. See [26, Section 7.7.1.3].

The sequential modular composition theorem is an important tool for analyzing the security of a protocol in a modular way. Assume that π_f is a protocol that securely computes a function f that uses a subprotocol π_g, which in return securely computes some functionality g. Instead of showing directly that π_f securely computes f, one can consider a protocol π_f^g that does not use the subprotocol π_g but instead uses a trusted party that ideally computes g (this is called a protocol for f in the g-hybrid model). Then, by showing that (1)

π_g securely implements g, and; (2) π_f^g securely implements f, we obtain that the protocol π_f securely implements f in the plain model. See [10] for further discussion.

Remark 3.2 (Input assumption). *We sometimes present functionalities in which we assume that the inputs satisfy some guarantee, for instance, that all points of the honest parties lie on the same degree-t polynomial. We remark that if the input assumption does not hold, then no security guarantees are obtained. This can be formalized as follows: In case that the condition does not hold (and the functionality can easily verify that), then it gives all the honest parties' inputs to the adversary and let the adversary singlehandedly determine all of the outputs of the honest parties. Clearly, any protocol can then be simulated. Note, however, that we always invoke the sub-protocols when the input assumptions are satisfied.*

3.2   Robust Secret Sharing

Let $\mathbb{F}$ be a finite field of order greater than n, let $\alpha_1, \ldots, \alpha_n$ be any distinct non-zero elements from $\mathbb{F}$ and denote $\vec{\alpha} = (\alpha_1, \ldots, \alpha_n)$. For a polynomial q, denote $\mathsf{Eval}_{\vec{\alpha}}(q) = (q(\alpha_1), \ldots, q(\alpha_n))$. The Shamir's $t+1$ out of n sharing scheme [37] consists of two procedure Share and Reconstruct as follows:

- Share(s). The algorithm is given $s \in \mathbb{F}$, then it chooses t independent uniformly random elements from $\mathbb{F}$, denoted $q_1, \ldots, q_t$, and defines the polynomial $q(x) = s + \sum_{i=1}^{t} q_t x^t$. Finally, it outputs $\mathsf{Eval}_{\vec{\alpha}}(q) = (q(\alpha_1), \ldots, q(\alpha_n))$. Define $s_i = q(\alpha_i)$ as the share of party P_i.
- Reconstruct($\vec{s}$). For a set $J \subseteq [n]$ of cardinality at least $t+1$, let $\vec{s} = \{s_i\}_{i \in J}$. Then, the algorithm reconstructs the secret s.

Correctness requires that every secret can be reconstructed from the shares for every subset of shares of cardinality $t+1$, and secrecy requires that every set of less than t shares is distributed uniformly in $\mathbb{F}$. We refer to [2] for a formal definition.

Reed Solomon Code. Recall that a linear $[n, k, d]$-code over a field $\mathbb{F}$ is a code of length n, dimension k and distance d. That is, each codeword is a sequence of n field elements, there are in total $|\mathbb{F}|^k$ different codewords, and the Hamming distance of any two codewords is at least d. Any possible corrupted codeword $\hat{c}$ can be corrected to the closest codeword c as long as $d(c, \hat{c}) < (d-1)/2$, where $d(x, y)$ denote the Hamming distance between the words $x, y \in \mathbb{F}^n$.

In Reed Solomon code, let $m = (m_0, \ldots, m_t)$ be the message to be encoded, where each $m_i \in \mathbb{F}$. The encoding of the message is essentially the evaluation of the degree-t polynomial $p_m(x) = m_0 + m_1 x + \ldots + m_t x^t$ on some distinct non-zero field elements $\alpha_1, \ldots, \alpha_n$. That is, $\mathsf{Encode}(m) = (p(\alpha_1), \ldots, p(\alpha_n))$. The distance of this code is $n - t$. This is because any two distinct polynomials of degree-t can agree at most t points. We have the following fact:

Fact 3.3. *The Reed-Solomon code is a linear $[n, t + 1, n - t]$ code over $\mathbb{F}$. In addition, there exists an efficient decoding algorithm that corrects up to $(n - t - 1)/2$ errors. That is, for every $m \in \mathbb{F}^{t+1}$ and every $x \in \mathbb{F}^n$ such that $d(x, C(m)) \leq (n - t - 1)/2$, the decoding algorithm returns m.*

For the case of $t < n/3$ we get that is is possible to efficiently correct up to $(3t + 1 - t - 1)/2 = t$ errors. Putting it differently, when sharing of a polynomial of degree-t, if during the reconstruction t errors were introduced by corrupted parties, it is still possible to recover the correct value.

3.3 Bivariate Polynomial

We call a bivariate polynomial of degree q in x and degree t in y as (q, t)-bivariate polynomial. If $q = t$ then we simply call the polynomial as degree-t bivariate polynomial. Such a polynomial can be written as follows:

$$S(x, y) = \sum_{i=0}^{q} \sum_{j=0}^{t} a_{i,j} x^i y^j \ .$$

Looking ahead, in our protocol we will consider degree-t bivariate polynomials and degree $(2t, t)$-bivariate polynomials. The proof of the following claim is given in the full version of this paper:

Claim 3.4 (Interpolation). *Let t be a nonnegative integer, and let $\alpha_1, \ldots, \alpha_{t+1}$ distinct elements in $\mathbb{F}$, and let $f_1(x), \ldots, f_{t+1}(x)$ be $t + 1$ univariate polynomials of degree at most q. Then, there exists a unique (q, t) bivariate polynomial $S(x, y)$ such that for every $k = 1, \ldots, t + 1$: $S(x, \alpha_k) = f_k(x)$.*

Symmetrically, one can interpolate the polynomial $S(x, y)$ from a set of $q + 1$ polynomials $g_i(y)$. The proof is similar to Claim 3.4.

Claim 3.5 (Interpolation). *Let t be a nonnegative integer, and let $\alpha_1, \ldots, \alpha_{q+1}$ distinct elements in $\mathbb{F}$, and let $g_1(y), \ldots, g_{q+1}(y)$ be $q + 1$ univariate polynomials of degree at most t each. Then, there exists a unique (q, t) bivariate polynomial $S(x, y)$ such that for every $k = 1, \ldots, t + 1$ it holds that $S(\alpha_k, y) = g_k(y)$.*

Hiding. The following is the "hiding" claim, showing that if a dealer wishes to share some polynomial $h(x)$ of degree-q, it can choose a random (q, t)-polynomial $S(x, y)$ that satisfies $S(x, 0) = h(x)$ and give each party P_i the shares $S(x, \alpha_i), S(\alpha_i, y)$. The adversary cannot learn any information about h besides $\{h(\alpha_i)\}_{i \in I}$, when it corrupts the set $I \subset [n]$. We prove the following two claims in the full version of this paper:

Claim 3.6 (Hiding). *Let $h(x)$ be an arbitrary univariate polynomial of degree q, and let $\alpha_1, \ldots, \alpha_k$ with $k \leq t$ be arbitrary distinct non-zero points in $\mathbb{F}$. Consider the following distribution $\mathsf{Dist}(h)$:*

- *Choose a random (q, t)-bivariate polynomial $S(x, y)$ under the constraint that $S(x, 0) = h(x)$.*

  – *Output* $\{(i, S(x, \alpha_i), S(\alpha_i, y))\}_{i \in [k]}$.

Then, for every two arbitrary degree-q polynomials $h_1(x), h_2(x)$ for which $h_1(\alpha_i) = h_2(\alpha_i)$ for every $i \in [k]$ it holds that $\mathsf{Dist}(h_1) \equiv \mathsf{Dist}(h_2)$.

Claim 3.7 (Hiding II). *Same as Claim 3.6, except that it holds that $h_1(0) = h_1(0) = \beta$ for some publicly known $\beta \in \mathbb{F}$. The output of the distribution is $\{(i, S(x, \alpha_i), S(\alpha_i, y))\}_{i \in [k]} \cup \{S(0, y)\}$.*

4 Weak Verifiable Secret Sharing and Extensions

In this section we show how to adapt the verifiable secret sharing protocol of [7] to allow weak secret sharing of a polynomial degree-t. We start with a description of the verifiable secret sharing protocol and highlight the main differences for getting a weak verifiable secret sharing protocol (sometimes we may omit the 'verifiable' and write only 'weak secret sharing'). We formally define the weak verifiable secret sharing in Sect. 4.2 and then strong VSS in Sect. 4.4. In our formalization of weak secret sharing, not all parties are happy with their shares. The set of parties that are happy with their shares is known to all parties, and is part of the output of all parties. Their shares also uniquely define the polynomial. Only parties that are happy with their shares will take part in the reconstruction. Thus, the output of WSS is a set K of all parties that are happy with their shares, where parties in $k \in K$ also output their shares (i.e., a pair $f_k(x), g_k(y)$), where parties $i \notin K$ just hold $g_i(y)$.

We remind that in BGW, after the parties verify the shares and obtain $f_i(x), g_i(y)$, they just project the bivariate shares to univariate shares by outputting $f_i(0)$. As mentioned, we will maintain bivariate sharing and the output $(f_i(x), g_i(y))$ in the strong VSS variant of the protocol.

4.1 Verifying Shares of a (q, t)-Bivariate Polynomial

Protocol 4.1: Weak/Strong Verifiable Secret Sharing of a Polynomial

– **Input:** The dealer holds a bivariate polynomial $S(x, y)$.
– **Common input:** The description of a field $\mathbb{F}$ and n non-zero distinct elements $\alpha_1, \ldots, \alpha_n \in \mathbb{F}$.
– **The protocol:**
  1. **Sharing – the dealer:**
     (a) Send to each party P_i the shares $(f_i(x), g_i(y))$ defined as $f_i(x) \overset{\text{def}}{=} S(x, \alpha_i)$, $g_i(y) \overset{\text{def}}{=} S(\alpha_i, y)$.
  2. **Initial checks – each party P_i:**
     (a) If (1) $f_i(x)$ has degree greater than q; or (2) $g_i(y)$ has degree greater than t; or (3) $f_i(\alpha_i) \neq g_i(\alpha_i)$ then broadcast $\mathsf{complaint}(i)$ and proceed to step 5.
     (b) Let $R = \{k \mid P_k \text{ broadcast } \mathsf{complaint}(k)\}$.

3. **Exchange subshares – each party P_i for $i \notin R$:**
   (a) Send $(f_i(\alpha_j), g_i(\alpha_j))$ to P_j for each $j \notin R$.
   (b) Let (u_j, v_j) be the values received from P_j, for $j \notin R$. If no value was received, then use $(\perp, \perp)$. If $u_j \neq g_i(\alpha_j)$ or $v_j \neq f_i(\alpha_j)$ then broadcast complaint$(i, j, f_i(\alpha_j), g_i(\alpha_j))$.
   (c) If no party broadcasts complaint$(i, j, \cdot, \cdot)$ and $R = \emptyset$, then[2]
       VSS: *Output $(f_i(x), g_i(y))$ and halt.*
       WSS: *Output $(f_i(x), g_i(y), [n])$ and halt.*
4. **Resolve complaints – the dealer:**
   (a) If P_i that broadcasted complaint(i) in Step 2a, or broadcasted complaint(i, j, u, v) with $u \neq S(\alpha_j, \alpha_i)$ or $v \neq S(\alpha_i, \alpha_j)$ then
       VSS: *Broadcast reveal$(i, S(x, \alpha_i), S(\alpha_i, y))$.*
       WSS: *Broadcast reveal$(i, S(\alpha_i, y))$.*
5. **Evaluate complaint resolutions – each party P_i:**
   (a) Add to R all indices k for which the dealer broadcasted reveal$(k, \dots)$. If $i \in R$, then replace $g_i(y)$ with the one provided in the broadcasted in reveal$(i, \cdot, \cdot)$.

       VSS: *If $i \in R$, then rewrite also $f_i(x)$.*
       If $i \in R$ then proceed to Step 6.
   (b) Verify that the dealer replied to each complaint(k) message from Step 2a with reveal$(k, \dots)$. If not, proceed to Step 6.
   (c) Upon viewing complaint(k, j, u_1, v_1) and complaint(j, k, u_2, v_2) broadcast by P_k and P_j, respectively, with $u_1 \neq v_2$ or $v_1 \neq u_2$, mark (j, k) as a joint complaint. If the dealer did not broadcast reveal$(k, \cdot)$ or reveal$(j, \cdot)$, then go to Step 6.
   (d) For every $j \in R$ verify that $f_i(\alpha_j) = g_j(\alpha_i)$,
       VSS: *and that $g_i(\alpha_j) = f_j(\alpha_i)$.*
       If the verification does not hold for some $j \in R$, then go to Step 6.
   (e) Broadcast the message good.
6. **Output:** Let K be the set of of all parties that broadcast good and are not in R. If $|K| < 2t + 1$, then output $\perp$. Otherwise,
   VSS: *Output $(f_i(x), g_i(y))$.*
   WSS: *Each party P_k for $k \in K$ outputs $(f_i(x), g_i(y), K)$. All other parties output $(g_i(y), K)$.*

It is easy to see that in the optimistic case, when there are no cheats, the protocol ends at Step 3c and incurs a communication overhead of $O(n^2)$ point-to-point messages and no broadcast. In the pessimistic (worst) case, however, there may be $O(n)$ and $O(n^2)$ complaints (broadcasts) in Steps 2a and 3b, respectively. Then, in step 4, there are $O(n)$ messages of total size $O(n^2)$ that are broadcasted

---

[2] We use two rounds of silence as an optimistic early stopping agreement on no complaints. We then combine this with a standard termination protocol that uses either the fast decision or the broadcast decision. It is easy to see that there will be no conflict between the two.

by the dealer (i.e. in order to reveal the polynomials of at most t parties who placed their complaint). Finally, there are $O(n)$ broadcast of the message good if the secret sharing is successfully verified. Overall, the pessimistic case incurs a communication overhead of $O(n^2)$ point-to-point messages and $O(n^2)$ broadcast messages.

4.2   Weak Verifiable Secret Sharing

In weak verifiable secret sharing, the dealer wishes to distribute shares to all parties, and then allow reconstruction only if it takes part in the reconstruction. The result of the reconstruction can be either a unique, well-defined polynomial which was determined in the sharing phase, or $\perp$.

Functionality 4.2: F_{WSS} – Weak Verifiable Secret Sharing Functionality

---

The functionality receives a set of indices $I \subset [n]$ and works as follows:

- If the dealer is honest $(1 \notin I)$:
  1. Receive a polynomial $S(x, y)$ of degree (q, t) from the dealer P_1.
  2. Send to the ideal adversary the shares $\{S(x, \alpha_i), S(\alpha_i, y)\}_{i \in I}$.
  3. Receive back from the adversary the set $I' \subseteq I$ and define $K = ([n] \setminus I) \cup I'$.
- If the dealer is corrupted $(1 \in I)$:
  1. Receive a polynomial $S(x, y)$ of degree (q, t) from the dealer P_1.
  2. Receive a set $K \subseteq [n]$ of cardinality at least $2t + 1$.
  3. Verify that $S(x, y)$ is of degree (q, t). If verification fails, overwrite $K = \perp$.
- **Output:** Send K to all parties. Moreover, for every $k \in K$, send $S(x, \alpha_k), S(\alpha_k, y)$ to P_k. For every $j \notin K$, send P_j the polynomial $S(\alpha_k, y)$.

Theorem 4.3. *Let $t < n/3$. Then, Protocol 4.1: when using the **WSS** branch is t-secure for the f_{WSS} functionality (Functionality 4.2) in the presence of a static malicious adversary. The protocol incurs $O(n^2)$ point-to-point messages in the optimistic case and additional $O(n^2)$ broadcast messages in the pessimistic case.*

Proof. Let $\mathcal{A}$ be an adversary in the real world. We have two cases, depending on whether the dealer is corrupted or not. We note that the protocol is deterministic, as well as the functionality.

Case 1: The Dealer is Honest. In this case in the ideal execution, the honest parties always hold shares of a polynomial $S(x, y)$ that is of degree (q, t). We describe the simulator $\mathcal{SIM}$.

The simulator $\mathcal{SIM}$.

  1. $\mathcal{SIM}$ invokes the adversary $\mathcal{A}$ on the auxiliary input z.
  2. $\mathcal{SIM}$ receives from the trusted party the polynomials of the corrupted parties, that is, $f_i(x), g_i(y)$, and the simulates the protocol execution for $\mathcal{A}$:
    (a) **Sharing:** *Simulate sending the shares $f_i(x), g_i(y)$ to each P_i, $i \in I$, as coming from the dealer P_1.*
    (b) **Initial checks:** *Initialize $R = \emptyset$. An honest party never broadcasts* complaint(i). *If the adversary broadcast* complaint(i), *then add i to R.*
    (c) **Exchange subshares:** *send to the adversary $\mathcal{A}$ the shares $g_i(\alpha_j), f_i(\alpha_j)$ from each honest party P_j, for each corrupted party $i \in I \backslash R$. Receive from the adversary $\mathcal{A}$ the points $(u_{i,j}, v_{i,j})$ that are supposed to be sent from P_i to P_j, for $i \in I \setminus R$ and $j \notin I$.*
    (d) **Broadcast complaints:** *The simulator checks the points $(u_{i,j}, v_{i,j})$ that the adversary sent in the previous step. If $u_{i,j} \neq f_i(\alpha_j)$ or $v_{i,j} \neq g_i(\alpha_j)$ then $\mathcal{SIM}$ simulates a broadcast of* complaint$(j, i, g_i(\alpha_j), f_i(\alpha_j))$ *as coming from party P_j.*
    Moreover, receive complaint(i, j, u, v) *broadcast messages from the adversary.*
    If the adversary does not broadcast any reveal *message and no* complaint *message was broadcasted by any party, then send I to the trusted party, and halt.*
    (e) **Resolve complaints – the dealer:** *The dealer never reveals the shares of honest parties. For every* complaint(i, j, u, v) *message received from the adversary, check that $u = f_i(\alpha_j)$ and $v = g_i(\alpha_j)$.*
    If not, then broadcast reveal$(i, g_i(y))$ *as coming from the dealer, and add $i \in R$. Moreover, if there was a* complaint(i) *in the initial checks step, then broadcast* reveal$(i, g_i(y))$.
    (f) **Evaluate complaint resolutions:** *Simulate all honest parties broadcast* good. *Let I' be the set of corrupted parties that broadcast* good.
  3. The simulator sends $I' \setminus R$ to the trusted party.

It is easy to see by inspection of the protocol, and by inspection of the simulation, and since the two are deterministic, that the view of the adversary in the real and ideal execution is *equal*. Our next goal is to show that the output of the honest parties is the same in the real and ideal executions.

In the optimistic case, where no reveal(i) messages are broadcasted by the dealer, and there are no complaint messages by any party, then in the real execution the output of all honest parties is $[n]$ and likewise, in the simulation the simulator sends I to the trusted party, which then sends $[n]$ to all parties.
We now consider the case where there are complaints and there is a vote. An honest party P_j broadcasts good if all the following conditions are met:

1. The polynomial $f_j(x)$ has degree at most $2t$, $g_j(y)$ has degree at most t and $f_j(\alpha_j) = g_j(\alpha_j)$. An honest party P_j therefore never broadcasts complaint(j).
2. While resolving complaints, the dealer never broadcasts reveal(j).
3. Each complaint(k) message is replied by the dealer with reveal$(k, \cdot)$ message.

4. All reveal$(i, g_i(y))$ messages broadcasted by the dealer satisfy $f_j(\alpha_i) = g_i(\alpha_j)$.
5. The dealer resolves all joint complaints.

It is easy to see that all those conditions are met in the case of an honest dealer. In particular: (1) is true by the assumption on the inputs; (2) An honest party never broadcasts complaint with the values it received from the dealer; As a result, according to our input assumption, the dealer never broadcasts reveal(j); (3) True by inspection of the code of the dealer; (4) When the dealer broadcasts a polynomial it always agrees with $f_j(x)$ initially given to P_j; (5) By the dealer's code specifications, it resolves all joint complaints.

Therefore, in the real execution all honest parties broadcast good, and some additional parties $I' \subseteq I$ that the adversary controls might also broadcast good. Then, all honest parties exclude from this set the parties in R, and output it. Since the view of the adversary is equal in the ideal execution, the same parties in the simulated ideal execution broadcast good. Let $I' \subseteq I$ be the set of corrupted parties that broadcast good. The simulator sends $I' \setminus R$ to the trusted party, which then defines K to be $([n] \setminus I) \cup (I' \setminus R)$, i.e., all honest parties and all corrupted parties that broadcast good, excluding those that are in R. Thus, the outputs of the honest parties in the real and ideal are identical.

Case 2: The Dealer is Corrupted. The proof of this case is deferred to the full version of this paper.

$\square$

4.3   Evaluation with the Help of the Dealer

We show how the parties can recover the secret polynomial using the help of the dealer. Towards that end, we show how the parties can evaluate polynomial $g_\beta(y)$ for every $\beta \in E$, where E is a set of elements in $\mathbb{F}$. By taking E to be of cardinality $q + 1$, it is possible to completely recover S (see Claim 3.5). When we are only interested in the constant term of S, we take $E = \{0\}$ to obtain $g(y) = S(0, y)$ and then output $g(0)$. The polynomial can be recovered with the help of the dealer. Looking ahead, in Protocol 5.2: in the optimistic case we will use just $E = \{0\}$. In the pessimistic case, E will contain another indices of parties that raised a complaint against the dealer.

Functionality 4.4: F_{WEval}: Evaluation of a polynomial in Weak VSS

The functionality receives a set of indices $I \subseteq [n]$ and works as follows:

1. The functionality receives the sets (K, E) from all honest parties, where E is a set of elements in $\mathbb{F}$. Moreover, for every $k \in ([n] \setminus I) \cap K$ it receives the polynomial $f_k(x)$ from P_k. The dealer holds a polynomial S' of degree (q, t). When the dealer is honest, it is guaranteed that the indices of all honest parties are included in K.

2. The functionality reconstructs the unique (q, t) bivariate polynomial S that agrees with the shares of the honest parties. When the dealer is honest it always holds that $S' = S$. Note that if the shares do not define a unique polynomial, then no security is guaranteed[3].
3. If the dealer is honest $(1 \notin I)$ then send $S(x, \alpha_i), S(\alpha_i, y)$ for every $i \in I$ together with the set E to the ideal adversary. Moreover, send the set of polynomials $\{S(\beta, y)\}_{\beta \in E}$ to all parties (and the ideal adversary).
4. If the dealer is corrupted $(1 \in I)$ then:
   (a) Send the polynomial $S(x, y)$ to the ideal adversary together with $(K, \{S(\beta, y)\}_{\beta \in E})$.
   (b) Receive either ok or $\perp$ from the ideal adversary.
   (c) If ok, then send $\{S(\beta, y)\}_{\beta \in E}$ to all parties, and otherwise, send $\perp$ to all parties.

Protocol 4.5: Evaluation of a polynomial in Weak VSS

- **Input:** All parties hold a set $K \subseteq [n]$ and a set E of elements in $\mathbb{F}$. Each party P_k with $k \in K$ holds $f_k(x)$. The dealer holds also a polynomial $S(x, y)$.
- **Input guarantees:** When the dealer is honest, the indices of all honest parties are included in K.
- **The protocol:**
  1. The dealer broadcasts $\{S(\beta, y)\}_{\beta \in E}$.
  2. Each party P_k with $k \in K$ checks that the broadcasted polynomials are of degree at most t, and that $S(\beta, \alpha_k) = f_k(\beta)$ for every $\beta \in E$. If so, it broadcast good.
  3. **Output:** If $2t + 1$ parties in K broadcast good, then output the message broadcasted by the dealer. Otherwise, output $\perp$.

We prove the following theorem in the full version of this paper:

Theorem 4.6. *Let $t < n/3$. Protocol 4.5: is t-secure for the F_{WEval} functionality (Functionality 4.4:) in the presence of a static malicious adversary. The protocol incurs $O(n \cdot |E|)$ broadcast field elements.*

Remark 4.7. (On the optimistic case of Protocol 4.5:). *In the optimistic case, we can implement Protocol 4.5: without any broadcast messages and with $O(n^2)$ field elements over the point-to-point channels. Specifically, in the optimistic case of the entire protocol (Protocol 5.2:) we have that $K = [n]$ and $E = \{0\}$. Each party P_k can send on the point-to-point channel to every other party P_j the message $f_k(0)$. Then, each party P_j uses the Reed Solomon decoding procedure to obtain the unique degree-t polynomial $g_\beta(y)$ satisfying $g_0(\alpha) = \gamma_k$, where γ_k is the point received from party P_k. Since there are $2t + 1$ honest parties in K, and since $S(0, y)$ is guaranteed to be a polynomial of degree-t, reconstruction works.*

---

[3] In that case, we simply give the adversary all inputs of all honest parties which makes any protocol vacuously secure as anything can be easily simulated, see Remark 3.2.

4.4 Strong Verifiable Secret Sharing

We provide the functionality for strong verifiable secret sharing, and prove its security. The main difference from [2] is that the output is the two univariate polynomials and not the projection to univariate sharing, and we therefore provide a proof for completeness in the full version of this paper.

Functionality 4.8: Strong Verifiable Secret Sharing

- **Input:** Receive $S(x, y)$ from the dealer P_1.
- **Output:** If $S(x, y)$ is of degree-t in both variables, then send $(S(x, \alpha_i), S(\alpha_i, y))$ to each party P_i. Otherwise, send $\perp$.

Theorem 4.9. *Let $t < n/3$. Then, Protocol 4.1: when using the **VSS** branch and with $q = t$ is t-secure for the f_{VSS} functionality (Functionality 4.8:) in the presence of a static malicious adversary. The protocol incurs $O(n^2)$ field elements in the point-to-point channels in the optimistic case and additional $O(n^2)$ field elements on the broadcast channel in the pessimistic case.*

Evaluation. Once a polynomial was shared using strong VSS, we use Functionality 4.4: to evaluate points on the polynomial with the help of the dealer. Note that in this case we have that $q = t$. Moreover, the parties use $K = [n]$. Note that K might now not be the same group of parties that broadcast good when the polynomial was shared, yet, since all honest parties hold shares $(f_j(x), g_j(y))$ it is safe to use $K = [n]$. Thus, to evaluate points E on a polynomial that was shared with VSS can be implemented using $O(n|E|)$ field messages broadcasted, as in Theorem 4.6.

4.5 Extending Univariate Sharing to Bivariate Sharing with a Dealer

Sometimes each party P_i holds a share $h(\alpha_i)$ of some univariate degree-t polynomial $h(x)$. The following functionality allows a dealer, who holds h, to distribute shares of a bivariate polynomial $S(x, y)$ satisfying $S(x, 0) = h(x)$. The protocol is very simple, demonstrating the advantage for working with bivariate sharing. This is the functionality $\tilde{F}_{extend}$ from [3]:

Functionality 4.10: F_{Extend}: Extending Univariate Sharing to Bivariate Sharing

The functionality receives the set of corrupted parties $I \subset [n]$ and works as follows:

- **Input:** The functionality receives the shares of the honest parties $\{u_j\}_{j \notin I}$. Let $h(x)$ be the unique degree-t polynomial determined by the points (α_j, u_j) for every $j \notin I$. If no such polynomial exists then no security is guaranteed.

- If the dealer is corrupted then send $h(x)$ to the ideal adversary.
- Receive $S(x,y)$ from the dealer. Check that $S(x,y)$ is of degree-t and that $S(x,0) = h(x)$.
- If both conditions hold, then send to $S(x,\alpha_i), S(\alpha_i, y)$ to P_i for every i. Otherwise, send $\perp$ to everyone.

Protocol 4.11: Implementing F_{Extend} in the F_{VSS}-hybrid model

---

- **Input:** Each party holds u_j. The dealer holds $S(x,y)$ and $h(x)$.
- **The protocol:**
    1. The dealer uses F_{VSS} to distribute $S(x,y)$.
    2. Each party P_i receives $(f_i(x), g_i(y)) \overset{\text{def}}{=} (S(x,\alpha_i), S(\alpha_i, y))$. If instead $\perp$ was received, then output $\perp$ and halt.
    3. Each party P_i verifies that $g_i(0) = u_j$. If not, it broadcast complaint(i).
    4. **Output:** If there are more than t complaints, then output $\perp$. Otherwise, output $(f_i(x), g_i(y))$.

The communication cost of the protocol is the same as Protocol 4.1: for VSS. Note that in the optimistic case there are no complaints, and thus there are no additional broadcast messages. We provide a proof of the following theorem in the full version paper.

Theorem 4.12. *Let $t < n/3$. Then, Protocol 4.11: is t-secure for the F_{Extend} functionality (Functionality 4.10:) for in the presence of a static malicious adversary, in the F_{VSS}-hybrid model. The protocol incurs $O(n^2)$ point-to-point messages in the optimistic case and additional $O(n^2)$ broadcast messages in the pessimistic case.*

5   Multiplication with a Constant Number of VSSs and WSSs

We now turn to the multiplication protocol. The multiplication protocol is reduced to multiplication with a dealer, i.e., when one dealer holds two univariate polynomials $f^a(x), f^b(x)$, each party holds a share on those polynomials, and the dealer wishes to distribute a polynomial $C(x,y)$ of degree-t in both variables in which $C(0,0) = f^a(0) \cdot f^b(0)$. We refer the reader to the full version of this paper to see how this functionality suffices to compute any multiplication gate (i.e., when there is no dealer). In Sect. 5.1 we show the functionality of this building block, in Sect. 5.2 we show the protocol that realizes it.

5.1   Functionality – Multiplication with a Dealer

Functionality 5.1: Functionality F_{VSS}^{mult} for sharing a product of shares

F_{VSS}^{mult} receives a set of indices $I \subseteq [n]$ and works as follows:

---

1. Receive a pair of points $(u_j, v_j) \in \mathbb{F}^2$ from P_j.
2. Compute the unique degree-t univariate polynomials $f^a(x)$ and $f^b(x)$ satisfying $f^a(\alpha_j) = u_j$ and $f^b(\alpha_j) = v_j$ for every $j \notin I$. (if no such polynomials f^a or f^b exist, then no security is guaranteed).
3. If the dealer P_1 is honest $(1 \notin I)$, then:
   (a) choose a random degree-t bivariate polynomial $C(x,y)$ under the constraint that $C(0,0) = f^a(0) \cdot f^b(0)$.
   (b) *Output for honest:* send $C(x,y)$ to P_1, and $C(x, \alpha_j)$, $C(\alpha_j, y)$ to P_j for every $j \notin I$.
   (c) *Output for adversary:* send $f^a(\alpha_i), f^b(\alpha_i), C(x, \alpha_i), C(\alpha_i, y)$ to the (ideal) adversary, for every $i \in I$.
4. If the dealer P_1 is corrupted $(1 \in I)$, then:
   (a) Send $f^a(x), f^b(x)$ to the (ideal) adversary.
   (b) Receive a bivariate polynomial C as input from the (ideal) adversary.
   (c) If either $\deg(C) > t$ or $C(0,0) \neq f^a(0) \cdot f^b(0)$, then reset $C(x,y) = f^a(0) \cdot f^b(0)$; that is, $C(x,y)$ is a constant polynomial that equals $f^a(0) \cdot f^b(0)$ everywhere.
   (d) *Output for honest:* send $C(x, \alpha_j), C(\alpha_j, y)$ to P_j, for every $j \notin I$. (There is no more output for the adversary in this case.)

5.2   The Protocol

As mentioned in the introduction, in our protocol the dealer distributes $C(x,y)$ using verifiable secret sharing, and then also distributes a random $(2t,t)$-polynomial $D(x,y)$ under the constraint that $D(x,0) = f^a(x) \cdot f^b(x) - C(x,0)$ and that $D(0,0) = 0$ by reconstructing the univariate polynomial $D(0,y)$.

To verify that $D(x,y)$ indeed satisfies this constraint, each party P_i verifies that $D(\alpha_i, 0) = f^a(\alpha_i) \cdot f^b(\alpha_i) - C(\alpha_i, 0)$ using the shares it received from P_1. If the verification fails, it broadcasts a complaint and all parties reconstruct the share of P_i. Since all polynomials are shared, it is possible to see whether the complaint is justified. Moreover, if for all honest parties the verification holds, then it must be that the two degree-$2t$ polynomials, $D(x,0)$ and $f^a(x) \cdot f^b(x) - C(x,0)$ are equal, as they agree on $2t + 1$ points.

Protocol 5.2: Computing F_{VSS}^{mult} in the $(F_{VSS}, F_{WSS}, F_{\text{Extend}}, F_{\text{WEval}})$ - hybrid model

---

– **Input:**
   1. The dealer P_1 holds two degree-t polynomials $f^a(x), f^b(x)$.
   2. Each party P_i holds two points $(u_i, v_i) = (f^a(\alpha_i), f^b(\alpha_i))$.
– **Common input:** A field $\mathbb{F}$ and distinct non-zero elements $\alpha_1, \ldots, \alpha_n \in \mathbb{F}$.
– **The protocol:**
   1. **Sharing phase:**
      (a) P_1 chooses a degree-t bivariate polynomial $C(x,y)$ under the constraint that $C(0,0) = f^a(0) \cdot f^b(0)$.

(b) P_1 chooses a random degree $(2t, t)$-bivariate polynomial $D(x, y)$ under the constraint that $D(x, 0) = f^a(x) \cdot f^b(x) - C(x, 0)$.

(c) Invoke F_{VSS} to share $C(x, y)$, and let $(f_i^c(x), g_i^c(y))$ be the output of P_i.

(d) Invoke F_{WSS} to share $D(x, y)$. Let $K \subseteq [n]$ be the output of F_{WSS}, such that each P_k for $k \in K$ also receives $(f_k^d(x), g_k^d(y))$, and each party P_j for $j \notin K$ receives $g_j^d(y)$.

(e) If $\perp$ was received in any of the above, then proceed to Step 5b.

2. **Verifying that $D(x, 0) = f^a(x) \cdot f^b(x) - C(x, 0)$:**

   (a) Each party P_i verifies that $g_i^d(0) = u_i \cdot v_i - g_i^c(0)$. If no, broadcast $\mathsf{complaint}(i)$.

   (b) If no party broadcasts a complaint, then proceed to Step 4.

3. **Complaint resolution (only in pessimistic case):**

   (a) Let R be the set of all parties broadcast $\mathsf{complaint}(i)$, and let $E = \{\alpha_i\}_{i \in R}$.

   (b) P_1 chooses two random degree-t bivariate polynomials, A, B under the constraint that $A(x, 0) = f^a(x)$ and $B(x, 0) = f^b(x)$. The parties run the F_{Extend} functionality twice, where each party P_i inputs u_i and the dealer inputs $A(x, y)$ in the first execution, and each party P_i inputs v_i and the dealer inputs $B(x, y)$ in the second execution.

   (c) The parties call to F_{WEval} where each party P_i inputs $(f_i^a(x), g_i^a(y), E, [n])$. Let $(f_j^a(x), g_j^a(y))$ be the result for every $j \in R$. Likewise, reconstruct $(f_j^b(x), g_j^b(y))$, $(f_j^c(x), g_j^c(y))$. If F_{WEval} returned $\perp$ in any one of the invocations, then proceed to Step 5b.

   (d) The parties call to F_{WEval} where all parties input K, E and each party P_k for $k \in K$ inputs also $(f_k^d(x), g_k^d(y))$. The output of F_{WEval} is $g_i^d(y)$ for every $i \in R$. If F_{WEval} returned $\perp$, then proceed to Step 5b.

   (e) For every $j \notin K$, all parties verify that $g_j^d(0) = g_j^a(0) \cdot g_j^b(0) - g_j^c(0)$. If not, then proceed to Step 5b.

4. **Verifying that $D(0, 0) = 0$:**

   (a) The parties call to F_{WEval} where all parties input $K, \{0\}$ and each party P_k for $k \in K$ inputs also $(f_k^d(x), g_k^d(y))$. The output of F_{WEval} is $g_0^d(y) = D(0, y)$ to all parties. If F_{WEval} returned $\perp$, then proceed to Step 5b.

   (b) Verify that $g_0^d(0) = 0$. If not, proceed to Step 5b.

5. **Finalization:**

   (a) *Accept:* If the dealer was not rejected, then each party P_i outputs $(f_i^c(x), g_i^c(y))$.

   (b) *Reject:* If the dealer is rejected, then each party P_i sends to P_j its points u_i, v_i. The parties reconstruct the polynomials $f^a(x), f^b(x)$ using Reed-Solomon decoding, and define their output shares $f_i^c(x) = g_i^c(y) = f^a(0) \cdot f^b(0)$.

The communication cost of the entire sharing phase (Step 1) is equal to the cost of a VSS/WSS, since it calls to F_{VSS} for C and F_{WSS} for D. Thus, it completes with communication overhead of $O(n^2)$ over the point-to-point channels in the optimistic case and additional overhead of $O(n^2)$ over the broadcast channel in the pessimistic case.

In Step 2, the optimistic case we have no complaints, no evaluation is required, therefore, there is no communication cost. On the other hand, the size of E may be $O(n)$ in the worst case, which leads to $O(n \cdot |E|) = O(n^2)$ broadcasted field elements.

Finally, in Step 4 there is a reconstruction of $D(0, y)$. In the optimistic case, this can be done using $O(n^2)$ words over the point-to-point channels and no broadcast (see Remark 4.5:). In the pessimistic case, this requires a broadcast of $O(n)$ field elements.

Overall, the optimistic case incurs a communication overhead of $O(n^2)$ over the point-to-point channels, and the pessimistic case incurs an additional communication overhead of $O(n^2)$ over the broadcast channel.

Theorem 5.3. *Let $t < n/3$. Then, Protocol 5.2: is t-secure for the F_{VSS}^{mult} functionality in the presence of a static malicious adversary, in the $(F_{VSS}, F_{WSS}, F_{Extend}, F_{WEval})$-hybrid model. The optimistic case incurs $O(n^2)$ point-to-point field elements, and the pessimistic case incurs additional $O(n^2)$ broadcast messages of field elements.*

The proof is provided in the full version of this paper.

By combining Theorems 4.9, 4.3, 4.12 and 4.6 with Theorem 5.3 we obtain the following Corollary:

Corollary 5.4. *Let $t < n/3$. Then, there exists a protocol that is t-secure for the F_{VSS}^{mult} functionality in the presence of a static malicious adversary in the plain model.*

6 Extension: Arbitrary Gates with Multiplicative Depth-1

We show how to extend the protocol in Sect. 5 to allow the dealer distributing any shares $b_1, \ldots, b_L$ given input shares $a_1, \ldots, a_M$ such that $(b_1, \ldots, b_L) = G(a_1, \ldots, a_M)$ where G is some circuit of multiplicative depth 1. Section 5 is a special case where $G(a_1, a_2) = a_1 \cdot a_2$.

Functionality 6.1: Functionality F^G_{VSS} for sharing a result of an evaluation of G

F^G_{VSS} receives a set of indices $I \subseteq [n]$ and works as follows, where P_1 is the dealer:

1. Receive a sequence of points $u_{j,1}, \ldots, u_{j,M} \in \mathbb{F}^M$ from P_j.
2. Compute the unique degree-t univariate polynomials $f^{a_1}(x), \ldots, f^{a_M}(x)$ satisfying $f^{a_m}(\alpha_j) = u_{j,m}$ for every $j \notin I$ and $m \in [M]$ (if no such polynomials $f^{a_m}(x)$ exist, then no security is guaranteed).
3. Let $(a_1, \ldots, a_m) \overset{\text{def}}{=} (f^{a_1}(0), \ldots, f^{a_m}(0))$. Evaluate $(b_1, \ldots, b_L) = G(a_1, \ldots, a_m)$.
4. If the dealer P_1 is honest $(1 \notin I)$ then:
   (a) For every $\ell \in [L]$, choose a random degree-t bivariate polynomial C_ℓ under the constraint that $C_\ell(0,0) = b_\ell$.
   (b) *Output for honest:* send C_ℓ to P_1 and $(C_\ell(x, \alpha_j), C_\ell(\alpha_j, y))$ to P_j for every $j \notin I$ and $\ell \in [L]$.
   (c) *Output for adversary:* send to the (ideal) adversary: (1) $f^{a_1}(\alpha_i), \ldots, f^{a_m}(\alpha_i)$ for every $i \in I$; (2) $(C_\ell(x, \alpha_i), C_\ell(\alpha_i, y))$ for every $i \in I$.
5. If the dealer P_1 is corrupted $(1 \in I)$, then:
   (a) Send $f^a(x), f^b(x)$ to the (ideal) adversary.
   (b) Receive bivariate polynomials $C_1, \ldots, C_L$ as input from the (ideal) adversary.
   (c) If either $\deg(C_\ell) > t$ or $C_\ell(0,0) \neq b_\ell$ for some $\ell \in [L]$, then reset $C_\ell(x,y) = b_\ell$ for every $\ell \in [L]$.
   (d) *Output for honest:* send $C_\ell(x, \alpha_j), C_\ell(\alpha_j, y)$ to P_j, for every $j \notin I$ and $\ell \in [L]$. (There is no more output for the adversary in this case.)

The protocol is similar to Protocol 5.2:. Given such a circuit G with L outputs, we let $G_1, \ldots, G_L$ be the circuits that define each outputs. That is, for $(b_1, \ldots, b_L) = G(a_1, \ldots, a_m)$ we let $b_\ell = G_\ell(a_1, \ldots, a_m)$ for every $\ell \in [L]$. In the protocol, the dealer distributes polynomials $C_1(x,y), \ldots, C_L(x,y)$ using VSS that are supposed to hide $b_1, \ldots, b_L$. Then, it defines L bivariate polynomials of degree$(2t, t)$, $D_1, \ldots, D_L$ such that for every $\ell \in [L]$ it holds that $D_\ell(x,0) = G(f^{a_1}(x), \ldots, f^{a_m}(x)) - C_\ell(x,0)$. The dealer distributes them using F_{WSS}. The parties then check from the shares they received that each one of the polynomials $C_1, \ldots, C_L$ is correct, and that $D_\ell(0,0)$ for every $\ell \in [L]$. When a party P_i complains the parties open the shares of P_i and publicly verify the complaint.

Protocol 6.2: Computing F^G_{VSS} **in the** $(F_{VSS}, F_{WSS}, F_{\text{Extend}}, F_{\text{WEval}})$-**hybrid model**

- **Input:**
    1. The dealer P_1 holds M degree-t polynomials $\{f^{a_m}(x)\}_{m \in [M]}$.
    2. Each party P_i holds a point $u_{i,m}$ for every $m \in [M]$ (where $u_{i,m} = f^{a_m}(\alpha_i)$).
- **Common input:** A field $\mathbb{F}$ and distinct non-zero elements $\alpha_1, \ldots, \alpha_n \in \mathbb{F}$.
- **The protocol:**
    1. **Sharing phase:**
        (a) P_1 computes $(b_1, \ldots, b_L) = G(f^{a_1}(0), \ldots, f^{a_M}(0))$.
        (b) For every $\ell \in [L]$, P_1 chooses a random degree-t bivariate polynomials, $C_\ell(x, y)$ such that $C_\ell(0, 0) = b_\ell$.
        (c) For every $\ell \in [L]$, P_1 chooses a random degree $(2t, t)$-bivariate polynomial $D_\ell(x, y)$ under the constraint that $D_\ell(x, 0) = G_\ell(f^{a_1}(x), \ldots, f^{a_M}(x)) - C_\ell(x, 0)$.
        (d) For every $\ell \in [L]$, invoke F_{VSS} to share $C_\ell(x, y)$ and let $(f_i^{b_\ell}(x), g_i^{b_\ell}(y))$ be the resulting share of P_i.
        (e) For every $\ell \in [L]$, invoke F_{WSS} to share $D_\ell(x, y)$. Let $K_\ell \subseteq [n]$ be the output of F_{WSS}, such that each P_j for $k \in K_\ell$ also receives $(f_k^{d_\ell}(x), g_k^{d_\ell}(y))$, and each party P_j for $j \notin K_\ell$ receives $g_j^{d_\ell}(y)$.
        (f) If $\perp$ was received in any of the above F_{VSS} or F_{WSS} invocations, then proceed to Step 5b.
    2. **Verifying that** $D_\ell(x, 0) = G_\ell((f^{a_1}(x), \ldots, f^{a_M}(x))) - C_\ell(x, 0)$ **for all** $\ell \in [L]$:[4]
        (a) For every $\ell \in [L]$, each party P_i verifies that $g_i^{d_\ell}(0) = G_\ell(u_{i,1}, \ldots, u_{i,M}) - g_i^{c_\ell}(0)$. If not, broadcast complaint(i)
        (b) If no party broadcast a complaint, proceed to Step 4.
    3. **Complaint resolution (only in pessimistic case):**
        (a) Let R be the set of all parties broadcast complaint(i), and let $E = \{\alpha_i\}_{i \in R}$.
        (b) For every $m \in [M]$, the dealer chooses a random bivariate polynomial of degree-t polynomial A_m such that $A_m(x, 0) = f^{a_m}(x)$. The parties run F_{Extend} where each party P_i inputs $u_{i,m}$ and P_1 inputs A_m. Let $(f_i^{a_m}(x), g_i^{a_m}(y))$ be the output share of P_i.
        (c) For every $m \in [M]$, the parties call to F_{WEval} where each party P_i inputs $(f_i^{a_m}(x), g_i^{a_m}(y), E, [n])$ and the dealer inputs A_m. Let $(f_j^{a_m}(x), g_j^{a_m}(y))$ be the result for every $j \in R$. Likewise, reconstruct $(f_j^{b_\ell}(x), g_j^{b_\ell}(y))$ for every $\ell \in [L]$. If F_{WEval} returned $\perp$ in any of those invocations, then proceed to Step 5b.

---

[4] We abuse notation and write $G_\ell((f^{a_1}(x), \ldots, f^{a_M}(x)))$ to denote a univariate polynomial in the variable x. Specifically, we take all polynomials $f^{a_1}(x), \ldots, f^{a_M}(x)$ and perform the same arithmetic operations as in G_ℓ on those input polynomials to receive a univariate polynomial in x.

(d) For every $\ell \in [L]$, the parties call to F_{WEval} where all parties input K_ℓ, E and each party P_k for $k \in K_\ell$ inputs also $(f_k^{d_\ell}(x), g_k^{d_\ell}(y))$. The output of F_{WEval} is $g_j^{d_\ell}(y)$ for every $j \in R$. If F_{WEval} returned $\bot$, then proceed to Step 5b.

(e) For every $j \in R$, $\ell \in [L]$, all parties verify that $g_j^{d_\ell}(0) = G(g_j^{a_1}(0), \ldots, g_j^{a_M}(0)) - g_j^{c_\ell}(0)$. If not, then proceed to Step 5b.

4. **Verifying that $D_\ell(0, 0) = 0$ for all $\ell \in [L]$:**

(a) For every $\ell \in [L]$, the parties call to F_{WEval} where all parties input $K_\ell, \{0\}$ and each party P_j for $j \in K_\ell$ inputs also $(f_j^{d_\ell}(x), g_j^{d_\ell}(y))$. The output of F_{WEval} is $g_0^{d_\ell}(y) = D_\ell(0, y)$ to all parties. If F_{WEval} returned $\bot$, then proceed to Step 5b.

(b) Verify that $g_0^{d_\ell}(0) = 0$. If not, proceed to Step 5b.

5. **Finalization:**

(a) *Accept:* If the dealer was not rejected, then each party P_i outputs $(f_i^{c_\ell}(x), g_i^{c_\ell}(y))$ for every $\ell \in [L]$.

(b) *Reject:* If the dealer is rejected, then each party P_i sends to P_j its points $u_{i,m}$ for every $m \in [M]$. The parties reconstruct the polynomials $f^{a_m}(x)$ using Reed-Solomon decoding, and output $G(f^{a_1}(0), \ldots, f^{a_M}(0))$.

Theorem 6.3. *Let $t < n/3$. Then, Protocol 6.2: is t-secure for the F_{VSS}^G functionality in the presence of a static malicious adversary, in the $(F_{VSS}, F_{WSS}, F_{\mathsf{Extend}}, F_{\mathsf{WEval}})$-hybrid model. The communication complexity of the protocol is just $O(L)$ VSSs in the optimistic case. In the pessimistic case, it corresponds to $O(L + M)$ VSSs.*

The proof is provided in the full version of this paper.

Acknowledgments. Gilad Asharov would like to thank Ilan Komargodski and Ariel Nof for helpful discussions.

References

1. Abraham, I., Pinkas, B., Yanai, A.: Blinder: MPC based scalable and robust anonymous committed broadcast (2020)
2. Asharov, G., Lindell, Y.: A full proof of the BGW protocol for perfectly secure multiparty computation. J. Cryptol. **30**(1), 58–151 (2017)
3. Asharov, G., Lindell, Y., Rabin, T.: Perfectly-secure multiplication for any t¡n/3. In: Rogaway, P. (ed.) Advances in Cryptology - CRYPTO 2011–31st Annual Cryptology Conference, Santa Barbara, CA, USA, 14–18, August 2011. Proceedings. Lecture Notes in Computer Science, vol. 6841, pp. 240–258. Springer, Berlin (2011). https://doi.org/10.1007/978-3-642-22792-9_14
4. Barak, A., Escudero, D., Dalskov, A.P.K., Keller, M.: Secure evaluation of quantized neural networks. IACR Cryptol. ePrint Arch. **2019**, 131 (2019)

5. Beaver, D.: Efficient multiparty protocols using circuit randomization. In: CRYPTO, pp. 420–432 (1991)
6. Beerliová-Trubíniová, Z., Hirt, M.: Perfectly-Secure MPC with Linear Communication Complexity. In: Canetti, R. (ed.) TCC 2008. LNCS, vol. 4948, pp. 213–230. Springer, Heidelberg (2008). https://doi.org/10.1007/978-3-540-78524-8_13
7. Ben-Or, M., Goldwasser, S., Wigderson, A.: Completeness theorems for non-cryptographic fault-tolerant distributed computation (extended abstract). In: Simon, J. (ed.) STOC, pp. 1–10. ACM (1988)
8. Berman, P., Garay, J.A., Perry, K.J.: Bit optimal distributed consensus, In: Baeza-Yates, R., Manber, U. (eds) Computer Science. Springer, Boston (1992). https://doi.org/10.1007/978-1-4615-3422-8_27
9. Anirudh, C., Choudhury, A., Patra, A.: A survey on perfectly-secure verifiable secret-sharing. IACR Cryptol. ePrint Arch. **2021**, 445 (2021). https://eprint.iacr.org/2021/445
10. Canetti, R.: Security and composition of multiparty cryptographic protocols. J. Cryptol. **13**(1), 143–202 (2000)
11. Canetti, R.: Universally composable security: a new paradigm for cryptographic protocols. In: FOCS, pp. 136–145. IEEE Computer Society (2001)
12. Canetti, R., Damgård, I., Dziembowski, S., Ishai, Y., Malkin, T.: Adaptive versus non-adaptive security of multi-party protocols. J. Cryptol. **17**(3), 153–207 (2004)
13. Chen, H., Kim, M., Razenshteyn, I.P., Rotaru, D., Song, Y., Wagh, S.: Maliciously secure matrix multiplication with applications to private deep learning. IACR Cryptol. ePrint Arch. **2020**, 451 (2020)
14. Chida, K., et al.: Fast large-scale honest-majority MPC for malicious adversaries. In: CRYPTO, pp. 34–64 (2018)
15. Chor, B., Goldwasser, S., Micali, S., Awerbuch, B.: Verifiable secret sharing and achieving simultaneity in the presence of faults (extended abstract). In: FOCS, pp. 383–395. IEEE Computer Society (1985)
16. Coan, B.A., Welch, J.L.: Modular construction of a byzantine agreement protocol with optimal message bit complexity. Inf. Comput. **97**(1), 61–85 (1992)
17. Cohen, R., Coretti, S., Garay, J.A., Zikas, V.: Probabilistic termination and composability of cryptographic protocols. J. Cryptol. **32**(3), 690–741 (2019)
18. Cramer, R., Damgård, I., Maurer, U.M.: General secure multi-party computation from any linear secret-sharing scheme. In: EUROCRYPT, pp. 316–334 (2000)
19. Damgård, I., Nielsen, J.B.: Scalable and Unconditionally Secure Multiparty Computation. In: Menezes, A. (ed.) CRYPTO 2007. LNCS, vol. 4622, pp. 572–590. Springer, Heidelberg (2007). https://doi.org/10.1007/978-3-540-74143-5_32
20. Damgård, I., Nielsen, J.B., Polychroniadou, A., Raskin, M.: On the Communication Required for Unconditionally Secure Multiplication. In: Robshaw, M., Katz, J. (eds.) CRYPTO 2016. LNCS, vol. 9815, pp. 459–488. Springer, Heidelberg (2016). https://doi.org/10.1007/978-3-662-53008-5_16
21. Damgård, I., Schwartzbach, N.I.: Communication lower bounds for perfect maliciously secure MPC. IACR Cryptol. ePrint Arch. **2020**, 251 (2020). https://eprint.iacr.org/2020/251
22. Dodis, Y., Micali, S.: Parallel Reducibility for Information-Theoretically Secure Computation. In: Bellare, M. (ed.) CRYPTO 2000. LNCS, vol. 1880, pp. 74–92. Springer, Heidelberg (2000). https://doi.org/10.1007/3-540-44598-6_5
23. Feldman, P.: Optimal algorithms for byzantine agreement (1988)
24. Feldman, P., Micali, S.: An optimal probabilistic protocol for synchronous byzantine agreement. SIAM J. Comput. **26**(4), 873–933 (1997)

25. Gennaro, R., Rabin, M.O., Rabin, T.: Simplified VSS and fast-track multiparty computations with applications to threshold cryptography. In: Coan, B.A., Afek, Y. (eds.) PODC, pp. 101–111. ACM (1998)
26. Goldreich, O.: The Foundations of Cryptography. Basic Applications, vol. 2. Cambridge University Press, Cambridge (2004)
27. Goldreich, O., Micali, S., Wigderson, A.: How to play any mental game or a completeness theorem for protocols with honest majority. In: Aho, A.V. (ed.) STOC, pp. 218–229. ACM (1987)
28. Goyal, V., Liu, Y., Song, Y.: Communication-Efficient Unconditional MPC with Guaranteed Output Delivery. In: Boldyreva, A., Micciancio, D. (eds.) CRYPTO 2019. LNCS, vol. 11693, pp. 85–114. Springer, Cham (2019). https://doi.org/10.1007/978-3-030-26951-7_4
29. Hirt, M., Maurer, U., Przydatek, B.: Efficient Secure Multi-party Computation. In: Okamoto, T. (ed.) ASIACRYPT 2000. LNCS, vol. 1976, pp. 143–161. Springer, Heidelberg (2000). https://doi.org/10.1007/3-540-44448-3_12
30. Hirt, M., Nielsen, J.B.: Robust Multiparty Computation with Linear Communication Complexity. In: Dwork, C. (ed.) CRYPTO 2006. LNCS, vol. 4117, pp. 463–482. Springer, Heidelberg (2006). https://doi.org/10.1007/11818175_28
31. Katz, J., Koo, C.: On expected constant-round protocols for byzantine agreement. J. Comput. Syst. Sci. **75**(2), 91–112 (2009)
32. Kushilevitz, E., Lindell, Y., Rabin, T.: Information-theoretically secure protocols and security under composition. SIAM J. Comput. **39**(5), 2090–2112 (2010)
33. Liu, J., Juuti, M., Lu, Y., Asokan, N.: Oblivious neural network predictions via minionn transformations. In: ACM CCS, pp. 619–631 (2017)
34. Mohassel, P., Rindal, P.: Aby3: a mixed protocol framework for machine learning. In: CCS, pp. 35–52 (2018)
35. Mohassel, P., Zhang, Y.: Secureml: a system for scalable privacy-preserving machine learning. In: SP, pp. 19–38 (2017)
36. Rabin, T., Ben-Or, M.: Verifiable secret sharing and multiparty protocols with honest majority (extended abstract). In: Johnson, D.S. (ed.) Proceedings of the 21st Annual ACM Symposium on Theory of Computing, 14–17, May 1989, Seattle, Washigton, USA, pp. 73–85. ACM (1989)
37. Shamir, A.: How to share a secret. Commun. ACM **22**(11), 612–613 (1979). https://doi.org/10.1145/359168.359176
38. Verma, A., Qassim, H., Feinizmer, D.: Residual squeeze CNDS deep learning CNN model for very large scale places image recognition. In: UEMCON, pp. 463–469 (2017)
39. Wagh, S., Gupta, D., Chandran, N.: Securenn: 3-party secure computation for neural network training. Proc. Priv. Enhancing Technol. **2019**(3), 26–49 (2019)
40. Yao, A.C.: How to generate and exchange secrets (extended abstract). In: FOCS, pp. 162–167. IEEE Computer Society (1986)

On Communication Models and Best-Achievable Security in Two-Round MPC

Aarushi Goel[1(✉)], Abhishek Jain[1], Manoj Prabhakaran[2], and Rajeev Raghunath[2]

[1] Johns Hopkins University, Baltimore, USA
{aarushig,abhishek}@cs.jhu.edu
[2] IIT Bombay, Mumbai, India
{mp,mrrajeev}@cse.iitb.ac.in

Abstract. Recently, a sequence of works have made strong advances in two-round (i.e., round-optimal) secure multi-party computation (MPC). In the *honest-majority* setting – the focus of this work – Ananth et al. [CRYPTO'18, EC'19], Applebaum et al. [TCC'18, EC'19] and Garg et al. [TCC'18] have established the feasibility of general two-round MPC in standard communication models involving broadcast ($\mathcal{BC}$) and private point-to-point ($\mathcal{P2P}$) channels.

In this work, we set out to understand what features of the communication model are necessary for these results, and more broadly the design of two-round MPC. Focusing our study on the plain model – the most natural model for honest-majority MPC – we obtain the following results:

- **Dishonest majority from Honest majority:** In the two round setting, honest-majority MPC and dishonest-majority MPC are surprisingly close, and often *equivalent*. This follows from our results that the former implies 2-message oblivious transfer, in many settings. (i) We show that without private point-to-point ($\mathcal{P2P}$) channels, i.e., when we use only broadcast ($\mathcal{BC}$) channels, *honest-majority MPC implies 2-message oblivious transfer*. (ii) Furthermore, this implication holds even when we use both $\mathcal{P2P}$ and $\mathcal{BC}$, provided that the MPC protocol is robust against "fail-stop" adversaries.

- **Best-Achievable Security:** While security with guaranteed output delivery (and even fairness) against malicious adversaries is impossible in two rounds, nothing is known with regards to the "next best" security notion, namely, security with identifiable abort (IA). We show that IA is also *impossible* to achieve with honest-majority even if we use both $\mathcal{P2P}$ and $\mathcal{BC}$ channels. However, if we replace $\mathcal{P2P}$ channels with a "bare" (i.e., untrusted) public-key infrastructure ($\mathcal{PKI}$), then even security with guaranteed output delivery (and hence IA) is possible to achieve.

These results "explain" that the reliance on $\mathcal{P2P}$ channels (together with $\mathcal{BC}$) in the recent two-round protocols in the plain model was in fact *necessary*, and that these protocols *couldn't* have achieved a stronger security guarantee, namely, IA. Overall, our results (put together with prior works) fully determine the best-achievable security for honest-majority

© International Association for Cryptologic Research 2021
K. Nissim and B. Waters (Eds.): TCC 2021, LNCS 13043, pp. 97–128, 2021.
https://doi.org/10.1007/978-3-030-90453-1_4

MPC in different communication models in two rounds. As a consequence, they yield the following hierarchy of communication models:

$$\mathcal{BC} < \mathcal{P2P} < \mathcal{BC} + \mathcal{P2P} < \mathcal{BC} + \mathcal{PKI}.$$

This shows that $\mathcal{BC}$ channel is the *weakest* communication model, and that $\mathcal{BC} + \mathcal{PKI}$ model is strictly stronger than $\mathcal{BC} + \mathcal{P2P}$ model.

1   Introduction

Recently, a sequence of works [1–4,9,12,18,19,30] have made strong advances in *two-round* secure multi-party computation (MPC). These works have established the feasibility of general two-round (i.e., round-optimal) MPC, relying on essentially minimal computational assumptions.

Such round optimality is of both theoretical and practical interest. In particular, it opens up the possibility of using MPC in scenarios where more rounds of interaction leads to significant costs, or in tools where a third round is simply inadmissible (e.g., if the communication is over blockchains, or if the first round messages are to be interpreted as "public keys" used to create "ciphertexts" in the second round). On the theoretical front, the separation between 1, 2 or more round protocols is arguably as fundamental as the separation between minicrypt, cryptomania or obfustopia, in that they admit only some cryptographic tools and not others. Indeed, the round complexity of protocols (e.g., of zero-knowledge proofs [23] and MPC) has always been a central theoretical question.

The practical and theoretical significance of round complexity is intertwined with the specific communication models employed. There are two major models of communication channels – *broadcast* ($\mathcal{BC}$) channels and secure *point-to-point* ($\mathcal{P2P}$) channels – that have been central in the MPC literature, starting from early results in the multi-party setting [8,11,21,31]. In the *honest-majority* setting – the focus of this work – these channels can provide varying "powers": e.g., $\mathcal{P2P}$ channels are necessary for achieving information-theoretic security [8,11], and broadcast channels are necessary for achieving security against $t > n/3$ corruptions [17]. They can also provide different use cases, e.g., a protocol that solely uses $\mathcal{BC}$ would be applicable in scenarios where, say, the first round messages are to be interpreted as public keys.

Our Work. The focus of this work is on understanding the role of these channels in the two-round setting with honest majority, where their differences come into sharper contrast. We ask:

> *In two-round honest-majority MPC, in the different communication models involving $\mathcal{BC}$ and $\mathcal{P2P}$, what levels of security are achievable for general computation, and under what assumptions?*

That is, we seek to understand the best-achievable security and the necessary assumptions in different communication models. We focus our study on the *plain* model – the most natural model for honest-majority MPC.[1] We sometimes

---

[1] Typically, the honest-majority assumption is viewed as an alternative to trusted setup assumptions such as a common reference string (CRS).

augment our model to include a "bare" (i.e., untrusted) public-key infrastructure (PKI) as a means for emulating $\mathcal{P}2\mathcal{P}$ channels over $\mathcal{BC}$.[2] Throughout this work, we use $\mathcal{PKI}$ to refer to a bare PKI setup.

Background on Security Notions. Before presenting our results, we provide a brief discussion on the prominent security notions studied in the literature. The weakest of them all is *semi-honest* (SH) security that guarantees privacy against semi-honest (a.k.a. honest but curious) adversaries. The case of malicious adversaries is more complex, and a variety of security notions have been studied.[3]

- **Security with abort:** A suite of three increasingly stronger security notions allows a malicious adversary to prevent the honest parties from learning the output by prematurely aborting the protocol: (a) *selective abort* (SA), where the adversary may selectively force a subset of honest parties to abort,(b) *unanimous abort* (UA), where all the honest parties agree on whether or not to abort, and (c) *identifiable abort* (IA) [29], where the honest parties agree on the identity of a corrupted party in the case of an abort.
- **Security with guaranteed output delivery:** Security with *guaranteed output delivery* ensures that an adversary cannot prevent the honest parties from learning the output via premature aborts. This notion is meaningful, both against fully malicious adversaries, and *fail-stop* adversaries who behave like semi-honest adversaries, except that they may prematurely abort. We refer to security in these two cases as M-GoD and FS-GoD, respectively.

The relationship between all of these notions can be summarized as follows: SH < SA < UA < IA < M-GoD, and SH < FS-GoD < M-GoD (note that FS-GoD is incomparable to SA, UA and IA).

Summary of Our Contributions. We start by providing a high-level statement of the key conclusions from our study, while omitting some finer points and results. We sketch an overview (omitting the specifics of the computational assumptions involved) in Fig. 1, which shows how our results fill in the gaps from prior work with regards to the feasibility of different security notions. A detailed description of our results in different communication models is given in Sect. 1.1.

- **Necessity of Oblivious Transfer:** While honest-majority MPC without any round restrictions is possible information-theoretically, our first set of results show that in many cases two-round MPC implies the existence of a two-message two-party *oblivious transfer* (OT) protocol:

---

[2] In a *bare* PKI setup, an adversarial party does not need to register its key prior to protocol; specifically, it does not need to prove knowledge of its secret key.

[3] The list of notions we discuss here is not exhaustive and some other notions have been studied that lie "in-between" the primary notions. This includes, e.g., semi-malicious security [5], which is a slight strengthening of SH, and fairness, which is a weakening of M-GoD. The lower and upper bounds for these notions tend to be similar to their respective "closest" notions; hence we do not explicitly discuss them.

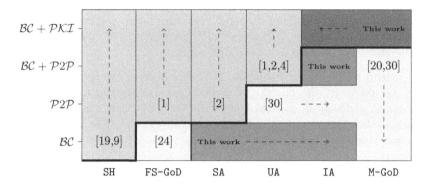

Fig. 1. Hierarchy of communication models in two-round honest-majority MPC without trusted setup. Green denotes feasibility of a security level and red denotes impossibility. The security notions featured in the columns are explained below. (Color figure online)

- When the two-round honest-majority MPC protocol is over a $\mathcal{BC}$ channel only (no $\mathcal{P2P}$ channels), then it implies a two-message OT protocol. If the original MPC protocol is semi-honest or malicious secure, and if it is in the plain model or uses a setup like a common reference string, the OT protocol inherits the same properties.
- Even if the honest-majority MPC protocol uses *both* a $\mathcal{BC}$ channel and $\mathcal{P2P}$ channels, if it offers FS-GoD security, then it implies two-message semi-honest OT. Interestingly, this holds only when the corruption threshold is $n/3 \leq t < n/2$; for $t < n/3$, we show that minicrypt assumptions are in fact sufficient.

- **Equivalence of Honest Majority and Dishonest Majority:** An interesting consequence of the first of the above results is that it removes the qualitative difference between honest-majority and dishonest-majority in the two-round $\mathcal{BC}$-only setting. Specifically, in the semi-honest setting, an honest-majority protocol implies two-message semi-honest OT, which in turn implies two-round dishonest-majority MPC [9,19]. On the other hand, in the malicious adversary setting, two-message OT is impossible in the plain model, and it follows that achieving malicious security is *impossible* in the honest-majority setting without $\mathcal{P2P}$ channels (as was already known for dishonest majority [22]). In other words, removing $\mathcal{P2P}$ channels "strips off" the advantages of the honest-majority model and places it on equal footing with dishonest-majority MPC – both in terms of necessary assumptions and feasibility.
- **Best-Achievable Security:** In the plain model, M-GoD and fairness are known to be impossible in two rounds even in the $\mathcal{BC} + \mathcal{P2P}$ setting [20,30].[4] Yet, nothing is known with regards to the "next best" security notion, namely, IA.

---

[4] There is a corner case of exactly one corruption (i.e., $t = 1$) and $n \geq 4$ where this impossibility result can be circumvented in the plain model [26,28].

We first prove that IA is also *impossible* in the plain model in the $\mathcal{BC} + \mathcal{P}2\mathcal{P}$ setting. However, if we replace $\mathcal{P}2\mathcal{P}$ channels with a bare $\mathcal{PKI}$ setup, then we observe that M-GoD (and hence, fairness and IA) is in fact *possible*. Previously, two-round protocols achieving M-GoD relied on a CRS setup in addition to bare $\mathcal{PKI}$ [24].

These results "explain" that the reliance on $\mathcal{P}2\mathcal{P}$ channels (together with $\mathcal{BC}$) in the recent constructions of two-round honest-majority MPC protocols [1–4,18,30] was in fact *necessary*, and that these protocols *couldn't* have achieved the stronger security guarantee of IA or achieved security with FS-GoD under weaker assumptions.

Overall, our results (put together with prior works) fully determine the best-achievable security notions in different communication models in two rounds in the honest-majority setting. Referring to Fig. 1, we obtain the following hierarchy of communication models:

$$\mathcal{BC} \ < \ \mathcal{P}2\mathcal{P} \ < \ \mathcal{BC} + \mathcal{P}2\mathcal{P} \ < \ \mathcal{BC} + \mathcal{PKI}.$$

This shows that $\mathcal{BC}$ channel is the weakest communication model, and that $\mathcal{BC} + \mathcal{PKI}$ model is strictly stronger than $\mathcal{BC} + \mathcal{P}2\mathcal{P}$ model.

1.1   Our Results in Detail

We conduct a comprehensive study of the role of communication channels in two-round honest-majority MPC. There are four natural communication models that one can consider: (i) $\mathcal{BC}$ *only*, i.e., where the protocol only uses $\mathcal{BC}$ channels, (ii) $\mathcal{P}2\mathcal{P}$ *only*, i.e., where the protocol only uses $\mathcal{P}2\mathcal{P}$ channels, (iii) $\mathcal{BC} + \mathcal{P}2\mathcal{P}$, where protocol uses both $\mathcal{BC}$ and $\mathcal{P}2\mathcal{P}$ channels, and (iv) $\mathcal{BC} + \mathcal{PKI}$, where we replace $\mathcal{P}2\mathcal{P}$ channels with a "bare" public-key infrastructure. Out of these four, the $\mathcal{P}2\mathcal{P}$ only model is already pretty well-understood from prior work. Hence, we primarily focus on the remaining three models.

For each of these models, we obtain new results for two-round honest-majority MPC that we elaborate on below. See Fig. 2 for a summary.

I. **Broadcast only.** We first investigate the feasibility of two-round honest-majority MPC without $\mathcal{P}2\mathcal{P}$ channels, i.e., by relying only on $\mathcal{BC}$. In this model, we show that *two-round honest-majority MPC is equivalent to two-round dishonest-majority MPC*. In other words, without $\mathcal{P}2\mathcal{P}$ channels, achieving security against dishonest minority is as hard as against dishonest majority.

Specifically, we show that any two-round honest-majority MPC for general functions in the $\mathcal{BC}$ only model can be transformed into two-round oblivious transfer (OT). Starting with an MPC with SH security yields semi-honest OT (sh-OT), while starting with one with SA (or stronger malicious) security yields malicious-receiver OT (mR-OT), where the view of a malicious receiver can be simulated.

Overall, in Sect. 4, we establish that sh-OT (resp., mR-OT) is *necessary* for SH (resp., SA, UA, IA), thereby yielding the following corollaries:

- SA, UA and IA are *impossible* in the plain model. This follows from the impossibility of two-round mR-OT in the plain model.

  Recently, two-round honest-majority MPC protocols with SH [1–3,18], SA [2,4] and UA [1,2,4] security were constructed for general circuits based on one-way functions (OWF) and for $\mathbf{NC}^1$ circuits unconditionally, i.e., with information-theoretic (IT) security. These protocols use (only) $\mathcal{P}2\mathcal{P}$ channels for achieving SH and SA security, and $\mathcal{BC} + \mathcal{P}2\mathcal{P}$ channels for achieving UA security. The above result establishes that the reliance on $\mathcal{P}2\mathcal{P}$ channels in these protocols is *necessary*.

- We observe that our transformation in fact also works in the CRS model. In the CRS model, two-round dishonest-majority MPC with SA and UA security was established in [9,19] based on mR-OT.[5] Recently, [12] extended these results to also capture IA security. A natural question is whether one could obtain similar feasibility results in the CRS model from weaker assumptions by assuming an honest majority. We establish that this is not the case; in particular, mR-OT is *necessary* even when we assume an honest majority.

II. **Broadcast + P2P.** We next investigate how the above landscape changes when we use $\mathcal{P}2\mathcal{P}$ channels together with $\mathcal{BC}$. Recent works have already shown that SH, SA, UA and FS-GoD are achievable in this model. Our contribution here is in providing a more complete picture, both with regards to best-achievable security and the necessary computational assumptions.

	SH	SA	UA	IA	FS-GoD		M-GoD
	$t < n/2$			$t < n/2$	$t < n/3$	$t < n/2$	$t < n/2$
$\mathcal{BC}$	sh-OT [19,9] ▼ Thm 1	✗ Cor 1			✗ [24]		
$\mathcal{P}2\mathcal{P}$	OWF/IT [1,3,18,2,4]	OWF/IT [2,4]	✗ [30]		OWF/IT Cor 2	sh-OT [1] ▼ Thm 3	✗ [20,30]
$\mathcal{BC} + \mathcal{P}2\mathcal{P}$	OWF/IT [1,3,18,2,4]			✗ Thm 2			
$\mathcal{BC} + \mathcal{PKI}$	PKE [1,3,18,2,4]			PKE+ m-NIZK Cor 3	PKE [1]		PKE+ m-NIZK Cor 3

Fig. 2. Feasibility of two-round honest-majority MPC. The symbol ✗ denotes impossibility and ▼ denotes necessity of an assumption.

---

[5] These works in fact rely on mR-OT in the CRS model with universally composable security [10].

1. **Identifiable Abort.** In light of the impossibility of M–GoD (as well as fairness), we investigate the feasibility of the "next best" security notion, namely, IA for which no prior results are known in the two-round setting (without trusted setup).

   In Sect. 5.1, we show that IA is *impossible* to achieve for general honest majority even in the $\mathcal{BC} + \mathcal{P2P}$ model.[6] This separates it from UA for which positive results are known in this model [1,2,4,30].

2. **Fail-Stop Guaranteed Output Delivery.** On the one hand, FS-GoD is known to be impossible in two rounds in the $\mathcal{BC}$ only model [24] due to implications to general-purpose program obfuscation [7]. On the other hand, it was recently shown to be achievable in the $\mathcal{P2P}$ only model based on sh-OT [1] for any $t < n/2$. A natural question is whether it is possible to base it on weaker assumptions, possibly in the stronger $\mathcal{BC} + \mathcal{P2P}$ model. We find that the answer is mixed:

   - For $n/3 \leq t < n/2$, in Sect. 5.2, we show that sh-OT is *necessary* for FS-GoD in the $\mathcal{BC} + \mathcal{P2P}$ model.
   - For $t < n/3$, in Sect. 5.2, we observe that FS-GoD can be easily achieved for general circuits based on only OWFs (and for $\mathbf{NC}^1$ circuits, with IT security) in the $\mathcal{P2P}$ only model.

III. **Broadcast + PKI.** Next, we consider the case where the protocol uses a bare $\mathcal{PKI}$ setup instead of $\mathcal{P2P}$ channels, together with $\mathcal{BC}$. It is easy to see that $\mathcal{BC} + \mathcal{PKI}$ model is at least as strong as $\mathcal{BC} + \mathcal{P2P}$ since private channels can be emulated over $\mathcal{BC}$ using public-key encryption (PKE). While it might be tempting to believe that these models are equivalent, this is not the case – $\mathcal{BC} + \mathcal{PKI}$ model is *strictly stronger* than $\mathcal{BC} + \mathcal{P2P}$.

- In Sect. 6, we observe that by leveraging a specially crafted bare $\mathcal{PKI}$, it is possible to achieve M–GoD against $t < n/2$ corruptions in two rounds in the $\mathcal{BC} + \mathcal{PKI}$ model.
- In the full version of this paper, we show that by using a bare $\mathcal{PKI}$ based on generic PKE, it is possible to achieve IA against $t < n/2$ corruptions in two rounds in the $\mathcal{BC} + \mathcal{PKI}$ model.

Both of these constructions rely on *multi*-CRS non-interactive zero-knowledge (m-NIZK) [25] proofs in addition to PKE. m-NIZK proof systems for NP are known based on Zaps [15] (which in turn can be constructed from various standard assumptions such as trapdoor permutations and assumptions on bilinear maps) or learning with errors [6].

We note that while the first protocol achieves a strictly stronger result, it is qualitatively different from the second in that it relies on a specially crafted bare $\mathcal{PKI}$ setup where the public keys contain CRSes of an m-NIZK proof system in addition to public keys of a PKE scheme. On a technical level, such a $\mathcal{PKI}$ allows for using m-NIZK proofs in the first round of the protocol which is instrumental

---

[6] In the weaker $\mathcal{P2P}$ only model, honest-majority protocols with IA security are known to be impossible even if we allow for arbitrary rounds [13].

for achieving M-GoD security. Without such a $\mathcal{PKI}$, however, we can still use m-NIZK proofs in the second round and we observe that this is sufficient for achieving IA security.

IV. **P2P Only.** The remaining case is when the parties have access to *only* P2P channels. A recent work of [30] established SA as the strongest achievable notion of security against malicious adversaries in this setting, and a matching positive result for computing general circuits was given by [2,4] based on OWFs (and for $\mathbf{NC}^1$ circuits, with IT security). For FS-GoD, [1] showed that it is achievable for $t < n/2$ based on sh-OT. We have further sharpened this result by showing that for $t < n/3$, OWFs suffice, and for $n/3 \le t < n/2$, sh-OT is necessary. Put together, these results complete the picture for the $\mathcal{P2P}$ only model as well.

1.2 Related Work

In this work, we show that any form of malicious security is impossible in the $\mathcal{BC}$ only setting in the plain model. In the CRS model, however, SA, UA and IA are possible to achieve in the $\mathcal{BC}$ only setting [9,12,19].

In a concurrent and independent work, Damgård et al. [14], explore a related (but different) question in the setting where parties have access to *both* a $\mathcal{PKI}$ and a trusted CRS setup. They investigate the necessity of $\mathcal{BC}$ in each individual round of a two-round honest-majority MPC protocol. In contrast, we consider a setting *without any trusted setup* (i.e., either the plain model or the plain model augmented with a bare $\mathcal{PKI}$). Hence, their results are incomparable to ours.

2   Technical Overview

In this section, we discuss the main ideas underlying our results.

2.1   Lower Bounds in the $\mathcal{BC}$ only Model

In the $\mathcal{BC}$ only model, we show that 2-round honest-majority MPC implies the existence of 2-message oblivious transfer (sh-OT or mR-OT, depending on the level of security of the honest-majority MPC). This is in sharp contrast to the general setting, where without any restriction on the number of rounds or communication channels, honest-majority MPC (even with M-GoD security) is possible *unconditionally*.

To understand the source of this requirement, we consider an n-party variant of OT, denoted as $\mathcal{F}_{n\text{-}OT}$, in which there is a sender, a receiver, and $(n-2)$ "helper parties" (who do not have any inputs or outputs). Interestingly, by relying on $\mathcal{P2P}$ channels, $\mathcal{F}_{n\text{-}OT}$ can be securely realized (with SH security) unconditionally in two rounds.[7] Further, even if we only use $\mathcal{BC}$ channels but allow for at least

---

[7] Specifically, it can be implemented as OLE over a large field, using a protocol in which each helper party receives degree t Shamir shares of a and x from sender and receiver respectively, and degree $2t$ shares of b from sender, and sends degree $2t$ shares of $ax + b$ to the receiver.

three rounds, then public-key encryption (rather than OT) is sufficient, by using the first round to send public keys for establishing private channels for the next two rounds. Thus the necessity of OT must stem from the combination of the two-round constraint and the restriction to $\mathcal{BC}$.

Our strategy is to build a two-message (two-party) OT protocol from an honest-majority two-round protocol Π for $\mathcal{F}_{n\text{-OT}}$, in the $\mathcal{BC}$ model. In this section, we only consider $n = 3$ (with the sender, the receiver and a single helper party), so that honest-majority translates to corruption of at most one party. The proof easily generalizes to an arbitrary number of parties and is shown in the technical section.

As a first attempt, one may hope that the helper party – who has no input and receives only publicly visible messages – can be implemented by either party (thus collapsing to a 2-party protocol), and the protocol will remain secure. Unfortunately, this is not true. For instance, suppose the receiver and the helper also broadcast a public key for encryption in the first round, and the sender's second round message also includes a 2-out-of-2 secret-sharing of its inputs, each share encrypted using one of these keys. In such a case, corrupting at most one party in Π does not reveal these inputs, but if the helper is implemented by the receiver, then the protocol is no longer secure. This attack is symmetric, and prevents clubbing the helper with either the sender or the receiver. On the other hand, the sender and the receiver *jointly* implementing the helper in a secure manner is not an option, as it leaves us with a harder problem than we set out to solve.

The key to resolving this conundrum is to *break the symmetry* between the receiver and the sender. We observe that Π can first be modified so that the receiver does not send any message in the second round. This is a legitimate modification, since the last round messages are only used for output generation, and the receiver is the only party with an output in the protocol. This modification to Π prevents the attack mentioned above *when the helper is implemented by the sender*. We go on to show that this in fact, leads to a protocol that is secure against all passive attacks. Clearly, security against corruption of the receiver follows from the same in Π. Security against corruption of the sender follows, informally, from the fact that even in Π, by corrupting the sender alone, the adversary can obtain the same view as in the transformed 2-party protocol, by internally simulating the helper party. Specifically, *since the honest receiver never responds to the helper's messages*, the internally simulated helper's view can be combined with the independently generated message of the receiver to obtain a valid simulation.

Thus the transformed protocol is a semi-honest secure 2-party OT protocol (i.e., sh-OT). Further, it can be cast as a *two message* protocol:

- **Round 1:** The first message from the receiver consists of its first round message in Π.
- **Round 2:** The second message from the sender consists of both first and second round messages from the sender and the helper in Π.

Note that we are able to "postpone" the first round messages of the sender and helper in Π to the second message of OT because an honest receiver is *non-rushing*; i.e., its first round message does not depend on the messages of the other parties.

This argument partly extends to the case when Π is secure against active corruptions. In this case, the transformed protocol will have the same security as Π against the corruption of the receiver, but only security against semi-honest corruption of the sender. When Π is secure w.r.t. straightline simulation (which is standard for security with honest majority) this yields a 2-party, 2-round OT protocol that is secure against passive corruption of senders, and active corruption of receivers, with straightline simulation in the latter case. We term such a protocol an mR-OT protocol.

These arguments readily extend to all $n \geq 3$. Thus two-round n-party honest-majority MPC over $\mathcal{BC}$ channels implies two-round sh-OT or two-round mR-OT, depending on the security level of the honest-majority protocol. In the latter case, we obtain an impossibility result for MPC in the plain model, by proving the impossibility of two-round mR-OT protocol (in the plain model), similar to the impossibility of UC security in the plain model. We give a formal proof in Sect. 4.

2.2 $\mathcal{BC} + \mathcal{P2P}$ Model

Impossibility of IA in $\mathcal{BC} + \mathcal{P2P}$ Model. We next describe our ideas for proving the impossibility of 2-round honest-majority MPC with IA security in the $\mathcal{BC} + \mathcal{P2P}$ model, without any setup. We focus on the case of $n = 3$ parties and $t = 1$ corruption.

From our first lower bound, we know that security with IA is impossible in two-rounds in the $\mathcal{BC}$ only model. In general, access to $\mathcal{P2P}$ channels can often help in overcoming such impossibilities. Indeed, recent two-round protocols [1,2,4] that achieve SA/UA security crucially rely on the use of $\mathcal{P2P}$ channels. An obvious advantage of using $\mathcal{P2P}$ channels in the honest majority setting is "easy" (straight-line) extraction of the adversary's inputs during simulation. However, there is also a *potential disadvantage*: an adversary may use $\mathcal{P2P}$ channels to create inconsistent views amongst the honest parties. For example, it may send honestly computed messages to one honest party, but not to the other.

While such attacks can usually be handled (by requiring the honest parties to output $\perp$ by default in case of any conflict or confusion) when we only require SA or UA security, it becomes a challenge in achieving IA security. Recall that in IA, if the honest parties output $\perp$, they *must* also be able to identify a corrupt party. In a *two round* protocol, even if an honest party – who does not receive a "valid" message in the first round from the adversary – tries to complain to another honest party in the second round, the latter party is left in a dilemma about whether the complaint is legitimate or fabricated (to frame the other party). As a result, it is unable to decide who amongst the other two parties is actually corrupt. This observation forms the basis of our impossibility result.

Consider a 3-party functionality $\mathcal{F}$ that takes inputs $b \in \{0,1\}$ from P_2 and (x_0, x_1) from P_3 and outputs x_b to P_1. That is, $\mathcal{F}(\bot, b, (x_0, x_1)) = (x_b, \bot, \bot)$. Consider an adversary who corrupts P_2 in the following manner: it behaves honestly, except that it does not send any protocol specified private channel message to P_1 (i.e., simply drops them).[8] We argue that no protocol can achieve IA security against such an attack.

In particular, we argue that in this case, the honest parties can neither output $\bot$ nor a non-$\bot$ value. As discussed earlier, if the honest parties output $\bot$, they must also be able to identify the corrupt party. However, P_3's view in this case is indistinguishable from another execution where a corrupt P_1 falsely accuses an honest P_2 of not sending private channel messages. It is easy to see that this inherent "conflict" for P_3 about who amongst P_1 and P_2 is the corrupt party is impossible to resolve. Hence, the output of the honest parties cannot be $\bot$.

This leaves the possibility of the output being non-$\bot$. Consider P_2 using an input b in the protocol execution. In case the output of the honest parties is a non-$\bot$ value, there are two possible outcomes, corresponding to what a simulator extracts as P_2's input: (1) the simulator extracts b with probability (almost) 1 or (2) with at least a non-negligible probability, it extracts $1 - b$.

- In the first case, note that the simulator's view of P_2's messages only involves messages visible to P_3. Then, since the simulator is a straight-line simulator, and the protocol is in the plain model, a corrupt P_3 can violate privacy by running the same simulator to extract an *honest* P_2's input. Hence this case is not possible.
- In the second case, consider another instance where P_1 is corrupt, while P_2 and P_3 are honest. Consider an execution where P_1 follows the protocol honestly and learns the output x_b. Later it launches an "offline reset attack," by recomputing its second round messages pretending that it did not receive a message from party P_2 in the first round. Upon recomputing the output using this alternate view (where P_2's private messages were not received), it learns, with non-negligible probability, x_{1-b}. Hence, P_1 can distinguish between the case $x_0 = x_1$ and $x_0 \neq x_1$ with a non-negligible advantage, thereby violating P_3's privacy. Hence, this case is also not possible.

We present a formal proof in Sect. 5.1.

Necessity of sh-OT for FS-GoD in the $\mathcal{BC} + \mathcal{P2P}$ Model. In the $\mathcal{BC} + \mathcal{P2P}$ model, we show that 2-round honest-majority that achieves FS-GoD security implies the existence of 2-message sh-OT. This implication holds for $n/3 \leq t < n/2$; for $t < n/3$, we describe a simple FS-GoD protocol in the technical sections based on weaker assumptions.

---

[8] If the protocol does not require any P2P message from P_2 to P_1, then the corrupted P_2 is simply behaving honestly since there is no message to be dropped. In this case, the protocol must result in a not-$\bot$ output. This case is addressed below.

Recall that in the transformation from a two-round $\mathcal{BC}$ only protocol for $\mathcal{F}_{3\text{-OT}}$ to a secure protocol for OT (discussed in Sect. 2.1), the sender implements the helper party. Security against a semi-honest sender follows from the fact that in the $\mathcal{BC}$ only model, the view of an adversary who corrupts the sender and the helper in the transformed protocol is no different from the view of an adversary who only corrupts the sender in the original protocol. It is easy to see that this argument *fails* (even in the semi-honest setting) when the protocol additionally uses $\mathcal{P}2\mathcal{P}$ channels. Consider, for example, the case where the receiver is required to send a private message to the helper in the first round. An adversary who corrupts both the sender and the helper now gets this additional information, which it does not get by corrupting the sender alone. Indeed, since two-round protocols [1–4,18] that achieve security with SA or UA in the $\mathcal{BC} + \mathcal{P}2\mathcal{P}$ model are already known, we know that the above approach *must* fail.

Our key insight is that if the two-round protocol achieves FS-GoD security, then it means that some private channel messages are "redundant," and can be removed if one only cares about security against semi-honest adversaries. This observation allows us to start with a "truncated" version of the underlying FS-GoD protocol (which only achieves SH security) and then use a similar strategy as in Sect. 2.1 to construct two-message sh-OT. We first focus on the setting with $n = 3$ parties and $t = 1$ corruption. Later we discuss how this argument can be extended for arbitrary n and $n/3 \le t < n/2$.

As earlier, we consider the functionality $\mathcal{F}_{3\text{-OT}}$ involving a sender, a receiver and a helper party. Let Π be a 3-party protocol for this functionality with FS-GoD security. Note that FS-GoD security implies that even if the helper does *not* send its second round message, the protocol must still remain (at the very least) semi-honest secure. Furthermore, if the helper is not required to send any messages in the second round, the sender and receiver do not need to send any messages to the helper in the first round (except the broadcast channel messages, which are received by everyone). Combining these observations with the observation from Sect. 2.1 that the receiver (by virtue of being the only output party) does not need to send a message in the second round, and that the sender and helper can send all their messages in the second round, we obtain the following two-message protocol:

- **Round 1:** The receiver computes and sends its first round broadcast message and its private message for the sender.
- **Round 2:** The sender computes and sends its first and second round broadcast messages and its private channel messages for the receiver. It also computes and sends the first round broadcast message and the private channel message of the helper for the receiver.

Security against a semi-honest sender and receiver in the transformed OT protocol can be argued similarly as before, although we need to be slightly more careful in handling private channel messages of each party in the underlying three-party protocol.

The above idea can be generalized to n parties and $n/3 \leq t < n/2$ corruptions for the n-party functionality $\mathcal{F}_{n\text{-OT}}$ (described earlier). In this case, the first $2t$ parties are emulated by the sender and the remaining $n - 2t$ are emulated by the receiver. Since $n/3 \leq t < n/2$, we know that $n - 2t \leq t$. Security against a semi-honest receiver in this case follows exactly as before. For security against a semi-honest sender, we rely on the fact that since t out of the $2t$ parties emulated by the sender do not send second round messages, the receiver parties do not need to send them private channel messages in the first round. We can now rely on the semi-honest security of (the truncated version of) Π to show that an adversary who corrupts the sender does not gain any more advantage over an adversary who corrupts the first t parties in Π. We defer further details to Sect. 5.2.

2.3 $\mathcal{BC} + \mathcal{PKI}$ Model

Positive Result for M-GoD. There exist two-round M-GoD protocols in the $\mathcal{BC} + \mathcal{PKI}$ model that rely on a trusted CRS setup [24]. We observe that there is simple way to eliminate the centralized CRS setup.

The CRS setup in existing two-round M-GoD protocols is only used for NIZK proofs. In the honest majority setting, it is easy to verify that standard NIZKs can be replaced with *multi*-CRS NIZKs (m-NIZKs) [25], where the setup consists of multiple CRS strings (as opposed to a single CRS) and soundness holds as long as a majority of the CRS are honestly generated. Our key observation is that a multi-CRS setup can in fact be embedded inside the bare $\mathcal{PKI}$ setup: start with any bare $\mathcal{PKI}$ setup and modify it such that the public key of each party also includes a CRS for a m-NIZK. This is still a valid bare $\mathcal{PKI}$ setup since the adversary in m-NIZK is allowed to choose its CRSes adaptively after looking at the honest parties' CRSes. Putting this together, we obtain a 2-round M-GoD protocol in the $\mathcal{PKI} + \mathcal{BC}$ model.

By using the same observation, the three-round M-GoD protocol of Ananth et al. [1] in the plain model can also be transformed into a two-round protocol in the $\mathcal{BC} + \mathcal{PKI}$ model by moving the entire first round of their protocol to a bare $\mathcal{PKI}$ setup. For the sake of completeness, in Sect. 6, we give a formal description of the resulting two-round M-GoD protocol. We in fact present a transformation from any two-round (semi-malicious) FS-GoD protocol in the $\mathcal{BC} + \mathcal{PKI}$ model (which is known from [1]) into a two-round M-GoD protocol using m-NIZKs.

Positive Result for IA. The above M-GoD protocol also implies a two-round protocol for IA in the $\mathcal{BC} + \mathcal{PKI}$ model and complements the IA impossibility result from Sect. 2.2. However, the protocol uses a specially crafted $\mathcal{PKI}$ where the public keys contain CRSes of an m-NIZK proof system in addition to public keys of a PKE scheme.

We present a separate protocol for IA in the $\mathcal{BC} + \mathcal{PKI}$ model, where the $\mathcal{PKI}$ can be instantiated from generic PKE. We obtain this protocol by devising a generic transformation from any two-round UA-secure protocol in the $\mathcal{BC} + \mathcal{P2P}$ model that achieves perfect correctness to a two-round IA-secure protocol in the $\mathcal{BC} + \mathcal{PKI}$ model.

Given a two-round protocol Π that achieves security with UA in the $\mathcal{BC}+\mathcal{P}2\mathcal{P}$ model, a natural idea to strengthen its security to IA (in the $\mathcal{BC}+\mathcal{PKI}$ model) is to simply require each party to prove honest behavior using the standard "commit and prove" approach: the parties encrypt their private channel messages under the public-keys of the recipient parties, broadcast them in the first round and attach a proof of having computed all of these messages honestly in each round. If a party cheats, then its proof will fail verification, and *all* the honest parties will be able to identify that corrupt party. While this idea can be easily implemented using NIZKs, it would result in a protocol in the CRS model.

Since we are in the honest majority setting, we can attempt to replace standard NIZKs with *multi*-CRS NIZKs (m-NIZKs) [25]. In our setting, the CRS strings can be generated by the parties in the first round of the protocol and the honest majority assumption implies that a majority of the CRS are computed honestly. Using m-NIZKs, the parties can still prove honest behavior in the second round of the protocol. However, a proof of honest behavior in the first round can no longer be sent in the first round itself (since the CRS strings are not known at that point); instead it can only be sent (belatedly) in the second round. In this case, we need to ensure that it is not "too late" for the honest parties to detect and identify a cheating party.

We implement this idea in the following manner. If the parties are able to compute their second round messages – given the first round messages from all the other parties – they give a single proof in the second round to prove that they computed all their (first and second round) messages honestly.

In case a corrupt party does not compute and encrypt its first round private channel messages honestly, there are two possibilities: (1) the honest recipient of the malformed private message is able to detect that the message is not "well-formed" (e.g. if the message is an empty string or it does not satisfy the syntax specified by underlying protocol, etc.) and is unable to use this message to compute its second round message, or (2) the honest recipient does not detect any issues with the message and is able to compute its second round message as per the specification of the underlying protocol. We handle these two scenarios differently.

In the first case, the recipient party simply reveals the decrypted malformed message to all other parties in the second round and gives a proof to convince them that its (respective) public key was honestly generated and that the corrupt party did indeed send them an encryption of this malformed message. Given the decrypted message, the remaining parties can perform the same (public) verification as the recipient party to determine whether or not the message is well-formed and identify the corrupt party. In the second case, we will rely on the soundness of the proof given by the corrupt party. In case the corrupt party did not encrypt its first round private channel messages honestly, it will not be able to give a convincing proof in the second round, and will be easily identified. The formal description of this construction is deferred to the full-version of this paper.

3   Preliminaries

Throughout the paper, we use λ to denote the security parameter. We recall some standard cryptographic definitions in this section. Apart from this, we also use the standard definitions of public key encryption and the different security notions in secure multiparty computation. We omit their definitions here.

3.1   Oblivious Transfer (OT)

In this paper, we consider the standard notion of 1-out-of-2 oblivious transfer [16]; where one party (the sender) has inputs (m_0, m_1) in some domain (say $\{0,1\}^*$), and another party (the receiver) has a choice bit $b \in \{0,1\}$. At the end, the receiver should learn m_b and nothing more while the sender should learn nothing about b.

We consider two variants of this OT protocol, a *semi-honest* version called sh-OT and one that is secure against a *malicious receiver* called mR-OT. For mR-OT, we require an efficient straight-line simulator for a maliciously corrupt receiver.

We define the syntax and the security guarantees of a two-message OT protocol in the plain model. The definition can be naturally extended to the CRS model.

Definition 1 (2 Message OT). *A two-message oblivious transfer between a receiver R and a sender S is defined by a tuple of 3 PPT algorithms* $(\mathsf{OT}_R, \mathsf{OT}_S, \mathsf{OT}_{\mathsf{out}})$. *Let λ be the security parameter. The receiver computes* msg_R, ρ *as the evaluation of* $\mathsf{OT}_R(1^\lambda, b)$, *where $b \in \{0,1\}$ is the receiver's input. The receiver sends msg_R to the sender. The sender computes msg_S as the evaluation of* $OT_S(1^\lambda, \mathsf{msg}_R, (m_0, m_1))$, *where $m_0, m_1 \in \{0,1\}^*$ are the sender's input. The sender sends msg_S to the receiver. Finally the receiver computes m_b by evaluating* $OT_{\mathsf{out}}(\rho, \mathsf{msg}_R, \mathsf{msg}_S)$.

A sh-OT protocol satisfies correctness, security against semi-honest receiver *and semi-honest sender, while a mR-OT satisfies* correctness, security against semi-honest sender and malicious receiver, *which are defined as follows:*

– **Correctness:** *For each $m_0, m_1 \in \{0,1\}^*$, $b \in \{0,1\}$, it holds that*

$$\Pr\left[\begin{array}{c} (\rho, \mathsf{msg}_R) \leftarrow \mathsf{OT}_R\left(1^\lambda, b\right) \\ \mathsf{msg}_S \leftarrow OT_S\left(1^\lambda, \mathsf{msg}_R, (m_0, m_1)\right) \end{array} \middle| \mathsf{OT}_{\mathsf{out}}\left(\rho, \mathsf{msg}_R, \mathsf{msg}_S\right) = m_b \right] = 1,$$

– **Security against Semi-Honest Sender:** *It holds that,*

$$\left\{ (\mathsf{msg}_R^0, \rho^0) \leftarrow \mathsf{OT}_R\left(1^\lambda, 0\right) \,\middle|\, \mathsf{msg}_R^0 \right\} \approx_c \left\{ (\mathsf{msg}_R^1, \rho^1) \leftarrow \mathsf{OT}_R\left(1^\lambda, 1\right) \,\middle|\, \mathsf{msg}_R^1 \right\}$$

– **Security against Semi-Honest Receiver:** *it holds that for each $b \in \{0,1\}$, $m_0, m_1, m_0', m_1' \in \{0,1\}^*$, and $m_b = m_b'$,*

$$\left\{ \mathsf{OT}_S\left(1^\lambda, \mathsf{msg}_R, (m_0, m_1)\right) \right\} \approx_c \left\{ \mathsf{OT}_S\left(1^\lambda, \mathsf{msg}_R, (m_0', m_1')\right) \right\}$$

where $(\mathsf{msg}_R, \rho) \leftarrow OT_R(1^\lambda, b)$.

– **Security against a Malicious Receiver**: *For every PPT adversary $\mathcal{A}$, there exists a PPT simulator $\mathcal{S}_R = (\mathcal{S}_R^1, \mathcal{S}_R^2)$ for any choice of $m_0, m_1 \in \{0,1\}^*$ such that the following holds*

$$\left| \Pr\left[\text{IDEAL}_{\mathcal{S}_R, \mathcal{F}_{\text{OT}}}(1^\lambda, m_0, m_1) = 1\right] - \Pr\left[\text{REAL}_{\mathcal{A}, \text{OT}}(1^\lambda, m_0, m_1) = 1\right] \right|$$

$$\leq \frac{1}{2} + \text{negl}(\lambda).$$

Where experiments $\text{IDEAL}_{\mathcal{S}_R, \mathcal{F}_{\text{OT}}}$ *and* $\text{REAL}_{\mathcal{A}, \text{OT}}$ *are defined as follows:*

Exp $\text{IDEAL}_{\mathcal{S}_R, \mathcal{F}_{\text{OT}}}(1^\lambda, m_0, m_1):$	**Exp** $\text{REAL}_{\mathcal{A}, \text{OT}}(1^\lambda, m_0, m_1):$
$\text{msg}_R \leftarrow \mathcal{A}\left(1^\lambda\right)$	$\text{msg}_R \leftarrow \mathcal{A}\left(1^\lambda\right)$
$b \leftarrow \mathcal{S}_R^1(1^\lambda, \text{msg}_R)$	
$m_b \leftarrow \mathcal{F}_{\text{OT}}(m_0, m_1, b)$	
$\text{msg}_S \leftarrow \mathcal{S}_R^2(1^\lambda, m_b, \text{msg}_R)$	$\text{msg}_S \leftarrow \text{OT}_S\left(1^\lambda, \text{msg}_R, (m_0, m_b)\right)$
Out $\mathcal{A}(\text{msg}_S)$	Out $\mathcal{A}(\text{msg}_S)$

3.2 Multi-CRS Non-interactive Zero Knowledge (m-NIZK)

We use the definition from [6], which is adapted from [25]. Let R be an efficiently computable binary relation and L an NP-language of statements x such that $(x, w) \in R$ for some witness w.

Definition 2 (Multi-CRS NIZK). *A multi-CRS NIZK for a language L is a tuple of PPT algorithms m-NIZK = (m-NIZK.Gen, m-NIZK.Prove, m-NIZK.Verify) satisfying the following specifications:*

– m-NIZK.Gen(1^λ): *It takes as input the security parameter λ and outputs a uniformly random string* crs.
– m-NIZK.Prove(crs, x, w): *It takes as input a set of n random strings $\overrightarrow{\text{crs}}$, a statement x, and a witness w and outputs a* proof.
– m-NIZK.Verify($\overrightarrow{\text{crs}}, x$, proof): *It takes as input a set of n random strings $\overrightarrow{\text{crs}}$, a statement x, and a* proof. *It outputs 1 if it accepts the* proof *and 0 if it rejects it.*

We require that the algorithms satisfy the following properties for all non uniform PPT adversaries $\mathcal{A}$:

- **Perfect Completeness**

$$\Pr\left[\begin{array}{c} s = \emptyset; (\overrightarrow{\mathsf{crs}}, x, w) \leftarrow \mathcal{A}^{\mathsf{m\text{-}NIZK.Gen}} \\ \mathsf{proof} \leftarrow \mathsf{m\text{-}NIZK.Prove}(\overrightarrow{\mathsf{crs}}, x, w) \end{array} \;\middle|\; \begin{array}{c} \mathsf{m\text{-}NIZK.Verify}(\overrightarrow{\mathsf{crs}}, x, \mathsf{proof}) = 0 \\ and \; (x, w) \in R \end{array}\right] = 0,$$

where m-NIZK.Gen *is an oracle that when queried, outputs* crs $\leftarrow$ m-NIZK.Gen(1^λ) *and sets* $\overrightarrow{\mathsf{crs}} = \overrightarrow{\mathsf{crs}} \cup \mathsf{crs}$. *Note that this says that even if the adversary arbitrarily picks all the random strings, perfect completeness still holds.*

- **Soundness**

$$\Pr\left[\begin{array}{c} S = \emptyset; \\ (\overrightarrow{\mathsf{crs}}, x, \mathsf{proof}) \leftarrow \mathcal{A}^{\mathsf{m\text{-}NIZK.Gen}} \end{array} \;\middle|\; \begin{array}{c} \mathsf{m\text{-}NIZK.Verify}(\overrightarrow{\mathsf{crs}}, x, \mathsf{proof}) = 0 \;\wedge \\ x \notin L \;\wedge\; |\overrightarrow{\mathsf{crs}} \cap S| > n/2 \end{array}\right] \leq \mathsf{negl}(\lambda)$$

where m-NIZK.Gen *is an oracle that when queried, outputs* crs $\leftarrow$ m-NIZK.Gen(1^λ) *and sets* $S = S \cup \mathsf{crs}_q$. *Note that this says that as long as at least half of the random strings are honestly generated, the adversary cannot forge a proof except with negligible probability.*

- **Zero-Knowledge.** *There exist PPT algorithms* $\mathcal{S}_{Gen}, \mathcal{S}_{Prove}$ *such that*

$$\Pr[\mathsf{crs} \leftarrow \mathsf{m\text{-}NIZK.Gen}(1^\lambda) \mid \mathcal{A}(\mathsf{crs}) = 1] \approx \Pr[(\mathsf{crs}, \tau) \leftarrow \mathcal{S}_{Gen}(1^\lambda) : \mathcal{A}(\mathsf{crs}) = 1]$$

and

$$\Pr\left[\begin{array}{c} s = \emptyset; (\overrightarrow{\mathsf{crs}}, x, \mathsf{proof}) \leftarrow \mathcal{A}^{\mathcal{S}_{Gen}} \\ \mathsf{proof} \leftarrow \mathsf{m\text{-}NIZK.Prove}(\overrightarrow{\mathsf{crs}}, x, w) \end{array} \;\middle|\; \begin{array}{c} \mathcal{A}(\mathsf{proof}) = 1 \; and \; (x, w) \in R \\ and \; |\overrightarrow{\mathsf{crs}} \cap S| > n/2 \end{array}\right]$$

$$\approx \Pr\left[\begin{array}{c} s = \emptyset; (\overrightarrow{\mathsf{crs}}, x, \mathsf{proof}) \leftarrow \mathcal{A}^{\mathcal{S}_{Gen}} \\ \mathsf{proof} \leftarrow \mathcal{S}_{Prove}(\overrightarrow{\mathsf{crs}}, x, \overrightarrow{\tau}) \end{array} \;\middle|\; \begin{array}{c} \mathcal{A}(\mathsf{proof}) = 1 \; and \; (x, w) \in R \\ and \; |\overrightarrow{\mathsf{crs}} \cap S| > n/2 \end{array}\right]$$

where $\overrightarrow{\tau}$ *is the set containing all simulation trapdoors* τ *generated by* $\mathcal{S}_{Gen}$.

4 Broadcast Model

In this section, we investigate the minimal assumptions required to enable two-round honest-majority secure MPC protocols over only a $\mathcal{BC}$ channel. In Sect. 4.1, we show that any two-round honest majority MPC for general functionalities that achieves either semi-honest security or security against malicious adversaries, over a $\mathcal{BC}$ channel can be transformed into a two-message oblivious transfer protocol. In the semi-honest case, this yields a semi-honest OT protocol (sh-OT), while in the malicious setting, this yields a malicious receiver OT protocol (mR-OT). Later in Sect. 4.2, we show that such a two-round malicious receiver OT is impossible in the plain model, thereby showing that maliciously secure, two-round MPC is impossible in the plain model given only broadcast channels.

4.1   Lower Bound for $t = 1$

We start by formally stating the observation that for functionalities where only a single party receives an output, the output party need not send any messages in the last round.

Observation 1. *Let $\mathcal{F}$ be any n-input functionality and let Π be a secure MPC protocol that computes $\mathcal{F}$, such that only one party P_{out} receives the output of $\mathcal{F}$. Then Π can be transformed into a protocol Π', where the output party does not send any message in the last round. Moreover, Π' achieves the same security as Π in the same communication/setup model.*

Indeed, the above observation holds w.l.o.g. If P_{out} simply drops its last round message, then by virtue of being the only output party, the output of all other parties remains unaffected. While P_{out} can still compute its output by first locally computing its last round message in Π and then running the output reconstruction algorithm of Π on the protocol transcript and this locally computed message. It is easy to see that the security of this modified protocol follows from the security of Π.

Given this observation, we now show that any two-round protocol in the $\mathcal{BC}$ model can be transformed into a two-message OT in the same setting.

Theorem 1. *If there exists a 2-round, n-party protocol over $\mathcal{BC}$ channels for general functions, in the plain model, that is secure against $t = 1$ semi-honest corruption, then there exists a 2-message semi-honest OT protocol in the plain model.*

If there exists a 2-round, n-party protocol over $\mathcal{BC}$ channels for general functions, in the plain model, that achieves security with abort (SA, UA, IA) against $t = 1$ malicious corruption, then there exists a 2-message malicious receiver OT protocol in the plain model.

Looking ahead, in Sect. 4.2, we show that two-message mR-OT in the plain model is impossible, thereby proving impossibility of SA, UA and IA in the plain model over only $\mathcal{BC}$ channels. We remark that while Theorem 1 is stated for the plain model, it will be easy to see that this implication from two-round $\mathcal{BC}$ only protocols to two-message OT also holds in the *CRS model*. As discussed in the Introduction, since mR-OT is achievable in two-rounds in the CRS model, this implication complements the two-round protocols based on two-message mR-OT for SA, UA and IA from [9,12,19] in the CRS model.

The proof of Theorem 1 is organised as follows: We first give a common transformation from an n-party protocol Π to a two-message OT protocol. Then in Lemma 1, we show that if Π is semi-honest secure, then the resulting OT protocol is also semi-honest secure. Finally, in Lemma 2, we show that if Π achieves security with abort (SA,UA,IA) against a malicious adversary, then the resulting OT protocol achieves malicious receiver security.

Proof (Proof of Theorem 1). Consider the following functionality involving a set of n parties, $\mathcal{P} = \{P_1, \dots, P_n\}$:

$$\mathcal{F}_{n\text{-OT}}((m_0, m_1), \{\perp\}_{i \in [n-2]}, b) = (\{\perp\}_{i \in [n-1]}, m_b)$$

where the input of the first party P_1 is $(m_0, m_1) \in \{0,1\}^*$, parties $P_2, \dots, P_{n-1}$ have no inputs and the input of the last party P_n is a bit $b \in \{0,1\}$. Party P_n is the only output party in this functionality.

Let Π be a protocol for $\mathcal{F}_{n\text{-OT}}$ that operates over a $\mathcal{BC}$ channel. From Observation 1, we know that any MPC protocol with a single output party can be transformed into one where the output party does not send any message in the last round. In Fig. 3, we show how such a protocol (where P_n does not participate in the second round) for $\mathcal{F}_{n\text{-OT}}$ can be used to design a two-message OT protocol Π_{OT} in the same setup/communication model as Π. We assume Π^r to be the rth round next message function in Π that takes the index of a party P_i among other values as input and outputs msg_i^r, ρ_i^r (internal state). We use $\overrightarrow{\mathsf{msg}}^r$ to denote the set of all the messages sent by the parties in round r. For simplicity of notation, we do not specify the randomness used in these functions explicitly. We specify the input of a party as part of the input to Π^1, and internal state as part of the input to Π^r, for $r > 1$.

Two-message OT from Two-round MPC for $\mathcal{F}_{n\text{-OT}}$ over $\mathcal{BC}$

Receiver Message

The receiver computes $(\mathsf{msg}_n^1, \rho_n^1) \leftarrow \Pi^1(n, b)$ and sends msg_n^1 to the sender.

Sender Message

The sender computes $(\mathsf{msg}_1^1, \rho_1^1) \leftarrow \Pi^1(1, (m_0, m_1))$, and for each $j \in [n-1] \setminus \{1\}$ it computes $(\mathsf{msg}_j^1, \rho_j^1) \leftarrow \Pi^1(j, \perp)$ and for each $j \in [n-1]$, it computes $\mathsf{msg}_j^2 \leftarrow \Pi^2(j, \rho_j^1, \overrightarrow{\mathsf{msg}}^1)$. It sends $\{\mathsf{msg}_j^1, \mathsf{msg}_j^2\}_{j \in [n-1]}$ to the receiver.

Receiver Output

The receiver computes and outputs $\mathsf{out} = \Pi^{\text{out}}(n, \rho_n^1, \overrightarrow{\mathsf{msg}}^1, \overrightarrow{\mathsf{msg}}^2)$, where $\overrightarrow{\mathsf{msg}}^1 = \{\mathsf{msg}_1^1, \dots, \mathsf{msg}_n^1\}$, and $\overrightarrow{\mathsf{msg}}^2 = \{\mathsf{msg}_1^2, \dots, \mathsf{msg}_{n-1}^2\}$.

Fig. 3. A transformation from a two-round MPC Π for $\mathcal{F}_{n\text{-OT}}$ that achieves SH/SA/UA/IA over a $\mathcal{BC}$ channel to a two-message OT protocol Π_{OT}.

Lemma 1. *Let Π be a two-round n-party protocol for $\mathcal{F}_{n\text{-OT}}$, secure against a single semi-honest corruption over $\mathcal{BC}$ in the plain (or CRS resp.) model, then the protocol Π_{OT} in Fig. 3 is a two-message sh-OT in the plain (or CRS resp.) model.*

Proof. Correctness of Π_{OT} follows directly from the correctness of the protocol Π for functionality $\mathcal{F}_{n\text{-}\mathsf{OT}}$. We now argue sender and receiver security. Let $\mathcal{E}$ be an execution of Π, where $P_1's$ input is (m_0, m_1) and $P_n's$ input is b.

1. **Security against semi-honest receiver:** From the semi-honest security of Π, we know that there exists a simulator $\mathcal{S}_n$ corresponding to the real world execution $\mathcal{E}$ where the adversary corrupts party P_n, such that the following holds:

$$\left\{\mathcal{S}_n(b, m_b), \{\bot\}_{i\in[n-1]}\right\} \approx_c \left\{\mathsf{view}_n(\mathcal{E}), \mathsf{out}_1(\mathcal{E}), \dots, \mathsf{out}_{n-1}(\mathcal{E})\right\}$$
$$\implies \left\{\mathcal{S}_n(b, m_b)\right\} \approx_c \left\{\mathsf{view}_n(\mathcal{E})\right\}$$

   where $\mathsf{view}_i(\mathcal{E}), \mathsf{out}_i(\mathcal{E})$ denote the view and output of party P_i in the real world execution $\mathcal{E}$.
   Let $\mathcal{E}'$ be another execution of Π, where $P_1's$ input is (m_0', m_1') and $P_n's$ input is b and let $m_b = m_b'$. Then it also holds that $\left\{\mathcal{S}_n(b, m_b)\right\} \approx_c \left\{\mathsf{view}_n(\mathcal{E}')\right\}$. From transitivity of the indistinguishability property,

$$\left\{\mathsf{view}_n(\mathcal{E})\right\} \approx_c \left\{\mathsf{view}_n(\mathcal{E}')\right\} \implies \left\{\mathsf{view}_R(\mathcal{E})\right\} \approx_c \left\{\mathsf{view}_R(\mathcal{E}')\right\}$$

   where $\mathsf{view}_n = \mathsf{view}_R$. Thus, sender security holds.
2. **Security against semi-honest sender:** From the semi-honest security of Π, we know that there exists a simulator $\mathcal{S}_1$ corresponding to $\mathcal{E}$ where the adversary corrupts party P_1, such that the following holds:

$$\left\{\mathcal{S}_1((m_0, m_1), \bot), \{\bot\}_{i\in[n-2]}, m_b\right\} \approx_c \left\{\mathsf{view}_1(\mathcal{E}), \mathsf{out}_2(\mathcal{E}), \dots, \mathsf{out}_n(\mathcal{E})\right\}$$
$$\left\{\overline{\mathsf{msg}}_n^1\right\} \approx_c \left\{\mathsf{msg}_n^1\right\}$$

   where $\overline{\mathsf{msg}}_n^1$ is the first round message of party P_n simulated by $\mathcal{S}_1((m_0, m_1), \bot)$.
   Let $\mathcal{E}'$ be another execution of Π, where $P_1's$ input is (m_0, m_1) and $P_n's$ input is $b' \neq b$. Then it also holds that $\left\{\overline{\mathsf{msg}}_n^1\right\} \approx_c \left\{\mathsf{msg}_n'^1\right\}$. Receiver security now follows from transitivity of the indistinguishability property

$$\left\{\mathsf{msg}_n^1\right\} \approx_c \left\{\mathsf{msg}_n'^1\right\} \implies \left\{\mathsf{view}_S(\mathcal{E})\right\} \approx_c \left\{\mathsf{view}_S(\mathcal{E}')\right\}$$

Lemma 2. *Let Π be a two-round n-party protocol for $\mathcal{F}_{n\text{-}\mathsf{OT}}$, that achieves security with abort ($\mathsf{SA}, \mathsf{UA}, \mathsf{IA}$) against a single malicious corruption over $\mathcal{BC}$ in the plain (or CRS resp.) model, then the protocol Π_{OT} in Fig. 3 is a two-message mR-OT in the plain (or CRS resp.) model.*

Proof. Correctness of the OT protocol follows directly from the correctness of the underlying protocol Π. Receiver security against a semi-honest sender follows exactly as in Lemma 1. We proceed to argue simulation-based sender security against a malicious receiver. Let the adversary corrupt party P_n in the underlying protocol Π. From security of Π, we know that there exists a stateful PPT simulator $\mathcal{S}_n$, that can simulate an indistinguishable view for this adversary in the ideal world.

Given $\mathcal{S}_n$, the simulator $\mathcal{S}_R$ for the OT protocol first computes $\{\mathsf{msg}_i^1\}_{i \in [n-1]} \leftarrow \mathcal{S}_n$. Upon receiving the OT receiver message $\mathsf{msg}_R = \mathsf{msg}_n^1$, it invokes $\mathcal{S}_n$ on this message. At some point, while running $\mathcal{S}_n$, when $\mathcal{S}_n$ queries the ideal functionality on input b of party P_n (receiver), the simulator $\mathcal{S}_R$ of the OT protocol forwards this query to its ideal functionality $\mathcal{F}_{\mathsf{OT}}$. Upon receiving the output m_b from its ideal functionality, it forwards it to the simulator $\mathcal{S}_n$. At the end, $\mathcal{S}_n$ also outputs simulated second round messages $\{\mathsf{msg}_i^2\}_{i \in [n-1]}$. It sends $\mathsf{msg}_S = \{\mathsf{msg}_i^1, \mathsf{msg}_i^2\}_{i \in [n-1]}$ to the adversary.

Indistinguishability of the real and ideal world executions of the OT protocol follow from security of protocol Π. We note that we do not need to explicitly consider the output of honest parties in the real and ideal experiments in this case, because the output of an honest sender in this case is $\perp$.

This completes the proof of Theorem 1.

4.2   Impossibility of Two-Message mR-OT in the Plain Model

In this section we show that a two-message malicious receiver OT is impossible in the plain model. We prove this impossibility by showing that if there exists a simulator that can simulate an indistinguishable view for a malicious receiver, then a malicious/semi-honest sender can run the same simulator to extract the input of an honest receiver.

Lemma 3. *There does not exist a 2-message* OT *with one-sided efficient straight-line simulation security against a corrupt receiver.*

Proof. Suppose there exists a 2-round protocol which securely realizes such an OT, i.e. for each PPT $\mathcal{A}$, there exists a PPT $\mathcal{S}_R = (\mathcal{S}_R^1, \mathcal{S}_R^2)$ s.t for each $m_0, m_1 \in \{0,1\}^*$:

$$\left| \Pr\left[\mathsf{IDEAL}_{\mathcal{S}_R, \mathcal{F}_{\mathsf{OT}}}(1^\lambda, m_0, m_1) = 1 \right] - \Pr\left[\mathsf{REAL}_{\mathcal{A},\mathsf{OT}}(1^\lambda, m_0, m_1) = 1 \right] \right|$$

$$\leq \frac{1}{2} + \mathsf{negl}(\lambda).$$

where experiments $\mathsf{IDEAL}_{\mathcal{S}_R, \mathcal{F}_{\mathsf{OT}}}$ and $\mathsf{REAL}_{\mathcal{A},\mathsf{OT}}$ are as defined in Definition 1. Let b be the input on which $\mathcal{S}_R$ queries the functionality $\mathcal{F}_{OT}(m_0, m_1)$. Then, we construct an adversary $\mathcal{A}_S$ who corrupts the sender as follows: $\mathcal{A}_S$ receives msg_R from an honest receiver, runs $\mathcal{S}_R^1(1^\lambda, \mathsf{msg}_R)$ and computes b. This enables $\mathcal{A}_S$ to extract an honest receiver's input with a high probability. Note that $\mathcal{A}_S$ is a semi-honest adversary since it does not need to send any message before extracting the receiver's input. This contradicts the assumption that the protocol is secure against a semi-honest sender.

Combining Theorem 1 with the above Lemma, we get the following corollary.

Corollary 1. *There exists a functionality $\mathcal{F} \in P/Poly$, for which there does not exist a two-round n-party protocol over $\mathcal{BC}$ that achieves security with* SA/UA/IA *against $t = 1$ malicious corruption with straight-line simulation in the plain model.*

We note that all known honest majority protocols have straight-line simulation.

Another interesting consequence of Theorem 1, is an equivalence between a two-round honest-majority MPC and a two-round dishonest majority MPC over broadcast channels. We note that the above reduction from 2-round honest majority MPC for general functionalities to mR-OT compliments the protocols in [9,19], where they show that OT is complete for two-round MPC over $\mathcal{BC}$ in the CRS model.

5 $\mathcal{BC} + \mathcal{P}2\mathcal{P}$ Model

In this section, we investigate the feasibility of a two round IA protocol with general honest majority in the $\mathcal{BC} + \mathcal{P}2\mathcal{P}$ model and investigate the minimal assumptions that are required for designing a two round FS-GoD protocol in the $\mathcal{BC} + \mathcal{P}2\mathcal{P}$ model.

5.1   Impossibility Result for Identifiable Result

In this section, we show that there does not exist a two-round IA protocol for general functionalities and general honest majority over $\mathcal{BC} + \mathcal{P}2\mathcal{P}$ in the plain model. To prove this result, it suffices to show that there exists a three-party functionality that cannot be securely realized with IA security, over $\mathcal{BC} + \mathcal{P}2\mathcal{P}$ in the plain model, in two-rounds, against a single corrupt party.

Theorem 2. *There exists a functionality $\mathcal{F} \in P/Poly$, for which there does not exist a three-party protocol that achieves security with* IA *against a single malicious corruption over $\mathcal{BC} + \mathcal{P}2\mathcal{P}$ with straight-line simulation in the plain model.*

Proof. Let $\mathcal{F}$ be a 3-party functionality in which party P_1 has no input, P_2's input is $b \in \{0, 1\}$ and P_3's input is (x_0, x_1). P_1 receives an output x_b, while P_2 and P_3 do not receive any output. That is, $\mathcal{F}(\bot, b, (x_0, x_1)) = (x_b, \bot, \bot)$. Let Π be a three-party protocol over $\mathcal{BC} + \mathcal{P}2\mathcal{P}$ channels, realises $\mathcal{F}$ with IA security and straight line simulation. Let $\mathcal{E}^1$ be an execution of the protocol Π computing $\mathcal{F}$. Also, let Π be such that the parties do not send any private messages in the second round (this holds w.l.o.g.). Let $\mathcal{A}$ be an adversary who corrupts party P_2 and works as follows; it behaves like an honest party except that it does not send its private channel message to party P_1 in the first round.

We consider the following three cases:

1. **Output of the honest parties is $\perp$:** We know that in security with IA, if the output of the honest parties is $\perp$, then they must identify at least one corrupted party. Since by assumption Π achieves security with IA, it must be the case that both P_1 and P_3 correctly identify P_2 as the corrupt party. Let $\mathsf{view}_3(\mathcal{E}^1)$ be the view of party P_3 in execution $\mathcal{E}^1$.

   Consider another execution $\mathcal{E}^2$ for the same functionality with the same set of inputs, where the adversary corrupts party P_1 and works as follows. It behaves honestly in the first round. In the second round, it lies about not having received a message from party P_2 in the first round and computes its second round messages accordingly. Let $\mathsf{view}_3(\mathcal{E}^2)$ be the view of party P_3 in execution $\mathcal{E}^2$. Clearly, the view of party P_3 in this case is indistinguishable from its view in execution $\mathcal{E}_\Pi^1$, i.e., $\mathsf{view}_3(\mathcal{E}^1) \approx_c \mathsf{view}_3(\mathcal{E}^2)$. Since the output of P_3 in $\mathcal{E}^1$ was $(\perp, P_2)$, it must be the case that the output of party P_3 in execution $\mathcal{E}^2$ is also $(\perp, P_2)$. However, since P_2 is an honest party, this violates the requirements of security with IA.

   Hence either Π does not achieve IA or the output of the honest parties in $\mathcal{E}^1$ cannot be $\perp$.

2. **The simulator extracts b as P_2's input with probability (almost) 1:** In this case, simulator $\mathcal{S}_2$'s view of P_2's messages only involves the broadcast message (say bmsg_2^1) and the private message (say $\mathsf{pmsg}_{2\to3}^1$) that was sent to P_3. The simulator $\mathcal{S}_2$, it straight-line, it is able to extract P_2's input b *only* using $(\mathsf{bmsg}_2^1, \mathsf{pmsg}_{2\to3}^1)$. Note that both of these messages are visible to P_3, i.e., $(\mathsf{bmsg}_2^1, \mathsf{pmsg}_{2\to3}^1) \in \mathsf{view}_3(\mathcal{E}^1)$.

   Consider another execution $\mathcal{E}^2$, where the adversary passively corrupts P_3 and all parties (including P_3) compute and send their messages honestly. Let $(\overline{\mathsf{bmsg}}_2^1, \overline{\mathsf{pmsg}}_{2\to3}^1)$ be the messages sent by an honest P_2 to P_3 in execution $\mathcal{E}^2$. Since the simulator $\mathcal{S}_2$ is straight-line, a corrupt P_3 can now simply run $\mathcal{S}_2$ on $(\overline{\mathsf{bmsg}}_2^1, \overline{\mathsf{pmsg}}_{2\to3}^1)$ to extract an honest P_2's input. This would clearly break privacy of an honest P_2's input. Hence, either Π does not achieve IA or there does not exist a straight-line simulator that extracts P_2's correct input b.

3. **The simulator extracts $1 - b$ as P_2's input with some non-negligible probability.** Consider another execution $\mathcal{E}^2$ for the same functionality $\mathcal{F}$, with the same set of inputs, where the adversary passively corrupts party P_1 and behaves honestly throughout the protocol execution. Let $\{\mathsf{bmsg}_i^1, \mathsf{bmsg}_i^2, \{\mathsf{pmsg}_{i\to j}^1\}_{j\in[3]}\}_{i\in[3]}$ be the set of messages exchanged between the parties. From correctness of protocol Π, it follows that P_1 learns the output $x_{b'}'$, where $x_{b'}'$ is P_3's input in $\mathcal{E}_2$ and b' is P_2's input.

   A semi-honest P_1 can now launch the following offline resetting attack: It computes a new second round message while assuming that it did not receive a message from P_2 in the first round, i.e.,

$$\overline{\mathsf{bmsg}}_1^2 \leftarrow \Pi^2(1, \overline{\mathsf{T}}_1^1),$$

   where $\overline{\mathsf{T}}_1^1$ is the truncated first round transcript $(\mathsf{bmsg}_2^1, \mathsf{bmsg}_3^1, \mathsf{pmsg}_{3\to1}^1)$ of party P_1. Note that the transcript of P_1 is now similar to the one in $\mathcal{E}^1$ and hence outcome of the protocol (output of P_1) in this case must be $x'_{1-b'}$ with non-negligible probability. As a result of this attack, P_1 is able to learn both $x'_{b'}$ and $x'_{1-b'}$, which clearly violates the privacy of P_3's input. Hence, either Π does not achieve IA or there does not exist a straight-line simulator that extracts $1 - b$ with non-negligible probability.

Since all 3 cases above are impossible, protocol Π cannot be a secure implementation of functionality $\mathcal{F}$, tolerating a single corruption with IA.

5.2   Fail-Stop Guaranteed Output Delivery

FS-GoD is known to be impossible [24] in the plain/CRS models in the absence of private channels in two rounds. In this section, we investigate the minimal assumptions that are required to a realize such protocols in the presence of private channels. More specifically, we show that for $n/3 \leq t < n/2$, sh-OT is necessary for achieving FS-GoD for general functionalities in the plain model,[9] while OWF suffice for $t < n/3$.

Necessity of sh-OT for ($t < n/2$). We first show that any n-party FS-GoD protocol for general functionalities with $n/3 \leq t < n/2$ implies sh-OT.

Theorem 3. *If there exists a 2-round n-party FS-GoD protocol for any $\mathcal{F} \in P/Poly$ in the plain model for $n/3 \leq t < n/2$, then there exists a two-message sh-OT protocol in the plain model.*

Proof. Let Φ be a n-party FS-GoD protocol over $\mathcal{BC} + \mathcal{P}2\mathcal{P}$ for the following functionality:

$$\mathcal{F}_{n\text{-}\mathsf{OT}}((m_0, m_1), \{\perp\}_{i \in [n-2]}, b) = (\{\perp\}_{i \in [n-1]}, m_b)$$

where, input of P_1 is $(m_0, m_1) \in \{0, 1\}^*$, parties $P_2, \ldots, P_{n-1}$ have no inputs, input of P_n is a bit $b \in \{0, 1\}$; and output of P_n is m_b.

From Observation 1, we assume that P_n does not send any message in the last round. Additionally, the remaining parties only need to send private channel messages to P_n in the second round. Now, since Φ achieves FS-GoD, even if t parties, say $P_{t+1}, \ldots, P_{2t}$ fail-stop after sending their first round messages, an honest P_n will still be able to learn the output. Let Π be a slightly modified version of Φ, which forces $P_{t+1}, \ldots, P_{2t}$ to stop after sending their first round messages, as follows:

- No messages are sent to $P_{t+1}, \ldots, P_{2t}$ in the first round.
- $P_{t+1}, \ldots, P_{2t}$ do not send any messages in the second round.

Note that Π is not only a correct protocol (based on FS-GoD security of Φ), but also a semi-honest secure protocol against corruption of any t parties. This

---

[9] We note that this lower bound complements the protocol designed by Ananth et al. in [1].

is true since an adversary in protocol Φ corrupting any t parties can further pretend to not have received the messages omitted in Π, thus simulating the view in protocol Π.

Two-message sh-OT from n-Party FS-GoD Protocol over $\mathcal{BC} + \mathcal{P2P}$

Receiver Message

- Compute $\left(\mathsf{bmsg}_n^1, \left\{\mathsf{pmsg}_{n \to j}^1\right\}_{j \in \{1,\ldots,t,2t+1,\ldots,n\}}\right) \leftarrow \Pi^1(n, b)$.
- For $i \in [2t+1, n]$, compute $\left(\mathsf{bmsg}_i^1, \left\{\mathsf{pmsg}_{i \to j}^1\right\}_{j \in \{1,\ldots,t,2t+1,\ldots,n\}}\right) \leftarrow \Pi^1(i, \perp)$.

Send $\left\{\mathsf{bmsg}_i^1, \mathsf{pmsg}_{i \to j}^1\right\}_{i \in [2t+1,n], j \in [1,t]}$ to the sender.

Sender Message

- Compute $\left(\mathsf{bmsg}_1^1, \left\{\mathsf{pmsg}_{1 \to j}^1\right\}_{j \in [n]}\right) \leftarrow \Pi^1(1, (m_0, m_1))$.
- For each $i \in [2t]$, compute $\left(\mathsf{bmsg}_i^1, \left\{\mathsf{pmsg}_{i \to j}^1\right\}_{j \in \{1,\ldots,t,2t+1,\ldots,n\}}\right) \leftarrow \Pi^1(i, \perp)$.
- For each $i \in [t]$, compute $\left(\mathsf{bmsg}_i^2, \mathsf{pmsg}_{i \to n}^2\right) \leftarrow \Pi^2(i, \mathsf{T}_i^1)$, where $\mathsf{T}_i^1 = \left\{\mathsf{bmsg}_j^1, \mathsf{pmsg}_{j \to i}^1\right\}_{j \in [n]}$.

Send $\left\{\mathsf{bmsg}_i^1, \mathsf{pmsg}_{i \to j}^1\right\}_{i \in [2t], j \in [2t+1,n]}, \left\{\mathsf{bmsg}_i^2, \mathsf{pmsg}_{i \to n}^2\right\}_{i \in [t]}$ to the receiver.

Receiver Output

- For each $i \in [2t+1, n]$, compute $\left(\mathsf{bmsg}_i^2, \mathsf{pmsg}_{i \to n}^2\right) \leftarrow \Pi^2(i, \mathsf{T}_i^1)$, where $\mathsf{T}_i^1 = \left\{\mathsf{bmsg}_j^1, \mathsf{pmsg}_{j \to i}^1\right\}_{j \in [n]}$.
- Compute and output $\mathsf{out} = \Pi^{\mathsf{out}}(n, \mathsf{T}_n^2)$, where $\mathsf{T}_n^2 = \left\{\mathsf{bmsg}_j^1, \mathsf{bmsg}_j^2, \mathsf{pmsg}_{j \to n}^1, \mathsf{pmsg}_{j \to n}^2\right\}_{j \in \{1,\ldots,t,2t+1,\ldots,n\}}$ ..

Fig. 4. A transformation from an n-party FS-GoD protocol Φ with $n/3 \leq t < n/2$ over $\mathcal{BC} + \mathcal{P2P}$ for $\mathcal{F}_{n\text{-OT}}$ to a two-message sh-OT. Π refers to a truncated SH variant of Φ, where parties $P_2, \ldots, P_{t+1}$ and P_n do not send any messages in the second round.

In Fig. 4, we show how Π for $\mathcal{F}_{n\text{-OT}}$ can be used to design a two-message sh-OT in the same setup/communication model as Π, where the first $2t$ parties act as the sender and the remaining parties act as the receiver. We use T_i^r to denote the transcript of party P_n, at the end of the round r. We borrow the remaining notations from previous sections. Correctness of the OT protocol in Fig. 4 follows directly from the correctness of the underlying protocol Π for functionality $\mathcal{F}_{n\text{-OT}}$. The proof for security against semi-honest receiver follows from semi-honest security of Π, since, any adversary corrupting the receiver in OT protocol can be viewed as an adversary corrupting the last $n - 2t$ parties in the underlying protocol Π (where $n - 2t < t$). We now argue security against semi-honest sender.

Security Against Semi-honest Sender. Recall that, we need to show that the distribution of the first message by the receiver on input $b = 0$ is indistinguishable from that on input $b = 1$. The message sent by the receiver is $\{\mathsf{bmsg}_j^1, \{\mathsf{pmsg}_{j\to i}^1\}_{i\in[2t]}\}_{j\in[2t+1,n]}$. But, since the parties do not send any messages to $P_t, \ldots, P_{2t}$ in the underlying protocol Π, the first message is in fact $\{\mathsf{bmsg}_j^1, \{\mathsf{pmsg}_{j\to i}^1\}_{i\in[t]}\}_{j\in[2t+1,n]}$. This however, is part of the view of a semi-honest adversary corrupting the first t parties in the underlying protocol Π. Hence by the semi-honest security guarantee of Π, this view remains indistinguishable between $b = 0$ and $b = 1$.

Positive Result for $(t < n/3)$. Now we construct a two-round FS-GoD protocol for $t < n/3$. Our construction is based on one-way functions for general functionalities in $P/Poly$ and achieves information-theoretic security for functions in $\mathbf{NC}^1$. We obtain this result by using the compiler from [4], who show that the task of securely computing any arbitrary polynomial function can be non-interactively reduced to securely computing arbitrary quadratic functions in the multi-party setting. An important property of their reduction is that the resulting protocol for arbitrary polynomial functions achieves the same security as the protocol for quadratic functions. We leverage this observation and focus on constructing an FS-GoD protocol for quadratic functionalities and prove the following theorem.

Theorem 4. *There exists a perfectly secure two-round FS-GoD protocol for quadratic functionalities with $t < n/3$ unbounded fail-stop corruptions over $\mathcal{P}2\mathcal{P}$ channels in the plain model.*

Instantiating the Master Theorem from [4] using the protocol from the above theorem, we get the following results.

Corollary 2. *Assuming the existence of OWF, there exists a two round FS-GoD protocol for $t < n/3$ over $\mathcal{P}2\mathcal{P}$ channels in the plain model for any $f \in P/Poly$.*

There exists a statistically secure two round FS-GoD protocol for $t < n/3$ over $\mathcal{P}2\mathcal{P}$ channels in the plain model for any $f \in \mathbf{NC}^1$.

Proof (Proof of Theorem 4). We observe that a slightly modified version of the semi-honest protocol in [27], achieves FS-GoD with $t < n/3$ for quadratic functionalities. The protocol in [27] is based on the standard "share-evaluate-reconstruct" approach, where the parties compute t-out-of-n threshold secret shares [32] of their inputs in the first round. In the second round all the parties evaluate the functionality (that they wish to compute) on their respective shares and send the evaluated share to all other parties, who can then run the reconstruction algorithm of the secret sharing scheme to reconstruct the output. We observe that pre-mature aborts by a fail-stop adversary can be handled in this protocol for $t < n/3$ as follows:

– **Abort in Round 1:** If a corrupt party P_i aborts in the first round and does not send any messages, the remaining parties can evaluate the functionality by simply setting the shares that they were expecting from P_i to 0 and proceed as normal, without any disruption.

– **Abort in Round 2:** Since there are $>2t$ honest parties and evaluated shares in the second round correspond to a $2t$-out-of-n secret sharing, the shares of the honest parties are sufficient to reconstruct the output. Therefore, aborts in the second round do not disrupt the computation.

For the sake of completeness, we give a description of this protocol in Fig. 5. The correctness and security of this modified protocol follows trivially and hence we omit it.

A two-round FS-GoD protocol for any quadratic functionality with $t < n/3$ over $\mathcal{P}2\mathcal{P}$ channels

Let $\mathcal{P} = \{P_1, \ldots, P_n\}$ be the set of parties and $\mathcal{F}$ be the function that they wish to jointly compute. Let X_i be the input held by party P_i. We say that a party is 'active', if it does not abort in the first round. Let $\mathsf{active} \subseteq [n]$ be the subset of parties that are active in the last round of the protocol. Let $(\mathsf{Share}, \mathsf{Recon})$ be a threshold secret sharing scheme [32].

$\boxed{\textbf{Party } P_i \textbf{ in Round 1}}$

1. Compute $\{[X_i]_1, \ldots, [X_i]_n\} \leftarrow \mathsf{Share}((t,n), X_i)$ and send $[X_i]_j$ to party P_j.
2. Compute $\{[Y_i]_1, \ldots, [Y_i]_n\} \leftarrow \mathsf{Share}((t,n), 0)$ and send $[Y_i]_j$ to party P_j.

$\boxed{\textbf{Party } P_i \textbf{ in Round 2}}$

Compute $[Z]_i = \mathcal{F}([X_1]_i, \ldots, [X_n]_i) + \sum_{j \in [n]} [Y_j]_i$, where $[X_j]_i = [Y_j]_i = 0$, if $P_j \notin$ active.

$\boxed{\textbf{Output Evaluation}}$

Compute and output $Z = \mathsf{Recon}((2t,n), \{[Z]_i\}_{i \in [n]})$.

Fig. 5. A two round FS-GoD protocol for quadratic functionalities with $t < n/3$ over $\mathcal{P}2\mathcal{P}$ channels.

6 $\mathcal{BC} + \mathcal{PKI}$ Model: Guaranteed Output Delivery

In this section, we give a generic compiler from any two-round (semi-malicious) FS-GoD protocol over $\mathcal{BC} + \mathcal{PKI}$ channels to a two-round M-GoD protocol over $\mathcal{BC} + \mathcal{PKI}$. Our transformation relies on multi-CRS non-interactive zero-knowledge (m-NIZK) proof systems and PKE. We refer the reader to Sect. 3.2 for a formal definition of m-NIZKs. This protocol is a simple adaptation of the three-round M-GoD protocol of Ananth et al. [1], with the only modification that the entire first round of their protocol is moved to the bare $\mathcal{PKI}$ setup in our protocol.

Theorem 5. *Assuming the existence of PKE and m-NIZK, there exists a generic transformation from any two round, n-party (semi-malicious) FS-GoD protocol in the $\mathcal{BC} + \mathcal{PKI}$ model for $t < n/2$, to a two-round n-party M-GoD protocol in the $\mathcal{BC} + \mathcal{PKI}$ model for $t < n/2$.*

Ananth et al. [1] present a two-round (semi-malicious) FS-GoD protocol in the $\mathcal{BC} + \mathcal{PKI}$ model based on public-key encryption (PKE) with perfect correctness. Instantiating the above theorem with this protocol, we get the following corollary.

Corollary 3. *Assuming the existence of PKE and m-NIZK, there exists an n-party protocol in the $\mathcal{BC} + \mathcal{PKI}$ model that achieves security with M-GoD against $t < n/2$ corruptions for any $\mathcal{F} \in P/Poly$.*

Protocol Description. Let $\mathcal{P} = \{P_1, \ldots, P_n\}$ be the set of parties with inputs $X_1, \ldots, X_n$. We start by listing the building blocks and establishing some notations:

1. **Protocol Π:** A two-round n-party MPC protocol $\Pi = (\Pi^{\mathcal{PKI}}, \Pi^1, \Pi^2, \Pi^{\text{out}})$ that operates in the $\mathcal{BC} + \mathcal{PKI}$ model and achieves (semi-malicious) FS-GoD security against $t < n/2$. Here, $\Pi^{\mathcal{PKI}}$ is the algorithm used by each party to compute its message in the bare $\mathcal{PKI}$ setup phase, Π^r is the rth round next-message function and Π^{out} is the output computation function of Π. We use msg_i^r to denote the broadcast message of party P_i in round r.
2. **PKE:** Public key encryption scheme (PKE.Gen, PKE.Enc, PKE.Dec) with perfect completeness.
3. **Secret Sharing:** A threshold secret sharing scheme (Share, Recon) [32].
4. **m-NIZK:** Multi-string NIZK (m-NIZK.Gen, m-NIZK.Prove, m-NIZK.Verify) (see Definitions 3.2). We assume the randomness used in these algorithms to be implicit and do not specify them.

At the start of the protocol, each party P_i samples a sufficiently long random tape ρ_i to use in the various sub-parts of the protocol; let ρ_i^{key} be the randomness used for generating keys $(\text{pk}_i, \text{sk}_i)$, $\rho_i^{\mathcal{PKI}}$ be the randomness used to generate the PKI in the underlying protocol Π, ρ_i^{Π} be the randomness for generating messages in protocol Π and $\rho_{i,j}^{\text{enc}}$ to encrypt the private message intended for P_j. We use the vector notation along with a $\bullet$ symbol to refer to a set of n messages, for instance, $\overrightarrow{\text{ct}}_{\bullet \to i} = \text{ct}_{1 \to i}, \ldots, \text{ct}_{n \to i}$. The remaining notations are borrowed from previous sections. A full description of our protocol appears in Fig. 6. We defer the security proof of this protocol to the full version of this paper.

Two-Round M-GoD Protocol for $t < n/2$ in the $\mathcal{BC} + \mathcal{PKI}$ Model

$\boxed{\textbf{Party } P_i \textbf{ for the Bare PKI Setup}}$

- **$\mathcal{PKI}$ for Protocol Π:** Compute $\mathsf{pk}_i^{\Pi} \leftarrow \Pi^{\mathcal{PKI}}(i; \rho_i^{\mathcal{PKI}})$.
- **PKE** Compute $(\mathsf{pk}_i, \mathsf{sk}_i) \leftarrow \mathsf{PKE.Gen}(; \rho_i^{\mathsf{key}})$
- **m-NIZK:** For each $j \in [n]$, compute $\mathsf{crs}_{i \to j} \leftarrow \mathsf{m\text{-}NIZK.Gen}$.
- Publish $\mathsf{PK}_i = (\mathsf{pk}_i^{\Pi}, \mathsf{pk}_i, \overrightarrow{\mathsf{crs}}_{i \to \bullet})$.

$\boxed{\textbf{Party } P_i \textbf{ in Round 1}}$

- **$\mathcal{PKI}$:** For each $j \in [n]$, parse $\mathsf{PK}_j = (\mathsf{pk}_j^{\Pi}, \mathsf{pk}_j, \overrightarrow{\mathsf{crs}}_{j \to \bullet})$.
- **Protocol Π:** Compute $\mathsf{msg}_i^1 \leftarrow \Pi^1\left(i, \mathsf{X}_i, \overrightarrow{\mathsf{pk}}_\bullet^{\Pi}; \rho_i^{\Pi}\right)$.
- **Secret Sharing:** Set $\mathsf{Y}_i = (\mathsf{X}_i, \rho_i^{\Pi})$ and compute $\{[\mathsf{Y}_i]_1, \dots, [\mathsf{Y}_i]_n\} \leftarrow \mathsf{Share}((t, n), \mathsf{Y}_i)$.
- **Ciphertexts:** For each $j \in [n]$, compute $\mathsf{ct}_{i \to j} \leftarrow \mathsf{PKE.Enc}(\mathsf{pk}_j, [\mathsf{Y}_i]_j ; \rho_{i,j}^{\mathsf{enc}})$.
- **m-NIZK:** Compute $\mathsf{proof}_i^1 \leftarrow \mathsf{m\text{-}NIZK.Prove}\left(\overrightarrow{\mathsf{crs}}_{\bullet \to i}, y_i, w_i\right)$, where $y_i^1 = \left(\overrightarrow{\mathsf{pk}}_\bullet^{\Pi}, \overrightarrow{\mathsf{pk}}_\bullet, \mathsf{msg}_i^1, \overrightarrow{\mathsf{ct}}_{i \to \bullet}\right)$ and $w_i^1 = \left(\mathsf{X}_i, \rho_i^{\Pi}, \rho_i^{\mathcal{PKI}}, \rho_i^{\mathsf{key}}, \overrightarrow{\rho}_{i,\bullet}^{\mathsf{enc}}\right)$, using language L_i^1 (see Figure 7)
- **Broadcast** $(\mathsf{msg}_i^1, \mathsf{proof}_i^1, \overrightarrow{\mathsf{ct}}_{i \to \bullet})$.

$\boxed{\textbf{Party } P_i \textbf{ in Round 2}}$

- **Proof Check:** For each $j \in [n]$, check if $\mathsf{m\text{-}NIZK.Verify}\left(\overrightarrow{\mathsf{crs}}_{\bullet \to j}, y_j^1, \mathsf{proof}_j^1\right) = 1$, where $y_j^1 = \left(\overrightarrow{\mathsf{pk}}_\bullet^{\Pi}, \overrightarrow{\mathsf{pk}}_\bullet, \mathsf{msg}_j^1, \overrightarrow{\mathsf{ct}}_{j \to \bullet}\right)$. If this check fails, set $\mathsf{msg}_j^1 = \bot$.
- **Protocol Π:** Compute $\mathsf{msg}_i^2 \leftarrow \Pi^2\left(i, \mathsf{X}_i, \overrightarrow{\mathsf{pk}}_\bullet^{\Pi}, \overrightarrow{\mathsf{msg}}_\bullet^1; \rho_i^{\Pi}\right)$.
- **m-NIZK:** Compute $\mathsf{proof}_i^2 \leftarrow \mathsf{m\text{-}NIZK.Prove}\left(\overrightarrow{\mathsf{crs}}_{\bullet \to i}, y_i^2, w_i^2\right)$, where $y_i^2 = \left(\overrightarrow{\mathsf{pk}}_\bullet^{\Pi}, \overrightarrow{\mathsf{pk}}_\bullet, \overrightarrow{\mathsf{ct}}_{i \to \bullet}, \mathsf{msg}_i^2, \overrightarrow{\mathsf{msg}}_\bullet^1\right)$ and $w_i^2 = \left(\mathsf{X}_i, \rho_i^{\Pi}, \overrightarrow{\rho}_{i,\bullet}^{\mathsf{enc}}\right)$, using language L_i^2 (see Figure 7)
- **Broadcast** $(\mathsf{msg}_i^2, \mathsf{proof}_i^2)$.

$\boxed{\textbf{Output Reconstruction.}}$

- For each $j \in [n]$, check if $\mathsf{m\text{-}NIZK.Verify}\left(\overrightarrow{\mathsf{crs}}_{\bullet \to j}, y_j^2, \mathsf{proof}_j^2\right) = 1$, where $y_j^2 = \left(\overrightarrow{\mathsf{pk}}_\bullet^{\Pi}, \overrightarrow{\mathsf{pk}}_\bullet, \overrightarrow{\mathsf{ct}}_{j \to \bullet}, \mathsf{msg}_j^2, \overrightarrow{\mathsf{msg}}_\bullet^1\right)$. If this check fails or if msg_j^1 was set to $\bot$, set $\mathsf{msg}_j^2 = \bot$.
- Compute and output $z = \Pi^{\mathsf{out}}\left(i, \mathsf{X}_i, \rho_i^{\Pi}, \rho_i^{\mathcal{PKI}}, \overrightarrow{\mathsf{pk}}_\bullet^{\Pi}, \overrightarrow{\mathsf{msg}}_\bullet^1, \overrightarrow{\mathsf{msg}}_\bullet^2\right)$.

Fig. 6. A transformation from a two-round (semi-malicious) FS-GoD protocol for $t < n/2$ in the $\mathcal{BC} + \mathcal{PKI}$ model to a two-round M-GoD protocol for $t < n/2$ in the $\mathcal{BC} + \mathcal{PKI}$ model.

L_i^1: **NP Language used in Round 1**	L_i^2: **NP Language used in Round 2**
Statement $y_i^1 = \left(\overrightarrow{\mathsf{pk}_\bullet^\Pi}, \overrightarrow{\mathsf{pk}_\bullet}, \mathsf{msg}_i^1, \overrightarrow{\mathsf{ct}}_{i \to \bullet} \right)$ **Witness** $w_i^1 = \left(\mathsf{X}_i, \rho_i^\Pi, \rho_i^{\mathcal{PKI}}, \rho_i^{\mathsf{key}}, \overrightarrow{\rho}_{i,\bullet}^{\mathsf{enc}} \right)$ **Relation** $R_i^1(y_i^1, w_i^1) = 1$, if *all* of the following conditions hold:	**Statement** $y_i^2 =$ $\left(\overrightarrow{\mathsf{pk}_\bullet^\Pi}, \overrightarrow{\mathsf{pk}_\bullet}, \overrightarrow{\mathsf{ct}}_{i \to \bullet}, \mathsf{msg}_i^2, \overrightarrow{\mathsf{msg}_\bullet^1} \right)$ **Witness** $w_i^2 = \left(\mathsf{X}_i, \rho_i^\Pi, \overrightarrow{\rho}_{i,\bullet}^{\mathsf{enc}} \right)$ **Relation** $R_i^2(y_i^2, w_i^2) = 1$, if *all* of the following conditions hold:
1. The public key pk_i was generated honestly using $\mathsf{PKE.Gen}()$ and randomness ρ_i^{key}. 2. The $\mathcal{PKI}$ pk_i^Π was generated honestly using $\Pi^{\mathcal{PKI}}$ with input i and randomness $\rho_i^{\mathcal{PKI}}$. 3. Shares $\{[\mathsf{Y}_i]_1, \ldots, [\mathsf{Y}_i]_n\}$ are honestly computed (t, n) threshold shares of $\mathsf{Y}_i = (\mathsf{X}_i, \rho_i^\Pi)$. 4. For each $j \in [n]$, the ciphertext $\mathsf{ct}_{i \to j}$ is an honest encryption of $[\mathsf{Y}_i]_j$ under the public key pk_j, using randomness $\rho_{i,j}^{\mathsf{enc}}$. 5. msg_i^1 is an honestly computed message using the next message function Π^1 with inputs $i, \mathsf{X}_i, \overrightarrow{\mathsf{pk}_\bullet^\Pi}$ and randomness ρ_i^Π.	1. msg_i^2 is an honestly computed message using the next message function Π^2 with inputs $i, \mathsf{X}_i, \overrightarrow{\mathsf{pk}_\bullet}, \overrightarrow{\mathsf{msg}_\bullet^1}$ and randomness ρ_i^Π. 2. Shares $\{[\mathsf{Y}_i]_1, \ldots, [\mathsf{Y}_i]_n\}$ are honestly computed (t, n) threshold shares of $\mathsf{Y}_i = (\mathsf{X}_i, \rho_i^\Pi)$. 3. 4. For each $j \in [n]$, the ciphertext $\mathsf{ct}_{i \to j}$ is an honest encryption of $[\mathsf{Y}_i]_j$ under the public key pk_j, using randomness $\rho_{i,j}^{\mathsf{enc}}$.

Fig. 7. NP Languages used in the protocol description in Fig. 6.

Acknowledgements. The first and second authors were supported in part by an NSF CNS grant 1814919, NSF CAREER award 1942789 and Johns Hopkins University Catalyst award. The second author was additionally supported in part by an Office of Naval Research grant N00014- 19-1-2294. The third author is supported by the joint Indo-Israel Project DST/INT/ISR/P-16/2017 and Ramanujan Fellowship of Dept. of Science and Technology, India.

References

1. Ananth, P., Choudhuri, A.R., Goel, A., Jain, A.: Round-optimal secure multiparty computation with honest majority. In: Shacham, H., Boldyreva, A. (eds.) CRYPTO 2018. LNCS, vol. 10992, pp. 395–424. Springer, Cham (2018). https://doi.org/10.1007/978-3-319-96881-0_14
2. Ananth, P., Choudhuri, A.R., Goel, A., Jain, A.: Two round information-theoretic MPC with malicious security. In: Ishai, Y., Rijmen, V. (eds.) EUROCRYPT 2019. LNCS, vol. 11477, pp. 532–561. Springer, Cham (2019). https://doi.org/10.1007/978-3-030-17656-3_19

3. Applebaum, B., Brakerski, Z., Tsabary, R.: Perfect secure computation in two rounds. In: Beimel, A., Dziembowski, S. (eds.) TCC 2018. LNCS, vol. 11239, pp. 152–174. Springer, Cham (2018). https://doi.org/10.1007/978-3-030-03807-6_6

4. Applebaum, B., Brakerski, Z., Tsabary, R.: Degree 2 is complete for the round-complexity of malicious MPC. In: Ishai, Y., Rijmen, V. (eds.) EUROCRYPT 2019. LNCS, vol. 11477, pp. 504–531. Springer, Cham (2019). https://doi.org/10.1007/978-3-030-17656-3_18

5. Asharov, G., Jain, A., López-Alt, A., Tromer, E., Vaikuntanathan, V., Wichs, D.: Multiparty computation with low communication, computation and interaction via threshold FHE. In: Pointcheval, D., Johansson, T. (eds.) EUROCRYPT 2012. LNCS, vol. 7237, pp. 483–501. Springer, Heidelberg (2012). https://doi.org/10.1007/978-3-642-29011-4_29

6. Badrinarayanan, S., Jain, A., Manohar, N., Sahai, A.: Secure MPC: laziness leads to GOD. Cryptology ePrint Archive, Report 2018/580 (2018). https://eprint.iacr.org/2018/580

7. Barak, B., et al.: On the (Im)possibility of obfuscating programs. In: Kilian, J. (ed.) CRYPTO 2001. LNCS, vol. 2139, pp. 1–18. Springer, Heidelberg (2001). https://doi.org/10.1007/3-540-44647-8_1

8. Ben-Or, M., Goldwasser, S., Wigderson, A.: Completeness theorems for non-cryptographic fault-tolerant distributed computation (extended abstract). In: 20th ACM STOC, pp. 1–10. ACM Press, May 1988

9. Benhamouda, F., Lin, H.: k-round multiparty computation from k-round oblivious transfer via garbled interactive circuits. In: Nielsen, J.B., Rijmen, V. (eds.) EURO-CRYPT 2018. LNCS, vol. 10821, pp. 500–532. Springer, Cham (2018). https://doi.org/10.1007/978-3-319-78375-8_17

10. Canetti, R.: Universally composable security: a new paradigm for cryptographic protocols. In: 42nd FOCS, pp. 136–145. IEEE Computer Society Press, October 2001

11. Chaum, D., Crépeau, C., Damgård, I.: Multiparty unconditionally secure protocols (abstract). In: Pomerance, C. (ed.) CRYPTO 1987. LNCS, vol. 293, pp. 462–462. Springer, Heidelberg (1988). https://doi.org/10.1007/3-540-48184-2_43

12. Cohen, R., Garay, J., Zikas, V.: Broadcast-optimal two-round MPC. In: Canteaut, A., Ishai, Y. (eds.) EUROCRYPT 2020. LNCS, vol. 12106, pp. 828–858. Springer, Cham (2020). https://doi.org/10.1007/978-3-030-45724-2_28

13. Cohen, R., Lindell, Y.: Fairness versus guaranteed output delivery in secure multiparty computation. In: Sarkar, P., Iwata, T. (eds.) ASIACRYPT 2014. LNCS, vol. 8874, pp. 466–485. Springer, Heidelberg (2014). https://doi.org/10.1007/978-3-662-45608-8_25

14. Damgård, I., Magri, B., Siniscalchi, L., Yakoubov, S.: Broadcast-optimal two round MPC with an honest majority. Cryptology ePrint Archive, Report 2020/1254 (2020). https://eprint.iacr.org/2020/1254

15. Dwork, C., Naor, M.: Zaps and their applications. In: 41st FOCS, pp. 283–293. IEEE Computer Society Press, November 2000

16. Even, S., Goldreich, O., Lempel, A.: A randomized protocol for signing contracts. In: Chaum, D., Rivest, R.L., Sherman, A.T. (eds.) CRYPTO'82, pp. 205–210. Plenum Press, New York (1982)

17. Fischer, M.J., Lynch, N.A., Merritt, M.: Easy impossibility proofs for distributed consensus problems. In: Malcolm, M.A., Strong, H.R. (eds.) 4th ACM PODC, pp. 59–70. ACM, August 1985

18. Garg, S., Ishai, Y., Srinivasan, A.: Two-round MPC: information-theoretic and black-box. In: Beimel, A., Dziembowski, S. (eds.) TCC 2018. LNCS, vol. 11239, pp. 123–151. Springer, Cham (2018). https://doi.org/10.1007/978-3-030-03807-6_5

19. Garg, S., Srinivasan, A.: Two-round multiparty secure computation from minimal assumptions. In: Nielsen, J.B., Rijmen, V. (eds.) EUROCRYPT 2018. LNCS, vol. 10821, pp. 468–499. Springer, Cham (2018). https://doi.org/10.1007/978-3-319-78375-8_16

20. Gennaro, R., Ishai, Y., Kushilevitz, E., Rabin, T.: On 2-round secure multiparty computation. In: Yung, M. (ed.) CRYPTO 2002. LNCS, vol. 2442, pp. 178–193. Springer, Heidelberg (2002). https://doi.org/10.1007/3-540-45708-9_12

21. Goldreich, O., Micali, S., Wigderson, A.: How to play any mental game or a completeness theorem for protocols with honest majority. In: Aho, A. (ed.) 19th ACM STOC, pp. 218–229. ACM Press, May 1987

22. Goldreich, O., Oren, Y.: Definitions and properties of zero-knowledge proof systems. J. Cryptol. 7(1), 1–32 (1994). https://doi.org/10.1007/BF00195207

23. Goldwasser, S., Micali, S., Rackoff, C.: The knowledge complexity of interactive proof-systems (extended abstract). In: 17th ACM STOC, pp. 291–304. ACM Press, May 1985

24. Dov Gordon, S., Liu, F.-H., Shi, E.: Constant-round MPC with fairness and guarantee of output delivery. In: Gennaro, R., Robshaw, M. (eds.) CRYPTO 2015. LNCS, vol. 9216, pp. 63–82. Springer, Heidelberg (2015). https://doi.org/10.1007/978-3-662-48000-7_4

25. Groth, J., Ostrovsky, R.: Cryptography in the multi-string model. In: Menezes, A. (ed.) CRYPTO 2007. LNCS, vol. 4622, pp. 323–341. Springer, Heidelberg (2007). https://doi.org/10.1007/978-3-540-74143-5_18

26. Ishai, Y., Kumaresan, R., Kushilevitz, E., Paskin-Cherniavsky, A.: Secure computation with minimal interaction, revisited. In: Gennaro, R., Robshaw, M. (eds.) CRYPTO 2015. LNCS, vol. 9216, pp. 359–378. Springer, Heidelberg (2015). https://doi.org/10.1007/978-3-662-48000-7_18

27. Ishai, Y., Kushilevitz, E.: Randomizing polynomials: a new representation with applications to round-efficient secure computation. In: 41st FOCS, pp. 294–304. IEEE Computer Society Press, November 2000

28. Ishai, Y., Kushilevitz, E., Paskin, A.: Secure multiparty computation with minimal interaction. In: Rabin, T. (ed.) CRYPTO 2010. LNCS, vol. 6223, pp. 577–594. Springer, Heidelberg (2010). https://doi.org/10.1007/978-3-642-14623-7_31

29. Ishai, Y., Ostrovsky, R., Zikas, V.: Secure multi-party computation with identifiable abort. In: Garay, J.A., Gennaro, R. (eds.) CRYPTO 2014. LNCS, vol. 8617, pp. 369–386. Springer, Heidelberg (2014). https://doi.org/10.1007/978-3-662-44381-1_21

30. Patra, A., Ravi, D.: On the exact round complexity of secure three-party computation. In: Shacham, H., Boldyreva, A. (eds.) CRYPTO 2018. LNCS, vol. 10992, pp. 425–458. Springer, Cham (2018). https://doi.org/10.1007/978-3-319-96881-0_15

31. Rabin, T., Ben-Or, M.: Verifiable secret sharing and multiparty protocols with honest majority (extended abstract). In: 21st ACM STOC, pp. 73–85. ACM Press, May 1989

32. Shamir, A.: How to share a secret. Commun. ACM 22(11), 612–613 (1979)

Generalized Pseudorandom Secret Sharing and Efficient Straggler-Resilient Secure Computation

Fabrice Benhamouda[1](✉), Elette Boyle[2], Niv Gilboa[3], Shai Halevi[1], Yuval Ishai[4], and Ariel Nof[4]

[1] Algorand Foundation, Boston, USA
fabrice.benhamouda@normalesup.org, shaih@alum.mit.edu
[2] IDC Herzliya, Herzliya, Israel
eboyle@alum.mit.edu
[3] Ben-Gurion University, Beersheba, Israel
gilboan@bgu.ac.il
[4] Technion, Haifa, Israel
{yuvali,ariel.nof}@cs.technion.ac.il

Abstract. Secure multiparty computation (MPC) enables n parties, of which up to t may be corrupted, to perform joint computations on their private inputs while revealing only the outputs. Optimizing the asymptotic and concrete costs of MPC protocols has become an important line of research. Much of this research focuses on the setting of an honest majority, where $n \geq 2t + 1$, which gives rise to concretely efficient protocols that are either information-theoretic or make a black-box use of symmetric cryptography. Efficiency can be further improved in the case of a *strong* honest majority, where $n > 2t + 1$.

Motivated by the goal of minimizing the communication and latency costs of MPC with a strong honest majority, we make two related contributions.

- **Generalized pseudorandom secret sharing (PRSS).** Linear correlations serve as an important resource for MPC protocols and beyond. PRSS enables secure generation of many pseudorandom instances of such correlations without interaction, given replicated seeds of a pseudorandom function. We extend the PRSS technique of Cramer et al. (TCC 2005) for sharing degree-d polynomials to new constructions leveraging a particular class of combinatorial designs. Our constructions yield a dramatic efficiency improvement when the degree d is higher than the security threshold t, not only for standard degree-d correlations but also for several useful generalizations. In particular, correlations for locally converting between slot configurations in "share packing" enable us to avoid the concrete overhead of prior works.
- **Cheap straggler resilience.** In reality, communication is not fully synchronous: protocol executions suffer from variance in communication delays and occasional node or message-delivery failures. We explore the benefits of PRSS-based MPC with a strong honest majority toward robustness against such failures, in turn yielding improved

© International Association for Cryptologic Research 2021
K. Nissim and B. Waters (Eds.): TCC 2021, LNCS 13043, pp. 129–161, 2021.
https://doi.org/10.1007/978-3-030-90453-1_5

latency delays. In doing so we develop a novel technique for defending against a subtle "double-dipping" attack, which applies to the best existing protocols, with almost no extra cost in communication or rounds.

Combining the above tools requires further work, including new methods for batch verification via distributed zero-knowledge proofs (Boneh et al., CRYPTO 2019) that apply to packed secret sharing. Overall, our work demonstrates new advantages of the strong honest majority setting, and introduces new tools—in particular, generalized PRSS—that we believe will be of independent use within other cryptographic applications.

1   Introduction

Protocols for secure multiparty computation (MPC) [5,16,30,52] enable a set of parties with private inputs to compute a joint function of their inputs while revealing nothing but the output. MPC provides a general-purpose tool for distributed computation on sensitive data, as well as for eliminating single points of failure. As a result, a major research effort focused on improving the asymptotic and concrete efficiency of MPC.

Efficient honest-majority MPC. The most practical MPC protocols rely on an *honest majority* assumption, namely security is guaranteed as long as $t < n/2$ out of the n parties are corrupted, and provide "security with abort" in the presence of malicious parties. Such protocols can be either information-theoretic, or alternatively achieve better communication cost by making a black-box use of a pseudorandom function. The latter is mainly useful for non-interactive generation of pseudorandom shared secrets via a pseudorandom secret sharing (PRSS) technique [18,28]. Moreover, the most efficient protocols in this setting follow the blueprint of Damgård and Nielsen (DN) [22], where each layer of a circuit is evaluated by having a designated "leader" party send messages to all other parties and receive a message from each party in return.

In almost all of this line of research, one assumes the weakest honest majority assumption of $n = 2t+1$ parties. However, assuming that up to half of the parties can be corrupted may sometimes be overly *pessimistic*, and small relaxations of corruption threshold can be highly preferred in favor of boosting performance. On the other hand, existing honest-majority protocols are also overly *optimistic* in that they assume all messages arrive on time and are not robust to transient delays or failures. We will revisit this issue later.

The potential for savings in the "strong honest majority" regime of $n > 2t+1$ has been asserted within the context of *asymptotic* efficiency [4,19–21,24,27,36]. In a sense, existing MPC protocols for $n = 2t+1$ parties are analogous to using a repetition code, which increases the total cost by a factor of n, whereas the latter protocols are analogous to asymptotically good codes that provide a constant or near-constant amortized asymptotic overhead. However, the techniques in these theory-oriented works incur large concrete overheads placing them quite far from practical efficiency, and their asymptotic efficiency benefits kick in only for large computations.

In the context of *concretely* efficient MPC, the potential gains of a strong honest majority remain relatively untapped—both in the sense that asymptotic benefits of prior works do not currently translate to concrete wins, and that potential for concrete gains outside the standard theoretical models or (asymptotic) goals have not been well explored. One exception to this is a recent line of works leveraging a larger number of honest parties for the purpose of closing the efficiency gap between security against *malicious* (or active) adversaries and security against *semi-honest* (or passive) adversaries [26,31]. However, recent works [8,11,12,37] have successfully closed this gap even given a minimal honest majority $n = 2t + 1$, in which case this advantage no longer applies.

In this work, we initiate a deeper study of *concretely efficient* MPC with *strong honest majority* $n > 2t+1$. We focus on developing general-purpose primitives and techniques to alleviate the concrete costs of existing theory-oriented solutions, as well as exploring new directions for improved latency in realistic networks. Our primary focus is on the case where the corruption threshold t is small. This enables the use of PRSS techniques that give rise to simpler and more efficient protocols, but incur (an offline) cost that scales exponentially with t. We are motivated by two main limitations of current techniques.

The Overhead of Packed Secret Sharing. A major source of concrete overhead in the aforementioned theory-oriented works is the use of a "share packing" technique [24] in which secret-shared values are arranged into blocks, and a set of shares can simultaneously encode several values at the same per-party cost. This technique natively supports computing a single circuit on many inputs in parallel (also known as a "SIMD computation"), by computing operations simultaneously on all values within a block. However, it requires a costly routing mechanism for general computations. This overhead applies even in the semi-honest setting, but introduces additional challenges in the malicious setting. While the initial $O(\log n)$ overhead of the routing-based technique from [20] was recently improved to a constant [36], this comes at the cost of poor concrete efficiency.

Extending the ideas of these works, one may observe that existence of certain useful linear correlations across parties would enable avoiding these routing overheads altogether. The desired correlations correspond to sets of packed shares of secret random values, where different sets include the same random values in different computation "slot" positions, in line with the routing of wires within the computation circuit. But, unlocking these savings demands a large number of *different* rerouting patterns, whose generation would destroy the optimization savings in existing works. Much of the effort in previous works [4,19–21,27,33,36] was spent on efficient distributed protocols for generating these linear correlations.

Tolerating Stragglers. One advantage of MPC with a strong honest majority, which serves as a primary motivation for the current work, is the potential for better robustness, in turn leading to *reduced latency* in realistic network environments. Existing MPC protocols with $n = 2t+1$ parties require at least one of the parties to wait for messages from *all other parties* before proceeding to the next round. In particular, in protocols that follow the DN blueprint, the leader needs to wait until it hears back from all other parties. But in reality, communication is not fully synchronous. Even in a semi-honest setting, protocol executions suffer from variance in communication delays and occasional message-delivery failures. This is sometimes referred to as the problem of *stragglers*. To deal with this problem, practical distributed systems typically employ redundancy to allow proceeding with the computation as long as "sufficiently many" messages were received. See [42] for empirical studies of the impact of stragglers on realistic network.

Interestingly, achieving robustness to stragglers becomes more challenging when some parties can be malicious. Standard secure protocols with good concrete efficiency do not have this feature even when $n > 3t$. While such protocols are able to terminate in the face of up to t stragglers, this occurs at the cost of labeling these parties as corrupt, and their secrets are no longer protected. Alternatively, attempting to run DN-style protocols in an "optimistic mode," by simply having the leader wait for the first $2t$ messages to arrive, gives rise to a subtle "double-dipping" attack that allows a malicious leader to learn private information. Previous solutions for this attack(see [26,35]) require significantly more interaction and are not suitable for efficiently dealing with transient faults; See Sect. 5.1 for more details.

1.1 Our Contributions

Motivated by the above opportunities and challenges, we present new techniques for MPC within the setting of a *strong honest majority*, $n > 2t + 1$, focusing on the case of small[1] values of t that enable efficient use of PRSS. We make the following two main contributions.

Contribution 1: Generalized pseudorandom secret sharing (PRSS). As noted above, PRSS enables a secure non-interactive generation of (pseudo)random values that are uniformly distributed over some linear vector space. It relies on a low-communication setup, where independent pseudorandom function (PRF) seeds are distributed to different subsets of the parties. The prominent cost metric of a PRSS scheme is the number of such seeds required for the parties to each compute their entry within the sampled vector. Following a general framework of Gilboa and Ishai [28], Cramer et al. [18] described PRSS techniques for sharing degree-d polynomials between n parties using $\binom{n}{d}$ seeds, $\binom{n-1}{d}$ per party, targeting the typical use-case where the security threshold t is equal to d. Motivated by the fact that in MPC with strong honest majority we have $t < d$, we present new PRSS constructions exploiting this gap.

Our constructions leverage suitable combinatorial designs, and yield a dramatic efficiency improvement when $t \ll d$, not only for standard degree-d correlations but also for several useful generalizations. This includes correlations for locally converting between slot configurations in "share packing," which enable

---

[1] More precisely, our protocols have storage and (offline) computation costs that grow exponentially in t but linearly in the number of parties n. Thus, when t is a small constant, they can be practical even for a large n.

us to avoid the concrete overhead of prior works on MPC based on share packing [20,27,33]. We remark that our PRSS results are independently motivated by other applications beyond the context of MPC, including threshold cryptography, advanced cryptographic primitives, and targeted multi-party protocols (e.g., [6,7,13,15,23]).

We provide a general transformation yielding PRSS schemes from any instance of a so-called "covering design" with appropriate parameters. An (n, m, t)-*cover* is a collection of size-m subsets $S_i \subset [n]$, such that every subset of t elements of $[n]$ is covered by some set S_i. The goal is to do so with the fewest number of such sets S_i. Construction of covering designs is a topic of combinatorial research, where bounds are known for small parameters, and several results are known in the larger parameter regime (see Sect. 3.3 for discussion). While it is not hard to see that the seed replication pattern of a PRSS must induce a covering design, the converse direction is less obvious. Indeed, our transformation incurs a small overhead that leaves a $(d + 1)$ multiplicative gap between the upper and lower bounds on the number of seeds for the case of degree-d polynomials.

The following theorem summarizes our general transformation from covering designs to PRSS for degree-d polynomials, as well as some corollaries obtained by plugging in existing covering designs from the literature (cf. [32]).

Theorem 1.1 (PRSS for degree-d polynomials from covering designs, informal). *Let n, d, t be positive integers such that $t < d < n$. Given an $(n, d + 1, t)$-cover of size k, one can construct a PRSS scheme for sharing random degree-d polynomials between n parties with security threshold t, requiring $k(d + 1)(n - d)/n$ PRF seeds per party. As a special case, plugging in existing covering designs for small t, we obtain the following:*

- *For $t = 1$, any n:* $\left\lceil \frac{n}{d+1} \right\rceil \frac{(d+1)(n-d)}{n}$ *PRF seeds per party (or just $n - d$ when $(d + 1)|n$).*
- *For $t = 2$, any $n \leq 3(d + 1)$: $13(d + 1)$ PRF seeds per party.*

We further obtain PRSS for "double Shamir sharing" (i.e. two random polynomials of degrees d and $2d$ with the same evaluations on given $d - t + 1$ points) with roughly twice as many PRF seeds.

In comparison to the parameters above, the naive baseline from [18] is $\binom{n-1}{d}$ seeds per party, which in the case that $t < d$ can be improved to $\binom{n-1}{t}$ seeds per party (we show the details in the full version of this paper). Plugging in explicit covering design constructions from the literature, the PRSS solutions obtained via Theorem 1.1 provide significant savings to even this improved baseline. For example:

- $(n, d, t) = (48, 15, 4)$ requires $2,772$ seeds per party, versus baseline $\binom{47}{4} = 178,365$.
- $(n, d, t) = (49, 23, 4)$ requires 484 seeds per party, versus baseline $\binom{48}{4} = 194,580$.

– $(n, d, t) = (49, 23, 8)$ requires $57, 281$ seeds per party, versus baseline $\binom{48}{8} \approx 3.7 \cdot 10^8$.

For additional data points, see the full version. Our PRSS constructions go beyond basic Shamir or double-Shamir shares, to a generalized form of PRSS that allows local generation of packed pseudorandom secrets with an arbitrary replication pattern. We achieve this with with additional redundancy of seeds to parties. However, the resulting complexity still provides significant savings as an alternative to existing approaches within motivated regimes. We refer the reader to Sect. 3.6 for a detailed treatment.

Contribution 2: Cheap Straggler Resilience. We propose a novel technique for dealing with the "straggler" problem of delayed messages, allowing the protocol to continue the execution once sufficiently many messages are received. In doing so, we need to defend against the subtle "double-dipping" attack mentioned above. In contrast to alternative approaches for defending against this attack [26, 35], our approach has no extra cost to the round complexity of the protocol and only a sublinear additive communication overhead. Our protocol makes black-box use of our PRSS construction to produce the required randomness without interaction.

Combining the above tools to obtain efficient MPC protocols with security against malicious parties requires additional ideas. In particular, we need to adapt the distributed zero-knowledge proof techniques of Boneh et al. [8] to the setting of MPC based on packed secret sharing. See additional discussion below.

The features of our final protocol are captured by the following theorem.

Theorem 1.2 (Malicious security with straggler resilience, informal).
Let $t \geq 1$ be a security threshold, $\ell \geq 1$ a packing parameter, $n \geq 2t + 2\ell - 1$ a number of parties, and $\mathbb{F}$ be a finite field such that $|\mathbb{F}| > n + t + 2\ell$. Then, for any arithmetic circuit C over $\mathbb{F}$ with S multiplication gates and depth D, there is an n-party protocol for C with the following efficiency and security features:

– *The protocol makes a black-box use of any pseudorandom function;*
– *Excluding $O(1)$ rounds of preprocessing and postprocessing, the protocol consists of D epochs, where in each epoch P_1 sends a message to each other party P_i and receives a message back from each P_i;*
– *It achieves security with abort in presence of t malicious parties even if $\tau = n - (2t + 2\ell - 1)$ messages, chosen by the adversary, are dropped in each epoch;*
– *If the parties follow the protocol, it terminates successfully even if τ messages, chosen by the adversary, are dropped in each epoch;*
– *Communication cost is $\left(\frac{3}{\ell} - \frac{2t+2\ell+1}{n \cdot \ell} \right) S + o(S)$ elements of $\mathbb{F}$ sent per party.*

We further discuss the communication, computation, and storage costs in the following remarks.

Remark 1.1 (Sensitivity to the topology of C.). As in other protocols based on packed secret sharing, the communication complexity bound in Theorem 1.2 assumes that the circuit C is "non-pathological" in the sense that its width is bigger than the packing parameter ℓ. (Otherwise there is an extra communication cost resulting from empty slots.) Since we typically expect ℓ to be much smaller than the circuit size, this condition is met for almost all natural instances of big circuits.

Remark 1.2 (On the cost of PRSS.). The generalized PRSS primitive influences the local storage and computational cost, which can be performed offline and are practical for small t even for large values of ℓ and n; see the full version of this paper for concrete numbers. By increasing the degree parameter d of the generalized PRSS construction beyond the minimum required by t and ℓ, we get better PRSS complexity at the cost of a lower straggler resilience threshold τ.

Remark 1.3 (On communication complexity.). When $\ell = 2$, the amortized communication cost in Theorem 1.2 is always less than 1.5 elements per party per gate, and when $\ell = 3$ it goes below 1 element per party. We present concrete efficiency analysis of our protocol in the full version of the paper, showing that as we increase n and ℓ, our protocol not only can withstand stragglers, but also achieves *lower total communication* than the best known semi-honest protocols with $n = 2t + 1$ parties. In particular, whenever $\ell = \Omega(n)$ the total communication complexity (ignoring lower order additive terms) is $O(s)$.

Technical Challenges and Contributions. Our final MPC protocol builds on new solutions for the following main challenges:

- *Generalized pseudorandom secret sharing (PRSS)* based on combinatorial designs that take advantage of the gap between the polynomial degree d and the security threshold t to reduce computation and storage costs.
- *Packed secret sharing beyond SIMD*, without the asymptotic or concrete overhead of previous techniques [20,27,33]. Our solution relies on generalized PRSS for cheaper batch generation of useful linear correlations, for "repacking" secret shared values in different orders.
- *Preventing "double-dipping" attacks*, identified by [26,35], which exploit the redundancy of encoding across parties in a strong honest majority to obtain related secret values under the same random mask (see below; note that this attack arises even without share packing). The works of [26,35] protect against the attack using methods that require participation from *all* parties and increase the round complexity by 2x or more; we do so while supporting resilience to stragglers, and with essentially no extra online cost.
- *Applying sublinear distributed zero knowledge [8] on packed shares*, as well as achieving batched verification with missing shares (due to stragglers). The former challenge arises again from the non-SIMD structure of general computation, here relating to the statements to be efficiently *verified*. The latter issue pertains to verifying consistency of several robustly secret shared values, when each secret has a *different* subset of shares missing, corresponding to different sets of straggling parties.

1.2 Related Work

We mention here specific recent works relating to our second contribution, of MPC in the strong honest majority setting achieving concrete efficiency and straggler resilience.

PRSS-Based vs. Interactive Correlated Randomness Generation. In this work, we use non-interactive PRSS to generate the double sharing required for the DN multiplication protocol. While we improve the efficiency of PRSS dramatically (when the polynomial degree d is higher than the corruption threshold t), the computational overhead still limits the practical use of this method to a relatively small number of corrupted parties t. See the full version for concrete estimates of computational cost. An alternative to the PRSS-based approach is using an interactive protocol, but with computation that scales polynomially with the number of parties. The state-of-the-art protocol by Goyal *et al.* [34] shows how to generate the double sharing with communication of just 0.5 field element sent per party. This implies that our method requires approximately 25% less overall communication. More importantly, the method of [34] does not support straggler resilience and applies only to gate-by-gate evaluations. While it can be easily extended to SIMD circuits, it does not extend to general non-SIMD circuits with packed secrets. Finally, the correlated randomness generation procedure from [34] requires interaction between all parties, which can be prohibitive in other applications scenarios.

MPC with Strong Honest Majority. Concretely efficient MPC in the strong honest majority setting has gained recent focus, including the works of Gordon *et al.* [33] and Beck *et al.* [27]. In comparison, their protocols scale to a larger number of parties, while our approach provides better efficiency for the regime of small corruptions t. This is due largely to our ability to generate the necessary setup correlations with minimal interaction via generalized PRSS. In addition, our protocols provide straggler resilience (yielding savings in settings with latency variance), whereas [27,33] assume a fully synchronous network. Finally, in these works, malicious security comes with a multiplicative overhead, whereas in our protocol, the overhead is sublinear in the size of the circuit.

A very recent work of Goyal *et al.* [36] shows how to achieve asymptotic constant communication cost per party in this setting for general non-SIMD circuits with information-theoretic security, but with poor concrete efficiency and without stragglers resilience.

MPC with Partial Synchrony. A number of works have studied MPC with various (stronger) flavors of partial synchrony from the perspective of feasibility, without focus on concrete efficiency. For example, the work of Zikas *et al.* [53] provides unconditionally secure protocols in a model where parties can additionally be send-omission or receive-omission corrupted. Guo *et al.* [38] consider a model where parties can periodically go offline and return. In Badrinarayanan *et al.* [3] parties can turn non-adversarially "lazy." Both of the latter rely on heavy cryptographic tools, such as (multi-key) fully homomorphic encryption.

Finally, a handful of works have considered concretely efficient MPC with forms of partial synchrony, with incomparable conclusions. Hirt and Maurer [41] consider a mixed model of malicious and fail-stop adversaries, achieve perfect security, but with larger overall cost (e.g., without the savings of share packing). The "Fluid MPC" work of Choudhuri et al. [17] builds efficient protocols within a very different model, designed for long computations, where in each period of time, a different set of parties carry-out the computation.

2   Preliminaries

Notation. Let $P_1, \ldots, P_n$ be the set of parties and let t, ℓ, d be integers such that $d \geq t + \ell - 1$ and $n \geq 2d + 1$. The parameter t bounds the number of parties that can be corrupted, the parameter ℓ denotes the size of the block of secrets that are evaluated together, and d will be the degree of the polynomial defined below. We use $[n]$ to denote the set $\{1, \ldots, n\}$ and denote by $\mathbb{F}$ a finite field.

2.1   Threshold Secret Sharing

Definition 2.1. *A d-out-of-n secret sharing scheme is a protocol for a dealer holding a secret value v and n parties $P_1, \ldots, P_n$. The scheme consists of two interactive algorithms:* share(v), *which outputs shares* $(v_1, \ldots, v_n)$ *and* reconstruct($\{v_j\}_{j \in T}, i$), *which given the shares $v_j, j \in T \subseteq [n]$ outputs v or $\perp$. The dealer runs* share(v) *and provides P_i with a share v_i of the secret v. A subset of users T run* reconstruct($\{v_j\}_{j \in T}, i$) *to reveal the secret to party P_i. The scheme must ensure that no subset of d shares provide any information on v, while $v =$* reconstruct($\{v_j\}_{j \in T}, i$) *for T only if $|T| \geq d+1$. We say that a sharing is* consistent *if* reconstruct($\{v_j\}_{j \in T}, i$) = reconstruct($\{v_j\}_{j \in T'}, i$) *for any two sets of honest parties $T, T' \subseteq \{1, \ldots, n\}$, and $|T|, |T'| \geq d + 1$.*

Packed Shamir Secret Sharing In Shamir's secret sharing scheme [48], the dealer defines a random polynomial $p(x)$ of degree d over a finite field $\mathbb{F}$ such that the constant term is the secret. Each party is associated with a distinct non-zero field element $\alpha \in \mathbb{F}$ and receives $p(\alpha)$ as its share of the secret. Since the degree of the polynomial is d, any $d + 1$ points are sufficient to compute the secret. We use the notation $[\![x]\!]_d$ to denote a sharing of x via a polynomial of degree d.

Two properties of this scheme that are very useful for MPC are: (1) linear operations on secrets can be computed locally on the shares, since polynomial interpolation is a linear operation; (2) given shares of x and y, the parties can locally multiply their shares to obtain a sharing of degree $2d$ of $x \cdot y$.

In this work, we use a generalization of Shamir's sharing scheme where multiple secrets are being encoded together, introduced by Franklin and Yung [24] and known as "packed secret sharing". This is achieved by storing the secrets on multiple points. Note however that if we pack ℓ secrets together on a polynomial of degree d, then the corruption threshold is being reduced to $t = d - \ell + 1$.

Throughout this paper, we will use the notation $[\![x_1 \cdots x_\ell]\!]_d$ to denote a sharing of the block $x_1, \ldots, x_\ell$ using a polynomial of degree d, and assume that $x_1, \ldots, x_\ell$ are stored at points $0, -1, \ldots, -\ell+1$ respectively and that the share of P_i is the value at the point i. Observe that the properties mentioned above apply to packed secret sharing as well. Namely, given a constant $\alpha, \beta \in \mathbb{F}$ and two sharings $[\![x_1 \cdots x_\ell]\!]_d$, $[\![y_1 \cdots y_\ell]\!]_d$, the following are local operations over the shares: (1) $[\![(\alpha x_1 + \beta y_1) \cdots (\alpha x_\ell + \beta y_\ell)]\!]_d = \alpha [\![x_1 \cdots x_\ell]\!]_d + \beta [\![y_1 \cdots y_\ell]\!]_d$; (2) $[\![x_1 y_1 \cdots x_\ell y_\ell]\!]_{2d} = [\![x_1 \cdots x_\ell]\!]_d \cdot [\![y_1 \cdots y_\ell]\!]_d$.

We say that a sharing $[\![x]\!]_d$ or $[\![x_1 \cdots x_\ell]\!]_d$ is inconsistent if all points do not lie on the same polynomial of degree d. Given all shares, this can be easily checked by using $d+1$ points to reconstruct the polynomial and checking whether the remaining points lie on this polynomial

2.2 Computation Model: Layered Straight-Line Programs

In this work, we present a multi-party protocol for performing arithmetic computations over a finite field. In the MPC literature, arithmetic computations are usually represented by a circuit or a straight line program (SLP) with addition and multiplication gates/operations. We use the notion of SLP, but choose a slightly different representation, with one instruction, which we call "bi-linear", that captures the two operations together. This model will allow us a simple and more clearer description of our protocols, and in particular, make the trick to achieve "free-addition" easier to describe.

Definition 2.2 (Layered straight-line program (SLP)). *A straight-line programs (SLP) over $\mathbb{F}$ is defined by an arbitrary sequence of the following kinds of instructions:*

- *Load an input into memory: $R_j \leftarrow x_i$.*
- *Bilinear instruction: $R_j \leftarrow (\sum_{\omega=1}^{w} a_\omega \cdot R_\omega) \cdot (\sum_{\omega=1}^{w} b_\omega \cdot R_\omega)$*
- *Output value from memory, as element of $\mathbb{F}$: $O_i \leftarrow R_j$.*

Here $x_1 \ldots, x_n$ are inputs, $R_1, \ldots, R_w$ are registers and $a_1, \ldots, a_w, b_1, \ldots, b_w$ are public constants in $\mathbb{F}$. We define the size of an SLP to be the number of instructions. A layered SLP is an SLP where the instructions are partitioned into sets called layers such that the inputs to instructions in layer j were computed in layer $k < j$. An ℓ-layered SLP is a layered SLP in which the number of instructions in each layer is a multiple of ℓ.

For simplicity, we assume in our MPC protocols for SLP that each party holds one input and receives one output at the end. However, the protocols naturally extend to the general case of multiple inputs or outputs per party.

Remark 2.1 (Simulating arithmetic circuits by layered SLPs). Every arithmetic circuit of size S (counting only multiplication gates, inputs, and outputs) can be converted into an SLP of size S by sorting its gates in an arbitrary topological order. The "ℓ-layered" notion of SLP intuitively corresponds to a lower bound on the circuit width. In particular, an SIMD circuit computing $k \geq \ell$ copies of a size-S circuit C on k distinct inputs can be written as an ℓ-layered SLP of size kS. Any layered SLP can be converted into an ℓ-layered one by naively adding dummy gates if needed, where the latter adds $(\ell - 1)$ times the depth in the worst case. But almost all "natural" instances of big circuits can be compiled into ℓ-layered SLPs with no overhead.

3 Generalized Pseudorandom Secret Sharing

An important resource for our main protocol is a packed secret sharing of blocks of ℓ secrets that are randomly sampled from a given linear subspace. In this section, we show how the parties can securely generate arbitrarily many such blocks of secrets without any interaction, assuming a short setup step where they distribute seeds for a Pseudorandom Function (PRF). Subsequently, shares are obtained by local computation on the seeds. We refer to this problem as generalized pseudorandom secret sharing (PRSS). This primitive is useful beyond the context of this work, and our results are useful even without any share packing (i.e., when $\ell = 1$).

More abstractly, we can view the problem as that of efficiently realizing a *linear correlation*, namely an ideal functionality that picks a random vector from a public linear space and delivers one or more entries of this vector to each party. To be applicable in an MPC protocol, even with a semi-honest adversary, the linear correlations must be generated *securely*. Loosely speaking, an adversary should not get any information on the shares of honest parties beyond what follows from the public linear correlation, even given the information that the adversary holds.

The ideal functionality $\mathcal{F}_{\text{LinRand}}$. We will make security arguments relative to an ideal functionality $\mathcal{F}_{\text{LinRand}}$ for sharing instances of *linear correlated randomness*. More concretely, $\mathcal{F}_{\text{LinRand}}$ is parametrized by some linear subspace, and in each invocation it picks a random vector from that linear subspace and distributes one or more entries to each party. Both the linear space and the assignment of which entry goes to what party are public. It is only the actual vector sampled from the linear subspace that should remain secret.

Security is defined with respect to a *static* adversary who may corrupt up to t parties. Concretely, the real world view of the adversary together with the outputs of honest parties should be indistinguishable from an ideal world in which the adversary chooses the corrupted parties' shares, and then the honest parties' shares are sampled from the target correlation conditioned on this choice. This can be formally viewed as a multiparty instance of a Pseudorandom Correlation Function (PCF), recently defined by Boyle et al. [10], applied to *linear correlations*. The notion of PCF naturally extends the notion of a Pseudorandom Correlation Generators (PCG) [9], analogously to the way a standard PRF extends a standard PRG.

We are interested in t-secure realizations of $\mathcal{F}_{\text{LinRand}}$ that have the following structure: (1) During an offline setup phase, a trusted dealer picks random and independent PRF seeds, and distributes each seed to a subset of the parties.[2] (2) Next, to realize a fresh invocation of $\mathcal{F}_{\mathrm{LinRand}}$ with common identifier id, each party *locally* evaluates the PRF with each seed it owns on one or more inputs derived from id, and outputs a *fixed linear combination* of the PRF outputs. (The linear combination is fixed and does not change from one id to the next.)

3.1   Overview

Following prior work, we reduce the goal of secure realization of $\mathcal{F}_{\mathrm{LinRand}}$ to an information-theoretic problem where the PRF seeds are replaced with true randomness. Namely, we consider locally generating an instance of the target correlation with perfect t-security given independently random field elements that are replicated between the parties. In the PRF-based computational realization of $\mathcal{F}_{\mathrm{LinRand}}$, the random field elements will be pseudorandomly sampled using the PRF. Security under the above PCF-style definition reduces to information-theoretic security via a standard hybrid argument.

The PRSS problem was first implicitly studied by Gilboa and Ishai [28]. Cramer, Damgård, and Ishai [18] made this notion explicit and described a simple construction for the case of generating t-out-of-n Shamir sharing of random values. This construction is a useful building block in many cryptographic applications. Here we extend the notion and construction of PRSS to more general settings that are motivated (among other applications) by MPC with strong honest majority. We show that a gap between the degree d and the security threshold t can give rise to dramatic efficiency improvements. Concretely:

- We start by extending the standard PRSS problem to the case where the degree of the Shamir-sharing polynomial can be larger than the security threshold t, and reduce this problem to a well-studied combinatorial design problem. This construction can be used for example to implement efficient distribution of *packed Shamir sharing* [24] of random values, and can be useful for many other applications.
- We show how to use the above construction in a black-box fashion to get efficient implementation of the kind of "double sharing" needed for protocols that follow the approach of Damgård-Nielsen (DN) [22]. Specifically, we implement the target correlation of two secret-sharing of the same (possibly packed) random values, one with a degree-d polynomial and the other with a degree-$2d$ polynomial.
- We show an extension of this technique to the harder case where we have degree-$2d$ sharings of random values, and degree-d sharings of *arbitrary linear combinations* of those random values. This is used to generate random packed secrets that satisfy given replicated constraints, as needed by efficient MPC protocols for *general circuits* based on packed secret sharing [19,20].

We note that our techniques can be used to improve the efficiency of even more general forms of linear correlation, but leave systematic study of their application to future work.

---

[2] This setup can alternatively be implemented by a secure MPC protocol.

3.2   The Gilboa-Ishai Framework

The functionality that we want to implement distributes linearly correlated random variables over some field $\mathbb{F}$ to n parties. The functionality is parameterized by a matrix $C \in \mathbb{F}^{N \times K}$ whose columns span a linear code (i.e., linear subspace of $\mathbb{F}^N$), and by a mapping $\rho : [N] \to [n]$ saying which party gets what entry of the output vector. The functionality chooses a random vector $\boldsymbol{v}$ in the code (by choosing a uniformly random $\boldsymbol{u} \leftarrow \mathbb{F}^K$ and setting $\boldsymbol{v} := C\boldsymbol{u}$), then privately sends to each party i' all the entries indexed by $\rho^{-1}(i')$.

Implementing this functionality without any interaction (beyond pre-distribution of PRF seeds) was studied by Gilboa and Ishai [28], in the information-theoretic setting where the PRF seeds are replaced by true randomness. In their framework, implementation of the linear-correlation functionality consists of:

- Input distribution, where an honest dealer draws $x_1, x_2, \ldots, x_k \in \mathbb{F}$ uniformly at random, and distributes each x_j to some subset of parties $S_j \subset [n]$;
- Local output computation, where each party i locally computes and outputs its entries of $\boldsymbol{v}$ from the x_j's that it received.

The complexity measures of interest for such a solution are:

- The number of distinct subsets S_j, corresponding to the number of PRF seeds to be distributed, and
- The sum $\sum_{j=1}^{k} |S_j|$, corresponding to the total number of pseudorandom field elements to be derived from these PRF seeds, across all the parties.

All the known implementations, including the ones that we describe here, rely on "small-support codewords" and the Gilboa-Ishai security criteria: A solution is specified by a "sparse" matrix $M \in \mathbb{F}^{N \times k}$ (typically $k \gg K$), whose columns span the same code as C. The output is computed by choosing a random vector $\boldsymbol{x} = (x_1, \ldots, x_k)$ and setting $\boldsymbol{v} := M\boldsymbol{x}$, and each party gets all the x_j'es that it needs in order to carry out this computation. Specifically, for an entry $\boldsymbol{v}[i]$ that belongs to party $\rho(i)$, we give that party the random elements x_j for which $M[i, j] \neq 0$, making it possible for this party to compute the inner product between $\boldsymbol{x}$ and the i'th row of M. Hence the sets $S_1, \ldots, S_k$ are defined

$$S_j = \{i' \in [n] : \exists i \in [N],\ M[i, j] \neq 0 \text{ and } i' = \rho(i)\}, \tag{1}$$

(For example, if the mapping ρ assigns entries 1 through 10 in $\boldsymbol{v}$ to Party 1 then the only x_j values that *are not given to this party* correspond to columns of M where the top 10 entries are all zero.) Clearly, the sparser the matrix M is, the fewer x_j values that must be distributed and the smaller we can make the sets S_j.

Gilboa and Ishai proved a necessary and sufficient criterion for security within this framework. Fix a code which is generated by the columns of the matrix C, and a solution matrix M whose columns span the same code. For a subset of parties $T \subset [n]$, let I_T be all the rows that belong to parties in T, and J_T be all the indices of x_j's that members of T get to see. That is, with the S_j's defined as in Eq. 1, we have

$$I_T = \bigcup_{i' \in T} \rho^{-1}(i'), \text{ and } J_T = \{j \in [k] : S_j \cap T \neq \emptyset\}.$$

Denote by $C_{\bar{T}}$ the restriction of $\mathsf{span}(C)$ to only the codewords that are zero in all the coordinates I_T. Also denote by $M'_{\bar{T}}$ the submatrix of M consisting of the rows in the complement $I_{\bar{T}} = [N] \setminus I_T$ and the columns in the complement $J_{\bar{T}} = [k] \setminus J_T$ (i.e., the ones corresponding to x_j's that *none of the parties in T receives*).

Lemma 3.1 ([28]). *Let $C \in \mathbb{F}^{N \times K}$ and $M \in \mathbb{F}^{N \times k}$ be two matrices with the same column space (so M describes a solution to the distribution of a codeword from $\mathsf{span}(C)$).*

For a subset of parties $T \subset [n]$, the solution specified by M is secure against a corrupted T iff the rank of $M'_{\bar{T}}$ equals the dimension of $C_{\bar{T}}$.

3.3 Technical Tool: Covering Designs

The main technical tool that we use in our construction is the following notion of covering designs:

Definition 3.1 ((n, m, t)-**cover**). *Fix integers $n \geq m \geq t > 0$, and let $\mathcal{C} = (S_1, \ldots, S_k)$ be a collection of k different subsets $S_j \subset [n]$, all of size $|S_j| = m$. $\mathcal{C}$ is said to be an (n, m, t)-cover if for every size-t subset $T \subset [n], |T| = t$, there is a set $S_j \in \mathcal{C}$ that covers it, $T \subseteq S_j$. We will refer to an (n, m, t)-cover as a t-cover when n, m are clear from the context.*

This notion is equivalent to the notion of t-immunity of Alon et al. [2], in which for every subset T there is a set S_j in the collection such that $T \cap S_j = \emptyset$. The collection $\mathcal{C}$ is an (n, m, t)-cover iff the complement sets $[n] \setminus S_j$ form an ($n, n - m, t$)-immune collection. The smallest number of subsets in an (n, m, t)-cover is also known as the hypergraph Turán number $\mathcal{T}(n, n - t, n - m)$ in honor of Paul Turán who initiated the study of these objects in [50,51].

The parameters of covering designs have been studied extensively, e.g. see [25,49] for surveys, but the exact value is still an open problem in the general case. The best known analytical bounds for small values of t are summarized in a Handbook of Combinatorial Designs chapter by Gordon and Stinson [32]. A good online resource that collects the best known bounds for concrete values of n, m, t with $t \leq 8$, including ones found via computer search, is Gordon's covering designs web page [1].

For general values of t, Micali and Sidney [44] proposed to construct an (n, m, t)-cover by randomly choosing $\binom{n}{t} / \binom{m}{t} \ln \binom{n}{t}$ subsets of size m from $[n]$ and used a probabilistic argument to show that with good probability this collection is an (n, m, t)-cover. Pieprzyk and Wang [39] construct a deterministic, greedy algorithm that achieves the same bound on the size of the collection.

Both works were motivated by variants of the PRSS problem where the seeds are stored in a replicated form, without the compressing share conversion step from [18, 28]

A range of parameters which is especially appealing for our MPC protocol is constant t, and m which is a linear fraction of n, e.g., $m = n/3$. In this case, the protocol can cope with a large number of stragglers and reduce communication by packing. When t is constant, the constructions in [39, 44] have collections of size $O(\log n)$.

We next describe a simple construction that achieves a constant-sized collection for $t = O(1)$ and $m = \Omega(n)$, when t divides m and m divides n. Denote $c = n/m$ and partition $[n]$ into ct subsets $R_1, \ldots, R_{ct}$ of equal size. Let the collection $S_1, \ldots, S_k$ be all the possible choices of t subsets $R_{i_1} \cup \cdots \cup R_{i_t}$. Obviously, each $|S_j| = t(n/ct) = m$ and for every $T \subseteq [n], |T| = t$ there exists some S_j such that $T \subseteq S_j$. The size of the collection is $\binom{ct}{t}$, which for constant t and c is constant, improving over the construction of [39, 44].

Taking for each parameter set (n, m, t) the minimal cover size between the simple construction and the construction in [39] provides a baseline construction for t-covers. This baseline achieves an upper bound for the cover size, which is bigger than the minimal possible size by a factor of at most $O(\log n)$, due to a simple lower bound of $\binom{n}{t}/\binom{m}{t}$ on this size (see, e.g., Theorem 11.19 in [32]). Both the upper bound of the baseline construction and the simple lower bound are generally not tight. Improved bounds for certain parameter ranges can be found in [1].

3.4   Generalized PRSS for Degree-d Polynomials

It is easy to see (see Theorem 3.2) that t-covers are necessary for t-secure distribution in the Gilboa-Ishai framework, since any corrupted subset must miss at least some of the x_j's. Here we observe that the other direction is also useful, establishing a close connection between the size of the best $(n, d+1, t)$-cover and the complexity of PRSS for distributing random degree-d polynomials between n parties with security against t-collusions.

Theorem 3.1 (Generalized PRSS for degree-d polynomials). *Fix integers $n \geq d > t > 0$. A size-k' $(n, d + 1, t)$-cover can be used to construct a generalized PRSS solution for t-secure distribution of degree-d polynomials, with the following complexity measures:*

- *The number of distinct subsets (or PRSS seeds) is $k = k'(d + 1)$, and*
- *The total subset size (storage) is $\sum_i |S_i| = k'(d+1)(n-d)$ and*
- *The total number of PRF calls is $k'(d + 1)(n - d)$.*

Proof: Let $\mathcal{C}' = (S'_1, \ldots, S'_{k'})$ be a size-k' $(n, d+1, t)$-cover, i.e. it consists of k' subsets, each of size $d + 1$, that cover all the t-subsets. We then consider all the subsets that are obtained by removing one element from any of the S'_j's,

$$\bar{\mathcal{C}} = \left\{ S' \setminus \{j\} : \ S' \in \mathcal{C}', j \in S' \right\}.$$

Clearly, there are at most $k \leq k'(d+1)$ distinct subsets in $\bar{\mathcal{C}}$, each of size d. Let us denote the subsets in $\bar{\mathcal{C}}$ by $\bar{S}_1, \bar{S}_2, \ldots, \bar{S}_k$, and we use these subsets in the CDI construction to distribute a random degree-d polynomial. We let $P_{\bar{S}_j}$ be the unique polynomial of degree d interpolated from

$$P_{\bar{S}_j}(X) = \begin{cases} 0 & \text{if } X \in \bar{S}_j \\ 1 & \text{if } X = 0 \end{cases}$$

As before, $P_{\bar{S}}$ is a nonzero degree-d polynomial, whose zeros are exactly all the parties in $\bar{S}_j$. A random vector $\boldsymbol{x} \in \mathbb{F}^k$ therefore defines the polynomial $Q_{\boldsymbol{x}}(X) = \sum_j x_j \cdot P_{\bar{S}_j}(X)$, and each party $i \in [n]$ gets the x_j's corresponding to the $\bar{S}_j$'s *that do not include* i, and can compute $Q_{\boldsymbol{x}}(i)$ from these x_j's. Thus, there are $k'(d+1)$ distinct subsets, each of cardinality $n - d$. This implies that the total stroage is $k'(d+1)(n-d)$ as the theorem states. Since each seed is used once, the total number of PRF calls is also the same.

In the language of the Gilboa-Ishai framework, the matrix $M \in \mathbb{F}^{n \times k}$ is defined by $M[i,j] = P_{\bar{S}_j}(i)$, and the distribution sets are exactly the complementing sets $S_j = [n] \setminus \bar{S}_j$ (namely we distribute each x_j to the complement of some $S' \in \mathcal{C}'$, together with one more element). The complexity measures are obvious.

It remains therefore to show security against a collusion of t parties, which for degree-d polynomials means showing that for every t-subset T, the submatrix $M'_{\bar{T}}$ has rank at least $d+1-t$. Fix a t-subset $T \subset [n]$, so there is a subset $S' \in \mathcal{C}'$ that covers it. Consider now the sub-matrix corresponding to the subsets $\bar{S}$ that were obtained by removing from S' one element *which is not in T* (hence those sets $\bar{S}$ still all cover T). That is, we consider the sub-matrix $M_{T,S'}$ of $M[i,j] = P_{\bar{S}_j}(i)$, consisting of the rows for $[n] \setminus T$ and the columns for $S_j = ([n] \setminus S') \cup \{j'\}$ for all $j' \in S' \setminus T$. Clearly $M_{T,S'}$ is a sub-matrix of $M'_{\bar{T}}$, it has $n - t$ rows and $d + 1 - t$ columns (since S' covers T), and it has the form

$$M_{T,S'} = \begin{bmatrix} * & * & \cdots & * \\ \vdots & \vdots & \ddots & \vdots \\ * & * & \cdots & * \\ * & & & \\ & \ddots & & \\ & & & * \end{bmatrix},$$

where the $*$'s are non-zero and everywhere else there are zeros. The top rows $* \cdots *$ correspond to $[n] \setminus S'$ and the bottom rows correspond to $S' \setminus T$. The last $d + 1 - t$ rows of this matrix are linearly independent, hence the rank of $M_{T,S'}$ is $d + 1 - t$, as needed for the Gilboa-Ishai condition. ∎

Corollary 3.1. *Fix integers $n \geq d > 1$. Then, the following holds for generalized PRSS solutions for t-secure distribution of degree-d polynomials with $t = 1, 2$:*

1. *There exists a solution for $t = 1$ with $\left\lceil \frac{n}{d+1} \right\rceil (d + 1)$ total seeds, $\left\lceil \frac{n}{d+1} \right\rceil \frac{(d+1)(n-d)}{n}$ seeds stored by each party and $\left\lceil \frac{n}{d+1} \right\rceil \frac{(d+1)(n-d)}{n}$ calls to the PRF made by each party.*
2. *If $n \leq 3(d+1)$ then there exists a solution for $t = 2$ with $13(d+1)$ total seeds, $13(d+1)(n-d)/n$ seeds stored by each party and $13(d+1)(n-d)/n$ calls to the PRF made by each party.*

We can also prove a nearly-matching lower bound Theorem 3.1 on the solution complexity for t-secure distribution of degree-d polynomials, in terms of the achievable size for $(n, d + 1, t)$-covers. This naturally generalizes a similar negative result for standard PRSS from [18]. The proof is in the full version.

Theorem 3.2 (Necessity of cover designs). *Any generalized PRSS solution for t-secure distribution of degree-d polynomials that has k distinct subsets implies an $(n, d + 1, t)$-cover of size $k' \leq k$.*

The combination of Theorems 3.1 and 3.2 prove that the best $(n, d + 1, t)$-cover implies a nearly optimal number of distinct subsets, up to a factor of at most $d + 1$.

3.5 Double Shamir Sharing

A useful resource for efficient honest-majority MPC protocols is a so-called "double Shamir sharing" of a random secret, where the parties are given two random polynomials of degrees d and $2d$ that share the same random secrets. Here we consider the case of packed secret sharing. Letting $\ell = d - t + 1$ be the packing parameter, we want to generate a random degree-d polynomial P_1, and another polynomial P_2 of degree-$2d$ which is random subject to $P_1(x) = P_2(x)$ for all $x \in \{0, -1, -2, \ldots, -\ell + 1\}$. It is easy to see that this task reduces to generating two independent random polynomials $P_1(X)$ of degree d and $R(X)$ of degree $2d - \ell$, then setting $P_2(X) = P_1(X) + R(X) \cdot X(X + 1)(X + 2) \cdots (X + \ell - 1)$.

Indeed, the polynomial on the right side is a random degree-$2d$ polynomial, under the constraint that its values at the points $\{0, -1, \ldots, \ell + 1\}$ are 0. Since $P_1(x)$ and $R(x)$ are random independent polynomials, we can use the construction from the previous section in a black-box way. Specifically, we can generate $P_1(x)$ using a $(n, d+1, t)$-cover and generate $R(x)$ using an $(n, 2d-\ell+1, t)$-cover.

Theorem 3.3 (Generalized PRSS for packed double sharing). *Fix integers $d > t > 0$ and $n > 2d$ and let $\ell = d - t + 1$. A size-k' $(n, d + 1, t)$-cover and a size-k'' $(n, 2d - \ell + 1, t)$-cover can be used to construct a solution for t-secure distribution of double-Sharing of degree-d and degree-$2d$ polynomials, both packing the same ℓ elements, with the following complexity measures:*

- *The number of distinct subsets (seeds) is at most $k \leq k'(d+1)+k''(2d-\ell+1) \leq k'(2d + t + 1)$;*
- *The total subset size (storage) is $\sum_j |S_j| \leq k'(d + 1)(n - d) + k''(d + t)(n - d - t + 1)$.*
- *The total number of PRF calls is $k'(d+1)(n - d) + k''(d + t)(n - d - t + 1)$.*

The proof is in the full version. This construction is already strong enough to support DN-type secure computation protocols, even while packing ℓ elements in each polynomial. (Hence it can be used to compute the same circuit on ℓ different inputs at once, in a SIMD fashion.)

As an alternative to the above, we can use an $(n, d+1, t)$-cover to construct both polynomials, by increasing the number of pseudorandom elements derived from each seed. This will reduce the number of seeds stored by the parties (by some factor smaller than two), but will increase the number of pseudorandom elements that must be derived from these seeds. We provide the construction in the full version of this paper. We use a similar idea in the construction in the next section.

3.6 Beyond Double Sharing

In some applications, including the protocol that we describe in Sect. 4, we must generate double-Shamir-sharing of linearly correlated packed values (rather than the same values twice). While we don't know how to use the random-polynomial construction in a black-box manner to achieve this, we show here how to modify that construction in order to distribute this more general linear correlation in a t-secure manner.

This extension, however, comes with some loss of efficiency. Specifically, we need to start from covers with smaller subsets, and moreover we no longer distribute only a single random element to each subset. Fix $n > d > t > 0$ and $\ell \leq d - t$ (allowing $\ell < d - t$ is useful to mitigate the parameter loss). The goal in this section is to share two types of polynomials:

- m polynomials $R_1, \ldots, R_m$ of degree $2d$, each packing ℓ "free variables" (i.e. unconstrained) in positions $0, -1, \ldots, -\ell + 1$.
- m' additional polynomials $U_1, \ldots, U_{m'}$ of degree d, each packing ℓ constrained variables, which are set as some fixed linear combinations of the free variables.

Denote the positions where these values are packed by $L = \{0, -1, \ldots, -\ell + 1\}$, and also denote the linear correlation above by $\mathcal{L}[n, d, \ell, m, m']$. In the full version, we show the following:

Theorem 3.4 (Generalized PRSS for replicated packed secrets). *Fix integers $n \geq d > t > 0$, $\ell \leq d - t$, $m, m' > 1$. A size-k' $(n, d - \ell + 1, t)$-cover can be used to construct a solution for t-secure distribution of the linear correlation $\mathcal{L}[n, d, \ell, m, m']$ above. The complexity is at most:*

- *The number of distinct subsets (seeds) is at most $k \leq k'(d - \ell + 1)$;*
- *The total subset size (storage) is $\sum_j |S_j| \leq k'(d - \ell + 1)(n - d + \ell)$;*
- *The total number of PRF calls is at most $k(n - d + \ell)(m(d + \ell + 1) + m')$.*

Parameters. We remark that the parameters of this construction behave differently than those of the previous constructions. For the constructions from Sects. 3.4 and 3.5, increasing ℓ (and d) was a double-win, not so for the current construction. Here we need to start from a $(n, d - \ell + 1, t)$-cover, so setting

$\ell = d - t$ we hardly get any slackness in the size of the sets in our t-cover (they will be of size only $t + 1$). To improve parameters (the cover size in particular), it is better to choose a smaller value of ℓ, thereby working with larger subsets and hence being able to find smaller covers. It is likely that setting $\ell \approx (d-t)/2$ will be a sweet spot for this construction in terms of complexity.

4   Constructions for Semi-honest Security

In this section, we present protocols to compute a layered straight-line program over a finite field $\mathbb{F}$, that is secure in the presence of a *semi-honest* adversary who controls t parties, and with straggler-resilience. Recall that we have $n \geq 2d + 1$ parties, where $d \geq t + \ell - 1$.

The starting point of our constructions is the DN protocol [22], which is the fastest protocol known to this date for $n > 3$ parties. We begin in Sect. 4.1 with recalling the baseline DN protocol. In Sect. 4.2, we introduce straggler resilience and show how to adapt the DN protocol accordingly. Then in Sect. 4.3 we provide our solutions for improving the communication and computation requirements of the protocol.

4.1   Baseline Protocol (with $\ell = 1$)

Recall that in the DN protocol [22], the parties compute linear operations without any interaction and compute multiplication operations with small constant communication cost per party. Given shares $[\![x]\!]_d$ and $[\![y]\!]_d$, the parties compute $[\![x \cdot y]\!]_d$ in the following way. The parties prepare random sharings $[\![r]\!]_d$ and $[\![r]\!]_{2d}$ in an offline step which are consumed as follows. First, the parties locally compute $[\![x \cdot y - r]\!]_{2d} = [\![x]\!]_d \cdot [\![y]\!]_d - [\![r]\!]_{2d}$ and send their shares to P_1. Then, party P_1 computes $x \cdot y - r$ and shares the result to the parties as $[\![xy - r]\!]_d$. Finally, the parties locally compute $[\![x \cdot y]\!]_d = [\![r]\!]_d + [\![xy - r]\!]_d$.

As the random sharings can be generated non-interactively (in the way described in Sect. 3), the communication cost is derived from parties sending one field element to P_1 and P_1 secret sharing $xy - r$ to the parties. Note that $2d$ shares are sufficient for P_1 to reconstruct $xy - r$ (together with its own share). Also, it is possible to reduce communication in the second round by setting the shares of d parties to be 0, and having P_1 define its own share and the remaining $n - d$ parties' shares, given the value of $xy - r$ and the d zero shares. This is possible since $xy - r$ is not secret (P_1 could send it in the clear to the parties) and since $[\![xy - r]\!]_d$ is shared via a polynomial of degree d, and so $d+1$ points are sufficient to define it. Overall, we have that the communication cost per party per bilinear gate is $\frac{2d+n-d-1}{n} = 1 + \frac{d-1}{n}$ field elements. When $n > 2d + 1$, it is possible to improve this by having the parties secret sharing their inputs to $2d + 1$ parties who perform the computation. In this case, the communication cost per party per bilinear gate reduces to $\frac{2d+d}{n} = \frac{3d}{n}$ elements.

We denote by $\Pi_{\mathrm{SH}}^{\mathrm{base}}$ the base protocol, which thus works as follows:

Protocol $\Pi_{\mathrm{SH}}^{\mathrm{base}}$:

The parties hold a description of a layered SLP over $\mathbb{F}$. Denote by S the set of parties $P_1, \ldots, P_{2d+1}$

- **Pre-processing**: The parties call $\mathcal{F}_{\mathrm{LinRand}}$ to obtain a pair of random sharings $[\![r]\!]_d$ and $[\![r]\!]_{2d}$ for each bilinear instruction.
- **The protocol**:
  1. *Input sharing:* for each instruction $R_j \leftarrow x_i$, party P_i run $[\![x_i]\!]_d \leftarrow \mathsf{share}(x_i)$ and sends the resulting shares to the parties in S.
  2. *Evaluating the jth bilinear instruction $R_j \leftarrow (\sum \alpha_\omega R_\omega) \cdot (\sum \beta_\omega R_\omega)$:* Let $[\![r]\!]_d, [\![r]\!]_{2d}$ be the next unused pair of random sharings. Then:
     (a) The parties in S locally compute $[\![x]\!]_d = \sum_{\omega=1}^{w} \alpha_\omega \cdot [\![R_\omega]\!]_d$ and $[\![y]\!]_d = \sum_{\omega=1}^{w} b_\omega \cdot [\![R_\omega]\!]_d$, where $[\![R_\omega]\!]_d$ denotes sharing of the ω-index memory value R_ω (stored from previous operations).
     (b) The parties in S locally compute $[\![xy - r]\!]_{2d} = [\![x]\!]_d \cdot [\![y]\!]_d - [\![r]\!]_{2d}$ and send the result to P_1.
     (c) P_1 locally reconstructs $xy - r$ and then computes a sharing $[\![xy - r]\!]_d$ such that the shares of $P_2 \ldots, P_{d+1}$ are 0. Then, it sends the non-zero shares to parties $P_{d+2}, \ldots, P_{2d+1}$.
     (d) The parties in S set $[\![z]\!]_d \leftarrow [\![r]\!]_d + [\![xy - r]\!]_d$, and define $[\![z]\!]_d$ as their share of the output.
  3. *Output reconstruction:* For each instruction $O_i \leftarrow R_j$, the parties in S send their shares of the value in R_j to P_i, who uses them to reconstruct the output O_i.

Security of $\Pi_{\mathrm{SH}}^{\mathrm{base}}$ against a semi-honest adversary $\mathcal{A}$ controlling d parties follows from the fact that $\mathcal{A}$'s view consists of d random shares in the input sharing step, and masked intermediate values when performing multiplication operations.

4.2   Straggler Resilience

The classical communication model for secure multi-party computation considers parties who advance in the same pace in a fully synchronous manner. However, in real world scenarios, it is unreasonable to assume that all messages arrive at the same time. A protocol which can proceed without having to wait for all the parties' messages to arrive in each round, has thus the potential to reduce the overall latency of the execution.

We consider a model of *straggler resilience*, to account for the fact that communication channels exhibit a distribution over latency times, each of which may incur long delays with small probability. Instead of requiring parties to block and wait in every communication round until the last messages arrive, we build into the protocol design that the computation may proceed even in the absence of a small number of messages per round, which have not yet successfully been delivered. We say that a protocol that terminates successfully even when τ messages are dropped in each round, is resilient to τ stragglers. As for privacy, following the standard definition of multi-party computation [29], we consider an adversary who controls t parties and, in addition, is allowed to choose τ messages to be dropped in each round.

Definition 4.1 (Straggler resilience, semi-honest security). *Let f be an n-party functionality. We say that protocol Π computes f with t-semi-honest-security and τ-straggler-resilience if it satisfies the following properties:*

- STRAGGLER-ROBUST CORRECTNESS: *Π terminates successfully (i.e. each party receives its prescribed output $f_i(\boldsymbol{x})$), even if in each communication round, τ messages, chosen adaptively by the adversary, are not delivered.*
- SEMI-HONEST SECURITY WITH STRAGGLERS: *For every real-world semi-honest adversary $\mathcal{A}$ controlling a set I of parties with $|I| \leq t$ and, in addition, can choose adaptively τ messages to drop in each communication round, there exists an ideal-world simulator $\mathcal{S}$ such that for every vector of inputs $\boldsymbol{x}$ it holds: $\{\mathcal{S}(I, \boldsymbol{x}_I, f_I(\boldsymbol{x}))\} \equiv \{\mathsf{view}^{\pi}_{\mathcal{A}}(\boldsymbol{x})\}$, where $\boldsymbol{x}_I$ is the inputs of the parties in I, $f_I(\boldsymbol{x})$ is the output intended to the parties in I, and $\mathsf{view}^{\pi}_{\mathcal{A}}(\boldsymbol{x})$ is $\mathcal{A}$'s view in a real execution of π.*

Remark 4.1 (Straggler resilience)

1. *Round vs. epoch.* Our protocol constructions have a very specific structure, common to concretely efficient n-party computation protocols (à la DN [22]), where execution is divided into phases, or "epochs." In each epoch, a fixed designated party sends messages to the other parties, and then receives back messages from the parties. Within such structure, a somewhat more natural notion of straggler resilience will correspond to a given number of dropped messages per *epoch* (i.e., 2 rounds). However, our notion of τ dropped messages per round is more generally applicable, while still capturing the setting of bounded number of messages dropped per epoch (in this case 2τ, for the two rounds).

2. *Message vs. node drop.* We choose to model latency behavior as embodied by failure of delivery of individual *messages*. This captures settings where delays are caused by network channels, each exhibiting some distribution of latency. This further shares similarities to the "message omission" model, where messages sent to/from affected parties may never be delivered, as considered in, e.g., [40,45,46].

   An alternative approach is to consider temporary *node* failures per epoch (as considered in, e.g., [43,47,53]). This models settings where delays are caused centrally by the node itself. On one hand, our model can be more fine-grained; on the other hand, failure of a node corresponds to failure of potentially many incoming/outgoing communication messages. We remark that achieving straggler resilience against node failures poses a challenge within protocols following a star-topology communication structure as in DN and successors since failure of the designated "central" party prevents forward progression of the protocol. Seeing as this protocol structure lies at the core of concretely efficient n-party protocols to date, it remains an interesting open direction to explore whether such node-straggler resilience notion can additionally be achieved with good concrete efficiency.

Observe that the DN protocol $\Pi_{\text{SH}}^{\text{base}}$ from the previous section is not resilient to any straggler. Since it chooses a set S of $2d+1$ parties *in advance* to carry-out the computation, and then the server cannot proceed without all $2d$ messages arriving to him in each multiplication, then an adversary who chooses to drop the messages of even one party in the set S will cause the execution to get stuck. Note that choosing a different set S in each step will not solve the problem, since the adversary is allowed to adaptively choose a different set in each epoch (not to mention the communication cost incurred by resharing intermediate values to the new set of parties).

Next, consider a protocol, where we let all the parties participate in the execution and send their $2d$-degree shares of $xy - r$ to P_1, who then uses the *first $2d$ shares* it receives (together with its own share) to compute $xy - r$. Then, P_1 shares $xy - r$ to the parties, with the optimization outlined above, which allows him to send shares to $n - d - 1$ parties only (d shares are always 0).

Note that now the cost is $\frac{n-1+n-d-1}{n} = 2 - \frac{d+2}{n}$ field elements sent per party. We denote by $\Pi_{\text{SH}}^{\text{single}}$ a protocol that is identical to $\Pi_{\text{SH}}^{\text{base}}$, with the difference that the input is shared to *all* the parties and multiplication operations are carried-out in the way described above. While the communication cost of $\Pi_{\text{SH}}^{\text{single}}$ is higher than of $\Pi_{\text{SH}}^{\text{base}}$, it does allow $(n - 2d - 1)$ messages in each epoch to be dropped, since P_1 needs only $2d$ shares in order to compute its message to the parties. For the input sharing and output reconstruction steps, note that $d+1$ shares suffices to compute shared secrets, and so even if $(n - 2d - 1)$ messages are dropped, there are enough shares to proceed. We thus have:

Theorem 4.1. *Let f be a n-ary functionality over a finite field $\mathbb{F}$ represented by a layered SLP, let t be a security threshold, let d be a parameter such that $d \geq t$, $n \geq 2d + 1$ and $|\mathbb{F}| > n + d + 1$. Then, Protocol $\Pi_{\text{SH}}^{\text{single}}$ computes f in the $\mathcal{F}_{\text{LinRand}}$-hybrid model, with t-semi-honest-security, $(n - 1 - 2d)$-stragglers-resilience and communication of $2 - \frac{d+2}{n}$ field elements sent per party for each bilinear instruction.*

Observe that setting the d parameter gives rise to trade-offs between communication cost, stragglers-resilience and storage cost. Specifically, increasing d reduces communication and also the amount of PRSS keys needed for producing the correlated randomness (see Sect. 3). In contrast, keeping d small (e.g., setting $d = t$) provides more room for stragglers.

4.3   Reducing Communication and Computation

In this section, we show how to reduce communication and computation cost while still providing resilience to stragglers. This is achieved by taking the app-roach of packed secret sharing: encoding ℓ secrets over the same polynomial and evaluating ℓ bilinear instructions together, at the cost of a single instruction. We begin with a construction that is designed for SIMD programs, and then show how to extend our techniques to general programs.

Computing SIMD Programs. A program which evaluates the same sub-program many times in parallel is called a SIMD ("same-instruction-multiple-data") straight-line program. Note that a program P which consists of ℓ copies of the same sub-program can be viewed as a program which evaluates each time *a bundle of ℓ identical instructions*. Following works in this area, our idea is to store the ℓ inputs to each bundle on the same polynomial, reducing both communication and computation by a factor of ℓ. Details can be found in the full version.

Computing General Layered Straight-Line Programs. We next show how use packing to reduce cost when computing any straight-line program. In the protocol, the parties will process in each round ℓ instructions together at the cost of evaluating a single instruction. For a general-structured program this clearly raises several difficulties. Recall that an instruction in our program consists of taking a linear combination of two sets of inputs and multiply them together. The goal is to carry-out this by packing the "left" inputs on one polynomial and the "right" inputs on a second polynomial and multiply them together, to obtain a polynomial encoding the outputs of ℓ instructions. However, it is now not clear how to proceed to the next batch of ℓ instructions. In particular, when we move from one batch of instructions to the next, the outputs should be reorganized into new blocks of inputs corresponding to the ordering of the inputs in the next ℓ instructions. Moreover, it is possible that an output is used as an input to more than one instruction in the next batch. In this case, we need to ensure that the same value appears in several blocks and possibly in different positions. We call this ordering the "repetition pattern" induced by the program. To overcome this challenge, we leverage the fact that in the semi-honest multiplication protocol, party P_1 sees all outputs in the clear, masked using random values. Thus, we can ask P_1 to reshare all values according the ordering of the next batch of instructions. Moreover, to achieve free-addition, we will ask P_1 to first compute the linear combinations over the masked outputs and only then reshare it to the other parties in blocks. The parties, who receive block of masked values, will unmask these values, using correlated randomness they hold, and proceed to the multiplication operation.

In our protocol, the parties hold a sharing of two blocks of ℓ inputs: $[\![x_1 \cdots x_\ell]\!]_d$ and $[\![y_1 \cdots y_\ell]\!]_d$. As in the DN protocol, they locally multiply their shares and add shares of a random block $[\![r_1 \cdots r_\ell]\!]_{2d}$ to obtain a sharing $[\![(x_1 \cdot y_1 + r_1) \cdots (x_\ell \cdot y_\ell + r_\ell)]\!]_{2d}$. Then, the parties send their shares to P_1 who reconstructs $x_1 \cdot y_1 + r_1, \ldots, x_\ell \cdot y_\ell + r_\ell$. However, instead of sending these back to the parties, we let P_1 proceed to the next batch of instructions and compute the linear combinations of the inputs over the masked secrets. Only then P_1 shares the left block of masked inputs and right block of masked inputs to the parties, to perform the next multiplication operation. Once the shares of the blocks of masked inputs are received from P_1, the parties unmask these by adding a block of shared random secret that correspond to the repetition pattern. That is, if we have in the kth position of, say, the left input, a linear combination $(\sum_{\omega=1}^{w} a_{k,\omega} \cdot R_\omega)$ and the value in R_ω was masked using r_ω, then the parties need here a sharing $[\![r`_1 \cdots r`_\ell]\!]_d$ where $r`_k = (\sum_{\omega=1}^{w} a_{k,\omega} \cdot r_\omega)$. For-tunately, our pre-processing protocol from Sect. 3 can produce these types of random blocks. As before, P_1 proceed once $2d$ shares have been received, which means that, as before, the protocol is resilient to $n - 1 - 2d$ stragglers. We stress that our trick to let P_1 compute the linear operations over the masked inputs and only then reshare it back to parties, is crucial for achieving addition for free - a property that is not trivial to achieve for non-SIMD circuits.

We formally describe our semi-honest protocol in the full version. Note that for each batch of ℓ bilinear instruction, $n - 1$ parties send an element to P_1, whereas P_1 need to share the inputs of the two inputs blocks, thus send-ing $2(n - 1 - d)$ elements. Overall, per a single instruction, each party sends $\frac{n-1+2(n-1-d)}{n \cdot \ell} = \frac{3}{\ell} - \frac{2d+3}{n \cdot \ell}$ field elements, where $d \geq t + \ell - 1$.

Theorem 4.2. *Let f be a n-party functionality over a finite field $\mathbb{F}$ represented by a ℓ-layered SLP, let t be a security threshold parameter and let d be a param-eter such that $d \geq t + \ell - 1$, $n \geq 2d + 1$ and $|\mathbb{F}| > n + d + \ell + 1$. Then, our protocol computes f in the $\mathcal{F}_{\mathrm{LinRand}}$-hybrid model with t-semi-honest-security, $(n - (2d + 1))$-stragglers-resilience and communication of $\frac{3}{\ell} - \frac{2d+3}{n \cdot \ell}$ field elements sent per party for each bilinear instruction.*

The proof in the full version. Observe that when $\ell \geq 3$ (i.e., packing at least 3 secrets on each polynomial), we have $\frac{3}{\ell} - \frac{2d+3}{n \cdot \ell} < 1$, which means that each party sends *less than one field element* for each bilinear instruction. When $\ell = 2$, then the cost is less than 1.5 elements sent per party. We thus obtain a protocol which provide the best of both worlds: it achieves both minimal communication and stragglers resilience. This is in contrast to $\Pi_{\mathrm{SH}}^{\mathrm{base}}$ which achieves minimal communication without any resilience to stragglers, and $\Pi_{\mathrm{SH}}^{\mathrm{single}}$ which can handle stragglers but at the cost of (at least) doubling the communication cost. We provide exact cost analysis with concrete numbers in the full version.

5   From Semi-honest to Malicious Security

In this section, we show how to augment our protocol from the previous section to malicious security (with abort). Our goal is to achieve malicious security without increasing the amortized communication cost per instruction, and while maintaining the resilience to stragglers.

We begin by defining the meaning of security and resilience to stragglers in the presence of malicious adversaries. Note that unlike the definition with semi-honest adversaries, we no longer guarantee a successful termination of the protocol, but rather provide security with abort. The straggler-robust correct-ness, however, will still require that the protocol ends successfully if the parties act honestly, even if in each round τ messages, chosen by the adversary, are dropped. In addition to this requirement, we also need the protocol to be secure in the presence of an adversary who controls t parties and, in addition, can drop any τ messages in each round of communication.

Following the standard ideal-world vs. real-world paradigm of MPC [14,29], let $\mathcal{A}$ be an adversary who chooses a set of parties before the beginning of the execution and corrupts them. We assume that the adversary is *rushing*, meaning that it first receives the messages sent by the honest parties in each round, and only then determines the corrupted parties' messages in this round. Let $\mathrm{REAL}_{\Pi,\mathcal{A},I}^{f}(1^{\kappa}, \boldsymbol{x})$ be a random variable that consists of the view of the adversary $\mathcal{A}$ controlling a set of parties I, and the honest parties' outputs, following an execution of Π over a vector of inputs $\boldsymbol{x}$ to compute f with security parameter κ. Similarly, we define an ideal-world execution with an ideal-world adversary $\mathcal{S}$, where $\mathcal{S}$ and the honest parties interact with a trusted party who computes f for them. We consider secure computation *with abort*, meaning that $\mathcal{S}$ is allowed to send the trusted party computing f a special command abort. Specifically, $\mathcal{S}$ can send an abort command instead of handing the corrupted parties' inputs to the trusted party (causing all parties to abort the execution), or, hand the inputs and then, after receiving the corrupted parties' outputs from the trusted party, send the abort command, and prevent them from receiving their outputs. We denote by $\mathrm{IDEAL}_{f,\mathcal{S},I}(1^{\kappa}, \boldsymbol{x})$, the random variable that consists of the output of $\mathcal{S}$ and the honest parties in an ideal execution to compute f, over a vector of inputs $\boldsymbol{x}$, where $\mathcal{S}$ controls a set of parties I. The security definition states that a protocol Π securely computes f with statistical error ε, if for every real-world adversary there exists an ideal-world adversary, such that the statistical distance between the two random variables is less than ε.

Definition 5.1 (Straggler resilience, malicious security). *Let f be an n-party functionality and let $\varepsilon = \varepsilon(\kappa)$ be a statistical error bound. We say that Π computes f with t-malicious-security-with-abort and τ-straggler-resilience with statistical error ε if it satisfies the following properties:*

- STRAGGLER-ROBUST CORRECTNESS: *If all parties act honestly, then Π terminates successfully (i.e. each party receives its prescribed output $f_i(\boldsymbol{x})$) even if in each communication round, τ messages, chosen adaptively by the adversary, are not delivered.*
- SECURITY WITH STRAGGLERS: *For every real-world malicious adversary $\mathcal{A}$ who controls a set of parties I with $|I| \leq t$ and, in addition, can choose adaptively any τ messages to drop in each round of communication, there exists an ideal-world simulator $\mathcal{S}$, such that for every κ and every vector of inputs $\boldsymbol{x}$ it holds that $SD\left(\mathrm{REAL}_{\Pi,\mathcal{A},I}^{f}(1^{\kappa}, \boldsymbol{x}), \mathrm{IDEAL}_{f,\mathcal{S},I}(1^{\kappa}, \boldsymbol{x})\right) \leq \varepsilon$ where $SD(X, Y)$ is the statistical distance between X and Y[3].*

---

[3] Note that we prove statistical security of our protocol in a hybrid model where parties hold correlated randomness. The resulting combined protocol provides computational security when this setup is instantiated using PRSS.

To construct a protocol that satisfies the definition, we work in two steps. First, we present a protocol to compute the program until (and not including) the output-revealing stage, that provides privacy in the presence of malicious adversaries. As we will see, maybe somewhat contrary to intuition, our semi-honest protocol from the previous section may leak private data to a malicious adversary. We thus show how to fix this without changing the communication cost or the round complexity and whilst providing the same resilience to stragglers.

Then, we add a step, before the revealing of the output, in which the parties verify the correctness of the computation, and abort with high probability if cheating took place. The properties of this step are: (i) it has sublinear communication (in the size of the program) and so the overall amortized communication cost per instruction remains the same, (ii) it requires a small constant number of rounds and so does not increase the round complexity of our protocol.

We note that although the protocol we describe only guarantees security with *selective* abort, it can be easily augmented to *unanimous* abort as required by the definition above with small constant cost, by running a single Byzantine agreement before the end of the execution. For simplicity, we omit this step from the description.

Before proceeding, we briefly describe two building blocks required by our protocol:

The $\mathcal{F}_{\text{coin}}$ ideal functionality. In our protocol, the parties will sometimes need to produce fresh random coins. The $\mathcal{F}_{\text{coin}}$ functionality, when called by the parties, hands them such coins. To compute $\mathcal{F}_{\text{coin}}$ with abort, the parties can simply generate a random sharing $[\![r]\!]_d$ and open it. In the honest majority setting, there is nothing the adversary can do here beyond causing an abort. We note that to generate any number of coins with constant communication cost, it suffices to call $\mathcal{F}_{\text{coin}}$ once to obtain a seed, and expand it to many pseudo-random coins.

Consistency Check. To check that m sharings $\{[\![x_{j,1} \cdots x_{j,\ell}]\!]_d\}_{j=1}^{m}$ are consistent, we use the well-known method of taking a random linear combination of these sharings, mask the result by adding a random sharing $[\![r_1 \cdots r_\ell]\!]_d$, and open it. For the random linear combination, the parties call $\mathcal{F}_{\text{coin}}$ to obtain the random coefficients.

5.1   Privacy in the Presence of Malicious Adversaries

In this section, we show how to compute a straight-line program with privacy in the presence of a malicious adversary. We begin by showing that DN-style semi-honest protocols which we consider in this work, may leak private information to a malicious adversary in the strong honest majority setting. Recall that in the semi-honest protocol, to carry-out a multiplication between shared inputs $[\![x]\!]_d$ and $[\![y]\!]_d$, the parties send $[\![x \cdot y - r]\!]_{2d}$ to P_1, who reconstruct $x \cdot y - r$ and shares it as $[\![x \cdot y - r]\!]_d$ to the parties. Then, the parties compute $[\![x \cdot y]\!]_d = [\![x \cdot y - r]\!]_d + [\![r]\!]_d$ and obtain a sharing of the output.

The "double-dipping" attack [35]. We now describe an attack that can be carried out by a malicious P_1, when $n > 2d + 1$. This attack was shown in [35] for the setting of $d < n/3$ and works over two multiplication gates/instructions as follows. Assume that the parties multiply $[\![x]\!]_d$ with $[\![y]\!]_d$. Thus, after receiving the masked shares from the parties, P_1 reconstructs $xy - r$ and computes a random sharing $[\![x \cdot y - r]\!]_d$. Then, P_1 sends the correct shares to all parties except for P_n, to whom it adds 1 to the intended share. Thus, all the parties, except for P_n, can compute the correct share of $x \cdot y$ by adding $[\![r]\!]_d$. Denote the share of $x \cdot y$ held by P_i by α_i. This means that P_n will hold $\alpha_n + 1$. Next, assume that the parties proceed to the next multiplication, where they need to multiply $[\![xy]\!]_d$ with $[\![z]\!]_d$, and denote the share of z held by P_i by z_i. Note that once P_1 receives $2d$ shares, it can not only reconstruct $xyz - r'$, where r' is the random masking for this multiplication, but also can compute the remaining $n - 1 - 2d$ shares that should be sent. In particular, after receiving shares from any subset of $2d$ parties that does not contain P_n, it can compute the correct share that should be sent by P_n, i.e., $\alpha_n \cdot z_n - r'_n$, where r'_n is P_n's share of r'. However, P_n will send the share $(\alpha_n + 1) \cdot z_n - r'_n$, which means that P_1 can compute $(\alpha_n \cdot z_n - r'_n) - ((\alpha_n + 1) \cdot z_n - r'_n) = z_n$, obtaining the secret share z_n of P_n.

Previous Solutions. The main reason for the above attack is that in the strong honest majority setting, there is redundancy in the masking. Indeed, the solution suggested in [35] is to use as masking the sharing $[\![r]\!]_{n-1}$, which means that $x \cdot y - r$ can be reconstructed only given the shares of all parties. A different solution was given in [26], where a consistency check was carried-out between each two layers of the program. This prevents the above attack, since by sending an incorrect share to P_n, the resulting sharing of $x \cdot y$ becomes inconsistent. Thus, a consistency check will detect this type of cheating and prevents P_1 from proceeding with the attack to the multiplication in the next layer. However, these solutions are not sufficient in our case, since either they require all parties to participate, preventing any resilience to stragglers, or, double the round complexity of the protocol.

A New Solution with Straggler Resilience. We thus need a new solution that achieves privacy, while allowing P_1 to proceed without requiring all parties' shares of $x \cdot y - r$. Our idea is to have a *different independent masking value for each subset of $2d + 1$ parties*. In particular, for each subset T of $2d + 1$ parties, we want the parties to hold a pair $([\![r_T]\!]_d, [\![r_T]\!]_{2d})$ which can be used in the multiplication protocol. This however raises a question. If each subset of parties have a different masking, then which masking share should a party use when it sends its message to P_1? To overcome this, we add an additional constraint: the parties should hold a pair $([\![r_T]\!]_d, [\![r_T]\!]_{2d})$ for each subset T under the constraint that each P_i's share in $[\![r_T]\!]_{2d}$ will be *identical* for all subsets. If this holds, then only one possible message exists for each P_i to send to P_1 (i.e., $x_i \cdot y_i - r_i$ where r_i is the random share used by P_i as a mask). We will see later how to generate such correlated randomness in an efficient way (without requiring the parties to store $\binom{n}{2d+1}$ different polynomials). Assuming the parties have a way to generate such random sharings, our private protocol to multiply $[\![x]\!]_d$ and $[\![y]\!]_d$ is:

$\Pi_{\text{mult}}^{\text{priv}}$:

- **Inputs**: Each P_i holds two inputs shares x_i, y_i and a random share r_i. For each subset $T \subset \{P_1, \ldots, P_n\}$ such that $|T| = 2d + 1$, the parties hold a sharing $[\![r_T]\!]_d$, where $r_T = \sum_{j|P_j \in T} \lambda_j \cdot r_j$, with λ_j being the corresponding Lagrange coefficient for the $2d$-polynomial q_T defined such that $q_T(j) = r_j$, for each j for which $P_j \in T$.
- **The protocol**:
  1. Each party P_i locally computes $e_i = x_i \cdot y_i - r_i$ and sends it to P_1.
  2. Let $e_{i_1}, \ldots, e_{i_{2d}}$ be the first $2d$ messages received by P_1 and let T be a subset of parties defined as $T = \{P_1, P_{i_1}, \ldots, P_{i_{2d}}\}$. Then, P_1 view $e_1, e_{i_1}, \ldots, e_{i_{2d}}$ as points on a polynomial p of $2d$-degree such that $p(1) = e_1$ and $\forall j \in [2d] : p(i_j) = e_{i_j}$ and uses them to compute (via Lagrange interpolation) the value $e_0 = p(0)$.
  3. P_1 chooses a new random sharing $[\![e_0]\!]_d$, under the constraint that d shares equal to 0, and sends each party P_i, with a non-zero share, its share. In addition, it sends T to all parties.
  4. The parties locally compute $[\![x \cdot y]\!]_d = [\![e_0]\!]_d + [\![r_T]\!]_d$.

It is easy to see that if the parties follow the protocol, then they will obtain $[\![x \cdot y]\!]_d$. Privacy is achieved since now there is no redundancy in the secret sharing of the masking random element, and each random share held by each party is independent from the other parties' random shares. We show this formally in the full version.

Efficient Generation of the Correlated Randomness. Recall that our protocol requires that for each multiplication, each P_i will hold a random independent r_i and a sharing $[\![r_T]\!]_d$ for each subset of parties T of size $2d + 1$, such that $r_T = \sum_{j|P_j \in T} \lambda_j \cdot r_j$. A simple way to achieve this, is to let each P_i choose a random r_i and share it to the other parties as $[\![r_i]\!]_d$. Upon holding $[\![r_i]\!]_d$ for each $i \in [n]$, the parties can locally compute $[\![r_T]\!]_d = \sum_{j|P_j \in T} \lambda_j \cdot [\![r_j]\!]_d$ for each subset T of size $2d + 1$. We note that in order to save cost, the parties can defer the last step of computing $[\![r_T]\!]_d$ until they receive the subset T from P_1. This is significant since now the parties need to compute just a single sharing of degree d and not $\binom{n}{2d+1}$.

To generate any number of such correlated randomness without any interaction but a short setup step, each party P_i can distribute a set of seeds to the other parties. As explained in Sect. 3, it is possible to non-interactively generate any number of Shamir's secret sharings $[\![r_i]\!]_d$ from these seeds and then continue as above. Note that since P_i knows all seeds, it can locally compute r_i and use it as its mask in the multiplication operation as required.

In the full version of this paper we show how to extend the solution when multiple secrets are packed together.

5.2   Verifying Correctness of the Computation

In the previous section, we showed how to prevent leakage of private data during the computation of the program. However, nothing prevents a malicious adversary from cheating by sending false messages, causing the output to be incorrect. To achieve correctness, we add a step to our protocol, before the output is revealed, where the parties verify the correctness of the computation, and abort if cheating is detected. This additional step satisfies two desired properties: (i) it is a short constant-round protocol; (ii) it has *sublinear communication* in the size of the program, which means that *amortized* over the program, the communication cost remains the same.

We define the ideal functionality $\mathcal{F}_{\mathsf{vrfy}}$ to verify that multiplications were carried out correctly. $\mathcal{F}_{\mathsf{vrfy}}$ receives from the honest parties their shares of all inputs, the inputs to multiplications operations and all outputs of the program. Then, it reconstructs the secrets and check for each value, that it is correct *given* the values held by the parties as inputs for the multiplications that precede it. We stress that it suffices for only the honest parties to send their shares, since they fully define the secrets (as we will see, a consistency check is carried out before calling $\mathcal{F}_{\mathsf{vrfy}}$ in our main protocol and so we are guaranteed at this stage that all sharings are consistent).

The formal description appears in the full version of the paper. We show how to realize $\mathcal{F}_{\mathsf{vrfy}}$ using distributed zero-knowledge proofs from [8], adapted to our setting, in the full version.

5.3   Putting It All Together - The Main Protocol

We are now ready the present our main protocol with security against malicious adversaries. The protocol works by having the parties run the private protocol to compute the program, and then, before revealing the output, call the ideal functionality $\mathcal{F}_{\mathsf{vrfy}}$ to verify that the sharings they obtained throughout the execution, are correct. Since $\mathcal{F}_{\mathsf{vrfy}}$ requires the sharings it receives to be consistent, then the parties run a batch consistency check before calling $\mathcal{F}_{\mathsf{vrfy}}$.

STRAGGLERS RESILIENCE. We show what resilience our protocol guarantees:

- *Input sharing step*: In this step, we require the parties to send a masked input $\hat{x}_i = x_i + r$ to all parties and not only to P_1. Looking on an epoch that consists of parties sending their masked input to the other parties, and then sending messages to P_1 in the first layer of bi-linear instructions, it is easy to see that even if $n - (2d + 1)$ messages are lost, party P_1 will receive $2d$ messages and will be able to proceed to the next epoch.
- *Private computation of the program*: Our new protocol in Sect. 5.1 can handle $n - (2d + 1)$ dropped messages in each epoch.
- *Verification step*: A subtle issue that arises here is the effect of stragglers existence in the private protocol, on the consistency check and $\mathcal{F}_{\mathsf{vrfy}}$. Specifically, if different subset of parties participate in each epoch, then the sharings used in the consistency check and $\mathcal{F}_{\mathsf{vrfy}}$ are held by different subset of parties,

which seems problematic. Nevertheless, we observe that the number of such subsets is bounded by the depth of the program. Hence, we have three possible solutions. If the depth of the program is low, then the parties can run these two steps for each subset separately (recall that each such subset is of size $2d + 1$ and so an honest majority required by the protocols is guaranteed). Since the cost in these final steps is anyway low and sublinear in the size of the program, we can afford running them several times. If the depth is larger than the number of possible subsets $\binom{n}{\tau}$ (with τ being the number of stragglers), then we can simply go over all possible subsets. Alternatively, if the program is very deep, then one can simply assume that all messages that were delayed during the computation, arrive by the time the parties reach the final steps. While this seems as a slight weakening of our stragglers-resilience model, note that even with this assumption, our protocol has a huge advantage over protocols with no resilience to stragglers, where the parties need to wait for all messages to arrive when computing *each layer*, and not only at the end of the entire computation.

Note that in the former solution we need to assume that no messages are dropped inside this step, since in each subset of $2d + 1$ parties, if a message is lost, we might lose the honest majority and hence the security guarantees. Since this step is a short constant-round protocol, this seems as a mild assumption.

– *Output Reconstruction*: If $2d + 1$ shares arrive to each party, then at least $d + 1$ shares are sent by honest parties and so are correct. This implies that the party can either reconstruct its correct output or abort if cheating took place. Thus, this step can also withstand $n - (2d + 1)$ stragglers.

The formal description appears in the full version of the paper. We thus obtain a maliciously-secured protocol, with the same (amortized) communication cost and same stragglers resilience as for semi-honest adversaries (with a small caveat for the short verification step). This is summarized in the following Theorem (the proof can be found in the full version):

Theorem 5.1. *Let $\mathbb{F}$ be a finite field, let f be a n-party functionality represented by a ℓ-layered straight-line program over $\mathbb{F}$ with S bilinear instructions, let t be a security threshold parameter and let d be a parameter such that $d \geq t + \ell - 1$, $n \geq 2d + 1$ and $|\mathbb{F}| > n + d + \ell + 1$. Then, our protocol computes f in the $(\mathcal{F}_{\mathrm{LinRand}}, \mathcal{F}_{\mathrm{coin}}, \mathcal{F}_{\mathrm{vrfy}})$-hybrid model with t-malicious-security-with-abort, $(n - (2d + 1))$-stragglers-resilience, with statistical error $\frac{1}{|\mathbb{F}|}$, and communication cost of $\left(\frac{3}{\ell} - \frac{2d+3}{n \cdot \ell}\right) S + o(S)$ field elements sent per party.*

The protocol has statistical error of $\frac{1}{|\mathbb{F}|}$ due to the consistency check that may fail. For small fields the error can be reduced by repeating the check with independent randomness.

Acknowledgements. We thank Tuvi Etzion for helpful pointers to the literature on covering designs. E. Boyle supported by ISF grant 1861/16, AFOSR Award FA9550-17-1–0069, and ERC Project HSS (852952). N. Gilboa supported by ISF grant 2951/20,

ERC grant 876110, and a grant by the BGU Cyber Center. Y. Ishai supported by ERC Project NTSC (742754), NSF-BSF grant 2015782, BSF grant 2018393, and ISF grant 2774/20. A. Nof supported by ERC Project NTSC (742754).

References

1. Covering Designs. www.dmgordon.org/cover//
2. Alon, N., Merritt, M., Reingold, O., Taubenfeld, G., Wright, R.N.: Tight bounds for shared memory systems accessed by byzantine processes. Distrib. Comput. (2005)
3. Badrinarayanan, S., Jain, A., Manohar, N., Sahai, A.: Secure MPC: laziness leads to GOD. In: ASIACRYPT (2020)
4. Baron, J., El Defrawy, K., Lampkins, J., Ostrovsky, R.: How to withstand mobile virus attacks, revisited. In: ACM PODC (2014)
5. Ben-Or, M., Goldwasser, S., Wigderson, A.: Completeness theorems for non-cryptographic fault-tolerant distributed computation (extended abstract). In: ACM STOC (1988)
6. Bendlin , R., Damgård, I.: Threshold decryption and zero-knowledge proofs for lattice-based cryptosystems. In: TCC (2010)
7. Bonawitz, K.A., et al.: Practical secure aggregation for privacy-preserving machine learning. In: ACM CCS (2017)
8. Boneh, D., Boyle, E., Corrigan-Gibbs, H., Gilboa, N., Ishai, Y.: Zero-knowledge proofs on secret-shared data via fully linear PCPs. In: Boldyreva, A., Micciancio, D. (eds.) CRYPTO 2019. LNCS, vol. 11694, pp. 67–97. Springer, Cham (2019). https://doi.org/10.1007/978-3-030-26954-8_3
9. Boyle, E., Couteau, G., Gilboa, N., Ishai, Y., Kohl, L., Scholl, P.: Efficient pseudorandom correlation generators: silent OT extension and more. In: CRYPTO (2019)
10. Boyle, E., et al.: Correlated pseudorandom functions from variable-density LPN. In: FOCS (2020)
11. Boyle, E., Gilboa, N., Ishai, Y., Nof, A.: Practical fully secure three-party computation via sublinear distributed zero-knowledge proofs. In: ACM CCS (2019)
12. Boyle, E., Gilboa, N., Ishai, Y., Nof, A.: Efficient fully secure computation via distributed zero-knowledge proofs. In: ASIACRYPT (2020)
13. Brakerski, Z., Chandran, N., Goyal, V., Jain, A., Sahai, A., Segev, G.: Hierarchical functional encryption. In: ITCS (2017)
14. Canetti, R.: Security and composition of multiparty cryptographic protocols. J. Cryptol. 13(1), 143–202 (2000)
15. Canetti, R., Goldwasser, S.: An efficient Threshold public key cryptosystem secure against adaptive chosen ciphertext attack. In: EUROCRYPT (1999)
16. Chaum, D., Crépeau, C., Damgård, I.: Multiparty unconditionally secure protocols (extended abstract). In: ACM STOC (1988)
17. Choudhuri, A. R., Goel, A., Green, M., Jain, A., Kaptchuk, G.: Fluid MPC: secure multiparty computation with dynamic participants. In: CRYPTO (2021)
18. Cramer, R., Damgård, I., Ishai, Y.: Share conversion, pseudorandom secret-sharing and applications to secure computation. In: TCC (2005)
19. Damgård, I., Ishai, Y.: Scalable secure multiparty computation. In: CRYPTO (2006)
20. Damgård, I., Ishai, Y., Krøigaard, M.: Perfectly secure multiparty computation and the computational overhead of cryptography. In: EUROCRYPT (2010)
21. Damgård, I., Ishai, Y., Krøigaard, M., Nielsen, J.B., Smith, A.D.: Scalable multiparty computation with nearly optimal work and resilience. In: CRYPTO (2008)

22. Damgård, I., Buus Nielsen, J.: Scalable and unconditionally secure multiparty computation. In: CRYPTO (2007)
23. Damgård, I., Thorbek, R.: Non-interactive proofs for integer multiplication. In: EUROCRYPT (2007)
24. Franklin, M.K., Yung, M.: Communication complexity of secure computation (extended abstract). In: ACM STOC (1992)
25. Füredi, Z.: Turán type problems. surveys in combinatorics **166**, 253–300 (1991)
26. Furukawa, J., Lindell, Y.: Two-thirds honest-majority MPC for malicious adversaries at almost the cost of semi-honest. In: ACM CCS (2019)
27. Beck, G., Goel, A., Jain, A., Kaptchuk, G.: Order-c secure multiparty computation for highly repetitive circuits. In: EUROCRYPT (2021)
28. Gilboa, N., Ishai, Y.: Compressing cryptographic resources. In: CRYPTO (1999)
29. Goldreich, O.: The foundations of cryptography, vol. 2, Cambridge University Press (2004)
30. Goldreich, O., Micali, S., Wigderson, A.: How to play any mental game or A completeness theorem for protocols with honest majority. In: ACM STOC (1987)
31. Gordon, D., Ranellucci, S., Wang, X.: Secure computation with low communication from cross-checking. In: ASIACRYPT (2018)
32. Gordon, D.M., Stinson, D.R.: Coverings. In: Handbook of Combinatorial Designs, pp. 391–398 (2006)
33. Gordon, S.D., Starin, D., Yerukhimovich, A.: The more the merrier: reducing the cost of large scale MPC. In: EUROCRYPT (2021)
34. Goyal, V., Li, H., Ostrovsky, R., Polychroniadou, A., Song, Y.: ATLAS: efficient and scalable MPC in the honest majority setting. In: CRYPTO (2021)
35. Goyal, V., Liu, Y., Song, Y.: Communication-efficient unconditional MPC with guaranteed output delivery. In: CRYPTO (2019)
36. Goyal, V., Polychroniadou, A., Song, Y.: Unconditional communication-efficient MPC via hall's marriage theorem. In: CRYPTO (2021)
37. Goyal, V., Song, Y., Zhu, C.: Guaranteed output delivery comes free in honest majority MPC. In: CRYPTO (2020)
38. Guo, Y., Pass, R., Shi, E.: Synchronous, with a chance of partition tolerance. In: CRYPTO (2019)
39. Wang, H., Pieprzyk, J.: Shared generation of pseudo-random functions with cumulative maps. In: CT-RSA (2003)
40. Hadzilacos, V.: Issues of fault tolerance in concurrent computations (databases, reliability, transactions, agreement protocols, distributed computing). PhD thesis (1985)
41. Hirt, M., Mularczyk, M.: Efficient MPC with a mixed adversary. In: Information-Theoretic Cryptography ITC (2020)
42. Keidar, I., Shraer, A.: How to choose a timing model. IEEE Trans. Parallel Distrib. Syst. **19**, 1367–1380 (2008)
43. Koo, C.Y.: Secure computation with partial message loss. In: TCC (2006)
44. Micali, S., Sidney, R.: A simple method for generating and sharing pseudo-random functions, with applications to clipper-like key escrow systems. In: CRYPTO (1995)
45. Raipin Parvédy, P., Raynal, M.: Uniform agreement despite process omission failures. In: International Parallel and Distributed Processing Symposium (IPDPS) (2003)
46. Perry, K.J., Toueg, S.: Distributed agreement in the presence of processor and communication faults. IEEE Trans. Softw. Eng. **12**, 477–482 (1986)
47. Raynal, M.: Consensus in synchronous systems: a concise guided tour. In: Symposium on Dependable Computing (PRDC) (2002)

48. Shamir, A.: How to share a secret. ACM, Commun. (1979)
49. Sidorenko, A.: What we know and what we do not know about turán numbers. Graphs and Combinatorics **11**(2), 179–199 (1995)
50. Turán, P.: On an external problem in graph theory. Mat. Fiz. Lapok **48**, 436–452 (1941)
51. Wills, J.M.: Research problems. periodica mathematica hungarica **14**(2), 189–191 (1983). https://doi.org/10.1007/BF01855430
52. Chi-Chih Yao, A.: How to generate and exchange secrets (extended abstract). In: FOCS (1986)
53. Zikas, V., Hauser, S., Maurer, U.: Realistic failures in secure multi-party computation. In: TCC (2009)

Blockchains Enable Non-interactive MPC

Vipul Goyal[1,2], Elisaweta Masserova[1(✉)], Bryan Parno[1], and Yifan Song[1]

[1] Carnegie Mellon University, Pittsburgh, USA
{goyal,parno}@cmu.edu, elisawem@cs.cmu.edu, yifans2@andrew.cmu.edu
[2] NTT Research, Palo Alto, USA

Abstract. We propose to use blockchains to achieve MPC which does not require the participating parties to be online simultaneously or interact with each other. Parties who contribute inputs but do not wish to receive outputs can go offline after submitting a single message. In addition to our main result, we study combined communication- and state-complexity in MPC, as it has implications for the communication complexity of our main construction. Finally, we provide a variation of our main protocol which additionally provides guaranteed output delivery.

1 Introduction

Secure Multiparty Computation (MPC) [Yao82, GMW87] enables parties to evaluate an arbitrary function in a secure manner, i.e., without revealing anything besides the outcome of the computation. MPC is increasingly important in the modern world and allows people to securely accomplish a number of difficult tasks. Obtaining efficient MPC protocols is thus a relevant problem and it has indeed been extensively studied [Yao82, GMW87, GMPP16]. One important question is the round complexity of MPC schemes. In the semi-honest case, in 1990, Beaver et al. [BMR90] gave the first constant-round MPC protocol for three or more parties. A number of works [KOS03, Pas04, Goy11] aiming to analyze and reduce round complexity followed, both in the semi-honest and fully malicious models. In 2016, Garg et al. [GMPP16] proved that four rounds are necessary to achieve secure MPC in the fully malicious case in the plain model. Four round MPC protocols have been recently proposed [BHP17, BGJ+18, CCG+20], resolving the questions of round complexity.

Unfortunately, solutions that achieve even the optimal round complexity are still problematic for many applications since these solutions typically require synchronous communication from the participants – imagine for example the U.S. voting process. If the voting is conducted via secure multi-party computation, all participants are required to be online at the same time. It is unrealistic to assume that all of the eligible U.S. voters can be persuaded to be online for an *entire Election Day*. In this work, we rely on blockchains to achieve MPC that *does not require participants to be online at the same time or interact with each other.*

K. Nissim and B. Waters (Eds.): TCC 2021, LNCS 13043, pp. 162–193, 2021.
https://doi.org/10.1007/978-3-030-90453-1_6

Such non-interactive solutions advance the state of the art of secure multi-party computation, opening up a whole new realm of possible applications. For example, *passive data collection* for privacy preserving collaborative machine learning becomes possible. Federated learning is already used to train machine learning models for the keyboards of mobile devices for the purposes of autocorrect and predictive typing [Go17]. Unfortunately, using off-the-shelf MPC protocols to perform such training securely is not straight-forward. Not all smartphones are online at the same time and it might even be unknown how many devices will end up participating. In contrast, off-the-shelf MPC protocols typically assume that all (honest) participants are indeed online during some time period, and the number of participants is known. This leads us to the following question:

Can we construct a secure MPC protocol which does not require the parties to be online at the same time and guarantees privacy and correctness even if all but one of the parties are fully malicious? Furthermore, is it possible to design such a protocol under the constraint that only a single message is required from the parties supplying the inputs, and the parties can go offline after submitting this message if they are not interested in learning the output?

Consider such a protocol in the use case outlined above – each smartphone could independently send a single message to a server, and at the end of the collection period the server would obtain the model trained on the submitted inputs, all while preserving the privacy of the gathered inputs.

1.1 Our Results

In our work, we provide a solution for MPC which achieves the property that each MPC participant who supplies inputs but does not wish to receive the output is not required to interact with other such participants and can go offline after sending only a single message. We additionally provide variations of our protocol that offer further desirable properties.

Before we provide the formal theorem statements, we discuss the protocol execution model and the notation.

In our work, we assume the existence of append-only bulletin boards that allow parties to publish data and receive a confirmation that the data was published in return. Furthermore, we assume a public key infrastructure (PKI). Finally, we rely on conditional storage and retrieval systems (CSaRs, see Sect. 2 for details). Roughly, CSaR systems allow a user to submit a secret along with a release condition. Later, if a (possibly different) user is able to satisfy this release condition, the secret is privately sent to this user. Intuitively, during the process, the secrets cannot be modified and no information is leaked about the secrets. We require that CSaRs are used as ideal functionalities. We note that due to the fact that existing CSaR systems [GKM+20,BGG+20] rely on blockchains, and bulletin boards can be realized using blockchains as well [GG17,CGJ+17,Kap20], relying on bulletin boards in our construction effectively does not add extra assumptions. In the following, for simplicity, we will state that we design our protocols in the blockchain model. Finally, we assume IND-CCA secure public key encryption, and digital signatures.

In our construction, we distinguish between parties who supply inputs (dubbed *MPC contributors*) and parties who wish to receive outputs (dubbed *evaluators*).

We are now ready to introduce our first result:

Theorem 1 (Informal). *Any MPC protocol π secure against fully-malicious adversaries can be transformed into another MPC protocol π' in the blockchain model that provides security with abort against fully-malicious adversaries and does not require participants to be online at the same time. Only a single message is required from the MPC contributors (the evaluators might be required to produce multiple messages). The adversary is allowed to corrupt as many MPC contributors in π' as is supported by the protocol π.*

In addition to this result, we discuss ways to optimize our construction. To this end, we explain why the *combined communication- and state complexity* of the underlying MPC protocol is of a particular importance in our construction. Briefly, both the communication- and state complexities of the underlying MPC translate directly into the number of CSaR storage- and retrieval requests (and thus communication complexity) in our overall construction. We describe a protocol in the plain model which relies on multi-key fully homomorphic encryption (MFHE). Its combined communication- and state complexity is independent of the function that we are computing. While optimizing communication complexity has received considerable attention in the community in the past few years, optimizing internal state complexity has been largely overlooked. We believe that this particular problem might be exciting on its own. In our construction which optimizes the combined communication and state complexity, we assume multi-key fully homomorphic encryption, probabilistically checkable proofs, collision-resistant hash functions, and IND-CPA secure public key encryption. The result that we achieve here is the following:

Theorem 2 (Informal). *Let f be an N-party function. Protocol 6 is an MPC protocol computing f in the standard model and secure against fully malicious adversaries corrupting up to $t < N$ parties. Its communication and state complexity depend only on security parameters, number of parties, and input and output sizes. In particular, the combined communication- and state complexity is independent of the function f.*

Using this MPC protocol in combination with our first construction, under the assumptions that we rely on in our main construction and in the MPC construction with optimized communication- and state complexity, we achieve the following:

Corollary 1 (Informal). *There exists an MPC protocol π' in the blockchain model which provides security with abort against fully-malicious adversaries and does not require participants to be online at the same time. Only a single message is required from the MPC contributors (the evaluators might be required to* *produce multiple messages). Furthermore, the communication complexity of this protocol is independent of the function that is being computed using this MPC protocol.*

Finally, we achieve an MPC protocol which requires only a single message from MPC contributors with the additional property of *guaranteed output delivery*, meaning that adversarial parties cannot prevent honest parties from receiving the output. For this, we in particular rely on the underlying protocol having guaranteed output delivery as well (and thus requiring the majority of the MPC contributors to be honest). We rely on the same assumptions (PKI, CSaRs, append-only bulletin boards etc.) as the ones used in our main construction. The formal result that we achieve is the following:

Theorem 3 (Informal). *Any MPC protocol π that is secure against fully-malicious adversaries and provides guaranteed output delivery can be transformed into another MPC protocol π' in the blockchain model that provides security with guaranteed output delivery against fully-malicious adversaries and does not require participants to be online at the same time. Only a single message is required from the MPC contributors (the evaluators might be required to produce multiple messages). The adversary is allowed to corrupt as many MPC contributors in π' as is supported by the protocol π.*

1.2   Technical Overview

In this work, we propose an MPC protocol that does not require participants to be present at the same time. In order to do so, we rely on the following cryptographic building blocks – garbled circuits [Yao82, Yao86, BHR12b], a primitive which we dub conditional storage and retrieval systems (*CSaRs*) and bulletin boards with certain properties. Before we introduce the construction idea, we elaborate on each of these primitives.

Roughly, a garbling scheme allows one to "encrypt" (garble) a circuit and its inputs such that when evaluating the garbled circuit only the output is revealed. In particular, no information about the inputs of other parties or intermediate values is revealed by the garbled circuit or during its evaluation. In our construction we use Yao's garbled circuits [Yao82, Yao86].

In our construction, we rely on bulletin boards which allow parties to publish strings on an append-only log. It must be hard to modify or erase contents from this log. Additionally, we require that parties receive a confirmation ("proof of publish") that the string was published and that other parties can verify this proof. Such bulletin boards have been extensively used in prior works [GG17, CGJ+17, Kap20] and as pointed out by these works can be realized both from centralized systems such as the Certificate Transparency project [tra20] and decentralized systems such as proof-of-stake or proof-of-work blockchains.

Finally, we define a primitive which we call conditional storage and retrieval systems (CSaRs). Roughly, this primitive allows for the distributed and secure storage- and retrieval of secrets and realizes the following ideal functionality:

– Upon receiving a secret along with a release condition and an identifier, if the identifier was not used before, the secret is stored and all participants are notified of a valid secret storage request. The release condition is simply an NP statement.
– Upon receiving an (identifier, witness) from a user, the ideal functionality checks whether a secret with this identifier exists and if so, whether the given witness satisfies the release condition of this secret record. If so, the secret is sent to the user who submitted the release request.

While systems that provide a similar primitive has been proposed in the past [GKM+20, BGG+20] we provide a clean definition that captures the essence of this functionality. We instantiate the CSaR with eWEB [GKM+20][1], which stands for "Extractable Witness Encryption on a Blockchain". Roughly, it allows users to encode a secret along with a release condition and store the secret on a blockchain. Once a user proves that they are able to satisfy the release condition, blockchain miners jointly and privately release the secret to this user. Along the way, no single party is able to learn any information about the secret.

Our Construction. By relying on bulletin boards, Yao's garbled circuits and CSaRs, we are able to *transform any secure MPC protocol π into another secure MPC protocol π' that provides security with abort and does not require participants to be online at the same time.* At a high level, our idea is as follows: first, each contributor (party who supplies inputs in the protocol) P in the MPC protocol π garbles the next-message function for each round of π. Then, P stores the garbled circuits as well as the garbled keys with a CSaR using carefully designed release conditions. Note that each party P is able to do so individually, without waiting for any information from other parties and can go offline afterwards. Once all contributors have stored their data with the CSaR, one or more "evaluators" (parties who wish to receive the output) interact with the CSaR and use the information stored by the MPC contributors in order to retrieve the garbled circuits and execute the original protocol π. The group of the contributors and the group of evaluators do not need to be the same – in fact, these groups can even be disjoint. The evaluators might change from round to round.

Note that while the high-level overview is simple, there are a number of technical challenges that we must overcome in the actual construction due to its non-interactive nature. For example, since the security of Yao's construction relies on the fact that for each wire only a single key is revealed, we must ensure that each honest garbled circuit is executed only on a *single* set of inputs. The adversary also must not trick a garbled circuit of some honest party A into thinking that a message broadcast by some party C is message m, and tricking a garbled circuit of another honest party B into thinking that C in fact broadcast message $m' \neq m$. Furthermore, we must ensure that it is hard to execute the protocol "out of order", i.e., an adversary cannot execute some round i prior to round j where $i > j$. Such issues do not come up in the setting where parties are

---

[1] Other instantiations are possible, see Sect. 2 for details.

online during the protocol execution and able to witness messages broadcast by other parties.

We solve these issues by utilizing bulletin boards, carefully constructing the release conditions for the garbled circuits and the wire keys, and modifying the next-message functions which must be garbled by the contributors.

Note that the next-message functions from round two onward take as inputs messages produced by the garbled circuits in prior rounds. At the time when the MPC contributors are constructing their circuits, the inputs of other parties are not known, and thus it is not possible to predict which wire key (the one corresponding to 0 or the one corresponding to 1) will be needed during the protocol execution. At the same time, one cannot simply make both wire keys public since the security of the garbled circuit crucially relies on the fact that for each wire only a single wire key can be revealed. We solve this problem by storing both wire keys with the CSaR, utilizing bulletin boards, and requiring the evaluators to publish the output of the garbled circuits of each round. Then, (part of) the CSaR release condition for the wire key corresponding to bit b on some wire w of some party's garbled circuit for round i is that the message from round $i - 1$ is published and contains bit b at position w. This way we ensure that while both options for wire w are "obtainable", only the wire key for bit b (the one that is needed for the execution) is revealed.

Next, note that in our construction we specifically rely on Yao's garbled circuits. Yao's construction satisfies the so-called "selective" notion of security, which requires the adversary to choose its inputs before it sees the garbled circuit (in contrast to the stronger "adaptive" notion of security which would allow the adversary to choose its inputs *after* seeing the garbled circuits [BHR12a]). We ensure that the selective notion of security is sufficient for our construction by requiring that not only the wire keys, but also the garbled circuits are stored with the CSaR. The release conditions both for the garbled circuit for some round i and all its wire keys require a proof that all messages for rounds 1 up to and including round $i - 1$ are published by the evaluators. This way, the evaluators are required to "commit" to the inputs before receiving the selectively secure garbled circuits, which achieves the same effect as adaptive garbled circuits.

As outlined above, we must ensure that it is hard for the adversary to trick the garbled circuit produced by some honest party A into accepting inputs from another honest party B that were not produced by B's circuits. We accomplish this by modifying the next-message function of every party A as follows: in addition to every message m that is produced by some party B, the next-message function takes as input a signature σ on m as well and verifies that the signature is correct. If this is not the case for any of the input messages, the next-message function outputs $\bot$. Otherwise, the next-message function proceeds as usual and in addition to outputting the resulting message it outputs the signature of party A on this message.

Our end goal is to reduce the security of our construction to the security of the underlying MPC protocol π. While utilizing bulletin boards and introducing signatures is a good step forward, we must be careful when designing the CSaR release conditions. The adversary could sign multiple messages for each corrupted contributor in π, publish these messages on the bulletin board and thus receive multiple keys for some wires. To prevent this, the CSaR release condition must consider only the *very first* message published for round $i - 1$ on the bulletin board. This way, we ensure that there is only a single instance of the MPC running (only a single wire key is released for each circuit): even if the adversary is able to sign multiple messages on behalf of various MPC contributors, only the very first message published on the bulletin board for a specific round will be used by the CSaR system to release the wire keys for the next round.

The ideas outlined above are the main ideas in our protocol. We now elaborate on a few additional details:

Note that the next-message function of the protocol typically outputs not only the message for the next round, but also the state which is used in the next round. It is assumed that this state is kept private by the party. In our case, the output of the next-message function will be output by the garbled circuit and thus made available to the evaluator. To ensure that the state is kept private, we further modify the next-message function to add an encryption step at the end: the state is encrypted under the public key of the party who is executing this next-message function. To ensure that the state can be used by the garbled circuit of the party in the next round, we add a state decryption step at the beginning of the next-message function of that round. Similar to the public output of the next-message function, we compute a signature on the encryption of the state and verify this signature in the garbled circuit of the next round.

Finally, note that in the construction outlined above, we use some secret information which does not depend on the particular execution but still must be kept private (secret keys of the parties used for the decryption of the state, signing keys used to sign the output of the next-message function etc.). This information is hard-coded in the garbled circuits. We explain how this can be done in Sect. 3.

We provide all protocol details and outline optimizations in Sect. 3 and give the formal construction in Protocols 1, 2 and 3. The formal security proof is done by providing a simulator for the construction and proving that an interaction with the simulator in the ideal world is indistinguishable from the interaction with an adversary in the real world.

To summarize, using the construction sketched above we achieve the following result:

Theorem 4 (Informal). *Protocols 1, 2 and 3 transform any MPC protocol π secure against fully-malicious adversaries into another MPC protocol π' in the blockchain model that provides security with abort against fully-malicious adversaries and does not require participants to be online at the same time. Only a single message is required from the MPC contributors (the evaluators might be required to produce multiple messages). The adversary is allowed to corrupt as many MPC contributors in π' as is supported by the protocol π.*

In addition to our main protocol that requires only one message from the MPC contributors and does not require any additional functionality from the

CSaR participants apart from the core CSaR functionality itself (storing and releasing secrets), we provide a number of variations that have further desirable properties, such as guaranteed output delivery. We now outline these further contributions.

Improving Efficiency. The efficiency of our construction is strongly tied to the efficiency of the underlying MPC protocol π. Note that in our construction each input wire key of each garbled circuit is stored with the CSaR, and the inputs of the garbled circuits are exactly messages exchanged between the parties *as well as the state information passed from previous rounds*. Thus, the communication- and state complexities translate directly into the number of CSaR store- and release operations that the MPC contributors, as well as later the evaluators, must make. In order to reduce the number of CSaR invocations, we describe an MPC protocol which optimizes the *combined communication and internal-state complexity*. While communication complexity is typically considered to be one of the most important properties of an MPC protocol, state complexity receives relatively little attention. Our main construction shows that there are indeed use cases where *both* the communication and the state complexity matter, and we initiate a study of the combined state- and communication complexity.

Specifically, we introduce an MPC protocol in which the combined communication- and state complexity is independent of the function we are computing. We achieve it in two steps: we start with a protocol secure against semi-malicious adversaries[2] which at the same time has communication- and state complexity which is independent of the function that is being computed. Then, we extend it to provide fully malicious security while taking care to retain the attractive communication- and state complexity properties in the process.

In more detail, we start with the MPC construction by Brakerski et al. [BHP17] which is based on multi-key fully homomorphic encryption (MFHE) and achieves semi-malicious security. We chose this construction in particular because its communication and state complexity depends only on the security parameters, the number of parties, and the input- and output sizes. In particular, note that the construction's combined communication- and state complexity is independent of the function we are computing.

Our next step is to extend this construction so that it provides security against malicious adversaries. For this, we propose to use the zero-knowledge protocol proposed by Kilian [Kil92] that relies on probabilistically checkable proofs (PCPs) and allows a party P to prove the correctness of some statement x to the prover V using a witness w. Along the way, we need to make minor adjustments to Kilian's construction because its state complexity is unfortunately too high for our purposes – in particular, in the original construction, the entire PCP string is stored by the prover to be used in later rounds. After making a minor adjustment – recomputing the PCP instead of storing it – to the construction to address this issue, we use this scheme after each round of

---

[2] Intuitively, semi-malicious adversaries can be viewed as semi-honest adversaries which are allowed to freely choose their random tapes.

the construction by Brakerski et al. in order to prove the correct execution of the protocol by the parties. The resulting construction achieves fully malicious security, and its communication and state complexities are still independent of the function that we are computing.

We provide the details of the construction and analyse its security and communication/state complexity properties in Sect. 5 with the formal protocol description in Protocol 6. In this protocol, we assume the existence of an MFHE scheme with circular security and the existence of a collision-resistant hash functions. We are able to achieve the following result which may be of independent interest:

Lemma 1. *Let f be an N-party function. Protocol 6 is an MPC protocol computing f in the plain model and secure against fully malicious adversaries corrupting up to $t < N$ parties. Its communication and state complexity depend only on security parameters, number of parties, and the input and output sizes. In particular, the communication and state complexity of Protocol 6 is independent of the function f.*

Using this MPC protocol in combination with our first construction, under the assumptions that we rely on in our main construction and in the MPC construction with optimized communication- and state complexity, we achieve the following:

Corollary 2 (Informal). *There exists an MPC protocol π' in the blockchain model that has adversarial threshold $t < N$, provides security with abort against fully-malicious adversaries and does not require participants to be online at the same time. Only a single message is required from the MPC contributors (the evaluators might be required to produce multiple messages). Furthermore, the communication complexity of this protocol is independent of the function that is being computed using this MPC protocol.*

Non-interactive MPC with Guaranteed Output Delivery (GoD). We need to modify our construction in order to provide guaranteed output delivery. In order to achieve GoD, we require the protocol π to have the GoD property as well (thus, the majority of the MPC contributors must be honest). While making this change (in addition to a few minor adjustments) would be enough to guarantee GoD in our construction in the setting with only a single evaluator, it is certainly not sufficient when there are multiple evaluators, some of them dishonest. This is due to the following issue: since we must prevent an adversary from executing honest garbled circuits on multiple different inputs, we cannot simply allow each evaluator to execute garbled circuits on the inputs of its choosing. In particular, the CSaR release conditions must ensure that for each wire only a *single* key is revealed. In our first construction this results in the malicious evaluator being able to prevent an honest evaluator from executing the garbled circuits as intended by submitting an invalid first message for any round. Thus, to ensure guaranteed output delivery while maintaining secrecy, we must ensure that a malicious evaluator posting a wrong message does *not* prevent an honest evaluator from posting a correct message and using it for the key reveal. In particular, we will ensure that only a *correct* (for a definition of "correctness" explained below) message can be used for the wire key reveal.

Note that the inputs to the garbled circuits depend on the evaluators' outputs from the previous rounds. Checking the "correctness" of the evaluators' outputs is not entirely straight-forward since an honest execution of a garbled circuit which was submitted by a dishonest party might produce outputs which look incorrect (for example, have invalid signatures). Thus, simply letting the CSaR system check the signatures on the messages supplied by the evaluators might result in an honest evaluator being denied the wire keys for the next round.

In our GoD construction we overcome this issue largely using the following adjustments:

- all initial messages containing garbled circuits and wire keys are required to be posted before some deadline.
- we use a CSaR with public release (whenever a secret is released, it is released publicly and the information can be viewed by anyone).
- we ensure that it is possible to distinguish between the case where the evaluator is being dishonest, and the case where the evaluator is being honest, but the contributor in π supplied invalid garbled circuits or keys, or did not supply some required piece of information.

We achieve the last point by letting the CSaR system check every output of the evaluator that appears to be of an invalid form (e.g., missing a signature, having an unexpected length, etc.) and verify that the evaluator's output can be explained by the information stored by the contributors in π. In particular, as part of the CSaR's release condition, we require a proof of correct execution for the incorrect-looking garbled circuit outputs. The relation that the CSaR system is required to check in this case is roughly as follows: "The execution of the garbled circuit GC on the wire keys $\{k_i\}_{i \in I}$ results in the output provided by E. Here, the garbled circuit GC is the circuit, and $\{k_i\}_{i \in I}$ are the keys for this circuit reconstructed using the values published by the CSaR which are present on the proof of publish supplied by E". Note that due to the switch to the CSaR with public release, the wire keys used for the computation are indeed accessible to the CSaR system after their first release.

Similar to our first construction, we eventually reduce the security of the new protocol to the security of the original protocol. In addition to our first construction however, since the CSaR system is now able to verify incorrect-looking messages submitted by the evaluators, honest evaluators are always able to advance in the protocol execution. This insight allows us to ensure that honest evaluators do not need to abort with more than a negligible probability along the way. Thus, if the underlying protocol π achieves guaranteed output delivery, the protocol we propose achieves guaranteed output delivery as well.

We give full details of the GoD construction in Sect. 6. The statement about our GoD construction is given below.

Lemma 2 (Informal). *Any MPC protocol π which is secure against fully-malicious adversaries and provides guaranteed output delivery can be transformed into another MPC protocol π' in the blockchain model that provides security with guaranteed output delivery against fully-malicious adversaries and does not require participants to be online at the same time. Only a single message is required from the MPC contributors (the evaluators might be required to produce multiple messages). The adversary is allowed to corrupt as many MPC contributors in π' as is supported by the protocol π.*

1.3 Related Work

Closest to our work is the line of research that studies non-interactive multiparty computation [HIJ+17, FKN94, HLP11], initiated in 1994 by Feige et al. [FKN94], in which a number of parties submit a single message to a server (evaluator) that, upon receiving all of the messages, computes the output of the function. In their work, Feige et al. allow the messages of the parties to be dependent on some shared randomness that must be unknown to the evaluator. Unfortunately, this means that if the evaluator is colluding with one or more of the participants, the scheme becomes insecure. Overcoming this restriction, Halevi et al. [HLP11] started a line of work on non-interactive *collusion-resistant* MPC. Their model of computation required parties to interact *sequentially* with the evaluator (in particular, the order in which the clients connect to the evaluator is known beforehand). Beimel et al. [BGI+14] and Halevi et al. [HIJ+16] subsequently removed the requirement of sequential interaction. Further improving upon these results, the work of Halevi et al. [HIJ+17] removed the requirement of a complex correlated randomness setup that was present in a number of previous works [BGI+14, HIJ+16, GGG+14]. Halevi et al. [HIJ+17] work in a public-key infrastructure (PKI) model in combination with a common random string. As the authors point out, PKI is the minimal possible setup that allows one to achieve the best-possible security in this setting, where the adversary is allowed to corrupt the evaluator and an arbitrary number of parties and learn nothing more than the so-called "residual function", which is the original function restricted to the inputs of the honest parties. In particular, this means that the adversary is allowed to learn the outcome of the original function on *every possible* choice of adversarial inputs.

   Our work differs from the line of work on non-interactive MPC described above in a number of aspects. In contrast to those works, our construction is not susceptible to the adversary learning the residual function – roughly because the adversary must effectively "commit" to its input, and the CSaR system ensures that the adversary only receives a single set of wire keys per honest garbled circuit (the set of wire keys that aligns with the adversarial input). Additionally, in our work the parties do not need to directly communicate with the evaluator. In fact, in our construction that ensures guaranteed output delivery, any party can *spontaneously* decide to become an evaluator and still receive the result – there is no need to rerun the protocol in this case.

Related to us are also the works on reusable non-interactive secure computation (NISC) [AMPR14, BGI+17, BJOV18, CDI+19, CJS14], initiated by Ishai et al. [IKO+11]. Intuitively, reusable NISC allows a receiver to publish a reusable encoding of its input x in a way that allows any sender to let the receiver obtain $f(x, y)$ for any f by sending only a single message to the receiver. In our work, we focus on a multi-party case, where a party that does not need the output is not required to wait for other parties to submit their inputs.

Recently, Benhamouda and Lin [BL20] proposed a model called *multiparty reusable Non-Interactive Secure Computation (mrNISC) Market* that beautifully extends reusable NIZC to the multiparty setting. In this model, parties first commit their inputs to a public bulletin board. Later, the parties can compute a function on-the-fly by sending a public message to an evaluator. An adversary who corrupts a subset of parties learns nothing more about the secret inputs of honest parties than what it can derive from the output of the computation. Importantly, the bulletin board commitments are reusable, and the security guarantee continues to hold even if there are multiple computation sessions. In their work, Benhamouda and Lin mention that any one-round construction is susceptible to the residual attacks and thus slightly relax the non-interactive requirement in order to solve this problem. Indeed, their construction can be viewed as a 2-round MPC protocol with the possibility to reuse messages of the first round for multiple computations. Our scheme shows that when using blockchains it is indeed possible to provide a construction that requires only a single round of interaction from the parties supplying the input and is nonetheless not susceptible to residual attacks. Furthermore, in contrast to the work of Benhamouda and Lin, our construction does not require any trusted setup[3] even in the fully malicious model.

Concurrent to our work, Almashaqbeh et al. [ABH+21] recently published a manuscript which focuses on designing non-interactive MPC protocols which use blockchains to provide *short term* security without residual leakage. They focus on the setting where the inputs of all but one of the parties are public. In this setting, designing one-round MPC can be done easily by having all parties send their input to the only party which holds the secret input. This party can then compute the output and distribute it to other parties. The authors are able to extend the setting to the two-party semi-honest private input setting where one round protocols for the party not getting the output can be easily designed as well. While our protocol provides a worst-case security guarantee, they focus on an incentive-based notion of security. While both constructions bypass the residual leakage issue, their security guarantees might degrade with time. The key challenge in their setting is fairness/guaranteed output delivery which they solve using an incentive-based model of security. Hence their work is essentially unrelated to ours.

Finally, recently two works ([CGG+21] and [GHK+21]) appeared which are inspired by blockchains and focus on improving the flexibility of the MPC protocols. Choudhuri et al. [CGG+21] proposed the notion of *fluid* MPC which allows

---

[3] Other than a PKI.

parties to dynamically join and leave the computation. Gentry et al. [GHK+21] proposed the YOSO ("You Only Speak Once") model which focuses on stateless parties which can only send a single message. Similar to us, their constructions allow the MPC participants to leave after the first round if they are not interested in learning the output. However, to execute the MPC protocol both Choudhuri et al. and Gentry et al. require a number of committees of different parties which interact with each other, and each committee must provide honest majority. Our protocol preserves privacy of inputs even if there is a single evaluator who is dishonest.

2   Preliminaries – CSaRs

In our work, we rely on what we call *conditional storage and retrieval systems* (*CSaRs*) that allow for a secure storage- and retrieval of secrets. In more detail, the user who stores the secret with a CSaR specifies a release condition, and the secret is released if and only if this condition is satisfied. While such systems could be realised via a trusted third party, they can also be realised using a set of parties with the guarantee that some sufficiently large subset of these parties is honest. A user can then distribute its secret between the set of parties, and the CSaR's security guarantee ensures that no subset of parties that is smaller than a defined threshold can use its secret shares to gain information about the secret. Recently, multiple independent works appeared that use blockchains to provide such functionality [GKM+20, BGG+20]. We provide a clean definition of the core functionality that these works aim to provide (without fixating on blockchains) and outline why the eWEB system [GKM+20] satisfies this definition. Note that the system proposed by Benhamouda et al. does not formally explain how the secrets can be stored to- and retrieved from the blockchain given a specific release condition. While this requires further research, it should be possible to take the same approach as is used by the eWEB system. Thus the system by Benhamouda et al. is also a viable candidate for a CSaR instantiation.

Formally, the ideal CSaR functionality is described in Fig. 1. The security of a CSaR system is then defined as follows:

CSaR Security. For any PPT adversary $\mathcal{A}$ there exists a PPT simulator $\mathcal{S}$ with access to our security model $\mathsf{Ideal}_{\mathrm{CSaR}}$ (described in Ideal CSaR), such that the view of $\mathcal{A}$ interacting with $\mathcal{S}$ is computationally indistinguishable from the view in the real execution.

3   Our Non-interactive MPC Construction

We now present our first construction - given an MPC protocol π, we use Yao's garbled circuits as well as a CSaR to transform it into an MPC protocol π' that does not require parties to be online at the same time. The contributors in π do not need to interact with each other. First, we briefly outline the assumptions we make and define the adversarial model.

1. **SecretStore** Upon receiving an (identifier, release condition, secret) tuple $\tau = (id, F, s)$ from a client P, $\mathsf{Ideal}_{\mathrm{CSaR}}$ checks whether id was already used. If not, $\mathsf{Ideal}_{\mathrm{CSaR}}$ stores τ and notifies all participants that a valid storage request with the identifier id and the release condition F has been received from a client P. Here, the release condition is an NP statement.
2. **SecretRelease** Upon receiving an (identifier, witness) tuple (id, w) from some client C, $\mathsf{Ideal}_{\mathrm{CSaR}}$ checks whether there exists a record with the identifier id. If so, $\mathsf{Ideal}_{\mathrm{CSaR}}$ checks whether $F(w) = true$, where F is the release condition corresponding to the secret with the identifier id. If so, $\mathsf{Ideal}_{\mathrm{CSaR}}$ sends the corresponding secret s to client C.

Fig. 1. Ideal CSaR: $\mathsf{Ideal}_{\mathrm{CSaR}}$

Assumptions. We assume a public-key infrastructure and the existence of a CSaR. To distinguish between concurrent executions of the protocol, we give each computation a unique identifier id, and we assume that the evaluators know the public keys of the parties eligible to contribute in the protocol π. We assume the existence of a bulletin board modeled as an append-only log that provides a *proof of publish* which cannot be (efficiently) forged. Such bulletin boards can be implemented in practice via a blockchain. Finally, we assume IND-CCA secure public key encryption, and digital signatures.

For the ease of presentation, we assume the following about the MPC protocol π: (a) it is in a broadcast model, and (b) it has a single output which is made public to all participants in the last round[4].

Adversary Model. We consider a computationally bounded, fully malicious, static adversary $\mathcal{A}$. Once an adversary corrupts a party it remains corrupted: the adversary is not allowed to adaptively corrupt previously honest parties.

3.1   Construction Overview

Intuitively, there are two main steps in the protocol. In the first step, the parties (dubbed "contributors") prepare the garbled circuits (and keys) and store these with the CSaR. In the second step, one or more parties (we dub them "evaluators") use the garbled circuits to execute the original protocol π.

---

[4] Note that these are not real limitations: if a protocol has several outputs, some of which cannot be made public, each party simply broadcasts the encryption of its output under this party' public key. Each party then outputs the concatenation of these ciphertexts. Additionally, later in this section we discuss how protocols with point-to-point channels can be supported in the broadcast model.

Step 1. Preparing Garbled Circuits and Keys. Each party P_j that wishes to participate (contribute inputs) in π starts by garbling the slightly modified next-message functions of each round of π. Typically, the next-message function takes as input some subset of the following: the secret input of the party, local randomness of the party for that particular round, the messages received in the previous rounds, some secret state passed along from the previous round. The output consists of the message that is broadcast as well as the state that is passed to the next round. We make the following modifications: in each round i, instead of the state s_j^i that is passed to the next round, the function outputs the encryption c_j^i of the state as well as a signature $sigpr_j^i$ over this encryption. Additionally, the modified next-message function outputs the public message m_j^i that is supposed to be broadcast by P_j in this round, as well as the signature $sigpub_j^i$ over this message. The secret key as well as the signature key of P_j are hard-coded in the circuit (we explain how it can be done later in this section). Prior to executing the original next-message function, the modified function decrypts the state using the hard-coded secret key of P_j and verifies the signatures on each public message as well as the signature on the state passed in from previous round. Intuitively, these modifications are due to the following reasons:

- The state of the party is passed in an *encrypted state* because the state information is assumed to be private in the original MPC construction.
- The parties need to *sign* their messages (and *verify* signatures on the messages passed as inputs) since we must prevent the adversary from tricking an honest party into acceptance of a message that is supposedly generated by another honest party, but in reality is mauled by the adversary.

Once the garbled circuits are prepared, P_j stores the garbled circuits with CSaR. Note that the next-round functions in particular take messages produced by *other parties* as inputs. Thus, there is no way for the party to know at the time the garbled circuits are constructed, whether the key corresponding to bit 0 or the key corresponding to bit 1 will be chosen for some wire w. To allow an evaluator to execute the garbled circuits anyway, P_j additionally stores both wire keys for each input wire with CSaR, each with a separate CSaR request. This needs to be done for every single round, since in any particular round the inputs will depend on the messages produced by the garbled circuits of other parties in the previous round.

Intuitively, in order to be able to reduce the security of this protocol to the security of the original MPC protocol, we need to ensure not only that the adversary is not able to maul messages of the honest parties and see the parties' private information, but also that the protocol is executed in order and there is only a single instance of the protocol running. This is ensured by carefully constructing conditions that must be met in order to release the garbled circuits and wire keys. In order to release a garbled circuit for some round i, a party needs to provide a proof that the execution of the protocol up to and including round $i - 1$ is finalized. In order to release a wire key corresponding to bit b on a wire corresponding to position p of the input to some garbled circuit, a party needs to additionally provide a proof that the input bit to position p in this circuit is indeed bit b. In the following, we first explain how the protocol is executed, and then explain how exactly the release conditions look like.

Step 2. Executing π. Once all required information is stored, an evaluator E can execute the original MPC protocol π. It is not required that E is one of the parties participating in the protocol π and in fact, there can be multiple evaluators (for simplicity, we refer to all of them as "E"). E executes the garbled circuits round-by-round. Once E has executed all garbled circuits for a certain round, E publishes the concatenation of the output of these circuits on a the bulletin board. Then, E uses the proof of publishing of this message in order to release the garbled circuits as well as the wire keys of the next round.

First Round Optimization. Note that the message broadcast by the parties in the first round of the protocol π does not require any information from the other participants in the MPC protocol. Thus, instead of storing the garbled circuits for the first round, we let the parties publish their first message (and the signature on it) directly. The secret state that needs to be passed to the second round is hard-coded in the garbled circuit of the second round.

Release Conditions. As described above, after the execution of all garbled circuits of the certain round, the evaluator is tasked with publishing the (concatenation of the) outputs of these circuit. This published message servers as a commitment to the evaluator's execution of this round, and this is what is needed to release the gabled circuits of the next round. We additionally require that the length of each published message is the same as expected by the protocol (corresponds to the number of input wires), and the correct length requirement holds for every part of this message (i.e., the public message, the signature over it, the state, and the signature over the state for each contributing party). In order to ensure that there is only a *single* evaluation of the original MPC running, only the *very first* published message that is of a correct form (i.e., satisfies the length requirements) can be used as the witness to release garbled circuits and keys of a certain round. We call such messages *authoritative* messages. Formally, the authoritative message of round $d > 1$ is a published message that satisfies the following conditions:

- Message is of the form (id, d, m), where m is of the form $(m_1^d \parallel \cdots \parallel m_n^d \parallel sigpub_1^d \parallel \cdots \parallel sigpub_n^d \parallel c_1^d \parallel \cdots \parallel c_n^d \parallel sigpr_1^d \parallel \cdots \parallel sigpr_n^d)$. This corresponds to the concatenated output of the garbled circuits of round d: public messages followed by signatures over each public message, and encryptions of state followed by signatures over each ciphertext.
- each m_j^d, c_j^d, $sigpub_j^d$, $sigpr_j^d$ has correct length.
- This is the first published message that satisfies the requirements above.

Due to our first round optimization the authoritative message of the first round is slightly different. In particular, there are up to n authoritative messages for the first round – one for each contributing party. Formally, an authoritative message of round $d = 1$ from party P_k is a published message that satisfies the following conditions:

- Message is of the form $(id, 1, k, m_k^1, sigpub_k^1)$.
- m_k^1 and $sigpub_k^1$ both have correct length.
- This is the first published message that satisfies the requirements above.

In terms of authoritative messages, the release conditions can be now defined as follows: in order to release the garbled circuits for round i, we require that all authoritative messages for rounds 1 up to and including round $i - 1$ are published. In order to release the wire key for some bit b of an input wire w of a garbled circuit the authoritative message of the previous round must contain bit b at the same position w.

Removing Point-to-Point Channels. While in our construction we assume that the original MPC protocol is in a broadcast model, it is very common for MPC protocols to assume secure point-to-point channels. We can handle such protocols as well since an MPC protocol that assumes point-to-point channels can be easily converted to a protocol in a broadcast model. A generic transformation is outlined in the eWEB paper (Protocols 1 and 2 in [GKM+20]), it requires using a protocol to "package" a message that must be sent and another protocol to "unpack" a message received by a party. Intuitively, these protocols rely on authenticated communication channels (which can be realized via signatures). The packaging is done via appending the id of the sender to the message and IND-CCA encrypting the resulting string. The unpacking is done via decrypting and verifying that the party id specified in the message corresponds to the id of the party who sent this message via the authenticated communication channel.

Hardcoding Secret Inputs. As mentioned above, some of the information used in the modified next-message function (such as the secrets of the parties, their secret keys etc.) is hardcoded in the circuit. Say the hardcoded input wire is w, and its value is (bit) b. Then, the party preparing the garbled circuit that uses w does so as follows: whenever one of the inputs to a gate is w, the party removes the wire corresponding to w from the circuit and computes the values in the ciphertexts using bit b only (instead of computing the output both for $w = 0$ and $w = 1$). We give an example for the computation of the AND-Gate in Fig. 2. For security purposes, it is important that we do *not* perform any circuit optimizations based on the value of w.

Notation. In the following, we denote party P_j's public- and secret encryption key pair as (pk_j, sk_j). We denote party P_j's signature and verification keys as $sigk_j$ and $verk_j$. By m_j^i we denote messages that are generated by the party P_j in the i-th round.

x	w	out
0	0	K_0
0	1	K_0
1	0	K_0
1	1	K_1

x	out
0	K_0
1	K_0

Fig. 2. On the left, we show the computation of the AND-gate in Yao's construction. Given the garbled keys of x and w, depending on whether they correspond to zero or one, the doubly-encrypted ciphertext contains K_0 or K_1. On the right, we show the computation for the AND-gate if $w = 0$. In this case, both ciphertexts contain K_0.

Further Details. Note that eWEB, the construction that we use as the instantiation of the CSaR, assumes a CRS. This requirement can be removed in our case by simply allowing each participant in the protocol π to prepare the CRS on its own. From a security standpoint, this is unproblematic – we only wish to protect the secrets of honest clients, and if a client is honest, it will generate the CRS honestly as well[5].

Additionally, we note that in eWEB the party storing the secret is required to send multiple messages. In order to ensure that in our MPC protocol a single message from the MPC participant is sufficient and the parties can go offline after sending this message, we slightly modify the eWEB construction. Roughly, in eWEB miners are tasked with jointly preparing a random value r s.t. each miner knows a share of r. The user then publishes the value $s + r$ (where s denotes the secret to be stored), and the miners compute their shares ob s by subtracting their shares of r from $s + r$. Along the way, the commitments to the sharing of s are made public. We modify it as follows: the user simply publishes the commitments to the sharing of s and sends shares of s (along with the witnesses) to the miners who then verify the correctness of the shares and witnesses.

The full construction is given in Protocols 1 and 2 (preparation of the garbled circuits and keys), as well as Protocol 3 (execution phase).

Security Analysis. Intuitively, correctness of the construction as well as the secrecy of the honest parties' inputs follow from the correctness as well as security properties of the underlying cryptographic primitives as well as the original protocol π. We formally show security by providing a simulator that does not have access to the parties' secrets. No PPT adversary can distinguish between interaction with the simulator and the interaction with the honest parties. We rely on the security of the cryptographic primitives used in our construction to show that the adversary is not able to use a garbled circuit from an honest party in a "wrong" way. In particular, the adversary cannot trick an honestly produced garbled circuit into accepting wrong inputs from other honest parties i.e.,

---

[5] Note that this change reduces the efficiency of the eWEB system – instead of batching secrets from different clients, only secrets from a single client can be processed together now.

Protocol 1. Non-Interactive MPC – $Circuit Preparation Phase$

1. P_j computes the output (m_j^1, s_j^1) of the first round of π. P_j computes the signature $sigpub_j^1$ on the message $(id, 1, j, m_j^1)$ using its signing key $sigk_j$. P_j posts $(id, 1, j, m_j^1, sigpub_j^1)$ on chain.
2. P_j produces Yao's garbled circuits $\{GC_j^i\}$ for each round i based on the circuit C_j^i of the next-message function f^i of the original MPC protocol π. The circuit C_j^i for which P_j does the garbling takes as input messages $\{m_k^{i-1}\}_{k=1}^n$ published by the parties in the previous round along with the signatures $\{sigpub_k^{i-1}\}_{k=1}^n$ of these messages, and the encryption c_j^{i-1} of the secret state passed by P_j from the previous round as well as the signature $sigpr_j^{i-1}$ over this ciphertext. All of P_j's keys, input x_j and randomness r_j^i are hardcoded in the circuit. The verification- and public keys of other participants are also hardcoded in the circuit. For the circuit of the second round, the secret state passed from the first round is also hardcoded in the circuit. The circuit decrypts the secret state and, if the ciphertext was correctly authenticated, executes the next message function of the current round:
   (a) If $i = 2$, proceed to step 2.(c).
   (b) Verify the signature on the encryption of the state c_j^{i-1} using $verk_j$. If this check fails, stop the execution and output $\perp$.
   (c) Verify the signature on each public message m_z^{i-1} from party P_z. If any verification check fails, stop the execution and output $\perp$.
   (d) Compute $s_j^{i-1} = Dec_{sk_j}(c_j^{i-1})$.
   (e) Obtain (m_j^i, s_j^i) by executing $f^i(x_j, r_j^i, m^i, s_j^{i-1})$, where $m^i = m_1^{i-1} \| \cdots \| m_n^{i-1}$.
   (f) Compute the signature $sigpub_j^i$ on the public message (id, i, j, m_j^i) using the signing key $sigk_j$.
   (g) Compute the encryption of the state $c_j^i = Enc_{pk_j}(s_j^i)$.
   (h) Compute the signature $sigpr_j^i$ on the tuple (id, i, j, c_j^i) including the encryption of state using the signing key $sigk_j$.
   (i) Output $(m_j^i, sigpub_j^i, c_j^i, sigpr_j^i)$.
3. P_j securely stores garbled tables for all of the rounds using a CSaR. The witness needed to release the garbled circuit of round i is a valid proof of publishing of all authoritative messages from round 1 and up to and including round $i-1$.

Protocol 2. Non-Interactive MPC – $Key Storage Phase$

1. Securely store input wire keys for the circuit of the second round using CSaR. For each party P_k whose first round message is needed for the computation, the witness required to decrypt the wire key corresponding to the i-th bit of the input being 0 (resp. 1) is a **valid proof of publishing** of the following:
   (a) All of the authoritative messages of the first round are published.
   (b) i-th bit of the authoritative message of round 1 of Party P_k is 0 (resp. 1).
2. Securely store input wire keys for the circuit of the d-th ($d \geq 3$) round using CSaR. The witness needed to decrypt the wire key corresponding to the i-th bit of the input being 0 (resp. 1) is a **valid proof of publishing** of the following:
   (a) All of the authoritative messages of the first $d-1$ rounds are published.
   (b) i-th bit of the authoritative message of round $d-1$ is 0 (resp. 1).

Protocol 3. NON-INTERACTIVE MPC − *ExecutionPhase*

1. The evaluator E uses messages $(id, 1, z, m_z^1, sigpub_z^1)$ posted on the bulletin board by each party P_z as the proof of publishing to get the garbled circuits (and keys) for the second round stored in CSaR by each participant in π. Then, E computes the outputs $(m_j^2, sigpub_j^2, c_j^2, sigpr_j^2)$ of the second round by executing the garbled circuits.

2. If an authoritative message of the second round was not published on the bulletin board yet, set $m = (m_1^2 \| \cdots \| m_n^2 \| sigpub_1^2 \| \cdots \| sigpub_n^2 \| c_1^2 \| \cdots \| c_n^2 \| sigpr_1^2 \| \cdots \| sigpr_n^2)$, publish $(id, 2, m)$ and use the proof of publish as the witness to decrypt the wire keys of the next round. If an authoritative message $(id, 2, m)$ was published on the bulletin board, use it as witness to compute the outputs of the next round if $m = m_1^2 \| \cdots \| m_n^2 \| sigpub_1^2 \| \cdots \| sigpub_n^2 \| c_1^2 \| \cdots \| c_n^2 \| sigpr_1^2 \| \cdots \| sigpr_n^2$. Otherwise, stop the execution and output $\perp$.

3. In each following round $d \geq 3$, E executes each garbled circuit published by party P_z for round $d - 1$. Then, E concatenates the outputs and checks if there is a message on the bulletin board for this round. If there is no such message, E posts the computed output $(id, d, m_1^{d-1} \| \cdots \| m_n^{d-1} \| sigpub_1^{d-1} \| \cdots \| sigpub_n^{d-1} \| c_1^{d-1} \| \cdots \| c_n^{d-1} \| sigpr_1^{d-1} \| \cdots \| sigpr_n^{d-1})$ and uses the proof of publishing as witness to decrypt input keys of the next round. Otherwise, if it is the same message as the one computed by E, E uses the proof of publishing of this message as a witness to decrypt the input keys of the next round. If it is not the same message as the one computed by E, E aborts the execution.

4. E outputs the concatenation of the outputs of the garbled circuits of the last round as the result.

---

inputs that were not produced using the garbled circuits or published (for the first message) by those parties directly, or claim that a required message from some honest party is missing. Additionally, there is no way for the adversary to execute honest garbled circuits for the same round on inconsistent inputs (or execute a single honest garbled circuit multiple times on a different inputs) since only the authoritative message published for a single round is considered valid. We then rely on the security of the original protocol π.

4   Optimizations

Our next goal is to minimize the number of CSaR invocations in our construction. For this, we will focus on our main construction (Protocols 1, 2 and 3), but the optimizations are applicable to our guaranteed output delivery construction (which will be introduced later) as well.

Let n denote the number of parties participating in the original MPC protocol π, n_{rounds} denote the number of rounds in π, $n_{wires,j}^i$ denote the number of input wires of a garbled circuit of the next-message function for round i of party P_j.

Then, the number of CSaR secret store operations is upper bounded by:

$$N_{store} = n * (n_{rounds} - 1) + \sum_{i=2}^{n_{rounds}} \sum_{j=1}^{n} 2 * n_{wires,j}^i$$

The term $n * (n_{rounds} - 1)$ is due to the fact that each party needs to store a garbled circuit for each round, except for the very first one. The term $\sum_{i=2}^{n_{rounds}} \sum_{i=1}^{n} 2 * n_{wires,j}^i$ is added because each party also needs to store two wire keys for each input wire of each garbled circuit it publishes.

The number of CSaR secret release operations for each evaluator is upper bounded by:

$$N_{release} = n * (n_{rounds} - 1) + \sum_{i=2}^{n_{rounds}} \sum_{j=1}^{n} n_{wires,j}^i$$

This is because the evaluator needs all of the garbled circuits, as well as a single wire key for each input wire of each garbled circuit, to perform the computation.

Note that the dominant factor in both of the equations is $\sum_{i=2}^{n_{rounds}} \sum_{j=1}^{n} n_{wires,j}^i$. This term is precisely the combined communication- and (encrypted) state complexity of the original MPC protocol π, minus the messages of the first round and plus the signatures on the public messages and the state. Thus, in order to minimize the number of eWEB invocations, we must first and foremost optimize the combined communication- and state complexity of the original MPC scheme. We discuss a possible way to do this in the next section.

5   Optimizing Communication and State Complexity in MPC

Our goal in this section is to design an MPC protocol in the plain model such that its combined communication- and state complexity is independent of the function that it is computing. While a number of works have focused on optimizing communication complexity, we are not aware of any construction optimizing both the communication- and state complexity.

We achieve it in two steps, starting with a protocol secure against *semi-malicious* adversaries. Semi-malicious security, introduced by Asharov et al. [AJLA+12], intuitively means that the adversary must follow the protocol, but can choose its random coins in an arbitrary way. The adversary is assumed to have a special witness-tape and is required to write a pair of input and randomness (x, r) that explains its behavior. We specifically start with a semi-malicious MPC protocol that has attractive communication- and state complexity (i.e., independent of the function being computed). Then, we extend it so that the resulting construction is secure against not only semi-malicious, but also fully malicious adversaries.

5.1   Step. 1: MPC with Semi-malicious Security

Our starting point is the solution proposed in the work of Brakerski et al. [BHP17] based on multi-key fully homomorphic encryption (MFHE) that achieves semi-malicious security[6]. The construction is for deterministic functionalities where all the parties receive the same output, however it can be easily extended using standard techniques to randomized functionalities with individual outputs for different parties [AJLA+12]. For technical details behind the construction and the security proof we refer to Brakerski et al., and Mukherjee and Wichs.

We note that while Brakerski et al. do not explicitly explain how to handle circuits of arbitrary depth, the *bootstrapping* approach outlined by Mukherjee and Wichs [MW16] can be used here. Informally, the bootstrapping is done as follows: each party encrypts their secret key bit-by-bit using their public key and broadcasts the resulting ciphertext. These ciphertexts are used to evaluate the decryption circuit, thus reducing the noise. To do so, the parameters of the MFHE scheme must be set in a way that allows it to handle the evaluation of the decryption circuit. We assume circular security that ensures that it is secure to encrypt a secret key under its corresponding public key and refer to Mukherjee and Wichs [MW16] for details.

To summarize, the construction in Protocol 4 is an MPC protocol secure against semi-malicious adversaries and can handle functions of arbitrary depth[7].

The communication complexity in Protocol 4 depends only on the security parameters, the number of parties, and input- and output sizes [BHP17]. Note that for a party P_i the state that is passed between the rounds in Protocol 4 consists of the following data:

- params_k (passed from round one to round two and round three)
- params, $(\mathsf{pk}_k, \mathsf{sk}_k)$, $\{c_{k,j}\}_{j \in [l_{in}]}$, $\{\tilde{c}_{k,j}\}_{j \in [l_{key}]}$ (passed from round two to round three)
- $\{ev_{k,j}\}_{j \in l_{out}}$ (passed from round three to round four)

Note that this data depends only on security parameters, number of parties, and input- and output sizes. Thus, the communication- and state complexity of the semi-malicious protocol does not depend on the circuit we are computing.

---

[6] Their scheme is secure when exactly all but one parties are corrupted. To transform it into a scheme that is secure against any number of corruptions, Brakerski et al. suggest to extend it by a protocol proposed by Mukherjee and Wichs (Sect. 6.2 in [MW16]) that relies on an so-called *extended function*. For simplicity, we skip this technical detail in our protocol. We note, however, that the additional communication and state complexity incurred due to the transformation depend only on the security parameter, as well as the parties' input- and output sizes.

[7] Again, this construction is secure against exactly $N - 1$ corruptions (where N is the total number of parties). When used with the extended function transformation by Mukherjee and Wichs (which we skip here for readability purposes), the construction becomes secure against arbitrary many corruptions.

Protocol 4. Optimizing MPC

---

1. Let P_k be the party executing this protocol.
2. Run $\mathsf{params}_k \leftarrow \mathsf{MFHE.DistSetup}(1^\kappa, 1^N, k)$. Broadcast params_k.
3. Set $\mathsf{params} = (\mathsf{params}_1, \ldots, \mathsf{params}_N)$, and do the following:
   - Generate a key-pair $(pk_k, sk_k) \leftarrow \mathsf{MFHE.Keygen}(\mathsf{params}, k)$
   - Let l_{in} denote the length of the party's input. Let $x_k[j]$ denote the j-th bit of P_k's input x_k. Let l_{key} denote the length of the party's secret key.
   - Encrypt the input bit-by-bit:

$$\{c_{k,j} \leftarrow \mathsf{MFHE.Encrypt}(pk_k, \mathsf{x}_k[j])_{j \in [l_{in}]}$$

   - Encrypt the secret key bit-by-bit:

$$\{\tilde{c}_{k,j} \leftarrow \mathsf{MFHE.Encrypt}(pk_k, sk_k[j])_{j \in [l_{key}]}$$

   - Broadcast the public key and the ciphertexts $(pk_k, \{c_{k,j}\}_{j \in [l_{in}]}, \{\tilde{c}_{k,j}\}_{j \in [l_{key}]})$
4. On receiving values $\{pk_i, c_{i,j}\}_{i \in [N] \setminus \{k\}, j \in [l_{in}]}$ execute the following steps:
   - Let f_j be the boolean function for j-th bit of the output of f. Let l_{out} denote the length of the output of f.
   - Run the evaluation algorithm to generate the evaluated ciphertext bit-by-bit:

$$\{c_j \leftarrow \mathsf{MFHE.Eval}(\mathsf{params}, f_j, (c_{1,1}, \ldots, c_{N,l_{in}}))\}_{j \in [l_{out}]},$$

   while performing a bootstrapping (using the previously broadcasted encryptions of the secret keys) whenever needed.
   - Compute the partial decryption for all $j \in [l_{out}]$:

$$ev_{k,j} \leftarrow \mathsf{MFHE.PartDec}(sk_k, c_j)$$

   - Broadcasts the values $\{ev_{k,j}\}_{j \in l_{out}}$
5. On receiving all the values $\{ev_{i,j}\}_{i \in [N], j \in [l_{out}]}$ run the final decryption to obtain the j-th output bit: $\{y_j \leftarrow \mathsf{MFHE.FinDec}(ev_{1,j}, \ldots, ev_{N,j}, c_j)\}_{j \in [l_{out}]}$. Output $y = y_1 \cdots y_{l_{out}}$.

5.2 Step. 2: MPC with Fully Malicious Security

In order to protect from fully malicious adversaries, we extend the construction above with the zero-knowledge protocol proposed by Kilian [Kil92]. In the following, we first elaborate on Kilian's protocol and some changes we need to make to it in order to keep the combined communication- and state complexity low. Then, we elaborate on how Kilian's protocol is used in the overall MPC construction.

Kilian's Zero-Knowledge Protocol. Kilian's construction [Kil92] relies on probabilistically checkable proofs (PCPs) and allows a party P to prove the correctness of some statement x using a witness w to the prover V. We specifically chose Kilian's construction because of its attractive communication- and state complexities. Note that we make a minor change to Kilian's construction (Protocol 5) – instead of storing the PCP string that was computed in round two to use it in round four (as is done in the Kilian's original scheme), P recomputes the string (using the same randomness) in round four. Clearly, this changes nothing in terms of correctness and security. However, it allows us to drastically cut the state complexity of Kilian's original construction since the storage of the PCP becomes unnecessary.

Protocol 5. Optimizing MPC - Kilian's construction

---

1. Verifier V chooses a collision-resistant hash function h and sends its description to the prover P.
2. Prover P uses the PCP prover P' to construct a PCP string $\psi \leftarrow P(x, w)$. Denote by r_p the randomness used by the prover in the generation of ψ. P computes the root of the Merkle tree (using the hash function h) on ψ, and sends the commitment to the Merkle tree root to the verifier V.
3. V chooses a randomness r_v and sends it to P.
4. P recomputes the PCP string $\psi \leftarrow P(x, w)$ using the randomness r_p and sends PCP answers to the set of queries generated according to the PCP verifier V' (executed on randomness r_v) to V.
5. V checks the validity of the answers, and accepts if all answers are valid and consistent with the previously received Merkle tree root. Otherwise, V outputs $\bot$.

Full Construction. The MPC construction secure against fully malicious adversaries is effectively the same as the semi-malicious one, except that additionally Kilian's construction is executed by each party P_k after each of the first three rounds of Protocol 4. In more detail:

We assume that there exists some ordering of parties participating in Protocol 4. Following the approach outlined by Gilad et al. [AJLA+12], in each round d of Protocol 4 we use Kilian's construction as follows:

For each pair of parties (P_i, P_j), P_i acts as a prover to the verifier P_j in order to prove the statement

$$\mathsf{NextMessage}_d(x_i, r_i^d, \{m^k\}_{k=1}^d, c_i^{d-1}) = m_i^d.$$

Here, $\mathsf{NextMessage}$ is the function executed by P_i in this round according to Protocol 4, x_i is the secret input of P_i, r_i^d is the randomness used by P_i in round d, $\{m_k\}_{k=1}^d$ are (concatenations of) the messages broadcast by all parties participating in Protocol 4 in rounds 1 to d, and m_i^d is the message broadcast by P_i in round d. If a check fails, P_j broadcasts $\bot$ and aborts. These proofs are done sequentially (starting a new one only after the previous is fully finished), following the ordering of the (pairs of) parties. If at least one party has broadcasted $\bot$, all parties abort.

Protocol 6. Optimizing MPC - handling fully malicious adversaries

---

1. Let P_z denote the party executing this protocol.
2. Let $\mathsf{NextMessage}_d(\cdot)$ denote the next message function of Protocol 4.
3. For each round $d = 1, \ldots, 3$.
   (a) Let $m^d = m_1^{d-1}, \ldots, m_n^{d-1}$.
   (b) Compute $\mathsf{NextMessage}_d(x_z, r_z, \{m^k\}_{k=1}^d, c_z^{d-1}) = (m_z^d, c_z^d)$.
   (c) Broadcast m_z^d.
   (d) For each ordered pair of parties (P_i, P_j):
       i. If $P_i = P_z$, P_z acts as a Prover in Protocol 5 and uses the witness (x_z, r_z, c_z^{d-1}) to prove that the following holds:
       $$\mathsf{NextMessage}_d(x_z, r_z, \{m^k\}_{k=1}^d, c_z^{d-1}) = m_z^d.$$
       ii. If $P_j = P_z$, P_z acts as a Verifier in Protocol 5 to verify that there exist (x_i, r_i, c_i^{d-1}) such that the following holds:
       $$\mathsf{NextMessage}_d(x_i, r_i, \{m^k\}_{k=1}^d, c_i^{d-1}) = m_i^d.$$
       If this verification check fails, broadcast $\perp$ and abort.
   (e) If any party party broadcast $\perp$, abort.
4. Output $\mathsf{NextMessage}_4(x_z, r_z, \{m^k\}_{k=1}^4, c_z^3) = m_z^d$.

5.3 Properties of the Resulting MPC Construction

We now discuss the properties of the scheme constructed above. Specifically, we show the following:

Theorem 5. *Let f be an N-party function. Protocol 6 is an MPC protocol computing f in the plain model which is secure against fully malicious adversaries corrupting up to $t < N$ parties. Its communication and state complexity depend only on security parameters, number of parties, and input and output sized. In particular, the complexity is independent of the function f.*

Correctness. Correctness of the overall construction follows directly from the completeness of Kilian's scheme [Kil92] as well as the correctness of the protocol of Brakerski et al. [BHP17].

Security. We outline why this construction is secure. Intuitively, in order to prove security we construct the simulator S as follows: S uses the zero-knowledge simulator S_{zk} of Kilian's protocol to simulate proofs on behalf of the honest parties. S honestly checks the proofs submitted by the adversary, aborting whenever a proof is invalid. Note that for the correctly chosen PCP, Kilian's construction is extractable, and thus there exists an extractor Ext. S uses Ext to retrieve the witness (x, r) used by the adversary in each valid proof. Finally, S uses the simulator S_{sm} of the semi-malicious scheme (writing witnesses (x, r) extracted by Ext on the adversary's witness tape) to simulate the execution of the underlying semi-malicious construction.

Communication- and State Complexity Analysis. As we mentioned above, the communication complexity of Protocol 4 depends only on security parameters, number of parties, and input- and output sizes. In particular, the communication- and state complexity of the semi-malicious protocol does not depend on the circuit we are computing.

The communication complexity of Kilian's protocol depends on the security parameter as well as the length of the statement. In our case, the statement consists of the messages sent by the parties participating in the semi-malicious MPC protocol in the previous round as well as the message output by the party in the current round. Since the communication complexity of the semi-malicious MPC protocol is independent of the function being computed, the communication complexity of the overall construction is also independent of the function being computed. As for the state complexity, recall that we made a minor change to Kilian's original protocol – instead of storing the PCP, the prover simply recomputes (using the same randomness) it whenever it is needed. Due to this simple modification the PCP string does not contribute to the state complexity. The only other things contributing to the state complexity is the hash function h and the randomness r_v, both independent of the function being computed by the MPC[8].

Thus, we have shown that the communication- and state complexity of our MPC construction that is secure against fully malicious adversaries with arbitrary number of corruptions is independent of the function the MPC protocol is tasked with computing.

Integrating Communication- and State Optimized MPC. As we showed in Sect. 4, the number of CSaR secret store operations in our main construction (Protocols 1, 2 and 3) is upper bounded by:

$$N_{store} = n * (n_{rounds} - 1) + \sum_{i=2}^{n_{rounds}} \sum_{j=1}^{n} 2 * n_{wires,j}^i$$

The number of CSaR secret release operations for each evaluator is upper bounded by:

$$N_{release} = n * (n_{rounds} - 1) + \sum_{i=2}^{n_{rounds}} \sum_{j=1}^{n} n_{wires,j}^i$$

As we pointed out in Sect. 4, the term $\sum_{i=2}^{n_{rounds}} \sum_{j=1}^{n} n_{wires,j}^i$ is precisely the combined communication- and (encrypted) state complexity of the underlying MPC protocol π, minus the messages of the first round and plus signatures on the public messages and the state. Thus, when using Protocol 6 as the underlying protocol π in our main non-interactive MPC construction (Protocols 1, 2 and

---

[8] Additionally, they can be chosen by V independently of any messages from P, and thus they can be hardcoded in the garbled circuits and do not add to the state complexity of the non-interactive construction.

3), we obtain a construction which number of CSaR store and release operations depends only on the number of rounds in π, security parameters, number of parties, and input- and output sizes. All of these parameters are independent of the function that π is tasked with computing.

Apart from the CSaR store- and release requests the only other data that is contributing to the communication complexity of the overall construction is the data that is being posted on the bulletin board:

– messages (as well as signatures) on these of the first round – MPC contributors are tasked with posting these on the bulletin board.
– outputs of the garbled circuits – evaluators are tasked with posting these on the bulletin board.

The outputs of the garbled circuits consist of the messages exchanged by the parties in π, the signatures on these messages, the encrypted state information, and the signatures on the encrypted state. Thus, the size of this data depends only on the combined communication- and (encrypted) state complexity of the underlying MPC protocol π. When using Protocol 6 as the underlying protocol π, the size of this data is independent of the function which is being computed.

Thus, we get the following result:

Corollary 3. *There exists an MPC protocol π' in the blockchain model that has adversarial threshold $t < N$, provides security with abort against fully-malicious adversaries and does not require participants to be online at the same time. Only a single message is required from the MPC contributors (the evaluators might be required to produce multiple messages). Furthermore, the communication complexity of this protocol is independent of the function that is being computed using this MPC protocol.*

6   Guaranteed Output Delivery

In this section, we provide an extension of our main construction that ensures guaranteed output delivery, meaning that the corrupted parties cannot prevent honest parties from receiving their output.

In order to provide guaranteed output delivery, the first step is to build upon an MPC protocol π that also has this property. However, note that this change by itself is not sufficient – a malicious evaluator could still disrupt the execution of our original construction by simply providing an authoritative message that contains an invalid signature and thus forcing honest garbled circuits to abort. It is clear that we cannot simply accept such invalid signatures. Thus, further modifications are required. In general, compared to our main protocol we make the following changes:

– The original MPC protocol must have the guaranteed output delivery property.
– We introduce a deadline by which all initial messages must be posted. In the following, we denote this deadline by τ.

- Signatures on the messages are verified not by the garbled circuits, but rather by the CSaR parties as part of the CSaR request. The signature is computed on the whole message, rather than separately for the public- and state parts of the next-message function's output.
- We use CSaR with public release, which is similar to CSaR, but instead of privately releasing secret shares to the user, the parties release the shares publicly (e.g., by posting them on the bulletin board).
- Whenever a message posted by the evaluator is of an invalid length or missing a valid signature, the miners use the garbled circuits and wire keys of the current round (that were previously published on the bullet board) to check whether the message posted by the evaluator is indeed the output of the garbled circuit in question. Only if this is the case (i.e., the evaluator acted honestly) is the evaluator allowed to receive the next wire keys. The evaluator uses a proof of publishing of the garbled circuits and the wire keys released by the CSaR parties to prove the correctness of the computation. The relation that the miners then check is roughly as follows: "The execution of the garbled circuit GC on the wire keys $\{k_i\}_{i \in I}$ results in the output provided by E. Here, the garbled circuit GC is the circuit, and $\{k_i\}_{i \in I}$ are the keys for this circuit reconstructed using the published values of the CSaR participants present on the proof of publish supplied by E".
- If a message from the first round was not published, or a garbled circuit or wire key from some party was not stored with CSaR, the evaluator needs to prove that with respect to the genesis block, by deadline τ indeed no such message was stored. We call such proof a "proof of missing message".
- In the cases described in the last two points, the miners release default wire keys (encoding "$\bot$") for each garbled circuit that is supposed to use the missing message.

In order to allow for an easy verification of the evaluator's claims of invalid garbled circuits, we use CSaR with public release (CSaR-PR), which is the same as CSaR, except that the witness is supplied by the client that wishes to receive the secrets publicly, and the secrets (garbled circuits and wire keys in our case) are released publicly as well (as long as the release condition is satisfied). Such CSaR-PR can be instantiated with the PublicWitness construction presented in the eWEB work. For simplicity, in the following we assume that the public release of the computation result is permitted. If the application requires that only the evaluator obtains the function result, it can be easily supported by changing the output of the function that is being computed to the *encryption* of this output under the evaluator's public key.

The definition of the *authoritative* message for this construction is a bit different to account for the fact that the signatures are checked by the CSaR parties. Formally, the authoritative message of round $d > 1$ is a published message that satisfies the following conditions:

- Message is of the form (id, d, m), where m is of the form $(m_1^d \| \cdots \| m_n^d \| c_1^d \| \cdots \| c_n^d \| sig_1^d \| \cdots \| sig_n^d)$.

– each m_j^d has correct length, and each sig_j^d is a valid signature of P_k on the tuple (id, d, j, m_j^d, c_j^d), with the following exceptions allowed:

1. if a required message from some party P_j is missing, the evaluator must prove that P_j failed to post some of the messages needed for the computation and the deadline τ has passed ("proof of missing message"). In this case, wire keys for the default value $\bot$ are released by the CSaR participants as wire keys corresponding to that message.
2. if the signature of some party P_j is invalid, or m_j^d (or c_j^d) has invalid length, the evaluator must prove that the output of the garbled circuit posted by P_j in the previous round is indeed what the evaluator claims this output to be. In this case, wire keys for the default value $\bot$ are released as wire keys corresponding to that messages.

– This is the first published message that satisfies the requirements above.

Same in our main construction, there are up to n authoritative messages for the first round – one for each contributing party. Formally, an authoritative message of round $d = 1$ from party P_k is a published message that satisfies the following conditions:

– Message is of the form $(id, 1, k, m_k^1, sig_k^1)$.
– sig_k^1 is a P_k's correct signature over m_k^1.
– m_k^1 has correct length.
– This is the first published message that satisfies the requirements above.

Just as in our main construction, we show security by providing a simulator that does not have access to the honest parties' secrets and showing that no PPT adversary is able to distinguish the interaction with the simulator from the interaction with the honest parties[9].

References

[Go17] Google AI Blog. Brendan McMahan and Daniel Ramage. Federated Learning: Collaborative Machine Learning without Centralized Training Data (2017). https://ai.googleblog.com/2017/04/federated-learning-collaborative.html

[ABH+21] Almashaqbeh, G., et al.: Gage MPC: bypassing residual function leakage for non-interactive MPC. Cryptology ePrint Archive, Report 2021/256 (2021). https://eprint.iacr.org/2021/256

[AJLA+12] Asharov, G., Jain, A., López-Alt, A., Tromer, E., Vaikuntanathan, V., Wichs, D.: Multiparty computation with low communication, computation and interaction via threshold FHE. In: Pointcheval, D., Johansson, T. (eds.) EUROCRYPT 2012. LNCS, vol. 7237, pp. 483–501. Springer, Heidelberg (2012). https://doi.org/10.1007/978-3-642-29011-4_29

---

[9] This time we additionally prove that the guaranteed output delivery property holds for our construction.

[AMPR14] Afshar, A., Mohassel, P., Pinkas, B., Riva, B.: Non-interactive secure computation based on cut-and-choose. In: Nguyen, P.Q., Oswald, E. (eds.) EUROCRYPT 2014. LNCS, vol. 8441, pp. 387–404. Springer, Heidelberg (2014). https://doi.org/10.1007/978-3-642-55220-5_22

[BGG+20] Benhamouda, F., et al.: Can a public blockchain keep a secret? In: Pass, R., Pietrzak, K. (eds.) TCC 2020. LNCS, vol. 12550, pp. 260–290. Springer, Cham (2020). https://doi.org/10.1007/978-3-030-64375-1_10

[BGI+14] Beimel, A., Gabizon, A., Ishai, Y., Kushilevitz, E., Meldgaard, S., Paskin-Cherniavsky, A.: Non-interactive secure multiparty computation. In: Garay, J.A., Gennaro, R. (eds.) CRYPTO 2014. LNCS, vol. 8617, pp. 387–404. Springer, Heidelberg (2014). https://doi.org/10.1007/978-3-662-44381-1_22

[BGI+17] Badrinarayanan, S., Garg, S., Ishai, Y., Sahai, A., Wadia, A.: Two-message witness indistinguishability and secure computation in the plain model from new assumptions. In: Takagi, T., Peyrin, T. (eds.) ASIACRYPT 2017. LNCS, vol. 10626, pp. 275–303. Springer, Cham (2017). https://doi.org/10.1007/978-3-319-70700-6_10

[BGJ+18] Badrinarayanan, S., Goyal, V., Jain, A., Kalai, Y.T., Khurana, D., Sahai, A.: Promise zero knowledge and its applications to round optimal MPC. In: Shacham, H., Boldyreva, A. (eds.) CRYPTO 2018. LNCS, vol. 10992, pp. 459–487. Springer, Cham (2018). https://doi.org/10.1007/978-3-319-96881-0_16

[BHP17] Brakerski, Z., Halevi, S., Polychroniadou, A.: Four round secure computation without setup. In: Kalai, Y., Reyzin, L. (eds.) TCC 2017. LNCS, vol. 10677, pp. 645–677. Springer, Cham (2017). https://doi.org/10.1007/978-3-319-70500-2_22

[BHR12a] Bellare, M., Hoang, V.T., Rogaway, P.: Adaptively secure garbling with applications to one-time programs and secure outsourcing. In: Wang, X., Sako, K. (eds.) ASIACRYPT 2012. LNCS, vol. 7658, pp. 134–153. Springer, Heidelberg (2012). https://doi.org/10.1007/978-3-642-34961-4_10

[BHR12b] Bellare, M., Hoang, V.T., Rogaway, P.: Foundations of garbled circuits. In: Proceedings of the 2012 ACM Conference on Computer and Communications Security, pp. 784–796 (2012)

[BJOV18] Badrinarayanan, S., Jain, A., Ostrovsky, R., Visconti, I.: Non-interactive secure computation from one-way functions. In: Peyrin, T., Galbraith, S. (eds.) ASIACRYPT 2018. LNCS, vol. 11274, pp. 118–138. Springer, Cham (2018). https://doi.org/10.1007/978-3-030-03332-3_5

[BL20] Benhamouda, F., Lin, H.: Mr NISC: multiparty reusable non-interactive secure computation. In: Pass, R., Pietrzak, K. (eds.) TCC 2020. LNCS, vol. 12551, pp. 349–378. Springer, Cham (2020). https://doi.org/10.1007/978-3-030-64378-2_13

[BMR90] Beaver, D., Micali, S., Rogaway, P.: The round complexity of secure protocols. In: Proceedings of the Twenty-Second Annual ACM Symposium on Theory of Computing, pp. 503–513 (1990)

[CCG+20] Rai Choudhuri, A., Ciampi, M., Goyal, V., Jain, A., Ostrovsky, R.: Round optimal secure multiparty computation from minimal assumptions. In: Pass, R., Pietrzak, K. (eds.) TCC 2020. LNCS, vol. 12551, pp. 291–319. Springer, Cham (2020). https://doi.org/10.1007/978-3-030-64378-2_11

[CDI+19] Chase, M., et al.: Reusable non-interactive secure computation. In: Boldyreva, A., Micciancio, D. (eds.) CRYPTO 2019. LNCS, vol. 11694, pp. 462–488. Springer, Cham (2019). https://doi.org/10.1007/978-3-030-26954-8_15

[CGG+21] Choudhuri, A.R., Goel, A., Green, M., Jain, A., Kaptchuk, G.: Fluid MPC: secure multiparty computation with dynamic participants. In: Malkin, T., Peikert, C. (eds.) CRYPTO 2021. LNCS, vol. 12826, pp. 94–123. Springer, Cham (2021). https://doi.org/10.1007/978-3-030-84245-1_4

[CGJ+17] Choudhuri, A.R., Green, M., Jain, A., Kaptchuk, G., Miers, I.: Fairness in an unfair world: fair multiparty computation from public bulletin boards. In: Proceedings of the 2017 ACM SIGSAC Conference on Computer and Communications Security, pp. 719–728 (2017)

[CJS14] Canetti, R., Jain, A., Scafuro, A.: Practical UC security with a global random oracle. In: Proceedings of the 2014 ACM SIGSAC Conference on Computer and Communications Security, pp. 597–608 (2014)

[FKN94] Feige, U., Killian, J., Naor, M.: A minimal model for secure computation. In: Proceedings of the Twenty-Sixth Annual ACM Symposium on Theory of Computing, pp. 554–563 (1994)

[GG17] Goyal, R., Goyal, V.: Overcoming cryptographic impossibility results using blockchains. In: Kalai, Y., Reyzin, L. (eds.) TCC 2017. LNCS, vol. 10677, pp. 529–561. Springer, Cham (2017). https://doi.org/10.1007/978-3-319-70500-2_18

[GGG+14] Goldwasser, S., et al.: Multi-input functional encryption. In: Nguyen, P.Q., Oswald, E. (eds.) EUROCRYPT 2014. LNCS, vol. 8441, pp. 578–602. Springer, Heidelberg (2014). https://doi.org/10.1007/978-3-642-55220-5_32

[GHK+21] Gentry, C., et al.: YOSO: you only speak once. In: Malkin, T., Peikert, C. (eds.) CRYPTO 2021. LNCS, vol. 12826, pp. 64–93. Springer, Cham (2021). https://doi.org/10.1007/978-3-030-84245-1_3

[GKM+20] Goyal, V., Kothapalli, A., Masserova, E., Parno, B., Song, Y.: Storing and retrieving secrets on a blockchain. Cryptology ePrint Archive, Report 2020/504 (2020). https://eprint.iacr.org/2020/504

[GMPP16] Garg, S., Mukherjee, P., Pandey, O., Polychroniadou, A.: The exact round complexity of secure computation. In: Fischlin, M., Coron, J.-S. (eds.) EUROCRYPT 2016. LNCS, vol. 9666, pp. 448–476. Springer, Heidelberg (2016). https://doi.org/10.1007/978-3-662-49896-5_16

[GMW87] Goldreich, O., Micali, S., Wigderson, A.: How to play any mental game. In: Proceedings of the Nineteenth ACM Symposium on Theory of Computing, STOC, pp. 218–229. ACM (1987)

[Goy11] Goyal, V.: Constant round non-malleable protocols using one way functions. In: Proceedings of the Forty-Third Annual ACM Symposium on Theory of Computing, pp. 695–704 (2011)

[HIJ+16] Halevi, S., Ishai, Y., Jain, A., Kushilevitz, E., Rabin, T.: Secure multiparty computation with general interaction patterns. In: Proceedings of the 2016 ACM Conference on Innovations in Theoretical Computer Science, pp. 157–168 (2016)

[HIJ+17] Halevi, S., Ishai, Y., Jain, A., Komargodski, I., Sahai, A., Yogev, E.: Non-interactive multiparty computation without correlated randomness. In: Takagi, T., Peyrin, T. (eds.) ASIACRYPT 2017. LNCS, vol. 10626, pp. 181–211. Springer, Cham (2017). https://doi.org/10.1007/978-3-319-70700-6_7

[HLP11] Halevi, S., Lindell, Y., Pinkas, B.: Secure computation on the web: computing without simultaneous interaction. In: Rogaway, P. (ed.) CRYPTO 2011. LNCS, vol. 6841, pp. 132–150. Springer, Heidelberg (2011). https://doi.org/10.1007/978-3-642-22792-9_8

[IKO+11] Ishai, Y., Kushilevitz, E., Ostrovsky, R., Prabhakaran, M., Sahai, A.: Efficient non-interactive secure computation. In: Paterson, K.G. (ed.) EUROCRYPT 2011. LNCS, vol. 6632, pp. 406–425. Springer, Heidelberg (2011). https://doi.org/10.1007/978-3-642-20465-4_23

[Kap20] Kaptchuk, G.: Giving state to the stateless: augmenting trustworthy computation with ledgers. In: Network and Distributed Systems Seminar, vol. 1 (2020)

[Kil92] Kilian, J.: A note on efficient zero-knowledge proofs and arguments. In: Proceedings of the Twenty-Fourth Annual ACM Symposium on Theory of Computing, pp. 723–732 (1992)

[KOS03] Katz, J., Ostrovsky, R., Smith, A.: Round efficiency of multi-party computation with a dishonest majority. In: Biham, E. (ed.) EUROCRYPT 2003. LNCS, vol. 2656, pp. 578–595. Springer, Heidelberg (2003). https://doi.org/10.1007/3-540-39200-9_36

[MW16] Mukherjee, P., Wichs, D.: Two round multiparty computation via multikey FHE. In: Fischlin, M., Coron, J.-S. (eds.) EUROCRYPT 2016. LNCS, vol. 9666, pp. 735–763. Springer, Heidelberg (2016). https://doi.org/10.1007/978-3-662-49896-5_26

[Pas04] Pass, R.: Bounded-concurrent secure multi-party computation with a dishonest majority. In: Proceedings of the Thirty-Sixth Annual ACM Symposium on Theory of Computing, pp. 232–241 (2004)

[tra20] Certificate transparency (2020). https://www.certificate-transparency.org/

[Yao82] Yao, A.C.: Protocols for secure computations. In: 23rd Annual Symposium on Foundations of Computer Science (SFCS 1982), pp. 160–164. IEEE (1982)

[Yao86] Yao, A.C.: How to generate and exchange secrets. In: 27th Annual Symposium on Foundations of Computer Science (SFCS 1986), pp. 162–167. IEEE (1986)

Multi-party PSM, Revisited:
Improved Communication and Unbalanced Communication

Léonard Assouline[1] and Tianren Liu[2(✉)]

[1] École Normale Supérieure, Paris, France
`leonard.assouline@ens.fr`
[2] University of Washington, Seattle, USA
`tianrenl@uw.edu`

Abstract. We improve the communication complexity in the Private Simultaneous Messages (PSM) model, which is a minimal model of non-interactive information-theoretic multi-party computation. The state-of-the-art PSM protocols were recently constructed by Beimel, Kushilevitz and Nissim (EUROCRYPT 2018).

We present new constructions of k-party PSM protocols. The new protocols match the previous upper bounds when $k = 2$ or 3 and improve the upper bounds for larger k. We also construct 2-party PSM protocols with unbalanced communication complexity. More concretely,

- For infinitely many k (including all $k \leq 20$), we construct k-party PSM protocols for arbitrary functionality $f : [N]^k \to \{0, 1\}$, whose communication complexity is $O_k(N^{\frac{k-1}{2}})$. This improves the former best known upper bounds of $O_k(N^{\frac{k}{2}})$ for $k \geq 6$, $O(N^{7/3})$ for $k = 5$, and $O(N^{5/3})$ for $k = 4$.
- For all rational $0 < \eta < 1$ whose denominator is ≤ 20, we construct 2-party PSM protocols for arbitrary functionality $f : [N] \times [N] \to \{0, 1\}$, whose communication complexity is $O(N^\eta)$ for one party, $O(N^{1-\eta})$ for the other. Previously the only known unbalanced 2-party PSM has communication complexity $O(\log(N)), O(N)$.

1 Introduction

Private Simultaneous Messages (PSM) is a minimal model of secure multi-party computation. It was introduced by Feige, Kilian and Naor [10], and was generalized to the multi-party setting by Ishai and Kushilevitz [12].

In a PSM protocol for evaluating a k-ary functionality $f : [N]^k \to \{0, 1\}$, there are k parties. They all share a common random string. For all $i \in [k]$, the i-th party holds a private input x_i. There is additionally a special party, called the *referee*. The referee receives one message from each party and is able to compute $f(x_1, \ldots, x_k)$, and should learn no other information about $x_1, \ldots, x_k$.

PSM is studied as an information-theoretic primitive. The key complexity measure is the communication complexity. The common random string is crucial for the model as the common random string is the only mean to protect the

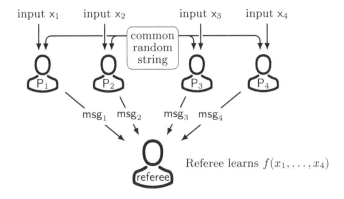

input x_1 input x_2 input x_3 input x_4

common
random
string

P_1 P_2 P_3 P_4

msg_1 msg_2 msg_3 msg_4

referee   Referee learns $f(x_1, \ldots, x_4)$

Fig. 1. Illustration of a multi-party PSM protocol

privacy against an unbounded adversarial referee, when the k parties cannot communicate with each other (Fig. 1).

In the PSM model, there are relatively efficient PSM protocols for computing non-deterministic branching programs [10] and modular branching programs [12]. But for general functionalities, little is known regarding their communication complexity in the PSM model. Assuming every party holds an input in $[N]$, the best known lower bound of 2-party PSM is $3 \log N - O(\log \log N)$ [4]. In k-party PSM where each party holds a 1-bit input, Ball et al. showed an $\Omega(k^2/\log k)$ lower bound [5]. Though the lower bounds are at most polynomial in the total input length, all known upper bounds are exponential, leaving an exponential gap between upper and lower bounds. For any functionality $f : [N]^k \to \{0,1\}$, a "naïve" k-party PSM requires $O(N^{k-1})$ communication (the 2-party version was presented in [10]). The first novel upper bound is $O(\sqrt{N})$ for 2-party PSM [6], and it was recently generalized to an $O_k(N^{k/2})$ upper bound for k-party PSM [8]. In the same paper, Beimel, Kushilevitz and Nissim also further optimize the communication complexity for small $k = 3, 4, 5$. In particular, they obtain an $O(N)$ upper bound for 3-party PSM. For $k = 4$ or 5, they improve the protocol by letting parties jointly emulate their 3-party PSM. Their results are summarized in Table 1 (Table 2).

1.1   Our Contributions

In the paper, we present two classes of results: We present new k-party PSM protocols that improve the communication complexity for infinitely many k. We introduce the notion of *unbalanced* 2-party PSM protocols, which allows a flexible repartition of the communication complexity among the two parties, and we such protocols.

k -party PSM Protocols. We present a framework for constructing multi-party PSM. The new framework improves the communication complexity upper bounds for infinitely many k. To compute any k-ary functionality $f : [N]^k \to \{0,1\}$,

Table 1. The communication complexity of computing general $f : [N]^k \rightarrow \{0,1\}$ in multi-party PSM model

Number of parties	BIKK [6]	BKN [8]	This work
2	$O(N^{1/2})$	$O(N^{1/2})$	$O(N^{1/2})$
3		$O(N)$	$O(N)$
4		$O(N^{5/3})$	$O(N^{3/2})$
5		$O(N^{7/3})$	$O(N^2)$
$k \geq 6$		$O(\text{poly}(k) \cdot N^{k/2})$	$2^{O(k)} \cdot N^{\frac{k-1}{2}}$ for infinitely many k including all $k \leq 20$

Table 2. The unbalanced communication complexity of general $f : [N] \times [N] \rightarrow \{0,1\}$ in 2-party PSM model

	Communication complexity of one party	Communication complexity of the other party
FKN [10]	$O(\log N)$	N
BIKK [6]	$O(N^{1/2})$	$O(N^{1/2})$
This work	$O(N^\eta)$	$O(N^{1-\eta})$

– For all $k \leq 20$, our framework yields a k-party PSM protocol of communication complexity $O(N^{\frac{k-1}{2}})$.
– For all k such that $k + 1$ is a prime or a prime power, our framework yields a k-party PSM protocol of communication complexity $O_k(N^{\frac{k-1}{2}})$.
– For all k, we *conjecture* that our framework will yield a k-party PSM protocol of communication complexity $O_k(N^{\frac{k-1}{2}})$.

2-party Unbalanced PSM Protocols. We also present a framework for constructing 2-party PSM protocols with unbalanced communication complexity. The new framework allows us to reduce the message length of one party at the cost of increasing the communication of the other party. We offer an almost smooth trade-off between the communication complexity of the two parties. To compute any functionality $f : [N] \times [N] \rightarrow \{0,1\}$,

– For every rational $\eta \in (0,1)$ whose denominator is no more than 20, our framework yields a 2-party PSM protocol, where one party sends $O(N^\eta)$ bits and the other sends $O(N^{1-\eta})$ bits.
– For every rational $\eta \in (0,1)$, we *conjecture* that our framework will yield a 2-party PSM protocol, where one party sends $O_\eta(N^\eta)$ bits and the other sends $O_\eta(N^{1-\eta})$ bits.

To some extent, such a trade-off was known in the literature when $\eta = 0$. The first 2-party PSM protocol is of communication complexity $O(N)$ but is strongly unbalanced: one of the two parties only sends $O(\log N)$ bits [10].

1.2   Proof Overview

This section presents the main ideas behind our new multi-party PSM protocols. We start with a warm-up example of a 3-party PSM, which is originally constructed by [8]. We present it in a way that matches the framework we will later introduce. Then we present a new 5-party PSM to demonstrate the power of our framework. The 5-party PSM example relies on new technique such as "hard terms cancelling". It can be easily generalized into a framework for constructing k-party PSM protocols for any odd k. But we do not formally present this framework in the paper.

Instead, in Sect. 3, we develop a modified framework that supports odd as well as even values of k. The modified framework evenly divides every party's input into two halves, this idea was first introduced in [6]. When we formally present the modified framework in Sect. 3.1, we use a 4-party PSM as an example.

In Sect. 4, we develop another framework for constructing unbalanced 2-party PSM protocols. Most terminologies and techniques are shared between the framework for k-party and the framework for unbalanced 2-party. Informally, the unbalanced 2-party PSM framework is the "tensor product" of two copies of the k-party framework. When we present the new framework in Sect. 4.1, we use as an example a 2-party PSM with unbalanced communication $O(N^{1/3}), O(N^{2/3})$.

Background: 3-Party PSM [8]. In this 3-party PSM protocol, three parties hold $x_1, x_2, x_3 \in [N]$ respectively. The protocol takes $O(N)$ communication and allows the referee to learn $f(x_1, x_2, x_3)$.

Fix a finite field $\mathbb{F}$. Let the i-th party locally computes a unit vector $\mathbf{x}_i \in \mathbb{F}^N$. That is, all entries in $\mathbf{x}_i$ are zero except for $\mathbf{x}_i[x_i] = 1$. Let $\mathbf{F}$ be the truth table of f represented as an $N \times N \times N$ array, we have $f(x_1, x_2, x_3) = \langle \mathbf{F}, \mathbf{x}_1 \otimes \mathbf{x}_2 \otimes \mathbf{x}_3 \rangle$, where $\otimes$ denotes the tensor product and $\langle \cdot, \cdot \rangle$ denotes the inner product.

Therefore, it is sufficient to construct a 3-party PSM protocol, where the i-th party has input $\mathbf{x}_i \in \mathbb{F}^N$ (not necessarily being an unit vector) and the referee learns $\langle \mathbf{F}, \mathbf{x}_1 \otimes \mathbf{x}_2 \otimes \mathbf{x}_3 \rangle$ for some public $\mathbf{F} \in \mathbb{F}^{N \times N \times N}$.

We start by letting the i-th party sample random $\mathbf{r}_i \in \mathbb{F}^N$ and send the one-time padded $\bar{\mathbf{x}}_i := \mathbf{x}_i + \mathbf{r}_i$ to the referee. Then the referee can compute $\langle \mathbf{F}, \bar{\mathbf{x}}_1 \otimes \bar{\mathbf{x}}_2 \otimes \bar{\mathbf{x}}_3 \rangle$. We call this term a *"masked term"*, because it is computed from the masked inputs $\bar{\mathbf{x}}_1, \bar{\mathbf{x}}_2, \bar{\mathbf{x}}_3$. This masked term can be decomposed as the sum of several *"pure terms"*

$$
\begin{aligned}
\langle \mathbf{F}, \bar{\mathbf{x}}_1 \otimes \bar{\mathbf{x}}_2 \otimes \bar{\mathbf{x}}_3 \rangle = &\langle \mathbf{F}, \mathbf{x}_1 \otimes \mathbf{x}_2 \otimes \mathbf{x}_3 \rangle + \\
&\langle \mathbf{F}, \mathbf{x}_1 \otimes \mathbf{x}_2 \otimes \mathbf{r}_3 \rangle + \langle \mathbf{F}, \mathbf{x}_1 \otimes \mathbf{r}_2 \otimes \mathbf{x}_3 \rangle + \langle \mathbf{F}, \mathbf{r}_1 \otimes \mathbf{x}_2 \otimes \mathbf{x}_3 \rangle + \\
&\langle \mathbf{F}, \mathbf{x}_1 \otimes \mathbf{r}_2 \otimes \mathbf{r}_3 \rangle + \langle \mathbf{F}, \mathbf{r}_1 \otimes \mathbf{x}_2 \otimes \mathbf{r}_3 \rangle + \langle \mathbf{F}, \mathbf{r}_1 \otimes \mathbf{r}_2 \otimes \mathbf{x}_3 \rangle + \\
&\langle \mathbf{F}, \mathbf{r}_1 \otimes \mathbf{r}_2 \otimes \mathbf{r}_3 \rangle.
\end{aligned}
\tag{1}
$$

We classify the pure terms into two categories:

Target Term. The term $\langle \mathbf{F}, \mathbf{x}_1 \otimes \mathbf{x}_2 \otimes \mathbf{x}_3 \rangle$. It is the term that the referee should learn as a consequence of the 3-party PSM protocol.

Easy Term. All the other terms fall into this category. As the name suggested, there also exist "hard terms", which will be introduced in the next example of 5-party PSM.

The easy terms are called "easy" because each of them can be securely revealed to the referee using only $O(N)$ communication. More formally, let the parties additionally sample random $r_1, \ldots, r_7 \in \mathbb{F}$ from their common random string such that $r_1 + \cdots + r_7 = 0$. There exist sub-protocols revealing each of

$$r_1 + \langle \mathbf{F}, \mathbf{x}_1 \otimes \mathbf{x}_2 \otimes \mathbf{r}_3 \rangle, \ r_2 + \langle \mathbf{F}, \mathbf{x}_1 \otimes \mathbf{r}_2 \otimes \mathbf{x}_3 \rangle, \ r_3 + \langle \mathbf{F}, \mathbf{r}_1 \otimes \mathbf{x}_2 \otimes \mathbf{x}_3 \rangle,$$
$$r_4 + \langle \mathbf{F}, \mathbf{x}_1 \otimes \mathbf{r}_2 \otimes \mathbf{r}_3 \rangle, \ r_5 + \langle \mathbf{F}, \mathbf{r}_1 \otimes \mathbf{x}_2 \otimes \mathbf{r}_3 \rangle, \ r_6 + \langle \mathbf{F}, \mathbf{r}_1 \otimes \mathbf{r}_2 \otimes \mathbf{x}_3 \rangle, \quad (2)$$
$$r_7 + \langle \mathbf{F}, \mathbf{r}_1 \otimes \mathbf{r}_2 \otimes \mathbf{r}_3 \rangle$$

to the referee without leaking any other information, taking at most $O(N)$ communication.

Assume that such sub-protocols exist, we can easily finish the 3-party PSM: The i-th party sends $\bar{\mathbf{x}}_i := \mathbf{x}_i + \mathbf{r}_i$, they use the aforementioned sub-protocols to reveal (2). The correctness follows almost directly from (1).

The only missing piece is to construct sub-protocols for computing the terms in (2). Let us discuss them individually:

- For the last term $r_7 + \langle \mathbf{F}, \mathbf{r}_1 \otimes \mathbf{r}_2 \otimes \mathbf{r}_3 \rangle$, any party (e.g. the first party) can compute it and send it to the referee.
- For the term $r_4 + \langle \mathbf{F}, \mathbf{x}_1 \otimes \mathbf{r}_2 \otimes \mathbf{r}_3 \rangle$, the first party computes it and sends it to the referee. Similarly for $r_5 + \langle \mathbf{F}, \mathbf{r}_1 \otimes \mathbf{x}_2 \otimes \mathbf{r}_3 \rangle$ and $r_6 + \langle \mathbf{F}, \mathbf{r}_1 \otimes \mathbf{r}_2 \otimes \mathbf{x}_3 \rangle$.
- For the term $r_1 + \langle \mathbf{F}, \mathbf{x}_1 \otimes \mathbf{x}_2 \otimes \mathbf{r}_3 \rangle$, both first and second party need to participate. Since the first party knows $\mathbf{F}, \mathbf{x}_1, \mathbf{r}_3$, it can locally compute a vector $\mathbf{g} \in \mathbb{F}^N$ such that

$$r_1 + \langle \mathbf{F}, \mathbf{x}_1 \otimes \mathbf{x}_2 \otimes \mathbf{r}_3 \rangle = r_1 + \langle \mathbf{g}, \mathbf{x}_2 \rangle.$$

Then they can jointly reveal it to the referee using the PSM for inner product (more details are provided in Sect. B.1). Similarly for $r_2 + \langle \mathbf{F}, \mathbf{x}_1 \otimes \mathbf{r}_2 \otimes \mathbf{x}_3 \rangle$ and $r_3 + \langle \mathbf{F}, \mathbf{r}_1 \otimes \mathbf{x}_2 \otimes \mathbf{x}_3 \rangle$.

Example: 5-Party PSM. We will sketch a 5-party PSM protocol for any $f : [N]^5 \to \{0, 1\}$ with communication complexity $O(N^2)$.

Let $\mathbb{F}$ be a finite field. Following the same observation we made in the 3-party PSM example, it is sufficient to construct a PSM protocol for any function of the form $(\mathbf{x}_1, \ldots, \mathbf{x}_5) \mapsto \langle \mathbf{F}, \mathbf{x}_1 \otimes \cdots \otimes \mathbf{x}_5 \rangle$, where $\otimes$ denotes the *tensor product*, the i-th party having input $\mathbf{x}_i \in \mathbb{F}^N$, $\mathbf{F}$ is public and fixed being the truth table of f.

For each $\Omega \subseteq \{1, 2, 3, 4, 5\}$, parties sample a dimension-$|\Omega|$ tensor $\mathbf{R}_\Omega \in \mathbb{F}^{N^{|\Omega|}}$ from the common random string. Define $\bar{\mathbf{X}}_\Omega := \mathbf{R}_\Omega + \bigotimes_{i \in \Omega} \mathbf{x}_i$. For example, $\bar{\mathbf{X}}_{\{2\}} := \mathbf{R}_{\{2\}} + \mathbf{x}_2$ and $\bar{\mathbf{X}}_{\{3,4\}} := \mathbf{R}_{\{3,4\}} + \mathbf{x}_3 \otimes \mathbf{x}_4$. Since the communication budget is $O(N^2)$, they can perform a PSM sub-protocol so that the referee learns $\bar{\mathbf{X}}_\Omega$ for all Ω such that $|\Omega| \leq 2$.

Learning those tensors allows the referee to compute many terms, including $\langle \mathbf{F}, \bar{\mathbf{X}}_{\{1,2\}} \otimes \bar{\mathbf{X}}_{\{3,4\}} \otimes \bar{\mathbf{X}}_{\{5\}} \rangle$. This term can be decomposed into the sum of the following 8 terms:

$$
\begin{aligned}
\langle \mathbf{F}, &\bar{\mathbf{X}}_{\{1,2\}} \otimes \bar{\mathbf{X}}_{\{3,4\}} \otimes \bar{\mathbf{X}}_{\{5\}} \rangle \\
= &\langle \mathbf{F}, \mathbf{x}_1 \otimes \mathbf{x}_2 \otimes \mathbf{x}_3 \otimes \mathbf{x}_4 \otimes \mathbf{x}_5 \rangle + \langle \mathbf{F}, \mathbf{x}_1 \otimes \mathbf{x}_2 \otimes \mathbf{x}_3 \otimes \mathbf{x}_4 \otimes \mathbf{R}_{\{5\}} \rangle \\
&+ \langle \mathbf{F}, \mathbf{x}_1 \otimes \mathbf{x}_2 \otimes \mathbf{R}_{\{3,4\}} \otimes \mathbf{x}_5 \rangle + \langle \mathbf{F}, \mathbf{x}_1 \otimes \mathbf{x}_2 \otimes \mathbf{R}_{\{3,4\}} \otimes \mathbf{R}_{\{5\}} \rangle \qquad (3) \\
&+ \langle \mathbf{F}, \mathbf{R}_{\{1,2\}} \otimes \mathbf{x}_3 \otimes \mathbf{x}_4 \otimes \mathbf{x}_5 \rangle + \langle \mathbf{F}, \mathbf{R}_{\{1,2\}} \otimes \mathbf{x}_3 \otimes \mathbf{x}_4 \otimes \mathbf{R}_{\{5\}} \rangle \\
&+ \langle \mathbf{F}, \mathbf{R}_{\{1,2\}} \otimes \mathbf{R}_{\{3,4\}} \otimes \mathbf{x}_5 \rangle + \langle \mathbf{F}, \mathbf{R}_{\{1,2\}} \otimes \mathbf{R}_{\{3,4\}} \otimes \mathbf{R}_{\{5\}} \rangle.
\end{aligned}
$$

Any term that is formed in the same way as the left-hand side of (3), i.e. $\langle \mathbf{F}, \bar{\mathbf{X}}_{S_1} \otimes \cdots \otimes \bar{\mathbf{X}}_{S_t} \rangle$ for some $S_1 + \cdots + S_t = \{1, 2, 3, 4, 5\}$, is called a *masked term*. It can be computed by the referee if $|S_i| \leq 2$ for all i.

Any term that is formed in the same way as the right-hand side of (3), i.e. $\langle \mathbf{F}, \mathbf{R}_{S_1} \otimes \cdots \otimes \mathbf{R}_{S_t} \otimes \mathbf{x}_{i_1} \otimes \cdots \otimes \mathbf{x}_{i_w} \rangle$ for some $S_1 + \cdots + S_t + \{i_1, \ldots, i_w\} = \{1, 2, 3, 4, 5\}$, is called a *pure term*. As hinted by Eq. (3), every masked term is equal to the sum of 2^t pure terms.

The pure terms fall naturally into three categories. In particular, we introduce a new category called *hard terms*.

Target term. The term $\langle \mathbf{F}, \mathbf{x}_1 \otimes \mathbf{x}_2 \otimes \mathbf{x}_3 \otimes \mathbf{x}_4 \otimes \mathbf{x}_5 \rangle$ is called the target term.

Easy term. A pure term $\langle \mathbf{F}, \mathbf{R}_{S_1} \otimes \cdots \otimes \mathbf{R}_{S_t} \otimes \mathbf{x}_{i_1} \otimes \cdots \otimes \mathbf{x}_{i_w} \rangle$ is easy if $w \leq 3$. Every easy term can be computed using a PSM protocol with communication complexity $O(N^2)$. For example, $\langle \mathbf{F}, \mathbf{R}_{\{1,2\}} \otimes \mathbf{x}_3 \otimes \mathbf{x}_4 \otimes \mathbf{x}_5 \rangle$ is an easy term. The 5th party, based on its view, can compute a tensor $\mathbf{G} \in \mathbb{F}^{N^2}$ such that $\langle \mathbf{F}, \mathbf{R}_{\{1,2\}} \otimes \mathbf{x}_3 \otimes \mathbf{x}_4 \otimes \mathbf{x}_5 \rangle = \langle \mathbf{G}, \mathbf{x}_3 \otimes \mathbf{x}_4 \rangle$. And $\langle \mathbf{G}, \mathbf{x}_3 \otimes \mathbf{x}_4 \rangle$ can be computed using a PSM protocol (Sect. B.1) with communication complexity $O(N^2)$.

Hard term. Any pure term that is neither the target term nor an easy term.

Let us ignore the easy terms for now. Then Eq. (3) can be rewritten as

$$
\begin{aligned}
\langle \mathbf{F}, &\bar{\mathbf{X}}_{\{1,2\}} \otimes \bar{\mathbf{X}}_{\{3,4\}} \otimes \bar{\mathbf{X}}_{\{5\}} \rangle \\
= &\langle \mathbf{F}, \mathbf{x}_1 \otimes \cdots \otimes \mathbf{x}_5 \rangle + \langle \mathbf{F}, \mathbf{x}_1 \otimes \mathbf{x}_2 \otimes \mathbf{x}_3 \otimes \mathbf{x}_4 \otimes \mathbf{R}_{\{5\}} \rangle + \text{easy terms}.
\end{aligned}
$$

There is only one hard term left. We would like to cancel out the hard term by combining a few masked terms. Let us consider the following masked terms: $\langle \mathbf{F}, \bar{\mathbf{X}}_{\{1,2\}} \otimes \bar{\mathbf{X}}_{\{3\}} \otimes \bar{\mathbf{X}}_{\{4,5\}} \rangle$, $\langle \mathbf{F}, \bar{\mathbf{X}}_{\{1,2\}} \otimes \bar{\mathbf{X}}_{\{3,5\}} \otimes \bar{\mathbf{X}}_{\{4\}} \rangle$ and $\langle \mathbf{F}, \bar{\mathbf{X}}_{\{1,2\}} \otimes \bar{\mathbf{X}}_{\{3\}} \otimes \bar{\mathbf{X}}_{\{4\}} \otimes \bar{\mathbf{X}}_{\{5\}} \rangle$.

$$
\begin{aligned}
\langle \mathbf{F}, &\bar{\mathbf{X}}_{\{1,2\}} \otimes \bar{\mathbf{X}}_{\{3\}} \otimes \bar{\mathbf{X}}_{\{4,5\}} \rangle \\
= &\langle \mathbf{F}, \mathbf{x}_1 \otimes \cdots \otimes \mathbf{x}_5 \rangle + \langle \mathbf{F}, \mathbf{x}_1 \otimes \mathbf{x}_2 \otimes \mathbf{R}_{\{3\}} \otimes \mathbf{x}_4 \otimes \mathbf{x}_5 \rangle + \text{easy terms}, \\
\langle \mathbf{F}, &\bar{\mathbf{X}}_{\{1,2\}} \otimes \bar{\mathbf{X}}_{\{3,5\}} \otimes \bar{\mathbf{X}}_{\{4\}} \rangle \\
= &\langle \mathbf{F}, \mathbf{x}_1 \otimes \cdots \otimes \mathbf{x}_5 \rangle + \langle \mathbf{F}, \mathbf{x}_1 \otimes \mathbf{x}_2 \otimes \mathbf{x}_3 \otimes \mathbf{R}_{\{4\}} \otimes \mathbf{x}_5 \rangle + \text{easy terms},
\end{aligned}
$$

$$\langle \mathbf{F}, \bar{\mathbf{X}}_{\{1,2\}} \otimes \bar{\mathbf{X}}_{\{3\}} \otimes \bar{\mathbf{X}}_{\{4\}} \otimes \bar{\mathbf{X}}_{\{5\}} \rangle$$
$$= \langle \mathbf{F}, \mathbf{x}_1 \otimes \cdots \otimes \mathbf{x}_5 \rangle + \langle \mathbf{F}, \mathbf{x}_1 \otimes \mathbf{x}_2 \otimes \mathbf{R}_{\{3\}} \otimes \mathbf{x}_4 \otimes \mathbf{x}_5 \rangle$$
$$+ \langle \mathbf{F}, \mathbf{x}_1 \otimes \mathbf{x}_2 \otimes \mathbf{x}_3 \otimes \mathbf{R}_{\{4\}} \otimes \mathbf{x}_5 \rangle + \langle \mathbf{F}, \mathbf{x}_1 \otimes \mathbf{x}_2 \otimes \mathbf{x}_3 \otimes \mathbf{x}_4 \otimes \mathbf{R}_{\{5\}} \rangle$$
$$+ \text{ easy terms.}$$

By carefully combining these masked tensors, we have

$$\langle \mathbf{F}, \bar{\mathbf{X}}_{\{1,2\}} \otimes \bar{\mathbf{X}}_{\{3,4\}} \otimes \bar{\mathbf{X}}_{\{5\}} \rangle + \langle \mathbf{F}, \bar{\mathbf{X}}_{\{1,2\}} \otimes \bar{\mathbf{X}}_{\{3\}} \otimes \bar{\mathbf{X}}_{\{4,5\}} \rangle$$
$$+ \langle \mathbf{F}, \bar{\mathbf{X}}_{\{1,2\}} \otimes \bar{\mathbf{X}}_{\{3,5\}} \otimes \bar{\mathbf{X}}_{\{4\}} \rangle - \langle \mathbf{F}, \bar{\mathbf{X}}_{\{1,2\}} \otimes \bar{\mathbf{X}}_{\{3\}} \otimes \bar{\mathbf{X}}_{\{4\}} \otimes \bar{\mathbf{X}}_{\{5\}} \rangle \quad (4)$$
$$= 2 \cdot \langle \mathbf{F}, \mathbf{x}_1 \otimes \cdots \otimes \mathbf{x}_5 \rangle + \text{ easy terms.}$$

Equation (4) shows us how to construct the desired PSM protocol. All of the masked tensors on the left-hand side of (4) can be computed by the referee. The parties perform a PSM sub-protocol so that the referee learns the sum of these easy terms. (The details are demonstrated in the last example of 3-party PSM, and are explained in Sect. 3.2.) Then from Eq. (4), the referee learns $2 \cdot \langle \mathbf{F}, \mathbf{x}_1 \otimes \cdots \otimes \mathbf{x}_5 \rangle$.

As long as $\mathbb{F}$ is a finite field in which $2 \neq 0$, the referee has learned the target term. The protocol takes a communication cost of $O(N^2)$ field elements.   □

1.3 Related Works

Besides [6,8], our construction of PSM protocols is also inspired by the progress in Conditional Disclosure of Secrets (CDS). Until recently, CDS had a similar exponential gap between known upper and lower bounds. CDS can be viewed as a variant of PSM where the referee knows all but 1 bit of the input: Consider the 2-party case and let $[N]$ be the input domain for both parties. The upper bounds of $O(\sqrt{N})$ is conserved [6,11]. A similar lower bound of $\Omega(\log N)$ is known [2,11]. Recently, Liu, Vaikuntanathan and Wee improved the CDS upper bound for arbitrary function to $2^{\tilde{O}\sqrt{\log N}}$ [14]. In a slightly different setting, the amortized CDS upper bound per party is improved to $\Theta(1)$ [1,2].

Gay, Kerenidis and Wee constructed 2-party CDS with smooth communication complexity trade-off between the two party [11]. In particular, for any $\eta \in [0, 1]$, they constructed a 2-party CDS protocol where one party sends $O(N^\eta)$ bits and the other sends $O(N^{1-\eta})$ bits.

In [3,9], constructions of *ad hoc* PSM are presented. In this framework, there are k parties, but only a subset of them will perform the computation. This notion, expanded in [7], was shown to imply obfuscation.

2 Preliminaries

Let $\mathbb{N} := \{0, 1, \ldots\}$ denote the set of all natural numbers, and let $[n] := \{1, \ldots, n\}$. In this paper, $\mathbb{F}$ denotes a field, $\mathcal{R}$ denotes a finite commutative ring. For some prime power p, let $\mathbb{F}_p$ denote the unique finite field of order p. A vector will be denoted by a bold face lowercase letter. For a vector $\mathbf{v}$, let $\mathbf{v}[i]$ denote its i-th entry.

2.1   Tensor

A *tensor* refers to the generalization of vectors and matrices which have multiple indices. Roughly speaking, a tensor is a multi-dimensional array. In the paper, a tensor will be denoted by a bold face capital letter. A k-dimensional tensor $\mathbf{T} \in \mathbb{F}^{n_1 \times n_2 \times \cdots \times n_k}$ is essentially an array of size $n_1 \times n_2 \times \cdots \times n_k$. The entries in $\mathbf{T}$ are indexed by $(i_1, \ldots, i_k) \in [n_1] \times \cdots \times [n_k]$, and denoted by $\mathbf{T}[i_1, \ldots, i_k]$. A tensor can also be viewed as a representation of a multi-linear function: any k-linear function $f : \mathbb{F}^{n_1} \times \mathbb{F}^{n_2} \times \ldots \times \mathbb{F}^{n_k} \to \mathbb{F}$ can be uniquely determined by its coefficient tensor $\mathbf{F} \in \mathbb{F}^{n_1 \times \cdots \times n_k}$, such that

$$f(\mathbf{v}_1, \ldots, \mathbf{v}_k) = \sum_{i_1 \in [n_1], \cdots, i_k \in [n_k]} \mathbf{F}[i_1, \ldots, i_k] \cdot \mathbf{v}_1[i_1] \cdot \ldots \cdot \mathbf{v}_k[i_k]. \tag{5}$$

The inner product of two tensors $\mathbf{S}, \mathbf{T} \in \mathbb{F}^{n_1 \times n_2 \times \cdots \times n_k}$ is defined as

$$\langle \mathbf{S}, \mathbf{T} \rangle := \sum_{i_1 \in [n_1], \cdots, i_k \in [n_k]} \mathbf{S}[i_1, \ldots, i_k] \cdot \mathbf{T}[i_1, \ldots, i_k].$$

Given two tensors $\mathbf{S} \in \mathbb{F}^{n_1 \times \cdots \times n_k}$ and $\mathbf{T} \in \mathbb{F}^{m_1 \times \cdots \times m_\ell}$, we define $\mathbf{S} \otimes \mathbf{T}$, their tensor product. It is a tensor in $\mathbb{F}^{n_1 \times \cdots \times n_k \times m_1 \times \cdots \times m_\ell}$ such that

$$(\mathbf{S} \otimes \mathbf{T})[i_1, \ldots, i_k, j_1, \ldots, j_\ell] = \mathbf{S}[i_1, \ldots, i_k] \cdot \mathbf{T}[j_1, \ldots, j_\ell].$$

Using the notation of inner product and tensor product, Eq. (5) can also be written as $f(\mathbf{v}_1, \ldots, \mathbf{v}_k) = \langle \mathbf{F}, \mathbf{v}_1 \otimes \ldots \otimes \mathbf{v}_k \rangle$.

2.2   Private Simultaneous Messages

Definition 1 (private simultaneous message). *A k-party functionality is a mapping $f : \mathcal{X}_1 \times \ldots \times \mathcal{X}_k \to \mathcal{Y}$, where $\mathcal{X}_1, \ldots, \mathcal{X}_k$ are its input spaces and $\mathcal{Y}$ is its output space.*

A private simultaneous message (PSM) protocol for a functionality f consists of a randomness space $\mathcal{W}$ and a tuple of deterministic functions $(\mathsf{M}_1, \ldots, \mathsf{M}_k, \mathsf{R})$

$$\mathsf{M}_i : \mathcal{X}_i \times \mathcal{W} \to \{0,1\}^{\mathsf{cc}_i}, \quad \text{for all } i \in [k],$$
$$\mathsf{R} : \{0,1\}^{\mathsf{cc}_1} \times \ldots \{0,1\}^{\mathsf{cc}_k} \to \{0,1\},$$

where cc_i is the communication complexity of the i-th party, $\mathsf{cc} := \mathsf{cc}_1 + \ldots + \mathsf{cc}_k$ is the total communication complexity.

A perfectly secure PSM protocol for f satisfies the following properties:

(correctness.) *For all input tuple $(x_1, \ldots, x_k) \in \mathcal{X}_1 \times \ldots \times \mathcal{X}_k$ and randomness $w \in \mathcal{W}$,*

$$\mathsf{R}(\mathsf{M}_1(x_1, w), \ldots, \mathsf{M}_k(x_k, w)) = f(x_1, \ldots, x_k)$$

(privacy.) *There exists a randomized simulator S, such that for any input $(x_1, \ldots, x_k) \in \mathcal{X}_1 \times \ldots \times \mathcal{X}_k$, the joint distribution of $\mathsf{M}_1(x_1, w), \ldots, \mathsf{M}_k(x_k, w)$ is the same as the distributions of $\mathsf{S}(f(x_1, \ldots, x_k))$, where the distributions are taken over $w \leftarrow \mathcal{W}$ and the coin tosses of S.*

2.3   Randomized Encoding

Randomized encoding is a primitive closely relate to PSM. The randomized encoding of a function f is a randomized function $\hat{f}$. The output $\hat{f}(x, w)$, where w denotes the randomness, contains sufficient information to recover $f(x)$ and no other information about x.

Definition 2 (randomized encoding). *A randomized encoding for a function* $f : \mathcal{X} \to \mathcal{Y}$ *consists of a randomized encoding function* $\hat{f} : \mathcal{X} \times \mathcal{W} \to \hat{\mathcal{Y}}$ *and a deterministic decoding function* $\mathsf{R} : \hat{\mathcal{Y}} \to \mathcal{Y}$, *where* $\mathcal{W}$ *denotes the randomness space and* $\hat{\mathcal{Y}}$ *denotes the coding space.*

A perfectly secure randomized encoding satisfies the following properties:

(correctness.) *For all* $x \in \mathcal{X}$ *and randomness* $w \in \mathcal{W}$,

$$\mathsf{R}(\hat{f}(x, w)) = f(x)$$

(privacy.) *There exists a randomized simulator* S, *such that for any input* $x \in \mathcal{X}$, *the joint distribution of* $\hat{f}(x, w)$ *is the same as the distributions of* $\mathsf{S}(f(x))$, *where the distributions are taken over* $w \leftarrow \mathcal{W}$ *and the coin tosses of* S.

Follows directly from the definitions, $(\mathsf{M}_1, \ldots, \mathsf{M}_k, \mathsf{R})$ is a PSM protocol for f if and only if $(\hat{f}, \mathsf{R})$ is a randomized encoding for f, where $\hat{f}(x_1, \ldots, x_k, w) := (\mathsf{M}_1(x_1, w), \ldots, \mathsf{M}_k(x_k, w))$.

In other words, PSM is a special form of randomized encoding, where the input is divided into a few portions, and each bit of the encoding only depends on the randomness and one portion of the input.

3   New Multi-party PSM Protocols

In this section, we present one of our main results: for many k, every functionality $f : [N]^k \to \{0, 1\}$ admits a PSM protocol of communication complexity $O_k(N^{\frac{k-1}{2}})$.

Theorem 1. *Let* $f : [N]^k \to \{0, 1\}$ *be an arbitrary* k-party functionality.

- *There is a* k-party PSM protocol for f with communication and randomness complexity $O(N^{\frac{k-1}{2}})$, if $k \leq 20$.
- *There is a* k-party PSM protocol for f with communication and randomness complexity $O_k(N^{\frac{k-1}{2}})$, if $k + 1$ is a prime or a prime power.

In this section, we prove a stronger statement. Let $\mathbb{F}$ be a finite field, consider the following auxiliary k-party functionality Aux_N^k:

---

k-party functionality Aux_N^k

- The i-th party has input $\mathbf{x}_{2i-1}, \mathbf{x}_{2i} \in \mathbb{F}^{\sqrt{N}}$
- The output is $\langle \mathbf{F}, \mathbf{x}_1 \otimes \cdots \otimes \mathbf{x}_{2k} \rangle$, where $\mathbf{F}$ is public and fixed

---

As shown in the beginning of Sect. 3.1, a PSM protocol for Aux_N^k implies a PSM for $f : [N]^k \to \{0,1\}$ with the same communication complexity. The reduction consists of having $\mathbf{F}$ be the truth table of f.

We will present a framework of constructing k-party PSM for Aux_N^k, whose communication complexity is $O_k(N^{\frac{k-1}{2}})$. Roughly speaking, the framework reduces the problem to a system of linear equations. A solution of the system implies a PSM protocol with the desired communication complexity. Therefore, we should rule out the possibility that the induced system has no solution. We partially achieve such a goal. We solve the induced system for infinitely many k:

- For all $k \leq 20$, we checked that the induced system of linear equations is solvable. For small k we solve the system by hand, and for larger k we verified it with a computer program.
- For all k such that $k+1$ is a prime power, we prove that the system is solvable.

Backed by the above observations, we strongly believe the induced system is solvable for all k.

Conjecture 1. *Let $f : [N]^k \to \{0,1\}$ be an arbitrary k-party functionality. There is a k-party PSM protocol for f with communication and randomness complexity $O_k(N^{\frac{k-1}{2}})$.*

Organization. Section 3.1 presents our framework for constructing multi-party PSM, introduces new notations, and gives a 4-party PSM as a concrete example. The following Sects. 3.2, 3.3, 3.4 are independent. Section 3.2 provides more technical detail of the PSM protocols yielded by our framework. Section 3.3 shows how the framework works for small k, and Sect. 3.4 shows how the framework works for any integer k such that $k + 1$ is a prime power.

3.1   A Framework for Multi-party PSM

As mentioned in the beginning of Sect. 3, the functionality $f : [N]^k \to \{0,1\}$ can be reduced to functionality Aux_N^k. The reduction works as follows: Let $x_1, \ldots, x_k$ be the input, the j-th party has input $x_j \in [N]$. We evenly divide x_j into $x'_{2j-1}, x'_{2j} \in [\sqrt{N}]$. For each $i \in [2k]$, let $\mathbf{x}_i := \mathbf{e}_{x'_i} \in \mathbb{F}^{\sqrt{N}}$ be the x'_i-th standard unit vector. We reduce f to Aux_N^k:

$$f(x_1, \ldots, x_{2k}) = \langle \mathbf{F}, \mathbf{x}_1 \otimes \ldots \otimes \mathbf{x}_{2k} \rangle$$

where $\mathbf{F}$ is the truth-table of f. For the remainder of the section, it is thus sufficient to construct a PSM protocol for Aux_N^k.

For each non-empty $\Omega \subseteq [2k]$, our protocol will sample a random dimension-$|\Omega|$ tensor $\mathbf{R}_\Omega \in \mathcal{R}^{(\sqrt{N})^{|\Omega|}}$ from the common random string[1]. Define $\bar{\mathbf{X}}_\Omega := \mathbf{R}_\Omega + \bigotimes_{i \in \Omega} \mathbf{x}_i$. E.g., $\bar{\mathbf{X}}_{\{2\}} := \mathbf{R}_{\{2\}} + \mathbf{x}_2$, $\bar{\mathbf{X}}_{\{3,4\}} := \mathbf{R}_{\{3,4\}} + \mathbf{x}_3 \otimes \mathbf{x}_4$.

---

[1] A note on the randomness complexity: The final protocol uses $\mathbf{R}_\Omega$ only if $|\Omega| \leq k - 1$.

Within the communication complexity budget $O(N^{\frac{k-1}{2}})$, we can let the referee learn $\bar{\mathbf{X}}_\Omega$ for all Ω such that $|\Omega| \leq k - 1$ (more details in Sect. 3.2). The referee does not learn extra information as $\bar{\mathbf{X}}_\Omega$ is one-time padded by $\mathbf{R}_\Omega$. For example when $k = 4$, we can let the referee learn tensors $\bar{\mathbf{X}}_{\{1\}}, \bar{\mathbf{X}}_{\{2\}}, \ldots, \bar{\mathbf{X}}_{\{8\}}$, $\bar{\mathbf{X}}_{\{1,2\}}, \bar{\mathbf{X}}_{\{1,3\}}, \ldots, \bar{\mathbf{X}}_{\{7,8\}}, \bar{\mathbf{X}}_{\{1,2,3\}}, \bar{\mathbf{X}}_{\{1,2,4\}}, \ldots, \bar{\mathbf{X}}_{\{6,7,8\}}$. The referee learns those tensor by having *subsets of the parties* recursively perform PSM ptocols with a smaller number of parties, so that the referee learns the required information. Learning those tensors allows the referee to compute many terms including $\langle \mathbf{F}, \bar{\mathbf{X}}_{\{1,2,3\}} \otimes \bar{\mathbf{X}}_{\{4,5,6\}} \otimes \bar{\mathbf{X}}_{\{7,8\}} \rangle$, which equals to the sum of the following 8 terms,

$$
\begin{aligned}
\langle \mathbf{F}, & \bar{\mathbf{X}}_{\{1,2,3\}} \otimes \bar{\mathbf{X}}_{\{4,5,6\}} \otimes \bar{\mathbf{X}}_{\{7,8\}} \rangle \\
= & \langle \mathbf{F}, \mathbf{x}_1 \otimes \mathbf{x}_2 \otimes \mathbf{x}_3 \otimes \mathbf{x}_4 \otimes \mathbf{x}_5 \otimes \mathbf{x}_6 \otimes \mathbf{x}_7 \otimes \mathbf{x}_8 \rangle \\
& + \langle \mathbf{F}, \mathbf{x}_1 \otimes \mathbf{x}_2 \otimes \mathbf{x}_3 \otimes \mathbf{x}_4 \otimes \mathbf{x}_5 \otimes \mathbf{x}_6 \otimes \mathbf{R}_{\{7,8\}} \rangle \\
& + \langle \mathbf{F}, \mathbf{x}_1 \otimes \mathbf{x}_2 \otimes \mathbf{x}_3 \otimes \mathbf{R}_{\{4,5,6\}} \otimes \mathbf{x}_7 \otimes \mathbf{x}_8 \rangle \\
& + \langle \mathbf{F}, \mathbf{x}_1 \otimes \mathbf{x}_2 \otimes \mathbf{x}_3 \otimes \mathbf{R}_{\{4,5,6\}} \otimes \mathbf{R}_{\{7,8\}} \rangle \\
& + \langle \mathbf{F}, \mathbf{R}_{\{1,2,3\}} \otimes \mathbf{x}_4 \otimes \mathbf{x}_5 \otimes \mathbf{x}_6 \otimes \mathbf{x}_7 \otimes \mathbf{x}_8 \rangle \\
& + \langle \mathbf{F}, \mathbf{R}_{\{1,2,3\}} \otimes \mathbf{x}_4 \otimes \mathbf{x}_5 \otimes \mathbf{x}_6 \otimes \mathbf{R}_{\{7,8\}} \rangle \\
& + \langle \mathbf{F}, \mathbf{R}_{\{1,2,3\}} \otimes \mathbf{R}_{\{4,5,6\}} \otimes \mathbf{x}_7 \otimes \mathbf{x}_8 \rangle \\
& + \langle \mathbf{F}, \mathbf{R}_{\{1,2,3\}} \otimes \mathbf{R}_{\{4,5,6\}} \otimes \mathbf{R}_{\{7,8\}} \rangle.
\end{aligned}
\tag{6}
$$

Before we continue, let us introduce a few notations to describe the terms appearing in (6). The term (tensor) on the left hand side of the equation will be called a *masked term* (masked tensor). The terms (tensors) on the right hand side of the equation will be called *pure terms* (pure tensors).

Definition (masked tensor & masked term). A masked tensor is a tensor product $\bar{\mathbf{X}}_{\Omega_1} \otimes \ldots \otimes \bar{\mathbf{X}}_{\Omega_t}$ [2] such that $\Omega_1, \ldots, \Omega_t$ are disjoint and their union equals $[2k]$. The *shape* of a masked tensor $\bar{\mathbf{X}}_{\Omega_1} \otimes \ldots \otimes \bar{\mathbf{X}}_{\Omega_t}$ is the multiset $\{|\Omega_1|, \ldots, |\Omega_t|\}$. The inner product of a masked tensor and $\mathbf{F}$ is called a masked term.

For any multiset P such that $\mathrm{sum}(P) = 2k$, let $\sum \bar{\mathbf{X}}(P)$ denote the sum of all masked tensors of shape P, let $\sum \langle \mathbf{F}, \bar{\mathbf{X}}(P) \rangle$ denote the sum of all masked terms of shape P. We thus have $\sum \langle \mathbf{F}, \bar{\mathbf{X}}(P) \rangle = \langle \mathbf{F}, \sum \bar{\mathbf{X}}(P) \rangle$.

Definition (pure tensor & pure term). A pure tensor is a tensor product $\mathbf{R}_{\Omega_1} \otimes \ldots \otimes \mathbf{R}_{\Omega_t} \otimes \mathbf{x}_{i_1} \otimes \ldots \otimes \mathbf{x}_{i_w}$ such that $\{i_1, \ldots, i_w\}, \Omega_1, \ldots, \Omega_t$ are disjoint and their union equals $[2k]$. The *shape* of a pure tensor $\mathbf{R}_{\Omega_1} \otimes \ldots \otimes \mathbf{R}_{\Omega_t} \otimes \mathbf{x}_{i_1} \otimes \ldots \otimes \mathbf{x}_{i_w}$ is the multiset $\{|\Omega_1|, \ldots, |\Omega_t|\}$. The inner product of a pure tensor and $\mathbf{F}$ is called a pure term.

---

[2] We implicitly exchange the order of indices in tensor product. E.g. when $k = 2$, the masked tensor $\bar{\mathbf{X}}_{\{1,4\}} \otimes \bar{\mathbf{X}}_{\{2,3\}}$ is defined by $(\bar{\mathbf{X}}_{\{1,4\}} \otimes \bar{\mathbf{X}}_{\{2,3\}})[j_1, j_2, j_3, j_4] = \bar{\mathbf{X}}_{\{1,4\}}[j_1, j_4] \cdot \bar{\mathbf{X}}_{\{2,3\}}[j_2, j_3]$.

For any multiset P such that $\text{sum}(P) \leq 2k$, let $\sum \mathbf{R}(P)$ denote the sum of all pure tensors of shape P, let $\sum \langle \mathbf{F}, \mathbf{R}(P) \rangle$ denote the sum of all pure terms of shape P. We thus have $\sum \langle \mathbf{F}, \mathbf{R}(P) \rangle = \langle \mathbf{F}, \sum \mathbf{R}(P) \rangle$.

The pure terms (pure tensors) can be grouped into 3 natural categories:

target term (target tensor) $\langle \mathbf{F}, \mathbf{x}_1 \otimes \ldots \otimes \mathbf{x}_{2k} \rangle$ is called the target term as it is desired functionality output. The corresponding tensor $\mathbf{x}_1 \otimes \ldots \otimes \mathbf{x}_{2k}$ is called the target tensor.

easy terms (easy tensors) A pure tensor $\mathbf{R}_{\Omega_1} \otimes \ldots \otimes \mathbf{R}_{\Omega_t} \otimes \mathbf{x}_{i_1} \otimes \ldots \otimes \mathbf{x}_{i_w}$ is called an easy tensor if at most $k+1$ out of the $2k$ dimensions are contributed by vector $\mathbf{x}_i$'s (i.e., $w \leq k+1$). The corresponding term is called an easy term. Every easy term admits a PSM protocol with communication complexity no more than $O(\text{poly}(k) \cdot N^{\frac{k-1}{2}})$ field elements (more details in Sect. 3.2).

hard terms (hard tensors) The rest.

With this terminology, we can give *an overview of our PSM protocol*. As the referee can learn $\bar{\mathbf{X}}_\Omega$ for all Ω such that $|\Omega| \leq k - 1$, the referee can compute any masked term of shape P if $\max(P) \leq k - 1$. As suggested by Eq. (6), every masked term is the linear combination of a few pure terms. Ideally, the referee only has to combine some computable masked terms, so that all the hard terms cancel out, resulting a linear combination of the target term and easy terms:

$$a \text{ } linear \text{ } combination \text{ } of \text{ } masked \text{ } terms = target \text{ } term + some \text{ } easy \text{ } terms. \quad (7)$$

Once we are in this ideal case, the easy terms can be easily removed by standard techniques, resulting the desired k-party PSM protocol for Aux_N^k. (More details are presented in Sect. 3.2.) Therefore, the task is reduced to a linear algebra problem: *is the target term (resp. tensor) spanned by the referee-computable masked terms (resp. tensors) and easy terms (resp. tensors)?*

When solving such linear algebra problem, it is fair to assume that the solution is symmetric. (Otherwise, assume that a solution that looks like (7) is asymmetric, it can be symmetrized by applying the symmetric sum on both sides.)

We have defined the (symmetric) sum of terms or tensors of the same shape. For example when $k = 4$, $\sum \bar{\mathbf{X}}(3, 3, 2)$ is defined as the sum of all masked tensors $\bar{\mathbf{X}}_{\Omega_1} \otimes \bar{\mathbf{X}}_{\Omega_2} \otimes \bar{\mathbf{X}}_{\Omega_3}$ such that the multiset $\{|\Omega_1|, |\Omega_2|, |\Omega_3|\}$ equals $\{3, 3, 2\}$, i.e.

$$\begin{aligned}
\sum \bar{\mathbf{X}}(3,3,2) := \text{ } & \bar{\mathbf{X}}_{\{1,2,3\}} \otimes \bar{\mathbf{X}}_{\{4,5,6\}} \otimes \bar{\mathbf{X}}_{\{7,8\}} + \bar{\mathbf{X}}_{\{1,2,3\}} \otimes \bar{\mathbf{X}}_{\{4,5,7\}} \otimes \bar{\mathbf{X}}_{\{6,8\}} \\
& + \bar{\mathbf{X}}_{\{1,2,3\}} \otimes \bar{\mathbf{X}}_{\{4,5,8\}} \otimes \bar{\mathbf{X}}_{\{5,6\}} + \bar{\mathbf{X}}_{\{1,2,3\}} \otimes \bar{\mathbf{X}}_{\{4,6,7\}} \otimes \bar{\mathbf{X}}_{\{5,8\}} \\
& + \ldots + \bar{\mathbf{X}}_{\{3,4,5\}} \otimes \bar{\mathbf{X}}_{\{6,7,8\}} \otimes \bar{\mathbf{X}}_{\{1,2\}}.
\end{aligned}$$

Let's revisit Eq. (6),

$$\underbrace{\langle \mathbf{F}, \bar{\mathbf{X}}_{\{1,2,3\}} \otimes \bar{\mathbf{X}}_{\{4,5,6\}} \otimes \bar{\mathbf{X}}_{\{7,8\}} \rangle}_{\text{a masked term of shape } \{3,3,2\}}$$

$$= \underbrace{\langle \mathbf{F}, \mathbf{x}_1 \otimes \cdots \otimes \mathbf{x}_8 \rangle}_{\text{a pure term of shape } \{\}} + \underbrace{\langle \mathbf{F}, \mathbf{x}_1 \otimes \cdots \otimes \mathbf{x}_6 \otimes \mathbf{R}_{\{7,8\}} \rangle}_{\text{a pure term of shape } \{2\}}$$

$$+ \underbrace{\langle \mathbf{F}, \mathbf{x}_1 \otimes \mathbf{x}_2 \otimes \mathbf{x}_3 \otimes \mathbf{R}_{\{4,5,6\}} \otimes \mathbf{x}_7 \otimes \mathbf{x}_8 \rangle + \langle \mathbf{F}, \mathbf{R}_{\{1,2,3\}} \otimes \mathbf{x}_4 \otimes \cdots \otimes \mathbf{x}_8 \rangle}_{\text{pure terms of shape } \{3\}}$$

$$+ \underbrace{\langle \mathbf{F}, \mathbf{x}_1 \otimes \mathbf{x}_2 \otimes \mathbf{x}_3 \otimes \mathbf{R}_{\{4,5,6\}} \otimes \mathbf{R}_{\{7,8\}} \rangle + \langle \mathbf{F}, \mathbf{R}_{\{1,2,3\}} \otimes \mathbf{x}_4 \otimes \mathbf{x}_5 \otimes \mathbf{x}_6 \otimes \mathbf{R}_{\{7,8\}} \rangle}_{\text{pure terms of shape } \{3,2\}}$$

$$+ \underbrace{\langle \mathbf{F}, \mathbf{R}_{\{1,2,3\}} \otimes \mathbf{R}_{\{4,5,6\}} \otimes \mathbf{x}_7 \otimes \mathbf{x}_8 \rangle}_{\text{a pure term of shape } \{3,3\}} + \underbrace{\langle \mathbf{F}, \mathbf{R}_{\{1,2,3\}} \otimes \mathbf{R}_{\{4,5,6\}} \otimes \mathbf{R}_{\{7,8\}} \rangle}_{\text{a pure term of shape } \{3,3,2\}}.$$

By applying a symmetric sum on both sides, we get

$$\sum \langle \mathbf{F}, \bar{\mathbf{X}}(3,3,2) \rangle = \underbrace{280 \cdot \sum \langle \mathbf{F}, \mathbf{R}() \rangle}_{\text{the target term}} + \underbrace{10 \cdot \sum \langle \mathbf{F}, \mathbf{R}(2) \rangle}_{\text{hard pure terms}}$$

$$+ \underbrace{10 \cdot \sum \langle \mathbf{F}, \mathbf{R}(3) \rangle + \sum \langle \mathbf{F}, \mathbf{R}(3,2) \rangle + \sum \langle \mathbf{F}, \mathbf{R}(3,3) \rangle + \sum \langle \mathbf{F}, \mathbf{R}(3,3,2) \rangle}_{\text{easy pure terms}}.$$

As another example of the symmetric sum of masked term that the referee can compute,

$$\sum \langle \mathbf{F}, \bar{\mathbf{X}}(2,2,2,2) \rangle = \underbrace{105 \cdot \sum \langle \mathbf{F}, \mathbf{R}() \rangle}_{\text{target term}} + \underbrace{15 \cdot \sum \langle \mathbf{F}, \mathbf{R}(2) \rangle}_{\text{hard pure terms}}$$

$$+ \underbrace{3 \cdot \sum \langle \mathbf{F}, \mathbf{R}(2,2) \rangle + \sum \langle \mathbf{F}, \mathbf{R}(2,2,2) \rangle + \sum \langle \mathbf{F}, \mathbf{R}(2,2,2,2) \rangle}_{\text{easy pure terms}}.$$

By carefully combining the above two equations, we get

$$3 \cdot \sum \langle \mathbf{F}, \bar{\mathbf{X}}(3,3,2) \rangle - 2 \cdot \sum \langle \mathbf{F}, \bar{\mathbf{X}}(2,2,2,2) \rangle = 630 \cdot \sum \langle \mathbf{F}, \mathbf{R}() \rangle + \text{easy terms}, \quad (8)$$

which induces a 4-party PSM whose communication complexity is $O(N^{3/2})$, if we let $\mathbb{F}$ to be any field in which $630 \neq 0$. (Section 3.2 explains how Eq. (8) implies a 4-party PSM with desired communication complexity.)

In the general k-party case, for each legit shape P of masked term (i.e., P is a multiset consisting of positive integers and $\text{sum}(P) = 2k$),

$$\sum \langle \mathbf{F}, \bar{\mathbf{X}}(P) \rangle = \sum_{Q \subseteq P} \alpha(Q) \cdot \sum \langle \mathbf{F}, \mathbf{R}(P \setminus Q) \rangle, \quad (9)$$

where $P \setminus Q$ is the multiset subtraction and

$$\alpha(Q) := \frac{(\text{sum}(Q))!}{\prod_{i \in Q} i! \cdot \prod_{m \in \mathbb{Z}^+}(\text{number of } m\text{'s in } Q)!} \quad (10)$$

is the following combinatoric number: $\alpha(Q)$ is the number of ways to partition $\text{sum}(Q)$ distinct elements into some unordered subsets $S_1, \ldots, S_t$ such that $Q = \{|S_1|, \ldots, |S_t|\}$. Equations (9), (10) are proved in Appendix A.

3.2   The Induced PSM Protocol

In order to develop the previous section smoothly, we skipped some technique details in Sect. 3.1. In this section, we will show how to construct a k-party PSM protocol assuming that the target term is spanned by referee-computable masked terms and easy pure terms.

By our assumption, there are referee-computable masked terms $\bar{\mathbf{X}}^{(1)}, \ldots, \bar{\mathbf{X}}^{(t)}$, easy pure terms $\mathbf{R}^{(1)}, \ldots, \mathbf{R}^{(s)}$, and coefficients $a_1, \ldots a_t, b_1, \ldots, b_s \in \mathbb{F}$ such that

$$\langle \mathbf{F}, \mathbf{x}_1 \otimes \cdots \otimes \mathbf{x}_{2k} \rangle = \sum_{j=1}^{t} a_j \bar{\mathbf{X}}^{(j)} + \sum_{j=1}^{s} b_j \mathbf{R}^{(j)}. \tag{11}$$

A k-party PSM for f, together with its correctness and security, is yielded by the following facts:

- Fact I: $\sum_{j=1}^{s} b_j \mathbf{R}^{(j)}$ and $\bar{\mathbf{X}}_\Omega$ for all $0 < |\Omega| \leq k - 1$ form a randomized encoding of $\langle \mathbf{F}, \mathbf{x}_1 \otimes \cdots \otimes \mathbf{x}_{2k} \rangle$. That is, they contain the sufficient information to recover $\langle \mathbf{F}, \mathbf{x}_1 \otimes \cdots \otimes \mathbf{x}_{2k} \rangle$, and they are garbled with additional randomness so that no other information can be recovered.
- Fact II: For every $\Omega \subseteq [2k]$ such that $0 < |\Omega| \leq k-1$, there is a PSM protocol for $\bar{\mathbf{X}}_\Omega$ with communication complexity $\text{poly}(k) \cdot N^{\frac{k-1}{2}}$ field elements.
- Fact III: There is a PSM protocol for $\sum_{j=1}^{s} b_j \mathbf{R}^{(j)}$ with communication complexity $\text{poly}(k) \cdot s \cdot N^{\frac{k-1}{2}}$ field elements.

The k-party PSM for f works as the follows: For each $\Omega \subseteq [2k]$ such that $0 < |\Omega| \leq k-1$, use the PSM guaranteed by Fact II to reveal $\bar{\mathbf{X}}_\Omega$ to the referee. Use the PSM guaranteed by Fact III to reveal $\sum_{j=1}^{s} b_j \mathbf{R}^{(j)}$ to the referee. Then Fact I allows the referee to compute the output from Eq. (11).

Proof of Fact I. Equation (11) shows that $\langle \mathbf{F}, \mathbf{x}_1 \otimes \cdots \otimes \mathbf{x}_{2k} \rangle$ can be computed from the encoding. Moreover, the distribution of the encoding is perfectly simulatable: The joint distribution of tensors $\bar{\mathbf{X}}_\Omega$ for $0 < |\Omega| \leq k - 1$ is uniform distribution, as they are independently one-time padded. Then the value of $\sum_{j=1}^{s} b_j \mathbf{R}^{(j)}$ is uniquely determined by Eq. (11).

Proof of Fact II. Each coordinate of $\mathbf{X}_\Omega$ is defined as

$$\bar{\mathbf{X}}_{\{j_1, \ldots, j_t\}}[i_1, \ldots, i_t] = \mathbf{R}_{\{j_1, \ldots, j_t\}}[i_1, \ldots, i_t] + \mathbf{x}_{j_1}[i_1] \cdot \ldots \cdot \mathbf{x}_{j_t}[i_t],$$

which is an arithmetic formula of size $O(k)$. Thus each coordinate has a PSM protocol with communication complexity $\text{poly}(k)$ field elements [13].

Proof of Fact III. Sample random $c_1, \ldots, c_s \in \mathbb{F}$ from the common random string such that $c_1 + \ldots + c_s = 0$. Then it's sufficient to construct a PSM protocol for computing $b_j \mathbf{R}^{(j)} + c_j$ for each j. Say this easy pure term $\mathbf{R}^{(j)}$ is $\langle \mathbf{F}, \mathbf{R}_{\Omega_1} \otimes \ldots \otimes \mathbf{x}_{i_1} \otimes \ldots \otimes \mathbf{x}_{i_w} \rangle$. By our definition of an easy term, $w \leq k+1$. There exists a special party, such that the other parties hold at most $k-1$ of $\mathbf{x}_{i_1}, \ldots, \mathbf{x}_{i_w}$. When $w = k+1$, the special party is the one who holds two of $\mathbf{x}_{i_1}, \ldots, \mathbf{x}_{i_w}$ (the existence is guaranteed by the pigeonhole principle). W.l.o.g. assume that the other parties hold $\mathbf{x}_{i_1}, \ldots, \mathbf{x}_{i_{w'}}$ such that $w' \leq k-1$. Then the special party knows a dimension-w' tensor $\mathbf{G}$ (which is determined by its input and $b_j, \mathbf{R}_{\Omega_1}, \mathbf{R}_{\Omega_2}, \ldots$) such that

$$b_j \mathbf{R}^{(j)} + c_j = \langle \mathbf{G}, \mathbf{x}_{i_1} \otimes \ldots \otimes \mathbf{x}_{i_{w'}} \rangle + c_j,$$

which admits a PSM protocol (presented in Sect. B.1) with communication complexity $O(\text{poly}(k) \cdot N^{w'/2})$ field elements.

3.3 When k is Small

As shown in Sect. 3.1, to construct PSM protocol for Aux_N^k with communication complexity $O_k(N^{\frac{k-1}{2}})$, it is sufficient to prove the target term is spanned by the referee-computable masked terms and easy pure terms. In this section, we verify the condition holds for all $k \leq 20$, which proves the first bullet of Theorem 1. However, we do not have a general construction of such linenar systems of equations for an arbitrary k.

The case when $k = 2$ was solved by [6]. Our framework yields the same protocol from

$$\sum \langle \mathbf{F}, \bar{\mathbf{X}}(1,1,1,1) \rangle = \sum \langle \mathbf{F}, \mathbf{R}() \rangle + \text{easy terms}.$$

The case when $k = 3$ was solved by [8]. Our framework yields a similar protocol from

$$\sum \langle \mathbf{F}, \bar{\mathbf{X}}(2,2,2) \rangle = \sum \langle \mathbf{F}, \mathbf{R}() \rangle + \text{easy terms}.$$

The case when $k = 4$ is solved in Sect. 3.1.

For $k = 5$, consider the following two masked terms,

$$\sum \langle \mathbf{F}, \bar{\mathbf{X}}(4,4,2) \rangle = 1575 \cdot \sum \langle \mathbf{F}, \mathbf{R}() \rangle + 35 \cdot \sum \langle \mathbf{F}, \mathbf{R}(2) \rangle + \text{easy terms},$$
$$\sum \langle \mathbf{F}, \bar{\mathbf{X}}(4,2,2,2) \rangle = 3150 \cdot \sum \langle \mathbf{F}, \mathbf{R}() \rangle + 210 \cdot \sum \langle \mathbf{F}, \mathbf{R}(2) \rangle + \text{easy terms}.$$

We have $6 \cdot \sum \langle \mathbf{F}, \bar{\mathbf{X}}(4,4,2) \rangle - \sum \langle \mathbf{F}, \bar{\mathbf{X}}(4,2,2,2) \rangle = 6300 \cdot \sum \langle \mathbf{F}, \mathbf{R}() \rangle + \text{easy terms}$, which induces a 5-party PSM with communication complexity $O(N^2)$.

For $k = 6$, consider the following masked terms

$$\begin{bmatrix} \sum \langle \mathbf{F}, \bar{\mathbf{X}}(5,4,3) \rangle \\ \sum \langle \mathbf{F}, \bar{\mathbf{X}}(4,4,4) \rangle \\ \sum \langle \mathbf{F}, \bar{\mathbf{X}}(3,3,3,3) \rangle \end{bmatrix} = \begin{bmatrix} 27720 & 126 & 56 \\ 5775 & & 35 \\ 15400 & 280 & \end{bmatrix} \begin{bmatrix} \sum \langle \mathbf{F}, \mathbf{R}() \rangle \\ \sum \langle \mathbf{F}, \mathbf{R}(3) \rangle \\ \sum \langle \mathbf{F}, \mathbf{R}(4) \rangle \end{bmatrix} + \text{easy terms}$$

Therefore, $100 \cdot \sum \langle \mathbf{F}, \bar{\mathbf{X}}(5,4,3) \rangle - 160 \cdot \sum \langle \mathbf{F}, \bar{\mathbf{X}}(4,4,4) \rangle - 45 \cdot \sum \langle \mathbf{F}, \bar{\mathbf{X}}(3,3,3,3) \rangle = 1155000 \cdot \sum \langle \mathbf{F}, \mathbf{R}() \rangle$ + easy terms, which induces a 6-party PSM with communication complexity $O(N^{2.5})$.

For $k = 7$, consider the following masked terms

$$
\begin{bmatrix} \sum \langle \mathbf{F}, \bar{\mathbf{X}}(4,4,4,2) \rangle \\ \sum \langle \mathbf{F}, \bar{\mathbf{X}}(6,6,2) \rangle \\ \sum \langle \mathbf{F}, \bar{\mathbf{X}}(6,4,4) \rangle \end{bmatrix} = \begin{bmatrix} 525525 & 5775 & 1575 \\ 42042 & 462 & \\ 105105 & & 210 \end{bmatrix} \begin{bmatrix} \sum \langle \mathbf{F}, \mathbf{R}() \rangle \\ \sum \langle \mathbf{F}, \mathbf{R}(2) \rangle \\ \sum \langle \mathbf{F}, \mathbf{R}(4) \rangle \end{bmatrix} + \text{easy terms}
$$

Therefore, $14 \cdot \sum \langle \mathbf{F}, \bar{\mathbf{X}}(4,4,4,2) \rangle - 175 \cdot \sum \langle \mathbf{F}, \bar{\mathbf{X}}(6,6,2) \rangle - 105 \cdot \sum \langle \mathbf{F}, \bar{\mathbf{X}}(6,4,4) \rangle = -11036025 \cdot \sum \langle \mathbf{F}, \mathbf{R}() \rangle$ + easy terms, which induces a 7-party PSM with communication complexity $O(N^3)$.

For larger k, we wrote a simple program[3] to check if the target term can be spanned by referee-computable masked terms and easy terms. For simplicity, our program requires specifying the finite field in advance. Our program verifies that the framework yields a PSM protocol with c.c. $O(N^{\frac{k-1}{2}})$ for every $k \le 20$. For example when $k = 20$, our program found:

$\sum \langle \mathbf{F}, \mathbf{R}() \rangle = 2895 \cdot \sum \langle \mathbf{F}, \bar{\mathbf{X}}(19,19,2) \rangle + 1902 \cdot \sum \langle \mathbf{F}, \bar{\mathbf{X}}(19,17,4) \rangle + 2843 \cdot \sum \langle \mathbf{F}, \bar{\mathbf{X}}(19,16,5) \rangle + 1025 \cdot \sum \langle \mathbf{F}, \bar{\mathbf{X}}(19,16,3,2) \rangle + 691 \cdot \sum \langle \mathbf{F}, \bar{\mathbf{X}}(19,15,6) \rangle + 2507 \cdot \sum \langle \mathbf{F}, \bar{\mathbf{X}}(19,15,4,2) \rangle + 1923 \cdot \sum \langle \mathbf{F}, \bar{\mathbf{X}}(19,14,7) \rangle + 1836 \cdot \sum \langle \mathbf{F}, \bar{\mathbf{X}}(19,14,5,2) \rangle + 2385 \cdot \sum \langle \mathbf{F}, \bar{\mathbf{X}}(19,13,8) \rangle + 2073 \cdot \sum \langle \mathbf{F}, \bar{\mathbf{X}}(19,13,6,2) \rangle + 1312 \cdot \sum \langle \mathbf{F}, \bar{\mathbf{X}}(19,12,9) \rangle + 2963 \cdot \sum \langle \mathbf{F}, \bar{\mathbf{X}}(19,12,7,2) \rangle + 568 \cdot \sum \langle \mathbf{F}, \bar{\mathbf{X}}(19,11,10) \rangle + 975 \cdot \sum \langle \mathbf{F}, \bar{\mathbf{X}}(19,11,8,2) \rangle + 2445 \cdot \sum \langle \mathbf{F}, \bar{\mathbf{X}}(19,10,9,2) \rangle + 2047 \cdot \sum \langle \mathbf{F}, \bar{\mathbf{X}}(19,9,8,4) \rangle + 318 \cdot \sum \langle \mathbf{F}, \bar{\mathbf{X}}(19,9,8,2,2) \rangle + 2118 \cdot \sum \langle \mathbf{F}, \bar{\mathbf{X}}(19,9,6,6) \rangle + 2189 \cdot \sum \langle \mathbf{F}, \bar{\mathbf{X}}(19,9,6,4,2) \rangle + 1271 \cdot \sum \langle \mathbf{F}, \bar{\mathbf{X}}(19,9,6,2,2,2) \rangle + 1557 \cdot \sum \langle \mathbf{F}, \bar{\mathbf{X}}(19,9,4,4,4) \rangle + 2482 \cdot \sum \langle \mathbf{F}, \bar{\mathbf{X}}(19,9,4,4,2,2) \rangle + 173 \cdot \sum \langle \mathbf{F}, \bar{\mathbf{X}}(19,9,4,2,2,2,2) \rangle + 1943 \cdot \sum \langle \mathbf{F}, \bar{\mathbf{X}}(19,9,2,2,2,2,2,2) \rangle + 29 \cdot \sum \langle \mathbf{F}, \bar{\mathbf{X}}(18,18,4) \rangle + 1247 \cdot \sum \langle \mathbf{F}, \bar{\mathbf{X}}(18,17,5) \rangle + 1768 \cdot \sum \langle \mathbf{F}, \bar{\mathbf{X}}(18,17,3,2) \rangle + 2735 \cdot \sum \langle \mathbf{F}, \bar{\mathbf{X}}(18,16,6) \rangle + 416 \cdot \sum \langle \mathbf{F}, \bar{\mathbf{X}}(18,16,4,2) \rangle + 1009 \cdot \sum \langle \mathbf{F}, \bar{\mathbf{X}}(18,15,7) \rangle + 130 \cdot \sum \langle \mathbf{F}, \bar{\mathbf{X}}(18,15,5,2) \rangle + 138 \cdot \sum \langle \mathbf{F}, \bar{\mathbf{X}}(18,14,8) \rangle + 52 \cdot \sum \langle \mathbf{F}, \bar{\mathbf{X}}(18,14,6,2) \rangle + 2661 \cdot \sum \langle \mathbf{F}, \bar{\mathbf{X}}(18,13,9) \rangle + 26 \cdot \sum \langle \mathbf{F}, \bar{\mathbf{X}}(18,13,7,2) \rangle + 731 \cdot \sum \langle \mathbf{F}, \bar{\mathbf{X}}(18,12,10) \rangle + 16 \cdot \sum \langle \mathbf{F}, \bar{\mathbf{X}}(18,12,8,2) \rangle + 145 \cdot \sum \langle \mathbf{F}, \bar{\mathbf{X}}(18,11,11) \rangle + 12 \cdot \sum \langle \mathbf{F}, \bar{\mathbf{X}}(18,11,9,2) \rangle + 818 \cdot \sum \langle \mathbf{F}, \bar{\mathbf{X}}(18,10,8,4) \rangle + 1728 \cdot \sum \langle \mathbf{F}, \bar{\mathbf{X}}(18,10,8,2,2) \rangle + 2676 \cdot \sum \langle \mathbf{F}, \bar{\mathbf{X}}(18,10,6,6) \rangle + 1533 \cdot \sum \langle \mathbf{F}, \bar{\mathbf{X}}(18,10,6,4,2) \rangle + 2490 \cdot \sum \langle \mathbf{F}, \bar{\mathbf{X}}(18,10,6,2,2,2) \rangle + 760 \cdot \sum \langle \mathbf{F}, \bar{\mathbf{X}}(18,10,4,4,4) \rangle + 747 \cdot \sum \langle \mathbf{F}, \bar{\mathbf{X}}(18,10,4,4,2,2) \rangle + 2752 \cdot \sum \langle \mathbf{F}, \bar{\mathbf{X}}(18,10,4,2,2,2,2) \rangle + 83 \cdot \sum \langle \mathbf{F}, \bar{\mathbf{X}}(18,10,2,2,2,2,2,2) \rangle + \text{easy terms} \mod 3001$

which induces a PSM protocol with c.c. $O(N^{9.5})$.

3.4 When $k + 1$ is a Prime Power

As shown in Sect. 3.1, to construct PSM protocol for Aux_N^k with communication complexity $O_k(N^{\frac{k-1}{2}})$, it is sufficient to prove the target term is spanned by the referee-computable masked terms and easy pure terms. In this section, we prove that the condition holds for all k such that $k + 1$ is a prime power, which proves the second bullet of Theorem 1.

When $k + 1$ is a prime p or a prime power p^e, we obtain a simple k-party PSM, by doing computations in the finite field $\mathbb{F}_p$.

---

[3] The source code can be downloaded from https://github.com/tianren/psm.

Proof. Consider the symmetric sum of all masked terms of shape $\{k-1, 1, \ldots, 1\}$

$$\sum \langle \mathbf{F}, \bar{\mathbf{X}}(k-1, \underbrace{1, \ldots, 1}_{k+1 \text{ 1's}}) \rangle$$

$$= \sum_{i=0}^{k+1} \alpha(k-1, \underbrace{1, \ldots, 1}_{k+1-i \text{ 1's}}) \cdot \sum \langle \mathbf{F}, \mathbf{R}(\underbrace{1, \ldots, 1}_{i \text{ 1's}}) \rangle$$

$$+ \sum_{i=0}^{k+1} \alpha(\underbrace{1, \ldots, 1}_{k+1-i \text{ 1's}}) \cdot \sum \langle \mathbf{F}, \mathbf{R}(k-1, \underbrace{1, \ldots, 1}_{i \text{ 1's}}) \rangle \quad (12)$$

$$= \alpha(k-1, \underbrace{1, \ldots, 1}_{k+1 \text{ 1's}}) \cdot \sum \langle \mathbf{F}, \mathbf{R}() \rangle$$

$$+ \sum_{i=1}^{k-2} \alpha(k-1, \underbrace{1, \ldots, 1}_{k+1-i \text{ 1's}}) \cdot \sum \langle \mathbf{F}, \mathbf{R}(\underbrace{1, \ldots, 1}_{i \text{ 1's}}) \rangle + \text{easy terms.}$$

(Recall that a pure term of shape P is easy iff $\text{sum}(P) \geq k-1$.)
W.l.o.g. assume $k > 2$. By definition, $\alpha(k-1, \underbrace{1, \ldots, 1}_{t \text{ 1's}}) = \binom{k-1+t}{k-1}$. Lemma 2 shows that $\alpha(k-1, \underbrace{1, \ldots, 1}_{k+1 \text{ 1's}}) = \binom{2k}{k-1} \equiv 1 \mod p$, while $\alpha(k-1, \underbrace{1, \ldots, 1}_{k+1-i \text{ 1's}}) = \binom{2k-i}{k-1}$ is a multiple of p for all $1 \leq i \leq k-2$. Therefore,

$$\sum \langle \mathbf{F}, \bar{\mathbf{X}}(k-1, \underbrace{1, \ldots, 1}_{k+1 \text{ 1's}}) \rangle = \sum \langle \mathbf{F}, \mathbf{R}() \rangle + \text{easy terms} \mod p,$$

which induces a k-party PSM protocol with c.c. $O_k(N^{\frac{k-1}{2}})$. □

Lemma 1. *For any prime p and positive integer e, $\binom{p^e}{t}$ is a multiple of p for all $0 < t < p^e$.*

Proof.

$$\binom{p^e}{t} = \frac{p^e}{t} \cdot \binom{p^e - 1}{t - 1}.$$

  □

Lemma 2. *For any prime p and positive integer e, binomial coefficient $\binom{p^e+t}{p^e-2}$ is a multiple of p for all $0 \leq t \leq p^e - 3$, while binomial coefficient $\binom{2p^e-2}{p^e-2} \equiv 1$ mod p.*

Proof. For every $0 \leq t \leq p^e - 3$,

$$\binom{p^e + t}{p^e - 2} = \sum_{j=0}^{t} \binom{t}{j} \underbrace{\binom{p^e}{p^e - 2 - j}}_{\text{multiple of } p}$$

is a multiple of p. While

$$\binom{2p^e-2}{p^e-2} = \underbrace{\sum_{j=0}^{p^e-3}\binom{p^e-2}{j}\binom{p^e}{p^e-2-j}}_{\text{multiple of }p} + \binom{p^e-2}{p^e-2}\binom{p^e}{0} \equiv 1 \mod p.$$

$\square$

4   Unbalanced 2-Party PSM Protocols

The two parties in 2-party PSM are conventionally called Alice and Bob. Let $x \in [N]$ denote Alice's and $y \in [N]$ denote Bob's input. In this section, we show that every functionality $f : [N] \times [N] \to \{0,1\}$ admits a 2-party PSM protocol, where Alice sends $O(N^\eta)$ bits and Bob sends $O(N^{1-\eta})$ bits.

Theorem 2. *For any functionality* $f : [N] \times [N] \to \{0,1\}$, *and any* $\eta = d/k$ *such that* d, k *are integers and* $0 < d < k \leq 20$, *there is a 2-party PSM protocol for* f *with unbalanced communication complexity* $O(N^\eta), O(N^{1-\eta})$.

In this section, we prove a stronger statement. Let $\mathbb{F}$ be a finite field, consider the following auxiliary 2-party functionality $\mathsf{Aux}^2_{k,N}$:

2-party functionality $\mathsf{Aux}^2_{k,N}$

- Alice has input $\mathbf{x}_1, \ldots, \mathbf{x}_k \in \mathbb{F}^{\sqrt[k]{N}}$
- Bob has input $\mathbf{y}_1, \ldots, \mathbf{y}_k \in \mathbb{F}^{\sqrt[k]{N}}$
- The output is $\langle \mathbf{F}, \mathbf{x}_1 \otimes \ldots \otimes \mathbf{x}_k \otimes \mathbf{y}_1 \otimes \ldots \otimes \mathbf{y}_k \rangle$, where $\mathbf{F}$ is public and fixed

---

A PSM protocol for $\mathsf{Aux}^2_{k,N}$ implies a PSM for $f : [N] \times [N] \to \{0,1\}$ with the same communication complexity of each party. The reduction consists of having $\mathbf{F}$ be the truth table of f.

We present a framework for the construction of 2-party PSM protocols for $\mathsf{Aux}^2_{k,N}$, where Alice sends $O_\eta(N^\eta)$ bits and Bob sends $O_\eta(N^{1-\eta})$ bits, for all $\eta \in \{\frac{1}{k}, \ldots, \frac{k-1}{k}\}$. Similar to the framework in Sect. 3, the framework in this section also reduces the problem to a system of linear equations. A solution of the system implies a 2-party PSM protocol with the desired communication complexity. By verifying with a computer, we find that our framework works well for all η whose denominator is no larger than 20. Backed by those observations, we believe that our framework allows for a smooth trade-off between the communication complexity of Alice and Bob:

Conjecture 2. *For any functionality* $f : [N] \times [N] \to \{0,1\}$, *and any* $0 < \eta < 1$, *there is a 2-party PSM protocol for* f *with unbalanced communication complexity* $O_\eta(N^\eta), O_\eta(N^{1-\eta})$.

Organization. Section 4.1 presents our framework for constructing multi-party PSM, introduces new notations, and gives as a concrete example a 2-party PSM with communication $O(N^{1/3}), O(N^{2/3})$. The following Sects. 4.2, 4.3 are independent. Section 4.2 provides more technical detail of the PSM protocols yielded by our framework. Section 4.3 shows how the framework works for small k.

4.1 A Framework for 2-Party PSM

Consider a rational $\eta = \frac{d}{k} \in (0,1)$. Let $\mathbb{F}$ be a finite commutative ring that we will fix later. All the operations are within ring $\mathbb{F}$ unless otherwise specified.

As mentioned in the beginning of Sect. 4, there is an non-interactive reduction from the functionality $f : [N] \times [N] \rightarrow \{0,1\}$ to functionality $\mathsf{Aux}_{k,N}^2$. The reduction works as follows: Let $x, y \in [N]$ be the input of Alice and Bob respectively. Evenly divide x into $x_1, \ldots, x_k \in [\sqrt[k]{N}]$, similarly divide y into $y_1, \ldots, y_k \in [\sqrt[k]{N}]$. For each $j \in [k]$, let $\mathbf{x}_j := \mathbf{e}_{x_j} \in \mathbb{F}^{\sqrt[k]{N}}$ be the x_j-th standard unit vector. Similarly let $\mathbf{y}_i := \mathbf{e}_{y_i} \in \mathbb{F}^{\sqrt[k]{N}}$ for every $i \in [k]$. The functionality f can be reduced to $\mathsf{Aux}_{k,N}^2$ by doing:

$$f(x_1, \ldots, x_k, y_1, \ldots, y_k) = \langle \mathbf{F}, \mathbf{x}_1 \otimes \ldots \otimes \mathbf{x}_k \otimes \mathbf{y}_1 \otimes \ldots \otimes \mathbf{y}_k \rangle.$$

where $\mathbf{F}$ is the truth-table of f. For the remainder of the section, it is thus sufficient to construct a PSM protocol for $\mathsf{Aux}_{k,N}^2$.

For every $\Omega \subseteq [k]$, our protocol will sample random $\mathbf{R}_\Omega, \mathbf{S}_\Omega \in \mathbb{F}^{(\sqrt[k]{N})^{|\Omega|}}$ from the common random string. Let $\bar{\mathbf{X}}_\Omega := \mathbf{R}_\Omega + \bigotimes_{i \in \Omega} \mathbf{x}_i$ and $\bar{\mathbf{Y}}_\Omega := \mathbf{S}_\Omega + \bigotimes_{i \in \Omega} \mathbf{y}_i$.

As the communication complexity of Alice is $O_\eta(N^{\frac{d}{k}})$, she can send $\bar{\mathbf{X}}_\Omega$ to the referee for every Ω that $|\Omega| \leq d$. So far no information is leaked as $\bar{\mathbf{X}}_\Omega$ is one-time padded by $\mathbf{R}_\Omega$. Similarly, Bob can send $\bar{\mathbf{Y}}_\Omega$ for every Ω that $|\Omega| \leq k-d$.

There are many meaningful terms that the referee can compute once he receives $(\bar{\mathbf{X}}_\Omega)_{|\Omega| \leq d}$ and $(\bar{\mathbf{Y}}_\Omega)_{|\Omega| \leq k-d}$. For example, when $\eta = d/k = 1/3$, the referee can compute:

$$\begin{aligned}
&\langle \mathbf{F}, \bar{\mathbf{X}}_{\{1\}} \otimes \bar{\mathbf{X}}_{\{2\}} \otimes \bar{\mathbf{X}}_{\{3\}} \otimes \bar{\mathbf{Y}}_{\{1,2\}} \otimes \bar{\mathbf{Y}}_{\{3\}} \rangle \\
&= \langle \mathbf{F}, \mathbf{x}_1 \otimes \mathbf{x}_2 \otimes \mathbf{x}_3 \otimes \mathbf{y}_1 \otimes \mathbf{y}_2 \otimes \mathbf{y}_3 \rangle \\
&\quad + \langle \mathbf{F}, \mathbf{x}_1 \otimes \mathbf{x}_2 \otimes \mathbf{x}_3 \otimes \mathbf{y}_1 \otimes \mathbf{y}_2 \otimes \mathbf{S}_{\{3\}} \rangle \\
&\quad + \langle \mathbf{F}, \mathbf{x}_1 \otimes \mathbf{x}_2 \otimes \mathbf{x}_3 \otimes \mathbf{S}_{\{1,2\}} \otimes \mathbf{S}_{\{3\}} \rangle \\
&\quad + \ldots \quad (28 \text{ other terms}) \\
&\quad + \langle \mathbf{F}, \mathbf{R}_{\{1\}} \otimes \mathbf{R}_{\{2\}} \otimes \mathbf{R}_{\{3\}} \otimes \mathbf{S}_{\{1,2\}} \otimes \mathbf{S}_{\{3\}} \rangle.
\end{aligned} \tag{13}$$

Before we continue, we have to introduce a few notations. We will define shape, masked tensor, pure tensor, easy & hard tensor, etc., in the same way as in Sect. 3.1.

Definition (masked tensor & masked term). An Alice-side masked tensor is a tensor product $\bar{\mathbf{X}}_{\Omega_1} \otimes \ldots \otimes \bar{\mathbf{X}}_{\Omega_t}$ such that $\Omega_1, \ldots, \Omega_t$ are disjoint and their union equals $[k]$. The *shape* of an Alice-side masked tensor $\bar{\mathbf{X}}_{\Omega_1} \otimes \ldots \otimes \bar{\mathbf{X}}_{\Omega_t}$ is the multiset $\{|\Omega_1|, \ldots, |\Omega_t|\}$. Bob-side masked tensors are defined symmetrically.

The tensor product of an Alice-side masked tensor and a Bob-side masked tensor is called a *masked tensor*. The inner product of $\mathbf{F}$ and a masked tensor is called a *masked term*.

An Alice-side masked tensor of shape P is referee-computable if $\max(P) \leq d$. A Bob-side masked tensor of shape Q is referee-computable if $\max(Q) \leq k-d$. An masked tensor (and its corresponding masked term) is called *referee-computable* if it's the tensor product of a referee-computable Alice-side masked tensor and a referee-computable Bob-side masked tensor.

Definition (pure tensor & pure term). An Alice-side pure tensor is a tensor product $\mathbf{R}_{\Omega_1} \otimes \ldots \otimes \mathbf{R}_{\Omega_t} \otimes \mathbf{x}_{i_1} \otimes \ldots \otimes \mathbf{x}_{i_w}$ such that $\{i_1, \ldots, i_w\}, \Omega_1, \ldots, \Omega_t$ are disjoint and their union equals $[k]$. The *shape* of an Alice-side masked tensor $\mathbf{R}_{\Omega_1} \otimes \ldots \otimes \mathbf{R}_{\Omega_t} \otimes \mathbf{x}_{i_1} \otimes \ldots \otimes \mathbf{x}_{i_w}$ is the multiset $\{|\Omega_1|, \ldots, |\Omega_t|\}$. Bob-side pure tensors are defined symmetrically.

The tensor product of an Alice-side pure tensor and a Bob-side pure tensor is called a *pure tensor*. The inner product of a pure tensor and $\mathbf{F}$ is called a *pure term*.

For any legit shape, let $\sum \mathbf{R}(P)$ denote the sum of all Alice-side pure tensor whose shape is P. Similarly, define Bob-side pure tensor sum $\sum \mathbf{S}(P)$.

Let's go back to the example when $\eta = 1/3$: examine the pure terms on the right side of Eq. (13), and check which of them has a 2-party PSM with communication complexity $O(N^{\frac{1}{3}}), O(N^{\frac{2}{3}})$.

- The term $\langle \mathbf{F}, \mathbf{x}_1 \otimes \mathbf{x}_2 \otimes \mathbf{x}_3 \otimes \mathbf{y}_1 \otimes \mathbf{y}_2 \otimes \mathbf{y}_3 \rangle$ is the desired functionality.
- The term $\langle \mathbf{F}, \mathbf{x}_1 \otimes \mathbf{x}_2 \otimes \mathbf{x}_3 \otimes \mathbf{S}_{\{1,2\}} \otimes \mathbf{y}_3 \rangle$ has a PSM protocol with communication complexity $O(N^{\frac{1}{3}})$. Because Alice knows a vector $\mathbf{g}$ (which is determined by $\mathbf{F}$, Alice's input and randomness $(\mathbf{R}_\Omega)_\Omega, (\mathbf{S}_\Omega)_\Omega$) such that $\langle \mathbf{F}, \mathbf{x}_1 \otimes \mathbf{x}_2 \otimes \mathbf{x}_3 \otimes \mathbf{S}_{\{1,2\}} \otimes \mathbf{y}_3 \rangle = \langle \mathbf{g}, \mathbf{y}_3 \rangle$.
- The term $\langle \mathbf{F}, \mathbf{S}_{\{1\}} \otimes \mathbf{x}_2 \otimes \mathbf{x}_3 \otimes \mathbf{y}_1 \otimes \mathbf{y}_2 \otimes \mathbf{y}_3 \rangle$ admits a PSM protocol with unbalanced communication complexity $O(N^{\frac{1}{3}})$, $O(N^{\frac{2}{3}})$. Because Bob knows a dimension-2 tensor $\mathbf{G}$ such that $\langle \mathbf{F}, \mathbf{S}_{\{1\}} \otimes \mathbf{x}_2 \otimes \mathbf{x}_3 \otimes \mathbf{y}_1 \otimes \mathbf{y}_2 \otimes \mathbf{y}_3 \rangle = \langle \mathbf{x}_2 \otimes \mathbf{x}_3, \mathbf{G} \rangle$. (This PSM is presented in Sect. B.2.)

The discussion above hints at the right classification of pure tensors.

target tensor. The only Alice-side target tensor is $\mathbf{x}_1 \otimes \cdots \otimes \mathbf{x}_k$. The only Bob-side target tensor is $\mathbf{y}_1 \otimes \cdots \otimes \mathbf{y}_k$. The only target tensor is $\mathbf{x}_1 \otimes \cdots \otimes \mathbf{x}_k \otimes \mathbf{y}_1 \otimes \cdots \otimes \mathbf{y}_k$.

easy tensor. An Alice-side pure tensor of shape P is called easy if $\mathrm{sum}(P) \geq d$. A Bob-side pure tensor of shape Q is called easy if $\mathrm{sum}(Q) \geq k - d$. A pure tensor $\mathbf{R} \otimes \mathbf{S}$ is called easy if either $\mathbf{R}$ or $\mathbf{S}$ is easy.

hard tensor. The rest.

The inner product of $\mathbf{F}$ and a target/easy/hard tensor is called a target/easy/hard term.

Then, Eq. (13) can be rewritten by grouping and ignoring the easy terms:

$$
\begin{aligned}
\langle \mathbf{F}, \bar{\mathbf{X}}_{\{1\}} &\otimes \bar{\mathbf{X}}_{\{2\}} \otimes \bar{\mathbf{X}}_{\{3\}} \otimes \bar{\mathbf{Y}}_{\{1,2\}} \otimes \bar{\mathbf{Y}}_{\{3\}} \rangle \\
&= \langle \mathbf{F}, \mathbf{x}_1 \otimes \mathbf{x}_2 \otimes \mathbf{x}_3 \otimes \mathbf{y}_1 \otimes \mathbf{y}_2 \otimes \mathbf{y}_3 \rangle \\
&\quad + \langle \mathbf{F}, \mathbf{x}_1 \otimes \mathbf{x}_2 \otimes \mathbf{x}_3 \otimes \mathbf{y}_1 \otimes \mathbf{y}_2 \otimes \mathbf{S}_{\{3\}} \rangle + \text{easy terms}
\end{aligned}
$$

By a symmetric sum, we get

$$
\begin{aligned}
\langle \mathbf{F}, \sum \bar{\mathbf{X}}(1,1,1) &\otimes \sum \bar{\mathbf{Y}}(2,1) \rangle \\
&= 3 \cdot \underbrace{\langle \mathbf{F}, \sum \mathbf{R}() \otimes \sum \mathbf{S}() \rangle}_{\text{target}} + \langle \mathbf{F}, \sum \mathbf{R}() \otimes \sum \mathbf{S}(1) \rangle + \text{easy terms}.
\end{aligned}
$$

Similarly, we have decomposed another referee-computable term

$$
\begin{aligned}
\langle \mathbf{F}, \sum \bar{\mathbf{X}}(1,1,1) &\otimes \sum \bar{\mathbf{Y}}(1,1,1) \rangle \\
&= \underbrace{\langle \mathbf{F}, \sum \mathbf{R}() \otimes \sum \mathbf{S}() \rangle}_{\text{target}} + \langle \mathbf{F}, \sum \mathbf{R}() \otimes \sum \mathbf{S}(1) \rangle + \text{easy terms}.
\end{aligned}
$$

Combine them to cancel out the hard terms:

$$
\begin{aligned}
\langle \mathbf{F}, \sum \bar{\mathbf{X}}(1,1,1) &\otimes \sum \bar{\mathbf{Y}}(2,1) \rangle - \langle \mathbf{F}, \sum \bar{\mathbf{X}}(1,1,1) \otimes \sum \bar{\mathbf{Y}}(1,1,1) \rangle \\
&= 2 \cdot \langle \mathbf{F}, \sum \mathbf{R}() \otimes \sum \mathbf{S}() \rangle + \text{easy terms}.
\end{aligned}
$$

Thus, by setting $\mathbb{F}$ to be any finite field where $2 \neq 0$, the above equation induces a 2-party PSM protocol with unbalanced communication complexity $O(N^{\frac{1}{3}}), O(N^{\frac{2}{3}})$.

In general, a masked term $\langle \mathbf{F}, \sum \bar{\mathbf{X}}(P) \otimes \sum \bar{\mathbf{Y}}(Q) \rangle$ can be decomposed into pure terms by

$$
\sum \bar{\mathbf{X}}(P) = \sum_{P' \subseteq P} \alpha(P') \sum \bar{\mathbf{X}}(P \setminus P'),
$$

$$
\sum \bar{\mathbf{Y}}(Q) = \sum_{Q' \subseteq Q} \alpha(Q') \sum \bar{\mathbf{Y}}(Q \setminus Q'),
$$

$$
\langle \mathbf{F}, \sum \bar{\mathbf{X}}(P) \otimes \sum \bar{\mathbf{Y}}(Q) \rangle = \sum_{\substack{P' \subseteq P \\ Q' \subseteq Q}} \alpha(P') \alpha(Q') \langle \mathbf{F}, \sum \bar{\mathbf{X}}(P \setminus P') \otimes \sum \bar{\mathbf{Y}}(Q \setminus Q') \rangle.
$$

with the combinatoric number α defined as in Sect. 3.1. The first two equations are essentially the same as Eq. (9) and they imply the third equation.

To construct a PSM protocol of the desired unbalanced communication complexity, it is sufficient to show the target term is spanned by the referee-computable masked terms and the easy terms. Namely,

the target term = a linear combination of referee-computable masked terms +

a linear combination of easy terms. (14)

The details of how this sufficient condition implies a PSM with desired communication complexity is presented in Sect. 4.2.

This sufficient condition of form (14) is unfortunately too combinatorically hard to use in practice, especially since we are going to use a program to search for the proof for different values of η. There are too many distinct masked terms and pure terms – their number is equal to the number of pairs of legit shapes (P, Q).

Fortunately, we come up with a simpler sufficient condition. A PSM protocol of the desired unbalanced communication complexity exists if both of the following hold:

– The Alice-side target tensor is spanned by referee-computable Alice-side masked tensors and Alice-side easy tensors;
– The Bob-side target tensor is spanned by referee-computable Bob-side masked tensors and Bob-side easy tensors.

The proof is quite straight-forward: Assume the new sufficient condition,

> *a linear combination of referee-computable Alice-side masked tensors*
> $= \sum \mathbf{R}() + \text{Alice-side easy tensors,}$
> *a linear combination of referee-computable Bob-side masked tensors*
> $= \sum \mathbf{S}() + \text{Bob-side easy tensors.}$

The tensor product of the above two equations is

> *a linear combination of referee-computable masked tensors*
> $= \sum \mathbf{R}() \otimes \sum \mathbf{S}() + \text{a linear combination of easy tensors.}$

Multiplying both sides of the above equation with $\mathbf{F}$ yields the desired sufficient condition of form (14). $\qquad\square$

4.2   The Induced PSM Protocol

In order to develop the previous section smoothly, we skipped the technique details on how the condition (14) implies a 2-party PSM of the desired communication complexity. In this section, we will show how to construct such a 2-party PSM protocol assuming that the target term is spanned by referee-computable masked terms and easy pure terms.

By the condition (14), there are referee-computable masked terms $\bar{\mathbf{Z}}^{(1)}, \ldots,$ $\bar{\mathbf{Z}}^{(t)}$, easy pure terms $\mathbf{T}^{(1)}, \ldots, \mathbf{T}^{(s)}$, and coefficients $a_1, \ldots a_t, b_1, \ldots, b_s \in \mathbb{F}$ such that

$$\langle \mathbf{F}, \mathbf{x}_1 \otimes \cdots \otimes \mathbf{x}_k \otimes \mathbf{y}_1 \otimes \cdots \otimes \mathbf{y}_k \rangle = \sum_{j=1}^{t} a_j \bar{\mathbf{Z}}^{(j)} + \sum_{j=1}^{s} b_j \mathbf{T}^{(j)}. \qquad (15)$$

A 2-party PSM for f, together with its correctness and security, is yielded by the following facts:

- Fact I: $\sum_{j=1}^{s} b_j \mathbf{T}^{(j)}$ together with $\bar{\mathbf{X}}_\Omega$ for all $0 < |\Omega| \leq d$ and $\bar{\mathbf{Y}}_\Omega$ for all $0 < |\Omega| \leq k - d$ form a randomized encoding of the functionality output.
- Fact II: There is a PSM protocol for $\sum_{j=1}^{s} b_j \mathbf{T}^{(j)}$, in which Alice sends $k \cdot s \cdot N^{\frac{d}{k}}$ field elements, Bob sends $k \cdot s \cdot N^{1-\frac{d}{k}}$ field elements.

The 2-party PSM for f works as the follows: For each $\Omega \subseteq [k]$ such that $0 < |\Omega| \leq d$, Alice sends $\bar{\mathbf{X}}_\Omega$ to the referee. Symmetrically, for $\Omega \subseteq [k]$ such that $0 < |\Omega| \leq k - d$, Bob sends $\bar{\mathbf{Y}}_\Omega$ to the referee. Use the PSM guaranteed by Fact II to reveal $\sum_{j=1}^{s} b_j \mathbf{T}^{(j)}$ to the referee. Then Fact I allows the referee to compute the output from Eq. (15).

Proof of Fact I. (Similar to the proof of Fact I in Sect. 3.2.) Equation (15) shows that $\langle \mathbf{F}, \mathbf{x}_1 \otimes \cdots \otimes \mathbf{x}_k \otimes \mathbf{y}_1 \otimes \cdots \otimes \mathbf{y}_k \rangle$ can be computed from the encoding. Moreover, the distribution of the encoding is perfectly simulatable: The joint distribution of tensors $\bar{\mathbf{X}}_\Omega$ for $0 < |\Omega| \leq d$ and $\bar{\mathbf{Y}}_\Omega$ for $0 < |\Omega| \leq k-d$ is uniform, as they are independently one-time padded. Then the value of $\sum_{j=1}^{s} b_j \mathbf{T}^{(j)}$ is uniquely determined by Eq. (15).

Proof of Fact II. Sample random $c_1, \ldots, c_s \in \mathbb{F}$ from the common random string such that $c_1 + \ldots + c_s = 0$. Then it's sufficient to construct a PSM protocol for computing $b_j \mathbf{T}^{(j)} + c_j$ for each j.

Because $\mathbf{T}^{(j)}$ is an easy term, we have $\mathbf{T}^{(j)} = \langle \mathbf{F}, \mathbf{R}^{(j)} \otimes \mathbf{S}^{(j)} \rangle$, where $\mathbf{R}^{(j)}$ is an Alice-side pure tensor, $\mathbf{S}^{(j)}$ is a Bob-side pure tensor, and either $\mathbf{R}^{(j)}$ is an Alice-side easy tensor, $\mathbf{S}^{(j)}$ is a Bob-side easy tensor. W.l.o.g., assume $\mathbf{R}^{(j)}$ is an Alice-side easy tensor.

Say this Alice-side easy pure term $\mathbf{R}^{(j)}$ is $\mathbf{R}_{\Omega_1} \otimes \ldots \otimes \mathbf{x}_{i_1} \otimes \ldots \otimes \mathbf{x}_{i_w}$. By the definition of an Alice-side easy term, $w \leq k - d$. Then Bob knows a dimension-w tensor $\mathbf{G}$ (which is determined by $\mathbf{S}^{(j)}, b_j, \mathbf{R}_{\Omega_1}, \mathbf{R}_{\Omega_2}, \ldots$) such that

$$b_j \mathbf{T}^{(j)} + c_j = \langle \mathbf{G}, \mathbf{x}_{i_1} \otimes \ldots \otimes \mathbf{x}_{i_w} \rangle + c_j,$$

which admits a PSM protocol (presented in Sect. B.2) in which Alice sends $O(w \cdot N^{1/k})$ field elements, Bob sends $N^{w/k}$ field elements.

4.3   When η Has a Small Denominator

Section 4.1 proves a sufficient condition that implies 2-party PSM protocols with the desired unbalanced communication complexity. In this section, we will verify that the sufficient condition holds for all rational $\eta \in (0, 1)$ whose denominator is no larger than 20. Theorem 2 follows as a consequence.

For $\eta = 1/3$, the 2-party PSM protocol in Sect. 4.1 is also induced by

$$\sum \bar{\mathbf{X}}(1,1,1) = \sum \mathbf{R}() + \text{Alice-side easy tensors,}$$
$$\sum \bar{\mathbf{Y}}(2,1) - \sum \bar{\mathbf{Y}}(1,1,1) = 2 \cdot \sum \mathbf{S}() + \text{Bob-side easy tensors.}$$

For $\eta = 1/4$, a 2-party PSM protocol with c.c. $O(N^{1/4})$, $O(N^{3/4})$ is induced by

$$\sum \bar{\mathbf{X}}(1,1,1,1) = \sum \mathbf{R}() + \text{Alice-side easy tensors},$$

$$\sum \bar{\mathbf{Y}}(1,1,1,1) + 2 \cdot \sum \bar{\mathbf{Y}}(3,1)$$
$$+ \sum \bar{\mathbf{Y}}(2,2) - \sum \bar{\mathbf{Y}}(2,1,1) = 6 \cdot \sum \mathbf{S}() + \text{Bob-side easy tensors}.$$

For $\eta = 1/5$, a 2-party PSM protocol with desired c.c. is induced by

$$\sum \bar{\mathbf{X}}(1,1,1,1,1) = \sum \mathbf{R}() + \text{Alice-side easy tensors},$$

$$6 \cdot \sum \bar{\mathbf{Y}}(4,1) + 2 \cdot \sum \bar{\mathbf{Y}}(3,2)$$
$$- 2 \cdot \sum \bar{\mathbf{Y}}(3,1,1) - \sum \bar{\mathbf{Y}}(2,2,1)$$
$$+ \sum \bar{\mathbf{Y}}(2,1,1,1) - \sum \bar{\mathbf{Y}}(1,1,1,1,1) = 24 \cdot \sum \mathbf{S}() + \text{Bob-side easy tensors}.$$

For $\eta = 2/5$, a 2-party PSM protocol with desired c.c. is induced by

$$2 \cdot \sum \bar{\mathbf{X}}(2,2,1) - \sum \bar{\mathbf{X}}(2,1,1,1) = 20 \cdot \sum \mathbf{R}() + \text{Alice-side easy tensors},$$

$$3 \cdot \sum \bar{\mathbf{Y}}(3,2) + \sum \bar{\mathbf{Y}}(3,1,1)$$
$$- \sum \bar{\mathbf{Y}}(2,2,1) - \sum \bar{\mathbf{Y}}(1,1,1,1,1) = 24 \cdot \sum \mathbf{S}() + \text{Bob-side easy tensors}.$$

For larger denominators, we wrote a computer program (See footnote 2) to assist us in the proof. For example, for $\eta = 7/20$, a 2-party PSM with desired c.c. is induced by

$\sum \mathbf{R}() = $ Alice-side easy tensors $+ 18 \cdot \Sigma \bar{\mathbf{X}}(7,7,6) + 10 \cdot \Sigma \bar{\mathbf{X}}(7,7,5,1) + 14 \cdot \Sigma \bar{\mathbf{X}}(7,7,4,2) + 14 \cdot \Sigma \bar{\mathbf{X}}(7,7,4,1,1) + 17 \cdot \Sigma \bar{\mathbf{X}}(7,7,3,3) + 20 \cdot \Sigma \bar{\mathbf{X}}(7,7,3,2,1) + 20 \cdot \Sigma \bar{\mathbf{X}}(7,7,3,1,1,1) + 10 \cdot \Sigma \bar{\mathbf{X}}(7,7,2,2,2) + 10 \cdot \Sigma \bar{\mathbf{X}}(7,7,2,2,1,1) + 10 \cdot \Sigma \bar{\mathbf{X}}(7,7,2,1,1,1,1) + 10 \cdot \Sigma \bar{\mathbf{X}}(7,7,1,1,1,1,1,1) + 6 \cdot \Sigma \bar{\mathbf{X}}(7,6,6,1) + 19 \cdot \Sigma \bar{\mathbf{X}}(7,6,5,2) + 19 \cdot \Sigma \bar{\mathbf{X}}(7,6,5,1,1) + 21 \cdot \Sigma \bar{\mathbf{X}}(7,6,4,3) + 22 \cdot \Sigma \bar{\mathbf{X}}(7,6,4,2,1) + 22 \cdot \Sigma \bar{\mathbf{X}}(7,6,4,1,1,1) + 7 \cdot \Sigma \bar{\mathbf{X}}(7,6,3,3,1) + 15 \cdot \Sigma \bar{\mathbf{X}}(7,6,3,2,2) + 15 \cdot \Sigma \bar{\mathbf{X}}(7,6,3,2,1,1) + 15 \cdot \Sigma \bar{\mathbf{X}}(7,6,3,1,1,1,1) + 19 \cdot \Sigma \bar{\mathbf{X}}(7,6,2,2,2,1) + 19 \cdot \Sigma \bar{\mathbf{X}}(7,6,2,2,1,1,1) + 19 \cdot \Sigma \bar{\mathbf{X}}(7,6,2,1,1,1,1,1) + 19 \cdot \Sigma \bar{\mathbf{X}}(7,6,1,1,1,1,1,1,1) \mod 23$

$\sum \mathbf{S}() = $ Bob-side easy tensors $+ 13 \cdot \Sigma \bar{\mathbf{Y}}(13,7) + 20 \cdot \Sigma \bar{\mathbf{Y}}(13,6,1) + 2 \cdot \Sigma \bar{\mathbf{Y}}(13,5,2) + 22 \cdot \Sigma \bar{\mathbf{Y}}(13,5,1,1) + 1 \cdot \Sigma \bar{\mathbf{Y}}(13,4,3) + 17 \cdot \Sigma \bar{\mathbf{Y}}(13,4,2,1) + 3 \cdot \Sigma \bar{\mathbf{Y}}(13,4,1,1,1) + 19 \cdot \Sigma \bar{\mathbf{Y}}(13,3,3,1) + 21 \cdot \Sigma \bar{\mathbf{Y}}(13,3,2,2) + 1 \cdot \Sigma \bar{\mathbf{Y}}(13,3,2,1,1) + 11 \cdot \Sigma \bar{\mathbf{Y}}(13,3,1,1,1,1) + 12 \cdot \Sigma \bar{\mathbf{Y}}(13,2,2,2,1) + 17 \cdot \Sigma \bar{\mathbf{Y}}(13,2,2,1,1,1) + 3 \cdot \Sigma \bar{\mathbf{Y}}(13,2,1,1,1,1,1) + 10 \cdot \Sigma \bar{\mathbf{Y}}(13,1,1,1,1,1,1,1) + 11 \cdot \Sigma \bar{\mathbf{Y}}(12,8) + 17 \cdot \Sigma \bar{\mathbf{Y}}(12,7,1) + 1 \cdot \Sigma \bar{\mathbf{Y}}(12,6,2) + 11 \cdot \Sigma \bar{\mathbf{Y}}(12,6,1,1) + 17 \cdot \Sigma \bar{\mathbf{Y}}(11,9) + 14 \cdot \Sigma \bar{\mathbf{Y}}(11,8,1) + 6 \cdot \Sigma \bar{\mathbf{Y}}(11,7,2) + 20 \cdot \Sigma \bar{\mathbf{Y}}(11,7,1,1) + 7 \cdot \Sigma \bar{\mathbf{Y}}(11,6,3) + 4 \cdot \Sigma \bar{\mathbf{Y}}(11,6,2,1) + 21 \cdot \Sigma \bar{\mathbf{Y}}(11,6,1,1,1) + 2 \cdot \Sigma \bar{\mathbf{Y}}(10,10) + 4 \cdot \Sigma \bar{\mathbf{Y}}(10,9,1) + 15 \cdot \Sigma \bar{\mathbf{Y}}(10,8,2) + 4 \cdot \Sigma \bar{\mathbf{Y}}(10,8,1,1) + 1 \cdot \Sigma \bar{\mathbf{Y}}(10,7,3) + 17 \cdot \Sigma \bar{\mathbf{Y}}(10,7,2,1) + 3 \cdot \Sigma \bar{\mathbf{Y}}(10,7,1,1,1) + 21 \cdot \Sigma \bar{\mathbf{Y}}(10,6,4) + 8 \cdot \Sigma \bar{\mathbf{Y}}(10,6,3,1) + 4 \cdot \Sigma \bar{\mathbf{Y}}(10,6,2,2) + 21 \cdot \Sigma \bar{\mathbf{Y}}(10,6,2,1,1) + 1 \cdot \Sigma \bar{\mathbf{Y}}(10,6,1,1,1,1) + 20 \cdot \Sigma \bar{\mathbf{Y}}(9,9,2) + 13 \cdot \Sigma \bar{\mathbf{Y}}(9,9,1,1) + 4 \cdot \Sigma \bar{\mathbf{Y}}(9,8,3) + 22 \cdot \Sigma \bar{\mathbf{Y}}(9,8,2,1) + 12 \cdot \Sigma \bar{\mathbf{Y}}(9,8,1,1,1) + 14 \cdot \Sigma \bar{\mathbf{Y}}(9,7,4) + 13 \cdot \Sigma \bar{\mathbf{Y}}(9,7,3,1) + 18 \cdot \Sigma \bar{\mathbf{Y}}(9,7,2,2) + 14 \cdot \Sigma \bar{\mathbf{Y}}(9,7,2,1,1) + 16 \cdot \Sigma \bar{\mathbf{Y}}(9,7,1,1,1,1) + 11 \cdot \Sigma \bar{\mathbf{Y}}(9,6,5) + 13 \cdot \Sigma \bar{\mathbf{Y}}(9,6,4,1) + 12 \cdot \Sigma \bar{\mathbf{Y}}(9,6,3,2) + 17 \cdot \Sigma \bar{\mathbf{Y}}(9,6,3,1,1) + 20 \cdot \Sigma \bar{\mathbf{Y}}(9,6,2,2,1) + 13 \cdot \Sigma \bar{\mathbf{Y}}(9,6,2,1,1,1) + 5 \cdot \Sigma \bar{\mathbf{Y}}(9,6,1,1,1,1,1) + 19 \cdot \Sigma \bar{\mathbf{Y}}(8,8,4) + 16 \cdot \Sigma \bar{\mathbf{Y}}(8,8,3,1) + 8 \cdot \Sigma \bar{\mathbf{Y}}(8,8,2,2) + 19 \cdot \Sigma \bar{\mathbf{Y}}(8,8,2,1,1) + 2 \cdot \Sigma \bar{\mathbf{Y}}(8,8,1,1,1,1) + 17 \cdot \Sigma \bar{\mathbf{Y}}(8,7,5) + 18 \cdot \Sigma \bar{\mathbf{Y}}(8,7,4,1) + 6 \cdot \Sigma \bar{\mathbf{Y}}(8,7,3,2) + 20 \cdot \Sigma \bar{\mathbf{Y}}(8,7,3,1,1) + 10 \cdot \Sigma \bar{\mathbf{Y}}(8,7,2,2,1) + 18 \cdot \Sigma \bar{\mathbf{Y}}(8,7,2,1,1,1) + 14 \cdot \Sigma \bar{\mathbf{Y}}(8,7,1,1,1,1,1) + 18 \cdot \Sigma \bar{\mathbf{Y}}(8,6,6) + 6 \cdot \Sigma \bar{\mathbf{Y}}(8,6,5,1) + 13 \cdot \Sigma \bar{\mathbf{Y}}(8,6,4,2) + 5 \cdot \Sigma \bar{\mathbf{Y}}(8,6,4,1,1) + 1 \cdot \Sigma \bar{\mathbf{Y}}(8,6,3,3) + 17 \cdot \Sigma \bar{\mathbf{Y}}(8,6,3,2,1) + 3 \cdot \Sigma \bar{\mathbf{Y}}(8,6,3,1,1,1) + 20 \cdot \Sigma \bar{\mathbf{Y}}(8,6,2,2,2) + 13 \cdot \Sigma \bar{\mathbf{Y}}(8,6,2,2,1,1) + 5 \cdot \Sigma \bar{\mathbf{Y}}(8,6,2,1,1,1,1) + 9 \cdot \Sigma \bar{\mathbf{Y}}(8,6,1,1,1,1,1,1) + 5 \cdot \Sigma \bar{\mathbf{Y}}(7,7,6) + 1 \cdot \Sigma \bar{\mathbf{Y}}(7,7,5,1) + 6 \cdot \Sigma \bar{\mathbf{Y}}(7,7,4,2) + 20 \cdot \Sigma \bar{\mathbf{Y}}(7,7,4,1,1) + 4 \cdot \Sigma \bar{\mathbf{Y}}(7,7,3,3) + 22 \cdot \Sigma \bar{\mathbf{Y}}(7,7,3,2,1) + 12 \cdot \Sigma \bar{\mathbf{Y}}(7,7,3,1,1,1) + 11 \cdot \Sigma \bar{\mathbf{Y}}(7,7,2,2,2) + 6 \cdot \Sigma \bar{\mathbf{Y}}(7,7,2,2,1,1) + 20 \cdot \Sigma \bar{\mathbf{Y}}(7,7,2,1,1,1,1) + 13 \cdot \Sigma \bar{\mathbf{Y}}(7,7,1,1,1,1,1,1) + 15 \cdot \Sigma \bar{\mathbf{Y}}(7,6,6,1) + 13 \cdot \Sigma \bar{\mathbf{Y}}(7,6,5,2) + 5 \cdot \Sigma \bar{\mathbf{Y}}(7,6,5,1,1) + 18 \cdot \Sigma \bar{\mathbf{Y}}(7,6,4,3) + 7 \cdot \Sigma \bar{\mathbf{Y}}(7,6,4,2,1) + 8 \cdot \Sigma \bar{\mathbf{Y}}(7,6,4,1,1,1) + 20 \cdot \Sigma \bar{\mathbf{Y}}(7,6,3,3,1) + 10 \cdot \Sigma \bar{\mathbf{Y}}(7,6,3,2,2) + 18 \cdot \Sigma \bar{\mathbf{Y}}(7,6,3,2,1,1) + 14 \cdot \Sigma \bar{\mathbf{Y}}(7,6,3,1,1,1,1) + 9 \cdot \Sigma \bar{\mathbf{Y}}(7,6,2,2,2,1) + 7 \cdot \Sigma \bar{\mathbf{Y}}(7,6,2,2,1,1,1) + 8 \cdot \Sigma \bar{\mathbf{Y}}(7,6,2,1,1,1,1,1) + 19 \cdot \Sigma \bar{\mathbf{Y}}(7,6,1,1,1,1,1,1,1) \mod 23$

We checked every rational $\eta = d/k$ such that $k \leq 20$, and verified that our framework does in fact yield a 2-party PSM protocol with unbalanced communication complexity $O(N^\eta)$, $O(N^{1-\eta})$.

5   Open Problems

This paper presents two frameworks: a framework of constructing k-party PSM protocols for general $f : [N]^k \to \{0,1\}$ with c.c. $O_k(N^{\frac{k-1}{2}})$, and a framework of constructing 2-party PSM protocols for general $f : [N] \times [N] \to \{0,1\}$ where one party sends $O_\eta(N^\eta)$ bits and the other party sends $O_\eta(N^{1-\eta})$ bits. An immediate open problem is to prove our frameworks work for all integer k and all rational η. Currently, we can only prove it works for some k and η.

For simplicity, our analysis only considers the symmetric sum of terms. The symmetric sum incurs a blow-up exponential on k. Thus the communication complexity of our k-party PSM protocols is $\exp(k) \cdot N^{\frac{k-1}{2}}$. While [8] achieves communication complexity $\mathrm{poly}(k) \cdot N^{\frac{k}{2}}$. Our protocols are less efficient in the domain where $\log N < k$. A possible approach of getting rid of the exponential dependency in k is to break the symmetry. The potential of such an approach is evidenced by the 5-party PSM protocol in Sect. 1.2, which is asymmetric.

There is no clear reason why our framework will not yields more efficient PSM protocols. Can our multi-party framework yield PSM protocols with communication complexity $O_k(N^{\frac{k}{2}-1})$, when k is sufficiently large? Can our 2-party framework might yield PSM protocol with communication $O_\eta(N^\eta)$ for some rational $\eta < \frac{1}{2}$? Our technique transfers such questions into some linear systems. Each question has an affirmative answer (for a given k or η) if and only if the corresponding linear system is solvable. We have modified our program to generate and solve these linear systems, but all the system we have tried are unsolvable. The failure suggests that our new upper bounds might be tight, or are tight for a natural class of PSM protocols.

The question of the communication complexity trade-off for multi-party PSM remains widely open. In our k-party PSM protocol, every party sends $O_k(N^{\frac{k-1}{2}})$ bits. A variant of [10] provides a k-party PSM protocol where the i-th party sends $\tilde{O}_k(N^{i-1})$ bits, whose geometric average is $\tilde{O}_k(N^{\frac{k-1}{2}})$. Should a future work achieves the smooth trade-off between the two, there is little doubt that it will bring us a deep insight into PSM.

Finally, this work belongs to a not-fully-successful attempt at constructing PSM with sub-exponential communication complexity, which is probably the moonshot open problem in the PSM literature.

Acknowledgements. We would like to thank Hoeteck Wee, Vinod Vaikuntanathan amd Michel Abdalla for helpful discussions. TL was supported by NSF grants CNS-1528178, CNS-1929901, CNS-1936825 (CAREER), CNS-2026774, a JP Morgan AI research Award, and a Simons Foundation Collaboration Grant on Algorithmic Fairness. Part of this work was performed while TL was in MIT, during which he was supported in part by NSF Grants CNS-1350619, CNS-1414119 and CNS-1718161, an MIT-IBM grant and a DARPA Young Faculty Award. LA was supported by a doctoral grant from the French Ministère de l'Enseignement Supérieur et de la Recherche.

A   Proof of Eq. (9) and (10)

Proof (Proof of Eq. (9)). By definition:

$$\sum_{(*)} \langle \mathbf{F}, \bar{\mathbf{X}}(P) \rangle = \sum_{(*)} \langle \mathbf{F}, \bar{\mathbf{X}}_{S_1} \otimes \ldots \otimes \bar{\mathbf{X}}_{S_t} \rangle$$

where $(*)$ denotes "for all unordered $E = \{S_1, \ldots, S_t\}$ being a partition of $[2k]$ such that $\{|S_1|, \ldots, |S_t|\} = P$". Thus,

$$\sum \langle \mathbf{F}, \bar{\mathbf{X}}(P) \rangle = \sum_{(*)} \left\langle \mathbf{F}, \bigotimes_{i \in [t]} \left(\mathbf{R}_{S_i} + \bigotimes_{j \in S_i} \mathbf{x}_j \right) \right\rangle$$

$$= \sum_{(*)} \sum_{G \subseteq E} \left\langle \mathbf{F}, \bigotimes_{S \in G} \mathbf{R}_S \otimes \bigotimes_{\substack{j \notin \bigcup_{S \in G} S}} \mathbf{x}_j \right\rangle$$

$$= \sum_{Q \subseteq P} \sum_{\substack{G = \{S_1, \ldots, S_t\} \text{ s.t.} \\ \{|S_1|, \ldots, |S_t|\} = P \setminus Q}} \beta(P, G) \cdot \left\langle \mathbf{F}, \bigotimes_{i \in [t]} \mathbf{R}_{S_i} \otimes \bigotimes_{\substack{j \notin \bigcup_{i \in [t]} S_i}} \mathbf{x}_j \right\rangle,$$

where $\beta(P, G)$ accounts for the redundancy: define $\beta(P, G)$ as the number of unordered partitions E of $[2k]$ such that $G \subseteq E$ and P is the shape of E. It is equivalent to count the number of $F := E \setminus G$. That is, $\beta(P, G)$ also equals the number of unordered partitions F of $[2k] \setminus \bigcup_{S \in G} S$ such that Q is the shape of F.
Thus by definition, $\beta(P, G) = \alpha(Q)$. The proof is concluded by

$$\sum \langle \mathbf{F}, \bar{\mathbf{X}}(P) \rangle = \sum_{Q \subseteq P} \sum_{\substack{G = \{S_1, \ldots, S_t\} \text{ s.t.} \\ \{|S_1|, \ldots, |S_t|\} = P \setminus Q}} \alpha(Q) \cdot \left\langle \mathbf{F}, \bigotimes_{i \in [t]} \mathbf{R}_{S_i} \otimes \bigotimes_{\substack{j \notin \bigcup_{i \in [t]} S_i}} \mathbf{x}_j \right\rangle$$

$$= \sum_{Q \subseteq P} \alpha(Q) \cdot \sum \langle \mathbf{F}, \mathbf{R}(P \setminus Q) \rangle.$$

$\square$

Proof (Proof of Eq. (10)). Let $n = \text{sum}(Q)$. By definition, $\alpha(Q)$ is the number of unsorted partitions $E = \{S_1, \ldots, S_t\}$ of $[n]$ such that the multiset $\{|S_1|, \ldots, |S_t|\}$ (i.e. the shape of E) equals Q.
   To compute $\alpha(Q)$, we count the number of ways to arranging $1, \ldots, n$ into a sequence.

- First, pick an unsorted partitions E of $[n]$ s.t. the shape of E equals Q. The number of choices is $\alpha(Q)$.
- Then, sort the sets in the partion $E = \{S_1, \ldots, S_t\}$. Sort them by their sizes, i.e. $|S_1| \leq |S_2| \leq \cdots \leq |S_t|$. For any m, if several sets are of the size m, their order has to be specified, the number of such choices is (number of m's in Q)!.
- Finally, arrange the elements in each S_i into a sub-sequence, the number of possible sequences is $|S_i|!$. Concatenate these sub-sequences in order.

$$\alpha(Q) \cdot \prod_{m \in \mathbb{Z}^+} (\text{number of m's in } Q)! \cdot \prod_{i \in Q} i! = n! \qquad \square$$

B   Auxiliary PSM Protocols for $\langle \mathbf{x}_1 \otimes \ldots \otimes \mathbf{x}_k, \mathbf{Y} \rangle + s$

B.1   The Multi-party Variant

In this section, we present an auxiliary PSM protocol that is used as a subroutine by our multi-party PSM in Sect. 3.

The functionality is $\langle \mathbf{x}_1 \otimes \ldots \otimes \mathbf{x}_k, \mathbf{Y} \rangle + s$. It is a $(k+1)$-party functionality where the i-th party has as input $\mathbf{x}_i \in \mathbb{F}^N$ for $i \in [k]$, and the $(k+1)$-th party has as inputs $\mathbf{Y} \in \mathbb{F}^{\underbrace{N \times \cdots \times N}_{k \text{ times}}}$ and $s \in \mathbb{F}$. We will present a PSM protocol for this functionality with a communication complexity of $O(\text{poly}(k) \cdot N^k)$ field elements. This protocol is implicitly used in [8].

First, we consider the special case when $k = 1$. That is, there are only two parties. Say we call them Alice and Bob. Alice has $\mathbf{x} \in \mathbb{F}^N$, Bob has $\mathbf{y} \in \mathbb{F}^N, s \in \mathbb{F}$. The functionality output is $\langle \mathbf{x}, \mathbf{y} \rangle + s$. The PSM protocol works as follows:

- Random $\mathbf{a}, \mathbf{b} \in \mathbb{F}^N, c \in \mathbb{F}$ are sampled from the common random string, which is known by both Alice and Bob.
- Alice sends $\bar{\mathbf{x}} := \mathbf{x} + \mathbf{a}, z := c - \langle \mathbf{b}, \mathbf{x} \rangle$ to the referee.
- Bob sends $\bar{\mathbf{y}} := \mathbf{y} + \mathbf{b}, w := s - c - \langle \mathbf{a}, \mathbf{y} \rangle - \langle \mathbf{a}, \mathbf{b} \rangle$ to the referee.
- The referee outputs $\langle \bar{\mathbf{x}}, \bar{\mathbf{y}} \rangle + z + w$.

For the case $k \geq 2$, the first k parties need to jointly emulate Alice. The protocol works as follows:

- Random $\mathbf{A}, \mathbf{B}, \mathbf{C} \in \mathbb{F}^{N \times \cdots \times N}$ are sampled from the common random string. Define $c \in \mathbb{F}$ as the sum of entries in $\mathbf{C}$.
- The $(k+1)$-th party sends $\bar{\mathbf{Y}} := \mathbf{Y} + \mathbf{B}, z := s - c - \langle \mathbf{A}, \mathbf{Y} \rangle - \langle \mathbf{A}, \mathbf{B} \rangle$ to the referee.
- The first k parties jointly reveal $\bar{\mathbf{X}} := \mathbf{x}_1 \otimes \ldots \otimes \mathbf{x}_k + \mathbf{A}, w := c - \langle \mathbf{B}, \mathbf{x}_1 \otimes \ldots \otimes \mathbf{x}_k \rangle$ to the referee.
  Since every coordinate of $\bar{\mathbf{X}}$ can be computed by an arithmetic formula of size $O(k)$, each of these coordinates can be computed by the referee by using a PSM protocol with communication complexity of $O(\text{poly}(k))$ field elements [13]. The referee learns $\bar{\mathbf{X}}$ after receiving $O(\text{poly}(k) \cdot N^k)$ field elements.
  The term $w := c - \langle \mathbf{B}, \mathbf{x}_1 \otimes \ldots \otimes \mathbf{x}_k \rangle$ equals the sum of all entries in $\mathbf{W} := \mathbf{C} - \mathbf{B} \circ_{\text{p.w.}} (\mathbf{x}_1 \otimes \ldots \otimes \mathbf{x}_k)$, where $\circ_{\text{p.w.}}$ denotes the point-wise product. In other words, we defines $\mathbf{W} \in \mathbb{F}^{N \times \cdots \times N}$ as

$$\mathbf{W}[i_1, \ldots, i_k] = \mathbf{C}[i_1, \ldots, i_k] - \mathbf{B}[i_1, \ldots, i_k] \mathbf{x}_1[i_1] \ldots \mathbf{x}_k[i_k].$$

Due to the randomness of $\mathbf{C}$, we know $\mathbf{W}$ is a randomized encoding of w. Thus, it is equivalent for the first k parties to jointly reveal $\mathbf{W}$ to the referee.

Since every coordinate of $\mathbf{W}$ can be computed by an arithmetic formula of size $O(k)$, each of them can be revealed by using the Ishai-Kushilevitz PSM protocol [13], which has a communication complexity of $O(\mathrm{poly}(k))$ field elements. The referee learns w after receiving $O(\mathrm{poly}(k) \cdot N^k)$ field elements.
- The referee outputs $\langle \bar{\mathbf{X}}, \bar{\mathbf{Y}} \rangle + z + w$.

The correctness of the protocol can be verified in the following equation:

$$
\begin{aligned}
&\langle \bar{\mathbf{X}}, \bar{\mathbf{Y}} \rangle + z + w \\
&= \langle \mathbf{x}_1 \otimes \ldots \otimes \mathbf{x}_k + \mathbf{A}, \mathbf{Y} + \mathbf{B} \rangle + s - c - \langle \mathbf{A}, \mathbf{Y} \rangle - \langle \mathbf{A}, \mathbf{B} \rangle + \\
&\quad c - \langle \mathbf{B}, \mathbf{x}_1 \otimes \ldots \otimes \mathbf{x}_k \rangle \\
&= \langle \mathbf{x}_1 \otimes \ldots \otimes \mathbf{x}_k, \mathbf{Y} \rangle + s.
\end{aligned}
$$

The privacy is guaranteed by the following simulator:

- Simulate $\bar{\mathbf{X}}, \bar{\mathbf{Y}}, \mathbf{W}$ as uniform random, since they are one-time-padded by $\mathbf{A}, \mathbf{B}, \mathbf{C}$.
- Given $\bar{\mathbf{X}}, \bar{\mathbf{Y}}, \mathbf{W}$ and the function output, w, z are uniquely determined since $w = \sum(\mathbf{W})$ and $\langle \bar{\mathbf{X}}, \bar{\mathbf{Y}} \rangle + z + w = \text{output}$.
- Simulate the transcripts of the inner Ishai-Kushilevitz PSM protocols using its own simulator, which takes $\bar{\mathbf{X}}, \mathbf{W}$ as input.

B.2   The 2-party Variant

In this section, we present an auxiliary PSM protocol that is used as a subroutine by our unbalanced 2-party PSM in Sect. 4.

The functionality is $\langle \mathbf{x}_1 \otimes \ldots \otimes \mathbf{x}_k, \mathbf{Y} \rangle + s$. It is a 2-party functionality where the first party, namely Alice, has as inputs $\mathbf{x}_1, \ldots, \mathbf{x}_k \in \mathbb{F}^N$ and the second party, namely Bob, has as inputs $\mathbf{Y} \in \mathbb{F}^{N \times \cdots \times N}_{k \text{ times}}$ and $s \in \mathbb{F}$. We will present a PSM protocol for this functionality with unbalanced communication complexity, where Alice sends $O(kN)$ field elements and Bob sends $(N+1)^k$ field elements.

As the first step, we consider a harder problem instead. Bob's input is replaced by a multi-affine function $f : \mathbb{F}^N \times \cdots \times \mathbb{F}^N \to \mathbb{F}$. Corresponding, the functionality is replaced by $f(\mathbf{x}_1, \ldots, \mathbf{x}_k)$. Every multi-affine function f can be uniquely represented by its coefficient tensor $\mathbf{F} \in \mathbb{F}^{(N+1) \times \cdots \times (N+1)}$ such that for any $\mathbf{z}_1, \ldots, \mathbf{z}_k \in \mathbb{F}^N$,

$$
f(\mathbf{z}_1, \ldots, \mathbf{z}_k) = \langle \mathbf{z}_1 \| 1 \otimes \cdots \otimes \mathbf{z}_k \| 1, \mathbf{F} \rangle.
$$

Here $\mathbf{z}_i \| 1$ denotes the concatenation of $\mathbf{z}_i$ and 1, which is a dimension-$(N+1)$ vector. Notice that, if we let the "first" $N \times \cdots \times N$ subtensor of $\mathbf{F}$ equal $\mathbf{Y}$, let its "last" entry $\mathbf{F}[N+1, \ldots, N+1] = s$, and let all other entries in $\mathbf{F}$ be 0, we have

$$
f(\mathbf{x}_1, \ldots, \mathbf{x}_k) = \langle \mathbf{x}_1 \| 1 \otimes \cdots \otimes \mathbf{x}_k \| 1, \mathbf{F} \rangle = \langle \mathbf{x}_1 \otimes \ldots \otimes \mathbf{x}_k, \mathbf{Y} \rangle + s.
$$

The protocol works as follows:

- Random $\mathbf{r}_1, \ldots, \mathbf{r}_k \in \mathbb{F}^N$ and a random multi-affine function g are sampled from the common random string.
- Alice sends $\bar{\mathbf{x}}_i = \mathbf{x}_i + \mathbf{r}_i$ to the referee, for all $i \in [k]$.
- Bob computes the multi-affine function g, such that

$$g(\mathbf{z}_1, \ldots, \mathbf{z}_k) := f(\mathbf{z}_1 - \mathbf{r}_1, \ldots, \mathbf{z}_k - \mathbf{r}_k).$$

Bob sends $\bar{g} = g + h$ to the referee.
- Alice additionally sends $s = h(\bar{\mathbf{x}}_1, \ldots, \bar{\mathbf{x}}_k)$ to the referee.
- The referee outputs $\bar{g}(\bar{\mathbf{x}}_1, \ldots, \bar{\mathbf{x}}_k) - s$.

The correctness follows directly from the following equation:

$$\begin{aligned}
\bar{g}(\bar{\mathbf{x}}_1, \ldots, \bar{\mathbf{x}}_k) - s &= g(\bar{\mathbf{x}}_1, \ldots, \bar{\mathbf{x}}_k) + h(\bar{\mathbf{x}}_1, \ldots, \bar{\mathbf{x}}_k) - h(\bar{\mathbf{x}}_1, \ldots, \bar{\mathbf{x}}_k) \\
&= g(\bar{\mathbf{x}}_1, \ldots, \bar{\mathbf{x}}_k) \\
&= f(\mathbf{x}_1 - \mathbf{r}_1 + \mathbf{r}_1, \ldots, \mathbf{x}_k - \mathbf{r}_k + \mathbf{r}_k) \\
&= f(\mathbf{x}_1, \ldots, \mathbf{x}_k).
\end{aligned}$$

The privacy is guaranteed by the following simulator:

- Simulate $\bar{\mathbf{x}}_1, \ldots, \bar{\mathbf{x}}_k, \bar{g}$ as uniform random, since they are one-time padded by $\mathbf{r}_1, \ldots, \mathbf{r}_k, h$.
- Given $\bar{\mathbf{x}}_1, \ldots, \bar{\mathbf{x}}_k, \bar{g}$ and the function output, simulate s by computing s from the equation $\bar{g}(\bar{\mathbf{x}}_1, \ldots, \bar{\mathbf{x}}_k) - s = $ output.

References

1. Applebaum, B., Arkis, B.: On the power of amortization in secret sharing: d-uniform secret sharing and CDS with constant information rate. In: Beimel, A., Dziembowski, S. (eds.) TCC 2018, Part I. LNCS, vol. 11239, pp. 317–344. Springer, Cham (2018). https://doi.org/10.1007/978-3-030-03807-6_12

2. Applebaum, B., Arkis, B., Raykov, P., Vasudevan, P.N.: Conditional disclosure of secrets: amplification, closure, amortization, lower-bounds, and separations. Electronic Colloquium on Computational Complexity (ECCC) **24**, 38 (2017). https://eccc.weizmann.ac.il/report/2017/038

3. Applebaum, B., Beimel, A., Farràs, O., Nir, O., Peter, N.: Secret-sharing schemes for general and uniform access structures. In: Ishai, Y., Rijmen, V. (eds.) EURO-CRYPT 2019, Part III. LNCS, vol. 11478, pp. 441–471. Springer, Cham (2019). https://doi.org/10.1007/978-3-030-17659-4_15

4. Applebaum, B., Holenstein, T., Mishra, M., Shayevitz, O.: The communication complexity of private simultaneous messages, revisited. J. Cryptol. **33**(3), 917–953 (2020)

5. Ball, M., Holmgren, J., Ishai, Y., Liu, T., Malkin, T.: On the complexity of decomposable randomized encodings, or: how friendly can a garbling-friendly PRF be? In: Vidick, T. (ed.) 11th Innovations in Theoretical Computer Science Conference, ITCS 2020, Seattle, Washington, USA, 12–14 January 2020. LIPIcs, vol. 151, pp. 86:1–86:22. Schloss Dagstuhl - Leibniz-Zentrum für Informatik (2020). https://doi.org/10.4230/LIPIcs.ITCS.2020.86

6. Beimel, A., Ishai, Y., Kumaresan, R., Kushilevitz, E.: On the cryptographic complexity of the worst functions. In: TCC, pp. 317–342 (2014)

7. Beimel, A., Ishai, Y., Kushilevitz, E.: Ad hoc PSM protocols: secure computation without coordination. In: Coron, J.-S., Nielsen, J.B. (eds.) EUROCRYPT 2017, Part III. LNCS, vol. 10212, pp. 580–608. Springer, Cham (2017). https://doi.org/10.1007/978-3-319-56617-7_20

8. Beimel, A., Kushilevitz, E., Nissim, P.: The complexity of multiparty PSM protocols and related models. In: Nielsen, J.B., Rijmen, V. (eds.) EUROCRYPT 2018, Part II. LNCS, vol. 10821, pp. 287–318. Springer, Cham (2018). https://doi.org/10.1007/978-3-319-78375-8_10

9. Ciampi, M., Goyal, V., Ostrovsky, R.: Threshold garbled circuits and ad hoc secure computation. Cryptology ePrint Archive, Report 2021/308 (2021). https://eprint.iacr.org/2021/308

10. Feige, U., Kilian, J., Naor, M.: A minimal model for secure computation (extended abstract). In: Leighton, F.T., Goodrich, M.T. (eds.) Proceedings of the Twenty-Sixth Annual ACM Symposium on Theory of Computing, 23–25 May 1994, Montréal, Québec, Canada, pp. 554–563. ACM (1994). https://doi.org/10.1145/195058.195408. http://doi.acm.org/10.1145/195058.195408

11. Gay, R., Kerenidis, I., Wee, H.: Communication complexity of conditional disclosure of secrets and attribute-based encryption. In: Gennaro, R., Robshaw, M. (eds.) CRYPTO 2015. LNCS, vol. 9216, pp. 485–502. Springer, Heidelberg (2015). https://doi.org/10.1007/978-3-662-48000-7_24

12. Ishai, Y., Kushilevitz, E.: Private simultaneous messages protocols with applications. In: Fifth Israel Symposium on Theory of Computing and Systems, ISTCS 1997, Ramat-Gan, Israel, 17–19 June 1997, Proceedings, pp. 174–184. IEEE Computer Society (1997). https://doi.org/10.1109/ISTCS.1997.595170

13. Ishai, Y., Kushilevitz, E.: Randomizing polynomials: a new representation with applications to round-efficient secure computation. In: 41st Annual Symposium on Foundations of Computer Science, FOCS 2000, 12–14 November 2000, Redondo Beach, California, USA, pp. 294–304. IEEE Computer Society (2000). https://doi.org/10.1109/SFCS.2000.892118

14. Liu, T., Vaikuntanathan, V., Wee, H.: Conditional disclosure of secrets via non-linear reconstruction. In: Katz, J., Shacham, H. (eds.) CRYPTO 2017, Part I. LNCS, vol. 10401, pp. 758–790. Springer, Cham (2017). https://doi.org/10.1007/978-3-319-63688-7_25

Multi-Party Functional Encryption

Shweta Agrawal[1]($\boxtimes$), Rishab Goyal[2], and Junichi Tomida[3]

[1] IIT Madras, Chennai, India
shweta.a@cse.iitm.ac.in
[2] MIT, Cambridge, MA, USA
goyal@utexas.edu
[3] NTT Corporation, Tokyo, Japan
junichi.tomida.vw@hco.ntt.co.jp

Abstract. We initiate the study of *multi-party functional encryption* (MPFE) which unifies and abstracts out various notions of functional encryption which support distributed ciphertexts or secret keys, such as multi-input FE, multi-client FE, decentralized multi-client FE, multi-authority FE, dynamic decentralized FE, adhoc multi-input FE and such others. Using our framework, we identify several gaps in the literature and provide some constructions to fill these:

1. **Multi-Authority ABE with Inner Product Computation.** The recent work of Abdalla et al. (ASIACRYPT'20) constructed a novel "composition" of Attribute Based Encryption (ABE) and Inner Product Functional Encryption (IPFE), namely functional encryption schemes that combine the access control functionality of attribute based encryption with the possibility of performing linear operations on the encrypted data. In this work, we extend the access control component to support the much more challenging multi-authority setting, i.e. "lift" the primitive of ABE in their construction to multi-authority ABE for the same class of access control policies (LSSS structures). This yields the first construction of a nontrivial multi-authority FE beyond ABE from simple assumptions on pairings to the best of our knowledge.

Our techniques can also be used to generalize the decentralized attribute based encryption scheme of Michalevsky and Joye (ESORICS'18) to support inner product computation on the message. While this scheme only supports inner product predicates which is less general than those supported by the Lewko-Waters (EUROCRYPT'11) construction, it supports policy hiding which the latter does not. Our extension inherits these features and is secure based on the k-linear assumption, in the random oracle model.

S. Agrawal—Research supported by the DST "Swarnajayanti" fellowship, an Indo-French CEFIPRA project and the CCD Centre of Excellence.

R. Goyal—Research supported in part by NSF CNS Award #1718161, an IBM-MIT grant, and by the Defense Advanced Research Projects Agency (DARPA) under Contract No. HR00112020023. Any opinions, findings and conclusions or recommendations expressed in this material are those of the author(s) and do not necessarily reflect the views of the United States Government or DARPA. Work done in part while at the Simons Institute for the Theory of Computing, supported by Simons-Berkeley research fellowship.

K. Nissim and B. Waters (Eds.): TCC 2021, LNCS 13043, pp. 224–255, 2021.
https://doi.org/10.1007/978-3-030-90453-1_8

2. **Function Hiding** DDFE. The novel primitive of *dynamic* decentralized functional encryption (DDFE) was recently introduced by Chotard et al. (CRYPTO'20), where they also provided the first construction for inner products. However, the primitive of DDFE does not support function hiding, which is a significant limitation for several applications. In this work, we provide a new construction for inner product DDFE which supports function hiding. To achieve our final result, we define and construct the first function hiding *multi-client* functional encryption (MCFE) scheme for inner products, which may be of independent interest.

3. **Distributed Ciphertext-Policy** ABE. We provide a distributed variant of the recent ciphertext-policy attribute based encryption scheme, constructed by Agrawal and Yamada (EUROCRYPT'20). Our construction supports $\mathbf{NC}^1$ access policies, and is secure based on "Learning With Errors" and relies on the generic bilinear group model as well as the random oracle model.

Our new MPFE abstraction predicts meaningful new variants of functional encryption as useful targets for future work.

1   Introduction

Functional encryption (FE) [14,32] is a powerful generalization of public key encryption which enables a user to learn a function of the encrypted data. Concretely, in FE, a secret key SK_f is associated with a function f and the ciphertext $\mathsf{CT}_\mathbf{x}$ is associated with a message $\mathbf{x}$ (in the domain of f). And, by combining SK_f with $\mathsf{CT}_\mathbf{x}$, the decryptor learns $f(\mathbf{x})$ and nothing else.

The original motivation behind the concept of functional encryption, as discussed in [14], was to put forth a *new broad vision of encryption systems*. Since its introduction, the concept of FE has been massively impactful in several aspects: (i) it helped unify the existing literature on encryption systems (such as identity-based encryption [12,33], attribute-based encryption [26,32], predicate encryption [15,27] and more) and place them under a single umbrella which enabled clear comparisons, (ii) it helped in predicting new natural encryption primitives that had not been studied before, such as partially hiding predicate/functional encryption [25], and (iii) it served as the right abstraction to understand the relationship of this broad concept with other notions in cryptography, such as to indistinguishability obfuscation [9,11].

Supporting Multiple Users. Subsequently, many new primitives arose to generalize FE to the multi-user setting – multi-input functional encryption [24], multi-client functional encryption [20], decentralized multi-client functional encryption, adhoc multi-input functional encryption [5], multi-authority attribute based encryption [17], dynamic decentralized functional encryption [22] and such others. Similar to the many special cases of functional encryption, these notions are related yet different and it is often difficult to understand how they compare to one-another, whether they use related techniques, and what is known in terms of feasibility. Moreover, each new variant that springs up acquires a different name, leading to a plethora of acronyms which clutter the landscape, often adding to confusion rather than clarity.

In this work, we initiate the study of "Multi-Party Functional Encryption" (MPFE) which unifies and abstracts out various notions of multi-user functional encryption, such as those described above. Our starting point is the observation that all above notions of FE support some form of distributed ciphertexts or distributed keys or both. In more detail, we summarize the state of affairs as:

1. **Distributed Ciphertexts.** The primitives of multi-input functional encryption (MIFE) [24] and multi-client functional encryption (MCFE) [20] generalize FE to support distributed inputs. Both notions permit different parties $P_1, \ldots, P_n$ each with inputs $x_1, \ldots, x_n$ to compute joint functions on their data, namely $f(x_1, \ldots, x_n)$. Each party encrypts its input x_i to obtain CT_i, a key authority holding a master secret MSK generates a functional key SK_f and these enable the decryptor to compute $f(x_1, \ldots, x_n)$.

   The main difference between these definitions lies in the way the inputs can be combined. In multi-*client* functional encryption (MCFE), inputs x_i are additionally associated with public "labels" lab_i and inputs can only be combined with other inputs that share the same label. On the other hand, multi-input functional encryption does not restrict the way that inputs are combined and permits all possible combinations of inputs. Both primitives are defined as *key policy* systems – namely, the access control policy or function is embedded in the secret key rather than the ciphertext.

2. **Distributed Keys.** Distribution or decentralization of keys in the context of FE has also been considered in various works, to achieve two primary objectives (not necessarily simultaneously) – a) handling the *key escrow* problem, so that there is no single entity in the system that holds a powerful master secret against which no security can hold, and b) *better fitting real world* scenarios where different authorities may be responsible for issuing keys corresponding to different attributes of a user, such as offices for passport, drivers license and such others. We summarize some relevant primitives next.

   (a) *Decentralized Attribute Based Encryption with Policy Hiding* (DABE): A decentralized policy-hiding ABE, denoted by DABE [31] was proposed by Michalevsky and Joye to handle the key escrow problem. In a DABE scheme, there are n key authorities, each of which run a local setup to generate their private and public keys. An encryptor encrypts a message m along with a general access structure C, while secret keys corresponding to (the same) attribute x are issued by independent authorities. Decryption recovers m if $C(x) = 1$. The access policy in the ciphertext is hidden.

   (b) *Multi-Authority Functional Encryption* (MAFE): The notion of Multi-Authority FE/ABE [16,17,29] emerged to address the second objective, i.e. handling the case where different authorities are responsible for different sets of attributes. Since ABE is a special case of FE, we focus on MAFE. A MAFE scheme is defined as a ciphertext-policy scheme, namely the policy/function is embedded in the ciphertext as against the function keys. In MAFE, n key authorities may independently generate their private and public keys, without any interaction. An encryptor computes a ciphertext for a message m along with a policy f over the various authorities. Any authority i, can generate a token for a user P for attributes lab_i. A decryptor with tokens for lab_i from authority $i \in [n]$, can decrypt the ciphertext to recover $f(\mathsf{lab}_1, \ldots, \mathsf{lab}_n, m)$.

3. **Distributed Ciphertexts and Keys.** Some primitives allow to distribute both ciphertexts and keys. Some examples below.

   (a) *Decentralized Multi-Client Functional Encryption* (D-MCFE): The notion of decentralized multi-client FE was defined by Chotard et al. [2,20,30] in order to handle the key escrow problem in an MCFE scheme. D-MCFE is defined as a key policy primitive, and adapts MCFE as described above to ensure that there is no single master secret held by any entity – the parties participate in an interactive setup protocol to establish their individual (correlated) master secret keys. In more detail, there are n parties, each holding PK_i for $i \in [n]$, that compute ciphertexts for their inputs $(\mathsf{lab}_i, \mathbf{x}_i)$ as well as generate partial decryption keys $\mathsf{SK}_{i,f}$ for a given function f. The decryptor can combine the partial secret keys and individual ciphertexts to compute $f(\mathbf{x}_1, \ldots, \mathbf{x}_n)$ if and only if all the labels are equal.

   (b) *Ad Hoc MIFE* (aMIFE): Similar to D-MCFE, this notion was introduced in [5] to handle the key escrow problem in MIFE. This notion is key policy, and offers some additional features as compared to D-MCFE—non-interactive setup and dynamic choice of function arity as well as parties that participate in a computation. This notion does not differentiate between key authorities and users, and lets users generate their own partial decryption keys along with ciphertexts. Thus, for $i \in [n]$, party i computes a ciphertext for $\mathbf{x}_i$ and partial key $\mathsf{SK}_{f,i}$ which can be combined by the decryptor to obtain $f(\mathbf{x}_1, \ldots, \mathbf{x}_n)$.

   (c) *Dynamic Decentralized FE* (DDFE): This primitive was introduced very recently in [22] to further generalize aMIFE – it requires non-interactive, local setup and allows dynamic choice of function arity as in aMIFE, but additionally allows partial decryption keys provided by users to be combined in more general ways than in aMIFE. Also, unlike aMIFE, it supports the public key setting.

1.1   Unifying the View: Multi-Party Functional Encryption

While the above notions enable controlled manipulation of encrypted data in increasingly expressive ways, they are too related to warrant independent identities. To unify and extend the above primitives, we propose the notion of multi-party functional encryption (MPFE). All the above examples (and more) can be cast as examples of MPFE with a suitable choice of parameters: this clarifies the connections between these primitives. MPFE allows for both distributed ciphertexts and distributed keys, and specifies how these may be combined for function evaluation. To avoid bifurcating key-policy and ciphertext-policy schemes, we allow either ciphertext or key inputs to encode functions. To better capture attribute and function hiding, we allow every message or function being encoded to have a public and private part. To support schemes with interactive, independent or centralized setup, we allow the setup algorithm of MPFE to function in any of these modes.

A bit more formally, let n_x be the number of ciphertext inputs and n_y be the number of key inputs. Let $\mathcal{X} = \mathcal{X}_{\mathrm{pub}} \times \mathcal{X}_{\mathrm{pri}}$ be the space of ciphertext inputs and $\mathcal{Y} = \mathcal{Y}_{\mathrm{pub}} \times \mathcal{Y}_{\mathrm{pri}}$ be the space of key inputs. We define two aggregation functions as $\mathsf{Agg}_x : \mathcal{X}^{n_x} \to \mathcal{X}$, and $\mathsf{Agg}_y : \mathcal{Y}^{n_y} \to \mathcal{Y}$, which specify how these inputs may be combined to capture a given primitive. The definitions of the algorithms that constitute an MPFE scheme are the same as in all prior work:

- a Setup algorithm outputs the encryption keys for n_x encryptors and master keys for n_y key authorities. This algorithm[1] may now run in one of three modes (Central, Local, Decentralized), which captures centralized setup, local/independent setup or decentralized/interactive setup.
- an Encrypt algorithm which is run independently by n_x users, each encoding their own message $x_i = (x_{\mathrm{pub},i}, x_{\mathrm{pri},i})$ with their own encryption key EK_i.
- a key-generation algorithm KeyGen which is run independently by all n_y key authorities, each generating its own partial key for an input $y_j = (y_{\mathrm{pub},j}, y_{\mathrm{pri},j})$ of its choice using its own master secret key PK_j.
- a decryption algorithm Decrypt, which given input the partial keys $\{\mathsf{SK}_i\}_{i \leq n_y}$ and partial ciphertexts $\{\mathsf{CT}_j\}_{j \leq n_x}$ can combine them to compute $\mathcal{U}\left(\mathsf{Agg}_x(\{x_i\}), \mathsf{Agg}_y(\{y_j\})\right)$, where $\mathcal{U}$ is the universal circuit.

Note that either x_i or y_j can be descriptions of functions, capturing both key and ciphertext policy schemes. By suitably choosing n_x, n_y, Agg_x, Agg_y and the mode of setup, namely (mode $\in \{\mathsf{Central}, \mathsf{Local}, \mathsf{Decentralized}\}$), the above abstraction lets us specify all the aforementioned primitives in a unified manner, and also allows us to instantiate these parameters in different ways to yield new, meaningful primitives. Please see Sect. 2 for the formal definition and the full version [6] for details on how the above primitives can be expressed as instances of MPFE.

Dynamic MPFE. In the above description, we assume that the number of parties as well as the aggregation functions are input to the setup algorithm. A more powerful definition could support full dynamism, where the parties generate their own keys, join the protocol dynamically without prior agreement, and choose the functionality (in our case Agg_x and Agg_y) dynamically so that it can change for every instance of the protocol.

While dynamism is obviously desirable, it is significantly harder to instantiate since it necessitates a local setup algorithm without any co-ordination between the parties. While there do exist some constructions for dynamic FE supporting

---

[1] If the setup mode is decentralized/interactive, then the description of setup could correspond to an interactive multi-round protocol instead of an algorithm. However, for ease of exposition we abuse the notation and use setup algorithm to refer to the corresponding protocol description.

multiple users, such as adhoc MIFE [5] and DDFE [22], most constructions in the literature are "static" and rely on centralized or interactive setup [1,2,4, 19–21,24,30]. Thus, a definition which is inherently dynamic would preclude representation of most constructions in the literature.

For simplicity of notation and ease of workability, we define MPFE with and without dynamism separately. We provide the definition of the static variant in Sect. 2 and the dynamic variant in the full version. We note that these two variants may be condensed to a single one using additional notation but this makes the definitions harder to work with.

Feasibility. In the full version, we provide a general feasibility of MPFE for circuits from the minimal assumption of MIFE for circuits.

1.2 Comparison with Prior Work

The notions of D-MCFE, aMIFE and DDFE are most closely related to our work, since they allow combining both ciphertexts and keys simultaneously. However, our notion differs from these in important ways. To begin, the setup algorithms of the above primitives have a fixed format – in D-MCFE, this is interactive, while for aMIFE and DDFE, it is decentralized and non-interactive. Thus, aMIFE and DDFE cannot capture D-MCFE and vice versa. Moreover, neither of these can capture most existing constructions in the literature which have trusted, centralized setup as discussed above. In contrast, we allow setup to have either of these, as well as other formats, allowing us to capture all the above primitives and more. Next, D-MCFE, aMIFE require partial keys to represent the same function. While DDFE does allow partial keys to be combined in expressive ways, it does not support any function hiding. Even the support for partial input hiding in these primitives is less than complete: for instance, aMIFE does not support public input in the ciphertext, and while DDFE allows for some part of the input to be public, this is via a separate empty key ϵ. In contrast, MPFE captures public and private input in both the ciphertext and the function key directly, making it feasible (in the case of function inputs) and simpler (in the case of ciphertext inputs) to capture partial hiding.

The most important feature of MPFE is that is captures existing constructions using a uniform, simple notation, allowing to place all prior work on the same map, making these constructions easier to compare and allowing to identify gaps between these. Using our MPFE framework, we interpolate the space in prior work to predict several new, natural and useful primitives. Then, we provide multiple new constructions from simple, standard assumptions to address these limitations (described next), as well as identify novel new primitives (described in Sect. 1.5) to be constructed in future work.

1.3   New Constructions

We next describe the new constructions we provide in this work.

Multi-Authority ABE ∘ IPFE. The recent work of Abdalla et al. [4] (ACGU20) constructed a novel "composition" of ABE and IPFE, namely functional encryption schemes that combine the access control functionality of attribute based encryption with the possibility of performing linear operations on the encrypted data. In more detail, the message space contains a policy predicate $\phi \in \mathsf{NC}_1$ and a message vector $\mathbf{v} \in \mathbb{Z}_q^\ell$, while decryption keys are jointly associated with an attribute vector $\mathbf{x} \in \{0,1\}^n$ and a key vector $\mathbf{u} \in \mathbb{Z}_q^\ell$. The functionality provided by such a system is that a decryptor recovers the inner product value $\langle \mathbf{u}, \mathbf{v} \rangle$ if $\phi(\mathbf{x}) = 1$. Thus, it provides a fine-grained access control on top of inner product functional encryption (IPFE) capability. For ease of exposition, we denote this primitive, which is called "IPFE with fine-grained access control" in [4] by ABE ∘ IPFE in our work[2]. Abdalla et al. [4] provide a construction leveraging state of the art ABE from pairings to support predicates represented by Linear Secret Sharing Schemes (LSSS) in the above functional encryption scheme.

Seen from the lens of MPFE, the ACGU20 construction has $n_x = n_y = 1$, with $(x_{\mathrm{pub}}, x_{\mathrm{pri}}) = (\phi, \mathbf{v})$, $(y_{\mathrm{pub}}, y_{\mathrm{pri}}) = ((f_{\mathbf{x}}, \mathbf{u}), \perp)$ where $f_{\mathbf{x}}$ is a function that takes as input three arguments $(\phi, \mathbf{v}, \mathbf{u})$ and outputs $\langle \mathbf{u}, \mathbf{v} \rangle$ if $\phi(\mathbf{x}) = 1$. The aggregation functions are trivial as there is only a single encryptor and key generator. In this work, we extend the ACGU20 construction to the multiparty setting. In more detail, we support $n_y = n$ for some fixed, polynomial n and Local mode of setup algorithm, so that each key generator generates its key components locally and independently. The number of encryptors n_x as well as the $(x_{\mathrm{pub}}, x_{\mathrm{pri}})$ remain unchanged. However, each of the n key generators now has input $(y_{\mathrm{pub}}, y_{\mathrm{pri}}) = ((\mathsf{GID}_i, x_i, \mathbf{u}_i), \perp)$ where $\mathsf{GID}_i \in \{0,1\}^*$ is a global identifier, $x_i \in \{0,1\}$ is an attribute bit, and $\mathbf{u}_i \in \mathbb{Z}_q^\ell$ is the key vector for $i \in [n]$. The Agg_x function remains trivial as before but the Agg_y function checks if all the global identifiers match $\mathsf{GID}_1 = \ldots = \mathsf{GID}_n$, key vectors are consistent $\mathbf{u}_1 = \ldots = \mathbf{u}_n$, and sets $(y_{\mathrm{pub}}, y_{\mathrm{pri}}) = ((f_{\mathbf{x}}, \mathbf{u}), \perp)$ if so, where $\mathbf{x} = (x_1, \ldots, x_n)$ and $f_{\mathbf{x}}$ is as above.

The above generalization has been studied in the literature in the context of ABE under the name *multi-authority* ABE, or MA-ABE – here, we extend the access control component of ACGU20 to support the multi-authority setting, i.e. "lift" the primitive of ABE ∘ IPFE to MA-ABE ∘ IPFE. Our construction departs significantly from ACGU20 in details – our starting point is the MA-ABE construction of Lewko and Waters [29] which we extend to support inner product computation. This yields the first construction of a nontrivial multi-authority FE beyond ABE from simple assumptions on pairings to the best of our knowledge.

Using our techniques, we also extend the decentralized attribute based encryption (DABE) scheme of Michalevsky and Joye [31] to support inner product computations. While [31] only supports inner product predicates unlike [29], it supports policy hiding unlike the latter – our extension inherits these features.

---

[2] We caution the reader that the notation ABE ∘ IPFE is for readability and does not denote a formal composition.

Function Hiding DDFE. The novel primitive of *dynamic* decentralized inner product functional encryption (IP-DDFE) was recently introduced by Chotard et al. [22], where they also provided the first construction. As discussed above, DDFE is an instance of dynamic MPFE. Using the notation of MPFE, we have the setup algorithm in the Local mode, so that each party i can dynamically join the system by generating a public key PK_i and a master secret key PK_i. For encryption, party i sets $(x_{\mathrm{pub}}, x_{\mathrm{pri}}) = ((\mathcal{U}_M, \mathsf{lab}_M), \mathbf{x}_i)$ where $\mathcal{U}_M$ is the set of parties whose inputs will be combined and lab_M is a label which imposes a constraint on which values can be aggregated together. For key generation, party i sets $(y_{\mathrm{pub}}, y_{\mathrm{pri}}) = ((\mathbf{y}_i, \mathcal{U}_K, \mathbf{y}), \bot)$ where $\mathcal{U}_K$ is a set of public keys that defines the support of the inner product, and $\mathbf{y}$ is an agreed upon vector $\mathbf{y} = \{\mathbf{y}_i\}_{i \in \mathcal{U}_K}$. The function Agg_x checks if the public inputs $(\mathcal{U}_M, \mathsf{lab}_M)$ match for all parties and that all the ciphertexts are provided for the set $\mathcal{U}_M$. If so, outputs $(\mathcal{U}_M, \mathbf{x})$ where $\mathbf{x} = (\mathbf{x}_1 \| \ldots \| \mathbf{x}_{n_x})$. The function Agg_y checks that all values $\mathcal{U}_K$ and $\mathbf{y}$ are the same for all parties, and that value $\mathbf{y}_i$ matches with its corresponding component in the agreed vector. If so, it outputs the function $f_{\mathcal{U}_K, \mathbf{y}}$ which takes as input $(\mathcal{U}_M, \mathbf{x})$, checks that $\mathcal{U}_M = \mathcal{U}_K$ and if so, outputs $\langle \mathbf{x}, \mathbf{y} \rangle$.

However, as discussed before, the primitive of DDFE does not support function hiding. We see this as a significant limitation of this notion. Function hiding is a well studied and very useful property with many applications – for instance, it allows parties to securely delegate computation to an untrusted server without the server being able to learn the functionality. In some cases, knowing the functionality and the output (which the server computes in the clear) may leak information about the underlying data. In other cases, the functionality itself may be private and protected by copyright laws. In our work, we provide a new construction for IP-DDFE which supports function hiding. In more detail, the key generator, similar to the encryptor associates a label lab_K with its vector $\mathbf{y}_i$ and combining partial keys is only possible when their labels match. Importantly, the key vector $\mathbf{y}_i$ may now be *hidden* analogously to the vector $\mathbf{x}_i$ in the ciphertext.

In more detail, for key generation, party i sets $(y_{\mathrm{pub}}, y_{\mathrm{pri}}) = ((\mathcal{U}_K, \mathsf{lab}_K), \mathbf{y}_i)$ where $\mathcal{U}_K, \mathsf{lab}_K$ have the same roles as $\mathcal{U}_M, \mathsf{lab}_M$, respectively. The function Agg_y, analogously to Agg_x checks that all values $\mathcal{U}_K$ and lab_K are the same for all parties. If so, it outputs the function $f_{\mathcal{U}_K, \mathbf{y} = (\mathbf{y}_1 \| \ldots \| \mathbf{y}_{n_y})}$ which takes as input $(\mathcal{U}_M, \mathbf{x})$, checks that $\mathcal{U}_M = \mathcal{U}_K$ and if so, outputs $\langle \mathbf{x}, \mathbf{y} \rangle$.

To achieve our final result, we define and construct the first *function hiding* MCFE scheme for inner products, which may be of independent interest.

Ciphertext-Policy ABE with Distributed Key Generation. We provide a multiparty variant of the recent ciphertext-policy attribute based encryption scheme, constructed by Agrawal and Yamada [8]. In our scheme, the setup algorithm is run in the Local mode and key generation is distributed amongst $n_y = n$ parties for any polynomial n. As in single-party ABE, we have $n_x = 1$ (hence Agg_x is trivial) where $(x_{\mathrm{pub}}, x_{\mathrm{pri}}) = (C, m)$ where C is a circuit in NC_1 and m is a hidden bit. For key generation, the ith party produces a key for $(y_{\mathrm{pub}}, y_{\mathrm{pri}}) = ((\mathbf{y}, \mathsf{GID}, y_i), \bot)$ where GID is a global identifier, and $\mathbf{y}$ is an agreed upon vector $\mathbf{y} = (y_1, \ldots, y_n)$. The aggregation function Agg_y checks if all the values GID and $\mathbf{y}$ are the same, and that value y_i matches with its corresponding component in the agreed vector $\mathbf{y}$. It then outputs a function $f_{\mathbf{y}}$ which takes as input a circuit C and message m and outputs m if $C(\mathbf{y}) = 1$. Our construction is secure based on "Learning With Errors" and relies on the generic bilinear group model as well as the random oracle model. We show that as long as at least one authority is honest, the scheme remains secure.

1.4 Technical Overview

In this section, we provide an overview of the techniques used for our constructions. We begin with our two constructions that extend multi-authority schemes [29,31] to support inner products.

Multi-Authority ABE ∘ IPFE **for LSSS Access Structures.** We described the functionality of MA-ABE∘IPFE in Sect. 1.3. Security is defined in a multifold setting where: (1) adversary is allowed to corrupt the key authorities, (2) make key queries that do not satisfy the challenge policy predicate ϕ^*, and (3) also make key queries that satisfy the challenge policy predicate ϕ^* but decrypt to the same value for both challenge vectors (that is, $\langle \mathbf{u}, \mathbf{v}_0^* \rangle = \langle \mathbf{u}, \mathbf{v}_1^* \rangle$).

A natural first line of attack is to consider whether such a scheme can generically be built from combining these two primitives. As it turns out, any such generic construction suffers from the common problem of mix and match attacks, that is, we must prevent an authorized MA-ABE portion of the key from being used along with an IPFE portion of an unauthorized key. Another idea is to extend the ABE ∘ IPFE construction of [4] to support multiple authorities. However, this work relies on the predicate encoding framework which is not suitable as-is for our application. Instead, our approach is to start with the multi-authority ABE construction by Lewko and Waters [29] for LSSS access structures, and show how to leverage it's intrinsic algebraic structure to add an inner product functionality "on top" of the multi-authority ABE construction.

To begin, we provide an informal sketch of a simplified version of our construction. Recall that an access policy corresponding to a linear secret sharing scheme access structure contains a share generating matrix $\mathbf{A}$ and a row index to party index mapping function ρ.

LSetup: The i-th authority samples a length ℓ masking vector $\boldsymbol{\alpha}_i$ as its secret key, and publishes its encoding $[\boldsymbol{\alpha}_i]_T$ in the target group as the public key.

KeyGen: To generate a secret key for key vector $\mathbf{u}$, the i-th authority projects $\boldsymbol{\alpha}_i$ on the vector space defined by key vector $\mathbf{u}$. That is, if the attribute bit x_i is 1^3, then the partial decryption key is simply $[\langle \boldsymbol{\alpha}_i, \mathbf{u} \rangle]$.

Enc: For encrypting a message vector $\mathbf{v}$ under an access policy $(\mathbf{A}, \rho)$, the encryptor first secret shares the message vector $\mathbf{v}$ using the access policy $\mathbf{A}$ into a share matrix $\mathbf{S_v}$. That is, $\mathbf{S_v}$ is a random matrix with the property that for each accepting attribute $\mathbf{x}$ there exists a reconstruction vector $\mathbf{z_x}$ such that

---

[3] As in prior ABE schemes based on bilinear maps, the key is empty when $x_i = 0$.

$\mathbf{z}_{\mathbf{x}}^{\top} \cdot \mathbf{S_v} = \mathbf{v}^{\top}$. It next arranges the authority public keys $[\boldsymbol{\alpha}_i]_T$ row-wise in a matrix $\boldsymbol{\Delta}$ as per the function ρ, that is i-th row on $\boldsymbol{\Delta}$ is $\rho(i)$-th public key $[\boldsymbol{\alpha}_{\rho(i)}]_T$. Finally, it output the ciphertext as the following matrix

$$\mathsf{CT}_0 = \left[\mathbf{S_v} + \boldsymbol{\Delta} \odot (\mathbf{r} \otimes \mathbf{1}^{\top})\right]_T, \quad \mathsf{CT}_1 = [\mathbf{r}],$$

where $\mathbf{r}$ is a random vector of appropriate dimension and $\odot$ denotes the component-wise multiplications between two matrices of same dimensions.

Dec: A decryptor then simply left-multiplies CT_0 with the reconstruction vector $\mathbf{z}_{\mathbf{x}}$ and right-multiplies with the key vector $\mathbf{u}$ to compute the following:

$$
\begin{aligned}
\mathbf{z}_{\mathbf{x}}^{\top} \cdot \mathsf{CT}_0 \cdot \mathbf{u} &= \mathbf{z}_{\mathbf{x}}^{\top} \cdot \left[\mathbf{S_v} + \boldsymbol{\Delta} \odot (\mathbf{r} \otimes \mathbf{1}^{\top})\right]_T \cdot \mathbf{u} \\
&= \left[\mathbf{v}^{\top} \cdot \mathbf{u} + \mathbf{z}_{\mathbf{x}}^{\top} \cdot (\boldsymbol{\Delta} \odot (\mathbf{r} \otimes \mathbf{1}^{\top})) \cdot \mathbf{u}\right]_T \\
&= \left[\mathbf{v}^{\top} \cdot \mathbf{u} + \mathbf{z}_{\mathbf{x}}^{\top} \cdot (\boldsymbol{\Delta} \odot (\mathbf{r} \otimes \mathbf{u}^{\top}))\right]_T
\end{aligned}
$$

It next arranges the partial decryption keys $[\langle \boldsymbol{\alpha}_i, \mathbf{u}\rangle]$ row-wise in a vector $\mathbf{K}$ as per the function ρ, that is i-th element of $\mathbf{K}$ is $\rho(i)$-th decryption key $[\langle \boldsymbol{\alpha}_{\rho(i)}, \mathbf{u}\rangle]$. It performs the component pairing between $\mathbf{K}$ and CT_1, and then takes the linear combination as specified by $\mathbf{z}_{\mathbf{x}}$ which can be simplified as follows:

$$\mathbf{z}_{\mathbf{x}}^{\top} \cdot e(\mathbf{K}, \mathsf{CT}_1) = \left[\mathbf{z}_{\mathbf{x}}^{\top} \cdot (\boldsymbol{\Delta} \odot (\mathbf{r} \otimes \mathbf{u}^{\top}))\right]_T$$

Finally, it can recover $[\mathbf{v}^{\top} \cdot \mathbf{u}]_T$ from the above two terms, and learn the exponent value by brute force search.

Now in the above sketch we ignored the global identifier GID that is necessary for tying together the partial decryption keys provided by each authority, and we also ignore the modifications necessary for proving security under standard bilinear assumptions. At a very high level, for proving security we rely on ideas from the dual system paradigm [34] as in the multi-authority ABE scheme of [29]. However, we must deal with several new challenges to adapt this paradigm to our setting, as we describe next.

In the dual system paradigm, the intuition is that the reduction algorithm first switches all the secret keys to semi-functional keys, and thereafter it also switches the challenge ciphertext to a semi-functional ciphertext, and after both these changes security follows directly from the property that semi-functional secret keys and ciphertexts are not compatible for decryption. In IPFE, we cannot hope to execute the same strategy directly since now we cannot switch all secret keys to semi-functional keys since some secret keys might allow decrypting the challenge ciphertext (but they still would not help in distinguishing by admissibility constraints on the attacker). At this point, we define the concept of *partial* semi-functional ciphertexts such that (at a high level) we first switch all the rejecting secret keys to semi-functional while leaving the accepting keys as is, and thereafter we switch the challenge ciphertext to be a "partial" semi-functional ciphertext such that this hides the non-trivial information about the encrypted message vectors.

Although this intuition seems to work at a high level, it is still insufficient since it is unclear how to switch the entire ciphertext to semi-functional in the standard model. To that end, our idea is to switch all the accepting secret keys (including the ones for satisfying predicates) to their semi-functional counterparts as well, but now ensure that the challenge ciphertext components that the accepting keys interact with are only *nominally* semi-functional. Here the difference between a regular ciphertext, a nominally semi-functional, and a standard semi-functional ciphertext is that – regular ciphertexts lie in a special subgroup with no special blinding terms; while nominally semi-functional ciphertexts have structured blinding factors outside the special subgroup but it does not affect decryption irrespective of the type of secret key being used; and a standard semi-functional ciphertext has unstructured blinding factors outside the special subgroup such that it affects decryption when using semi-functional keys. Now switching portions of the challenge ciphertext as nominally semi-functional is necessary because of two reasons: first, making the entire challenge ciphertext semi-functional will affect decryption w.r.t. accepting keys which will be distinguishable for the adversary; second, it is unclear how to sample the challenge ciphertext in which only one component is semi-functional while other are regular sub-encryptions due to the fact that these different ciphertext components are significantly correlated. Thus, we get around this barrier by ensuring that the challenge ciphertext is sampled as what we call a partial semi-functional ciphertext (which has nominally semi-functional components along with a standard semi-functional component).

Please see Sect. 3 for the formal construction and proof. Our construction relies on standard assumptions over composite-order bilinear groups, but could be also be easily adapted to prime-order groups with a security proof in the generic group model as in [29].

DABE ∘ IPFE for Inner Product Predicates, with Policy Hiding. Next, we extend the construction of decentralized attribute based encryption by Michalevsky and Joye [31] to incorporate inner product functional encryption. Observe that [31] supports only inner product predicates but allows for hiding the policy in the ciphertext. While our extension to the scheme of [31] also yields a multi-authority ABE extended to support inner products as above, the details of the transformation are quite different. We observe that the algebraic structure of [31] makes it amenable to incorporating the IPFE functionality using ideas developed in the literature for constructing IPFE generically from public-key encryption which have special structural and homomorphic properties [3,7,10]. We proceed to describe this transformation next.

In an overly simplified version of the Michalevsky-Joye construction, one could interpret the i-th key authority as simply sampling a pair of secret exponents $\delta_i, w_i \leftarrow \mathbb{Z}_p$, where δ_i is regarded as the partial message masking term, while w_i is considered the i-th attribute bit binding term. Now each authority's public key is simply set as the group encodings $[\delta_i]$ and $[w_i]$. Implicitly, the scheme uses the linear combination of partial message masking terms $\delta = \sum_i \delta_i$ to derive the main message masking term (used for deriving the secret key encapsulating the message, or the KEM key in short).

To encrypt a message m under attribute $\mathbf{x}$, the user chooses randomness $r \leftarrow \mathbb{Z}_p$ and computes $[r\delta]_T$ to be used as the KEM key, and binds each attribute bit to a ciphertext component as $[(x_i\alpha + w_i)r]$ (where $[\alpha]$ is taken from the CRS). It sets the ciphertext to be $C_0 = [r]$, $C_m = m \cdot [r\delta]_T$, and $C_i = [(x_i\alpha + w_i)r]$ for $i \in [n]$. While a partial secret key for policy vector $\mathbf{y}$ for user GID is simply generated as $K_{i,\mathbf{y}} = [\delta_i - y_i w_i h]$ where $[h]$ is computed as $H(\text{GID})$ so as to bind the different authorities' secret keys. The decryption can be simply performed given the bilinear operation as:

$$\text{Dec}(\{K_{i,\mathbf{y}}\}_i, \text{CT}) = \frac{C_m}{\prod_i e(C_i, H(\text{GID})^{y_i}) \cdot \prod_i e(K_{i,\mathbf{y}}, C_0)}$$

$$= \frac{m \cdot [r\delta]_T}{\left[\langle \mathbf{x}, \mathbf{y} \rangle \alpha r h + \sum_i w_i h y_i r\right]_T \cdot \left[\delta r - \sum_i y_i w_i h r\right]_T} = \frac{m}{\left[\langle \mathbf{x}, \mathbf{y} \rangle \alpha r h\right]_T}$$

As discussed above, we upgrade the [31] construction using ideas from [3,7,10] as follows. During key generation, each authority now samples a vector of partial masking terms instead of a single element, i.e. $\boldsymbol{\delta}_i \leftarrow \mathbb{Z}_p^\ell$, and appropriately sets the public key too. Implicitly, the main message masking term is now set as $\boldsymbol{\delta} = \sum_i \boldsymbol{\delta}_i$. To encrypt a message vector $\mathbf{u}$ under attribute vector $\mathbf{x}$, the user chooses randomness $r \leftarrow \mathbb{Z}_p$ and computes $[r\boldsymbol{\delta}]_T$ to be used as the KEM key for encrypting $\mathbf{u}$ index-by-index, and binds the attribute bit as before. Thus, only the message binding ciphertext component changes to $C_m = [r\boldsymbol{\delta} + \mathbf{u}]_T$. Looking ahead, it will be decryptor's job to first homomorphically take an inner product between the C_m vector and the inner product key vector $\mathbf{v}$. Next, a partial secret key for policy vector $\mathbf{y}$ and inner-product vector $\mathbf{v}$ for user GID is generated as $K_{i,\mathbf{y},\mathbf{v}} = [\sum_j \delta_{i,j} v_j - y_i w_i h]$. In words, the idea here is that the partial secret key now uses a linear combination of its partial (un)masking term $\sum_j \delta_{i,j} v_j$ depending on the underlying inner-product vector $\mathbf{v}$. The decryption can be naturally extended by performing inner products via the bilinear operations.

As in the case of our first construction, the proof techniques in [31] do not apply directly as they were specially designed for ABE which is an all-or-nothing encryption primitive, and do not translate directly to IPFE. Again, we solve this issue by a careful analysis in the dual system paradigm [34]. We refer the reader to the full version for more details.

Function-Hiding DDFE for Inner Products. In this section, we describe the main ideas in the construction of our function hiding DDFE for inner products. The functionality of IP-DDFE was discussed in Sect. 1.3. Informally, the security of DDFE requires that the adversary cannot distinguish two sets $\{\text{CT}_i^0\}$ and $\{\text{CT}_i^1\}$ of ciphertexts even given a set $\{\text{SK}_i\}$ of secret keys and a set $\{\text{PK}_i\}$ of master secret keys of corrupted parties as long as two sets of values are the same that are legitimately obtained from $\{\text{CT}_i^0\}$ and $\{\text{CT}_i^1\}$ using $\{\text{SK}_i\}$ and $\{\text{PK}_i\}$. Let us recall dynamic decentralized inner product functional encryption (IP-DDFE) by Chotard et al. [22].

The starting point of the IP-DDFE scheme of [22] is the multi-client inner product functional encryption (IP-MCFE) scheme in [20], where participants

$\{1, ..., n\}$ in the system are a priori fixed, and there is an authority who generates encryption keys mcEK_i for each party and a master secret key mcMSK, which is used to generate secret keys mcSK. Here, $\mathsf{mcMSK} = \{\mathsf{mcMSK}_i\}_{i \in [n]}$ and $\mathsf{mcEK}_i = \mathsf{mcMSK}_i$ (and we denote an encryption key for i by mcMSK_i in what follows). We also recall that in MCFE, only a set of ciphertexts with the same label can be decrypted. Chotard et al. [22] lifted the IP-MCFE scheme to an IP-DDFE scheme via following steps. First, each party joins the system dynamically by generating a key K_i of a pseudorandom function (PRF) as a master secret key PK_i. In encryption and key generation for party set $\mathcal{U}$, party $i \in \mathcal{U}$ generates $\mathsf{mcMSK}_{i,\mathcal{U}}$ on the fly, which corresponds to mcMSK_i of the IP-MCFE scheme for participants $\mathcal{U}$. Then, it can generate $\mathsf{mcCT}_{i,\mathcal{U}}$ and $\mathsf{mcSK}_{i,\mathcal{U}}$ with $\mathsf{mcMSK}_{i,\mathcal{U}}$, which corresponds to CT_i and SK_i of the IP-DDFE scheme. Second, they introduce a class of DDFE called DSum, which allows a decryptor to securely obtain $\mathsf{mcSK}_{\mathcal{U}} = \sum_{i \in \mathcal{U}} \mathsf{mcSK}_{i,\mathcal{U}}$ from encryption of partial secret keys $\{\mathsf{mcSK}_{i,\mathcal{U}}\}_{i \in \mathcal{U}}$. Then, the decryptor can compute $\mathsf{mcDec}(\mathsf{mcSK}_{\mathcal{U}}, \{\mathsf{mcCT}_{i,\mathcal{U}}\}_{i \in \mathcal{U}})$. DSum also plays a role in preventing combination of partial secret keys for which the agreed vectors are inconsistent.

Our Function-Hiding IP-DDFE. Our approach is to lift function-hiding IP-MCFE to function-hiding IP-DDFE following their blueprint. Unfortunately, there are no function-hiding IP-MCFE schemes, and we need to start with constructing this. Our first idea is to leverage the recent conversion by Abdalla et al. [1] from IPFE to IP-MCFE. However, this idea does not work since all parties share the same encryption key of an IPFE scheme in their converted schemes, and once a single party is corrupted, the adversary can learn the entire function (or vector) in secret keys. Thus, we could not achieve a function-hiding IP-MCFE scheme even if we apply the conversion to a function-hiding IPFE scheme.

To address this challenge, we devise a new technique to convert function-hiding IPFE to function-hiding IP-MCFE, which is inspired by the function-hiding multi-input IPFE scheme by Datta et al. [23]. In their scheme, each party i has a master secret key iMSK_i of a function-hiding IPFE scheme, the ciphertext miCT_i of $\mathbf{x}_i$ is $\mathsf{iCT}_i[(\mathbf{x}_i, 1)]$, and the secret key miSK of $\{\mathbf{y}_i\}_{i \in [n]}$ is $\{\mathsf{iSK}_i[(\mathbf{y}_i, r_i)]\}_{i \in [n]}$ where r_i are randomly chosen so that $\sum_{i \in [n]} r_i = 0$. $\mathsf{iCT}_i[\mathbf{x}]$ and $\mathsf{iSK}_i[\mathbf{y}]$ denotes the ciphertext of $\mathbf{x}$ and the secret key of $\mathbf{y}$ in the function-hiding IPFE scheme, respectively. To lift their MIFE to MCFE, we need to add the label checking mechanism and security against corruption of parties. Fortunately, we can achieve the latter almost for free since each party uses independent master secret key and corruption of a party does not affect other parties' ciphertexts and secret keys. We can achieve the former by changing miCT_i to $\mathsf{iCT}_i[(\mathbf{x}_i, t_i)]$ where $t_i = H(\mathsf{lab})$ is a hash of a label. Then, a decryptor can learn $\sum(\langle \mathbf{x}_i, \mathbf{y}_i \rangle + t_i r_i)$, which reveals $\sum \langle \mathbf{x}_i, \mathbf{y}_i \rangle$ only when $t_1 = \cdots = t_n$. We can prove the masking term $t_i r_i$ hides $\langle \mathbf{x}_i, \mathbf{y}_i \rangle$ under the SXDH assumption in the random oracle model.

Our next step is to lift function-hiding IP-MCFE to function-hiding IP-DDFE. To do so, we must address additional technical challenges as described next. In the original definition of IP-DDFE, recall that each secret key is associated with $(\mathbf{y}_i, \mathcal{U}, \mathbf{y} = \{\mathbf{y}_{i'}\}_{i' \in \mathcal{U}})$ where the first element $\mathbf{y}_i$ is a vector for a linear function while the third element $\mathbf{y}$ is an agreed vector that controls combination of partial secret keys. More precisely, a decryptor can combine partial secret keys to obtain a full secret key for $\mathbf{y}$ only when it has $\{\mathsf{SK}_i\}_{i \in \mathcal{U}}$ associated with $\mathbf{y}$. However, $\mathbf{y}$ cannot be hidden in the blueprint by Chotard et al. To tackle this, we observe that the role of the agreed vector is analogous to a label in the ciphertext, controlling combination of partial secret keys. Thus, we alternatively use an independent label lab_K to create a natural symmetry between inputs for encryption and key generation. Now, since the vector $\mathbf{y}_i$ for a linear function can be hidden by function-hiding IP-MCFE, we obtain function-hiding IP-DDFE.

Another deviation from their blueprint arises in the part that securely generates $\mathsf{mcSK}_{\mathcal{U}}$ from $\mathsf{mcSK}_{i,\mathcal{U}}$. In our IP-MCFE construction, $\mathsf{mcSK}_{i,\mathcal{U}} = \mathsf{iSK}_i[(\mathbf{y}_i, r_i)]$ and $\mathsf{mcSK}_{\mathcal{U}} = \{\mathsf{iSK}_i[(\mathbf{y}_i, r_i)]\}_{i \in \mathcal{U}}$. Thus, we do not need to sum up $\mathsf{mcSK}_{i,\mathcal{U}}$ to obtain $\mathsf{mcSK}_{\mathcal{U}}$, instead, each party has to somehow generate a secret share r_i without interaction such that $\sum_{i \in [\mathcal{U}]} r_i = 0$ only when all $\mathsf{mcSK}_{i,\mathcal{U}}$ are generated on behalf of the same label. To handle this issue, we employ a technique by Chase and Chow [18] to generate such shares via pseudorandom function. Please see Sect. 4 for more details.

Distributed Ciphertext-Policy ABE. The recent construction of Agrawal-Yamada [8] proposed a succinct ciphertext-policy ABE for log-depth circuits provably secure under LWE in the bilinear generic group model. In our work, we extend the setup and key generation in [8] among a polynomial number of authorities that are working completely *non-interactively* and asynchronously. We start by describing the syntax of a distributed CP-ABE scheme. In a fully distributed setting, the authorities run their local setup algorithms individually to generate a fresh master public-secret key pair $(\mathsf{PK}, \mathsf{PK})$ per authority such that given a sequence of, say N, master public keys $\{\mathsf{PK}_i\}_{i \in [N]}$, an encryptor could encrypt a message μ for a predicate circuit F of its choice. Such ciphertexts can be decrypted after obtaining a partial predicate key from all N authorities for a consistent identifier GID, and attribute vector $\mathbf{x}$ such that $F(\mathbf{x}) = 1$. Note that here the key generation algorithm is run locally (and independently) by each authority, which on input its master key PK_i along with GID and attribute $\mathbf{x}$, computes a partial key $\mathsf{SK}_{i,\mathsf{GID},\mathbf{x}}$. While correctness is natural, security must be defined carefully.

In this work, we consider the strongest form of corruption, where we allow the adversary to pick the key parameters for all corrupt authorities, and also allow it to query honest authorities on identifier-attribute pairs $(\mathsf{GID}, \mathbf{x})$ such that $F^*(\mathbf{x}) = 1$ (where F^* is the challenge predicate circuit) as long as there is at least one honest authority to which the adversary did not query the pair $(\mathsf{GID}, \mathbf{x})$. All other queries are unconstrained since if $F^*(\mathbf{x}) = 0$, then such keys should not be useful for decryption to begin with. The intuition behind allowing the queries to honest authorities such that $F^*(\mathbf{x}) = 1$ is that we want to prevent partial secret keys for two distinct accepting attributes provided by two distinct authorities to be usable for decryption.

To describe our construction, we recall the high level structure of the Agrawal-Yamada scheme [8], which in turn uses the BGG$^+$ ABE construction [13].

Roughly, a BGG^+ ciphertext is sampled in two steps—first, it samples a sequence of 2ℓ encodings $\{\psi_{i,b}\}_{i,b}$; second, depending upon the attribute $\mathbf{x}$ the final ciphertext consists of ℓ encodings $\{\psi_{i,x_i}\}_i$. (Note that BGG^+ is a key-policy scheme, whereas we are building a ciphertext-policy system.) The main idea behind the ciphertext-policy ABE of [8] is as follows:

Setup: Sample 2ℓ random exponents $w_{i,b}$, store it as master secret key, and give its encoding $\{[w_{i,b}]_1\}_{i,b}$ as the public key.

KeyGen: To generate a secret key for attribute $\mathbf{x} \in \{0,1\}^\ell$, first sample a random exponent δ and then given out $[\delta/w_{i,x_i}]_2$ for $i \in [\ell]$ as the secret key.

Enc: To encrypt under predicate F, the encryptor samples all 2ℓ BGG^+ encodings $\{\psi_{i,b}\}_{i,b}$, and also samples a random exponent γ. It then gives out the ciphertext as a BGG^+ secret key for predicate C along with encodings $[\gamma w_{i,b}\psi_{i,b}]_1$ for $i \in [\ell], b \in \{0,1\}$.

Dec: A decryptor pairs the encodings $[\gamma w_{i,x_i}\psi_{i,x_i}]_1$ with $[\delta/w_{i,x_i}]_2$ to learn $[\gamma\delta\psi_{i,x_i}]_T$, and then it performs the BGG^+ decryption in the exponent to learn the plaintext.

For the multi-authority extension, each authority samples its own sequence of 2ℓ random exponents $w_{i,b}^{(j)}$ for $j \in [N]$. Then during encryption, the encryptor N-out-of-N (additively) secret shares the BGG^+ encodings $\{\psi_{i,b}\}_{i,b}$ into $\{\phi_{i,b}^{(j)}\}_{i,b}$ for $j \in [N]$. Now it encodes each sequence of $\{\phi_{i,b}^{(j)}\}_{i,b}$ terms under the corresponding authority's master public key as above. During decryption, a decryptor will first recover $\{\phi_{i,x_i}^{(j)}\}_i$ for all j in the exponent, then add them to reconstruct the actual BGG^+ ciphertext $\{\psi_{i,x_i}\}_i$ which it can decrypt as before. In order to let multiple independent authorities sample the same δ, we rely on a hash function which we model as a ROM, and set $[\delta]_2 = H(\mathsf{GID})$.

Although our multi-authority transformation is natural, the proof does not follow trivially from [8]. This is primarily due to the fact that in the distributed setting, the adversary could potentially make key queries on accepting attributes as long as there is at least one honest party that does not receive the same query. Such queries did not exist in the single-authority setting. However, we can extend the single-authority proof to the multi-authority setting by a careful analysis of the additional "bad" zero-test queries that an adversary can make. Please see the full version for more details.

1.5 Predicting New and Useful Primitives via MPFE

One of the most exciting benefits of MPFE is that it provides the right framework to pose new, compelling questions that have not been studied before. For example, a very interesting question is what new kinds of dynamic key accumulation are possible, namely how to combine keys of different users chosen dynamically. So far, most existing literature on FE systems that enable aggregation of multiple decryption keys still consider very restricted scenarios: (i) each partial decryption key corresponds to a portion of a much larger decryption key of a single user (e.g., distributed/decentralized/multi-authority FE etc.), (ii) each partial decryption key corresponds to a function and many such keys may be combined if they each encode the *same* function (e.g. adhoc MIFE, D-MCFE).

However, the ability to combine keys in much more creative ways can enable several cool new applications. As an example, consider the following notion of "reputation point based encryption" – in this setting, each user key is associated with a subject tag T (say math, history etc.) and a reputation value v (that is, a point score denoted as an integer). Now an encryptor specifies a tag T' along with a threshold reputation value w, and hides its message m under it. That is, $\mathsf{CT}(T', w, m)$ denotes such a ciphertext, and we require the functionality that such a ciphertext should be decryptable by any sequence of user keys $\mathsf{SK}(T_1, v_1), \ldots \mathsf{SK}(T_\ell, v_\ell)$ where all the subject tags match $(T' = T_1 \cdots = T_\ell)$ and the combined reputation value of the group $\sum_{i \le \ell} v_i$ is greater than threshold w. For example, an encryption of a message under subject 'math' and minimum reputation value of 1000 points can be decrypted by not only a single user with 1000 reputation points in 'math' but also by say a group of three users with 400, 250, 350 reputation points (respectively) in 'math', but not by a group of users who satisfy either the subject check or the reputation point check *but not both*. To the best of our knowledge, such an encryption framework has not been studied before, but our MPFE framework enables expressing and introducing such an encryption functionality.

2   Multi-Party Functional Encryption

In this section, we define our notion of multi-party functional encryption (MPFE). Let n_x be the number of ciphertext inputs and n_y be the number of key inputs. Let $\mathcal{X} = \mathcal{X}_{\mathrm{pub}} \times \mathcal{X}_{\mathrm{pri}}$ be the space of ciphertext inputs and $\mathcal{Y} = \mathcal{Y}_{\mathrm{pub}} \times \mathcal{Y}_{\mathrm{pri}}$ be the space of key inputs. We define two aggregation functions as $\mathsf{Agg}_x : \mathcal{X}^{n_x} \to \mathcal{X}^*$, and $\mathsf{Agg}_y : \mathcal{Y}^{n_y} \to \mathcal{Y}^*$.

An MPFE scheme is defined as a tuple of 4 algorithms/protocols $\mathsf{MPFE} = (\mathsf{Setup}, \mathsf{KeyGen}, \mathsf{Encrypt}, \mathsf{Decrypt})$. To suitably capture existing primitives, we define our Setup algorithm/protocol to run in three modes, described next.

Setup modes. The Setup algorithm/protocol can be run in different modes: central, local, or interactive. For mode $\in \{\mathsf{Central}, \mathsf{Local}, \mathsf{Interactive}\}$, consider the following.

Central: Here the Setup algorithm is run by one trusted third party which outputs the master secret keys and encryption keys for all users in the system.

Local: Here it is run independently by different parties without any interaction, and each party outputs its own encryption key and/or master secret key.

Interactive: Here it is an interactive protocol run by a set of users, at the end of which, each user has its encryption key and/or master secret key. We note that these keys may be correlated across multiple users.

A multi-party functional encryption (MPFE) consists of the following:

Setup $\left(1^\lambda, n_x, n_y, \mathsf{Agg}_x, \mathsf{Agg}_y\right)$: This algorithm/protocol can be executed in any one of the three modes described above.[4] Given input the security parameter, number of ciphertext inputs n_x, number of key inputs n_y and two aggregation functions Agg_x, Agg_y as defined above, this algorithm outputs a set of encryption keys $\{\mathsf{EK}_i\}_{i \leq n_x}$, master secret keys $\{\mathsf{PK}_i\}_{i \leq n_y}$ and public key PK.

KeyGen $(\mathsf{PK}, \mathsf{PK}, j, y = (y_{\mathrm{pub}}, y_{\mathrm{pri}}))$: Given input the public key PK, a master secret key PK, user index $j \in [n_y]$ and a function input $y = (y_{\mathrm{pub}}, y_{\mathrm{pri}})$, this algorithm outputs a secret key SK_y.

Encrypt $(\mathsf{PK}, \mathsf{EK}, i, x = (x_{\mathrm{pub}}, x_{\mathrm{pri}}))$: Given input the public key PK, an encryption key EK, user index $i \in [n_x]$, an input $x = (x_{\mathrm{pub}}, x_{\mathrm{pri}})$, this algorithm outputs a ciphertext CT_x.

Decrypt $\left(\mathsf{PK}, \{\mathsf{SK}_j\}_{j \leq n_y}, \{\mathsf{CT}_i\}_{i \leq n_x}\right)$: Given input the public key PK, a set of secret keys $\{\mathsf{SK}_j\}_{j \leq n_y}$ and a set of ciphertexts $\{\mathsf{CT}_i\}_{i \leq n_x}$, this algorithm outputs a value z or $\perp$.

We remark that in the *local* setup mode, it will be helpful to separate the setup algorithm into a global setup, denoted by GSetup along with a local setup, denoted by LSetup, where the former is used only to generate common parameters of the system, such as group descriptions and such.

Correctness. We say that an MPFE scheme is *correct* if, $\forall (n_x, n_y) \in \mathbb{N}^2$, ciphertext inputs $x_i \in \mathcal{X}$ for $i \in [n_x]$, key inputs $y_j \in \mathcal{Y}$ for $j \in [n_y]$, message and function aggregation circuits Agg_x and Agg_y, it holds that:

$$\Pr \left[z = z' : \begin{array}{l} (\mathsf{PK}, \{\mathsf{EK}_i\}, \{\mathsf{PK}_j\}) \leftarrow \mathsf{Setup}(1^\lambda, n_x, n_y, \mathsf{Agg}_x, \mathsf{Agg}_y) \\ \mathsf{CT}_i \leftarrow \mathsf{Encrypt}(\mathsf{PK}, \mathsf{EK}_i, i, x_i) \; \forall i \in [n_x] \\ \mathsf{SK}_j \leftarrow \mathsf{KeyGen}(\mathsf{PK}, \mathsf{PK}_j, j, y_j) \; \forall j \in [n_y] \\ z \leftarrow \mathsf{Decrypt}\left(\mathsf{PK}, \{\mathsf{SK}_j\}_{j \leq n_y}, \{\mathsf{CT}_i\}_{i \leq n_x}\right) \\ z' = \mathcal{U}\left(\mathsf{Agg}_x(\{x_i\}), \mathsf{Agg}_y(\{y_j\})\right) \end{array} \right] = 1.$$

Recall that $\mathcal{U}$ is the universal circuit with appropriate input and output size.

Indistinguishability Based Security. Next, we define security of MPFE. The security definition is modelled in a similar fashion to MIFE security [24, §2.2] while taking into account corruption queries.

For any choice of parameters λ, n_x, n_y, aggregation functions $\mathsf{Agg}_x, \mathsf{Agg}_y$, and master keys $\mathsf{K} = (\mathsf{PK}, \{\mathsf{EK}_i\}_{i \in [n_x]}, \{\mathsf{PK}_j\}_{j \in [n_y]}) \leftarrow \mathsf{Setup}(1^\lambda, n_x, n_y, \mathsf{Agg}_x, \mathsf{Agg}_y)$, we define the following list of oracles:

Corrupt$^{\mathsf{K}}(\cdot)$, upon a call to this oracle for any $i \in [n_x]$ or $j \in [n_y]$, the adversary gets the corresponding encryption key EK_i or master secret key PK_j. In the case of a local setup, the adversary could instead also supply the oracle with adversarially generated keys for the corresponding user; whereas in case of an interactive setup, the adversary could simulate the behavior of the queried

---

[4] We omit specifying the mode in the syntax for notational brevity.

user index in the setup protocol. (Let $\mathcal{S}_x \subseteq [n_x]$ and $\mathcal{S}_y \subseteq [n_y]$ denote the set of user indices for which the corresponding encryption and master keys have been corrupted.)[5]

$\mathsf{Key}^{\mathsf{K},\beta}(\cdot,\cdot)$, upon a call to this oracle for an honest user index $j \in [n_y]$, function inputs $(y_j^{k,0}, y_j^{k,1})$ (where $y_j^{k,b} = \left(y_{j,\mathrm{pub}}^{k,b}, y_{j,\mathrm{pri}}^{k,b}\right)$ for $b \in \{0,1\}$), the challenger first checks whether the user j was already corrupted or not. That is, if $j \in \mathcal{S}_y$, then it sends nothing, otherwise it samples a decryption key for function input $y_j^{k,\beta}$ using key PK_j and sends it to the adversary. (Here β is the challenge bit chosen at the start of the experiment.).

$\mathsf{Enc}^{\mathsf{K},\beta}(\cdot,\cdot)$, upon a call to this oracle for an honest user index $i \in [n_x]$, message inputs $(x_i^{\ell,0}, x_i^{\ell,1})$ (where $x_i^{\ell,b} = \left(x_{i,\mathrm{pub}}^{\ell,b}, x_{i,\mathrm{pri}}^{\ell,b}\right)$ for $b \in \{0,1\}$), the challenger first checks whether the user i was already corrupted or not. That is, if $i \in \mathcal{S}_x$, then it sends nothing, otherwise it samples a ciphertext for input $x_i^{\ell,\beta}$ using key EK_i and sends it to the adversary.

We let Q_x and Q_y be the number of encryption and key generation queries (respectively) that had non-empty responses. Let $\mathcal{Q}_x = \{(i, (x^{\ell,0}, x^{\ell,1}))\}_{\ell \in [Q_x]}$ be the set of ciphertext queries and $\mathcal{Q}_y = \{(j, (y_j^{k,0}, y_j^{k,1}))\}_{k \in [Q_y]}$ be the set of key queries.

We say that an adversary $\mathcal{A}$ is *admissible* if:

1. For each of the encryption and key challenges, the public components of the two challenges are equal, namely $x_{\mathrm{pub}}^{\ell,0} = x_{\mathrm{pub}}^{\ell,1}$ for all $\ell \in [Q_x]$, and $y_{\mathrm{pub}}^{k,0} = y_{\mathrm{pub}}^{k,1}$ for all $k \in [Q_y]$.
2. For each of the encryption and key challenges, the *private* components of the two challenges are also equal, namely $x_{\mathrm{pri}}^{\ell,0} = x_{\mathrm{pri}}^{\ell,1}$ for all $\ell \in [Q_x]$ whenever $(i, (x^{\ell,0}, x^{\ell,1})) \in \mathcal{Q}_x$ and $i \in \mathcal{S}_x$, and $y_{\mathrm{pri}}^{k,0} = y_{\mathrm{pri}}^{k,1}$ for all $k \in [Q_y]$ whenever $(j, (y^{\ell,0}, y^{\ell,1})) \in \mathcal{Q}_y$ and $j \in \mathcal{S}_y$. That is, the private components must be the same as well if the user index i or j, that the query was made for, was corrupted during the execution.
3. There do not exist two sequences $(\overrightarrow{x}^0, \overrightarrow{y}^0)$ and $(\overrightarrow{x}^1, \overrightarrow{y}^1)$ such that:

$$\mathcal{U}\left(\mathsf{Agg}_x(\{x_i^0\}), \mathsf{Agg}_y(\{y_j^0\})\right) \neq \mathcal{U}\left(\mathsf{Agg}_x(\{x_i^1\}), \mathsf{Agg}_y(\{y_j^1\})\right)$$

and i) for every $i \in [n_x]$, either x_i^b was queried or EK_i was corrupted, and ii) for every $j \in [n_y]$, either y_j^b was queried or PK_j was corrupted, and iii) at least one of inputs $\{x_i^b\}, \{y_j^b\}$ were queried and indices i, j were not corrupted.

---

[5] Note that in case EK_i is completely contained in some PK_j then make a master secret corruption query for j will also add the corresponding index i to $\mathcal{S}_x$, and vice versa. At a very high level, although having separate aggregation functions for partial secret key and ciphertexts as part of the framework allows us to capture a highly expressive class of encryption scheme; defining the most general notion of security for MPFE that captures all different types of setup and key distribution settings could be very dense. To that end, here we provide a clean security game which captures the existing encryption primitives. Capturing security for each setup mode and corruption model individually would be more precise in certain settings.

(Note that if $i \in [n_x]$ or $j \in [n_y]$ were queried to the Corrupt oracle, the adversary can generate partial keys or ciphertexts for any value of its choice.)

An MPFE scheme (Setup, KeyGen, Encrypt, Decrypt) is said to be IND secure if for any *admissible* PPT adversary $\mathcal{A}$, all length parameters $n_x, n_y \in \mathbb{N}$, and aggregation functions $\mathsf{Agg}_x, \mathsf{Agg}_y$, there exists a negligible function $\mathsf{negl}(\cdot)$ such that for all $\lambda \in \mathbb{N}$, the following holds

$$\Pr\left[\mathcal{A}^{\mathsf{Corrupt}^{\mathsf{K}}(\cdot),\mathsf{Key}^{\mathsf{K},\beta}(\cdot),\mathsf{Enc}^{\mathsf{K},\beta}(\cdot)}(1^\lambda, \mathsf{PK}) = \beta : \begin{matrix} \mathsf{K} \leftarrow \mathsf{Setup}(1^\lambda, n_x, n_y, \mathsf{Agg}_x, \mathsf{Agg}_y), \\ \mathsf{K} = (\mathsf{PK}, \{\mathsf{EK}_i\}_i, \{\mathsf{PK}_j\}_j), \\ \beta \leftarrow \{0,1\} \end{matrix}\right] \leq \frac{1}{2} + \mathsf{negl}(\lambda).$$

Remark 2.1 (Weaker notions of security). We say the scheme is selective IND secure if the adversary outputs the challenge message and function pairs at the very beginning of the game, before it makes any queries or receives the PK. One may also consider the semi-honest setting, where the Corrupt oracle is not provided, or the case of static corruptions where the adversary provides all its corruptions once and for all at the start of the game.

Due to space constraints, we provide our definition of dynamic MPFE in the full version, and also provide a general feasibility of MPFE for circuits from the minimal assumption of MIFE for circuits.

3   Multi-Authority **ABE ∘ IPFE** for LSSS Access Structures

In this section, extend the construction of Abdalla et al. [4] (ACGU20) to the multiparty setting. As discussed in Sect. 1, we support $n_y = n$ for some fixed, polynomial n and Local mode of setup algorithm, so that each key generator generates its key components locally and independently. The number of encryptors $n_x = 1$ and public, private input $(\phi, \mathbf{v})$. Each of the n key generators has public inputs $(\mathsf{GID}_i, x_i, \mathbf{u}_i)$ where $x_i \in \{0,1\}$ and $\mathbf{u}_i \in \mathbb{Z}_q^\ell$ for $i \in [n]$. The ciphertext aggregation function remains trivial but the key aggregation function checks if $\mathsf{GID}_1 = \mathsf{GID}_2 = \ldots = \mathsf{GID}_n$, $\mathbf{u}_1 = \mathbf{u}_2 = \ldots = \mathbf{u}_n$, and outputs $(f_\mathbf{x}, \mathbf{u})$ if so, where $\mathbf{x} = (x_1, \ldots, x_n)$ and $f_\mathbf{x}$ is a function that takes as input three arguments $(\phi, \mathbf{v}, \mathbf{u})$ and outputs $\langle \mathbf{u}, \mathbf{v} \rangle$ if $\phi(\mathbf{x}) = 1$.

In other words, we build a multi-authority attribute-based inner product functional encryption (MA-AB-IPFE) scheme for linear secret sharing schemes (LSSS) access structures. We rely on simple assumptions over bilinear maps.

3.1   Specializing the MPFE Syntax

Since our framework of MPFE described in Sect. 2 is general enough to capture a large family of functionalities, using the general syntax as-is would result in a cumbersome definition in which multiple parameters are non-functional. Hence, we specialize the general framework to the specific functionality of interest here for ease of exposition.

Syntax. A MA-AB-IPFE scheme for predicate class $\mathcal{C} = \{\mathcal{C}_n : \mathcal{X}_n \to \{0,1\}\}_{n \in \mathbb{N}}$ and inner product message space $\mathcal{U} = \{\mathcal{U}_\ell\}_{\ell \in \mathbb{N}}$ consists of the following PPT algorithms:

$\mathsf{GSetup}(1^\lambda) \to \mathsf{PP}$. On input the security parameter λ, the setup algorithm outputs public parameters PP.

$\mathsf{LSetup}(\mathsf{PP}, 1^n, 1^\ell, i) \to (\mathsf{PK}, \mathsf{PK})$. On input the public parameters PP, attribute length n, message space index ℓ, and authority's index $i \in [n]$, the authority setup algorithm outputs a pair of master public-secret key $(\mathsf{PK}, \mathsf{PK})$ for the i-th authority.

$\mathsf{KeyGen}(\mathsf{PK}_j, \mathsf{GID}, b, \mathbf{u}) \to \mathsf{SK}_{j,\mathsf{GID},b,\mathbf{u}}$. The key generation algorithm takes as input the authority master secret key PK_j, global identifier GID, an attribute bit $b \in \{0,1\}$, and key vector $\mathbf{u} \in \mathcal{U}_\ell$. It outputs a partial secret key $\mathsf{SK}_{j,\mathsf{GID},b,\mathbf{u}}$.

$\mathsf{Enc}(\{\mathsf{PK}_i\}_{i \in [n]}, C, \mathbf{v}) \to \mathsf{CT}$. The encryption algorithm takes as input the list of public keys $\{\mathsf{PK}_i\}_i$, predicate circuit C, and a message vector $\mathbf{v} \in \mathcal{U}_\ell$, and outputs a ciphertext CT.

$\mathsf{Dec}(\{\mathsf{SK}_{i,\mathsf{GID},\mathbf{x},\mathbf{u}}\}_{i \in [n]}, \mathsf{CT}) \to m/\perp$. On input a list of n partial secret keys $\{\mathsf{SK}_{i,\mathsf{GID},\mathbf{x},\mathbf{u}}\}_i$ and a ciphertext CT, the decryption algorithm either outputs a message m (corresponding to the inner product value) or a special string $\perp$ (to denote decryption failure).

Correctness. A MA-AB-IPFE scheme is said to be correct if for all $\lambda, n, \ell \in \mathbb{N}$, $C \in \mathcal{C}_n$, $\mathbf{u}, \mathbf{v} \in \mathcal{U}_\ell$, $\mathbf{x} \in \mathcal{X}_n$, GID, if $C(\mathbf{x}) = 1$, the following holds:

$$\Pr\left[\mathsf{Dec}(\mathsf{SK}, \mathsf{CT}) = \langle \mathbf{u}, \mathbf{v} \rangle : \begin{array}{l} \mathsf{PP} \leftarrow \mathsf{GSetup}(1^\lambda) \\ \forall i \in [n] : (\mathsf{PK}_i, \mathsf{PK}_i) \leftarrow \mathsf{LSetup}(\mathsf{PP}, 1^n, 1^\ell, i) \\ \forall j \in [n] : \mathsf{SK}_{j,\mathsf{GID},x_j,\mathbf{u}} \leftarrow \mathsf{KeyGen}(\{\mathsf{PK}_i\}_i, \mathsf{PK}_j, \mathsf{GID}, x_j, \mathbf{u}) \\ \mathsf{CT} \leftarrow \mathsf{Enc}(\{\mathsf{PK}_i\}_i, C, \mathbf{v}), \mathsf{SK} = \{\mathsf{SK}_{i,\mathsf{GID},x_i,\mathbf{u}}\}_i \end{array}\right] = 1.$$

Security. In terms of security, a MA-AB-IPFE provides powerful notion of encrypted message vector indistinguishability where the adversary is allowed to corrupt the key generation authorities and also make key queries for message vector distinguishing key vectors (as long as the attribute does not satisfy the encrypted predicate). Below we provide the selective security variant of the corresponding property.[6]

Definition 3.1 (Selective *MA-AB-IPFE* security with static corruptions).
A MA-AB-IPFE *scheme is selectively secure with static corruptions if for every*

---

[6] In this work, we only focus on standard semantic security, but one could also amplify to its CCA counterpart by relying on the generic CPA-to-CCA amplification techniques [28].

stateful admissible PPT adversary $\mathcal{A}$, there exists a negligible function $\mathsf{negl}(\cdot)$ such that for all $\lambda \in \mathbb{N}$, the following holds

$$\Pr \left[\mathcal{A}^{O(\mathsf{key}, \cdot, \cdot, \cdot)}(\{\mathsf{PK}_i\}_{i \in [n] \setminus S^*}, \mathsf{CT}) = b : \begin{array}{l} \mathsf{PP} \leftarrow \mathsf{GSetup}(1^\lambda) \\ (1^n, 1^\ell, S^*, C, (\mathbf{v}_0, \mathbf{v}_1), \{\mathsf{PK}_i\}_{i \in S^*}) \leftarrow \mathcal{A}(1^\lambda, \mathsf{PP}) \\ \forall i \in [n] \setminus S^* : (\mathsf{PK}_i, \mathsf{PK}_i) \leftarrow \mathsf{LSetup}(\mathsf{PP}, 1^n, 1^\ell, i) \\ b \leftarrow \{0, 1\}, \mathsf{CT} \leftarrow \mathsf{Enc}(\{\mathsf{PK}_i\}_{i \in [n]}, C, \mathbf{v}_b) \\ \mathsf{key} = \{(\mathsf{PK}_i, \mathsf{PK}_i)\}_{i \in [n] \setminus S^*} \end{array} \right]$$

$$\leq \frac{1}{2} + \mathsf{negl}(\lambda),$$

where the oracle $O(\mathsf{key}, \cdot, \cdot, \cdot)$ has the master key for honest authorities hard-wired. The oracle on input a tuple of a global identifier GID, an authority index $j \in [n] \setminus S^*$, and an attribute-key vector pair $(b, \mathbf{u})$, responds with a partial secret key computed as $\mathsf{SK}_{j, \mathsf{GID}, b, \mathbf{u}} \leftarrow \mathsf{KeyGen}(\mathsf{PK}_j, \mathsf{GID}, b, \mathbf{u})$. Note that the adversary is only allowed to submit key queries for non-corrupt authorities (i.e., $j \notin S^*$). Also, the adversary $\mathcal{A}$ is admissible as long as every secret key query made by $\mathcal{A}$ to the key generation oracle O satisfies the condition that—(1) either $\langle \mathbf{u}, \mathbf{v}_0 \rangle = \langle \mathbf{u}, \mathbf{v}_1 \rangle$, or (2) C does not accept any input $\mathbf{x}$ such that $x_j = b$ for $(b, j) \in Q_{\mathsf{GID}}$ where Q_{GID} contains the attribute bits queries for GID[7].

3.2   Construction

Let Gen be a composite-order bilinear group generator. Also, let $\mathbb{G}$ and $\mathbb{G}_T$ be the source and target groups, respectively. Additionally, we rely on a hash function $H : \{0, 1\}^* \to \mathbb{G}$ that maps global identities GID to elements of $\mathbb{G}$ and we later model it as a random oracle in the proof. Below we provide our MA-AB-IPFE scheme based on composite-order bilinear maps for the predicates described as an access policy for a linear secret sharing scheme.

$\mathsf{GSetup}(1^\lambda) \to \mathsf{PP}$. The setup algorithm samples a bilinear group as follows

$$(p_1, p_2, p_3, \mathbb{G}, \mathbb{G}_T, e(\cdot, \cdot)) \leftarrow \mathsf{Gen}(1^\lambda, 3).$$

It samples a random generator $g_1 \in \mathbb{G}_1$, and sets the global public parameters as $\mathsf{PP} = (g_1, N = p_1 p_2 p_3, \mathbb{G}, \mathbb{G}_T, e(\cdot, \cdot))$.

(**Notation.** Here and throughout, we use the 'bracket' notation for representing group elements. Where $[1]_1 := g_1$, and $[1]_{T,1} := e(g_1, g_1)$.)

$\mathsf{LSetup}(\mathsf{PP}, 1^n, 1^\ell, i) \to (\mathsf{PK}, \mathsf{PK})$. The algorithm samples two random vectors $\boldsymbol{\alpha}, \mathbf{w} \leftarrow \mathbb{Z}_N^\ell$, and sets the authority public-secret key pair as $\mathsf{PK} = (\mathsf{PP}, [\boldsymbol{\alpha}]_{T,1}, [\mathbf{w}]_1)$ and $\mathsf{PK} = (\boldsymbol{\alpha}, \mathbf{w})$. (Here and throughout, note that $[\mathbf{w}]_1$ and similar terms can be computed as $g_1^{\mathbf{w}}$.)

$\mathsf{KeyGen}(\mathsf{PK}_j, \mathsf{GID}, b, \mathbf{u}) \to \mathsf{SK}_{j, \mathsf{GID}, b, \mathbf{u}}$. It parses the authority key as described above. If $b = 0$, it sets the secret key as empty string. Otherwise, it first

---

[7] Note that in general this could be a non-falsifiable condition to check if S^* is $\omega(\log \lambda)$ and the predicate class contains general non-monotonic functions.

hashes the GID to create a masking term $[\mu] \in \mathbb{G}$ as $[\mu] = H(\mathsf{GID})$. It then outputs the secret key as

$$\mathsf{SK}_{j,\mathsf{GID},b,\mathbf{u}} = \left[\langle \boldsymbol{\alpha}, \mathbf{u} \rangle\right]_1 \cdot \left[\mu \cdot \langle \mathbf{w}, \mathbf{u} \rangle\right].$$

Note that since the vectors $\mathbf{u}, \mathbf{w}, \boldsymbol{\alpha}$ are known to the algorithm in the clear, thus the above key term can be computed efficiently.

$\mathsf{Enc}(\{\mathsf{PK}_i\}_{i \in [n]}, (\mathbf{A}, \rho), \mathbf{v}) \to \mathsf{CT}$. The encryption algorithm first parses the keys PK_i as $(\mathsf{PP}, [\boldsymbol{\alpha}_i]_{T,1}, [\mathbf{w}_i]_1)$, and the predicate contains an $m_1 \times m_2$ access matrix $\mathbf{A}$ with function ρ mapping the rows to the attribute positions. It samples a $m_2 \times \ell$ matrix $\mathbf{S}$ and $(m_2 - 1) \times \ell$ matrix $\mathbf{T}'$ uniformly at random as $\mathbf{S} \leftarrow \mathbb{Z}_N^{m_2 \times \ell}$ and $\mathbf{T}' \leftarrow \mathbb{Z}_N^{(m_2-1) \times \ell}$. It sets a $m_2 \times \ell$ matrix $\mathbf{T}$, and arranges two $m_1 \times \ell$ matrices $\boldsymbol{\Delta}$ and $\boldsymbol{\Gamma}$ as

$$\mathbf{T} = \begin{pmatrix} \mathbf{0}^\top \\ \mathbf{T}' \end{pmatrix}, \qquad \boldsymbol{\Delta} = \begin{pmatrix} \boldsymbol{\alpha}^\top_{\rho(1)} \\ \vdots \\ \boldsymbol{\alpha}^\top_{\rho(m_1)} \end{pmatrix}, \qquad \boldsymbol{\Gamma} = \begin{pmatrix} \mathbf{w}^\top_{\rho(1)} \\ \vdots \\ \mathbf{w}^\top_{\rho(m_1)} \end{pmatrix}.$$

That is, the matrix $\mathbf{T}$ contains all zeros in the first row and is random otherwise. It also samples a random vector as $\mathbf{r} \leftarrow \mathbb{Z}_N^{m_1}$, and computes the ciphertext $\mathsf{CT} = (C_0, C_1, C_2, C_3)$ as:

$$C_0 = \left[\mathbf{s}_1 + \mathbf{v}\right]_{T,1}, \qquad C_1 = \left[\mathbf{A} \cdot \mathbf{S} + \boldsymbol{\Delta} \odot (\mathbf{r} \otimes \mathbf{1}^\top)\right]_{T,1},$$

$$C_2 = \left[\mathbf{r}\right]_1, \qquad C_3 = \left[\mathbf{A} \cdot \mathbf{T} + \boldsymbol{\Gamma} \odot (\mathbf{r} \otimes \mathbf{1}^\top)\right]_1.$$

Here the vector $\mathbf{s}_1$ is the first column vector of matrix $\mathbf{S}^\top$ (that is, $\mathbf{s}_1 = \mathbf{S}^\top \cdot \mathbf{e}_1$ where $\mathbf{e}_1$ is the first fundamental basis vector of $\mathbb{Z}_N^{m_2}$).

$\mathsf{Dec}(\{\mathsf{SK}_{i,\mathsf{GID},x_i,\mathbf{u}}\}_{i \in [n]}, \mathsf{CT}) \to M$. It parses the secret key and ciphertext as described above. Let $(\mathbf{A}, \rho)$ be the access policy associated with the ciphertext, and $\mathbf{u}$ be the key vector associated with the partial secret keys. (This could either be explicitly addded to the ciphertext and secret keys above, or passed as an auxiliary input.)

The decryptor first computes the LSSS reconstruction vector $\mathbf{z}$ such that $\mathbf{z}^\top \cdot \mathbf{A} = \mathbf{e}_1^\top = (1, 0, \dots, 0)$. The decryptor then arranges the key terms as

$$K = \begin{pmatrix} \mathsf{SK}_{\rho(1),\mathsf{GID},x_{\rho(1)},\mathbf{u}} \\ \vdots \\ \mathsf{SK}_{\rho(m_1),\mathsf{GID},x_{\rho(m_1)},\mathbf{u}} \end{pmatrix}$$

and recovers the inner product message value M by computing the discrete log of the following the following:

$$[M]_{T,1} = \frac{\langle C_0, \mathbf{u} \rangle}{(\mathbf{z}^\top \cdot C_1 \cdot \mathbf{u})} \cdot \frac{\mathbf{z}^\top \cdot e\,(K, C_2)}{e\,(H(\mathsf{GID}), \mathbf{z}^\top \cdot C_3 \cdot \mathbf{u})}$$

where the matrix vector operations involving group elements and exponents are performed by first raising the exponent of each term (component-by-component) for performing multiplication in the exponent, and then followed by multiplication of the resulting encodings to simulate addition being performed in the exponent. Also, the operation $e(K, C_2)$ performs the pairing operation element-by-element for each element of the vector.

3.3 Correctness and Security

Due to space constraints, the proof is provided in the full version [6].

4 Function-Hiding DDFE for Inner Products

In this section, we present our function-hiding decentralized dynamic inner product functional encryption (IP-DDFE) scheme. As described in Sect. 1, we have the setup algorithm in the Local mode, so that each party i can dynamically join the system by generating a public key PK_i and a master secret key PK_i. For encryption, party i sets $(x_{\mathrm{pub}}, x_{\mathrm{pri}}) = ((\mathcal{U}_M, \mathsf{lab}_M), \mathbf{x}_i)$ where $\mathcal{U}_M$ is the set of parties whose inputs will be combined and lab_M is a label which imposes a constraint on which values can be aggregated together. For key generation, party i sets $(y_{\mathrm{pub}}, y_{\mathrm{pri}}) = ((\mathcal{U}_K, \mathsf{lab}_K), \mathbf{y}_i)$ where $\mathcal{U}_K, \mathsf{lab}_K$ have the same roles as $\mathcal{U}_M, \mathsf{lab}_M$, respectively. The function Agg_x checks if the public inputs $(\mathcal{U}_M, \mathsf{lab}_M)$ match for all parties and that all the ciphertexts are provided for the set $\mathcal{U}_M$. If so, outputs $(\mathcal{U}_M, \mathbf{x})$ where $\mathbf{x} = (\mathbf{x}_1 \| \dots \| \mathbf{x}_{n_x})$. The function Agg_y checks that all values $\mathcal{U}_K$ and lab_K are the same for all parties. If so, it outputs the function $f_{\mathcal{U}_K, \mathbf{y}=(\mathbf{y}_1 \| \dots \| \mathbf{y}_{n_y})}$ which takes as input $(\mathcal{U}_M, \mathbf{x})$, checks that $\mathcal{U}_M = \mathcal{U}_K$ and if so, outputs $\langle \mathbf{x}, \mathbf{y} \rangle$.

As discussed in the introduction, we first obtain a function-hiding multi-client inner product functional encryption (IP-MCFE) scheme, and then lift it to a function-hiding IP-DDFE scheme in a non-black box manner. We first define necessary notions to describe our IP-MCFE and IP-DDFE scheme. As before, we will specialize the MPFE syntax for ease of exposition.

4.1 Specializing the MPFE Syntax

Syntax of MCFE. Let $\mathcal{F}$ be a function family such that, for all $f \in \mathcal{F}$, $f : \mathcal{M}_1 \times \dots \times \mathcal{M}_n \to \mathcal{Z}$. Let $\mathcal{L}$ be a label space. An MCFE scheme for $\mathcal{F}$ and $\mathcal{L}$ consists of four algorithms.

Setup($1^\lambda, 1^n$): It takes a security parameter 1^λ and a number 1^n of slots, and outputs a public parameter PK, encryption keys $\{\mathsf{EK}_i\}_{i \in [n]}$, a master secret key PK. The other algorithms implicitly take PK.

KeyGen(PK, f): It takes PK and $f \in \mathcal{F}$, and outputs a secret key SK.

Enc($i, \mathsf{EK}_i, x_i, \mathsf{lab}$): It takes PK, an index $i \in [n]$, $x_i \in \mathcal{M}_i$, and a label lab and outputs a ciphertext CT_i.

Dec($\mathsf{CT}_1, \dots, \mathsf{CT}_n, \mathsf{SK}$): It takes $\mathsf{CT}_1, \dots, \mathsf{CT}_n$ and SK, and outputs a decryption value $d \in \mathcal{Z}$ or a symbol $\perp$.

Correctness. An MCFE scheme is correct if it satisfies the following condition. For all $\lambda, n \in \mathbb{N}$, $(x_1, ..., x_n) \in \mathcal{M}_1 \times \cdots \times \mathcal{M}_n$, $f \in \mathcal{F}$, lab $\in \mathcal{L}$, we have

$$\Pr \left[d = f(x_1, ..., x_n) : \begin{array}{l} (\mathsf{PK}, \{\mathsf{EK}_i\}, \mathsf{PK}) \leftarrow \mathsf{Setup}(1^\lambda, 1^n) \\ \mathsf{CT}_i \leftarrow \mathsf{Enc}(i, \mathsf{EK}_i, x_i, \mathsf{lab}) \\ \mathsf{SK} \leftarrow \mathsf{KeyGen}(\mathsf{PK}, f) \\ d = \mathsf{Dec}(\mathsf{CT}_1, ..., \mathsf{CT}_n, \mathsf{SK}) \end{array} \right] = 1.$$

Security. We basically adopt the security definition for MCFE in [2] and extend it to function-hiding security. We also introduce a selective vatiant because our final goal is IP-DDFE with selective security, and selectively secure IP-MCFE is sufficient for the security analysis of our IP-DDFE scheme.

Definition 4.1 (Function-hiding security of MCFE**).** An MCFE scheme is Leak_y-xx-yy-function-hiding (xx $\in \{\mathsf{sel}, \mathsf{sta}, \mathsf{adt}\}$, yy $\in \{\mathsf{any}, \mathsf{pos}\}$) if for every stateful PPT adversary $\mathcal{A}$, there exists a negligible function $\mathsf{negl}(\cdot)$ such that for all $\lambda, n \in \mathbb{N}$, the following holds

$$\Pr \left[\beta \leftarrow \mathcal{A}^{\mathsf{QCor}(), \mathsf{QEnc}^\beta(), \mathsf{QKeyGen}^\beta()}(\mathsf{PK}) : \begin{array}{l} \beta \leftarrow \{0, 1\} \\ (\mathsf{PK}, \{\mathsf{EK}_i\}, \mathsf{PK}) \leftarrow \mathsf{Setup}(1^\lambda, 1^n) \end{array} \right] \leq \frac{1}{2} + \mathsf{negl}(\lambda)$$

where $\mathsf{QCor}(i)$ outputs EK_i, $\mathsf{QEnc}^\beta(i, x_i^0, x_i^1, \mathsf{lab})$ outputs $\mathsf{Enc}(i, \mathsf{EK}_i, x_i^\beta, \mathsf{lab})$, and $\mathsf{QKeyGen}^\beta(f^0, f^1)$ outputs $\mathsf{KeyGen}(\mathsf{PK}, f^\beta)$. Let $q_{c,i,\mathsf{lab}}$ be the numbers of queries of the forms of $\mathsf{QEnc}^\beta(i, *, *, \mathsf{lab})$. Let $\mathcal{HS}$ be the set of parties on which the adversary has not queried QCor at the end of the game, and $\mathcal{CS} = [n] \backslash \mathcal{HS}$. Then, the adversary's queries must satisfy the following conditions.

- For $i \in \mathcal{CS}$, the queries $\mathsf{QEnc}^\beta(i, x_i^0, x_i^1, \mathsf{lab})$ and $\mathsf{QKeyGen}^\beta(f^0, f^1)$ must satisfy $x_i^0 = x_i^1$ and $\mathsf{Leak}_y(i, f^0) = \mathsf{Leak}_y(i, f^1)$, respectively.[8]
- There are no sequences $(x_1^0, ..., x_n^0, f^0, \mathsf{lab})$ and $(x_1^1, ..., x_n^1, f^1, \mathsf{lab})$ that satisfy all the conditions:
  - For all $i \in [n]$, [$\mathsf{QEnc}^\beta(i, x_i^0, x_i^1, \mathsf{lab})$ is queried and $i \in \mathcal{HS}$] or [$x_i^0 = x_i^1 \in \mathcal{M}_i$ and $i \in \mathcal{CS}$].
  - $\mathsf{QKeyGen}^\beta(f^0, f^1)$ are queried.
  - $f^0(x_1^0, ..., x_n^0) \neq f^1(x_1^1, ..., x_n^1)$.
- When xx = sta: the adversary cannot query QCor after querying QEnc or $\mathsf{QKeyGen}$ even once.
- When xx = sel: the adversary must make all queries in one shot. That is, first it outputs $(\mathcal{CS}, \{i, x_i^0, x_i^1, \mathsf{lab}\}, \{f^0, f^1\})$ and obtains the response: $(\{\mathsf{EK}_i\}_{i \in \mathcal{CS}}, \{\mathsf{Enc}(i, \mathsf{EK}_i, x_i^\beta, \mathsf{lab})\}, \{\mathsf{KeyGen}(\mathsf{PK}, f^\beta)\})$.
- When yy = pos: for each $\mathsf{lab} \in \mathcal{L}$, either $q_{c,i,\mathsf{lab}} > 0$ for all $i \in \mathcal{HS}$ or $q_{c,i,\mathsf{lab}} = 0$ for all $i \in \mathcal{HS}$.

---

[8] The leakage function captures information that EK_i reveals from SK.

Syntax of DDFE. We define the syntax of DDFE. Note that we use an identifier $i \in \mathcal{ID}$ to specify each party while they use PK for identifier in the original definition [22], since it allows more precise indexing than the indexing by PK^9. We assume that the correspondence between id i and public key PK_i is publicly known, or it could be supplied as an input to the local setup algorithm. We describe the syntax of DDFE in the context of MPFE and change some expressions from the original definition. For instance, we use PK instead of SK for secret keys of each party, public/private inputs for Enc and KeyGen instead of using empty keys, and so on.

Let $\mathcal{ID}, \mathcal{K}, \mathcal{M}$ be an ID space, a key space, and a message space, respectively. $\mathcal{K}, \mathcal{M}$ consist of a public part and a private part, that is, $\mathcal{K} = \mathcal{K}_{\mathrm{pri}} \times \mathcal{K}_{\mathrm{pub}}, \mathcal{M} = \mathcal{M}_{\mathrm{pri}} \times \mathcal{M}_{\mathrm{pub}}$. Let f be a function such that $f : \bigcup_{i \in \mathbb{N}} (\mathcal{ID} \times \mathcal{K})^i \times \bigcup_{i \in \mathbb{N}} (\mathcal{ID} \times \mathcal{M})^i \to \mathcal{Z}$. A DDFE scheme for f consists of five algorithms.

$\mathsf{GSetup}(1^\lambda)$: It takes a security parameter 1^λ and outputs a public parameter PP. The other algorithms implicitly take PP.

$\mathsf{LSetup}(\mathsf{PP})$: It takes PP and outputs local public parameter PK_i and a master secret key PK_i. The following three algorithms implicitly take PK_i.

$\mathsf{KeyGen}(\mathsf{PK}_i, k = (k_{\mathrm{pri}}, k_{\mathrm{pub}}))$: It takes PK_i and $k \in \mathcal{K}$, and outputs a secret key SK_i.

$\mathsf{Enc}(\mathsf{PK}_i, m = (m_{\mathrm{pri}}, m_{\mathrm{pub}}))$: It takes PK_i and $m \in \mathcal{M}$, and outputs a ciphertext CT_i.

$\mathsf{Dec}(\{\mathsf{SK}_i\}_{i \in \mathcal{U}_K}, \{\mathsf{CT}_i\}_{i \in \mathcal{U}_M})$: It takes $\{\mathsf{SK}_i\}_{i \in \mathcal{U}_K}, \{\mathsf{CT}_i\}_{i \in \mathcal{U}_M}$ and outputs a decryption value $d \in \mathcal{Z}$ or a symbol $\perp$ where $\mathcal{U}_K \subseteq \mathcal{ID}$ and $\mathcal{U}_M \subseteq \mathcal{ID}$ are any sets.

Correctness. An DDFE scheme for f is correct if it satisfies the following condition. For all $\lambda \in \mathbb{N}$, $\mathcal{U}_K \subseteq \mathcal{ID}$, $\mathcal{U}_M \subseteq \mathcal{ID}$, $\{i, k_i\}_{i \in \mathcal{U}_K} \in \bigcup_{i \in \mathbb{N}} (\mathcal{ID} \times \mathcal{K})^i$, $\{i, m_i\}_{i \in \mathcal{U}_M} \in \bigcup_{i \in \mathbb{N}} (\mathcal{ID} \times \mathcal{M})^i$, we have

$$\Pr\left[d = f(\{i, k_i\}_{i \in \mathcal{U}_K}, \{i, m_i\}_{i \in \mathcal{U}_M}) : \begin{array}{l} \mathsf{PP} \leftarrow \mathsf{GSetup}(1^\lambda) \\ \mathsf{PK}_i, \mathsf{PK}_i \leftarrow \mathsf{LSetup}(\mathsf{PP}) \\ \mathsf{CT}_i \leftarrow \mathsf{Enc}(\mathsf{PK}_i, m_i) \\ \mathsf{SK}_i \leftarrow \mathsf{KeyGen}(\mathsf{PK}_i, k_i) \\ d = \mathsf{Dec}(\{\mathsf{SK}_i\}_{i \in \mathcal{U}_K}, \{\mathsf{CT}_i\}_{i \in \mathcal{U}_M}) \end{array}\right] = 1.$$

Note that we can consider the case where $\mathcal{U}_K$ and $\mathcal{U}_M$ are multisets as in the original definition in [22]. However, we do not consider the case here since it induces ambiguity that can be also found in $[22]^{10}$. We assume that $\mathbb{N}$ contains 0 here and $(\mathcal{ID} \times \mathcal{K})^0 = \{i, k_i\}_{i \in \emptyset} = \emptyset$. That is, $\mathcal{U}_K$ and $\mathcal{U}_M$ can be an empty set,

---

[9] In [22], some definitions have ambiguity that seems to stem from the indexing by pk. For instance, correctness of DDFE in Definition 1 implicitly assumes that $\mathsf{sk}_{\mathrm{pk}}$ is uniquely decided by pk, while the syntax does not require such a condition. Another example is the IP-DDFE construction in [22, § 7.2].

[10] Concretely, when $\mathcal{U}_K$ is a multiset, and $i' \in \mathcal{U}_K$ has multiplicity 2, how to treat $k_{i'} \in \{k_i\}_{i \in \mathcal{U}_K}$ is unclear.

which corresponds to the case where Dec does not take secret keys/ciphertexts as input.

Security. We naturally extend the security definition for DDFE in [22] to the function-hiding setting as follows.

Definition 4.2 (Function-hiding security of DDFE). An DDFE scheme is xx-yy-function-hiding (xx $\in$ {sel, adt}, yy $\in$ {sym, asym}) if for every stateful PPT adversary $\mathcal{A}$, there exists a negligible function negl($\cdot$) such that for all $\lambda \in \mathbb{N}$, the following holds

$$\Pr\left[\beta \leftarrow \mathcal{A}^{\mathsf{QHonestGen}(),\mathsf{QCor}(),\mathsf{QEnc}^{\beta}(),\mathsf{QKeyGen}^{\beta}()}(\mathsf{PP}) : \begin{array}{l} \beta \leftarrow \{0,1\} \\ \mathsf{PP} \leftarrow \mathsf{GSetup}(1^{\lambda}) \end{array}\right] \leq \frac{1}{2} + \mathsf{negl}(\lambda).$$

Each oracle works as follows. For $i \in \mathcal{ID}$, QHonestGen(i) runs $(\mathsf{PK}_i, \mathsf{PK}_i) \leftarrow$ LSetup(PP) and returns PK_i. For i such that QHonestGen(i) was queried, the adversary can make the following queries: QCor(i) outputs PK_i, $\mathsf{QEnc}^{\beta}(i, m^0, m^1)$ outputs Enc(PK_i, m^{β}), and $\mathsf{QKeyGen}^{\beta}(i, k^0, k^1)$ outputs KeyGen(PK_i, k^{β}). Note that k^{β} and m^{β} consist of the private elements $k_{\mathrm{pri}}^{\beta}, m_{\mathrm{pri}}^{\beta}$ and the public elements $k_{\mathrm{pub}}, m_{\mathrm{pub}}$, respectively (we always require that $k_{\mathrm{pub}}^0 = k_{\mathrm{pub}}^1 = k_{\mathrm{pub}}$ and $m_{\mathrm{pub}}^0 = m_{\mathrm{pub}}^1 = m_{\mathrm{pub}}$ as the public elements are not hidden in SK or CT). Let $\mathcal{S}$ be the set of parties on which QHonestGen(i) is queried, $\mathcal{HS}$ be the set of parties on which the adversary has not queried QCor at the end of the game, and $\mathcal{CS} = \mathcal{S} \backslash \mathcal{CS}$. Then, the adversary's queries must satisfy the following conditions.

- There are no sequences $(\{i, k_i^0\}_{i \in \mathcal{U}_K}, \{i, m_i^0\}_{i \in \mathcal{U}_M})$ and $(\{i, k_i^1\}_{i \in \mathcal{U}_K}, \{i, m_i^1\}_{i \in \mathcal{U}_M})$ that satisfy all the conditions:
  - For all $i \in \mathcal{U}_K$, [$\mathsf{QKeyGen}^{\beta}(i, k_i^0, k_i^1)$ is queried and $i \in \mathcal{HS}$] or [$k_i^0 = k_i^1 \in \mathcal{K}$ and $i \in \mathcal{CS}$].
  - For all $i \in \mathcal{U}_M$, [$\mathsf{QEnc}^{\beta}(i, m_i^0, m_i^1)$ is queried and $i \in \mathcal{HS}$] or [$m_i^0 = m_i^1 \in \mathcal{M}$ and $i \in \mathcal{CS}$].
  - $f(\{i, k_i^0\}_{i \in \mathcal{U}_K}, \{i, m_i^0\}_{i \in \mathcal{U}_M}) \neq f(\{i, k_i^1\}_{i \in \mathcal{U}_K}, \{i, m_i^1\}_{i \in \mathcal{U}_M})$.
- When xx = sel: the adversary first generates a set $\mathcal{S}$ of honest users in one shot. After that it makes the corruption, key generation, encryption queries in one shot to obtain $\{\mathsf{PK}_i\}, \{\mathsf{KeyGen}(\mathsf{PK}_i, k^{\beta})\}, \{\mathsf{Enc}(\mathsf{EK}_i, m^{\beta})\}$.
- When yy = sym: for $i \in \mathcal{CS}$, the queries $\mathsf{QKeyGen}^{\beta}(i, k^0, k^1)$ and $\mathsf{QEnc}^{\beta}(i, m^0, m^1)$ must satisfy $k^0 = k^1$ and $m^0 = m^1$, respectively[11].

Definition 4.3 (Inner Product Functional Encryption (IPFE)). Let $\Pi = (p, \mathbb{G}_1, \mathbb{G}_2, \mathbb{G}_T, e, g_1, g_2)$ be bilinear groups. IPFE for Π is a class of FE where $\mathcal{M} = \mathbb{G}_1^N$, and function $f \in \mathcal{F}$ is represented by $[\mathbf{y}]_2 \in \mathbb{G}_2^N$ where $\mathbf{y} \in \mathbb{Z}_p^N$ and defined as $f([\mathbf{x}]_1) = [\langle \mathbf{x}, \mathbf{y} \rangle]_T$. We say IPFE is function-hiding if it has both message and function privacy.

Definition 4.4 (IP-MCFE). Let $B \in \mathbb{N}$ be a bound of the infinity norm of vectors. IP-MCFE is a class of MCFE where $\mathcal{M}_i = [-B, B]^N$, $\mathcal{Z} = \mathbb{Z}$, and $\mathcal{L} = \{0, 1\}^*$. The function f is represented by $\mathbf{y} \in [-B, B]^{nN}$ and defined as $f(\mathbf{x}_1, ..., \mathbf{x}_n) = \langle (\mathbf{x}_1 || ... || \mathbf{x}_n), \mathbf{y} \rangle$.

---

[11] The symmetric setting captures the case where PK_i can be used to not only encrypt/key generation but also decryption/decoding of $\mathsf{CT}_i / \mathsf{SK}_i$.

Definition 4.5 (IP-DDFE). Let $B \in \mathbb{N}$ be a bound of the infinity norm of vectors. IP-DDFE is a class of DDFE where $\mathcal{ID} = \{0,1\}^*$, $\mathcal{K}_{\mathrm{pri}} = \mathcal{M}_{\mathrm{pri}} = [-B, B]^{\mathsf{N}}$, $\mathcal{K}_{\mathrm{pub}} = \mathcal{M}_{\mathrm{pub}} = 2^{\mathcal{ID}} \times \mathcal{L}$, $\mathcal{Z} = \mathbb{Z}$ for label space $\mathcal{L} = \{0,1\}^*$. The function f is defined as, for $\{k_i = (\mathbf{y}_i, \mathcal{U}_{K,i}, \mathsf{lab}_{K,i})\}_{i \in \mathcal{U}'_K}$ and $\{m_i = (\mathbf{x}_i, \mathcal{U}_{M,i}, \mathsf{lab}_{M,i})\}_{i \in \mathcal{U}'_M}$,

$$f(\{i, k_i\}_{i \in \mathcal{U}'_K}, \{i, m_i\}_{i \in \mathcal{U}'_M}) = \begin{cases} \sum_{i \in \mathcal{U}'_K} \langle \mathbf{x}_i, \mathbf{y}_i \rangle & \text{the condition below is satisfied} \\ \bot & \text{otherwise} \end{cases}$$

- $\mathcal{U}'_K = \mathcal{U}'_M$, and $\forall i \in \mathcal{U}'_K, \mathcal{U}_{K,i} = \mathcal{U}_{M,i} = \mathcal{U}'_K$.
- $\exists (\mathsf{lab}_K, \mathsf{lab}_M) \in \mathcal{L}^2, \forall i \in \mathcal{U}'_K, \mathsf{lab}_{K,i} = \mathsf{lab}_K, \mathsf{lab}_{M,i} = \mathsf{lab}_M$.

Definition 4.6 (One key-label restriction for IP-DDFE). We define an additional restriction for the adversary in the security game for IP-DDFE. We say an IP-DDFE scheme is xx-yy-function-hiding under the one key-label restriction if it satisfies Definition 4.2 where the adversary's queries additionally satisfy the following condition: QKeyGen with respect to user $i \in \mathcal{ID}$ and label $\mathsf{lab}_K \in \mathcal{L}$ (the query of the form of QKeyGen$(i, *, *, *, \mathsf{lab}_K)$) can be made only once for each pair (i, lab_K).

Definition 4.7 (All-or-nothing encryption (AoNE)). AoNE is a class of DDFE where $\mathcal{ID} = \{0,1\}^*$, $\mathcal{M}_{\mathrm{pri}} = \{0,1\}^L$ for some $L \in \mathbb{N}$, $\mathcal{M}_{\mathrm{pub}} = 2^{\mathcal{ID}} \times \mathcal{L}$, $\mathcal{K} = \emptyset$, $\mathcal{Z} = \{0,1\}^*$. The function f is defined as, for $\mathcal{U}'_K \in 2^{\mathcal{ID}}$ and $\{m_i = (x_i, \mathcal{U}_{M,i}, \mathsf{lab}_{M,i})\}_{i \in \mathcal{U}'_M}$,

$$f(\{i\}_{i \in \mathcal{U}'_K}, \{i, m_i\}_{i \in \mathcal{U}'_M}) = \begin{cases} \{x_i\}_{i \in \mathcal{U}'_M} & \text{the condition below is satisfied} \\ \bot & \text{otherwise} \end{cases}$$

- $\forall i \in \mathcal{U}'_M, \mathcal{U}'_M = \mathcal{U}_{M,i}$.
- $\exists \mathsf{lab}_M \in \mathcal{L}, \forall i \in \mathcal{U}'_M, \mathsf{lab}_{M,i} = \mathsf{lab}_M$.

This means that KeyGen is unnecessary, and Dec works without taking secret keys as input in AoNE (recall that $\mathcal{U}'_K$ can be an empty set).

Chotard et al. showed that sel-sym-IND-secure AoNE can be generically constructed from identity-based encryption [22][12]. We also use pseudorandom functions and non-interactive key exchange with quite simple requirements, which can be realized by the original Diffie-Hellman key exchange. We formally define it in the full version.

4.2 Construction of Function-Hiding IP-MCFE

We first construct a function-hiding IP-MCFE scheme as a step to a function-hiding IP-DDFE scheme. Let $\Pi = (p, \mathbb{G}_1, \mathbb{G}_2, \mathbb{G}_T, e, g_1, g_2)$ be bilinear groups. Let iFE = (iSetup, iKeyGen, iEnc, iDec) be a function-hiding IPFE scheme (recall

---

[12] In AoNE, there are no secret keys and thus the IND-security defined in [22] is exactly the same as function-hiding security in our paper.

that $\mathsf{iKeyGen}, \mathsf{iEnc}$ take a group-element vector as input instead of a $\mathbb{Z}_p$-element vector (see Definition 4.3)) and $H : \mathcal{L} \to \mathbb{G}_1$ be a hash function modeled as a random oracle. The construction of function hiding IP-MCFE for vector length N is provided in Fig. 1.

$\mathsf{Setup}(1^\lambda, 1^n)$: On input the security parameter 1^λ, the number of slots 1^n, the setup algorithm outputs $(\mathsf{PK}, \mathsf{EK}_i, \mathsf{MSK})$ as follows.

$$\{\mathsf{iMSK}_i\}_{i \in [n]} \leftarrow \mathsf{iSetup}(1^\lambda, 1^{2N+2})$$
$$\mathsf{PK} = \varPi, \mathsf{EK}_i = \mathsf{iMSK}_i, \mathsf{MSK} = \{\mathsf{EK}_i\}_{i \in [n]}.$$

$\mathsf{KeyGen}(\mathsf{MSK}, \{\mathbf{y}_i\}_{i \in [n]})$: The key generation algorithm takes as input the master secret key MSK, and vectors $\{\mathbf{y}_i\}_{i \in [n]}$ and outputs SK as follows. It randomly chooses $r_i \in \mathbb{Z}_p$ so that $\sum_{i \in [n]} r_i = 0$ and compute

$$\widehat{\mathbf{y}}_i = (\mathbf{y}_i, 0^\mathsf{N}, r_i, 0), \ \mathsf{iSK}_i \leftarrow \mathsf{iKeyGen}(\mathsf{iMSK}_i, \widehat{\mathbf{y}}_i), \ \mathsf{SK} = \{\mathsf{iSK}_i\}_{i \in [n]}.$$

$\mathsf{Enc}(i, \mathsf{EK}_i, \mathbf{x}_i, \mathsf{lab})$: The encryption algorithm takes as input user index $i \in [n]$, an encryption key EK_i, an input vector $\mathbf{x}_i$, a label lab and outputs CT_i as follows.

$$[t_{\mathsf{lab}}]_1 = H(\mathsf{lab}), \ \widehat{\mathbf{x}}_i = (\mathbf{x}_i, 0^\mathsf{N}, t_{\mathsf{lab}}, 0), \ \mathsf{CT}_i = \mathsf{iCT}_i \leftarrow \mathsf{iEnc}(\mathsf{iMSK}_i, [\widehat{\mathbf{x}}_i]_1).$$

$\mathsf{Dec}(\mathsf{SK}, \mathsf{CT}_1, ..., \mathsf{CT}_n)$: The decryption algorithm takes as input the secret key SK, ciphertexts $\mathsf{CT}_1, ..., \mathsf{CT}_n$ and outputs d as follows.

$$[d]_T = \prod_{i \in [n]} \mathsf{iDec}(\mathsf{iSK}_i, \mathsf{iCT}_i).$$

Fig. 1. Function-Hiding IP-MCFE

Correctness and Security. For correctly generated $(\mathsf{SK}, \mathsf{CT}_1, ..., \mathsf{CT}_n)$ for $\{\mathbf{y}_i, \mathbf{x}_i\}$, we have

$$\prod_{i \in [n]} \mathsf{iDec}(\mathsf{iSK}_i, \mathsf{iCT}_i) = [\sum_{i \in [n]} \langle \mathbf{x}_i, \mathbf{y}_i \rangle]_T = [\sum_{i \in [n]} \langle \mathbf{x}_i, \mathbf{y}_i \rangle]_T.$$

In our scheme, EK_i has a power to decode both CT_i and SK_i since EK_i is a part of PK. This is captured as the function Leak_y below.

Theorem 4.8. *If the SXDH assumption holds in $\mathbb{G}_1$ and iFE is function-hiding, then our IP-MCFE scheme is Leak_y-sel-pos-function-hiding in the random oracle model, where $\mathsf{Leak}_y(i, \{\mathbf{y}_i\}_{i \in [n]}) = \mathbf{y}_i$.*

Due to limited space, we present the proof in the full version.

4.3 Construction of Function-Hiding IP-DDFE

We next construct our function-hiding IP-DDFE scheme. Intuitively, our IP-DDFE scheme instantiates our IP-MCFE scheme in parallel per each party set via a pseudorandom function in a non-black box manner. Nevertheless, in the security proof, we can delete the information of the challenge bit β in a hybrid sequence similarly to the security proof of IP-MCFE.

Let iFE $=$ (iSetup, iKeyGen, iEnc, Dec) be a function-hiding IPFE scheme with the length of the random tape for iSetup($1^\lambda, 1^{2N+2}$) being $p(\lambda, N)$, AoNE $=$ (aGSetup, aLSetup, aEnc, aDec) be an all-or-nothing encryption scheme, NIKE $=$ (nSetup, nKeyGen, nSharedKey) be a non-interactive key exchange scheme, $\{\mathsf{PRF}_1^K\} : \mathcal{L} \to \mathbb{Z}_p$, $\{\mathsf{PRF}_2^K\} : 2^{\mathcal{ID}} \to \{0,1\}^{p(\lambda,N)}$ be families of pseudorandom functions where $\mathcal{ID}$ denotes an identity space, and $H : 2^{\mathcal{ID}} \times \mathcal{L} \to \mathbb{G}_1$ is a hash function modeled as a random oracle. Let $\mathcal{K}_1, \mathcal{K}_2$ be key spaces of $\mathsf{PRF}_1, \mathsf{PRF}_2$. We assume that the range of nSharedKey and the key space for PRF_1 are the same, namely, $\mathcal{K}_1$. Our construction for vector length N is provided in Fig. 2.

Correctness and Security. Thanks to the correctness of AoNE, we have $\widetilde{\mathsf{iCT}}_i = \mathsf{iCT}_i$, $\widetilde{\mathsf{iSK}}_i = \mathsf{iSK}_i$. For all $\mathsf{lab}_K, \{\mathsf{K}_{i,j,1}\}, \mathcal{U}$, we have

$$\sum_{i\in\mathcal{U}} r_i = \sum_{i\in\mathcal{U}} \sum_{\substack{j\in\mathcal{U}\\i\neq j}} (-1)^{j<i} \mathsf{PRF}_1^{\mathsf{K}_{i,j,1}}(\mathsf{lab}_K) = 0$$

since $\mathsf{K}_{i,j,1} = \mathsf{K}_{j,i,1}$. For all $i \in \mathcal{U}$, iSK_i and iCT_i are generated under the same iMSK_i since they are generated using the same random tape $\mathsf{PRF}_2^{\mathsf{K}_{i,2}}(\mathcal{U})$. Thus, thanks to the correctness of iFE, we have $\sum_{i\in\mathcal{U}} \mathsf{iDec}(\widetilde{\mathsf{iSK}}_i, \widetilde{\mathsf{iCT}}_i) = [\sum_{i\in\mathcal{U}} \langle \mathbf{x}_i, \mathbf{y}_i\rangle]_T = [\sum_{i\in\mathcal{U}} \langle \mathbf{x_i}, \mathbf{y_i}\rangle]_T$.

We show security via the following theorem.

Theorem 4.9. *If* $\{\mathsf{PRF}_1^K\}, \{\mathsf{PRF}_2^K\}$ *are families of pseudorandom functions,* NIKE *is IND-secure,* AoNE *is sel-sym-IND-secure, the SXDH assumption holds in* $\mathbb{G}_1$, *and* iFE *is function-hiding, then our* IP-DDFE *scheme is sel-sym-function-hiding under the one key-label restriction in the random oracle model.*

Due to space constraints, we present the proof in the full version.

GSetup(1^λ): On input the security parameter 1^λ, the setup algorithm outputs PK as follows.

$$\Pi = (p, \mathbb{G}_1, \mathbb{G}_2, \mathbb{G}_T, e, g_1, g_2) \leftarrow \mathsf{Gen}(1^\lambda)$$

$$\mathsf{aPP} \leftarrow \mathsf{aGSetup}(1^\lambda), \ \mathsf{nPP} \leftarrow \mathsf{nSetup}(1^\lambda), \ \mathsf{PP} = (\Pi, \mathsf{aPP}, \mathsf{nPP}).$$

LSetup(PP): On input PP, user $i \in \mathcal{ID}$ generates $(\mathsf{PK}_i, \mathsf{MSK}_i)$ via the setup algorithm as follows.

$$(\mathsf{nPK}_i, \mathsf{nSK}_i) \leftarrow \mathsf{nKeyGen}(\mathsf{nPP}), \ (\mathsf{aPK}_i, \mathsf{aMSK}_i) \leftarrow \mathsf{aLSetup}(\mathsf{aPP}), \ \mathsf{K}_{i,2} \leftarrow \mathcal{K}_2$$

$$\mathsf{PK}_i = (\mathsf{nPK}_i, \mathsf{aPK}_i), \ \mathsf{MSK}_i = (\mathsf{nSK}_i, \mathsf{aMSK}_i, \mathsf{K}_{i,2}).$$

KeyGen(MSK_i, k): The key generation algorithm takes the master secret key MSK_i, and an input $k = (\mathbf{y}_i, \mathcal{U}_K, \mathsf{lab}_K)$ such that $i \in \mathcal{U}_K$ and outputs SK_i as follows.

$$\mathsf{rt}_i = \mathsf{PRF}_2^{\mathsf{K}_{i,2}}(\mathcal{U}_K), \ \mathsf{iMSK}_i = \mathsf{iSetup}(1^\lambda, 1^{2\mathsf{N}+2}; \mathsf{rt}_i), \ \mathsf{K}_{i,j,1} \leftarrow \mathsf{nSharedKey}(\mathsf{nSK}_i, \mathsf{nPK}_j)$$

$$r_i = \sum_{\substack{j \in \mathcal{U}_K \\ i \neq j}} (-1)^{j<i} \mathsf{PRF}_1^{\mathsf{K}_{i,j,1}}(\mathsf{lab}_K), \ \widehat{\mathbf{y}}_i = (\mathbf{y}_i, 0^\mathsf{N}, r_i, 0), \ \mathsf{iSK}_i \leftarrow \mathsf{iKeyGen}(\mathsf{iMSK}_i, \widehat{\mathbf{y}}_i)$$

$$\text{(4.1)}$$

$$\mathsf{aCT}_i \leftarrow \mathsf{aEnc}(\mathsf{aMSK}_i, (\mathsf{iSK}_i, \mathcal{U}_K, \mathsf{lab}_K)), \ \mathsf{SK}_i = (\mathsf{aCT}_i, \mathcal{U}_K, \mathsf{lab}_K). \qquad \text{(4.2)}$$

Enc(MSK_i, m): The encryption algorithm takes as input the public parameters PK, the master secret key MSK_i, and an input $m = (\mathbf{x}_i, \mathcal{U}_M, \mathsf{lab}_M)$ such that $i \in \mathcal{U}_M$ and outputs CT_i as follows.

$$\mathsf{rt}_i = \mathsf{PRF}_2^{\mathsf{K}_{i,2}}(\mathcal{U}_M), \ \mathsf{iMSK}_i = \mathsf{iSetup}(1^\lambda, 1^{2\mathsf{N}+2}; \mathsf{rt}_i), \ [t]_1 = H(\mathcal{U}_M, \mathsf{lab}_M)$$

$$\widehat{\mathbf{x}}_i = (\mathbf{x}_i, 0^\mathsf{N}, t, 0), \ \mathsf{iCT}_i \leftarrow \mathsf{iEnc}(\mathsf{iMSK}_i, [\widehat{\mathbf{x}}_i]_1) \qquad \text{(4.3)}$$

$$\mathsf{aCT}_i \leftarrow \mathsf{aEnc}(\mathsf{aMSK}_i, (\mathsf{iCT}_i, \mathcal{U}_M, \mathsf{lab}_M)), \ \mathsf{CT}_i = (\mathsf{aCT}_i, \mathcal{U}_M, \mathsf{lab}_M). \qquad \text{(4.4)}$$

Dec($\{\mathsf{SK}_i\}_{i \in \mathcal{U}_K}, \{\mathsf{CT}_i\}_{i \in \mathcal{U}_M}$): The decryption algorithm takes as input the public parameters PK, secret keys $\{\mathsf{SK}_i\}_{i \in \mathcal{U}_K}$, ciphertexts $\{\mathsf{CT}_i\}_{i \in \mathcal{U}_M}$ such that $\mathcal{U} = \mathcal{U}_K = \mathcal{U}_M$ and outputs d as follows. Perse $\mathsf{SK}_i = (\mathsf{aCT}_i, \mathcal{U}_K, \mathsf{lab}_K)$ and $\mathsf{CT}_i = (\mathsf{aCT}'_i, \mathcal{U}_M, \mathsf{lab}_M)$. Compute

$$\widetilde{\mathsf{iSK}}_i = \mathsf{aDec}(\{\mathsf{aCT}_i\}_{i \in \mathcal{U}}), \ \widetilde{\mathsf{iCT}}_i = \mathsf{aDec}(\{\mathsf{aCT}'_i\}_{i \in \mathcal{U}}), \ [d]_T = \prod_{i \in \mathcal{U}} \mathsf{iDec}(\widetilde{\mathsf{iSK}}_i, \widetilde{\mathsf{iCT}}_i).$$

Fig. 2. Function Hiding IP-DDFE

References

1. Abdalla, M., Benhamouda, F., Gay, R.: From single-input to multi-client inner-product functional encryption. In: Galbraith, S.D., Moriai, S. (eds.) ASIACRYPT 2019. LNCS, vol. 11923, pp. 552–582. Springer, Cham (2019). https://doi.org/10.1007/978-3-030-34618-8_19
2. Abdalla, M., Benhamouda, F., Kohlweiss, M., Waldner, H.: Decentralizing inner-product functional encryption. In: Lin, D., Sako, K. (eds.) PKC 2019. LNCS, vol. 11443, pp. 128–157. Springer, Cham (2019). https://doi.org/10.1007/978-3-030-17259-6_5

3. Abdalla, M., Bourse, F., De Caro, A., Pointcheval, D.: Simple functional encryption schemes for inner products. In: Katz, J. (ed.) PKC 2015. LNCS, vol. 9020, pp. 733–751. Springer, Heidelberg (2015). https://doi.org/10.1007/978-3-662-46447-2_33

4. Abdalla, M., Catalano, D., Gay, R., Ursu, B.: Inner-product functional encryption with fine-grained access control. In: Moriai, S., Wang, H. (eds.) ASIACRYPT 2020. LNCS, vol. 12493, pp. 467–497. Springer, Cham (2020). https://doi.org/10.1007/978-3-030-64840-4_16

5. Agrawal, S., Clear, M., Frieder, O., Garg, S., O'Neill, A., Thaler, J.: Ad hoc multi-input functional encryption. In: ITCS 2020 (2020)

6. Agrawal, S., Goyal, R., Tomida, J.: Multi-party functional encryption. Cryptology ePrint Archive, Report 2020/1266 (2020). https://ia.cr/2020/1266

7. Agrawal, S., Libert, B., Stehle, D.: Fully secure functional encryption for linear functions from standard assumptions, and applications. In: Crypto (2016)

8. Agrawal, S., Yamada., S.: Optimal broadcast encryption from pairings and LWE. In: Proceedings of EUROCRYPT (2020)

9. Ananth, P., Jain, A.: Indistinguishability obfuscation from compact functional encryption. In: Gennaro, R., Robshaw, M. (eds.) CRYPTO 2015. LNCS, vol. 9215, pp. 308–326. Springer, Heidelberg (2015). https://doi.org/10.1007/978-3-662-47989-6_15

10. Bishop, A., Jain, A., Kowalczyk, L.: Function-hiding inner product encryption. In: Iwata, T., Cheon, J.H. (eds.) ASIACRYPT 2015. LNCS, vol. 9452, pp. 470–491. Springer, Heidelberg (2015). https://doi.org/10.1007/978-3-662-48797-6_20

11. Bitansky, N., Vaikuntanathan, V.: Indistinguishability obfuscation from functional encryption. FOCS 2015, 163 (2015). http://eprint.iacr.org/2015/163

12. Boneh, D., Franklin, M.: Identity-based encryption from the weil pairing. In: Kilian, J. (ed.) CRYPTO 2001. LNCS, vol. 2139, pp. 213–229. Springer, Heidelberg (2001). https://doi.org/10.1007/3-540-44647-8_13

13. Boneh, D., et al.: Fully key-homomorphic encryption, arithmetic circuit ABE and compact garbled circuits. In: Nguyen, P.Q., Oswald, E. (eds.) EUROCRYPT 2014. LNCS, vol. 8441, pp. 533–556. Springer, Heidelberg (2014). https://doi.org/10.1007/978-3-642-55220-5_30

14. Boneh, D., Sahai, A., Waters, B.: Functional encryption: definitions and challenges. In: Ishai, Y. (ed.) TCC 2011. LNCS, vol. 6597, pp. 253–273. Springer, Heidelberg (2011). https://doi.org/10.1007/978-3-642-19571-6_16

15. Boneh, D., Waters, B.: Conjunctive, subset, and range queries on encrypted data. In: Vadhan, S.P. (ed.) TCC 2007. LNCS, vol. 4392, pp. 535–554. Springer, Heidelberg (2007). https://doi.org/10.1007/978-3-540-70936-7_29

16. Brakerski, Z., Chandran, N., Goyal, V., Jain, A., Sahai, A., Segev, G.: Hierarchical functional encryption. In: ITCS 2017 (2017)

17. Chase, M.: Multi-authority attribute based encryption. In: Vadhan, S.P. (ed.) TCC 2007. LNCS, vol. 4392, pp. 515–534. Springer, Heidelberg (2007). https://doi.org/10.1007/978-3-540-70936-7_28

18. Chase, M., Chow, S.S.M.: Improving privacy and security in multi-authority attribute-based encryption. In: ACM CCS 2009 (2009)

19. Chen, Y., Zhang, L., Yiu, S.M.: Practical attribute based inner product functional encryption from simple assumptions. Cryptology ePrint Archive (2019)

20. Chotard, J., Dufour Sans, E., Gay, R., Phan, D.H., Pointcheval, D.: Decentralized multi-client functional encryption for inner product. In: Peyrin, T., Galbraith, S. (eds.) ASIACRYPT 2018. LNCS, vol. 11273, pp. 703–732. Springer, Cham (2018). https://doi.org/10.1007/978-3-030-03329-3_24

21. Chotard, J., Dufour-Sans, E., Gay, R., Phan, D.H., Pointcheval, D.: Multi-client functional encryption with repetition for inner product. Cryptology ePrint Archive, Report 2018/1021 (2018)

22. Chotard, J., Dufour-Sans, E., Gay, R., Phan, D.H., Pointcheval, D.: Dynamic decentralized functional encryption. In: Micciancio, D., Ristenpart, T. (eds.) CRYPTO 2020. LNCS, vol. 12170, pp. 747–775. Springer, Cham (2020). https://doi.org/10.1007/978-3-030-56784-2_25

23. Datta, P., Okamoto, T., Tomida, J.: Full-hiding (unbounded) multi-input inner product functional encryption from the k-linear assumption. In: Abdalla, M., Dahab, R. (eds.) PKC 2018. LNCS, vol. 10770, pp. 245–277. Springer, Cham (2018). https://doi.org/10.1007/978-3-319-76581-5_9

24. Goldwasser, S., et al.: Multi-input functional encryption. In: Nguyen, P.Q., Oswald, E. (eds.) EUROCRYPT 2014. LNCS, vol. 8441, pp. 578–602. Springer, Heidelberg (2014). https://doi.org/10.1007/978-3-642-55220-5_32

25. Gorbunov, S., Vaikuntanathan, V., Wee, H.: Predicate encryption for circuits from LWE. In: Gennaro, R., Robshaw, M. (eds.) CRYPTO 2015. LNCS, vol. 9216, pp. 503–523. Springer, Heidelberg (2015). https://doi.org/10.1007/978-3-662-48000-7_25

26. Goyal, V., Pandey, O., Sahai, A., Waters, B.: Attribute-based encryption for fine-grained access control of encrypted data. In: CCS (2006)

27. Katz, J., Sahai, A., Waters, B.: Predicate encryption supporting disjunctions, polynomial equations, and inner products. In: Smart, N. (ed.) EUROCRYPT 2008. LNCS, vol. 4965, pp. 146–162. Springer, Heidelberg (2008). https://doi.org/10.1007/978-3-540-78967-3_9

28. Koppula, V., Waters, B.: Realizing chosen ciphertext security generically in attribute-based encryption and predicate encryption. In: Boldyreva, A., Micciancio, D. (eds.) CRYPTO 2019. LNCS, vol. 11693, pp. 671–700. Springer, Cham (2019). https://doi.org/10.1007/978-3-030-26951-7_23

29. Lewko, A., Waters, B.: Decentralizing attribute-based encryption. In: Paterson, K.G. (ed.) EUROCRYPT 2011. LNCS, vol. 6632, pp. 568–588. Springer, Heidelberg (2011). https://doi.org/10.1007/978-3-642-20465-4_31

30. Libert, B., Țițiu, R.: Multi-client functional encryption for linear functions in the standard model from LWE. In: Galbraith, S.D., Moriai, S. (eds.) ASIACRYPT 2019. LNCS, vol. 11923, pp. 520–551. Springer, Cham (2019). https://doi.org/10.1007/978-3-030-34618-8_18

31. Michalevsky, Y., Joye, M.: Decentralized policy-hiding ABE with receiver privacy. In: Lopez, J., Zhou, J., Soriano, M. (eds.) ESORICS 2018. LNCS, vol. 11099, pp. 548–567. Springer, Cham (2018). https://doi.org/10.1007/978-3-319-98989-1_27

32. Sahai, A., Waters, B.: Fuzzy identity-based encryption. In: Cramer, R. (ed.) EUROCRYPT 2005. LNCS, vol. 3494, pp. 457–473. Springer, Heidelberg (2005). https://doi.org/10.1007/11426639_27

33. Shamir, A.: Identity-based cryptosystems and signature schemes. In: Blakley, G.R., Chaum, D. (eds.) CRYPTO 1984. LNCS, vol. 196, pp. 47–53. Springer, Heidelberg (1985). https://doi.org/10.1007/3-540-39568-7_5

34. Waters, B.: Dual system encryption: realizing fully secure IBE and HIBE under simple assumptions. In: Halevi, S. (ed.) CRYPTO 2009. LNCS, vol. 5677, pp. 619–636. Springer, Heidelberg (2009). https://doi.org/10.1007/978-3-642-03356-8_36

Succinct LWE Sampling, Random Polynomials, and Obfuscation

Lalita Devadas[1]([✉]), Willy Quach[2], Vinod Vaikuntanathan[1], Hoeteck Wee[3], and Daniel Wichs[2,3]

[1] Massachusetts Institute of Technology, Cambridge, MA 02139, USA
{lali,vinodv}@mit.edu
[2] Northeastern University, Boston, MA 02115, USA
quach.w@northeastern.edu, wichs@ccs.neu.edu
[3] NTT Research, Sunnyvale, CA 94085, USA
wee@di.ens.fr

Abstract. We present a construction of indistinguishability obfuscation (iO) that relies on the learning with errors (LWE) assumption together with a new notion of succinctly sampling pseudorandom LWE samples. We then present a candidate LWE sampler whose security is related to the hardness of solving systems of polynomial equations. Our construction improves on the recent iO candidate of Wee and Wichs (Eurocrypt 2021) in two ways: first, we show that a much weaker and simpler notion of LWE sampling suffices for iO; and secondly, our candidate LWE sampler is secure based on a compactly specified and falsifiable assumption about random polynomials, with a simple error distribution that facilitates cryptanalysis.

Keywords: Indistinguishability obfuscation · Learning with errors

1 Introduction

Indistinguishability obfuscation (iO) [BGI+01, GR07] is a probabilistic polynomial-time algorithm $\mathcal{O}$ that takes as input a circuit C and outputs an (obfuscated) circuit $C' = \mathcal{O}(C)$ satisfying two properties: (a) *functionality*: C and C' compute the same function; and (b) *security*: for any two circuits C_1 and C_2 that compute the same function (and have the same size), $\mathcal{O}(C_1)$ and $\mathcal{O}(C_2)$ are computationally indistinguishable. Since the first candidate for iO was introduced in [GGH+13], a series of works have shown that iO would have a huge impact on cryptography.

In this work, we build upon the recent line of works on lattice-inspired iO candidates [Agr19, CHVW19, AP20, BDGM20b, BDGM20a, WW21, GP21] that are plausibly post-quantum secure. The dream goal here is to ultimately base iO on the hardness of the learning with errors (LWE) problem together with an assumption about simple Boolean or integer pseudorandom generators (PRGs). Such a result would, in particular, eliminate pairings from the recent breakthrough result basing iO on well-founded assumptions [JLS21].

© International Association for Cryptologic Research 2021
K. Nissim and B. Waters (Eds.): TCC 2021, LNCS 13043, pp. 256–287, 2021.
https://doi.org/10.1007/978-3-030-90453-1_9

1.1   Our Contributions

We present a candidate construction of iO that relies on LWE together with a new notion of succinctly sampling pseudorandom LWE samples. In addition, we present a candidate sampler whose security is related to the hardness of solving systems of polynomial equations. Our construction improves on the recent iO candidate of Wee and Wichs [WW21] (henceforth referred to as the WW construction) in two ways:

- First, our new notion of succinct LWE sampling simplifies and relaxes the notion of oblivious LWE sampling from WW. Instead of a simulation-based definition as in WW, we have a simple indistinguishability-based definition, where the generated LWE sample can be used to drown out the differences between certain error distributions. Furthermore, we put forth two variants of succinct LWE sampling, and provide a general amplification from a weak (falsifiable) notion that refers to a specific error distribution to a strong (non-falsifiable) notion that refers to general error distributions.
- Next, our candidate succinct LWE sampler is easy to describe and is based on random polynomials. It yields an LWE sample with a simple error distribution that facilitates cryptanalysis. This is in contrast to WW, where the LWE sampler involved complex FHE evaluation, and the resulting error distribution in the samples was dependent on the concrete implementation of the circuit being evaluated. Indeed, a recent work of [HJL21] carefully crafted circuit implementations that would render the WW candidate as well as the related candidate in [GP21] insecure (see Sect. 1.3 for a more detailed discussion).

1.2   Technical Overview

The starting point of our construction is essentially the same as that of the Wee-Wichs (WW) iO candidate, which in turn builds on [BDGM20a]. We begin by describing a notion of succinct randomized encoding (SRE), which can be seen as a relaxation of the notions of split FHE and functional encodings used in prior works. It is also very related to the notion of exponentially efficient iO (XiO) from [LPST16], and is easily seen to imply it, but we find the SRE abstraction easier to work with in the context of our work. By leveraging prior results on XiO [LPST16], our notion of SRE implies iO under the LWE assumption.

Succinct Randomized Encodings. A succinct randomized encoding[1] [BGL+15, LPST16] of a function $f : \{0,1\}^\ell \to \{0,1\}^N$ is an efficient probabilistic algorithm Encode such that:

- <u>functionality</u>: we can efficiently recover $f(x)$ given f and $\mathsf{Encode}(f, x)$;

---

[1] Our notion of succinct randomized encodings is weaker than prior works: indeed, [BGL+15] required the encoder to run in time sublinear in N, whereas we allow the encoder run-time to be polynomial in N.

- security: for any x_0, x_1 such that $f(x_0) = f(x_1)$, we have $\mathsf{Encode}(f, x_0) \approx_c$ $\mathsf{Encode}(f, x_1)$; and
- succinctness: $\mathsf{Encode}(f, x)$ is shorter than the output length of f. That is, $|\mathsf{Encode}(f, x)| = \widetilde{O}(N^\delta)$ for some constant $\delta < 1$, ignoring factors polynomial in ℓ and the security parameter.

Henceforth, we will focus on building SRE for circuits.

Base Scheme. We start with a base scheme for succinct randomized encodings implicit in WW, which is insecure, but serves as the basis of our eventual construction. The base scheme uses a variant of the homomorphic encryption/commitment schemes of [GSW13, GVW15], along with the "packing" techniques in [PVW08, MW16, BTVW17, PS19, GH19, BDGM19]. Given a commitment $\mathbf{C}$ to an input $x \in \{0, 1\}^\ell$, along with a circuit $f : \{0, 1\}^\ell \to \{0, 1\}^N$, this scheme allows us to homomorphically compute a commitment $\mathbf{C}_f$ to the output $f(x)$. Moreover, the opening for the output commitment is shorter than the output size N. Concretely, we define $\mathbf{C}, \mathbf{C}_f$ as follows:

- We treat the function $f : \{0, 1\}^\ell \to \{0, 1\}^N$ as a function $f : \{0, 1\}^\ell \to \{0, 1\}^{M \times K}$, where M and K are parameters we shall specify shortly, such that $MK = N$.
- Given a public random matrix $\mathbf{A} \in \mathbb{Z}_q^{M \times w}$ where $M \gg w$, we define a commitment $\mathbf{C}$ to an input x as

$$\mathbf{C} := \mathbf{AR} + x \otimes \mathbf{G} + \mathbf{E}$$

where $\mathbf{A} \leftarrow \mathbb{Z}_q^{M \times w}, \mathbf{R} \leftarrow \mathbb{Z}_q^{w \times \ell M \log q}$ are uniformly random, $\mathbf{E} \leftarrow \chi^{M \times \ell M \log q}$ has its entries chosen from an error distribution χ, $\mathbf{G} \in \mathbb{Z}_q^{M \times M \log q}$ is the gadget matrix [MP12], and we treat x as a row vector of length ℓ in $x \otimes \mathbf{G}$.
- Homomorphic evaluation of f on $\mathbf{C}$ yields $\mathbf{C}_f$ satisfying

$$\mathbf{C}_f = \mathbf{AR}_{f,x} + \mathbf{E}_{f,x} + f(x) \cdot \frac{q}{2} \in \mathbb{Z}_q^{M \times K} \tag{1}$$

where $f(x) \in \{0, 1\}^{M \times K}$, $\mathbf{R}_{f,x} \in \mathbb{Z}_q^{w \times K}$ and $\mathbf{E}_{f,x}$ has small entries.

Our base scheme[2] simply outputs

$$\mathbf{A}, \; \mathbf{C} := \mathbf{AR} + x \otimes \mathbf{G} + \mathbf{E}, \; \mathbf{R}_{f,x}$$

---

[2] In the WW terminology, this would be a candidate K-sim functional encoding for $f_1, \ldots, f_K : \{0, 1\}^\ell \to \{0, 1\}^M$.

as the encoding of x. Decoding computes $\mathbf{C}_f$ given $(\mathbf{C}, f)$, subtracts $\mathbf{A} \cdot \mathbf{R}_{f,x}$ to obtain $f(x) \cdot \frac{q}{2}$ plus error (following Eq. 1) and rounds to obtain $f(x)$.

The encoding is also succinct: The total size of the encoding (in bits) is

$$O((Mw + M^2\ell + wK) \cdot \log q).$$

Setting $M = N^{1/3}, K = N^{2/3}, w = O(\lambda)$ yields encoding size $\widetilde{O}(N^{2/3})$, where $\widetilde{O}(\cdot)$ hides polynomial factors in λ, ℓ and the depth of the circuit computing f.

The scheme is, however, *completely insecure* as written because, given $\mathbf{C}, \mathbf{R}_{f,x}$ and a "guess" for x, we can recover $\mathbf{R}$ by solving a system of linear equations, and test if our guess was correct (see WW). This allows us to easily distinguish between encodings of any x_0 and x_1.

"Pseudorandom" LWE Sampling. Following [WW21], we fix the insecurity of the base scheme by masking $\mathbf{R}_{f,x}$ using a "pseudorandom" LWE sample; similar ideas were used in several prior works [BDGM20a, GP21, JLS21, AR17, Agr19, JLMS19, AJL+19] with "pseudorandom" noise. That is, we generate a "pseudorandom" LWE sample $\mathbf{B}^* = \mathbf{A}\mathbf{S}^* + \mathbf{E}^* \in \mathbb{Z}_q^{M \times K}$ and output

$$\mathsf{seed}_{\mathbf{B}^*}, \ \mathbf{A}, \ \mathbf{A}\mathbf{R} + x \otimes \mathbf{G} + \mathbf{E}, \ \mathbf{R}_{f,x} + \mathbf{S}^* \tag{2}$$

where $\mathsf{seed}_{\mathbf{B}^*}$ is a succinct description of $\mathbf{B}^*$, with $|\mathsf{seed}_{\mathbf{B}^*}| \leq (MK)^\delta$ for some $\delta < 1$. Correctness now relies on the fact that

$$\mathbf{A} \cdot (\mathbf{R}_{f,x} + \mathbf{S}^*) \approx \mathbf{B}^* + \mathbf{C}_f + f(x) \cdot \frac{q}{2}.$$

WW's security requirement for the pseudorandom LWE sample, "oblivious LWE sampling", was cumbersome to define, required a simulator, and only made sense in the common reference string model. The reliance on a simulator means the definition did not have an inherently falsifiable format that enables demonstrating insecurity by constructing an efficient attacker. Here, we reformulate a simpler and falsifiable variant that we call "succinct LWE sampling".[3]

Defining pseudorandom LWE sampling, in WW and in our work, is difficult because we want $\mathbf{B}^* = \mathbf{A}\mathbf{S}^* + \mathbf{E}^*$ to look like a random LWE sample, but this is impossible since it is succinctly described in $\mathsf{seed}_{\mathbf{B}^*}$. Instead, we essentially want $\mathbf{E}^*$ to drown out the difference between any two sufficiently small error distributions $\mathbf{Z}_0$ and $\mathbf{Z}_1$, in the sense that $\mathsf{seed}_{\mathbf{B}^*}, \mathbf{E}^* - \mathbf{Z}_b$ hides b. Unfortunately, this too is impossible, since $\mathsf{seed}_{\mathbf{B}^*}$ lets us get $\mathbf{B}^* = \mathbf{A}\mathbf{S}^* + \mathbf{E}^*$ from which we can then derive $\mathbf{A}\mathbf{S}^* + \mathbf{Z}_b$; this allows us to distinguish between (say) $\mathbf{Z}_0 = 0$ and $\mathbf{Z}_1$ being a small Gaussian by checking rank. Our main observation is that we don't need indistinguishability to hold for worst-case distributions $\mathbf{Z}_b$, but rather only for ones where an LWE sample $\mathbf{A}\mathbf{R} + \mathbf{Z}_b$ with the error $\mathbf{Z}_b$ and a truly random $\mathbf{R}$ would hide the bit b. Formally, the definition says that for any two distributions of $(\mathbf{Z}_b, \mathsf{aux}_b)$ where $\mathbf{Z}_b$ is sufficiently short:

---

[3] It is simpler in terms of syntax, since we do not refer to LWE trapdoors for $\mathbf{A}$, and in terms of the security requirement since we do not require a simulator, but instead have a simple indistinguishability criterion.

If $$(\mathsf{aux}_0, \mathbf{A}, \mathbf{AR} + \mathbf{Z}_0) \approx_c (\mathsf{aux}_1, \mathbf{A}, \mathbf{AR} + \mathbf{Z}_1), \tag{3}$$

then $$(\mathsf{seed}_{\mathbf{B}^*}, \mathsf{aux}_0, \mathbf{A}, \mathbf{E}^* - \mathbf{Z}_0) \approx_c (\mathsf{seed}_{\mathbf{B}^*}, \mathsf{aux}_1, \mathbf{A}, \mathbf{E}^* - \mathbf{Z}_1). \tag{4}$$

Note that, since $\mathsf{seed}_{\mathbf{B}^*}$ defines $\mathbf{AS}^* + \mathbf{E}^*$, giving $\mathbf{E}^* - \mathbf{Z}_b$ in (4) is equivalent to giving $\mathbf{AS}^* + \mathbf{Z}_b$, and hence we use these interchangeably in the definition.

The above definition is not falsifiable since it quantifies over all $(\mathsf{aux}_b, \mathbf{Z}_b)$ satisfying the pre-condition (3). However, we also consider a weaker, falsifiable definition, where we fix a specific $(\mathsf{aux}_b^*, \mathbf{Z}_b^*)$ that satisfies the pre-condition (3). We then show a generic transformation that lifts any scheme realizing the weak definition into one that realizes the general definition. Specifically, in the weak definition, we fix $\mathsf{aux}_b^* = (\widehat{\mathbf{B}}, \mathbf{C})$ to consist of a commitment $\widehat{\mathbf{B}}$ to 0, along with a commitment $\mathbf{C}$ to $-b$. We then homomorphically evaluate an AND operation (multiplication) on the commitments $\widehat{\mathbf{B}}, \mathbf{C}$, which results in a commitment to 0, and we define $\mathbf{Z}_b^*$ to be the error term for this commitment. Formally,

$$\mathsf{aux}_b^* = \left(\widehat{\mathbf{B}} = \mathbf{AS}_0 + \mathbf{F}, \quad \mathbf{C} = \mathbf{AR} + \mathbf{E} - b\mathbf{G} \right) \quad \text{and} \quad \mathbf{Z}_b^* = \mathbf{EG}^{-1}(\widehat{\mathbf{B}}) - b\mathbf{F},$$

where $\mathbf{E}$ and $\mathbf{F}$ are matrices with small entries. The transformation is inspired by a trick employed in WW to frame the security of their candidate oblivious LWE sampler construction as a falsifiable assumption. Here, we are able to abstract this trick out and formally prove that it amplifies a weak definition of security to a strong one. Therefore, we get a simple and falsifiable definition of succinct LWE sampling as our target. We refer to the full version for more details.

Our final definition introduces additional relaxations. Instead of a uniformly random matrix $\mathbf{A}$, we allow the use of matrices $\mathbf{A}^*$, which may not be uniformly random and can have some additional structure, as long as LWE still holds w.r.t. $\mathbf{A}^*$. We also allow the succinct sampler to rely on a non-succinct common reference string (CRS) of length $\mathsf{poly}(N)$. This is analogous to the reliance on a CRS in WW (as well as [BDGM20a, GP21]) and suffices for iO.

Our Succinct Randomized Encoding. To go from succinct LWE sampling to SRE, we essentially follow WW, and replace $\mathbf{A}$ with $\mathbf{A}^*$ in (2). The SRE consists of:

$$\mathsf{seed}_{\mathbf{B}^*}, \quad \mathbf{A}^*, \quad \mathbf{A}^*\mathbf{R} + x \otimes \mathbf{G} + \mathbf{E}, \quad \mathbf{R}_{f,x} + \mathbf{S}^* . \tag{5}$$

Correctness and succinctness follow readily as before. To prove security, we need to argue as follows that $\mathsf{Encode}(f, x_b)$ hides b as long as $f(x_0) = f(x_1)$.

- As long as $\mathbf{A}^*$ is full-rank, $(\mathbf{R}_{f,x_b} + \mathbf{S}^*)$ can be computed from $\mathbf{A}^*$ and $\mathbf{A}^* \cdot (\mathbf{R}_{f,x_b} + \mathbf{S}^*)$, so it suffices to argue that:

$$\mathsf{seed}_{\mathbf{B}^*}, \quad \mathbf{A}^*, \quad \mathbf{A}^*\mathbf{R} + x_b \otimes \mathbf{G} + \mathbf{E}, \quad \mathbf{A}^* \cdot (\mathbf{R}_{f,x_b} + \mathbf{S}^*)$$

  hides b.
- Using $\mathbf{C}_f = \mathbf{A}^*\mathbf{R}_{f,x_b} + \mathbf{E}_{f,x_b} + f(x_b) \cdot \frac{q}{2}$ and deriving $\mathbf{B}^* = \mathbf{A}^*\mathbf{S}^* + \mathbf{E}^*$ from $\mathsf{seed}_{\mathbf{B}^*}$, we can write

$$\mathbf{A}^* \cdot (\mathbf{R}_{f,x_b} + \mathbf{S}^*) = \mathbf{C}_f - f(x_b) \cdot \frac{q}{2} + \mathbf{B}^* - \mathbf{E}^* - \mathbf{E}_{f,x_b},$$

so it suffices to argue that

$$\mathsf{seed}_{\mathbf{B}^*}, \quad \mathbf{A}^*, \quad \mathbf{A}^*\mathbf{R} + x_b \otimes \mathbf{G} + \mathbf{E}, \quad \mathbf{E}^* + \mathbf{E}_{f,x_b}$$

hides b.
– At this point, we will invoke security of our succinct LWE sampler with

$$\mathsf{aux}_b = \mathbf{A}^*\mathbf{R} + x_b \otimes \mathbf{G} + \mathbf{E}, \qquad \mathbf{Z}_b = \mathbf{E}_{f,x_b}$$

For this step, we need to show that the pre-condition (3) holds:

$$(\mathbf{A}^*\mathbf{R} + x_0 \otimes \mathbf{G} + \mathbf{E}, \ \mathbf{A}^*, \ \mathbf{A}^*\mathbf{S}' + \mathbf{E}_{f,x_0}) \approx_c (\mathbf{A}^*\mathbf{R} + x_1 \otimes \mathbf{G} + \mathbf{E}, \ \mathbf{A}^*, \ \mathbf{A}^*\mathbf{S}' + \mathbf{E}_{f,x_1}).$$

This follows from LWE w.r.t. $\mathbf{A}^*$ and the fact that $\mathbf{A}^*\mathbf{S}' + \mathbf{E}_{f,x_b} \equiv \mathbf{A}^*\mathbf{S}' + \mathbf{C}_f - f(x_b) \cdot \frac{q}{2}$, where $f(x_0) = f(x_1)$.

Note that, in the above, we only relied on the security of the LWE sampler for the special case where aux_b is an encryption of x_b and $\mathbf{Z}_b$ is the error in the ciphertext one gets by homomorphically computing $f(x_b)$ for some function f such that $f(x_0) = f(x_1)$. However, as mentioned previously, we can also rely on an even more restricted form of $(\mathsf{aux}_b, \mathbf{Z}_b)$, essentially corresponding to the extremely simple case where f just computes the AND of b and 0, and generically lift security to the completely general case.

Our Candidate Succinct LWE Sampler. We want to design a succinct LWE sampler generating $\mathbf{B}^* = \mathbf{A}^*\mathbf{S}^* + \mathbf{E}^*$. The security requirement in Eq. (4) implies that $\mathbf{E}^* - \mathbf{Z}_b$ hides b for any short matrices $\mathbf{Z}_0, \mathbf{Z}_1$ satisfying some additional properties which we shall ignore in the rest of this overview. In addition, we want $\mathbf{B}^*$ to admit a short description $\mathsf{seed}_{\mathbf{B}^*}$, which means that $\mathbf{E}^* \in \mathbb{Z}^{M \times K}$ should compute a "pseudorandom" noise-flooding distribution.

Following [JLMS19, AJL+19], a good candidate for $\mathbf{E}^*$ is to evaluate MK random degree-d polynomials in dmk variables drawn from independent Gaussian distributions, where $MK \ll (dmk)^{d/2}$ to avoid linearization and potential sum-of-squares-based attacks; the ensuing distribution is plausibly indistinguishable from MK independent samples from a "noise-flooding" distribution $\mathcal{D}$ for a suitable choice of parameters. Concretely, thinking of d as a small constant, we sample "secret" Gaussian matrices $\mathbf{E}_1, \ldots, \mathbf{E}_d \leftarrow \chi^{m \times k}$ and public Gaussian matrices $\mathbf{P} \leftarrow \chi^{M \times m^d}$ and $\mathbf{P}' \leftarrow \chi^{k^d \times K}$ and we define

$$\mathbf{E}^* := \mathbf{P}(\mathbf{E}_1 \otimes \mathbf{E}_2 \otimes \cdots \otimes \mathbf{E}_d)\mathbf{P}' \in \mathbb{Z}^{M \times K}$$

where $\mathbf{P}, \mathbf{P}'$ are published in the CRS. In the special case of $m = M = 1$ and $\mathbf{P} = 1$, the distribution of $\mathbf{E}^* \in \mathbb{Z}^K$ corresponds roughly to the evaluation of K random (i.e. Gaussian) degree-d (multilinear) polynomials in dk variables (where the dk variables are the entries of the $\mathbf{E}_1, \ldots, \mathbf{E}_d$ and the coefficients of the polynomial are specified by $\mathbf{P}'$). In the general case, we have a collection of polynomials, where each one looks at a certain structured set of monomials. For more details, see Sect. 4.5.

Next, we specify $(\mathbf{B}^*, \mathbf{A}^*, \mathbf{S}^*, \mathsf{seed}_{\mathbf{B}^*})$, starting with $\mathsf{seed}_{\mathbf{B}^*}$. Following [JLMS19], we additionally sample $\mathbf{A}_i \leftarrow \mathbb{Z}_q^{m \times w}, \mathbf{S}_i \leftarrow \mathbb{Z}_q^{w \times k}$ for $i = 1, \ldots, d$ and some $w \ll m, k$, and we define:

$$\mathsf{seed}_{\mathbf{B}^*} := (\mathbf{B}_1 := \mathbf{A}_1\mathbf{S}_1 + \mathbf{E}_1 \, , \, \ldots \, , \, \mathbf{B}_d := \mathbf{A}_d\mathbf{S}_d + \mathbf{E}_d) \in (\mathbb{Z}_q^{m \times k})^d.$$

Inspired by the homomorphic operations of the Brakerski-Vaikuntanathan FHE [BV11], we want to relate $\mathbf{E}^*$ to $\mathbf{B}_1 \otimes \cdots \otimes \mathbf{B}_d$ and from there, derive $\mathbf{B}^*, \mathbf{A}^*, \mathbf{S}^*$ such that $\mathbf{B}^* = \mathbf{A}^*\mathbf{S}^* + \mathbf{E}^*$ (we will discuss succinctness after that). We start with $d = 2$ for simplicity. By the mixed product property:

$$\mathbf{B}_1 \otimes \mathbf{B}_2 = \mathbf{A}_1\mathbf{S}_1 \otimes \mathbf{B}_2 \, + \, \mathbf{E}_1 \otimes \mathbf{A}_2\mathbf{S}_2 \, + \, \mathbf{E}_1 \otimes \mathbf{E}_2$$

$$= [\mathbf{A}_1 \otimes \mathbf{I}_m \mid \mathbf{I}_m \otimes \mathbf{A}_2]\begin{pmatrix} \mathbf{S}_1 \otimes \mathbf{B}_2 \\ \mathbf{E}_1 \otimes \mathbf{S}_2 \end{pmatrix} \, + \, \mathbf{E}_1 \otimes \mathbf{E}_2.$$

We start by defining $\mathbf{B}^*$ and "pre-cursor" values $\overline{\mathbf{A}}^*, \overline{\mathbf{S}}^*$, which we will use to derive the final $\mathbf{A}^*, \mathbf{S}^*$ later, via:

$$\overbrace{\mathbf{P} \cdot (\mathbf{B}_1 \otimes \mathbf{B}_2) \cdot \mathbf{P}'}^{\mathbf{B}^*} = \overbrace{\mathbf{P}[\mathbf{A}_1 \otimes \mathbf{I}_m \mid \mathbf{I}_m \otimes \mathbf{A}_2]}^{\overline{\mathbf{A}}^*} \cdot \overbrace{\begin{pmatrix} \mathbf{S}_1 \otimes \mathbf{B}_2 \\ \mathbf{E}_1 \otimes \mathbf{S}_2 \end{pmatrix} \mathbf{P}'}^{\overline{\mathbf{S}}^*} + \overbrace{\mathbf{P}(\mathbf{E}_1 \otimes \mathbf{E}_2)\mathbf{P}'}^{\mathbf{E}^*}$$

For general d, we have:

$$\mathbf{B}^* = \mathbf{P} \cdot (\mathbf{B}_1 \otimes \cdots \otimes \mathbf{B}_d) \cdot \mathbf{P}' \in \mathbb{Z}_q^{M \times K}, \quad \mathbf{E}^* = \mathbf{P}(\mathbf{E}_1 \otimes \mathbf{E}_2 \otimes \cdots \otimes \mathbf{E}_d)\mathbf{P}' \in \mathbb{Z}_q^{M \times K},$$

$$\overline{\mathbf{A}}^* = \mathbf{P} \cdot (\mathbf{A}_1 \otimes \mathbf{I}_m \otimes \cdots \otimes \mathbf{I}_m \| \cdots \cdots \| \mathbf{I}_m \otimes \cdots \otimes \mathbf{I}_m \otimes \mathbf{A}_d) \in \mathbb{Z}_q^{M \times dwm^{d-1}},$$

$$\overline{\mathbf{S}}^* = \begin{pmatrix} \mathbf{S}_1 \otimes \mathbf{B}_2 \otimes \cdots \otimes \mathbf{B}_d \\ \mathbf{E}_1 \otimes \mathbf{S}_2 \otimes \cdots \otimes \mathbf{B}_d \\ \vdots \\ \mathbf{E}_1 \otimes \mathbf{E}_2 \otimes \cdots \otimes \mathbf{S}_d \end{pmatrix} \cdot \mathbf{P}' \in \mathbb{Z}_q^{dwm^{d-1} \times K}, \text{ which we show satisfy}$$

$$\mathbf{B}^* = \overline{\mathbf{A}}^* \cdot \overline{\mathbf{S}}^* + \mathbf{E}^*.$$

Note that while the width of $\mathbf{A}$ in both the base scheme and WW is $w = \mathrm{poly}(\lambda)$, the width of $\overline{\mathbf{A}}^*$ is much larger and will in fact grow with N.

As mentioned above, it seems reasonable to conjecture that $\mathbf{E}^*$ on its own is pseudo-iid. However, $\overline{\mathbf{S}}^*$ is structured and does not look random on its own, which is problematic since we want $\overline{\mathbf{S}}^* + \mathbf{R}_{f,x}$ to drown out differences in the distribution of $\mathbf{R}_{f,x}$. Therefore, we will rely on a variant of Kilian randomization [Kil88] to hide the structure of $\overline{\mathbf{A}}^*, \overline{\mathbf{S}}^*$. We compute a random basis $\mathbf{A}^*$ of the column span of $\overline{\mathbf{A}}^*$ and then solve for $\mathbf{S}^*$ subject to $\mathbf{A}^*\mathbf{S}^* = \overline{\mathbf{A}}^* \cdot \overline{\mathbf{S}}^*$. This ensures that $\mathbf{A}^*, \mathbf{S}^*$ essentially do not reveal more than the product $\overline{\mathbf{A}}^*\overline{\mathbf{S}}^*$.

Succinctness. With the above implementation of succinct LWE sampling, from (5), the encodings of the resulting SRE have size

$$|\mathsf{Encode}(f,x)| = \widetilde{O}\left(\underbrace{M^2}_{\mathbf{A}^*\mathbf{R}+x\otimes\mathbf{G}+\mathbf{E}} + \underbrace{dmk}_{\mathsf{seed}_{\mathbf{B}^*}} + \underbrace{Mdwm^{d-1}}_{\mathbf{A}^*} + \underbrace{Kdwm^{d-1}}_{\mathbf{S}^*+\mathbf{R}_{f,x}} \right)$$

where $\widetilde{O}(\cdot)$ hides $\mathrm{poly}(\lambda,\log q,\ell)$ factors, which is in turn polynomial in λ,ℓ and circuit depth of f. We set

$$
\begin{aligned}
w &= \mathrm{poly}(\lambda), \\
m &= N^{\frac{1}{2d}}, \qquad M = m^{d-1/2} = N^{\frac{1}{2}-\frac{1}{4d}}, \\
k &= m^5 = N^{\frac{5}{2d}}, \qquad K = m^{d+1/2} = N^{\frac{1}{2}+\frac{1}{4d}}.
\end{aligned}
$$

Then, $|\mathsf{Encode}(f,x)| = \widetilde{O}(m^{2d-1/6}) = \widetilde{O}(N^{1-\frac{1}{12d}})$, that is, our scheme achieves $(1 - \frac{1}{12d})$-succinctness, which can then be lifted to iO using [AJ15,BV15, LPST16].

Our Final Assumption: Subspace Flooding. Combined with the transformation discussed earlier, we only need our sampler to satisfy weak security, which boils down to the following *subspace flooding* assumption: that

$$\mathbf{P}, \mathbf{P}', \mathsf{seed}_{\mathbf{B}^*}, \mathbf{A}^*, \widehat{\mathbf{B}} = \mathbf{A}^*\mathbf{S}_0 + \mathbf{F}, \ \mathbf{C} = \mathbf{A}^*\mathbf{R} + \mathbf{E} - b\mathbf{G}, \ \mathbf{E}^* + \mathbf{E}\cdot\mathbf{G}^{-1}(\widehat{\mathbf{B}}) - b\mathbf{F} \tag{6}$$

hides b where $\mathbf{P} \in \mathbb{Z}^{M\times m^d}$, $\mathbf{P}' \in \mathbb{Z}^{k^d\times K}$, $\mathbf{E} \in \mathbb{Z}^{M\times M\log q}$, and $\mathbf{F} \in \mathbb{Z}^{M\times K}$ and $\{\mathbf{E}_i\}_{i\in[d]}$ are sampled from small distributions;

$$\mathbf{E}^* = \mathbf{P}(\mathbf{E}_1 \otimes \mathbf{E}_2 \otimes \cdots \otimes \mathbf{E}_d)\mathbf{P}' \in \mathbb{Z}^{M\times K};$$

for $i = 1,\ldots,d$, $\mathbf{A}_i$ is sampled from $\mathbb{Z}_q^{m\times w}$ and $\mathbf{S}_i$ is sampled from $\mathbb{Z}_q^{w\times k}$;

$$\mathsf{seed}_{\mathbf{B}^*} = \{\mathbf{B}_i = \mathbf{A}_i\mathbf{S}_i + \mathbf{E}_i\}_{i\in[d]} \in (\mathbb{Z}_q^{m\times w})^d;$$

$\mathbf{S}_0$ is sampled from $\mathbb{Z}_q^{dwm^{d-1}\times K}$ and $\mathbf{R}$ is sampled from $\mathbb{Z}_q^{dwm^{d-1}\times M\log q}$ so $\widehat{\mathbf{B}} \in \mathbb{Z}_q^{M\times K}$ and $\mathbf{C} \in \mathbb{Z}_q^{M\times M\log q}$; and $\mathbf{A}^*$ is the result of the Kilian randomization process described above.

Note that the columns of $\mathbf{E}\cdot\mathbf{G}^{-1}(\widehat{\mathbf{B}}) \in \mathbb{Z}^{M\times K}$ live in a low-rank subspace defined by the columns of $\mathbf{E} \in \mathbb{Z}^{M\times M\log q}$ where $K \gg M\log q$ and $\mathbf{F}$ is sampled independently from a small distribution. Thus, the assumption states that $\mathbf{E}^*$ masks whether the error $\mathbf{EG}^{-1}(\widehat{\mathbf{B}}) - b\mathbf{F} \in \mathbb{Z}^{M\times K}$ lives in this low-rank subspace, hence the name "subspace flooding".

A different, less syntactic, perspective on the subspace flooding assumption tells us that to protect arbitrary computations, it is sufficient to protect a single homomorphic multiplication. Indeed, consider $\mathbf{C}$ to be a GSW encryption of $-b$ and $\widehat{\mathbf{B}}$ to be a GSW encryption of 0. Their homomorphic multiplication gives us

$$\mathbf{C}\cdot\mathbf{G}^{-1}(\widehat{\mathbf{B}}) = \mathbf{A}^*(\mathbf{R}\mathbf{G}^{-1}(\widehat{\mathbf{B}}) - b\mathbf{S}_0) + (\mathbf{E}\cdot\mathbf{G}^{-1}(\widehat{\mathbf{B}}) - b\mathbf{F})$$

Subspace flooding says that adding $\mathbf{E}^*$ "protects" the error $\mathbf{E}\cdot\mathbf{G}^{-1}(\widehat{\mathbf{B}}) - b\mathbf{F}$ in the evaluated ciphertext in the sense of hiding b.

Theorem 1 (Informal). *Under the (subexponential hardness of the) learning with errors assumption and the subspace flooding assumption (Eq. 6 above), there exists an indistinguishability obfuscation scheme.*

1.3   Discussion

Noise Distribution in Prior Works. The sampler in WW sampler works by homomorphically generating pseudorandom LWE samples using an encrypted (weak) pseudorandom function, such as that given by $k, u \mapsto \mathsf{round}(\langle k, u \rangle)$ for key k and random input u. Prior works used the GSW FHE for homomorphic evaluation, but did not specify the circuit implementation for the PRF. Hopkins, Jain and Lin (HJL) [HJL21] presented attacks on these prior LWE samplers that "exploit the flexibility to choose specific implementations of circuits and LWE error distributions in the Gay-Pass and Wee-Wichs assumptions." Specifically, they showed how to introduce redundancy into the circuit used in homomorphic evaluation following the GSW FHE so that the last two bits of $\mathbf{E}^* + \mathbf{Z}_b$ leak b.

Note that the above attack can be circumvented by fixing some natural choice of a concrete weak PRF, such as the aforementioned, which corresponds to FHE decryption; and a circuit evaluation of it, such as [AP14], which is in fact a read-once branching program with k hardwired. Unfortunately, writing down an explicit expression for the error distribution in the pseudorandom LWE sample is far from straightforward, which in turn impedes any cryptanalytic efforts. In this work, we avoid such considerations by directly considering succinct LWE samplers, as opposed to homomorphically evaluated weak PRFs.

Relation to the "LWE with Leakage" Assumption of [JLMS19]. Our assumption basically asserts that for small $\mathbf{Z}_0, \mathbf{Z}_1$ satisfying some precondition:

$$\mathbf{A}_1, \ldots, \mathbf{A}_d, \quad (\mathbf{B}_i := \mathbf{A}_i \mathbf{S}_i + \mathbf{E}_i)_{i \in [d]}, \quad \mathbf{P}, \mathbf{P}', \quad \mathbf{P}(\mathbf{E}_1 \otimes \cdots \otimes \mathbf{E}_d)\mathbf{P}' - \mathbf{Z}_b$$

hides b. (In fact, we do not give away $\mathbf{A}_1, \ldots, \mathbf{A}_d$, rather a random basis for the column span of $\mathbf{A}^*$. We ignore this difference for the rest of the comparison.)

The LWE with leakage assumption of [JLMS19] basically asserts that for small $\mathbf{z}_0, \mathbf{z}_1$, and $\mathbf{A}_i \in \mathbb{Z}_q^{m \times w}$, $\mathbf{s}_i \in \mathbb{Z}_q^{w \times 1}$, $\mathbf{e}_i \in \chi^{m \times 1}$:

$$\mathbf{A}_1, \ldots, \mathbf{A}_{d-2}, \quad (\mathbf{b}_i := \mathbf{A}_i \mathbf{s}_i + \mathbf{e}_i)_{i \in [d-2]}, \quad \mathbf{P}, \quad \mathbf{P}(\mathbf{e}_1 \otimes \cdots \otimes \mathbf{e}_d) + \mathbf{z}_b$$

hides b.

The LWE with leakage assumption of [JLMS19] can be viewed as a variant of our flooding assumption. Syntactically, their definition can be recovered from ours with three modifications:

1. Set $k = 1$ as opposed to our assumption where $k \gg m$;
2. Set $\mathbf{P}$ to be very compressing, namely, the output has length $M \ll m^{d/2}$, whereas in our case $M \approx m^{d-1/2}$; and
3. Do not release $\mathbf{A}_{d-1}, \mathbf{A}_d, \mathbf{B}_{d-1}, \mathbf{B}_d$ to the distinguisher, ensuring that the only leakage about $\mathbf{e}_{d-1}, \mathbf{e}_d$ comes from $\mathbf{E}^*$.

These syntactic differences have the following consequences:

- With $k = 1$ and $M \approx m^{d-1/2}$, the assumption can indeed be broken with sum-of-squares attacks (see, e.g., [BHJ+19].) Thus, our source of security comes from the fact that k is large. Semantically, this means that we take multiple, albeit correlated, instances of the [JLMS19] problem, defined by the k^d columns of our matrix $\mathbf{E}_1 \otimes \cdots \otimes \mathbf{E}_d$, and output a "few", namely, $K \ll k^{d/2}$ linear combinations of them.
- An adversary in our setting can check the rank of

$$\mathbf{P}(\mathbf{B}_1 \otimes \cdots \otimes \mathbf{B}_d)\mathbf{P}' - \mathbf{E}^* + \mathbf{Z}_b \bmod q$$

which is something that cannot be computed in the [JLMS19] assumption since $\mathbf{B}_{d-1}, \mathbf{B}_d$ are not given to the distinguisher. This allows the latter to plausibly handle *worst-case small* $\mathbf{z}_b$, whereas we require an additional precondition on $\mathbf{Z}_b$.

Their final iO scheme additionally assume bilinear groups (in addition to LWE), which we do not.

Cryptanalytic Challenges. A central open problem from this work is to design succinct LWE samplers based on weaker assumptions and to carry out cryptanalysis of our candidate succinct LWE sampler. To facilitate the latter, we describe concrete cryptanalytic challenges in Sect. 4.6. Thanks to our amplification theorem, in order to base iO on our candidate LWE sampler, it suffices for security to hold for a specific pair of distributions $(\mathbf{Z}_0, \mathbf{Z}_1)$. On the other hand, the heuristic underlying our candidate sampler (related to random polynomials being indistinguishable from independent copies of a noise-flooding distribution $\mathcal{D}$) does not refer to properties of the specific distribution. For this reason, our cryptanalytic challenges also refer to more general distributions $\mathbf{Z}_0, \mathbf{Z}_1$ that may not correspond to those which are sufficient for iO.

2 Preliminaries

2.1 Notations

We will denote by λ the security parameter. The notation $\mathrm{negl}(\lambda)$ denotes any function f such that $f(\lambda) = \lambda^{-\omega(1)}$, and $\mathrm{poly}(\lambda)$ denotes any function f such that $f(\lambda) = \mathcal{O}(\lambda^c)$ for some $c > 0$. For a probabilistic algorithm $\mathsf{alg}(\mathsf{inputs})$, we might explicitly refer to its random coins by writting $\mathsf{alg}(\mathsf{inputs};\mathsf{coins})$. We will denote vectors by bold lower case letters (e.g. $\mathbf{a}$) and matrices by bold upper cases letters (e.g. $\mathbf{A}$). We will denote by $\mathbf{a}^\top$ and $\mathbf{A}^\top$ the transposes of $\mathbf{a}$ and $\mathbf{A}$, respectively. We will denote by $\lfloor x \rceil$ the nearest integer to x, rounding towards 0 for half-integers. For matrices $\mathbf{A}, \mathbf{B}$ of appropriate dimensions, we will denote by $(\mathbf{A}\|\mathbf{B})$ their horizontal concatenation and $\binom{\mathbf{A}}{\mathbf{B}}$ their vertical concatenation. For an integer $n \geq 1$, we denote by $\mathbf{I}_n$ the identity matrix of dimension n. For integral vectors and matrices (i.e., those over $\mathbb{Z}$), we use the notation $\|\mathbf{r}\|, \|\mathbf{R}\|$ to denote the maximum absolute value over all the entries.

For matrices $\mathbf{A}, \mathbf{B}$, we denote by $\mathbf{A} \otimes \mathbf{B}$ their tensor (or Kronecker) product. We'll use the following mixed-product property: for matrices $\mathbf{A}, \mathbf{B}, \mathbf{C}, \mathbf{D}$ of appropriate dimensions, we have $(\mathbf{AB}) \otimes (\mathbf{CD}) = (\mathbf{A} \otimes \mathbf{C}) \cdot (\mathbf{B} \otimes \mathbf{D})$.

For $p \in \mathbb{Q}$, we write $\mathsf{Round}_p(x) = \lfloor x \cdot 1/p \rfloor$. If $\mathbf{X}$ is a matrix, $\mathsf{Round}_p(\mathbf{X})$ denotes the rounded value applied component-wise. We denote by $\lceil x \rceil$ the smallest integer larger or equal to x.

For a finite set S, $s \leftarrow S$ denotes sampling uniformly in S. We define the statistical distance between two random variables X and Y over some domain Ω as: $\mathsf{SD}(X, Y) = \frac{1}{2} \sum_{w \in \Omega} |X(w) - Y(w)|$. We say that two ensembles of random variables $X = \{X_\lambda\}$, $Y = \{Y_\lambda\}$ are *statistically indistinguishable*, denoted $X \approx_s Y$, if $\mathsf{SD}(X_\lambda, Y_\lambda) \leq \mathsf{negl}(\lambda)$.

We say that two ensembles of random variables $X = \{X_\lambda\}$, and $Y = \{Y_\lambda\}$ are *computationally indistinguishable*, denoted $X \approx_c Y$, if, for all (non-uniform) PPT distinguishers $\mathcal{A}$, we have $|\Pr[\mathcal{A}(X_\lambda) = 1] - \Pr[\mathcal{A}(Y_\lambda) = 1]| \leq \mathsf{negl}(\lambda)$. We also refer to sub-exponential security, meaning that there exists some $\varepsilon > 0$ such that the distinguishing advantage is at most $2^{-\lambda^\varepsilon}$.

2.2 Learning with Errors

Definition 1 (B-bounded distribution). *We say that a distribution χ over $\mathbb{Z}$ is B-bounded if*

$$\Pr[\chi \in [-B, B]] = 1.$$

We recall the definition of the (decision) *Learning with Errors* problem, introduced by Regev [Reg05].

Definition 2 ((Decision) Learning with Errors ([Reg05])). *Let $n = n(\lambda)$ and $q = q(\lambda)$ be integer parameters and $\chi = \chi(\lambda)$ be a distribution over $\mathbb{Z}$. The Learning with Errors (LWE) assumption $LWE_{n,q,\chi}$ states that for all polynomials $m = \mathrm{poly}(\lambda)$ the following distributions are computationally indistinguishable:*

$$(\mathbf{A}, \mathbf{As} + \mathbf{e}) \approx_c (\mathbf{A}, \mathbf{u})$$

where $\mathbf{A} \leftarrow \mathbb{Z}_q^{m \times n}, \mathbf{s} \leftarrow \mathbb{Z}_q^n, \mathbf{e} \leftarrow \chi^m, \mathbf{u} \leftarrow \mathbb{Z}_q^m$.

Just like many prior works, we rely on LWE security with the following range of parameters. We assume that for any polynomial $p = p(\lambda) = \mathrm{poly}(\lambda)$ there exists some polynomial $n = n(\lambda) = \mathrm{poly}(\lambda)$, some $q = q(\lambda) = 2^{\mathrm{poly}(\lambda)}$ and some $B = B(\lambda)$-bounded distribution $\chi = \chi(\lambda)$ such that $q/B \geq 2^p$ and the $LWE_{n,q,\chi}$ assumption holds. Throughout the paper, the *LWE assumption* without further specification refers to the above parameters. The *sub-exponentially secure LWE* assumption further assumes that $LWE_{n,q,\chi}$ with the above parameters is sub-exponentially secure, meaning that there exists some $\varepsilon > 0$ such that the distinguishing advantage of any polynomial-time distinguisher is $2^{-\lambda^\varepsilon}$.

The works of [Reg05, Pei09] showed that the (sub-exponentially secure) LWE assumption with the above parameters follows from the worst-case (sub-exponential) quantum hardness SIVP and classical hardness of GapSVP with sub-exponential approximation factors.

2.3   Lattice Tools

Noise Flooding. We will use the following fact.

Lemma 1 (Flooding Lemma (e.g., [AJL+12])). *Let $B = B(\lambda), B' = B'(\lambda) \in \mathbb{Z}$ be parameters and let $U([-B, B])$ be the uniform distribution over the integer interval $[-B, B]$. Then for any $e \in [-B', B']$, the statistical distance between $U([-B, B])$ and $U([-B, B]) + e$ is B'/B.*

Gadget Matrix [MP12]. For an integer $q \geq 2$, define: $\mathbf{g} = (1, 2, \cdots, 2^{\lceil \log q \rceil - 1}) \in \mathbb{Z}_q^{1 \times \lceil \log q \rceil}$. The *gadget matrix* $\mathbf{G}$ is defined as $\mathbf{G} = \mathbf{g} \otimes \mathbf{I}_n \in \mathbb{Z}_q^{n \times m}$ where $n \in \mathbb{N}$ and $m = n\lceil \log q \rceil$. There exists an efficiently computable deterministic function $\mathbf{G}^{-1} : \mathbb{Z}_q^n \to \{0, 1\}^m$ such for all $\mathbf{u} \in \mathbb{Z}_q^n$ we have $\mathbf{G} \cdot \mathbf{G}^{-1}(\mathbf{u}) = \mathbf{u}$. We let $\mathbf{G}^{-1}(\$)$ denote the distribution obtained by sampling $\mathbf{u} \leftarrow \mathbb{Z}_q^n$ uniformly at random and outputting $\mathbf{t} = \mathbf{G}^{-1}(\mathbf{u})$. These extend directly to matrices: $\mathbf{G}^{-1} : \mathbb{Z}_q^{n \times k} \to \{0, 1\}^{m \times k}$ by concatenating the outputs.

2.4   Homomorphic Operations

In this section, we describe how to perform homomorphic operations over certain encodings of inputs. For readers familiar with lattice-based primitives, these essentially are packed versions of the GSW homomorphism.

Our operations follow readily from [WW21] (building on [GSW13,GVW15], along with the "packing" techniques in [PVW08,MW16,BTVW17,PS19,GH19, BDGM19]), who build homomorphic operations for $f : \{0,1\}^\ell \to \{0,1\}^M$, producing some vector $\mathbf{c}_f \in \mathbb{Z}_q^M$. We extend these operations to functions $f : \{0,1\}^\ell \to \{0,1\}^{M \times K}$ to produce some matrix $\mathbf{C}_f \in \mathbb{Z}_q^{M \times K}$, obtained by concatenating K vectors $\mathbf{c}_{f_i}$. This yields the following.

Definition 3 (Homomorphic operations). *Let M, W, q, ℓ, K, t be parameters. We define the following efficient algorithms:*

- *$\mathsf{Eval}(f : \{0,1\}^\ell \to \{0,1\}^{M \times K}, \mathbf{C} \in \mathbb{Z}_q^{M \times \ell M \log q})$: deterministically outputs a matrix $\mathbf{C}_f \in \mathbb{Z}_q^{M \times Q}$.*
- *$\mathsf{Eval}_{\mathsf{open}}(f, \mathbf{A} \in \mathbb{Z}_q^{M \times W}, x \in \{0,1\}^\ell, \mathbf{R} \in \mathbb{Z}_q^{W \times \ell M \log q}, \mathbf{E} \in \mathbb{Z}^{M \times \ell M \log q})$: deterministically outputs two matrices $(\mathbf{R}_{f,x} \in \mathbb{Z}_q^{W \times Q}, \mathbf{E}_{f,x} \in \mathbb{Z}^{M \times Q})$.*

These operations have the following property. For all $f : \{0,1\}^\ell \to \{0,1\}^{M \times K}$ of depth t, $\mathbf{x} \in \{0,1\}^\ell$, $\mathbf{A} \in \mathbb{Z}_q^{M \times W}$, $\mathbf{R} \in \mathbb{Z}_q^{W \times \ell M \log q}$ and $\mathbf{E} \in \mathbb{Z}^{M \times \ell M \log q}$, if

$$\mathbf{C} = \mathbf{AR} + x^\top \otimes \mathbf{G} + \mathbf{E} \in \mathbb{Z}_q^{M \times \ell M \log q},$$

$$\mathbf{C}_f = \mathsf{Eval}(f, \mathbf{C}),$$

$$(\mathbf{R}_{f,x}, \mathbf{E}_{f,x}) = \mathsf{Eval}_{\mathsf{open}}(f, \mathbf{A}, x, \mathbf{R}, \mathbf{E}),$$

where we view x as a row vector $x \in \{0,1\}^{1 \times \ell}$, then

$$\mathbf{C}_f = \mathbf{AR}_{f,x} + q/2 \cdot f(x) + \mathbf{E}_{f,x} \in \mathbb{Z}_q^{M \times K},$$

where $f(x) \in \{0,1\}^{M \times K}$. Furthermore $\|\mathbf{E}_{f,x}\| = \|\mathbf{E}\| \cdot M^{g(t)}$ for some efficiently computable g such that $g(t) = \mathcal{O}(t)$.

Similarly to [WW21], these algorithms extend to functions f with outputs in $\mathbb{Z}_q$.

- $\mathsf{Eval}^q(f : \{0,1\}^\ell \to \mathbb{Z}_q^{M \times K}, \mathbf{C} \in \mathbb{Z}_q^{M \times \ell M \log q})$: deterministically outputs a matrix $\mathbf{C}_f \in \mathbb{Z}_q^{M \times Q}$.
- $\mathsf{Eval}_{\mathsf{open}}^q(f, \mathbf{A} \in \mathbb{Z}_q^{M \times W}, x \in \{0,1\}^\ell, \mathbf{R} \in \mathbb{Z}_q^{W \times \ell M \log q}, \mathbf{E} \in \mathbb{Z}^{M \times \ell M \log q})$: deterministically outputs two matrices $(\mathbf{R}_f \in \mathbb{Z}_q^{W \times Q}, \mathbf{E}_f \in \mathbb{Z}^{M \times Q})$.

The correctness requirement becomes:

$$\mathbf{C}_f = \mathbf{A}\mathbf{R}_{f,x} + f(x) + \mathbf{E}_{f,x} \in \mathbb{Z}_q^{M \times K},$$

where $\mathbf{C} = \mathbf{A}\mathbf{R} + x \otimes \mathbf{G} + \mathbf{E} \in \mathbb{Z}_q^{M \times \ell M \log q}$, x being again seen as a row vector, $\mathbf{C}_f = \mathsf{Eval}^q(f, \mathbf{C})$ and $(\mathbf{R}_{f,x}, \mathbf{E}_{f,x}) = \mathsf{Eval}_{\mathsf{open}}^q(f, \mathbf{A}, x, \mathbf{R}, \mathbf{E})$, and $f(x) \in \mathbb{Z}_q^{M \times K}$. Again, $\|\mathbf{E}_{f,x}\| = \|\mathbf{E}\| \cdot M^{g(t)}$.

2.5   Succinct Randomized Encodings

Next, we define succinct randomized encodings [BGL+15, BCG+18, LPST16].

Definition 4. *A succinct randomized encoding scheme (SRE) for the function family $\mathcal{F}_{\ell,N,t} = \{f : \{0,1\}^\ell \to \{0,1\}^N\}$ of circuits of depth at most t, is a tuple of PPT algorithms* $(\mathsf{CRSGen}, \mathsf{Encode}, \mathsf{Decode})$ *with the following syntax:*

- $\mathsf{CRSGen}(1^\lambda, \mathcal{F}_{\ell,N,t}) \to \mathsf{crs}$: *on input the security parameter and a function family, outputs* crs.
- $\mathsf{Encode}(\mathsf{crs}, f, x) \to C$: *on input* crs, *a function* $f \in \mathcal{F}_{\ell,N,t}$ *and* $x \in \{0,1\}^\ell$, *outputs an encoding* C.
- $\mathsf{Decode}(\mathsf{crs}, C, f) \to y$: *a deterministic algorithm which, on input* crs, *an encoding* C, *and a function* $f \in \mathcal{F}_{\ell,N,t}$, *outputs a value* $y \in \{0,1\}^N$.

We require the following properties:

Correctness: For $f \in \mathcal{F}_{\ell,N,t}$ *and any* $x \in \{0,1\}^\ell$:

$$\Pr\left[\mathsf{Decode}(\mathsf{crs}, \mathsf{Encode}(\mathsf{crs}, f, x), f) = f(x)\right] \geq 1 - \mathsf{negl}(\lambda),$$

where $\mathsf{crs} \leftarrow \mathsf{CRSGen}(1^\lambda, \mathcal{F}_{\ell,N,t})$ *(over the randomness of* $\mathsf{CRSGen}, \mathsf{Encode}$*).*

δ-*Succinctness: There exists a constant* $\delta < 1$ *such that, for all* $\mathsf{crs} \leftarrow \mathsf{CRSGen}(1^\lambda, \mathcal{F}_{\ell,N,t})$, $C \leftarrow \mathsf{Encode}(\mathsf{crs}, f, x)$, *we have:*

$$|C| = N^\delta \cdot \mathsf{poly}(\lambda, \ell, t).$$

Indistinguishability-Based Security: For all PPT $\mathcal{A}$, *all* $x_0, x_1 \in \ell$, *and all* $f \in \mathcal{F}_{t,\ell,N}$ *such that* $f(x_0) = f(x_1)$, *the following distributions are indistinguishable for* $b = 0$ *and* $b = 1$:

- $\mathcal{D}_b$: *Sample* $\mathsf{crs} \leftarrow \mathsf{CRSGen}(1^\lambda, \mathcal{F}_{t,\ell,N})$, $C_b \leftarrow \mathsf{Encode}(\mathsf{crs}, f, x_b)$. *Output* (crs, C_b).

Relation to XiO. Our notion of SRE is also very related to the notion of exponentially efficient iO (XiO) from [LPST16]. An XiO scheme obfuscates a circuit $C : \{0,1\}^{\log N} \to \{0,1\}$ with the same security guarantee as iO, but the runtime of the obfuscator can be as high as $\mathrm{poly}(\lambda, |C|, N)$ and the only constraint that makes the problem non-trivial is that the obfuscated circuit is succinct, of size at most $N^\delta \mathrm{poly}(\lambda, |C|)$ for $\delta < 1$. An SRE scheme immediately yields an XiO scheme by thinking of f as the universal circuit that takes as input a circuit $x = C$ an evaluates it on all N inputs in $\{0,1\}^{\log N}$. The output size of f is N and the depth of f can be bounded by $t = \mathrm{poly}(|C|)$, so the succinctness of the SRE yields the corresponding succinctness of the XiO. Therefore, by leveraging the prior work of [LPST16] that shows how to go from XiO (in the CRS model) to iO via LWE, we get the following theorem.

Theorem 2 [AJ15, BV15, LPST16]. *Assuming sub-exponentially secure SRE exist and sub-exponentially secure LWE, there exists an iO scheme.*

3   Succinct LWE Sampler: Definition and Amplification

In Sect. 3.1, we define the notion of succinct LWE samplers. In Sect. 3.2, we describe a seemingly weaker notion of LWE sampler, and prove that it implies the first (and stronger) notion.

3.1   Definition and Discussion

Definition 5 (Succinct LWE Sampler). *A succinct LWE sampler is a tuple of PPT algorithms* (SampCRSGen, LWEGen, Expand) *with the following syntax:*

- SampCRSGen$(1^\lambda, 1^N, \alpha)$: *on input the security parameter λ, a size parameter N and a blow-up factor α, samples a common reference string* crs, *which include parameters* params $= (q, M, K, \overline{\chi}, \overline{B})$.
- LWEGen(crs): *samples* $(\mathrm{seed}_{\mathbf{B}^*}, \mathbf{A}^*, \mathbf{S}^*)$.
- Expand(crs, $\mathrm{seed}_{\mathbf{B}^*}$) *is a deterministic algorithm that outputs a matrix $\mathbf{B}^*$.*

Domains and Parameters. The outputs of LWEGen *and* Expand *satisfy:*

$$\mathbf{A}^* \in \mathbb{Z}_q^{M \times W}, \quad \mathbf{S}^* \in \mathbb{Z}_q^{W \times K}, \quad \mathbf{B}^* \in \mathbb{Z}_q^{M \times K},$$

for some integer W. We require that:

- $N = MK$;
- $\overline{B} = \mathrm{poly}(N)$;
- $\overline{\chi}$ *is a $\overline{B}$-bounded noise distribution; and*
- $q \geq 8 \cdot 2^\lambda \cdot \alpha \cdot \overline{B}$.

Correctness. We require that

$$||\mathbf{B}^* - \mathbf{A}^*\mathbf{S}^*|| := \beta \leq q/8$$

where crs $\leftarrow$ SampCRSGen$(1^\lambda, 1^N, \alpha)$, $(\mathrm{seed}_{\mathbf{B}^*}, \mathbf{A}^*, \mathbf{S}^*) \leftarrow$ LWEGen(crs) *and* $\mathbf{B}^* :=$ Expand(crs, $\mathrm{seed}_{\mathbf{B}^*}$). *Furthermore, we require that $\mathbf{A}^*$ is full-rank with overwhelming probability over the randomness of* SampCRSGen *and* LWEGen.

δ-Succinctness. We require the total bit length of the output of LWEGen *is small. That is,*

$$\text{bitlength}(\text{seed}_{\mathbf{B}^*}, \mathbf{A}^*, \mathbf{S}^*) \leq N^\delta \cdot \text{poly}(\lambda, \log q) = (MK)^\delta \cdot \text{poly}(\lambda, \log q) ,$$

where $\delta < 1$ is a constant. When we omit δ, it means succinctness holds for some constant $\delta < 1$.

LWE with respect to $\mathbf{A}^*$. We require that

$$(\text{coins}_{\text{crs}}, \text{coins}_{\text{seed}}, \mathbf{A}^* \mathbf{s}' + \mathbf{e}') \approx_c (\text{coins}_{\text{crs}}, \text{coins}_{\text{seed}}, \mathbf{b}),$$

where crs $= \text{SampCRSGen}(1^\lambda, 1^N, \alpha; \text{coins}_{\text{crs}})$, $(\text{seed}_{\mathbf{B}^*}, \mathbf{A}^*, \mathbf{S}^*) \leftarrow \text{LWEGen}(\text{crs};$ $\text{coins}_{\text{seed}})$, $\mathbf{s}' \leftarrow \mathbf{Z}_q^W$, *and* $\mathbf{e}' \leftarrow \overline{\chi}^M$.

Security (or β_0-Flooding). Let D_0, D_1 be any two polynomial-time samplable distributions such that $(\text{aux}_b, \mathbf{Z}_b) \leftarrow D_b(\mathbf{A}^*)$ satisfies $\mathbf{Z}_b \in \mathbb{Z}^{M \times K}$, $\|\mathbf{Z}_b\| \leq \beta_0$ where $\beta_0 \cdot 2^\lambda \leq \beta$ and

$$(\text{coins}_{\text{crs}}, \text{coins}_{\text{seed}}, \mathbf{A}^* \mathbf{S}' + \mathbf{Z}_0, \text{aux}_0) \approx_c (\text{coins}_{\text{crs}}, \text{coins}_{\text{seed}}, \mathbf{A}^* \mathbf{S}' + \mathbf{Z}_1, \text{aux}_1)$$

where crs $= \text{SampCRSGen}(1^\lambda, 1^N, \alpha; \text{coins}_{\text{crs}})$, $(\text{seed}_{\mathbf{B}^*}, \mathbf{A}^*, \mathbf{S}^*) = \text{LWEGen}(\text{crs};$ $\text{coins}_{\text{seed}})$ *and* $\mathbf{S}' \leftarrow \mathbb{Z}_q^{W \times K}$. *Then,*

$$(\text{crs}, \text{seed}_{\mathbf{B}^*}, \mathbf{A}^*, \mathbf{A}^* \mathbf{S}^* + \mathbf{Z}_0, \text{aux}_0) \approx_c (\text{crs}, \text{seed}_{\mathbf{B}^*}, \mathbf{A}^*, \mathbf{A}^* \mathbf{S}^* + \mathbf{Z}_1, \text{aux}_1).$$

We will refer to the assumption on D_0, D_1 as the pre-condition *for security, and the resulting indistinguishability the* post-condition.
Furthermore, as we will later describe a relaxed notion of security, we will sometimes refer to the notion above as **strong security** *to avoid ambiguity.*

Remark 1 (Alternate formulation). Since the sampler allows us to compute $\text{Expand}(\text{crs}, \text{seed}_{\mathbf{B}^*}) = \mathbf{B}^* = \mathbf{A}^* \mathbf{S}^* + \mathbf{E}^*$, the security post-condition can be equivalently stated as:

$$(\text{crs}, \text{seed}_{\mathbf{B}^*}, \mathbf{A}^*, \mathbf{E}^* - \mathbf{Z}_0, \text{aux}_0) \approx_c (\text{crs}, \text{seed}_{\mathbf{B}^*}, \mathbf{A}^*, \mathbf{E}^* - \mathbf{Z}_1, \text{aux}_1).$$

Remark 2 (Implied Statements). The randomness $\text{coins}_{\text{crs}}$ and $\text{coins}_{\text{seed}}$ respectively used by SampCRSGen and LWEGen allow us to compute crs, $\text{seed}_{\mathbf{B}^*}, \mathbf{A}^*, \mathbf{S}^*$. In particular, LWE with respect to $\mathbf{A}^*$ implies that

$$(\text{crs}, \text{seed}_{\mathbf{B}^*}, \mathbf{A}^*, \mathbf{S}^*, \mathbf{A}^* \mathbf{s}' + \mathbf{e}) \approx_c (\text{crs}, \text{seed}_{\mathbf{B}^*}, \mathbf{A}^*, \mathbf{S}^*, \mathbf{b}),$$

and the pre-condition on D_0, D_1 for security implies that

$$(\text{crs}, \text{seed}_{\mathbf{B}^*}, \mathbf{A}^*, \mathbf{S}^*, \text{aux}_0, \mathbf{A}^* \mathbf{S}' + \mathbf{Z}_0) \approx_c (\text{crs}, \text{seed}_{\mathbf{B}^*}, \mathbf{A}^*, \mathbf{S}^*, \text{aux}_1, \mathbf{A}^* \mathbf{S}' + \mathbf{Z}_1).$$

Remark 3 (Restrictions on $\mathbf{Z}_0, \mathbf{Z}_1$). We note that security (namely, the post-conditionition) cannot hold for arbitrary $\mathbf{Z}_0, \mathbf{Z}_1$, for which the pre-condition does not hold. Even if one only required that $\mathbf{Z}_0$ and $\mathbf{Z}_1$ had small entries, one can efficiently distinguish $\mathbf{Z}_0 = \mathbf{0}$ from any $\mathbf{Z}_1$ not in the column span of $\mathbf{A}^*$. In particular, the rank of $\mathbf{A}^*\mathbf{S}^* + \mathbf{Z}_b$ would leak b: this is because $\mathbf{A}^*\mathbf{S}^*$ is rank-deficient by succinctness. We can rule out such distinguishers simply by requiring that $\mathbf{Z}_0 - \mathbf{Z}_1$ lies in the column span of $\mathbf{A}^*$; our pre-condition is in some sense a "distributional" or "computational" relaxation of such a requirement.

Remark 4 (Triviality without succinctness). We remark that it is easy to build a succinct LWE sampler if there are no restrictions on the bit-length of $\mathsf{seed}_{\mathbf{B}^*}$ (looking ahead, such a sampler would not be sufficient to build iO). Indeed, without any succinctness requirement, we could set:

$$\mathsf{crs} = \emptyset, \quad \mathsf{seed}_{\mathbf{B}^*} = \mathbf{A}^*\mathbf{S}^* + \mathbf{E}^* \in \mathbb{Z}_q^{M \times K}$$

where $\mathbf{S}^*$ is random and $\mathbf{E}^*$ has small entries, but large enough to "noise-flood" $\mathbf{Z}_b$ (namely, $\beta_0/\beta = 2^{-\lambda}$).

For convenience, we consider the equivalent notion of security from Remark 1. We claim that this construction (unconditionally) satisfies security. To see this, first note that for all $b \in \{0, 1\}$:

$$(\mathsf{seed}_{\mathbf{B}^*}, \mathbf{A}^*, \mathbf{E}^* - \mathbf{Z}_b, \mathsf{aux}_b) \approx_s (\mathbf{A}^*\mathbf{S}^* + (\mathbf{E}^* + \mathbf{Z}_b), \mathbf{A}^*, \mathbf{E}^*, \mathsf{aux}_b)$$

by noise flooding, where we use that $\mathbf{E}^*$ is sampled independently of $\mathsf{aux}_b, \mathbf{Z}_b$. The pre-condition then implies that

$$(\mathbf{A}^*, (\mathbf{A}^*\mathbf{S}^* + \mathbf{Z}_0) + \mathbf{E}^*, \mathbf{E}^*, \mathsf{aux}_0) \approx_c (\mathbf{A}^*, (\mathbf{A}^*\mathbf{S}^* + \mathbf{Z}_1) + \mathbf{E}^*, \mathbf{E}^*, \mathsf{aux}_1),$$

where we again use that $\mathbf{E}^*$ is sampled independently of $\mathsf{aux}_b, \mathbf{Z}_b, \mathbf{S}^*$, and that $\mathbf{S}^*$ is sampled uniformly at random independently of the other components (and takes the role of $\mathbf{S}'$ in the pre-condition).

Remark 5 (Heuristic necessity of a CRS). We heuristically show that security requires a (long) CRS if $\mathsf{seed}_{\mathbf{B}^*}$ is required to be short, namely the CRS needs to be of length $\approx N$ for any δ-succinct scheme with $\delta < 1$.

Suppose for contradiction that there is such a sampler that expands some short input $(\mathsf{crs}, \mathsf{seed}_{\mathbf{B}^*})$ of length at most $N^\delta \cdot \mathrm{poly}(\lambda, \log q)$ to some $\mathsf{Expand}(\mathsf{seed}_{\mathbf{B}^*}) = \mathbf{B}^* = \mathbf{A}^*\mathbf{S}^* + \mathbf{E}^*$ of bit-length $N \log q$. Let $\mathbf{Z}_b$ be a random LWE error and let aux_b be an obfuscation of the following program:

$P_{b, \mathbf{A}^*, \mathbf{Z}_b}$: on input $(\mathsf{crs}, \mathsf{seed}_{\mathbf{B}^*})$ of bit-length $N^\delta \cdot \mathrm{poly}(\lambda, \log q)$, and $\widetilde{\mathbf{B}}$ of bit-length $N \log q$,
 – Check that $\widetilde{\mathbf{B}} - \mathbf{Z}_b$ is in the column span of $\mathbf{A}^*$, and output $\perp$ if not.
 – Compute $\mathbf{B}^* = \mathsf{Expand}(\mathsf{crs}, \mathsf{seed}_{\mathbf{B}^*}) = \mathbf{A}^*\mathbf{S}^* + \mathbf{E}^*$. Output b if $\|\mathbf{B}^* - \widetilde{\mathbf{B}} + \mathbf{Z}_b\| \leq \beta$, and output $\perp$ otherwise.

Then $(\mathsf{crs}, \mathsf{seed}_{\mathbf{B}^*}, \widetilde{\mathbf{B}} = \mathbf{A}^*\mathbf{S}^* + \mathbf{Z}_0, \mathsf{aux}_0)$ is efficiently distinguishable from $(\mathsf{crs}, \mathsf{seed}_{\mathbf{B}^*}, \widetilde{\mathbf{B}} = \mathbf{A}^*\mathbf{S}^* + \mathbf{Z}_1, \mathsf{aux}_1)$, by running aux_b on input $((\mathsf{crs}, \mathsf{seed}_{\mathbf{B}^*}), \widetilde{\mathbf{B}})$ and using the fact that $(\mathsf{crs}, \mathsf{seed}_{\mathbf{B}^*})$ has bit-length at most $\widetilde{O}(N^\delta)$ by assumption, that $\|\mathbf{E}^*\| \le \beta$, that $\mathbf{A}^*\mathbf{S}^*$ has low rank by succinctness, and that $\mathbf{A}^*\mathbf{S}^* + \mathbf{Z}_0 - \mathbf{Z}_1$ has high rank w.h.p.

Furthermore, suppose heuristically that aux_b acts like an ideal obfuscation of $P_{b,\mathbf{Z}_b}$, meaning that it does not reveal more than black-box access to the program. Then, the pre-condition would hold since given $(\mathsf{coins}_{\mathsf{crs}}, \mathsf{coins}_{\mathsf{seed}}, \mathbf{B}_b = \mathbf{A}^*\mathbf{S}' + \mathbf{Z}_b)$ and black-box access to $P_{b,\mathbf{Z}_b}$, one cannot distinguish $b = 0$ vs $b = 1$. The idea is that the only way to learn anything about b is to provide a "good" input to $P_{b,\mathbf{Z}_b}$ that makes it output something other than $\bot$. Any good input must be of the form $((\mathsf{crs}', \mathsf{seed}'_{\mathbf{B}^*}), \mathbf{B}_b + \mathbf{A}^*\mathbf{S})$ for some $\mathbf{S} \in \mathbb{Z}_q^{W \times K}$. But if $\mathbf{B}_b$ was uniform, there would be no inputs of this form, where $(\mathsf{crs}', \mathsf{seed}'_{\mathbf{B}^*})$ is short, such that $\|\mathsf{Expand}(\mathsf{crs}', \mathsf{seed}'_{\mathbf{B}^*}) - \mathbf{B}_b + \mathbf{A}^*\mathbf{S}\|$ is also small, meaning that $P_{b,\mathbf{Z}_b}$ would always output $\bot$ in this case. This follows by a counting argument, where the sizes of crs', $\mathsf{seed}'_{\mathbf{B}^*}$ and $\mathbf{S}$ are much smaller than the size of $\mathbf{B}_b$ whenever δ is sufficiently small, and β is relatively small compared to q. Therefore finding a good input to $P_{b,\mathbf{Z}_b}$ would require breaking LWE with respect to $\mathbf{A}^*$.

3.2 Weak Succinct LWE Samplers

We now present a weaker security notion for succinct LWE samplers. Instead of quantifying over all $(\mathbf{Z}_b, \mathsf{aux}_b)$ that satisfy the specified pre-condition as we did previously, we now fix one particular and simple choice of $(\mathbf{Z}_b, \mathsf{aux}_b)$. In particular, this makes the definition falsifiable. We then show in Theorem 3 that there is a generic compiler that upgrades this type of weak security to the previous definition of strong security (Definition 5).

Definition 6. *Weak Security (or Weak β_0-Flooding). Define D_0, D_1 as follows.*

$$D_b: \quad \mathsf{aux}_b = \left(\widehat{\mathbf{B}} := \mathbf{A}^*\widehat{\mathbf{S}} + \widehat{\mathbf{E}}, \quad \mathbf{C} = \mathbf{A}^*\mathbf{R} + \mathbf{E} - b \cdot \mathbf{G}\right)$$
$$\mathbf{Z}_b = \mathbf{E}\mathbf{G}^{-1}(\widehat{\mathbf{B}}) - b\widehat{\mathbf{E}},$$

where

- SampCRSGen *defines* $(q, M, K, \overline{\chi}, \overline{B}) = $ params*;*
- LWEGen *defines* $\mathbf{A}^* \in \mathbb{Z}_q^{M \times W}$*;*
- $\widehat{\mathbf{B}} \in \mathbb{Z}_q^{M \times K}$, $\widehat{\mathbf{S}} \leftarrow \mathbb{Z}_q^{W \times K}$, *and* $\widehat{\mathbf{E}} \leftarrow [-B_{\mathsf{flood}}, B_{\mathsf{flood}}]^{M \times K}$, *where* $B_{\mathsf{flood}} = (\beta_0 + \overline{B}) \cdot 2^\lambda$*;*
- $\mathbf{C} \in \mathbb{Z}_q^{M \times M \log q}$, $\mathbf{R} \leftarrow \mathbb{Z}_q^{W \times M \log q}$, *and* $\mathbf{E} \leftarrow \overline{\chi}^{M \times M \log q}$.

We say that the sampler (SampCRSGen, LWEGen, Expand) *is weakly secure if*

$$(\mathsf{crs}, \mathsf{seed}_{\mathbf{B}^*}, \mathbf{A}^*, \mathbf{A}^*\mathbf{S}^* + \mathbf{Z}_0, \mathsf{aux}_0) \approx_c (\mathsf{crs}, \mathsf{seed}_{\mathbf{B}^*}, \mathbf{A}^*, \mathbf{A}^*\mathbf{S}^* + \mathbf{Z}_1, \mathsf{aux}_1).$$

Remark 6 (Alternate formulation of security). Similar to Remark 1, as the sampler allows us to compute $\mathsf{Expand}(\mathsf{crs}, \mathsf{seed}_{\mathbf{B}^*}) = \mathbf{B}^* = \mathbf{A}^* \mathbf{S}^* + \mathbf{E}^*$, weak security equivalently states that:

$$(\mathsf{crs}, \mathsf{seed}_{\mathbf{B}^*}, \mathbf{A}^*, \mathbf{E}^* - \mathbf{Z}_0, \mathsf{aux}_0) \approx_c (\mathsf{crs}, \mathsf{seed}_{\mathbf{B}^*}, \mathbf{A}^*, \mathbf{E}^* - \mathbf{Z}_1, \mathsf{aux}_1).$$

Remark 7 (Pre-condition from LWE). We note that the distributions D_0, D_1 satisfy the pre-condition for security of Definition 5, assuming LWE, namely:

$$(\mathsf{coins}_{\mathsf{crs}}, \mathsf{coins}_{\mathsf{seed}}, \mathbf{A}^* \mathbf{S}' + \mathbf{Z}_0, \mathsf{aux}_0) \approx_c (\mathsf{coins}_{\mathsf{crs}}, \mathsf{coins}_{\mathsf{seed}}, \mathbf{A}^* \mathbf{S}' + \mathbf{Z}_1, \mathsf{aux}_0), \quad (7)$$

where $(\mathsf{aux}_b, \mathbf{Z}_b) \leftarrow D_b$ and $\mathbf{S}' \leftarrow \mathbb{Z}_q^{W \times K}$.

This is true because one can efficiently sample $\mathbf{A}^* \mathbf{S}' + \mathbf{Z}_b$ given only $(\mathbf{A}^*, \mathsf{aux}_b)$, as follows:

- Compute $\mathbf{C}_{\widehat{\mathbf{B}}} = \mathbf{C}\mathbf{G}^{-1}(\widehat{\mathbf{B}}) \in \mathbb{Z}_q^{M \times K}$; and
- Output $\mathbf{C}_{\widehat{\mathbf{B}}} + \mathbf{A}^* \mathbf{S}$ for some random $\mathbf{S} \leftarrow \mathbb{Z}_q^{W \times K}$.

Indeed,

$$\begin{aligned}
\mathbf{C}_{\widehat{\mathbf{B}}} + \mathbf{A}^* \mathbf{S} &= (\mathbf{A}^* \mathbf{R} + \mathbf{E} - b\mathbf{G})\mathbf{G}^{-1}(\widehat{\mathbf{B}}) + \mathbf{A}^* \mathbf{S} \\
&= \mathbf{A}^* (\mathbf{R}\mathbf{G}^{-1}(\widehat{\mathbf{B}}) - b\widehat{\mathbf{S}} + \mathbf{S}) + (\mathbf{E}\mathbf{G}^{-1}(\widehat{\mathbf{B}}) - b\widehat{\mathbf{E}})
\end{aligned}$$

and the latter term is distributed identically to $\mathbf{A}^* \mathbf{S}' + \mathbf{Z}_b$ with a random $\mathbf{S}'$.

Therefore, to show the precondition Eq. (7), it suffices to prove that $(\mathsf{coins}_{\mathsf{crs}}, \mathsf{coins}_{\mathsf{seed}}, \mathsf{aux}_b)$ hides b. But this follows from LWE with respect to $\mathbf{A}^*$ (Definition 5) with noise distribution $\overline{\chi}$.

3.3 Amplification

The following theorem allows to lift weak security (Definition 6) to strong security (Definition 5).

Theorem 3. *Suppose there exists a weakly secure, δ-succinct LWE sampler (Definition 6). Suppose furthermore that it satisfies $M^2 \leq N^\delta \cdot \mathrm{poly}(\lambda, \log q)$. Then, assuming LWE, there exists a secure δ-succinct LWE sampler, satisfying strong security (Definition 5). Moreover, with the parameters of Definition 6, there exists such a sampler that is (strongly) β_0-flooding.*

We refer to the full version for a construction and a proof.

4 Candidate Succinct LWE Sampler

In Sect. 4.1, we present the template of our main candidate. In Sect. 4.2, we state correctness and succinctness (and refer to the full version for proofs). In Sect. 4.3, we explain how to setup parameters, and state our conjectured security. Last, we discuss the plausibility of our conjecture in Sect. 4.5.

4.1   A Basic Framework

We describe a basic template to build succinct LWE samplers. Looking ahead, the SRE construction in Sect. 5 requires an additional succinctness requirement, namely, that additional encodings produced by the SRE are succinct. We make sure that our template and the parameters we propose are compatible with that constraint.

We now describe our framework. It uses a set of parameters:

$$\mathsf{parameters} := (d, m, k, w, M, K, \overline{\chi}, \chi, \beta, q)$$

which in particular includes $\mathsf{params} = (q, M, K, \overline{\chi}, \overline{B}, \chi)$ directly output by $\mathsf{SampCRSGen}$. Informally,

- the security of our sampler is related to the hardness of solving systems of random degree d polynomials;
- q is the underlying LWE modulus;
- m, k, w define the dimensions of the "seed" LWE samples $\mathbf{A}_i, \mathbf{S}_i, \mathbf{E}_i$, which together with d, determine M, K, which are the dimensions for "expanded" sample $\mathbf{B}^*$;
- χ is the noise distribution for $\mathbf{E}_i$; it is B-bounded over $\mathbb{Z}$;
- $\overline{\chi}$ is the noise distribution used for LWE w.r.t $\mathbf{A}^*$; it is $\overline{B}$-bounded over $\mathbb{Z}$;
- D_P a σ-bounded distribution over $\mathbb{Z}$. We will take $D_P = \chi$ for simplicity.

We now describe our candidate $(\mathsf{SampCRSGen}, \mathsf{LWEGen}, \mathsf{Expand})$.

- $\mathsf{SampCRSGen}(1^\lambda, 1^N, \alpha)$: Derive $\mathsf{parameters} = (d, m, k, w, M, K, \overline{\chi}, \overline{B}, \chi, \beta, q)$ from $(1^\lambda, 1^N, \alpha)$ as described later in Sect. 4.3. Set $\mathsf{params} = (q, M, K, \overline{\chi}, \overline{B}, \chi)$. Sample $\mathbf{P}' \leftarrow \chi^{k^d \times K}$ and $\mathbf{P} \leftarrow \chi^{M \times m^d}$. Output

$$\mathsf{crs} = (\mathsf{params}, \mathbf{P}, \mathbf{P}').$$

- $\mathsf{LWEGen}(\mathsf{crs})$: On input $\mathsf{crs} = (\mathsf{params}, \mathbf{P}, \mathbf{P}')$, sample, for $i \in [d]$, $\mathbf{A}_i \leftarrow \mathbb{Z}_q^{m \times w}$, $\mathbf{S}_i \leftarrow \mathbb{Z}_q^{w \times k}$, $\mathbf{E}_i \leftarrow \chi^{m \times k}$ where χ is specified in params. Compute:

$$\mathbf{B}_i = \mathbf{A}_i \mathbf{S}_i + \mathbf{E}_i \in \mathbb{Z}_q^{m \times k}.$$

Set:

$$\overline{\mathbf{A}}^* = \mathbf{P} \cdot \Big(\mathbf{A}_1 \otimes \mathbf{I}_m \otimes \cdots \otimes \mathbf{I}_m \,\|\, \mathbf{I}_m \otimes \mathbf{A}_2 \otimes \mathbf{I}_m \otimes \cdots \otimes \mathbf{I}_m \,\|\, \cdots$$
$$\cdots \,\|\, \mathbf{I}_m \otimes \cdots \otimes \mathbf{I}_m \otimes \mathbf{A}_d \Big) \in \mathbb{Z}_q^{M \times dwm^{d-1}}$$

$$\overline{\mathbf{S}}^* = \begin{pmatrix} \mathbf{S}_1 \otimes \mathbf{B}_2 \otimes \cdots \otimes \mathbf{B}_d \\ \mathbf{E}_1 \otimes \mathbf{S}_2 \otimes \cdots \otimes \mathbf{B}_d \\ \vdots \\ \mathbf{E}_1 \otimes \mathbf{E}_2 \otimes \cdots \otimes \mathbf{S}_d \end{pmatrix} \cdot \mathbf{P}' \in \mathbb{Z}_q^{dwm^{d-1} \times K}.$$

Sample a random basis $\mathbf{A}^* \in \mathbb{Z}_q^{M \times W}$ of the column space of $\overline{\mathbf{A}}^*$, and solve for $\mathbf{S}^* \in \mathbb{Z}_q^{W \times K}$ such that $\mathbf{A}^*\mathbf{S}^* = \overline{\mathbf{A}}^* \cdot \overline{\mathbf{S}}^*$. Output:

$$\mathsf{seed}_{\mathbf{B}^*} = \{\mathbf{B}_i\}_{i \in [d]}, \quad \mathbf{A}^*, \mathbf{S}^*.$$

- Expand($\mathsf{crs}, \mathsf{seed}_{\mathbf{B}^*}$): On input $\mathsf{crs} = (\mathsf{params}, \mathbf{P}, \mathbf{P}')$ and $\mathsf{seed}_{\mathbf{B}^*} = \{\mathbf{B}_i\}_{i \in [d]}$, output:
$$\mathbf{B}^* = \mathbf{P} \cdot (\mathbf{B}_1 \otimes \cdots \otimes \mathbf{B}_d) \cdot \mathbf{P}' \in \mathbb{Z}_q^{M \times K}.$$

4.2   Correctness, Succinctness, and LWE with Respect to A*

We show that for appropriate parameters, the sampler described above is correct and succinct.

Claim 1. *Assume $\beta \geq B^2(mkB)^d$. Then the sampler* (SampCRSGen, LWEGen, Expand) *described above satisfies correctness (Definition 5).*

Claim 2. *Suppose there exists $\delta < 1$ such that*

$$(dmk + MW + WK) \leq N^\delta \cdot \mathrm{poly}(\lambda, \log q),$$

where W is the width of $\mathbf{A}^*$. Then (SampCRSGen, LWEGen, Expand) *described above is δ-succinct.*

Proof. This follows as $\mathsf{bitlength}(\{\mathbf{B}_i\}_{i \in [d]}, \mathbf{A}^*, \mathbf{S}^*) = (dmk + MW + WK) \cdot \log q$.

Next, we show that LWE holds with respect to $\mathbf{A}^*$ (assuming standard LWE), for our candidate sampler. We first show that it holds with respect to $\overline{\mathbf{A}}^*$.

Lemma 2 (LWE with respect to $\overline{\mathbf{A}}^*$). *Let $\chi(\lambda)$ be a $B(\lambda)$-bounded distribution. Let D_P be a σ-bounded distribution over $\mathbb{Z}$ such that if $\mathbf{P} = D_P^{M \times m^d}(\mathsf{coins}_P)$ is sampled using randomness coins_P, then with overwhelming probability over coins_P, $\mathbf{P}$ is full-rank. Suppose furthermore that $M \leq m^d$.*
  Suppose $\mathrm{LWE}_{w,q,\chi}$ holds. Let $\overline{\chi} = \mathcal{U}([-\overline{B}, \overline{B}])$ be the uniform distribution in $[-\overline{B}, \overline{B}]$, where $\overline{B} \geq \sigma m^d B \cdot 2^\lambda$. Then:

$$\left(\mathsf{coins}_P, \mathbf{P}, \{\mathbf{A}_i\}_{i \in [d]}, \overline{\mathbf{A}}^*, \overline{\mathbf{A}}^* \cdot \mathbf{s} + \mathbf{e}\right) \approx_c \left(\mathsf{coins}_P, \mathbf{P}, \{\mathbf{A}_i\}_{i \in [d]}, \overline{\mathbf{A}}^*, \mathbf{b}\right),$$

where $\mathbf{P} = D_P^{M \times m^d}(\mathsf{coins}_P)$, $\mathbf{b} \leftarrow \mathbb{Z}_q^M$, $\mathbf{s} \leftarrow \mathbb{Z}_q^{dwm^{d-1}}$, $\mathbf{e} \leftarrow \overline{\chi}^M$.

Corollary 1 (LWE with respect to A*). *Let $\chi(\lambda)$ be a $B(\lambda)$-bounded distribution. Suppose furthermore that $M \leq m^d$. Then, assuming $\mathrm{LWE}_{w,\chi,q}$,* (SampCRSGen, LWEGen, Expand) *satisfies LWE with respect to $\mathbf{A}^*$ with noise distribution $\overline{\chi} = \mathcal{U}([-\overline{B}, \overline{B}])$ where $\overline{B} = B^2 \cdot m^d \cdot 2^\lambda$.*

We refer to the full version for proofs of Claim 1, Lemma 2, and Corollary 1.

4.3   Instantiating the Parameters

Parameters. We first go through our parameters, and show that they satisfy the constraints of Definition 5.

Our candidate is a "degree-d" sampler, where $d \geq 2$ is a fixed constant integer. It expands LWE samples $\mathbf{B}_i \in \mathbb{Z}_q^{m \times k}$ to a matrix $\mathbf{B}^* \in \mathbb{Z}_q^{M \times K}$, using matrices $\mathbf{P} \leftarrow \chi^{M \times m^d}$ and $\mathbf{P}' \leftarrow \chi^{k^d \times K}$.[4] This expansion has stretch γ, in the sense that $MK = (mk)^\gamma$. w and W are the respective widths of the underlying matrices $\mathbf{A}_i \in \mathbb{Z}_q^{m \times w}$ and $\mathbf{A}^* \in \mathbb{Z}_q^{M \times W}$. δ is the succinctness parameter of our sampler.

χ denotes a B-bounded distribution used to sample $\mathsf{seed}_{\mathbf{B}^*}$, namely the matrices $\{\mathbf{E}_i\}_{i \in [d]}$, and we assume that $\mathrm{LWE}_{w,q,\chi}$ holds. β is a bound on $\|\mathbf{E}^*\|$ which depends on B.

$\overline{\chi}$ denotes a $\overline{B}$-bounded distribution such that LWE with respect to $\mathbf{A}^*$ holds (assuming LWE holding for some fixed parameters only dependent on the security parameter λ). α denotes a blow-up factor that defines the noise bound β_0 that the sampler is masking in the security property, namely $\beta_0 = \alpha \overline{B}$.

We gather the constraints on our parameters below:

- $N = MK$ //constraint of the sampler
- $(dmk + MW + WK) \leq N^\delta \cdot \mathrm{poly}(\lambda, \log q)$ for some $\delta < 1$ //δ-succinctness
- $M^2 \leq N^\delta \cdot \mathrm{poly}(\lambda, \log q)$ //for SRE succinctness
- $M \leq m^d$ //LWE with respect to $\mathbf{A}^*$ (Corollary 1)
- χ is a B-bounded distribution s.t. $\mathrm{LWE}_{w,q,\chi}$ holds. //base LWE assumption
- $\overline{B} = B^2 m^d \cdot 2^\lambda$ //LWE with respect to $\mathbf{A}^*$ (Corollary 1)
- $\beta = B^2 (mkB)^d$ //bound on $\|\mathbf{E}^*\|$
- B large enough s.t. $\beta \geq \beta_0 \cdot 2^\lambda$ where $\beta_0 = \alpha \overline{B}$. //constraint of the sampler
- $q \geq 8\beta$.   //constraint of the sampler

We additionally add the following constraints to ensure security:

- $\gamma < d/2$ //to avoid SOS attacks (Sect. 4.5).
- $M \leq m^d, K \leq k^d$ //to avoid rank attacks[5] (Sect. 4.5).

Next, we show our candidate sampler satisfies these constraints. Given the security parameter λ, fix a degree $d = \mathcal{O}(1)$, a dimension $w = w(\lambda)$, and a bound $B = B(\lambda)$. Given additional parameters $N \geq w^{6d}$ and α as input, our candidate sets the following parameters.

It fixes a stretch parameter $\gamma \in \left[\frac{2d}{2d - 1/6}, d/2 \right)$.

Set $m = N^{1/2d} \geq w^3$. It then defines the following "dimension" parameters k, M, K:

$$k = m^{\frac{2d}{\gamma} - 1}, \quad M = m^{d-1/2}, \quad K = m^{d+1/2}$$

---

[4] In general, we can use a different (small) distributions D_P and D_P' for $\mathbf{P}, \mathbf{P}'$. We only set $D_P = D'_P = \chi$ to minimize the number of distributions and parameters.

[5] The first constraint is redundant with the constraints of Corollary 1.

and $wm^{d-1} \le W = \operatorname{rank}\left(\overline{\mathbf{A}}^*\right) \le m^d - (m-w)^d < dwm^{d-1} = \operatorname{width}\left(\overline{\mathbf{A}}^*\right)$ by construction of $\mathbf{A}^*$.[6] Note that the second inequality is strict as $m > w$,[7] that is, $\overline{\mathbf{A}}^*$ is rank deficient.

It then defines the following "bound" parameters $\overline{B}, \beta$:

$$\overline{B} = B^2 m^d \cdot 2^\lambda, \quad \beta = B^2 (mkB)^d,$$

where we assume that χ is B-bounded with $B \ge \frac{(\alpha \cdot 2^{2\lambda})^{1/d}}{k}$ such that $\mathrm{LWE}_{w,q,\chi}$ holds.[8]

Let $\overline{\chi} = \mathcal{U}([-\overline{B}, \overline{B}])$ be the uniform distribution over $[-\overline{B}, \overline{B}]$. It finally sets the modulus q as

$$q = 8\beta.$$

We show that the setting of parameters satisfy all the constraints described above. First, by definition, $N = m^{2d} = MK$. Furthermore:

$$\begin{aligned}
\mathsf{bitlength}(\mathsf{seed}_{\mathbf{B}^*}, \mathbf{A}^*, \mathbf{S}^*) &= dmk \log q \ + \ M \cdot W \log q \ + \ W \cdot K \log q \\
&< \left(dm^{2d/\gamma} + dwm^{2d-3/2} + dwm^{2d-1/2}\right) \cdot \log q \\
&= \left(m^{2d-\frac{1}{6}} + dm^{2d/\gamma}\right) \cdot \log q \\
&= N^\delta \cdot \mathrm{poly}(\lambda, \log q)
\end{aligned}$$

with $\delta = 1 - \frac{1}{12d} = \frac{2d-1/6}{2d}$, where we used $W < dwm^{d-1}$, $w \le m^{1/3}$, which follows as $N \ge w^{6d}$ and $m = N^{1/2d}$, and $1/\gamma \le \delta$.

We furthermore have $M^2 = m^{2d-1} \le N^\delta$.

We have by construction: $\overline{B} = B^2 m^d \cdot 2^\lambda$, $\beta_0 = \alpha \overline{B}$, $\beta = \beta_0 \cdot 2^\lambda$, $\beta \ge B^2 (mkB)^d$ and $q = 8\beta$, so that the constraint $\beta \ge \beta_0 \cdot 2^\lambda$ can be rewritten as:

$$B^2 (mkB)^d \ge \alpha \cdot 2^\lambda \cdot (B^2 m^d 2^\lambda),$$

which is exactly our constraint on B.

Last, we have $\gamma < d/2$ by definition, $M = m^{d-1/2} \le m^d$, and $K = m^{d+1/2} \le (m^3)^d$.

Remark 8 (Length of the CRS). As noted in Remark 5, a long CRS is required for security to hold if we allow arbitrary auxiliary information aux. We note this is the case for the parameters of Conjecture 1. Indeed: $\mathsf{bitlength}(\mathbf{P}') = k^d K \ \log q \ge m^{4d+1/2} \ \log q \ge N \ \mathrm{poly}(\lambda, \log q) = m^{2d} \ \mathrm{poly}(\lambda, \log q)$.

---

[6] We prove that $\operatorname{rank}\left(\overline{\mathbf{A}}^*\right) \le m^d - (m-w)^d$ in Sect. 4.5, paragraph Rank of $\mathbf{A}^*\mathbf{S}^*$.

[7] Writing $m = m' + w$ where $m' > 0$, the difference $(m' + w)^d - (m'^d + dw(m' + w)^{d-1})$ is the sum of monomials in m', w with positive coefficients.

[8] This is without loss of generality by defining for instance $\chi' = \chi + [-B, B]$ where B' is large enough to satisfy the previous constraint. A direct reduction ensures that if LWE holds with χ, then it holds with χ'.

Remark 9 (Parameters as a function of γ). Our construction induces different parameters, according the choice of γ. The main affected parameter is k, which goes from $k = m^{3+o(1)}$ to $k \approx m^{2d}$. We note here that it also makes sense to use a constant $\gamma \in \left(1, \frac{2d}{2d-1/6}\right]$ for our construction. The only difference is that the succinctness of the scheme then becomes $1/\gamma$ as opposed to $1 - \mathcal{O}(1/d)$.

We gather some example parameters in the table below. In all cases, we set $d \geq 4$ be a constant, $m \geq w^3$ so that $N = m^{2d}$, $M = m^{d-1/2}$ and $K = m^{d+1/2}$. The third column represent the components that should have size bounded by N^δ to satisfy δ-succinctness (Fig. 1).

Stretch γ	Dimension k	$M^2 + \text{bitlength}(\text{seed}_{\mathbf{B}^*}, \mathbf{A}^*, \mathbf{S}^*)$	Succinctness δ
$\gamma = d/3$	$k = m^5$	$\mathcal{O}(m^{2d-1/6})$	$\delta = 1 - \frac{1}{12d}$
$\gamma = \frac{2d}{2d-1/6}$	$k = m^{2d-7/6}$	$\mathcal{O}(m^{2d-1/6})$	$\delta = 1 - \frac{1}{12d} = 1/\gamma$
$\gamma = \frac{2d}{2d-\epsilon}$	$k = m^{2d-\epsilon-1}$	$\mathcal{O}(m^{2d-\epsilon})$	$\delta = 1/\gamma$

Fig. 1. Example parameters. In the above, we fix a constant $d \geq 4$ and $w = w(\lambda)$. The output size is $N = m^{2d}$ where $N \geq w^{6d}$.

Next, we state our main conjecture for our candidate, namely that it satisfies the weak notion of security of Definition 6. Looking ahead, thanks to Theorem 3, this suffices to imply iO.

Conjecture 1 (Conjectured security). Let χ be a B-bounded distribution, and assume $\text{LWE}_{w,q,\chi}$ holds. Then $(\text{SampCRSGen}, \text{LWEGen}, \text{Expand})$ with any of the parameters above satisfies weak β_0-flooding (Definition 6), where $\beta_0 = \alpha\overline{B}$.

Remark 10 (Security as a function of d). Our constructions decouples the stretch γ, defined as $(\text{bitlength}(\{\mathbf{B}_i\}_{i\in[d]}))^\gamma = \text{bitlength}(\mathbf{B}^*)$ (up to polynomial factors in $\lambda, \log q$), from the degree d. In particular, for a fixed (constant) stretch $\gamma \geq \frac{2d}{2d-1/6}$, we expect Conjecture 1 to be weaker as d increases.

Next, combining the above with Theorem 3, we describe two distributions whose indistinguishability would imply the existence of succinct LWE sampler with θ-flooding (Definition 5) for some parameter θ. Looking ahead, combined with Theorem 4, this suffices to imply an iO scheme.

Conjecture 2 (Stand-alone θ-flooding). Let $\beta_0 = \theta \cdot 2^\lambda$. With any of the parameters params described above, the following distributions Δ_b are indistinguishable:

$$\Delta_b = \Big(\mathbf{P}, \mathbf{P}', \text{seed}_{\mathbf{B}^*}, \mathbf{A}^*, \quad \widehat{\mathbf{B}} = \mathbf{A}^*\mathbf{S}_0 + \mathbf{F},$$

$$\mathbf{C} = \mathbf{A}^*\mathbf{R} + \mathbf{E} - b\mathbf{G}, \quad \mathbf{E}^* + \mathbf{E} \cdot \mathbf{G}^{-1}(\widehat{\mathbf{B}}) - b\mathbf{F}\Big)$$

where

$$\mathbf{P} \leftarrow \chi^{M \times m^d}, \quad \mathbf{P}' \leftarrow \chi^{k^d \times K},$$

$$\mathsf{seed}_{\mathbf{B}^*} = \{\mathbf{B}_i\}_{i \in [d]} \in (\mathbb{Z}_q^{m \times w})^d$$

$$\widehat{\mathbf{B}} \in \mathbb{Z}_q^{M \times K}, \quad \text{where} \quad \mathbf{S}_0 \leftarrow \mathbb{Z}_q^{W \times K}, \quad \mathbf{F} \leftarrow \chi_{\mathsf{flood}}^{M \times K}$$

$$\mathbf{C} \in \mathbb{Z}_q^{M \times M \log q}, \quad \text{where} \quad \mathbf{R} \leftarrow \mathbb{Z}_q^{W \times M \log q}, \quad \mathbf{E} \leftarrow \overline{\chi}^{M \times M \log q}$$

where $(\mathsf{seed}_{\mathbf{B}^*}, \mathbf{A}^*, \mathbf{S}^*) \leftarrow \mathsf{LWEGen}(\mathsf{params}, \mathbf{P}, \mathbf{P}')$, $\mathbf{B}^* = \mathsf{Expand}(\mathsf{params}, \mathbf{P}, \mathbf{P}', \mathsf{seed}_{\mathbf{B}^*})$, and $\mathbf{E}^* = \mathbf{B}^* - \mathbf{A}^* \mathbf{S}^*$. Furthermore, $\overline{\chi}$ is a noise distribution such that LWE with respect to $\mathbf{A}^*$ holds, and χ_{flood} is a β_0-bounded distribution that floods θ-bounded distributions.

4.4 Alternate Candidate Construction

In the full version, we present a variant of the construction in Sect. 4.1. The main intuition is that this new variant sums T copies of the candidate of Sect. 4.1, but reusing the same matrices $\mathbf{A}_i$ across all copies. We refer to the full version for a complete description of that candidate.

4.5 Cryptanalysis

Recall that security of a succinct LWE sampler requires

$$(\mathsf{crs}, \mathsf{seed}_{\mathbf{B}^*}, \mathbf{A}^*, \mathbf{E}^* - \mathbf{Z}_b, \mathsf{aux}_b)$$

to hide b for appropriate aux_b and small $\mathbf{Z}_b$.

Ignoring the auxiliary information related to the sampler for now, the crucial requirement is that $\mathbf{E}^* - \mathbf{Z}_b$ (or, equivalently, $\mathbf{A}^* \mathbf{S}^* + \mathbf{Z}_b$) hides b for sufficiently small $\mathbf{Z}_b$. As noted in the technical overview, pseudorandomness of $\mathbf{E}^*$ cannot hold given $\mathsf{seed}_{\mathbf{B}^*}$: one can compute $\mathbf{B}^* - \mathbf{E}^*$ and check that it is low rank. Nonetheless, as a sanity check, we would like to ensure that the marginal distribution of $\mathbf{E}^*$ is pseudorandom *by itself*, i.e. in the absence of $\mathsf{seed}_{\mathbf{B}^*}$. We first describe some attacks on the pseudorandomness of $\mathbf{E}^*$, and their influence on our parameters in Sect. 4.3.

Linearization Attacks. A strong break for the pseudorandomness of $\mathbf{E}^*$ is to recover the initial errors $\mathbf{E}_i \in \mathbb{Z}^{m \times k}$ such that $\mathbf{P} \left(\bigotimes_{i=1}^d \mathbf{E}_i \right) \mathbf{P}' = \mathbf{E}^*$. This would be enough to break pseudorandomness: only a small fraction of small $\mathbf{E}^* \in \mathbb{Z}^{M \times K}$ have such a succinct description as long as $N = MK$ is large enough compared to m and k (say $MK = (mk)^\gamma$ for some constant $\gamma > 1$).

One way of recovering the $\mathbf{E}_i$'s given $\mathbf{E}^*$, $\mathbf{P}$ and $\mathbf{P}'$ is to view the equation

$$\mathbf{P} \left(\bigotimes_{i=1}^d \mathbf{E}_i \right) \mathbf{P}' = \mathbf{E}^*$$

as a set of *linear* equations with the $(mk)^d$ variables

$$X_{i_1,j_1,\cdots,i_d,j_d} = \mathbf{E}_1^{i_1,j_1} \times \cdots \times \mathbf{E}_d^{i_d,j_d}$$

where $i_1,\cdots,i_d \in [m]$ and $j_1,\cdots,j_d \in [k]$, and where $\mathbf{E}^{i,j}$ denotes the (i,j)th component of $\mathbf{E}$. In particular, this is solvable as long as the number of equations is no smaller than the number of variables, that is:

$$MK \geq (mk)^d.$$

Our choice of parameters reflects security against linearization attacks. We also note that the linearization attack (in contrast to the sum of squares attack) works just as well over any finite field as it does over the integers.

Low-Degree Polynomials and Sum of Squares. The recovery attack described above can be generically improved using the more refined *sum of squares* (SOS) attacks. These ensure that pseudorandomness of $\mathbf{E}^*$ cannot hold whenever

$$MK \geq (mk)^{d/2}.$$

We refer the reader to [BHJ+19] for more details on sum of squares attacks. In our scheme, we explicitly require that the stretch of our sampler, namely γ such that $MK = (mk)^\gamma$, is smaller than $d/2$.

Security when $m = 1$. When $m = 1$, $\mathbf{P}$ is a scalar that we will ignore. We are given

$$\mathbf{e}^* = \left(\bigotimes_{i=1}^{d} \mathbf{e}_i\right) \mathbf{P}'$$

which is a vector of length K. Since $\bigotimes_{i=1}^{d} \mathbf{e}_i$ is simply the set of all degree-d multilinear monomials with a variable from each of the $\mathbf{e}_i$, this can be interpreted as evaluating K degree-d polynomials with Gaussian coefficients on the dk variables in $\mathbf{e}_1,\ldots,\mathbf{e}_d$. Since $K \ll k^{d/2}$, neither linearization nor sum of squares seems to apply [BHJ+19].

The work of Kosov [Kos20] tells us each entry in $\mathbf{E}^*$ by itself, namely a polynomial with Gaussian coefficients evaluated on Gaussian inputs, comes from a noise-flooding distribution (for mild choices of parameters).

This analysis also points to the qualitative distinction between our assumption and the analysis above for $m = 1$. When $m = 2$, for example, we obtain MK polynomials evaluated on a number of correlated random variables. That is, setting the two rows of $\mathbf{E}_i$ to be $\mathbf{e}_{i1}$ and $\mathbf{e}_{i2}$,

$$\mathbf{E}^* = \mathbf{P} \begin{bmatrix} \mathbf{e}_{11} \otimes \mathbf{e}_{21} \otimes \cdots \otimes \mathbf{e}_{d1} \\ \mathbf{e}_{12} \otimes \mathbf{e}_{21} \otimes \cdots \otimes \mathbf{e}_{d1} \\ \vdots \\ \mathbf{e}_{12} \otimes \mathbf{e}_{22} \otimes \cdots \otimes \mathbf{e}_{d2} \end{bmatrix} \mathbf{P}'$$

To the best of our knowledge, all attacks described above still fail. In fact, we don't even have an attack if $\mathbf{P} = \mathbf{I}_{2^d}$ was the identity and $M = 2^d$. However, this is certainly a cryptanalytic avenue worth pursuing in the future.

Rank Attacks. Towards analyzing the case of larger m, we attempt another class of attacks which consist of looking at the *rank* of the various matrices that arise in the assumption.

Rank Attack on $\mathbf{E}^*$. Note that a random (e.g. Gaussian) $\mathbf{E}^*$ would be full-rank with overwhelming probability. In particular, as

$$\mathbf{E}^* = \mathbf{P} \left(\bigotimes_{i=1}^{d} \mathbf{E}_i \right) \mathbf{P}',$$

where $\mathbf{P} \in \mathbb{Z}^{M \times m^d}$ and $\mathbf{P}' \in \mathbb{Z}^{k^d \times K}$, the rank of $\mathbf{E}^*$ is at most the rank of $\mathbf{P}, \mathbf{P}'$. In particular, $\mathbf{P}$ and $\mathbf{P}'$ need to be full-rank and compressing, meaning that $M \le m^d$ and $K \le k^d$, respectively. Our setting of parameters (see Sect. 4.3) ensure these restrictions hold.

The rank of $\bigotimes_{i=1}^{d} \mathbf{E}_i$ is the product of the ranks of $\mathbf{E}_i$, and is therefore, $\min(m^d, k^d)$ with high probability. Heuristically, then, the rank of $\mathbf{E}^*$ is exactly $\min(K, M)$ with high probability, as long as the Gaussians have sufficiently large width, a statement that we verified experimentally.

Rank Attack on $\mathbf{A}^*\mathbf{S}^*$. Note that if $\mathbf{A}^*\mathbf{S}^*$ is computationally indistinguishable from $\mathbf{A}^*\mathbf{S}'$ for a uniformly random $\mathbf{S}'$ given $\mathsf{crs}, \mathsf{seed}_{\mathbf{B}^*}, \mathbf{A}^*, \mathsf{aux}_b$, then the precondition implies the post-condition in Definition 5, guaranteeing security. Thus, we evaluate possible distinguishers between $\mathbf{A}^*\mathbf{S}^*$ and $\mathbf{A}^*\mathbf{S}'$.

One such class of attacks consist in comparing the rank of $\mathbf{A}^*\mathbf{S}^*$ to the rank of $\mathbf{A}^*$. We heuristically and experimentally analyzed the ranks of $\mathbf{A}^*$ and $\mathbf{A}^*\mathbf{S}^*$ to reason about these attacks.

First, note that $\overline{\mathbf{A}}^* \overline{\mathbf{S}}^* = \mathbf{A}^*\mathbf{S}^*$. Recall that the matrices $\mathbf{A}_i \in \mathbb{Z}_q^{m \times w}$ are random and therefore w.h.p. full-rank (i.e., rank w). Let $\mathbf{A}_i^\perp \in \mathbb{Z}_q^{(m-w) \times m}$ be a basis for the left-kernel of $\mathbf{A}_i$, that is, they are rank-$(m-w)$ matrices such that

$$\mathbf{A}_i^\perp \mathbf{A}_i = 0 \pmod{q}$$

We note that w.h.p. the rank of the matrix

$$(\mathbf{A}_1 \otimes \mathbf{I}_m \otimes \cdots \otimes \mathbf{I}_m \,\|\, \mathbf{I}_m \otimes \mathbf{A}_2 \otimes \mathbf{I}_m \otimes \cdots \otimes \mathbf{I}_m \,\|\, \cdots \,\|\, \mathbf{I}_m \otimes \cdots \otimes \mathbf{I}_m \otimes \mathbf{A}_d)$$

is at most $m^d - (m-w)^d \approx dwm^{d-1} - d^2 w^2 m^{d-2}/2$ (the approximation assumes that $m \gg w$ which is the case for us) since the row-span of $\mathbf{A}^*$ is contained in the right kernel of $(\mathbf{A}_1^\perp \otimes \cdots \otimes \mathbf{A}_d^\perp)$, and the latter has rank $m^d - (m-w)^d$. Our experiments indicate that the rank is indeed $m^d - (m-w)^d$ w.h.p. In other words, this matrix is *rank-deficient* by approximately $d^2 w^2 m^{d-2}/2$.

Heuristically,

$$\overline{\mathbf{A}}^* = \mathbf{P} \cdot (\mathbf{A}_1 \otimes \mathbf{I}_m \otimes \cdots \otimes \mathbf{I}_m \,\|\, \mathbf{I}_m \otimes \mathbf{A}_2 \otimes \mathbf{I}_m \otimes \cdots \otimes \mathbf{I}_m \,\|\, \mathbf{I}_m \otimes \cdots \otimes \mathbf{I}_m \otimes \mathbf{A}_d)$$

has the same rank since $\mathbf{P} \in \mathbb{Z}^{M \times m^d}$ is Gaussian and nearly full-rank, i.e., rank $M \approx m^{d-1/2}$. That is, w.h.p., (heuristically)

$$\mathsf{rank}(\overline{\mathbf{A}}^*) = m^d - (m-w)^d$$

Also, heuristically, $\overline{\mathbf{A}}^*\overline{\mathbf{S}}^*$ has this rank as long as $\overline{\mathbf{S}}^*$ has sufficiently many columns, i.e. as long as K is large enough compared to $\mathsf{rank}(\overline{\mathbf{A}}^*)$. (Note that the entries of $\overline{\mathbf{A}}^*$ and $\overline{\mathbf{S}}^*$ are correlated.)

To test these heuristic statements, we ran experiments for $d = 3$ and a range of values of m, k and q. We found that $\overline{\mathbf{A}}^*$ had rank $m^d - (m-w)^d$ as expected (in all the runs of our experiment, suggesting a high probability statement). We also found that when $k \geq m$ and K is large enough so that $\mathbf{S}^*$ is wide, $\overline{\mathbf{A}}^*\overline{\mathbf{S}}^* = \mathbf{A}^*\mathbf{S}^*$ also had rank $m^d - (m - w)^d$ with high probability. This is the same as one would expect from $\mathbf{A}^*\mathbf{S}'$ for a random $\mathbf{S}'$, suggesting that rank attacks fail.

4.6   Cryptanalytic Challenges

We describe a few cryptanalytic challenges and how they relate to our candidate and our assumptions. For each of these problems, we can also consider easier challenges where (a) the challenger also gets $\mathbf{A}^*$; and (b) we replace $\mathbf{P}$ with the identity matrix.

Pseudo-flooding in the Absence of $\mathsf{seed}_{\mathbf{B}^*}$. Our intuition says that for any two low-norm matrices $\mathbf{Z}_0$ and $\mathbf{Z}_1$, $\mathbf{E}^* + \mathbf{Z}_b$ hides b. Concretely, let χ be a discrete Gaussian of sufficiently large parameter σ. A challenge is to come up with matrices $\mathbf{Z}_0$ and $\mathbf{Z}_1$ where $||\mathbf{Z}_b|| < \sigma/2^\lambda$ such that the bit b can be recovered given

$$\mathbf{P}\left(\bigotimes_{i=1}^{d} \mathbf{E}_i\right)\mathbf{P}' + \mathbf{Z}_b .$$

We note that when $m = 1$ and $\mathbf{P} = 1$, as argued above, this seems to follow from the noise-flooding properties of random (e.g. Gaussian) polynomials [BHJ+19].

Pseudo-flooding in the Presence of $\mathsf{seed}_{\mathbf{B}^*}$. Our stronger notion of security (Definition 5) would imply that it would be hard to recover b from

$$(\mathsf{seed}_{\mathbf{B}^*}, \ \mathbf{A}^*\mathbf{S}^* + \mathbf{Z}_b, \ \mathbf{E}^* - \mathbf{Z}_b), \quad b \leftarrow \{0,1\}$$

for the following concrete distributions of $\mathbf{Z}_0, \mathbf{Z}_1$:

- (norm and ideal membership) $\mathbf{Z}_0$ is drawn from a Gaussian, and $\mathbf{Z}_1 = 2\mathbf{Z}_0$, and q is odd. In particular, an attacker that manages to learn the parity of $\mathbf{Z}_b$ or accurately approximate the norm of $\mathbf{Z}_b$ will be able to learn b.
- (subspace membership) $\mathbf{Z}_b = \mathbf{E}_0\mathbf{M} + b\hat{\mathbf{E}}$ where $||\mathbf{E}_0|| \gg ||\hat{\mathbf{E}}||$ and $\mathbf{M}$ is a public low-norm matrix. The distribution here is closely related to that for weak flooding. Here, $||\mathbf{Z}_0|| \approx ||\mathbf{Z}_1||$, but an attacker that manages to learn whether $\mathbf{Z}_b$ lies in the row span of $\mathbf{M}$ will be able to learn b.

In both cases, an attacker could try to exploit the leakage on b from $\mathbf{A}^*\mathbf{S}^* + \mathbf{Z}_b$ or from $\mathbf{E}^* - \mathbf{Z}_b$. For instance, an efficient algorithm that recovers $\mathbf{E}^*$ from $\mathsf{seed}_{\mathbf{B}^*}$ or one that recovers b from $\mathbf{E}^* - \mathbf{Z}_b$ solves this problem.

Distinguishing $\mathbf{A}^*\mathbf{S}^*$ *from* $\mathbf{A}^*\mathbf{S}'$. As described above, we think the following claim is plausible:

$$\mathbf{A}^*\mathbf{S}^* \approx_c \mathbf{A}^*\mathbf{S}'$$

where $\mathbf{S}' \leftarrow \mathbb{Z}_q^{W \times K}$. As $\mathbf{A}^*\mathbf{S}^* = \overline{\mathbf{A}}^* \cdot \overline{\mathbf{S}}^*$ (where $\overline{\mathbf{A}}^*, \overline{\mathbf{S}}^*$ are defined in Sect. 4.1), and given that $\mathbf{A}^*$ and $\overline{\mathbf{A}}^*$ have the same column span, this is equivalent to

$$\overline{\mathbf{A}}^* \cdot \overline{\mathbf{S}}^* \approx_c \overline{\mathbf{A}}^* \cdot \mathbf{S}''$$

where $\mathbf{S}'' \leftarrow \mathbb{Z}_q^{dwm^{d-1} \times K}$, and $\overline{\mathbf{A}}^*, \overline{\mathbf{S}}^*$ have closed form expressions described in Sect. 4.1.

A distinguisher here does not immediately break strong or weak-flooding, but we believe it constitutes strong evidence that strong-flooding is false.

5   Our Succinct Randomized Encoding Construction

Let (SampCRSGen, LWEGen, Expand) be a succinct LWE sampler (Definition 5) with parameters to be determined later.

We now describe our SRE for the family $\mathcal{F}_{\ell,N,t} = \{f : \{0,1\}^\ell \to \{0,1\}^N\}$ of depth-t circuits. Let q be a modulus and $\overline{\chi}$ be a $\overline{B}$-bounded distribution to be determined later.

Let $g(t) = \mathcal{O}(t)$ be the function defined in Definition 3.

- CRSGen$(1^\lambda, \mathcal{F}_{\ell,N,t})$: Output crs $\leftarrow$ SampCRSGen$(1^\lambda, 1^N, N^{g(t)})$. It in particular includes parameters params $= (q, M, K, \overline{\chi}, \overline{B})$.
- Encode(crs, f, x): Compute $(\text{seed}_{\mathbf{B}^*}, \mathbf{A}^*, \mathbf{S}^*) \leftarrow \text{LWEGen}(\text{crs})$, where $\mathbf{A}^* \in \mathbb{Z}_q^{M \times W}, \mathbf{S}^* \in \mathbb{Z}_q^{W \times K}$.
  Sample $\mathbf{R} \leftarrow \{0,1\}^{W \times \ell M \log q}$, and $\mathbf{E} \leftarrow \overline{\chi}^{M \times \ell M \log q}$. Compute

$$\mathbf{C} = \mathbf{A}^*\mathbf{R} + x \otimes \mathbf{G} + \mathbf{E} \in \mathbb{Z}_q^{M \times \ell M \log q},$$

where we view $x \in \{0,1\}^{1 \times \ell}$ as a row vector, and compute $(\mathbf{R}_{f,x}, \mathbf{E}_{f,x}) = \text{Eval}_{\text{open}}(f, \mathbf{A}^*, x, \mathbf{R}, \mathbf{E})$.
  Output:

$$C = (\text{seed}_{\mathbf{B}^*}, \mathbf{C}, \mathbf{A}^*, (\mathbf{R}_{f,x} + \mathbf{S}^*)).$$

- Decode$(\text{crs}, C, f))$: On input $C = (\text{seed}_{\mathbf{B}^*}, \mathbf{C}, \mathbf{A}^*, \mathbf{V})$, compute $\mathbf{C}_f = \text{Eval}(f, \mathbf{C})$, and $\mathbf{B}^* = \text{Expand}(\text{crs}, \text{seed}_{\mathbf{B}^*})$. Output

$$f(x) = \text{Round}_{q/2}\left(\mathbf{C}_f + \mathbf{B}^* - \mathbf{A}^* \cdot \mathbf{V}\right) \in \{0,1\}^{M \times K}.$$

Theorem 4. *Suppose* (SampCRSGen, LWEGen, Expand) *is a succinct LWE sampler satisfying δ-succinctness and β_0-flooding (Definition 5) with $\beta_0 = \overline{B} \cdot N^{g(t)}$. Suppose furthermore that:*

$$M^2 = N^\delta \cdot \text{poly}(\lambda, \ell, t).$$

Then (CRSGen, Encode, Decode) *is an SRE for $\mathcal{F}_{\ell,N,t}$ satisfying δ-succinctness.*

Next, we show that the construction above satisfies correctness and succinctness.

Claim 3 (Correctness). *Suppose* (SampCRSGen, LWEGen, Expand) *satisfy the parameters constraints and correctness Definition 5. Then* (CRSGen, Encode, Decode) *is correct.*

Proof. Define $\mathbf{V} = (\mathbf{R}_{f,x} + \mathbf{S}^*)$. By Definition 3, we have

$$\mathbf{C}_f + \mathbf{B}^* - \mathbf{A}^* \cdot (\mathbf{R}_{f,x} + \mathbf{S}^*) = f(x) \cdot q/2 + \mathbf{E}_{f,x} + \mathbf{E}^*.$$

Let $\beta_0 = \overline{B} \cdot N^{g(t)}$. The setting of parameters β, $\overline{B}$ and q from (SampCRSGen, LWEGen, Expand) imply $\|\mathbf{E}\| \leq \overline{B}$ and therefore $\|\mathbf{E}_{f,x}\| \leq \overline{B}M^{g(t)} \leq N^{g(t)} = \beta_0$ by definition of g (Definition 3), and using $M \leq N$. Furthremore $\beta \geq \beta_0 \cdot 2^\lambda$ and $q \geq 8\beta$ so that $\|\mathbf{E}_{f,x} + \mathbf{E}^*\| < q/4$, and therefore

$$\mathsf{Round}_{q/2}\left(\mathbf{C}_f + \mathbf{B}^* - \mathbf{A}^* \cdot \mathbf{V}\right) = \mathsf{Round}_{q/2}\left(f(x) \cdot q/2 + \mathbf{E}_{f,x} + \mathbf{E}^*\right) = f(x).$$

Claim 4. *Suppose the sampler* (SampCRSGen, LWEGen, Expand) *is δ-succinct (Definition 5), and suppose that the sampler furthermore satisfies*

$$M^2 = N^\delta \cdot \mathrm{poly}(\lambda, \ell, t).$$

Then (CRSGen, Encode, Decode) *is δ-succinct.*

Proof. The setting of the parameters implies $\log q = \mathrm{poly}(\lambda, t)$. Then $\ell M^2 \log^2 q = N^\delta \cdot \mathrm{poly}(\lambda, \ell, t)$.

Furthermore $\mathbf{V} = (\mathbf{R}_{f,x} + \mathbf{S}^*) \in \mathbb{Z}_q^{W \times K}$ and therefore bitlength(seed$_{\mathbf{B}^*}$, $\mathbf{C}$, $\mathbf{A}^*$, $\mathbf{V}$) $\leq N^\delta \cdot \mathrm{poly}(\lambda, \ell, t)$ by δ-succinctness of (SampCRSGen, LWEGen, Expand). Therefore the SRE is δ-succinct.

5.1 Security

Claim 5 (Indistinguishability-based security.). *Let $f : \{0,1\}^\ell \to \{0,1\}^N$ of depth t, and $x_0, x_1 \in \{0,1\}^\ell$ such that $f(x_0) = f(x_1)$. Suppose* (SampCRSGen, LWEGen, Expand) *is secure (Definition 5), and LWE hold. Then:*

$$(\mathsf{crs}, \mathsf{Encode}(\mathsf{crs}, f, x_0)) \approx_c (\mathsf{crs}, \mathsf{Encode}(\mathsf{crs}, f, x_1)),$$

where $\mathsf{crs} \leftarrow \mathsf{CRSGen}(1^\lambda, \mathcal{F}_{\ell, N, t})$.

We refer to the full version for a proof of Claim 5. Combining Theorem 4 with our candidate succinct LWE sampler (Sects. 4.1 and 4.3), noting that our proposed parameters in Sect. 4.3 satisfy $M^2 = N^\delta \cdot \mathrm{poly}(\lambda, \ell, t)$, gives a candidate SRE. Invoking Theorem 2, we obtain the following.

Corollary 2. *Assuming Conjecture 1 and sub-exponential LWE, there exists an iO scheme.*

We can furthermore use Theorem 3 to relax the requirement on our candidate succinct LWE sampler (Sect. 4.1), and only rely on weak security Definition 6), thus obtaining the following.

Corollary 3. *Assuming Conjecture 2 and sub-exponential LWE, there exists an iO scheme.*

Acknowledgements. We thank Pravesh Kothari for his pointers to and conversations about the literature on SOS and low-degree polynomial attacks. LD and VV were supported by DARPA under Agreement No. HR00112020023, a grant from the MIT-IBM Watson AI, a grant from Analog Devices, a Microsoft Trustworthy AI grant, and a DARPA Young Faculty Award. WQ completed part of this work during an internship at NTT Research. DW was supported by NSF grant CNS-1750795, CNS-2055510, and the Alfred P. Sloan Research Fellowship.

References

[Agr19] Agrawal, S.: Indistinguishability obfuscation without multilinear maps: new methods for bootstrapping and instantiation. In: Ishai, Y., Rijmen, V. (eds.) EUROCRYPT 2019, Part I. LNCS, vol. 11476, pp. 191–225. Springer, Cham (2019). https://doi.org/10.1007/978-3-030-17653-2_7

[AJ15] Ananth, P., Jain, A.: Indistinguishability obfuscation from compact functional encryption. In: Gennaro, R., Robshaw, M. (eds.) CRYPTO 2015, Part I. LNCS, vol. 9215, pp. 308–326. Springer, Heidelberg (2015). https://doi.org/10.1007/978-3-662-47989-6_15

[AJL+12] Asharov, G., Jain, A., López-Alt, A., Tromer, E., Vaikuntanathan, V., Wichs, D.: Multiparty computation with low communication, computation and interaction via threshold FHE. In: Pointcheval, D., Johansson, T. (eds.) EUROCRYPT 2012. LNCS, vol. 7237, pp. 483–501. Springer, Heidelberg (2012). https://doi.org/10.1007/978-3-642-29011-4_29

[AJL+19] Ananth, P., Jain, A., Lin, H., Matt, C., Sahai, A.: Indistinguishability obfuscation without multilinear maps: new paradigms via low degree weak pseudorandomness and security amplification. In: Boldyreva, A., Micciancio, D. (eds.) CRYPTO 2019, Part III. LNCS, vol. 11694, pp. 284–332. Springer, Cham (2019). https://doi.org/10.1007/978-3-030-26954-8_10

[AP14] Alperin-Sheriff, J., Peikert, C.: Faster bootstrapping with polynomial error. In: Garay, J.A., Gennaro, R. (eds.) CRYPTO 2014, Part I. LNCS, vol. 8616, pp. 297–314. Springer, Heidelberg (2014). https://doi.org/10.1007/978-3-662-44371-2_17

[AP20] Agrawal, S., Pellet-Mary, A.: Indistinguishability obfuscation without maps: attacks and fixes for noisy linear FE. In: Canteaut, A., Ishai, Y. (eds.) EUROCRYPT 2020, Part I. LNCS, vol. 12105, pp. 110–140. Springer, Cham (2020). https://doi.org/10.1007/978-3-030-45721-1_5

[AR17] Agrawal, S., Rosen, A.: Functional encryption for bounded collusions, revisited. In: Kalai, Y., Reyzin, L. (eds.) TCC 2017, Part I. LNCS, vol. 10677, pp. 173–205. Springer, Cham (2017). https://doi.org/10.1007/978-3-319-70500-2_7

[BCG+18] Bitansky, N., et al.: Indistinguishability obfuscation for RAM programs and succinct randomized encodings. SIAM J. Comput. **47**(3), 1123–1210 (2018)

[BDGM19] Brakerski, Z., Döttling, N., Garg, S., Malavolta, G.: Leveraging linear decryption: rate-1 fully-homomorphic encryption and time-lock puzzles. In: Hofheinz, D., Rosen, A. (eds.) TCC 2019, Part II. LNCS, vol. 11892, pp. 407–437. Springer, Cham (2019). https://doi.org/10.1007/978-3-030-36033-7_16

[BDGM20a] Brakerski, Z., Döttling, N., Garg, S., Malavolta, G.: Candidate iO from homomorphic encryption schemes. In: Canteaut, A., Ishai, Y. (eds.) EUROCRYPT 2020, Part I. LNCS, vol. 12105, pp. 79–109. Springer, Cham (2020). https://doi.org/10.1007/978-3-030-45721-1_4

[BDGM20b] Brakerski, Z., Döttling, N., Garg, S., Malavolta, G.: Factoring and pairings are not necessary for iO: circular-secure LWE suffices. Cryptology ePrint Archive, Report 2020/1024 (2020)

[BGI+01] Barak, B., et al.: On the (im)possibility of obfuscating programs. In: Kilian, J. (ed.) CRYPTO 2001. LNCS, vol. 2139, pp. 1–18. Springer, Heidelberg (2001). https://doi.org/10.1007/3-540-44647-8_1

[BGL+15] Bitansky, N., Garg, S., Lin, H., Pass, R., Telang, S.: Succinct randomized encodings and their applications. In: Servedio, R.A., Rubinfeld, R. (eds.) 47th ACM STOC, pp. 439–448. ACM Press, June 2015

[BHJ+19] Barak, B., Hopkins, S.B., Jain, A., Kothari, P., Sahai, A.: Sum-of-squares meets program obfuscation, revisited. In: Ishai, Y., Rijmen, V. (eds.) EUROCRYPT 2019, Part I. LNCS, vol. 11476, pp. 226–250. Springer, Cham (2019). https://doi.org/10.1007/978-3-030-17653-2_8

[BTVW17] Brakerski, Z., Tsabary, R., Vaikuntanathan, V., Wee, H.: Private constrained PRFs (and more) from LWE. In: Kalai, Y., Reyzin, L. (eds.) TCC 2017, Part I. LNCS, vol. 10677, pp. 264–302. Springer, Cham (2017). https://doi.org/10.1007/978-3-319-70500-2_10

[BV11] Brakerski, Z., Vaikuntanathan, V.: Efficient fully homomorphic encryption from (standard) LWE. In: Ostrovsky, R. (ed.) 52nd FOCS, pp. 97–106. IEEE Computer Society Press, October 2011

[BV15] Bitansky, N., Vaikuntanathan, V.: Indistinguishability obfuscation from functional encryption. In: Guruswami, V. (ed.) 56th FOCS, pp. 171–190. IEEE Computer Society Press, October 2015

[CHVW19] Chen, Y., Hhan, M., Vaikuntanathan, V., Wee, H.: Matrix PRFs: constructions, attacks, and applications to obfuscation. In: Hofheinz, D., Rosen, A. (eds.) TCC 2019, Part I. LNCS, vol. 11891, pp. 55–80. Springer, Cham (2019). https://doi.org/10.1007/978-3-030-36030-6_3

[GGH+13] Garg, S., Gentry, C., Halevi, S., Raykova, M., Sahai, A., Waters, B.: Candidate indistinguishability obfuscation and functional encryption for all circuits. In: 54th FOCS, pp. 40–49. IEEE Computer Society Press, October 2013

[GH19] Gentry, C., Halevi, S.: Compressible FHE with applications to PIR. In: Hofheinz, D., Rosen, A. (eds.) TCC 2019, Part II. LNCS, vol. 11892, pp. 438–464. Springer, Cham (2019). https://doi.org/10.1007/978-3-030-36033-7_17

[GP21] Gay, R., Pass, R.: Indistinguishability obfuscation from circular security. In: STOC (2021)

[GR07] Goldwasser, S., Rothblum, G.N.: On best-possible obfuscation. In: Vadhan, S.P. (ed.) TCC 2007. LNCS, vol. 4392, pp. 194–213. Springer, Heidelberg (2007). https://doi.org/10.1007/978-3-540-70936-7_11

[GSW13] Gentry, C., Sahai, A., Waters, B.: Homomorphic encryption from learning with errors: conceptually-simpler, asymptotically-faster, attribute-based. In: Canetti, R., Garay, J.A. (eds.) CRYPTO 2013, Part I. LNCS, vol. 8042, pp. 75–92. Springer, Heidelberg (2013). https://doi.org/10.1007/978-3-642-40041-4_5

[GVW15] Gorbunov, S., Vaikuntanathan, V., Wichs, D.: Leveled fully homomorphic signatures from standard lattices. In: Servedio, R.A., Rubinfeld, R., (eds.) 47th ACM STOC, pp. 469–477. ACM Press, June 2015

[HJL21] Hopkins, S., Jain, A., Lin, H.: Counterexamples to new circular security assumptions underlying iO. In: Malkin, T., Peikert, C. (eds.) CRYPTO 2021, Part II. LNCS, vol. 12826, pp. 673–700. Springer, Cham (2021). https://doi.org/10.1007/978-3-030-84245-1_23

[JLMS19] Jain, A., Lin, H., Matt, C., Sahai, A.: How to leverage hardness of constant-degree expanding polynomials over $\mathbb{R}$ to build $i\mathcal{O}$. In: Ishai, Y., Rijmen, V. (eds.) EUROCRYPT 2019, Part I. LNCS, vol. 11476, pp. 251–281. Springer, Cham (2019). https://doi.org/10.1007/978-3-030-17653-2_9

[JLS21] Jain, A., Lin, H., Sahai, A.: Indistinguishability obfuscation from well-founded assumptions. In: STOC (2021)

[Kil88] Kilian, J.: Founding cryptography on oblivious transfer. In: 20th ACM STOC, pp. 20–31. ACM Press, May 1988

[Kos20] Kosov, E.: Distributions of polynomials in Gaussian random variables under structural constraints (2020)

[LPST16] Lin, H., Pass, R., Seth, K., Telang, S.: Indistinguishability obfuscation with non-trivial efficiency. In: Cheng, C.-M., Chung, K.-M., Persiano, G., Yang, B.-Y. (eds.) PKC 2016, Part II. LNCS, vol. 9615, pp. 447–462. Springer, Heidelberg (2016). https://doi.org/10.1007/978-3-662-49387-8_17

[MP12] Micciancio, D., Peikert, C.: Trapdoors for lattices: simpler, tighter, faster, smaller. In: Pointcheval, D., Johansson, T. (eds.) EUROCRYPT 2012. LNCS, vol. 7237, pp. 700–718. Springer, Heidelberg (2012). https://doi.org/10.1007/978-3-642-29011-4_41

[MW16] Mukherjee, P., Wichs, D.: Two round multiparty computation via multi-key FHE. In: Fischlin, M., Coron, J.-S. (eds.) EUROCRYPT 2016, Part II. LNCS, vol. 9666, pp. 735–763. Springer, Heidelberg (2016). https://doi.org/10.1007/978-3-662-49896-5_26

[Pei09] Peikert, C.: Public-key cryptosystems from the worst-case shortest vector problem: extended abstract. In: Mitzenmacher, M. (ed.) 41st ACM STOC, pp. 333–342. ACM Press, May/June 2009

[PS19] Peikert, C., Shiehian, S.: Noninteractive zero knowledge for NP from (plain) learning with errors. In: Boldyreva, A., Micciancio, D. (eds.) CRYPTO 2019, Part I. LNCS, vol. 11692, pp. 89–114. Springer, Cham (2019). https://doi.org/10.1007/978-3-030-26948-7_4

[PVW08] Peikert, C., Vaikuntanathan, V., Waters, B.: A framework for efficient and composable oblivious transfer. In: Wagner, D. (ed.) CRYPTO 2008. LNCS, vol. 5157, pp. 554–571. Springer, Heidelberg (2008). https://doi.org/10.1007/978-3-540-85174-5_31

[Reg05] Regev, O.: On lattices, learning with errors, random linear codes, and cryptography. In: Gabow, H.N., Fagin, R. (eds.) 37th ACM STOC, pp. 84–93. ACM Press, May 2005

[WW21] Wee, H., Wichs, D.: Candidate obfuscation via oblivious LWE sampling. In: Canteaut, A., Standaert, F.-X. (eds.) EUROCRYPT 2021, Part III. LNCS, vol. 12698, pp. 127–156. Springer, Cham (2021). https://doi.org/10.1007/978-3-030-77883-5_5

ABE for DFA from LWE Against Bounded Collusions, Revisited

Hoeteck Wee[✉]

NTT Research, Sunnyvale, CA, USA
wee@di.ens.fr

Abstract. We present a new public-key ABE for DFA based on the LWE assumption, achieving security against collusions of a-priori bounded size. Our scheme achieves ciphertext size $\tilde{O}(\ell + B)$ for attributes of length ℓ and collusion size B. Prior LWE-based schemes has either larger ciphertext size $\tilde{O}(\ell \cdot B)$, or are limited to the secret-key setting. Along the way, we introduce a new technique for lattice trapdoor sampling, which we believe would be of independent interest. Finally, we present a simple candidate public-key ABE for DFA for the unbounded collusion setting.

1 Introduction

Attribute-based encryption (ABE) [19,24] is a generalization of public-key encryption to support fine-grained access control for encrypted data. Here, ciphertexts are associated with a description value x and keys with a policy M, and decryption is possible when $M(x) = 1$. One important class of policies we would like to support are those specified using deterministic finite automata (DFA). Such policies capture many real-world applications involving simple computation on data of unbounded size, such as network monitoring and logging, pattern matching in gene sequences, and processing tax returns. Since the seminal work of Waters [26] introducing ABE for DFA and providing the first instantiation from pairings, substantial progress has been made in the study of pairing-based ABE for DFA [2,4,7,8,13], culminating in adaptively secure public-key ABE for DFA against unbounded collusions based on the k-Lin assumption [14,21].

In this work, we look at ABE for DFA based on the LWE assumption, which has seen fairly limited progress in spite of the exciting progress we have made in obtaining expressive ABE for circuits [9,16]. Here, the state of the art is as follows:

- a public-key scheme secure against collusions of a-prior bounded size (that is, the adversary gets to see a bounded number of secret keys), by combining the scheme of Agrawal and Singh [5] –henceforth AS17– for collusions of size one with generic amplification techniques for bounded collusions in [6,15,20];
- a secret-key scheme for DFA (and NFA) secure against unbounded collusions [3].

Henceforth, we focus on the setting studied in AS17, namely public-key ABE for DFA secure against bounded collusions (indeed, most of the ABE literature consider the public-key setting). From a practical stand-point, the bounded collusion setting already captures a fairly realistic attack scenario. From a

K. Nissim and B. Waters (Eds.): TCC 2021, LNCS 13043, pp. 288–309, 2021.
https://doi.org/10.1007/978-3-030-90453-1_10

reference	hardness	|ct|	|sk|	remarks
AS17 [5]	$\lambda^{\mathsf{poly}(\log \lambda)}$	$B\ell$	Q	extends to FE
AMY19 [3]	$\lambda^{\mathsf{poly}(\log \lambda)}$	$\mathsf{poly}(\ell)$	$\mathsf{poly}(Q)$	secret-key, unbounded B
this work	$\lambda^{\omega(1)}$	$\ell + B$	Q	

Fig. 1. Summary of LWE-based ABE schemes for DFA, secure against collusions of size B (cf. Sect. 2.1). In the table, Q is the number of states in the DFA M associated with sk and ℓ is the length of x associated with ct, and $Q, \ell < \lambda^{\omega(1)}$. Hardness refers to the modulus-to-noise ratio for the LWE assumption, for $\lambda^{\omega(1)}$-security and $\lambda^{-\omega(1)}$ decryption error. We ignore factors polynomial in the security parameter λ, $|\Sigma|$, and $\log \ell$.

theoretical stand-point, it often already requires interesting and insightful techniques. In particular, the core technical novelty in the recent works on ABE for DFA from k-Lin [13,14,21] –both in the selective and the adaptive settings– lies in solving the problem in the one-collusion setting; amplification to unbounded collusions is achieved via the dual system encryption methodology [7,25,27], which unfortunately, we do not know how to instantiate from LWE.

1.1 Our Contributions

Our main result is a new public-key ABE for DFA based on the LWE assumption, in the bounded collusion setting:

- Our scheme achieves ciphertext size $\tilde{O}(\ell + B)$ for attributes of length ℓ and collusion size B and only requires a $\lambda^{\omega(1)}$ modulus-to-noise ratio, whereas the AS17 scheme achieves ciphertext size $\tilde{O}(\ell \cdot B)$ and requires a larger $\lambda^{\mathsf{poly}(\log \lambda)}$ modulus-to-noise ratio; see Fig. 1 for a comparison.
- As in AS17, our scheme achieves sk-selective security, where all the key queries are made before the adversary sees the public key or the ciphertext.

Our construction and its analysis are inspired by the pairing-based ABE for DFA in [13,14,26,26], and is simpler than prior LWE-based schemes in [3,5] in that we do not require an ABE for circuits [9,16] as an intermediate building block. Our construction is very algebraic and entails the use of multiple LWE secrets in the ABE ciphertext, whereas the prior LWE-based schemes are more combinatorial. Along the way, we introduce a new technique for lattice trapdoor sampling, which we believe to be of independent interest. Finally, we present a simple candidate public-key ABE for DFA for the unbounded collusion setting (no such heuristic post-quantum candidate was known before, without assuming post-quantum iO).

ABE for DFA. Our ABE scheme follows the high-level structure of the pairing-based schemes in [13,26]:

- encryption of $x \in \{0,1\}^\ell$ picks $\ell + 1$ fresh LWE secrets $\mathbf{s}_0, \mathbf{s}_1, \ldots, \mathbf{s}_\ell$ (row vectors);
- a secret key for a DFA with Q states is associated with Q random row vectors $\tilde{\mathbf{d}}_1, \ldots, \tilde{\mathbf{d}}_Q$;

– during decryption, we compute $\mathbf{s}_i \tilde{\mathbf{d}}_{u_i}^\top$ (approximately), where u_i denotes the state reached upon the first i bits of x, for $i = 0, 1, \ldots, \ell$ (i.e., u_0 is the DFA start state).

In a bit more detail,

– the master public key specifies a pair of matrices $\mathbf{A}_0, \mathbf{A}_1$ as well as $\tilde{\mathbf{d}}_{u_0}^\top$;
– the ciphertext contains $\mathbf{s}_0 \tilde{\mathbf{d}}_{u_0}^\top$ and $\mathbf{c}_i \approx (\mathbf{s}_{i-1} \| - \mathbf{s}_i) \mathbf{A}_{x_i}$, $i = 1, \ldots, \ell$;
– the secret key contains $\mathbf{k}_{u,\sigma}^\top \leftarrow \mathbf{A}_\sigma^{-1} \binom{\tilde{\mathbf{d}}_u^\top}{\tilde{\mathbf{d}}_v^\top}$ for all state transitions $(u, \sigma) \in [Q] \times \{0, 1\} \mapsto v \in [Q]$, where $\mathbf{A}_\sigma^{-1}(\cdot)$ denotes a Gaussian pre-image;
– in order to compute $\mathbf{s}_i \tilde{\mathbf{d}}_{u_i}^\top$, it suffices to compute the successive differences $\mathbf{s}_{i-1} \tilde{\mathbf{d}}_{u_{i-1}}^\top - \mathbf{s}_i \tilde{\mathbf{d}}_{u_i}^\top$ as follows[1]:

$$\mathbf{c}_i \cdot \mathbf{k}_{u_i, x_i}^\top \approx (\mathbf{s}_{i-1} \| - \mathbf{s}_i) \mathbf{A}_{x_i} \cdot \mathbf{A}_{x_i}^{-1} \binom{\tilde{\mathbf{d}}_{u_{i-1}}^\top}{\tilde{\mathbf{d}}_{u_i}^\top} = \mathbf{s}_{i-1} \tilde{\mathbf{d}}_{u_{i-1}}^\top - \mathbf{s}_i \tilde{\mathbf{d}}_{u_i}^\top$$

In the proof of security, we will modify the ciphertext distribution in a way that traces the DFA computation path while keeping the secret key distribution unchanged. In contrast, prior ABE for DFA based on k-Lin modifies both the ciphertext and secret key distribution in the security proof (even for collusions of size one). Our proof strategy requires knowing the DFA while simulating the challenge ciphertext, and for that reason, we only achieve sk-selective security.

Lattice Trapdoor Sampling. We introduce a new lattice trapdoor notion and sampling technique for our proof of security. Given a wide LWE matrix $\mathbf{A}$, the Micciancio-Peikert (MP) trapdoor [22] is a low-norm matrix $\mathbf{T}$ such that $\mathbf{A} \cdot \mathbf{T} = \mathbf{G}$, where $\mathbf{G}$ is the gadget matrix. Such a matrix $\mathbf{T}$ allows us to sample a random Gaussian preimage $\mathbf{A}^{-1}(\mathbf{z})$ for all $\mathbf{z}$, but it also breaks the LWE assumption with respect to $\mathbf{A}$ (in fact, we can use $\mathbf{T}$ to recover $\mathbf{s}$ given $\mathbf{sA} + \mathbf{e}$).

In this work, we consider a "half trapdoor", namely a low-norm matrix $\mathbf{T}_{1/2}$ such that

$$\mathbf{A} \cdot \mathbf{T}_{1/2} = \binom{\mathbf{0}}{\mathbf{G}}, \quad \mathbf{A} \in \mathbb{Z}_q^{2n \times m}, \mathbf{T}_{1/2} \in \mathbb{Z}^{m \times n \log q}, \mathbf{G} \in \mathbb{Z}_q^{n \times n \log q}, m > 2n \log q$$

That is, let $\overline{\mathbf{A}}, \underline{\mathbf{A}} \in \mathbb{Z}_q^{n \times m}$ denote the top and bottom halves of $\mathbf{A}$. Then, $\overline{\mathbf{A}} \cdot \mathbf{T}_{1/2} = \mathbf{0}$ and $\underline{\mathbf{A}} \cdot \mathbf{T}_{1/2} = \mathbf{G}$, which means $\mathbf{T}_{1/2}$ is a MP trapdoor for $\underline{\mathbf{A}}$. We show that $\mathbf{T}_{1/2}$ satisfies the following properties:

---

[1] To facilitate comparison with Waters' pairing-based scheme, we note that the terms corresponding to $\mathbf{c}_i$ and $\mathbf{k}_{u,\sigma}$ there-in are given by:

$$(g_1^{s_{i-1}}, g_1^{s_{i-1}z + s_i w_{x_i}}, g_1^{s_i}), \quad (g_2^{-\tilde{d}_u + zr}, g_2^r, g_2^{-\tilde{d}_v + w_\sigma r})$$

where g_1, g_2 are the respective generators the group $\mathbb{G}_1, \mathbb{G}_2$ in a bilinear group $e : \mathbb{G}_1 \times \mathbb{G}_2 \to \mathbb{G}_T$. We can then compute a pairing-product over these terms to derive $e(g_1, g_2)^{s_{i-1}\tilde{d}_{u_{i-1}} - s_i \tilde{d}_{u_i}}$.

– restricted trapdoor sampling: Given $\mathbf{Z} \in \mathbb{Z}_q^{n \times Q}, \mathbf{M} \in \{0,1\}^{Q \times Q}$, we can efficiently sample (using $\mathbf{A}, \mathbf{T}_{1/2}$) a random Gaussian pre-image

$$\mathbf{A}^{-1}\begin{pmatrix} \mathbf{D} \\ \mathbf{DM} + \mathbf{Z} \end{pmatrix}, \text{ for random } \mathbf{D} \leftarrow \mathbb{Z}_q^{n \times Q} \tag{1}$$

These Gaussian pre-images appear in the secret keys with $\mathbf{D} = [\tilde{\mathbf{d}}_1^\top \mid \cdots \mid \tilde{\mathbf{d}}_Q^\top]$, $\mathbf{M} \in \{0,1\}^{Q \times Q}$ being a DFA transition matrix, and $\mathbf{Z} = \mathbf{0}$.

– LWE given $\mathbf{T}_{1/2}$: We also require computational hardness of the form $(\mathbf{A}, s\overline{\mathbf{A}} + \mathbf{e})$ is pseudorandom given $\mathbf{T}_{1/2}$. However, such a statement is false since $(s\overline{\mathbf{A}} + \mathbf{e}) \cdot \mathbf{T}_{1/2} \approx \mathbf{0}$. Instead, we require that $(\mathbf{A}, s\overline{\mathbf{A}} + \mathbf{e})$ is pseudorandom even if the distinguisher gets adaptive queries to the restricted trapdoor sampling oracle in (1); we refer to this as $\mathbf{T}_{1/2}$-LWE.

As a sanity check for restricted trapdoor sampling, observe that it is easy to sample from each of $\overline{\mathbf{A}}^{-1}(\mathbf{D})$ and $\underline{\mathbf{A}}^{-1}(\mathbf{DM} + \mathbf{Z})$, the latter since $\mathbf{T}_{1/2}$ is a MP-trapdoor for $\underline{\mathbf{A}}$. However, what we need is to sample from the "intersection" of these two distributions. With regards to $\mathbf{T}_{1/2}$-LWE, prior works [10,18] showed that LWE implies $\mathbf{T}_{1/2}$-LWE for the special case where the oracle queries are restricted to $\mathbf{M} = \mathbf{0}$; these in turn generalize a classic result in [12] showing pseudorandomness of $(\mathbf{A}, s\overline{\mathbf{A}} + \mathbf{e})$ given $\overline{\mathbf{A}}^{-1}(\mathbf{D})$ for random $\mathbf{D}$.

1.2 Technical Overview I: $\mathbf{T}_{1/2}$

In the first part of the technical overview, we address the properties of $\mathbf{T}_{1/2}$.

Restricted Trapdoor Sampling. We show how to sample from the distribution in (1) given $\mathbf{T}_{1/2}$. Our sampler combines two ideas:
Step 1. First, we describe how to use $\mathbf{T}_{1/2}$ to sample from a related distribution, namely:

$$\mathbf{A}^{-1}\begin{pmatrix} \mathbf{D} \\ \mathbf{MD} + \mathbf{z} \end{pmatrix}, \text{ for random } \mathbf{D} \leftarrow \mathbb{Z}_q^{n \times Q} \tag{2}$$

where we replaced $\mathbf{DM}, \mathbf{M} \in \{0,1\}^{Q \times Q}$ with $\mathbf{MD}, \mathbf{M} \in \{0,1\}^{n \times n}$. We begin by writing (2) as

$$\mathbf{A}^{-1}\begin{pmatrix} \mathbf{D} \\ \mathbf{MD} + \mathbf{z} \end{pmatrix} \approx_s \begin{pmatrix} \overline{\mathbf{A}} \\ \underline{\mathbf{A}} - \mathbf{M}\overline{\mathbf{A}} \end{pmatrix}^{-1} \begin{pmatrix} \mathbf{D} \\ \mathbf{z} \end{pmatrix} \approx_s (\underline{\mathbf{A}} - \mathbf{M}\overline{\mathbf{A}})^{-1}(\mathbf{Z})$$

where the first $\approx_s$ holds for all $\mathbf{D}$, and the second $\approx_s$ uses the fact that $\mathbf{D}$ is random and a statistical lemma shown in [10,18]. Next, observe that $(\underline{\mathbf{A}} - \mathbf{M}\overline{\mathbf{A}}) \cdot \mathbf{T}_{1/2} = \mathbf{G}$, which means we can use the MP trapdoor sampling algorithm [22] with $\mathbf{T}_{1/2}$ as a trapdoor to sample from the distribution $(\underline{\mathbf{A}} - \mathbf{M}\overline{\mathbf{A}})^{-1}(\mathbf{Z})$.

Step 2. We rely on the vectorization operator $\text{vec}(\cdot)$ for matrices from linear algebra (see Sect. 2) to relate the distributions in (2) and (1). The vectorization of a matrix $\mathbf{Z}$, denoted by $\text{vec}(\mathbf{Z})$, is the column vector obtained by stacking the columns of the matrix $\mathbf{Z}$ on top off one another. Using a standard vectorization identity $\text{vec}(\mathbf{XYZ}) = (\mathbf{Z}^\top \otimes \mathbf{X})\text{vec}(\mathbf{Y})$, we have

$$\text{vec}(\mathbf{DM}) = (\mathbf{M}^\top \otimes \mathbf{I}_n)\text{vec}(\mathbf{D})$$

This basically says that we can sample from the desired distribution in (1) by sampling from the distribution in (2) with $(\mathbf{M}^\top \otimes \mathbf{I}_n)\text{vec}(\mathbf{D})$ in place of $\mathbf{MD}$.

LWE Implies $\mathbf{T}_{1/2}$-LWE. Next, we sketch a proof of the statement LWE implies $\mathbf{T}_{1/2}$-LWE, that is, $(\mathbf{A}, \mathbf{s}\overline{\mathbf{A}} + \mathbf{e})$ is pseudorandom given the restricted trapdoor sampling oracle in (1). In the reduction, we sample $\mathbf{A}$ as

$$\mathbf{A} := \left[\mathbf{A}' \mid \mathbf{A}'\mathbf{R} + \begin{pmatrix} \mathbf{0} \\ \mathbf{G} \end{pmatrix}\right]$$

where $\mathbf{A}' \leftarrow \mathbb{Z}_q^{2n \times (m - n \log q)}, \mathbf{R} \leftarrow \{0,1\}^{(m-n \log q) \times n \log q}$.

- Note that $\mathbf{T}_{1/2} = \begin{pmatrix} -\mathbf{R} \\ \mathbf{I} \end{pmatrix}$ satisfies $\mathbf{A} \cdot \mathbf{T}_{1/2} = \begin{pmatrix} \mathbf{0} \\ \mathbf{G} \end{pmatrix}$. This means that we can use $\mathbf{R}$ to compute $\mathbf{T}_{1/2}$ and to implement the restricted trapdoor sampling oracle in (1).
- By LWE w.r.t. the public matrix $\overline{\mathbf{A}}'$, we have

$$\mathbf{s}\overline{\mathbf{A}} + \mathbf{e} \approx_s (\mathbf{s}\overline{\mathbf{A}}' + \mathbf{e}', (\mathbf{s}\overline{\mathbf{A}}' + \mathbf{e}')\mathbf{R} + \mathbf{e}'') \approx_c (\mathbf{c}, \mathbf{c}\mathbf{R} + \mathbf{e}''), \ \mathbf{c} \leftarrow \mathbb{Z}_q^{m-n \log q}$$

  This holds even if the distinguisher gets $\mathbf{R}$, which we need to implement the oracle.
- Now, observe that the oracle in (1) leaks no information about $\mathbf{R}$ beyond $\overline{\mathbf{A}}'\mathbf{R}$. By the left-over hash lemma, $\mathbf{c}\mathbf{R}$ is statistically random given $\mathbf{c}, \overline{\mathbf{A}}', \overline{\mathbf{A}}'\mathbf{R}$. (A similar argument first appeared in [1].)

1.3   Technical Overview II: ABE for DFA

We proceed to provide a technical overview of our ABE for DFA. In this work, it is convenient to specify a DFA using vector-matrix notation. That is, a DFA M is a tuple $(Q, \Sigma, \{\mathbf{M}_\sigma\}_{\sigma \in \Sigma}, \mathbf{u}_0, \mathbf{f})$ where Σ is the alphabet and

$$Q \in \mathbb{N}; \quad \mathbf{M}_\sigma \in \{0,1\}^{Q \times Q}, \forall \sigma \in \Sigma; \quad \mathbf{u}_0, \mathbf{f} \in \{0,1\}^{1 \times Q}.$$

The DFA accepts an input $x = (x_1, \ldots, x_\ell) \in \Sigma^\ell$, denoted by $M(x) = 1$, if

$$\mathbf{f}\mathbf{M}_{x_\ell} \cdots \mathbf{M}_{x_2}\mathbf{M}_{x_1}\mathbf{u}_0^\top = 1 \tag{3}$$

ABE for $B = 1$. We begin with our ABE scheme for collusions of size one:

$$\mathsf{mpk} = \big(\mathbf{d}_0, \{\mathbf{A}_\sigma\}_{\sigma \in \Sigma}, \mathbf{A}_{\mathrm{end}}, \mathbf{d}_{\mathrm{end}}\big), \ \mathbf{A}_\sigma \leftarrow \mathbb{Z}_q^{2n \times m}, \ \mathbf{A}_{\mathrm{end}} \leftarrow \mathbb{Z}_q^{n \times m} \tag{4}$$

$$\mathsf{ct} = \big(\overbrace{\mathbf{s}_0 \mathbf{d}_0^\top + \mathbf{e}_0}^{c_0}, \ \overbrace{\{\mathbf{s}_{i-1}\overline{\mathbf{A}}_{x_i} - \mathbf{s}_i\underline{\mathbf{A}}_{x_i} + \mathbf{e}_i\}_{i \in [\ell]}}^{c_i}, \ \overbrace{\mathbf{s}_\ell \mathbf{A}_{\mathrm{end}} + \mathbf{e}_{\ell+1}}^{c_{\ell+1}}, \ \overbrace{\mathbf{s}_\ell \mathbf{d}_{\mathrm{end}}^\top + e_{\ell+2} + \mu \cdot \lfloor \tfrac{q}{2} \rfloor}^{c_{\ell+2}}\big)$$

$$\mathsf{sk}_M = \big(\mathbf{K}_{\mathrm{end}}, \{\mathbf{K}_\sigma\}_{\sigma \in \Sigma}\big),$$

where $\mathbf{D} \leftarrow \mathbb{Z}_q^{n \times Q}$ s.t. $\mathbf{D} \cdot \mathbf{u}_0^\top = \mathbf{d}_0$, $\mathbf{K}_{\mathrm{end}} \leftarrow \mathbf{A}_{\mathrm{end}}^{-1}(\mathbf{D} - \mathbf{d}_{\mathrm{end}}^\top \otimes \mathbf{f})$, $\mathbf{K}_\sigma \leftarrow \mathbf{A}_\sigma^{-1}\big(\begin{smallmatrix}\mathbf{D}\\\mathbf{DM}_\sigma\end{smallmatrix}\big)$

In the rest of this overview, we assume $\Sigma = \{0, 1\}$, and mostly ignore the error terms $e_0, \mathbf{e}_i$ for notational simplicity. To see how decryption works, we first let

$$\mathbf{u}_i^\top := \mathbf{M}_{x_i} \cdots \mathbf{M}_{x_2} \mathbf{M}_{x_1} \mathbf{u}_0^\top$$

That is, $\mathbf{u}_i^\top$ is the characteristic vector for the state reached upon reading $x_1, \ldots, x_i$. In addition, let $\mathbf{d}_i^\top := \mathbf{D} \cdot \mathbf{u}_i^\top$ denote the corresponding column in $\mathbf{D}$ (denoted by $\tilde{\mathbf{d}}_{u_i}^\top$ in Sect. 1.1). It is straight-forward (though a little tedious) to verify that

$$- \overbrace{c_0}^{\approx \mathbf{s}_0 \mathbf{d}_0^\top} + \bigg(\sum_{i=1}^\ell \overbrace{\mathbf{c}_i \cdot \mathbf{K}_{x_i} \cdot \mathbf{u}_{i-1}^\top}^{\approx \mathbf{s}_{i-1}\mathbf{d}_{i-1}^\top - \mathbf{s}_i \mathbf{d}_i^\top}\bigg) + \overbrace{\mathbf{c}_{\ell+1} \cdot \mathbf{K}_{\mathrm{end}} \cdot \mathbf{u}_\ell^\top}^{\approx \mathbf{s}_\ell(\mathbf{d}_\ell^\top - M(x)\mathbf{d}_{\mathrm{end}}^\top)} \approx -M(x) \cdot \mathbf{s}_\ell \mathbf{d}_{\mathrm{end}}^\top \tag{5}$$

In particular, whenever $M(x) = 1$, we can recover μ from $\mathbf{c}_{\ell+2}$. Note that the noise growth in (5) grows with ℓ, and since we can only bound ℓ by $\lambda^{\omega(1)}$, we require a $\lambda^{\omega(1)}$ modulus-to-noise ratio for decryption correctness. The security proof additionally uses noise smudging, which also requires a $\lambda^{\omega(1)}$ modulus-to-noise ratio.

Security. The main tool we have for the proof of security is $\mathbf{T}_{1/2}$-LWE, which we want to use to replace $\mathbf{s}_{i-1}\overline{\mathbf{A}}_{x_i}$ in $\mathbf{c}_i$ with random (while relying the oracle for restricted trapdoor sampling to simulate the corresponding secret keys). We cannot do so directly, since each $\mathbf{s}_{i-1}$ also appears in $\mathbf{c}_{i-1}$ (c_0, in the case $i = 1$). To resolve this issue, we start by using (5), which tells us that when $M(x) = 0$ as is the case for unauthorized keys in the proof of security, we have:

$$-c_0 + \bigg(\sum_{i=1}^\ell \mathbf{c}_i \cdot \mathbf{K}_{x_i} \cdot \mathbf{u}_{i-1}^\top\bigg) + \mathbf{c}_{\ell+1} \cdot \mathbf{K}_{\mathrm{end}} \cdot \mathbf{u}_\ell^\top \approx 0$$

This allows us to write c_0 as a function of $\mathbf{c}_1, \ldots, \mathbf{c}_\ell, \mathbf{c}_{\ell+1}$ and $\mathbf{K}_0, \mathbf{K}_1$ from sk_M, thereby "eliminating" $\mathbf{s}_0$ from c_0. (Here, we use the fact that we are in the sk-selective setting.) At this point, we can replace $\mathbf{s}_0 \overline{\mathbf{A}}_{x_1}$ in $\mathbf{c}_1$ with random, and thus $\mathbf{c}_1$ with random. This in "eliminates" $\mathbf{s}_1$ from $\mathbf{c}_1$, upon which we can replace $\mathbf{s}_1 \overline{\mathbf{A}}_{x_2}$ in $\mathbf{c}_2$ and thus $\mathbf{c}_2$ with random. This continues until we have replaced $\mathbf{c}_\ell$ with random. At this point, it suffices to argue that

$$\mathbf{s}_\ell \mathbf{A}_{\mathrm{end}}, \ \mathbf{s}_\ell \mathbf{d}_{\mathrm{end}}^\top + \mu \cdot \lfloor \tfrac{q}{2} \rfloor, \mathbf{K}_{\mathrm{end}}$$

hides μ, which can be handled using fairly standard techniques.

Handling B Collusions. Our basic scheme extends naturally to handle B collusions by sampling a fresh $\mathbf{D}$ per secret key except one important caveat: the encryptor needs to know $\mathbf{d}_0 = \mathbf{D} \cdot \mathbf{u}_0^\top$ in order to compute $\mathbf{s}_0 \mathbf{d}_0$, and for the security proof, we need a fresh $\mathbf{d}_0$ per secret key. To solve this problem, we modify the scheme as follows:

- during set-up, we sample and publish $\mathbf{d}_{0,j}, j \in [B]$ in mpk;
- the encryptor includes $\{\, \mathbf{c}_{0,j} := \mathbf{s}_0 \mathbf{d}_{0,j} \,\}_{j \in [B]}$ in ct, which increases the ciphertext size by an additive factor of $B \cdot \mathsf{poly}(\lambda)$ (independent of ℓ);
- when issuing the j'th key, we sample a random $\mathbf{D}$ such that $\mathbf{D} \cdot \mathbf{u}_0^\top = \mathbf{d}_{0,j}$.

The security proof is similar to that for $B = 1$, except we start by using (5) to rewrite each $\mathbf{c}_{0,j}$ in terms of $\mathbf{c}_1, \ldots, \mathbf{c}_{\ell+1}$.

Candidate ABE for DFA Against Unbounded Collusions. We start with our ABE for $B = 1$ in (4) and make the following modifications:

- replace $\mathbf{d}_0$ in mpk with a random matrix $\mathbf{A}_{\mathsf{st}}$;
- replace $\mathbf{s}_0 \mathbf{d}_0^\top$ in ct with $\mathbf{s}_0 \mathbf{A}_{\mathsf{st}}$;
- add $\mathbf{k}_{\mathsf{st}} \leftarrow \mathbf{A}_{\mathsf{st}}^{-1}(\mathbf{D}\mathbf{u}_0^\top)$ to the secret key, where a fresh random $\mathbf{D} \leftarrow \mathbb{Z}_q^{n \times Q}$ is chosen for each key.

Correctness follows as before, except we first compute $\mathbf{s}_0 \mathbf{d}_0^\top$ using $\mathbf{s}_0 \mathbf{A}_{\mathsf{st}} \cdot \mathbf{k}_{\mathsf{st}}$. We believe that our candidate sheds new insights into both avenues and concrete difficulties for realizing a public-key ABE for DFA against unbounded collusions from LWE.

1.4 Prior Works

We provide a brief overview of prior LWE-based scheme, along with a folklore construction based on general circuits. We will refer to constructions secure against collusions of size 1 as a one-key scheme, and we use $Q_{\max}$ to denote an upper bound on the number of DFA states.

A Folklore Construction via General Circuits. We can get bounded-collusion ABE for DFA by using bounded-collusion ciphertext-policy ABE for circuits; the latter can be constructed based on any semantically secure public-key encryption scheme –and thus LWE with $\mathsf{poly}(\lambda)$ hardness– via garbled circuits [15,23]. Concretely, we encode the DFA M as a bit string of length $O(Q \log Q)$ and the DFA input $x \in \{0,1\}^\ell$ as a circuit of size $O(\ell \cdot Q)$ that on input M, outputs $M(x)$. The main draw-back is that the ciphertext size grows with $Q_{\max}$, which we want to avoid.

The Agrawal-Singh AS17 Scheme. The AS17 scheme is a one-key sk-selective functional encryption (FE) scheme for DFA based on LWE. The construction uses the GKPVZ compact one-key FE cFE for circuits, a symmetric-key encryption scheme SE, and a PRF PRF (the AS17 scheme uses a pairwise-independent hashing instead of a PRF). We sketch a simplified variant of the AS17 scheme in the ABE setting:

- Encryption of $x \in \{0,1\}^\ell$ picks ℓ PRF keys $K_1, \ldots, K_\ell$. During decryption, the decryptor computes $\mathsf{PRF}(K_i, u_i)$ for $i = 1, \ldots, \ell$, where u_i denotes the state reached upon the first i bits of x.
- In order to go from $\mathsf{PRF}(K_i, u_i)$ to $\mathsf{PRF}(K_{i+1}, u_{i+1})$, the decryptor would need to compute

$$\mathsf{SE.Enc}_{\mathsf{PRF}(K_i, u_i)}(\mathsf{PRF}(K_{i+1}, u_{i+1}))$$

  To compute the quantity above, the decryptor first computes $\mathsf{cFE.Enc}$ (x_i, u_i, K_i, K_{i+1}). The ABE secret key then contains cFE secret keys that decrypts the cFE-ciphertext to $\mathsf{SE.Enc}_{\mathsf{PRF}(K_i, u_i)}(\mathsf{PRF}(K_{i+1}, u_{i+1}))$. This requires generating cFE secret keys for circuits of depth $O(\log Q)$, and hence a noise-to-modulus ratio $\lambda^{O(\log Q_{\max})} = \lambda^{\mathsf{poly}(\log \lambda)}$.[2]
- One question remains: how does the decryptor compute $\mathsf{cFE.Enc}(x_i, u_i, K_i, K_{i+1})$? Note that the encryptor cannot compute this quantity because it does not know u_i. The naive solution would be for the encryptor to publish in the ciphertext:

$$\left\{ \mathsf{SE.Enc}_{\mathsf{PRF}(K_i, u)}(\mathsf{cFE.Enc}(x_i, u, K_i, K_{i+1})) : u \in [Q_{\max}] \right\}$$

  However, this would mean that the final ABE ciphertext size grows with $Q_{\max}$ instead of $\log Q_{\max}$. Instead, AS17 shows how to compress the above quantity, using the fact that the cFE ciphertext is "decomposable".

An open problem is whether our techniques extend to functional encryption for DFA, as achieved in AS17.

The Agrawal-Maitra-Yamada AMY19 Scheme. The AMY19 scheme is a private-key ABE for NFA based on LWE; the scheme achieves ct, sk-selective security against unbounded ciphertext queries and against unbounded collusions. The AMY19 scheme uses two special ABE schemes:

(i) a public-key ABE for the relation $M(x) \wedge (|x| \overset{?}{\leq} |M|)$;
(ii) a secret-key ABE for the relation $M(x) \wedge (|x| \overset{?}{>} |M|)$.

These two ABE schemes are constructed using the BGGHNSVV ABE for circuits [9] and using the fact that an NFA M for inputs of length ℓ can be simulated using a circuit of size $O(\ell \cdot |M|)$ and depth $\mathsf{poly}(\log \ell, \log |M|)$. The final ABE scheme for NFA contains BGGHNSVV ciphertexts into both the ciphertexts and the secret keys, and since the BGGHNSVV scheme is sk-selective, the AMY19 scheme is ct, sk-selective.

Prior k-Lin Based Schemes. As mentioned in the first step of our security proof, we essentially embed the DFA computation into the challenge ciphertext. In contrast, prior k-Lin based schemes embed the DFA computation into the secret key, which in turn requires using a computational assumption over the secret key space.

---

[2] It seems plausible (with some considerable changes to the scheme and the proof) that we can replace cFE for depth $O(\log Q)$ circuits with an ABE for branching programs of size $\mathsf{poly}(Q)$. The latter can realized from LWE with a polynomial modulus-to-noise ratio [16, 17].

1.5   Discussion

ABE for DFA and More. In this work, we present new constructions and techniques for LWE-based ABE for DFA, achieving some improvements over prior works of AS17 and AMY19 along the way. Our techniques are largely complementary to those in AS17 and AMY19, and we believe there is much more to be gained by combining the techniques and insights from all three works. We conclude with two open problems:

– Find an attack on our candidate ABE against unbounded collusions. Or, use the candidate as a starting point to design a simple secret-key ABE for DFA against unbounded collusions based on the LWE assumption, possibly by leveraging additional insights from AMY19.
– It seems quite plausible that we can combine our techniques with ideas from [21] to obtain a simple one-collusion ABE for Turing machines M running in time T and space S, where $|\mathsf{ct}| = \mathsf{poly}(\ell) \cdot T \cdot S \cdot 2^S$ and $|\mathsf{sk}| = O(|M|)$. A more interesting problem is to design a simple and algebraic one-collusion ABE for Turing machines running in time T where $|\mathsf{ct}| = \mathsf{poly}(\ell, T)$ and $|\mathsf{sk}| = \mathsf{poly}(|M|)$, as achieved in AS17.

LWE-based ABE with Multiple LWE Secrets. More broadly, we see this work as also taking a first step towards exploring the use of multiple LWE secrets in LWE-based ABE as well as bringing design ideas from more complex pairing-based schemes to the LWE setting. While the use of multiple LWE secrets is implicit also in AS17 and AMY19 (where the ciphertext contains multiple ciphertexts from some existing LWE-based scheme), our construction makes the connection more explicit.

2   Preliminaries

Notations. We use boldface lower case for row vectors (e.g. $\mathbf{r}$) and boldface upper case for matrices (e.g. $\mathbf{R}$). For integral vectors and matrices (i.e., those over $\mathbb{Z}$), we use the notation $|\mathbf{r}|, |\mathbf{R}|$ to denote the maximum absolute value over all the entries. We use $v \leftarrow \mathcal{D}$ to denote a random sample from a distribution $\mathcal{D}$, as well as $v \leftarrow S$ to denote a uniformly random sample from a set S. We use $\approx_s$ and $\approx_c$ as the abbreviation for statistically close and computationally indistinguishable.

Matrix Operations. The vectorization of a matrix $\mathbf{Z}$, denoted by $\mathrm{vec}(\mathbf{Z})$, is the column vector obtained by stacking the columns of the matrix $\mathbf{Z}$ on top off one another. For instance, for the 2×2 matrix $\mathbf{Z} = \begin{pmatrix} a & b \\ c & d \end{pmatrix}$, we have

$$\mathrm{vec}(\mathbf{Z}) = \begin{pmatrix} a \\ c \\ b \\ d \end{pmatrix}$$

We use $\text{vec}^{-1}(\cdot)$ to denote the inverse operator so that $\text{vec}^{-1}(\text{vec}(\mathbf{Z})) = \mathbf{Z}$. For all matrices $\mathbf{X}, \mathbf{Y}, \mathbf{Z}$ of the appropriate dimensions, we have $\text{vec}(\mathbf{XYZ}) = (\mathbf{Z}^\top \otimes \mathbf{X})\text{vec}(\mathbf{Y})$.

The tensor product (Kronecker product) for matrices $\mathbf{A} = (a_{i,j}) \in \mathbb{Z}^{\ell \times m}$, $\mathbf{B} \in \mathbb{Z}^{n \times p}$ is defined as

$$\mathbf{A} \otimes \mathbf{B} = \begin{bmatrix} a_{1,1}\mathbf{B}, & \ldots, & a_{1,m}\mathbf{B} \\ \ldots, & \ldots, & \ldots \\ a_{\ell,1}\mathbf{B}, & \ldots, & a_{\ell,m}\mathbf{B} \end{bmatrix} \in \mathbb{Z}^{\ell n \times mp}.$$

The mixed-product property for tensor product says that

$$(\mathbf{A} \otimes \mathbf{B})(\mathbf{C} \otimes \mathbf{D}) = (\mathbf{AC}) \otimes (\mathbf{BD})$$

DFA. We use $M = (Q, \Sigma, \{\mathbf{M}_\sigma\}_{\sigma \in \Sigma}, \mathbf{u}_0, \mathbf{f})$ to describe deterministic finite automata (DFA for short), where $\mathbf{u}_0, \mathbf{f} \in \{0,1\}^Q, \mathbf{M}_\sigma \in \{0,1\}^{Q \times Q}$, and both $\mathbf{u}_0$ and every column of $\mathbf{M}_\sigma$ contains exactly one 1. For any $x = (x_1, \ldots, x_\ell) \in \Sigma^\ell$, we have:

$$M(x) = \mathbf{f}\mathbf{M}_{x_\ell} \cdots \mathbf{M}_{x_1} \mathbf{u}_0^\top$$

2.1 Attribute-Based Encryption

Syntax. An attribute-based encryption (ABE) scheme for some class $\mathcal{C}$ consists of four algorithms:

Setup$(1^\lambda, \mathcal{C}) \to (\mathsf{mpk}, \mathsf{msk})$. The setup algorithm gets as input the security parameter 1^λ and class description $\mathcal{C}$. It outputs the master public key mpk and the master secret key msk.

Enc$(\mathsf{mpk}, x, \mu) \to \mathsf{ct}_x$. The encryption algorithm gets as input mpk, an input x and a message $\mu \in \{0,1\}$. It outputs a ciphertext ct_x. Note that x is public given ct_x.

KeyGen$(\mathsf{mpk}, \mathsf{msk}, M) \to \mathsf{sk}_M$. The key generation algorithm gets as input mpk, msk and $M \in \mathcal{C}$. It outputs a secret key sk_M. Note that M is public given sk_M.

Dec$(\mathsf{mpk}, \mathsf{sk}_M, \mathsf{ct}_x) \to m$. The decryption algorithm gets as input sk_M and ct_x such that $M(x) = 1$ along with mpk. It outputs a message μ.

Correctness. For all inputs x and M with $M(x) = 1$ and all $\mu \in \{0,1\}$, we require

$$\Pr\left[\mathsf{Dec}(\mathsf{mpk}, \mathsf{sk}_M, \mathsf{ct}_x) = \mu : \begin{array}{l} (\mathsf{mpk}, \mathsf{msk}) \leftarrow \mathsf{Setup}(1^\lambda, \mathcal{C}) \\ \mathsf{sk}_M \leftarrow \mathsf{KeyGen}(\mathsf{mpk}, \mathsf{msk}, M) \\ \mathsf{ct}_x \leftarrow \mathsf{Enc}(\mathsf{mpk}, x, \mu) \end{array} \right] = 1 - \mathrm{negl}(\lambda).$$

Security Definition. For a stateful adversary $\mathcal{A}$, we define the advantage function

$$\mathsf{Adv}^{\mathrm{ABE}}_{\mathcal{A}}(\lambda) := \Pr \left[\beta = \beta' : \begin{array}{l} (\mathsf{mpk}, \mathsf{msk}) \leftarrow \mathsf{Setup}(1^\lambda, \mathcal{C}) \\ \mathcal{A}^{\mathsf{KeyGen}(\mathsf{mpk},\mathsf{msk},\cdot)}(1^\lambda) \\ (x^*, \mu_0, \mu_1) \leftarrow \mathcal{A}(\mathsf{mpk}) \\ \beta \leftarrow \{0,1\}; \ \mathsf{ct}_{x^*} \leftarrow \mathsf{Enc}(\mathsf{mpk}, x^*, \mu_\beta) \\ \beta' \leftarrow \mathcal{A}(\mathsf{ct}_{x^*}) \end{array} \right] - \frac{1}{2}$$

with the restriction that all queries M that $\mathcal{A}$ sent to $\mathsf{KeyGen}(\mathsf{mpk}, \mathsf{msk}, \cdot)$ satisfy $M(x^*) = 0$. An ABE scheme is sk-selectively secure if for all PPT adversaries $\mathcal{A}$, the advantage $\mathsf{Adv}^{\mathrm{ABE}}_{\mathcal{A}}(\lambda)$ is a negligible function in λ. Note that $\mathcal{A}$ only gets oracle access to KeyGen at the beginning of the experiment before it sees mpk. (The security experiment starts with $(\mathsf{mpk}, \mathsf{msk}) \leftarrow \mathsf{Setup}$ to generate the first two inputs to the KeyGen oracle.)

Bounded-Collusion Setting. We say that an ABE scheme is B-bounded secure if Setup gets an additional input 1^B, and the adversary is only allowed to make at most B queries to KeyGen. For simplicity, we focus on tag-based B-bounded security (sometimes referred to as stateful key generation in the literature) where:

- KeyGen takes an additional tag $j \in [B]$ and correctness holds for all $j \in [B]$;
- In the security game, the queries made to KeyGen must correspond to distinct tags.

It is easy to see that we can construct a tag-based B-bounded scheme from any 1-bounded scheme by running B independent copies of the 1-bounded scheme; this incurs a factor B blow-up in $|\mathsf{mpk}|, |\mathsf{ct}|$ while $|\mathsf{sk}|$ remains the same. Furthermore, we can construct a B-bounded scheme from a tag-based $O(B)$-bounded scheme [6,15,20], with an additional $O(\lambda^2 (\log B)^2)$ multiplicative blow-up in $|\mathsf{mpk}|, |\mathsf{ct}|$. We sketch a construction from [20] for removing tags with a bigger blow-up: take a tag-based $O(B^2)$-bounded scheme and generate secret keys for a random tag. Now, if the adversary gets at most B keys, then by a birthday bound, the advantage of the adversary is bounded by $1/4$, and then we can apply hardness amplification to reduce the advantage to negligible.

2.2   Lattices Background

Learning with Errors. Given $n, m, q, \chi \in \mathbb{N}$, the $\mathsf{LWE}_{n,m,q,\chi}$ assumption states that

$$(\mathbf{A}, \mathbf{sA} + \mathbf{e}) \approx_c (\mathbf{A}, \mathbf{c})$$

where

$$\mathbf{A} \leftarrow \mathbb{Z}_q^{n \times m}, \mathbf{s} \leftarrow \mathbb{Z}_q^n, \mathbf{e} \leftarrow \mathcal{D}_{\mathbb{Z}^m, \chi}, \mathbf{c} \leftarrow \mathbb{Z}_q^m$$

Trapdoor and Preimage Sampling. Given any $\mathbf{z} \in \mathbb{Z}_q^n$, $s > 0$, we use $\mathbf{A}^{-1}(\mathbf{z}, s)$ to denote the distribution of a vector $\mathbf{y}$ sampled from $\mathcal{D}_{\mathbb{Z}^m, s}$ conditioned on $\mathbf{Ay} = \mathbf{z}$ (mod q). We sometimes suppress s when the context is clear.

There is a p.p.t. algorithm $\mathsf{TrapGen}(1^n, 1^m, q)$ that, given the modulus $q \geq 2$, dimensions n, m such that $m \geq 2n \log q$, outputs $\mathbf{A} \approx_s U(\mathbb{Z}_q^{n \times m})$ with a trapdoor τ. Moreover, there is a p.p.t. algorithm that for $s \geq 2\sqrt{n \log q}$, given $(\mathbf{A}, \tau) \leftarrow \mathsf{TrapGen}(1^n, 1^m, q)$, $\mathbf{z} \in \mathbb{Z}_q^n$, outputs a sample from $\mathbf{A}^{-1}(\mathbf{z}, s)$.

3 Trapdoor Sampling with $\mathbf{T}_{1/2}$ and a Computational Lemma

We describe our new computational lemma, which we coin the "$\mathbf{T}_{1/2}$-LWE assumption" and which says that LWE holds in the presence of some oracle $\mathcal{O}_\mathbf{A}(\cdot)$. Then, we show that the $\mathbf{T}_{1/2}$-LWE assumption follows from the LWE assumption.

3.1 LWE Implies $\mathbf{T}_{1/2}$-LWE

Theorem 1 ($\mathbf{T}_{1/2}$-LWE assumption). *Fix parameters n, m, q. Under the* $\mathsf{LWE}_{n, m-n \log q, \chi}$ *assumption, we have that*

$$(\mathbf{A}, \mathbf{s}\overline{\mathbf{A}} + \mathbf{e}) \approx_c (\mathbf{A}, \mathbf{c})$$

where

$$\mathbf{A} \leftarrow \mathbb{Z}_q^{2n \times m}, \mathbf{s} \leftarrow \mathbb{Z}_q^n, \mathbf{e} \leftarrow \mathcal{D}_{\mathbb{Z}^m, \hat{\chi}}, \mathbf{c} \leftarrow \mathbb{Z}_q^m, \hat{\chi} = \chi \cdot n^{\omega(1)}$$

and where the distinguisher gets unbounded, adaptive queries to an oracle $\mathcal{O}_\mathbf{A}(\cdot)$ that on input $\mathbf{M} \in \mathbb{Z}_q^{Q \times Q}, \mathbf{Z} \in \mathbb{Z}_q^{n \times Q}$, outputs a sample from

$$\left[\mathbf{A}^{-1}\left(\begin{pmatrix} \mathbf{D} \\ \mathbf{DM} + \mathbf{Z} \end{pmatrix}, s \right) \mid \mathbf{D} \leftarrow \mathbb{Z}_q^{n \times Q} \right]$$

where $s^2 \geq O(m) + \omega(\log mQ + \log n)$.

Proof. We sample $\mathbf{A}$ as

$$\mathbf{A} := \left[\mathbf{A}' \mid \mathbf{A}'\mathbf{R} + \begin{pmatrix} \mathbf{0} \\ \mathbf{G} \end{pmatrix} \right]$$

where $\mathbf{A}' \leftarrow \mathbb{Z}_q^{2n \times (m-n \log q)}, \mathbf{R} \leftarrow \{0, \pm 1\}^{(m-n \log q) \times n \log q}$.[3] Setting $\mathbf{T}_{1/2} := \begin{pmatrix} -\mathbf{R} \\ \mathbf{I} \end{pmatrix}$, we have $\mathbf{A} \cdot \mathbf{T}_{1/2} = \begin{pmatrix} \mathbf{0} \\ \mathbf{G} \end{pmatrix}$. We show in the next section that using $\mathbf{A}, \mathbf{T}_{1/2}$, we can efficiently simulate the oracle $\mathcal{O}_\mathbf{A}$. We can then complete the current proof in two steps:

---

[3] Following [22, Section 5.2], we choose each entry of $\mathbf{R}$ to be 0 with probability $1/2$, and ± 1 each with probability $1/4$. This yields $|\mathbf{R}| = 1$ and $s_1(\mathbf{R}) = O(\sqrt{m})$ w.h.p. Moreover, $(\mathbf{A}, \mathbf{AR}) \approx_s$ uniform.

– By the LWE assumption, we have:

$$(\mathbf{A}', \mathbf{s}\mathbf{A}' + \mathbf{e}') \approx_c (\mathbf{A}', \mathbf{c}')$$

where $\mathbf{c}' \leftarrow \mathbb{Z}_q^{m-n\log q}, \mathbf{e}' \leftarrow \mathcal{D}_{\mathbb{Z}^{m-n\log q}, \chi}$. This means that

$$\mathbf{s}\overline{\mathbf{A}} + \mathbf{e} \approx_s (\mathbf{s}\overline{\mathbf{A}}' + \mathbf{e}' + \mathbf{e}''_0, (\mathbf{s}\overline{\mathbf{A}}' + \mathbf{e}')\mathbf{R} + \mathbf{e}'') \approx_c (\mathbf{c} + \mathbf{e}''_0, \mathbf{c}\mathbf{R} + \mathbf{e}''), \quad \mathbf{c} \leftarrow \mathbb{Z}_q^{m-n\log q}$$

even given $\mathbf{A}, \mathbf{R}$, where the first $\approx_s$ uses noise smudging. We can then use $\mathbf{R}$ to simulate $\mathcal{O}_\mathbf{A}(\cdot)$.
– By left-over hash lemma, we can replace $\mathbf{c}'\mathbf{R}$ with random, even given $(\mathbf{A}', \mathbf{c}', \mathbf{A}'\mathbf{R})$. Here, we crucially rely on the fact that the distribution $\mathcal{O}_\mathbf{A}(\cdot)$ depends only on $\mathbf{A}$ (and thus $\mathbf{A}', \mathbf{A}'\mathbf{R}$) and leaks no additional information about $\mathbf{R}$.

3.2   Trapdoor Sampling with $\mathbf{T}_{1/2}$

Additional Notation. We adopt additional notation from [11]. We use $\eta_\epsilon(\cdot)$ to denote the smoothing parameter of a lattice, and $\Lambda^\perp(\cdot)$ to denote the q-ary kernel lattice. We use $[\![\cdot]\!]$ for probability distributions.

Lemma 1 ([10, Lemma 4.1, 4.2]). *Fix parameters ϵ, s, n, m, q such that $m > 18n\log q$. For all $\mathbf{A} \in \mathbb{Z}_q^{2n\times m}$ satisfying $\mathbf{A} \cdot \{0,1\}^m = \mathbb{Z}_q^{2n}$, and for all $\mathbf{z} \in \mathbb{Z}_q^n$ and $s > \eta_\epsilon(\Lambda^\perp(\mathbf{A}))$, the distributions:*

$$\left[\!\!\left[\mathbf{A}^{-1}\left(\begin{pmatrix} \mathbf{d} \\ \mathbf{z} \end{pmatrix}, s \right) \mid \mathbf{d} \leftarrow \mathbb{Z}_q^n \right]\!\!\right] \quad and \quad \left[\!\!\left[\underline{\mathbf{A}}^{-1}(\mathbf{z}, s) \right]\!\!\right]$$

are 2ϵ-statistically close.

Note that the difference from the notation in [10] in that we switched the roles of $\overline{\mathbf{A}}, \underline{\mathbf{A}}$. Also, the condition in $\mathbf{A}$ as stated in [10] is that $\{ \overline{\mathbf{A}} \cdot \mathbf{x} \mid \mathbf{x} \in \{0,1\}^m \cap \Lambda^\perp(\underline{\mathbf{A}}) \} = \mathbb{Z}_q^n$, which is implied by $\mathbf{A} \cdot \{0,1\}^m = \mathbb{Z}_q^{2n}$.

Theorem 2. *Fix parameters $n, q, m \geq O(n\log q)$. There is an efficient algorithm that on input $\mathbf{A} \in \mathbb{Z}_q^{2n\times m}, \mathbf{T}_{1/2} \in \mathbb{Z}^{m\times n\log q}, \mathbf{M} \in \mathbb{Z}_q^{Q\times Q}, \mathbf{Z} \in \mathbb{Z}_q^{n\times Q}, s \in \mathbb{N}$ such that $\mathbf{A} \cdot \mathbf{T}_{1/2} = \begin{pmatrix} \mathbf{0} \\ \mathbf{G} \end{pmatrix}$, outputs a sample statistically close to the distribution*

$$\left[\!\!\left[\mathbf{A}^{-1}\left(\begin{pmatrix} \mathbf{D} \\ \mathbf{D}\mathbf{M} + \mathbf{Z} \end{pmatrix}, s \right) \mid \mathbf{D} \leftarrow \mathbb{Z}_q^{n\times m} \right]\!\!\right]$$

if the following conditions are satisfied:

$$\mathbf{A} \cdot \{0,1\}^m = \mathbb{Z}_q^{2n}, \quad \lambda_m(\Lambda^\perp(\mathbf{A})) = O(1), \quad s^2 \geq O(1) \cdot s_1(\mathbf{T}_{1/2})^2 + \omega(\log mQ + \log n)$$

As shown in [12], the conditions $\mathbf{A} \cdot \{0,1\}^m = \mathbb{Z}_q^{2n}$ and $\lambda_m(\Lambda^\perp(\mathbf{A})) = O(1)$ are satisfied for all but a $1 - 2q^{-2n}$ fraction of $\mathbf{A}$.

Proof. We start by specifying the algorithm:

Algorithm. Output

$$\mathrm{vec}^{-1}((\mathbf{I}_Q \otimes \underline{\mathbf{A}} - \mathbf{M}^\top \otimes \overline{\mathbf{A}})^{-1}(\mathrm{vec}(\mathbf{Z}), s))$$

where $(\mathbf{I}_Q \otimes \underline{\mathbf{A}} - \mathbf{M}^\top \otimes \overline{\mathbf{A}})^{-1}(\cdot)$ is computed using MP trapdoor sampling [22] with $\mathbf{I}_Q \otimes \mathbf{T}_{1/2}$ as a trapdoor.

The analysis proceeds in three steps:

Step 1. We show that for all $\mathbf{M}, \mathbf{Z}$:

$$\left[\!\!\left[\, \mathrm{vec}\left(\mathbf{A}^{-1}\begin{pmatrix}\mathbf{D} \\ \mathbf{DM} + \mathbf{Z}\end{pmatrix}\right) : \mathbf{D} \leftarrow \mathbb{Z}_q^{n \times Q}\,\right]\!\!\right] \approx_s (\mathbf{I}_Q \otimes \underline{\mathbf{A}} - \mathbf{M}^\top \otimes \overline{\mathbf{A}})^{-1}(\mathrm{vec}(\mathbf{Z}))$$

To show this, first observe that for all $\mathbf{A}, \mathbf{D}, \mathbf{M}, \mathbf{Z}$ and all $\mathbf{K}$, we have:

$$\mathbf{A} \cdot \mathbf{K} = \begin{pmatrix}\mathbf{D} \\ \mathbf{DM} + \mathbf{Z}\end{pmatrix}$$

$$\iff \overline{\mathbf{A}}\mathbf{K} = \mathbf{D}, \quad \underline{\mathbf{A}}\mathbf{K} - \overline{\mathbf{A}}\mathbf{K}\mathbf{M} = \mathbf{Z}$$

$$\iff \begin{pmatrix}\mathbf{I}_Q \otimes \overline{\mathbf{A}} \\ \mathbf{I}_Q \otimes \underline{\mathbf{A}} - \mathbf{M}^\top \otimes \overline{\mathbf{A}}\end{pmatrix} \cdot \mathrm{vec}(\mathbf{K}) = \begin{pmatrix}\mathrm{vec}(\mathbf{D}) \\ \mathrm{vec}(\mathbf{Z})\end{pmatrix}$$

where the second $\iff$ uses

$$\mathrm{vec}(\overline{\mathbf{A}}\mathbf{K}) = (\mathbf{I}_Q \otimes \overline{\mathbf{A}}) \cdot \mathrm{vec}(\mathbf{K}), \;\; \mathrm{vec}(\underline{\mathbf{A}}\mathbf{K}) = (\mathbf{I}_Q \otimes \underline{\mathbf{A}}) \cdot \mathrm{vec}(\mathbf{K}), \;\; \mathrm{vec}(\overline{\mathbf{A}}\mathbf{K}\mathbf{M}) = (\mathbf{M}^\top \otimes \overline{\mathbf{A}}) \cdot \mathrm{vec}(\mathbf{K}).$$

This means that for all $\mathbf{A}, \mathbf{D}, \mathbf{M}, \mathbf{Z}$ and all s, the two distributions

$$\mathrm{vec}\left(\mathbf{A}^{-1}\left(\begin{pmatrix}\mathbf{D} \\ \mathbf{DM} + \mathbf{Z}\end{pmatrix}, s\right)\right) \quad \text{and} \quad \begin{pmatrix}\mathbf{I}_Q \otimes \overline{\mathbf{A}} \\ \mathbf{I}_Q \otimes \underline{\mathbf{A}} - \mathbf{M}^\top \otimes \overline{\mathbf{A}}\end{pmatrix}^{-1}\left(\begin{pmatrix}\mathrm{vec}(\mathbf{D}) \\ \mathrm{vec}(\mathbf{Z})\end{pmatrix}, s\right)$$

are identically distributed.

Applying Lemma 1 to

$$\mathbf{A}' := \begin{pmatrix}\mathbf{I}_Q \otimes \overline{\mathbf{A}} \\ \mathbf{I}_Q \otimes \underline{\mathbf{A}} - \mathbf{M}^\top \otimes \overline{\mathbf{A}}\end{pmatrix}$$

we have

$$\left[\!\!\left[\,\begin{pmatrix}\mathbf{I}_Q \otimes \overline{\mathbf{A}} \\ \mathbf{I}_Q \otimes \underline{\mathbf{A}} - \mathbf{M}^\top \otimes \overline{\mathbf{A}}\end{pmatrix}^{-1}\begin{pmatrix}\mathrm{vec}(\mathbf{D}) \\ \mathrm{vec}(\mathbf{Z})\end{pmatrix} : \mathbf{D} \leftarrow \mathbb{Z}_q^{n \times Q}\,\right]\!\!\right] \approx_s \left[\!\!\left[\,(\mathbf{I}_Q \otimes \underline{\mathbf{A}} - \mathbf{M}^\top \otimes \overline{\mathbf{A}})^{-1}(\mathrm{vec}(\mathbf{Z}))\,\right]\!\!\right]$$

In Step 3, we check that $\mathbf{A}'$ satisfies the conditions for Lemma 1.

Step 2. Observe that

$$(\mathbf{I}_Q \otimes \underline{\mathbf{A}} - \mathbf{M}^\top \otimes \overline{\mathbf{A}}) \cdot (\mathbf{I}_Q \otimes \mathbf{T}_{1/2}) = (\mathbf{I}_Q \otimes \mathbf{G} - \mathbf{M}^\top \otimes \mathbf{0}) = \mathbf{I}_Q \otimes \mathbf{G}$$

which means that we can use $\mathbf{I}_Q \otimes \mathbf{T}_{1/2}$ as a MP-trapdoor to sample from the distribution $(\mathbf{I}_Q \otimes \underline{\mathbf{A}} - \mathbf{M}^\top \otimes \overline{\mathbf{A}})^{-1}(\mathrm{vec}(\mathbf{Z}))$.

Step 3. To complete the analysis, we need to bound $\eta_\epsilon(\mathbf{A}')$ and show that $\mathbf{A}' \cdot \{0,1\}^{mQ} = \mathbb{Z}_q^{2nQ}$ (in order to invoke Lemma 1). Observe that

$$\mathbf{A}' = \begin{pmatrix} \mathbf{I}_Q \otimes \mathbf{I}_n & \mathbf{0} \\ -\mathbf{M}^\top \otimes \mathbf{I}_n & \mathbf{I}_Q \otimes \mathbf{I}_n \end{pmatrix} \begin{pmatrix} \mathbf{I}_Q \otimes \overline{\mathbf{A}} \\ \mathbf{I}_Q \otimes \underline{\mathbf{A}} \end{pmatrix}$$

This means that $\Lambda^\perp(\mathbf{A}') = \Lambda^\perp(\mathbf{I}_Q \otimes \mathbf{A})$, and that we can bound $\eta_\epsilon(\Lambda^\perp(\mathbf{I}_Q \otimes \mathbf{A}))$ using $\lambda_m(\Lambda^\perp(\mathbf{A})) = O(1)$. In addition, we have:

$$\mathbf{A} \cdot \{0,1\}^m = \mathbb{Z}_q^{2n} \;\Rightarrow\; (\mathbf{I}_Q \otimes \mathbf{A}) \cdot \{0,1\}^{mQ} = \mathbb{Z}_q^{2nQ} \;\Rightarrow\; \mathbf{A}' \cdot \{0,1\}^{mQ} = \mathbb{Z}_q^{2nQ}$$

This completes the proof.   □

4   ABE for DFA Against Bounded Collusions

In this section, we present our ABE scheme for DFA against bounded collusions.

4.1   Our Scheme

– Setup$(1^n, \Sigma, 1^B)$: Sample

$$(\mathbf{A}_\sigma, \tau_\sigma) \leftarrow \mathsf{TrapGen}(1^{2n}, 1^m, q),\; \sigma \in \Sigma,\; (\mathbf{A}_{\mathrm{end}}, \tau_{\mathrm{end}}) \leftarrow \mathsf{TrapGen}(1^n, 1^m, q),\; \mathbf{d}_{0,j}, \mathbf{d}_{\mathrm{end}} \leftarrow \mathbb{Z}_q^n, j \in [B]$$

Output

$$\mathsf{mpk} := \big(\{\mathbf{d}_{0,j}\}_{j \in [B]}, \{\mathbf{A}_\sigma\}_{\sigma \in \Sigma}, \mathbf{A}_{\mathrm{end}}, \mathbf{d}_{\mathrm{end}} \big), \quad \mathsf{msk} := \big(\{\tau_\sigma\}_{\sigma \in \Sigma}, \tau_{\mathrm{end}} \big)$$

– Enc$(\mathsf{mpk}, (x_1, \ldots, x_\ell) \in \Sigma^\ell, \mu \in \{0,1\})$. Sample

$$\mathbf{s}_0, \mathbf{s}_1, \ldots, \mathbf{s}_\ell \leftarrow \mathbb{Z}_q^n, \quad e_{0,j}, e_{\ell+2} \leftarrow \mathcal{D}_{\mathbb{Z}, \hat{\chi}},\; j \in [B], \quad \mathbf{e}_1, \ldots, \mathbf{e}_\ell, \mathbf{e}_{\ell+1} \leftarrow \mathcal{D}_{\mathbb{Z}^m, \chi}$$

Output

$$\mathsf{ct} := (\{ \overbrace{\mathbf{s}_0 \mathbf{d}_{0,j}^\top + e_{0,j}}^{c_{0,j}} \}_{j \in [B]}, \{ \overbrace{(\mathbf{s}_{i-1} \overline{\mathbf{A}}_{x_i} - \mathbf{s}_i \underline{\mathbf{A}}_{x_i} + \mathbf{e}_i}^{\mathbf{c}_i} \}_{i \in [\ell]}, \overbrace{\mathbf{s}_\ell \mathbf{A}_{\mathrm{end}} + \mathbf{e}_{\ell+1}}^{\mathbf{c}_{\ell+1}}, \overbrace{\mathbf{s}_\ell \mathbf{d}_{\mathrm{end}}^\top + e_{\ell+2} + \mu \cdot \lfloor \tfrac{q}{2} \rfloor}^{c_{\ell+2}})$$

– KeyGen(msk, M_j, j): Parse $M_j = (Q_j, \Sigma, \{\mathbf{M}_{\sigma,j}\}_{\sigma \in \Sigma}, \mathbf{u}_{0,j}, \mathbf{f}_j)$. Sample

$$\mathbf{D}_j \leftarrow \mathbb{Z}_q^{n \times Q_j} \text{ s.t. } \mathbf{D}_j \cdot \mathbf{u}_{0,j}^\top = \mathbf{d}_{0,j}^\top, \quad \mathbf{K}_{\mathrm{end},j} \leftarrow \mathbf{A}_{\mathrm{end}}^{-1}(\mathbf{D}_j - \mathbf{d}_{\mathrm{end}}^\top \otimes \mathbf{f}_j), \quad \mathbf{K}_{\sigma,j} \leftarrow \mathbf{A}_\sigma^{-1}\begin{pmatrix} \mathbf{D}_j \\ \mathbf{D}_j \mathbf{M}_{\sigma,j} \end{pmatrix}, \sigma \in \Sigma$$

using trapdoors $\tau_{\mathrm{end}}, \{\tau_\sigma\}_{\sigma \in \Sigma}$. Output

$$\mathsf{sk}_{M_j} := \big(\mathbf{K}_{\mathrm{end},j}, \{\mathbf{K}_{\sigma,j}\}_{\sigma \in \Sigma} \big)$$

– Dec$(\mathsf{sk}, \mathsf{ct}, j)$: For $i = 1, \ldots, \ell$, compute $\mathbf{u}_{i,j}^\top := \mathbf{M}_{x_i,j} \cdots \mathbf{M}_{x_1,j} \mathbf{u}_{0,j}^\top$. Output

$$\mathsf{round}_{q/2}\big(c_{0,j} + (\sum_{i=1}^{\ell} \mathbf{c}_i \cdot \mathbf{K}_{x_i,j} \cdot \mathbf{u}_{i-1,j}^\top) + \mathbf{c}_{\ell+1} \cdot \mathbf{K}_{\mathrm{end},j} \cdot \mathbf{u}_{\ell,j}^\top + c_{\ell+2} \big)$$

where $\mathsf{round}_{q/2} : \mathbb{Z}_q \to \{0,1\}$ denotes rounding to the nearest multiple of $q/2$.

Parameters. The Gaussians in $\mathbf{A}_\sigma^{-1}(\cdot)$, $\mathbf{A}_{\mathrm{end}}^{-1}(\cdot)$ have parameters $O(m + \log Q)$. The choice of n, m, q, χ comes from the LWE assumption subject to

$$n = O(\lambda), \quad m = O(n \log q), \quad \hat{\chi} = \chi \cdot (\ell + 1)m \cdot \lambda^{\omega(1)}, \quad q = O((\hat{\chi} + \ell \cdot \chi) \cdot m \cdot (m + \log Q))$$

In particular, this means

$$|\mathsf{ct}| = O((B + \ell)m \log q) = \tilde{O}((B + \ell)), \quad |\mathsf{sk}| = O(|\Sigma|Qm \log q) = \tilde{O}(|\Sigma|Q\lambda)$$

where $\tilde{O}(\cdot)$ hides $\mathsf{poly}(\log \lambda, \log \ell, \log \log Q)$ factors. To handle general a-prior unbounded ℓ, Q as is necessarily the case in ABE for DFA, we just bound ℓ, Q by $\lambda^{\omega(1)}$.

Correctness. Fix x, j, M_j such that $M_j(x) = 1$. Write $\mathbf{d}_{i,j} := \mathbf{D}_j \cdot \mathbf{u}_{i,j}^\top$, for $j = 0, \ldots, \ell$. First, we show that

$$- c_{0,j} + \left(\sum_{i=1}^\ell \mathbf{c}_i \cdot \mathbf{K}_{x_i,j} \cdot \mathbf{u}_{i-1,j}^\top \right) + \mathbf{c}_{\ell+1} \cdot \mathbf{K}_{\mathrm{end},j} \cdot \mathbf{u}_{\ell,j}^\top \approx -\mathbf{s}_\ell \mathbf{d}_{\mathrm{end}}^\top \otimes \mathbf{f}_j \mathbf{u}_{\ell,j}^\top \quad (6)$$

This follows readily from

$$(\mathbf{s}_{i-1}\overline{\mathbf{A}}_{x_i} - \mathbf{s}_i \underline{\mathbf{A}}_{x_i}) \cdot \mathbf{K}_{x_i,j} \cdot \mathbf{u}_{i-1,j}^\top = \mathbf{s}_{i-1}\mathbf{d}_{i,j}^\top - \mathbf{s}_i \mathbf{d}_{i,j}^\top$$
$$\mathbf{s}_\ell \mathbf{A}_{\mathrm{end}} \cdot \mathbf{K}_{\mathrm{end},j} \cdot \mathbf{u}_{\ell,j}^\top = \mathbf{s}_\ell \mathbf{d}_{\ell,j}^\top - \mathbf{s}_\ell \mathbf{d}_{\mathrm{end}}^\top \otimes (\mathbf{f}_j \mathbf{u}_{\ell,j}^\top)$$

which in turns follows from

$$\mathbf{A}_{x_i} \cdot \mathbf{K}_{x_i,j} \cdot \mathbf{u}_{i-1,j} = \begin{pmatrix} \mathbf{D}_j \\ \mathbf{D}_j \mathbf{M}_{x_i} \end{pmatrix} \cdot \mathbf{u}_{i-1,j} = \begin{pmatrix} \mathbf{d}_{i-1,j} \\ \mathbf{d}_{i,j} \end{pmatrix}$$
$$\mathbf{A}_{\mathrm{end}} \cdot \mathbf{K}_{\mathrm{end},j} \cdot \mathbf{u}_{\ell,j}^\top = (\mathbf{D}_j - \mathbf{d}_{\mathrm{end}}^\top \otimes \mathbf{f}_j)\mathbf{u}_{\ell,j}^\top = \mathbf{d}_{\ell,j}^\top - \mathbf{d}_{\mathrm{end}}^\top \otimes (\mathbf{f}_j \mathbf{u}_{\ell,j}^\top)$$

Next, since $M_j(x) = 1$, we have $\mathbf{f}_j \mathbf{u}_{\ell,j}^\top = 1$. It follows from (6) that

$$\underbrace{- c_{0,j} + \left(\sum_{i=1}^\ell \mathbf{c}_i \cdot \mathbf{K}_{x_i,j} \cdot \mathbf{u}_{i-1,j}^\top \right) + \mathbf{c}_{\ell+1} \cdot \mathbf{K}_{\mathrm{end},j} \cdot \mathbf{u}_{\ell,j}^\top}_{\approx -\mathbf{s}_\ell \mathbf{d}_{\mathrm{end}}^\top} + \underbrace{\mathbf{c}_{\ell+2}}_{\approx \mathbf{s}_\ell \mathbf{d}_{\mathrm{end}}^\top + \mu \cdot \lfloor \frac{q}{2} \rfloor} \approx \mu \cdot \lfloor \tfrac{q}{2} \rfloor$$

In particular, the error term is bounded by $\hat{\chi} + (\ell + 1)\chi$.

4.2 sk-Selective Security

We assume that the adversary always makes exactly B key queries; this is WLOG, since we can always repeat some of the queries.

Game Sequence. The proof of security follows a sequence of games:

- H_0: Real game where

$$\mathsf{ct} := (\; \{\; \overbrace{\mathbf{s}_0 \mathbf{d}_{0,j}^\top + e_{0,j}}^{c_{0,j}} \;\}_{j\in[B]}, \; \{\; \overbrace{(\mathbf{s}_{i-1}\overline{\mathbf{A}}_{x_i} - \mathbf{s}_i \underline{\mathbf{A}}_{x_i} + \mathbf{e}_i}^{\mathbf{c}_i} \;\}_{i\in[\ell]}, \; \overbrace{\mathbf{s}_\ell \mathbf{A}_{\mathrm{end}} + \mathbf{e}_{\ell+1}}^{\mathbf{c}_{\ell+1}}, \; \overbrace{\mathbf{s}_\ell \mathbf{d}_{\mathrm{end}}^\top + e_{\ell+2} + \mu_\beta \cdot \lfloor \tfrac{q}{2} \rfloor}^{c_{\ell+2}})$$

- H_0': same as H_0, except we replace every $c_{0,j}$ with

$$\left(\sum_{i=1}^{\ell} \mathbf{c}_i \cdot \mathbf{K}_{x_i,j} \cdot \mathbf{u}_{i-1,j}^\top \right) + \mathbf{c}_{\ell+1} \cdot \mathbf{K}_{\mathrm{end},j} \cdot \mathbf{u}_{\ell,j}^\top + e_{0,j} \tag{7}$$

This game is well-defined because the adversary fixes all key queries (M_j, j) before it chooses x in the sk-selective setting.

- $\mathsf{H}_i', i = 1, \ldots, \ell$: same as H_0', except we sample $\mathbf{c}_1, \ldots, \mathbf{c}_i \leftarrow \mathbb{Z}_q^m$. Note that this also changes the distribution of $\{c_{0,j}\}_{j\in[B]}$, since they depend on $\mathbf{c}_1, \ldots, \mathbf{c}_i$ as defined in (7).
- $\mathsf{H}_{\ell+1}$: same as H_ℓ, except we replace $c_{\ell+2}$ in H_ℓ with $c_{\ell+2}' \leftarrow \mathbb{Z}_q$.

Lemma 2. $\mathsf{H}_0 \approx_s \mathsf{H}_0'$.

Proof. It suffices to show that The only difference in the two games lies in the distribution of $\{c_{0,j}\}_{j\in[B]}$. Since $M_j(x) = 0$, we have $\mathbf{f}_j \mathbf{d}_{\ell,j}^\top = 0$. It follows from (6) that

$$c_{0,j} \approx \left(\sum_{i=1}^{\ell} \mathbf{c}_i \cdot \mathbf{K}_{x_i,j} \cdot \mathbf{u}_{i-1,j}^\top\right) + \mathbf{c}_{\ell+1} \cdot \mathbf{K}_{\mathrm{end},j} \cdot \mathbf{u}_{\ell,j}^\top$$

Combined with noise smudging using $e_{0,j}$, namely

$$e_{0,j} \approx_s e_{0,j} + \left(\sum_{i=1}^{\ell} \mathbf{e}_i \cdot \mathbf{K}_{x_i,j} \cdot \mathbf{u}_{i-1,j}^\top\right) + \mathbf{e}_{\ell+1} \cdot \mathbf{K}_{\mathrm{end},j} \cdot \mathbf{u}_{\ell,j}^\top$$

which in turn follows from $\hat{\chi} \geq \chi \cdot (\ell+1)m \cdot \lambda^{\omega(1)}$, we have

$$\{c_{0,j}\}_{j\in[B]} \approx_s \left\{ -\left(\sum_{i=1}^{\ell} \mathbf{c}_i \cdot \mathbf{K}_{x_i,j} \cdot \mathbf{u}_{i-1,j}^\top\right) - \mathbf{c}_{\ell+1} \cdot \mathbf{K}_{\mathrm{end},j} \cdot \mathbf{u}_{\ell,j}^\top + e_{0,j} \right\}_{j\in[B]}$$

The lemma follows readily. □

Lemma 3. *For* $i = 1, \ldots, \ell$, $\mathsf{H}_{i-1}' \approx_c \mathsf{H}_i'$.

Proof. Observe that the only difference between H_{i-1}' and H_i' lies in the distribution of $\mathbf{c}_i$:

- in H_{i-1}', we have $\mathbf{c}_i = \mathbf{s}_{i-1}\overline{\mathbf{A}}_{x_i} - \mathbf{s}_i \underline{\mathbf{A}}_{x_i} + \mathbf{e}_i$;
- in H_i', we have $\mathbf{c}_i \leftarrow \mathbb{Z}_q^m$.

We show that $\mathsf{H}'_{i-1} \approx_c \mathsf{H}'_i$ follows from the $\mathbf{T}_{1/2}$-LWE assumption.

As a simplifying assumption, we assume that the reduction knows x_i from the start. In the more general setting, the reduction simply guesses x_i at random at the beginning of the experiment, and aborts if the guess is wrong; this incurs a loss of $|\Sigma|$ in the security reduction.

By the $\mathbf{T}_{1/2}$-LWE assumption applied to secret $\mathbf{s}_{i-1}$ and public matrix $\mathbf{A}_{x_i}$, we have:

$$\boxed{\mathbf{s}_{i-1}\overline{\mathbf{A}}_{x_i}} \approx_c \mathbf{c} \ , \quad \mathbf{c} \leftarrow \mathbb{Z}_q^m$$

given $\mathbf{A}_{x_i}$ and oracle access to $\mathcal{O}_{\mathbf{A}_{x_i}}(\cdot)$.

The reduction on input $\mathbf{A}_{x_i}, \tilde{\mathbf{c}} \in \{\mathbf{s}_{i-1}\overline{\mathbf{A}}_{x_i}, \mathbf{c}\}, \mathbf{K}_{x_i,j}$ and oracle access to $\mathcal{O}_{\mathbf{A}_{x_i}}(\cdot)$:

– samples

$$(\mathbf{A}_\sigma, \tau_\sigma) \leftarrow \mathsf{TrapGen}(1^{2n}, 1^m, q), \sigma \neq x_i \quad (\mathbf{A}_{\mathsf{end}}, \tau_{\mathsf{end}}) \leftarrow \mathsf{TrapGen}(1^n, 1^m, q), \quad \mathbf{d}_{\mathsf{end}} \leftarrow \mathbb{Z}_q^n$$

– when $\mathcal{A}$ makes a key query (M_j, j) where $M_j = (Q_j, \Sigma, \{\mathbf{M}_{\sigma,j}\}_{\sigma \in \Sigma}, \mathbf{u}_{0,j}, \mathbf{f}_j)$:
  • queries $\mathcal{O}_{\mathbf{A}_{x_i}}(\mathbf{M}_{x_i,j}, \mathbf{0})$ to get $\mathbf{K}_{x_i,j} \leftarrow \mathbf{A}_{x_i}^{-1}\binom{\mathbf{D}_j}{\mathbf{D}_j\mathbf{M}_{x_i,j}}$;
  • computes $\mathbf{D}_j = \overline{\mathbf{A}}_{x_i} \cdot \mathbf{K}_{x_i,j}$;
  • for all $\sigma \neq x_i$, uses τ_σ to compute $\mathbf{K}_{\sigma,j}$ as in KeyGen;
  • uses τ_{end} to compute $\mathbf{K}_{\mathsf{end},j}$ as in KeyGen;
  • outputs $\mathsf{sk}_{M_j} := \left(\mathbf{K}_{\mathsf{end},j}, \{\mathbf{K}_{\sigma,j}\}_{\sigma \in \Sigma}\right)$
– computes $\mathsf{mpk} = \left(\{\mathbf{D}_j\mathbf{u}_{0,j}^\top\}_{j \in [B]}, \{\mathbf{A}_\sigma\}_{\sigma \in \Sigma}, \mathbf{A}_{\mathsf{end}}, \mathbf{d}_{\mathsf{end}}\right)$
– runs $x = (x_1, \ldots, x_\ell), \mu_0, \mu_1 \leftarrow \mathcal{A}(\mathsf{mpk})$
– picks $\beta \leftarrow \{0,1\}$ and computes ct as follows:
  • samples random $\mathbf{s}_0, \ldots, \mathbf{s}_{\ell-1}, \mathbf{s}_\ell$ except $\mathbf{s}_{i-1}$;
  • computes $\mathbf{c}_i := \tilde{\mathbf{c}} - \mathbf{s}_i\underline{\mathbf{A}}_{x_i}$;
  • computes the rest of ct as in H'_{i-1};
– outputs $\mathcal{A}(\mathsf{ct})$.

Now, observe that when

– if $\tilde{\mathbf{c}} = \mathbf{s}_{i-1}\overline{\mathbf{A}}_{x_i} + \mathbf{e}_i$, this matches H'_{i-1}.
– if $\tilde{\mathbf{c}} = \mathbf{c}$, this matches H'_i since $\mathbf{c} - \mathbf{s}_i\underline{\mathbf{A}}_{x_i}$ is uniformly random.

This completes the proof.   □

Lemma 4 (final transition). $\mathsf{H}'_\ell \approx_c \mathsf{H}_{\ell+1}$.

Proof. By the LWE assumption, we have

$$\mathbf{A}_{\mathsf{end}}, \mathbf{d}_{\mathsf{end}}, \overbrace{\mathbf{s}_\ell\mathbf{A}_{\mathsf{end}} + \mathbf{e}_{\ell+1}}^{\mathbf{c}_{\ell+1}}, \boxed{\mathbf{s}_\ell\mathbf{d}_{\mathsf{end}}^\top + e_{\ell+2}}$$

$$\approx_c \mathbf{A}_{\mathsf{end}}, \mathbf{d}_{\mathsf{end}}, \overbrace{\mathbf{s}_\ell\mathbf{A}_{\mathsf{end}} + \mathbf{e}_{\ell+1}}^{\mathbf{c}_{\ell+1}}, c'_{\ell+2}$$

The reduction on input $\mathbf{A}_{\mathsf{end}}, \mathbf{d}_{\mathsf{end}}, \mathbf{c}_{\ell+2}, \tilde{c}$, where $\tilde{c} \in \{\mathbf{s}_\ell\mathbf{d}_{\mathsf{end}}^\top + e_{\ell+2}, c'_{\ell+2}\}$,

– samples
$$(\mathbf{A}_\sigma, \tau_\sigma) \leftarrow \mathsf{TrapGen}(1^{2n}, 1^m, q), \sigma \in \Sigma$$

– when $\mathcal{A}$ makes a key query (M_j, j) where $M_j = (Q_j, \Sigma, \{\mathbf{M}_{\sigma,j}\}_{\sigma \in \Sigma}, \mathbf{u}_{0,j}, \mathbf{f}_j)$:
  • samples $\mathbf{K}_{\mathrm{end},j} \leftarrow \mathcal{D}_{\mathbb{Z}^{m \times Q_j}}$
  • programs $\mathbf{D}_j = \mathbf{A}_{\mathrm{end}}\mathbf{K}_{\mathrm{end},j} + \mathbf{d}_{\mathrm{end}}^\top \otimes \mathbf{f}_j$;
  • for all $\sigma \in \Sigma$, computes $\mathbf{K}_{\sigma,j}$ using τ_σ as in KeyGen;
  • outputs $\mathsf{sk}_{M_j} := \left(\mathbf{K}_{\mathrm{end},j}, \{\mathbf{K}_{\sigma,j}\}_{\sigma \in \Sigma}\right)$
– computes $\mathsf{mpk} = \left(\{\mathbf{D}_j \mathbf{u}_{0,j}^\top\}_{j \in [B]}, \{\mathbf{A}_\sigma\}_{\sigma \in \Sigma}, \mathbf{A}_{\mathrm{end}}, \mathbf{d}_{\mathrm{end}}\right)$
– runs $x = (x_1, \ldots, x_\ell), \mu_0, \mu_1 \leftarrow \mathcal{A}(\mathsf{mpk})$
– picks $\beta \leftarrow \{0,1\}$ and computes ct as follows:
  • samples random $\mathbf{c}_1, \ldots, \mathbf{c}_\ell$;
  • for all $j \in [B]$, compute $c_{0,j}$ using (7) except replacing $\mathbf{s}_\ell \mathbf{d}_{\ell,j}^\top$ with
  $$\mathbf{c}_{\ell+1} \cdot \mathbf{K}_{\mathrm{end},j} \cdot \mathbf{u}_{\ell,j}^\top$$
  • outputs $\mathsf{ct} := (\{c_{0,j}\}_{j \in [B]}, \mathbf{c}_1, \ldots, \mathbf{c}_\ell, \mathbf{c}_{\ell+1}, \tilde{c} + \mu_\beta \cdot \lfloor \frac{q}{2} \rfloor)$.
– outputs $\mathcal{A}(\mathsf{ct})$.

Here, we use

$$\mathbf{D}_j \leftarrow \mathbb{Z}_q^{n \times Q_j}, \mathbf{K}_{\mathrm{end},j} \leftarrow \mathbf{A}_{\mathrm{end}}^{-1}(\mathbf{D}_j - \mathbf{d}_{\mathrm{end}}^\top \otimes \mathbf{f}_j) \approx_s \mathbf{A}_{\mathrm{end}}\mathbf{K}_{\mathrm{end},j} + \mathbf{d}_{\mathrm{end}}^\top \otimes \mathbf{f}_j, \mathbf{K}_{\mathrm{end},j} \leftarrow \mathcal{D}_{\mathbb{Z}^{m \times Q_j}}$$

This completes the proof.   □

5   Candidate ABE for DFA Against Unbounded Collusions

In this section, we describe a candidate ABE scheme for DFA against unbounded collusions:

– Setup$(1^n, \Sigma)$: Sample

$$(\mathbf{A}_\sigma, \tau_\sigma) \leftarrow \mathsf{TrapGen}(1^{2n}, 1^m, q), \sigma \in \Sigma, \quad (\mathbf{A}_{\mathrm{end}}, \tau_{\mathrm{end}}) \leftarrow \mathsf{TrapGen}(1^n, 1^m, q),,$$
$$(\mathbf{A}_{\mathrm{st}}, \tau_{\mathrm{st}}) \leftarrow \mathsf{TrapGen}(1^n, 1^m, q), \quad \mathbf{d}_{\mathrm{end}} \leftarrow \mathbb{Z}_q^n,$$

Output

$$\mathsf{mpk} := \left(\{\mathbf{A}_\sigma\}_{\sigma \in \Sigma}, \mathbf{A}_{\mathrm{end}}, \mathbf{A}_{\mathrm{st}}, \mathbf{d}_{\mathrm{end}}\right), \quad \mathsf{msk} := \left(\{\tau_\sigma\}_{\sigma \in \Sigma}, \tau_{\mathrm{end}}\right)$$

– Enc$(\mathsf{mpk}, (x_1, \ldots, x_\ell) \in \Sigma^\ell, \mu \in \{0,1\})$. Sample

$$\mathbf{s}_0, \mathbf{s}_1, \ldots, \mathbf{s}_\ell \leftarrow \mathbb{Z}_q^n, \quad e_{\ell+2} \leftarrow \mathcal{D}_{\mathbb{Z}, \hat{\chi}}, j \in [B], \quad \mathbf{e}_0, \mathbf{e}_1, \ldots, \mathbf{e}_\ell, \mathbf{e}_{\ell+1} \leftarrow \mathcal{D}_{\mathbb{Z}^m, \chi}$$

Output

$$\mathsf{ct} := (\overbrace{\mathbf{s}_0 \mathbf{A}_{\mathrm{st}} + \mathbf{e}_0}^{c_0}, \overbrace{\{(\mathbf{s}_{i-1}\overline{\mathbf{A}}_{x_i} - \mathbf{s}_i \underline{\mathbf{A}}_{x_i} + \mathbf{e}_i\}_{i \in [\ell]}}^{c_i}, \overbrace{\mathbf{s}_\ell \mathbf{A}_{\mathrm{end}} + \mathbf{e}_{\ell+1}}^{c_{\ell+1}}, \overbrace{\mathbf{s}_\ell \mathbf{d}_{\mathrm{end}}^\top + e_{\ell+2} + \mu \cdot \lfloor \frac{q}{2} \rfloor}^{c_{\ell+2}})$$

– KeyGen(msk, M): Parse $M = (Q, \Sigma, \{\mathbf{M}_\sigma\}_{\sigma \in \Sigma}, \mathbf{u}_0, \mathbf{f})$. Sample

$$\mathbf{D} \leftarrow \mathbb{Z}_q^{n \times Q}, \quad \mathbf{k}_{st}^\top \leftarrow \mathbf{A}_{st}^{-1}(\mathbf{D} \cdot \mathbf{u}_0^\top), \quad \mathbf{K}_{end} \leftarrow \mathbf{A}_{end}^{-1}(\mathbf{D} - \mathbf{d}_{end}^\top \otimes \mathbf{f}), \quad \mathbf{K}_\sigma \leftarrow \mathbf{A}_\sigma^{-1}\begin{pmatrix} \mathbf{D} \\ \mathbf{DM}_\sigma \end{pmatrix}, \sigma \in \Sigma$$

using trapdoors $\tau_{st}, \tau_{end}, \{\tau_\sigma\}_{\sigma \in \Sigma}$. Output

$$\mathsf{sk}_M := \left(\mathbf{k}_{st}, \mathbf{K}_{end}, \{\mathbf{K}_\sigma\}_{\sigma \in \Sigma} \right)$$

– Dec(sk, ct): For $i = 1, \ldots, \ell$, compute $\mathbf{u}_i^\top := \mathbf{M}_{x_i} \cdots \mathbf{M}_{x_1} \mathbf{u}_0^\top$. Output

$$\mathsf{round}_{q/2}\left(\mathbf{c}_0 \mathbf{k}_{st}^\top + \sum_{i=1}^{\ell} \mathbf{c}_i \cdot \mathbf{K}_{x_i} \cdot \mathbf{u}_{i-1}^\top + \mathbf{c}_{end} \cdot \mathbf{K}_{end} \cdot \mathbf{u}_\ell^\top + \mathbf{c}_{\ell+2} \right)$$

where $\mathsf{round}_{q/2} : \mathbb{Z}_q \to \{0, 1\}$ denotes rounding to the nearest multiple of $q/2$.

Preliminary Cryptanalysis. We make two small observations:

– Given unbounded keys, the adversary can recover a full short basis for the matrices

$$[\mathbf{A}_{st} \mid \overline{\mathbf{A}}_\sigma], \forall \sigma$$

This follows from the fact that for each key,

$$[\mathbf{A}_{st} \mid \overline{\mathbf{A}}_\sigma]\begin{pmatrix} \mathbf{k}_{st} \\ -\mathbf{K}_\sigma \mathbf{u}_0^\top \end{pmatrix} = \mathbf{D} \cdot \mathbf{u}_0^\top - \mathbf{D} \cdot \mathbf{u}_0^\top = 0$$

However, we do not know how to use such a collection of short basis to break security of the scheme.

– Suppose we replace each $\mathbf{k}_{st}^\top$ with $\mathbf{c}_0 \mathbf{k}_{st}^\top + \mathbf{e}_0'$ for some fresh $\mathbf{e}_0'$, then the scheme is indeed sk-selective secure, via essentially the same analysis as our bounded-collusion scheme. (Recall that the role of $\mathbf{k}_{st}^\top$ for correctness is indeed only to compute $\mathbf{c}_0 \mathbf{k}_{st}^\top$, so this change does not ruin functionality.) This means that any attack on our candidate scheme must crucially exploit access to $\mathbf{k}_{st}^\top$ (beyond approximating $\mathbf{c}_0 \mathbf{k}_{st}^\top$), for instance, to recover a short basis as in the previous bullet.

Acknowledgments. I would like to thank Yilei Chen and Vinod Vaikuntanathan for illuminating discussions on lattice trapdoor sampling, as well as the reviewers for meticulous and constructive feedback.

References

1. Agrawal, S., Boneh, D., Boyen, X.: Efficient lattice (H)IBE in the standard model. In: Gilbert, H. (ed.) EUROCRYPT 2010. LNCS, vol. 6110, pp. 553–572. Springer, Heidelberg (2010). https://doi.org/10.1007/978-3-642-13190-5_28

2. Agrawal, S., Chase, M.: Simplifying design and analysis of complex predicate encryption schemes. In: Coron, J.-S., Nielsen, J.B. (eds.) EUROCRYPT 2017. LNCS, vol. 10210, pp. 627–656. Springer, Cham (2017). https://doi.org/10.1007/978-3-319-56620-7_22

3. Agrawal, S., Maitra, M., Yamada, S.: Attribute based encryption (and more) for nondeterministic finite automata from LWE. In: Boldyreva, A., Micciancio, D. (eds.) CRYPTO 2019. LNCS, vol. 11693, pp. 765–797. Springer, Cham (2019). https://doi.org/10.1007/978-3-030-26951-7_26

4. Agrawal, S., Maitra, M., Yamada, S.: Attribute based encryption for deterministic finite automata from DLIN. In: Hofheinz, D., Rosen, A. (eds.) TCC 2019. LNCS, vol. 11892, pp. 91–117. Springer, Cham (2019). https://doi.org/10.1007/978-3-030-36033-7_4

5. Agrawal, S., Singh, I.P.: Reusable garbled deterministic finite automata from learning with errors. In: Chatzigiannakis, I., Indyk, P., Kuhn, F., Muscholl, A. (eds.) ICALP 2017, volume 80 of LIPIcs, pp. 36:1–36:13. Schloss Dagstuhl, July 2017

6. Ananth, P., Vaikuntanathan, V.: Optimal bounded-collusion secure functional encryption. In: Hofheinz, D., Rosen, A. (eds.) TCC 2019. LNCS, vol. 11891, pp. 174–198. Springer, Cham (2019). https://doi.org/10.1007/978-3-030-36030-6_8

7. Attrapadung, N.: Dual system encryption via doubly selective security: framework, fully secure functional encryption for regular languages, and more. In: Nguyen, P.Q., Oswald, E. (eds.) EUROCRYPT 2014. LNCS, vol. 8441, pp. 557–577. Springer, Heidelberg (2014). https://doi.org/10.1007/978-3-642-55220-5_31

8. Attrapadung, N.: Dual system encryption framework in prime-order groups via computational pair encodings. In: Cheon, J.H., Takagi, T. (eds.) ASIACRYPT 2016. LNCS, vol. 10032, pp. 591–623. Springer, Heidelberg (2016). https://doi.org/10.1007/978-3-662-53890-6_20

9. Boneh, D., et al.: Fully key-homomorphic encryption, arithmetic circuit ABE and compact garbled circuits. In: Nguyen, P.Q., Oswald, E. (eds.) EUROCRYPT 2014. LNCS, vol. 8441, pp. 533–556. Springer, Heidelberg (2014). https://doi.org/10.1007/978-3-642-55220-5_30

10. Chen, Y., Vaikuntanathan, V., Wee, H.: GGH15 beyond permutation branching programs: proofs, attacks, and candidates. In: Shacham, H., Boldyreva, A. (eds.) CRYPTO 2018. LNCS, vol. 10992, pp. 577–607. Springer, Cham (2018). https://doi.org/10.1007/978-3-319-96881-0_20

11. Genise, N., Micciancio, D., Peikert, C., Walter, M.: Improved discrete Gaussian and subgaussian analysis for lattice cryptography. In: Kiayias, A., Kohlweiss, M., Wallden, P., Zikas, V. (eds.) PKC 2020. LNCS, vol. 12110, pp. 623–651. Springer, Cham (2020). https://doi.org/10.1007/978-3-030-45374-9_21

12. Gentry, C., Peikert, C., Vaikuntanathan, V.: Trapdoors for hard lattices and new cryptographic constructions. In: Ladner, R.E., Dwork, C. (eds.) 40th ACM STOC, pp. 197–206. ACM Press, May 2008

13. Gong, J., Waters, B., Wee, H.: ABE for DFA from k-Lin. In: Boldyreva, A., Micciancio, D. (eds.) CRYPTO 2019. LNCS, vol. 11693, pp. 732–764. Springer, Cham (2019). https://doi.org/10.1007/978-3-030-26951-7_25

14. Gong, J., Wee, H.: Adaptively secure ABE for DFA from k-Lin and more. In: Canteaut, A., Ishai, Y. (eds.) EUROCRYPT 2020. LNCS, vol. 12107, pp. 278–308. Springer, Cham (2020). https://doi.org/10.1007/978-3-030-45727-3_10

15. Gorbunov, S., Vaikuntanathan, V., Wee, H.: Functional encryption with bounded collusions via multi-party computation. In: Safavi-Naini, R., Canetti, R. (eds.) CRYPTO 2012. LNCS, vol. 7417, pp. 162–179. Springer, Heidelberg (2012). https://doi.org/10.1007/978-3-642-32009-5_11

16. Gorbunov, S., Vaikuntanathan, V., Wee, H.: Attribute-based encryption for circuits. In: Boneh, D., Roughgarden, T., Feigenbaum, J. (eds.) 45th ACM STOC, pp. 545–554. ACM Press, June 2013

17. Gorbunov, S., Vinayagamurthy, D.: Riding on asymmetry: efficient ABE for branching programs. In: Iwata, T., Cheon, J.H. (eds.) ASIACRYPT 2015. LNCS, vol. 9452, pp. 550–574. Springer, Heidelberg (2015). https://doi.org/10.1007/978-3-662-48797-6_23

18. Goyal, R., Koppula, V., Waters, B.: Collusion resistant traitor tracing from learning with errors. In: Diakonikolas, I., Kempe, D., Henzinger, M. (eds.) 50th ACM STOC, pp. 660–670. ACM Press, June 2018

19. Goyal, V., Pandey, O., Sahai, A., Waters, B.: Attribute-based encryption for fine-grained access control of encrypted data. In: Juels, A., Wright, R.N., De Capitani di Vimercati, S. (eds.) ACM CCS 2006, pp. 89–98. ACM Press, October/November 2006. Available as Cryptology ePrint Archive Report 2006/309

20. Itkis, G., Shen, E., Varia, M., Wilson, D., Yerukhimovich, A.: Bounded-collusion attribute-based encryption from minimal assumptions. In: Fehr, S. (ed.) PKC 2017. LNCS, vol. 10175, pp. 67–87. Springer, Heidelberg (2017). https://doi.org/10.1007/978-3-662-54388-7_3

21. Kowalczyk, L., Wee, H.: Compact adaptively secure ABE for NC^1 from k-Lin. J. Cryptol. **33**(3), 954–1002 (2019). https://doi.org/10.1007/s00145-019-09335-x

22. Micciancio, D., Peikert, C.: Trapdoors for lattices: simpler, tighter, faster, smaller. In: Pointcheval, D., Johansson, T. (eds.) EUROCRYPT 2012. LNCS, vol. 7237, pp. 700–718. Springer, Heidelberg (2012). https://doi.org/10.1007/978-3-642-29011-4_41

23. Sahai, A., Seyalioglu, H.: Worry-free encryption: functional encryption with public keys. In: Al-Shaer, E., Keromytis, A.D., Shmatikov, V. (eds.) ACM CCS 2010, pp. 463–472. ACM Press, October 2010

24. Sahai, A., Waters, B.: Fuzzy identity-based encryption. In: Cramer, R. (ed.) EUROCRYPT 2005. LNCS, vol. 3494, pp. 457–473. Springer, Heidelberg (2005). https://doi.org/10.1007/11426639_27

25. Waters, B.: Dual system encryption: realizing fully secure IBE and HIBE under simple assumptions. In: Halevi, S. (ed.) CRYPTO 2009. LNCS, vol. 5677, pp. 619–636. Springer, Heidelberg (2009). https://doi.org/10.1007/978-3-642-03356-8_36

26. Waters, B.: Functional encryption for regular languages. In: Safavi-Naini, R., Canetti, R. (eds.) CRYPTO 2012. LNCS, vol. 7417, pp. 218–235. Springer, Heidelberg (2012). https://doi.org/10.1007/978-3-642-32009-5_14

27. Wee, H.: Dual system encryption via predicate encodings. In: Lindell, Y. (ed.) TCC 2014. LNCS, vol. 8349, pp. 616–637. Springer, Heidelberg (2014). https://doi.org/10.1007/978-3-642-54242-8_26

Distributed Merkle's Puzzles

Itai Dinur[✉] and Ben Hasson

Department of Computer Science, Ben-Gurion University, Beersheba, Israel
dinuri@cs.bgu.ac.il

Abstract. Merkle's puzzles were proposed in 1974 by Ralph Merkle as a key agreement protocol between two players based on symmetric-key primitives. In order to agree on a secret key, each player makes T queries to a random function (oracle), while any eavesdropping adversary has to make $\Omega(T^2)$ queries to the random oracle in order to recover the key with high probability. The quadratic gap between the query complexity of the honest players and the eavesdropper was shown to be optimal by Barak and Mahmoody [CRYPTO'09].

We consider Merkle's puzzles in a distributed setting, where the goal is to allow *all* pairs among M honest players with access to a random oracle to agree on secret keys. We devise a protocol in this setting, where each player makes T queries to the random oracle and communicates at most T bits, while any adversary has to make $\Omega(M \cdot T^2)$ queries to the random oracle (up to logarithmic factors) in order to recover *any one* of the keys with high probability. Therefore, the amortized (per-player) complexity of achieving secure communication (for a fixed security level) decreases with the size of the network.

Finally, we prove that the gap of $T \cdot M$ between the query complexity of each honest player and the eavesdropper is optimal.

1 Introduction

In 1974 Merkle proposed a protocol that allows a pair of players to agree on a shared secret key without any secret shared in advance (the work was published in 1978 [17]). We describe an idealized variant of the protocol, assuming that player 1 (Alice), player 2 (Bob) and the adversary have access to a cryptographic hash function $H : [N] \to [N']$ (where $[N] = \{1, \dots, N\}$) that is hard to invert, modeled as a random function (oracle). Alice begins by selecting $\sqrt{N}$ elements in $[N]$ independently and uniformly at random $(x_1, \dots, x_{\sqrt{N}})$, and sends $(H(x_1), \dots, H(x_{\sqrt{N}}))$ to Bob. Then, Bob attempts to invert one of the elements by selecting $\sqrt{N}$ elements in $[N]$ independently and uniformly at random $(y_1, \dots, y_{\sqrt{N}})$, computing $(H(y_1), \dots, H(y_{\sqrt{N}}))$, and comparing with the hashed elements received from Alice. By a birthday paradox-like argument, with high probability, the query sets $\{x_1, \dots, x_{\sqrt{N}}\}$ and $\{y_1, \dots, y_{\sqrt{N}}\}$ intersect, namely,

I. Dinur—This research was supported by the Israel Science Foundation (grants no. 573/16 and 1903/20). The first author was additionally supported by the European Research Council under the ERC starting grant agreement no. 757731 (LightCrypt).

K. Nissim and B. Waters (Eds.): TCC 2021, LNCS 13043, pp. 310–332, 2021.
https://doi.org/10.1007/978-3-030-90453-1_11

there exist i, j such that $x_i = y_j$. Thus, Bob sends i to Alice and the players agree on x_i as the shared secret key. The properties of H should guarantee that collisions (i.e., different inputs that hash to the same output) are unlikely inside query sets of this size, and thus the players agree on the same key with high probability. In terms of security, as H is a random oracle, an eavesdropping adversary has to query it on essentially the entire domain $[N]$ in order to recover x_i with high probability.

The quadratic gap between the query complexity of the honest players and the eavesdropper was shown to be optimal by Barak and Mahmoody [2,3] (tightening the previous bound of Impagliazzo and Rudich [13]), assuming the symmetric-key primitive is used as a black box. This stands in contrast to various key-agreement protocols (notably, the Diffie–Hellman protocol [7]) that achieve a super-polynomial gap between the complexity of the honest players and the eavesdropper, based on stronger assumptions which imply that public-key encryption schemes exist (refer to [1] for more details about such protocols). Clearly, the security of Merkle's puzzles is far from the ideal exponential security. However, Biham, Goren and Ishai [4] pointed out that it is not completely unacceptable, since the ratio between the work of the honest players and the adversary grows as technology advances and the honest players can afford more computation.

Key agreement protocols based on black-box use of symmetric-key primitives are still subject to active research. For example, the recent work [12] by Haitner et al. studied the communication complexity of such protocols. In this work we propose a distributed model for Merkle's puzzles and show that in this model the gap in query complexity between each honest player and the eavesdropper can be super-quadratic.

1.1 Distributed Key Agreement Based on Symmetric-Key Primitives

We study key agreement protocols in a generalized (distributed) model in which there are M honest players $p_1, \ldots, p_M$ that form a fully connected network.[1] The goal is to allow *all* pairs of players to agree on secret keys. We assume that all honest players and the eavesdropping adversary have access to a random oracle H. We measure the query and communication complexity of the players and the query complexity of the adversary. The problem can be easily solved if the players already have secure communication channels with a trusted party, which can use the channels to distribute all keys. However, in this work we do not assume any pre-existing secure channels.

Motivation. We do not expect our protocol to be used in practice for the purpose of key agreement, largely due to the small gap between the complexity of the honest players and the eavesdropper. However, we believe that the distributed

---

[1] Our protocol can also be made to work with small overhead in a sparse, but well-connected network such as the hypercube or the butterfly networks [18, Chapter 4.5].

model is a natural generalization of the basic problem of pairwise key agreement using symmetric-key primitives, and is worth studying. Moreover, techniques used in the protocol could potentially be useful in other settings as well. For example, they may be used to optimize key pre-distribution schemes in highly connected networks (see Sect. 1.4 for details about these schemes).

Basic Protocol. In the most straightforward distributed protocol, each of the $\binom{M}{2}$ pairs of players independently carry out the standard 2-player Merkle's puzzles protocol. However, a closer examination reveals that this is wasteful and it is sufficient to form $O(M)$ secure links or edges (i.e., shared keys between player pairs) such that the secure communication graph is connected. Thus, in order for an arbitrary pair of players p_i, p_j to agree on a key, p_i chooses a key $k_{i,j}$ and sends it encrypted on a path to p_j in the secure link graph. Namely, if (ℓ, m) is a secure link in the graph, then p_ℓ sends $k_{i,j}$ to p_m encrypted with the key shared by p_ℓ and p_m. Player p_m decrypts $k_{i,j}$ and then sends it encrypted on the next secure link.

This protocol has the disadvantage that $k_{i,j}$ is not kept private from the other players (and is thus insecure in a model which does not assume all players are perfectly honest). It can be (partially) mitigated by p_i splitting $k_{i,j}$ into different secret shares, and sending the shares to p_j on non-intersecting paths.

In this improved protocol, it is sufficient for each player to agree on secret keys with $O(1)$ other players via standard Merkle's puzzles. Thus, every player makes $O(T)$ queries to H and an eavesdropping adversary has to make $\Omega(T^2)$ queries to recover any particular key with high probability. However, a key is now used to encrypt (shares of) other keys, and thus if the adversary is able to recover a few keys, the security of the entire network may collapse. Thus, we would like security guarantees against recovering *any one* of the keys with high probability. In order to achieve this, we can split the domain of H (assuming it is sufficiently large) among the different executions of Merkle's puzzles, such that they are completely independent.

The main question we consider in this work is whether the quadratic gap in query complexity in the distributed model (obtained by the basic protocol above) between the honest players and the eavesdropping adversary is optimal.

1.2 Our Results

We show that the quadratic gap obtained by the basic protocol in the distributed model is suboptimal.

Theorem 1 (informal). *For parameters M and T such that $T = \tilde{\Omega}(M)$,[2] there is a key agreement protocol based on symmetric-key primitives in the distributed model, where each honest player makes T queries to the random oracle and communicates at most $\tilde{O}(T)$ bits, while any adversary has to make $\tilde{\Omega}(M \cdot T^2)$*

---

[2] Throughout this paper, the notation $\tilde{O}(\cdot)$ and $\tilde{\Omega}(\cdot)$ hide poly-logarithmic factors in T.

queries to the random oracle in order to recover any one of the keys with high probability.

We further note that the computational complexity (in the standard word RAM model) of each honest player in our protocol is $\tilde{O}(T)$. Consequently, up to small factors, a group of about 2^{20} players can communicate with 100-bit security after each player performs 2^{40} work. The complexity of the basic protocol above is 2^{50}, which is much higher.

More generally, if we fix the number of queries of the adversary (i.e., the security level of the protocol) to T_A, then the query and communication complexity of each player in our protocol is about $\sqrt{T_A/M}$. This gives the following (informal) property of our protocol.

Property 1. The complexity per player for securely connecting a network decreases with the size of the network.

This property may seem counterintuitive, as the number of targets (secure links) available to the adversary increases with the size of the network, so one may be tempted to conclude that each player must work at least as hard.

We also show that the gap of $T \cdot M$ obtained in our protocol between the query complexity of each player and the adversary is optimal (up to logarithmic factors). In fact, we show that this gap is the best possible even if we set a presumably weaker goal of establishing a single key between p_1 (or any other fixed player) and *any* other player p_j for $j \in [M]\backslash\{1\}$. In other words, we obtain the following property of the distributed model.

Property 2. The complexity per player for securely connecting p_1 to any one of the other players is essentially the same as for securely connecting the entire network.

Property 1 and Property 2 are due to a combination of the birthday paradox and properties of random graphs, as described next.

1.3   Overview of the Protocol and Its Analysis

Setup Protocol. Instead of trying to create pre-fixed secure links between pairs of players (as in the basic protocol described above), we start by creating arbitrary secure links based on a setup protocol via a distributed variant of Merkle's puzzles. Fixing the parameters T and M, every player selects T elements uniformly at random from $[N]$ (the domain of $H : [N] \rightarrow [N']$) and queries H to obtain the corresponding T images. If we choose $N \approx M \cdot T^2$, a birthday paradox-like argument shows that with high probability, the T elements chosen by any player p_i intersect the $(M - 1) \cdot T \approx M \cdot T$ elements chosen by the other players. As in standard Merkle's puzzles, two players with intersecting query sets can agree on a shared key. However, it is not yet clear how the players can detect such intersections with limited communication.

One way to detect intersections is to have each player send its T query images to p_1 (or any designated player) that acts as an intermediate and informs all player pairs about the matches. However, this requires that p_1 communicates $\Omega(M \cdot T)$ bits. In order to get around this problem, we distribute the role of the intermediate among the different players: for each query $x \in [N]$, $H(x)$ is sent to player number $H(x) \bmod M$. This guarantees that each player receives about T images (with high probability), and can detect matches among them and then inform the corresponding players.

Choosing $N \approx M \cdot T^2 / \log M$, ensures that the secure network formed by the setup protocol is connected with high probability. However, in terms of security, an adversary may invert any one of the $\Omega(M)$ images (i.e., recover any one of the secret keys) and can succeed with high probability in doing so after making about $N/M \approx T^2 / \log M$ queries. Therefore, we have not yet improved upon the basic protocol.

Amplification. In order to strengthen the security of the protocol, we perform amplification. The goal is to connect the network via "strong links" (keys) that the adversary has negligible probability (e.g., less than $2/N$) of recovering unless making (about) $N/2$ queries. For this purpose, for a (small) parameter L, we perform L independent executions of the setup protocol (with independent random oracles that can be derived by splitting the domain of H). Assume we wish to connect p_i and p_j by a strong link. Then, p_i selects $k_{i,j}$ (from a sufficiently large space), computes an L-out-of-L secret sharing of $k_{i,j}$ and sends the ℓ'th share on a path to p_j, encrypted using the keys of the ℓ'th execution. In terms of security, in order to recover $k_{i,j}$, the adversary has to recover one setup key on each of the L paths. For a fixed number of queries, the probability of the adversary to recover a setup key on a path depends on its length (which defines the number of targets). If the paths are too long then we need to select a large value of L to achieve the required security level, resulting in an inefficient protocol (in terms of both query and communication complexity).

Fortunately, the secure link graph formed by an execution of the setup protocol has diameter (i.e., maximal distance between two nodes) of $O(\log M)$ with high probability, and thus the paths are short. A similar phenomenon occurs in the $G(n, p)$ graph model [6] (in which each edge in the n-node graph is present independently with probability $p \approx \frac{\log n}{n}$). We note, however, that the edges of the secure link graph formed by the setup protocol are not independent.

Extension to the Semi-honest Model. Our basic protocol assumes that all players are perfectly honest. However, using similar techniques used for amplification, the protocol can be extended with logarithmic overhead to the semi-honest model (in which some players are honest but curious), where an adversary controls a fraction of $O(1/\log M)$ of the players.

Analysis. The main contribution of this work is proposing a distributed key agreement model based on symmetric-key primitives and devising a protocol in this model. On the other hand, the analysis of the protocol is elementary and mainly consists of basic concentration inequalities (it is easy to check that the protocol "works on average"). The proof of optimality follows by reduction from a 2-player protocol and is based on the result of Barak and Mahmoody [3]. Throughout the paper we aim for simplicity and make little effort to optimize low-order terms. In particular, it seems that a logarithmic improvement can be obtained by running the setup protocol only once with appropriate parameters, such that it is possible to select sufficiently many short disjoint paths in the secure link graph for the purpose of amplification. However, the analysis of such a protocol is substantially more complicated.

We chose to analyze our protocol in an idealized (information-theoretic) model as it simplifies the protocol and its analysis, and emphasizes its most important differences compared to previous works. An idealized model is also necessary for the proof of optimality. Alternatively, we could have investigated the minimal complexity-theoretic assumptions under which our protocol could be proven secure. Based on the analysis of [4] for 2-player protocols, it seems that we similarly need a one-way function of exponential strength and a "dream version" of Yao's XOR lemma [11]. We leave the formal treatment of this subject to future work.

1.4   Previous Work

Since Merkle's seminal work [17], various aspects of key agreement protocols based on symmetric-key primitives have been studied (c.f., [2–4,12,13]).

Key agreement protocols among a group of players have been investigated in numerous previous works, many of which make use of asymmetric-key primitives (c.f., [14]).

Various works also investigated the problem of key agreement among a group of players without using asymmetric-key primitives in models that are fundamentally different from ours. Among these we mention [16] by Leighton and Micali, that studied the problem in a model where keys are pre-assigned to players by a trusted dealer. Another example is [10] by Fischer and Wright, where it is assumed that the players have access to a particular type of correlated randomness (specifically, each player is given a secret set of cards that are not given to any other player).

The key agreement problem among a group of players is also related to secure message transmission (c.f., [8]), but our adversarial model is completely different and the relation is mostly indirect.

To the best of our knowledge, key agreement protocols among a group of players based on symmetric-key primitives have not been previously investigated in our (i.e., Merkle's) model, perhaps because it is not obvious that they offer any advantage compared to 2-player protocols. Below we elaborate on the line of work that seems to be the closest to ours (and is also related to [16]).

Random Key Pre-distribution Schemes. In random key pre-distribution schemes each player (node) is initialized with a set of symmetric keys (chosen randomly from a group of keys, unknown to the adversary) prior to the key agreement protocol in order to bootstrap it. This model has been mostly studied in the context of sensor networks which have limited computational power (c.f., [5,9] and many followup works).

The random key pre-distribution model is related to ours, as our goal is also to connect a network via secure links using symmetric-key cryptography. However, there are important differences between the models, as in random key pre-distribution schemes, there is no random oracle (keys are pre-distributed) and the adversarial model allows the attacker to compromise nodes and discover their keys (but not to break cryptography). On the other hand, in our model the adversary may break the cryptography by querying the random oracle after eavesdropping. In addition, the network topology assumed in key pre-distribution scheme is different than ours and it has a substantial effect on the protocols.

To demonstrate the effect of the different models, note that in key pre-distribution schemes we can trivially establish a pre-shared key between any (fixed) pair of nodes, and the difficulty is in deploying a large-scale system with pre-shared keys where the adversary can compromise some of the nodes. Hence, Properties 1 and 2 do not hold for these schemes. On the other hand, in our case, a larger network allows us to make use of its collective power to agree on keys with reduced amortized complexity, resulting in Property 1 (and indirectly, in Property 2).

Despite the different models and analysis, there are similarities between key pre-distribution protocols and our protocol. In particular, our setup protocol is analogous to the initial phase in key pre-distribution protocols, where each node discovers its neighbors by communicating identifiers of keys that it holds. However, the setup protocol of [5,9] is similar to the basic (undistributed) protocol we considered in which suboptimal parameters are selected (each pair of nodes share a common key with high probability). On the other hand, our advantage comes from the distributed variant of Merkle's puzzles in which each player shares a key only with a few other players not selected in advance. This allows to increase the key space (and the complexity of exhaustive search) by a factor of about M. Additionally, unlike [5,9], we match player couples (i.e., discover immediate neighbors in the secure link graph) via intermediate players in order to minimize communication.

The amplification we use is similar to the multipath-reinforcement protocol of [5] that strengthens the security of a link between two nodes by leveraging other secure links. However, we use paths of length about $\log M$, while [5] mainly uses paths of length 2, which are unlikely to exist in our case.

Open Problems. An interesting open problem deals with an extended security model in which the goal of the adversary is to recover κ of the keys (where $\kappa \geq 1$ is an integer parameter). In our protocol, the adversary has to query the random oracle about $M \cdot T^2$ times in order to recover one key with high probability, yet roughly the same number of queries suffice for recovering all keys. We conjecture that this is essentially optimal, namely, in any protocol where the players agree on $\Omega(M)$ pairwise keys, the adversary can recover a constant fraction of them with $O(M \cdot T^2)$ queries.

Structure of Paper. Next, we describe some preliminaries in Sect. 2 and then formally define our model in Sect. 3. Our setup and main protocols are described and analyzed in Sects. 4 and 5, respectively. In Sect. 6 we prove the optimality of our protocol with respect to query complexity. Finally, we discuss the extension to the semi-honest model and a communication-security tradeoff in Sect. 7.

2   Preliminaries

For numbers x and b, we denote by $\log x$, $\log_b x$ and $\ln x$ the logarithm of x with basis 2, b and e, respectively.

Given positive integers n, t, denote $[n] = \{1, \ldots, n\}$ and $[n]^t = \underbrace{[n] \times [n] \times \ldots \times [n]}_{t}$.

We will use the following inequalities. For every positive integer n, $n! > \left(\frac{n}{e}\right)^n$, while for every positive integers n, t (such that $n \geq t$),

$$\binom{n}{t} \leq \frac{n^t}{t!} < \left(\frac{e \cdot n}{t}\right)^t.$$

2.1   Graphs

Let $G = (V, E)$ be an undirected graph. The *distance* between two vertices $v, u \in V$ in G is the length of the shortest path between them. The *diameter* of G is the maximal distance between any two vertices of G.

The vertex v is a *neighbor* of u if $(v, u) \in E$. Let $U \subseteq V$. We define the *neighborhood* of U as $N_G(U) \triangleq \{v \in V \backslash U \mid v \text{ has neighbor in } U\}$.

We will use the notion of (vertex) expander graphs.

Definition 1 (Expander graphs). *Let $G = (V, E)$ be an undirected graph with n vertices and let $\delta > 0$. The graph G is a δ-expander if $|N_G(U)| \geq \delta \cdot |U|$ for every vertex subset $U \subset V$ with $|U| \leq n/2$.*

The following result is considered folklore (c.f., [15, Corollary 3.2]).

Proposition 1 (Diameter of expander graphs). *Let $G = (V, E)$ be an undirected graph with n vertices that is a δ-expander. Then, $diam(G) \leq 2\lceil \log_{1+\delta}(n/2) \rceil + 1 = O_\delta(\log n)$.*

Proof. Let $v \in V$. For an integer $t \geq 0$, denote by $B_t(v)$ the set of vertices within distance t from v in G. We prove by induction on t that

$$|B_t(v)| \geq \min(n/2, (1 + \delta)^t).$$

For $t = 0$, we have $B_t(v) = \{v\}$ and $|B_t(v)| = 1$. For the induction step, assume that $|B_{t-1}(v)| \geq \min(n/2, (1 + \delta)^{t-1})$ and note that $B_{t-1}(v) \subseteq B_t(v)$.

If $|B_{t-1}(v)| \geq n/2$, we are done. Otherwise, $|B_{t-1}(v)| \geq (1+\delta)^{t-1}$ and $|B_{t-1}(v)| < n/2$. Denote $U = B_{t-1}(v)$. We have $B_t(v) = U \cup N_G(U)$ and $|N_G(U)| \geq \delta \cdot |U|$ since G is a δ-expander. Therefore, $|B_t(v)| \geq (1+\delta)|U| \geq (1+\delta)^t$ as claimed.

In particular, for $t = \lceil \log_{1+\delta}(n/2) \rceil$, for any $v, u \in V$ we have $B_t(v) \geq n/2$ and $B_t(u) \geq n/2$. Thus, $B_{t+1}(v) > n/2$ intersects $B_t(u)$, proving the result. ■

2.2   Random Functions and Encryption

A random function (oracle) can be thought of as an idealization of a cryptographic hash function. For positive integers N, N', a random function $H : [N] \to [N']$ is random variable, where for each $x \in [N]$, $H(x)$ is selected independently uniformly at random from $[N']$.

We also make use of an idealization of an encryption scheme using a random function. There are various ways to implement such an encryption scheme and we choose the following one that resembles the counter mode-of-operation: let $F : [N] \to [N']$ be a random function such that $N = N_1 \times N_2$ (i.e., we can write $F : [N_1] \times [N_2] \to [N']$). Given a key $k \in [N_1]$ and a counter $ct \in [N_2]$, a message $m \in [N']$ is encrypted as $F(k, ct) + m \mod N'$. Decryption is performed by computing $F(k, ct)$ and subtracting it modulo N' from the ciphertext.

Assuming a pair (k, ct) is not reused to encrypt different messages and the adversary does not query F with the key k, then the scheme essentially acts as a one-time pad and no information is revealed about the encrypted messages from the ciphertexts and the values of F queried to the adversary.

3   Distributed Key Agreement Protocols Based on Random Oracles

We consider a complete network with M players $p_1, \ldots, p_M$ that have access to a random oracle H. The players run a protocol whose the goal is to establish keys between a fixed set of pairs of players $E_s \subseteq [M] \times [M]$. We do not assume a broadcast channel, and thus broadcasting a bit requires M bits of communication. We note that if a broadcast channel is assumed, then the communication restrictions in the protocols we devise are essentially trivial to satisfy.

All probabilities are computed with respect to the random oracle and the coin tosses of the players and adversary (whenever relevant).

Definition 2 (Distributed key agreement protocol). *A (M, α, T, β)-DKAP is a protocol between M players $p_1, \ldots, p_M$ with access to a random oracle H. Each player receives as input the same set of edges $E_s \subseteq [M] \times [M]$. For $i \in [M]$, denote the total number of queries of player p_i to H by T_i and the total communication of p_i by C_i. The protocol satisfies the following properties:*

- *For each $(i, j) \in E_s$, player p_i outputs $k_{i,j}$ and player p_j outputs $k_{j,i}$ such that $\Pr[\forall (i, j) \in E_s : k_{i,j} = k_{j,i}] \geq \alpha$.*

– $\Pr[\forall i \in [M] : T_i \leq T] = 1$, and $\Pr[\forall i \in [M] : C_i \leq T] \geq \beta$.

A variant of this definition places a worst-case upper bound on the communication complexity of each player. For sufficiently large α and β this variant is essentially equivalent to the one above, since a (M, α, T, β)-DKAP can easily be converted into a $(M, \alpha + \beta - 1, T, 1)$-DKAP: a player that exceeds the communication bound simply aborts and outputs a random value.

Another potential variant also places a bound of $\tilde{O}(T)$ on the total computation performed by each player (in some standard computational model). Our protocol satisfies this additional constraint.

As in standard Merkle's puzzles, security is defined with respect to a passive adversary that has access to the complete transcript of the protocol. The adversary makes a bounded number of queries to H and outputs a string of the form $((i, j), k)$. The adversary wins if $(i, j) \in E_s$ and $k = k_{i,j}$.

Definition 3 (Security of a distributed key agreement protocol). *A (M, α, T, β)-DKAP is (T_A, α_A)-secure if for any adversary $\mathcal{A}$ with access to the communication (transcript) of the protocol Λ that makes at most T_A queries to H, $\Pr[(i, j) \in E_s \wedge k = k_{i,j} \mid \mathcal{A}^H(\Lambda) \to ((i, j), k)] \leq \alpha_A$.*

The security definition does not restrict the keys on which the players agree. In particular, a protocol in which all players agree on the same key can potentially satisfy the definition. However, in our specific protocol the players agree on independent keys. This allows to easily extend it to the semi-honest model, as described in Sect. 7.

Supporting $E_s = [M] \times [M]$. In general, the parameters of a key agreement protocol may depend on (be a function of) E_s. Ultimately, we would like to design a protocol that allows all pairs of players to exchange keys, namely, $E_s = [M] \times [M]$. However, as we outline below, a protocol for $E_s = [M] \times [M]$ can be easily obtained (with a small loss in parameters) from a protocol in which E_s is much sparser.

Specifically, assume we have a protocol that supports inputs E_s where $G = (V, E_s)$ is a sparse network with $|E_s| = \tilde{O}(M)$ for which there exist routing protocols with small congestion (such as the hypercube or the butterfly networks [18, Chapter 4.5]). Then, we can extend it to allow all $\binom{M}{2}$ pairs of players to agree on keys such that each player performs $\tilde{O}(M)$ additional encryptions (i.e. oracle queries) and communicates additional $\tilde{O}(M)$ bits almost surely: for each $(i, j) \in [M] \times [M]$ such that $i < j$, p_i picks a key $k'_{i,j}$ uniformly at random and sends it encrypted to p_j along a short path in (V, E_s).[3] If the exchanged keys are in a sufficiently large space (of size $\tilde{\Omega}(M \cdot T^2)$ in our case) and perfect encryption with domain separation is used (as described in Sect. 2), then recovering any $k'_{i,j}$ requires recovering at least one key in E_s and hence the advantage

---

[3] This exposes $k'_{i,j}$ to the players along the path, and is therefore insecure in the semi-honest model. However, the protocol can be patched by secret sharing $k'_{i,j}$ and sending multiple shares encrypted along disjoint paths. We use a somewhat similar protocol for the purpose of amplification.

of an adversary (with a fixed upper bound on the number of queries) does not increase due to the additional key agreements. Therefore, we may restrict ourselves to designing distributed key agreement protocols in which $|E_s| = \tilde{O}(M)$.

4   The Setup Protocol

Algorithm 1 describes the setup protocol for player p_i (for any $i \in [M]$), assuming the M players have access to a random oracle $H : [N] \to [N']$. The protocol first establishes keys between various pairs of players and then propagates the information about which players share keys.

Algorithm 1: Setup protocol (p_i's algorithm)

Parameters: M, T, N, N', D

1 For all $j \in [M]\setminus\{i\}$, set $k_{i,j} = \perp$
2 Choose $(x_1, \ldots, x_T) \in [N]^T$ uniformly at random (with replacement)
3 Compute $(H(x_1), \ldots, H(x_T)) \in [N']^T$ and store the T pairs $(x_j, H(x_j))$ in a table $\mathcal{T}_1$, sorted by the second column
4 For each $j \in [T]$, send $(i, H(x_j))$ to player number $H(x_j) \bmod M \in [M]$
5 Receive messages from other players: $(u_1, y_1), (u_2, y_2), \ldots$ and store them in a table $\mathcal{T}_2$, sorted by the second column
6 **forall the** *collisions in $\mathcal{T}_2$*: $\{(u_j, y_j), (u_\ell, y_\ell) \mid y_j = y_\ell \wedge u_j \neq u_\ell\}$ **do**
7   send (u_ℓ, y_j) to player number u_j
8   send (u_j, y_j) to player number u_ℓ
9 Receive messages from other players: $(v_1, z_1), (v_2, z_2), \ldots$
10 For each message (v_j, z_j), search for z_j in $\mathcal{T}_1$. If there exists an entry $(x_\ell, H(x_\ell))$ in $\mathcal{T}_1$ such that $z_j = H(x_\ell)$, set

$$k_{i,v_j} = \begin{cases} x_\ell & \text{if } k_{i,v_j} = \perp \text{ or } H(k_{i,v_j}) < H(x_\ell), \\ k_{i,v_j} & \text{otherwise} \end{cases}$$

▷ **Distribute secure link graph**
11 Broadcast the elements of the set $\{(i, j) \mid k_{i,j} \neq \perp \wedge i < j\}$
12 Receive and store messages $(f_1, g_1), (f_2, g_2), \ldots$ from other players
13 Construct a graph $G = (V, E)$, where $V = [M]$, $E = \{(f_1, g_1), (f_2, g_2), \ldots\}$
14 Run breadth-first search on G from node i and calculate the minimal distance to each $j \in [V]$. If there exists $j \in [V]$ whose distance from i is larger than D, broadcast "fail" and output $\perp$.
15 If a "fail" message is received, then output $\perp$. Otherwise, output G and $\{(j, k_{i,j}) \mid k_{i,j} \neq \perp\}$

Parameter Selection. We assume for simplicity that M divides N'. We choose $N = \lfloor \frac{T^2 \cdot M}{25 \ln M} \rfloor$, $N' = T^6$ and $D = 4 \log M$. We further denote $R \triangleq \frac{T^2 \cdot M}{N}$.

We assume that $M \geq 64, T \geq 20000$ and note that $25 \ln M \leq R \leq 26 \ln M$. Moreover, we assume $M \leq T$, which is reasonable as otherwise, iterating over the list of players requires more than T time (and broadcasting a bit has communication complexity of M bits).

We now analyze the setup protocol with respect to correctness, query and communication complexity, connectivity of the secure link graph G and security.

4.1   Correctness

Proposition 2. *Assume that for all* $(i,j) \in E_s$, p_i *outputs* $k_{i,j}$ *player* p_j *outputs* $k_{j,i}$. *Then,* $\Pr[\forall (i,j) \in E_s : k_{i,j} = k_{j,i}] \geq 1 - T^{-2}$.

Proof. Note that if the players output $\perp$ the protocol is still formally correct. Therefore, the only event that may cause a pair of players to output non-matching keys is that their joint query set contains a collision in H, namely a pair of elements $q_i, q_j \in [N]$ such that $H(q_i) = H(q_j)$ but $q_i \neq q_j$.

Based on the randomness of H, a pair of different queries collide with probability $1/N'$. By a union bound over all query pairs, the probability of a collision in the $M \cdot T$ queries made by the players is bounded by $\frac{(T \cdot M)^2}{N'} \leq \frac{T^4}{N'} = T^{-2}$. ∎

4.2   Query and Communication Complexity

Proposition 3. *Each player makes at most* T *queries to* H *and communicates* $\tilde{O}(T)$ *bits, except with probability at most* $M \cdot 2^{-T} + (36 \log T \cdot T)^{-1} + T^{-2}$.

Clearly, each player makes T queries to H. It remains to bound the communication complexity by $\tilde{O}(T)$. First, all the messages are in a space of size polynomial in T, hence the length of each message is $\tilde{O}(1)$ bits. Propositions 4 and 5 below bound the number of messages sent and received by each player. Given that G contains $\tilde{O}(T)$ edges (which is guaranteed with high probability by Proposition 5), then the communication of all players for propagating the edges is bounded by $\tilde{O}(T)$. Therefore, it remains to prove Propositions 4 and 5 in order to complete the proof of Proposition 3.

Proposition 4. *In lines 4–5 of the setup protocol, each player communicates at most* $8T$ *messages, except with probability at most* $M \cdot 2^{-T}$.

Proposition 5. *In lines 6–9 of the setup protocol, all players (collectively) communicate at most* $130 \log T \cdot T$ *messages, except with probability at most* $(36 \log T \cdot T)^{-1} + T^{-2}$.

The probability bound in Proposition 5 is rather loose, but it is sufficient for our purpose.

Proof (of Proposition 4). In Line 4, each player sends at most T messages. It remains to analyze the number of messages each player receives in Line 5.

The number of received messages by p_i is determined by the number of images of H computed by the M players that are equal to i modulo M. As we assume that M divides N' and each image of H is uniform in $[N']$, the probability that each query to H results in a message sent to p_i is $1/M$.

Overall, the players make $M \cdot T$ queries to H, each is uniform in $[N]$. We order them arbitrarily and denote them by $q_1, \ldots, q_{M \cdot T}$. The query q_ℓ results in a message to p_i if $H(q_{j_\ell}) \bmod M = i$ and we bound the probability that this happens for many queries below.

Claim. Consider any ordered subset of $7T$ queries $q_{j_1}, \ldots, q_{j_{7T}}$. Then,

$$\Pr[\forall \ell \in [7T] : H(q_{j_\ell}) \bmod M = i] < \left(\tfrac{2}{M}\right)^{7T}.$$

Proof. For some positive integer $r < 7T$, assume that $H(q_{j_r}) \bmod M = i$ for all $\ell \in [r]$. Then, $H(q_{j_{r+1}}) \bmod M = i$ holds if either $q_{j_{r+1}} \in \{q_{j_1}, \ldots, q_{j_r}\}$ (which occurs with probability at most r/N), or $q_{j_{r+1}} \notin \{q_{j_1}, \ldots, q_{j_r}\}$ and $H(q_{j_{r+1}}) \bmod M = i$ (which occurs with probability at most $1/M$). Therefore $H(q_{j_{r+1}}) \bmod M = i$ holds with probability at most

$$\tfrac{1}{M} + \tfrac{r}{N} \le \tfrac{1}{M} + \tfrac{7T}{N} < \tfrac{1}{M} + \tfrac{1}{M} = \tfrac{2}{M},$$

as $N = \tfrac{M \cdot T^2}{R} \ge 7M \cdot T$ (given that $T \ge 20000$). The claim follows by induction on r. □

There are

$$\binom{M \cdot T}{7T} \le \left(\tfrac{e \cdot M \cdot T}{7T}\right)^{7T} = \left(\tfrac{e \cdot M}{7}\right)^{7T}$$

different query subsets of size $7T$. By a union bound over all of them, the probability that at least $7T$ messages are sent to p_i in Line 5 is at most

$$\left(\tfrac{e \cdot M}{7}\right)^{7T} \cdot \left(\tfrac{2}{M}\right)^{7T} < 2^{-T}.$$

The results follows by a union bound over all M players. ∎

Proof (of Proposition 5). The number of messages sent in lines 6–8 and received in Line 9 is upper bounded by twice the number of collisions in the tables of the players. Consider the queries made by the players in arbitrarily order $q_1, \ldots, q_{M \cdot T}$. We will make a distinction between two types of collisions. A collision in H was shown in Proposition 3 to occur with probability at most T^{-2}. We assume such a collusion does not occur and use a union bound to obtain the final result. A query collision occurs if $q_j = q_\ell$ for $j \ne \ell$ and it results in a shared key (assuming the queries are issued by different players).

We denote the total number of query collisions by Col and bound $\Pr[Col \ge 65 \log T \cdot T]$ to finish the proof.

For all $j, \ell \in [M \cdot T]$ such that $j \ne \ell$, define an indicator random variable $C_{j,\ell}$ that is equal to 1 if $q_j = q_\ell$. We have

$$\mathrm{E}[C_{j,\ell}] = \Pr[C_{j,\ell} = 1] = N^{-1}, \text{ and}$$
$$\mathrm{Var}[C_{j,\ell}] = \mathrm{E}[(C_{j,\ell})^2] - (\mathrm{E}[C_{j,\ell}])^2 = N^{-1} - N^{-2} < N^{-1}.$$

Hence,

$$\mathrm{E}[Col] = \mathrm{E}\left[\sum_{j,\ell} C_{j,\ell}\right] = \sum_{j,\ell} \mathrm{E}[C_{j,\ell}] < \frac{(M \cdot T)^2}{N} = R \cdot M.$$

Note that the random variables $\{C_{j,\ell}\}$ are pairwise independent. Hence,

$$\mathrm{Var}[Col] = \mathrm{Var}\left[\sum_{j,\ell} C_{j,\ell}\right] = \sum_{j,\ell} \mathrm{Var}[C_{j,\ell}] < \frac{(M \cdot T)^2}{N} = R \cdot M.$$

For a parameter $c > 0$, Chebyshev's inequality gives

$$\Pr\left[Col - \mathrm{E}[Col] \geq c \cdot \sqrt{\mathrm{Var}[Col]}\right] \leq c^{-2}.$$

Recalling that $T \geq M$ and $25 \log M \leq R \leq 26 \log M$, we obtain

$$\Pr\left[Col \geq 65 \log T \cdot T\right] \leq \Pr\left[Col - R \cdot M \geq 39 \log T \cdot T\right]$$
$$\leq \Pr\left[Col - R \cdot M \geq 6\sqrt{\log T \cdot T} \cdot \sqrt{R \cdot M}\right] \leq (36 \log T \cdot T)^{-1},$$

as required. ∎

4.3 Connectivity

We prove that the secure link graph formed by the setup protocol is a good expander with high probability, and therefore it has small diameter.

Let U be a group of players of size $k > 0$. We call U *useful* if the players in U make at least $T \cdot k/2$ distinct queries to H.

Proposition 6. *Any group of players is useful, except with probability at most* 2^{-2T}.

Proof. Fix a group U of size k. There are $k \cdot T$ queries made by the players in U. Consider them in some order. We call the j'th query useful if it does not collide with the previous $j - 1$ queries (and not useful otherwise). For each $j \in [k \cdot T]$, the probability that query number j is not useful is at most $\frac{k \cdot T}{N}$.

Consider an arbitrary subset of $\frac{k \cdot T}{2}$ queries made by players in U. The probability that they are all not useful is at most $\left(\frac{k \cdot T}{N}\right)^{(k \cdot T)/2}$. Taking a union bound over all such sets (whose number is less than $2^{k \cdot T}$), the probability that there is a set of size $k \cdot T/2$ of non-useful queries is at most $2^{k \cdot T} \cdot \left(\frac{k \cdot T}{N}\right)^{k \cdot T/2} = \left(\frac{4 \cdot k \cdot T}{N}\right)^{k \cdot T/2} \leq 2^{-2T}$, given that $N = \frac{M \cdot T^2}{R} \geq 64 M \cdot T$ (as $T \geq 20000$). Hence U is useful, except with probability at most 2^{-2T}. ∎

Proposition 7. *Consider the secure link graph $G = (V, E)$ formed by the setup protocol. Let $U \subset V$ be a set of size k for $1 \leq k \leq M/2$. Then,*

$$\Pr[|N_G(U)| \leq \tfrac{k}{2}] \leq e^{-R \cdot k/12} + 2^{-2T}.$$

Proof. We first prove that

$$\Pr[|N_G(U)| \le \tfrac{k}{2} \mid U \text{ is useful}] \le e^{-R \cdot k/12} \tag{1}$$

Combined with Proposition 6, this implies

$$\Pr[|N_G(U)| \le \tfrac{k}{2}] \le$$
$$\Pr[|N_G(U)| \le \tfrac{k}{2} \mid U \text{ is useful}] + \Pr[U \text{ is not useful}] \le e^{-R \cdot k/12} + 2^{-2T},$$

as required.

We now prove (1). Given that U is useful, we fix a set Q of $T \cdot k/2$ distinct queries made by the players in this group.

Note that if $|N_G(U)| \le \tfrac{k}{2}$ then there exists a set $V' \subseteq V \backslash U$ of size at least $M - k - \tfrac{k}{2} = M - 3k/2 \ge M/4$ such that $V' \cap N_G(U) = \emptyset$. Hence the intersection of the queries of the players in V' (whose number is at least $T \cdot M/4$) with Q is empty. The probability of a query hitting Q is $|Q|/N$. Since all the $T \cdot (M - 3k/2)$ queries are independent, the probability none of them hits Q is at most

$$\left(1 - \tfrac{|Q|}{N}\right)^{T \cdot M/4} \le e^{-|Q| \cdot T \cdot M/4N} = e^{-T^2 \cdot k \cdot M/8N} = e^{-R \cdot k/8}.$$

where for the inequality we have used in inequality $1 - x \le e^{-x}$ (which holds for any real x).

The number of sets $V' \subseteq V \backslash U$ of size $M - 3k/2$ is

$$\binom{M-k}{M-3k/2} = \binom{M-k}{k/2} \le \binom{M}{k/2} \le \left(\tfrac{2eM}{k}\right)^{k/2} = e^{k(1+\ln 2 + \ln M - \ln k)/2}.$$

Taking a union bound over all of them, we conclude

$$\Pr[|N_G(U)| \le \tfrac{k}{2} \mid U \text{ is useful}] \le e^{-R \cdot k/8 + k(1 + \ln 2 + \ln M - \ln k)/2} \le$$
$$e^{-k(R/8 - 1 - \ln M/2)} \le e^{-R \cdot k/12},$$

where the last inequality follows since $R \ge 25 \ln M$. ∎

Proposition 8. *The secure link graph $G = (V, E)$ formed by the setup protocol satisfies $\Pr[diam(G) > 4 \log M] \le 2e \cdot M^{-1}$.*

Proof. We show that G is a δ-expander for $\delta = 1/2$, except with probability at most $2e \cdot M^{-1}$. Then, by Proposition 1, $diam(G) \le 2\lceil \log_{3/2}(M/2) \rceil + 1 \le 2 \log_{3/2}(M/2) + 3 \le 3.42 \log_2 M + 3 \le 4 \log M$ (as $M \ge 64$).

Let $U \subset V$ be of size $k \le M/2$. By Proposition 7, $|N_G(U)| > k/2$ except with probability at most $e^{-R \cdot k/12} + 2^{-2T}$. Taking union bound over all subsets of size k, whose number is $\binom{M}{k} \le \left(\tfrac{eM}{k}\right)^k = e^{k(\ln M + 1 - \ln k)}$, we conclude that for all of them $|N_G(U)| > k/2$, except with probability at most

$$e^{k(\ln M + 1 - \ln k - R/12)} + \binom{M}{k} 2^{-2T}$$
$$\le e^{k(\ln M + 1 - \ln k - 24 \ln M/12)} + \binom{M}{k} 2^{-2T}$$
$$\le M^{-k} \cdot e^{k(-\ln k + 1)} + \binom{M}{k} 2^{-2T}$$
$$\le e \cdot M^{-k} + \binom{M}{k} 2^{-2T},$$

where we have used the inequality $R \geq 25 \ln M \geq 24 \ln M$.

Taking a union bound over all $k \in [M/2]$, we conclude that all groups U of size at most $M/2$ satisfy $|N_G(U)| > k/2$, except with probability at most $2^M \cdot 2^{-2T} + \sum_{k=1}^{M/2} e \cdot M^{-k} \leq 2e \cdot M^{-1}$, since $M \geq 64$ and $T \geq M$.   ∎

4.4   Security

Proposition 9. *Fix any pair of players* (p_i, p_j) *for which* $k_{i,j} \neq \perp$. *Then, any adversary (with access to the full transcript of the protocol) that makes at most* T_A *queries to* H, *makes the query* $k_{i,j}$ *with probability at most* $\frac{T_A}{N}$.

The security proof is essentially identical to the proof for standard Merkle's puzzles.

Proof. Let Λ be a random variable for the transcript of the protocol, which includes $H(k_{i,j})$, as well as other images. The query sets of the players are uniform, and H is a random function for which images do not give any information about their preimages.[4] Consequently, $k_{i,j} \mid \Lambda = \lambda$ is uniformly distributed in $[N]$ for any λ (for which the images of H computed by p_i and p_j intersect).

Fix an adversary for Algorithm 1 that receives Λ as input. Let Γ_t be a random variable for the first t (adaptive) queries of the adversary and their answers. Since H is a random function, any query $q \neq k_{i,j}$ to H may only give the information that $q \neq k_{i,j}$ (in case $H(q) \neq H(k_{i,j})$). Thus, by induction on the number of queries t, they either hit $k_{i,j}$ with probability at most t/N, or $k_{i,j} \mid \Lambda = \lambda, \Gamma_t = \gamma$ remains uniformly distributed in a set which contains (at least) the remaining $N - t$ inputs to H. Setting $t = T_A$ gives the result.   ∎

5   The Distributed Key Agreement Protocol

We describe our key agreement protocol in Algorithm 2, where every player receives as input the same set of edges E_s. We set $L = \lceil 16 \log T \rceil$ (the other parameters are set as in the setup protocol).

It remains to describe the strong secure link protocol. We assume that the players have access to a perfect encryption scheme: for $\ell \in [L]$ given access to an (independent) random function $F^{(\ell)} : [N] \times [M] \times [M] \times [T^2] \rightarrow [N]$, players f, g that share a key $k_{f,g}^{(\ell)} \in [N]$, encrypt the ct'th message $m \in [N]$ as $F^{(\ell)}(k_{i,j}^{(\ell)}, f, g, ct) + m \bmod N$. We embed f and g into the input of F in order to make sure that it is not invoked twice on the same input.

In the protocol, p_i chooses L independent and uniform values $r_1, \ldots, r_L \in [N]$ and computes $k_{i,j} = \sum_{\ell=1}^{L} r_\ell \bmod N$ (i.e., $k_{i,j}$ is split into L shares using a standard additive L-out-of-L secret sharing scheme). Then, p_i sends the ℓ'th

---

[4] The transcript reveals information about the equalities (and inequalities) among different queries made by the players, yet any individual query remains uniform in $[N]$.

Algorithm 2: Distributed key agreement protocol

Parameters: M, T, N, N', D, L
Input: E_s
1 Run the setup protocol (with parameters M, T, N, N', D) $2L$ times with independent random oracles (derived from H)
2 If more than L executions fail (i.e., output $\perp$), then each player outputs an independent and uniform value in $[N]$. Otherwise, for the first L successful executions, denote the corresponding random oracles and secure graphs by $H^{(1)}, \ldots, H^{(L)}$ and $G^{(1)}, \ldots, G^{(L)}$
3 For each $(i, j) \in E_s$, run the strong secure link protocol (Algorithm 3), after which p_i outputs $k_{i,j}$ and p_j outputs $k_{j,i}$

---

share r_ℓ on a short path to p_j, encrypted with the keys of $G^{(\ell)}$. Specifically, for each edge (f, g) on the selected path, p_f encrypts r_ℓ with counter ct as $F^{(\ell)}(k_{f,g}^{(\ell)}, f, g, ct) + r_\ell \bmod N$ (p_f and p_g then increment the counter). Player g decrypts the message (by subtracting $F^{(\ell)}(k_{f,g}^{(\ell)}, f, g, ct)$ modulo N from the encryption) and encrypts it using the next key on the path. Finally, p_j receives the (encrypted) values $r_1, \ldots, r_L$ and computes $k_{j,i}$ (which should equal $k_{i,j}$) by decrypting and summing the values mod N.

The algorithm of p_i is given below.

Algorithm 3: Strong secure link protocol (p_i's algorithm)

Parameters: M, N, L
Input: j such that $(i, j) \in E_s$
1 Select L uniform and independent values $r_1, \ldots, r_L \in [N]$ and define $k_{i,j} = \sum_{\ell=1}^{L} r_\ell \bmod N$.
2 **forall the** $\ell \in [L]$ **do**
3   Find the shortest path between i and j in $G^{(\ell)}$ via breadth-first search, and send r_ℓ on that path (encrypted with the corresponding keys of $G^{(\ell)}$)

5.1 Security Analysis

Proposition 10. *Fix an adversary $\mathcal{A}$ that makes $T_A \leq N/4$ queries to $H^{(1)}, \ldots, H^{(L)}$ and $F^{(1)}, \ldots, F^{(L)}$. Then, given the view of the adversary $\text{view}_\mathcal{A}$ (the transcript of the protocol of Algorithm 2 and the oracle queries and answers), each $k_{i,j}$ for $(i, j) \in E_s$ is uniformly distributed in $[N]$, except with probability at most T^{-6}. Namely, $\Pr[(\forall (i, j) \in E_s : k_{i,j}$ is uniformly distributed in $[N]) \mid \text{view}_\mathcal{A}] \leq T^{-6}$.*

Proof. Let Λ be a random variable for the transcript of Algorithm 2. The adversary for Algorithm 2 receives Λ as input. Let Γ be a random variable for the (adaptive) queries of the adversary to $H^{(1)}, \ldots, H^{(L)}$, and $F^{(1)}, \ldots, F^{(L)}$ and their answers.

Fix $(i, j) \in E_s$. For $\ell \in [L]$, let $K^{(\ell)}$ be the set of keys under which r_ℓ is encrypted in Algorithm 3. Namely, $K^{(\ell)}$ contains $k_{f,g}^{(\ell)}$ for all edges (f, g) on the path in $G^{(\ell)}$ selected by p_i. Define the random variable $\mathcal{E}_\ell$ as an indicator for the event that Γ contains a query $F^{(\ell)}(k_{f,g}^{(\ell)}, f, g, ct)$ for some $k_{f,g}^{(\ell)} \in K^{(\ell)}$ and counter ct.

Claim. For any values λ, γ (that occur with positive probability),

$$k_{i,j} \mid \Lambda = \lambda, \Gamma = \gamma, \wedge_{\ell \in [L]} \mathcal{E}_\ell = 0$$

is distributed uniformly in $[N]$.

In other words, if $\wedge_{\ell \in [L]} \mathcal{E}_\ell = 0$ occurs, then $k_{i,j}$ is distributed uniformly in $[N]$ given the view of the adversary.

Proof. Given that $\wedge_{\ell \in [L]} \mathcal{E}_\ell = 0$, then there exists $\ell \in [L]$ such that $\mathcal{E}_\ell = 0$. We fix any such ℓ.

For each $k_{f,g}^{(\ell)} \in K^{(\ell)}$, denote by $c_{f,g}^{(\ell)} = F^{(\ell)}(k_{f,g}^{(\ell)}, f, g, ct) + r_\ell \bmod N$ the encryption (ciphertext) of r_ℓ, and denote $C^{(\ell)} = \{c_{f,g}^{(\ell)} \mid k_{f,g}^{(\ell)} \in K^{(\ell)}\}$. Since we assume the adversary did not query $F^{(\ell)}(k_{f,g}^{(\ell)}, f, g, ct)$ for any $k_{f,g}^{(\ell)} \in K^{(\ell)}$, and since $F^{(\ell)}$ is a random function, then $r_\ell \mid C^{(\ell)}, \mathcal{E}_\ell = 0$ remains uniformly distributed in $[N]$. As the additional values in the adversary's view are independent of r_ℓ (and of all $F^{(\ell)}(k_{f,g}^{(\ell)}, f, g, ct)$), then

$$r_\ell \mid \Lambda = \lambda, \Gamma = \gamma, \mathcal{E}_\ell = 0$$

is also uniform in $[N]$. Recall that $k_{i,j} = \sum_{\ell=1}^{L} r_\ell \bmod N$, where each share is selected independently and uniformly at random from $[N]$. Since r_ℓ is uniform in $[N]$ given the view of the adversary, then $k_{i,j}$ is uniform in $[N]$ given the view of the adversary regardless of the other shares. $\square$

It remains to upper bound $\Pr[\wedge_{\ell \in [L]} \mathcal{E}_\ell = 1]$. A bound on this quantity in the information theoretic model essentially follows from Proposition 9.

Recall that for each $\ell \in [L]$, the path length in $G^{(\ell)}$ between i and j is at most $D = 4 \log M$, and hence $|K^{(\ell)}| \leq 4 \log M$.

Assume without loss of generality that the adversary makes exactly T_A queries to $H^{(\ell)}$ (and $F^{(\ell)}$) for each $\ell \in [L]$. Recall that the L executions of the setup protocol are independent. Therefore, as in the proof of Proposition 9, by induction on the number of queries to $H^{(\ell)}$ (and $F^{(\ell)}$) (denoted by t), they either hit $K^{(\ell)}$ with probability at most $|K^{(\ell)}| \cdot t/N \leq 4 \log M \cdot t/N$, or only give the information that $K^{(\ell)}$ does not intersect these queries. Hence, $\Pr[\mathcal{E}_\ell = 1] \leq \left(\frac{4 \log M \cdot T_A}{N}\right)$ holds for each $\ell \in L$ independently of all $\mathcal{E}_f$ for $f \neq \ell$. Thus,

$$\Pr[\wedge_{\ell \in [L]} \mathcal{E}_\ell = 1] = \prod_{\ell \in [L]} \Pr[\mathcal{E}_\ell = 1 \mid \wedge_{f \in [\ell-1]} \mathcal{E}_f = 1] \leq \left(\frac{4 \log M \cdot T_A}{N}\right)^L. \quad (2)$$

Remark 1. We also need to condition on the success of the protocol that constructs $G^{(\ell)}$, i.e., on the event that the graph $G^{(\ell)}$ is of diameter at most $D = 4 \log M$. However, the diameter of the graph (or its structure in general) does not reveal any information about the individual queries of the players to $H^{(\ell)}$ (each one remains uniformly distributed). Hence the event is independent of the success probability of the adversary.

We can obtain a slightly better bound as follows. Consider a restricted adversary that before making any query to the oracles, fixes some subset $L' \subseteq L$ of size $L/2$ and makes at most $2T_A/L$ queries to $H^{(\ell)}$ (and $F^{(\ell)}$) for each $\ell \in L'$. For such an adversary,

$$\Pr[\wedge_{\ell \in [L]} \bar{\mathcal{E}}_\ell = 1] \leq \Pr[\wedge_{\ell \in [L']} \bar{\mathcal{E}}_\ell = 1] \leq \left(\frac{8 \log M \cdot T_A}{L \cdot N} \right)^{L/2}$$

similarly to (2) (where $\bar{\mathcal{E}}_\ell$ are random variables associated with the restricted adversary). For an arbitrary adversary that makes a total of at most T_A queries, there is always such a subset $L' \subseteq L$ of size $L/2$, but L' may depend on the oracle queries. Yet, we can build a restricted adversary from an arbitrary one by guessing the subset L' uniformly at random in advance. Since our guess is correct with probability at least 2^{-L}, we have

$$\Pr[\wedge_{\ell \in [L]} \mathcal{E}_\ell = 1] \leq 2^L \cdot \Pr[\wedge_{\ell \in [L]} \bar{\mathcal{E}}_\ell = 1] \leq 2^L \left(\frac{8 \log M \cdot T_A}{L \cdot N} \right)^{L/2} = \left(\frac{32 \log M \cdot T_A}{L \cdot N} \right)^{L/2}.$$

Since $L \geq 16 \log T$ and $T_A \leq N/4$, we get $\Pr[\wedge_{\ell \in [L]} \mathcal{E}_\ell = 1] \leq 2^{-L/2} \leq T^{-8}$.

The proposition follows by a union bound over all $(i,j) \in E_s$ (whose size is less than $M^2 \leq T^2$). ∎

5.2 Main Theorem

The formal version of Theorem 1 is given below.

Theorem 2. *Assume that $M \geq 64$, $T \geq 20000$, $T \geq M$ and $|E_s| = \tilde{O}(M)$. Let $\hat{T} = \tilde{O}(T)$ be sufficiently large. Then, Protocol 2 is a*

$$\left(M, \alpha = 1 - \tilde{O}(\hat{T}^{-1}), \hat{T}, \beta = 1 - \tilde{O}(\hat{T}^{-1}) \right) \text{-DKAP}$$

which is

$$\left(T_A = \tilde{\Theta}(M \cdot \hat{T}^2), \alpha_A = \tilde{O}\left(\frac{1}{M \cdot \hat{T}^2} \right) \right) \text{-secure.}$$

Proof. We prove the equivalent statement that Protocol 2 is a

$$\left(M, \alpha = 1 - \tilde{O}(T^{-1}), \tilde{O}(T), \beta = 1 - \tilde{O}(T^{-1}) \right) \text{-DKAP}$$

which is

$$\left(T_A = \tilde{\Theta}(M \cdot T^2), \alpha_A = \tilde{O}\left(\frac{1}{M \cdot T^2} \right) \right) \text{-secure.}$$

Correctness. The protocol is correct if at least L of the setup protocol executions do not fail and all pairs of players agree on consistent keys. By Proposition 2 and a union bound over the $2L$ executions, a pair of players output inconsistent keys with probability at most $2L \cdot T^{-2}$.

By Proposition 8, each execution of the setup protocol fails (the players output $\perp$) with probability at most $2e \cdot M^{-1} \leq 1/8$ (since $M \geq 64$). In a sequence of L independent executions, all fail with probability at most 2^{-3L}. Hence, there exists such a sequence among the $2L$ executions of the protocol with probability at most $2^{2L} \cdot 2^{-3L} = 2^{-L}$.

Therefore, the protocol is correct, except with probability at most

$$2L \cdot T^{-2} + 2^{-L} \leq T^{-1} = \tilde{O}(T^{-1})$$

(as $T \geq 20000$).

Queries and Communication. The setup protocol is executed $2L = 2\lceil 16 \log T \rceil < 34 \log T$ times. By Proposition 3, in each execution each player makes at most T queries with probability 1 and communicates $\tilde{O}(T)$ bits, except with probability $M \cdot 2^{-T} + (36 \log T \cdot T)^{-1} + T^{-2}$. Moreover, each edge in E_s results in at most L additional queries (and L messages) per player in the strong secure link protocol (Algorithm 3).

Thus, each player makes less than

$$34 \log T \cdot T + 17 \log T \cdot |E_s| = \tilde{O}(T)$$

queries, and communicates $\tilde{O}(T)$ bits, except with probability at most

$$2L \cdot (M \cdot 2^{-T} + (36 \log T \cdot T)^{-1} + T^{-2}) \leq T^{-1} = \tilde{O}(T^{-1})$$

(since $T \geq 20000$).

Security. By Proposition 10, any adversary that makes at most

$$T_A = \frac{N}{8} \geq \frac{M \cdot T^2}{208 \ln M} = \tilde{\Theta}(M \cdot T^2)$$

queries to the random oracle outputs $((i,j), k_{i,j})$ for $(i,j) \in E_s$ with probability at most

$$T^{-6} \cdot 1 + (1 - T^{-6}) \cdot 1/N \leq \frac{2}{N} \leq \frac{52 \ln M}{M \cdot T^2} = \tilde{O}\left(\frac{1}{M \cdot T^2}\right).$$

∎

6   Optimality of the Distributed Key Agreement Protocol

We prove the optimality of our key agreement protocol (up to logarithmic factors) with respect to the ratio of the number of queries made by each honest player and the adversary. We use the following result.

Theorem 3 ([3], Theorem 3.1, adapted). *Let Π be a 2-player key agreement protocol between p_1 and p_2 using a random oracle H in which:*

- *p_1 makes at most T_1 queries to H and outputs $k_{1,2}$.*
- *p_2 makes at most T_2 queries to H and outputs $k_{2,1}$.*
- *$\Pr[k_{1,2} = k_{2,1}] \geq \alpha$*

Then, for every $0 < \delta < \alpha$, there is an adversary with access to the transcript of the protocol that makes at most $400 \cdot T_1 \cdot T_2/\delta^2$ queries to H and outputs $k_{2,1}$ with probability at least $\alpha - \delta$.

Proposition 11. *Let Π be a protocol between M players using a random oracle H in which:*

- *Every player makes at most T queries to H.*
- *p_1 outputs $j \in [M]\setminus\{1\}$ and $k_{1,j}$, and p_j outputs $k_{j,1}$.*
- *$\Pr[k_{1,j} = k_{j,1}] \geq \alpha$.*

Then, for every $0 < \delta < \alpha$, there is an adversary with access to the transcript of the protocol that makes at most $400 \cdot M \cdot T^2/\delta^2$ queries to H and outputs $k_{j,1}$ with probability at least $\alpha - \delta$.

Proof. Given an M-player protocol Π as above with players $p_1, \ldots, p_M$, we devise a 2-player protocol Π' with players p_1' and p_2' as follows: player p_1' simulates p_1 by sending all messages intended for $p_2, \ldots, p_M$ to p_2'. Player p_2' simulates $p_2, \ldots, p_M$ by sending all messages intended for p_1 to p_1' (messages sent among $p_2, \ldots, p_M$ do not require communication). Finally, if p_1 outputs j and $k_{1,j}$, then p_1' outputs $k_{1,2}' = k_{1,j}$ and sends j to p_2' that outputs $k_{2,1}' = k_{j,1}$.

We have $\Pr[k_{1,j} = k_{j,1}] \geq \alpha$, and hence $\Pr[k_{1,2}' = k_{2,1}'] \geq \alpha$. Moreover, p_1' makes at most T queries to H, while p_2' makes at most $(M-1) \cdot T < M \cdot T$ queries to H. Therefore, by Theorem 3, there exists an adversary $\mathcal{A}'$ with access to the transcript of Π' that makes at most $400 \cdot M \cdot T^2/\delta^2$ queries to H and outputs $k_{2,1}'$ with probability at least $\alpha - \delta$.

We devise an adversary $\mathcal{A}$ for Π using $\mathcal{A}'$: $\mathcal{A}$ gives to $\mathcal{A}'$ only the messages sent and received by p_1 (so that the transcript is identical to the corresponding execution of Π') and outputs the same value. Thus, $\mathcal{A}$ makes at most $400 \cdot M \cdot T^2/\delta^2$ queries to H and outputs $k_{j,1} = k_{2,1}'$ with probability at least $\alpha - \delta$. ∎

Theorem 4. *Any (M, α, T, β)-DKAP that is (T_A, α_A)-secure for non-empty $E_s \subseteq [M] \times [M]$ such that $\alpha \geq 3/4$ and $T_A \geq 6400M \cdot T^2$, satisfies $\alpha_A \geq 1/2$.*

Proof. Apply Proposition 11 for an edge $(j, 1) \in E_s$ (by renaming the players) and $\delta = 1/4$. Since $\Pr[k_{1,j} = k_{j,1}] \geq 3/4$, and $T_A \geq 6400M \cdot T^2 = 400M \cdot T^2/\delta^2$, there exists an adversary that makes at most T_A queries to H and outputs $k_{j,1}$ with probability at least $3/4 - 1/4 = 1/2$. ∎

7   Extensions

We briefly discuss two extensions of the protocol.

7.1   The Semi-honest Model

We consider security in a model where adversarial players execute the protocol as designed, but try to learn the secret keys of the honest players.

With small overhead, the protocol can be extended to provide resistance against an adversary that controls a fraction of $O(1/\log M)$ of the players in the semi-honest model, which are chosen in advance (i.e., static corruptions). In particular, such an extension allows any two honest players to communicate securely, except with negligible probability (unless the adversary makes $\tilde{\Omega}(M \cdot T^2)$ queries to the random oracle).

The extension is simple. Fix some edge $(i, j) \in E_s$ between two honest players. Note that the only advantage of the corrupted players (over an eavesdropping adversary) is in the strong secure link protocol. Specifically, in this protocol p_i chooses $k_{i,j}$ and sends each of its shares on a path to p_j, encrypted using secure links created by a setup protocol execution. In order to maintain security, we must ensure that with high probability, there is at least one path in which all players are honest.

Recall that each path chosen by p_i to encrypt $k_{i,j}$ is of length at most $D = 4 \log M$. Therefore, each path does not include any corrupted player with constant probability. Repeating the setup protocol independently $\Omega(\log T)$ times (while choosing among shortest paths independently via randomization), ensures that $\Omega(\log T)$ paths do not include a corrupted player (except with small probability) and the analysis of the original protocol applies to these paths with small modifications. Thus, the only change required is to repeat the setup protocol according to the fraction of adversarial players we wish to tolerate. On the other hand, we conjecture that it is not possible to tolerate a constant fraction of adversarial players with a small overhead of $\tilde{O}(1)$ in query complexity.

7.2   Communication-Security Tradeoff

For a parameter $B \geq 1$ such that $T = \tilde{\Omega}(M \cdot B)$, it is possible to extend the protocol such that each player makes T queries and communicates $\tilde{O}(T/B)$ bits, while any adversary has to make $\tilde{\Omega}\left(\frac{M \cdot T^2}{B}\right)$ queries to recover any key with high probability. As for standard Merkle's puzzles, this can done by defining a new random oracle H' based on H by partitioning its domain into groups of size B. The output of a query to H' is computed by summing (modulo N') the outputs of the corresponding group (consisting of B queries to H).

References

1. Barak, B.: The complexity of public-key cryptography. In: Tutorials on the Foundations of Cryptography. ISC, pp. 45–77. Springer, Cham (2017). https://doi.org/10.1007/978-3-319-57048-8_2
2. Barak, B., Mahmoody-Ghidary, M.: Merkle puzzles are optimal — an $O(n^2)$-query attack on any key exchange from a random oracle. In: Halevi, S. (ed.) CRYPTO 2009. LNCS, vol. 5677, pp. 374–390. Springer, Heidelberg (2009). https://doi.org/10.1007/978-3-642-03356-8_22

3. Barak, B., Mahmoody-Ghidary, M.: Merkle's key agreement protocol is optimal: an $O(n^2)$ attack on any key agreement from random oracles. J. Cryptol. **30**(3), 699–734 (2017)
4. Biham, E., Goren, Y.J., Ishai, Y.: Basing weak public-key cryptography on strong one-way functions. In: Canetti, R. (ed.) TCC 2008. LNCS, vol. 4948, pp. 55–72. Springer, Heidelberg (2008). https://doi.org/10.1007/978-3-540-78524-8_4
5. Chan, H., Perrig, A., Song, D.X.: Random key predistribution schemes for sensor networks. In: 2003 IEEE Symposium on Security and Privacy (S&P 2003), 11–14 May 2003, Berkeley, CA, USA, p. 197. IEEE Computer Society (2003)
6. Chung, F., Lu, L.: The diameter of sparse random graphs. Adv. Appl. Math. **26**(4), 257–279 (2001)
7. Diffie, W., Hellman, M.E.: New directions in cryptography. IEEE Trans. Inf. Theory **22**(6), 644–654 (1976)
8. Dolev, D., Dwork, C., Waarts, O., Yung, M.: Perfectly secure message transmission. J. ACM **40**(1), 17–47 (1993)
9. Eschenauer, L., Gligor, V.D.: A key-management scheme for distributed sensor networks. In: Atluri, V. (ed.) Proceedings of the 9th ACM Conference on Computer and Communications Security, CCS 2002, Washington, DC, USA, 18–22 November 2002, pp. 41–47. ACM (2002)
10. Fischer, M.J., Wright, R.N.: Multiparty secret key exchange using a random deal of cards. In: Feigenbaum, J. (ed.) CRYPTO 1991. LNCS, vol. 576, pp. 141–155. Springer, Heidelberg (1992). https://doi.org/10.1007/3-540-46766-1_10
11. Goldreich, O., Nisan, N., Wigderson, A.: On Yao's XOR-Lemma. In: Goldreich, O. (ed.) Studies in Complexity and Cryptography. Miscellanea on the Interplay between Randomness and Computation. LNCS, vol. 6650, pp. 273–301. Springer, Heidelberg (2011). https://doi.org/10.1007/978-3-642-22670-0_23
12. Haitner, I., Mazor, N., Oshman, R., Reingold, O., Yehudayoff, A.: On the communication complexity of key-agreement protocols. In: Blum, A. (ed.) 10th Innovations in Theoretical Computer Science Conference, ITCS 2019, San Diego, California, USA, 10–12 January 2019, vol. 124, pp. 40:1–40:16. LIPIcs, Schloss Dagstuhl - Leibniz-Zentrum für Informatik (2019)
13. Impagliazzo, R., Luby, M.: One-way functions are essential for complexity based cryptography (extended abstract). In: 30th Annual Symposium on Foundations of Computer Science, Research Triangle Park, North Carolina, USA, 30 October–1 November 1989, pp. 230–235. IEEE Computer Society (1989)
14. Ingemarsson, I., Tang, D.T., Wong, C.K.: A conference key distribution system. IEEE Trans. Inf. Theory **28**(5), 714–719 (1982)
15. Krivelevich, M.: Expanders - how to find them, and what to find in them (2019)
16. Leighton, T., Micali, S.: Secret-key agreement without public-key cryptography. In: Stinson, D.R. (ed.) CRYPTO 1993. LNCS, vol. 773, pp. 456–479. Springer, Heidelberg (1994). https://doi.org/10.1007/3-540-48329-2_39
17. Merkle, R.C.: Secure communications over insecure channels. Commun. ACM **21**(4), 294–299 (1978)
18. Mitzenmacher, M., Upfal, E.: Probability and Computing: Randomized Algorithms and Probabilistic Analysis. Cambridge University Press, Cambridge (2005)

Continuously Non-malleable Secret Sharing: Joint Tampering, Plain Model and Capacity

Gianluca Brian[1(✉)], Antonio Faonio[2], and Daniele Venturi[1]

[1] Sapienza University of Rome, Rome, Italy
brian@di.uniroma1.it
[2] EURECOM, Biot, France

Abstract. We study non-malleable secret sharing against *joint leakage* and *joint tampering* attacks. Our main result is the first *threshold* secret sharing scheme in the *plain model* achieving resilience to noisy-leakage and continuous tampering. The above holds under (necessary) minimal computational assumptions (*i.e.*, the existence of one-to-one one-way functions), and in a model where the adversary commits to a fixed partition of all the shares into non-overlapping subsets of at most $t-1$ shares (where t is the reconstruction threshold), and subsequently jointly leaks from and tampers with the shares within each partition.

We also study the *capacity* (*i.e.*, the maximum achievable asymptotic information rate) of continuously non-malleable secret sharing against joint continuous tampering attacks. In particular, we prove that whenever the attacker can tamper jointly with $k > t/2$ shares, the capacity is at most $t - k$. The rate of our construction matches this upper bound.

An important corollary of our results is the first non-malleable secret sharing scheme against *independent tampering* attacks breaking the rate-one barrier (under the same computational assumptions as above).

Keywords: Secret sharing · Non-malleability · Leakage resilience

1 Introduction

A t-out-of-n secret sharing scheme [5,28] allows to distribute a message into n shares in such a way that: (i) given t or more shares we can reconstruct the original message; and (ii) any attacker corrupting strictly less than t share holders has no information about the message. The parameter t is called the reconstruction threshold, and a scheme with the above properties is called a *threshold* secret sharing. An important efficiency parameter of secret sharing is the so-called *information rate*, which equals the ratio between the length of the message and the maximum length of a share.

Goyal and Kumar [18] introduced *non-malleable* secret sharing, which further satisfies the following guarantee: (iii) no attacker tampering with possibly all of

The first and last author acknowledge support by Sapienza University under the grant SPECTRA.

K. Nissim and B. Waters (Eds.): TCC 2021, LNCS 13043, pp. 333–364, 2021.
https://doi.org/10.1007/978-3-030-90453-1_12

the shares can generate a valid secret sharing of a message which is related to the original shared value. This notion was inspired by the related concept of non-malleable codes defined by Dziembowski, Pietrzak and Wichs [14], and by similar notions in the setting of non-malleable cryptography [12,13].

Clearly, we must put some restriction on how the attacker can tamper with the shares (as if she can tamper with all of them in a joint manner she can reconstruct the message and compute a valid secret sharing of a related value). The original paper by Goyal and Kumar constructed threshold secret sharing schemes both against *independent tampering* attacks (*i.e.*, each share can be tampered arbitrarily yet independently) and *joint tampering* attacks (*i.e.*, the attacker can partition any set of t shares into two non-empty subsets and tamper jointly with the shares contained in each subset). This initial result spurred further research on the subject, yielding non-malleable secret sharing schemes with additional properties and with resilience to stronger tampering attacks. We review the state of the art for joint tampering (which is the focus of this paper) below, and in Table 1, and refer the reader to Sect. 1.4 for additional related work.

1.1 Non-malleability Against Joint Tampering

In a follow-up paper, Goyal and Kumar [19] constructed n-out-of-n non-malleable secret sharing in a stronger tampering model where the attacker can partition the n shares into two (possibly overlapping) subsets of its choice, and then jointly tamper with the shares in each of the subsets independently. Similarly to the construction in [18], the information rate of this scheme asymptotically reaches zero (when the message length goes to infinity).

Brian, Faonio and Venturi [7] showed how to compile any *leakage-resilient* secret sharing into a *continuously* non-malleable one [15,16] using a trusted setup (and computational assumptions). Here, leakage resilience refers to the guarantee that the secret remains hidden even given leakage from the shares. Continuous non-malleability refers to the ability of the attacker to adaptively tamper polymany[1] times with the same target secret sharing.

When the initial secret sharing is resilient to joint-leakage attacks, the compiled scheme tolerates continuous joint-tampering and joint-leakage attacks in a model where the adversary commits to a partition $\mathcal{B} = (\mathcal{B}_1, \ldots, \mathcal{B}_m)$ of $[n]$ into m disjoint subsets of size at most k at the beginning of the experiment, and subsequently can tamper with and leak from the shares within each subset in an adaptive fashion. The reconstruction set $\mathcal{T}$ (with cardinality $|\mathcal{T}| \geq t$) associated to each tampering query can be chosen adaptively, a feature sometimes known under the name of *adaptive concurrent reconstruction* [1]. In this work, we dub secret sharing schemes that are secure in the above setting as leakage-resilient continuously non-malleable under *selective* k-joint leakage and tampering attacks. By plugging recent constructions of leakage-resilient secret sharing under joint-leakage attacks [9,22,23], we get rate-zero schemes satisfying this notion either for arbitrary access structures with $k = O(\log n)$, or for threshold access structures with $k = t - 1$ (which is optimal).

---

[1] The only (necessary) restriction is that the experiment self-destructs after the first tampering query yielding an invalid secret sharing.

Brian *et al.* [6] showed how to compile any leakage-resilient one-time non-malleable secret sharing scheme with *statistical security* under selective k-joint leakage and tampering attacks into a p-time *computationally* non-malleable secret sharing under selective k-joint tampering attacks in the plain model (assuming one-to-one one-way functions). Here, p-time non-malleability means that the number of tolerated tampering queries is a-priori bounded (and the length of the shares depends on it). Moreover, when the initial secret sharing is secure under *adaptive* k-joint leakage and tampering attacks (*i.e.*, the attacker can change the partition adaptively within each leakage/tampering query), the compiled scheme satisfies p-time non-malleability under *semi-adaptive*[2] k-joint tampering attacks too. Combined with [9,18,19,22,23], the results of [6] ultimately yield rate-zero schemes satisfying the latter notion either for arbitrary access structures with $k = O(\log n)$, or for threshold access structures with $k = O(t/\log t)$ (and $k = t - 1$ in case of selective partitioning).

Finally, Goyal, Srinivasan and Zhu [20] obtain rate-zero one-time non-malleable threshold secret sharing with statistical security against t-cover free tampering, which intuitively requires that every share is tampered together with at most $t-2$ other shares (this model includes disjoint tampering as a special case).

1.2   Our Results

A major drawback of [6] is that it only satisfies computational p-time non-malleability. This is far from optimal, as the notion could in principle be obtained information theoretically. On the other hand, [7] achieves continuous non-malleability under selective partitioning of the shares at the price of assuming a trusted setup (and minimal, inherent, computational assumptions).

Our main contribution is a construction of leakage-resilient *continuously* non-malleable t-out-of-n secret sharing under *selective* k-joint leakage and tampering attacks in the *plain model* (assuming one-to-one one-way functions), for any $k < t$ and $t \geq 2n/3$. Furthermore, our scheme achieves the following features:

- The information rate asymptotically reaches 1, which we show to be optimal.
- Leakage resilience holds in the stronger (and more practical) model where the length of the leakage (from each subset in the fixed partition of the shares) is arbitrary, so long as it does not decrease the min-entropy of the shares by more than ℓ bits (where $\ell \geq 0$ is called the *noisy-leakage* parameter).

An interesting corollary of our results is the first non-malleable t-out-of-n secret sharing under *independent* tampering attacks in the plain model (assuming one-to-one one-way functions) breaking the rate-one barrier (for $t \geq 2n/3$). In particular, we obtain asymptotic rate $t/2$.

All previous non-malleable secret sharing schemes against joint tampering had rate zero, and the only scheme with rate one was secure in the much weaker setting of independent tampering [15]. In this vein, our result shows that the

---

[2] In this setting, once a subset of shares has been tampered with jointly, that subset is always either tampered jointly or not modified by future tampering queries.

Table 1. State-of-the-art non-malleable secret sharing schemes tolerating joint tampering and leakage attacks. The value n denotes the number of parties, $|\mu|$ is the size of the message, ℓ denotes the leakage parameter, p is the number of tampering queries, λ denotes the security parameter, t is the reconstruction threshold, and k is the maximal number of shares that can be tampered jointly. Semi-adaptive partitioning refers to the ability of the attacker to change the way the target shares are partitioned within each leakage/tampering query in a somewhat restricted manner [6]. OWFs stands for "one-way functions", TDPs for "(doubly-enhanced) trapdoor permutations", CRHs for "collision-resistant hash functions", CRS for "common reference string", ROM for "random oracle model", and AGM for "algebraic group model". For readability, in the last two rows the values for the rates are displayed as lower bounds.

Reference	Access Structure	Non-Malleability	Leakage	Rate	Assumptions	Partitioning
[18]	Threshold $(t \geq 2)$	1-Time $(k < t)$	✗	$\Theta(|\mu|^{-9})$	—	Disjoint
[19]	Threshold $(t = n)$	1-Time $(k < t)$	✗	$\Theta(|\mu|^{-6})$	—	Overlapping
[7]	General	Continuous $(k \leq O(\log n))$	Bounded	$\mathsf{poly}(|\mu|, n, \ell, \lambda)^{-1}$	TDPs, CRHs, CRS	Selective, Disjoint
	Threshold $(t \geq 2)$	Continuous $(k < t)$	Bounded	$\mathsf{poly}(|\mu|, n, \ell, \lambda)^{-1}$	TDPs, CRHs, CRS	Selective, Disjoint
	Threshold $(t = n)$	Continuous $(k \leq 0.99n)$	Bounded	$\mathsf{poly}(|\mu|, n, \ell, \lambda)^{-1}$	TDPs, CRHs, CRS	Selective, Disjoint
[6]	Threshold $(t \geq 2)$	p-Time $(k < t)$	✗	$\mathsf{poly}(|\mu|, n, p, \lambda)^{-1}$	1-to-1 OWFs	Selective, Disjoint
	Threshold $(t = n)$	p-Time $(k < t)$	✗	$\mathsf{poly}(|\mu|, n, p, \lambda)^{-1}$	1-to-1 OWFs	Selective, Disjoint
	General	p-Time $(k \leq O(\log n))$	✗	$\mathsf{poly}(|\mu|, n, p, \lambda)^{-1}$	1-to-1 OWFs	Semi-Adaptive, Disjoint
	Threshold $(t \geq 2)$	p-Time $(k \leq O(t/\log t))$	✗	$\mathsf{poly}(|\mu|, n, p, \lambda)^{-1}$	1-to-1 OWFs	Semi-Adaptive, Disjoint
	Threshold $(t = n)$	p-Time $(k \leq 0.99n)$	✗	$\mathsf{poly}(|\mu|, n, p, \lambda)^{-1}$	1-to-1 OWFs	Semi-Adaptive, Disjoint
[20]	Threshold $(t \geq 2)$	1-Time $(k < t)$	✗	$\mathsf{poly}(|\mu|, n, \ell, \lambda)^{-1}$	—	Overlapping
[8], Sect. 6.1	Threshold $(t \geq 2)$	1-Time $(k < t)$	Noisy	$\mathsf{poly}(|\mu|, n, \ell, \lambda)^{-1}$	—	Disjoint
Section 6.2	Threshold $(t \geq 2n/3)$	Continuous $(k < t)$	Noisy	$1 - \mathsf{poly}(n, \ell, \lambda) \cdot |\mu|^{-1}$	1-to-1 OWFs	Selective, Disjoint
[8], Sect. 6.2	Threshold $(t \geq 2n/3)$	Continuous $(k < t)$	Noisy	$t - \mathsf{poly}(n, \ell, \lambda) \cdot |\mu|^{-1}$	ROM/AGM	Selective, Disjoint
Section 6.3	Threshold $(t \geq 2n/3)$	1-Time $(k = 1)$	Noisy	$t/2 - \mathsf{poly}(n, \ell, \lambda) \cdot |\mu|^{-1}$	1-to-1 OWFs	—

lower bounds on the rate of leakage-resilient and non-malleable secret sharing [6,25] can be circumvented in the computational setting. We stress that cryptographic assumptions are inherent for continuous non-malleability [15,16,29].

1.3 Overview of Techniques

The construction of our secret sharing schemes consists of two main steps. First, we show how to obtain leakage-resilient continuously non-malleable t-out-of-n secret sharing under selective $(t - 1)$-joint leakage and tampering attacks in the plain model, with asymptotic rate zero. Second, we show how to boost the asymptotic rate to one generically.

Rate-Zero Construction. In order to explain our techniques, it will be useful to recall the construction of leakage-resilient continuously non-malleable t-out-of-n secret sharing under independent[3] tampering attacks in the plain model, by Brian, Faonio and Venturi [7] (which in turn builds on the construction by Ostrovsky *et al.* [26]). For simplicity, let us focus on the case $t = n = 2$ (*i.e.*, so-called leakage-resilient non-malleable *split-state codes*).

Here, one takes the message μ and commits to it via a non-interactive (perfectly binding) commitment scheme using random coins ρ, yielding a commitment γ. Hence, the string $\mu\|\rho$ is secret shared using a leakage-resilient one-time

---

[3] i.e., one-joint leakage and tampering attacks.

non-malleable 2-out-of-2 secret sharing scheme. This yields shares (σ_1, σ_2), so that the final shares become $\sigma_1^* = (\gamma, \sigma_1)$ and $\sigma_2^* = (\gamma, \sigma_2)$. In the following, we will refer to σ_1^* as the left share and to σ_2^* as the right share. The reconstruction algorithm proceeds naturally by first checking that the left and right commitment are the same value γ, and thus reconstructing the string $\mu||\rho$ from the shares (σ_1, σ_2) and outputting μ if and only if (μ, ρ) is a valid opening for the commitment.

The security analysis crucially relies on the assumption that the underlying one-time non-malleable secret sharing scheme has statistical security. In particular, the main hurdle in the proof is to reduce continuous non-malleability to one-time non-malleability. Brian et al. overcome this obstacle using the following strategy. First, they move to a mental[4] experiment in which (σ_1, σ_2) is a secret sharing of $\mu||\rho'$, where ρ' is random and independent of the random coins ρ used to compute the commitment γ. Second, they reduce a distinguisher between the real and mental experiment to an (inefficient) attacker against statistical leakage-resilient one-time non-malleability. The key idea of this reduction is to simulate multiple tampering queries by leaking the commitments $\tilde{\gamma}_1$ and $\tilde{\gamma}_2$ contained in the tampered shares $\tilde{\sigma}_1$ and $\tilde{\sigma}_2$. If $\tilde{\gamma}_1 \neq \tilde{\gamma}_2$ the reduction outputs $\perp$ and self-destructs, and otherwise it brute forces the commitment and outputs the corresponding message.

In order for the reduction to go through, one needs to argue that it does not ask too much leakage. Here is where noisy-leakage resilience kicks in. Brian et al. assume that the underlying secret sharing satisfies an additional property known as conditional independence: For any message, the right (resp. left) share drops the conditional average min-entropy of the left (resp. right) share by some (possibly small) parameter $d \in \mathbb{N}$. This property is satisfied by existing leakage-resilient one-time non-malleable t-out-of-n secret sharing schemes in the independent leakage and tampering model [7,26]. Now, the point is that, so long as the commitments $\tilde{\gamma}_1$ and $\tilde{\gamma}_2$ are equal, the leakage on the left (resp. right) share can be thought of as a function of the right (resp. left share), and thus the overall leakage does not drop the min-entropy by more than $d + |\gamma| + O(\log \lambda)$ where the additional loss $|\gamma|$ corresponds to the tampering query in which $\tilde{\gamma}_1 \neq \tilde{\gamma}_2$ (and the term $O(\log \lambda)$ corresponds to the index of such query). Luckily, the latter happens only once because after that a self-destruct is triggered, which ultimately allows the reduction to go through.

1st Barrier: Leakage-Resilient One-Time Non-malleability. The first (obvious) difficulty in order to generalize the above construction to the joint-tampering setting is that we need a leakage-resilient one-time non-malleable t-out-of-n secret sharing under joint leakage and tampering attacks, which was not known. We overcome this difficulty by suitably modifying a recent construction by Goyal, Srinivasan and Zhu [20], which we briefly recall below.

---

[4] In the hybrid experiment, one also needs to adjust the reconstruction algorithm so that an attacker cannot distinguish between the hybrid and the original experiment by mauling σ_1, σ_2 without changing the underlying shared value. In the description, we omit these details to simplify the exposition.

The sharing procedure first shares the message μ using a t-out-of-n secret sharing scheme Π. Then, given the resulting shares $(\sigma_1, \ldots, \sigma_n)$, it encodes each σ_i into a codeword $(\sigma_{\mathsf{L},i}, \sigma_{\mathsf{R},i})$ using a t-time non-malleable split-state code Π'. Finally, it uses again the t-out-of-n secret sharing scheme Π to obtain shares $(\sigma_{\mathsf{R},i}^{(1)}, \ldots, \sigma_{\mathsf{R},i}^{(n)})$ of the right part of the codeword $\sigma_{\mathsf{R},i}$ for each $i \in [n]$. This yields shares $(\sigma_{\mathsf{L},i})_{i \in [n]}$ and $(\sigma_{\mathsf{R},i}^{(j)})_{i,j \in [n]}$, which are distributed to the players by letting $\sigma_i^* = (\sigma_{\mathsf{L},i}, (\sigma_{\mathsf{R},j}^{(i)})_{j \in [n]})$ for all $i \in [n]$.

Goyal et $al.$ proved that the construction is a t-out-of-n one-time non-malleable secret sharing scheme with statistical security under k-joint tampering[5] attacks for any $k < t$. The original analysis did not consider leakage resilience. However, it is not too hard to lift the proof to the setting in which the attacker is also allowed to perform noisy-leakage attacks, so long as the secret sharing scheme Π' is noisy-leakage-resilient t-time non-malleable. See the full version [8] for a formal treatment.

2nd Barrier: Conditional Independence. The second barrier is more subtle. One may think that after obtaining leakage-resilient one-time non-malleable t-out-of-n secret sharing under joint leakage and tampering attacks we would be done by using this scheme instead of the t-out-of-n one-time non-malleable secret sharing under independent leakage and tampering attacks in the construction by Brian, Faonio and Venturi [7].

Unfortunately, generalizing their analysis based on conditional independence to the case of joint leakage and tampering attacks is not straightforward. Recall that the reduction cannot perform too much noisy leakage. In our case, the reduction needs to leak the tampered commitments $(\tilde{\gamma}_i)_{i \in [m]}$, $i.e.$ one commitment for each set of tampered shares.[6]

For concreteness, let us focus on the leakage performed on the shares within a fixed subset $\mathcal{B}_i$ of the partition. While it is still true that, before self-destruct, the tampered commitment $\tilde{\gamma}_i$ corresponding to a tampering query $(\mathcal{T}, (f_1, \ldots, f_m))$ can be thought of as a function of the shares within $\mathcal{T} \backslash \mathcal{B}_i$, the fact that the reconstruction set $\mathcal{T}$ can change across different tampering queries would require the following flavor of conditional independence: For any message and any unauthorized subset $\mathcal{U}$, the shares within $[n] \backslash \mathcal{U}$ drop the conditional average min-entropy of the shares within $\mathcal{U}$ by some (possibly small) parameter $d \in \mathbb{N}$.

However, the leakage-resilient one-time non-malleable t-out-of-n secret sharing under joint leakage and tampering attacks we described in the previous paragraph does not satisfy such a strong flavor of conditional independence. This is because, $e.g.$, in Shamir's secret sharing with $t < n$, the conditional average min-entropy of the first share conditioned on all other shares is zero (as given any t shares we can interpolate the polynomial used to determine the shares). In Sect. 4, we show how to circumvent this problem by leaving off one level of

---

[5] Actually, Goyal et $al.$ prove security in the more general setting of t-cover-free tampering, in which, intuitively, the subsets of the partition of the shares may overlap.

[6] Note that in case the tampered commitments within one of the subsets $\mathcal{B}_i$ are not equal, the reduction can immediately self-destruct.

abstraction. Namely, we analyze the compiler from [7] when instantiated with (our leakage-resilient variant of) the secret sharing scheme from [20]. Intuitively, this allows us to perform an hybrid argument where at each step we reduce to leakage-resilient t-time non-malleability of the underlying 2-out-of-2 secret sharing schemes, and thus to only assume the standard flavor of conditional independence for such kind of secret sharing schemes, which is much easier to achieve.

Capacity of Continuously Non-malleable Secret Sharing. The above construction still has shares of length polynomial in the number of parties, the leakage parameter, the security parameter, and the message size, thus yielding information rate asymptotically reaching 0. Motivated by this limitation, we study the *capacity* (*i.e.*, the best achievable rate) of continuously non-malleable threshold secret sharing against joint tampering. As our main negative result, in Sect. 5.1, we establish that whenever the attacker can tamper jointly with $k > t/2$ shares, the capacity is at most $t - k$.

The latter can be seen as follows. Let Π be any continuously non-malleable threshold secret sharing scheme against joint tampering with at most k shares. Consider the non-interactive commitment scheme whose commit procedure does a secret sharing of the message μ obtaining $(\sigma_1, \ldots, \sigma_n)$ using a continuous non-malleable secret sharing scheme, and finally outputs $\gamma = (\sigma_1, \ldots, \sigma_{t-k})$. If we can show that this commitment is perfectly binding then $|\mu| \leq |\gamma| = (t - k) \cdot s$ (where s is the size of a single share), and thus the rate of Π must be at most $t - k$. Assume the commitment scheme is not perfectly binding, namely, there exist two distinct messages $\mu^{(0)}$ and $\mu^{(1)}$, along with openings ρ_0 and ρ_1, such that $\gamma = (\sigma_1, \ldots, \sigma_{t-k})$ is consistent with both $(\mu^{(0)}, \rho_0)$ and $(\mu^{(1)}, \rho_1)$.

We show how to construct an efficient adversary breaking continuous non-malleability of Π. Let $\sigma^* = (\sigma_1^*, \ldots, \sigma_n^*)$ be the target secret sharing. The adversary computes offline $\sigma^{(0)} = (\sigma_1^{(0)}, \ldots, \sigma_n^{(0)})$ and $\sigma^{(1)} = (\sigma_1^{(1)}, \ldots, \sigma_n^{(1)})$ by secret sharing $\mu^{(0)}$ with coins ρ_0 and $\mu^{(1)}$ with coins ρ_1. Note that, by construction, the first $t - k$ shares of $\sigma^{(0)}$ and $\sigma^{(1)}$ are identical. Hence, the attacker tampers repeatedly with σ^* as described below:

- It fixes the partition $\mathcal{B}$ of $[n]$ to be $\mathcal{B} = (\mathcal{B}_1, \mathcal{B}_2, \mathcal{B}_3)$, such that $\mathcal{B}_1 = [t - k]$ and $\mathcal{B}_2 = [t] \setminus [t - k]$, and $\mathcal{B}_3$ is any k-sized partition of $[n] \setminus [t]$. The fact that $k > t/2$ ensures that $\mathcal{B}$ is a k-sized partition of $[n]$.
- It defines the tampering query f that replaces the first $t - k$ shares of σ^* with the corresponding shares of $\sigma^{(0)}$ (which are the same of $\sigma^{(1)}$), and the shares of σ^* within $\mathcal{B}_2$ with the corresponding shares of either $\sigma^{(0)}$ or $\sigma^{(1)}$ depending on whether the i-th bit of $\sigma_{\mathcal{B}_2}^*$ is either zero or one. The shares within $\mathcal{B}_3$ are unchanged.
- It submits $f = (f_1, f_2, f_3)$ to the tampering oracle along with the reconstruction set $\mathcal{T} = [t]$. Note that it is irrelevant how the shares within $\mathcal{B}_3$ were modified, as those are not included in $[t]$.

Using the above tampering query, the attacker learns the i-th bit of $\sigma_{\mathcal{B}_2}^*$. After all the shares $\sigma_{\mathcal{B}_2}^*$ are obtained, it is trivial to break non-malleability by hard-wiring those shares in the tampering function that is allowed to modify the shares within $\mathcal{B}_1$ (as $\mathcal{B}_1 \cup \mathcal{B}_2 = [t]$, which allows to reconstruct the target message).

Rate-One Construction (and More). The above upper bound shows that the best possible rate of continuously non-malleable secret sharing against $(t-1)$-joint tampering attacks is 1. As our last contribution, in Sect. 5.2, we show that such a rate is achievable under the same computational assumptions needed for our rate-zero construction. We do so by revisiting a paradigm originally due to Krawczyk [21] for boosting the rate of classical threshold secret sharing.

Let Π be a threshold secret sharing scheme with rate zero. The main idea is to use Π to share the private key κ of a symmetric encryption scheme, obtaining shares $(\kappa_1, \ldots, \kappa_n)$; hence, we encrypt the message μ and use an information dispersal in order to distribute the ciphertext γ (along with the shares of the key) to the parties. Namely, by denoting with γ_i the i-th share of the information dispersal, the final share of party i is going to be $\sigma_i = (\kappa_i, \gamma_i)$. Krawczyk proved that computational privacy of this construction follows easily from the privacy property of the underlying secret sharing scheme, along with semantic security of encryption. Moreover, let t^* be the reconstruction threshold of the information dispersal, by setting $t^* = t$, the rate of the scheme asymptotically reaches t (thus share size is smaller than the message size) the reason is that the size of the shares of the key do not depend on the size of the message. Such a rate is known to be optimal.

Unfortunately, our capacity upper bound immediately implies that the above construction cannot yield a continuously non-malleable secret sharing scheme against $(t-1)$-joint leakage and tampering attacks when $t^* = t$. In fact the best possible rate is one, which corresponds to setting the reconstruction threshold of the information dispersal to $t^* = 1$, essentially meaning that the same ciphertext must be repeated in every share, i.e. $\sigma_i = (\kappa_i, \gamma)$. The main step of the proof is to transition to a mental experiment in which the shares $(\sigma_1, \ldots, \sigma_n)$ are computed by sharing an unrelated key $\hat{\kappa}$, and reduce a distinguisher between this experiment and the original game to an adversary attacking leakage-resilient continuous non-malleability of the underlying secret sharing scheme. In particular, the reduction needs to obtain the tampered ciphertexts $(\tilde{\gamma}_i)_{i \in [m]}$, i.e. one ciphertext for each set of tampered shares,[7] so that it can either decrypt the ciphertext $\tilde{\gamma} := \tilde{\gamma}_1 = \cdots = \tilde{\gamma}_m$ with the tampered key $\tilde{\kappa}$ obtained from the challenger, or self-destruct in case the ciphertexts within the reconstruction set $\mathcal{T}$ specified by the distinguisher are not all equal.

One possibility would be to obtain each ciphertext $\tilde{\gamma}_i$ via leakage queries, and then to argue that this does not reduce the conditional average min-entropy by too much since, before self-destruct, the ciphertext $\tilde{\gamma}_i$ can be thought of as a function of the other shares. However, the possibility to change the reconstruction set $\mathcal{T}$ adaptively within each tampering query, would require us to assume

---

[7] Note that in case the tampered ciphertexts within one of the subsets $\mathcal{B}_i$ are not equal, the reduction can immediately self-destruct.

the strong flavor of conditional independence discussed in Sect. 1.3 (which we do not know how to achieve). Instead, we use a different technique, and obtain the tampered ciphertexts via multiple tampering queries (and thus with no leakage). In particular, given a tampering query from the adversary, our reduction sends $|\gamma| + 1$ different tampering queries. The first $|\gamma|$ queries extract the tampered ciphertext $\tilde{\gamma}$ one bit at a time, while the last tampering query extracts the secret key used to encrypt the message. To perform the first $|\gamma|$ queries we fix two valid secret sharing $(\sigma_1^{(0)}, \ldots, \sigma_n^{(0)})$ and $(\sigma_1^{(1)}, \ldots, \sigma_n^{(1)})$ for two distinct messages $\mu^{(0)}$ and $\mu^{(1)}$. The i-th tampering query coordinates its outputs using the i-th bits of the tampered ciphertexts. If the tampered ciphertexts are all the same then the shares produced by the i-th tampering function are either $(\sigma_1^{(0)}, \ldots, \sigma_n^{(0)})$ or $(\sigma_1^{(1)}, \ldots, \sigma_n^{(1)})$ (depending on the i-th bit of $\tilde{\gamma}$). On the other hand, if the tampered ciphertexts are not all the same, let j, j' be the indexes such that the ciphertexts $\tilde{\gamma}_j$ and $\tilde{\gamma}_{j'}$ differ on the i-th bit, then the tampering function outputs $(\sigma_k^{(0)})_{k \in \mathcal{B}_j}$ and $(\sigma_k^{(1)})_{k \in \mathcal{B}_{j'}}$, which triggers a self-destruct.

Finally, we show how to bypass the limitations imposed by our capacity upper bound by extending the ideas behind our rate compiler in two directions:

- First, we analyze the rate compiler assuming the reconstruction threshold of the information dispersal is any value $t^* \leq t-1$ and the adversary is limited to what we call t^*-*intersecting tampering*: Each tampering query $(\mathcal{T}, f)$ output by the attacker is such that, for all subsets $\mathcal{B}_i$ of the partition $\mathcal{B}$, either $\mathcal{B}_i \cap \mathcal{T} = \emptyset$ or $|\mathcal{B}_i \cap \mathcal{T}| \geq t^*$. Note that this yields asymptotic rate t^* for the final secret sharing scheme (without contradicting our capacity upper bound which does not consider t^*-intersecting tampering). An important consequence of this generalization is that it yields the first non-malleable secret sharing scheme against *independent* tampering attacks with positive rate $t/2$. We achieve this by setting $t^* = t/2$, and by reducing an attacker for independent tampering to a t^*-intersecting-tampering attacker that partitions the shares into two blocks of $t/2$ shares each.
- Second, in the full version [8], we show that optimal asymptotic rate t can be obtained both in the random oracle model (ROM) and in the algebraic group model (AGM). More in detail, we consider the same rate compiler but where the sharing procedure additionally appends to each of the shares a *cryptographic hash h* of the ciphertext γ. The reconstruction procedure checks that the hash values are consistent (*i.e.*, they are all the same and equal to the hash of γ). In the ROM, we model the hash function as a random oracle, while in the AGM we instantiate it using the so-called Pedersen's hash function. In the reductions, we show that one can extract the tampered ciphertext $\tilde{\gamma}$ from the tampered hash $\tilde{h}$ corresponding to each tampering query, without the need to rely on leakage resilience of the underlying t-out-of-n continuously non-malleable secret sharing scheme.

These results do not contradict our capacity upper bound which is for the plain model only. Informally, this is true because both in the ROM and in the AGM we can obtain extractable commitment schemes that are succinct (*i.e.*, where the size of a commitment is shorter than the size of the message).

Concrete Instantiations. Finally, in Sect. 6, we show how to instantiate the building blocks required for all of our constructions. We construct a leakage-resilient t-time non-malleable split-state code by generalizing the black-box transformation of Ball *et al.* [4] to the setting of noisy-leakage and multiple-tampering attacks. This construction satisfies the conditional independence property that is needed for the analysis of our secret sharing scheme from Sect. 4.

Putting everything together, for any $t \geq 2$ (resp. $t \geq 2n/3$) we obtain the first statistically-secure (resp. computationally-secure) t-out-of-n noisy-leakage-resilient one-time (resp. continuously) non-malleable secret sharing under selective $(t-1)$-joint leakage and tampering attacks with asymptotic rate zero (resp. one), as also highlighted in Table 1.

1.4   Related Work

Non-malleable secret sharing with security against one-time joint-tampering attacks further exists for certain restricted tampering classes including polynomials of bounded degree (see Ball *et al.* [3]) and affine tampering (see Lin *et al.* [24]), and for ramp secret sharing (see Chattopadhyay and Li [10]).

A series of papers focuses on constructing non-malleable secret sharing in the weaker setting of independent tampering attacks [1,2,7,15,18,19,29]. In particular, Faonio and Venturi [15], as well as Brian *et al.* [7], previously analyzed a simplified version of the rate compiler of Krawczyk [21] and the non-malleable code construction by Ostrovsky *et al.* [26] (generalized to threshold secret sharing) in the setting of both independent and joint leakage and tampering attacks. However, their analysis requires a non-standard[8] flavor of noisy-leakage resilience for the underlying rate-zero secret sharing scheme which we show to be not necessary in this work.

2   Standard Definitions

For a string $x \in \{0, 1\}^*$, we denote its length by $|x|$; if $x, y \in \{0, 1\}^*$ are two strings, we denote by $x \| y$ the concatenation of x and y. If $\mathcal{X}$ is a set, $|\mathcal{X}|$ represents the number of elements in $\mathcal{X}$. We denote by $[n]$ the set $\{1, \ldots, n\}$. For a set of indices $\mathcal{I} = (i_1, \ldots, i_t)$ and a vector $x = (x_1, \ldots, x_n)$, we write $x_{\mathcal{I}}$ to denote the vector $(x_{i_1}, \ldots, x_{i_t})$. When x is chosen randomly in $\mathcal{X}$, we write $x \leftarrow_\$ \mathcal{X}$. When A is a randomized algorithm, we write $y \leftarrow_\$ \mathsf{A}(x)$ to denote a run of A on input x (and implicit random coins ρ) and output y; the value y is a random variable and $\mathsf{A}(x; \rho)$ denotes a run of A on input x and randomness ρ. An algorithm A is *probabilistic polynomial-time* (PPT for short) if A is randomized and for any input $x, \rho \in \{0, 1\}^*$, the computation of $\mathsf{A}(x; \rho)$ terminates in a polynomial number of steps (in the size of the input).

---

[8] They require that the leakage on the i-th share does not drop the conditional average min-entropy of the share i *conditioned on all other shares $j \neq i$* by too much. This additional requirement makes their rate compiler incompatible with the non-malleable secret sharing scheme by Brian, Faonio, Obremski, Simkin and Venturi [6] which does not satisfy this property.

Negligible Functions. We denote with $\lambda \in \mathbb{N}$ the security parameter. A function p is *polynomial* (in the security parameter) if $p(\lambda) \in \Theta(\lambda^c)$ for some constant $c > 0$; we sometimes write $\mathsf{poly}(\lambda)$ for an unspecified polynomial. A function $\nu : \mathbb{N} \to [0, 1]$ is *negligible* (in the security parameter) if it vanishes faster than the inverse of any polynomial in λ, *i.e.* $\nu(\lambda) \in O(1/p(\lambda))$ for all positive polynomials $p(\lambda)$; we sometimes write $\mathsf{negl}(\lambda)$ to denote an unspecified negligible function. We assume that the security parameter is given as input (in unary) to all algorithms.

Random Variables. For a random variable $\mathbf{X}$, we write $\Pr[\mathbf{X} = x]$ for the probability that $\mathbf{X}$ takes on a particular value $x \in \mathcal{X}$, with $\mathcal{X}$ being the set where $\mathbf{X}$ is defined. The statistical distance between two random variables $\mathbf{X}$ and $\mathbf{Y}$ over the same set $\mathcal{X}$ is defined as

$$\Delta(\mathbf{X}, \mathbf{Y}) = \frac{1}{2} \sum_{x \in \mathcal{X}} |\Pr[\mathbf{X} = x] - \Pr[\mathbf{Y} = x]|.$$

Given two ensembles $\mathbf{X} = \{\mathbf{X}_\lambda\}_{\lambda \in \mathbb{N}}$ and $\mathbf{Y} = \{\mathbf{Y}_\lambda\}_{\lambda \in \mathbb{N}}$, we write $\mathbf{X} \equiv \mathbf{Y}$ to denote that they are identically distributed, $\mathbf{X} \overset{s}{\approx} \mathbf{Y}$ to denote that they are *statistically close*, *i.e.* $\Delta(\mathbf{X}_\lambda, \mathbf{Y}_\lambda) \leq \mathsf{negl}(\lambda)$, and $\mathbf{X} \overset{c}{\approx} \mathbf{Y}$ to denote that they are *computationally indistinguishable*, *i.e.* for every PPT distinguisher D:

$$|\Pr[\mathsf{D}(\mathbf{X}_\lambda) = 1] - \Pr[\mathsf{D}(\mathbf{Y}_\lambda) = 1]| \leq \mathsf{negl}(\lambda).$$

We extend the notion of computational indistinguishability to the case of interactive experiments (a.k.a. games) featuring an adversary A. In particular, let $\mathbf{G}_\mathsf{A}(\lambda)$ be the random variable corresponding to the output of A at the end of the experiment, where wlog. we may assume that A outputs a decision bit. Given two experiments $\mathbf{G}_\mathsf{A}(\lambda, 0)$ and $\mathbf{G}_\mathsf{A}(\lambda, 1)$, we write $\{\mathbf{G}_\mathsf{A}(\lambda, 0)\}_{\lambda \in \mathbb{N}} \overset{c}{\approx} \{\mathbf{G}_\mathsf{A}(\lambda, 1)\}_{\lambda \in \mathbb{N}}$ as a shorthand for

$$|\Pr[\mathbf{G}_\mathsf{A}(\lambda, 0) = 1] - \Pr[\mathbf{G}_\mathsf{A}(\lambda, 1) = 1]| \leq \mathsf{negl}(\lambda).$$

The above naturally generalizes to statistical distance, which we denote by $\Delta(\mathbf{G}_\mathsf{A}(\lambda, 0), \mathbf{G}_\mathsf{A}(\lambda, 1))$, in case of *unbounded* adversaries.

Average min-entropy. The min-entropy of a random variable $\mathbf{X}$ with domain $\mathcal{X}$ is $\mathbb{H}_\infty(\mathbf{X}) := -\log \max_{x \in \mathcal{X}} \Pr[\mathbf{X} = x]$, and intuitively it measures the best chance to predict $\mathbf{X}$ (by a computationally unbounded algorithm). For conditional distributions, unpredictability is measured by the conditional average min-entropy $\widetilde{\mathbb{H}}_\infty(\mathbf{X} \mid \mathbf{Y}) := -\log \mathbb{E}_y \left[2^{-\mathbb{H}_\infty(\mathbf{X} \mid \mathbf{Y}=y)} \right]$ [11]. The lemma below is sometimes known as the "chain rule" for conditional average min-entropy.

Lemma 1 ([11], Lemma 2.2). *Let* $\mathbf{X}, \mathbf{Y}, \mathbf{Z}$ *be random variables. If* $\mathbf{Y}$ *has at most* 2^ℓ *possible values, then* $\widetilde{\mathbb{H}}_\infty(\mathbf{X} \mid \mathbf{Y}, \mathbf{Z}) \geq \widetilde{\mathbb{H}}_\infty(\mathbf{X}, \mathbf{Y} \mid \mathbf{Z}) - \ell \geq \widetilde{\mathbb{H}}_\infty(\mathbf{X} \mid \mathbf{Z}) - \ell$. *In particular,* $\widetilde{\mathbb{H}}_\infty(\mathbf{X} \mid \mathbf{Y}) \geq \widetilde{\mathbb{H}}_\infty(\mathbf{X}, \mathbf{Y}) - \ell \geq \widetilde{\mathbb{H}}_\infty(\mathbf{X}) - \ell$.

Game $\mathbf{SKE}_{\Sigma,\mathsf{A}}^{\mathsf{ind\text{-}cca}}(\lambda, b)$:

$\kappa \leftarrow_\$ \mathcal{K}$

$(\mu_0, \mu_1, \alpha) \leftarrow_\$ \mathsf{A}_1^{\mathcal{O}_{\mathsf{enc}}(\kappa,\cdot),\mathcal{O}_{\mathsf{dec}}(\kappa,\cdot)}(1^\lambda)$

$\hat{\gamma} \leftarrow_\$ \mathsf{Enc}(\kappa, \mu_b)$

Return $\mathsf{A}_2^{\mathcal{O}_{\mathsf{enc}}(\kappa,\cdot),\mathcal{O}_{\mathsf{dec}}(\kappa,\cdot)}(\alpha, \hat{\gamma})$

Oracle $\mathcal{O}_{\mathsf{enc}}(\kappa, \mu)$:

Return $\mathsf{Enc}(\kappa, \mu)$

Oracle $\mathcal{O}_{\mathsf{dec}}(\kappa, \gamma)$:

If $\gamma = \hat{\gamma}$

Return $\bot$

Else

Return $\mathsf{Dec}(\kappa, \gamma)$

Fig. 1. Experiment defining security of SKE.

2.1   Non-interactive Commitment Schemes

A non-interactive commitment scheme Com is a randomized algorithm taking as input a message $\mu \in \mathcal{M}$ and random coins $\rho \in \mathcal{R}$ and outputting a value $\gamma = \mathsf{Com}(\mu; \rho)$ called *commitment*. The pair (μ, ρ) is called *opening*.

Intuitively, a secure commitment scheme satisfies two properties called binding and hiding. The first property says that it is hard to open a commitment in two different ways. The second property says that a commitment hides the underlying message. The formal definitions follows.

Definition 1 (Binding). *We say that a non-interactive commitment scheme* Com *is* computationally binding *if for all PPT adversaries* A *the following is negligible:*

$$\Pr\left[\mu' \neq \mu \wedge \mathsf{Com}(\mu'; \rho') = \mathsf{Com}(\mu; \rho) \mid (\mu, \rho, \mu', \rho') \leftarrow_\$ \mathsf{A}(1^\lambda)\right].$$

If the above holds even in the case of unbounded adversaries, we say that Com *is* statistically binding. *Finally, if the above probability is exactly 0 for all adversaries (i.e. each commitment can be opened to at most a single message), we say that* Com *is* perfectly binding.

Definition 2 (Hiding). *We say that a non-interactive commitment scheme* Com *is* computationally hiding *if for all messages* $\mu_0, \mu_1 \in \mathcal{M}$ *it holds that*

$$\left\{\mathsf{Com}(1^\lambda, \mu_0)\right\}_{\lambda \in \mathbb{N}} \stackrel{c}{\approx} \left\{\mathsf{Com}(1^\lambda, \mu_1)\right\}_{\lambda \in \mathbb{N}}.$$

In case the above ensembles are statistically close (resp. identically distributed), we say that Com *is* statistically *(resp. perfectly) hiding.*

2.2   Symmetric Encryption

A secret-key encryption (SKE) scheme is a tuple $\Sigma = (\mathsf{Enc}, \mathsf{Dec})$ of polynomial-time algorithms specified as follows.

- Enc is a randomized algorithm that takes as input a key $\kappa \in \mathcal{K}$ and a message $\mu \in \mathcal{M}$ and outputs a ciphertext $\gamma \in \mathcal{C}$, where $\mathcal{M}$ and $\mathcal{C}$ are the *message space* and the *ciphertext space* respectively.

- Dec is a deterministic algorithm that takes as input the key $\kappa \in \mathcal{K}$ and a ciphertext $\gamma \in \mathcal{C}$ and outputs a message $\mu \in \mathcal{M} \cup \{\bot\}$, where $\bot$ denotes an invalid ciphertext.

We say that Σ satisfies correctness if, for all $\kappa \in \mathcal{K}$ and all messages $\mu \in \mathcal{M}$, we have that $\mathsf{Dec}(\kappa, \mathsf{Enc}(\kappa, \mu)) = \mu$ with probability 1 over the randomness of Enc. As for security, we will need SKE schemes satisfying the standard notion of indistinguishability against chosen-ciphertext attacks (IND-CCA). Informally, this property states that it is hard to distinguish the encryption of any two messages even if the adversary has encryption/decryption capabilities under the target key. Formally, we have the following definition.

Definition 3 (Security of SKE). *We say that* $\Sigma = (\mathsf{Enc}, \mathsf{Dec})$ *is an IND-CCA secure SKE scheme if the following holds for the experiment in Fig. 1: For all PPT adversaries* A,

$$\left\{ \mathbf{SKE}_{\Sigma,\mathsf{A}}^{\mathsf{ind\text{-}cca}}(\lambda, 0) \right\}_{\lambda \in \mathbb{N}} \overset{c}{\approx} \left\{ \mathbf{SKE}_{\Sigma,\mathsf{A}}^{\mathsf{ind\text{-}cca}}(\lambda, 1) \right\}_{\lambda \in \mathbb{N}} .$$

2.3 Information Dispersal

Information dispersals are similar to secret sharing schemes but they do not guarantee privacy. Formally, let $n, t \in \mathbb{N}$, with $t \leq n$. A t-out-of-n information dispersal is a pair of (deterministic) polynomial-time algorithms $(\mathsf{IDisp}, \mathsf{IRec})$ defined as follows:

- IDisp takes as input a message $\mu \in \mathcal{M}$ and outputs n shares $\mu_1, \ldots, \mu_n$, where each $\mu_i \in \mathcal{M}_i$.
- IRec takes as input a certain subset of shares and outputs a value in $\mathcal{M} \cup \{\bot\}$.

We require the following correctness property: For all $\mu \in \mathcal{M}$ and all $\mathcal{I}$ with $|\mathcal{I}| \geq t$, it holds that $\mathsf{IRec}((\mathsf{IDisp}(\mu))_{\mathcal{I}}) = \mu$.

3 Secret Sharing Schemes

A n-party secret sharing scheme Π, with *message space* $\mathcal{M}$ and *share space* $\mathcal{S} = \mathcal{S}_1 \times \ldots \times \mathcal{S}_n$, consists of polynomial-time algorithms $(\mathsf{Share}, \mathsf{Rec})$ specified as follows:

- Share is a randomized algorithm that takes as input a message $\mu \in \mathcal{M}$ and outputs n shares $\sigma_1, \ldots, \sigma_n$, with $\sigma_i \in \mathcal{S}_i$.
- Rec is a deterministic algorithm that takes as input a certain subset of shares and outputs a value in $\mathcal{M} \cup \{\bot\}$.

The subset of parties allowed to reconstruct the secret by pulling their shares together form the so-called *access structure*. We consider the t-out-of-n access structure where any subset of shares of cardinality bigger or equal to t can reconstruct (we call such subsets *authorized*), while any subset of shares of cardinality less than t cannot (we call such subsets *unauthorized*). Subsets of cardinality exactly t are called *minimal authorized* sets.

Definition 4 (Threshold secret sharing scheme). *Let $n, t \in \mathbb{N}$ and $t \leq n$, we say that $\Pi = (\mathsf{Share}, \mathsf{Rec})$ is a t-out-of-n secret sharing scheme if the following two properties are satisfied.*

- ***Correctness:*** *for all $\lambda \in \mathbb{N}$, all $\mu \in \mathcal{M}$ and all $\mathcal{I}$ with $|\mathcal{I}| \geq t$, we have that $\mathsf{Rec}((\mathsf{Share}(1^\lambda, \mu))_\mathcal{I}) = \mu$ with overwhelming probability over the randomness of the sharing algorithm.*
- ***Perfect Privacy:*** *for all pairs of messages $\mu_0, \mu_1 \in \mathcal{M}$ and for any $\mathcal{U}$ with $|\mathcal{U}| < t$, we have that*

$$\{(\mathsf{Share}(1^\lambda, \mu_0))_\mathcal{U}\}_{\lambda \in \mathbb{N}} \equiv \{(\mathsf{Share}(1^\lambda, \mu_1))_\mathcal{U}\}_{\lambda \in \mathbb{N}},$$

If the above ensembles are statistically (resp. computationally) close, we speak of statistical (resp. computational) privacy.

Finally, when considering the length of the shares, we define the *information rate* of a secret sharing scheme as the ratio between the length of the secret message and the maximal length of a share.

Definition 5 (Asymptotic rate). *Let Π be an n-party secret sharing scheme with message space $\mathcal{M} = \{0, 1\}^*$ and share space $\mathcal{S}_1 \times \ldots \times \mathcal{S}_n$. Let $s(|\mu|, \lambda) = \max_{i \in [n]} \log |\mathcal{S}_i(|\mu|, \lambda)|$ where $\mathcal{S}_1(|\mu|, \lambda) \times \ldots \times \mathcal{S}_n(|\mu|, \lambda)$ is the share space for messages μ of length $|\mu|$ and security parameter λ. The asymptotic information rate of Π is defined to be*

$$\varrho = \inf_{\lambda \in \mathbb{N}} \lim_{|\mu| \to \infty} \frac{|\mu|}{s(|\mu|, \lambda)}.$$

3.1   Tampering and Leakage Model

In our model the attacker partitions all of the shares into m (non-overlapping) blocks with size at most k, covering the entire set $[n]$. This is formalized through the notion of a k-sized partition.

Definition 6 (k-sized partition). *Let $k, m \in \mathbb{N}$. We call $\mathcal{B} = (\mathcal{B}_1, \ldots, \mathcal{B}_m)$ a k-sized partition of $[n]$ if: (i) $\bigcup_{i \in [m]} \mathcal{B}_i = [n]$; (ii) $\forall i_1, i_2 \in [m]$ such that $i_1 \neq i_2$, $\mathcal{B}_{i_1} \cap \mathcal{B}_{i_2} = \emptyset$; (iii) $\forall i \in [m], |\mathcal{B}_i| \leq k$.*

Fix $\mu \in \mathcal{M}$ and let $\mathcal{B}$ be a k-sized partition of $[n]$. To define our security model, we consider an adversary A interacting with a target secret sharing $\sigma = (\sigma_1, \ldots, \sigma_n)$ of μ as follows:

- **Leakage queries.** For each $i \in [m]$, the attacker can leak jointly from the shares $\sigma_{\mathcal{B}_i}$. This can be done repeatedly and in an adaptive fashion, so long as the leakage does not decrease the min-entropy of the shares by too much. Formally, for any $\mu \in \mathcal{M}$, for each $i \in [m]$ and for $\ell \geq 0$, we require that

$$\widetilde{\mathbb{H}}_\infty((\mathbf{\Sigma}_j)_{j \in \mathcal{B}_i} \mid \mathbf{\Lambda}_i) \geq \widetilde{\mathbb{H}}_\infty((\mathbf{\Sigma}_j)_{j \in \mathcal{B}_i}) - \ell, \tag{1}$$

where $(\mathbf{\Sigma}_1, \ldots, \mathbf{\Sigma}_n)$ is the r.v. corresponding to $\mathsf{Share}(\mu)$, and $\mathbf{\Lambda}_i$ is the r.v. corresponding to the total leakage performed within $\mathcal{B}_i$ (over all queries). An adversary obeying this restriction is called ℓ-*leakage admissible*.

$\textbf{LR-CNMSS}_{\Pi,A,\mathcal{B}}^{\mu_0,\mu_1}(\lambda, b)$:

$\sigma \leftarrow_\$ \mathsf{Share}(\mu_b)$
$\mathsf{stop} \leftarrow \mathsf{false}$
Return $A^{\mathcal{O}_{\mathsf{leak}}(\sigma,\cdot),\mathcal{O}_{\mathsf{tamp}}^{\mu_0,\mu_1}(\sigma,\cdot,\cdot)}$

Oracle $\mathcal{O}_{\mathsf{leak}}(\sigma,(g_1,\ldots,g_m))$:

If $\mathsf{stop} = \mathsf{true}$
   Return $\perp$
Else
   $\forall i \in [m]$, $\Lambda_i = g_i(\sigma_{\mathcal{B}_i})$
   Return $\Lambda = \Lambda_1 || \ldots || \Lambda_m$

Oracle $\mathcal{O}_{\mathsf{tamp}}(\sigma, \mathcal{T}, (f_1,\ldots,f_m))$:

If $\mathsf{stop} = \mathsf{true}$
   Return $\perp$
Else
   $\forall i \in [m]$, $\tilde{\sigma}_{\mathcal{B}_i} = f_i(\sigma_{\mathcal{B}_i})$
   $\tilde{\mu} = \mathsf{Rec}(\tilde{\sigma}_\mathcal{T})$
   If $\tilde{\mu} \in \{\mu_0, \mu_1\}$
      Return $\diamond$
   If $\tilde{\mu} = \perp$
      Return $\perp$, and $\mathsf{stop} \leftarrow \mathsf{true}$
   Else
      Return $\tilde{\mu}$

Fig. 2. Experiment defining leakage-resilient continuously non-malleable secret sharing against joint tampering. The tampering and leakage oracles are implicitly parameterized by set $\mathcal{B}$, messages μ_0, μ_1 and flag stop.

– **Tampering queries.** For each $i \in [m]$, the attacker can tamper jointly with the shares $\sigma_{\mathcal{B}_i}$. Each such query yields tampered shares $\tilde{\sigma}_1, \ldots, \tilde{\sigma}_n$, for which the adversary is allowed to choose a *different* reconstruction set $\mathcal{T} \subseteq [n]$, with $|\mathcal{T}| \geq t$, and see the corresponding reconstructed message. This can be done repeatedly and in an adaptive fashion, the only restriction being that after the first tampering query yielding an invalid message, the answer to all future tampering (and leakage) queries is automatically set to $\perp$ (the so-called *self-destruct* feature). This restriction is well-known to be necessary when an arbitrary polynomial number of tampering queries is allowed [15,29].

Now we are ready to give the formal notion of security. Intuitively, leakage-resilient continuous non-malleability states that, given two[9] messages $\mu_0, \mu_1 \in \mathcal{M}$, no admissible adversary, as defined above, can distinguish whether it is interacting with a secret sharing of μ_0 or of μ_1.

Definition 7 (Leakage-resilient continuous non-malleability [7]). *Let n, $t, k \in \mathbb{N}$ and $\ell \geq 0$ be parameters. A t-out-of-n secret sharing scheme Π is ℓ-noisy-leakage-resilient continuously non-malleable under selective k-joint leakage and tampering attacks $((k,\ell)$-LR-CNMSS, for short), if for all messages $\mu_0, \mu_1 \in \mathcal{M}$, all k-sized partitions of $[n]$, and all PPT ℓ-leakage admissible attackers A, the following holds for the experiment of Fig. 2:*

$$\left\{\textbf{LR-CNMSS}_{\Pi,A,\mathcal{B}}^{\mu_0,\mu_1}(\lambda, 0)\right\}_{\lambda \in \mathbb{N}} \stackrel{c}{\approx} \left\{\textbf{LR-CNMSS}_{\Pi,A,\mathcal{B}}^{\mu_0,\mu_1}(\lambda, 1)\right\}_{\lambda \in \mathbb{N}}. \quad (2)$$

When no leakage is allowed (i.e. $\ell = 0$), we simply say that Π is a k-CNMSS.

---

[9] Goyal and Kumar [18] originally gave a simulation-based definition of non-malleability (for the case of one-time tampering). It is folklore that this flavor of non-malleability can be shown to be equivalent to the indistinguishability-based notion we define (even in the setting of continuous tampering), so long as the message length is super-logarithmic in the security parameter.

3.2   Related Notions

By adapting the above definition, we obtain several notions as special cases, as detailed below.

Leakage-Resilient One-Time Non-malleability. Let $\mathbf{LR\text{-}NMSS}_{\varPi,\mathsf{A},\mathcal{B}}^{\mu_0,\mu_1}(\lambda,b)$ be the experiment that is defined identically to $\mathbf{LR\text{-}CNMSS}_{\varPi,\mathsf{A},\mathcal{B}}^{\mu_0,\mu_1}(\lambda,b)$, except that the attacker is allowed a *single* tampering query and all the leakage happens before such query. In this case, Definition 7 can be achieved information theoretically (*i.e.*, for all unbounded adversaries). In particular, Eq. (2) now becomes

$$\Delta\left(\mathbf{LR\text{-}NMSS}_{\varPi,\mathsf{A},\mathcal{B}}^{\mu_0,\mu_1}(\lambda,0);\mathbf{LR\text{-}NMSS}_{\varPi,\mathsf{A},\mathcal{B}}^{\mu_0,\mu_1}(\lambda,1)\right)\le\epsilon \qquad (3)$$

for some $\epsilon\in[0,1)$, and we speak of ℓ-noisy-leakage-resilient one-time statistically ϵ-non-malleable secret sharing under selective k-joint leakage and tampering attacks ((k,ℓ,ϵ)-LR-NMSS, for short).

Asymmetric p-time Non-malleable Codes. When the number of parties is $n=2$, *i.e.* in case $\varPi$ is a 2-out-of-2 secret sharing, we obtain the notion of leakage-resilient split-state continuously non-malleable codes [16,26] as a special case. Here, it will be useful to consider asymmetric shares and possibly to tolerate different amounts of leakage from each side; towards this, when we explicitly need the size of the shares, we speak of $(s_\mathsf{L},s_\mathsf{R})$-asymmetric codes, where $s_\mathsf{L}=\log|\mathcal{S}_\mathsf{L}|$ is the size of the left share and $s_\mathsf{R}=\log|\mathcal{S}_\mathsf{R}|$ is the size of the right share. Moreover, it will suffice for us to consider an attack scenario where the adversary performs all the leakage *before* tampering, and can only send p tampering queries (where p is fixed *a priori*). Notice that, when the number of tampering queries is bounded, then we can obtain security even without assuming self-destruct (*i.e.*, the self-destruct flag `stop` is never set to true in the experiment of Fig. 2).

An adversary A is called $(\ell_\mathsf{L},\ell_\mathsf{R})$-leakage and p-time tampering admissible, so long as it makes at most p tampering queries and performs all leakage queries before the first tampering query, with the restriction that:

$$\widetilde{\mathbb{H}}_\infty(\mathbf{\Sigma}_\mathsf{L}\mid\mathbf{\Lambda}_\mathsf{L})\ge\widetilde{\mathbb{H}}_\infty(\mathbf{\Sigma}_\mathsf{L})-\ell_\mathsf{L},$$
$$\widetilde{\mathbb{H}}_\infty(\mathbf{\Sigma}_\mathsf{R}\mid\mathbf{\Lambda}_\mathsf{R})\ge\widetilde{\mathbb{H}}_\infty(\mathbf{\Sigma}_\mathsf{R})-\ell_\mathsf{R},$$

where $\mathbf{\Sigma}=(\mathbf{\Sigma}_\mathsf{L},\mathbf{\Sigma}_\mathsf{R})$ is the r.v. corresponding to the target secret sharing, and $\mathbf{\Lambda}_\mathsf{L},\mathbf{\Lambda}_\mathsf{R}$ are the r.v. corresponding to the total leakage performed on $\mathbf{\Sigma}_\mathsf{L},\mathbf{\Sigma}_\mathsf{R}$ (over all queries). In this case, we say that $\varPi$ is an asymmetric $(\ell_\mathsf{L},\ell_\mathsf{R})$-leakage-resilient p-time ϵ-non-malleable split-state code (asymmetric $(\ell_\mathsf{L},\ell_\mathsf{R},p,\epsilon)$-LR-NMC, for short). We denote the corresponding experiment as $\mathbf{LR\text{-}NMC}_{\varPi,\mathsf{A}}^{\mu_0,\mu_1}(\lambda,b)$.

When no leakage is allowed (*i.e.*, $\ell_\mathsf{L},\ell_\mathsf{R}=0$), we simply speak of asymmetric p-time ϵ-non-malleable split-state codes (asymmetric (p,ϵ)-NMC for short); similarly, when no tampering is allowed (*i.e.* $p=0$), we speak of asymmetric $(\ell_\mathsf{L},\ell_\mathsf{R},\epsilon)$-leakage-resilient split-state code (asymmetric $(\ell_\mathsf{L},\ell_\mathsf{R})$-LRC for short).

Finally, in the latter case, we also need the existence of an efficiently computable algorithm $\overline{\mathsf{Share}}$ such that, for all $\sigma_\mathsf{R} \in \mathcal{S}_\mathsf{R}$ and $\mu \in \mathcal{M}$, it holds that $\mathsf{Rec}(\overline{\mathsf{Share}}(\mu, \sigma_\mathsf{R}), \sigma_\mathsf{R}) = \mu$ and moreover the distributions of the left shares sampled from $\overline{\mathsf{Share}}$ is equivalent to the distribution of the left shares of Share conditioned on the right share being σ_R and the message being μ. In other words, given as input the message μ and a right share σ_R, the algorithm $\overline{\mathsf{Share}}$ produces a left share σ_L such that $(\sigma_\mathsf{L}, \sigma_\mathsf{R})$ is a valid and properly distributed encoding of μ. We refer the reader to Sect. 6 for concrete examples of leakage-resilient split-state codes meeting the above property.

4   Rate-Zero Continuously Non-malleable Secret Sharing

In this section, we give a construction of a leakage-resilient continuously non-malleable secret sharing scheme against selective joint tampering. We refer the reader to Sect. 1.3 for an overview of our scheme (and its security) and here directly provide a formal treatment.

Let $\varPi = (\mathsf{Share}, \mathsf{Rec})$ be the t-out-of-n Shamir's secret sharing scheme. For simplicity we assume that $\varPi$ can support messages of variable length, namely the sharing procedure chooses a field that is large enough to encode the input message μ for n parties (for simplicity, we assume that $|\mu| \geq \log n$), and we denote such field as $\mathbb{F}(|\mu|)$, or simply $\mathbb{F}$ when the message is clear from the context. A share σ_i of $\varPi$ is a tuple (i, x) where $i \in [n]$ and $x \in \mathbb{F}$ is a field element; in particular, if p is the polynomial chosen by the Share algorithm, for all $i \in [n]$, $\sigma_i = (i, p(i))$. Let $\mathcal{S}_i(|\mu|) := \{(i, x) : x \in \mathbb{F}(|\mu|)\}$, clearly a secret sharing of μ has support $\mathcal{S}_1(|\mu|) \times \cdots \times \mathcal{S}_n(|\mu|)$. Consider the function idx that, upon input a tuple $\sigma = (i^*, x)$, outputs the first component $\mathsf{idx}(\sigma) = i^*$; in particular, for a share σ_i generated by the sharing function Share, it holds that $\mathsf{idx}(\sigma_i) = i$. Finally, let $\varPi' = (\mathsf{Share}', \mathsf{Rec}')$ be a split-state code with codeword space $\mathcal{S}_\mathsf{L} \times \mathcal{S}_\mathsf{R}$ and Com be a non-interactive commitment scheme. Consider the following derived scheme $\varPi^* = (\mathsf{Share}^*, \mathsf{Rec}^*)$.

- **Algorithm Share^*:** upon input μ, first sample randomness $\rho \leftarrow_\$ \mathcal{R}$ and compute $\gamma \leftarrow \mathsf{Com}(\mu; \rho)$ and $(\sigma_1, \dots, \sigma_n) \leftarrow_\$ \mathsf{Share}(\mu||\rho)$. Then, for each $i \in [n]$, compute $(\sigma_{\mathsf{L},i}, \sigma_{\mathsf{R},i}) \leftarrow_\$ \mathsf{Share}'(\sigma_i)$ and $(\sigma_{\mathsf{R},i}^{(1)}, \dots, \sigma_{\mathsf{R},i}^{(n)}) \leftarrow_\$ \mathsf{Share}(\sigma_{\mathsf{R},i})$. Finally, set $\sigma_i^* = (\gamma, \sigma_{\mathsf{L},i}, (\sigma_{\mathsf{R},j}^{(i)})_{j \in [n]})$ for all $i \in [n]$ and output $(\sigma_1^*, \dots, \sigma_n^*)$.
- **Algorithm Rec^*:** upon input shares $(\sigma_i^*)_{i \in \mathcal{I}}$, parse $\sigma_i = (\gamma_i, \sigma_{\mathsf{L},i}, (\sigma_{\mathsf{R},j}^{(i)})_{j \in [n]})$ for all $i \in \mathcal{I}$. Check that all the commitments $(\gamma_i)_{i \in \mathcal{I}}$ are the same; if not output $\bot$, and else let γ be the commitment contained in each share. Compute $\sigma_{\mathsf{R},i} = \mathsf{Rec}((\sigma_{\mathsf{R},i}^{(j)})_{j \in \mathcal{I}})$ and $\sigma_i = \mathsf{Rec}'(\sigma_{\mathsf{L},i}, \sigma_{\mathsf{R},i})$; check that there exist no distinct $i_1, i_2 \in \mathcal{I}$ such that $\mathsf{idx}(\sigma_{i_1}) = \mathsf{idx}(\sigma_{i_2})$ (and output $\bot$ otherwise). Finally, reconstruct $\mu||\rho = \mathsf{Rec}((\sigma_i)_{i \in \mathcal{I}})$ and output μ if $\gamma = \mathsf{Com}(\mu; \rho)$ and $\bot$ otherwise.

We are now ready to state the following theorem.

LR-CNMSS$_{\Pi^*,A,B}^{\mu_0,\mu_1}(\lambda,b)$ **Hyb**$_r^{\mu_0,\mu_1}(\lambda,b)$:

$\rho \leftarrow_\$ \mathcal{R}$

$\gamma := \mathsf{Com}(\mu_b;\rho)$

$(\sigma_1,\ldots,\sigma_n) \leftarrow_\$ \mathsf{Share}(\mu_b\|\rho)$

$(\sigma_1',\ldots,\sigma_n') \leftarrow_\$ \times_{i\in[n]} \mathcal{S}_i(|\mu_b|+|\rho|)$

$\forall i > r, \sigma_i' := \sigma_i$

$\forall i \in [n]:$

$\quad (\sigma_{\mathsf{L},i},\sigma_{\mathsf{R},i}) \leftarrow_\$ \mathsf{Share}'(\sigma_i)$

$\quad \boxed{(\sigma_{\mathsf{L},i},\sigma_{\mathsf{R},i}) \leftarrow_\$ \mathsf{Share}'(\sigma_i')}$

$\quad (\sigma_{\mathsf{R},i}^{(1)},\ldots,\sigma_{\mathsf{R},i}^{(n)}) \leftarrow_\$ \mathsf{Share}(\sigma_{\mathsf{R},i})$

$\quad \sigma_i^* := (\gamma,\sigma_{\mathsf{L},i},(\sigma_{\mathsf{R},j}^{(i)})_{j\in[n]})$

$\sigma^* := (\sigma_1^*,\ldots,\sigma_n^*)$

$\mathbf{stop} \leftarrow \mathbf{false}$

Return $A^{\mathcal{O}_{\mathsf{tamp}}(\sigma^*,\cdot),\mathcal{O}_{\mathsf{leak}}(\sigma^*,\cdot)}(1^\lambda)$

Algorithm $\mathsf{Split}((\sigma_i^*)_{i\in\mathcal{T}})$:

$\sigma_{\mathsf{R},i} = \mathsf{Rec}((\sigma_{\mathsf{R},i}^{(j)})_{j\in\mathcal{T}})$

$\sigma_i = \mathsf{Rec}'(\sigma_{\mathsf{L},i},\sigma_{\mathsf{R},i})$

Output $(\sigma_i)_{i\in\mathcal{T}}$

Oracle $\mathcal{O}_{\mathsf{tamp}}(\sigma^*,\mathcal{T},(f_1,\ldots,f_m))$:

If $\mathbf{stop} = \mathbf{true}$, return $\bot$

$\forall i \in [m]: \tilde{\sigma}_{\mathcal{B}_i}^* := f_i(\sigma_{\mathcal{B}_i}^*)$

$\tilde{\sigma}^* = (\tilde{\sigma}_1^*,\ldots,\tilde{\sigma}_n^*)$

$\forall i \in \mathcal{T}, \tilde{\sigma}_i^* = (\tilde{\gamma}_i,\tilde{\sigma}_{\mathsf{L},i},(\tilde{\sigma}_{\mathsf{R},j}^{(i)})_{j\in[n]})$

If $\exists i_1,i_2 \in \mathcal{T}: \tilde{\gamma}_{i_1} \neq \tilde{\gamma}_{i_2}$

$\quad \mathbf{stop} \leftarrow \mathbf{true}$ and return $\bot$

Else, let $\tilde{\gamma} := \tilde{\gamma}_i$

$(\tilde{\sigma}_i)_{i\in\mathcal{T}} = \mathsf{Split}((\tilde{\sigma}_i^*)_{i\in\mathcal{T}})$

If $\exists i_1,i_2 \in \mathcal{T}: \mathsf{idx}(\tilde{\sigma}_{i_1}) = \mathsf{idx}(\tilde{\sigma}_{i_2})$

$\quad \mathbf{stop} \leftarrow \mathbf{true}$ and return $\bot$

$\forall i_1,i_2 \in \mathcal{T}: \tilde{\sigma}_{i_1} = \sigma_{i_2}'$

$\quad \text{Let } \tilde{\sigma}_{i_1} := \sigma_{i_2}$

$\tilde{\mu}\|\tilde{\rho} = \mathsf{Rec}((\tilde{\sigma}_i)_{i\in\mathcal{T}})$

If $\tilde{\gamma} \neq \mathsf{Com}(\tilde{\mu};\tilde{\rho})$,

$\quad \mathbf{stop} \leftarrow \mathbf{true}$ and return $\bot$

If $\tilde{\mu} \in \{\mu_0,\mu_1\}$, return $\diamond$

Return $\tilde{\mu}$

Oracle $\mathcal{O}_{\mathsf{leak}}(\sigma^*,(g_1,\ldots,g_m))$:

If $\mathbf{stop} = \mathbf{true}$, return $\bot$

Else, return $g_1(\sigma_{\mathcal{B}_1}^*),\ldots,g_m(\sigma_{\mathcal{B}_m}^*)$

Fig. 3. Experiments in the proof of Theorem 1. The instructions boxed in red are the modifications introduced by the hybrid experiment. For compactness, we denote by Split the algorithm that reconstructs the shares σ_i from the shares $(\sigma_{\mathsf{L},i},(\sigma_{\mathsf{R},j}^{(i)})_{j\in[n]})$. (Color figure online)

Theorem 1. *Let $n,t \in \mathbb{N}$, with $t > 2n/3$, and $\ell_\mathsf{L},\ell_\mathsf{R} \geq 0$. Assume that Com is a perfectly binding and computationally hiding commitment and Π' is an asymmetric $(\ell_\mathsf{L},\ell_\mathsf{R},\mathsf{negl}(\lambda),t)$-LR-NMC satisfying the following properties:*

(i) *There exists $\sigma_\mathsf{L}^* \in \mathcal{S}_\mathsf{L}$ such that, for any μ, there exists $\sigma_\mathsf{R} \in \mathcal{S}_\mathsf{R}$ such that $\mathsf{Rec}'(\sigma_\mathsf{L}^*,\sigma_\mathsf{R}) = \mu$.*

(ii) *There exists $d \geq 0$ such that, for any μ, it holds that $\widetilde{\mathbb{H}}_\infty(\mathbf{\Sigma}_\mathsf{L}\,|\,\mathbf{\Sigma}_\mathsf{R}) \geq \mathbb{H}_\infty(\mathbf{\Sigma}_\mathsf{L}) - d$ and $\widetilde{\mathbb{H}}_\infty(\mathbf{\Sigma}_\mathsf{R}\,|\,\mathbf{\Sigma}_\mathsf{L}) \geq \mathbb{H}_\infty(\mathbf{\Sigma}_\mathsf{R}) - d$, where $(\mathbf{\Sigma}_\mathsf{L},\mathbf{\Sigma}_\mathsf{R})$ is the r.v. corresponding to $\mathsf{Share}'(\mu)$.*

Then, the above secret sharing scheme Π^* is a t-out-of-n $(t-1,\ell^*)$-LR-CNMSS so long as:

$$\ell_\mathsf{R} \geq (t-1)\cdot\ell^* + |\mu| + |\gamma| + d + 1 + \log(\lambda)$$
$$\ell_\mathsf{L} \geq \ell^* + n\cdot(t-1)\cdot s_\mathsf{R} + |\gamma| + d + 1 + \log(\lambda),$$

where $|\mu| \in \mathbb{N}$ is the length of the message, $|\gamma|$ is the length of a commitment and $s_\mathsf{R} = \log|\mathcal{S}_\mathsf{R}|$ is the size of a right share under Π'.

The privacy property of Π^* follows readily by privacy of Π and the computational hiding property of Com. In what follows, we focus on the proof of leakage-resilient continuous non-malleability. Wlog., we are going to assume that each reconstruction set $\mathcal{T}$ queried by the adversary is minimal.[10] Furthermore, we will make the simplifying assumption that the partition $\mathcal{B}$ fixed by the attacker only contains two subsets, i.e. $\mathcal{B}_1$ and $\mathcal{B}_2$. Note that this restriction is wlog. whenever $t > 2n/3$: in fact, for any partition $\mathcal{B} = (\mathcal{B}_1, \ldots, \mathcal{B}_m)$, it is always possible to find a set of indices $\mathcal{I} \subseteq [m]$ such that $t/2 \leq |\bigcup_{i \in \mathcal{I}} \mathcal{B}_i| < t$ and then consider the two subsets to be $\hat{\mathcal{B}}_1 = \bigcup_{i \in \mathcal{I}} \mathcal{B}_i$ (which contains less than t elements by construction) and $\hat{\mathcal{B}}_2 = \bigcup_{i \notin \mathcal{I}} \mathcal{B}_i$ (which contains $n - |\bigcup_{i \in \mathcal{I}} \mathcal{B}_i| < 3t/2 - t/2 = t$ elements).

Remark 1. Note that if we restrict the adversary to only choose partitions of two subsets, i.e. $\mathcal{B}_1, \mathcal{B}_2 \subseteq [n]$ s.t. $\mathcal{B}_1 \cap \mathcal{B}_2 = \emptyset$ and $\mathcal{B}_1 \cup \mathcal{B}_2 = [n]$, then it only suffices to require $t \geq n/2 + 1$. This is because we can put $\hat{\mathcal{B}}_1 := \mathcal{B}_1$ and $\hat{\mathcal{B}}_2 := \mathcal{B}_2$, while the restriction on t comes from the fact that both $\mathcal{B}_1$ and $\mathcal{B}_2$ must be unauthorized, i.e. $|\mathcal{B}_1|, |\mathcal{B}_2| \leq t - 1$, and therefore $n = |\mathcal{B}_1| + |\mathcal{B}_2| \leq 2t - 2$, that is, $t \geq n/2 + 1$.

For $r \in [n]$, consider the auxiliary hybrid experiments $\mathbf{Hyb}_r(\lambda, b)$ described in Fig. 3 along with the original experiment in order to highlight the main differences. In particular, in $\mathbf{Hyb}_r(\lambda, b)$, we replace the first r shares $(\sigma_1, \ldots, \sigma_r)$ from the first application of Π with random and independent values $(\sigma'_1, \ldots, \sigma'_r)$, letting the remaining shares $\sigma'_{r+1}, \ldots, \sigma'_n$ the same as the original experiment. Note that, when $r = 0$, we do not replace any share, hence, for all $b \in \{0, 1\}$, $\mathbf{Hyb}_0(\lambda, b) \equiv \mathbf{LR\text{-}CNMSS}_{\Pi^*, \mathsf{A}, \mathcal{B}}^{\mu_0, \mu_1}(\lambda, b)$. For all $r \in [n]$, we will prove by induction over the number of tampering queries that the experiments $\mathbf{Hyb}_{r-1}(\lambda, b)$ and $\mathbf{Hyb}_r(\lambda, b)$ are statistically close. Towards this, for all $r \in [n] \cup \{0\}$, let us denote by $\mathbf{Hyb}_r(\lambda, b, p)$ the experiment $\mathbf{Hyb}_r(\lambda, b)$ where the adversary A is limited to ask exactly p tampering queries.

4.1   Induction Basis

The lemma below constitutes the basis of the induction.

Lemma 2. *For all $b \in \{0, 1\}$, and all $r \in [n]$, it holds that*

$$\left\{\mathbf{Hyb}_{r-1}(\lambda, b, 1)\right\}_{\lambda \in \mathbb{N}} \stackrel{s}{\approx} \left\{\mathbf{Hyb}_r(\lambda, b, 1)\right\}_{\lambda \in \mathbb{N}}.$$

Proof. The difference between the two hybrids is that in $\mathbf{Hyb}_r(\lambda, b, 1)$ the share σ'_r is uniformly random, whereas in $\mathbf{Hyb}_{r-1}(\lambda, b, 1)$ the share σ'_r is set to be σ_r (as defined in the original experiment). For any $j \in [n]$, let $\xi(j) \in \{1, 2\}$ be the index such that $j \in \mathcal{B}_{\xi(j)}$. The proof proceeds by reduction to leakage-resilient t-time non-malleability of Π'. In more detail, for a fixed choice of $b \in \{0, 1\}$ and $r \in [n]$, let A be an adversary telling apart the two hybrids with probability at least $1/\mathsf{poly}(\lambda)$. Consider the following (possibly inefficient) adversary A' attacking Π'.

---

[10] It is always possible to modify the reconstruction algorithm Rec so that, upon input more than t shares, say $\sigma_{i_1}, \ldots, \sigma_{i_t}, \ldots$, with $i_1 < i_2 < \ldots < i_t < \ldots$, it only considers the first t shares $\sigma_{i_1}, \ldots, \sigma_{i_t}$ in order to reconstruct the message.

1. **Setup.** Set the challenge messages to be σ_r and σ'_r sampled as in $\mathbf{Hyb}_r(\lambda, b, 1)$, and let γ be the commitment corresponding to the message μ_b.

2. **Shared randomness.** For every $i \in [n] \setminus \{r\}$, sample $\sigma_{\mathsf{L},i}, (\sigma_{\mathsf{R},i}^{(j)})_{j \in [n]}$ according to $\mathbf{Hyb}_r(\lambda, b)$. Then, let $i_\mathsf{L} = \xi(r)$ and $i_\mathsf{R} = 3 - i_\mathsf{L} \in \{1, 2\}$. Let $\mathcal{J}$ be any set such that $\mathcal{B}_{i_\mathsf{L}} \subseteq \mathcal{J} \subseteq [n]$ and $|\mathcal{J}| = t - 1$. For all $j \in \mathcal{J}$, sample the shares $\sigma_{\mathsf{R},r}^{(j)}$ uniformly at random. Finally, sample the left share σ_L^* given by property (i) of Π'.

   After this step, the reduction A' knows σ_L^* and the following values:

$$\forall i \in [n] \setminus \mathcal{J} : \quad \gamma, \qquad \sigma_{\mathsf{L},i}, \qquad (\sigma_{\mathsf{R},j}^{(i)})_{j \in [n] \setminus \{r\}} \tag{4}$$

$$\forall i \in \mathcal{J} \setminus \{r\} : \quad \gamma, \qquad \sigma_{\mathsf{L},i}, \qquad (\sigma_{\mathsf{R},j}^{(i)})_{j \in [n]} \tag{5}$$

$$\text{For } i = r : \quad \gamma, \qquad (\sigma_{\mathsf{R},j}^{(i)})_{j \in [n]} \tag{6}$$

3. **Leakage queries.** Upon receiving a leakage query $g = (g_1, g_2)$ from A, construct the following leakage functions.
   (a) Let g_L be the leakage function which takes as input the value $\sigma_{\mathsf{L},r}$, plugs it in Eq. (6) and appends the values of Eq. (5) to obtain $(\sigma_i^*)_{i \in \mathcal{B}_{i_\mathsf{L}}}$ (recall that $\mathcal{B}_{i_\mathsf{L}} \subseteq \mathcal{J}$), and finally outputs $\Lambda_{i_\mathsf{L}} = g_{i_\mathsf{L}}((\sigma_i^*)_{i \in \mathcal{B}_{i_\mathsf{L}}})$.
   (b) Let g_R be the leakage function which takes as input the value $\sigma_{\mathsf{R},r}$, computes the values $(\sigma_{\mathsf{R},r}^{(i)})_{i \in [n] \setminus \mathcal{J}}$ using $\sigma_{\mathsf{R},r}$ and the values $(\sigma_{\mathsf{R},r}^{(i)})_{i \in \mathcal{J}}$ and plugs them in Eq. (4) in order to obtain $(\sigma_i^*)_{i \in [n] \setminus \mathcal{J}}$; then, appends the values of Eq. (5) to obtain $(\sigma_i^*)_{i \in \mathcal{B}_{i_\mathsf{R}}}$, and finally outputs $\Lambda_{i_\mathsf{R}} = g_{i_\mathsf{R}}((\sigma_i^*)_{i \in \mathcal{B}_{i_\mathsf{R}}})$.
   Send $(g_\mathsf{L}, g_\mathsf{R})$ to the leakage oracle and forward the answer $\Lambda_1 \| \Lambda_2$ to A.

4. **Tampering query.** Upon receiving the tampering query $(\mathcal{T}, f = (f_1, f_2))$ from A, construct the following leakage and tampering functions.
   (a) Let $\hat{g}_\mathsf{L}$ be the leakage function which takes as input the value $\sigma_{\mathsf{L},r}$, plugs it in Eq. (6) and appends the values of Eq. (5) to obtain $(\sigma_i^*)_{i \in \mathcal{B}_{i_\mathsf{L}}}$, computes the tampered shares $(\tilde{\sigma}_i^*)_{i \in \mathcal{B}_{i_\mathsf{L}}} = f_{i_\mathsf{L}}((\sigma_i^*)_{i \in \mathcal{B}_{i_\mathsf{L}}})$, checks if all the tampered commitments within $\mathcal{T} \cap \mathcal{B}_{i_\mathsf{L}}$ agree on a single value $\tilde{\gamma}_\mathsf{L}$ (and outputs $\perp$ if not), and finally outputs the values $\tilde{\gamma}_\mathsf{L}, (\tilde{\sigma}_{\mathsf{R},j}^{(i)})_{i \in \mathcal{B}_{i_\mathsf{L}}, j \in \mathcal{T}}$.
   (b) Let $\hat{g}_\mathsf{R}$ be the leakage function which takes as input the value $\sigma_{\mathsf{R},r}$, computes the values $(\sigma_{\mathsf{R},r}^{(i)})_{i \in [n] \setminus \mathcal{J}}$ using $\sigma_{\mathsf{R},r}$ and the values $(\sigma_{\mathsf{R},r}^{(i)})_{i \in \mathcal{J}}$ and plugs them in Eq. (4) in order to obtain $(\sigma_i^*)_{i \in [n] \setminus \mathcal{J}}$; then, appends the values of Eq. (5) to obtain $(\sigma_i^*)_{i \in \mathcal{B}_{i_\mathsf{R}}}$, applies f_{i_R} to $(\sigma_i^*)_{i \in \mathcal{B}_{i_\mathsf{R}}}$, thus obtaining $(\tilde{\sigma}_i^*)_{i \in \mathcal{B}_{i_\mathsf{R}}}$, checks if all the tampered commitments within $\mathcal{T} \cap \mathcal{B}_{i_\mathsf{R}}$ agree on a single value $\tilde{\gamma}_\mathsf{R}$ (and outputs $\perp$ if not), and finally outputs $\tilde{\gamma}_\mathsf{R}$.
   (c) For all $i \in \mathcal{T}$, let $f_{\mathsf{L},i}$ be the function which takes as input the value $\sigma_{\mathsf{L},r}$, obtains $(\sigma_j^*)_{j \in \mathcal{B}_{i_\mathsf{L}}}$ by appending the values of Eq. (5) and plugging $\sigma_{\mathsf{L},r}$ into Eq. (6), and then computes the tampered shares $(\tilde{\sigma}_j^*)_{j \in \mathcal{B}_{i_\mathsf{L}}} = f_{i_\mathsf{L}}((\sigma_j^*)_{j \in \mathcal{B}_{i_\mathsf{L}}})$ and outputs $\tilde{\sigma}_{\mathsf{L},i}$ if $i \in \mathcal{B}_{i_\mathsf{L}}$ and the special share σ_L^* otherwise.
   (d) For all $i \in \mathcal{T}$, let $f_{\mathsf{R},i}$ be the function which takes as input the value $\sigma_{\mathsf{R},r}$, computes the values $(\sigma_{\mathsf{R},r}^{(i)})_{i \in [n] \setminus \mathcal{J}}$ using $\sigma_{\mathsf{R},r}$ and the values $(\sigma_{\mathsf{R},r}^{(i)})_{i \in \mathcal{J}}$ and

plugs them in Eq. (4) in order to obtain $(\sigma_i^*)_{i\in[n]\setminus\mathcal{J}}$; then, appends the values of Eq. (5) to obtain $(\sigma_i^*)_{i\in\mathcal{B}_{i_R}}$, applies f_{i_R} to $(\sigma_i^*)_{i\in\mathcal{B}_{i_R}}$, thus obtaining $(\tilde{\sigma}_i^*)_{i\in\mathcal{B}_{i_R}}$, uses these values along with the values $(\tilde{\sigma}_{R,j}^{(i)})_{i\in\mathcal{B}_{i_L},j\in\mathcal{T}}$ obtained by $\hat{g}_L$ in order to reconstruct $\tilde{\sigma}_{R,i}$ for all $i\in\mathcal{T}$, and finally outputs $\tilde{\sigma}_{R,i}$ if $i\in\mathcal{B}_{i_L}$ and a share $\sigma_{R,i}^*$ such that $\mathsf{Rec}'(\sigma_L^*,\sigma_{R,i}^*)=\mathsf{Rec}'(\tilde{\sigma}_{L,i},\tilde{\sigma}_{R,i})$ otherwise.

Send the leakage query $(\hat{g}_L,\hat{g}_R)$, thus obtaining $((\tilde{\gamma}_L,(\tilde{\sigma}_{R,j}^{(i)})_{i\in\mathcal{B}_{i*},j\in[n]}),\tilde{\gamma}_R)$, return $\perp$ to A if $\tilde{\gamma}_L\neq\tilde{\gamma}_R$ and, otherwise, call $\tilde{\gamma}$ the tampered commitment obtained from such a query. Next, for all $i\in\mathcal{T}$, send the tampering query $(f_{L,i},f_{R,i})$, thus obtaining the tampered share $\tilde{\sigma}_i$ (or $\perp$, in which case return $\perp$ to A), and replace $\tilde{\sigma}_i$ with σ_r if $\tilde{\sigma}_i=\diamond$ or replace $\tilde{\sigma}_i$ with σ_j if there exists $j\in[n]$ such that $\tilde{\sigma}_i=\sigma_j'$. Finally, check that there exist no distinct $i_1,i_2\in\mathcal{T}$ s.t. $\mathsf{idx}(\sigma_{i_1})=\mathsf{idx}(\sigma_{i_2})$ (and output $\perp$ otherwise), reconstruct $\tilde{\mu}||\tilde{\rho}=\mathsf{Rec}((\tilde{\sigma}_i)_{i\in\mathcal{T}})$, check that $\tilde{\gamma}=\mathsf{Com}(\tilde{\mu};\tilde{\rho})$ (and return $\perp$ otherwise), replace $\tilde{\mu}$ with $\diamond$ if $\tilde{\mu}\in\{\mu_0,\mu_1\}$ and return $\tilde{\mu}$ to A.

5. **Guess.** Return the same distinguishing bit as that of A.

For the analysis, call $\mathbf{Bad}_i$ the event that one tampering query modifies the shares so that the tampered value $(\tilde{\sigma}_{L,i},\tilde{\sigma}_{R,i})$ is a valid encoding of σ_r' (i.e., the adversary purposely replaces $(\sigma_{L,i},\sigma_{R,i})$ with a valid encoding of σ_r'). Clearly, the probability of the event $\mathbf{Bad}_i$ in the hybrid experiment $\mathbf{Hyb}_{r-1}$ is $O(2^{-\lambda})$ as provoking the event corresponds to guessing the value σ_r' which is uniformly random over $\mathcal{S}_r(|\mu_b|+|\rho|)$. Furthermore, the reduction perfectly simulates $\mathbf{Hyb}_{r-1}(\lambda,b,1)$ if the target codeword encodes σ_r and conditioning on $\mathbf{Bad}=\bigcup_i\mathbf{Bad}_i$ not happening. On the other hand, if the target codeword encodes σ_r', the reduction perfectly simulates $\mathbf{Hyb}_r(\lambda,b,1)$. In particular, the latter holds because: (i) By perfect privacy of Shamir's secret sharing the distribution of the shares $(\sigma_i^*)_{i\in\mathcal{B}_{i_L}}$ and $(\sigma_i^*)_{i\in\mathcal{B}_{i_R}}$ computed inside the leakage and tampering oracles is identical to that of the target secret sharing of either $\mathbf{Hyb}_{r-1}(\lambda,b,1)$ or $\mathbf{Hyb}_r(\lambda,b,1)$; (ii) The auxiliary information leaked by the functions $(\hat{g}_L,\hat{g}_R)$, along with the answer to the tampering queries $(f_{L,i},f_{R,i})_{i\in[t]}$, yield a perfect simulation of A's tampering query.

Hence, to conclude the proof, it only remains to show that the constraints on the leakage hold. The amount of leakage performed by the reduction is exactly the one performed by A, plus the leakage used to obtain the tampered commitments $\tilde{\gamma}_L,\tilde{\gamma}_R$ and the tampered shares $(\tilde{\sigma}_{R,j}^{(i)})_{i\in\mathcal{B}_{i*},j\in[n]}$, therefore we need:

$$\ell_L\geq\ell^*+t\cdot(t-1)\cdot s_R+|\gamma| \qquad \text{and} \qquad \ell_R\geq\ell^*+|\gamma|.$$

The lemma follows.

4.2 Inductive Step

The lemma below constitutes the inductive step. The proof appears in the full version [8].

Lemma 3. *Fix any $p \in \text{poly}(\lambda)$ and assume that for all $b \in \{0,1\}$, and all $r \in [n]$, it holds:*

$$\left\{\mathbf{Hyb}_{r-1}(\lambda, b, p)\right\}_{\lambda \in \mathbb{N}} \overset{\text{s}}{\approx} \left\{\mathbf{Hyb}_r(\lambda, b, p)\right\}_{\lambda \in \mathbb{N}}.$$

Then,

$$\left\{\mathbf{Hyb}_{r-1}(\lambda, b, p+1)\right\}_{\lambda \in \mathbb{N}} \overset{\text{s}}{\approx} \left\{\mathbf{Hyb}_r(\lambda, b, p+1)\right\}_{\lambda \in \mathbb{N}}.$$

4.3   Putting It Together

By Lemmas 2 and 3, we get that, for all $b \in \{0,1\}$ and all $r \in [n]$,

$$\left\{\mathbf{Hyb}_{r-1}(\lambda, b)\right\}_{\lambda \in \mathbb{N}} \overset{\text{s}}{\approx} \left\{\mathbf{Hyb}_r(\lambda, b)\right\}_{\lambda \in \mathbb{N}}.$$

Hence, by repeatedly applying the triangular inequality, we have obtained

$$\left\{\mathbf{Hyb}_0(\lambda, b)\right\}_{\lambda \in \mathbb{N}} \overset{\text{s}}{\approx} \left\{\mathbf{Hyb}_n(\lambda, b)\right\}_{\lambda \in \mathbb{N}}.$$

The lemma below concludes the proof of the theorem. The proof appears in the full version [8].

Lemma 4. $\left\{\mathbf{Hyb}_n(\lambda, 0)\right\}_{\lambda \in \mathbb{N}} \overset{\text{c}}{\approx} \left\{\mathbf{Hyb}_n(\lambda, 1)\right\}_{\lambda \in \mathbb{N}}.$

5   Rate Compilers and Capacity Upper Bounds

In this section, we first establish an upper bound on the capacity of continuously non-malleable threshold secret sharing against joint tampering. We focus on secret sharing scheme that are not leakage resilient. Indeed, an upper bound on the capacity of this weaker primitive implies an upper bound on the capacity of leakage-resilient continuous non-malleable secret sharing schemes. Additionally, we exhibit a compiler for boosting the rate of our construction from the previous section so that it achieves the best possible rate in the plain model. For completeness, in the full version [8], we show that our upper bound on the capacity can be overcome both in the random oracle model (ROM) and in the algebraic generic group model (AGM).

5.1   Capacity Upper Bounds

We show the following upper bound on the maximal achievable rate of any continuously non-malleable secret sharing scheme against k-joint tampering, for $k > t/2$. Recall that computational assumptions are inherent for continuous non-malleability, and thus our negative results hold even in the computational setting.

Theorem 2. *Let Π be a t-out-of-n k-CNMSS scheme. If $k > t/2$, then Π cannot achieve better asymptotic rate than $\varrho \leq t - k$.*

Proof. We prove the slightly stronger statement that the capacity upper bound holds even if the attacker always uses the same reconstruction set $\mathcal{T}$ across all tampering queries. For simplicity, we assume that the share space of Π is $\mathcal{S} = \mathcal{S}_1 \times \cdots \times \mathcal{S}_n$ with $|\mathcal{S}_i| = |\mathcal{S}_j|$ for all $i, j \in [n]$. (A generalization is immediate.) Consider the following commitment scheme:

- The commitment procedure Com, upon input a message μ and random coins ρ, samples shares $(\sigma_1, \ldots, \sigma_n) := \mathsf{Share}(\mu; \rho)$ and outputs $\gamma = (\sigma_1, \ldots, \sigma_{t-k})$.
- The opening procedure, upon input an opening μ, ρ and a commitment γ, recomputes the shares $\sigma_1, \ldots, \sigma_n$ and checks that γ equals the first $t - k$ shares.

We now prove that the above defined commitment scheme is perfectly binding. Note that the latter implies that $|\mu| \leq |\gamma|$ because Com must be an injective function. Thus, by letting $s = \log |\mathcal{S}_1|$, the rate satisfies $\varrho = |\mu|/s \leq |\gamma|/s \leq t - k$ (as desired).

Towards a contradiction, assume that Com is not perfectly binding. Namely, there exist a commitment γ and two openings $(\mu^{(0)}, \rho_0)$ and $(\mu^{(1)}, \rho_1)$ such that both openings are valid for γ and $\mu^{(0)} \neq \mu^{(1)}$. Consider the following PPT attacker against continuous non-malleability, with the values $\mu^{(0)}, \rho_0, \mu^{(1)}, \rho_1$ hard-coded in:

1. Let μ_0^* and μ_1^* be any two distinct messages, and denote by $(\sigma_1, \ldots, \sigma_n)$ the target secret sharing of μ_b^* in the experiment defining continuous non-malleability. For better readability, set $\ell = |(\sigma_{t-k+1}||\cdots||\sigma_t)|$.
2. Compute the shares $(\sigma_0^{(0)}, \ldots, \sigma_n^{(0)}) := \mathsf{Share}(\mu^{(0)}; \rho_0)$ and $(\sigma_0^{(1)}, \ldots, \sigma_n^{(1)}) := \mathsf{Share}(\mu^{(1)}; \rho_1)$. By validity of the openings, we have that $\sigma_i^{(0)} = \sigma_i^{(1)}$ for all $i \in [t - k]$.
3. Set $\mathcal{T} := [t]$, $\mathcal{B}_1 := [t - k]$, and $\mathcal{B}_2 := [t] \setminus [t - k]$.
4. For each $j \in [\ell]$, the j-th tampering query is defined to be $(\mathcal{T}, (f_1, f_2^{(j)}))$ where the tampering functions are specified as follows:
   - $f_1((\sigma_i)_{i \in \mathcal{B}_1}) := (\sigma_i^{(0)})_{i \in \mathcal{B}_1}$.
   - $f_2^{(j)}((\sigma_i)_{i \in \mathcal{B}_2})$ is the function that outputs $(\sigma_i^{(0)})_{i \in \mathcal{B}_2}$ if and only if the j-th bit of the string $(\sigma_i)_{i \in \mathcal{B}_2}$ equals 0 (and outputs $(\sigma_i^{(1)})_{i \in \mathcal{B}_2}$ otherwise).
   Let $\tilde{\mu}$ be the output of the j-th tampering query. Set $\alpha_j := 0$ if and only if $\tilde{\mu} = \mu^{(0)}$ (and $\alpha_j := 1$ otherwise).
5. Parse the string $\alpha_1, \ldots, \alpha_\ell$ as $\sigma_{t-k+1}, \ldots, \sigma_t$. Forward the query $(\mathcal{T}, (f_1', f_2'))$ to the tampering oracle, where f_1' takes as input $(\sigma_i)_{i \in \mathcal{B}_1}$, reconstructs the message μ_b^* (using the values $\sigma_{t-k+1}, \ldots, \sigma_t$), and finally either does nothing (say, if the reconstructed message is μ_0^*) or outputs garbage.
6. Output $b' = 0$ if and only if the output of the last tampering query is $\diamond$ (and otherwise output $b' = 1$).

Note that $t - k < k$ as $k > t/2$, and thus $\mathcal{B} = (\mathcal{B}_1, \mathcal{B}_2)$ is a k-sized partition of $\mathcal{T} = [t]$. Moreover, the above reduction clearly breaks continuous non-malleability of Π with overwhelming probability. This concludes the proof.

$\mathbf{LR\text{-}CNMSS}^{\mu_0,\mu_1}_{\Pi^*,\mathsf{A},\mathcal{B}}(\lambda,b)$ $\mathbf{Hyb}^{\mu_0,\mu_1}_{\Pi^*,\mathsf{A},\mathcal{B}}(\lambda,b)$:

$\kappa \leftarrow_\$ \mathcal{K}$

$\hat{\kappa} \leftarrow_\$ \mathcal{K}$

$(\kappa_1,\ldots,\kappa_n) \leftarrow_\$ \mathsf{Share}(\kappa)$

$(\hat{\kappa}_1,\ldots,\hat{\kappa}_n) \leftarrow_\$ \mathsf{Share}(\hat{\kappa})$

$\gamma \leftarrow_\$ \mathsf{Enc}(\kappa,\mu_b)$

$(\gamma_1,\ldots,\gamma_n) = \mathsf{IDisp}(\gamma)$

$\forall i \in [n]:$

$\quad \sigma_i := (\kappa_i,\gamma_i)$

$\sigma := (\sigma_1,\ldots,\sigma_n)$

$\mathtt{stop} \leftarrow \mathtt{false}$

Return $\mathsf{A}^{\mathcal{O}_{\mathsf{tamp}}(\sigma,\cdot),\mathcal{O}_{\mathsf{leak}}(\sigma,\cdot)}(1^\lambda)$

Oracle $\mathcal{O}_{\mathsf{leak}}(\sigma,(g_1,\ldots,g_m))$:

If $\mathtt{stop} = \mathtt{true}$, return $\bot$

Else, return $g_1(\sigma_{\mathcal{B}_1}),\ldots,g_m(\sigma_{\mathcal{B}_m})$

Oracle $\mathcal{O}_{\mathsf{tamp}}(\sigma,\mathcal{T},(f_1,\ldots,f_m))$:

If $\mathtt{stop} = \mathtt{true}$, return $\bot$

$\forall i \in [m] : \tilde{\sigma}_{\mathcal{B}_i} := f_i(\sigma_{\mathcal{B}_i})$

$\tilde{\sigma} = (\tilde{\sigma}_1,\ldots,\tilde{\sigma}_n)$

$\forall i \in \mathcal{T}, \tilde{\sigma}_i = (\tilde{\kappa}_i,\tilde{\gamma}_i)$

$\tilde{\gamma} = \mathsf{IRec}((\tilde{\gamma}_i)_{i\in\mathcal{T}})$

If $\mathsf{IDisp}(\tilde{\gamma})_{\mathcal{T}} \neq (\tilde{\gamma}_i)_{i\in\mathcal{T}}$

$\quad \mathtt{stop} \leftarrow \mathtt{true}$ and return $\bot$

$\tilde{\kappa} = \mathsf{Rec}((\tilde{\kappa}_i)_{i\in\mathcal{T}})$

If $\tilde{\kappa} = \bot$, $\mathtt{stop} \leftarrow \mathtt{true}$ and return $\bot$

If $\tilde{\kappa} = \hat{\kappa}$, $\tilde{\kappa} \leftarrow \kappa$

$\tilde{\mu} = \mathsf{Dec}(\tilde{\kappa},\tilde{\gamma})$

If $\tilde{\mu} = \bot$, $\mathtt{stop} \leftarrow \mathtt{true}$ and return $\bot$

If $\tilde{\mu} \in \{\mu_0,\mu_1\}$, return $\diamond$

Else return $\tilde{\mu}$

Fig. 4. Experiments in the proof of Theorem 3. The instructions boxed in red are the modifications introduced by the hybrid experiment. (Color figure online)

5.2 Rate Compiler (Plain Model)

Let $(\mathsf{IDisp},\mathsf{IRec})$ be an information dispersal, $\Pi = (\mathsf{Share},\mathsf{Rec})$ be a secret sharing scheme and $\Sigma = (\mathsf{Enc},\mathsf{Dec})$ be a secret-key encryption scheme. Consider the following derived secret sharing scheme $\Pi^* = (\mathsf{Share}^*,\mathsf{Rec}^*)$.

- **Algorithm** Share*: upon input a message μ, sample a random key $\kappa \leftarrow_\$ \mathcal{K}$ and compute $\gamma \leftarrow_\$ \mathsf{Enc}(\kappa,\mu)$, $(\gamma_1,\ldots,\gamma_n) = \mathsf{IDisp}(\gamma)$ and $(\kappa_1,\ldots,\kappa_n) \leftarrow_\$ \mathsf{Share}(\kappa)$; finally, for all $i \in [n]$, let $\sigma_i = (\kappa_i,\gamma_i)$ and output $(\sigma_1,\ldots,\sigma_n)$.
- **Algorithm** Rec*: upon input a set $(\sigma_i)_{i\in\mathcal{I}}$ of at least t shares parse $\sigma_i = (\kappa_i,\gamma_i)$ for all $i \in \mathcal{I}$, reconstruct $\kappa = \mathsf{Rec}((\kappa_i)_{i\in\mathcal{I}})$ and $\gamma = \mathsf{IRec}((\gamma_i)_{i\in\mathcal{I}})$, check that $\mathsf{IDisp}(\gamma)_{\mathcal{I}} = (\gamma_i)_{i\in\mathcal{I}}$ (and return $\bot$ if not), and finally output $\mu = \mathsf{Dec}(\kappa,\gamma)$.

The construction above was first proposed and analyzed by Krawczyk [21] in the setting of plain threshold secret sharing. The theorem below states its security in the setting of continuous joint tampering and leakage attacks.

Theorem 3. *Let $n,t,t^*,\ell \in \mathbb{N}$ be parameters such that $t^* \leq t-1$. Assume that:*

- *$(\mathsf{IDisp},\mathsf{IRec})$ is a t^*-out-of-n information dispersal;*
- *$(\mathsf{Share},\mathsf{Rec})$ is a t-out-of-n $(\ell,t-1)$-LR-CNMSS;*
- *$(\mathsf{Enc},\mathsf{Dec})$ is an IND-CCA secure secret-key encryption scheme.*

Then, Π^* is a t-out-of-n $(\ell,t-1)$-LR-CNMSS under the following restriction: Each tampering query $(\mathcal{T},f)$ output by the attacker is such that, for all subsets $\mathcal{B}_i$ of the partition $\mathcal{B}$, either $\mathcal{B}_i \cap \mathcal{T} = \emptyset$ or $|\mathcal{B}_i \cap \mathcal{T}| \geq t^*$. Moreover, the asymptotic rate of Π^* is $\varrho = t^*$.

Proof. The proof proceeds by a hybrid argument. In particular, we argue that the original experiment is computationally close to a mental experiment in which we replace the secret sharing of the key κ with a secret sharing of an unrelated random key $\hat{\kappa}$. The mental experiments is depicted in Fig. 4 along with the original experiment in order to highlight the main differences. The lemma below states that the two experiments are computationally indistinguishable. The proof appears in the full version [8].

Lemma 5. *For all $\mu_0, \mu_1 \in \mathcal{M}$, all $(t-1)$-sized partitions $\mathcal{B}$ of $[n]$, and all $b \in \{0,1\}$, it holds that:*

$$\left\{\mathbf{LR\text{-}CNMSS}^{\mu_0,\mu_1}_{\Pi^*,\mathsf{A}}(\lambda,b)\right\}_{\lambda \in \mathbb{N}} \stackrel{c}{\approx} \left\{\mathbf{Hyb}^{\mu_0,\mu_1}_{\Pi^*,\mathsf{A},\mathcal{B}}(\lambda,b)\right\}_{\lambda \in \mathbb{N}}.$$

The lemma below concludes the proof of continuous non-malleability in Theorem 3.

Lemma 6. *For all $\mu_0, \mu_1 \in \mathcal{M}$, and all $(t-1)$-sized partitions $\mathcal{B}$ of $[n]$, it holds that:*

$$\left\{\mathbf{Hyb}^{\mu_0,\mu_1}_{\Pi^*,\mathsf{A},\mathcal{B}}(\lambda,0)\right\}_{\lambda \in \mathbb{N}} \stackrel{c}{\approx} \left\{\mathbf{Hyb}^{\mu_0,\mu_1}_{\Pi^*,\mathsf{A},\mathcal{B}}(\lambda,1)\right\}_{\lambda \in \mathbb{N}}.$$

Proof. By reduction to IND-CCA security of the symmetric encryption scheme. Suppose that there exist two messages $\mu_0, \mu_1 \in \mathcal{M}$, a $(t-1)$-sized partition $\mathcal{B}$ of $[n]$, and a PPT adversary A that is able to distinguish between the two experiments with non-negligible probability. Consider the following reduction A' attacking IND-CCA security of Σ.

1. **Setup.** Set the challenge messages to be μ_0 and μ_1, obtain the challenge ciphertext γ, sample a key $\hat{\kappa} \leftarrow_\$ \mathcal{K}$ and compute $(\gamma_1, \ldots, \gamma_n) = \mathsf{IDisp}(\hat{\gamma})$, and $(\kappa_1, \ldots, \kappa_n) \leftarrow_\$ \mathsf{Share}(\hat{\kappa})$. Finally, for all $i \in [n]$, construct the share $\sigma_i^* := (\kappa_i, \gamma_i)$.
2. **Leakage queries.** Answer leakage queries as in the hybrid experiment.
3. **Tampering queries.** Upon input a tampering query $(\mathcal{T}, (f_1, \ldots, f_m))$, for all $i \in [m]$, compute $(\tilde{\sigma}_j)_{j \in \mathcal{B}_i} = f_i((\sigma_j)_{j \in \mathcal{B}_i})$, perform the consistency checks on the tampered ciphertext $\tilde{\gamma}$ (and output $\perp$ if any of these checks fails), and then reconstruct the tampered key $\tilde{\kappa} \in \mathcal{K}$. If $\tilde{\kappa} = \hat{\kappa}$, obtain the tampered message $\tilde{\mu} \in \mathcal{M} \cup \{\perp\}$ by sending $\tilde{\gamma}$ to the decryption oracle; otherwise, compute $\tilde{\mu} = \mathsf{Dec}(\tilde{\kappa}, \tilde{\gamma})$. If $\tilde{\mu} \in \{\mu_0, \mu_1\}$, set $\tilde{\mu} = \diamond$. Finally, return $\tilde{\mu}$ to A (and self-destruct if $\tilde{\mu} = \perp$).
4. **Guess.** Output the same distinguishing bit as A does.

For the analysis, note that the reduction is perfect and, in particular, for $b \in \{0,1\}$, it perfectly simulates $\mathbf{Hyb}^{\mu_0,\mu_1}_{\Pi^*,\mathsf{A},\mathcal{B}}(\lambda,b)$ whenever the challenge ciphertext γ is an encryption of μ_b. This concludes the proof.

It only remains to discuss the rate of the construction. Towards this, note that the length of the key κ for the SKE scheme Σ, and thus the size of the shares of the secret sharing scheme Π, only depends on the security parameter

λ, the number of parties n and the tolerated leakage ℓ (but not on the length $|\mu|$ of the message); call $s_0(\lambda, n, \ell)$ the length of this portion of the final shares (namely, κ_i). On the other hand, it is possible to achieve length of the ciphertext $|\gamma| = |\mu| + O(\lambda)$, hence the length of each share γ_i of the information dispersal amounts to $|\gamma_i| = \frac{|\gamma|}{t^*} = \frac{|\mu| + O(\lambda)}{t^*}$. Putting it together, we have obtained:

$$s(\lambda, n, \ell, |\mu|) = s_0(\lambda, n, \ell) + \frac{|\mu| + O(\lambda)}{t^*},$$

that translates into

$$\begin{aligned}
\varrho &= \inf_{\lambda \in \mathbb{N}} \lim_{|\mu| \to \infty} \frac{|\mu|}{s(\lambda, n, \ell, |\mu|)} \\
&= \inf_{\lambda \in \mathbb{N}} \lim_{|\mu| \to \infty} \frac{t^* \cdot |\mu|}{|\mu| + t^* \cdot \mathsf{poly}(\lambda, n, \ell)} \\
&= t^*.
\end{aligned}$$

This completes the proof of Theorem 3.

Rate Optimality. We stress that when $k = t - 1$, Theorem 2 says that the capacity of continuously non-malleable secret sharing against joint tampering with at most $t - 1$ shares is 1. This is not in contrast with the fact that our rate compiler from Theorem 3 achieves rate larger than 1, as the latter only holds under an additional restriction on the way the attacker can manipulate the shares. Nevertheless, it is possible to adapt the proof of Theorem 2 in order to show that our rate compiler achieves the best possible rate whenever $t^* < t/2$.

Theorem 4. *Let Π be a t-out-of-n $(t-1)$-CNMSS scheme under the restriction that each tampering query (T, f) output by the attacker must be such that, for all subsets $\mathcal{B}_i$ of the partition $\mathcal{B}$, either $\mathcal{B}_i \cap T = \emptyset$ or $|\mathcal{B}_i \cap T| \geq t^*$. If $t^* \leq t/2$, then Π cannot achieve better rate than $\varrho \leq t^*$.*

Proof. The proof is almost identical to that of Theorem 2, and thus we only highlight the main differences. We change the definition of Com so that it now outputs the value $\gamma = (\sigma_1, \ldots, \sigma_{t^*})$, and we adjust the opening procedure accordingly. Hence, the goal is to prove, again, that Com is perfectly binding, so that the rate of Π must satisfy $\varrho \leq t^*$.

The reduction is identical to that in the proof of Theorem 2, except that now we define $\ell := |\sigma_{t^*+1}|| \cdots ||\sigma_t|$ and moreover the adversary attacking continuous non-malleability sets $\mathcal{B}_1 := [t^*]$ and $\mathcal{B}_2 := [t] \backslash [t^*]$ in step 3., and parses the string $\alpha_1, \ldots, \alpha_\ell$ as $\sigma_{t^*+1}, \ldots, \sigma_t$ in step 5.. Note that $|\mathcal{B}_1| = t^*$ and $|\mathcal{B}_2| = t - t^* \geq 2t^* - t^* = t^*$. Since $t^* \leq t - 1$, the adversary is admissible which concludes the proof.

Remark 2. More generally, Theorem 4 holds for t-out-of-n k-CNMSS so long as $k \geq t - t^*$.

6 Instantiations

In this section, we show how to instantiate the building blocks required by the abstract constructions of Theorems 1 and 3.

6.1 Leakage-Resilient p-time Non-malleable Code

Here, we explain how to obtain noisy-leakage-resilient p-time non-malleable asymmetric split-state codes with the additional properties stated in Theorem 1. Our construction exploits leakage-resilient asymmetric split-state codes as defined in Sect. 3.2, as recently introduced by Ball, Guo, and Wichs [4] and generalized to the noisy-leakage setting by Brian, Faonio and Venturi [7].

Let $\Pi = (\mathsf{Share}, \mathsf{Rec})$, $\Pi_\mathsf{L} = (\mathsf{Share}_\mathsf{L}, \mathsf{Rec}_\mathsf{L})$ and $\Pi_\mathsf{R} = (\mathsf{Share}_\mathsf{R}, \mathsf{Rec}_\mathsf{R})$ be split-state codes. Consider the following split-state code $\Pi^* = (\mathsf{Share}^*, \mathsf{Rec}^*)$.

- **Algorithm Share^*:** upon input a message μ, compute $(\sigma_\mathsf{L}, \sigma_\mathsf{R}) \leftarrow_\$ \mathsf{Share}(\mu)$, and $(\sigma_{\mathsf{L},\mathsf{L}}, \sigma_{\mathsf{L},\mathsf{R}}) \leftarrow_\$ \mathsf{Share}_\mathsf{L}(\sigma_\mathsf{L})$ and $(\sigma_{\mathsf{R},\mathsf{L}}, \sigma_{\mathsf{R},\mathsf{R}}) \leftarrow_\$ \mathsf{Share}_\mathsf{R}(\sigma_\mathsf{R})$. Set $\sigma_\mathsf{L}^* = (\sigma_{\mathsf{L},\mathsf{L}}, \sigma_{\mathsf{R},\mathsf{R}})$ and $\sigma_\mathsf{R}^* = (\sigma_{\mathsf{R},\mathsf{L}}, \sigma_{\mathsf{L},\mathsf{R}})$, and output $\sigma_\mathsf{L}^*, \sigma_\mathsf{R}^*$.
- **Algorithm Rec^*:** upon input two shares $(\sigma_\mathsf{L}^*, \sigma_\mathsf{R}^*)$, parse $\sigma_\mathsf{L}^* = (\sigma_{\mathsf{L},\mathsf{L}}, \sigma_{\mathsf{R},\mathsf{R}})$ and $\sigma_\mathsf{R}^* = (\sigma_{\mathsf{R},\mathsf{L}}, \sigma_{\mathsf{L},\mathsf{R}})$, compute the shares $\sigma_\mathsf{L} = \mathsf{Rec}_\mathsf{L}(\sigma_{\mathsf{L},\mathsf{L}}, \sigma_{\mathsf{L},\mathsf{R}})$ and $\sigma_\mathsf{R} = \mathsf{Rec}_\mathsf{R}(\sigma_{\mathsf{R},\mathsf{L}}, \sigma_{\mathsf{R},\mathsf{R}})$, and output $\mu = \mathsf{Rec}(\sigma_\mathsf{L}, \sigma_\mathsf{R})$.

Theorem 5. *For all $i, j \in \{\mathsf{L}, \mathsf{R}\}$, let $p, s_i, s_{i,j} \in \mathbb{N}$, $\ell_i, \ell_{i,j} \geq 0$, and $\epsilon, \epsilon_i \in [0, 1]$ be parameters such that:*

- *$s_\mathsf{R} < s_\mathsf{L}$;*
- *$s_{\mathsf{L},\mathsf{R}} < s_{\mathsf{L},\mathsf{L}}$, $\ell_{\mathsf{L},\mathsf{L}} \geq \ell_\mathsf{L} + p \cdot s_{\mathsf{R},\mathsf{R}}$ and $\ell_{\mathsf{L},\mathsf{R}} \geq \ell_\mathsf{R}$;*
- *$s_{\mathsf{R},\mathsf{R}} < s_{\mathsf{R},\mathsf{L}}$, $\ell_{\mathsf{R},\mathsf{L}} \geq \ell_\mathsf{R} + p \cdot s_{\mathsf{L},\mathsf{R}}$ and $\ell_{\mathsf{R},\mathsf{R}} \geq \ell_\mathsf{L}$.*

Assume that:

- *Π is an $(s_\mathsf{L}, s_\mathsf{R})$-asymmetric (p, ϵ)-NMC;*
- *Π_L is an $(s_{\mathsf{L},\mathsf{L}}, s_{\mathsf{L},\mathsf{R}})$-asymmetric $(\ell_{\mathsf{L},\mathsf{L}}, \ell_{\mathsf{L},\mathsf{R}}, \epsilon_\mathsf{L})$-LRC;*
- *Π_R is an $(s_{\mathsf{R},\mathsf{L}}, s_{\mathsf{R},\mathsf{R}})$-asymmetric $(\ell_{\mathsf{R},\mathsf{L}}, \ell_{\mathsf{R},\mathsf{R}}, \epsilon_\mathsf{R})$-LRC.*

Then, Π^* is an $(s_\mathsf{L}^*, s_\mathsf{R}^*)$-asymmetric $(\ell_\mathsf{L}, \ell_\mathsf{R}, p, \epsilon + 2(\epsilon_\mathsf{L} + \epsilon_\mathsf{R}))$-LR-NMC, where $s_\mathsf{L}^* = s_{\mathsf{L},\mathsf{L}} + s_{\mathsf{R},\mathsf{R}}$ and $s_\mathsf{R}^* = s_{\mathsf{L},\mathsf{R}} + s_{\mathsf{R},\mathsf{L}}$.

The proof to the above theorem (which appears in the full version [8]) goes along the same lines of the proof of Theorem 7 in [7] for the case of 2-out-of-2 secret sharing. The only difference is that Π is a p-time NMC instead of a one-time NMC, and we use different parameters for Π_L and Π_R. In particular, all the hybrid experiments are the same as in [7] with the only difference that we have to leak $2p$ tampered values (namely, $\tilde{\sigma}_{\mathsf{R},\mathsf{R}}^{(j)}, \tilde{\sigma}_{\mathsf{L},\mathsf{R}}^{(j)}$ for $j \in [p]$) instead of only two; however, our choice of the leakage parameters allows us to do so, since

$$\ell_{\mathsf{L},\mathsf{L}} \geq \ell_\mathsf{L} + p \cdot s_{\mathsf{R},\mathsf{R}} \quad \text{and} \quad \ell_{\mathsf{R},\mathsf{L}} \geq \ell_\mathsf{R} + p \cdot s_{\mathsf{L},\mathsf{R}}.$$

Finally, we show that the scheme Π^* of Theorem 5 is able to achieve the properties (i)–(ii) needed to instantiate Theorem 1. The lemma below states that if the underlying NMC Π satisfies the additional property (i), so does the scheme Π^*.

Lemma 7. *Suppose that there exists σ_L such that, for all $\mu \in \mathcal{M}$, there exists σ_R such that $\mathsf{Rec}(\sigma_L, \sigma_R) = \mu$. Then, there exists σ_L^* such that, for all $\mu \in \mathcal{M}$, there exists σ_R^* such that $\mathsf{Rec}^*(\sigma_L^*, \sigma_R^*) = \mu$.*

Proof. Let σ_L be such that, for all $\mu \in \mathcal{M}$, there exists σ_R such that $\mathsf{Rec}(\sigma_L, \sigma_R) = \mu$. Then, we can fix $\sigma_{R,R}$ and $\sigma_{L,R}$ and compute $\sigma_{L,L} \leftarrow_\$ \overline{\mathsf{Share}}_L(\sigma_L, \sigma_{L,R})$. The new left share will be $\sigma_L^* = (\sigma_{L,L}, \sigma_{R,R})$ and, once fixed σ_L^* and $\mu \in \mathcal{M}$, in order to obtain the right share it suffices to compute $\sigma_{R,L} \leftarrow_\$ \overline{\mathsf{Share}}_R(\sigma_R, \sigma_{R,R})$ and set $\sigma_R^* = (\sigma_{R,L}, \sigma_{L,R})$.

The property (ii) is a bit more delicate because, even if Π_L, Π_R achieve it, the random variables $(\Sigma_{L,L}, \Sigma_{R,R})$ and $(\Sigma_{R,L}, \Sigma_{L,R})$ are defined by $(\Sigma_{L,L}, \Sigma_{R,R}) = \mathsf{Share}_L(\Sigma_L)$ and $(\Sigma_{R,L}, \Sigma_{R,R}) = \mathsf{Share}_R(\Sigma_R)$, and Σ_L and Σ_R are related distributions. Instead, here we use a non-blackbox approach and prove that the asymmetric code given by Appendix A of [7], which we describe below, allows Π^* to achieve property (ii).

Let Ext be a seeded extractor with d-bits source, r-bit seed and m-bit output and let $\mathsf{2Ext}$ be a two-source extractor with s_2-bits sources and r-bit output. Consider the following secret sharing scheme Π_{LRC} with message space $\mathcal{M} = \{0,1\}^m$ and shares space $\mathcal{S} = \{0,1\}^{s_1} \times \{0,1\}^{s_2}$:

- **Algorithm Share:** upon input the message μ, randomly sample $\sigma_2 \leftarrow_\$ \{0,1\}^{s_2}, x \leftarrow_\$ \{0,1\}^d, y \leftarrow_\$ \{0,1\}^{s_2}$, compute $\rho := \mathsf{2Ext}(\sigma_2, y)$ and $z := \mathsf{Ext}(x, \rho) \oplus \mu$ and finally output (σ_1, σ_2), where $\sigma_1 = (x, y, z)$.
- **Algorithm Rec:** upon input the shares (σ_1, σ_2), parse $\sigma_1 = (x, y, z)$ and output $\mu := z \oplus \mathsf{Ext}(x, \mathsf{2Ext}(\sigma_1, y))$.

For all $\epsilon, \ell_1, \ell_2 \geq 0$ there exists an appropriate choice of the parameters d and r such that the above is an $(\ell_1, \ell_2, \epsilon)$-LRC (see [4,7] for the details) and, moreover, the above admits the following alternative sharing algorithm $\overline{\mathsf{Share}}$:

- **Algorithm $\overline{\mathsf{Share}}$:** upon input the message μ and the value σ_2, randomly sample $x \leftarrow_\$ \{0,1\}^d, y \leftarrow_\$ \{0,1\}^{s_2}$, compute $\rho := \mathsf{2Ext}(\sigma_2, y)$ and $z := \mathsf{Ext}(x, \rho) \oplus \mu$ and finally output (σ_1, σ_2), where $\sigma_1 = (x, y, z)$.

The following lemma proves that the above scheme allows our construction Π^* to achieve property (ii) of Theorem 1. The proof appears in the full version [8].

Lemma 8. *Instantiating Π_L and Π_R with the asymmetric LRC Π_{LRC}, for all $\mu \in \mathcal{M}$ it holds that*

$$\widetilde{\mathbb{H}}_\infty(\Sigma_L^* \mid \Sigma_R^*) \geq \mathbb{H}_\infty(\Sigma_L^*) - d \qquad \widetilde{\mathbb{H}}_\infty(\Sigma_R^* \mid \Sigma_L^*) \geq \mathbb{H}_\infty(\Sigma_R^*) - d,$$

where $d = s_L + s_R$ and $(\Sigma_L^*, \Sigma_R^*) = \mathsf{Share}^*(\mu)$ is the distribution of the shares of μ using the scheme Π^*.

Corollary 5.7 of [20] shows that, for all $n_1, n_2 \in \mathbb{N}$ and all polynomials p', there exists a two-source p-time ϵ-non-malleable extractor for sources of full-entropy of size n_1, n_2, where $p = n_2^{\Omega(1)}$, $n_1 = 4n_2 + p'(n_2)$ and $\epsilon = 2^{-n_2^{\Omega(1)}}$. This scheme has efficient pre-image sampleability and further satisfies the additional property described in the hypothesis of Lemma 7. By the known connection between (leakage-resilient) non-malleable extractors with efficient pre-image sampleability and (leakage-resilient) non-malleable codes, we obtain a $(p, \epsilon \cdot 2^{p|\mu|+1})$-NMC. Additionally, we note that by our setting of the parameters in Theorem 5 we can have $\ell_L \geq s_R^*$ so long as the underlying schemes Π_L and Π_R allow to arbitrarily set the parameters of leakage and of the codeword size of the left shares and right shares, which is the case thanks to Theorem 6 of [7].

Hence, together with Lemmas 7 and 8, we have obtained the following corollary:

Corollary 1. *For any $s_L, s_R, \ell_L, \ell_R, p \in \mathbb{N}, \epsilon \in [0, 1]$, there is a construction of an (s_L, s_R)-asymmetric (ℓ_L, ℓ_R)-noisy leakage-resilient p-time ϵ-non-malleable code satisfying the additional properties stated in Theorem 1.*

6.2 Leakage-Resilient Continuously Non-malleable Secret Sharing

By instantiating Theorem 1, we obtain the following.

Corollary 2. *Assuming the existence of one-to-one one-way functions, for any $n, t, \ell \in \mathbb{N}$ with $t > 2n/3$, there is a construction of a t-out-of-n secret sharing scheme satisfying noisy-leakage resilient continuous non-malleability under selective k-joint leakage and tampering attacks, where $k = t - 1$.*

Proof. The proof follows by instantiating the inner non-malleable code using Corollary 1 and recalling that perfectly binding and computationally hiding commitment schemes can be instantiated from one-to-one one-way functions [17]. □

Furthermore, by instantiating Theorem 3 with $t^* = 1$, we obtain the following.

Corollary 3. *Assuming the existence of one-to-one one-way functions, for any $n, t, \ell \in \mathbb{N}$ with $t > 2n/3$, there is a construction of a t-out-of-n secret sharing scheme satisfying noisy leakage-resilient continuous non-malleability under selective k-joint leakage and tampering attacks; moreover, the scheme achieves asymptotic rate 1, which is optimal.*

Proof. It is well known that IND-CCA secure SKE schemes can be constructed in a black-box way from any OWF, whereas the information dispersal can be instantiated using linear algebra over finite fields [27]; as for the continuously non-malleable secret sharing scheme we can take the one given by Corollary 2. Finally, when applying Theorem 3 with $t^* = 1$, the restriction on the tampering queries disappears (any subset either contains at least $t^* = 1$ share in $\mathcal{T}$ or does not contain any share in $\mathcal{T}$) and we obtain the standard definition of continuous non-malleability against $(t - 1)$-joint tampering attacks; since $t^* = 1$, the asymptotic rate[11] of the construction is one, which, by Theorem 2, is optimal.

---

[11] For the information dispersal, it suffices to define $\mathsf{IDisp}(\mu) := (\mu, \ldots, \mu)$ (*i.e.*, the same message repeated n times) and $\mathsf{IRec}(\mu) := \mu$.

6.3   Breaking the Rate-One Barrier

Finally, Theorem 3 also allows to obtain the first non-malleable secret sharing scheme against independent tampering attacks with rate larger than one.

Corollary 4. *Assuming the existence of one-to-one one-way functions, for any $n, t \in \mathbb{N}$ with $t > 2n/3$, there is a construction of a t-out-of-n secret sharing scheme satisfying one-time non-malleability under independent tampering attacks; moreover, the scheme achieves asymptotic rate $t/2$.*

Proof. The construction is the same of Theorem 3 with $t^* = t/2$,[12] therefore the concrete instantiation follows by Corollary 3.

   The proof of security follows by a simple reduction to non-malleability against joint tampering. In particular, assume that there exists an adversary A which is able to break one-time non-malleability by submitting an independent tampering query $(\mathcal{T}, f)$ to the tampering oracle. Then, it is possible to construct a reduction $\hat{\mathsf{A}}$ which partitions $\mathcal{T}$ into two subsets $\mathcal{B}_1, \mathcal{B}_2$ of $t/2$ shares each, runs A, forwards the tampering query $(\mathcal{T}, f)$ to the tampering oracle (recall that any independent tampering query is also a k-joint tampering query for all $k \geq 1$), and finally returns the tampered message $\tilde{\mu}$ to A and outputs the same distinguishing bit of A. Clearly, the attacker $\hat{\mathsf{A}}$ perfectly simulates the view of A, and moreover the condition $|\mathcal{B}_1 \cup \mathcal{T}| = |\mathcal{B}_2 \cup \mathcal{T}| = t/2$ is satisfied.

Remark 3. Corollary 4 can be trivially extended to include noisy-leakage resilience. Moreover, it can also be extended to continuous non-malleability if we assume that the reconstruction set $\mathcal{T}$ is the same across all tampering queries.

Acknowledgments. We thank Mark Simkin and Maciej Obremski for their valuable comments.

References

1. Aggarwal, D., et al.: Stronger leakage-resilient and non-malleable secret sharing schemes for general access structures. In: Boldyreva, A., Micciancio, D. (eds.) CRYPTO 2019. LNCS, vol. 11693, pp. 510–539. Springer, Cham (2019). https://doi.org/10.1007/978-3-030-26951-7_18
2. Badrinarayanan, S., Srinivasan, A.: Revisiting non-malleable secret sharing. In: Ishai, Y., Rijmen, V. (eds.) EUROCRYPT 2019. LNCS, vol. 11476, pp. 593–622. Springer, Cham (2019). https://doi.org/10.1007/978-3-030-17653-2_20
3. Ball, M., Chattopadhyay, E., Liao, J.J., Malkin, T., Tan, L.Y.: Non-malleability against polynomial tampering. Cryptology ePrint Archive, Report 2020/147 (2020). https://ia.cr/2020/147
4. Ball, M., Guo, S., Wichs, D.: Non-malleable codes for decision trees. In: CRYPTO 2019, Part I, pp. 413–434 (2019)
5. Blakley, G.R.: Safeguarding cryptographic keys. In: Proceedings of AFIPS 1979 National Computer Conference, pp. 313–317 (1979)

---

[12] For the sake of simplicity, assume t even. When t is odd, we obtain $t^* = (t-1)/2$.

6. Brian, G., Faonio, A., Obremski, M., Simkin, M., Venturi, D.: Non-malleable secret sharing against bounded joint-tampering attacks in the plain model. In: CRYPTO 2020, Part III, pp. 127–155 (2020)
7. Brian, G., Faonio, A., Venturi, D.: Continuously non-malleable secret sharing for general access structures. In: TCC 2019, Part II, pp. 211–232 (2019)
8. Brian, G., Faonio, A., Venturi, D.: Continuously non-malleable secret sharing: joint tampering, plain model and capacity. Cryptology ePrint Archive, Report 2021/1128 (2021). https://ia.cr/2021/1128
9. Chattopadhyay, E., Goodman, J., Goyal, V., Li, X.: Leakage-resilient extractors and secret-sharing against bounded collusion protocols. Cryptology ePrint Archive, Report 2020/478 (2020). https://ia.cr/2020/478
10. Chattopadhyay, E., Li, X.: Non-malleable codes, extractors and secret sharing for interleaved tampering and composition of tampering. Cryptology ePrint Archive, Report 2018/1069 (2018). https://ia.cr/2018/1069
11. Dodis, Y., Ostrovsky, R., Reyzin, L., Smith, A.: Fuzzy extractors: how to generate strong keys from biometrics and other noisy data. Cryptology ePrint Archive, Report 2003/235 (2003). http://ia.cr/2003/235
12. Dolev, D., Dwork, C., Naor, M.: Non-malleable cryptography (extended abstract). In: 23rd ACM STOC, pp. 542–552 (1991)
13. Dolev, D., Dwork, C., Naor, M.: Nonmalleable cryptography. SIAM J. Comput. **2**, 391–437 (2000)
14. Dziembowski, S., Pietrzak, K., Wichs, D.: Non-malleable codes. In: ICS 2010, pp. 434–452 (2010)
15. Faonio, A., Venturi, D.: Non-malleable secret sharing in the computational setting: adaptive tampering, noisy-leakage resilience, and improved rate. In: Boldyreva, A., Micciancio, D. (eds.) CRYPTO 2019. LNCS, vol. 11693, pp. 448–479. Springer, Cham (2019). https://doi.org/10.1007/978-3-030-26951-7_16
16. Faust, S., Mukherjee, P., Nielsen, J.B., Venturi, D.: Continuous non-malleable codes. In: Lindell, Y. (ed.) TCC 2014. LNCS, vol. 8349, pp. 465–488. Springer, Heidelberg (2014). https://doi.org/10.1007/978-3-642-54242-8_20
17. Goldreich, O., Micali, S., Wigderson, A.: How to play any mental game or a completeness theorem for protocols with honest majority. In: 19th ACM STOC, pp. 218–229 (1987)
18. Goyal, V., Kumar, A.: Non-malleable secret sharing. In: 50th ACM STOC, pp. 685–698 (2018)
19. Goyal, V., Kumar, A.: Non-malleable secret sharing for general access structures. In: Shacham, H., Boldyreva, A. (eds.) CRYPTO 2018. LNCS, vol. 10991, pp. 501–530. Springer, Cham (2018). https://doi.org/10.1007/978-3-319-96884-1_17
20. Goyal, V., Srinivasan, A., Zhu, C.: Multi-source non-malleable extractors and applications. IACR Cryptology ePrint Archive 2020/157 (2020). https://ia.cr/2020/157
21. Krawczyk, H.: Secret sharing made short. In: Stinson, D.R. (ed.) CRYPTO 1993. LNCS, vol. 773, pp. 136–146. Springer, Heidelberg (1994). https://doi.org/10.1007/3-540-48329-2_12
22. Kumar, A., Meka, R., Sahai, A.: Leakage-resilient secret sharing against colluding parties. In: 60th FOCS, pp. 636–660 (2019)
23. Kumar, A., Meka, R., Zuckerman, D.: Bounded collusion protocols, cylinder-intersection extractors and leakage-resilient secret sharing. Cryptology ePrint Archive, Report 2020/473 (2020). https://ia.cr/2020/473
24. Lin, F., Cheraghchi, M., Guruswami, V., Safavi-Naini, R., Wang, H.: Leakage-resilient non-malleable secret sharing in non-compartmentalized models. CoRR abs/1902.06195 (2019). http://arxiv.org/abs/1902.06195

25. Nielsen, J.B., Simkin, M.: Lower bounds for leakage-resilient secret sharing. In: Canteaut, A., Ishai, Y. (eds.) EUROCRYPT 2020. LNCS, vol. 12105, pp. 556–577. Springer, Cham (2020). https://doi.org/10.1007/978-3-030-45721-1_20

26. Ostrovsky, R., Persiano, G., Venturi, D., Visconti, I.: Continuously non-malleable codes in the split-state model from minimal assumptions. In: Shacham, H., Boldyreva, A. (eds.) CRYPTO 2018. LNCS, vol. 10993, pp. 608–639. Springer, Cham (2018). https://doi.org/10.1007/978-3-319-96878-0_21

27. Rabin, M.O.: Efficient dispersal of information for security, load balancing, and fault tolerance. J. ACM **36**(2), 335–348 (1989). https://doi.org/10.1145/62044.62050

28. Shamir, A.: How to share a secret. Commun. Assoc. Comput. Mach. **11**, 612–613 (1979)

29. Srinivasan, A., Vasudevan, P.N.: Leakage resilient secret sharing and applications. In: Boldyreva, A., Micciancio, D. (eds.) CRYPTO 2019. LNCS, vol. 11693, pp. 480–509. Springer, Cham (2019). https://doi.org/10.1007/978-3-030-26951-7_17

Disappearing Cryptography
in the Bounded Storage Model

Jiaxin Guan[1,2(✉)] and Mark Zhandry[1,2]

[1] Princeton University, Princeton, USA
jiaxin@guan.io, mzhandry@princeton.edu
[2] NTT Research, Palo Alto, USA

Abstract. In this work, we study *disappearing cryptography* in the bounded storage model. Here, a component of the transmission, say a ciphertext, a digital signature, or even a program, is streamed bit by bit. The stream is too large for anyone to store in its entirety, meaning the transmission effectively disappears once the stream stops.

We first propose the notion of online obfuscation, capturing the goal of disappearing programs in the bounded storage model. We give a negative result for VBB security in this model, but propose candidate constructions for a weaker security goal, namely VGB security. We then demonstrate the utility of VGB online obfuscation, showing that it can be used to generate disappearing ciphertexts and signatures. All of our applications are *not* possible in the standard model of cryptography, regardless of computational assumptions used.

1 Introduction

The bounded storage model [Mau92] leverages bounds on the adversary's storage ability to enable secure applications. A typical bounded storage model scheme will involve transmitting more information than what the adversary can possibly store. One approach is then to use some small piece of the transmission to perform, say, a one-time pad or other tasks. Since the adversary cannot record the entire transmission, they most likely will not be able to recover the small piece that is used, preventing attacks. Other approaches, say those based on taking parities [Raz16, GZ19], are also possible. In any case, the honest users' space requirements are always much less than the adversary's storage bound; usually, if the honest parties have space N, the adversary is assumed to have space up to roughly $O(N^2)$.

The bounded storage model has mostly been used to achieve information-theoretic, unconditional, and everlasting security; in contrast, the usual time-bounded adversary model generally requires computational assumptions.

This Work: Disappearing Cryptography. A critical feature of the bounded storage model is that the large transmission cannot be entirely stored by the adversary. This large transmission is then subsequently used in such a way that whatever

K. Nissim and B. Waters (Eds.): TCC 2021, LNCS 13043, pp. 365–396, 2021.
https://doi.org/10.1007/978-3-030-90453-1_13

space-limited information the adversary managed to record about the transmission will become useless. In this way, the large transmission is ephemeral, effectively disappearing immediately after it is sent.

Most work in the bounded storage model uses this disappearing communication to achieve information-theoretic security for primitives such as key agreement, commitments, or oblivious transfer, for which computational assumptions are necessary in the standard model. However, apart from insisting on statistical security, the security goals are typically the same as standard-model schemes.

The goal of this work, in contrast, is to use such "disappearing" communication to realize never-before-possible security goals, especially those that are *impossible* in the standard model.

Remark 1. The usual bounded storage model as defined in [Mau92] envisions a trusted third party broadcasting a large stream of uniformly random bits, which is assumed to be too large to store. All other communication remains short. In this work, we operate in a slightly different setting where there is no trusted third party, but the large streams are instead generated by the users themselves. Additionally, we allow the stream of bits to be structured. However, we emphasize that we still require all parties to be low space.

1.1 Motivating Examples

Example 1: Deniable Encryption. Deniable encryption [CDNO97] concerns the following scenario: Alice has the secret key sk for a public key encryption scheme. At some point, Bob sends a ciphertext ct encrypting message m to Alice. Charlie observes the ciphertext ct.

Later, Charlie obtains the ability to force that Alice reveals sk (say, through a warrant), so that he can decrypt ct and learn the message m. Alice wants to maintain the privacy of the message m in this scenario, so she reveals a fake decryption key sk′, such that decrypting ct with sk′ will result in a fake message $m′$. This version of deniable encryption is called *receiver* deniable encryption.

Unfortunately, as shown in [BNNO11], such receiver deniable encryption is impossible for "normal" encryption where the ciphertext is just a single (concise) transmission from Bob to Alice[1]. Prior works [CDNO97, CPP20] therefore consider a more general notion of encryption that involves back-and-forth communication between the parties.

In this work, we consider a different solution: what if the ciphertext is so large that it cannot be recorded by Charlie? Alice also cannot store the ciphertext in its entirety, but she will be able to decrypt it live using her secret key. Charlie, who does not know the secret key, will be unable to decrypt during the transmission. Then we may hope that, even if Alice subsequently reveals the *true* secret key sk, that Charlie will not be able to learn the message m since he no longer has

---

[1] The deniable encryption literature often refers to such a scheme as having two-messages, as they consider the transmission of the public key from Alice to Bob as the first message.

access to ct. Such a scheme would immediately be deniable: Alice can claim that ct encrypted any arbitrary message m', and Charlie would have no way to verify whether or not she was telling the truth. Relative to the solution in prior work, such a scheme would then require only one-way communication, but at the expense of greatly increased communication in order to ensure that Charlie cannot record all of ct. Such a scheme might make sense in a setting where Bob is unable to receive incoming communication, or Alice is unable to broadcast.

Example 2: Second-hand Secret Keys. Consider an encrypted broadcast service where a user may buy a decoder box which decrypts broadcasts. The content distributor wants to enforce that for each decoder box, only one individual at a time can decrypt broadcasts. Specifically, the content distributor is concerned about several users trying to share a single decoder box. During broadcast time, each user records the encrypted broadcast individually. Then they pass the decoder box around to the various users, allowing them to decrypt their locally-stored broadcast one at a time. Of course, once one user decrypts the broadcast, they can simply send the decrypted contents to the other users. We imagine, however, that the contents are very large, and it is easier to send the decoder box than to transmit the large decrypted contents.

Our solution, again, is to imagine the ciphertexts being so long that they cannot be stored. As such, Alice's decoder box will be completely useless to Bob after the broadcast occurs.

Example 3: Non-interactive Security Against Replay Attacks. Consider a scenario where instructions are being broadcast from a command center to a number of recipients. Suppose that the recipients are low-power embedded devices with limited capabilities; in particular, they cannot keep long-term state nor transmit outgoing messages. We are concerned that an attacker may try to issue malicious instructions to the recipients.

The natural solution is to authenticate the instructions, say by signing them. However, this still opens up the possibility of a replay attack, where the adversary eavesdrops on some signed instruction, and then later on sends the same instruction a second time, causing some adverse behavior.

In the classical model with stateless recipients, the only way to prevent replay attacks is with an interactive protocol, since a stateless recipient cannot distinguish the command center's original message and signature from the adversary's replay. In a broadcast scenario, interacting with each recipient may be impractical. Moreover, interaction requires the recipients themselves to send messages, which may be infeasible for weak devices.

As before, our idea is to have the signatures be so large that the adversary cannot record them in their entirety. The recipients can nonetheless validate the signatures, but an adversary will be unable to ever generate a valid signature, even after witnessing many authenticated instructions from the command center. The result is non-interactive security against replay attacks.

Example 4: Software Subscription. The traditional software model involves the software company sending the software to users, who then run the software for themselves. Software-as-a-Service, instead, hosts the software centrally and allows the users to run remotely. The centralized model allows for subscription-based software services—where the user can only have access to the program by making recurring payments—that are impossible with traditional software.

On the other hand, software-as-a-service requires the user to send their inputs to the software company. While many technologies exist to protect the user data, this model inherently requires interaction with the users.

We instead imagine the company sends its software to the users, but the transmissions are so large that the users cannot record the entire program. Nevertheless, the users have the ability to run the program entirely locally *during* the transmission, without sending any information to the software company. Then, once the transmission ends, the user will be unable to further run the program.

Example 5: Overcoming Impossibility Results for Obfuscation. Program obfuscation is a form of intellectual property protection whereby a program is transformed so that (1) all implementation details are hidden, but (2) the program can still be run by the recipient. Virtual Black Box (VBB) obfuscation, as defined by Barak et al. [BGI+01], is the ideal form of obfuscation: it informally says that having the obfuscated code is "no better than" having black box access to the functionality. Unfortunately, Barak et al. show that such VBB obfuscation is impossible. The counter-example works by essentially running the program on its own description, something that is not possible just given oracle access. As a consequence, other weaker notions have been used, including indistinguishability obfuscation (iO), differing inputs obfuscation [BGI+01], and virtual grey box obfuscation (VGBO) [BCKP14]. These notions have proven tremendously useful for cryptographic applications, where special-purpose programs are designed to be compatible with the weaker obfuscation notions. However, for securing intellectual property, these weaker notions offer only limited guarantees.

Our model for transmitting programs above may appear to give hope for circumventing this impossibility. Namely, if the obfuscated program is so large that it cannot be recorded in its entirety, then maybe it also becomes impossible to run the program on its own description.

1.2   Our Results

In this work, we explore the setting of disappearing cryptography, giving both negative and positive results.

Online Obfuscation. First, we propose a concrete notion of online obfuscation, which is streamed to the recipient. We then explore what kinds of security guarantees we can hope for, motivated by Examples 4 and 5 above.

We demonstrate that, under the Learning With Errors (LWE) assumption, VBB obfuscation is still impossible. The proof closely follows Barak et al.'s proof for circuits, adapting it for online obfuscation. This rules out Example 5.

This still leaves open the hope that online obfuscation can yield something interesting that is not possible classically. We next define a useful notion of online obfuscation, motivated by the goal of classically-impossible tasks. We note that differing inputs obfuscation is known to be a problematic definition [GGH+13b] in the standard model. We also observe that indistinguishability obfuscation appears to offer no advantages in the streaming setting over the classical setting. We therefore settle on a notion of virtual grey box (VGB) obfuscation for online obfuscation. We formulate a definition of VGB obfuscation which allows the recipient to evaluate the program while it is being transmitted, but then loses access to the program after the transmission completes.

We give two candidate VGB online obfuscators based on very different ideas, and leave a provable secure scheme as an interesting open question.

Applications of Online Obfuscation. Next we turn to applications, establishing VGB online obfuscation as a central tool in the study of disappearing cryptography, and providing techniques for its use. We show how to use VGB online obfuscation to realize each of the Examples 1–3.

Specifically, assuming VGB online obfuscation (and other comparatively mild computational assumptions), we define and construct the following:

- Public key encryption with *disappearing ciphertext security* in the bounded storage model. Here, ciphertexts are streamed to the recipient, and message secrecy holds against adversaries with bounded storage[2], *even if the adversary later learns the secret key*. This solves Examples 1 and 2.
- We generalize to functional encryption with disappearing ciphertext security, which combines the disappearing security notion above with the expressive functionality of functional encryption. This allows, for example, to combine the advantages of disappearing ciphertext security with traditional functional encryption security goals of fine-grained access control.
- Digital signatures with *disappearing signature security*, where signatures are streamed, and the recipient loses the ability to verify signatures after the stream is complete. This solves Example 3.

In the following, we expand and explain our results in more detail.

1.3   Defining Obfuscation in the Bounded Storage Model

We first study obfuscation in the bounded storage model. We specifically imagine that obfuscated programs are too large to store, but can be streamed and run in low space while receiving the stream.

Negative Result for VBB Obfuscation. We show that virtual black box (VBB) security remains impossible, even for this model. Recall that VBB security requires that anything which can be efficiently learned from the obfuscated code can be efficiently learned given just oracle access. We follow the

---

[2] We also require the usual polynomial *time* constraint on the adversary.

Barak et al. [BGI+01] impossibility, but take care to show that it still works for online obfuscation.

The idea is that, the version of Barak et al.'s impossibility that works for circuit obfuscation already has to contend with the fact that circuits cannot be evaluated on themselves, since a circuit is almost always larger than its input size. In order to get an impossibility result for online obfuscation, we show that their attack works in low storage. The full proof is given in the full version.

One issue that comes up in the naive adaptation of Barak et al.'s attack is that it requires the obfuscation to be streamed multiple times. We explain how to make the attack work with just a single stream using Compute-and-Compare obfuscation [GKW17, WZ17], following ideas from [AP20].

Defining Online Obfuscation. Above, we only considered the standard notions of security, but for online obfuscation. We now seek to formulate a definition which captures the goal of having the obfuscated program "disappear" after the stream is complete. Concretely, we want that, after the stream is complete, it is impossible to evaluate the program on any "new" inputs.

Our formalization of this is roughly as follows: we imagine the attacker gets the program stream, and then later learns some additional information. We ask that any such attacker can be simulated by an oracle algorithm. This algorithm makes queries to the program, and then receives the same additional information the original adversary received. Importantly, after the additional information comes in, the simulator can no longer query the program any more.

Some care is needed with the definition. VBB security, which requires the simulator to be computationally bounded, is impossible for the reasons discussed above. Indistinguishability obfuscation (iO) allows for a computationally unbounded simulator, which avoids the impossibility. While iO is immensely useful in the standard model, we observe that there is little added utility to considering iO in the online model. Indeed, an unbounded simulator can query the entire function on all inputs during the query phase, and thus has no need to make additional queries after receiving the additional information[3].

We therefore give a virtual *grey* box (VGB) notion of security [BCKP14], where the simulator is computationally unbounded, but can only make a polynomial number of queries. The computationally unbounded simulator then receives the additional information, but can make no more queries. Our full definition is in Sect. 3. We note that it may be possible to also consider a version of differing inputs obfuscation (diO) in our setting, but there is evidence that diO may be impossible [GGHW14]. So we therefore stick to VGB obfuscation.

---

[3] The usual way indistinguishability approach to defining iO does not use a simulator, but is equivalent in the standard model to the simulation definition. In the online model, the indistinguishability and simulation models may not be equivalent. Nevertheless, the indistinguishability version of iO still appears to offer no advantages in the online setting, since in this version the adversary knows the programs in the clear from the very beginning.

1.4   Applications

Before giving our candidate online obfuscation schemes, we discuss applications.

Disappearing Ciphertext Security. We first demonstrate how to use online obfuscation to construct public key encryption where ciphertexts effectively disappear after being transmitted. Concretely, we say that a public key encryption scheme has *disappearing ciphertext security* if the contents of a ciphertext remain hidden, even if the attacker subsequently learns the secret key.

Our first attempt is to use an online obfuscator as a witness encryption scheme [GGSW13]: the public key pk is set, say, to be the output of a one-way function f on the secret key sk. To encrypt a message m to pk, generate an online obfuscation of the program $P(sk')$ which outputs m if and only if $f(sk') = pk$. Decryption just evaluates the program on the secret key.

For security, the key difficulty is that we cannot switch to a hybrid where the secret key does not exist, as would be used to prove the standard CPA security of the scheme using witness encryption. After all, the adversary eventually sees the secret key, so it must always exist!

Toward a proof, we note that, by the one-wayness of f, an attacker who just knows pk and sees the ciphertext cannot evaluate the ciphertext program on any input that will reveal m. Hence, m presumably remains hidden. Moreover, even if the attacker learns sk after seeing the ciphertext, it should not help the attacker learn m, since the attacker no longer has access to the program stream.

Security would be trivial with online obfuscation with VBB security. However, difficulties arise with trying to formalize this intuition with our notion of VGB security. Suppose we have an adversary $\mathcal{A}$ for the encryption scheme. We would like to use $\mathcal{A}$ to reach a contradiction. To do so, we invoke the security of the online obfuscator to arrive at a simulator $\mathcal{S}$ that can only query the ciphertext program, but does not have access to the program stream. Unfortunately, this simulator is computationally unbounded, meaning it can invert f to recover sk at the beginning of the experiment, and then query the program on sk.

Our solution is to replace f with a lossy function [PW08], which is a function with two modes: an injective mode (where f is injective) and a lossy mode (where the image of f is small). The security requirement is that the two modes are indistinguishable. Lossy functions can be build under various standard assumptions such as DDH or LWE.

We start with f being in the injective mode. In the proof, we first switch the ciphertext program to output m if and only if $sk' = sk$; by the injectivity of f this change does not affect the functionality of the program. Hence, the simulator cannot detect the change (even though it can invert f and learn sk for itself), meaning the adversary cannot detect the change either.

In the next step, we switch f to being lossy, which cannot be detected by a computationally bounded attacker. We next change the ciphertext program again, this time to never output m. This only affects the program's behavior on a single point sk. But notice that for lossy f, sk is statistically hidden from the attacker, who only knows pk when the ciphertext is streamed. This means the simulator, despite being computationally unbounded, will be unable to query on sk, and thus cannot detect the change. This holds true even though the simulator later learns sk, since at this point it can no longer query the ciphertext program. Since indistinguishability holds relative to the simulator, it also holds for the original attacker. The result is the following, proved in Sect. 4:

Theorem 1 (Informal). *Assuming the existence of VGB online obfuscation and lossy functions, there exists a public key encryption scheme with disappearing ciphertext security.*

Extension to Functional Encryption. We can also extend disappearing ciphertext security to functional encryption. Functional encryption allows users to obtain secret keys for functions g, which allow them to learn $g(m)$ from a ciphertext encrypting m. The usual requirement for functional encryption is that an attacker, who has secret keys for functions g_i such that $g_i(m_0) = g_i(m_1)$ for all i, cannot distinguish encryptions of m_0 from encryptions of m_1.

In Sect. 6, we consider a disappearing ciphertext security variant, where the requirement that $g_i(m_0) = g_i(m_1)$ only holds for secret keys in possession when the ciphertext is transmitted. Even if the attacker later obtains a secret key for a function g such that $g(m_0) \neq g(m_1)$, indistinguishability will still hold. Analogous to the case of plain public key encryption, this captures the intuition that the ciphertext disappears, becoming unavailable once the transmission ends.

We show how to combine standard-model functional encryption with online VGB obfuscation to obtain functional encryption with such disappearing ciphertext security. The basic idea is as follows. To encrypt a message m, first compute an encryption c of m under the standard-model functional encryption scheme. Then compute an online obfuscation of the program which takes as input the secret key sk_g for a function g, and decrypts c using sk_g, the result being $g(m)$.

This construction seems like it should work, but getting the proof to go through using computationally unbounded simulators is again non-trivial. In Sect. 6, we show how to modify the sketch above to get security to go through, yielding the following:

Theorem 3 (Informal). *Assuming the existence of VGB online obfuscation, NIZKs, non-uniform secure PRFs, and* standard-model *functional encryption, there exists a functional encryption scheme with disappearing ciphertext security.*

Disappearing Signatures. We next turn to constructing disappearing signatures, signatures that are large streams that can be verified online, but then the signature disappears after the transmission ends. We formalize this notion by modifying the usual chosen message security notion to give *disappearing signature security*, where the attacker (who does not know the signing key) cannot produce a signature on *any* message, even messages that it previously saw signatures for.

We show how to construct disappearing signatures in Sect. 5, using online obfuscation. An additional building block we need is a *prefix puncturable signature*. This is a scheme where, given the signing key sk, it is possible to produce a "punctured" signing key sk_{x^*} which can sign any message of the form (x, m)

such that $x \neq x^*$, but sk_{x^*} is incapable of signing messages of the form (x^*, m). Such prefix puncturable signatures can be built from standard tools [BF14].

We construct a signature scheme with disappearing signatures by setting the signature on a message m to be an online obfuscation of the following program P. P has sk hardcoded, and on input x outputs a signature on (x, m). To verify, simply run the streamed program on a random prefix to obtain a signature, and then verify the obtained signature.

We then prove that an attacker cannot produce a valid signature stream on any message, even messages for which it already received signature streams. For simplicity, consider the case where the attacker gets to see a signature on a single message m. Let x^* be the prefix that the verifier will use to test the adversary's forgery. Note that x^* is information-theoretically hidden to the adversary at the time it produces its forgery. We will switch to having the signature program for m reject the prefix x^*. Since the program no longer needs to sign the prefix x^*, it can use the punctured key sk_{x^*} to sign instead. The only point where the program output changes is on x^*. The simulator will be unable to query on x^* (since it is information-theoretically hidden), meaning the simulator, and hence the original adversary, cannot detect this change.

Now we rely on the security of the puncturable signature to conclude that the adversary's forgery program cannot output a signature on any message of the form (x^*, m), since the entire view of the attacker is simulated with the punctured key sk_{x^*}. But such a signature is exactly what the verifier expects to see; hence the verifier will reject the adversary's program. The result is the following theorem:

Theorem 2 (Informal). *Assuming the existence of VGB online obfuscation and one-way functions, there exists a disappearing signature scheme.*

1.5 Constructing Online Obfuscation

We finally turn to giving two candidate constructions of online obfuscation. We unfortunately do not know how to prove the security of either construction, which we leave as an interesting open problem. However, we discuss why the constructions are presumably resistant to attacks.

Construction 1: Large Matrix Branching Programs. Our first construction is based on standard-model obfuscation techniques, starting from [GGH+13a]. As in [GGH+13a], we first convert an NC^1 circuit into a matrix branching program using Barrington's theorem [Bar86]. In [GGH+13a], the program is then "re-randomized" following Kilian [Kil88] by left and right multiplying the various branching program components with random matrices, such that the randomization cancels out when evaluating the program. We instead first pad the matrices to be very large, namely so large that honest users can record a single column, but the adversary cannot write down the entire matrix. We then re-randomize the large padded matrix.

We show that, if the matrix components are streamed in the correct order, honest users can evaluate the program in space proportional to N, the height of the matrices. However, recording even a single matrix from the program requires space N^2, and so for adversaries with space somewhat less than N^2, it may be reasonable to conjecture that the program "disappears" after the stream concludes.

We note that in the standard model, re-randomizing the branching program is not enough to guarantee security. Indeed, linear algebra attacks on the program matrices are possible, as well as "mixed-input" attacks where multiple reads of the same input bit are set to different values. Garg et al. [GGH+13a] and follow-up works block these attacks by placing the branching program matrices "in the exponent" of a cryptographic multilinear map.

In our setting, the large matrices presumably prevent linear algebra attacks, since an adversary with space somewhat less than N^2 will be unable to even record a single matrix from the program. Moreover, we show how to block mixed-input attacks by choosing the matrix padding to have a special structure, which is inspired by the classical obfuscation techniques. While we are unable to prove the security of our multilinear-map-less scheme, we conjecture that it nevertheless remains secure. The result is a plausible VGB online obfuscator for NC^1 circuits. Details are given in Sect. 7.

Remark 2. The re-randomization of $N \times N$ matrices samples random $N \times N$ matrices, and must compute their inverses. Inverting a random $N \times N$ matrix is impossible with space $o(N^2)$, a consequence of [Raz16]. Our basic construction thus has the sender use $O(N^2)$ space, while the receiver requires only $O(N)$ space. We show, however, how to reduce the space requirements of the sender to $O(N)$ by generating the re-randomization matrices and their inverses using PRFs. The resulting low-sender-space obfuscation scheme is secure, provided the basic construction is a secure (with large sender space) online obfuscation, and the PRF is secure. Details are given in Sect. 7.2.

Construction 2: Time-Stamping. Our second construction is based on time-stamping [MST04] in the bounded storage model. Here, a large stream is sent. Anyone listening can use the stream to compute a time-stamp on any message. However, once the stream concludes, it will be impossible to time-stamp a "new" message. The concrete security notion guarantees a fixed (polynomial-sized) upper bound on the total number of stamped messages any adversary can produce.

Our construction uses time-stamping, together with standard-model obfuscation. To obfuscate a program P, first generate and send a random stream for time-stamping. Afterward, compute and send a standard-model obfuscation of the program P', which takes as input x together with a time-stamp, verifies the time-stamp is valid for x, and then runs P if and only if the stamp is valid.

The intuition for security is that we can invoke the standard-model security of P' to get a simulator S' which just makes black box queries to P'. We then use the security of the time-stamping protocol to conclude that the accepting queries from the simulator, which are those containing valid time stamps, must have been "known" when the time-stamping stream was sent. For any inputs derived from new information sent after the stream concludes, the adversary will not be able to produce a valid time stamp, and thus P' will reject any such inputs. The result is that S' should be simulatable just by making queries to P, and these queries are all made prior to receiving any additional post-stream information.

Unfortunately, turning the above intuition into a full proof appears challenging. One issue is that the obfuscation of P' serves as a verification oracle for checking the validity of time stamps. Existing time stamping security notions offer no guarantees in the presence of a verification oracle, and we do not know if the existing constructions are secure in this setting.

If we were to assume the time-stamping protocol secure even with verification queries, there are still potential problems, mostly revolving around formalizing that the simulator "knows" its input when the time-stamping stream is sent. Indeed, to prove security we need to convert our simulator S' into a simulator S which makes all of its queries by the time the stream concludes, before receiving any additional information. The above intuition would show that S' "knew" these inputs before the stream concludes, but perhaps the inputs (and their time stamps) were hidden inside of the code of S' and only revealed later, after more information is received.

We conjecture that such an S can nevertheless be constructed from S'. The idea is to have S run S' until the time-stamping stream concludes. Then S will try to extract the queries from the state of S' by simulating many possible executions of the remaining security experiment for S' and collecting the queries S' makes to P'. It then uses its assumed time-stamping verification oracle to check which queries have valid time stamps. Since S' can only know a polynomial number of valid time stamps, it seems S should eventually collect all of them. Then it can make these queries to its own oracle for P, and run S' one more time using the answers to P. Unfortunately, formalizing this idea appears tricky, and we leave it as a direction for future work.

1.6 Related Work, Discussion, and Future Directions

Never-Before-Possible Results. The bounded storage model is most often used to eliminate computational assumptions. Time-stamping in the bounded storage model [MST04], as discussed above, is perhaps the first application of the bounded storage model beyond achieving information-theoretic security. We note, however, that non-interactive time-stamping was recently achieved in the standard model using appropriate computational assumptions [LSS19].

Our work shows that there is potentially a rich landscape of applications which leverage the bounded storage model to give results that are *impossible* in the standard model. Our particular applications can all be seen as achieving versions of *forward* security, where a key revealed does not affect the security of prior sessions. Forward security has been studied in numerous standard-model contexts (e.g. [DvW92]). However, standard-model constructions of forward secure (non-interactive) encryption such as [CHK03] always involve updating the secret keys. Our constructions do not require the secret key to be updated. We note that Dziembowski [Dzi06] considers a notion of forward-secure storage, which is very similar to our notion of disappearing ciphertext security for encryption. A key difference is that their work only considers the secret key case, and it is unclear how to adapt their constructions to the public key setting. A natural direction for future work is to explore other potential areas besides forward security which may be impossible classically but are achievable in the bounded storage model.

Obfuscation in the Bounded Storage Model. We also initiate the study of obfuscation in the bounded storage model. Just as standard-model obfuscation has proven to be a central tool in the study of standard-model cryptography, our work demonstrates online obfuscation is analogously a central tool in the study of disappearing cryptography. Just as standard-model obfuscation schemes started out as conjectures, with security gradually improved culminating with [JLS20], we hope that future work will improve the status of our candidates.

Besides achieving never-before-possible applications, one advantage of our setting is that we may be able to leverage the bounded storage model to achieve security under milder assumptions than is known for obfuscation in the standard model. Indeed, online obfuscation could plausibly exist *information-theoretically*, and our first construction could plausibly be an instantiation[4]. This gives hope that security can actually be proved unconditionally, without requiring the strong algebraic assumptions needed in the standard model. We leave exploring such information-theoretic security as a fascinating open question.

The Quadratic Gap. All prior information-theoretic results in the bounded storage model achieve at best an adversary storage that is quadratic in the honest users' storage. Our first candidate construction of an online obfuscator, being plausibly information-theoretic, inherits this quadratic gap. While some negative results are known [DM04], it remains open whether this quadratic "gap" is necessary. While our constructions are probably impractical due to the reliance on obfuscation techniques, such a quadratic gap may be meaningful in practice: for example, if the honest users' storage is 16 GB, then security would be maintained against adversaries with ~5ZB, which is on the order of the total data center storage capacity world-wide in 2021 [Mli21]. On the other hand, using computational assumptions, it is possible to get an improved "gap" for time-stamping, and our second construction built from time-stamping can similarly be obtained with an arbitrarily-large polynomial gap.

Other Computational Models. It is possible to achieve classically-impossible results using either hardware assumptions (e.g. [GKR08]) or non-classical laws of physics such as quantum mechanics (e.g. [BB84]). However, as far as we are

---

[4] The basic large-sender-space version would be purely information-theoretic, whereas the version with low sender space requires only the information-theoretic conjecture together with the existence of one-way functions.

aware, none of these models besides the bounded storage model allows for sending messages that effectively disappear after the transmission is over.

2   Preliminaries

Different sections of this paper rely on different cryptographic primitives. To minimize the page-turning effort of our reader, we will introduce the related notions and definitions separately in each section. Here we will just state the notations that are used throughout this paper.

We use capital bold letters to denote a matrix $\mathbf{M}$. Lowercase bold letters denote vectors $\mathbf{v}$. For $n \in \mathbb{N}$ we let $[n]$ denote the ordered set $\{1, 2, \ldots, n\}$. For a bit-string $x \in \{0, 1\}^n$, we let x_i denote the i-th bit of x. We use $\mathsf{diag}(\mathbf{M}_1, \ldots, \mathbf{M}_n)$ to denote a matrix with block diagonals $\mathbf{M}_1, \ldots, \mathbf{M}_n$.

3   Defining Obfuscation in the Bounded Storage Model

In this section we will formally define online obfuscation ($o\mathcal{O}$) and its corresponding security notions, but before we start, we will first introduce an idea called a *stream*. It is similar to the publicly-accessible random string as in [Mau92], but now it is created and sent by one of the parties, and it does not need to be random.

A *stream* $s_\gg$ is a long sequence of bits sent sequentially from one party to another. Generally, we require that the length of the stream, denoted as $|s_\gg|$, to be greater than the memory bound of the users and adversaries[5]. This means that a properly constructed stream can *not* be stored in its entirety. However, algorithms or programs can still take a stream as an input, reading the bits one-by-one. This means that the algorithm or program would operate in an online manner - as the streaming happens, it actively reads the stream bit by bit, performs the computation simultaneously, and produces the output in one pass. Since the outputs of such algorithms or programs could have significantly smaller sizes than the stream, while $s_\gg$ itself is too large to write down, the short outputs can be reasonably stored. We denote a variable as a stream by putting a "$\gg$" in the subscript.

Definition 1 (Online Obfuscator). *Let* λ, n *be security parameters. An online obfuscator* $o\mathcal{O}$ *for a circuit class* $\{\mathcal{C}_\lambda\}$ *consists of a pair of uniform PPT machines* $(\mathsf{Obf}, \mathsf{Eval})$ *that satisfy the following conditions:*

- Obf *takes as input a circuit* $C \in \mathcal{C}_\lambda$*, uses up to* $O(n)$ *memory bits, and produces a stream* $s_\gg \leftarrow \mathsf{Obf}(C)$*.*
- Eval *takes as input a stream* $s_\gg$ *and an input* x*, uses up to* $O(n)$ *memory bits, and outputs* $y \leftarrow \mathsf{Eval}(s_\gg, x)$*.*
- *For all* $C \in \mathcal{C}_\lambda$*, for all inputs* x*, we have that*

$$\Pr\left[C(x) = y : s_\gg \leftarrow \mathsf{Obf}(C), y \leftarrow \mathsf{Eval}(s_\gg, x)\right] = 1.$$

---

[5] Notice that generating such a stream could still be done using a low memory bound.

To define security for an online obfuscator $o\mathcal{O} = (\mathsf{Obf}, \mathsf{Eval})$, consider the following two experiments:

1. $\mathsf{ExpAdv}_{\mathcal{A},\mathsf{ch},o\mathcal{O}}(C \in \mathcal{C}_\lambda, k)$:
   - The experiment consists of an arbitrary number of rounds. At each round, one of the following two scenarios happens:
     - At an *interaction round*, the adversary $\mathcal{A}$ interacts arbitrarily with the challenger ch.
     - At a *stream round*, the adversary $\mathcal{A}$ receives a fresh stream[6] of the obfuscated circuit $s_\gg \leftarrow \mathsf{Obf}(C)$. The challenger ch will receive a special tag notifying it that a streaming has happened.
   - The challenger ch may choose to terminate the experiment at any time by outputting a bit $b \in \{0, 1\}$, and b will be the output of the program.
   - Whenever the number of stream rounds is greater than k, the challenger ch immediately outputs 0 and terminates the experiment.
2. $\mathsf{ExpSim}_{\mathcal{S},\mathsf{ch},o\mathcal{O}}(C \in \mathcal{C}_\lambda, k, q)$:
   - The experiment consists of an arbitrary number of rounds:
     - At an *interaction round*, the simulator $\mathcal{S}$ interacts arbitrarily with the challenger ch.
     - At a *stream round*, the simulator $\mathcal{S}$ may send up to q adaptive oracle queries to the circuit C and receive corresponding responses. The challenger ch will receive a special tag notifying it that a streaming has happened.
   - The challenger ch may choose to terminate the experiment at any time by outputting a bit $b \in \{0, 1\}$, and b will be the output of the program.
   - Whenever the number of stream rounds is greater than k, the challenger ch immediately outputs 0 and terminates the experiment.

The purpose of the interaction round is to allow the challenger to obtain auxiliary information about the circuit C, such as an accepting input. The key feature is that this auxiliary information can be obtained *after* seeing the obfuscated stream, at which point the stream effectively disappears and the adversary can no longer query the program.

We note that in the stream round, we allow the simulator to make adaptive queries. One could also imagine a stronger variant where the simulator can only send a single round of *non-adaptive* queries to the circuit in the stream round. We focus on the weaker version since it suffices for our applications and our VBB impossibility already applies in this setting.

---

[6] Notice that a fresh stream is sampled every time, so that no single stream is sent repeatedly. One could also imagine a stronger version where the same stream is sent repeatedly, but to achieve that the randomness used must be small. It has also been shown that for learning parities, even just two-pass learning, where the same stream is repeated only once more, has a weaker time-space lower bound than the one-pass one [GRT19] ($\Omega(n^{1.5})$ vs. $\Omega(n^2)$). Therefore, applications are far less plausible in the setting where the same stream is repeated many more times.

Definition 2 (k-time Virtual Grey-Box (VGB) Security). *Let λ, n be security parameters. Let k be a fixed positive integer. For an online obfuscator $o\mathcal{O}$ to satisfy k-time Virtual Grey-Box security under memory bound $S(n)$, we require that for any challenger* ch, *and any adversary $\mathcal{A}$ that uses up to $S(n)$ memory bits, there exists a computationally unbounded simulator $\mathcal{S}$ s.t. for all circuits $C \in \mathcal{C}_\lambda$:*

$$|\Pr[\mathsf{ExpAdv}_{\mathcal{A},\mathsf{ch},o\mathcal{O}}(C, k) = 1] - \Pr[\mathsf{ExpSim}_{\mathcal{S},\mathsf{ch},o\mathcal{O}}(C, k, q) = 1]| \leq \mathsf{negl}(\lambda),$$

where $q = \mathsf{poly}(\lambda)^7$.

The definitions for Indistinguishability Obfuscation (iO) security and Virtual Black-Box (VBB) security are obtained analogously by applying minor changes to the VGB security definition.

Remark 3 (k-time iO Security). We modify Definition 2 to allow $q = \mathsf{superpoly}(\lambda)$ to obtain the definition for k-time iO Security.

Remark 4 (k-time VBB Security). We modify Definition 2 to restrict $\mathcal{S}$ to be a PPT simulator to obtain the definition for k-time VBB Security. We show in the full version of the paper that online obfuscators with VBB security do not exist.

Remark 5 (1-time VBB/VGB/iO Security). Under the special case where $k = 1$, we obtain the definitions for 1-time VBB/VGB/iO security correspondingly.

Remark 6 (Unbounded VBB/VGB/iO Security). Under the special case where $k = \mathsf{superpoly}(\lambda)$, we obtain the definitions for unbounded VBB/VGB/iO security correspondingly.

4   Public Key Encryption with Disappearing Ciphertext Security

4.1   Definition

We will start by defining a security notion for public key encryption that we name *Disappearing Ciphertext Security*.

Essentially, it captures the security game where the adversary is given the private key after all of its queries but before it outputs a guess for the bit b. In traditional models, this definition does not make much sense, as the adversary can simply store the query responses, and then later use the received private

---

[7] A space $S(n)$ attacker can always run the honest evaluation procedure $S(n)/O(n)$ times in parallel on different inputs, thereby evaluating the program on $S(n)/O(n)$ different points. Thus, the number of queries q the simulator makes must be at least this quantity. One could imagine an alternative definition that sets q to be *exactly* this value. We instead opt for a weaker notion where the simulator is allowed to make an arbitrarily large polynomial number of queries in order to simulate, potentially much larger than S.

key to decrypt. However, in the bounded storage model, the adversary cannot possibly store the ciphertexts, so even if the adversary is handed the private key afterwards, it cannot possibly use it to decrypt anything.

Put formally, for security parameters λ and n, a public key encryption scheme in the bounded storage model is a tuple of PPT algorithms $\Pi = (\mathsf{Gen}, \mathsf{Enc}, \mathsf{Dec})$ that each uses up to $O(n)$ memory bits. The syntax is identical to that of a classical PKE, except that now the ciphertexts are streams $\mathsf{ct}_{\gg}$. For the security definition, consider the following experiment:

Disappearing Ciphertext Security Experiment $\mathsf{Dist}_{\mathcal{A},\Pi}^{\mathsf{DisCt}}(\lambda, n)$:

- Run $\mathsf{Gen}(1^\lambda, 1^n)$ to obtain keys $(\mathsf{pk}, \mathsf{sk})$.
- Sample a uniform bit $b \in \{0, 1\}$.
- The adversary $\mathcal{A}$ is given the public key pk.
- The adversary $\mathcal{A}$ submits two messages m_0 and m_1, and receives $\mathsf{ct}_{\gg} \leftarrow \mathsf{Enc}(\mathsf{pk}, m_b)$, which is a stream.
- The adversary $\mathcal{A}$ is given the private key sk.
- The adversary $\mathcal{A}$ outputs a guess b' for b. If $b' = b$, we say that the adversary succeeds and the output of the experiment is 1. Otherwise, the experiment outputs 0.

Using this experiment, we are now able to formally define disappearing ciphertext security.

Definition 3 (Disappearing Ciphertext Security). *Let λ, n be security parameters. A public key encryption scheme $\Pi = (\mathsf{Gen}, \mathsf{Enc}, \mathsf{Dec})$ has disappearing ciphertext security under memory bound $S(n)$ if for all PPT adversaries $\mathcal{A}$ that use at most $S(n)$ memory bits:*

$$\Pr\left[\mathsf{Dist}_{\mathcal{A},\Pi}^{\mathsf{DisCt}}(\lambda, n) = 1\right] \leq \frac{1}{2} + \mathsf{negl}(\lambda).$$

Now we will show how to use online obfuscation to construct a public key encryption scheme with disappearing ciphertext security. One important tool that we will take advantage of is lossy functions, which we will introduce in the following.

4.2   Lossy Function

Lossy functions are a subset of Lossy Trapdoor Functions due to Peikert and Waters [PW08] that do not require the existence of a trapdoor for the injective mode. To put formally:

Definition 4 (Lossy Function). *Let λ be the security parameter. For $\ell(\lambda) = \mathsf{poly}(\lambda)$ and $k(\lambda) \leq \ell(\lambda)$ (k is referred to as the "lossiness"), a collection of (ℓ, k)-lossy functions is given by a tuple of PPT algorithms (S, F) with the following properties. As short-hands, we have $S_{inj}(\cdot)$ denote $S(\cdot, 1)$ and $S_{lossy}(\cdot)$ denote $S(\cdot, 0)$.*

- **Easy to sample an injective function:** S_{inj} outputs a function index s, and $F(s, \cdot)$ computes an injective (deterministic) function $f_s(\cdot)$ over the domain $\{0,1\}^\ell$.
- **Easy to sample a lossy function:** S_{lossy} outputs a function index s, and $F(s, \cdot)$ computes a (deterministic) function $f_s(\cdot)$ over the domain $\{0,1\}^\ell$ whose image has size at most $2^{\ell-k}$.
- **Hard to distinguish injective mode from lossy mode:** Let X_λ be the distribution of s sampled from S_{inj}, and let Y_λ be the distribution of s sampled from S_{lossy}, the two distributions should be computationally indistinguishable, i.e. $\{X_\lambda\} \overset{c}{\approx} \{Y_\lambda\}$.

4.3   Construction

Here we present our construction of a PKE scheme with disappearing ciphertext security, using online obfuscation and lossy function as building blocks.

Construction 1. Let λ, n be the security parameters. Let $\mathsf{LF} = (S, F)$ be a collection of (ℓ, k)-lossy functions, and $o\mathcal{O} = (\mathsf{Obf}, \mathsf{Eval})$ an online obfuscator with 1-time VGB security under $S(n)$ memory bound. The construction $\Pi = (\mathsf{Gen}, \mathsf{Enc}, \mathsf{Dec})$ works as follows:

- $\mathsf{Gen}(1^\lambda, 1^n)$: Sample an injective function index f_s from S_{inj}, and a uniform $\mathsf{sk} \leftarrow \{0,1\}^\ell$. Compute $y = F(s, \mathsf{sk}) = f_s(\mathsf{sk})$, and set $\mathsf{pk} = (s, y)$. Output $(\mathsf{pk}, \mathsf{sk})$.
- $\mathsf{Enc}(\mathsf{pk}, m)$: Construct the program $P_{f_s, y, m}$ as follows:

$$P_{f_s, y, m}(x) = \begin{cases} m & \text{if } f_s(x) = y \\ \bot & \text{otherwise} \end{cases}.$$

   Obfuscate the above program to obtain a stream $\mathsf{ct}_{\gg} \leftarrow \mathsf{Obf}(P_{f_s, y, m})$. The ciphertext is simply the stream $\mathsf{ct}_{\gg}$.
- $\mathsf{Dec}(\mathsf{sk}, \mathsf{ct}_{\gg})$: Simply evaluate the streamed obfuscation using sk as input. An honest execution yields $\mathsf{Eval}(\mathsf{ct}_{\gg}, \mathsf{sk}) = P_{f_s, y, m}(\mathsf{sk}) = m$ as desired.

4.4   Proof of Security

Now we show that if LF is a collection of (ℓ, k)-lossy functions with a lossiness $k = \mathsf{poly}(\lambda)$, and $o\mathcal{O}$ is an online obfuscator with 1-time VGB security under $S(n)$ memory bound, then the above construction has disappearing ciphertext security under $S(n)$ memory bound.

We organize our proof into a sequence of hybrids. In the very first hybrid, the adversary plays the disappearing ciphertext security game $\mathsf{Dist}_{\mathcal{A},\Pi}^{\mathsf{DisCt}}(\lambda, n)$ where b is fixed to be 0. Then we gradually modify the hybrids to reach the case where $b = 1$. We show that all pairs of adjacent hybrids are indistinguishable from each other, and therefore by a hybrid argument the adversary cannot distinguish between $b = 0$ and $b = 1$. This then directly shows disappearing ciphertext security.

Sequence of Hybrids

- H_0: The adversary plays the original disappearing ciphertext security game $\mathsf{Dist}_{A,\Pi}^{\mathsf{DisCt}}(\lambda, n)$ where $b = 0$, i.e. it always receives $\mathsf{Enc}(\mathsf{pk}, m_0)$.
- H_1: The same as H_0, except that in $\mathsf{Enc}(\mathsf{pk}, m_b)$, we replace P_{f_s,y,m_b} with P'_{sk,m_b} such that

$$P'_{\mathsf{sk},m_b}(x) = \begin{cases} m_b & \text{if } x = \mathsf{sk} \\ \perp & \text{otherwise} \end{cases}.$$

So now instead of checking the secret key by checking its image in the injective function, the program now directly checks for sk.
- H_2: The same as H_1, except that instead of sampling f_s from S_{inj}, we now use $f_{s'}$ sampled from S_{lossy}.
- H_3: The same as H_2, except that now we set $b = 1$ instead of 0.
- H_4: Switch back to using injective f_s instead of the lossy $f_{s'}$.
- H_5: Switch back to using the original program P_{f_s,y,m_b} instead of P'_{sk,m_b}.

Theorem 1. *If LF is a collection of (ℓ, k)-lossy functions with lossiness $k = \mathsf{poly}(\lambda)$, and $o\mathcal{O}$ is an online obfuscation with 1-time VGB security under $S(n)$ memory bound, then Construction 1 has disappearing ciphertext security under $S(n)$ memory bound.*

For the proofs of the hybrid arguments and the Theorem, please refer to the full version of the paper.

5   Disappearing Signature Scheme

5.1   Definition

In this section, we define a public-key signature scheme in the bounded storage model which we call *Disappearing Signatures*. The idea is that we make the signatures be streams such that one can only verify them on the fly, and cannot possibly store them. The security game requirement is also different. Traditionally, for an adversary to win the signature forgery game, the adversary would need to produce a signature on a fresh new message. However, in the disappearing signature scheme, the adversary can win even by producing a signature on a message that it has previously queried. The catch here is that even though the message might have been queried by the adversary before, the adversary has no way to store the valid signature on the message due to its sheer size.

Put formally, for security parameters λ and n, a disappearing signature scheme consists of a tuple of PPT algorithms $\Pi = (\mathsf{Gen}, \mathsf{Sign}, \mathsf{Ver})$ that each uses up to $O(n)$ memory bits. The syntax is identical to that of a classical public key signature scheme, except that now the signatures are streams $\sigma_{\gg}$. In addition to the standard model signature security (where the adversary has unbounded space), we also require *disappearing signature security* that utilizes the following experiment:

Signature Forgery Experiment $\mathsf{SigForge}_{\mathcal{A},\Pi}(\lambda, n)$:

- Run $\mathsf{Gen}(1^\lambda, 1^n)$ to obtain keys $(\mathsf{pk}, \mathsf{sk})$.
- The adversary $\mathcal{A}$ is given the public key pk.
- For $q = \mathsf{poly}(\lambda)$ rounds, the adversary $\mathcal{A}$ submits a message m, and receives $\sigma_\gg \leftarrow \mathsf{Sign}(\mathsf{sk}, m)$, which is a stream.
- The adversary $\mathcal{A}$ outputs m' and streams a signature $\sigma'_\gg$. The output of the experiment is $\mathsf{Ver}(\mathsf{pk}, m', \sigma'_\gg)$.

Notice that traditionally, we would require m' to be distinct from the messages m's queried before, but here we have no such requirement. With this experiment in mind, we now define the additional security requirement for a disappearing signature scheme.

Definition 5 (Disappearing Signature Security). *Let λ, n be security parameters. A disappearing signature scheme $\Pi = (\mathsf{Gen}, \mathsf{Sign}, \mathsf{Ver})$ has disappearing signature security under memory bound $S(n)$, if for all PPT adversaries $\mathcal{A}$ that use up to $S(n)$ memory bits,*

$$\Pr\left[\mathsf{SigForge}_{\mathcal{A},\Pi}(\lambda, n) = 1\right] \leq \mathsf{negl}(\lambda).$$

To construct such a disappearing signature scheme, one tool that we will use alongside online obfuscation is a *prefix puncturable signature*.

5.2 Prefix Puncturable Signature

A *prefix puncturable signature* is similar to a regular public key signature scheme that works for messages of the form (x, m), where x is called the *prefix*. Additionally, it has a puncturing procedure Punc that takes as input the secret key sk and a prefix x^*, and outputs a punctured secret key sk_{x^*}. sk_{x^*} allows one to sign any message of the form (x, m) with $x \neq x^*$. The security requirement is that, given sk_{x^*}, one cannot produce a signature on any message of the form (x^*, m).

To put formally, in addition to the usual correctness and security requirements of a signature scheme, we also have a correctness requirement and a security requirement for the punctured key.

Definition 6 (Correctness of the Punctured Key). *Let λ be the security parameter. We require that for all $m \in \{0,1\}^*$ and $x, x^* \in \{0,1\}^\lambda$ s.t. $x \neq x^*$:*

$$\Pr\left[\sigma = \sigma' : \begin{array}{l} (\mathsf{pk}, \mathsf{sk}) \leftarrow \mathsf{Gen}(1^\lambda) \\ \sigma \leftarrow \mathsf{Sign}(\mathsf{sk}, (x, m)) \\ \mathsf{sk}_{x^*} \leftarrow \mathsf{Punc}(\mathsf{sk}, x^*) \\ \sigma' \leftarrow \mathsf{Sign}(\mathsf{sk}_{x^*}, (x, m)) \end{array}\right] = 1.$$

Definition 7 (Security of the Punctured Key). *Let λ be the security parameter. We require that for all $x^* \in \{0,1\}^\lambda$ and $m \in \{0,1\}^*$, for all PPT adversaries $\mathcal{A}$, we have*

$$\Pr\left[\mathsf{Ver}(\mathsf{pk}, (x^*, m), \sigma) = 1 : \begin{array}{l} (\mathsf{pk}, \mathsf{sk}) \leftarrow \mathsf{Gen}(1^\lambda) \\ \mathsf{sk}_{x^*} \leftarrow \mathsf{Punc}(\mathsf{sk}, x^*) \\ \sigma \leftarrow \mathcal{A}(\mathsf{sk}_{x^*}, \mathsf{pk}, (x^*, m)) \end{array}\right] \leq \mathsf{negl}(\lambda).$$

Bellare and Fuchsbauer [BF14] have shown that a puncturable signature can be built from any one-way function using certificates, though their basic construction does not satisfy the strong correctness we require: their punctured key yields valid signatures, but not necessarily identical signatures. Nevertheless, it is straightforward to modify the ideas to yield a scheme with the desired correctness. Our modified scheme for prefix puncturable signature can be found in the full version of the paper.

5.3   Construction

We now present our construction of the disappearing signature scheme.

Construction 2. Let λ, n be the security parameters. Let $\mathsf{PPS} = (\mathsf{Gen}, \mathsf{Sign}, \mathsf{Ver}, \mathsf{Punc})$ be a prefix puncturable signature scheme, and $o\mathcal{O} = (\mathsf{Obf}, \mathsf{Eval})$ be an online obfuscator with 1-time VGB security under $S(n)$ memory bound. The construction $\Pi = (\mathsf{Gen}, \mathsf{Sign}, \mathsf{Ver})$ works as follows:

- $\mathsf{Gen}(1^\lambda, 1^n)$: Run $(\mathsf{pk}, \mathsf{sk}) \leftarrow \mathsf{PPS.Gen}(1^\lambda)$, and output $(\mathsf{pk}, \mathsf{sk})$.
- $\mathsf{Sign}(\mathsf{sk}, m)$: Construct the program P as follows:

$$P_{\mathsf{sk}, m}(x) = \mathsf{PPS.Sign}(\mathsf{sk}, (x, m)).$$

Obfuscate the above program to obtain a stream $\sigma_\gg \leftarrow \mathsf{Obf}(P)$. The signature is simply the stream $\sigma_\gg$.
- $\mathsf{Ver}(\mathsf{pk}, m, \sigma_\gg)$: Sample a random prefix $x^* \in \{0,1\}^\lambda$, and evaluate the streamed obfuscated program using x^* as input. This yields

$$\sigma^* = \mathsf{Eval}(\sigma_\gg, x^*) = \mathsf{PPS.Sign}(\mathsf{sk}, (x^*, m)).$$

Then, output $\mathsf{PPS.Ver}(\mathsf{pk}, (x^*, m), \sigma^*)$ as the result.

The correctness of the construction comes directly from the correctness of the underlying prefix puncturable signature scheme.

Theorem 2. *If PPS is a correct and secure prefix puncturable signature scheme, and $o\mathcal{O}$ is an online obfuscator with 1-time VGB security under $S(n)$ memory bound, then Construction 2 is secure under $S(n)$ memory bound.*

The proof of this theorem uses some similar techniques as that of Theorem 1 and can be found in the full version of the paper.

6   Functional Encryption

6.1   Definition

The concept of Functional Encryption (FE) is first raised by Sahai and Waters [SW05] and later formalized by Boneh, Sahai, Waters [BSW11] and O'Neill [O'N10]. Here we review the syntax and security definition of functional encryption and how they would translate to the bounded storage model.

Syntax of Functional Encryption. Let λ be the security parameter. Let $\{\mathcal{C}_\lambda\}$ be a class of circuits with input space $\mathcal{X}_\lambda$ and output space $\mathcal{Y}_\lambda$. A functional encryption scheme for the circuit class $\{\mathcal{C}_\lambda\}$ is a tuple of PPT algorithms $\Pi =$ (Setup, KeyGen, Enc, Dec) defined as follows:

- Setup$(1^\lambda) \to$ (pk, msk) takes as input the security parameter λ, and outputs the public key pk and the master secret key msk.
- KeyGen(msk, C) $\to$ sk$_C$ takes as input the master secret key msk and a circuit $C \in \{\mathcal{C}_\lambda\}$, and outputs a function key sk$_C$.
- Enc(pk, m) $\to$ ct takes as input the public key pk and a message $m \in \mathcal{X}_\lambda$, and outputs the ciphertext ct.
- Dec(sk$_C$, ct) $\to y$ takes as input a function key sk$_C$ and a ciphertext ct, and outputs a value $y \in \mathcal{Y}_\lambda$.

We require correctness and security of a functional encryption scheme.

Definition 8 (Correctness). *A functional encryption scheme* $\Pi =$ (Setup, KeyGen, Enc, Dec) *is said to be correct if for all* $C \in \{\mathcal{C}_\lambda\}$ *and* $m \in \mathcal{X}_\lambda$:

$$
\Pr\left[y = C(m) : \begin{array}{l} (\text{pk}, \text{msk}) \leftarrow \text{Setup}(1^\lambda) \\ \text{sk}_C \leftarrow \text{KeyGen}(\text{msk}, C) \\ \text{ct} \leftarrow \text{Enc}(\text{pk}, m) \\ y \leftarrow \text{Dec}(\text{sk}_C, \text{ct}) \end{array} \right] \geq 1 - \text{negl}(\lambda).
$$

For the security definition, consider the following experiment:

Functional Encryption Security Experiment $\text{Dist}_{\mathcal{A},\Pi}^{\text{FE}}(\lambda)$:

- Run Setup(1^λ) to obtain keys (pk, msk) and sample a uniform bit $b \in \{0, 1\}$.
- The adversary $\mathcal{A}$ is given the public key pk.
- For a polynomial number of rounds, the adversary submits a circuit $C \in \{\mathcal{C}_\lambda\}$, and receives sk$_C \leftarrow$ KeyGen(msk, C).
- The adversary $\mathcal{A}$ submits the challenge query consisting of 2 messages m_0 and m_1 s.t. $C(m_0) = C(m_1)$ for any circuit C that has been queried before, and receives Enc(pk, m_b).
- For a polynomial number of rounds, the adversary submits a circuit $C \in \{\mathcal{C}_\lambda\}$ s.t. $C(m_0) = C(m_1)$, and receives sk$_C \leftarrow$ KeyGen(msk, C).
- The adversary $\mathcal{A}$ outputs a guess b' for b. If $b' = b$, we say that the adversary succeeds and the output of the experiment is 1. Otherwise, the experiment outputs 0.

Definition 9 (Adaptive Security). *A functional encryption scheme* $\Pi =$ (Setup, KeyGen, Enc, Dec) *is said to be secure if for all PPT adversaries* $\mathcal{A}$:

$$
\Pr\left[\text{Dist}_{\mathcal{A},\Pi}^{\text{FE}}(\lambda) = 1 \right] \leq \frac{1}{2} + \text{negl}(\lambda).
$$

Now we discuss how these definitions would need to be modified for defining functional encryption in the bounded storage model. As we have seen in the PKE with disappearing ciphertext security construction, the core idea here is similar: we now produce ciphertexts that are *streams*.

Concretely, for security parameters λ and n, a functional encryption scheme in the bounded storage model consists of a tuple of PPT algorithms $\Pi = (\mathsf{Setup}, \mathsf{KeyGen}, \mathsf{Enc}, \mathsf{Dec})$ that each uses up to $O(n)$ memory bits. The rest of the syntax is identical to that of the classical FE scheme, except that now the ciphertexts $\mathsf{ct}_{\gg}$ are streams. The correctness requirement remains unchanged apart from the syntax change, but the security definition would need to be supplemented with a memory bound for the adversary and a slightly different security experiment $\mathsf{Dist}_{\mathcal{A},\Pi}^{\mathsf{FE\text{-}BSM}}$. $\mathsf{Dist}_{\mathcal{A},\Pi}^{\mathsf{FE\text{-}BSM}}$ is identical (apart from syntax changes) to $\mathsf{Dist}_{\mathcal{A},\Pi}^{\mathsf{FE}}$ except that for function key queries submitted after the challenge query, we no longer require that $C(m_0) = C(m_1)$.

Definition 10 (Adaptive Security in the Bounded Storage Model). *A functional encryption scheme* $\Pi = (\mathsf{Setup}, \mathsf{KeyGen}, \mathsf{Enc}, \mathsf{Dec})$ *is said to be secure under memory bound* $S(n)$ *if for all PPT adversaries* $\mathcal{A}$ *that use at most* $S(n)$ *memory bits:*

$$\Pr\left[\mathsf{Dist}_{\mathcal{A},\Pi}^{\mathsf{FE\text{-}BSM}}(\lambda, n) = 1\right] \leq \frac{1}{2} + \mathsf{negl}(\lambda).$$

With these definitions in mind, we now present how one can construct a secure functional encryption scheme in the bounded storage model using online obfuscation. The construction will also be based on three classical cryptographic primitives: a Non-Interactive Zero Knowledge (NIZK) proof system, a secure classical functional encryption scheme, and a Pseudo-Random Function (PRF).

6.2   Construction

Construction 3. Let λ, n be the security parameters. Let $\mathsf{NIZK} = (\mathcal{P}, \mathcal{V})$ be a non-interactive zero knowledge proof system, $\mathsf{FE} = (\mathsf{Setup}, \mathsf{KeyGen}, \mathsf{Enc}, \mathsf{Dec})$ a functional encryption scheme, $\mathsf{PRF} : \{0,1\}^w \times \{0,1\}^* \to \{0,1\}^w$ a pseudorandom function for $w = \mathsf{poly}(\lambda)$, and $o\mathcal{O} = (\mathsf{Obf}, \mathsf{Eval})$ an online obfuscator with 1-time VGB security under memory bound $S(n)$. We construct the functional encryption scheme $\Pi = (\mathsf{Setup}, \mathsf{KeyGen}, \mathsf{Enc}, \mathsf{Dec})$ as follows:

- $\mathsf{Setup}(1^\lambda, 1^n)$: Sample $(\mathsf{pk}, \mathsf{msk}) \leftarrow \mathsf{FE.Setup}(1^\lambda)$. Sample the common reference string crs for the NIZK system. Output $(\mathsf{pk}, \mathsf{crs})$ as the overall public key. Output msk as the master secret key.
- $\mathsf{KeyGen}(\mathsf{msk}, C)$: Sample random $x, y \in \{0,1\}^w$. Consider the following function:

$$F_{C,x,y}(m, k) = \begin{cases} C(m) & \text{if } k = \bot \text{ or } \mathsf{PRF}(k, (C, y)) \neq x \\ \bot & \text{otherwise} \end{cases}.$$

Compute $\mathsf{sk}_F \leftarrow \mathsf{FE.KeyGen}(\mathsf{msk}, F_{C,x,y})$. Also, produce a NIZK proof π that sk_F is correctly generated, i.e. the tuple $(\mathsf{pk}, C, x, y, \mathsf{sk}_F)$ is in the language

$$\mathcal{L}_{\mathsf{pk},C,x,y,\mathsf{sk}_F} := \left\{ (\mathsf{pk}, C, x, y, \mathsf{sk}_F) \middle| \begin{array}{l} (\mathsf{pk}, \mathsf{msk}) \leftarrow \mathsf{FE.Setup}(1^\lambda) \\ \mathsf{sk}_F \leftarrow \mathsf{FE.KeyGen}(\mathsf{msk}, F_{C,x,y}) \end{array} \right\}.$$

Output the function key as $\mathsf{sk}_C = (C, x, y, \mathsf{sk}_F, \pi)$.
- $\mathsf{Enc}((\mathsf{pk}, \mathsf{crs}), m)$: Compute $c \leftarrow \mathsf{FE.Enc}(\mathsf{pk}, (m, \bot))$. Then consider the following program that takes as input a function key $\mathsf{sk}_C = (C, x, y, \mathsf{sk}_F, \pi)$:

$$P_{c,\mathsf{pk},\mathsf{crs}}(\mathsf{sk}_C) = \begin{cases} \mathsf{FE.Dec}(\mathsf{sk}_F, c) & \text{if } \mathsf{NIZK}.\mathcal{V}(\mathsf{crs}, (\mathsf{pk}, C, x, y, \mathsf{sk}_F), \pi) = 1 \\ \bot & \text{otherwise} \end{cases}.$$

Obfuscate the above program to obtain a stream $\mathsf{ct}_\gg \leftarrow \mathsf{Obf}(P)$. The ciphertext is simply the stream $\mathsf{ct}_\gg$.
- $\mathsf{Dec}(\mathsf{sk}_C, \mathsf{ct}_\gg)$: Simply output $\mathsf{Eval}(\mathsf{ct}_\gg, \mathsf{sk}_C)$.

It should be easy to verify that an honest execution yields

$$P_{c,\mathsf{pk},\mathsf{crs}}(C, x, y, \mathsf{sk}_F, \pi) = \mathsf{FE.Dec}(\mathsf{sk}_F, c) = F_{C,x,y}(m, \bot) = C(m)$$

as desired.

Theorem 3. *If* NIZK *is zero-knowledge and statistically sound,* PRF *is a secure pseudorandom function against non-uniform attackers,* FE *is a secure functional encryption scheme, and the online obfuscator* $o\mathcal{O}$ *has 1-time VGB security under* $S(n)$ *memory bound, then Construction 3 is secure under* $S(n)$ *memory bound.*

The proof of this theorem uses some similar techniques as that of Theorem 1 and can be found in the full version of the paper.

7 Candidate Construction 1

Here, we give a candidate online obfuscation scheme, for NC^1 circuits. This suffices for our applications, provided the underlying building blocks can be computed in NC^1. Note that we might heuristically be able to bootstrap our scheme to all circuits using FHE, but such bootstrapping (e.g. [GGH+13a]) is not known to provably apply to VGB obfuscation. In Sect. 8, we give a very different construction that directly yields VGB obfuscation.

7.1 Matrix Branching Programs

A *matrix branching program* BP of length h, width w, and input length ℓ consists of an input selection function $\mathsf{inp} : [h] \rightarrow [\ell]$, $2h$ matrices $\{\mathbf{M}_{i,b} \in \{0,1\}^{w \times w}\}_{i \in [h]; b \in \{0,1\}}$, a left bookend that is a row matrix $\mathbf{s} \in \{0,1\}^{1 \times w}$, and a right bookend that is a column matrix $\mathbf{t} \in \{0,1\}^{w \times 1}$. BP is evaluated on input $x \in \{0,1\}^\ell$ by computing $\mathsf{BP}(x) = \mathbf{s} \left(\prod_{i \in [h]} \mathbf{M}_{i,x_{\mathsf{inp}(i)}} \right) \mathbf{t}$.

We say that a family of matrix branching programs are *input-oblivious* if all programs in the family share the same parameters h, w, ℓ, and the input selection function inp.

Lemma 1 (Barrington's Theorem [Bar86]**).** *For a circuit C of depth d where each gate takes at most 2 inputs, we can construct a corresponding matrix branching program* BP *with width* 5 *and* $h = 4^d$.

7.2   The Basic Framework

Here we present the basic framework of an online obfuscator based on matrix branching programs. Our framework will be parameterized by a randomized procedure Convert, which takes as input a log-depth circuit C and width w, and produces a branching program of length $h = \text{poly}(\lambda)$ and width w. w will be chosen so that the honest parties only need $O(w)$ space to evaluate the program as it is streamed, while security is maintained even if the adversary has up to γw^2 space, for some small constant γ.

Since the branching program BP will be too large for a space bounded obfuscator to write down, we will need to provide a local, space-efficient way to compute each entry of the branching program, given the circuit C and the random coins of Convert.

Note that Barrington's theorem implies, for log-depth circuits, that $h = \text{poly}(\lambda)$ and that w can be taken as small as 5. Convert can be thought of as some procedure to expand the width to match the desired space requirements, and also enforce other security properties, as discussed in Sect. 7.3, where we discuss our particular instantiation of the framework.

Our basic framework actually consists of three schemes. As we will demonstrate, the three schemes have equivalent security, under the assumed existence of a pseudorandom function. The first scheme is much simpler, highlights the main idea of our construction, and allows us to more easily explore security. The downside of the first scheme is that the obfuscator requires significant space, namely more than the adversary. We therefore present two additional schemes with equivalent security, where the final scheme allows the obfuscator to run in space $O(w)$, while having equivalent security to the original scheme.

Construction with Kilian Randomization. We start with the first and simpler scheme, denoted $\mathcal{O}_{\text{Kil}}$, that uses randomization due to Kilian [Kil88] to construct a matrix branching program BP′ as follows.

Sample random invertible matrices $\mathbf{R}_i \in \{0,1\}^{w \times w}$ for $i = 0, 1, \ldots, h$. Compute $\mathbf{M}'_{i,b} = \mathbf{R}_{i-1}^{-1} \mathbf{M}_{i,b} \mathbf{R}_i$ for $i \in [h]$ and $b \in \{0,1\}$. Additionally, compute new bookends $\mathbf{s}' = \mathbf{s} \cdot \mathbf{R}_0$, and $\mathbf{t}' = \mathbf{R}_h^{-1} \cdot \mathbf{t}$. The new randomized matrix branching program is now BP′ $= (\text{inp}, \{\mathbf{M}'_{i,b}\}_{i \in [h]; b \in \{0,1\}}, \mathbf{s}', \mathbf{t}')$. Notice that when we compute BP′(x), these random matrices will cancel each other out and hence the output of the program should be unchanged.

Now to turn BP′ into an online obfuscator, all we need to do is to properly stream the branching program. Here we specify the order that the matrices will be streamed:

$$\mathbf{s}', \mathbf{M}'_{1,0}, \mathbf{M}'_{1,1}, \mathbf{M}'_{2,0}, \mathbf{M}'_{2,1}, \ldots, \mathbf{M}'_{h,0}, \mathbf{M}'_{h,1}, \mathbf{t}'.$$

When streaming a matrix $\mathbf{M}$, we require that the matrix $\mathbf{M}$ is streamed column by column, i.e. we start by sending the first column of $\mathbf{M}$, followed by the second column, then the third, so on and so forth.

Now let's take a look at how to evaluate the obfuscated program, i.e. the matrix branching program sent over the stream. Notice that we would need to do this using only space linear to w.

To evaluate the program, we will keep a row matrix $\mathbf{v} \in \{0,1\}^{1\times w}$ as our partial result. When the streaming begins, we will set $\mathbf{v} = \mathbf{s}'$ received over the stream.

For $i \in [h]$, we will compute $b = x_{\mathsf{inp}(i)}$ and listen to the stream of $\mathbf{M}'_{i,b}$. Let the columns of $\mathbf{M}'_{i,b}$ be $\mathbf{c}_1, \mathbf{c}_2, \ldots, \mathbf{c}_w$. Since $\mathbf{M}'_{i,b}$ is streamed column by column, we will receive on the stream $\mathbf{c}_1, \mathbf{c}_2, \ldots, \mathbf{c}_w$. As the columns are being streamed, we will compute an updated partial result $\mathbf{v}' = (v_1, v_2, \ldots, v_w)$ on the fly. As we receive $\mathbf{c}_j$ for $j \in [w]$, we would compute $v_j = \mathbf{v} \cdot \mathbf{c}_j$. After all the columns of $\mathbf{M}'_{i,b}$ have been streamed and that $\mathbf{v}'$ has been fully computed, we set $\mathbf{v} = \mathbf{v}'$.

In the end after we receive $\mathbf{t}'$, we output $\mathsf{BP}'(x) = \mathbf{v} \cdot \mathbf{t}'$.

Notice that throughout the evaluation process, we use at most $2w$ memory bits, which is linear to w.

However, one issue with this construction is that running the obfuscator requires computing products of matrices of size $w \times w$, and this inherently requires $O(w^2)$ space. In the full version of the paper, we show two additional schemes that eventually help us carry out the randomization process using only $O(w)$ space. The security of these schemes are equivalent to the security of the construction above, assuming the existence of pseudorandom functions. Therefore, it suffices to analyze the security of the construction above. Next, we will explain how to instantiate Convert in a way that presumably gives security.

7.3   Instantiating Convert

Now we will discuss how we specifically instantiate Convert, constructing the branching program BP for a circuit C that we plug into our framework.

To motivate our construction, we recall that Barrington's theorem [Bar86] plus Kilian randomization [Kil88] already provides *some* very mild security: given the matrices corresponding to an evaluation on any chosen input x (which selects one matrix from each matrix pair), the set of matrices information-theoretically hides the entire program, save for the output of the program on x.

This one-time security, however, is clearly not sufficient for full security. For starters, the adversary can perform *mixed-input* attacks, where it selects a single matrix from each pair, but for multiple reads of the same input, it chooses different matrices. This allows the attacker to treat the branching program as a read-once branching program. It may be that, by evaluating on such inputs, the adversary learns useful information about the program.

Another problem is linear-algebraic attacks. The rank of each matrix is preserved under Kilian randomization. Assuming all matrices are full-rank (which is true of Barrington's construction), the eigenvalues of $\mathbf{M}_{i,0} \cdot \mathbf{M}_{i,1}^{-1}$ are preserved under Kilian randomization.

In branching program obfuscation starting from [GGH+13a], multi-linear maps are used to block these attacks. In our setting, we will instead use the storage bounds on the attacker. First, we observe that Raz [Raz16] essentially shows that linear-algebraic attacks are impossible if the attacker cannot even record the matrices being streamed. While we do not know how to apply Raz's result to analyze our scheme, we conjecture that for appropriately chosen matrices, it will be impossible to do linear-algebraic attacks.

The next main problem is to enforce input consistency to prevent mixed-input attacks. To accomplish this, we will do the following. We will first run Barrington's theorem to get a branching program consisting of 5×5 matrices. We will then construct an "input consistency check" branching program, and glue the two programs together.

As a starting point, we will construct a *read-once* matrix branching program BP_1 (one that reads each input bit exactly once) that outputs 0 on an all-zero or all-one input string, and outputs 1 on all other inputs. Looking forward, we will insert this program into the various reads of a single input bit: any honest evaluation will cause the branching program to output 0, whereas an evaluation that mixes different reads of this bit will cause the program to output 1.

Matrix Branching Program BP_1:

- The width, the length, and the input length of the branching program are all L.
- inp is the identity function, i.e. $\mathbf{M}_{i,b}$ reads x_i as input.
- For $i \in [L]$, $\mathbf{M}_{i,0} = \mathbf{I}_L$ where $\mathbf{I}_L$ is the $L \times L$ identity matrix. $\mathbf{M}_{i,1}$ is the $L \times L$ permutation matrix representing shifting by 1. Specifically,

$$\mathbf{M}_{i,1} = \begin{pmatrix} 0^{(L-1)\times 1} & \mathbf{I}_{L-1} \\ 1 & 0^{1\times(L-1)} \end{pmatrix}.$$

- The left bookend is $\mathbf{s} = \begin{pmatrix} 1\,0\,0\,\cdots\,0 \end{pmatrix}$ and the right bookend is $\mathbf{t} = \begin{pmatrix} 0\,1\,1\,\cdots\,1 \end{pmatrix}^T$.

We now briefly justify why BP_1 works as desired. Let $0 \le \mathsf{w}(x) \le L$ be the Hamming weight of the input x. Notice that when evaluating $\mathsf{BP}_1(x)$, the number of $\mathbf{M}_{i,1}$ matrices chosen is exactly $\mathsf{w}(x)$, and the rest of the chosen matrices are all $\mathbf{M}_{i,0}$, the identity matrix. Therefore, the product of all the $\mathbf{M}$ matrices is equivalent to a permutation matrix representing shifting by $\mathsf{w}(x)$. When this product is left-multiplied by $\mathbf{s} = \begin{pmatrix} 1\,0\,0\,\cdots\,0 \end{pmatrix}$, we get a resulting row matrix $\mathbf{s}'$ that is equivalent to $\mathbf{s}$ right-shifted by $\mathsf{w}(x)$. Notice that $\mathbf{s}'$ has a single 1 at position $(\mathsf{w}(x) \bmod L) + 1$. When multiplying $\mathbf{s}'$ by the right bookend $\mathbf{t}$, the result will always be 1, unless $(\mathsf{w}(x) \bmod L) + 1 = 1$. The only $\mathsf{w}(x)$ values that satisfy $(\mathsf{w}(x) \bmod L) + 1 = 1$ are $\mathsf{w}(x) = 0$ and $\mathsf{w}(x) = L$, which correspond to $x = 0^L$ and $x = 1^L$ respectively. Hence BP_1 gives us the desired functionality.

Next up, we will expand BP_1 to a read-once matrix branching program BP_2 with the following functionality: for a set S of input bits, BP_2 outputs 0 if and only if all the input bits within S are identical (the input bits outside of S can be arbitrary). This is accomplished by simply setting the matrices for the inputs in S to be from BP_1, while the matrices for all other inputs are just identity matrices.

Next, we describe a simple method of taking the "AND" of two matrix branching programs with the same length, input length and input function. Given matrix branching programs $\mathsf{BP}^A = (\mathsf{inp}, \{\mathbf{M}^A_{i,b}\}_{i\in[h];b\in\{0,1\}}, \mathbf{s}^A, \mathbf{t}^A)$ and $\mathsf{BP}^B = (\mathsf{inp}, \{\mathbf{M}^B_{i,b}\}_{i\in[h];b\in\{0,1\}}, \mathbf{s}^B, \mathbf{t}^B)$ with length h and input length ℓ, we construct a new brancing program BP^C such that $\mathsf{BP}^C = \mathsf{BP}^A(x) \cdot \mathsf{BP}^B(x)$ for all inputs x:

Constructing $\mathsf{BP}^C = \mathsf{AND}(\mathsf{BP}^A, \mathsf{BP}^B)$:

- The length, the input length, and the input function of BP^C are also h, ℓ and inp, respectively. The width of BP^C is $w_C = w_A \cdot w_B$, where w_A and w_B are the widths of BP^A and BP^B, respectively.
- For all $i \in [h]$ and $b \in \{0,1\}$, compute $\mathbf{M}^C_{i,b} = \mathbf{M}^A_{i,b} \otimes \mathbf{M}^B_{i,b}$ where $\otimes$ denotes the matrix tensor product (Kronecker product). Notice that the widths of $\mathbf{M}^A_{i,b}, \mathbf{M}^B_{i,b}$, and $\mathbf{M}^C_{i,b}$ are w_A, w_B, and $w_A w_B$ as desired.
- The left bookend is $\mathbf{s}^C = \mathbf{s}^A \otimes \mathbf{s}^B$, and the right bookend is $\mathbf{t}^C = \mathbf{t}^A \otimes \mathbf{t}^B$.

Using the mixed-product property of matrix tensor products, it should be easy to verify that $\mathsf{BP}^C(x) = \mathsf{BP}^A(x) \cdot \mathsf{BP}^B(x)$ as desired.

Next, let BP_* be a random read-once matrix branching program with input length L and width $m = \mathsf{poly}(\lambda)$. We can sample such a branching program by uniformly sampling each of its matrices and bookends.[8]

We will assume that the program computed by BP_* gives a pseudo-random function. This is, unfortunately not strictly possible: write $x = (x_1, x_2)$ for two contiguous chunks of input bits x_1, x_2. Then the matrix $\left(\mathsf{BP}_*(x_1, x_2)\right)_{x_1\in X_1, x_2\in X_2}$ for any sets X_1, X_2 will have rank at most m. By setting X_1, X_2 to be larger than m, one can distinguish this matrix consisting of outputs of BP_* from a uniformly random one. The good news is that this attack requires a large amount of space, namely m^2. If the attacker's space is limited to be somewhat less than m^2, this plausibly leads to a pseudorandom function. We leave justifying this conjecture as an interesting open question.

Now consider the branching program $\mathsf{BP}_3 = \mathsf{AND}(\mathsf{BP}_2, \mathsf{BP}_*)$. Notice that BP_3 has width nm and is equal to 0 on inputs x where $\forall i, j \in S, x_i = x_j$, and is equal to $\mathsf{BP}_*(x)$ on all other x.

---

[8] When this is later put through the basic framework, we would need to generate these random matrices using a PRF. This allows us to reconstruct it at a later point.

With these tools in hand, we are now ready to show how to enforce input consistency on an existing matrix branching program.

Given a matrix branching program $\mathsf{BP} = (\mathsf{inp}, \{\mathbf{M}_{i,b}\}_{i \in [h]; b \in \{0,1\}}, \mathbf{s}, \mathbf{t})$ with length h, width w and input length ℓ, we construct the branching program BP' as follow:

Input Consistent Branching Program BP':

- BP' has the same length h, input length ℓ, and input function inp as BP. The width is now $w + mh$ where $m = \mathsf{poly}(\lambda)$.
- For all $j \in [\ell]$, let S_j be the set of all reads of x_j, i.e. $S_j = \{i | i \in [h], \mathsf{inp}(i) = j\}$. Construct the branching program $\mathsf{BP}_2^{(j)}$ using the BP_2 construction with input length h and $S = S_j$. Overwrite the input function of $\mathsf{BP}_2^{(j)}$ with inp so that it now takes $x \in \{0,1\}^\ell$ as input. Notice that $\mathsf{BP}_2^{(j)}(x) = 0$ if and only if all reads of the j-th bit of x are identical. Sample a fresh random matrix branching program $\mathsf{BP}_*^{(j)}$ with length h, width m, input length ℓ and input function inp. Compute $\mathsf{BP}_3^{(j)} = \mathsf{AND}(\mathsf{BP}_2^{(j)}, \mathsf{BP}_*^{(j)})$. Denote the matrices in $\mathsf{BP}_3^{(j)}$ as $\{\mathbf{M}_{i,b}^{(j)}\}_{i \in [h]; b \in \{0,1\}}$, and the bookends as $\mathbf{s}^{(j)}, \mathbf{t}^{(j)}$.
- For all $i \in [h]$, and $b \in \{0,1\}$, construct the matrix $\mathbf{M}_{i,b}'$ by adding all the $\mathbf{M}_{i,b}^{(j)}$'s to the diagonal as $\mathbf{M}_{i,b}' = \mathsf{diag}(\mathbf{M}_{i,b}, \mathbf{M}_{i,b}^{(1)}, \ldots, \mathbf{M}_{i,b}^{(\ell)})$. Notice that the width of $\mathbf{M}_{i,b}'$ is $w + \sum_{j \in [\ell]} m|S_j| = w + mh$.
- The left bookend is now $\mathbf{s}' = \begin{pmatrix} \mathbf{s} & \mathbf{s}^{(1)} & \mathbf{s}^{(2)} & \cdots & \mathbf{s}^{(\ell)} \end{pmatrix}$ and the right bookend is now $\mathbf{t}' = \left(\mathbf{t}^T \ \left(\mathbf{t}^{(1)}\right)^T \ \left(\mathbf{t}^{(2)}\right)^T \ \cdots \ \left(\mathbf{t}^{(\ell)}\right)^T \right)^T$.

Notice that we have

$$\mathsf{BP}'(x) = \mathsf{BP}(x) + \sum_{j \in [\ell]} \mathsf{BP}_3^{(j)}(x) = \mathsf{BP}(x) + \sum_{j \in [\ell]} \mathsf{BP}_2^{(j)}(x)\mathsf{BP}_*^{(j)}(x).$$

If all reads of the input x are consistent, then we have $\mathsf{BP}_2^{(j)}(x) = 0$ for all j, and the program outputs the original output $\mathsf{BP}'(x) = \mathsf{BP}(x)$.

If the reads of the input x are not consistent, then $\mathsf{BP}_2^{(j)}(x) = 1$ for some j, and consequently $\mathsf{BP}_*^{(j)}(x)$ will be added to the program output. By our conjecture that $\mathsf{BP}_*^{(j)}(x)$ acts as a PRF to space-bounded attackers, we thus add a pseudorandom value to $\mathsf{BP}(x)$, hiding its value. Thus, we presumably force input consistency. BP' will be the output of $\mathsf{Convert}$, which we then plug into our framework.

8   Candidate Construction 2

Now we present the second candidate construction from digital time-stamping and standard-model obfuscation. The concept of a digital time-stamp was first introduced by Haber and Stornetta [HS91], and since then we have seen various instantiations of digital time-stamping systems. One construction of particular interest is by Moran, Shaltiel and Ta-Shma [MST04], where they construct a non-interactive time-stamping scheme in the bounded storage model using a randomness beacon. A slightly modified definition that uses a stream instead of a randomness beacon will be what we base our candidate construction on.

Definition 11 (Non-Interactive Digital Time-stamp in the Bounded Storage Model). *Let λ, n be the security parameters. A non-interactive digital time-stamp scheme in the bounded storage model with stamp length $\ell = O(n)$ consists of a tuple of PPT algorithms $\Pi = (\mathsf{Stream}, \mathsf{Stamp}, \mathsf{Ver})$ that each uses up to $O(n)$ memory bits:*

- $\mathsf{Stream}(1^\lambda, 1^n) \to (s_\gg, k)$ *takes as input security parameters λ, n and outputs a stream $s_\gg$ and a short sketch k of the stream.*
- $\mathsf{Stamp}(s_\gg, x) \to \sigma$ *takes as input the stream $s_\gg$ and an input $x \in \{0, 1\}^*$, and outputs a stamp $\sigma \in \{0, 1\}^\ell$.*
- $\mathsf{Ver}(k, x, \sigma) \to 0/1$ *takes as input the sketch k, an input $x \in \{0, 1\}^*$ and a stamp σ and outputs a single bit 0 or 1.*

We require correctness and security of the digital time-stamp scheme.

Definition 12 (Correctness). *We require that for all $x \in \{0, 1\}^*$, we have*

$$\Pr\left[\mathsf{Ver}(k, x, \sigma) = 1 : (s_\gg, k) \leftarrow \mathsf{Stream}(1^\lambda, 1^n), \sigma \leftarrow \mathsf{Stamp}(s_\gg, x)\right] = 1.$$

For security, we ideally want that an adversary cannot produce a valid time-stamp on an input x that the adversary did not run Stamp on. Instead, [MST04] notice that an adversary with $S(n)$ memory bits can store at most $S(n)/\ell$ time-stamps, and therefore define security as upper bounding the number of time-stamps an adversary can produce. While not the same as the ideal goal, it at least implies the adversary cannot produce arbitrary time-stamped messages.

Definition 13 (Security). *We require that for all adversary $\mathcal{A}$ that uses up to $S(n)$ memory bits, we have*

$$\Pr\left[\forall (x, \sigma) \in M, \mathsf{Ver}(k, x, \sigma) = 1 \,\middle|\, \begin{array}{c} (s_\gg, k) \leftarrow \mathsf{Stream}(1^\lambda) \\ M \leftarrow \mathcal{A}^{\mathsf{Stamp}(\cdot)}(s_\gg) \\ |M| > \frac{S(n)}{\ell} \\ \forall (x_1, \sigma_1), (x_2, \sigma_2) \in M, x_1 \neq x_2 \end{array}\right] \leq \mathsf{negl}(\lambda).$$

Now we show how we can use such a digital time-stamping scheme to construct an online obfuscator.

Construction 4. Let λ, n be the security parameters. Let TSP be a digital time-stamping scheme in the bounded storage model. Let VGB = (Obf, Eval) be a classical VGB obfuscator for all circuits. We construct our online obfuscator for the circuit class $\{\mathcal{C}_\lambda\}$ as follows:

- Obf(C): Run TSP.Stream($1^\lambda, 1^n$) to stream $s_\gg$ and obtain the sketch k. Consider the following program $P_{C,k}$:

$$P_{C,k}(x, \sigma) = \begin{cases} C(x) & \text{if TSP.Ver}(k, x, \sigma) = 1 \\ \bot & \text{otherwise} \end{cases}.$$

Let $\mathcal{P} \leftarrow \text{VGB.Obf}(P_{C,k})$ be the *standard-model* VGB obfuscation of $P_{C,k}$. The obfuscated program is simply the stream $s_\gg$ followed by $\mathcal{P}$.
- Eval($(s_\gg, \mathcal{P}), x$): To evaluate the obfuscated program, first compute $\sigma \leftarrow$ TSP.Stamp($s_\gg, x$) when $s_\gg$ is being streamed. Then the output is simply VGB.Eval($\mathcal{P}, (x, \sigma)$).

Correctness is straightforward. One detail is that, using the basic time-stamping protocol of [MST04], the sketch k, and thus $P_{C,k}$ will be of size $O(n)$ bits. Thus, we need to use an obfuscator such that VGB.Obf only expands the input circuit by a constant factor. While no such constructions are currently known, there are also no known impossibilities. Alternatively, one can use branching-program based obfuscation directly from multilinear maps, for example [GGH+13a] and follow-ups. [BCKP14] even gives evidence that these constructions may be VGB secure. The difficulty is that the constructions blow up the input program by a polynomial factor, and therefore cannot be written down. However, as they have the form of a branching program, they can be streamed much the same way as we stream Candidate Construction 1. Finally, another option is to use the computational time-stamping protocol from [MST04], which shrinks the size of the sketch and the proof, at the cost of relying on computational assumptions. We therefore conjecture that some instantiation of VGB.Obf will lead to a secure online VGB obfuscator that can also be streamed in low space. We leave proving or disproving this conjecture as an open question.

References

[AP20]   Ananth, P., La Placa, R.L.: Secure software leasing. In: Canteaut, A., Standaert, F.-X. (eds.) EUROCRYPT 2021. LNCS, vol. 12697, pp. 501–530. Springer, Cham (2021). https://doi.org/10.1007/978-3-030-77886-6_17

[Bar86] Barrington, D.A.M.: Bounded-width polynomial-size branching programs recognize exactly those languages in NC^1. In: 18th ACM STOC, pp. 1–5. ACM Press, May 1986

[BB84]   Bennett, C.H., Brassard, G.: Quantum cryptography: Public key distribution and coin tossing. In: Proceedings of IEEE International Conference on Computers, Systems, and Signal Processing (1984)

[BCKP14] Bitansky, N., Canetti, R., Kalai, Y.T., Paneth, O.: On virtual grey box obfuscation for general circuits. In: Garay, J.A., Gennaro, R. (eds.) CRYPTO 2014. LNCS, vol. 8617, pp. 108–125. Springer, Heidelberg (2014). https://doi.org/10.1007/978-3-662-44381-1_7

[BF14] Bellare, M., Fuchsbauer, G.: Policy-based signatures. In: Krawczyk, H. (ed.) PKC 2014. LNCS, vol. 8383, pp. 520–537. Springer, Heidelberg (2014). https://doi.org/10.1007/978-3-642-54631-0_30

[BGI+01] Barak, B., et al.: On the (im)possibility of obfuscating programs. In: Kilian, J. (ed.) CRYPTO 2001. LNCS, vol. 2139, pp. 1–18. Springer, Heidelberg (2001). https://doi.org/10.1007/3-540-44647-8_1

[BNNO11] Bendlin, R., Nielsen, J.B., Nordholt, P.S., Orlandi, C.: Lower and upper bounds for deniable public-key encryption. In: Lee, D.H., Wang, X. (eds.) ASIACRYPT 2011. LNCS, vol. 7073, pp. 125–142. Springer, Heidelberg (2011). https://doi.org/10.1007/978-3-642-25385-0_7

[BSW11] Boneh, D., Sahai, A., Waters, B.: Functional encryption: definitions and challenges. In: Ishai, Y. (ed.) TCC 2011. LNCS, vol. 6597, pp. 253–273. Springer, Heidelberg (2011). https://doi.org/10.1007/978-3-642-19571-6_16

[CDNO97] Canetti, R., Dwork, C., Naor, M., Ostrovsky, R.: Deniable encryption. In: Kaliski, B.S. (ed.) CRYPTO 1997. LNCS, vol. 1294, pp. 90–104. Springer, Heidelberg (1997). https://doi.org/10.1007/BFb0052229

[CHK03] Canetti, R., Halevi, S., Katz, J.: A forward-secure public-key encryption scheme. In: Biham, E. (ed.) EUROCRYPT 2003. LNCS, vol. 2656, pp. 255–271. Springer, Heidelberg (2003). https://doi.org/10.1007/3-540-39200-9_16

[CPP20] Canetti, R., Park, S., Poburinnaya, O.: Fully deniable interactive encryption. In: Micciancio, D., Ristenpart, T. (eds.) CRYPTO 2020. LNCS, vol. 12170, pp. 807–835. Springer, Cham (2020). https://doi.org/10.1007/978-3-030-56784-2_27

[DM04] Dziembowski, S., Maurer, U.: On generating the initial key in the bounded-storage model. In: Cachin, C., Camenisch, J.L. (eds.) EUROCRYPT 2004. LNCS, vol. 3027, pp. 126–137. Springer, Heidelberg (2004). https://doi.org/10.1007/978-3-540-24676-3_8

[DvW92] Diffie, W., van Oorschot, P.C., Wiener, M.J.: Authentication and authenticated key exchanges. Des. Codes Crypt. 2(2), 107–125 (1992)

[Dzi06] Dziembowski, S.: On forward-secure storage. In: Dwork, C. (ed.) CRYPTO 2006. LNCS, vol. 4117, pp. 251–270. Springer, Heidelberg (2006). https://doi.org/10.1007/11818175_15

[GGH+13a] Garg, S., Gentry, C., Halevi, S., Raykova, M., Sahai, A., Waters, B.: Candidate indistinguishability obfuscation and functional encryption for all circuits. In: 54th FOCS, pp. 40–49. IEEE Computer Society Press, October 2013

[GGH+13b] Garg, S., Gentry, C., Halevi, S., Sahai, A., Waters, B.: Attribute-based encryption for circuits from multilinear maps. In: Canetti, R., Garay, J.A. (eds.) CRYPTO 2013. LNCS, vol. 8043, pp. 479–499. Springer, Heidelberg (2013). https://doi.org/10.1007/978-3-642-40084-1_27

[GGHW14] Garg, S., Gentry, C., Halevi, S., Wichs, D.: On the implausibility of differing-inputs obfuscation and extractable witness encryption with auxiliary input. In: Garay, J.A., Gennaro, R. (eds.) CRYPTO 2014. LNCS, vol. 8616, pp. 518–535. Springer, Heidelberg (2014). https://doi.org/10.1007/978-3-662-44371-2_29

[GGSW13] Garg, S., Gentry, C., Sahai, A., Waters, B.: Witness encryption and its applications. In: Boneh, D., Roughgarden, T., Feigenbaum, J. (eds.) 45th ACM STOC, pp. 467–476. ACM Press, June 2013

[GKR08] Goldwasser, S., Kalai, Y.T., Rothblum, G.N.: One-time programs. In: Wagner, D. (ed.) CRYPTO 2008. LNCS, vol. 5157, pp. 39–56. Springer, Heidelberg (2008). https://doi.org/10.1007/978-3-540-85174-5_3

[GKW17] Goyal, R., Koppula, V., Waters, B.: Lockable obfuscation. In: Umans, C. (ed.) 58th FOCS, pp. 612–621. IEEE Computer Society Press, October 2017

[GRT19] Garg, S., Raz, R., Tal, A.: Time-space lower bounds for two-pass learning. In: 34th Computational Complexity Conference (CCC 2019). Schloss Dagstuhl-Leibniz-Zentrum fuer Informatik (2019)

[GZ19] Guan, J., Zhandary, M.: Simple schemes in the bounded storage model. In: Ishai, Y., Rijmen, V. (eds.) EUROCRYPT 2019. LNCS, vol. 11478, pp. 500–524. Springer, Cham (2019). https://doi.org/10.1007/978-3-030-17659-4_17

[HS91] Haber, S., Stornetta, W.S.: How to time-stamp a digital document. In: Menezes, A.J., Vanstone, S.A. (eds.) CRYPTO 1990. LNCS, vol. 537, pp. 437–455. Springer, Heidelberg (1991). https://doi.org/10.1007/3-540-38424-3_32

[JLS20] Jain, A., Lin, H., Sahai, A.: Indistinguishability obfuscation from well-founded assumptions. Cryptology ePrint Archive, Report 2020/1003 (2020). https://eprint.iacr.org/2020/1003

[Kil88] Kilian, J.: Founding cryptography on oblivious transfer. In: 20th ACM STOC, pp. 20–31. ACM Press, May 1988

[LSS19] Landerreche, E., Stevens, M., Schaffner, C.: Non-interactive cryptographic timestamping based on verifiable delay functions. Cryptology ePrint Archive, Report 2019/197 (2019). https://eprint.iacr.org/2019/197

[Mau92] Maurer, U.M.: Conditionally-perfect secrecy and a provably-secure randomized cipher. J. Cryptol. 5(1), 53–66 (1992)

[Mli21] Mlitz, K.: Data center storage capacity worldwide from 2016 to 2021, by segment (2021). https://www.statista.com/statistics/638593/worldwide-data-center-storage-capacity-cloud-vs-traditional/

[MST04] Moran, T., Shaltiel, R., Ta-Shma, A.: Non-interactive timestamping in the bounded storage model. In: Franklin, M. (ed.) CRYPTO 2004. LNCS, vol. 3152, pp. 460–476. Springer, Heidelberg (2004). https://doi.org/10.1007/978-3-540-28628-8_28

[O'N10] O'Neill, A.: Definitional issues in functional encryption. Cryptology ePrint Archive, Report 2010/556 (2010). https://eprint.iacr.org/2010/556

[PW08] Peikert, C., Waters, B.: Lossy trapdoor functions and their applications. In: Ladner, R.E., Dwork, C. (eds.) 40th ACM STOC, pp. 187–196. ACM Press, May 2008

[Raz16] Raz, R.: Fast learning requires good memory: a time-space lower bound for parity learning. In: Dinur, I. (ed.) 57th FOCS, pp. 266–275. IEEE Computer Society Press, October 2016

[SW05] Sahai, A., Waters, B.: Fuzzy identity-based encryption. In: Cramer, R. (ed.) EUROCRYPT 2005. LNCS, vol. 3494, pp. 457–473. Springer, Heidelberg (2005). https://doi.org/10.1007/11426639_27

[WZ17] Wichs, D., Zirdelis, G.: Obfuscating compute-and-compare programs under LWE. In: Umans, C. (ed.) 58th FOCS, pp. 600–611. IEEE Computer Society Press, October 2017

Trojan-Resilience Without Cryptography

Suvradip Chakraborty[2], Stefan Dziembowski[1], Małgorzata Gałązka[1(✉)],
Tomasz Lizurej[1], Krzysztof Pietrzak[2], and Michelle Yeo[2]

[1] University of Warsaw, Warsaw, Poland
[2] IST Austria, Klosterneuburg, Austria

Abstract. Digital hardware Trojans are integrated circuits whose implementation differ from the specification in an arbitrary and malicious way. For example, the circuit can differ from its specified input/output behavior after some fixed number of queries (known as "time bombs") or on some particular input (known as "cheat codes").

To detect such Trojans, countermeasures using multiparty computation (MPC) or verifiable computation (VC) have been proposed. On a high level, to realize a circuit with specification $\mathcal{F}$ one has more sophisticated circuits $\mathcal{F}^\diamond$ manufactured (where $\mathcal{F}^\diamond$ specifies a MPC or VC of $\mathcal{F}$), and then embeds these $\mathcal{F}^\diamond$'s into a *master circuit* which must be trusted but is relatively simple compared to $\mathcal{F}$. Those solutions impose a significant overhead as $\mathcal{F}^\diamond$ is much more complex than $\mathcal{F}$, also the master circuits are not exactly trivial.

In this work, we show that in restricted settings, where $\mathcal{F}$ has no evolving state and is queried on independent inputs, we can achieve a relaxed security notion using very simple constructions. In particular, we do not change the specification of the circuit at all (i.e., $\mathcal{F} = \mathcal{F}^\diamond$). Moreover the master circuit basically just queries a subset of its manufactured circuits and checks if they're all the same.

The security we achieve guarantees that, if the manufactured circuits are initially tested on up to T inputs, the master circuit will catch Trojans that try to deviate on significantly more than a $1/T$ fraction of the inputs. This bound is optimal for the type of construction considered, and we provably achieve it using a construction where 12 instantiations of $\mathcal{F}$ need to be embedded into the master. We also discuss an extremely simple construction with just 2 instantiations for which we conjecture that it already achieves the optimal bound.

T. Lizurej—Stefan Dziembowski, Małgorzata Gałązka, and Tomasz Lizurej were supported by the 2016/1/4 project carried out within the Team program of the Foundation for Polish Science co-financed by the European Union under the European Regional Development Fund.

K. Pietrzak—Suvradip and Krzysztof have received funding from the European Research Council (ERC) under the European Union's Horizon 2020 research and innovation programme (682815 - TOCNeT).

K. Nissim and B. Waters (Eds.): TCC 2021, LNCS 13043, pp. 397–428, 2021.
https://doi.org/10.1007/978-3-030-90453-1_14

1   Hardware Trojans

Preventing attacks on cryptographic hardware that are based on leakage and tampering has been a popular topic both in the theory in the practical research communities [6–10,15]. Despite being very powerful, the models considered in this area are restricted in the sense that it is typically assumed that a given device has been manufactured correctly, i.e., the adversary is present during the execution of the device, but not when it is produced. As it turns out, this assumption is not always justifiable, and in particular in some cases the adversary may be able to modify the device at the production time. This is because, for economic reasons, private companies and government agencies are often forced to use hardware that they did not produce themselves. The contemporary, highly-specialized digital technology requires components that are produced by many different enterprises, usually operating in different geographic locations. Even a single chip is often manufactured in a production cycle that involves different entities. In a very popular method of hardware production, called the *foundry model*, the product designer is only developing the abstract description of a device. The real hardware fabrication happens in *foundry*. Only few major companies (like Intel) still manufacture chips by themselves [16].

Modifications to the original circuit specification introduced during the manufacturing process (in a way that is hard to detect by inspection and simple testing) are called *hardware Trojans*, and can be viewed as the extreme version of hardware attacks. For more on the practical feasibility of such attacks the reader may consult, e.g., books [13,16], or popular-science articles [1,12]. Hardware Trojans can be loosely classified into *digital* and *physical* ones. Physical hardware Trojans can be triggered and/or communicate via a physical side-channel, while digital hardware Trojans only use the regular communication interfaces. In this paper we only consider digital hardware Trojans.

1.1   Detecting Digital Hardware Trojans

A simple non-cryptographic countermeasure to detect whether a circuit F contains a hardware Trojan or follows the specification $\mathcal{F}$ is testing: one samples inputs $x_1, \ldots, x_T$, queries $y_i \leftarrow \mathsf{F}(x_i)$ and checks whether $y_i = \mathcal{F}(x_i)$ for all i. Two types of digital hardware Trojans discussed in the literature that evade detection by such simple testing are time bombs and cheat codes (see, e.g., [5]). A *time bomb* is a hardware Trojan where the circuit starts deviating after a fixed number of queries. *Cheat codes* refer to hardware Trojans where the circuits deviate on a set of hard-coded inputs. To achieve some robustness against all digital hardware Trojans, solutions using cryptographic tools, in particular verifiable computation (VC) [2,17] and multiparty computation (MPC) [5] were suggested. In both cases the idea is to take the specification $\mathcal{F}$ of the desired circuit and replace it with a more sophisticated construction of one or more circuits $\mathcal{F}^{\diamond}$. The circuit(s) $\mathsf{F}^{\diamond}$ that (presumably) are manufactured according to specification $\mathcal{F}^{\diamond}$ are then embedded into a master circuit M to get a circuit $\mathsf{M}^{\mathsf{F}^{\diamond}}$

Method	Specification of circuit $\mathcal{F}^\diamond$ (to be manufactured by untrusted fab) to realize $\mathcal{F}$	Test and (trusted) Master Circuit	Security with Trojans	Functionality when no Trojans present
MPC [5]	**Different than $\mathcal{F}$:** Implements functionality $\mathcal{F}$ in terms of a 3-player MPC computation.	**Testing**: T test queries. **Master's computation** — **non-trivial**: Master secret shares inputs and reconstructs outputs. It needs lots of randomness.	Gives $n < T/2$ correct and guaranteed outputs with prob. $1 - \exp(-k)$. No restriction on $\mathcal{F}$.	**Limited**: Behaves like $\mathcal{F}$ for $n = T/2$ queries, then stops.
VC [17,2]	**Different than $\mathcal{F}$:** $\mathcal{F}$ plus succinct proof of correct computation	**Testing**: no test queries. **Master's computation** — **non-trivial**: Master verifies succinct proof.	No guarantee on number of outputs, but as long as outputs are provided they are correct. No restriction on $\mathcal{F}$	**Ideal**: behaves like $\mathcal{F}$ for unbounded number of outputs.
This work	Same as $\mathcal{F}$: 12 instantiations needed in our provable construction, 2 conjectured to be already sufficient.	**Testing**: T test queries. **Master's computation** — very simple: Master only does equality checks and Multiplexer. Needs tiny amount of randomness.	Either the Trojans will be detected with probability $1-o(1)$, or at most a $O(1/T)$ fraction of the outputs is wrong. Requires that $\mathcal{F}$ has no evolving state and inputs are independent.	**Ideal**: (as above)

Fig. 1. Comparison of cryptographic solutions with our new construction. We achieve weaker security, but with a *much* simpler construction.

which is proven to follow specification $\mathcal{F}$ with high probability as long as it produces outputs. The master circuit must be trusted, but hopefully can be much simpler than $\mathcal{F}$. We elaborate on these two methods below.

Using Verifiable Computation. Here the idea is to let $\mathcal{F}^\diamond(x)$ output a tuple (y, π) where $y = \mathcal{F}(x)$ and π is a succinct zero-knowledge proof (see [3]) that y is the correct output. In the compiled circuit $\mathsf{M}^{\mathsf{F}^\diamond}$ the master M in input x

invokes $(y, \pi) \leftarrow \mathsf{F}^{\diamond}$, then verifies the proof π and only outputs y if the check passes. If verification fails, the master aborts with a warning. As long as the compiled circuit provides outputs, they are guaranteed to be correct. If there are no Trojans, the number of outputs is unbounded; but if there is a Trojan, they can make the compiled circuit abort already at the first query. See [2,17] for the details.

Using Multiparty Computation. In this case, the idea is to use secure multiparty computation protocols (MPCs, see, e.g., [4]). The compiled circuit $\mathsf{M}^{\mathsf{F}^{\diamond}}$ contains some number of sub-components $\mathsf{F}^{\diamond}$ that communicate only via the master circuit. In [5], this number is $3k$ (where k is a parameter). The sub-components are grouped in triples, each of them executing a 3-party protocol. In order to avoid the "cheat code" attacks, the master secret shares the input between the 3 parties. To get assurance that the sub-components are not misbehaving they are tested before deployment. In order to avoid the "time bomb" attacks, the number of times each sub-component is tested is an independently chosen random number from 1 to T. The output of each triple is secret-shared between its sub-components. Each of them sends its share to the master circuit, who reconstructs the k secrets, and outputs the value that is equal to the majority of these secrets. For the details see [5].

Simple Schemes. In this work we consider compilers as discussed above, but only particularly simple ones which have the potential of being actually practical. In particular, we require that $\mathcal{F} \equiv \mathcal{F}^{\diamond}$. That is, the specification $\mathcal{F}^{\diamond}$ of the functionality given to the untrusted manufacturer is the actual functionality $\mathcal{F} : \mathcal{X} \rightarrow \mathcal{Y}$ we want to implement. Moreover, our master just invokes (a random subset of) the circuits on the input and checks if the outputs are consistent.

This restricted model has very appealing properties. For example, it means one can use our countermeasures with circuits that have already been manufactured. But there are also limitations on what type of security one can achieve. Informally, the security we prove for our construction roughly states that for any constant $c > 0$ there exists a constant c' such that no malicious manufacturer can create Trojans which (1) will not be detected with probability at least c, and (2) if not detected, will output a $\geq c'/T$ fraction of wrong outputs. Here T is an upper bound on the number of test queries we can make to the Trojans before they are released.

In particular, we only guarantee that most outputs are correct, and we additionally require that the inputs are iid. Unfortunately, it's not hard to see that for the simple class of constructions considered these assumptions are not far from necessary.[1] We will state the security of the VC and MPC solutions using our notion of Trojan-resilience in Sect. 2.7.

It's fair to ask whether our notion has any interesting applications at all. Two settings in which Trojan resilience might be required are (1) in settings where a computation is performed where false (or at least too many false) outputs would have serious consequences, and (2) cryptographic settings where the circuit holds a key or other secret values that should not leak.

For (1) our compiler would only be provably sufficient if the inputs are iid, and only useful if a small fraction of false outputs can be tolerated. This is certainly a major restriction, but as outlined above, if one doesn't have the luxury to manufacture circuits that are much more sophisticated than the required functionality, it's basically the best one can get. Depending on the setting, one can potentially use our compiler in some mode – exploiting redundancy or using repetition – to fix those issues. We sketch some measures in the cryptographic setting below.

For the cryptographic setting (2) our notion seems even less useful: if the adversary can learn outputs of the Trojans, he can use the $\Theta(1/T)$ fraction of wrong outputs to embed (and thus leak) its secrets. While using the compiler directly might not be a good idea, we see it as a first but major step towards simple and Trojan-resilient constructions in the cryptographic setting. As an example, consider a weak PRF $\mathcal{F} : \mathcal{K} \times \mathcal{X} \to \mathcal{Y}$ (a weak PRF is defined like a regular PRF, but the outputs are only pseudorandom if queried on random inputs). While implementing $\mathcal{F}(k, \cdot)$ using our compiler directly is not a good idea as discussed above,[2] we can compile $t > 1$ weak PRFs with independent keys and inputs and finally XOR the outputs of the t master circuits to implement a weak PRF $\mathcal{F}_3((k_1, \ldots, k_t), (x_1, \ldots, x_t)) = \oplus_{i=1}^{t} \mathcal{F}(k_i, x_i)$. Intuitively, the output can only leak significant information about the keys if *all* t outputs are wrong as otherwise the at least one pseudorandom output will mask everything. If each output is wrong with probability, say $1/T$ for a modest $T = 2^{30}$ and we use $t = 3$, then for each query we only have a probability of $1/T^3 = 2^{-90}$ that all $t = 3$ outputs deviate, which we can safely assume will never happen. Unfortunately, at this point we can't prove the above intuition and leave this for future work. For one thing, while we know that the XOR will not leak much if at least one of the t values is correct when the weak PRFs are modelled as ideal ciphers [11], we don't have a similar result in the computational setting. More importantly, we only

---

[1] We show that a small fraction of wrong outputs must be allowed in Sect. 2.4. The iid assumption can be somewhat relaxed, but as we don't have a clean necessary condition we will not discuss this further in this paper. Informally, a sufficient condition seems to just require that there is no (efficiently recognisable) subset of inputs which appear rarely (not more than with probability around $1/T$) but can come in "bursts", say two such inputs are consecutive with prob. $\gg 1/T^2$.

[2] It's acceptable by our construction if the inputs are iid conditioned on some secret, so the master on input x and key k can forward (k, x) to the circuits. Alternatively the key k can be hard-coded in the circuit (probably not a good idea if the manufacturer is not trusted in the first place) or, if the circuits have some storage, one can give them k after receiving the circuits from the manufacturer.

prove that at most a $1/T$ fraction of the outputs is wrong once a sufficiently large number of queries was made, but to conclude that in the above construction all t instances fail at the same time with probability at most $1/T^t$ we need a stronger statement saying that for each individual query the probability of failure is $1/T$ (we believe that this is indeed true for our construction, but the current proof does not imply this).

Weak PRFs are sufficient for many basic symmetric-key cryptographic tasks like authentication or encryption.[3] Even if a fraction of outputs can be wrong, as long as they don't leak the key (as it seems to be the case for the construction just sketched), this will only affect completeness, but not security. An even more interesting construction, and the original motivation for this work, is a trojan-resilient stream cipher. This could then be used to e.g., generate the high amount of randomness required in side-channel countermeasures like masking schemes. The appealing property of a stream-cipher in this setting is that we don't care about correctness at all, we just want the output to be pseudorandom. It's not difficult to come up with a candidate for such a stream-cipher based on our compiler, but again, a proof will require more ideas. One such construction would start with the weak PRF construction just discussed, and then use two instantiations of it in the leakage-resilient mode from [14].

2   Definition and Security of Simple Schemes

For $m \in \mathbb{N}$, an *m-redundant simple construction* $\Pi_m = (\mathsf{T}^*, \mathsf{M}^*)$ is specified by a master circuit $\mathsf{M}^* : \mathcal{X} \to \mathcal{Y} \cup \{\mathsf{abort}\}$ and a test setup $\mathsf{T}^* : \mathbb{N} \to \{\mathsf{fail}, \mathsf{pass}\}$.[4] The $*$ indicates that they expect access to some "oracles". The following oracles will be used: (a) $\mathsf{F}_1, \ldots, \mathsf{F}_m$—the Trojan circuits that presumably implement the functionality $\mathcal{F} : \mathcal{X} \to \mathcal{Y}$, (b) F—a trusted implementation of $\mathcal{F}$ (only available in the test phase), and (c) \$—a source of random bits (sometimes we will provide the randomness as input instead),

2.1   Test and Deployment

The construction Π_m which implements $\mathcal{F}$ in a Trojan-resilient way using the untrusted $\mathsf{F}_1, \ldots, \mathsf{F}_m$ is tested and deployed as follows.

Lab Phase (test): In this first phase we execute $\{\mathsf{pass}, \mathsf{fail}\} \leftarrow \mathsf{T}^{\mathsf{F}_1, \ldots, \mathsf{F}_m, \mathsf{F}, \$}(T)$
  The input T specifies that each F_i may be queried at most T times. If the output is fail, a Trojan was detected. Otherwise (i.e. the output is pass) we move to the next phase.
Wild Phase (deployment): If the test outputs pass, the F_i's are embedded into the master to get a circuit $\mathsf{M}^{\mathsf{F}_1, \ldots, \mathsf{F}_m, \$} : \mathcal{X} \to \mathcal{Y} \cup \mathsf{abort}$.

---

[3] To encrypt m sample a random r and compute the ciphertext $(r, \mathcal{F}(k, r) \oplus m)$.
[4] We consider much stronger $\mathsf{M}^*, \mathsf{T}^*$ for the lower bounds compared to what we require in the constructions as discussed in Sect. 2.5.

2.2   Completeness

The completeness requirement states that if every F_i correctly implements $\mathcal{F}$, then the test phase outputs pass with probability 1 and the master truthfully implements the functionality $\mathcal{F}$. That is, for every sequence $x_1, x_2, \ldots, x_q$ (of arbitrary length and potentially with repetitions) we have

$$\Pr[\forall i \in [q] \; : \; y_i = \mathcal{F}(x_i)] = 1 \text{ where for } i = 1 \text{ to } q \; : \; y_i := \mathsf{M}^{\mathsf{F}_1, \ldots, \mathsf{F}_m, \$}(x_i)$$

The reason we define completeness this way and not simply for all x we have $\Pr[\mathsf{M}^{\mathsf{F}_1, \ldots, \mathsf{F}_m, \$}(x) = \mathcal{F}(x)]$ is that the Trojan F_i can be stateful, so the order in which queries are made does matter.

2.3   Security of Simple Schemes

We consider a security game $\mathsf{TrojanGame}(\Pi, T, Q)$ where, for some $T, Q \in \mathbb{Z}$, an adversary Adv can choose the functionality $\mathcal{F}$ and the Trojan circuits $\mathsf{F}_1, \ldots, \mathsf{F}_m$. We first run the test phase $\tau \leftarrow \mathsf{T}^{\mathsf{F}_1, \ldots, \mathsf{F}_m, \mathsf{F}, \$}(T)$ We then run the wild phase by querying the master on Q iid inputs $x_1, \ldots, x_Q$.

$$\text{for } i = 1, \ldots, Q \; : \; y_i \leftarrow \mathsf{M}^{\mathsf{F}_1, \ldots, \mathsf{F}_m, \$}(x_i).$$

The goal of the adversary is two-fold:

1. They do not want to be caught, if either $\tau = \mathsf{fail}$ or $y_i = \mathsf{abort}$ for some $i \in [Q]$ we say the adversary was detected and define the predicate

$$\mathsf{detect} = \mathsf{false} \iff (\tau = \mathsf{pass}) \wedge (\forall i \in [Q] : y_i \neq \mathsf{abort})$$

2. They want the master to output as many wrong outputs as possible. We denote the number of wrong outputs by $Y \overset{\text{def}}{=} |\{i : \; y_i \neq \mathcal{F}(x_i)\}|$.

Informally, we call a compiler (like our simple schemes) $(\mathsf{win}, \mathsf{wrng})$-Trojan resilient, or simply $(\mathsf{win}, \mathsf{wrng})$-secure, if for every Trojan, the probability that it causes the master to output $\geq \mathsf{wrng}$ fraction of wrong outputs without being detected is at most win. In the formal definition win and wrng are allowed to be a function of the number of test queries T.

Definition 1 ($(\mathsf{win}, \mathsf{wrng})$-Trojan resilience). *And adversary $(\mathsf{win}, \mathsf{wrng})$-wins in $\mathsf{TrojanGame}(\Pi, T, Q)$ if the master outputs more than a wrng fraction of wrong values without the Trojans being detected with probability greater than win, i.e.,*

$$\Pr_{\mathsf{TrojanGame}(\Pi, T, Q)}[(\mathsf{detect} = \mathsf{false}) \wedge (Y/Q \geq \mathsf{wrng})] \geq \mathsf{win}$$

For $\mathsf{win} : \mathbb{N} \rightarrow [0, 1], \mathsf{wrng} : \mathbb{N} \rightarrow [0, 1], q : \mathbb{N} \rightarrow \mathbb{N}$, we say that Π is $(\mathsf{win}(T), \mathsf{wrng}(T), q(T))$-Trojan-resilient (or simply "secure") if there exists a constant T_0, such that for all $T \geq T_0$ and $Q \geq q(T)$ no adversary $(\mathsf{win}(T), \mathsf{wrng}(T))$-wins in $\mathsf{TrojanGame}(\Pi, T, Q)$.

We say Π is $(\mathsf{win}(T), \mathsf{wrng}(T))$ Trojan-resilient if it is $(\mathsf{win}(T), \mathsf{wrng}(T), q(T))$-Trojan-resilient for some (sufficiently large) polynomial $q(T) \in poly(T)$.

In all our simple constructions the test and master only use the outputs of the F_i (and for the test also F) oracles to check for equivalence. This fact will allow us to consider somewhat restricted adversaries in the security proof.

Definition 2 (Generic Simple Scheme). *A* **generic** *simple scheme* T^*, M^* *treats the outputs of the* F_i *(and for* T^* *additionally* F*) oracles like variables. Concretely, two or more oracles can be queried on the same input, and then one checks if the outputs are identical. Moreover the master can use the output of an* F_i *as its own output.*

By the following lemma, to prove security of generic simple schemes, it will be sufficient to consider restricted adversaries that always choose to attack the trivial functionality $\mathcal{F}(x) = 0$ and where the output range of the Trojans is a bit.

Lemma 1. *For any generic simple scheme* Π_m*, assume an adversary* Adv *exists that* (win, wrng)*-wins in* TrojanGame(Π_m, T, Q) *and let* $\mathcal{F} : \mathcal{X} \to \mathcal{Y}$*,* $F_1, \dots, F_m :$ $\mathcal{X} \to \mathcal{Y}$ *denote its choices for the attack. Then there exists an adversary* Adv$'$ *who also* (win, wrng)*-wins in* TrojanGame(Π_m, T, Q) *and chooses* $\mathcal{F}' : \mathcal{X} \to$ $\{0, 1\}$ *,* $F_1', \dots, F_m' : \mathcal{X} \to \{0, 1\}$ *where moreover* $\forall x \in \mathcal{X} : \mathcal{F}'(x) = 0$*.*

Proof. Adv$'$ firstly runs Adv to learn *(i)* the functionality $\mathcal{F} : \mathcal{X} \to \mathcal{Y}$ which it wants to attack and *(ii)* its Trojans $F_1, \dots, F_m$. It then outputs (as its choice of function to attack) an $\mathcal{F}'$ where $\forall x \in \mathcal{X} : \mathcal{F}'(x) = 0$ and, for every $i \in [m]$, it chooses the Trojan F_i' to output 0 if F_i would output the correct value, and 1 otherwise. More formally, $F_i'(x)$ invokes the original Trojan $y \leftarrow F_i(x)$ and outputs 0 if $\mathcal{F}(x) = y$ and 1 otherwise.

By construction, whenever one of the F_i''s deviates (i.e., outputs 1), also the original F_i would have deviated. And whenever the test or master detect an inconsistency in the new construction, they would also have detected an inconsistency with the original $\mathcal{F}$ and F_i.[5]   □

2.4   Lower Bounds

By definition, (win, wrng)-security implies (win$'$, wrng$'$)-security for any win$' \geq$ win, wrng$' \geq$ wrng. The completeness property implies that no scheme is $(1, 0)$-secure (as by behaving honestly an adversary can $(1, 0)$-win). And also no scheme is $(0, 1)$-secure (as $\Pr[E] \geq 0$ holds for every event E). Thus our (win, wrng)-security notion is only interesting if both, win and wrng are > 0. We will prove the following lower bound:

Lemma 2 (Lower bound for simple schemes). *For any* $c > 0$ *and* $m \in \mathbb{N}$ *there exists a constant* $c' = c'(c, m) > 0$ *such that no* m*-redundant simple scheme* Π_m *is* $(c, \frac{c'}{T})$*-Trojan-resilient.*

---

[5] Let us mention that the opposite is not true (it's possible that for some $i \neq j$ we have $F_i'(x) = F_j'(x) = 1$, while $F_i(x) \neq F_j(x)$). This just captures the observation that an adversary who wants to deviate as often as possible without being detected can wlog. always deviate to the same value.

Proof. Adv chooses the constant functionality $\mathcal{F}(x) = 0$ with a sufficiently large input domain $|\mathcal{X}| \gg (m \cdot T)^2$ (so that sampling $m \cdot T$ elements at random from $\mathcal{X}$ with or without repetition is basically the same). Now Adv samples a random subset $\mathcal{X}' \subset \mathcal{X}$, $|\mathcal{X}'|/|\mathcal{X}| = \frac{1.1 \cdot c'}{T}$ (for c' to be determined) and then defines Trojans which deviate on inputs from $\mathcal{X}'$

$$\forall i \in [m] \; : \; \mathsf{F}_i(x) = \begin{cases} 1 \text{ if } x \in \mathcal{X}' \text{ (deviate)} \\ 0 \text{ if } x \notin \mathcal{X}' \text{ (correct)} \end{cases}$$

Should the test pass, the master will deviate on each input with probability $1.1 \cdot c'/T$, if we set the number of queries Q large enough, the fraction of wrong outputs will be close to its expectation $1.1 \cdot c'/T$, and thus almost certainly larger than c'/T.

It remains to prove that the test passes with probability $\geq c$. By correctness, the testing procedure $\mathsf{T}^{\mathsf{F}_1,\dots,\mathsf{F}_m,\mathsf{F},\$}$ must output pass unless one of the total $\leq m \cdot T$ queries it made to the F_is falls into the random subset $\mathcal{X}'$. The probability that no such query is made is at least

$$\left(1 - \frac{1.1 \cdot c'}{T}\right)^{m \cdot T}$$

and this expression goes to 1 as c' goes to 0. We now choose $c' > 0$ sufficiently small so the expression becomes $> c$. To get a quantitative bound one can use the well known inequality $\lim_{T \to \infty}(1 - 1/T)^T = 1/e \approx 0.367879$. □

The (proof of) the previous lemma also implies the following.

Corollary 1. *If a simple scheme* Π_m *is* $(\mathsf{win}(T), \mathsf{wrng}(T))$ *secure with*

1. $\mathsf{win}(T) \in 1 - o(1)$ *then* $\mathsf{wrng}(T) \in o(1/T)$.
2. $\mathsf{wrng}(T) \in \omega(1/T)$ *then* $\mathsf{win}(T) \in o(1)$.

The first item means that if Adv wants to make sure the Trojan is only detected with sub-constant probability, then he can only force the master to output a $o(1/T)$ fraction of wrong outputs during deployment. The second item means that if Adv wants to deviate on a asymptotically larger than $1/T$ fraction of outputs, it will be detected with a probability going to 1.

Not Interesting Security for 1-Redundant Schemes. For $m = 1$ redundant circuits a much stronger lower bound compared to Lemma 2 holds. The following Lemma implies that no 1-redundant scheme is $(\epsilon(T), \delta(T))$-Trojan-resilient for any $\epsilon(T) > 0$ and $\delta(T) = 1/\mathsf{poly}(T)$ (say $\epsilon(T) = 2^{-T}, \delta(T) = T^{-100}$).

Lemma 3 (Lower bound for $m = 1$). *For any 1-redundant scheme* Π_1 *and any polynomial* $p(T) > 0$, *there is an adversary that* $(1, 1 - 1/p(T))$-*wins in the* $\mathsf{TrojanGame}(\Pi_1, T, Q)$ *game for* $Q \geq p(T) \cdot T$.

Proof. Consider an adversary who chooses a "time bomb" Trojan F_1 which correctly outputs $\mathcal{F}(x)$ for the first T queries and also stores those queries, so it can output the correct value if one of those queries is repeated in the future. From query $T + 1$ the Trojan outputs wrong values unless it is given one of the first T queries as input, in which case it outputs the correct value. This Trojan will pass any test making at most T invocations, while the master will deviate on almost all queries, i.e., all except the first T.

To see why we store the first T queries and do not deviate on them when they repeat in the future, consider a master which stores the outputs it observes on the first T queries so it can later detect inconsistencies.   □

2.5   Efficiency of Lower Bound vs. Constructions

For the lower bounds in the previous section, the *only* restriction on the test $\mathsf{T}^{\mathsf{F}_1,\ldots,\mathsf{F}_m,\mathsf{F},\$}(T)$ is that each F_i can only be queried at most T times. There are no restrictions on the master $\mathsf{M}^{\mathsf{F}_1,\ldots,\mathsf{F}_m,\$}(\cdot)$ at all. In particular, it can be stateful, computationally unbounded, use an arbitrary amount of randomness, and query the F_is on an unbounded number of inputs (as the Trojan F_is can be stateful this is not the same as learning the function table of the F_i's).

While the lack of any restrictions makes the lower bound stronger, we want our upper bounds, i.e., the actual constructions, to be as efficient (in terms of computational, query and randomness complexity) and simple as possible, and they will indeed be very simple.

Let us stress that one thing the definition does not allow is the test to pass a message to the master. If we would allow a message of unbounded length to be passed this way no non-trivial lower bound would hold as T could send the entire function table of $\mathcal{F}$ to M, which then could perfectly implement $\mathcal{F}$. Of course such a "construction" would get against the entire motivation for simple schemes where M^* should be much simpler and independent of $\mathcal{F}$. Still, constructions where the test phase sends a short message to the master (say, a few correct input/output pairs of $\mathcal{F}$ which the master could later use to "audit" the Trojans) could be an interesting relaxation to be considered.

2.6   Our Results and Conjectures

Our main technical result is a construction of a simple scheme which basically matches the lower bound from Lemma 2. Of course for any constant $c > 0$, the constant c' in the theorem below must be larger than in Lemma 2 so there's no contradiction.

Theorem 1 (Main, optimal security of Π_{12}). *For any constant $c > 0$ there is a constant c' such that the simple construction Π_{12} from Fig. 3 is $(c, \frac{c'}{T})$-Trojan resilient.*

While $(c, \frac{c}{T})$-Trojan-resilience matches our lower bound, the construction is $m = 12$-redundant (recall this means we need 12 instantiations of $\mathcal{F}$ manufactured to instantiate the scheme). While for $m = 1$ redundancy is not sufficient to get any interesting security, as we showed in Lemma 3, we conjecture that $m = 2$ is sufficient to match the lower bound, and give a candidate construction.

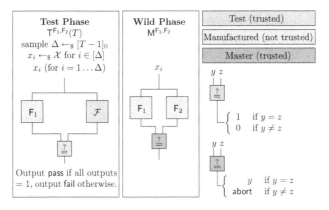

Fig. 2. Construction Π_2^* (discussed in Sect. 2.9), which is $(c, \frac{c'}{T})$ secure *for history-independent* Trojans.

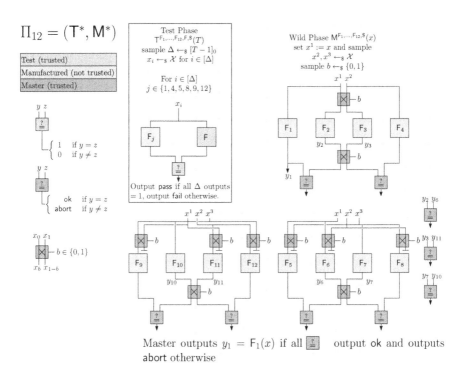

Fig. 3. Construction Π_{12} for which we prove optimal Trojan-resilience as stated in Theorem 1. Very informally, the security proof is by contradiction: via a sequence of hybrids an attack against Π_{12} is shown to imply an attack where the yellow part basically corresponds to Π_2^* with two history independent circuits. This attack contradicts the security of Π_2^* as stated in Theorem 2. (Color figure online)

Conjecture 1 (Optimal security of Π_2^ϕ). For any $0 < \phi < 1$ and any constant $c > 0$ there is a constant $c' = c'(c, \phi)$ such that the simple construction Π_2^ϕ from Sect. 3 is $(c, \frac{c'}{T})$-Trojan resilient.

The parameter ϕ in this construction basically specifies that the master will query both oracles F_1 and F_2 on a (random) $T^{-\phi}$ fraction of the input, and check consistency in this case. While the conjecture is wrong for $\phi = 0$ and $\phi \geq 1$, the $\phi = 0$ case (i.e., when we always query both, F_1 and F_2) will be of interest to us as security of the $\Pi_2^\star \overset{\text{def}}{=} \Pi_2^0$ construction against a limited adversary (termed history-independent and discussed in Sect. 2.9 below) will be a crucial step towards our proof of our main theorem.

2.7   Comparison with VC and MPC

Let us shortly compare the security we achieve with the more costly solutions based on verifiable computation (VC) [2,17] and multiparty computation (MPC) [5] discussed in the introduction. We can consider (win, wrng)-security as in Definition 1 also for the VC and MPC construction, here one would need change the TrojanGame(Π, T, Q) from Sect. 2.3 to allow the trojans F_i to implement a different functionality than the target $\mathcal{F}$ (for VC one needs to compute an extra succinct proof, for MPC the trojans implement the players in an MPC computation). For VC there's no test (so $T = 0$) and only one $m = 1$ Trojan, and for MPC and VC we can drop the requirement that the inputs are iid.

In the VC construction the master will catch *every* wrong output (except with negligible probability), so for any polynomial *poly* there is a negligible function *negl* (in the security parameter of the underlying succinct proof system), such that the scheme is $(1/poly, negl, Q)$ secure for any polynomial Q.

For the MPC construction the master will provide $Q < c_0 T$ outputs with probability c_1^m (where $c_0 \in [0, 1/2]$ and $c_1 \in [0, 1]$ are some constants), but while outputs are provided they are most likely correct, so for any polynomial Q, T we have $(1 - c_1^m, negl, Q)$ security.

2.8   Stateless Trojans

In our security definition we put no restriction on the Trojans F_i provided by the adversary (other than being *digital* hardware Trojans as discussed in the introduction), in particular, the F_i's can have arbitrary complex evolving state while honestly manufactured circuits could be stateless. We can consider a variant of our security definition (Definition 1) where the adversary is only allowed to choose *stateless* Trojan circuits F_i. Note that the lower bound from Lemma 2 still holds as in its proof we did only consider stateless F_i's. There's an extremely simple 1-redundant construction that matches the lower bound when the adversary is only allowed to chose stateless Trojans.

Consider a construction $\Pi_1 = (T^*, M^*)$ where the master is the simplest imaginable: it just forwards inputs/outputs to/from its oracle, if F_1 is stateless this simply means $M^{F_1}(\cdot) = F_1(\cdot)$. The test $T^{F_1,F,\$}(T)$ queries F_1 and the trusted F on T random inputs and outputs fail iff there is a mismatch.

Proposition 1 (Optimal security for 1-redundant scheme for *stateless* Trojans). *For any constant $c > 0$ there is a constant $c' > 0$ such that Π_1 is $(c, \frac{c'}{T})$-Trojan resilient if the adversary is additionally restricted to choose a stateless Trojan.*

Proof. If wrng' denotes the fraction of inputs on which the Trojan F_1 differs from the specification $\mathcal{F}$ (both chosen by an adversary Adv, note that wrng' is only well defined here as F_1 is stateless), then wrng' must satisfy $c > (1 - \text{wrng}')^T$ if the adversary wants to (c, wrng)-win for any wrng, as otherwise already the test catches the Trojan with probability $(1 - \text{wrng}')^T > c$. For $c > (1 - \text{wrng}')^T$ to hold wrng' $\in \Omega(1/T)$, in particular, wrng' $\geq c'/T$ for some $c' > 0$. □

2.9 History-Independent Trojans

A notion of in-between general (stateful) Trojans and stateless Trojans will play a central role in our security proof. We say a trojan F_i is *history-independent* if its only state is a counter which is incremented by one on every invocation, so it's answer to the i'th query can depend on the current index i, but not on any inputs it saw in the past.

We observe that Lemma 3 stating that no 1-redundant simple scheme can be secure still holds if we restrict the choice of the adversary to history-independent Trojans as the "time-bomb" Trojan used in the proof is history-independent. We will show a 2-redundant construction $\Pi_2^\star$ that achieves optimal security against history-independent Trojans.

Theorem 2 (History-Independent Security of $\Pi_2^\star$). *For any constant $c > 0$ there is a constant $c' = c'(c) > 0$ such that $\Pi_2^\star$ from Fig. 2 is $(c, \frac{c'}{T})$-Trojan resilient if the adversary is additionally restricted to choose a history-independent Trojans.*

The technical Lemma 4 we prove and which implies this theorem, actually implies a stronger statement: for any positive integer k, the above holds even if we relax the security notion and declare the adversary a winner as long a Trojan is detected by the test or master at most $k - 1$ times. What this exactly means is explained in Sect. 4.2. Note that this notion coincides with the standard notion for $k = 1$.

The $\Pi_2^\star$ scheme is just the Π_2^ϕ scheme from Conjecture 1 for $\phi = 0$, where we conjecture that Π_2^ϕ is (in some sense) optimally secure for $0 < \phi < 1$. For ϕ the conjecture is wrong, but somewhat ironically we are only able to *prove* security against history-independent Trojans for $\phi = 0$, and this result will be key towards proving the security of Π_{12} as stated in our main Theorem 1.

2.10   Proof Outline

The proof of our main Theorem 1 stating that Π_{12} is optimally Trojan-resilient is done in two steps. As just discussed, we first prove security of $\Pi_2^\star$ against *history-independent* Trojans, and in a second step we reduce the security of Π_{12} against general Trojans to the security of $\Pi_2^\star$ against history-independent Trojans. We outline the main ideas of the two parts below.

Part 1: Security of $\Pi_2^\star$ Against History-Independent Trojans (Theorem 2, Lemma 4). $\Pi_2^\star$ is a very simple scheme where the test $\mathsf{T}^{\mathsf{F}_1,\mathsf{F}_2,\mathsf{F},\$}$ just queries F_1 on a random number $\Delta, 0 \le \Delta < T$ of inputs and checks if they are correct (the test ignores F_2). The master $\mathsf{M}^{\mathsf{F}_1,\mathsf{F}_2,\$}(x)$ queries $y \leftarrow \mathsf{F}_1(x)$ and $y' \leftarrow \mathsf{F}_2(x)$ on x and aborts if they disagree.

In the proof of Lemma 4 we define p_i and q_i as the probability that F_1 and F_2 outputs a wrong value in the ith query on a random input, respectively. As $\mathsf{F}_1, \mathsf{F}_2$ are history independent, this is well defined as this probability only depends on i (but not previous queries).

Let the variable Φ_Δ denote the number of times the Trojans will be detected conditioned on the random number of test queries being Δ. This value is (below Q is the number of queries to the master and we use the convention $q_i = 0$ for $i < 0$)

$$\mathbb{E}[\Phi_\Delta] = \sum_{i=1}^{Q+\Delta} |p_i - q_{i-\Delta}| \tag{1}$$

In this sum, the first Δ terms account for the test, and the last Q terms for the wild-phase. Moreover let Y_Δ denote the number of times F_1 deviates (and thus the master outputs a wrong value), its expectation is

$$\mathbb{E}[Y_\Delta] = \sum_{i=\Delta+1}^{Q+\Delta} p_i$$

To prove Trojan-resilience of $\Pi_2^\star$ as stated in Lemma 4 boils down to proving that, for most Δ, whenever the probability of $\Phi_\Delta = 0$ (i.e., the Trojan is not detected) is constant, the fraction of wrong outputs Y_Δ/Q must be "small" (concretely, $O(1/T)$).

The core technical result establishing this fact is Lemma 5. Unfortunately, this Lemma only establishes this fact for the expectation, i.e., whenever $\mathbb{E}[\Phi_\Delta]$ is small, also $\mathbb{E}[Y_\Delta]$ is small. Here is where we use the fact that the $\mathsf{F}_1, \mathsf{F}_2$ are history independent: in the history independent case Φ_Δ and Y_Δ can be written as the sum of independent boolean variables, so using a Chernoff bound it follows that their actual value will be close to their expectation with high probability.

It is instructive to see why for example setting $p_i = q_i = \delta$ for some fixed $\delta > 0$ does not contradict Theorem 2. To contradict it, the fraction of wrong outputs (which here is simply δ) must be $\omega(1/T)$. In this case, $\mathbb{E}[\Phi_\Delta] = \Delta \cdot \delta = \omega(\Delta/T)$, which to contradict the lemma must be at least constant, which in turn means $\Delta \in o(T)$ must hold. As $\Delta, 0 \ge \Delta < T$ is uniform, t's $o(T)$ with $o(1)$ probability, but for a contradiction we also need this probability to be constant.

Part 2: Reducing the Security of Π_{12} Against General Trojans to the Security of $\Pi_2^\star$ Against History Independent Trojans (Theorem 1). While the random shift Δ makes $\Pi_2^\star$ secure against history-independent attacks (like time-bombs, where a Trojan starts deviating after some fixed number of queries), it succumbs to cheat codes: as the master always queries F_1, F_2 on the same inputs, a Trojan can specify some set of trigger inputs, and after receiving such a trigger the Trojans will deviate forever. By making the fraction of inputs that are triggers sparse, the Trojans will likely not be detected during testing (a $1/T$ fraction will survive testing with constant probability).

To prevent such a coordination via the inputs, in Π_{12} inputs are somewhat randomly assigned to the different Trojans. In particular, as emphasized in the yellow area in Fig. 3, the F_1 is always queried on the input x, and then the random bit b determines whether F_2 or F_3 are queried on x. If an input x were to trigger the Trojans to always deviate, F_1 and one of F_2 and F_3 will be triggered, say it's F_2. But now, as soon as F_3 is queried in a future round the master will abort as F_1 will deviate, but F_3 will not (except if this query also happens to be a trigger, which is unlikely as triggers must be sparse to survive the testing phase).

This just shows why a particular attack does not work on Π_{12}. But we want a proof showing security against all possible Trojans. Our proof proceeds by a sequence of hybrids, where we start with assuming a successful attack on Π_{12}, and then, by carefully switching some circuits and redefining them by hard coding "fake histories", we arrive at a hybrid game where there is still a successful attack, but now the circuits in the yellow area basically correspond to two the $\Pi_2^\star$ construction instantiated with history-independent Trojans, but such an attack contradicts our security proof for $\Pi_2^\star$ as stated in Lemma 4.

3 Conjectured Security of 2-Redundant Schemes

While the main technical result in this paper is a simple scheme Π_{12} that provably achieves optimal security as stated in Theorem 1, this construction is not really practical as it is 12-redundant. Recall that k-redundant means the master needs k instantiations of the functionality $\mathcal{F}$, so it's in some sense the hardware cost. For this section let us also define a computational cost: the **rate** of a simple construction is the average number of invocations to its F_i oracles the master $M^{F_1,\ldots,F_m,\$}(\cdot)$ makes with any query.

3.1   A 2-Redundant Scheme Π_2^ϕ

We will now define a scheme Π_2^ϕ which in terms of redundancy and rate is as efficient as we possibly could hope for a scheme with non-trivial security: it's 2-redundant and has a rate of slightly above (the trivial lower bound of) 1. The construction $\Pi_2^\phi = (M^*, T^*)$, where $\phi \in \mathbb{R}, \phi \geq 0$ is illustrated in Fig. 4.

test: In the test phase, $T^{F_1,F_2,F}(T)$ picks a random $\Delta, 0 \leq \Delta \leq T - 1$, then queries F_1 on Δ random inputs and checks if the outputs are correct by comparing with the trusted F.

master: With probability $1 - T^{-\phi}$ the master $\mathsf{M}^{\mathsf{F_1,F_2,\$}}(x)$ picks either $\mathsf{F_1}$ or $\mathsf{F_2}$ at random, queries it on x and uses the output as its output. Otherwise, with probability $T^{-\phi}$, the master queries both oracles and outputs abort if their outputs don't match, and forwards the output of $\mathsf{F_1}$ otherwise.

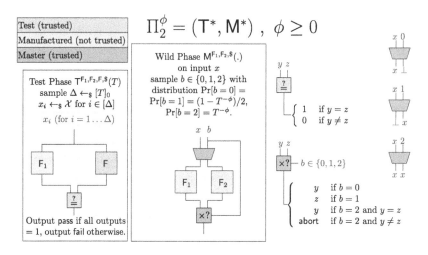

Fig. 4. Construction Π_2^ϕ from Conjecture 1.

Our Conjecture 1 states that this construction achieves optimal security (optimal in the sense of matching the lower bound from Lemma 2) for any $0 < \phi < 1$, i.e.,

For any $0 < \phi < 1$ and any constant $c > 0$ there is a constant c' such that Π_2^ϕ is $(c, \frac{c'}{T})$-Trojan resilient.

We discuss how Π_2^ϕ performs against typical Trojans like time-bombs and cheat codes. Our conjecture only talks about $(\mathsf{win}(T), \mathsf{wrng}(T))$-security where the winning probability $\mathsf{win}(T) = c$ is a constant, and here the exact value of ϕ does not seem to matter much as long as it is bounded away from 0 and 1. For $\mathsf{win}(T) = o(1)$ the parameter ϕ will matter as those attacks will illustrate. (the $o(1)$ always denotes any value that goes to 0 as $T \to \infty$).

Proposition 2 (Time Bomb against Π_2^ϕ). *For any ϕ, there exists an adversary that $(\Theta(T^{-\phi}), 1 - o(1))$-wins in* $\mathsf{TrojanGame}(\Theta(\Pi_2^\phi), T, \omega(T))$

Proof (sketch). Let Adv choose the constant functionality $\forall x \in \mathcal{X} : \mathcal{F}(x) = 0$, and a Trojan $\mathsf{F_1}$ which outputs the correct value 0 for the first T queries, and 1 for all queries $> T$, while $\mathsf{F_2}$ always outputs 1.

$\mathsf{F_1}$ will always pass the test. The master will abort iff one of its first $T - \Delta$ queries to $\mathsf{F_1}$ (where the output is 0) is a "$b = 2$" query (as then $\mathsf{F_1}(x) = 1 \neq 0 = \mathsf{F_2}(x)$). With probability $T^{-\phi}$ we have $\Delta \geq T - T^\phi$, and in this case such a bad

event only happens with constant probability (using $(1-\epsilon)^{1/\epsilon} \approx 1/e = 0.368\ldots$).
So the Trojan will not be detected with probability $T^{-\phi}/e$, and in this case also
almost all outputs will be wrong. $\qquad\square$

Proposition 3 (Cheat Code against Π_2^ϕ). *For any ϕ, there exists an adversary that $(\Theta(T^{\phi-1}), 1 - o(1))$-wins in* TrojanGame$(\Theta(\Pi_2^\phi), T, \omega(T))$

Proof (sketch). Let Adv choose the constant functionality $\forall x \in \mathcal{X} : \mathcal{F}(x) = 0$.
The Trojans $\mathsf{F}_1, \mathsf{F}_2$ output 0 until they get a query from a "trigger set" $\mathcal{X}' \subset \mathcal{X}$,
after this query they always deviate and output 1.

   If we set $|\mathcal{X}'|/|\mathcal{X}| = 1/T$, then the test will pass with constant probability
$(1 - 1/T)^\Delta \geq (1 - 1/T)^T \approx 1/e$. Assuming the Trojans passed the test phase,
the master will *not* catch the Trojans if the first trigger query to F_1 and F_2
happen in-between the same $b = 2$ queries (or in such a query). This happens
with probability $\approx T^{\phi-1}$. $\qquad\square$

The two propositions above imply that the adversary can always
$(T^{\max\{-\phi,\phi-1\}}, 1-o(1))$-win by either using a time-bomb or cheat-code depending on ϕ. The winning probability is minimized if $-\phi = \phi - 1$ which holds for
$\phi = 0.5$. We conjecture that the above two attacks are basically all one can do
to attack Π_2^ϕ.

Conjecture 2 (Security of $\Pi_2^{0.5}$ for low winning probabilities). For win$(T) \in$
$\omega(T^{-0.5})$, $\Pi_2^{0.5}$ is $(\mathsf{win}(T), \mathsf{wrng}(T))$-Trojan resilient for some $\mathsf{wrng}(T) \in o(1)$.

4   A Scheme for History-Independent Trojans

In this section we define the simple scheme $\Pi_2^\star$ and prove its security as claimed in
Theorem 2. Recall that a history-independent Trojan circuit is a stateless circuit,
except that it maintains a counter. We recall that a trojan is *history-independent*
if its state is a counter which is incremented by one on every invocation, so its
answer to the i'th query can depend on the current index i and current input
x_i, but not on any inputs it saw in the past.

4.1   Notation

For an integer n we define $[n] \overset{\text{def}}{=} \{1, \ldots, n\}$ and $[n]_0 \overset{\text{def}}{=} \{0, \ldots, n\}$. We will also
use the Chernoff bound.

4.2   Security of $\Pi_2^\star$

Relaxing the Winning Condition. We can think of the security experiment
TrojanGame$(\Pi_2^\star, T, Q)$ as proceeding in rounds. First, for a random $\Delta \in [T]$, we
run the test for Δ rounds (in each querying F_1 and F on a random input and
checking equivalence), and then Q rounds for querying the master (in each round
querying F_1 and F_2 and checking for equivalence). The adversary immediately

loses the game if a comparison fails (outputs 0 in the test or abort in the master) in any round.

We consider a relaxed notion of (win, wrng)-winning, "relaxed" as we make it easier for the adversary, and thus proving security against this adversary gives a stronger statement. We define (win, wrng)-k-winning like (win, wrng)-winning, but the adversary is allowed to be detected in up to $k-1$ rounds, so (win, wrng)-1-winning is (win, wrng)-winning.

This relaxed notion is not of practical interested, as one would immediately abort the moment a Trojan is detected. We consider this notion as we need it for the security proof of our main Theorem 1, where we will only be able to reduce security of Π_{12} to the security of $\Pi_2^\star$ (against history-independent Trojans) if $\Pi_2^\star$ satisfies this stronger notion.

Proof of Theorem 2. The following lemma implies Theorem 2 for $k = 1$, as discussed after the statement of the theorem the lemma below is somewhat more general as we'll need the stronger security for any k.

Lemma 4. *For any constant $c > 0$ and positive integer k, there exists a constant c', and integer T_0 and polynomial $q(.)$ such that no adversary* Adv *exists that only chooses* history-independent *Trojans and that for any*

$$T \geq T_0 \quad , \quad Q \geq q(T)$$

can $(c, c'/T)$-k-win TrojanGame$(\Pi_2^\star, T, Q)$.

Proof. For a given $c > 0$ define

$$c'' = \max\{64k, -256\ln(c/2)\}$$

we then set $c', q(T)$ and T_0 as

$$c' = c''/c^2 \ , \ q(T) = \frac{5 \cdot T^2 c}{c''} + 5T \ , \ T_0 = 1 \tag{2}$$

These values are just chosen so that later our inequalities work out nicely, we did not try to optimise them.

By Lemma 1 we can consider the security experiment where an adversary Adv chooses the constant functionality $\mathcal{F} : \mathcal{X} \to 0$ as target and the two (history-independent) Trojans $\mathsf{F}_1, \mathsf{F}_2 : \mathcal{X} \to \{0, 1\}$ output a bit (so they can either correctly output 0 or deviate by outputting 1). As the $\mathsf{F}_1, \mathsf{F}_2$ are history independent, we can think of F_1 as a sequence $\mathsf{F}_1^1, \mathsf{F}_1^2, \ldots$ of functions where F_1^i behaves like F_1 on the ith query. Let p_i and q_i denote the probability that F_1 and F_2 deviates on the ith query, respectively

$$p_i \overset{\text{def}}{=} \Pr_{x \leftarrow \mathcal{X}}[\mathsf{F}_1^i(x) = 1] \quad , \quad q_i \overset{\text{def}}{=} \Pr_{x \leftarrow \mathcal{X}}[\mathsf{F}_2^i(x) = 1]$$

In TrojanGame$(\Pi_2^\star, T, Q)$, for $\delta \in [T-1]_0$ let the variable Y_δ denote the number of wrong outputs by F_1 conditioned on the number of test queries $\Delta \leftarrow_\$ [T-1]_0$ being $\Delta = \delta$. The expectation is

$$\mathbb{E}(Y_\delta) = \sum_{i=1}^{Q} p_{i+\delta} \tag{3}$$

Let the variables Φ_δ^T and Φ_δ^M denote the number of times the test and the master "catch" a Trojan conditioned on $\Delta = \delta$.

$$\mathbb{E}[\Phi_\delta^T] = \sum_{i=1}^{\delta} |p_i| \quad , \quad \mathbb{E}[\Phi_\delta^M] \geq \sum_{i=1}^{Q} |p_{i+\delta} - q_i|$$

let $\Phi_\delta \stackrel{\text{def}}{=} \Phi_\delta^T + \Phi_\delta^M$ denote the total number of times the Trojans are detected, and Φ_δ' being the same but we ignore the last δ queries. With the convention that $q_i = 0$ for $i < 1$

$$\mathbb{E}[\Phi_\delta] \geq \sum_{i=1}^{Q+\delta} |p_i - q_{i-\delta}| \quad , \quad \mathbb{E}[\Phi_\delta'] \geq \sum_{i=1}^{Q} |p_i - q_{i-\delta}| \quad , \quad \mathbb{E}[\Phi_\delta] \geq \mathbb{E}[\Phi_\delta'] \tag{4}$$

As we consider *history-independent* Trojans the Y_δ, Φ_δ variables are sums of independent Bernoulli random variables. Using a Chernoff bound we will later be able to use the fact that for such variables are close to their expectation with high probability.

Claim. For any $\delta \in [T-1]_0, \tau \in [T-1-\delta]$ (so $\delta + \tau \leq T - 1$)

$$\mathbb{E}[\Phi_\delta] + \mathbb{E}[\Phi_{\delta+\tau}] \geq \tau \cdot \frac{\mathbb{E}[Y_\delta] - T}{Q + T} \tag{5}$$

Proof (of Claim). Assume for a moment that $p_1, \ldots, p_\tau = 0$ as required to apply Lemma 16, then

$$\mathbb{E}[\Phi_\delta] + \mathbb{E}[\Phi_{\delta+\tau}] \overset{(4)}{\geq} \mathbb{E}[\Phi_\delta'] + \mathbb{E}[\Phi_{\delta+\tau}'] \tag{6}$$

$$\geq \sum_{\Delta \in \{\delta, \delta+\tau\}} \sum_{i=1}^{Q} |p_i - q_{i-\Delta}| \tag{7}$$

$$\overset{\text{Lemma 5}}{\geq} \tau \cdot \frac{\sum_{i=1}^{Q} p_i}{Q} = \tau \cdot \frac{\mathbb{E}[Y_0]}{Q} \tag{8}$$

$$\geq \tau \cdot \frac{\mathbb{E}[Y_\delta] - T}{Q} \tag{9}$$

The last step used $\mathbb{E}[Y_0] + \delta \geq \mathbb{E}[Y_\delta]$ and $\delta \leq T$.

We now justify our assumption $p_1, \ldots, p_\tau = 0$. For this change the security experiment and replace the Trojans F_1, F_2 chosen by the adversary with Trojans that first behave correctly for the first T inputs, and only then start behaving like $\mathsf{F}_1, \mathsf{F}_2$ (technically, the new Trojans deviate with probabilities p'_i, q'_i satisfying $p'_1, \ldots, p'_T = 0, q'_1, \ldots, q'_T = 0$ and for $i > T$ :: $p'_i = p_{i-T}$ and $q'_i = q_{i-T}$). At the same time, we increase Q to $Q + T$. This change leaves $\mathbb{E}[Y_\delta]$ unaffected, while $\mathbb{E}[\varPhi'_\delta], \mathbb{E}[\varPhi'_{\delta+\tau}]$ can only increase. This proves the claim, note that in (5) the denominator is $Q + T$ not Q as in (9) to account for this shift.   △

Claim. For all but at most a $c/2$ fraction of the $\delta \in [T]_0$

$$\mathbb{E}[\varPhi_\delta] \geq \frac{c \cdot T}{8} \cdot \frac{\mathbb{E}[Y_\delta] - T}{Q + T} \tag{10}$$

Proof (of Claim). We use Eq. (5) which can be understood as stating that if $\mathbb{E}[\varPhi_\delta]$ is "small" for some δ, then all $\mathbb{E}[\varPhi_{\delta'}]$ with $|\delta - \delta'|$ large enough can't be small too. Concretely, consider any δ for which (if no such δ exists the claim already follows)

$$\mathbb{E}[\varPhi_\delta] < \frac{c \cdot T}{8} \cdot \frac{\mathbb{E}[Y_\delta] - T}{Q + T}$$

then for all $\delta' \in [T]_0$ for with $|\delta - \delta'| \geq \frac{c \cdot T}{4}$ (note this is at least a $c/2$ fraction) by Eq. (5)

$$\mathbb{E}[\varPhi_\delta] + \mathbb{E}[\varPhi_{\delta'}] \geq \frac{c \cdot T}{4} \cdot \frac{\mathbb{E}[Y_\delta] - T}{Q + T}$$

the two equations above now give

$$\mathbb{E}[\varPhi_{\delta'}] \geq \frac{c \cdot T}{8} \cdot \frac{\mathbb{E}[Y_\delta] - T}{Q + T}$$

as claimed.   △

To prove the lemma we need to show that when Q is sufficiently large, any adversary attacking at least c'/T fraction of times, can win at most k times with probability less than c. Since the duration of test phase δ is chosen randomly from the set $\{0, ..., T - 1\}$, we start with the following equation:

$$\frac{1}{T} \sum_{\delta=0}^{T-1} \Pr[(Y_\delta/Q \geq c'/T) \wedge (\varPhi_\delta < k)] < c \tag{11}$$

Let c_δ denote the probability the adversary k-wins conditioned on $\varDelta = \delta$

$$c_\delta \overset{\text{def}}{=} \Pr[(Y_\delta/Q \geq c'/T) \wedge (\varPhi_\delta < k)] \tag{12}$$

With this notation we need to show

$$\frac{1}{T} \sum_{\delta=0}^{T-1} c_\delta < c$$

which follow from the claim below

Claim. $c_\delta < c/2$ holds for all δ, except (the at most $c/2$ fraction of) the $\delta \in [T]_0$ for which (10) does not hold

Proof (of Claim). Consider any δ for which (10) holds. If for this δ $\Pr[Y_\delta \geq Q \cdot c'/T] < c/2$ we're done as by (12) also $c_\delta < c/2$ (using that $\Pr[a \wedge b] \leq \Pr[a]$ for all events a, b). To finish the proof of the claim we need to show that otherwise, i.e., if

$$\Pr[Y_\delta \geq Q \cdot c'/T] \geq c/2 \tag{13}$$

then

$$\Pr[\Phi_\delta < k] < c/2 \tag{14}$$

as this again implies $c_\delta < c/2$. Equation (13) (using $\Pr[V \geq x] \geq p \Rightarrow \mathbb{E}[V] \geq x \cdot p$ which follows from Markov's inequality) gives

$$\mathbb{E}[Y_\delta] \geq Q \cdot c' \cdot c/2T \tag{15}$$

Plugging this into (10), then using or choice (2) of $c' = c''/c^2$ and in the last step of $Q \geq q(T) = 5 \cdot T^2 \cdot c/c'' + 5T$ (this bound for $q(T)$ was just chosen so the last inequality below works out nice).

$$
\begin{aligned}
\mathbb{E}[\Phi_\delta] &\overset{(10)}{\geq} \frac{c \cdot T}{8} \cdot \frac{\mathbb{E}[Y_\delta] - T}{Q + T} \\
&\overset{(15)}{\geq} \frac{c \cdot T}{8} \cdot \frac{\frac{Q \cdot c' \cdot c}{2T} - T}{Q + T} \\
&\overset{(2)}{\geq} \frac{Q \cdot c'' - 2T^2 \cdot c}{16(Q + T)} \\
&\geq c''/32
\end{aligned}
$$

Using the Chernoff bound with $\epsilon = 1/2$ and $c'' \geq -256 \ln(c/2)$ (refer to Appendix in the extended technical report for details).

$$\Pr[\Phi_\delta < c''/64] \leq \Pr[\Phi_\delta < \mathbb{E}[\Phi_\delta]/2] \leq e^{-\mathbb{E}[\Phi_\delta]/8} \leq e^{-c''/256} \leq c/2$$

With our choice (2) of $c'' = \max\{64k, -256 \ln(c/2)\}$ we get the bound $\Pr[\Phi_\delta < k] \leq c/2$ claimed in (14). $\triangle$

$\square$

4.3   A Technical Lemma

Consider any $t, z \in \mathbb{N}$, $z > t$, $t = 0 \bmod 2$ and $p_1, \ldots, p_z \in [0, 1]$. Denote with $\bar{p} \overset{\mathsf{def}}{=} \frac{\sum_{i=1}^{z} p_i}{z}$ be the average value.

Lemma 5. *For any $q_1, \ldots, q_z \in [0, 1]$, (defining $q_i = 0$ for $i \leq 0$) and integers Δ', τ where $0 \geq \Delta', \tau \geq 0$, if $p_1 = p_2 = \ldots = p_\tau = 0$ then*

$$\sum_{\Delta \in \{\Delta', \Delta' + \tau\}} \sum_{i=1}^{z} |p_i - q_{i-\Delta}| \geq \tau \cdot \bar{p} \tag{16}$$

We refer the reader to our technical report for the full proof, but let us observe that for example it implies, that if $p_1 = p_2 = \ldots = p_t = 0$, then

$$\frac{1}{t}\sum_{\Delta=0}^{t-1}\sum_{i=1}^{z}|p_i - q_{i-\Delta}| = \frac{1}{t}\sum_{\Delta'=0}^{t/2-1}\underbrace{\sum_{\Delta\in\{\Delta',\Delta'+t/2\}}\sum_{i=1}^{z}|p_i - q_{i-\Delta}|}_{\geq t\cdot\bar{p}/2 \text{ by (16)}} \geq \frac{t}{4}\cdot\bar{p} \qquad (17)$$

Looking ahead, the lhs. of Eq. (17) will denote the expected number of times the master circuit detects an inconsistency in the experiment, while $\bar{p}$ denotes the fraction of outputs where F_1 diverts. So if the fraction of wrong outputs is larger than $4/t$, the master circuit will on average raise an alert once. To get a bound on the security the *expected* number of alerts is not relevant, only in the probability that it's larger than one, as this means that a Trojan was detected. The more fine grained statement Eq. (16) will be more useful to argue this.

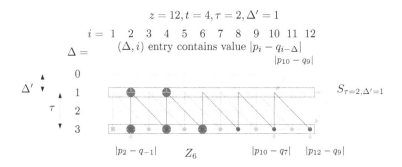

Fig. 5. Illustration of the main variables used in the proof of Lemma 5.

5   A 12-Redundant Scheme Π_{12}

In this section we define a scheme Π_{12} and we will show that the lower bound for achievable security for very simple schemes (shown in Lemma 2) is asymptotically tight. Our proof is constructive - the analysis of our Π_{12} construction shows that it is $(c, \frac{c}{T})$-Trojan resilient for suitable constants.

Our Π_{12} scheme operates with three independent input streams and one independent bit stream. On each query, every circuit in Π_{12} receives one of the three inputs and produces an output. The master circuit then checks the consistency of the outputs, i.e. verifies if there is no mismatch between any pair of circuits receiving the same input.

As stated in Sect. 1, digital Trojans mainly employ two types of strategies: time bombs (where time is measured in the number of usages) and cheat codes (as a part of the input). To counter these strategies, Π_{12} desynchronizes the circuits in two ways. First, some of the circuits are tested in the test phase for a randomly chosen time (already employed in the Π_2^* scheme). This effectively makes it difficult for time bomb Trojans to coordinate the time in which they start deviating. In Π_{12}, half of the circuits are tested for T times where T is a random variable with uniform distribution on $[t]$.

The second method of desynchronization involves using the value of the aforementioned input bit to *alternate* the way inputs are distributed among the circuits. Consequently, cheat code Trojans are rendered ineffective as only a subset of the circuits share the same input. Moreover, at any given point in time a circuit never "knows" which alternating state it is in (i.e. it does not know whether its output would be compared with deviating circuits or not).

$$x, x' \leftarrow_\$ \mathcal{X}, b \leftarrow_\$ \{0,1\}$$

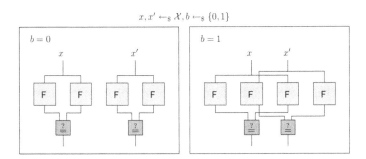

Fig. 6. In a given group of circuits, depending on the value of b, the leftmost and rightmost circuits (outer circuits) are paired with the circuits in the middle (inner circuits). Circuits in a pairing are given the same input, and their outputs are checked for equivalence.

The main building block of the Π_{12}-scheme is a group of four circuits: two outer ones and two inner ones (see Fig. 6). On each query, every group of circuits receives two inputs - the first is given to the outer circuit on the left and the second to the outer circuit on the right. Additionally, in every step a fresh decision/alternation bit b is sampled. According to its value these two inputs are given to the inner circuits. Π_{12} consists of three such groups. Crosschecks are performed whenever two distinct circuits receive the same input (both within a group and among groups).

The proof that the construction Π_{12} is actually Trojan-resilient starts with assuming that it is not secure, goes via a hybrid argument and leads to a contradiction with security of Π_2^* construction. In every hybrid we change the construction slightly by swapping some pairs of circuits, arguing that the advantage of the adversary does not change much between each successive hybrids. In the final hybrid we show that the modified construction contains Π_2^* as a subconstruction. It turns out, that any adversary who wins with reasonable good probability in the final hybrid can be used to build an adversary who breaks the security of Π_2^* which is a contradiction with Theorem 2.

5.1   The Π_{12} Scheme

We will now define our Π_{12} construction. It is illustrated in Fig. 3. We view our 12-circuit construction as three groups of four circuits each. Group 1 consists of circuits $F_1, \ldots, F_4$, group 2 consists of $F_5, \ldots, F_8$, and group 3 consists of $F_9, \ldots, F_{12}$. At the beginning the three independent and identically distributed sequences of inputs are sampled. Moreover, independent sequence of bits is sampled (it is used to alternate the inputs' distribution in the wild). For every query in the wild, the construction performs two steps: (i) the *querying step*, where the inputs are distributed to all the 12 circuits depending on the value of the corresponding bit (ii) the *cross-checking step*, where the master circuit checks the consistency of the outputs of the circuits who receive the same inputs.

Now we can take a closer look on our construction. There are three pairs of circuits that share the same input throughout the course of the game regardless of the value of the random bit (see Fig. 3). For instance, the circuit pairs (F_2, F_6), (F_3, F_{11}) and (F_7, F_{10}) share the exact same inputs throughout the game. The outer two circuits within each circuit group (circuits F_i for $i \equiv 0, 1 \mod 4$) are uniquely paired with exactly one of the middle circuits, i.e. given the same input, depending on the value of the random bit b_i sampled by the master circuit at each step of the game. For instance, in circuit group 1 if $b_i = 0$, F_1 is paired with F_2 and both circuits given x_i^1 as input, and F_4 is paired with F_3 and both given x_i^2 as input. After the querying phase, the master cross-checks the output of the circuits which share the same input streams. If any of the cross checks in any round fail, then the master aborts and the adversary looses. We now provide a more detailed description of the construction as follows:

test: In the test phase, $T^{F_1, \cdots, F_{12}, F}(T)$ picks a random Δ such that $0 \leq \Delta \leq T - 1$, then queries F_1, F_4, F_5, F_8, F_9 and F_{12} on Δ random and independent inputs $x_i^1, x_i^4, x_i^5, x_i^8, x_i^9$ and x_i^{12} respectively and checks if the outputs of the corresponding circuits are correct by comparing them with the trusted F.

master: The master samples three independent input streams $\vec{x_1} = (x_1^1, x_2^1, x_3^1, \cdots)$, $\vec{x_2} = (x_1^2, x_2^2, x_3^2, \cdots)$, $\vec{x_3} = (x_1^3, x_2^3, x_3^3, \cdots)$ and an independent bit string $\vec{b} = (b_1, b_2, \cdots)$. The operation of the master circuit is split into two phases: (i) querying phase and (ii) cross-checking phase.

Querying step. For all $i \in [Q]$, it queries the functions $F_1, F_2 \cdots, F_{12}$ as follows:

1. If $b_i = 0$,
   - The functions F_1, F_2, F_5, F_6 get x_i^1 as input,
   - The functions F_3, F_4, F_{11}, F_{12} get x_i^2 as input, and
   - The functions F_7, F_8, F_9, F_{10} get x_i^3 as input.
2. if $b_i = 1$,
   - The functions F_1, F_3, F_9, F_{11} get x_i^1 as input,
   - The functions F_2, F_4, F_6, F_8 get x_i^2 as input, and
   - The functions F_5, F_7, F_{10}, F_{12} get x_i^3 as input

Cross-Checking Step. For all $i \in [Q]$, the master circuit pairwise compares the outputs of the circuits that receive the same inputs (refer to the technical report for the details of the cross-checking phase). If at any round any of the checks fail, the master outputs abort and the adversary looses.

Output. If all the checks succeed in the cross-checking phase, the master outputs the output of the circuit F_1, i.e., $\vec{y} = F_1(\vec{x^1})$ as the output of Π_{12}.

5.2   Security of Π_{12}

In this section we prove Theorem 1, which states that the construction presented in Sect. 5.1 is $(c, \frac{c'}{T})$-secure for appropriate choice of constants c and c'. More precisely, we show that the security of the 2-circuit construction from Sect. 2.9 can be reduced to the security of the 12-circuit construction presented above. Before proceeding with the proof, we introduce some useful definitions and notations.

5.2.1 History Hardcoded Circuits and Plaits

We observe that the notation $F(x)$ for *stateful* circuits is ambiguous, since its value depends also on the *history* of queries to F (which is not provided as a parameter). We can thus assume that each F is associated with some stream $\mathbf{x} = (x_1, x_2, ...)$ and that $F(x_i) := F(x_i | x_1, x_2, ..., x_{i-1})$. This notation uniquely describes the i-th query to F given the stream $\mathbf{x}$.

In our proof we will however need a slightly different notion called *history-hardcoded circuits*. Given any stateful circuit F and two arbitrary streams $\mathbf{x} = (x_1, x_2, x_3, ...)$ and $\mathbf{w} = (w_1, w_2, w_3, ...)$, we say $F^{\mathbf{x}}$ is an $\mathbf{x}$-history-hardcoded circuit if at the i-th query it *hardcodes* the stream values $x_1, ..., x_{i-1}$ as its history and takes w_i from the stream $\mathbf{w}$ as the input to query i. Thus $F^{\mathbf{x}}$ on the i-th query with input w_i returns the value: $F^{\mathbf{x},i}(w_i) = F(w_i | x_1, x_2, ..., x_{i-1})$ and on the $i + 1$-th query returns $F^{\mathbf{x},i+1}(w_{i+1}) = F(w_{i+1} | x_1, x_2, ..., x_{i-1}, x_i)$. We call the stream $\mathbf{x}$ the *hardcoded history stream* and $\mathbf{w}$ the *input stream*.

For a random variable $\mathbf{X}$ which takes values from $\{X_1, X_2, ...\}$ and a circuit F we define another random variable $F^{\mathbf{X}}$ as follows. Its value for $\mathbf{X} = \mathbf{x}$ is simply $F^{\mathbf{x}}$. We will call this random variable an $\mathbf{X}$-*history-hardcoded* circuit. Note that as long as $F^{\mathbf{X}}$ receives inputs from a stream $\mathbf{W}$ *independent* from $\mathbf{X}$, we can say that $F^{\mathbf{x}}$ is a *history-independent* circuit.

We emphasize that when the hardcoded history stream is equal to the actual input stream, the history-hardcoded circuit returns the same results as the original stateful circuit receiving the same input stream. In other words:

$$F(X_i) = F^{\mathbf{X},i}(X_i), \tag{18}$$

for all $i \in \mathbb{N}$ with probability 1.

Another idea exploited in our construction is the concept of *alternating* inputs depending on the values of random bits. We will express this idea using the notion of $\mathbf{b}$-*plaits*, where $\mathbf{b}$ is a stream of random bits. A $\mathbf{b}$-plait of two streams $\mathbf{a}^0$ and $\mathbf{a}^1$ is a new stream $(\mathbf{a}^0 \mathbf{a}^1)_{\mathbf{b}}$, where its i-th value is either a_i^0 from stream $\mathbf{a}^0$ or a_i^1 from stream $\mathbf{a}^1$ depending on the i-th value of the *decision* stream $\mathbf{b}$. More precisely:

$$(\mathbf{a}^0 \mathbf{a}^1)_{\mathbf{b}} = (a_1^{b_1}, a_2^{b_2}, a_3^{b_3}, ...)$$

In our construction, there is only one decision stream used for every plait, therefore the $\mathbf{b}$ will be omitted for simplicity. Thus to express the plait of two streams $\mathbf{a}^0$, $\mathbf{a}^1$ we will simply write $\mathbf{a}^0\mathbf{a}^1$. A plait of two identical streams of say $\mathbf{s}$ will simply be written as $\mathbf{s}$, rather than $\mathbf{ss}$.

Similarly to $\mathbf{b}$-plaits of streams we can define the plaits of history-hardcoded circuits. Let $G_0^{\mathbf{x}^0}$ be an $\mathbf{x}^0$-history-hardcoded circuit and $G_1^{\mathbf{x}^1}$ be an $\mathbf{x}^1$-history-hardcoded circuit. We say $(G_0^{\mathbf{x}^0}G_1^{\mathbf{x}^1})_\mathbf{b}$ is $\mathbf{b}$-$plait$ for $G_0^{\mathbf{x}^0}, G_1^{\mathbf{x}^1}$ iff

$$(G_0^{\mathbf{x}^0}G_1^{\mathbf{x}^1})_\mathbf{b}^i(\mathsf{x}) = G_{b^i}^{\mathbf{x}^{b_i},i}(\mathsf{x}). \tag{19}$$

Note that the plaited circuit $(G_0^{\mathbf{x}^0}G_1^{\mathbf{x}^1})_\mathbf{b}$ can be expressed as a function of G_0, G_1 and streams $\mathbf{x}^0, \mathbf{x}^1$. Looking ahead, this notion of plaited circuits will be crucial in our final reduction of the security of Π_{12} to $\Pi_2^\star$

Finally, we define an operation on history-hardcoded circuits in the context of our construction:

$\mathsf{Swap}(F^{\mathsf{x}}, G^{\mathsf{t}})$: Given two history hardcoded circuits F^{x} and G^{t} in our construction, this operation physically exchanges the positions of both circuits. That is, that F^{t} physically replaces G^{x} and vice versa. Swapped circuits keep their histories, but since they change their place in the construction, they now receive potentially different inputs and are crosschecked with different circuits.

An important notion related to the Swap operation which we will exploit in a proof is a *red edge*. We say there is a *red edge* in the k-th query between two history hardcoded circuits F^{x} and G^{t} iff after performing the $\mathsf{Swap}(F, G)$ operation there is a change in either of the outputs of the swapped circuits on the k-th query compared to the outputs of the circuits if the Swap operation was not performed. Looking ahead, the notion of swaps and red edges would be used in our proof to show that modifying the original Π_{12} construction by some Swap operations does not change much the security parameters.

Now, given these definitions, we are ready to present an intuition that lies behind our construction. We might (and should) ask the authors "but why 12 circuits?". The reason is understandable: it is hard to perform any direct proof for history-dependent circuits; things become too complicated. Fortunately, there exist reductions. As long as we have a valid proof of Theorem 2 for history-independent circuits, we can try to find some construction of history-dependent circuits which can be reduced to it. The main goal is to design the crosschecks is such a way, that, informally speaking, making circuit *more history-dependent* make the whole construction *more secure*. It is not hard to believe in such a statement; thanks to the alternating random bit, you never know which of some two circuits will receive a specific input. If these two circuits are very history dependent and have independent histories, there is a high probability, that on the given input they would answer differently. Thank to crosschecks, the master may detect such inconsistency with high probability. To make a practical advantage of this remark, we need to perform many Swap operations and analyze the behaviour of various parameters describing our construction. We were able to handle such design and analysis for 12 circuits construction.

Now we will give a more detailed description of the intuition. As written a few lines before, the main idea of the proof is to reduce the construction which consists of (possibly) history-dependent circuits to $\Pi_2^\star$. $\Pi_2^\star$ consists of 2 history-independent circuits (alternatively speaking - pairs of circuits with different hardcoded histories, independent of the inputs that they receive). The Swap operation $\mathsf{Swap}(\mathsf{F}^\mathsf{x}, \mathsf{G}^\mathsf{t})$ is legit whenever either one of the conditions holds - the circuits F and G are engaged in the cross-checking process as pictured in the Fig. 6 (e.g. circuits F_1 and F_4 or circuits F_6 and F_7 in the Fig. 7 (Hyb_0) or the circuits received the same inputs before performing any swaps (e.g. circuits F_2 and F_7 swapped in Hyb_2 which are placed at the positions of F_2 and F_6 from Hyb_0 in the Fig. 7). Now, the main idea of the proof is that by performing a series of Swap operations on the setting with 3 rows of 4-circuit groups, we are able to end up with a setting Hyb_2 that contains 2 pairs of history-independent circuits at the place of cross-checked circuit pairs $(\mathsf{F}_1, \mathsf{F}_2)$ and $(\mathsf{F}_3, \mathsf{F}_4)$. We need just 1 Swap operation in the middle row to have history-independent circuits in the place of F_1 and F_4, but for F_2 (and F_2) we will need an additional input stream that goes with a new row.

We are now ready to proceed to the proof of Theorem 1.

5.2.2 Proof of Theorem 1

The proof of Theorem 1 proceeds in two parts. We ultimately want to prove a reduction from the security of Π_{12} to that of $\Pi_2^\star$. Nevertheless recall in Lemma 4 the security of $\Pi_2^\star$ crucially depends on history independent circuits. Thus the first part of our proof constructs a sequence of three hybrids, Hyb_0, Hyb_1, Hyb_2, to get a pair of history independent circuits, F_4^2 and $\mathsf{F}_7^3\mathsf{F}_{10}^3$, in the final hybrid. Hyb_0 is the original construction. To get from Hyb_0 to Hyb_1, we perform the Swap operation on the following pairs of circuits in Hyb_0: $(\mathsf{F}_1^1, \mathsf{F}_4^2)$; $(\mathsf{F}_6^{12}, \mathsf{F}_7^3)$; $(\mathsf{F}_{10}^3, \mathsf{F}_{11}^{21})$. To get from Hyb_1 to Hyb_2, we perform the Swap operation on the following pairs of circuits in Hyb_1: $(\mathsf{F}_2^{12}, \mathsf{F}_7^3)$; $(\mathsf{F}_3^{21}, \mathsf{F}_{10}^3)$ (refer to Fig. 7). Note that in the final hybrid Hyb_2, it is crucial that F_4^2 and $\mathsf{F}_7^3\mathsf{F}_{10}^3$ are not just history independent, but also take in the same inputs from input stream $\mathbf{1}$ regardless of the value of the random bit ($\mathsf{F}_7^3\mathsf{F}_{10}^3$ takes inputs from stream $\mathbf{1}$ due to the definition of plaited circuit in (19)). This will be necessary for the second part of our proof which uses F_4^2 and $\mathsf{F}_7^3\mathsf{F}_{10}^3$ in the final hybrid as the two history independent circuits needed for the $\Pi_2^\star$ construction and uses the $\Pi_2^\star$ construction with these circuits as a subroutine.

Proof. For a given $\mathsf{F}_1, ..., \mathsf{F}_{12}$, we can define some random variables as follows. Let $\phi_{\mathsf{F}_j^\mathsf{A};\mathbf{B}}$ be the total number of queries, where F_j^A gets input from a stream $\mathbf{B}$ and has a mismatch with any other circuit getting input from the same stream in this query. We will refer to random variables related to the i-th hybrid by adding a superscript i. For example, $\phi_{\mathsf{F}_1^1;\mathbf{2}}^0 = 0$, since in Hyb_0 no crosschecks are made between F_1^1 and the circuits receiving inputs from stream $\mathbf{2}$. Let Φ be the total number of mismatches detected by the master circuit. Recall from Sect. 2.3 that Y is the total number of mistakes the master circuit makes. The probability

Hyb$_0$

F_5^{13}	F_6^{12}	F_7^3	F_8^{32}
13	12	3	32
F_1^1	F_2^{12}	F_3^{21}	F_4^2
1	12	21	2
F_9^{31}	F_{10}^3	F_{11}^{21}	F_{12}^{23}
31	3	21	23

Hyb$_1$

F_5^{13}	F_7^3	F_6^{12}	F_8^{32}
13	12	3	32
F_4^2	F_2^{12}	F_3^{21}	F_1^1
1	12	21	2
F_9^{31}	F_{11}^{21}	F_{10}^3	F_{12}^{23}
31	3	21	23

Hyb$_2$

F_5^{13}	F_2^{12}	F_6^{12}	F_8^{32}
13	12	3	32
F_4^2	F_7^3	F_{10}^3	F_1^1
1	12	21	2
F_9^{31}	F_{11}^{21}	F_3^{21}	F_{12}^{23}
31	3	21	23

Fig. 7. Hybrids with the circuits and their corresponding plaited hardcoded history and input streams (above and below each circuit in black respectively). In Hyb$_2$, F_4^2 and the plaited circuit $F_7^3 F_{10}^3$ (in red) are history independent. (Color figure online)

space of these random variables is the set of all choices of a stream of random bits **b** and streams of random inputs **1, 2, 3** and a number of tests Δ.

We prove our statement by contradiction. To this end, we assume that

$$\exists_{c>0} \forall_{c'>0, T_0 \in \mathbb{N}, q \in poly} \exists_{T>T_0, Q>q(T)} \exists\mathsf{Adv} \text{ such that}$$
$$\mathsf{Adv}\left(c, \tfrac{c'}{T}\right) -\text{wins} \quad \mathsf{TrojanGame}(\Pi_{12}, T, Q) \tag{20}$$

Therefore for some c and for all c' there exists an infinite set $\mathcal{T} \subset \mathbb{N}$ such that for every $t \in \mathcal{T}$ there exists an infinite set $\mathcal{Q}_t \subset \mathbb{N}$ such that for every $t \in \mathcal{T}, z \in \mathcal{Q}_t$ there exists an adversary $\mathsf{Adv} = \mathsf{Adv}(c, c', z, t)$ such that the following formula is true:

$$\Pr\left[\Phi^0 = 0 \quad \text{and} \quad Y^0 \geq c' \cdot \left(\frac{z}{t}\right)\right] \geq c. \tag{21}$$

Now we will look what happens to inequality (21) as we move through each hybrid:

Hyb$_0$: Hybrid 0 corresponds to the original construction due to equality (18). Hence, the probability that the adversary $\mathsf{Adv}(c, c', z, t)$ wins in this hybrid is precisely that in Eq. (21).

Hyb$_1$: In this hybrid we simply perform three Swap operations on the following pairs of circuits: (F_1^1, F_4^2); (F_6^{12}, F_7^3); (F_{10}^3, F_{11}^{21}).

Claim. $\Pr\left[\phi_{F_4^2,1}^1, \phi_{F_7^3,12}^1, \phi_{F_{10}^3,21}^1 \leq k \wedge \Phi^0 = 0 \wedge Y^1 \geq c' \cdot (\frac{z}{t}) - 3k\right] \geq c - 3 \cdot 2^{-k}.$

Proof of the claim is in the technical report.

Hyb$_2$: In this hybrid we simply perform two Swap operations on the following pairs of circuits: (F_2^{12}, F_7^3); (F_3^{21}, F_{10}^3).

Claim.
$$\Pr\left[(\phi^2_{\mathsf{F}^2_4,1} \le 3k) \wedge (Y^2 \ge c'(\tfrac{z}{t}) - 5k)\right] \ge c - 3 \cdot 2^{-k}. \tag{22}$$

Proof. Every Swap operation performed in Hyb_2 changes the value of $Y^2, \phi^2_{\mathsf{F}^2_4,1}$ by at most k (since inequality (refer to our extended technical report for details) holds). The inequality is explicit. $\triangle$

Claim. For every $k \in \mathbb{N}$ and every adversary Adv who $(c, \tfrac{c'}{t})$-wins (Π_{12}, T, Q) − TrojanGame there exists an adversary Adv' who $(c - 3 \cdot 2^{-k}, \tfrac{c'}{t} - \tfrac{5k}{z})$-$(3k+1)$-wins the game $\mathsf{TrojanGame}(\Pi^\star_2, T, Q)$.

We want to conclude, that the above statement contradicts Lemma 4. So we want to show, that this incorrect statement is implied by our construction.

$$\exists_{\tilde{c}>0} \forall_{\tilde{c}'>0, T_0 \in \mathbb{N}, q \in poly} \exists_{T>T_0, Q>q(T)} \exists_{\widetilde{\mathsf{Adv}}} \text{ such that}$$
$$\widetilde{\mathsf{Adv}} \quad (\tilde{c}, \tfrac{\tilde{c}'}{T})-\text{wins} \quad \mathsf{TrojanGame}(\Pi^\star_2, T, Q). \tag{23}$$

Let $k = 2 + \log(\tfrac{1}{c})$ and $\tilde{c} = c - 3 \cdot 2^{-k} = \tfrac{c}{4} > 0$. Choose $\tilde{c}'$ arbitrarily and let $c' = \cdot\tilde{c}'$. Let $\tilde{T} = T$. Let

$$\widetilde{Q_t} = \{z \in Q_t : z > t\left(\frac{5k}{\tilde{c}'} + 1\right)\}.$$

Obviously $\widetilde{Q_t}$ is infinite. As a result, for every $q \in poly$ there exists $z \in \widetilde{Q_t}$ such that $z > q(t)$.

Now we can construct the adversary $\widetilde{\mathsf{Adv}}$ which would break the security of $\Pi^\star_2$ which lead us to contradiction. Thanks to the analysis of the hybrids we know, that for Adv the inequality (22) holds. Define the circuits $\widetilde{\mathsf{F}_1}, \widetilde{\mathsf{F}_2}$ given to $\widetilde{\mathsf{Adv}}$ in the following way:

$$\widetilde{\mathsf{F}_1} = \mathsf{F}^2_4, \quad \widetilde{\mathsf{F}_2} = \mathsf{F}^3_7\mathsf{F}^3_{10},$$

where the latter is a **b**-plait (as defined in Eq. (19)). Actual values of streams **2, 3, b** are sampled uniformly and independently by $\widetilde{\mathsf{Adv}}$, and hardcoded in $\widetilde{\mathsf{F}_1}, \widetilde{\mathsf{F}_2}$. Obviously $\widetilde{\mathsf{F}_1}, \widetilde{\mathsf{F}_2}$ are history independent, therefore $\widetilde{\mathsf{Adv}}$ meets the requirements for the $\Pi^\star_2$ scheme.

Now we can bound a random variable $\widetilde{\Phi}$ - the number of queries in a $(\Pi^\star_2, T, Q)$ − TrojanGame where the adversary is caught on deviating. If $\phi^2_{\mathsf{F}^2_4,1} \le 3k$, then $\widetilde{\Phi} \le 3k$, since if in the i-th query there was any inconsistency between $\widetilde{\mathsf{F}_1}, \widetilde{\mathsf{F}_2}$, there must had been a mismatch between F^3_4 and any other circuit receiving the same input. Which concludes in:

$$\tilde{c} = c - 3 \cdot 2^{-k} \le \Pr\left[(\phi^2_{\mathsf{F}^2_4,1} \le 3k) \wedge (Y^2 \ge c'(\tfrac{z}{t}) - 5k)\right]$$
$$\le \Pr\left[\widetilde{\Phi} \le 3k \wedge (\widetilde{Y} \ge c'(\tfrac{z}{t}) - 5k)\right]$$
$$\le \Pr\left[\widetilde{\Phi} \le 3k \wedge (\widetilde{Y} \ge \tilde{c}(\tfrac{5k}{\tilde{c}'} + 1) - 5k = \tilde{c}')\right].$$

Note that $\widetilde{Y}$ is the number of mistakes made by the master circuit in the $\mathsf{TrojanGame}(\Pi_2^\star, T, Q)$ and the last inequality comes from $z > t\left(\frac{5k}{c'} + 1\right)$. We conclude, that that there exists $\tilde{c}$, such that for *every* $\tilde{c}'$ there exists $\widetilde{\mathsf{Adv}}$ who $(\tilde{c}, \frac{\tilde{c}'}{t})$-$(3k+1)$-wins $\mathsf{TrojanGame}(\Pi_2^\star, T, Q)$. It is with contradiction with Lemma 4, which ends the proof. □

5.3 Reapplying the Hybrid Argument

In the previous section, we have used the outputs produced on the input stream **1** in place of F_1 as an output stream of the construction. By symmetry, the argument from the previous section works for the input stream **2** in place of F_4. Now we will show that in fact the outputs from F_5 or F_8 may be used as an output stream of the construction, which also implies the possibility of using input stream **3** to produce the output stream of the construction.

Now, in Hyb_0 (Fig. 7) firstly swapping the labels of the input streams **3** and **2** on the input bit 0 and the labels of the input streams **3** and **1** on the input bit 1 and secondly visually swapping the rows 1 and 2 does not change the setting. We achieve the Hyb_0'' construction as shown in Fig. 8.

Hyb_0''

F_1^{13} 13	F_2^{12} 12	F_3^{3} 3	F_4^{32} 32
F_5^{1} 1	F_6^{12} 12	F_7^{21} 21	F_8^{2} 2
F_9^{23} 23	F_{10}^{21} 21	F_{11}^{3} 3	F_{12}^{31} 31

Fig. 8. Hyb_0'' construction.

We can still reapply the hybrid argument from the previous section to the modified Hyb_0'' construction by applying the following swaps. $\mathsf{Hyb}_0'' \rightarrow \mathsf{Hyb}_1''$ *swaps* : $(\mathsf{F}_5^{\mathbf{1}}, \mathsf{F}_8^{\mathbf{2}})$; $(\mathsf{F}_2^{\mathbf{12}}, \mathsf{F}_3^{\mathbf{3}})$; $(\mathsf{F}_{11}^{\mathbf{3}}, \mathsf{F}_{10}^{\mathbf{21}})$. $\mathsf{Hyb}_1'' \rightarrow \mathsf{Hyb}_2''$ *swaps* : $(\mathsf{F}_3^{\mathbf{12}}, \mathsf{F}_6^{\mathbf{3}})$; $(\mathsf{F}_7^{\mathbf{21}}, \mathsf{F}_{11}^{\mathbf{3}})$. Finally we conclude that the output streams of either F_5 or F_8 (by symmetry) may be used as an output stream of the construction, what implies that by taking outputs from circuit F_8 on input bit 0 and circuit F_5 on input bit 1 could be used as an output of the construction produced with input stream **3**.

The above argument implies that in each round our construction may output 3 outputs produced by consuming inputs from the same number of 3 input streams.

6 Outlook and Open Problems

In this work we introduced countermeasures against hardware Trojans which compared to existing solutions based on multiparty or verifiable computation are extremely simple and efficient, but only achieve limited security guarantees (i.e., we only guarantee that *most* outputs are correct or the Trojan is detected with high probability) in a restricted setting (iid inputs and no evolving state).

Because of this, the scope of application for our schemes is limited, but as discussed in the introduction, we believe they will serve as a first but major step towards solving some of the main application targets like randomness generation. In particular, creating pseudorandomness for "randomness hungry" side-channel countermeasures like masking in a Trojan-resilient way is one of the main motivations for this work. The reason our simple schemes are a promising starting point towards Trojan-resilient pseudorandomness generation is the fact that in most settings (like masking) one does not need that the pseudorandomness is correctly generated, only that it is indistinguishable from uniform, so the relaxed security of our schemes is not a deal breaker. Another reason is the fact that one could use some of the pseudorandomness that is created to implement the master's randomness source, thus making it deterministic. Fleshing these ideas out will require a better understanding of amplification and circularity issues in this setting.

The main concrete technical question left open problem in this work is to prove the security of the "minimal" and thus really practical scheme Π_2^ϕ as stated in Conjecture 1. A positive resolution of the conjecture will need techniques that go beyond our proof via history-independence used in the proof for Π_{12}.

References

1. Adee, S.: The hunt for the kill switch, spectrum (2008). https://tinyurl.com/j95zbmxa
2. Ateniese, G., Kiayias, A., Magri, B., Tselekounis, Y., Venturi, D.: Secure outsourcing of cryptographic circuits manufacturing. In: Baek, J., Susilo, W., Kim, J. (eds.) ProvSec 2018. LNCS, vol. 11192, pp. 75–93. Springer, Cham (2018). https://doi.org/10.1007/978-3-030-01446-9_5
3. Bitansky, N., Canetti, R., Chiesa, A., Tromer, E.: From extractable collision resistance to succinct non-interactive arguments of knowledge, and back again. In: Goldwasser, S. (ed.) ITCS, pp. 326–349. ACM (2012). https://doi.org/10.1145/2090236.2090263
4. Cramer, R., Damgård, I., Nielsen, J.B.: Secure Multiparty Computation and Secret Sharing. Cambridge University Press, Cambridge (2015). http://www.cambridge.org/de/academic/subjects/computer-science/cryptography-cryptology-and-coding/secure-multiparty-computation-and-secret-sharing?format=HB&isbn=9781107043053
5. Dziembowski, S., Faust, S., Standaert, F.: Private circuits III: hardware trojan-resilience via testing amplification. In: Weippl, E.R., Katzenbeisser, S., Kruegel, C., Myers, A.C., Halevi, S. (eds.) ACM CCS, pp. 142–153. ACM (2016). https://doi.org/10.1145/2976749.2978419

6. Dziembowski, S., Pietrzak, K.: Leakage-resilient cryptography. In: FOCS, pp. 293–302. IEEE Computer Society (2008). https://doi.org/10.1109/FOCS.2008.56

7. Gennaro, R., Lysyanskaya, A., Malkin, T., Micali, S., Rabin, T.: Algorithmic Tamper-Proof (ATP) security: theoretical foundations for security against hardware tampering. In: Naor, M. (ed.) TCC 2004. LNCS, vol. 2951, pp. 258–277. Springer, Heidelberg (2004). https://doi.org/10.1007/978-3-540-24638-1_15

8. Ishai, Y., Sahai, A., Wagner, D.: Private circuits: securing hardware against probing attacks. In: Boneh, D. (ed.) CRYPTO 2003. LNCS, vol. 2729, pp. 463–481. Springer, Heidelberg (2003). https://doi.org/10.1007/978-3-540-45146-4_27

9. Kocher, P.C.: Timing attacks on implementations of Diffie-Hellman, RSA, DSS, and other systems. In: Koblitz, N. (ed.) CRYPTO 1996. LNCS, vol. 1109, pp. 104–113. Springer, Heidelberg (1996). https://doi.org/10.1007/3-540-68697-5_9

10. Kocher, P., Jaffe, J., Jun, B.: Differential power analysis. In: Wiener, M. (ed.) CRYPTO 1999. LNCS, vol. 1666, pp. 388–397. Springer, Heidelberg (1999). https://doi.org/10.1007/3-540-48405-1_25

11. Maurer, U., Pietrzak, K., Renner, R.: Indistinguishability amplification. In: Menezes, A. (ed.) CRYPTO 2007. LNCS, vol. 4622, pp. 130–149. Springer, Heidelberg (2007). https://doi.org/10.1007/978-3-540-74143-5_8

12. Mitra, S., Wong, H.S.P., Wong, S.: Stopping hardware trojans in their tracks, spectrum (2015). https://tinyurl.com/5emst8f2

13. Mukhopadhyay, D., Chakraborty, R.S.: Hardware Security: Design, Threats, and Safeguards, 1st edn. Chapman & Hall/CRC, Boca Raton (2014)

14. Pietrzak, K.: A leakage-resilient mode of operation. In: Joux, A. (ed.) EUROCRYPT 2009. LNCS, vol. 5479, pp. 462–482. Springer, Heidelberg (2009). https://doi.org/10.1007/978-3-642-01001-9_27

15. Standaert, F.-X., Malkin, T.G., Yung, M.: A unified framework for the analysis of side-channel key recovery attacks. In: Joux, A. (ed.) EUROCRYPT 2009. LNCS, vol. 5479, pp. 443–461. Springer, Heidelberg (2009). https://doi.org/10.1007/978-3-642-01001-9_26

16. Tehranipoor, M., Salmani, H., Zhang, X.: Integrated Circuit Authentication: Hardware Trojans and Counterfeit Detection. Springer, Cham (2013). https://doi.org/10.1007/978-3-319-00816-5

17. Wahby, R.S., Howald, M., Garg, S., Shelat, A., Walfish, M.: Verifiable ASICs. In: IEEE SP, pp. 759–778. IEEE Computer Society (2016). https://doi.org/10.1109/SP.2016.51

On Derandomizing Yao's Weak-to-Strong OWF Construction

Chris Brzuska[1]([✉]), Geoffroy Couteau[2], Pihla Karanko[1], and Felix Rohrbach[3]

[1] Aalto University, Espoo, Finland
{chris.brzuska,pihla.karanko}@aalto.fi
[2] IRIF, CNRS, Paris, France
geoffroy.couteau@ens.fr
[3] TU Darmstadt, Darmstadt, Germany
felix.rohrbach@cryptoplexity.de

Abstract. The celebrated result of Yao (Yao, FOCS'82) shows that concatenating $n \cdot p(n)$ copies of a weak one-way function (OWF) f, which can be inverted with probability $1 - \frac{1}{p(n)}$, suffices to construct a strong OWF g, showing that weak and strong OWFs are black-box equivalent. This direct product theorem for hardness amplification of OWFs has been very influential. However, the construction of Yao is not *security-preserving*, i.e., the input to g needs to be much larger than the input to f. Understanding whether a larger input is inherent is a long-standing open question.

In this work, we explore necessary features of constructions which achieve short input length by proving the following: for any *direct product* construction of a strong OWF g from a weak OWF f, which can be inverted with probability $1 - \frac{1}{p(n)}$, the input size of g must grow as $\Omega(p(n))$. By direct product construction, we refer to any construction with the following structure: the construction g executes some arbitrary pre-processing function (independent of f) on its input, obtaining a vector $(y_1, \cdots, y_l)$, and outputs $f(y_1), \cdots, f(y_l)$. Note that Yao's construction is obtained by setting the pre-processing to be the identity. Our result generalizes to functions g with post-processing, as long as the post-processing function is not too lossy. Thus, in essence, any weak-to-strong OWF hardness amplification must either (1) be very far from security-preserving, (2) use adaptivity, or (3) must be very far from a *direct-product* structure (in the sense of having a very lossy post-processing of the outputs of f).

On a technical level, we use ideas from lower bounds for secret-sharing to prove the impossibility of derandomizing Yao in a black-box way. Our results are in line with Goldreich, Impagliazzo, Levin, Venkatesan, and Zuckerman (FOCS 1990) who derandomize Yao's construction for *regular* weak OWFs by evaluating the OWF along a random walk on an expander graph—the construction is adaptive, since it alternates steps on the expander graph with evaluations of the weak OWF.

1 Introduction

In this work, we continue the study of constructions of strong one-way functions (OWFs) from weak OWFs. The classical weak-to-strong hardness amplification

© International Association for Cryptologic Research 2021
K. Nissim and B. Waters (Eds.): TCC 2021, LNCS 13043, pp. 429–456, 2021.
https://doi.org/10.1007/978-3-030-90453-1_15

technique, due to Yao [40], uses direct product amplification which is not security preserving[1]. Our main result shows that the increase in the input size is inherent for *direct product* constructions. Namely, any direct product black-box construction of a strong OWF from a $(1 - 1/p(n))$-weak OWF must have input length at least $\Omega(p(n))$.

Weak and Strong OWFs. An $\alpha(n)$-secure OWF $f : \{0,1\}^n \mapsto \{0,1\}$ is an efficiently computable function such that any probabilistic polynomial-time adversaries $\mathcal{A}$ can invert f with probability at most $\alpha(n)$. When α is a negligible function, we say that f is a *strong* OWF; when $\alpha(n) = 1-1/p(n)$ for a polynomial p, we say that f is a *weak* OWF. The seminal work of Yao [40] shows that weak OWFs imply strong OWFs, via a standard *direct product* hardness amplification: given a weak OWF f, define $g(x_1, ..., x_l) = f(x_1)||...||f(x_l)$. Then, Yao proved that g is a strong OWF for $l > |x_i| p(|x_i|)$.

Adaptive vs. Non-adaptive Construction. In this paper we study *non-adaptive* weak-to-strong OWF constructions, that is, constructions where the calls to the weak OWF can be made in parallel. I.e., a strong OWF construction g that makes calls to a weak OWF f is called *non-adaptive* if g's calls to f only depend on g's input, but not on the output of f on any of these inputs. Yao's construction is a simple, non-adaptive construction where each call to f is an independent chunk of the input. In general, non-adaptive constructions can make correlated calls to f though.

We say that a construction is *adaptive*, if the output of (at least) one call to f is used to determine the input to another f call. That is, adaptive constructions cannot compute all calls to f in parallel. For the toy constructions on the right, g_1 is non-adaptive (it does not matter whether g_1 computes $f(x)$ or $f(x + 1)$ first) and g_2 is adaptive (g_2 must make the inner f call first).

$$g_1(x) := f(x)||f(x + 1)$$
$$g_2(x) := f(f(x))$$

On the (in)efficiency of Yao's Construction. The construction of Yao is generic: it turns an *arbitrary* weak OWF f into a strong OWF g and just depends on the hardness of f. In addition, g has an appealing simple direct-product structure. In turn, g is suboptimal w.r.t. its computational complexity:

1. g makes a *large number of calls* to the underlying weak OWF, and
2. g is *not security preserving*, in that the input length of g is polynomially larger than the input length of f.

Many celebrated cryptographic reductions are similarly not security-preserving and have a high number of calls—the HILL construction of pseudorandom generator from any OWF being perhaps one of the most well-known examples [14].

---

[1] In a security-preserving construction, the input length of the strong OWF is linear in that of the weak OWF.

In beautiful works, a decade ago, Haitner, Reingold, Vadhan and Zheng [13,36] developed rich tools for computational entropy, and improved the original n^8 seed length by HILL to $\mathcal{O}(n^3)$, where n is the input length of the OWF—since further improvements seem extremely hard to obtain, it is natural to ask whether large lower bounds on the input size are inherent.

In a seminal result [19], Impagliazzo and Rudich [19] formalize the notions of *black-box* constructions/reductions, and develop methods to establish their limitations. Informally, a (fully) black-box construction of a primitive C from a primitive P treats both P and any adversary $\mathcal{A}$ against P in a black-box way. Following this breakthrough result, a long line of work (see [6,8,9,23,24, 26,27,38]) has been devoted to proving limitations on the *efficiency* of black-box reductions. Our work continues this successful line of work.

To our knowledge, three previous works study black-box limitations on the efficiency of Yao's construction. Lin, Trevisan, and Wee [24] address the first of the two limitations above: they show that any fully black-box construction of an $\varepsilon(n)$-secure OWF from a $(1 - \delta(n))$-secure OWF f must make at least $q = \Omega((1/\delta) \cdot \log(1/\varepsilon))$ calls to f. They also show that fully black-box construction cannot be perfectly security-preserving: if f has input size n, the input size of the strong OWF must be at least $n + \Omega(\log 1/\varepsilon) - O(\log q)$. The work of [26] showed that *non-adaptive* fully black-box construction (i.e., a construction where all the calls to f are made in parallel) cannot amplify security beyond $\mathsf{poly}(n)$ if the algorithm implementing the reduction has constant depth, and its size is below $2^{\mathsf{poly}(n)}$. Eventually, the work of [27] extended the results of [24] to the weakly black-box setting with bounded non-uniformity.

1.1   On Security-Preserving Amplification of Weak OWFs

The above result leaves open one of the most intriguing limitations of Yao's construction: the fact that it causes a polynomial blowup in the input size. While [24] shows that *some* blowup in the input size is available, it leaves a huge gap: starting with a $(1 - 1/p(n))$-secure OWF f with input length n, Yao's construction requires an input size $n^2 \cdot p(n)$ to build *any* strong OWF, while the result of [24] only shows that to build an *extremely strong* OWF, say a $2^{-\mu \cdot n}$-secure OWF (for some constant μ), one needs input size at least $(1+\mu) \cdot n - \log p$.

In a sense, the proof of [24] cannot do much better, because it also applies to the setting of *regular* one-way functions (where outputs have the same number of preimages), and rules out even *adaptive* fully black-box reductions. However, in this setting, it is actually known that we can do much better than Yao's construction and obtain an almost security-preserving construction, if we start from a regular weak OWF, and use adaptivity. Indeed, the work of [10] provides precisely such a construction, using random walks on expander graphs.

This leaves us in between two extremes: on the one hand, Yao's construction is non-adaptive (hence optimally parallelizable: if one starts with a parallelizable weak OWF, one ends up with a parallelizable strong OWF), extremely simple (it has a straightforward direct product structure) and works for arbitrary OWFs; however, it is not security-preserving. On the other hand, the construction of Goldreich, Impagliazzo, Levin, Venkatesan, and Zuckerman [10] is almost security-preserving, but is considerably more involved, requires adaptive calls, and works only for regular OWFs. Improving this state of affair is a long-standing and intriguing open problem.

1.2   Our Contribution

In this work, we make progress on this problem. Specifically, we show that any relativizing *direct product* black-box construction of strong OWF from a $(1 - 1/p(n))$-secure OWF cannot be security preserving, in a strong sense: it requires an input length of at least $\Omega(p(n))$. While this still leaves a gap with respect to Yao's construction, which has input length $O(n^2 \cdot p(n))$, this gap vanishes asymptotically when p grows. By *direct product* construction, we mean a construction g of strong OWF with the following structure: on input x, $g(x)$ outputs $(f(y_1), \cdots, f(y_\ell))$, where f is the weak OWF, and $(y_1, \cdots, y_\ell)$ are computed from x arbitrarily, but without calling f (we call the mapping from x to $(y_1, \cdots, y_\ell)$ the *pre-processing*). This is a natural generalization of *Yao-style* constructions of strong OWFs (we recover Yao's construction by letting the pre-processing be the identity function). Furthermore, our result generalizes to the setting where some post-processing (independent of f) is applied to the outputs $(f(y_1), \cdots, f(y_\ell))$, whenever this post-processing is *not too lossy*: we prove that whenever each output of the post-processing has at most polynomially many preimages, the same $\Omega(p(n))$ input length bound holds. We summarize the results in the following informal theorem:

Theorem 1. *Let f be a $(1 - 1/p(n))$-secure OWF (a weak OWF). Let g be any non-adaptive construction, with not-too-compressing post-processing, of input length $< cp(n)$, for certain constant c. Then, it is impossible to prove, in a relativizing fully black-box way, that g is a strong OWF.*

Observe that if we could generalize our result to arbitrary (f-independent) post-processing functions, the above would capture all non-adaptive constructions. Hence, in essence, our result says the following: any (fully black-box) construction of strong OWF from a weak OWF must either (1) be very far from security preserving, or (2) use adaptivity, or (3) compute a highly non-injective function of the outputs of the non-adaptive calls (i.e., be very far from a "direct product" structure).

1.3   Relation to Correlated-Product and Correlated-Input Security

Usually, parallel concatenation of cryptographic primitives on *independent* inputs preserves security. For example, if f and g are one-way functions, then so is $(x_1, x_2) \mapsto (f(x_1), g(x_2))$. However, things might potentially change radically when x_1 and x_2 are not sampled independently, but are instead *correlated*, e.g., sampled jointly from a high min-entropy source. Variants of this problem have been studied on many occasions in cryptography, and have profound connections to the feasibility of cryptography with weak sources of randomness, leakage-resilient cryptography, related-key attacks, or deterministic encryption (to name a few); see e.g. [39] for discussions on cryptography with correlated sources. In addition, security for correlated inputs has proven to be a very useful assumption by itself: one-wayness under correlated product (i.e., one-wayness of $f(x_1), \cdots, f(x_k)$ for $(x_1, \cdots, x_k)$ sampled from a joint distribution) has been used to build CCA secure cryptosystems [16,30], and correlated-input secure hash functions have found numerous applications such as OT extension [22], trapdoor hash function [7], constrained pseudorandom functions [1], password-based login [12], and many more.

A general and natural question to ask is: which type of constructions *preserve* hardness, when the inputs are jointly sampled from a high min-entropy source, rather than being sampled independently? This is a fundamental question in itself, because this setting occurs in real-life use of standard cryptographic construction (when they are misused, when the source of randomness is imperfect, or when the adversary has access to some leakage on the inputs), but also due to the many applications outlined above.

It is well-known that not all constructions will preserve security under correlated inputs. For example, even though the map $x \mapsto x^e \bmod n$ is believed to be one-way when n is a product of two large safe primes (this is the RSA assumption), the extended euclidean algorithm provides an efficient inverter for the map $x \mapsto (x^{e_1}, x^{e_2}) \bmod n$ whenever $\gcd(e_1, e_2) = 1$ (this example is taken from [16]). Hence, there are specific functions f_i (here, $f_i : x \mapsto x^{e_i}$) and specific correlations of the inputs (here, the equality correlation: the same input x is used for all functions) such that correlated-product security breaks down. However, this leaves open the possibility that some specific input correlations preserve correlated-product security (for example, this is the case when the correlated-inputs are indistinguishable from random, e.g. when sampled as the output of a PRG), or that some specific functions maintain correlated-product security for general correlations.

Our results can be cast in the context of correlated-product security: we show that even though Yao's construction of OWF, which is a very natural and seminal construction, is provably secure (with a black-box proof) when used with random and independent inputs, it breaks down for *any possible correlated source*, whenever the entropy of the source is below $p(n)$. This provides a natural example of a construction, from a weak OWF f, where correlated-product security cannot be generically shown to hold (in a black-box way) for *arbitrary* sources, unless they contain enough entropy such that all of the correlated inputs can have independent entropy. In contrast, [30] shows that when f is instantiated as a *lossy trapdoor function*, then $f(x_1), \cdots, f(x_k)$ is one-way for correlated inputs $(x_1, \cdots, x_k)$, and [16] shows that assuming OWFs, there *exists* a correlated-product secure function. Our results provide a partial complementary perspective to this line of work.

Comparison to [39]. Wichs [39] also studies, among other questions, the one-wayness of constructions of the form $(f(x_1), \cdots, f(x_k))$ for inputs $(x_1, \cdots, x_k)$ sampled from a correlated source. Our results are incomparable: we show that for a *generic weak OWF* f, and for any *fixed* distribution over the inputs $(x_1, \cdots, x_k)$ with $o(k)$ bits of entropy, the one-wayness of $f(x_1), \cdots, f(x_k)$ does not follow from that of f in a black-box way. In contrast, [39] shows that for an *arbitrary function* f, there is no black-box reduction (to any standard hardness assumption) of one-wayness of $(f(x_1), \cdots, f(x_k))$ when the x_i can come from *arbitrarily correlated distributions*, even with high per-input entropy. That is, [39] handles a considerably larger class of constructions and reductions to many possible assumptions, but only rules out a much more stringent security notion (where one-wayness must hold even when the input distributions are not fixed a priori and can be correlated arbitrarily).

1.4 Related Works

We already pointed out to numerous related works on bounding the efficiency of black-box reductions [6,8,9,23,24,26,27,38], including some specifically targeting hardness amplifications of one-way functions, and related works on correlated-product security. Besides, our black-box separations use some established tools (in addition to key new technical insights, which we cover afterwards) such as the two-oracle technique of [17,32] where one oracle implements the base primitive and the second oracle breaks all constructions built from this primitive. We use Borel-Cantelli style technique from [28] to extract a single oracle from a distribution of random oracles analogously to the seminal work on black-box separations by Impagliazzo and Rudich [19].

   Hardness amplification of functions, via direct products and related constructions, have a rich and dense history, which goes well beyond one-way functions and is too vast to be covered here. In particular, amplifying the hardness of *computing* boolean functions (rather than inverting functions) using direct product constructions is at the heart of rich lines of work on worst-case to average-case reductions, constructions of non-cryptographic pseudorandom generators, circuit lower bounds, and many more – see e.g. [2,3,11,15,18,21,25,31,33–35,37] and references therein.

1.5 Technical Overview

To prove our black-box separations, we exhibit an oracle relative to which there is a weak one-way function, yet all strong one-way functions with an appropriate structure can be inverted efficiently with constant probability. The standard method to do so is to design oracles relative to which the starting primitive (here, the weak one-way function) clearly exists and is the *only possible source of hardness*. For example, in the seminal work by Impagliazzo and Rudich (IR) on the separation of key exchange from OWFs [20], IR introduce a random oracle, which is a strong OWF with high probability, as well as assuming $\mathsf{P} = \mathsf{NP}$, thereby ruling out most other (stronger) cryptographic primitives. In our setting, we instantiate this intuition by choosing three oracles:

(1) A PSPACE oracle, which *destroys* all possible sources of hardness,

(2) a random oracle F, which instantiates the weak OWF, and
(3) an inverter INV, which inverts F on a (roughly) $1-1/p$ fraction of its inputs, effectively turning it into a weak OWF. Note that a random oracle F alone would already be a strong OWF, if we did not weaken it by adding INV.

In this oracle world, we consider *non-adaptive* constructions of strong OWFs g from the weak OWF F. Since we wish to rule out (relativizing) *fully black-box* reductions (as defined by Reingold, Trevisan and Vadhan [29]), we do not give g access to INV. In fact, this is inherent in our setting: observe that given access to INV, it is not too hard to build a strong OWF (e.g. the strong OWF can perform a random walk starting from the input x, until it lands on a hard input y – which can be tested using INV – and outputs $F(y)$). In general, whenever one can efficiently test which inputs are hard, constructing a security-preserving OWF becomes feasible – and it is precisely the lack of any such tester that makes it highly nontrivial to improve over Yao's seminal construction. Since we rule out fully black-box reductions, we do not let g access INV and thus, g does not know where the easy inputs are.

Modeling Non-adaptive Constructions. Non-adaptive construction can be thought of as a circuit which first has a pre-processing layer, followed by a layer of parallel calls to a weak OWFs and then some post-processing, see Fig. 1. When the construction omits the post-processing layer, as in Yao's construction, this corresponds to a *direct product* construction. The input size n of the construction might be different from the input size m of the weak OWF. As a starting point, we consider what happens when the construction does not use any post-processing, as is the case in Yao's construction. When there is no post-processing, the additional data d in Fig. 1 only reduces the input domain and does not add any security. Thus, w.l.o.g., we assume that there is no d.

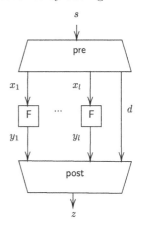

$g(s)$
_____
$x_1, ..., x_l, d \leftarrow \mathsf{pre}(s)$
for $i = 1..l$
  $y_i \leftarrow \mathsf{F}(x_i)$
$z \leftarrow \mathsf{post}(y_1, ..., y_l, d)$
return z

Fig. 1. (n, m)-non-adaptive construction. F is the weak OWF. Length of d can be arbitrary, $|x_i| = |y_i| = m$ and $|s| = n$.

Inverting Direct Product Constructions. Considering the simple case with no post-processing and no d, the first observation is that g must make more than $p(m)$ calls to the weak OWF, since otherwise *all* the calls will be easy to invert with constant probability. In that case the adversary could simply invert all the weak OWF calls and then use PSPACE to invert the pre-processing layer, thus inverting g with constant probability.

Now that g makes at least $p(m)$ calls to the weak OWF, we can make the main observation of the paper: if we can invert a $1-1/p(m)$ fraction of the weak

OWF calls and n is slightly smaller than $p(m)$, then the remaining entropy of the input s cannot be very high, on the average. This is formalized in Lemma 21. This is because the number of calls to the weak OWF is at least the same order of magnitude as the length of the input to the strong OWF. Hence, there is not enough entropy in the strong OWF input to distribute among all the weak OWF calls, so most of the calls will end up having very little entropy of their own, i.e. entropy that is not shared with other calls.

Now the probability that an adversary can indeed invert a $1 - 1/p(m)$ fraction of the weak OWF calls is high, since that is the expected fraction of easy calls. Since the entropy of the input s is low, given the easy calls, and the adversary has the PSPACE oracle, the adversary can guess s with high probability. Note that low entropy alone is not enough to guess s, since inverting pre-processing might be inefficient, hence we also need PSPACE.

To summarize, we know that there must be many calls to the underlying weak one-way function—and since we can also show that each of them must have a non-trivial amount of entropy (i.e., information about the input)—we can show that we can invert all non-adaptive constructions without post-processing, unless n is larger than a small constant times $p(m)$, establishing the first lower bound on the randomness efficiency of non-adaptive constructions. Note that Yao's construction consumes $n = m^2 p(m)$ many bits.

On Strong OWFs with Injectiveish Post-processing. We sketched above why constructions without post-processing (direct product constructions) cannot be strongly one-way. It is relatively easy to extend the above argument to constructions with *not too lossy* post-processing, i.e., constructions where any output of the post-processing has at most polynomially many preimages: the inverter chooses a uniformly random value amongst the (polynomial size) list of all possible preimages of the post-processing, and applies the previous inversion attack on the candidate. It then succeeds with probability $\frac{1}{\text{poly}}$ times the success probability of the previous attack.

1.6   Relation to Threshold Secret Sharing

The pre-processing pre in Fig. 1 is conceptually similar to a threshold secret sharing scheme, where the participants' shares correspond to the values x_i and the secret together with the dealer's randomness corresponds to the strong OWF input s. On average, we learn the 'shares' of all but a $\frac{1}{p(m)}$ fraction of the 'participants'. So effectively, we are interested in how long the secret and the dealer's randomness together must be in a $(1 - \frac{1}{p(m)} + \epsilon)$-threshold secret sharing scheme. The difference is that we allow a negligible failing probability for the secret sharing scheme and we do not distinguish which part of the input is the secret and which part of the input is the randomness of dealer in the secret sharing scheme.

To make the intuition concrete, our result can be formulated as a result on the threshold achievable by any *deterministic* threshold secret sharing schemes with short secret.

Definition 2 (Deterministic Threshold Secret Sharing Scheme). *We say that function* $S : \{0,1\}^n \to (\{0,1\}^m)^l$ *(i.e. S outputs l bitstrings of length m) is* (l,t)-*deterministic threshold secret sharing scheme if for all adversaries* $\mathcal{A}$:

$$\Pr_{\pi \leftarrow\$ \, permutations \; of \; (1,...,l), x \leftarrow\$ \{0,1\}^n} \left[x \leftarrow\$ \mathcal{A}(S(x)_{\pi(1)}, ..., S(x)_{\pi(t)}) \right] \leq negl(n),$$

where $S(x)_i$ *denotes the ith share, i.e., the ith length n bitstring of the output of S. The secret length n should be polynomial in the share length m (hence, negligible in n is also negligible in m).*

Note that any threshold secret sharing scheme can be made deterministic by considering the randomness as part of the secret – but then the randomness must be counted towards the secret length. The fact that Definition 2 uses probability over permutations of the shares only makes the definition cover a larger class of schemes, in particular, a scheme that is secure for all permutations is also secure by Definition 2.

Also, notice that Definition 2 relies on a very weak hiding notion: no subset of size less than t should be able to *fully recover* the secret (except with negligible probability). This sets our result apart from most known bounds on secret sharing, which apply to the indistinguishability setting.

In this language, our result states the following: let m be the share length and p be any polynomial. Consider any candidate (l,t)-threshold deterministic secret sharing scheme with $t \geq (1 - 1/p(m)) \cdot l$, now the scheme must have secret size $n > p(m)/c$, for a certain constant. For traditional (l,t)-threshold secret sharing schemes, this means that the combined length of the secret and the randomness used by the scheme must be $> p(m)/c$, if $t \geq (1 - 1/p(m)) \cdot l$. Naturally, in order to this result being meaningful, the number of shares l should be bigger than the polynomial $p(m)$.

The result follows from our main conceptual Lemma 21, which effectively states that the expected entropy of the remaining shares, when you know $(1 - 1/p(m))$ fraction of the shares, is small. Hence, the remaining shares can be guessed with non-negligible probability.

Our result stays the same even if we change Definition 2 to cover only *efficient*, i.e. probabilistic polynomial time, adversaries $\mathcal{A}$, provided that the scheme S is such that you can compute the secret in polynomial time, when you know *all* the shares. That is, we even rule out computational security if $t \geq (1-1/p(m)) \cdot l$ and $n < p(m)/c$.

More precisely, let us change the Definition 2 to a definition that covers an even larger class of schemes (the difference to Definition 2 is high-lighted in pink) and subsequently state our result in the secret-sharing terminology.

Definition 3 (Computational Deterministic Threshold Secret Sharing Scheme). *A function* $S : \{0,1\}^n \to (\{0,1\}^m)^l$ *(i.e. S outputs l bitstrings of length m) is* (l,t)-*computational deterministic threshold secret sharing scheme if for all probabilistic polynomial time adversaries* $\mathcal{A}$:

$$\Pr_{\pi \leftarrow\$ \, permutations \; of \; (1,...,l), x \leftarrow\$ \{0,1\}^n} \left[x \leftarrow\$ \mathcal{A}(S(x)_{\pi(1)}, ..., S(x)_{\pi(t)}) \right] \leq negl(n),$$

where $S(x)_i$ denotes the ith share, i.e., the ith length n bitstring of the output of S. The secret length n should be polynomial in the share length m. The function S^{-1} should be computable in polynomial time.

Theorem 4 (Threshold Secret Sharing View). *Fix a large enough m and a polynomial p. Consider a computational deterministic threshold secret sharing scheme where*

- *the dealer has an n bits secret;*
- *there are l participants, each getting a share of length m;*
- *the threshold t satisfies $t \geq (1 - \frac{1}{p(m)})l$.*

Then the secret must be long: $n > \frac{1}{c}p(m)$, where c is some constant.

Blundo, Santis, Vaccaro [5] discuss the minimum amount of randomness needed by an information theoretically secure secret sharing scheme. They prove that if the secret length is m and there are l participants, then the dealer needs to use $l \cdot m$ bits of randomness (to choose both the secret and the participants' shares). This is the same as the analogous number in Yao's weak to strong OWF construction (when number of weak OWF calls is $l > mp(m)$, we use lm input length) and it is close to the analogous number that we get in this paper (input length to strong OWF needs to be $\mathcal{O}(p(m))$, i.e. there is m^2 gap between our result and Yao's).

It is intuitive that some gap should exist between the information theoretically secure secret sharing scheme and our more relaxed "mostly secure secret sharing scheme", where the adversary is allowed to learn part of the secret as long as they cannot learn the whole input and additionally, the adversary is only allowed to run in polynomial time. However, the two secret sharing schemes are not really comparable (because we do not distinguish between randomness and secret) and a better lower bound, than what we present, might be possible.

2   Preliminaries

Definition 5 (One-Way Functions). *Let $f : \{0,1\}^* \rightarrow \{0,1\}^*$ be a polynomial-time computable function. f is called a (strong) one-way function (OWF), if for every probabilistic polynomial-time algorithm $\mathcal{A}$ there exists a negligible function $\epsilon : \mathbb{N} \rightarrow [0,1]$ such that for every n,*

$$\Pr\nolimits_{\mathcal{A}, x \leftarrow \{0,1\}^n} \left[\mathcal{A}(1^n, f(x)) \in f^{-1}(f(x)) \right] \leq \epsilon(n).$$

Further, f is called a weak one-way function, if there exists a polynomial $p(n)$ such that for every probabilistic polynomial-time algorithm $\mathcal{A}$ there exists a $N_0 \in \mathbb{N}$ such that for all $n \geq N_0$:

$$\Pr\nolimits_{\mathcal{A}, x \leftarrow \{0,1\}^n} \left[\mathcal{A}(1^n, f(x)) \in f^{-1}(f(x)) \right] \leq 1 - \frac{1}{p(n)}.$$

In this case we sometimes say that f is a p-weak OWF.

Definition 6 (Oracle Algorithms). *The complexity of an oracle algorithm (e.g., Turing Machine) is the number of steps it makes, where an oracle query is counted as one step.*

In particular, a probabilistic polynomial-time (PPT) oracle algorithm makes at most polynomial queries. Since our oracle algorithms have access to a PSPACE oracles, we usually limit the discussion to the number of oracle calls the algorithm makes.

We use the following Borel-Cantelli style theorem from [28, Lemma 2.9].

Theorem 7 *Let $(E_1, E_2, ...)$ be a sequence of events such that $\exists c \forall m \in \mathbb{N} : \Pr[E_m] \geq c$, where c is a constant strictly between 0 and 1. Then,*

$$\Pr\left[\bigwedge_{k=1}^{\infty} \bigvee_{m>k} E_m\right] \geq c \tag{1}$$

2.1 Entropy Toolbox

Throughout this paper, the term *entropy* refers to *Shannon entropy* which satisfies a *chain rule*.

Definition 8 (Shannon Entropy). *Let X be a random variable and let $dom(X)$ be its domain, then*

$$H(X) := -\sum_{z \in dom(X)} \Pr[X = z] \cdot \log_2(\Pr[X = z]),$$

is the Shannon entropy *of X.*

Lemma 9 (Chain Rule for Entropy). *Let $X_1, \ldots, X_n$ be random variables. Then the following holds*

$$H(X_1, \ldots, X_n) = H(X_1) + H(X_2|X_1) + \cdots + H(X_n|X_1, \ldots, X_{n-1}).$$

We use also other simple but useful properties of entropy. In particular, Definition 8 implies that entropy is non-negative. Also, the entropy $H(X)$ of a random variable X is always more or equal to the entropy $H(f(X))$ of the random variable $f(X)$ for any deterministic function f—if f is injective, the entropy is preserved, if f is not injective, it decreases. Finally, for any three random variables X, Y, Z, we have that $H(X|Y) \geq H(X|Y, Z)$, i.e., conditioning on additional information maintains or decreases the entropy of a random variable.

3 Main Results

In this section, we introduce different types of constructions of strong OWF from weak OWF which we study in this paper (Sect. 3.1) and state our main theorems (Sect. 3.2). In particular, we introduce non-adaptive constructions, non-adaptive constructions without post-processing and non-adaptive constructions with injective*ish* post-processing.

3.1   Black-Box Constructions and Reductions

Definition 10 (Non-adaptive). *A construction* $g = (\mathsf{pre}, \mathsf{post})$ *from a weak one-way function* F *is non-adaptive, if it computes its output as* $\mathsf{post}(\mathsf{F}(\mathsf{pre}(s)))$ *(see Fig. 1). The number of queries* l *is induced by* pre. (n, m)*-NA denotes a non-adaptive construction with input length* n *based on a weak OWF* F *whose input length is* m.

Definition 11 (Non-adaptive, no post-processing construction). *We say that a construction* $g = (\mathsf{pre}, \mathsf{post})$ *is a* (n, m)*-NANPP, if it is* (n, m)*-NA and the post-processing function is the identity function, i.e.,* $\mathsf{post}(y_1, ..., y_l, d) := y_1 || .. || y_l || d$.

Definition 12 (Non-adaptive, injectiveish post-processing constr). *We say that a construction* $g = (\mathsf{pre}, \mathsf{post})$ *is a* (n, m)*-NAIPP, if it is* (n, m)*-NA and the post-processing function is almost injective, that is, every image of* post *has at most a polynomial (in* n*) number of preimages.*

Note that the identity function is injective and thus, in particular, is injective*ish*. Therefore, every NANPP is also a NAIPP, but the converse does not hold. Likewise, both NANPP and NAIPP are NA constructions, but the converse does not hold. Since we are interested in ruling out negative results, whenever we rule out NAIPP, we also rule out NANPP.

We formalized the kind of constructions our negative results capture, and now specify which type of reduction proofs our theorems rule out. Namely, our results concern BBB-style proofs following the notation of [4] or fully black-box proofs following the notation of [29]. Since we consider parametrized definitions, we here state a customized version of fully black-box security which precisely captures the quantifiers our negative results capture.

Definition 13 (Fully Black-Box Proof). *We say that a proof that weak OWF implies strong OWF is* fully black-box *if it establishes a* relativizing *statement of the following type:*

$\forall poly\ p, \exists\ poly\text{-}time\ computable\ g, \forall poly\ q, \exists PPT\ \mathcal{R}\ \forall p\text{-}weak\ OWF\ \mathsf{F}, \mathcal{A}:$

$$\text{if } \Pr_{x \leftarrow\$ \{0,1\}^n} \left[g^\mathsf{F}(\mathcal{A}(1^n, g^\mathsf{F}(x))) = g^\mathsf{F}(x) \right] > \frac{1}{q(n)} \text{ for inf. many } n \in \mathbb{N}$$

$$\text{then } \Pr_{x \leftarrow\$ \{0,1\}^n} \left[\mathsf{F}(\mathcal{R}^{\mathcal{A},\mathsf{F}}(1^n, \mathsf{F}(x))) = \mathsf{F}(x) \right] > 1 - \frac{1}{p}(n) \text{ for inf. many } n \in \mathbb{N}.$$

In this case, we also refer to the construction g *as fully black-box.*

Note that typically, in the definition of fully black-box, the pink parts are omitted. That is, the polynomial p is considered as part of the definition of F and the polynomial q is considered as part of the definition of $\mathcal{A}$ (i.e. the adversary's success probability). We allow the construction g to depend on the polynomial p and the reduction $\mathcal{R}$ to depend on q, since we seek to cover a larger and meaningful class of proofs. In particular, Yao's original proof building strong OWFs from weak OWFs is fully black-box in the sense of Definition 13, but would not be covered if the construction were now allowed to depend on p or if the reduction were not allowed to depend on q.

3.2   Theorems

We now state our main theorems, all of which rely on the two-oracle technique. Namely, we construct a distribution over oracles $(\mathcal{O}_1, \mathcal{O}_2)$ such that $\mathcal{O}_1$ will be a weak one-way function and $\mathcal{O}_2$ will help to invert the strong one-way function. Since we rule out black-box reductions rather than provide an oracle separation, only the reduction has access to the oracle $\mathcal{O}_2$ while the construction does not (cf. Section 1.5). Note that in Corollary 16, we extract a single oracle from the oracle distribution, using the Borel-Cantelli style argument Theorem 7. However, we prefer to state our theorem in terms of oracle distributions since this more closely matches the technical core arguments of our separation results.

Theorem 14 (NANPP Impossibility). $\exists$ *constant* **c** *such that* $\forall poly\ p$, $\forall (n, m)$-*NANPP* g *with input length* $n \leq \frac{1}{c}p(m)$, $\exists$ *poly-query* $\mathcal{A}$, $\exists poly\ q(n) = n^c, c \in \mathbb{N}_+$, $\forall PPT\ \mathcal{R}$, $\exists$ *distribution* $\mathcal{D}$ *over pairs of oracles* $(\mathcal{O}_1, \mathcal{O}_2)$:

$$\Pr_{(\mathcal{O}_1, \mathcal{O}_2) \leftarrow \$ \mathcal{D}} \left[\mathsf{Bad}_m^{\mathcal{R}, \mathcal{A}, g} \right] = constant < 1$$

where $\mathsf{Bad}_m^{\mathcal{R}, \mathcal{A}, g}$ *is an indicator variable that is 1 iff at least one of the following is true:*

1. *Weak OWF breaks:*
   $$\Pr_{x \leftarrow \$ \{0,1\}^m, \mathcal{R}} \left[\mathcal{R}^{\mathcal{A}^{\mathcal{O}_1, \mathcal{O}_2}, \mathcal{O}_1, \mathcal{O}_2}(1^m, \mathcal{O}_1(x)) \in \mathcal{O}_1^{-1}(\mathcal{O}_1(x)) \right] \geq 1 - \frac{1}{p(m)}.$$
2. *Strong OWF is secure-ish:*
   $$\Pr_{s \leftarrow \$ \{0,1\}^n, \mathcal{A}} \left[\mathcal{A}^{\mathcal{O}_1, \mathcal{O}_2}(1^n, g^{\mathcal{O}_1}(s)) \in (g^{\mathcal{O}_1})^{-1}(g^{\mathcal{O}_1}(s)) \right] \leq \frac{1}{q(n)}.$$

We emphasize that in the definition of the bad event, the oracles are *fixed* and the randomness is taken only over the sampling of x as well as the internal randomness of $\mathcal{A}$ and $\mathcal{R}$, respectively.

Theorem 15 (NAIPP Impossibility). $\exists$ *constant* **c** $\forall poly\ p$, $\forall (n, m)$-*NAIPP* g *with input length* $n \leq \frac{1}{c}p(m)$, $\exists$ *poly-query* $\mathcal{A}$, $\exists poly\ q(n) = n^c, c \in \mathbb{N}_+$, $\forall PPT\ \mathcal{R}$, $\exists$ *distribution* $\mathcal{D}$ *over pairs of oracles* $(\mathcal{O}_1, \mathcal{O}_2)$:

$$\Pr_{(\mathcal{O}_1, \mathcal{O}_2) \leftarrow \$ \mathcal{D}} \left[\mathsf{Bad}_m^{\mathcal{R}, \mathcal{A}, g} \right] = constant < 1$$

where $\mathsf{Bad}_m^{\mathcal{R}, \mathcal{A}, g}$ *is the same indicator variable as in Theorem 14.*

We use the same oracle distribution for Theorem 15 and Theorem 14, see Sect. 4. Theorem 15 implies Theorem 14, so it would suffice to prove Theorem 15. However, we found the presentation to be easier to follow when presenting the proof of the weaker Theorem 14 first (Sect. 5.2) and then discussing the generalization to the proof of Theorem 15 (Sect. 6). For both theorems, we prove that relative to $\mathcal{O}_1, \mathcal{O}_2$, oracle $\mathcal{O}_1$ is a weak OWF. Before proving the theorems for oracle distributions, we now use the strengthened Borel-Cantelli lemma by Mahmoody, Mohammed, Nematihaji, Pass and Shelat [28] to extract a single oracle from the distribution where the bad event happens with *constant* probability, as opposed to less than $1/m^2$ required by standard Borel-Cantelli.

Corollary 16 (Main). *There is no fully black-box (n, m)-NAIPP construction of a OWF from a $p(m)$-weak OWF with $n \leq \frac{1}{c}p(m)$, where **c** is some constant.*

Proof. Recall that a black-box proof means the following:

$\forall$poly $p, \exists$ poly-time computable $g, \forall$poly $q, \exists$PPT $\mathcal{R} \, \forall p$-weak OWF F, $\mathcal{A}$:

$(\mathcal{A}$ inverts $g) \Rightarrow (\mathcal{R}^{\mathcal{A}}$ inverts F$)$ Formally:

$$\left(\Pr_{x \twoheadleftarrow \{0,1\}^n} \left[g^{\mathsf{F}}(\mathcal{A}(1^n, g^{\mathsf{F}}(x))) = g^{\mathsf{F}}(x) \right] > \tfrac{1}{q(n)} \text{ for inf. many } n \in \mathbb{N} \right)$$

$$\Rightarrow \left(\Pr_{x \twoheadleftarrow \{0,1\}^n} \left[\mathsf{F}(\mathcal{R}^{\mathcal{A},\mathsf{F}}(1^n, \mathsf{F}(x))) = \mathsf{F}(x) \right] > 1 - \tfrac{1}{p}(n) \text{ for inf. many } n \in \mathbb{N} \right)$$

In order to rule out a black-box proof, we thus define an oracle $\mathcal{O}_1$ (and an oracle $\mathcal{O}_2$ helping the adversary) such that the following holds:

$\color{gray}{\forall\text{poly } p,} \forall$ poly-time $g^{\mathcal{O}_1}, \exists$poly $q, \forall$PPT $\mathcal{R}^{\mathcal{O}_1, \mathcal{O}_2} \exists \mathcal{A}^{\mathcal{O}_1, \mathcal{O}_2}, \exists \mathcal{O}_1, \mathcal{O}_2$:

$\mathcal{A}$ breaks $g_1^{\mathcal{O}}$, but $\mathcal{R}$ does not p-invert $\mathcal{O}_1$. Formally:

$\Pr_{x \twoheadleftarrow \{0,1\}^n} \left[g^{\mathcal{O}_1}(\mathcal{A}^{\mathcal{O}_1, \mathcal{O}_2}(1^n, g^{\mathcal{O}_1}(x))) = g^{\mathcal{O}_1}(x) \right] > \tfrac{1}{q(n)}$ for inf. many $n \in \mathbb{N}$.

$\Pr_{x \twoheadleftarrow \{0,1\}^n} \left[\mathcal{O}_1(\mathcal{R}^{\mathcal{A}, \mathcal{O}_1, \mathcal{O}_2}(1^n, \mathcal{O}_1(x))) = \mathcal{O}_1(x) \right] < 1 - \tfrac{1}{p}(n)$

for all but finitely many $n \in \mathbb{N}$.

In order to rule out a fully black-box reduction, we would only need to show that statement with the $\color{magenta}{\text{pink}}$ universal quantifier being replaced by existential quantifier. However, proving the statement for all polynomials p is stronger without making the proof more complicated. Now, let us fix a polynomial p, a candidate NAIPP g, a polynomial q (s.t. it satisfies Theorem 15) and a candidate reduction $\mathcal{R}$ and show the existence of an adversary and a p-weak OWF F.

By Theorem 15, there is an oracle distribution over pairs $(\mathcal{O}_1, \mathcal{O}_2)$, and an adversary $\mathcal{A}$ such that the probability of the bad event $\mathsf{Bad}_m^{\mathcal{R}, \mathcal{A}, g}$ is constant in m. We show that there exists a *fixed* oracle pair $(\mathcal{O}_1, \mathcal{O}_2)$ for which the bad event $\mathsf{Bad}_m^{\mathcal{R}, \mathcal{A}, g}$ in Theorem 15 happens only for finitely many m. From that it follows that there is a fixed oracle pair for which $\mathcal{A}^{\mathcal{O}_1, \mathcal{O}_2}$ breaks the candidate strong OWF $g^{\mathcal{O}_1}$ infinitely many often, but the reduction $\mathcal{R}^{\mathcal{A}^{\mathcal{O}_1, \mathcal{O}_2}}$ inverts the weak OWF $\mathcal{O}_1$ well enough at most on finitely many m. Thus, it suffices to show via Theorem 7, that Theorem 15 implies that there is an oracle relative to which $\mathsf{Bad}_m^{\mathcal{R}, \mathcal{A}, g}$ happens only for finitely many m.

By Theorem 15, we have

$$\Pr_{(\mathcal{O}_1, \mathcal{O}_2) \twoheadleftarrow \mathcal{D}} \left[\mathsf{Bad}_m^{\mathcal{R}, \mathcal{A}, g} \right] = \text{constant} < 1.$$

Hence, the constant probability version of Borel-Cantelli (Theorem 7) yields

$$\Pr_{(\mathcal{O}_1, \mathcal{O}_2) \twoheadleftarrow \mathcal{D}} \left[\bigwedge_{m=1}^{\infty} \bigvee_{m > k} \mathsf{Bad}_m^{\mathcal{R}, \mathcal{A}, g} \right] = \text{constant} < 1,$$

which means that, with constant probability, there is a k for which no $m > k$ satisfies $\mathsf{Bad}_m^{\mathcal{R}, \mathcal{A}, g}$. Taking such an oracle pair $(\mathcal{O}_1, \mathcal{O}_2)$ concludes the proof of Corollary 16. $\square$

4   Oracle Distributions

In this section, we define the oracle (distribution)s we rely on. Firstly, a PSPACE creates a world where no one-way functions exist. Then, we add an oracle (distribution) F in order to create a world where weak one-way functions exist, and finally, we add an oracle (distribution) $\mathcal{O}_2$ which breaks NANPP and NAIPP constructions. The adversary will have access to $\mathcal{O}_2$, PSPACE and F while the candidate strong OWF construction only has access to PSPACE and F, but not to $\mathcal{O}_2$. We recall from Sect. 1.5 that it is *necessary* to not give the construction access to the information which parts of F are easy and which parts are hard, and not giving the construction access to $\mathcal{O}_2$ is related to this necessary restriction, since the adversary (modeled by $\mathcal{O}_2$) uses the information of which parts are easy. On a technical-conceptual level, it is meaningful to not give the construction access to the adversary (modeled by $\mathcal{O}_2$), since the adversary is *inefficient*, while the construction is efficient (in this (oracle) world where all algorithms have access to PSPACE and F). We consider an inefficient adversary since we rule out black-box reduction which work for *any* black-box adversary that breaks the strong OWF, including inefficient ones.

As mentioned before, we denote our adversary by $\mathcal{O}_2$. We encode the pair of oracles PSPACE and F into a single oracle $\mathcal{O}_1$ so that we are aligned with the terminology of a two-oracle separation result (and this is also convenient notation in the proof).

Definition 17 (Oracle Distributions). *Let* **p** *be any fixed polynomial. The oracle distribution* $D_\mathbf{p}$ *over oracles* $\mathcal{O}_1$ *and* $\mathcal{O}_2$ *samples permutations* Π_m *of the elements in* $\{0,1\}^m$ *for every* $m \in \mathbb{N}$ *and a random subset* $\mathsf{EASY}^m_{\mathsf{in}}$ *of* $\{0,1\}^m$ *s.t.* $|\mathsf{EASY}^m_{\mathsf{in}}| = \lceil (1 - 1/\mathbf{p}(m))2^m \rceil$. *We define*

$$\mathcal{O}_1 := (\mathsf{PSPACE}, \mathsf{F}) \text{ and } \mathcal{O}_2 := \mathsf{INV},$$

where F *and* INV *behave as follows:*

$\mathsf{F}(x)$	$\mathsf{INV}(y)$
$m \leftarrow |x|$	$m \leftarrow |y|$
$y \leftarrow \Pi_m(x)$	**if** $y \in \mathsf{EASY}^m_{\mathsf{out}}$
return y	**return** $\mathsf{F}^{-1}(y)$
	else return $\bot$

Here, we use $\mathsf{EASY}^m_{\mathsf{out}} := \Pi_m(\mathsf{EASY}^m_{\mathsf{in}})$.

Remark. Throughout this paper we treat $(1-1/\mathbf{p}(m))2^m$ as an integer, omitting the ceil function since the difference is negligible and does not affect our proofs.

5   Proof of Theorem 14

We split the proof of Theorem 14 into two parts. We first show that the probability of Case 1 (weak OWF breaks) of the bad event introduced in Theorem 14 is smaller than any constant (Sect. 5.1), and then we show that the probability of Case 2 (strong OWF is secure-ish) of the bad event introduced in Theorem 14 is a small constant (Sect. 5.2). Recall that both probabilities are (only) over the sampling of the oracles $\mathcal{O}_1$ and $\mathcal{O}_2$.

5.1 $\mathcal{R}^{\mathcal{A}}$ is Not a Successful Weak OWF Inverter

In this section, we show that the probability (over the oracle distributions) that F is not a $2\mathbf{cp}(m)$-weak OWF is small.

Theorem 18 (F is Weak OWF). *For all constants* $\mathbf{c}$, *for all polynomials* $\mathbf{p}$, *for all poly-query* $\mathcal{A}^{\mathsf{F},\mathsf{PSPACE},\mathsf{INV}}$, *for all adversaries* $\mathcal{R}$ *making polynomially many (in* m*) queries to the oracles* $\mathsf{F}, \mathsf{PSPACE}, \mathsf{INV}, \mathcal{A}^{\mathsf{F},\mathsf{PSPACE},\mathsf{INV}}$,

$$\Pr_{\mathsf{F},\mathsf{PSPACE},\mathsf{INV} \leftarrow\!\!\$\, D_{\mathbf{p}}} \left[\mathsf{SuccInv}_{\mathcal{A},\mathcal{R}}^{\mathsf{F},\mathsf{PSPACE},\mathsf{INV}} \geq 1 - \frac{1}{2\mathbf{cp}(m)} \right] \leq 1/\mathbf{c}$$

where $\mathsf{SuccInv}_{\mathcal{A},\mathcal{R}}^{\mathsf{F},\mathsf{PSPACE},\mathsf{INV}}$ *is defined as*

$$\Pr_{x \leftarrow\!\!\$\, \{0,1\}^m, \mathcal{R}} \left[\mathcal{R}^{\mathsf{F},\mathsf{PSPACE},\mathsf{INV},\mathcal{A}^{\mathsf{F},\mathsf{PSPACE},\mathsf{INV}}} (1^m, \mathsf{F}(x)) \in \mathsf{F}^{-1}(\mathsf{F}(x)) \right].$$

When we define $\mathbf{p}(m) := \frac{1}{2\mathbf{c}}p(m)$, *the above is equivalent to*

$$\Pr_{(\mathcal{O}_1,\mathcal{O}_2) \leftarrow\!\!\$\, \mathcal{D}} \left[\text{Case 1 of } \mathsf{Bad}_m^{\mathcal{R},\mathcal{A},g} \right] \leq 1/\mathbf{c},$$

where $\mathcal{D} := D_{\mathbf{p}}$, $\mathcal{O}_1 := \mathsf{F}, \mathsf{PSPACE}$, $\mathcal{O}_2 := \mathsf{INV}$ *and* $\mathsf{Bad}_m^{\mathcal{R},\mathcal{A},g}$ *is defined as in Theorem 14.*

We prove Theorem 18 in Appendix B.

5.2 $\mathcal{A}$ is a Successful Strong OWF Inverter

We prove that an adversary with access to the oracles F, INV and PSPACE (cf. Sect. 4), can break all short input NANPP constructions which have access to F and PSPACE only.

Theorem 19 (Inverting OWF Candidate). $\forall$ *poly* $\mathbf{p}$, $\forall (n, m)$-*NANPP* g *with input length* $n \leq \frac{1}{4}\mathbf{p}(m)$, $\exists$ *poly-query* $\mathcal{A}^{\mathsf{F},\mathsf{INV},\mathsf{PSPACE}}$, $\exists constant\ c > 0\ s.\ t.$

$$\Pr_{(\mathsf{F},\mathsf{INV}) \leftarrow\!\!\$\, D_{\mathbf{p}}} \left[\Pr_{s,\ coins\ of\ \mathcal{A}} \left[\mathcal{A}^{\mathsf{F},\mathsf{INV},\mathsf{PSPACE}}\ inverts\ g(s) \right] \leq c \right] = \text{constant} < 1$$

This implies that

$$\Pr_{(\mathcal{O}_1,\mathcal{O}_2) \leftarrow\!\!\$\, \mathcal{D}} \left[\text{Case 2 of } \mathsf{Bad}_m^{\mathcal{R},\mathcal{A},g} \right] = \text{constant} < 1$$

where $\mathcal{D} := D_{\mathbf{p}}$, $\mathcal{O}_1 := \mathsf{F}, \mathsf{PSPACE}$, $\mathcal{O}_2 := \mathsf{INV}$ *and* $\mathsf{Bad}_m^{\mathcal{R},\mathcal{A},g}$ *is defined as in Theorem 14.*

For the proof of Theorem 19, let $\mathbf{p}(m)$ be a fixed polynomial. We start by showing that Theorem 19 holds for constructions which make few queries. More precisely, we show that no matter what the input length to g is, g must make at least $l > \mathbf{cp}(m)$ calls to F, otherwise all the F calls are easy with constant probability, which makes inverting g trivial.

Proposition 20 (Easy inversion if few F-Calls). *Consider a NANPP $g =$ (pre, post) (where we recall that $\mathsf{post}(y_1, .., y_l, d) = y_1||..||y_l||d$). For all constants c, if $\mathsf{pre}(s) = (x_1, .., x_l, d)$ induces at most $l \leq \mathbf{cp}(m)$ (parallel) calls to F, then all $y_i := \mathsf{F}(x_i)$ are in $\mathsf{EASY}^m_{\mathrm{out}}$ with constant probability, more precisely*

$$\Pr_{\mathsf{F} \leftarrow\$ D_{\mathbf{p}}} [\Pr_s [\forall y_i \in g(s) : y_i \in \mathsf{EASY}^m_{\mathrm{out}}] > constant > 0] > constant > 0 \quad (2)$$

In particular, with constant probability over the choice of the oracle F, g can be inverted with non-negligible (constant) probability by a poly-query adversary.

Proof. Suppose there are $l \leq \mathbf{cp}(m)$ parallel calls to F. Denote by $y_1, ..., y_l$ the outputs of the parallel calls to F. Now, when considering the randomness of choosing $\mathsf{EASY}^m_{\mathrm{in}}$, we have

$$\Pr_{\mathsf{F} \leftarrow\$ D_{\mathbf{p}},s} [y_1, ..., y_l \in \mathsf{EASY}^m_{\mathrm{out}}]$$

$$\geq \underbrace{\sum_s 2^{-|s|} \Pr_{\mathsf{F} \leftarrow\$ D_{\mathbf{p}}} [y_1 \in \mathsf{EASY}^m_{\mathrm{out}} \mid s] \cdot ... \cdot \Pr_{\mathsf{F} \leftarrow\$ D_{\mathbf{p}}} [y_l \in \mathsf{EASY}^m_{\mathrm{out}} \mid s]}_{=1}$$

$$= \left(1 - \frac{1}{\mathbf{p}(m)}\right)^l \geq \left(1 - \frac{1}{\mathbf{p}(m)}\right)^{\mathbf{cp}(m)} \geq \left(\frac{1}{4}\right)^c \forall \mathbf{p}(m) > 2.$$

where the first inequality is an equality iff $y_i \neq y_j \forall i \neq j$ and the second inequality follows since $(1 - \frac{1}{x})^x$ converges monotonously to $\frac{1}{e}$ and is greater than $\frac{1}{4}$ whenever $x \geq 2$. Now since $\left(\frac{1}{4}\right)^c$ is constant, we can use a simple averaging argument (see Appendix A, Lemma 23) to prove (2).

In the case where all $y_1, ..., y_l$ are all easy, $\mathcal{A}$ can invert $y_1, ..., y_l$ using INV oracle. Note that there is only a single pre-image x_i per y_i and thus, given the list $x_1, ..., x_l$, $\mathcal{A}$ can use the PSPACE oracle to find an s such that $\mathsf{pre}(s) = x_1$, $..., x_l$. □

Due to Proposition 20, for the remainder of this section, we can focus on constructions where pre makes more than $c \cdot \mathbf{p}(m)$ calls. Also in the case where g makes many queries, we can always invert the easy fraction of $(y_1, .., y_l)$. However, if many queries are made, then (with high probability) some y_i will also be hard. Of course, if pre-processing $\mathsf{pre}(s) = (x_1, .., x_l)$ distributes the entropy well, then knowing some of the x_i might suffice to restrict the set of suitable candidate values s to a polynomial-sized set, and once a polynomial-sized set of candidates is obtained, a random candidate s is a suitable pre-image with high enough probability. How well does this strategy work when considering *arbitrary* pre-processing pre?

To analyze this strategy, we study the entropy of the hard values x_i given $(1 - \frac{1}{\mathbf{p}(m)})l$ many easy values x_i (note that in expectation, $(1 - \frac{1}{\mathbf{p}(m)})l$ many values are easy) and seek to prove that their entropy is low. Towards that goal, we fix a permutation π and look at the entropy of the $\frac{1}{\mathbf{p}(m)}l$ many first x_i under that permutation:

$$h(\pi) := H(X_{\pi(1)}, \ldots, X_{\pi\left(\frac{l}{\mathbf{p}(m)}\right)} | X_{\pi\left(\frac{l}{\mathbf{p}(m)}+1\right)}, \ldots, X_{\pi(l)}),$$

where X_i is the random variable defined as follows: sample a uniformly random s from $\{0,1\}^n$, compute $\mathsf{pre}(s)$ and take the ith output (i.e. the input to the ith F-call in g).

First, in Lemma 21 (Small Entropy Expectation), we show that the expectation of entropy $h(\pi)$ is small in our case. This is our main conceptual lemma.

Lemma 21 (Small Entropy Expectation). *Suppose* $\mathbf{p}(m)$ *divides* l. *Then,*

$$\mathbb{E}_{\pi \in \Pi(l)}[h(\pi)] \leq \frac{n}{\mathbf{p}(m)},$$

which is equivalent to

$$\mathbb{E}_{\pi \in \Pi(l)}\left[H(X_{\pi(1)}, \ldots, X_{\pi\left(\frac{l}{\mathbf{p}(m)}\right)} | X_{\pi\left(\frac{l}{\mathbf{p}(m)}+1\right)}, \ldots, X_{\pi(l)})\right] \leq \frac{n}{\mathbf{p}(m)}. \quad (3)$$

Proof. Let's consider a permutation π of the weak OWF inputs $x_{\pi(1)}, \ldots, x_{\pi(l)}$. Let's divide the inputs x_i into $\mathbf{p}(m)$ equal-sized blocks as follows:

$$\left(x_{\pi(1)}, \ldots, x_{\pi(l/\mathbf{p}(m))}, \underbrace{x_{\pi(l/\mathrm{p}(m)+1)}, \ldots, x_{\pi(2l/\mathbf{p}(m))}}_{\text{one block}}, x_{\pi(2l/\mathrm{p}(m)+1)}, \ldots, x_{\pi(l)} \right).$$

Each pink index starts a new block. Let's denote the set of the pink indices by $J := \{1, l/\mathbf{p}(m)+1, 2l/\mathbf{p}(m)+1, \ldots, (\mathbf{p}(m)-1)l/\mathbf{p}(m)+1\}$. Now consider the following sum

$$\sum_{j \in J} \mathbb{E}_{\pi \in \Pi(l)}\left[H\left(\underbrace{X_{\pi(j)}, \ldots, X_{\pi\left(j+\frac{l}{\mathbf{p}(m)}-1\right)}}_{\text{one block}} | \underbrace{X_{\pi\left(j+\frac{l}{\mathbf{p}(m)}\right)}, \ldots, X_{\pi(l)}}_{\text{all } X_i \text{ after the block}} \right) \right] \quad (4)$$

$$= \mathbb{E}_{\pi \in \Pi(l)}\left[\sum_{j \in J} H\left(X_{\pi(j)}, \ldots, X_{\pi\left(j+\frac{l}{\mathbf{p}(m)}-1\right)} | X_{\pi\left(j+\frac{l}{\mathbf{p}(m)}\right)}, \ldots, X_{\pi(l)} \right) \right] \quad (5)$$

$$= \mathbb{E}_{\pi \in \Pi(l)}\left[H\left(X_{\pi(1)}, \ldots, X_{\pi(l)} \right) \right] \quad (6)$$

$$\leq \mathbb{E}_{\pi \in \Pi(l)}\left[H\left(S \right) \right] \quad (7)$$

$$= n \quad (8)$$

where (5) holds by linearity of expectation and (6) holds by Lemma 9 (Chain Rule for Entropy). The inequality (7) is equality iff the pre-processing is injective (entropy of a random variable cannot increase when it is passed through a deterministic function). The equality (8) follows from the fact that $H(S) = |s| = n$.

Now, from (4), we have that n is greater or equal to

$$\sum_{j \in J} \mathbb{E}_{\pi \in \Pi(l)} \left[H \left(X_{\pi(j)}, .., X_{\pi\left(j+\frac{l}{\mathbf{p}(m)}-1\right)} | X_{\pi\left(j+\frac{l}{\mathbf{p}(m)}\right)}, .., X_l \right) \right] \tag{9}$$

$$\geq \sum_{j \in J} \mathbb{E}_{\pi \in \Pi(l)} \left[H \left(X_{\pi(j)}, .., X_{\pi\left(j+\frac{l}{\mathbf{p}(m)}-1\right)} | X_{\pi(i)}, i = 1, .., j-1, j+\frac{l}{\mathbf{p}(m)}, .., l \right) \right] \tag{10}$$

$$= \sum_{j \in J} \mathbb{E}_{\pi' \in \Pi(l)} \left[H \left(X_{\pi'(1)}, .., X_{\pi'\left(\frac{l}{\mathbf{p}(m)}\right)} | X_{\pi'\left(\frac{l}{\mathbf{p}(m)}+1\right)}, .., X_{\pi'(l)} \right) \right] \tag{11}$$

$$= \mathbf{p}(m) \, \mathbb{E}_{\pi' \in \Pi(l)} \left[H \left(X_{\pi'(1)}, .., X_{\pi'\left(\frac{l}{\mathbf{p}(m)}\right)} | X_{\pi'\left(\frac{l}{\mathbf{p}(m)}+1\right)}, .., X_{\pi'(l)} \right) \right] \tag{12}$$

where (10) follows from the general property of entropy: $\forall A, B, C : H(A|B) \geq H(A|B,C)$, i.e. conditioning the entropy on more random variables can only decrease the entropy. In this case, we condition additionally on all X_i for $i < \pi(j)$ and not only on those for $i \geq \pi(j + \frac{l}{\mathbf{p}(m)})$. At (11) we change to a more convenient indexing where we choose permutation $\pi'(1) = \pi(j), ..., \pi'(\frac{l}{\mathbf{p}(m)}) = \pi(j + \frac{l}{\mathbf{p}(m)} - 1)$. Now, consider any of the summands, i.e. the expectation for some fixed j. Now for that j, π' still goes through all possible permutations (like π did in (10)). At (12) we notice that the summands do not depend on j and recall that $|J| = \mathbf{p}(m)$. Dividing by $\mathbf{p}(m)$ proves the Lemma 21. $\qquad \square$

With Lemma 21 as a tool, we can now prove Theorem 19. Note that, interestingly, the result of Theorem 19, does not depend on the number of calls to F in the strong OWF construction g. That is, if the input length of the construction g is too short, then no number of calls to F can make it a strong OWF.

$$\underline{\mathcal{A}(y_1 || ... || y_l || d)}$$

for $i \in 1, ..., l$
$\quad x_i \leftarrow \mathsf{INV}(y_i)$
$\quad s \leftarrow_\$ \mathsf{pre}^{-1}(x_1, ..., x_l, d)$
return s

Proof of Theorem 19. Let g be a (n, m)-NANPP g with input length $n \leq \frac{1}{4}\mathbf{p}(m)$ and let l be the number of queries to F which g makes. The adversary $\mathcal{A}$ (described on the right) now tries to invert all $y_1, .., y_l$ using INV and put $\bot$ when inversion fails. $\mathcal{A}$ then computes a random pre-image of the pre-processing that matches the known x_is and d which is possible in polynomial-time when using the PSPACE oracle. We now argue that a random pre-image of the pre-processing, that matches the known x_is and d, is an actual preimage of $y_1||...||y_l||d$ under g with constant probability.

W.l.o.g., we assume that $|d| = 0$. This is because the data d is known to the adversary, so it cannot add entropy. From now on, we assume that there is no d. Further and also w.l.o.g., we assume that $\mathbf{p}(m)$ divides l for all m, n (if there was some remainder, we could add constant dummy F-calls until there is no remainder. Such F-calls would not make g weaker nor stronger, so our result would still hold.) Note that if $l \leq \mathbf{p}(m)$, then with constant probability all x_i are easy and INV inverts all of them (cf. Theorem 20). In that case $\mathcal{A}$ can use PSPACE oracle to find a correct preimage s with probability 1. Hence, we can assume that $l > \mathbf{p}(m)$.

First, in Lemma 21 (Small Entropy Expectation) establishes that the expectation of entropy $h(\pi)$ is small. Namely, since Theorem 19 assumes that $\mathbf{p}(m) > 4n$, we have

$$\mathbb{E}_{\pi \leftarrow\!\!\$\, \Pi(l)}[h(\pi)] \leq \frac{n}{\mathbf{p}(m)} < \frac{1}{4}.$$

Since the expectation of the entropy over π is small, an averaging argument (cf. Lemma 24 (Small Entropy w.h.p.) in Appendix A) yields that for at least half of the permutations, the entropy is small, i.e.,

$$\Pr_{\pi \in \Pi(l)}\left[h(\pi) < \frac{2n}{\mathbf{p}(m)}\right] \geq \frac{1}{2}. \tag{13}$$

We call a π such that $h(\pi) < \frac{2n}{\mathbf{p}(m)}$ *good*. If π is good, then the remaining entropy of the input is small and thus, some inputs are very likely (cf. Lemma 25 (Predictable Inputs) in Appendix A) and thus likely chosen by adversary $\mathcal{A}$ which chooses a random pre-image amongst the possible candidates.

With this high level intuition of the proof in mind, we can now lower-bound the probability of $\mathcal{A}$'s success.

$$\Pr_{\mathsf{F},s}[\mathcal{A} \text{ inverts } g(s)]$$
$$\geq \Pr_{\mathsf{F}}\left[\exists \pi : x_{\pi(1)}, ..., x_{\pi((1-\frac{1}{\mathbf{p}(m)})l)} \in \mathsf{EASY}_{\mathsf{in}}^m\right]$$
$$\cdot \Pr_s\left[\mathcal{A} \text{ inverts } g(s) \,\middle|\, \exists \pi : x_{\pi(1)}, ..., x_{\pi((1-\frac{1}{\mathbf{p}(m)})l)} \in \mathsf{EASY}_{\mathsf{in}}^m\right]$$
$$\geq \frac{1}{2}\Pr_s\left[\mathcal{A} \text{ inverts } g(s) \,\middle|\, \exists \pi : x_{\pi(1)}, ..., x_{\pi((1-\frac{1}{\mathbf{p}(m)})l)} \in \mathsf{EASY}_{\mathsf{in}}^m\right] \tag{14}$$

$$\geq \frac{1}{2} \Pr_s \underbrace{\left[H\left(X_{\pi(1)}, \ldots, X_{\pi\left(\frac{l}{\mathbf{p}(m)}\right)} \,\middle|\, X_{\pi\left(\frac{l}{\mathbf{p}(m)}+1\right)}, \ldots, X_{\pi(l)} \right) < \frac{2n}{\mathbf{p}(m)} \right]}_{=:C}. \tag{15}$$

$$\Pr_s \left[\Pr_{s'} \left[\begin{matrix} \forall k & \in & \forall j & \in \\ \pi(1),\ldots,\pi(l/\mathbf{p}(m)), & \pi(l/\mathbf{p}(m)+1),\ldots,\pi(l), \\ X_k = \mathsf{pre}(s')_k & X_j = \mathsf{pre}(s)_j \end{matrix} \right] > \frac{1}{4} \,\middle|\, C \right]. \tag{16}$$

$$\Pr_s \left[\mathcal{A} \text{ inverts } g(s) \,\middle|\, \Pr_{s'} \left[\begin{matrix} \forall k & \in & \forall j & \in \\ \pi(1),\ldots,\pi(l/\mathbf{p}(m)), & \pi(l/\mathbf{p}(m)+1),\ldots,\pi(l), \\ X_k = \mathsf{pre}(s')_k & X_j = \mathsf{pre}(s)_j \end{matrix} \right] > \frac{1}{4} \land C \right] \tag{17}$$

$$\geq \frac{1}{2} \cdot \frac{1}{2} \cdot \frac{3}{4} \cdot \frac{1}{4} = \text{constant} \tag{18}$$

where (14) follows from the fact that whether x_i is easy or not follows binomial distribution with $(1 - \frac{1}{\mathbf{p}(m)})l$ many easy values in expectation. Inequality (15) uses chain rule of probability. The fractions at (18) follow from the lemmas, namely, the probability on line (15) is less than $1/2$ by Lemma 21 (Small Entropy Expectation) and probability on line (16) is less than $3/4$ by Lemma 25 (Predictable Inputs). The last fraction follows from the definition of adversary $\mathcal{A}$ and the probability statement at (17). Namely, if adversary guesses a random s which is consistent with the known x_i, and we condition the probability on such s being correct $1/4$ of the time, adversary must be right $1/4$ of the time.

Now that we know that

$$\Pr_{\mathsf{F},s}[\mathcal{A} \text{ inverts } g(s)] \geq \text{const} > 0,$$

we can use a simple averaging argument (see Appendix A, Lemma 23) to show that $\Pr_{\mathsf{F}}[\Pr_s[\mathcal{A} \text{ inverts } g(s)] > \text{const} > 0] \geq \text{const} > 0$ which proves Theorem 19. $\square$

Theorem 14 follows from the Theorems 19 and 18 by union bound, namely

$$\Pr_{(\mathcal{O}_1,\mathcal{O}_2) \hookleftarrow_\$ \mathcal{D}} \left[\mathsf{Bad}_m^{\mathcal{R},\mathcal{A},g} \right] = \Pr \left[\text{Case 1 of } \mathsf{Bad}_m^{\mathcal{R},\mathcal{A},g} \text{ or Case 2 of } \mathsf{Bad}_m^{\mathcal{R},\mathcal{A},g} \right]$$
$$\leq 1/\mathbf{c} + \text{constant from Theorem 19} < 1$$

Note that since the constant $\mathbf{c}$ in Theorem 18 can be made arbitrarily large, in particular, it can be chosen s.t. $1/\mathbf{c}$ + constant from Theorem 19 is < 1.

6   Constructions with Post-processing

In this section, we prove Theorem 15. Towards this goal, we use the oracles F, INV and PSPACE (cf. Sect. 4), and show that there are no short input NAIPP constructions under the oracles.

Theorem 22 (No Strong OWFs with Injectiveish Post-Processing). $\forall$ *poly* $\mathbf{p}$, $\forall (n, m)$-*NAIPP* g *with input length* $n \leq \frac{1}{4}\mathbf{p}(m)$, $\exists poly\ q(n) = n^c, c \in \mathbb{N}_+$, $\exists$ *poly-query* $\mathcal{A}^{\mathsf{F},\mathsf{INV},\mathsf{PSPACE}}$ *such that*

$$\Pr_{(\mathsf{F},\mathsf{INV}) \leftarrow\!\$ D_{\mathbf{p}}} \left[\Pr_{s,\ coins\ of\ \mathcal{A}} \left[\mathcal{A}^{\mathsf{F},\mathsf{INV},\mathsf{PSPACE}}\ inverts\ g(s) \right] \leq q(n) \right] = \mathsf{constant} < 1$$

$$and\ thus\ \Pr_{(\mathcal{O}_1,\mathcal{O}_2) \leftarrow\!\$ \mathcal{D}} \left[Case\ 2\ of\ \mathsf{Bad}_m^{\mathcal{R},\mathcal{A},g} \right] = \mathsf{constant} < 1$$

where $\mathsf{Bad}_m^{\mathcal{R},\mathcal{A},g}$ *is defined as in Theorem 15.*

Theorems 18 and 22 together imply Theorem 15 by union bound analogously to the NANPP case. It thus remains to prove Theorem 22.

$\underline{\mathcal{A}(z)}$

$y_1, ..., y_l, d \leftarrow \mathsf{post}^{-1}(z)$

for $i \in 1, ..., l$

$\quad x_i \leftarrow \mathsf{INV}(y_i)$

$s \leftarrow\!\$ \mathsf{pre}^{-1}(x_1, ..., x_l, d)$

return s

Proof. Let g be (n, m)-NAIPP which makes l queries to F and let $\mathcal{A}$ be the adversary on the right which samples a uniformly random pre-image of z under post, then inverts the easy queries and returns a seed s which is consistent with the pre-image of the easy values. Firstly observe that $\mathcal{A}$ runs in polynomial-time since it can use the PSPACE oracle for inverting post. Moreover, it makes only a polynomial number of queries since l is a polynomial.

As the post-processing of g is almost injective, $y_1, ..., y_l, d \leftarrow\!\$ \mathsf{post}^{-1}(z)$ returns the values $y_1, ..., y_l, d$ which the one-wayness experiment used to compute z with probability $\frac{1}{\mathsf{poly}(n)}$. This probability is independent of F. If $y_1, ..., y_l, d$ are indeed the correct values, then adversary $\mathcal{A}$ also finds a pre-image s with constant probability by the same arguments as in Theorem 19. Thus, the overall success of $\mathcal{A}$ is $\frac{1}{\mathsf{poly}(n)} \cdot \mathsf{constant}$ which is inverse polynomial as required by Theorem 22. □

Acknowledgments. We thank the anonymous reviewers for valuable comments. Parts of this work have been funded by the Deutsche Forschungsgemeinschaft (DFG, German Research Foundation) - SFB 1119 - 236615297 and by the Academy of Finland.

A   Additional Lemmas and Proofs

Lemma 23 (Averaging Argument). *Let* A_n *and* B_n *be probability distributions that depend on natural number* n *(e.g. uniform distribution over* $\{0,1\}^n$ *). For convenience, we write* $A := A_n, B := B_n$. *Let* $E(\cdot, \cdot)$ *be any event.*

If $\Pr_{a \leftarrow\!\$ A, b \leftarrow\!\$ B}[E(a,b)] \geq c$, *where* $c > 0$ *constant, then there exist constants* $d, d' > 0$ *s.t.* $\Pr_{a \leftarrow\!\$ A}[\Pr_{b \leftarrow\!\$ B}[E(a,b)] \geq d] \geq d'$.

The proof is standard, we defer it to the full version.

Lemma 24 (Small Entropy w.h.p.). *If* $\mathbb{E}_{\pi \in \Pi(l)}[h(\pi)] \leq \frac{n}{\mathbf{p}(m)}$ *then*

$$\Pr_{\pi \in \Pi(l)}\left[h(\pi) < \frac{2n}{\mathbf{p}}\right] \geq 1/2,$$

where $h(\pi) = \mathrm{H}\left(X_{\pi(1)}, \ldots, X_{\pi\left(\frac{l}{\mathbf{p}(m)}\right)} \,\middle|\, X_{\pi\left(\frac{l}{\mathbf{p}(m)}+1\right)}, \ldots, X_{\pi(l)}\right).$

The proof is a direct application of Markov bound, we defer it to the full version.

Lemma 25 (Predictable Inputs). *If*

$$\mathrm{H}\left(X_{\pi(1)}, \ldots, X_{\pi\left(\frac{l}{\mathbf{p}(m)}\right)} \,\middle|\, X_{\pi\left(\frac{l}{\mathbf{p}(m)}+1\right)}, \ldots, X_{\pi(l)}\right) < \frac{2n}{\mathbf{p}(m)}$$

then

$$\Pr_{s'}\left[\Pr_s[X_k = \mathsf{pre}(s)_k \,\forall k \in \pi(1), \ldots, \pi\left(\tfrac{l}{\mathbf{p}(m)}\right) \mid X_j = \mathsf{pre}(s')_j \,\forall j \in \pi\left(\tfrac{l}{\mathbf{p}(m)}+1\right), \ldots, \pi(l)] > \tfrac{1}{4}\right] \geq \frac{3}{4}$$

Proof. Since $4n < \mathbf{p}(m)$, we get that

$$\mathrm{H}\left(X_{\pi(1)}, \ldots, X_{\pi\left(\frac{l}{\mathbf{p}(m)}\right)} \,\middle|\, X_{\pi\left(\frac{l}{\mathbf{p}(m)}+1\right)}, \ldots, X_{\pi(l)}\right) < \frac{2n}{\mathbf{p}(m)} < \frac{1}{2} \qquad (19)$$

Let $S_{h,e} \subseteq \{0,1\}^m$ be defined as

$$S_{h,e} = \{s' : \Pr_s[P_h = p_h(s') \mid P_e = p_e(s')] < \frac{1}{4}\},$$

where we define $\Pr_s[P_h = p_h(s') \mid P_e = p_e(s')]$ below. Using (19) and the definition of conditional Shannon entropy, we get that

$$\frac{1}{2} > \mathrm{H}\left(\underbrace{X_{\pi(1)}, \ldots, X_{\pi\left(\frac{l}{\mathbf{p}(m)}\right)}}_{=:P_h} \,\middle|\, \underbrace{X_{\pi\left(\frac{l}{\mathbf{p}(m)}+1\right)}, \ldots, X_{\pi(l)}}_{=:P_e}\right)$$

$$= \sum_{s' \in \{0,1\}^m} \Pr_s\left[P_h = p_h(s') \text{ and } P_e = p_e(s')\right] \cdot \left|\log \Pr_s\left[P_h = p_h(s') \mid P_e = p_e(s')\right]\right|$$

$$= \sum_{s' \in S_{h,e}} \Pr_s\left[P_h = p_h(s') \text{ and } P_e = p_e(s')\right] \cdot \left|\log \Pr_s\left[P_h = p_h(s') \mid P_e = p_e(s')\right]\right|$$

$$\quad + \sum_{s' \notin S_{h,e}} \Pr_s\left[P_h = p_h(s') \text{ and } P_e = p_e(s')\right] \cdot \left|\log \Pr_s\left[P_h = p_h(s') \mid P_e = p_e(s')\right]\right|$$

$$\geq \left(\sum_{s' \in S_{h,e}} \Pr_s\left[P_h = p_h(s') \text{ and } P_e = p_e(s')\right]\right) \cdot \left|\log \frac{1}{4}\right|$$

$$\quad + \left(\sum_{s' \notin S_{h,e}} \Pr_s\left[P_h = p_h(s') \text{ and } P_e = p_e(s')\right]\right) \cdot |\log 1|$$

$$\geq \Pr_{s'}\left[\Pr_s\left[P_h = p_h(s') \mid P_e = p_e(s')\right] < \frac{1}{4}\right] \cdot 2 + 0$$

where log is the base-2 logarithm and

$$p_e(s') := \mathsf{pre}(s')_{\pi\left(\frac{l}{\mathbf{p}(m)}+1\right)}, \ldots, \mathsf{pre}(s')_{\pi(l)}$$

and

$$p_h(s') := \mathsf{pre}(s')_{\pi(1)}, \ldots, \mathsf{pre}(s')_{\pi\left(\frac{l}{\mathbf{p}(m)}\right)}.$$

Now

$$\frac{1}{2} \geq \Pr_{s'}\left[\Pr_s[P_h = p_h(s') \mid P_e = p_e(s')] < \frac{1}{4}\right] \cdot 2$$

$$\Leftrightarrow \quad \frac{1}{4} \geq \Pr_{s'}\left[\Pr_s[P_h = p_h(s') \mid P_e = p_e(s')] < \frac{1}{4}\right]$$

$$\Rightarrow \Pr_{s'}\left[\Pr_s[P_h = p_h(s') \mid P_e = p_e(s')] \geq \frac{1}{4}\right]$$

$$= 1 - \Pr_{s'}\left[\Pr_s[P_h = p_h(s') \mid P_e = p_e(s')] < \frac{1}{4}\right]$$

$$> 1 - \frac{1}{4} = \frac{3}{4}$$

which proves the statement.   □

B   Proof of Theorem 18 (F is a weak OWF)

In order to prove Theorem 18, we need to show that F is weak OWF with inversion probability $1 - 1/2\mathbf{cp}(m)$ with all but small constant probability. Namely, we need to show that for all polynomials $\mathbf{p}$, for all poly-query $\mathcal{A}^{\mathsf{F},\mathsf{PSPACE},\mathsf{INV}}$, for all adversaries $\mathcal{R}$ making polynomially many (in m) queries to the oracles $\mathsf{F}, \mathsf{PSPACE}, \mathsf{INV}, \mathcal{A}^{\mathsf{F},\mathsf{PSPACE},\mathsf{INV}}$,

$$\Pr_{\mathsf{F},\mathsf{PSPACE},\mathsf{INV} \leftarrow_\$ D_{\mathbf{p}}}\left[\mathsf{SuccInv}_{\mathcal{A},\mathcal{R}}^{\mathsf{F},\mathsf{PSPACE},\mathsf{INV}} \geq 1 - \frac{1}{2\mathbf{cp}(m)}\right] \leq 1/\mathbf{c}, \quad (20)$$

where $\mathsf{SuccInv}_{\mathcal{A},\mathcal{R}}^{\mathsf{F},\mathsf{PSPACE},\mathsf{INV}}$ is defined as

$$\Pr_{x \leftarrow_\$ \{0,1\}^m, \mathcal{R}}\left[\mathcal{R}^{\mathsf{F},\mathsf{PSPACE},\mathsf{INV},\mathcal{A}^{\mathsf{F},\mathsf{PSPACE},\mathsf{INV}}}(1^m, \mathsf{F}(x)) \in \mathsf{F}^{-1}(\mathsf{F}(x))\right].$$

Proof. Fix $\mathbf{p}$, $\mathcal{R}$ and $\mathcal{A}$. Since $\mathcal{A}$ and $\mathcal{R}$ both make polynomially many queries to the same oracles, $\mathcal{R}$ can simply simulate $\mathcal{A}$. Thus, w.l.o.g., we can assume that $\mathcal{R}$ only makes queries to F, PSPACE and INV. Additionally, we consider $\mathcal{R}$ to be a computationally unbounded algorithm so that w.l.o.g., we can assume that it does not make queries to the PSPACE oracle.

Let q be a polynomial such that adversary $\mathcal{R}$ makes exactly $q(m)$ queries to the oracle F and an arbitrary number of queries to INV. Since we let the adversary $\mathcal{R}$ make an arbitrary number of queries to INV, that is, the adversary can be assumed to know the $\mathsf{EASY}_{\mathsf{in}}^m$ and $\mathsf{EASY}_{\mathsf{out}}^m$ and how F maps $\mathsf{EASY}_{\mathsf{in}}^m$ to $\mathsf{EASY}_{\mathsf{out}}^m$ completely. This only makes the adversary stronger. Importantly, using INV does not give the adversary any information on F on the *hard* values (only the fact that the values are hard).

Denote the preimages to F queries by $x_1, ..., x_{q(m)}$ and the adversary's guess for the pre-image of its input y by $x_{q(m)+1}$.

$$\Pr_{\mathsf{F},\mathsf{INV} \leftarrow_\$ D_{\mathbf{p}}, x \leftarrow_\$ \{0,1\}^m, \mathcal{R}} \left[\mathcal{R}(\mathsf{F}(x)) \in \mathsf{F}^{-1}(\mathsf{F}(x)) \right]$$

$$= \Pr\left[\mathcal{R}(\mathsf{F}(x)) \in \mathsf{F}^{-1}(\mathsf{F}(x)) \,\big|\, x \in \mathsf{EASY}_{\mathsf{in}}^m \right] \cdot \Pr\left[x \in \mathsf{EASY}_{\mathsf{in}}^m \right]$$
$$+ \Pr\left[\mathcal{R}(\mathsf{F}(x)) \in \mathsf{F}^{-1}(\mathsf{F}(x)) \,\big|\, x \notin \mathsf{EASY}_{\mathsf{in}}^m \right] \cdot \Pr\left[x \notin \mathsf{EASY}_{\mathsf{in}}^m \right]$$

$$\leq 1 \cdot \left(1 - \frac{1}{\mathbf{p}(m)} \right) + \Pr\left[\mathcal{R}(\mathsf{F}(x)) \in \mathsf{F}^{-1}(\mathsf{F}(x)) \,\big|\, x \notin \mathsf{EASY}_{\mathsf{in}}^m \right] \cdot \frac{1}{\mathbf{p}(m)}$$

$$\leq 1 - \frac{1}{\mathbf{p}(m)} + \frac{1}{\mathbf{p}(m)} \sum_{i=1}^{q(m)+1} \Pr\left[\mathsf{F}(x_i) = \mathsf{F}(x) \,\middle|\, \begin{array}{l} \mathsf{F}(x_1), ..., \mathsf{F}(x_{i-1}) \neq \mathsf{F}(x), \\ x \notin \mathsf{EASY}_{\mathsf{in}}^m \end{array} \right]$$

$$\leq 1 - \frac{1}{\mathbf{p}(m)} + \frac{1}{\mathbf{p}(m)} \sum_{i=1}^{q(m)+1} \frac{1}{\frac{1}{\mathbf{p}(m)} 2^m - i} \leq 1 - \frac{1}{2\mathbf{p}(m)} \quad \text{when } m \text{ is large enough.}$$

Next, we apply an averaging argument. Consider the random variable

$$\mathsf{SuccInv}_{\mathcal{A},\mathcal{R}}^{\mathsf{F},\mathsf{PSPACE},\mathsf{INV}}$$

which maps $\mathsf{F}, \mathsf{PSPACE}, \mathsf{INV} \leftarrow_\$ D_{\mathbf{p}}$ to the probability that

$$\mathcal{R}^{\mathsf{F},\mathsf{PSPACE},\mathsf{INV},\mathcal{A}^{\mathsf{F},\mathsf{PSPACE},\mathsf{INV}}}$$

inverts F over the randomness of $\mathcal{R}$, $\mathcal{A}$ and sampling x. Then, by the previous analysis, the expected value μ of $\mathsf{SuccInv}_{\mathcal{A},\mathcal{R}}^{\mathsf{F},\mathsf{PSPACE},\mathsf{INV}}$ is at most $1-\epsilon$ for $\epsilon := \frac{1}{2\mathbf{p}(m)}$. Using Markov inequality on $1 - \mathsf{SuccInv}_{\mathcal{A},\mathcal{R}}^{\mathsf{F},\mathsf{PSPACE},\mathsf{INV}}$, we obtain that

$$\Pr_{\mathsf{F},\mathsf{PSPACE},\mathsf{INV} \leftarrow_\$ D_{\mathbf{p}}} \left[\mathsf{SuccInv}_{\mathcal{A},\mathcal{R}}^{\mathsf{F},\mathsf{PSPACE},\mathsf{INV}} \geq 1 - c\epsilon \right] \leq \frac{1}{c}.$$

for any c. $\square$

References

1. Attrapadung, N., Matsuda, T., Nishimaki, R., Yamada, S., Yamakawa, T.: Constrained PRFs for NC^1 in traditional groups. In: Shacham, H., Boldyreva, A. (eds.) CRYPTO 2018, Part II. LNCS, vol. 10992, pp. 543–574. Springer, Heidelberg (2018)

2. Babai, L., Fortnow, L., Lund, C.: Non-deterministic exponential time has two-prover interactive protocols. Comput. Complex. **1**(1), 3–40 (1991)
3. Babai, L., Fortnow, L., Nisan, N., Wigderson, A.: BPP has subexponential time simulations unlessexptime has publishable proofs. Comput. Complex. **3**(4), 307–318 (1993)
4. Baecher, P., Brzuska, C., Fischlin, M.: Notions of black-box reductions, revisited. In: Sako, K., Sarkar, P. (eds.) ASIACRYPT 2013, Part I. LNCS, vol. 8269, pp. 296–315. Springer, Heidelberg (2013). https://doi.org/10.1007/978-3-642-42033-7_16
5. Blundo, C., Santis, A.D., Vaccaro, U.: Randomness in distribution protocols. Inf. Comput. **131**(2), 111–139 (1996)
6. Canetti, R., Rivest, R., Sudan, M., Trevisan, L., Vadhan, S., Wee, H.: Amplifying collision resistance: a complexity-theoretic treatment. In: Menezes, A. (ed.) CRYPTO 2007. LNCS, vol. 4622, pp. 264–283. Springer, Heidelberg (2007). https://doi.org/10.1007/978-3-540-74143-5_15
7. Döttling, N., Garg, S., Ishai, Y., Malavolta, G., Mour, T., Ostrovsky, R.: Trapdoor hash functions and their applications. In: Boldyreva, A., Micciancio, D. (eds.) CRYPTO 2019, Part III. LNCS, vol. 11694, pp. 3–32. Springer, Cham (2019). https://doi.org/10.1007/978-3-030-26954-8_1
8. Gennaro, R., Gertner, Y., Katz, J.: Lower bounds on the efficiency of encryption and digital signature schemes. In: 35th ACM STOC, pp. 417–425. ACM Press, June 2003
9. Gennaro, R., Trevisan, L.: Lower bounds on the efficiency of generic cryptographic constructions. In: 41st FOCS, pp. 305–313. IEEE Computer Society Press, November 2000
10. Goldreich, O., Impagliazzo, R., Levin, L.A., Venkatesan, R., Zuckerman, D.: Security preserving amplification of hardness. In: 31st FOCS, pp. 318–326. IEEE Computer Society Press, October 1990
11. Goldreich, O., Nisan, N., Wigderson, A.: On yao's xor lemma. Technical report TR95-050, Electronic Colloquium on Computational Complexity (1995)
12. Goyal, V., O'Neill, A., Rao, V.: Correlated-input secure hash functions. In: Ishai, Y. (ed.) TCC 2011. LNCS, vol. 6597, pp. 182–200. Springer, Heidelberg (2011). https://doi.org/10.1007/978-3-642-19571-6_12
13. Haitner, I., Reingold, O., Vadhan, S.P.: Efficiency improvements in constructing pseudorandom generators from one-way functions. In: Schulman, L.J. (ed.) 42nd ACM STOC, pp. 437–446. ACM Press, June 2010
14. Håstad, J., Impagliazzo, R., Levin, L.A., Luby, M.: A pseudorandom generator from any one-way function. SIAM J. Comput. **28**(4), 1364–1396 (1999)
15. Healy, A., Vadhan, S.P., Viola, E.: Using nondeterminism to amplify hardness. In: Babai, L. (ed.) 36th ACM STOC, pp. 192–201. ACM Press, June 2004
16. Hemenway, B., Lu, S., Ostrovsky, R.: Correlated product security from any one-way function. In: Fischlin, M., Buchmann, J., Manulis, M. (eds.) PKC 2012. LNCS, vol. 7293, pp. 558–575. Springer, Heidelberg (May 2012)
17. Hsiao, C.-Y., Reyzin, L.: Finding collisions on a public road, or do secure hash functions need secret coins? In: Franklin, M. (ed.) CRYPTO 2004. LNCS, vol. 3152, pp. 92–105. Springer, Heidelberg (2004). https://doi.org/10.1007/978-3-540-28628-8_6
18. Impagliazzo, R.: Hard-core distributions for somewhat hard problems. In: 36th FOCS, pp. 538–545. IEEE Computer Society Press, October 1995
19. Impagliazzo, R., Rudich, S.: Limits on the provable consequences of one-way permutations. In: 21st ACM STOC, pp. 44–61. ACM Press, May 1989

20. Impagliazzo, R., Rudich, S.: Limits on the provable consequences of one-way permutations. In: Goldwasser, S. (ed.) CRYPTO 1988. LNCS, vol. 403, pp. 8–26. Springer, New York (1990). https://doi.org/10.1007/0-387-34799-2_2
21. Impagliazzo, R., Wigderson, A.: P = BPP if E requires exponential circuits: derandomizing the XOR lemma. In: 29th ACM STOC, pp. 220–229. ACM Press, May 1997
22. Ishai, Y., Kilian, J., Nissim, K., Petrank, E.: Extending oblivious transfers efficiently. In: Boneh, D. (ed.) CRYPTO 2003. LNCS, vol. 2729, pp. 145–161. Springer, Heidelberg (2003). https://doi.org/10.1007/978-3-540-45146-4_9
23. Kim, J.H., Simon, D.R., Tetali, P.: Limits on the efficiency of one-way permutation-based hash functions. In: 40th FOCS, pp. 535–542. IEEE Computer Society Press, October 1999
24. Lin, H., Trevisan, L., Wee, H.: On hardness amplification of one-way functions. In: Kilian, J. (ed.) TCC 2005. LNCS, vol. 3378, pp. 34–49. Springer, Heidelberg (2005). https://doi.org/10.1007/978-3-540-30576-7_3
25. Lipton, R.: New directions in testing. Distrib. Comput. Cryptogr. **2**, 191–202 (1991)
26. Lu, C.-J.: On the complexity of parallel hardness amplification for one-way functions. In: Halevi, S., Rabin, T. (eds.) TCC 2006. LNCS, vol. 3876, pp. 462–481. Springer, Heidelberg (2006). https://doi.org/10.1007/11681878_24
27. Lu, C.-J.: On the security loss in cryptographic reductions. In: Joux, A. (ed.) EUROCRYPT 2009. LNCS, vol. 5479, pp. 72–87. Springer, Heidelberg (2009). https://doi.org/10.1007/978-3-642-01001-9_4
28. Mahmoody, M., Mohammed, A., Nematihaji, S., Pass, R., Shelat, A.: A note on black-box separations for indistinguishability obfuscation. Cryptology ePrint Archive, Report 2016/316 (2016). https://eprint.iacr.org/2016/316
29. Reingold, O., Trevisan, L., Vadhan, S.: Notions of reducibility between cryptographic primitives. In: Naor, M. (ed.) TCC 2004. LNCS, vol. 2951, pp. 1–20. Springer, Heidelberg (2004). https://doi.org/10.1007/978-3-540-24638-1_1
30. Rosen, A., Segev, G.: Chosen-ciphertext security via correlated products. In: Reingold, O. (ed.) TCC 2009. LNCS, vol. 5444, pp. 419–436. Springer, Heidelberg (2009). https://doi.org/10.1007/978-3-642-00457-5_25
31. Shaltiel, R., Viola, E.: Hardness amplification proofs require majority. In: Ladner, R.E., Dwork, C. (eds.) 40th ACM STOC, pp. 589–598. ACM Press, May 2008
32. Simon, D.R.: Finding collisions on a one-way street: can secure hash functions be based on general assumptions? In: Nyberg, K. (ed.) EUROCRYPT 1998. LNCS, vol. 1403, pp. 334–345. Springer, Heidelberg (1998). https://doi.org/10.1007/BFb0054137
33. Sudan, M., Trevisan, L., Vadhan, S.: Pseudorandom generators without the XOR lemma. J. Comput. Syst. Sci. **62**(2), 236–266 (2001)
34. Trevisan, L.: List-decoding using the XOR lemma. In: 44th FOCS, pp. 126–135. IEEE Computer Society Press, October 2003
35. Trevisan, L.: On uniform amplification of hardness in NP. In: Gabow, H.N., Fagin, R. (eds.) 37th ACM STOC, pp. 31–38. ACM Press, May 2005
36. Vadhan, S.P., Zheng, C.J.: Characterizing pseudoentropy and simplifying pseudorandom generator constructions. In: Karloff, H.J., Pitassi, T. (eds.) 44th ACM STOC, pp. 817–836. ACM Press, May 2012
37. Viola, E.: The complexity of constructing pseudorandom generators from hard functions. Comput. Complex. **13**(3–4), 147–188 (2005)
38. Wee, H.: One-way permutations, interactive hashing and statistically hiding commitments. In: Vadhan, S.P. (ed.) TCC 2007. LNCS, vol. 4392, pp. 419–433. Springer, Heidelberg (2007). https://doi.org/10.1007/978-3-540-70936-7_23

39. Wichs, D.: Barriers in cryptography with weak, correlated and leaky sources. In: Kleinberg, R.D. (ed.) ITCS 2013, pp. 111–126. ACM, January 2013
40. Yao, A.C.C.: Theory and applications of trapdoor functions (extended abstract). In: 23rd FOCS, pp. 80–91. IEEE Computer Society Press, November 1982

Simple Constructions from (Almost) Regular One-Way Functions

Noam Mazor[1]([envelope]) and Jiapeng Zhang[2]

[1] Tel-Aviv University, Tel Aviv-Yafo, Israel
noammazor@tauex.tau.ac.il
[2] University of Southern California, Los Angeles, USA
jiapengz@usc.edu

Abstract. Two of the most useful cryptographic primitives that can be constructed from one-way functions are *pseudorandom generators* (PRGs) and *universal one-way hash functions* (UOWHFs). In order to implement them in practice, the efficiency of such constructions must be considered. The three major efficiency measures are: the *seed length*, the *call complexity* to the one-way function, and the *adaptivity* of these calls. Still, the optimal efficiency of these constructions is not yet fully understood: there exist gaps between the known upper bound and the known lower bound for black-box constructions.

A special class of one-way functions called *unknown-regular* one-way functions is much better understood. Haitner, Harnik and Reingold (CRYPTO 2006) presented a PRG construction with semi-linear seed length and linear number of calls based on a method called *randomized iterate*. Ames, Gennaro and Venkitasubramaniam (TCC 2012) then gave a construction of UOWHF with similar parameters and using similar ideas. On the other hand, Holenstein and Sinha (FOCS 2012) and Barhum and Holenstein (TCC 2013) showed an almost linear call-complexity lower bound for black-box constructions of PRGs and UOWHFs from one-way functions. Hence Haitner et al. and Ames et al. reached *tight* constructions (in terms of seed length and the number of calls) of PRGs and UOWHFs from regular one-way functions. These constructions, however, are adaptive.

In this work, we present non-adaptive constructions for both primitives which match the optimal call-complexity given by Holenstein and Sinha and Barhum and Holenstein. Our constructions, besides being simple and non-adaptive, are robust also for *almost-regular* one-way functions.

Keywords: Pseudorandom generator · Universal one-way hash function

N. Mazor—Research supported by Israel Science Foundation grant 666/19 and the Blavatnik Interdisciplinary Cyber Research Center at Tel-Aviv University.

K. Nissim and B. Waters (Eds.): TCC 2021, LNCS 13043, pp. 457–485, 2021.
https://doi.org/10.1007/978-3-030-90453-1_16

1   Introduction

A wide class of cryptographic primitives can be constructed from *one-way functions*, which is the minimal assumption for cryptography. Informally, a function f is called a one-way function if it is easy to compute, but hard to invert by polynomial-time algorithms. Two important primitives that can be constructed from one-way functions are *pseudorandom generators* (PRGs) [5,22] and *universal one-way hash functions* (UOWHFs) [19]. These two primitives are useful for constructing even more powerful primitives such as encryption, digital signatures and commitments. Thus, an improvement in the efficiency of constructions for PRGs and UWOHFs would have an effect on other primitives. Yet, the optimal efficiency of these two basic primitives is not fully understood.

There are several important efficiency measures to account for when considering PRGs and UOWHFs. For PRG constructions, one aims to minimize the seed length and the number of calls to the one-way function f. For UOWHF constructions, there is a need to minimize the key length and the number of calls to f. Besides these two measurements, another important parameter is the *adaptivity* of the calls. That is, if the inputs for the one-way function are independent of the output of previous calls, then the construction can be implemented in parallel. By contrast, if the calls are adaptive, one must make them sequentially.

Constructions. Much progress was done since the notion of PRGs has been introduced. The first construction of pseudorandom generators was given by Blum and Micali [5] based on the assumption that a specific function is hard to invert. This construction was generalized by Yao [22] to work with any one-way permutation. Since then, many subsequent works made effort to construct PRGs based on arbitrary one-way functions. Notably, through introducing the *randomized iterate*[1] method, Goldreich, Krawczyk and Luby [8] gave a PRG construction from any *unknown-regular* one-way function. The notion of regular one-way function is a refinement of a one-way permutation: A one-way function f is called *regular* if for every n and x, x' with $|x| = |x'| = n$ it holds that $\left| f^{-1}(f(x)) \right| = \left| f^{-1}(f(x')) \right|$. We say that the function is *unknown-regular* if the *regularity parameter*, $\left| f^{-1}(f(x)) \right|$, may not be a computable function of n. More recently, the randomized iterate method was further studied by [11,23], who reached a construction of PRGs from any unknown-regular one-way functions, while having $O(n \log n)$ seed length and making $O(n/ \log n)$ calls to the one-way function. [25] improved the seed length up to $\omega(n)$ by using a transformation that converts any unknown-regular function into a function that is known-regular on its image.

For arbitrary one-way function, a seminal work by Håstad, Impagliazzo, Levin and Luby [15] gave the first PRG construction. Since then, the efficiency has been improved by many works [10,13,16,21]. Currently, the state-of-the-art construction of PRGs due to [21] uses $O(n^3)$ bits of random seed and $O(n^3)$

---

[1] For a one-way function f and pairwise independent hash functions $h_1, \ldots, h_k$, the k-th randomized iteration of f is $f \circ h_k \circ \cdots \circ f \circ h_1 \circ f$.

adaptive calls to the one-way function, or alternatively seed of size $O(n^4)$ with non-adaptive calls [13,21].[2]

The constructions of UOWHFs use similar ideas to the constructions of PRGs. Still, the best PRGs constructions from arbitrary one-way functions are more efficient than the best known UOWHFs constructions. Rompel [20] gave the first UOWHF construction from arbitrary one-way functions. The efficiency was improved by [12], who gave a construction of UOWHF using $O(n^6)$ adaptive calls with a key of size $O(n^7)$. Constructing a UOWHF using $O(n^3)$ calls to the one-way function is still an interesting open question.

The efficiency of UOWHF based on an unknown-regular one-way function is similar to the efficiency of the unknown-regular based PRGs. Interestingly, this was shown by [2] using the same method of randomized iterate, resulting in a construction that uses $\Theta(n)$ key length and $\Theta(n)$ calls. We stress that when the regularity of f is known (i.e., can be computed efficiently given n), there are much more efficient constructions for both PRGs and UOWHFs [7,9,19,23].

Lower Bounds. The lower bounds for black-box constructions are relatively far from the upper bounds. In this line of work, there are two incomparable types of results. The first type, due to [6] is stated with terms of the stretching and compression of the PRG and UOWHF, respectively. Specifically, [6] showed that any black-box PRG construction $G: \{0,1\}^m \rightarrow \{0,1\}^{m+s}$ from f must use $\Omega(s/\log n)$ calls to f. Similarly, any black box UWOHF construction with input size m and output size $m - s$ must use $\Omega(s/\log n)$ calls. In the second type of results [17] showed that any black-box PRG construction from f must use $\Omega(n/\log n)$ calls to f, even for 1-bit stretching. [3] showed similar results for 1-bit compressing UWOHF.

As mentioned, there is a substantial gap between the aforementioned lower and upper bounds. One explanation for that gap is that all of the above lower bounds hold even when the one-way function f is *unknown-regular.* For this case, these bounds are known to be tight with the mentioned above constructions, which are based on *randomized iterations.* These constructions, however, are adaptive.

1.1 Our Contribution

In this paper, we give *non-adaptive* constructions of tight call complexity for PRGs and UOWHFs from unknown-regular one-way functions. Both of our constructions are quite simple and are very similar to each other. Same as previous results, the security of our constructions holds also if f is only almost-regular [23], which means that for every $|x| = |x'|$, the ratio between $\left|f^{-1}(f(x))\right|$ and $\left|f^{-1}(f(x'))\right|$ is only bounded by a polynomial in $|x|$ (compared to a ratio of 1, in the case of regular functions).

---

[2] We ignore low order terms for this introduction.

The seed (or key) length in our construction for PRGs (or UOWHFs respectively) is $O(n^2)$, compared to $\tilde{O}(n)$ bits in the previous adaptive constructions. This seems unavoidable and raises an interesting open question.[3]

Our Constructions and Results. In this section, we present our constructions. The results here are stated for regular one-way functions but can be naturally expanded to almost-regular functions, as stated in Sects. 3 and 4. The main crux of the construction is the following observation. For regular f and i.i.d uniform random variables X_1, X_2 over $\{0,1\}^n$, given any fixing of $f(X_1)$, both the entropy and min-entropy of the pair $X_1, f(X_2)$ are exactly n. To see the above, recall that for regular f with (unknown) regularity parameter r, it holds that there are exactly r possible values for X_1 given $f(X_1)$, and exactly $2^n/r$ possible values for $f(X_2)$. Thus, the regularity parameter r "cancels out" when considering the number of possible values (given $f(X_1)$) of the pair $X_1, f(X_2)$, which is $r \cdot 2^n/r = 2^n$. In the PRG construction, we exploit this fact by using a universal family of hash functions $\mathcal{H}$ (and the Goldreich-Levin theorem) in order to extract pseudo-uniform bits. In the UOWHF construction, we use similar ideas in order to compress the pair $X_1, f(X_2)$ without creating too many collisions. For both constructions, we need additional properties from the universal family $\mathcal{H}$ that we ignore for this introduction. See more details in Sects. 3 and 4. We next present the constructions. The main ideas of the proofs for the following theorems are described in Sect. 1.2.

A Simple Construction of PRGs From Regular One-Way Functions. We start with a description of our PRG construction. Let $\mathcal{H} = \left\{h : \{0,1\}^{2n} \to \{0,1\}^{n+\log n}\right\}$ be a family of 2-universal hash functions. For a regular one-way function $f : \{0,1\}^n \to \{0,1\}^n$ and an integer $t \in \mathbb{N}$,[4] the generator $G_t : \mathcal{H} \times \{0,1\}^{n(t+1)} \to \mathcal{H} \times \{0,1\}^{t \cdot (n+\log n)}$ is given by

$$G_t(h, x_1, \ldots, x_{t+1}) = (h, h(x_1, f(x_2)), \ldots, h(x_t, f(x_{t+1})))$$

We show that for every polynomial t, the distribution $G_t(\mathcal{H}, X_1, \ldots, X_t)$ is pseudorandom. Note that the input length of G_t is $|h| + n \cdot (t+1)$ and the output length is $|h| + t \cdot (n + \log n)$. By making $t = \Theta(n/\log n)$ calls, we show that G_t is indeed a pseudorandom generator.

Theorem 1.1. *[Main theorem for PRG, informal] Let $f : \{0,1\}^n \to \{0,1\}^n$ be an unknown-regular one-way function and let $t(n) \geq n/\log n + 1$ be some polynomial. Then, G_t is a PRG with seed length $O(n^2 + n(t(n)+1))$. Furthermore, G_t makes $t(n)$ non-adaptive calls to f.*

---

[3] By [17], $\Omega(n)$ calls are necessary for any black-box construction. Since for non-adaptive constructions the uniformly random calls seem the only reasonable way to use the one-way function, such construction needs at least $\Omega(n^2)$ input bits. We admit it is only a vague explanation.

[4] The assumption that f is length-preserving is made for simplicity, and is not crucial for our constructions.

A Simple Construction of UOWHFs From Regular One-Way Functions. Now we introduce the construction of the UOWHFs. It is a well-known fact that in order to construct UWOHF, it is sufficient to construct a function for which it is hard to find a collision for a *random* input. Let f be a one-way function, let t be a parameter and let $\mathcal{H} = \left\{ h : \{0,1\}^{2n} \to \{0,1\}^{n-\log n} \right\}$ be a family of hash functions. We define the function $C_t : \mathcal{H} \times \{0,1\}^{n \cdot t} \to \mathcal{H} \times \{0,1\}^{(t-1)\cdot(n-\log n)+2n}$ as

$$C_t (h, x_1, \ldots, x_t) = (h, f(x_1), h(x_1, f(x_2)), \ldots, h(x_{t-1}, f(x_t)), x_t)$$

The main difference of this construction from the PRG one is that h is now a shrinking function. In addition, we also output $f(x_1)$ and the very last input of C_t. As before, since the output length of UOWHFs has to be shorter than the input length, we have to make up for the additional output $(f(x_1), x_t)$ by taking t to be $\Theta(n/\log n)$.

The OUWHF can now be defined using C_t. Let $k = \log |\mathcal{H}| + n \cdot t$ and for a string $z \in \{0,1\}^k$, let C_z be the function defined by $C_z(w) = C_t(w \oplus z)$ for every $w \in \{0,1\}^k$. Our main theorem for this part is stated as follows.

Theorem 1.2. *[Main theorem for UOWHF, informal] Let $f \colon \{0,1\}^n \to \{0,1\}^n$ be an unknown-regular one-way function and let $t(n) \geq n/\log n + 2$ be some polynomial. Then, $\{C_z\}_{z \in \{0,1\}^k}$ is a family of universal one-way hash functions with key length $k = O(n^2 + n \cdot t(n))$ and output length $O(n^2 + n \cdot t(n))$. Furthermore, for every $z \in \{0,1\}^k$, C_z makes t non-adaptive calls to f.*

1.2 Proof Overview

Here we give a short overview of our proofs. For both constructions, the proof boils down to showing that each input pair x_i, x_{i+1} induces a weak version of the desired primitive. For PRG, the main part of the security proof is showing that given $f(x_1)$ and h, it is hard to distinguish between $h(x_1, f(x_2))$ and a uniform string. For UOWHF, we prove the security by showing that given h, x_1, x_2, it is hard to find a collision h, x'_1, x'_2 to the function $C(h, x_1, x_2) = h, f(x_1), h(x_1, f(x_2))$. Note that it may be easy to find $x'_2 \neq x_2$ with $f(x'_2) = f(x_2)$. To solve this, we further demand that $f(x'_2) \neq f(x_2)$.[5] To show that this is enough, we prove that any collision in our UOWHF must contain a collision in the above form, for at least one input pair. Below we give short descriptions of the main ideas in more details.

The PRG Construction. We start by sketching the security proof for the PRG. Let X_1 and X_2 be uniform random variables over $\{0,1\}^n$, and let h be a hash function, uniformly sampled from a universal family of hash functions $\mathcal{H} = \left\{ h : \{0,1\}^{2n} \to \{0,1\}^{n+\log n} \right\}$. Recall that we want to show that given

---

[5] For this reason we need to output the last input x_t in our UOWHF construction.

h and $f(X_1)$, it holds that $h(X_1, f(X_2))$ is computationally indistinguishable from uniform $n + \log n$ bits. For simplicity, assume that we are only interested in proving that the distinguish advantage is at most n^{-c}, for some constant $c > 1$.

The main observation is that for regular f, given $f(X_1)$, the pair $X_1, f(X_2)$ has exactly n bits of min-entropy. Thus, by the leftover hash lemma, the $n - O(c \log n)$ first bits of $h(X_1, f(X_2))$ are $n^{-c}/2$ statistically close to uniform. To argue that the suffix of $h(X_1, f(X_2))$ looks uniform, we show that $g(x_1, y) = h, f(x_1), h(x_1, y)_{1,\ldots,n-O(c \log n)}$ is a one-way function,[6] and thus we can use Goldreich-Levin in order to extract additional $O(c \log n)$ pseudorandom bits from $X_1, f(X_2)$.

The UOWHF Construction. We now sketch the security proof for the UOWHF. Let $\mathcal{H}$ be a universal family of hash functions $\left\{ h : \{0,1\}^{2n} \to \{0,1\}^{n-\log n} \right\}$. We show that given random h and uniformly sampled x_1 and x_2 from $\{0,1\}^n$, it is hard to find $(x_1', x_2') \neq (x_1, x_2)$ such that $f(x_1) = f(x_1')$, $f(x_2) \neq f(x_2')$ and yet $h(x_1, f(x_2)) = h(x_1', f(x_2'))$. For $x_1, x_2 \in \{0,1\}^n$ and $h \in \mathcal{H}$ we define

$$\mathcal{G}_{h,x_1,x_2} := \{(x_1', y) : h(x_1, f(x_2)) = h(x_1', y) \ \wedge \ f(x_1) = f(x_1') \ \wedge \ y \in Im(f)\}.$$

That is, the set $\mathcal{G}_{h,x_1,x_2}$ contains all the pairs $(x_1', f(x_2'))$ for which h, x_1', x_2' collides with h, x_1, x_2. The main observation here is that, since h outputs $n - \log n$ bits, and there are exactly 2^n pairs (x_1', y) such that $y \in Im(f)$ and $f(x_1') = f(x_1)$, the expected size of $\mathcal{G}_{h,x_1,x_2}$ is at most $2^n/2^{n-\log n} = n$. Thus, we can use an algorithm A that finds a collision in the above function in order to invert f: Given input y, we choose random $x_1, x_2 \in \{0,1\}^n$ and *plant* y in $\mathcal{G}_{h,x_1,x_2}$. That is, we choose a random h conditioned on the event that $h(x_1, f(x_2)) = h(x_1', y)$ for some $x_1' \in f^{-1}(f(x_1))$. Since there are about n such pairs, we can hope that the planted pair (x_1', y) will be output by A with good probability.

However, we need to find x_1' for which the pair (x_1', y) has a good probability to be output by A. To do that, we also use A in order to find a pre-image x_1' of $f(x_1)$, and then show that x_1' has a good probability to be output again by A.[7] For more details, see Sect. 4.

1.3   Additional Related Work

Arbitrary One-Way Functions. In [12], the notion of inaccessible entropy (introduced in [14]) was used in order to construct UOWHF. Similar techniques were later used in [10] to construct PRG, where the notion of inaccessible entropy was replaced with next-block pseudoentropy. This construction was later simplified by [21], who also improved the seed length with the cost of adaptivity. Lately [1] pointed out that the notions of accessible entropy and next-block pseudoentropy are deeply related to each other.

---

[6] Actually, we need to show that the function g is hard to invert on outputs sampled from a specific distribution. This is sufficient for applying the Goldreich-Levin theorem, see Lemma 2.5.

[7] Such a "collision based" argument was also used in [2].

Regular One-Way Functions. As mentioned above, the construction from regular one-way functions are more efficient. Beside almost-regular, a few refinements of regularity were considered in past works. [4] showed a construction for UOWHF that uses $O(ns^6(n))$ key-length under the assumption that $f^{-1}(f(x))$ is concentrated in an interval of size $2^{s(n)}$. [24] considered unknown-weakly-regular functions. The last are functions for which the set of inputs with maximal number of siblings is of fraction at least n^{-c} for some constant c. For such functions, [24] presented PRG with $O(n \log n)$ seed-length and $O(n^{2c+1})$ calls. [23] considered known-almost-regular and unknown-weakly-regular functions. For the last, [23] showed a tight construction of UOWHF based on the randomized iterate method.

1.4   Paper Organisation

Formal definitions are given in Sect. 2. The PRG construction and proof of Theorem 1.1 are in Sect. 3. The UOWHF construction and proof of Theorem 1.2 are in Sect. 4.

2   Preliminaries

2.1   Notations

We use calligraphic letters to denote sets, uppercase for random variables, and lowercase for values and functions. For $n \in \mathbb{N}$, let $[n] := \{1, \ldots, n\}$. Given a vector $s \in \{0,1\}^n$, let s_i denote its i-th entry, and $s_{1,\ldots,i}$ denote its first i entries. For $s, w \in \{0,1\}^*$ we use $s \circ w$ to denote their concatenation and for $s, w \in \{0,1\}^n$, we use $s \oplus w \in \{0,1\}^n$ to denote their bit-wise XOR.

The support of a distribution P over a finite set $\mathcal{S}$ is defined by $\mathrm{Supp}(P) := \{x \in \mathcal{S} : P(x) > 0\}$. For a (discrete) distribution D let $d \leftarrow D$ denote that d was sampled according to D. Similarly, for a set $\mathcal{S}$, let $s \leftarrow \mathcal{S}$ denote that s is drawn uniformly from $\mathcal{S}$. For a function $f \colon \{0,1\}^n \rightarrow \{0,1\}^n$, let $y \leftarrow f(\{0,1\}^n)$ denote that y sampled from the following distribution: sample x uniformly from $\{0,1\}^n$, and let $y = f(x)$. Let $\mathsf{Im}(f) := \{f(x) \colon x \in \{0,1\}^n\}$ be the image of f. The statistical distance (also known as, variation distance) of two distributions P and Q over a discrete domain $\mathcal{X}$ is defined by $\mathrm{SD}(P, Q) := \max_{\mathcal{S} \subseteq \mathcal{X}} |P(\mathcal{S}) - Q(\mathcal{S})| = \frac{1}{2} \sum_{x \in \mathcal{S}} |P(x) - Q(x)|$. The min-entropy of a distribution X, denoted by $\mathrm{H}_\infty(X)$ is defined by $\mathrm{H}_\infty(X) := -\log(\max_{x \in \mathrm{Supp}(X)} \{\Pr[X = x]\})$.

Let poly denote the set of all polynomials, and let PPT stand for probabilistic polynomial time. A function $\nu \colon \mathbb{N} \rightarrow [0,1]$ is negligible, denoted $\nu(n) = neg(n)$, if $\nu(n) < 1/p(n)$ for every $p \in$ poly and large enough n. Lastly, we identify a matrix $M \in \{0,1\}^{n \times m}$ with a function $M \colon \{0,1\}^n \rightarrow \{0,1\}^m$ by $M(x) := x \cdot M$, thinking of $x \in \{0,1\}^n$ as a vector with dimension n.

2.2   One-Way Functions

We now formally define basic cryptographic primitives. We start with the definition of one-way function.

Definition 2.1 (One-way function). *A polynomial-time computable function* $f : \{0,1\}^* \to \{0,1\}^*$ *is called a* one-way *function if for every probabilistic polynomial time algorithm* A, *there is a negligible function* $\nu : \mathbb{N} \to [0,1]$ *such that for every* $n \in \mathbb{N}$

$$\Pr_{x \leftarrow \{0,1\}^n} \left[\mathsf{A}(f(x)) \in f^{-1}(f(x)) \right] \leq \nu(n)$$

For simplicity we assume that the one-way function f is length-preserving. That is, $|f(x)| = |x|$ for every $x \in \{0,1\}^*$. This can be assumed without loss of generality, and is not crucial for our constructions.

In this paper we focus on almost-regular one-way functions, formally defined below.

Definition 2.2 (Almost-regular function). *A function family* $f = \{f_n : \{0,1\}^n \to \{0,1\}^n\}$ *is* β-almost-regular *for* $\beta \geq 0$ *if for every* $n \in \mathbb{N}$ *and* $x \in \{0,1\}^n$ *it holds that*

$$\frac{2^n}{|\mathsf{Im}(f)|} \cdot n^{-\beta} \leq \left| f^{-1}(f(x)) \right| \leq \frac{2^n}{|\mathsf{Im}(f)|} \cdot n^{\beta}.$$

f *is* almost-regular *if there exists* $\beta \geq 0$ *such that* f *is* β-almost-regular, *and* regular *if it is* 0-almost-regular.

Note that we do not assume that the regularity of f can be computed efficiently. That is, we only assume that f is unknown-(almost)-regular.

Immediately from the definition of a one-way function, we get the following simple observation.

Claim 2.3. *For every one-way function* $f : \{0,1\}^n \to \{0,1\}^n$ *there exists a negligible function* $\nu(n)$ *such that for every input* $x \in \{0,1\}^n$ *it holds that* $\left| f^{-1}(f(x)) \right| \leq 2^n \cdot \nu(n)$.

2.3 Pseudorandom Generators

In Sect. 3 we use one-way functions in order to construct PRGs. The later are formally defined below.

Definition 2.4 (Pseudorandom generator). *Let* n *be a security parameter. A polynomial-time computable function* $G : \{0,1\}^n \to \{0,1\}^{m(n)}$ *is called a* pseudorandom generator *if for every* $n > 0$ *it holds that* $m(n) > n$ *and, for every probabilistic polynomial time algorithm* D, *there is a negligible function* $\nu : \mathbb{N} \to [0,1]$ *such that for every* $n > 0$,

$$\left| \Pr_{x \leftarrow \{0,1\}^n} [\mathsf{D}(G(x)) = 1] - \Pr_{x \leftarrow \{0,1\}^{m(n)}} [\mathsf{D}(x) = 1] \right| \leq \nu(n).$$

A key ingredient in the construction of PRG from one-way function is the Goldreich-Levin hardcore predicate. The following lemma follows almost directly from [9].

Lemma 2.5. *Let n be a security parameter. Let $f \colon \{0,1\}^n \to \{0,1\}^n$ be a function, and D a distribution on $\{0,1\}^n$, such that for every PPT A*

$$\Pr_{x \leftarrow D} \left[A(f(x)) \in f^{-1}(f(x)) \right] = neg(n).$$

Then for every PPT P,

$$\Pr_{x \leftarrow D, r \leftarrow \{0,1\}^n} \left[P(f(x), r) = GL(x, r) \right] \leq 1/2 + neg(n)$$

where $GL(x, r) := \langle x, r \rangle$ is the Goldreich-Levin predicate.

Proof. By the proof of Goldreich-Levin [9], for every $p \in$ poly there is an oracle-aided PPT algorithm A such that for every algorithm P and x with

$$\Pr_{r \leftarrow \{0,1\}^n} \left[P(f(x), r) = GL(x, r) \right] \geq 1/2 + 1/p(n)$$

it holds that

$$\Pr \left[A^P(f(x)) = x \right] \geq 1/p^2(n).$$

Thus, it holds for every $p \in$ poly that

$$\Pr_{x \leftarrow D} \left[\Pr_{r \leftarrow \{0,1\}^n} \left[P(f(x), r) = GL(x, r) \right] \geq 1/2 + 1/p(n) \right] = neg(n)$$

which implies that

$$\Pr_{x \leftarrow D, r \leftarrow \{0,1\}^n} \left[P(f(x), r) = GL(x, r) \right] \leq 1/2 + 1/p(n) + neg(n)$$

for every $p \in$ poly. $\qquad\square$

The next lemma, stated in [22], is useful for showing that a sequence of bits is pseudorandom. The proof of the lemma is given in Appendix A.

Lemma 2.6 (Distinguishability to prediction). *There exists an oracle-aided PPT algorithm P such that the following holds. Let Q be a distribution over $\{0,1\}^* \times \{0,1\}^n$, let D be an algorithm and $\alpha \in [0,1]$ such that,*

$$\Pr_{(x,y) \leftarrow Q, z \leftarrow \{0,1\}^n} \left[D(x, z) = 1 \right] - \Pr_{(x,y) \leftarrow Q} \left[D(x, y) = 1 \right] \geq \alpha.$$

Then there exists $i \in [n]$ such that

$$\Pr_{(x,y) \leftarrow Q} \left[P^D(x, y_{1,\dots,i-1}) = y_i \right] \geq 1/2 + \alpha/n.$$

2.4   Universal One Way Hash Function

Lastly, we formally define UOWHF.

Definition 2.7 (Universal one-way hash function)
   Let k be a security parameter. A family of functions
$\mathcal{F} = \left\{ f_z \colon \{0,1\}^{n(k)} \to \{0,1\}^{m(k)} \right\}_{z \in \{0,1\}^k}$ *is a family of universal one-way hash functions (UOWHFs) if it satisfies:*

1. *Efficiency: Given $z \in \{0,1\}^k$ and $x \in \{0,1\}^{n(k)}$, $f_z(x)$ can be evaluated in time $\mathrm{poly}(n(k), k)$.*
2. *Shrinking: $m(k) < n(k)$.*
3. *Target Collision Resistance: For every probabilistic polynomial-time adversary A, the probability that A succeeds in the following game is negligible in k:*
   (a) *Let $(x, state) \leftarrow \mathsf{A}(1^k) \in \{0,1\}^{n(k)} \times \{0,1\}^*$.*
   (b) *Choose $z \leftarrow \{0,1\}^k$.*
   (c) *Let $x' \leftarrow \mathsf{A}(state, z) \in \{0,1\}^{n(k)}$.*
   (d) *A succeeds if $x \neq x'$ and $f_z(x) = f_z(x')$.*

A relaxation of the target collision resistance property can be done by requiring the function to be collision resistant only on random inputs.

Definition 2.8 (Collision resistance on random inputs). *Let n be a security parameter. A function $f \colon \{0,1\}^n \to \{0,1\}^{m(n)}$ is collision resistant on random inputs if for every probabilistic polynomial-time adversary A, the probability that A succeeds in the following game is negligible in n:*

1. *Choose $x \leftarrow \{0,1\}^n$.*
2. *Let $x' \leftarrow \mathsf{A}(x) \in \{0,1\}^n$.*
3. *A succeeds if $x \neq x'$ and $f(x) = f(x')$.*

The following lemma states that it is enough to construct a function that is collision resistant on random inputs, in order to get UOWHF.

Lemma 2.9 (From random inputs to targets, folklore). *Let n be a security parameter. Let $F \colon \{0,1\}^n \to \{0,1\}^{m(n)}$ be a length-decreasing function. Suppose F is collision-resistant on random inputs.*
   Then $\{F_y \colon \{0,1\}^n \to \{0,1\}^m\}_{y \in \{0,1\}^n}$, for $F_y(x) := F(y \oplus x)$, is a family of target collision-resistant hash functions.

2.5   2-Universal Hash Families

2-universal families are an important ingredient in our constructions. In this section, we formally define this notion, together with some useful properties of such families.

Definition 2.10 (2-universal family). *A family of function* $\mathcal{F} = \left\{f\colon \{0,1\}^n \to \{0,1\}^\ell\right\}$ *is 2-universal if for every* $x \neq x' \in \{0,1\}^n$ *it holds that* $\Pr_{f \leftarrow \mathcal{F}}[f(x) = f(x')] = 2^{-\ell}$.

A universal a family is explicit *if given a description of a function* $f \in \mathcal{F}$ *and* $x \in \{0,1\}^n$, $f(x)$ *can be computed in polynomial time (in* n, ℓ*). Such family is* constructible *if it is explicit and there is a* PPT *algorithm that given* $x, x' \in \{0,1\}^n$ *outputs a uniform* $f \in \mathcal{F}$, *such that* $f(x) = f(x')$.

An important property of 2-universal families is that they can be used to construct a strong extractor. This is stated in the leftover hash lemma:

Lemma 2.11 (Leftover hash lemma [18]). *Let* $n \in \mathbb{N}$, $\epsilon \in [0,1]$, *and let* X *be a random variable over* $\{0,1\}^n$. *Let* $\mathcal{H} = \left\{h\colon \{0,1\}^n \to \{0,1\}^\ell\right\}$ *be a 2-universal hash family with* $\ell \leq H_\infty(X) - 2\log 1/\epsilon$. *Then,*

$$SD((H, H(X)), (H, U_\ell)) \leq \epsilon$$

for U_ℓ *being the uniform distribution over* $\{0,1\}^\ell$ *and* H *being the uniform distribution over* $\mathcal{H}$.

The family of all binary matrices of size $n \times \ell$, $\left\{m\colon m \in \{0,1\}^{n \times \ell}\right\}$, is a constructible 2-universal family. This family has an additional property that is useful in the proof. This property is defined below.

Definition 2.12 (Approximately flat family). *A family of functions* $\mathcal{H} = \left\{h\colon \{0,1\}^{2n} \to \{0,1\}^\ell\right\}$ *is* approximately-flat *if for every set* $\mathcal{Y} \subseteq \{0,1\}^n$, $x_1, x_2 \in \{0,1\}^n$ *and* $y_1 \in \mathcal{Y}$ *it holds that,*

$$\Pr_{h \leftarrow \mathcal{H}}[\exists y_2 \in \mathcal{Y} \text{ s.t. } h(x_1, y_1) = h(x_2, y_2)] \geq 2^{-10} \cdot \min\left\{|\mathcal{Y}| \cdot 2^{-\ell}, 1\right\}.$$

The proof of the next lemma is in Appendix A.

Lemma 2.13. *For every* $\ell, n \in \mathbb{N}$ *such that* $\ell \leq n$, *the family* $\left\{m\colon m \in \{0,1\}^{n \times \ell}\right\}$ *is approximately-flat.*

2.6 Useful Inequalities

The following well-known inequalities will be useful later on.

Lemma 2.14 (Jensen Inequality). *Let* X *be a distribution over* $\mathbb{R}$ *and let* $f\colon \mathbb{R} \to \mathbb{R}$ *be a convex function. It holds that*

$$f(\mathrm{E}\,[X]) \leq \mathrm{E}\,[f(X)]$$

Lemma 2.15 (Cauchy–Schwarz inequality). *Let* $n \in \mathbb{N}$ *and* $a_1, \ldots, a_n \in \mathbb{R}$ *be numbers. Then,*

$$\left(\sum_{i \in [n]} a_i\right)^2 \leq n \cdot \sum_{i \in [n]} a_i^2$$

Lastly, the following lemma will be useful in the security proof of the UOWHF. Let A be an algorithm such that for every x, the output of $A(x)$ is in some small set $\mathcal{S}_x$. Then the lemma roughly states the event of two executions of A returning the same value is not too rare.

Lemma 2.16. *Let $\Omega \subseteq \{0,1\}^n$ and $\mathcal{X}$ be some set, let X be a distribution over $\mathcal{X}$, and let $S \colon \mathcal{X} \to P(\Omega)$ be a function that maps elements in $\mathcal{X}$ to subsets of Ω. Let A be an algorithm, such that for every $x \in \mathcal{X}$, $A(x) \in S(x) \cup \{\bot\}$. Assume that for every $u \in \Omega$, it holds that $0 < \Pr_{x \leftarrow X}[u \in S(x)] \le \ell/|\Omega|$, and that $\Pr_{x \leftarrow X}[A(x) \in S(x)] \ge p$. Then*

$$\sum_{u \in \Omega} \Pr_{x \leftarrow X}[A(x) = u] \Pr_{x \leftarrow X}[A(x) = u \mid u \in S(x)] \ge p^2/\ell.$$

Proof. Using Cauchy–Schwarz inequality, it holds that:

$$\sum_{u \in \Omega} \Pr_{x \leftarrow X}[A(x) = u] \Pr_{x \leftarrow X}[A(x) = u \mid u \in S(x)]$$

$$= \sum_{u \in \Omega} \Pr_{x \leftarrow X}[A(x) = u]^2 / \Pr_{x \leftarrow X}[u \in S(x)]$$

$$\ge \sum_{u \in \Omega} \Pr_{x \leftarrow X}[A(x) = u]^2 \cdot |\Omega|/\ell$$

$$\ge \left(\sum_{u \in \Omega} \Pr_{x \leftarrow X}[A(x) = u] \right)^2 / \ell$$

$$\ge p^2/\ell.$$

3   The PRG Construction

In this section we prove the security of our PRG construction. We start with a description of the construction. Let $f \colon \{0,1\}^n \to \{0,1\}^n$ be an almost-regular one-way function, let t be a parameter and let $\mathcal{H} = \left\{ m \colon m \in \{0,1\}^{2n \times (n + \log n)} \right\}$ be the 2-universal family induced by the set of matrices of size $2n \times (n + \log n)$.[8] The generator $G \colon \mathcal{H} \times \{0,1\}^{n(t+1)} \to \mathcal{H} \times \{0,1\}^{t \cdot (n + \log n)}$ is given by

$$G(h, x_1, \ldots, x_{t+1}) = (h, h(x_1, f(x_2)), \ldots, h(x_t, f(x_{t+1}))).$$

The main theorem of this part is as follows.

---

[8] By taking $\mathcal{H} = \left\{ h_m \colon m \in \{0,1\}^{2n \times (\log^2 n + \log n)}, h \in \mathcal{G} \right\}$ where $\mathcal{G} = \left\{ g \colon \{0,1\}^{2n} \to \{0,1\}^{n - \log^2 n} \right\}$ is arbitrary 2-universal family, and $h_m(z) := h(z) \circ m(z)$, the seed of length can be reduced up to $O(n \cdot t)$.

Theorem 3.1. *[Main theorem for PRG] Let $f \colon \{0,1\}^n \to \{0,1\}^n$ be an almost-regular one-way function and let $t(n) \geq n/\log n + 1$ be some polynomial. Then G is a PRG with seed length $O(n^2 + n(t+1))$. Furthermore, G uses t non-adaptive calls to f.*

Note that the stretch of G is $t \cdot \log n - n$, which is tight with [6] for large values of t. We now prove Theorem 3.1. Our main lemma states that given h and $f(x_1)$, the hash $h(x_1, f(x_2))$ looks uniform for a computationally bounded algorithm.

Lemma 3.2. *Let $f \colon \{0,1\}^n \to \{0,1\}^n$ be an almost-regular one-way function. For any PPT algorithm D, it holds that*

$$\left| \Pr_{\substack{x_1 \leftarrow \{0,1\}^n, \\ h \leftarrow \mathcal{H}, \\ u \leftarrow \{0,1\}^{n+\log n}}} [\mathsf{D}(h, f(x_1), u) = 1] - \Pr_{\substack{x_1, x_2 \leftarrow \{0,1\}^n, \\ h \leftarrow \mathcal{H}}} [\mathsf{D}(h, f(x_1), h(x_1, f(x_2))) = 1] \right|$$

is a negligible function of n.

We prove Lemma 3.2 below, but first we use it in order to give the proof of Theorem 3.1, which is straight-forward.

Proof (Proof of Theorem 3.1). Let f and t be as in Theorem 3.1. By construction G makes t calls to f. Additionally, $t(n + \log n) > n(t + 1)$ when $t \geq n/\log n + 1$. We are left to show that the output of G is indistinguishable from uniform. The proof is by a hybrid argument. Let H be a uniform random variable over $\mathcal{H}$, and $X_1, \ldots, X_{t+1}$ be i.i.d. uniform random variables over $\{0,1\}^n$. Assume toward a contradiction that there is a PPT algorithm $\widehat{\mathsf{D}}$ that can distinguish $G(H, X_1, \ldots, X_{t+1})$ from uniform. Then we show that the following algorithm D contradicts Lemma 3.2.

Algorithm 3.3 (The distinguisher D)

Input: $h \in \mathcal{H}, y \in \{0,1\}^n, z \in \{0,1\}^{n+\log n}$.

Operation:

1. *Sample $\ell \leftarrow [t]$.*
2. *Sample $x_1, \ldots x_{\ell-1} \leftarrow (\{0,1\}^n)^{\ell-1}$ and $u \leftarrow \{0,1\}^{(t-\ell)n\log n}$.*
3. *Compute $w := h, h(x_1, f(x_2)), \ldots, h(x_{\ell-2}, f(x_{\ell-1})), h(x_{\ell-1}, y), z, u$.*
4. *Execute $\widehat{\mathsf{D}}(w)$ and output its output.*

For each $\ell \in [t+1]$, let the distribution Hyb_ℓ be defined as

$$Hyb_\ell := \Big(H, H(X_1, f(X_2)), \ldots, H(X_{\ell-1}, f(X_\ell)), U_{(t+1-\ell)n \cdot \log n} \Big)$$

where $U_{(t+1-\ell)n\cdot\log n}$ is the uniform distribution over $\{0,1\}^{(t+1-\ell)n\cdot\log n}$. That is, Hyb_ℓ is equal to $G(H, X_1, \ldots, X_{t+1})$ on the first $\ell - 1$ blocks, and uniform on the rest. Observe that for every fixing of ℓ in the algorithm, the distribution of w for input $h \leftarrow \mathcal{H}, y \leftarrow f(U_n), z \leftarrow \{0,1\}^{n+\log n}$ is exactly as the distribution Hyb_ℓ. Similarly, the distribution of w for input $h \leftarrow \mathcal{H}, y \leftarrow f(U_n)$ and $z = h(X', Y')$ for $X' \leftarrow f^{-1}(y)$ and $Y' \leftarrow f(\{0,1\}^n)$ is exactly as the distribution $Hyb_{\ell+1}$. Thus, it holds that,

$$
\left| \Pr_{\substack{x_1 \leftarrow \{0,1\}^n, \\ h \leftarrow \mathcal{H}, \\ u \leftarrow \{0,1\}^{n+\log n}}} [D(h, f(x_1), u) = 1] - \Pr_{\substack{x_1, x_2 \leftarrow \{0,1\}^n, \\ h \leftarrow \mathcal{H}}} [D(h, f(x_1), h(x_1, f(x_2))) = 1] \right|
$$

$$
= \left| 1/t \cdot \sum_{\ell=1}^{t} \left(\Pr_{w \leftarrow Hyb_\ell} \left[\widehat{D}(w) = 1 \right] - \Pr_{w \leftarrow Hyb_{\ell+1}} \left[\widehat{D}(w) = 1 \right] \right) \right|
$$

$$
= 1/t \cdot \left| \Pr_{w \leftarrow Hyb_1} \left[\widehat{D}(w) = 1 \right] - \Pr_{w \leftarrow Hyb_{t+1}} \left[\widehat{D}(w) = 1 \right] \right|
$$

$$
= 1/t \cdot \left| \Pr_{w \leftarrow \{0,1\}^{\log |\mathcal{H}| + (n+\log n) \cdot t}} \left[\widehat{D}(w) = 1 \right] - \Pr_{w \leftarrow G(H, X_1, \ldots, X_{t+1})} \left[\widehat{D}(w) = 1 \right] \right|.
$$

$$\tag{1}$$

Where the last equality holds since $Hyb_{t+1} \equiv G(H, X_1, \ldots, X_{t+1})$ and Hyb_1 is the uniform distribution. We conclude by Lemma 3.2 that the advantage probability of $\widehat{D}$ is negligible.

3.1   Proving Lemma 3.2

In the rest of this section we prove Lemma 3.2. Fix $\beta \geq 0$, any β-almost-regular one-way function $f : \{0,1\}^n \to \{0,1\}^n$ and $n \in \mathbb{N}$. Recall that we want to show that $h(x_1, f(x_2))$ looks uniform to computationally bounded algorithms, given h and $f(x_1)$. By the leftover hash lemma, every prefix $p(x_1, x_2)$ of the above hash $h(x_1, f(x_2))$ is somewhat close to uniform. In order to show that the suffix looks uniform as well, we prove that the concatenation of h, $f(x_1)$ and $p(x_1, x_2)$ is a one-way function, and then use Goldreich-Levin. The next claim states that the described function is indeed one-way on part of its domain.

Claim 3.4. *For every* $i \in [n+\log n]$, *let* $g_i \colon \mathcal{H} \times \{0,1\}^n \times \{0,1\}^n \to \mathcal{H} \times \{0,1\}^n \times \{0,1\}^{i-1}$ *be the following function*

$$
g_i(h, x_1, y) := (h, f(x_1), h(x_1, y)_{1, \ldots, i-1}).
$$

Then it holds that for every PPT A *and every function* $i = i(n)$

$$
\Pr_{\substack{h \leftarrow \mathcal{H}, x_1, x_2 \leftarrow \{0,1\}^n \\ z = (h, x_1, f(x_2))}} [A(g_i(z)) \in g_i^{-1}(g_i(z))] = neg(n). \tag{2}
$$

Proof. Assume toward contradiction that the claim does not hold. That is, there exists PPT algorithm A, a function $i(n)$ and a constant $d \in \mathbb{N}$ such that

$$\Pr_{\substack{h \leftarrow \mathcal{H}, x_1, x_2 \leftarrow \{0,1\}^n \\ z = (h, x_1, f(x_2))}} \left[A(g_i(z)) \in g_i^{-1}(g_i(z)) \right] \geq n^{-d} \tag{3}$$

for infinitely many $n \in \mathbb{N}$. Fix such n and consider the following algorithm $\widehat{A}$. In the following we show $\widehat{A}$ can be used to invert f.

Algorithm 3.5 (The inverter $\widehat{A}$)
Input: $h \in \mathcal{H}, y \in \{0,1\}^n$, $z \in \{0,1\}^{n-(4d+2\beta)\log n}$.
Operation:

1. *For every* $w \in \{0,1\}^{(4d+2\beta+1)\log n}$ *and* $j \in [n + \log n]$:
   (a) *Let* (h, x, y') *be the output of* $A(h, y, (z \circ w)_{1,\dots,j-1})$.
   (b) *If* $f(x) = y$, *output* x.

That is, $\widehat{A}$ tries to invert y using A and only a prefix of $h(x_1, f(x_2))$. It does so by iterating over all the possible values of the missing input bits

$$h(f^{-1}(y), f(x_2))_{n-(4d+2\beta)\log n+1,\dots,n+\log n}$$

and every possible index $j \in [n + \log n]$. Clearly $\widehat{A}$ runs in a polynomial time. Let x_1 be some preimage of y and let x_2 be some element in $\{0,1\}^n$. Note that when the guess w is equal to $h(x_1, f(x_2))_{n-(4d+2\beta)\log n+1,\dots,n+\log n}$, and when the index j is equal to i, the value of $h, y, (z \circ w)_{1,\dots,j-1}$ computed by the algorithm is equal to the output of $g_i(h, x_1, f(x_2))$. Thus, by definition it is clear that the success probability of $\widehat{A}$ is better than A's. Formally, we get that,

$$\Pr_{h \leftarrow \mathcal{H}, x_1, x_2 \leftarrow \{0,1\}^n} \left[\widehat{A}(h, f(x_1), h(x_1, f(x_2))_{1,\dots,n-(4d+2\beta)\log n}) \in f^{-1}(f(x_1)) \right]$$

$$\geq \Pr_{x_1, x_2 \leftarrow \{0,1\}^n} \left[A(g_i(h, x_1, f(x_2))) \in g_i^{-1}(g_i(h, x_1, f(x_2))) \right]$$

$$\geq n^{-d}. \tag{4}$$

Next, we show that $\widehat{A}$ can guess the value of $h(x_1, f(x_2))_{1,\dots,n-(4d+2\beta)\log n}$. Indeed, recall that by the β-almost-regularity of f, given any fixing of $f(x_1)$, the min-entropy of $x_1, f(x_2)$ is at least $n - 2\beta \log n$. Thus, by the left-over hash lemma, $h(x_1, f(x_2))_{1,\dots,n-(4d+2\beta)\log n}$ is $n^{-d}/2$ close to uniform given h and $f(x_1)$. Let $k = n - (4d + 2\beta) \log n$. Combining the above with Eq. (4),

$$\Pr_{h \leftarrow \mathcal{H}, x_1 \leftarrow \{0,1\}^n, u \leftarrow \{0,1\}^k} \left[\widehat{\mathsf{A}}(h, f(x_1), u) \in f^{-1}(f(x_1))\right]$$

$$= \underset{y \leftarrow f(\{0,1\}^n)}{\mathbb{E}} \left[\Pr_{\substack{h \leftarrow \mathcal{H}, x_1 \leftarrow f^{-1}(y), \\ u \leftarrow \{0,1\}^k}} \left[\widehat{\mathsf{A}}(h, y, u) \in f^{-1}(f(x_1))\right]\right]$$

$$\geq \underset{y}{\mathbb{E}} \left[\Pr_{\substack{h \leftarrow \mathcal{H}, x_1 \leftarrow f^{-1}(y), \\ x_2 \leftarrow \{0,1\}^n}} \left[\widehat{\mathsf{A}}(h, y, h(x_1, f(x_2))_{1,\dots,k}) \in f^{-1}(f(x_1))\right] - n^{-d}/2\right]$$

$$= \Pr_{h \leftarrow \mathcal{H}, x_1, x_2 \leftarrow \{0,1\}^n} \left[\widehat{\mathsf{A}}(h, f(x_1), h(x_1, f(x_2))_{1,\dots,k}) \in f^{-1}(f(x_1))\right] - n^{-d}/2$$

$$\geq n^{-d}/2. \tag{5}$$

Finally, let Inv be the algorithm that given $f(x_1)$ samples $h \leftarrow \mathcal{H}$ and $u \leftarrow \{0,1\}^{n-(4d+2\beta)\log n}$, and executes $\widehat{\mathsf{A}}$. By Eq. (5) Inv inverts $f(x_1)$ successfully with probability at least $n^{-d}/2$ for uniformly sampled $x_1 \in \{0,1\}^n$, for infinitely many $n \in \mathbb{N}$, which is a contradiction.

We are now ready to prove Lemma 3.2. The proof is straight-forward from Claim 3.4 together with Lemma 2.5 and Lemma 2.6.

Proof (Proof of Lemma 3.2.). Assume toward a contradiction that Lemma 3.2 does not hold. That is, there exists PPT algorithm D and a constant $c \in \mathbb{N}$ such that

$$\left| \Pr_{\substack{x_1 \leftarrow \{0,1\}^n, \\ h \leftarrow \mathcal{H}, \\ u \leftarrow \{0,1\}^{n+\log n}}} [\mathsf{D}(h, f(x_1), u) = 1] - \Pr_{\substack{x_1, x_2 \leftarrow \{0,1\}^n, \\ h \leftarrow \mathcal{H}}} [\mathsf{D}(h, f(x_1), h(x_1, f(x_2))) = 1] \right|$$
$$\geq n^{-c} \tag{6}$$

for infinitely many $n \in \mathbb{N}$. We assume without loss of generality that for infinitely many $n \in \mathbb{N}$ it holds that

$$\Pr_{\substack{x_1 \leftarrow \{0,1\}^n, \\ h \leftarrow \mathcal{H}, \\ u \leftarrow \{0,1\}^{n+\log n}}} [\mathsf{D}(h, f(x_1), u) = 1] - \Pr_{\substack{x_1, x_2 \leftarrow \{0,1\}^{2n}, \\ h \leftarrow \mathcal{H}}} [\mathsf{D}(h, f(x_1), h(x_1, f(x_2))) = 1]$$
$$\geq n^{-c} \tag{7}$$

as otherwise we can flip the output of D. By Lemma 2.6 there is a oracle-aided PPT algorithm P such that for infinitely many $n \in \mathbb{N}$ and $i = i(n)$ it holds that

$$\Pr_{\substack{x_1, x_2 \leftarrow \{0,1\}^{2n}, \\ h \leftarrow \mathcal{H}}} \left[\mathsf{P}^{\mathsf{D}}(h, f(x_1), h(x_1, f(x_2))_{1,\dots,i-1}) = h(x_1, f(x_2))_i\right] \geq 1/2 + n^{-c-4}.$$

Recall that, by definition, $h, f(x_1), h(x_1, f(x_2))_{1,...,i-1} = g_i(x_1, f(x_2))$. Additionally, by our choice of the family $\mathcal{H}$, $h(x_1, f(x_2)))_i$ is the GL predicate of the function $g_i(x_1, f(x_2))$.[9] Thus, the above contradicts Claim 3.4 and Lemma 2.5.

4   The UOWHF Construction

In this section we prove the security of our UOWHF construction. We start with a full description of the construction. Let $f\colon \{0,1\}^n \to \{0,1\}^n$ be an almost-regular one-way function, let t be a parameter and let $\mathcal{H} = \left\{m\colon m \in \{0,1\}^{2n \times (n - \log n)}\right\}$ be the 2-universal family induced by the set of matrices of size $2n \times (n - \log n)$.[10]

The function $C : \mathcal{H} \times \{0,1\}^{n \cdot t} \to \mathcal{H} \times \{0,1\}^{(t-1)\cdot(n-\log n)+2n}$ is given by

$$C(h, x_1, \ldots, x_t) = h, f(x_1), h(x_1, f(x_2)), \ldots, h(x_{t-1}, f(x_t)), x_t.$$

Let $k = \log |\mathcal{H}| + n \cdot t$. For a string $z \in \{0,1\}^k$, let $C_z(w) := C(w \oplus z)$. Our main theorem for this part is stated as follows.

Theorem 4.1 *[Main theorem for UOWHF] Let $f = f\colon \{0,1\}^n \to \{0,1\}^n$ be an almost-regular one-way function and let $t(n) \geq n/\log n + 2$ be some polynomial. Then $\mathcal{F}_k = \{C_z\}_{z \in \{0,1\}^k}$ is a family of universal one-way hash functions with key length $k = O(n^2 + n \cdot t(n))$ and output length $O(n^2 + n \cdot t(n))$. Furthermore, for every $z \in \{0,1\}^k$, C_z uses t non-adaptive calls to f.*

In the rest of this section we prove Theorem 4.1. Note that by Lemma 2.9 in order to prove Theorem 4.1, it is enough to show that it is hard to find a collision of C for a *random* input. The main lemma of this part is the following one, which essentially states that no efficient algorithm can find a collision in a simpler function, $\widehat{C}(h, x_1, x_2) = h, f(x_1), h(x_1, f(x_2))$. Note that $\widehat{C}$ is not UOWHF, as it is not shrinking, and, as we are only interested in collisions (h, x_1', x_2') in which $f(x_2) \neq f(x_2')$.

Lemma 4.2. *Let $f\colon \{0,1\}^n \to \{0,1\}^n$ be an almost-regular one-way function. For every PPT algorithm A, it holds that,*

$$\Pr_{\substack{h \leftarrow \mathcal{H}, x_1, x_2 \leftarrow \{0,1\}^n, \\ (x_1', x_2') \leftarrow A(h, x_1, x_2)}} [f(x_1) = f(x_1') \wedge f(x_2) \neq f(x_2') \wedge h(x_1, f(x_2)) = h(x_1', f(x_2'))]$$

is a negligible function of n.

---

[9] Note that if $i \leq n - \omega(\log n)$ there is no need in GL. Indeed, by the leftover hash lemma, the first bits of h are statistically close to uniform.

[10] Any approximately-flat, constructible, and 2-universal hash family will suffice. Such a family with a smaller size, if exists, can be used in order to reduce the key length up to $O(n \cdot t)$.

We prove Lemma 4.2 below, but first let us prove the security of C using Lemma 4.2. The proof is by reduction, stated in the next claim. Informally, we show that an algorithm that breaks the security of C can be used in order to find a collision in the function $\widehat{C}$ defined above.

Claim 4.3. *There exists an oracle-aided* PPT *algorithm* A *such that the following holds. Let f be a one-way function, $t \in$ poly and C be the function described above. Let $n \in \mathbb{N}$, $\alpha \in [0, 1]$ and let* ColFinder *be an algorithm such that*

$$\Pr_{w \leftarrow \mathcal{H} \times (\{0,1\}^n)^t, w' \leftarrow \mathsf{ColFinder}(w)} [w' \neq w \wedge C(w) = C(w')] = \alpha.$$

Then,

$$\Pr_{\substack{h \leftarrow \mathcal{H}, x_1, x_2 \leftarrow \{0,1\}^n, \\ (x_1', x_2') \leftarrow \mathsf{A}^{\mathsf{ColFinder}}(h, x_1, x_2)}} \left[\begin{array}{c} f(x_1) = f(x_1') \\ \wedge f(x_2) \neq f(x_2') \wedge h(x_1, f(x_2)) = h(x_1', f(x_2')) \end{array} \right] \geq (\alpha - \nu(n))/t,$$

where ν is a negligible function, depending only on f and t.

The proof of Theorem 4.1 is now immediate.

Proof (Proof of Theorem 4.1.). Let f, t and C_z be as in Theorem 4.1. It is clear that C_z is efficiently computable for every $z \in \{0, 1\}^k$, and that C is shrinking since $\log |H| + n \cdot t > \log |H| + (t - 1) \cdot (n - \log n) + 2n$ for $t \geq n/\log n + 2$.

Next, we show that it is collision-resistant for random input. Assume toward contradiction that there exists a PPT ColFinder and $p \in$ poly such that

$$\Pr_{\substack{w \leftarrow \mathcal{H} \times (\{0,1\}^n)^t, \\ w' \leftarrow \mathsf{ColFinder}(w)}} [w' \neq w \wedge C(w) = C(w')] \geq 1/p(n)$$

for infinitely many $n \in \mathbb{N}$. Then, by Claim 4.3, for infinitely many $n \in \mathbb{N}$ it holds that

$$\Pr_{\substack{h \leftarrow \mathcal{H}, x_1, x_2 \leftarrow \{0,1\}^n, \\ (x_1', x_2') \leftarrow \mathsf{A}^{\mathsf{ColFinder}}(h, x_1, x_2)}} \left[\begin{array}{c} f(x_1) = f(x_1') \wedge \\ f(x_2) \neq f(x_2') \wedge h(x_1, f(x_2)) = h(x_1', f(x_2')) \end{array} \right] \geq 1/(2t \cdot p(n)).$$

Note that by the choice of t, $1/(2t \cdot p(n))$ is not negligible, and that since both A and ColFinder are efficient, $\mathsf{A}^{\mathsf{ColFinder}}(\cdot)$ can be efficiently implemented. Thus, the above contradicts Lemma 4.2.

4.1   Proving Claim 4.3

We next prove Claim 4.3. The next simple claim will be useful in the proof, as it states that given $(h, x_1, \ldots, x_t)$, with high probability there is no collision $(h, x_1', \ldots, x_t')$ of C in which for some $j \in [t]$ it holds that $x_j \neq x_j'$ while $f(x_j) = f(x_j')$ and $f(x_{j+1}) = f(x_{j+1}')$.

Claim 4.4. *For every one-way function f and polynomial t, there exists a negligible function ν such that the following holds. For every $x_1, \ldots, x_t \in \{0,1\}^n$,*

$$\Pr_{h \leftarrow \mathcal{H}} \begin{bmatrix} \forall j \in [t-1], \ \forall x'_j \in f^{-1}(f(x_j)) \backslash \{x_j\} \text{ it holds that} \\ h(x'_j, f(x_{j+1})) \neq h(x_j, f(x_{j+1})) \end{bmatrix} \geq 1 - \nu(n).$$

Proof. Fix $x_1, \ldots, x_t \in \{0,1\}^n$, $j \in [t-1]$ and $x'_j \in f^{-1}(f(x_j)) \setminus \{x_j\}$. Since $\mathcal{H}$ is 2-universal, it holds that

$$\Pr_{h \leftarrow \mathcal{H}} \left[h(x'_j, f(x_{j+1})) = h(x_j, f(x_{j+1})) \right] = n/2^n.$$

By the union bound,

$$\Pr_{h \leftarrow \mathcal{H}} \begin{bmatrix} \exists j \in [t-1], x'_j \in f^{-1}(f(x_j)) \backslash \{x_j\} \text{ s.t.} \\ h(x'_j, f(x_{j+1})) = h(x_j, f(x_{j+1})) \end{bmatrix}$$

$$\leq \sum_{j \in [t-1]} \sum_{x'_j \in f^{-1}(f(x_j)) \backslash \{x_j\}} \Pr_{h \leftarrow \mathcal{H}} \left[h(x'_j, f(x_{j+1})) = h(x_j, f(x_{j+1})) \right]$$

$$\leq t(n) \cdot |f^{-1}(f(x_j))| \cdot n/2^n.$$

Since f is a one-way function, by Claim 2.3 it holds that $|f^{-1}(f(x_k))| \leq 2^n \cdot neg(n)$, and thus the claim follows.

Proof (Proof of Claim 4.3.). Let f, t n, α and ColFinder as in Claim 4.3. Let A be the following algorithm.

Algorithm 4.5 (The reduction A)
Input: $h \in \mathcal{H}$, $x_1, x_2 \in \{0,1\}$.
Oracle: ColFinder.
Operation:

1. *Sample $i \leftarrow [t-1]$, $z_1, \ldots, z_{i-1}, z_{i+2}, \ldots, z_t \leftarrow \{0,1\}^n$ and set $z_i = x_1, z_{i+1} = x_2$.*
2. *Apply ColFinder$(h, z_1, \ldots, z_t)$ to get $(h', z'_1, \ldots, z'_t)$.*
3. *Output z'_i, z'_{i+1}.*

We next show that with all but negligible probability over the choice of $w = (h, x_1, \ldots, x_t)$, the following must hold. For every $w' = (h', x'_1, \ldots, x'_t)$ with $w \neq w'$ and $C(w) = C(w')$, there exists some $i \in [t-1]$ such that $f(x_i) = f(x'_i)$ and $f(x_{i+1}) \neq f(x'_{i+1})$. The lemma then follows easily.

Indeed, fix such w and w'. First note that since $C(w) = C(w')$, it holds that $h = h'$. Let j be the first index for which $x_j \neq x'_j$, and observe that by the definition of C, $j \in [t-1]$. We split into cases:

– If $f(x_j) \neq f(x'_j)$, then $j > 1$ (since $C(w) = C(w')$ implies that $f(x_1) = f(x'_1)$) and for $i = j - 1$ it holds that $f(x_i) = f(x'_i)$ and $f(x_{i+1}) \neq f(x'_{i+1})$.

– For the other case, assume that $f(x_j) = f(x'_j)$. By Claim 4.4, with probability all but negligible over the choice of w, it holds that, $h(x_j, f(x_{j+1})) \neq h(x'_j, f(x_{j+1}))$, and thus it must hold that $f(x_{j+1}) \neq f(x'_{j+1})$. We get that for $i = j$, it holds that $f(x_i) = f(x'_i)$ and $f(x_{i+1}) \neq f(x'_{i+1})$.

Since i is chosen uniformly in Theorem 4.5, and since the distribution of $h, z_1, \ldots, z_t$ in Theorem 4.5 is uniform for every $i \in [t-1]$ and uniformly chosen input h, x_1, x_2, we conclude that the success probability of $\mathsf{A}^{\mathsf{ColFinder}}$ is at least $(\alpha - neg(n))/t$.

4.2 Proving Lemma 4.2

We now prove Lemma 4.2. For the rest of this section, fix $\beta \geq 0$, and a β-almost-regular one-way function f. In order to prove the lemma, we show how to invert the one-way function f using an algorithm that contradicts the lemma. Formally,

Claim 4.6. *There exists* PPT *oracle-aided algorithm* Inv *such that the following holds. Let* $n \in \mathbb{N}$, $\alpha \in [0,1]$ *and let* A *be an algorithm such that*

$$\Pr_{\substack{h \leftarrow \mathcal{H}, x_1, x_2 \leftarrow \{0,1\}^n, \\ (x'_1, x'_2) \leftarrow \mathsf{A}(h, x_1, x_2)}} \left[f(x_1) = f(x'_1) \wedge f(x_2) \neq f(x'_2) \wedge h(x_1, f(x_2)) = h(x'_1, f(x'_2)) \right] = \alpha.$$

Then,

$$\Pr_{x \leftarrow \{0,1\}} \left[\mathsf{Inv}^{\mathsf{A}}(f(x)) \in f^{-1}(f(x)) \right] \geq \alpha^2 \cdot n^{-2\beta - 2} \cdot 2^{-12}.$$

The proof of Lemma 4.2 is immediate from Claim 4.6, as $\Pr_{x \leftarrow \{0,1\}} \left[\mathsf{Inv}^{\mathsf{A}}(f(x)) \in f^{-1}(f(x)) \right]$ must be negligible.

Proof (Proof of Lemma 4.2.). Assume toward contradiction that there exists a PPT algorithm A and $p \in$ poly such that

$$\Pr_{\substack{h \leftarrow \mathcal{H}, x_1, x_2 \leftarrow \{0,1\}^n, \\ (x'_1, x'_2) \leftarrow \mathsf{A}(h, x_1, x_2)}} \left[\begin{array}{c} f(x_1) = f(x'_1) \wedge \\ f(x_2) \neq f(x'_2) \wedge h(x_1, f(x_2)) = h(x'_1, f(x'_2)) \end{array} \right] \geq 1/p(n)$$

for infinitely many $n \in \mathbb{N}$. Then, by Claim 4.6 it holds that

$$\Pr_{x \leftarrow \{0,1\}} \left[\mathsf{Inv}^{\mathsf{A}}(f(x)) \in f^{-1}(f(x)) \right] \geq 1/p(n)^2 \cdot n^{-2\beta - 2} \cdot 2^{-10}$$

for infinitely many $n \in \mathbb{N}$, which is a contradiction to f being a one-way function.

The rest of this part is dedicated for proving Claim 4.6. Let n, α and A be as in Claim 4.6. In the following we assume that A outputs a valid pair (x'_1, x'_2) with $(f(x_1) = f(x'_1) \wedge f(x_2) \neq f(x'_2) \wedge h(x_1, f(x_2)) = h(x'_1, f(x'_2)))$ or $(\bot, \bot)$. For x_1, x_2 and h, we define,

$$\mathcal{G}_{h,x_1,x_2} := \left\{ (x'_1, y) \in f^{-1}(f(x_1)) \times \mathsf{Im}(f) : h(x_1, f(x_2)) = h(x'_1, y) \right\}.$$

For ease of notation, we say that $x \in \mathcal{G}_{h,x_1,x_2}$ if there exists $y \in \mathsf{Im}(f)$ such that $(x,y) \in \mathcal{G}_{h,x_1,x_2}$. Let Inv be the following algorithm. Note that Inv can be implemented efficiently, by the constructibility of $\mathcal{H}$.

Algorithm 4.7 (The inverter Inv)
Input: $y \in \mathsf{Im}(f)$.
Oracle: A.
Operation:

1. Sample $x_1, x_2 \leftarrow \{0,1\}^n$ and $h \leftarrow \mathcal{H}$.
2. Apply $\mathsf{A}(h, x_1, x_2)$ to get (x_1', x_2'). If A outputs $(\perp, \perp)$, output $\perp$.
3. Sample $h' \leftarrow \mathcal{H}$ such that $h'(x_1, f(x_2)) = h'(x_1', y)$.
4. Apply $\mathsf{A}(h', x_1, x_2)$ to get (x_1'', x). Output x.

That is, in order to invert its input y, Inv samples x_1, x_2 and h. It then uses A in order to find x_1' with $f(x_1') = f(x_1)$. Lastly, it samples h' with $h'(x_1, f(x_2)) = h'(x_1', y)$ and uses A in order to find a collision to h', x_1, x_2. By the choice of h', a possible collision is $(h', x_1', f^{-1}(y))$. We observe that if A finds such a collision, Inv successfully inverted y.

For $x_1, x_2 \in \{0,1\}^n$, $x_1' \in f^{-1}(f(x))$ and $y \in \mathsf{Im}(f)$, let

$$p_{\mathsf{A}}(x_1, x_2, x_1', y)$$
$$:= \Pr_{h' \leftarrow \mathcal{H}} \left[\mathsf{A}(h', x_1, x_2) \in \{x_1'\} \times f^{-1}(y) \mid h'(x_1, f(x_2)) = h'(x_1', y) \right]$$
$$= \Pr_{h' \leftarrow \mathcal{H}} \left[\mathsf{A}(h', x_1, x_2) \in \{x_1'\} \times f^{-1}(y) \mid (x_1', y) \in \mathcal{G}_{h', x_1, x_2} \right]$$

and define $p_{\mathsf{A}}(x_1, x_2, \perp, y) = 0$. By the above observation, it holds that

$$\Pr_{x \leftarrow \{0,1\}^n} \left[\mathsf{Inv}^{\mathsf{A}}(f(x)) \in f^{-1}(f(x)) \right] \geq \mathop{\mathbb{E}}_{\substack{h \leftarrow \mathcal{H}, x_1, x_2 \leftarrow \{0,1\}^n \\ y \leftarrow f(\{0,1\}^n) \\ (x_1', x_2') \leftarrow \mathsf{A}(h, x_1, x_2)}} \left[p_{\mathsf{A}}(x_1, x_2, x_1', y) \right] \quad (8)$$

and thus it is enough to bound the latter. We bound it using the following two claims. The first shows that it is enough to bound the probability that A outputs $(x_1', \cdot)$. The second claim bounds the last probability.

Claim 4.8. *For every $x_1, x_2 \in \{0,1\}^n$ and $x' \in f^{-1}(f(x_1))$ the following holds.*

$$\mathop{\mathbb{E}}_{y \leftarrow f(\{0,1\}^n)} \left[p_{\mathsf{A}}(x_1, x_2, x', y) \right]$$
$$\geq \Pr_{h' \leftarrow \mathcal{H}} \left[\mathsf{A}(h', x_1, x_2) = (x', \cdot) \mid x' \in \mathcal{G}_{h', x_1, x_2} \right] \cdot n^{-\beta - 1} \cdot 2^{-10}.$$

Proof. Fix $x_1, x_2 \in \{0,1\}^n$ and $x' \in f^{-1}(f(x_1))$, and for every $h \in \mathcal{H}$, let $\mathsf{A}(h) := \mathsf{A}(h, x_1, x_2)$ and $\mathcal{G}_h := \mathcal{G}_{h, x_1, x_2}$. Then, by the definition of p_{A}, it holds that

$$\underset{y\leftarrow f(\{0,1\}^n)}{\mathrm{E}} [p_A(x_1, x_2, x', y)]$$

$$= \underset{y\leftarrow f(\{0,1\}^n)}{\mathrm{E}} \left[\Pr_{h'\leftarrow \mathcal{H}} \left[A(h') \in \{x'\} \times f^{-1}(y) \mid (x', y) \in \mathcal{G}_{h'} \right] \right]$$

$$= \underset{y\leftarrow f(\{0,1\}^n)}{\mathrm{E}} \left[\frac{\Pr_{h'\leftarrow \mathcal{H}} \left[(x', y) \in \mathcal{G}_{h'} \wedge A(h') \in \{x'\} \times f^{-1}(y) \mid x' \in \mathcal{G}_{h'} \right]}{\Pr_{h'\leftarrow \mathcal{H}} \left[(x', y) \in \mathcal{G}_{h'} \mid x' \in \mathcal{G}_{h'} \right]} \right]$$

$$= \underset{y\leftarrow f(\{0,1\}^n)}{\mathrm{E}} \left[\frac{\Pr_{h'\leftarrow \mathcal{H}} \left[A(h') \in \{x'\} \times f^{-1}(y) \mid x' \in \mathcal{G}_{h'} \right]}{\Pr_{h'\leftarrow \mathcal{H}} \left[(x', y) \in \mathcal{G}_{h'} \mid x' \in \mathcal{G}_{h'} \right]} \right]$$

$$= \underset{y\leftarrow f(\{0,1\}^n)}{\mathrm{E}} \left[\Pr_{h'\leftarrow \mathcal{H}} \left[A(h') \in \{x'\} \times f^{-1}(y) \mid x' \in \mathcal{G}_{h'} \right] \cdot \frac{\Pr_{h'\leftarrow \mathcal{H}} \left[x' \in \mathcal{G}_{h'} \right]}{\Pr_{h'\leftarrow \mathcal{H}} \left[(x', y) \in \mathcal{G}_{h'} \right]} \right]$$

Since by our assumption on A, for every (x', y) with $\Pr \left[A(h) \in \{x'\} \times f^{-1}(y) \right] > 0$ it holds that $(x', y) \neq (x_1, f(x_2))$, we get that for every such pair $\Pr_{h'\leftarrow \mathcal{H}} \left[(x', y) \in \mathcal{G}_{h'} \right] = n/2^n$. Continue,

$$\underset{y\leftarrow f(\{0,1\}^n)}{\mathrm{E}} [p_A(x_1, x_2, x', y)]$$

$$= \sum_{y\in\mathsf{Im}(f)} \Pr_{x\leftarrow\{0,1\}^n} [f(x) = y] \cdot \Pr_{h'\leftarrow \mathcal{H}} \left[A(h') \in \{x'\} \times f^{-1}(y) \mid x' \in \mathcal{G}_{h'} \right]$$

$$\cdot \frac{2^n}{n} \cdot \Pr_{h'\leftarrow \mathcal{H}} \left[x' \in \mathcal{G}_{h'} \right]$$

$$\geq \sum_{y\in\mathsf{Im}(f)} \frac{1}{|\mathsf{Im}(f)| \cdot n^\beta} \cdot \Pr_{h'\leftarrow \mathcal{H}} \left[A(h') \in \{x'\} \times f^{-1}(y) \mid x' \in \mathcal{G}_{h'} \right]$$

$$\cdot \frac{2^n}{n} \cdot \Pr_{h'\leftarrow \mathcal{H}} \left[x' \in \mathcal{G}_{h'} \right]$$

$$= \frac{1}{|\mathsf{Im}(f)| \cdot n^\beta} \cdot \frac{2^n}{n} \cdot \Pr_{h'\leftarrow \mathcal{H}} \left[x' \in \mathcal{G}_{h'} \right]$$

$$\cdot \sum_{y\in\mathsf{Im}(f)} \Pr_{h'\leftarrow \mathcal{H}} \left[A(h') \in \{x'\} \times f^{-1}(y) \mid x' \in \mathcal{G}_{h'} \right]$$

$$= \frac{2^n}{|\mathsf{Im}(f)| \cdot n^{\beta+1}} \cdot \Pr_{h'\leftarrow \mathcal{H}} \left[x' \in \mathcal{G}_{h'} \right] \cdot \Pr_{h'\leftarrow \mathcal{H}} \left[A(h') = (x', \cdot) \mid x' \in \mathcal{G}_{h'} \right]$$

where the inequality holds since f is β-almost-regular. Recall that the family $\mathcal{H}$ is approximately-flat. That is,

$$\Pr_{h'\leftarrow \mathcal{H}} [\exists y \in \mathsf{Im}(f) \text{ s.t. } h'(x_1, f(x_2)) = h'(x', y)]$$

$$\geq 2^{-10} \cdot \min \left\{ |\mathsf{Im}(f)| \cdot 2^{-(n-\log n)}, 1 \right\}.$$

Thus,

$$
\frac{2^n}{|\mathsf{Im}(f)| \cdot n^{\beta+1}} \cdot \Pr_{h' \leftarrow \mathcal{H}}[x' \in \mathcal{G}_{h'}] \cdot \Pr_{h' \leftarrow \mathcal{H}}[\mathsf{A}(h') = (x', \cdot) \mid x' \in \mathcal{G}_{h'}]
$$

$$
\geq \frac{2^n}{|\mathsf{Im}(f)| \cdot n^{\beta+1}} \cdot 2^{-10} \cdot \min\left\{|\mathsf{Im}(f)| \cdot 2^{-(n-\log n)}, 1\right\}
$$
$$
\cdot \Pr_{h' \leftarrow \mathcal{H}}[\mathsf{A}(h') = (x', \cdot) \mid x' \in \mathcal{G}_{h'}]
$$

$$
\geq n^{-\beta-1} \cdot 2^{-10} \cdot \Pr_{h' \leftarrow \mathcal{H}}[\mathsf{A}(h') = (x', \cdot) \mid x' \in \mathcal{G}_{h'}]
$$

and the claim holds.

The next claim uses Lemma 2.16 in order to show that in a random execution of Inv, A has a good probability to output the same element x'_1 in Items 2 and 4.

Claim 4.9. *For every* $x_1, x_2 \in \{0,1\}$ *the following holds. Let* $\alpha_{x_1,x_2} :=$ $\Pr_{h \leftarrow \mathcal{H}}[\mathsf{A}(h, x_1, x_2) \neq \bot]$. *Then,*

$$
\sum_{x'_1 \in f^{-1}(f(x_1))} \Pr_{h \leftarrow \mathcal{H}}[\mathsf{A}(h, x_1, x_2) = (x'_1, \cdot)]
$$
$$
\cdot \Pr_{h' \leftarrow \mathcal{H}}[\mathsf{A}(h', x_1, x_2) = (x'_1, \cdot) \mid x'_1 \in \mathcal{G}_{h', x_1, x_2}]
$$
$$
\geq \alpha^2_{x_1,x_2} \cdot n^{-\beta-1}/4.
$$

Proof. Fix $x_1, x_2 \in \{0,1\}^n$, and let α_{x_1,x_2} be as in Claim 4.9. Let $\alpha_1 := \Pr_{h \leftarrow \mathcal{H}}[\mathsf{A}(h, x_1, x_2) = (x_1, \cdot)]$ and let $\alpha_2 := \Pr_{h \leftarrow \mathcal{H}}[\mathsf{A}(h, x_1, x_2) \notin \{(x_1, \cdot), \bot\}]$. Notice that $\alpha_{x_1,x_2} = \alpha_1 + \alpha_2$.

Define $\widetilde{\mathsf{A}}(h)$ to be the algorithm that outputs the first coordinate of A's output $(\mathsf{A}(h, x_1, x_2)_1)$ if it is different from x_1, or $\bot$ otherwise. Let $\mathcal{G}_h := \mathcal{G}_{h, x_1, x_2}$. Note that by the assumption on A, $\widetilde{\mathsf{A}}$ always outputs elements in $S(h) = \{x \in \mathcal{G}_{h, x_1, x_2} : x \neq x_1\}$. We get that $\alpha_2 := \Pr_{h \leftarrow \mathcal{H}}\left[\widetilde{\mathsf{A}}(h) \neq \bot\right]$. Let $\Omega = f^{-1}(f(x_1)) \setminus \{x_1\}$. It holds that,

$$
\sum_{x'_1 \in f^{-1}(f(x_1))} \Pr_{h \leftarrow \mathcal{H}}[\mathsf{A}(h, x_1, x_2) = (x'_1, \cdot)]
$$
$$
\cdot \Pr_{h' \leftarrow \mathcal{H}}[\mathsf{A}(h', x_1, x_2) = (x'_1, \cdot) \mid x'_1 \in \mathcal{G}_{h', x_1, x_2}]
$$
$$
= \sum_{x'_1 \in \Omega} \Pr_{h \leftarrow \mathcal{H}}[\mathsf{A}(h, x_1, x_2) = (x'_1, \cdot)] \cdot \Pr_{h' \leftarrow \mathcal{H}}[\mathsf{A}(h', x_1, x_2) = (x'_1, \cdot) \mid x'_1 \in \mathcal{G}_{h', x_1, x_2}]
$$
$$
+ \Pr_{h \leftarrow \mathcal{H}}[\mathsf{A}(h, x_1, x_2) = (x_1, \cdot)] \cdot \Pr_{h' \leftarrow \mathcal{H}}[\mathsf{A}(h', x_1, x_2) = (x_1, \cdot) \mid x_1 \in \mathcal{G}_{h', x_1, x_2}]
$$
$$
= \sum_{x'_1 \in \Omega} \Pr_{h \leftarrow \mathcal{H}}\left[\widetilde{\mathsf{A}}(h) = x'_1\right] \cdot \Pr_{h' \leftarrow \mathcal{H}}\left[\widetilde{\mathsf{A}}(h) = x'_1 \mid x'_1 \in \mathcal{G}_{h', x_1, x_2}\right]
$$
$$
+ \Pr_{h \leftarrow \mathcal{H}}[\mathsf{A}(h, x_1, x_2) = (x_1, \cdot)] \cdot \Pr_{h' \leftarrow \mathcal{H}}[\mathsf{A}(h', x_1, x_2) = (x_1, \cdot)]
$$
$$
= \sum_{x'_1 \in \Omega} \Pr_{h \leftarrow \mathcal{H}}\left[\widetilde{\mathsf{A}}(h) = x'_1\right] \cdot \Pr_{h' \leftarrow \mathcal{H}}\left[\widetilde{\mathsf{A}}(h) = x'_1 \mid x'_1 \in S(h')\right] + \alpha^2_1,
$$

where the second equality holds by definition of $\widetilde{A}$ and since x_1 is always a member in $\mathcal{G}_{h,x_1,x_2}$. We next show that

$$\sum_{x_1' \in \Omega} \Pr_{h \leftarrow \mathcal{H}} \left[\widetilde{A}(h) = x_1' \right] \cdot \Pr_{h' \leftarrow \mathcal{H}} \left[\widetilde{A}(h) = x_1' \mid x_1' \in S(h') \right] \geq \alpha_2^2 \cdot n^{-\beta-1}. \quad (9)$$

Indeed, assume that Ω is not empty, as otherwise the above holds trivially. We observe that for every $x \in \Omega$,

$$0 < \Pr_{h' \leftarrow \mathcal{H}} [x \in S(h')] \leq |\mathsf{Im}(f)| \cdot n/2^n \leq n^{\beta+1}/|f^{-1}(f(x))| \leq n^{\beta+1}/|\Omega|. \quad (10)$$

Thus we can use Lemma 2.16, with $\mathcal{X} = \mathcal{H}$ in order to get Eq. (9).

Combining the above, we conclude that

$$\sum_{x_1' \in f^{-1}(f(x_1))} \Pr_{h \leftarrow \mathcal{H}} [A(h, x_1, x_2) = (x_1', \cdot)]$$
$$\cdot \Pr_{h' \leftarrow \mathcal{H}} [A(h', x_1, x_2) = (x_1', \cdot) \mid x_1' \in \mathcal{G}_{h', x_1, x_2}]$$
$$\geq \alpha_2^2 \cdot n^{-\beta-1} + \alpha_1^2.$$

The claim follows since either α_1 or α_2 is at least $\alpha_{x_1,x_2}/2$.

We are now ready to prove Claim 4.6.

Proof (Proof of Claim 4.6). For fixed x_1 and x_2 let α_{x_1,x_2} be as in Claim 4.9. We start by showing that

$$\Pr_{x \leftarrow \{0,1\}} \left[\mathsf{Inv}^A(f(x)) \in f^{-1}(f(x)) \right] \geq \mathop{\mathbb{E}}_{x_1,x_2 \leftarrow \{0,1\}^n} \left[\alpha_{x_1,x_2}^2 \right] \cdot n^{-2\beta-2} \cdot 2^{-12}. \quad (11)$$

Indeed, by Eq. (8),

$$\Pr_{x \leftarrow \{0,1\}} \left[\mathsf{Inv}^A(f(x)) \in f^{-1}(f(x)) \right] \geq \mathop{\mathbb{E}}_{\substack{h \leftarrow \mathcal{H}, x_1, x_2 \leftarrow \{0,1\}^n \\ y \leftarrow f(\{0,1\}^n) \\ (x_1', x_2') \leftarrow A(h, x_1, x_2)}} [p_A(x_1, x_2, x_1', y)]$$

$$= \mathop{\mathbb{E}}_{x_1, x_2 \leftarrow \{0,1\}^n} \left[\mathop{\mathbb{E}}_{\substack{h \leftarrow \mathcal{H}, y \leftarrow f(\{0,1\}^n), \\ (x_1', x_2') \leftarrow A(h, x_1, x_2)}} [p_A(x_1, x_2, x_1', y)] \right],$$

and thus it is enough to show that for every fixed $x_1, x_2 \in \{0,1\}^n$,

$$\mathop{\mathbb{E}}_{\substack{h \leftarrow \mathcal{H}, y \leftarrow f(\{0,1\}^n), \\ (x_1', x_2') \leftarrow A(h, x_1, x_2)}} [p_A(x_1, x_2, x_1', y)] \geq \alpha_{x_1,x_2}^2 \cdot n^{-2\beta-2} \cdot 2^{-12}.$$

Indeed, recall that by definition, $p_A(x_1, x_2, \perp, y) = 0$. Therefore,

$$\mathop{E}_{\substack{h \leftarrow \mathcal{H}, y \leftarrow f(\{0,1\}^n), \\ (x_1', x_2') \leftarrow A(h, x_1, x_2)}} [p_A(x_1, x_2, x_1', y)]$$

$$= \sum_{x_1' \in f^{-1}(f(x_1))} \mathop{Pr}_{h \leftarrow \mathcal{H}} [A(h, x_1, x_2) = (x_1', \cdot)] \cdot \mathop{E}_{y \leftarrow f(\{0,1\}^n)} [p_A(x_1, x_2, x_1', y)]$$

$$\geq \sum_{x_1' \in f^{-1}(f(x_1))} \mathop{Pr}_{h \leftarrow \mathcal{H}} [A(h, x_1, x_2) = (x_1', \cdot)]$$

$$\cdot \mathop{Pr}_{h' \leftarrow \mathcal{H}} [A(h', x_1, x_2) = (x_1', \cdot) \mid x_1' \in \mathcal{G}_{h', x_1, x_2}] \cdot n^{-\beta-1} \cdot 2^{-10}$$

$$\geq \alpha_{x_1, x_2}^2 \cdot n^{-2\beta-2} \cdot 2^{-12}.$$

Where the equality holds by the assumption that A always outputs a valid collision, or $\perp$. The first inequality holds by Claim 4.8 and the second by Claim 4.9.

We are now left to bound $E_{x_1, x_2 \leftarrow \{0,1\}^n} \left[\alpha_{x_1, x_2}^2 \right] \cdot n^{-2\beta-2} \cdot 2^{-12}$. Observe that by definition $E_{x_1, x_2 \leftarrow \{0,1\}^n} \left[\alpha_{x_1, x_2} \right] = \alpha$, and thus by the Jensen inequality, it holds that $E_{x_1, x_2 \leftarrow \{0,1\}^n} \left[\alpha_{x_1, x_2}^2 \right] \geq \alpha^2$, which concludes the proof.

Acknowledgement. We are thankful to Iftach Haitner and Salil Vadhan for very useful discussions. We also thank the anonymous reviewers for their comments.

A   Missing Proofs

A.1   Pseudorandom Generator

Lemma A.1 (Lemma *2.6*, restated). *There exists a* PPT *algorithm* P *such that the following holds. Let Q be a distribution over $\{0,1\}^* \times \{0,1\}^n$, and let* D *be an algorithm and $\alpha \in [0,1]$ such that,*

$$\mathop{Pr}_{(x,y) \leftarrow Q, z \leftarrow \{0,1\}^n} [D(x, z) = 1] - \mathop{Pr}_{(x,y) \leftarrow Q} [D(x, y) = 1] \geq \alpha.$$

Then there exists $i \in [n]$ such that

$$\mathop{Pr}_{(x,y) \leftarrow Q} \left[P^D(x, y_{1,\ldots,i-1}) = y_i \right] \geq 1/2 + \alpha/n.$$

Proof (Proof of Claim 2.6.). Let Q, D and α be as in Claim 2.6. We start by showing that D can be used in order to distinguish y_i from uniform bit given $x, y_{1,\ldots,i-1}$ for some index $i \in [n]$. Later we use this fact in order to predict y_i. Indeed, it holds that

$$\alpha \leq \mathop{Pr}_{(x,y) \leftarrow Q, z \leftarrow \{0,1\}^n} [D(x, z) = 1] - \mathop{Pr}_{(x,y) \leftarrow Q} [D(x, y) = 1]$$

$$\leq \sum_{i=1}^{n} (\mathop{Pr}_{(x,y) \leftarrow Q, z \leftarrow \{0,1\}^n} [D(x, y_{1,\ldots,i-1}, z_{i,\ldots,n}) = 1]$$

$$- \mathop{Pr}_{(x,y) \leftarrow Q, z \leftarrow \{0,1\}^n} [D(x, y_{1,\ldots,i}, z_{i+1,\ldots,n}) = 1]),$$

and thus there exists $i \in [n]$ such that

$$\epsilon := \Pr_{\substack{(x,y) \leftarrow Q, \\ b \leftarrow \{0,1\} \\ z \leftarrow \{0,1\}^{n-i}}} [D(x, y_{1,\ldots,i-1}, b, z) = 1] - \Pr_{\substack{(x,y) \leftarrow Q, \\ z \leftarrow \{0,1\}^{n-i}}} [D(x, y_{1,\ldots,i-1}, y_i, z) = 1]$$

$$\geq \alpha/n, \tag{12}$$

as we wanted to show. We now describe the predictor P. Consider the following algortihm.

Algorithm A.2 (The predictor P).
Input: $x \in \{0,1\}^*$, $y_{1,\ldots,i-1} \in \{0,1\}^{i-1}$.
Oracle: A distinguisher D.
Operation:

1. *Sample* $b \leftarrow \{0,1\}$, $z \leftarrow \{0,1\}^{n-i}$ *and execute* $D(x, y_{1,\ldots,i-1}, b, z)$.
2. *If* D *output* 1, *output* $1 - b$. *Otherwise, output* b.

We next show that the probability that P outputs y_i is at least $1/2 + \alpha/n$.
Let $p := \Pr_{(x,y) \leftarrow Q, z \leftarrow \{0,1\}^{n-i}} [D(x, y_{1,\ldots,i-1}, y_i, z) = 1]$. It holds that

$$p + \epsilon = \Pr_{\substack{(x,y) \leftarrow Q, b \leftarrow \{0,1\} \\ z \leftarrow \{0,1\}^{n-i}}} [D(x, y_{1,\ldots,i-1}, b, z) = 1]$$

$$= 1/2 \cdot (\Pr_{\substack{(x,y) \leftarrow Q, \\ z \leftarrow \{0,1\}^{n-i}}} [D(x, y_{1,\ldots,i-1}, y_i, z) = 1]$$

$$+ \Pr_{\substack{(x,y) \leftarrow Q, \\ z \leftarrow \{0,1\}^{n-i}}} [D(x, y_{1,\ldots,i-1}, 1 - y_i, z) = 1])$$

$$= 1/2 \cdot (p + \Pr_{\substack{(x,y) \leftarrow Q, \\ z \leftarrow \{0,1\}^{n-i}}} [D(x, y_{1,\ldots,i-1}, 1 - y_i, z) = 1])).$$

Thus, $\Pr_{(x,y) \leftarrow Q, z \leftarrow \{0,1\}^{n-i}} [D(x, y_{1,\ldots,i-1}, 1 - y_i, z) = 1] = p + 2\epsilon$. Continue, the probability that P outputs y_i is given by

$$\Pr_{b \leftarrow \{0,1\}^n} [b = y_i] \cdot (1 - p) + \Pr_{b \leftarrow \{0,1\}^n} [b = 1 - y_i]$$

$$\cdot \Pr_{\substack{(x,y) \leftarrow Q, \\ z \leftarrow \{0,1\}^{n-i}}} [D(x, y_{1,\ldots,i-1}, 1 - y_i, z) = 1]$$

$$= 1/2 \cdot (1 - p) + 1/2 \cdot (p + 2\epsilon)$$

$$= 1/2 + \epsilon$$

$$\geq 1/2 + \alpha/n$$

as needed.

A.2   Universal Hash Families

Lemma A.3 (Lemma *2.13,* **restated).** *For every $\ell, n \in \mathbb{N}$ such that $\ell \leq n$, the family $\left\{ m \colon m \in \{0,1\}^{n \times \ell} \right\}$ is approximately-flat.*

Proof (Proof of Lemma 2.13). Fix $\mathcal{Y}, x_1, x_2$ and y_1 as in Definition 2.12. We want to show that

$$\Pr_{M \leftarrow \{0,1\}^{2n \times \ell}} [\exists y_2 \in \mathcal{Y} \text{ s.t. } M(x_1, y_1) = M(x_2, y_2)] \geq 2^{-10} \cdot \min \left\{ |\mathcal{Y}| \cdot 2^{-\ell}, 1 \right\}.$$

We first assume that $x_1 \neq x_2$, as otherwise the lemma holds trivially. Next, we observe that M can be written as $M_{\mathcal{X}} \in \{0,1\}^{n \times \ell}$ and $M_{\mathcal{Y}} \in \{0,1\}^{n \times \ell}$, such that for every vectors $x, y \in \{0,1\}^n$ it holds that

$$M(x,y) = (x \cdot M_{\mathcal{X}}) \oplus (y \cdot M_{\mathcal{Y}}). \tag{13}$$

We want to bound the probability that there exists $y_2 \in \mathcal{Y}$ such that $M(x_1, y_1) = M(x_2, y_2)$, or equivalently,

$$(x_1 \oplus x_2) \cdot M_{\mathcal{X}} = (y_2 \oplus y_1) \cdot M_{\mathcal{Y}}. \tag{14}$$

Since $x_1 \neq x_2$, it holds that $(x_1 \oplus x_2) \cdot M_{\mathcal{X}}$ is a uniform element in $\{0,1\}^{\ell}$. Thus, we are interested in lower bounding the probability

$$\Pr_{M_{\mathcal{Y}} \leftarrow \{0,1\}^{n \times \ell}, z' \leftarrow \{0,1\}^{\ell}} [\exists y_2 \in \mathcal{Y} \text{ s.t. } z' = (y_2 \oplus y_1) \cdot M_{\mathcal{Y}}]$$

$$= \Pr_{M_{\mathcal{Y}} \leftarrow \{0,1\}^{n \times \ell}, z \leftarrow \{0,1\}^{\ell}} [\exists y_2 \in \mathcal{Y} \text{ s.t. } z = y_2 \cdot M_{\mathcal{Y}}]$$

where the equality holds since $z := z' \oplus y_1 \cdot M_{\mathcal{Y}}$ is a uniform element in $\{0,1\}^{\ell}$ which is independent from $M_{\mathcal{Y}}$. In the following we show that with probability at least $1/2$ over the choice of $M_{\mathcal{Y}}$, the size of the set $\mathcal{Y} \cdot M_{\mathcal{Y}} = \{y \cdot M_{\mathcal{Y}} \colon y \in \mathcal{Y}\}$ is at least $\min \left\{ |\mathcal{Y}|/2, 2^{\ell}/32 \right\}$, from which the lemma follows.

To see the above, first notice that for every vector $v \in \{0,1\}^n$ with $v \neq 0$, it holds that $\Pr_{M_{\mathcal{Y}}} [v \cdot M_{\mathcal{Y}} = 0] = 2^{-\ell}$, and thus,

$$\underset{M_{\mathcal{Y}}}{\mathrm{E}} [|\{y_1 \neq y_2 \in \mathcal{Y} \colon y_1 \cdot M_{\mathcal{Y}} = y_2 \cdot M_{\mathcal{Y}}\}|]$$

$$= \underset{M_{\mathcal{Y}}}{\mathrm{E}} [|\{y_1 \neq y_2 \in \mathcal{Y} \colon (y_1 \oplus y_2) \cdot M_{\mathcal{Y}} = 0\}|]$$

$$\leq |\mathcal{Y}|^2 \cdot 2^{-\ell}.$$

By Markov inequality, we get that with probability at least $1/2$ over the choice of $M_{\mathcal{Y}}$, it holds that

$$|\{y_1 \neq y_2 \in \mathcal{Y} \colon y_1 \cdot M_{\mathcal{Y}} = y_2 \cdot M_{\mathcal{Y}}\}| \leq 2 |\mathcal{Y}|^2 \cdot 2^{-\ell}. \tag{15}$$

In the following we show that for every matrix $M_{\mathcal{Y}}$ for which Eq. (15) holds, it holds that $\mathcal{Y} \cdot M_{\mathcal{Y}} \geq \min \left\{ |\mathcal{Y}|/2, 2^{\ell}/32 \right\}$.

Indeed, consider a graph $\mathcal{G}$, in which the set of vertices is $\mathcal{Y}$, and the set of edges E is the set $\{y_1 \neq y_2 \in \mathcal{Y} : y_1 \cdot M_{\mathcal{Y}} = y_2 \cdot M_{\mathcal{Y}}\}$. By assumption, $|E| \leq 2 |\mathcal{Y}|^2 \cdot 2^{-\ell}$. Furthermore, it is not hard to see that $\mathcal{G}$ is composed of disjoint cliques, and that the number of connected components in $\mathcal{G}$ is exactly the size of $\mathcal{Y} \cdot M_{\mathcal{Y}}$. To bound the number of connected components of $\mathcal{G}$, we first assume that $\mathcal{G}$ has no more than $|\mathcal{Y}|/2$ isolated vertices, as otherwise the bound trivially follows. We start with removing the isolated vertices from $\mathcal{G}$, to get a graph with at least $|\mathcal{Y}|/2$ vertices and at most $2 |\mathcal{Y}|^2 \cdot 2^{-\ell}$ edges. Let k be the number of connected components in the graph, and let $c_1, \ldots, c_k$ be the number of vertices in each component. Since $c_i > 1$ for every i, the number of edges in the i-th component is larger than $c_i^2/4$. By Cauchy–Schwarz inequality,

$$(|\mathcal{Y}|/2)^2 \leq (\sum_{i \in [k]} c_i)^2 \leq k \cdot \sum_{i \in [k]} c_i^2 \leq 4k |E| \leq 8k |\mathcal{Y}|^2 \cdot 2^{-\ell},$$

which implies that $k \geq 2^\ell/32$, and the lemma follows.

References

1. Agrawal, R., Chen, Y.-H., Horel, T., Vadhan, S.: Unifying computational entropies via Kullback–Leibler divergence. In: Boldyreva, A., Micciancio, D. (eds.) CRYPTO 2019. LNCS, vol. 11693, pp. 831–858. Springer, Cham (2019). https://doi.org/10.1007/978-3-030-26951-7_28
2. Ames, S., Gennaro, R., Venkitasubramaniam, M.: *The Generalized randomized iterate* and its application to new efficient constructions of UOWHFs from regular one-way functions. In: Wang, X., Sako, K. (eds.) ASIACRYPT 2012. LNCS, vol. 7658, pp. 154–171. Springer, Heidelberg (2012). https://doi.org/10.1007/978-3-642-34961-4_11
3. Barhum, K., Holenstein, T.: A cookbook for black-box separations and a recipe for UOWHFs. In: Sahai, A. (ed.) TCC 2013. LNCS, vol. 7785, pp. 662–679. Springer, Heidelberg (2013). https://doi.org/10.1007/978-3-642-36594-2_37
4. Barhum, K., Maurer, U.: UOWHFs from OWFs: trading regularity for efficiency. In: Hevia, A., Neven, G. (eds.) LATINCRYPT 2012. LNCS, vol. 7533, pp. 234–253. Springer, Heidelberg (2012). https://doi.org/10.1007/978-3-642-33481-8_13
5. Blum, M., Micali, S.: How to generate cryptographically strong sequences of pseudorandom bits. SIAM J. Comput. **13**(4), 850–864 (1984)
6. Gennaro, R., Gertner, Y., Katz, J., Trevisan, L.: Bounds on the efficiency of generic cryptographic constructions. SIAM J. Comput. **35**(1), 217–246 (2005)
7. Goldreich, O., Impagliazzo, R., Levin, L., Venkatesan, R., Zuckerman, D.: Security preserving amplification of hardness. In: Proceedings [1990] 31st Annual Symposium on Foundations of Computer Science, pp. 318–326. IEEE (1990)
8. Goldreich, O., Krawczyk, H., Luby, M.: On the existence of pseudorandom generators. SIAM J. Comput. **22**(6), 1163–1175 (1993)
9. Goldreich, O., Levin, L.A.: A hard-core predicate for all one-way functions. In: Proceedings of the Twenty-First Annual ACM Symposium on Theory of Computing, pp. 25–32 (1989)

10. Haitner, I., Harnik, D., Reingold, O.: Efficient pseudorandom generators from exponentially hard one-way functions. In: Bugliesi, M., Preneel, B., Sassone, V., Wegener, I. (eds.) ICALP 2006. LNCS, vol. 4052, pp. 228–239. Springer, Heidelberg (2006). https://doi.org/10.1007/11787006_20

11. Haitner, I., Harnik, D., Reingold, O.: On the power of the randomized iterate. In: Dwork, C. (ed.) CRYPTO 2006. LNCS, vol. 4117, pp. 22–40. Springer, Heidelberg (2006). https://doi.org/10.1007/11818175_2

12. Haitner, I., Holenstein, T., Reingold, O., Vadhan, S., Wee, H.: Universal one-way hash functions via inaccessible entropy. In: Gilbert, H. (ed.) EUROCRYPT 2010. LNCS, vol. 6110, pp. 616–637. Springer, Heidelberg (2010). https://doi.org/10.1007/978-3-642-13190-5_31

13. Haitner, I., Reingold, O., Vadhan, S.: Efficiency improvements in constructing pseudorandom generators from one-way functions. SIAM J. Comput. **42**(3), 1405–1430 (2013)

14. Haitner, I., Reingold, O., Vadhan, S., Wee, H.: Inaccessible entropy. In: Proceedings of the Forty-First Annual ACM Symposium on Theory of Computing, pp. 611–620 (2009)

15. Håstad, J., Impagliazzo, R., Levin, L.A., Luby, M.: A pseudorandom generator from any one-way function. SIAM J. Comput. **28**(4), 1364–1396 (1999)

16. Holenstein, T.: Pseudorandom generators from one-way functions: a simple construction for any hardness. In: Halevi, S., Rabin, T. (eds.) TCC 2006. LNCS, vol. 3876, pp. 443–461. Springer, Heidelberg (2006). https://doi.org/10.1007/11681878_23

17. Holenstein, T., Sinha, M.: Constructing a pseudorandom generator requires an almost linear number of calls. In: 2012 IEEE 53rd Annual Symposium on Foundations of Computer Science, pp. 698–707. IEEE (2012)

18. Impagliazzo, R., Levin, L.A., Luby, M.: Pseudo-random generation from one-way functions. In: Proceedings of the Twenty-First Annual ACM Symposium on Theory of Computing, pp. 12–24 (1989)

19. Naor, M., Yung, M.: Universal one-way hash functions and their cryptographic applications. In: Proceedings of the Twenty-First Annual ACM Symposium on Theory of Computing, pp. 33–43 (1989)

20. Rompel, J.: One-way functions are necessary and sufficient for secure signatures. In: Proceedings of the Twenty-Second Annual ACM Symposium on Theory of Computing, pp. 387–394 (1990)

21. Vadhan, S., Zheng, C.J.: Characterizing pseudoentropy and simplifying pseudorandom generator constructions. In: Proceedings of the Forty-Fourth Annual ACM Symposium on Theory of Computing, pp. 817–836 (2012)

22. Yao, A.C.: Theory and application of trapdoor functions. In: 23rd Annual Symposium on Foundations of Computer Science (SFCS 1982), pp. 80–91. IEEE (1982)

23. Yu, Yu., Gu, D., Li, X., Weng, J.: (Almost) optimal constructions of UOWHFs from 1-to-1, regular one-way functions and beyond. In: Gennaro, R., Robshaw, M. (eds.) CRYPTO 2015. LNCS, vol. 9216, pp. 209–229. Springer, Heidelberg (2015). https://doi.org/10.1007/978-3-662-48000-7_11

24. Yu, Yu., Gu, D., Li, X., Weng, J.: The randomized iterate, revisited - almost linear seed length PRGs from a broader class of one-way functions. In: Dodis, Y., Nielsen, J.B. (eds.) TCC 2015. LNCS, vol. 9014, pp. 7–35. Springer, Heidelberg (2015). https://doi.org/10.1007/978-3-662-46494-6_2

25. Yu, Y., Li, X., Weng, J.: Pseudorandom generators from regular one-way functions: new constructions with improved parameters. Theor. Comput. Sci. **569**, 58–69 (2015)

On Treewidth, Separators and Yao's Garbling

Chethan Kamath[1(✉)], Karen Klein[2], and Krzysztof Pietrzak[3]

[1] Tel Aviv University, Tel Aviv-Yafo, Israel
[2] ETH Zurich, Zurich, Switzerland
[3] IST, Klosterneuburg, Austria
pietrzak@ist.ac.at

Abstract. We show that Yao's garbling scheme is adaptively indistinguishable for the class of Boolean circuits of size S and treewidth w with only a $S^{O(w)}$ loss in security. For instance, circuits with constant treewidth are as a result adaptively indistinguishable with only a polynomial loss. This (partially) complements a negative result of Applebaum et al. (Crypto 2013), which showed (assuming one-way functions) that Yao's garbling scheme cannot be adaptively *simulatable*. As main technical contributions, we introduce a new pebble game that abstracts out our security reduction and then present a pebbling strategy for this game where the number of pebbles used is roughly $O(\delta w \log(S))$, δ being the fan-out of the circuit. The design of the strategy relies on separators, a graph-theoretic notion with connections to circuit complexity.

1 Introduction

Suppose that Alice, who holds a function represented as a Boolean circuit C, and Bob, who holds an input x to that function, want to jointly evaluate $y = C(x)$ such that Alice learns nothing about x while Bob learns nothing about C (except for some side-information that is unavoidable). Yao put forward[1] the following elegant solution:

1. Alice first sends $\tilde{C}$, a "garbling" of the circuit C, to Bob,

---

[1] According to [7], the idea was first presented by Yao in oral presentations on secure function-evaluation [42,43] but formally described only in [21].

Chethan, K—Supported by Azrieli International Postdoctoral Fellowship. Most of the work was done while the author was at Northeastern University and Charles University, funded by the IARPA grant IARPA/2019-19-020700009 and project PRIMUS/17/SCI/9, respectively.

Karen, K—Supported in part by ERC CoG grant 724307. Most of the work was done while the author was at IST Austria funded by the European Research Council (ERC) under the European Union's Horizon 2020 research and innovation programme (682815 - TOCNeT).

Krzysztof, P—Funded by the European Research Council (ERC) under the European Union's Horizon 2020 research and innovation programme (682815 - TOCNeT).

© International Association for Cryptologic Research 2021
K. Nissim and B. Waters (Eds.): TCC 2021, LNCS 13043, pp. 486–517, 2021.
https://doi.org/10.1007/978-3-030-90453-1_17

2. Bob then obtains $\tilde{x}$, a "garbling" of his input x, from Alice via oblivious transfer,
3. Bob finally evaluates $\tilde{\mathsf{C}}$ on $\tilde{x}$ to learn y and sends it over to Alice.

Yao showed how the garbling steps above can be carried out using a symmetric-key encryption (SKE) scheme (and hence one-way functions). This has been ever since referred to as Yao's garbling scheme, and is the focus of this work. We describe it next in slightly more details.

Yao's Garbling Scheme. Let $(\mathsf{Enc}, \mathsf{Dec})$ be a (special) SKE. To garble a circuit $\mathsf{C} : \{0,1\}^n \to \{0,1\}^\ell$ with fan-in 2 and arbitrary fan-out:

1. Alice first samples a pair of secret keys (k_w^0, k_w^1) for each wire w in C.
2. For every gate $g : \{0,1\}^2 \to \{0,1\}$ with left input wire u, right input wire v, and output wire w, she then computes a *garbling table* $\tilde{g}$ consisting of the four ciphertexts listed in Table 1(a) in random order.
3. Finally, she constructs the *output mapping* μ which, for each output wire w, maps each of the keys (k_w^0, k_w^1) to the bit it "encodes".

The *garbled circuit* $\tilde{\mathsf{C}}$ consists of all the garbling tables $\tilde{g}$ and the output map μ, Alice sends it over to Bob. This constitutes the *offline* phase of the protocol. To garble an input $x = x_1 \| \ldots \| x_n$, Alice simply gives out, for each input wire w_i, the key $k_{w_i}^{x_i}$ corresponding to the bit x_i. This constitutes the *online* phase of the protocol. To evaluate the garbled circuit on the garbled input, the encryption scheme must satisfy a *special correctness property*: for each cipher-text $c \leftarrow \mathsf{Enc}_k(m)$ there should exist a single key (i.e., k) such that decryption passes. Using the keys in the garbling input, Bob can now evaluate C "over the encryption" as follows:

1. Starting from the input level and in some topological order, he progressively decrypts each garbling table in $\tilde{\mathsf{C}}$ by trying the two keys in hand on all the four ciphertexts for each garbling table. Thus, in each step, he learns one of the secret keys corresponding to the output wire of the gate in consideration.
2. At the end of this process, Bob recovers exactly one of the two keys associated with each output wire of the circuit. This allows him to use the output map μ to "decode" the revealed output keys to the output string $y \in \{0,1\}^\ell$.

The scheme as described above is what is regarded to be the original formulation of Yao's garbling scheme [27,33]. A slight variant in which Alice defers sending the output map μ to the online phase (along with $\tilde{x}$) is also of interest [27], although it suffers from a higher online complexity compared to the original formulation. To avoid confusion, we refer to the original scheme as *Yao's offline garbling scheme* and the modified scheme as *Yao's online garbling scheme* or, in short, Online Yao and Offline Yao respectively. Our work concerns the security of Offline Yao.

Table 1. Garbling tables for (a) general gate g (b) constant-0 gate and (c) constant-1 gate. u and v denote the two input wires and w denotes the output wire. The two keys associated with (say) the wire u are denoted by k_u^0 and k_u^1.

$\mathsf{E}_{k_u^0}(\mathsf{E}_{k_v^0}(k_w^{g(0,0)}))$	$\mathsf{E}_{k_u^0}(\mathsf{E}_{k_v^0}(k_w^0))$	$\mathsf{E}_{k_u^0}(\mathsf{E}_{k_v^0}(k_w^1))$
$\mathsf{E}_{k_u^1}(\mathsf{E}_{k_v^0}(k_w^{g(1,0)}))$	$\mathsf{E}_{k_u^0}(\mathsf{E}_{k_v^1}(k_w^0))$	$\mathsf{E}_{k_u^0}(\mathsf{E}_{k_v^1}(k_w^1))$
$\mathsf{E}_{k_u^0}(\mathsf{E}_{k_v^1}(k_w^{g(0,1)}))$	$\mathsf{E}_{k_u^1}(\mathsf{E}_{k_v^0}(k_w^0))$	$\mathsf{E}_{k_u^1}(\mathsf{E}_{k_v^0}(k_w^1))$
$\mathsf{E}_{k_u^1}(\mathsf{E}_{k_v^1}(k_w^{g(1,1)}))$	$\mathsf{E}_{k_u^1}(\mathsf{E}_{k_v^1}(k_w^0))$	$\mathsf{E}_{k_u^1}(\mathsf{E}_{k_v^1}(k_w^1))$
(a)	(b)	(c)

Security. Even though garbling schemes found several applications (see [7]), its security was formally analysed much later in [33]. They consider a simulation-based notion[2] captured by the following experiment:

1. The adversary submits a circuit-input pair (C, x) to the challenger.
2. The challenger responds either with the real garbling $(\tilde{\mathsf{C}}, \tilde{x})$ (i.e., real game or Real) or with a "simulated" garbling where a constant-0 circuit is used instead of C (i.e., simulated game or Sim). The constant-0 circuit has the same topology as C but with all its gates replaced by constant-0 gates.
3. The adversary wins if it guesses which case it is.

Then they gave a reduction from the (special) indistinguishability of the underlying SKE for *offline* Yao. Note that the adversary in the above security game must *select* the garbling input x at the same time as the circuit C. This is in conflict with the online-offline nature of the actual scheme where Bob (a potential adversary) sees $\tilde{\mathsf{C}}$ *before* he commits to x. Hence Bob could have chosen the input, *adaptively*, based on $\tilde{\mathsf{C}}$. In fact, such a scenario does arise in applications such as one-time programs and secure outsourcing [6]. Therefore it is natural to consider strengthening the above selective definition of simulatability to an adaptive definition where A gets to choose the input after it sees the garbling of a circuit of its choice. Unfortunately, this is too strong a notion to attain for Offline Yao: it was shown in [4] that the *online complexity* of a garbling scheme (or, more generally, a randomised encoding scheme) in the adaptive setting *must* exceed the output-size of the circuit (given that one-way functions exist). Jafargholi and Wichs [27] observed that this negative result does not apply to Online Yao since the output map there gets sent in the online phase, and even managed to prove adaptive *simulatability* of Online Yao. Security of other variants of Yao's garbling scheme was also proved [22,26]. However, the case of Offline Yao was largely ignored.

---

[2] This is an equivalent formulation of the definition in [33] and is taken from [27]. Our overview of the proof in [33] to be discussed in Sect. 1.2 has been adapted accordingly.

1.1   Our Results

Although the negative result in [4] rules out adaptive *simulatability* of Offline Yao, it is not clear if it also applies to its adaptive *indistinguishability* [7], which is defined by the following experiment:

1. The adversary submits a pair of circuits (C_0, C_1) of the same topology to the challenger
2. The challenger. flips a coin b and responds with $\tilde{C}_b$.
3. The adversary then submits a pair of inputs (x_0, x_1) such that $C_0(x_0) = C_1(x_1)$ and the challenger responds with $\tilde{x}_b$.
4. The adversary wins if it guesses the bit b correctly.

Although it is a weaker notion of security, adaptive indistinguishability suffices for certain applications (e.g, adaptively-indistinguishable symmetric-key functional encryption [26]).

Table 2. Security of Yao garbling and its variants. The (only) negative result is highlighted in red.

	Selective		Adaptive	
	Offline Yao	Online Yao	Offline Yao	Online Yao
Simulatability	[33]		[4]	[27]
Indistinguishability			This work	

Our Results. We help (partially) complete the landscape for security of Yao's garbling (see Table 2). To this end, we characterise the adaptive indistinguishability of Offline Yao in terms of the treewidth[3] of the circuit. Our main results are informally stated below.

Theorem (main). Consider the class of Boolean circuits $\mathcal{C}$ of size S with treewidth $w = w(S)$. Offline Yao is adaptively indistinguishable for $\mathcal{C}$ with $S^{O(w)}$ loss in security.

For Boolean circuits of constant (resp., poly-logarithmic) treewidth, we obtain the following corollary.

Corollary. Offline Yao is adaptively indistinguishable for Boolean circuits of size S and $O(1)$ (resp., **polylog**(S)) treewidth with a polynomial (resp., quasi-polynomial) in S loss in security.

---

[3] Since treewidth is defined for undirected graphs, whenever we refer to the treewidth of a directed graph (or a circuit) we refer to the treewidth of the graph obtained by ignoring the direction of its edges.

Interpreting Our Results. Treewidth is a notion from algorithmic graph theory that has found several applications in parametrised and circuit complexity (see Sect. 1.3) Intuitively, it is a (graph) property that measures how "far" the circuit is from a formula (and, more generally, how far a graph is from a tree): in particular, the smaller the treewidth the closer the circuit is to a formula. Therefore, it is not surprising that having a low treewidth limits how powerful a circuit can be. A precise characterisation of this (from above) was given in [19]: every circuit of size S and treewidth $w = w(S)$ can be simulated in *depth* $w \log(S)$. Thus, e.g, circuits of constant treewidth can be simulated in $\mathbf{NC}^1$. Whether the converse is true in general – i.e., whether $\mathbf{NC}^i$ can be simulated using circuits with treewidth $O(\log^{i-1}(S))$ – is an open problem to the best of our knowledge.[4] However it is partially true: namely, $\mathbf{NC}^1$ circuits can be simulated using polynomial-sized Boolean formulae (which, by definition, have treewidth 1) [13,41]. Consequently, the first corollary applies to functions computable in $\mathbf{NC}^1$.

Given the aforementioned negative result from [4], we find any proof of adaptive security for Offline Yao rather surprising. Nevertheless, there are scenarios where our results also lead to improvements in concrete efficiency (even after the loss in security is taken into account). We describe one such scenario next. Recall from the discussion above that for functions computable in $\mathbf{NC}^1$, we show security of Offline Yao at only a polynomial loss. Moreover, the online complexity of garbling such a function using Offline Yao depends only on the input length n (times the security parameter λ). Now, note that PRGs of arbitrary stretch (say n^c for a constant $c \in \mathbb{N}$) exist in $\mathbf{NC}^1$ [15,23]. However, if one were to use Online Yao, then the online complexity is substantial ($n^c \times \lambda$). This example is particularly interesting since Offline Yao for such a function is not simulatable at all as a consequence of the negative result.

Finally, a remark on the optimality of our upper bound: it was recently shown in [30] that any *black-box* reduction that proves indistinguishability of Offline Yao (or, for that matter, Online Yao) must lose security by a factor that is sub-exponential in the depth of the circuit. Therefore, there remains a gap between the lower bound proved there and the upper bound shown here.

Implications to Simulatability of Online Yao. It is worth pointing out that our results may also imply tighter reductions for simulatability of Online Yao. The reduction for simulatability of Online Yao from [27] loses a factor that is exponential in the *width* of a circuit: our approach can be seen as an extension of their techniques. Since treewidth is bounded from above by width, in cases where there is a gap between treewidth and width for a circuit class, our approach would lead to a tighter reduction for simulatability of Online Yao compared to [27]. A more detailed explanation follows later in Remark 1.

Comparison with [26]. We conclude the section by comparing our result with [26], which is also concerned with adaptively-indistinguishable garbled circuits. The

---

[4] See this question (48504) posted on CSTheory, Stack Exchange.

construction in [26] builds on [22] and therefore has Offline Yao as its basis. However, it requires (i) applying an additional layer of *somewhere equivocal encryption* to the garbling table and (ii) modifying the circuit to be garbled in order to make the security proof go through. These modifications lead to their construction being less efficient compared to plain Offline Yao, but it does allow them to prove adaptive indistinguishability. It is not clear if any of the ideas employed there can be used to argue the indistinguishability of Offline Yao (this is, in fact, posed as an open question there).

1.2   Technical Overview

Outline. Our starting point is the reduction provinf adaptive simulatability of Online Yao [27]. The key idea in [27] is to abstract out the hybrid argument using a pebble game on the circuit, which we call the black-gray (BG) pebble game (Definition 8). To be precise, they showed that if a circuit allows a BG pebbling strategy of length τ that uses σ (black) pebbles, then there exists a reduction proving adaptive simulatability of Online Yao with a loss in security at most $O(\tau 2^\sigma)$. This allows us to shift the focus from security reductions to the conceptually-cleaner task of coming up with "pebble-efficient" strategies. We start off below by describing this connection and then explain why this approach falls short when it comes to arguing adaptive indistinguishability (or simulatability) of Offline Yao. Next we show how this issue can be remedied, key to it is a new pebble game, which we call the black-gray-red (BGR) pebble game (Definition 11). Analogous to [27], we prove that if there exists a BGR pebbling strategy of length τ that uses σ ("grayscale", i.e. black or gray) pebbles, then there exists a reduction for adaptive indistinguishability of Offline Yao where the loss in security is at most $O(\tau 2^\sigma)$ (Theorem 6). Finally to complete the proof – and as our main technical contribution – we describe a pebble-efficient strategy for the BGR pebble game in which the number of (grayscale) pebbles used grows only with the treewidth of the circuit (Theorem 5). The strategy has a divide-and-conquer flavour and crucially relies on the notion of *separators* from graph theory. We next elaborate on each of the steps above.

Pebble Game and Hybrids. The reduction in [27] builds on the reduction for selective simulatability of Offline Yao [33]. Both these works follow a sophisticated hybrid argument which can be described abstractly using a BG pebbling strategy.

Pebbles and Garbling Modes. The BG pebble game (formally defined in Definition 8), as its name suggests, uses two types of pebbles: black and gray. A pebble configuration $\mathcal{P}$ for a circuit C determines how the garbled circuit $\tilde{\mathsf{C}}$ is simulated in the hybrid $\mathsf{H}_\mathcal{P}$. To be more precise, the pebble configuration $\mathcal{P}$ can associate each gate g in C with a black or gray pebble. In order to translate $\mathcal{P}$ to the garbling $\tilde{\mathsf{C}}$, the simulator in hybrid $\mathsf{H}_\mathcal{P}$ does the following:

- if g carries no pebble in $\mathcal{P}$, then the corresponding garbling table in $\tilde{\mathsf{C}}$ consists of an honest garbling table of g (Table 1(a))
- if g carries a gray pebble, then the garbling table encodes a constant-0 gate (Table 1(b)).
- if g carries a black pebble then the garbling table encodes either a constant-0 or a constant-1 gate (Table 1(c)) *depending* on the value of (the output wire of) g when C is run on the garbling input x.

The three *modes* above of simulating individual gates are named real, simulated and input-dependent modes respectively or, in short, Real, Sim and Input, respectively (Table 3(a)). Note that the real garbling game corresponds to the empty pebble configuration (since all the gates are honestly garbled), whereas the simulated game will correspond to the all-gray configuration (since all the gates have been replaced by the constant-0 gate).

Pebbling Rules. Note that any arbitrary configuration of pebbles $\mathcal{P}$ describes a valid hybrid $\mathsf{H}_{\mathcal{P}}$. The role of the pebbling rules is to model indistinguishability of neighbouring hybrids. To be more precise, if a pebble configuration $\mathcal{Q}$ can be obtained from another configuration $\mathcal{P}$ by a valid pebbling move (or vice versa) then the hybrids $\mathsf{H}_{\mathcal{P}}$ and $\mathsf{H}_{\mathcal{Q}}$ should be indistinguishable. Consequently a BG pebbling strategy $\mathcal{P}$, which must start from an empty configuration and end with the all-gray configuration, leads to a valid sequence of hybrids that establishes that the real garbling game and simulated garbling game are indistinguishable, proving the security of the garbling scheme. In the BG pebble game, the following moves (see Fig. 1) are allowed:

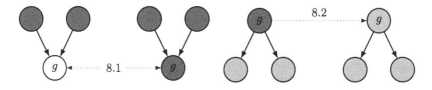

Fig. 1. Rules for BG pebble game.

1. a black pebble can be placed on or removed from a gate g if and only if g's predecessor gates are pebbled black; and
2. a black pebble on a gate g can be replaced by a gray pebble if g's *successor* gates are pebbled, either black or gray.

To understand the rationale behind the two rules, one needs to take a closer look at the structure of a garbling table in Yao's scheme. Since this is not that relevant to the current discussion, we refer the readers interested in more details to Sect. 3.

Selective Simulatability of Offline Yao. Observe that in order to simulate $\tilde{C}$ in a hybrid $H_{\mathcal{P}}$, the simulator only needs to know the output value of those gates that are pebbled black in $\mathcal{P}$ (i.e., the gates in Input mode). In the selective setting, since the adversary commits to the garbling input x in the offline phase, the value of *all* the gates is available beforehand. Hence, in this case the simulator has the luxury of using as many pebbles as it needs. Therefore the pebbling strategy (implicitly) employed in [33] is the following:

1. starting from the input gates, pebble the circuit completely black in some topological order, and then
2. starting from the output gates and in reverse topological order, replace each black pebble with a gray pebble.

To complete the description of the hybrid $H_{\mathcal{P}}$ in the selective setting, one thing remains to be addressed. For concreteness, let's consider the simulated game, which corresponds to the all-gray pebble configuration (the argument for other hybrids is analogous). Note that it is not possible to send the honestly-generated output map μ in $H_{\mathcal{P}}$ since this will lead to the output being mapped to the all-0 string. However, since x is available in the offline phase, [33] resolved this issue by *programming* the output map to map the zero-keys of the output wires to $C(x)$. The adversary cannot tell this from the honest output map since the change is information-theoretic.

Since the above pebbling strategy takes at most $2S$ moves (and uses S black pebbles) the corresponding hybrid argument only loses a $2S$ factor. It is possible to further reduce to adaptive simulatability via *random guessing*, but this incurs an additional loss in security that is exponential in the length of x.

Adaptive Simulatability of Online Yao. In order to avoid this exponential loss in the adaptive setting, [27] had to mainly tackle two issues, both arising from the fact that the garbling input x is now only available in the online phase.

1. Firstly, simulating the hybrids could not rely on the knowledge of the values of too many gates in C.
2. Secondly, the output map could no longer be programmed in the offline phase since the output $C(x)$ is only determined in the online phase.

The first issue was resolved in [27] by employing BG pebbling strategies that were more frugal in terms of the number of black pebbles used. To this end, they proved that if there exists a BG pebbling strategy of length τ that uses σ black pebbles, then the loss in the resulting security is at most $O(\tau 2^{\sigma})$. Here, loosely speaking, the 2^{σ} factor is the cost of randomly guessing the output values of the gates pebbled black, which they require in order to carry out the simulation of the hybrids (as well as the reduction).[5] To complete their proof, [27] described two (generic) pebbling strategies: one where σ grows only with the width of the circuit and another where σ grows only with the depth of the circuit.

---

[5] This is one of the earliest applications of the piecewise-guessing framework [24].

A consequence of the latter is the adaptive simulatability of log-depth (i.e., $\mathbf{NC}^1$) circuits with a *polynomial* loss in security.

The second issue, on the other hand, was basically side-stepped by *modifying* the garbling scheme to defer the sending of the output map to the online phase, i.e., by resorting to *online* Yao. This tweak allowed [27] to carry out a "deferred programming" of the output map since the garbling input is available in the online phase. The cost is an increased online complexity which is now dependent also on the output size.

Indistinguishability of Offline Yao: Our Approach. Unfortunately, given the negative result from [4], it is unlikely that a result as strong as [27] could be shown for adaptive simulatability of Offline Yao.[6] However, as we will see, relaxing the security requirement to adaptive indistinguishability offers some wiggle room. The key to exploiting this, as we explain next, is to discard the simulated garbling mode (Sim) in the hybrids altogether, which allows us to argue security *without* having to program the output map.

Bypassing the Simulated Mode. A standard way to show that a simulation-based definition implies an indistinguishability-based definition (e.g, think of semantic security and IND-CPA) is to use a two-step hybrid argument where the simulated game acts as an intermediary between the "left" and "right" indistinguishability games. If one attempts to use this approach in our context and use the result from [27] to argue adaptive indistinguishability of *offline* Yao garbling, we immediately run into the issue with programming the output map. Thus it seems that the necessity to program the output map is tied to the simulated game, and hence to the simulated mode of garbling. The main idea behind our reduction is therefore to avoid the simulated mode and instead only work with the real and input-dependent modes, which do not require programming the output map. Thus in all our hybrids, the output map is simply the honestly-generated output map and therefore can be generated in the offline phase itself.

Our Approach. Our idea is to directly replace – gate by gate – the honest garbling table of gates in C_0 (Real$_0$) with that of gates in C_1 (Real$_1$). Since the luxury of programming the output map is no longer available, it is crucial to ensure that the evaluation of the garbled circuit in all intermediate hybrids is correct at all times: even though $C_0(x_0) = C_1(x_1)$ holds (by definition) there is no guarantee that the output of the internal gates of C_0 and C_1 match. An error propagated as a result of one circuit influencing the computation of another may render the hybrids trivially distinguishable to the adversary (via evaluation of the garbling). To this end, we employ the input-dependent modes for (C_0, x_0) and (C_1, x_1) (resp., Input$_0$ and Input$_1$). In more details, in all our hybrids, we ensure

---

[6] Since pseudo-random generators (of arbitrary stretch) exist in $\mathbf{NC}^1$ [15,23], the result in [4] rules out reductions with polynomial loss for *offline* Yao. This is in stark contrast to the aforementioned positive result from [27] for *online* Yao for $\mathbf{NC}^1$ circuits.

that a gate in Real_0 mode is *never* adjacent to another gate in the Real_1 mode. This is accomplished by maintaining a "frontier" of gates in Input_0 and Input_1 mode in between the gates in real mode. This separation of the left (Real_0 and Input_0) and right (Real_1 and Input_1) modes guarantees that the computations belonging to the two circuits do not "corrupt" each other. We point out that this is reminiscent of (circuit) simulation strategies adopted in certain works in circuit complexity [19] (see Sect. 1.3).

The design of our black-gray-red (BGR) pebble game is carried out keeping the above blueprint in mind. Looking ahead, one can think of it as a symmetrised formulation of the BG pebble game. Our proof that a BGR strategy implies a valid sequence of hybrids is mostly similar to that in [27]: we show that if there exists a BGR pebbling strategy of length τ that uses σ grayscale (i.e. black or gray) pebbles, then there exists a reduction to adaptive indistinguishability of Offline Yao with a loss in security at most $O(\tau 2^\sigma)$ (Theorem 6).[7] The bulk of our technical work goes into coming up with pebble-efficient strategies for the BGR pebble game. This task turns out to be considerably more involved than for the BG pebble game (primarily due to the constraints introduced by the additional rules in the BGR game). The best strategy we could come up with exploits the treewidth w of the circuit, and as a result the number of (grayscale) pebbles used is roughly $\sigma := w\delta \log(S)$, where S is the size of the circuit and δ its fan-out. The strategy has a divide-and-conquer flavour and crucially relies on the notion of separators from graph theory [11,40]. In the remainder of the technical overview, we informally present the BGR pebble game and then briefly explain the treewidth-based BGR strategy.

BGR Pebble Game. Let g denote the location of a gate in $G := \Phi(\mathsf{C}_0) = \Phi(\mathsf{C}_1)$, the directed acyclic graph (DAG) underlying the circuits, and let g_0 (resp., g_1) denote the corresponding gate in C_0 (resp., C_1). The BGR pebble game (formally defined in Definition 11), as its name suggests, uses three types of pebbles: black, gray and red. In order to translate a BGR pebble configuration $\mathcal{P}$ to the garbling $\tilde{\mathsf{C}}$, the simulator in hybrid $\mathsf{H}_\mathcal{P}$ does the following for all internal gates g:

- if g carries no pebble in $\mathcal{P}$, then its garbling table in $\tilde{\mathsf{C}}$ will be the honest garbling table of g_0,
- if g carries a black pebble then the honest garbling table will be replaced by that of constant-0 or constant-1 gate *depending* on the output value of g_0 when C_0 is run on x_0,
- if g carries a gray pebble, then the simulation is the same as in previous case except that the garbling *depends* on the output value of g_1 when C_1 is run on x_1,
- if g carries a red pebble, then its garbling table in $\tilde{\mathsf{C}}$ will be the honest garbling table of g_1.

The input is then garbled as follows: For the i-th input gate, if this gate carries no pebble or a black pebble, then the i-th key in $\tilde{x}$ is the key corresponding to the ith

---

[7] We use the piecewise-guessing framework [24] instead of a direct argument as in [27].

bit of x_0, otherwise it is the key corresponding to the ith bit of x_1. (The pebbles on the output gates are simply ignored.) The four modes of simulation above are real and input-dependent modes for the left and right game respectively or, in short, Real_0, Input_0, Input_1 and Real_1 respectively (see Table 3(b)). Note that the semantics of gates that carry no pebble or a black pebble is the same as in the BG pebble game (if one sets $(\mathsf{C}_0, x_0) = (\mathsf{C}, x)$), but a gray pebble is now interpreted differently. A BGR pebbling strategy starts off with a configuration with all gates empty (i.e., honest garbling of C_0) but the goal is now to pebble them all red (i.e., honest garbling of C_1). Thus the extreme hybrids correspond to the left and right games in the adaptive indistinguishability game. The pebbling rules, listed below (see Fig. 2), are designed keeping the above discussion in mind and so that indistinguishability of neighbouring hybrids can be argued (Lemma 1):

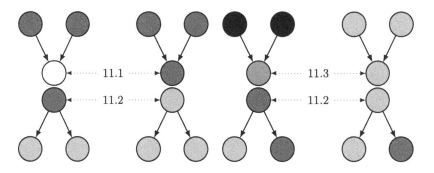

Fig. 2. Rules for BGR pebble game.

1. a black pebble can be placed on or removed from a gate g if and only if g's predecessor gates are pebbled black; and
2. a black pebble on a gate g can be *swapped* with a gray pebble if g's successor gates are pebbled, either black or gray; and
3. a gray pebble on a gate g can be *swapped* with a red pebble if g's predecessor gates are pebbled gray.

Note that the dynamic between no pebbles and black pebbles is similar to the dynamic between red and gray pebbles (hence the reason we consider it to be a symmetric version of the BG pebble game). Since the output values of gates which carry a black or gray pebble in $\mathcal{P}$ need to be known to carry out the simulation of $\mathsf{H}_{\mathcal{P}}$, the goal here is to minimise the number of such "grayscale" pebbles.

Treewidth, Separators and BGR Pebbling Strategies. Compared to the BG pebble game, pebble-efficient strategies for the BGR pebble game are harder to come by. (This is not surprising, in hindsight, given the negative result [4].) In particular, the generic pebbling strategies used in [27] no longer work without incurring a blow-up in the number of pebbles employed.[8] Below we briefly explain our treewidth-based strategy, the best (generic) strategy we could come up with.

Crucial to our strategy is the notion of *separators*. Informally, a separator for a circuit C of size S is a subset of gates $\mathcal{S}$ such that removing $\mathcal{S}$ (and the edges incident on it) from C partitions C into sub-circuits of "comparable" size. Slightly more formally, $\mathcal{S}$ partitions C into sub-circuits $C_1, \ldots, C_p$ such that for every sub-circuit C_i, $|C_i| \leq 2S/3$ (say). In a classical result from graph theory, it is shown that the size of separator of a graph (and therefore a circuit) is at most its treewidth [11,40]. Since treewidth is a monotonous property – i.e., removing wires or gates from C can only decrease its treewidth – the process of decomposition into sub-circuits using separators can be recursively carried out further (using a different separator each time) till one ends up with constant-size sub-circuits. Such a recursive decomposition is also carried out in the simulation in [19, Theorem 2] (also see [9,35]).

Our pebbling strategy exploits this recursive decomposition to minimise the number of grayscale pebbles used. To this end, the pebbling strategy maintains *long-term* grayscale pebbles only at the separators. These pebbles help reduce the task at hand to that of (recursively) pebbling the resulting sub-circuits, one at a time *reusing* pebbles in that process. Therefore, our pebbling strategy can be recursively described as follows:

- place grayscale pebbles at the separator $\mathcal{S}$ of G,
- recursively, one at a time, place red pebbles on each subcircuit C_i,
- replace the grayscale pebbles on $\mathcal{S}$ with red pebbles.

Since the depth of the recursion is bounded by $O(\log S)$ (thanks to the property of the separator), the hope would be that the number of grayscale pebbles maintained overall does not blow up. We show that this is indeed the case as our main technical contribution (Theorem 5).

Theorem (main). Any circuit C of size S, fan-out δ and treewidth w can be BGR pebbled using $O(\delta w \log(S))$ grayscale pebbles.

Translating the above divide-and-conquer approach into an actual pebbling strategy (Sect. 4) turns out to be tricky due to the intricate nature of the BGR pebbling rules. We refer the readers to Sect. 4 for the details.

Epilogue. It is instructive to review the above pebbling strategy in terms of the actual simulation. The (garbling tables of) circuit C_0 is being progressively, piece by piece, replaced by the (garbling tables of) circuit C_1 as dictated by the recursion, with the bulk of the replacement happening at the base of the recursion. It is exactly those long-term grayscale pebbles placed on the separators which act as the frontier between the pieces of C_0 and C_1. This ensures that computations of the two circuits are insulated from each other.

---

[8] The width-based BG strategy from [22,27] can be modified to obtain a comparable BGR strategy for *levelled* circuits. However, the resulting security bounds do not yield any advantage over simply guessing the input (which we want to avoid).

Remark 1. We remark that our result on the BGR pebbling complexity can also be used to prove tighter security bounds for simulatability of Online Yao for circuit classes where the treewidth is smaller as the width. This is true since any BGR sequence with complexity σ implies a BG sequence with complexity at most σ: simply consider the BG sequence obtained from a BGR sequence by substituting all the red pebbles with a gray pebble, and note that for BG pebbling only the number of black pebbles is counted.

1.3   Related Work

Garbling. Most of the works on garbling that are relevant to our paper have already been discussed in Sect. 1. In addition to them, [5,20,25,31] pertain to adaptively-secure garbling and are also worth pointing out. Besides, there are several constructions of garbling schemes which aim to exploit structured primitives to improve upon other aspects of garbling like, e.g, online complexity (e.g, [3,12]). We refer the readers to [7] for an excellent exposition on both the historial and technical aspects of Yao's garbling.

Treewidth, Separators and Computational Complexity. Treewidth [40] has its roots in algorithmic graph theory. Many hard graph-theoretic problems become tractable when one restricts to graphs of bounded treewidth. In some cases, this leads to even **NC** algorithms for problems which are otherwise known to be **NP**-complete (e.g, [9]). More often than not, this is because bounding the treewidth leads to divide-and-conquer algorithms, sometimes via separators (see [10] for an instructive survey). Unsurprisingly, this also has several consequences in circuit complexity (e.g, [1,2,34,36]), and perhaps the most relevant to our work are [19,28]. It was shown in [28] that circuits with constant treewidth can be simulated in $\mathbf{NC}^1$; [19] extended this result by using separators to show that circuits of size S and treewidth w can be simulated in depth $w \log(S)$. Both these results can be regarded to be a generalisation of Spira's theorem that Boolean formulae can be simulated by $\mathbf{NC}^1$ circuits [41].

Computing Separators. The problem of computing (balanced) separators in its full generality is **NP**-complete [18,37]; finding *minimal* separators is **NP**-hard [14]. The parameterised complexity of this problem is well-studied and it is $\mathbf{W}[1]$-hard (in both the size of the separator and size of the components) [37]. However, when restricted to *constant-degree* graphs, the problem becomes fixed-parameter tractable [37]. For results pertaining to approximation algorithms for computing (balanced) separators, see [16–18].

2   Preliminaries

2.1   Notation

By $[a, b]$, we denote the sequence of integers $a, a + 1, \ldots, b - 1, b$. All our logarithms are base two.

Notation for Graphs. For a graph $G = (\mathcal{V}, \mathcal{E})$ and a subset $\mathcal{S} \subseteq \mathcal{V}$, $G_{|\mathcal{S}}$ denotes the subgraph of G obtained by *restricting* to the set of vertices in $\mathcal{S}$. That is $G_{|\mathcal{S}} = (\mathcal{S}, \mathcal{E}_{|\mathcal{S}})$ where $\mathcal{E}_{|\mathcal{S}} := \{(u, v) \in \mathcal{E} : u, v \in \mathcal{S}\}$. For a directed graph G, a vertex $u \in \mathcal{V}$ is a predecessor (resp., successor) of another vertex $v \in \mathcal{V}$ if $(u, v) \in \mathcal{E}$ (resp., $(v, u) \in \mathcal{E}$). We say that u is adjacent to v if it is either a predecessor or a successor of v. These definitions can be naturally extended to a set of vertices $\mathcal{S}$ by taking a union over all the vertices in $\mathcal{S}$. The degree δ of a vertex is the number of vertices adjacent to it. The in-degree δ_{in} (resp., out-degree δ_{out}) of a vertex is its number of predecessors (resp., successors). The degree, in-degree and out-degree of a graph is obtained by taking the corresponding maximum over all its vertices.

Notation for Circuits. We consider Boolean circuits with explicit input and output gates, associated with the input and output wires respectively. For a circuit $\mathsf{C} : \{0, 1\}^n \to \{0, 1\}^\ell$ with S gates (including the n input and ℓ output gates) and W wires of which n (resp., ℓ) are input (resp., output) wires, we denote the DAG that represents the topology of the circuit C by $\Phi(\mathsf{C})$. That is, $\Phi(\mathsf{C})$ is a graph with $\mathcal{V} = [1, S]$ obtained by:

1. assigning the input (resp., output) gates to the vertices $[1, n]$ (resp., $[S - \ell + 1, S]$),
2. assigning the internal gates to the vertices $[n + 1, S - \ell]$, and
3. assigning the wires of the circuit to the edges.

The wires are assigned an index from $[1, W]$, with the input (resp., output) wires indexed from $[1, n]$ (resp., $[W - \ell + 1, W]$). An internal gate of a circuit is represented by a four-tuple (g, u, v, w) where $g : \{0, 1\}^2 \to \{0, 1\}$ denotes the predicate implemented, and u, v and w denote the left input, right input and output wires, respectively. We use $V_0(w)$ (resp., $V_1(w)$) as a short-hand for $V_0(\mathsf{C}_0, x_0, w)$ (resp., $V_1(\mathsf{C}_1, x_1, w)$), the function that returns the *value* of the wire w when the circuit C_0 (resp., C_1) is evaluated on the input x_0 (resp., x_1).

2.2 Garbling

The formal definition of syntax and security of garbling schemes is originally from [7]. Our definitions are taken mostly from [26].

Definition 1 (Indistinguishability). *A function $\epsilon : \mathbb{N} \to [0, 1]$ is negligible if for every polynomial $p(\lambda)$ there exists an $\lambda_0 \in \mathbb{N}$ such that $\epsilon(\lambda) \leq 1/p(\lambda)$ for all $\lambda \geq \lambda_0$. Let $X = \{X_\lambda\}_{\lambda \in \mathbb{N}}$ and $Y = \{Y_\lambda\}_{\lambda \in \mathbb{N}}$ be two distribution ensembles indexed by a security parameter λ. We say that X_λ and Y_λ are $(\epsilon(\lambda), T(\lambda))$-indistinguishable if for any adversary A of size at most $T(\lambda)$,*

$$|\mathsf{Pr}_{a \leftarrow X_\lambda}[\mathsf{A}(a) = 1] - \mathsf{Pr}_{a \leftarrow Y_\lambda}[\mathsf{A}(a) = 1]| \leq \epsilon(\lambda).$$

Definition 2 (Garbling Scheme). *A garbling scheme $\mathbf{GC}$ is a tuple of PPT algorithms* $(\mathsf{GCircuit}, \mathsf{GInput}, \mathsf{GEval})$ *with syntax and semantics defined as follows.*

$(\tilde{C},K) \leftarrow \mathsf{GCircuit}(1^{\lambda}, \mathsf{C})$. *On inputs a security parameter λ and a circuit C : $\{0,1\}^{n} \rightarrow \{0,1\}^{\ell}$, the garble-circuit algorithm $\mathsf{GCircuit}$ outputs the garbled circuit $\tilde{C}$ and key K.*

$\tilde{x} \leftarrow \mathsf{GInput}(K,x)$. *On input an input $x \in \{0,1\}^{n}$ and key K, the garble-input algorithm GInput outputs $\tilde{x}$.*

$y = \mathsf{GEval}(\tilde{C},\tilde{x})$. *On input a garbled circuit $\tilde{C}$ and a garbled input $\tilde{x}$, the evaluate algorithm GEval outputs $y \in \{0,1\}^{\ell}$.*

Correctness. There is a negligible function $\epsilon = \epsilon(\lambda)$ such that for any $\lambda \in \mathbb{N}$, any circuit C and input x it holds that

$$\Pr\left[\mathsf{C}(x) = \mathsf{GEval}(\tilde{C},\tilde{x})\right] = 1 - \epsilon(\lambda),$$

where $(\tilde{C}, K) \leftarrow \mathsf{GCircuit}(1^{\lambda}, \mathsf{C})$, $\tilde{x} \leftarrow \mathsf{GInput}(K,x)$.

Definition 3 (Adaptive Indistinguishability). *A garbling scheme **GC** is (ϵ, T)-adaptively-indistinguishable for a class of circuits $\mathcal{C}$, if for any probabilistic adversary A of size $T = T(\lambda)$,*

$$|\Pr\left[\mathsf{G}_{\mathsf{A},\mathbf{GC}}(1^{\lambda},0) = 1\right] - \Pr\left[\mathsf{G}_{\mathsf{A},\mathbf{GC}}(1^{\lambda},1) = 1\right]| \leq \epsilon(\lambda).$$

where the experiment $\mathsf{G}_{\mathsf{A},\mathbf{GC},\mathsf{S}}(1^{\lambda}, b)$ is defined as follows:

1. A *selects two circuits $\mathsf{C}_0, \mathsf{C}_1 \in \mathcal{C}$ such that $\Phi(\mathsf{C}_0) = \Phi(\mathsf{C}_1)$ and receives $\tilde{C}_b$ where $(\tilde{C}_b, K) \leftarrow \mathsf{GCircuit}(1^{\lambda}, \mathsf{C}_b)$.*
2. A *specifies x_0, x_1 such that $\mathsf{C}_0(x_0) = \mathsf{C}_1(x_1)$ and receives $\tilde{x}_b \leftarrow \mathsf{GInput}(K, x_b)$.*
3. *Finally, A outputs a bit b', which is the output of the experiment.*

In the selective counterpart of Definition 3, the adversary has to select (along with the circuit) the input also in the first step. For self-containment, we provide the definition of selective indistinguishability in Definition 4.

Definition 4 (Selective Indistinguishability). *A garbling scheme **GC** is (ϵ, T)-selective-indistinguishable for a class of circuits $\mathcal{C}$, if for any probabilistic adversary A of size $T = T(\lambda)$,*

$$|\Pr\left[\mathsf{H}_{\mathsf{A},\mathbf{GC}}(1^{\lambda},0) = 1\right] - \Pr\left[\mathsf{H}_{\mathsf{A},\mathbf{GC}}(1^{\lambda},1) = 1\right]| \leq \epsilon(\lambda).$$

where the experiment $\mathsf{G}_{\mathsf{A},\mathbf{GC},\mathsf{S}}(1^{\lambda}, b)$ is defined as follows:

1. A *selects two circuits $\mathsf{C}_0, \mathsf{C}_1 \in \mathcal{C}$ and two inputs x_0, x_1 such that $\Phi(\mathsf{C}_0) = \Phi(\mathsf{C}_1)$ and $\mathsf{C}_0(x_0) = \mathsf{C}_1(x_1)$. It receives $(\tilde{C}_b, \tilde{x}_b)$ where $(\tilde{C}_b, K) \leftarrow \mathsf{GCircuit}(1^{\lambda}, \mathsf{C}_b)$ and $\tilde{x}_b \leftarrow \mathsf{GInput}(K, x_b)$*
2. A *outputs a bit b', which is the output of the experiment.*

Remark 2. A few remarks concerning Definitions 3 and 4 are in order:

1. We call the experiments corresponding to $b = 0$ and $b = 1$ in Definitions 3 and 4 the "left" and "right" experiments, respectively.
2. When the context is clear, we use the simpler notation F^0 and F^1 to denote the experiments $\mathsf{F}_{\mathsf{A},\mathbf{GC},\mathsf{S}}(1^{\lambda},0)$ and $\mathsf{F}_{\mathsf{A},\mathbf{GC},\mathsf{S}}(1^{\lambda},1)$, respectively. Similarly, we use G^0, G^1, H^0 and H^1 for the experiments in Definitions 3 and 4.
3. We use $T_{\mathsf{G}} = T_{\mathsf{G}}(\lambda)$ (resp., $T_{\mathsf{H}} = T_{\mathsf{H}}(\lambda)$) to denote the time taken to run experiment G (resp., H).

Offline Yao. We formally describe Yao's original garbling scheme in the full version of the paper [29]. In addition to satisfying the standard notion of security for SKE (IND-CPA), the SKE needs to satisfy the following property for correctness of the garbling schemes to hold.

Definition 5 (Special Correctness [27]). *We say that an SKE* (Gen, Enc, Dec) *with message space $\mathcal{M}$ satisfies special correctness if for every security parameter λ, every key $k \leftarrow \mathsf{Gen}(1^\lambda)$, every message $m \in \mathcal{M}$, and encryption $c \leftarrow \mathsf{Enc}_k(m)$, $\mathsf{Dec}_{k'}(c) = \bot$ holds for all $k' \neq k$ with overwhelming probability.*

2.3 Pebble Games

In this section, we formally define the pebble games that are relevant to our discussion.

Definition 6 (Reversible black pebble game [8,38]). *Consider a DAG $G = (\mathcal{V}, \mathcal{E})$ with $\mathcal{V} = [1, S]$ and let $\mathcal{X}_B = \{\bot, B\}$. Let $\mathcal{T} \subseteq \mathcal{V}$ denote the sinks of G. Consider a sequence $\boldsymbol{P} := (\mathcal{P}_0, \ldots, \mathcal{P}_\tau)$ of pebble configurations for G, where $\mathcal{P}_i \in \mathcal{X}_B^{\mathcal{V}}$ for all $i \in [0, \tau]$. We call such a sequence a reversible black pebbling strategy[9] for G if (i) every vertex is empty in the initial configuration (i.e., $\mathcal{P}_0 = (\bot, \ldots, \bot)$), (ii) every sink is black-pebbled in the final configuration (i.e., $\mathcal{P}_\tau(j) = B$ for all $j \in \mathcal{T}$), and (iii) every configuration is obtained by applying the following rule to its preceding configuration:*

1. *$\bot \leftrightarrow B$: a black pebble can be placed on or removed from a vertex if its predecessors are black-pebbled. In particular, a black pebble can be placed on or removed from a source vertex at any time. More formally, $\exists! j^* \in \mathcal{V}$ such that*
   - *$(\mathcal{P}_{i+1}(j^*) = B$ and $\mathcal{P}_i(j^*) = \bot)$ or $(\mathcal{P}_{i+1}(j^*) = \bot$ and $\mathcal{P}_i(j^*) = B)$,*
   - *$\forall j \in \mathsf{pre}_G(j^*) : \mathcal{P}_i(j) = B$, and*
   - *$\forall j \in \mathcal{V} \setminus \{j^*\} : \mathcal{P}_{i+1}(j) = \mathcal{P}_i(j)$.*

The space-complexity *of a reversible black pebbling strategy $\boldsymbol{P} = (\mathcal{P}_0, \ldots, \mathcal{P}_\tau)$ for a DAG G is defined as the maximum number of black pebbles used at any point in the strategy:*

$$\sigma_G(\boldsymbol{P}) := \max_{i \in [0, \tau]} |\{j \in [1, S] : \mathcal{P}_i(j) = B\}|.$$

Definition 7. *If $\boldsymbol{P} = (\mathcal{P}_0, \ldots, \mathcal{P}_\tau)$ is a black pebbling strategy of space-complexity σ for a graph G, we say that $\boldsymbol{P}$ is a (σ, τ)-strategy for G. We say that a class of graphs $\mathcal{G}$ has a (σ, τ)-strategy if every graph $G \in \mathcal{G}$ has a (σ, τ)-strategy. Similarly, we say that a class of circuits $\mathcal{C}$ has a (σ, τ)-strategy if for every circuit $\mathsf{C} \in \mathcal{C}$, $\Phi(\mathsf{C})$ has a (σ, τ)-strategy.*

---

[9] To be precise, such a pebbling strategy is said to be *persistent* [38] since the final configuration consists of the sinks pebbled. In this paper, we only deal with persistent strategies.

Remark 3. Similar definitions apply to the rest of the pebble games considered in the paper.

Definition 8 (Black-gray (BG) pebble game [22,27]). *Consider a DAG* $G = (\mathcal{V}, \mathcal{E})$ *with* $\mathcal{V} = [1, S]$ *and let* $\mathcal{X}_{BG} = \{\perp, B, G\}$ *denote the set of colours of the pebbles. Consider a sequence* $\boldsymbol{\mathcal{P}} := (\mathcal{P}_0, \ldots, \mathcal{P}_\tau)$ *of pebble configurations for G, where* $\mathcal{P}_i \in \mathcal{X}_{BG}^{\mathcal{V}}$ *for all* $i \in [0, \tau]$. *We call such a sequence a black-gray pebbling strategy for G if (i) every vertex is empty in the initial configuration (i.e.,* $\mathcal{P}_0 = (\perp, \ldots, \perp))$, *(ii) every vertex is gray-pebbled in the final configuration (i.e.,* $\mathcal{P}_\tau = (G, \ldots, G))$ *and (iii) every configuration is obtained by applying one of the following rules to its preceding configuration (see Fig. 1):*

1. $\perp \leftrightarrow B$: *a black pebble can be placed on or removed from a vertex if its predecessors are black-pebbled. In particular, a black pebble can be placed on or removed from a source vertex at any time. More formally,* $\exists! j^* \in \mathcal{V}$ *such that*
   - $(\mathcal{P}_{i+1}(j^*) = B$ *and* $\mathcal{P}_i(j^*) = \perp)$ *or* $(\mathcal{P}_{i+1}(j^*) = \perp$ *and* $\mathcal{P}_i(j^*) = B)$,
   - $\forall j \in \mathsf{pre}_G(j^*) : \mathcal{P}_i(j) = B$, *and*
   - $\forall j \in \mathcal{V} \setminus \{j^*\} : \mathcal{P}_{i+1}(j) = \mathcal{P}_i(j)$.
2. $B \mapsto G$: *a black pebble on a vertex* $v \in \mathcal{V}$ *can be replaced with a gray pebble if v's successors are pebbled (either black or gray). In particular, a black pebble on a sink can be replaced by a gray pebble at any time. More formally,* $\exists! j^* \in \mathcal{V}$ *such that*
   - $\mathcal{P}_{i+1}(j^*) = G$ *and* $\mathcal{P}_i(j^*) = B$,
   - $\forall j \in \mathsf{suc}_G(j^*) : \mathcal{P}_i(j) \in \{B, G\}$, *and*
   - $\forall j \in \mathcal{V} \setminus \{j^*\} : \mathcal{P}_{i+1}(j) = \mathcal{P}_i(j)$.

The space-complexity *of a BG pebbling strategy* $\boldsymbol{\mathcal{P}} = (\mathcal{P}_0, \ldots, \mathcal{P}_\tau)$ *for a DAG G is defined as the maximum number of black pebbles used at any point in the strategy:*

$$\sigma_G(\boldsymbol{\mathcal{P}}) := \max_{i \in [0, \tau]} |\{j \in [1, S] : \mathcal{P}_i(j) = B\}|.$$

Remark 4. The rule to place or remove a black pebble in Definition 8 (Rule 8.1) is the same as in Definition 6 (Rule 6.1). Therefore the BG pebble game can be thought of as an extension of the RB pebble game (with a different goal).

2.4   Graph Theory

We recall the definition of treewidth and graph separators, and then state a crucial theorem connecting them, which will be exploited in our pebbling strategy. We emphasise that understanding the definition of treewidth is *not* essential to understanding our pebbling strategies: it is the notion of separators, along with Theorem 1, which is key.

Definition 9 ([11,40]). *A tree decomposition of a graph* $G = (\mathcal{V}, \mathcal{E})$ *is a tree, T, with nodes* $\mathcal{X}_1, \ldots, \mathcal{X}_p$, *where each* $\mathcal{X}_i \subseteq \mathcal{V}$, *satisfying the following properties:*

1. *Each graph vertex is contained in at least one tree node (i.e., $\cup_{i \in [1,p]} \mathcal{X}_i = \mathcal{V}$).*
2. *For every edge $(v, w) \in \mathcal{E}$, there exists a node $\mathcal{X}_i$ that contains both v and w.*
3. *The tree nodes containing a vertex v form a connected subtree of T.*

The width of a tree decomposition is the size of its largest node $\mathcal{X}_i$ minus one. Its treewidth $w(G)$ is the minimum width among all possible tree decompositions.

Definition 10 ([40])**.** *For a graph $G = (\mathcal{V}, \mathcal{E})$, a set $\mathcal{S} \subseteq \mathcal{V}$ is said to be a separator if the graph $G_{|\overline{\mathcal{S}}}$ has at least two components, and each of these components has size at most $2|\mathcal{V}|/3$.*[10]

Theorem 1 ([11,40])**.** *A graph G with treewidth $w(G)$ has a separator of size at most $w(G)$.*

3 Hybrid Argument and the BGR Pebble Game

In this section, we formally show that black-gray-red (BGR) pebbling strategies lead to security reductions for Offline Yao. We start off in Sect. 3.1 by formally defining the BGR pebble game and then explain the semantics of its pebbles, described already (albeit informally) in Sect. 1.2. This enables us to define a hybrid $H_{\mathcal{P}}$ in terms of a pebble configuration $\mathcal{P}$. Then, in Sect. 3.2, we justify the pebble rules by proving that neighbouring pebble configurations can indeed be proved indistinguishable (Lemma 1). Finally, we put these two steps together in Sect. 3.3 and show that BGR strategies imply adaptive indistinguishability of Offline Yao (Theorem 4) using the piecewise-guessing framework [24]. Since most of the ideas in Sects. 3.2 and 3.3 are similar to pre-existing works [24,27], we skip detailed proofs and resort to high-level sketches.

3.1 Pebble Configurations and Hybrids

The BGR pebble game is a symmetric version of the BG pebble game. In addition to the ones in BG pebble game (Rules 8.1 and 8.2), there are additional rules (Rules 11.2 and 11.3) which govern how the red pebbles interact with the gray pebbles. Intuitively speaking, the dynamic between no pebbles and black pebble (Rule 11.1) is similar to the dynamic between red pebbles and gray pebbles (Rule 11.3): see Remark 5. A more formal definition of the game is given next.

Definition 11 (Black-Gray-Red (BGR) pebble game). *Consider a DAG $G = (\mathcal{V}, \mathcal{E})$ with $\mathcal{V} = [1, S]$ and let $\mathcal{X}_{BGR} = \{\bot, B, G, R\}$ denote the set of colours of the pebbles. A pebble is called* grayscale *if it is black or gray. Consider a sequence $\boldsymbol{\mathcal{P}} := (\mathcal{P}_0, \ldots, \mathcal{P}_\tau)$ of pebble configurations for G, where $\mathcal{P}_i \in \mathcal{X}_{BGR}^{\mathcal{V}}$ for all $i \in [0, \tau]$. We call such a sequence a BGR pebbling strategy for G if (i) every vertex is empty in the initial configuration (i.e., $\mathcal{P}_0 = (\bot, \ldots, \bot)$), (ii) and every vertex is red-pebbled in the final configuration (i.e., $\mathcal{P}_\tau = (R, \ldots, R)$) and (iii) every configuration is obtained by applying one of the following rules to its preceding configuration (see Fig. 2):*

---

[10] To be precise, such a separator is called "balanced" [19]. In this paper, we only consider balanced separators.

1. $\perp \leftrightarrow B$: *a black pebble can be placed on or removed from a vertex if its predecessors are black-pebbled. In particular, a black pebble can be placed on or removed from a source vertex at any time. More formally, $\exists! j^* \in V$ such that*
   - $(\mathcal{P}_{i+1}(j^*) = B$ and $\mathcal{P}_i(j^*) = \perp)$ or $(\mathcal{P}_{i+1}(j^*) = \perp$ and $\mathcal{P}_i(j^*) = B)$,
   - $\forall j \in \mathsf{pre}_G(j^*) : \mathcal{P}_i(j) = B$, and
   - $\forall j \in V \setminus \{j^*\} : \mathcal{P}_{i+1}(j) = \mathcal{P}_i(j)$.
2. $B \leftrightarrow G$: *a black pebble on a vertex $v \in V$ can be swapped with a gray pebble if v's successors carry grayscale pebbles (i.e., either black or gray). In particular, a black pebble on a sink vertex can be swapped with a gray pebble at any time. More formally, $\exists! j^* \in V$ such that*
   - $(\mathcal{P}_{i+1}(j^*) = G$ and $\mathcal{P}_i(j^*) = B)$ or $(\mathcal{P}_{i+1}(j^*) = B$ and $\mathcal{P}_i(j^*) = G)$,
   - $\forall j \in \mathsf{suc}_G(j^*) : \mathcal{P}_i(j) \in \{B, G\}$, and
   - $\forall j \in V \setminus \{j^*\} : \mathcal{P}_{i+1}(j) = \mathcal{P}_i(j)$.
3. $G \leftrightarrow R$: *a gray pebble can be swapped with a red if its predecessors are gray-pebbled. In particular, a gray pebble on a source vertex can be swapped with a red pebble at any time. More formally, $\exists! j^* \in V$ such that*
   - $(\mathcal{P}_{i+1}(j^*) = G$ and $\mathcal{P}_i(j^*) = R)$ or $(\mathcal{P}_{i+1}(j^*) = R$ and $\mathcal{P}_i(j^*) = G)$,
   - $\forall j \in \mathsf{pre}_G(j^*) : \mathcal{P}_i(j) = G$, and
   - $\forall j \in V \setminus \{j^*\} : \mathcal{P}_{i+1}(j) = \mathcal{P}_i(j)$.

The space-complexity *of a BGR pebbling strategy $\boldsymbol{P} = (\mathcal{P}_0, \ldots, \mathcal{P}_\tau)$ for a DAG G is defined as the maximum number of* grayscale *pebbles used at any point in the strategy:*

$$\sigma_G(\boldsymbol{P}) := \max_{i \in [0,\tau]} |\{j \in [1, S] : \mathcal{P}_i(j) \in \{B, G\}\}|.$$

Remark 5. A few remarks on the BGR pebble game are in order:

1. Note that Rules 11.1 and 11.2 (the $B \mapsto G$ part) correspond to the rules in the BG pebble game. The end goals in the two games are however different.
2. When restricted to either black and empty (Rule 11.1) or gray and red pebbles (11.3), the BGR pebble game simplifies to the reversible black pebble game of Bennett [8] defined in Definition 6. This is obvious for the black pebbles since the BGR pebble game is an extension of the BG pebble game which, in turn, is an extension of the reversible black pebble game. To see why this is the case for gray and red pebbles, simply think of vertices with red pebbles as being empty (i.e., $R = \perp$) and gray pebbles as black pebbles (i.e., $G = B$), and note that Rule 11.3 is now the same as Rule 11.1. Therefore, if one starts with an all-red (i.e., empty) configuration, the gray pebbles can be placed using reversible pebbling rules. Some of the reversible pebbling strategies will serve as crucial subroutines in the BGR pebbling strategies in the coming sections.
3. When restricted to black and gray pebbles, the BGR pebble game again simplifies to the reversible pebble game played on the graph with the direction of the edges *flipped*. However, we do not make use of this observation.
4. Only black pebbles can be placed on empty vertices. Gray (resp., red) pebbles have to replace black or red (resp., gray) pebbles, respectively.

5. By the pebbling rules, in any strategy a vertex that is empty can *never* end up adjacent to another vertex with red pebble in any BGR pebbling strategy. Moreover, a vertex with gray (resp., black) pebble cannot be a predecessor of a vertex with no (resp.red) pebble; the converse is however possible. These properties will turn out to be important sanity checks in ensuring the validity of BGR pebbling strategies in the later sections. Moreover, they ensure correctness of the simulations they represent.

Table 3. (a) Garbling modes in [27]. The gate is denoted by g and the value of its output wire w when run on input x is denoted by $V(w)$. (b) Garbling modes in our case. The gates g_0 and g_1 are the gates in the same position in the circuits C_0 and C_1, respectively. The value $V_0(w)$ (resp., $V_1(w)$) denotes the bit going over the wire w in the computation $C_0(x_0)$ (resp., $C_1(x_1)$).

	Real ($\perp$)	Input (B)	Sim (G)
$c_{0,0}$	$E_{k_u^0}(E_{k_v^0}(k_w^{g(0,0)}))$	$E_{k_u^0}(E_{k_v^0}(k_w^{V(w)}))$	$E_{k_u^0}(E_{k_v^0}(k_w^0))$
$c_{0,1}$	$E_{k_u^0}(E_{k_v^1}(k_w^{g(0,1)}))$	$E_{k_u^0}(E_{k_v^1}(k_w^{V(w)}))$	$E_{k_u^0}(E_{k_v^1}(k_w^0))$
$c_{1,0}$	$E_{k_u^1}(E_{k_v^0}(k_w^{g(1,0)}))$	$E_{k_u^1}(E_{k_v^0}(k_w^{V(w)}))$	$E_{k_u^1}(E_{k_v^0}(k_w^0))$
$c_{1,1}$	$E_{k_u^1}(E_{k_v^1}(k_w^{g(1,1)}))$	$E_{k_u^1}(E_{k_v^1}(k_w^{V(w)}))$	$E_{k_u^1}(E_{k_v^1}(k_w^0))$

(a)

	Real$_0$ ($\perp$)	Input$_0$ (B)	Input$_1$ (G)	Real$_1$ (R)
$c_{0,0}$	$E_{k_u^0}(E_{k_v^0}(k_w^{g_0(0,0)}))$	$E_{k_u^0}(E_{k_v^0}(k_w^{V_0(w)}))$	$E_{k_u^0}(E_{k_v^0}(k_w^{V_1(w)}))$	$E_{k_u^0}(E_{k_v^0}(k_w^{g_1(0,0)}))$
$c_{0,1}$	$E_{k_u^0}(E_{k_v^1}(k_w^{g_0(0,1)}))$	$E_{k_u^0}(E_{k_v^1}(k_w^{V_0(w)}))$	$E_{k_u^0}(E_{k_v^1}(k_w^{V_1(w)}))$	$E_{k_u^0}(E_{k_v^1}(k_w^{g_1(0,1)}))$
$c_{1,0}$	$E_{k_u^1}(E_{k_v^0}(k_w^{g_0(1,0)}))$	$E_{k_u^1}(E_{k_v^0}(k_w^{V_0(w)}))$	$E_{k_u^1}(E_{k_v^0}(k_w^{V_1(w)}))$	$E_{k_u^1}(E_{k_v^0}(k_w^{g_1(1,0)}))$
$c_{1,1}$	$E_{k_u^1}(E_{k_v^1}(k_w^{g_0(1,1)}))$	$E_{k_u^1}(E_{k_v^1}(k_w^{V_0(w)}))$	$E_{k_u^1}(E_{k_v^1}(k_w^{V_1(w)}))$	$E_{k_u^1}(E_{k_v^1}(k_w^{g_1(1,1)}))$

(b)

Template for Hybrids. A pebble configuration $\mathcal{P} \in \mathcal{X}_{BGR}^V$ is used to encode a selective hybrid $H_\mathcal{P}$. For an *internal gate* v, the translation is carried out as described below:

- if v carries no pebble ($\perp$) in $\mathcal{P}$ then g is garbled as in the left game (Real$_0$),
- a black pebble (B) on v indicates that the garbling of g is input-dependant on x_0 and C_0, (Input$_0$)
- a gray pebble (G) on v indicates that the garbling of g is input-dependant on x_1 and C_1 (Input$_1$)
- a red pebble (R) on v indicates g is garbled as in the right game (Real$_1$).

The distributions corresponding to the four garbling modes – Real$_0$, Input$_0$, Input$_1$ and Real$_1$ – are formally defined in Table 3(b). (Note that the semantics of gray

pebbles is different from that in the BG pebble game.) This information is sufficient to construct the garbled circuit $\tilde{\mathsf{C}}$. What remains to complete the description of $\mathsf{H}_{\mathcal{P}}$, is describing how to generate the input garbling $\tilde{x}$ and the output
map. If an input gate carries no (resp., a red) pebble then the garbling key for
x_0 (resp., x_1) is selected in that hybrid. The output map, on the other hand, is
simply the default one prescribed in the scheme and therefore the pebbles on the
output gates are ignored. We refer the readers to the full version of the paper
[29] for a formal definition of $\mathsf{H}_{\mathcal{P}}$.

Sequence of Hybrids. A pebbling strategy $\mathcal{P} = \{\mathcal{P}_0, \ldots, \mathcal{P}_\tau\}$ will give rise to a
sequence of selective hybrids

$$\mathsf{H}^0 = \mathsf{H}_{\mathcal{P}_0}, \ldots, \mathsf{H}_{\mathcal{P}_\tau} = \mathsf{H}^1, \tag{1}$$

Note that the extreme games correspond to the left selective experiment
$\mathsf{H}^0 = \mathsf{H}_{\mathsf{A},\mathsf{GC}}(1^\lambda, 0)$ (since $\mathcal{P}_0 = (\bot, \ldots, \bot)$) and right selective experiment
$\mathsf{H}^1 = \mathsf{H}_{\mathsf{A},\mathsf{GC}}(1^\lambda, 1)$ (since $\mathcal{P}_\tau = (\mathsf{R}, \ldots, \mathsf{R})$), respectively. The exact pebbling
strategy will be discussed later in Sect. 4. In the next section, we prove the
indistinguishability of two neighbouring hybrids in such a sequence.

3.2   Indistinguishability of Neighbouring Hybrids

Lemma 1 (neighbouring indistinguishability). *Let $\mathcal{P}$ and $\mathcal{Q}$ denote two
neighbouring configurations in a BGR pebbling strategy. If the underlying encryp-
tion scheme* **SKE** *is (ϵ, T)-IND-CPA secure, then $\mathsf{H}_{\mathcal{P}}$ and $\mathsf{H}_{\mathcal{Q}}$ are $(3\epsilon, T - T_{\mathsf{H}})$-
indistinguishable, i.e., for any adversary* A *of size at most $T - T_{\mathsf{H}}$*

$$|\Pr[\langle \mathsf{A}, \mathsf{H}_{\mathcal{P}} \rangle = 1] - \Pr[\langle \mathsf{A}, \mathsf{H}_{\mathcal{Q}} \rangle = 1]| \le 3\epsilon.$$

Proof. Recall that hybrids correspond to pebble configurations and that two
neighbouring hybrids differ by a single pebble. We split the proof into three cases
which correspond to the pebbling moves $\bot \leftrightarrow \mathsf{B}$, $\mathsf{B} \leftrightarrow \mathsf{G}$ and $\mathsf{R} \leftrightarrow \mathsf{G}$ respectively.
The reduction in the first and last cases is similar, and relies on the indistin-
guishability of the underlying encryption scheme (similar to [27, Lemma 1]).
Therefore in the claim below we focus on the first case. In the second case, we
argue that the hybrids are identically distributed (similar to [27, Lemma 2]).
Moreover, since the proofs are similar to those in [27], we refer the reader to the
full version of the paper [29].

Claim (Rule 11.1: $\bot \leftrightarrow \mathsf{B}$). If the underlying encryption scheme **SKE** is (ϵ, T)-
IND-CPA secure, and if $\mathcal{Q}$ is obtained from $\mathcal{P}$ using Rule 11.1 then the hybrids
$\mathsf{H}_{\mathcal{P}}$ and $\mathsf{H}_{\mathcal{Q}}$ are $(3\epsilon, T - T_{\mathsf{H}})$-indistinguishable.

Claim (Rule 11.2: $\mathsf{B} \leftrightarrow \mathsf{G}$). If $\mathcal{Q}$ is obtained from $\mathcal{P}$ using Rule 11.2 then the
hybrids $\mathsf{H}_{\mathcal{P}}$ and $\mathsf{H}_{\mathcal{Q}}$ are identically distributed.

$\square$

Selective indistinguishability. Combining Lemma 1 with the semantics of the pebbles (Table 3) yields (via the standard hybrid argument) selective indistinguishability of Offline Yao.

Theorem 2. *Suppose that a class of circuits C has a (σ, τ)-BGR pebbling strategy. If the encryption scheme* **SKE** *is (ϵ, T)-secure then* **YGC$_{\text{SKE}}$** *is $(3\tau\epsilon, T - T_H)$-selectively-indistinguishable for C.*

3.3 Adaptive Indistinguishability via Piecewise Guessing

Observe that in the hybrid $H_{\mathcal{P}}$, the knowledge of the committed garbling inputs x_0 and x_1 is used to compute the output value of gates that carry grayscale pebbles in the configuration $\mathcal{P}$. So, in principle, the simulation of $H_{\mathcal{P}}$ can be carried out if this information is available as an "advice". Moreover, the indistinguishability of two successive hybrids can be shown (Lemma 1) if such advice for *both* the hybrids is available. In case the number of grayscale pebbles is small, the size of this advice could potentially be smaller than the size of garbling inputs x_0 and x_1. This means that it is possible to apply the piecewise-guessing framework [24]. We explain this in detail next.

Applying the Piecewise-Guessing Framework. The main theorem in [24] is stated below in Theorem 3 after having been simplified and tailored for our application to circuit garbling. The result of applying Theorem 3 to Offline Yao is stated in Theorem 4. Furthermore, exploiting the properties of the pebbling strategies we design, we provide an optimised version of Theorem 4 later in Sect. 4.2 (Theorem 6).

Theorem 3 (Theorem 2 in [24] tailored to Definitions 3 and 4). *Let G^0, G^1, H^0 and H^1 be as in Definitions 3 and 4. Furthermore, let $H^0 = H_{\mathcal{P}_0}, \ldots, H_{\mathcal{P}_\tau} = H^1$ be the sequence of hybrids from Equation (1) and suppose that every pebbling configuration $\mathcal{P}_i$ in the strategy $\mathcal{P}_0, \ldots, \mathcal{P}_\tau$ can be computed in time T_p. Assume that for each $i \in [0, \tau - 1]$, there exists a function $\alpha_i \colon \{0,1\}^{1=*} \to \{0,1\}^\sigma$ such that the hybrids $H_{\mathcal{P}_i}$ and $H_{\mathcal{P}_{i+1}}$ are (ϵ, T)-indistinguishable when A commits to $\alpha_i(C_0, C_1, x_0, x_1)$ as advice at the beginning of the experiment (instead of (x_0, x_1)). Then G^0 and G^1 are $(\epsilon \cdot \tau \cdot 2^\sigma, T - (T_\sigma + T_p))$-indistinguishable where T_σ denotes the time to sample a string in $\{0,1\}^\sigma$ uniformly at random.*

Theorem 4. *Suppose that a class of circuits C has a (σ, τ)-BGR pebbling strategy. If the encryption scheme* **SKE** *is (ϵ, T)-secure then* **YGC$_{\text{SKE}}$** *is $(\tau 2^\sigma \cdot 3\epsilon, T - (T_H + T_\sigma + T_p))$-adaptively-indistinguishable for C.*

Proof (Sketch). As already observed, the advice function α_i should return the values of the output wires of all those gates that carry grayscale pebbles in $\mathcal{P}_i$ and $\mathcal{P}_{i+1}$. Therefore, in Theorem 3 we set

$$\alpha_i(C_0, C_1, x_0, x_1) := (V_0(w) : (g, u, v, w) \in C_0 \text{ and } \mathcal{P}(g) = B) \|$$
$$(V_1(w) : (g, u, v, w) \in C_1 \text{ and } \mathcal{P}(g) = G) \tag{2}$$

where $\mathcal{P} := \mathcal{P}_{i+1}$ if $\mathcal{P}_{i+1}$ is obtained from $\mathcal{P}_i$ by adding a grayscale pebble; and $\mathcal{P} := \mathcal{P}_i$ otherwise.[11] The length of the advice is therefore smaller than in the selective hybrid in case the pebbling complexity of $G = \varPhi(\mathsf{C}_0) = \varPhi(\mathsf{C}_1)$ is smaller than the input length. What remains is to show that indistinguishability of two consecutive hybrids can be shown relying only on $\boldsymbol{\alpha}_i := \alpha_i(\mathsf{C}_0, \mathsf{C}_1, x_0, x_1)$. To see this note that the knowledge of the committed garbling inputs x_0 and x_1 is used to compute the output value of gates that carry grayscale pebbles in the configuration $\mathcal{P}$. Since these are already present in the hint, the reduction algorithm can simply extract these values from $\boldsymbol{\alpha}_i$ and use them instead of explicitly computing $V_0(\cdot)$ and $V_1(\cdot)$. Following the arguments in Lemma 1, we get that if the encryption scheme is (ϵ, T)-secure then the experiments $\mathsf{H}_{\mathcal{P}_i}$ and $\mathsf{H}_{\mathcal{P}_{i+1}}$ are $(3\epsilon, T - T_{\mathsf{H}})$-indistinguishable when A commits to $\boldsymbol{\alpha}_i$, and the proof now follows Theorem 3.

$\square$

4   BGR Pebbling Strategy

In this section, we describe our main strategy for the BGR pebble game. Then, we discuss the implications of our pebbling strategy to the security of Offline Yao (Sect. 4.2).

4.1   BGR Pebbling via Separators

The strategy we describe, BGRSwitch, is implicit in the simulation in [19]. As a consequence of Theorem 1, a graph G with treewidth $w(G)$ can be recursively decomposed using separators of size at most $w(G)$ into smaller and smaller "component" sub-graphs till the sub-graph is of a manageable (constant) size. As a result, one gets a "component tree" out of the graph, starting with the whole graph at the root and ending with manageable-sized sub-graphs as leaves. For a graph with S vertices and degree δ, the depth of the component tree is at most $O(\log S)$ and its out-degree is at most $\delta \cdot |\mathcal{S}|$ (since each vertex in $\mathcal{S}$ can be connected to at most δ components). The pebbling strategy using separators exploits this recursive structure to minimise the number of grayscale pebbles employed.

Remark 6. Note that Theorem 1 does not provide any guarantees on whether such a sequence of separators can be found *efficiently*. This becomes crucial when simulating the hybrids since it determines the factor T_p. We address this question at the end of this section.

---

[11] Recall from the proof of Lemma 1 that for pebbling configurations $\mathcal{P}_i$ and $\mathcal{P}_{i+1}$ that differ by a pebbling move $\mathsf{B} \leftrightarrow \mathsf{G}$, the corresponding hybrids $\mathsf{H}_{\mathcal{P}_1}$ and $\mathsf{H}_{\mathcal{P}_{i+1}}$ are *identically* distributed.

RB Pebbling via Separators. We first describe RBTreewidth, a space-efficient RB pebbling strategy that will be used as a subroutine in BGRSwitch. RBTreewidth places a black pebble on any vertex on a graph G of size S and treewidth w using $\sigma := O(w \log(S))$ pebbles. To the best of our knowledge, this strategy is new and might be of independent interest.[12] Since the strategy is reversible, by RBTreewidth^{-1} we denote the reverse strategy that *removes* a black pebble. This strategy, thanks to the observation in Remark 5.2, will also be used to both place or remove a gray pebble on an all-red-pebbled graph (RGRTreewidth).

Lemma 2. *Every node in a DAG G with S vertices, in-degree δ_{in} and treewidth w can be black-pebbled following the RB pebbling rules using at most $\sigma := O((\delta_{in} + w) \log(S))$ black pebbles in at most $\tau := (\delta_{in} w)^{O(\log(S))}$ steps.*

Lemma 3. *Starting from the all-red configuration, every node in a DAG G with S vertices, in-degree δ_{in} and treewidth w can be gray-pebbled following the BGR pebbling rules using at most $\sigma := O((\delta_{in} + w) \log(S))$ gray(scale) pebbles in at most $\tau := (\delta_{in} w)^{O(\log(S))}$ steps.*

Proof (of Lemma 2). We denote the pebbling strategy by RBTreewidth and it takes as input a graph (component) C and a vertex v^* to be pebbled. It uses the same recursive decomposition into components as will be in BGRSwitch (i.e., the component tree). The base case is when the graph C is of small enough size (i.e., with $O(1)$ vertices) and here RBTreewidth simply places a black pebble on v^* using as many black pebbles as needed; i.e.:

1. place black pebbles on all vertices in C in topological order (Rule 6.1); and then
2. remove the black pebbles on the ancestors of v^* in reverse topological order (Rule 6.1).

Otherwise, RBTreewidth splits C into smaller components using its separator, recursively places a black pebble on every vertex in the separator in *topological order*, places a black pebble on v^* by recursing on the component C^* that contains v^*. Finally, it recursively removes the black pebbles on the separator in *reverse* topological order. The details are given below.

1. Decomposes C into its components $C_1, \ldots, C_p$ using its separator $\mathcal{S} \subseteq \mathcal{C}$, where $\mathcal{C} = \mathcal{S} \cup \mathcal{C}_1 \cup \ldots \cup \mathcal{C}_p$ and $C_i := C_{|\mathcal{C}_i}$.

---

[12] It is possible to bound the space-complexity of RB pebbling on DAGs of treewidth w using existing results. First, use the fact that the RB pebbling number of a graph of size S is upper bounded by the *plain* black pebbling [39] number with a multiplicative $\log(S)$ factor [32]. Second, use the fact that the black pebbling number is upper bounded by treewidth w (via so-called pathwidth) with another multiplicative $\log(S)$ factor [11, Theorem 2, Corollary 24]. Consequently, we get that the RB pebbling number is at most $w \log^2(S)$. But this is a worse bound compared to what we show directly in Lemma 2.

2. Recursively place black pebbles on the vertices in S in topological order. That is, for each vertex $s \in S$ chosen in topological order:
   (a) recursively place a black pebble on each predecessor of s (unless it already carries a black pebble) in topological order,
   (b) place a black pebble on s (Rule 6.1), and
   (c) recursively remove the black pebbles on each predecessor of s that is not in S in reverse topological order.
3. Recursively pebble the component $C^* \in C_1, \ldots, C_p$ which contains v^*.
4. Undo Item 2 by recursively removing the black pebbles on the separator in reverse topological order. That is, for each vertex $s \in S$ chosen in reverse topological order:
   (a) recursively place a black pebble on each predecessor of s in topological order,
   (b) remove the black pebble on s (Rule 6.1), and
   (c) recursively remove the black pebbles on each predecessors of s in reverse topological order.

As we explain next, carrying out Items 2 and 4 in topological and reverse topological order, respectively, is crucial for the efficiency (and correctness) of RBTreewidth. Recall that the property of the separator S guarantees that the components $C_1, \ldots, C_p$ are themselves of small enough size (see Definition 10). Therefore, once S is pebbled black RBTreewidth can be called on all the resulting components as there are no edges between the components. However, pebbling a vertex s in S itself is tricky: the predecessors of s could very well be in different components (since there are no guarantees for the vertices in the separator). However, we do have the guarantee that all the predecessors of a predecessor (outside S) of s belong to the same component or the separator, and are reachable via either source vertices *or* vertices belonging to S. Therefore, as long as the vertices in S are black-pebbled in topological order, S can be completely pebbled in Item 2 by recursing on small enough components. A similar argument applies when the black pebbles on the separator are removed in Item 4.

With this in mind, we now analyse RBTreewidth. The reason this strategy requires at most $\sigma := O(w \log(S))$ black pebbles is similar to what we will see in the proof of Theorem 5. The number of pebbles is governed by the expression

$$\sigma(i) \leq (w + \delta_{in}) + \sigma(i+1), \tag{3}$$

where the index i is the depth of the recursion of RBTreewidth. The factor $(w + \delta_{in})$ is the cost of black pebbles placed on the separator in Item 2 and the factor $\sigma(i+1)$ is the cost of recursions in Items 2 to 4. Note that since the size of the components in each these recursive calls is at most $2/3$ of the size of the original component C, the overall depth of the recursion remains $O(\log(S))$. The upper bound on the number of pebbles claimed in the lemma follows on solving Eq. (3).

As for the number of steps, it is governed by the expression

$$\tau(i) \leq \tau(i+1)O(\delta_{in}w). \tag{4}$$

since RBTreewidth is recursively called at most $O(\delta_{in}w)$ times on the (sub-) components. As in the case of space-complexity, since we end up with constant-size components at the end of the recursion, the base cost is $O(1)$. The lemma follows on solving Eq. (4).   □

Recursive Switching. We are now primed to describe BGRSwitch. It takes as input:

1. the original graph $G = (\mathcal{V}, \mathcal{E})$ that is to be pebbled
2. the vertices $\mathcal{C} \subseteq \mathcal{V}$ that define the graph component $C = G_{|\mathcal{C}}$ being currently considered
3. the "higher" separator $\mathcal{U}$, which is the union of all the separators in the "higher" recursive calls that resulted in the creation of the current component C.

Note that $\mathcal{C}$ and $\mathcal{U}$ are disjoint sets by definition. Throughout the execution of BGRSwitch, we maintain a few pebbling properties as invariants:

– At the start of the execution of BGRSwitch on the current component C, it is guaranteed that the vertices in $\mathcal{U}$ are all black-pebbled. This, in some sense, "isolates" C from the rest of the graph and, as a result, it can be pebbled independently of the rest.
– At the end of the execution of BGRSwitch, we guarantee that the vertices $\mathcal{C}$ in C are red-pebbled (via black and then gray), *except* for the children of the higher separator $\mathcal{U}$, which will be left gray-pebbled.

Next, let's see what happens in BGRSwitch when called on $(G, \mathcal{C}, \mathcal{U})$ (in the first call $\mathcal{C} = \mathcal{V}$ and $\mathcal{U} = \emptyset$). The base case is when the current component $C := G_{|\mathcal{C}}$ is of small enough size (i.e., with $O(1)$ vertices). Here BGRSwitch simply switches C to red by using as many pebbles as needed; i.e.:

1. place black pebbles on all vertices in C (Rule 11.1),
2. replace them with gray pebbles (Rule 11.2), and
3. replace the gray pebbles with red pebbles (Rule 11.3) *except* if the vertex is a child of the upper separator $\mathcal{U}$.

Otherwise, BGRSwitch does the switching from no pebbles to red pebbles for C by recursively splitting into smaller components using the separator for C as follows .

1. Decompose $C = G_{|\mathcal{C}}$ into its components $C_1, \ldots, C_p$ using its separator $\mathcal{S} \subseteq \mathcal{C}$, where $\mathcal{C} = \mathcal{S} \cup \mathcal{C}_1 \cup \ldots \cup \mathcal{C}_p$ and $C_i := G_{|\mathcal{C}_i}$. (Midpoint-separator analogy)
2. Place black pebbles on the vertices in $\mathcal{S}$ using RBTreewidth. Note that this is possible only because all the vertices that are required to carry this out are either empty or belong to $\mathcal{U}$ and therefore are black-pebbled.
3. Recursively switch each component $C_1, \ldots, C_p$ using BGRSwitch. After all component are switched, all vertices in $\mathcal{C}$, except the ones that are children of $\mathcal{S}$, are red-pebbled; the children of $\mathcal{S}$ are left gray-pebbled.

4. Replace the black pebbles on the separator S with gray pebbles by using Rule 11.2.
5. Replace the gray pebbles on S and its adjacent vertices with red pebbles (except if the vertex is a child of the upper separator) using Rule 11.3 and RGRTreewidth.

Note that during the whole strategy, we maintain as invariant a black-gray frontier between the empty and red-pebbled vertices, and this frontier is exactly at the separators. That is, at any point of the pebbling *no* two vertices such that one is empty and the other is red-pebbled are related (see Remark 5.5.). As pointed out in the technical overview (Sect. 1.2), it is this frontier that insulates the computations in the two circuits and help ensure correctness at all times. In the following theorem we formally analyse its space- and time-complexity.

Theorem 5 (Main theorem). *Every DAG G with S vertices, degrees $\delta_{in}, \delta_{out} \leq \delta$ and treewidth w can be BGR-pebbled using at most $\sigma = O((\delta_{in} + w\delta_{out})\log(S))$ grayscale pebbles in at most $\tau := (\delta w)^{O(\log(S))}$ steps.*

Proof. To bound the space-complexity of BGRSwitch, first note that the algorithm indeed maintains the invariants stated above:

1. At the start of the execution of BGRSwitch on the current component C, it is guaranteed that the vertices in $\mathcal{U}$ are all black-pebbled. Hence, on input a component at depth of recursion $i \in [0, O(\log(S))]$, there are $|\mathcal{U}(i)| = O(iw)$ pebbles that remain black-pebbled.
2. At the end of the execution of BGRSwitch, all the vertices $\mathcal{C}$ in C are red-pebbled, *except* for children of the higher separator $\mathcal{U}$, which will be left gray-pebbled. Hence, after the execution of BGRSwitch on a component at depth $i > 0$ there are up to $\delta_{out} \cdot |\mathcal{U}(i)| = O(i\delta_{out}w)$ many gray pebbles on the graph.

Now, in Item 3 there are up to δw many components, among which some are already switched, some not, and one is currently processed. For the former set of components, all nodes within these which are children of $\mathcal{U} \cup \mathcal{S}$ are pebbled gray. Hence, by the above, there are up to $\delta_{out} \cdot (|\mathcal{U}(i)| + 1) + |\mathcal{U}(i)| = O(i\delta_{out}w)$ nodes that remain gray- or black-pebbled while BGRSwitch is processed on a lower component. Now, while some node on the separator $\mathcal{S}'$ in the currently-processed component is pebbled using RBTreewidth or RGRTreewidth (cf. Item 2), there are up to $|\mathcal{S}'| \leq w$ additional nodes that remain pebbled. By Lemmas 2 and 3, the space-complexity of RBTreewidth/RGRTreewidth is bounded by $O((\delta_{in} + w)\log(S))$. Thus, we arrive at

$$\sigma(i) \leq O(i\delta_{out}w) + w + O((\delta_{in} + w)\log(S)) = O((\delta_{in} + w\delta_{out})\log(S)).$$

As for the number of steps, on input a component at depth of recursion i, the time-complexity of BGRSwitch is governed by the expression

$$\tau(i) \leq (\delta_{in}w)^{O(\log(S))} \cdot w + \tau(i+1)\delta w. \tag{5}$$

The first factor is the cost of the subroutines used to pebble the separator black: the subroutine is called at most $|\mathcal{S}| \leq w$ times, each time incurring a cost of at most $(\delta_{in} w)^{O(\log(S))}$ (Lemma 2). The second factor is the cost of recursively calling BGRSwitch on at most δw (sub-)components. Since we end up with constant-size components at the end of the recursion, the base cost is $O(1)$. On solving Equation (5), the theorem follows.   □

Computing the Separators. Finally, let us return to the question of computing the sequence of separators underlying our pebbling strategy. While we are not aware of an efficient algorithm for computing balanced separators (see discussion in Sect. 1.3), it suffices for our purpose that a separator of size w can be found in time at most $S^{O(w)}$: since we anyway lose a similar factor in the distinguishing advantage, the overall (asymptotic) loss that the reduction incurs remains similar. Therefore, we simply enumerate all w-sized subsets of vertices till we find a balanced separator – note that given a separator it is easy to verify that it is indeed one, i.e., the problem lies in **NP**. Since computing any BGR pebbling configuration requires knowledge of at most $O(\log(S))$ many separators, the total time required to compute a pebbling configuration is at most $T_p = O(\log(S)S^w)$.

4.2   Optimised Piecewise Guessing

Recall that in Theorem 4, the loss in adaptive security is exponential in the BGR pebbling complexity. This is because the reduction requires as advice the value of the output wire of all the gates that are grayscale pebbled. Therefore when Theorem 4 is used in conjunction with Theorem 5, the loss is exponential in the treewidth *as well as* degree. First, note that for Yao's garbling scheme, we only consider Boolean circuits with fan-in 2. We argue next that the dependence on *out-degree* can be removed thanks to the structure of the configurations in the BGRSwitch pebbling strategy. The resulting theorem is stated in Theorem 6.

Let's return to the recursive step in Item 3 which is the cause of dependence on the degree. At the start of this step, all the vertices in the separator $\mathcal{S}$ have been pebbled. Then each component C_i is recursively switched to red one at a time. At the end of switching C_i, each vertex in C_i is pebbled red, *except* for those vertices that are children of $\mathcal{S}$ (or $\mathcal{U}$) which are left gray. Therefore we can restrict our focus on those vertices that have its predecessors in the separator – let's consider one such vertex v^*. Note that in any configuration where v^* carries a gray pebble, it is guaranteed that its predecessors in the separator are black-pebbled. Therefore, instead of requiring the value of the gate g^* corresponding to v^* as an advice, it can simply be computed as a function of the values of its predecessor gates (which *are* included in the advice). To sum up, instead of providing as advice the values of the output wires of *all* the gates that are grayscale pebbled as in Eq. (2), it suffices to provide a much smaller advice as outlined above. As a result of this observation, we get the following optimised version of Theorem 4. This leads to the corollaries stated in Sect. 1.1.

Theorem 6. *Suppose that a class of circuits $\mathcal{C}$ of size S, fan-in 2 has degree δ and treewidth w. If the encryption scheme* **SKE** *is (ϵ, T)-secure then* **YGC**$_{\mathbf{SKE}}$ *is $(3\tau 2^\sigma \epsilon, T - (T_{\mathsf{H}} + T_\sigma + T_p))$-adaptively-indistinguishable for $\mathcal{C}$ where*

$$\tau := (\delta w)^{O(\log(S))}, \quad \sigma := O(w \log(S)) \ \text{and} \ T_p := O(\log(S) S^w).$$

5   Conclusion and Open Problems

Yao's garbling scheme is one of the most fundamental cryptographic constructions. In this work, we took another step towards completing the landscape of its security. Our result leads to several interesting questions, the most natural being whether the upper bound on loss in security can be improved. To this end, one could look at other (orthogonal) graph properties. Another pressing question is whether there are other applications of treewidth in cryptography (which seems relatively overlooked compared to other fields such as circuit complexity or algorithmic graph theory). This closely concerns the divide-and-conquer approach employed in our security reduction: it seems that the approach of surgically replacing one circuit with another should find use in other scenarios. Our hope is that this work spurs further research in this direction.

Acknowledgements. We are grateful to Daniel Wichs for helpful discussions on the landscape of adaptive security of Yao's garbling. We would also like to thank Crypto 2021 and TCC 2021 reviewers for their detailed review and suggestions, which helped improve presentation considerably.

References

1. Alekhnovich, M., Razborov, A.: Satisfiability, branch-width and tseitin tautologies. Comput. Complex. **20**(4), 649–678 (2011)
2. Allender, E., Chen, S., Lou, T., Papakonstantinou, P.A., Tang, B.: Width-parametrized SAT: time-space tradeoffs. Theory Comput. **10**, 297–339 (2014)
3. Ananth, P., Lombardi, A.: Succinct garbling schemes from functional encryption through a local simulation paradigm. In: Beimel, A., Dziembowski, S. (eds.) TCC 2018. LNCS, vol. 11240, pp. 455–472. Springer, Cham (2018). https://doi.org/10.1007/978-3-030-03810-6_17
4. Applebaum, B., Ishai, Y., Kushilevitz, E., Waters, B.: Encoding functions with constant online rate or how to compress garbled circuits keys. In: Canetti, R., Garay, J.A. (eds.) CRYPTO 2013. LNCS, vol. 8043, pp. 166–184. Springer, Heidelberg (2013). https://doi.org/10.1007/978-3-642-40084-1_10
5. Bellare, M., Hoang, V.T., Keelveedhi, S.: Instantiating random oracles via UCEs. In: Canetti, R., Garay, J.A. (eds.) CRYPTO 2013. LNCS, vol. 8043, pp. 398–415. Springer, Heidelberg (2013). https://doi.org/10.1007/978-3-642-40084-1_23
6. Bellare, M., Hoang, V.T., Rogaway, P.: Adaptively secure garbling with applications to one-time programs and secure outsourcing. In: Wang, X., Sako, K. (eds.) ASIACRYPT 2012. LNCS, vol. 7658, pp. 134–153. Springer, Heidelberg (2012). https://doi.org/10.1007/978-3-642-34961-4_10

7. Bellare, M., Hoang, V.T., Rogaway, P.: Foundations of garbled circuits. In: Yu, T., Danezis, G., Gligor, V.D. (eds.) ACM CCS 2012: 19th Conference on Computer and Communications Security, pp. 784–796. ACM Press, Raleigh, NC, USA, Oct. 16–18 (2012)

8. Bennett, C.H.: Time/space trade-offs for reversible computation. SIAM J. Comput. **18**(4), 766–776 (1989)

9. Bodlaender, H.L.: NC-algorithms for graphs with small treewidth. In: van Leeuwen, J. (ed.) WG 1988. LNCS, vol. 344, pp. 1–10. Springer, Heidelberg (1989). https://doi.org/10.1007/3-540-50728-0_32

10. Bodlaender, H.L.: A tourist guide through treewidth. Acta Cybern. **11**(1–2), 1–21 (1993)

11. Bodlaender, H.L.: A partial k-arboretum of graphs with bounded treewidth. Theor. Comput. Sci. **209**(1), 1–45 (1998)

12. Boneh, D., et al.: Fully key-homomorphic encryption, arithmetic circuit abe and compact garbled circuits. In: Nguyen, P.Q., Oswald, E. (eds.) EUROCRYPT 2014. LNCS, vol. 8441, pp. 533–556. Springer, Heidelberg (2014). https://doi.org/10.1007/978-3-642-55220-5_30

13. Brent, R.P.: The parallel evaluation of general arithmetic expressions. J. ACM **21**(2), 201–206 (1974)

14. Bui, T.N., Jones, C.: Finding good approximate vertex and edge partitions is np-hard. Inf. Process. Lett. **42**(3), 153–159 (1992)

15. Cryan, M., Miltersen, P.B.: On pseudorandom generators in NC^0. In: Sgall, J., Pultr, A., Kolman, P. (eds.) MFCS 2001. LNCS, vol. 2136, pp. 272–284. Springer, Heidelberg (2001). https://doi.org/10.1007/3-540-44683-4_24

16. Even, G., Naor, J.S., Rao, S., Schieber, B.: Fast approximate graph partitioning algorithms. SIAM J. Comput. **28**(6), 2187–2214 (1999)

17. Feige, U., Hajiaghayi, M.T., Lee, J.R.: Improved approximation algorithms for minimum-weight vertex separators. In: Gabow, H.N., Fagin, R. (eds.) 37th Annual ACM Symposium on Theory of Computing, pp. 563–572. ACM Press, Baltimore, MA, USA, May 22–24 (2005)

18. Feige, U., Mahdian, M.: Finding small balanced separators. In: Kleinberg, J.M. (ed.) 38th Annual ACM Symposium on Theory of Computing, pp. 375–384. ACM Press, Seattle, WA, USA, May 21–23 (2006)

19. Gál, A., Jang, J.: A generalization of Spira's theorem and circuits with small segregators or separators. Inf. Comput. **251**, 252–262 (2016)

20. Garg, S., Srinivasan, A.: Adaptively secure garbling with near optimal online complexity. In: Nielsen, J.B., Rijmen, V. (eds.) EUROCRYPT 2018. LNCS, vol. 10821, pp. 535–565. Springer, Cham (2018). https://doi.org/10.1007/978-3-319-78375-8_18

21. Goldreich, O., Micali, S., Wigderson, A.: How to play any mental game or A completeness theorem for protocols with honest majority. In: Aho, A. (ed) 19th Annual ACM Symposium on Theory of Computing, pp. 218–229. ACM Press, New York City, NY, USA, May 25–27 (1987)

22. Hemenway, B., Jafargholi, Z., Ostrovsky, R., Scafuro, A., Wichs, D.: Adaptively secure garbled circuits from one-way functions. In: Robshaw, M., Katz, J. (eds.) CRYPTO 2016. LNCS, vol. 9816, pp. 149–178. Springer, Heidelberg (2016). https://doi.org/10.1007/978-3-662-53015-3_6

23. Impagliazzo, R., Naor, M.: Efficient cryptographic schemes provably as secure as subset sum. J. Cryptol. **9**(4), 199–216 (1996)

24. Jafargholi, Z., Kamath, C., Klein, K., Komargodski, I., Pietrzak, K., Wichs, D.: Be adaptive, avoid overcommitting. In: Katz, J., Shacham, H. (eds.) CRYPTO 2017. LNCS, vol. 10401, pp. 133–163. Springer, Cham (2017). https://doi.org/10.1007/978-3-319-63688-7_5

25. Jafargholi, Z., Oechsner, S.: Adaptive security of practical garbling schemes. In: Bhargavan, K., Oswald, E., Prabhakaran, M. (eds.) INDOCRYPT 2020. LNCS, vol. 12578, pp. 741–762. Springer, Cham (2020). https://doi.org/10.1007/978-3-030-65277-7_33

26. Jafargholi, Z., Scafuro, A., Wichs, D.: Adaptively indistinguishable garbled circuits. In: Kalai, Y., Reyzin, L. (eds.) TCC 2017. LNCS, vol. 10678, pp. 40–71. Springer, Cham (2017). https://doi.org/10.1007/978-3-319-70503-3_2

27. Jafargholi, Z., Wichs, D.: Adaptive security of yao's garbled circuits. In: Hirt, M., Smith, A. (eds.) TCC 2016. LNCS, vol. 9985, pp. 433–458. Springer, Heidelberg (2016). https://doi.org/10.1007/978-3-662-53641-4_17

28. Jansen, M.J., Sarma, J.: Balancing bounded treewidth circuits. Theory Comput. Syst. **54**(2), 318–336 (2014)

29. Kamath, C., Klein, K., Pietrzak, K.: On treewidth, separators and yao's garbling. Cryptology ePrint Archive, Report 2021/926 (2021)

30. Kamath, C., Klein, K., Pietrzak, K., Wichs, D.: Limits on the adaptive security of yao's garbling. In: Malkin, T., Peikert, C. (eds.) CRYPTO 2021. LNCS, vol. 12826, pp. 486–515. Springer, Cham (2021). https://doi.org/10.1007/978-3-030-84245-1_17

31. Kitagawa, F., Nishimaki, R., Tanaka, K., Yamakawa, T.: Adaptively secure and succinct functional encryption: improving security and efficiency, simultaneously. In: Boldyreva, A., Micciancio, D. (eds.) CRYPTO 2019. LNCS, vol. 11694, pp. 521–551. Springer, Cham (2019). https://doi.org/10.1007/978-3-030-26954-8_17

32. Levine, R.Y., Sherman, A.T.: A note on Bennett's time-space tradeoff for reversible computation. SIAM J. Comput. **19**(4), 673–677 (1990)

33. Lindell, Y., Pinkas, B.: A proof of security of Yao's protocol for two-party computation. J. Cryptol. **22**(2), 161–188 (2009)

34. Lipton, R.J., Tarjan, R.E.: A separator theorem for planar graphs. SIAM J. Appl. Math. **36**(2), 177–189 (1979)

35. Lipton, R.J., Tarjan, R.E.: Applications of a planar separator theorem. SIAM J. Comput. **9**(3), 615–627 (1980)

36. Lokshtanov, D., Mikhailin, I., Paturi, R., Pudlák, P.: Beating brute force for (quantified) satisfiability of circuits of bounded treewidth. In: Czumaj, A. (ed.) 29th Annual ACM-SIAM Symposium on Discrete Algorithms, pp. 247–261. ACM-SIAM, New Orleans, LA, USA, Jan. 7–10 (2018)

37. Marx, D.: Parameterized graph separation problems. In: Downey, R., Fellows, M., Dehne, F. (eds.) IWPEC 2004. LNCS, vol. 3162, pp. 71–82. Springer, Heidelberg (2004). https://doi.org/10.1007/978-3-540-28639-4_7

38. Nordström, J.: New Wine into Old Wineskins: A Survey of Some Pebbling Classics with Supplemental Results (2015)

39. Paterson, M.S., Hewitt, C.E.: Record of the project mac conference on concurrent systems and parallel computation. Chapter Comparative Schematology, pp. 119–127. ACM, New York, NY, USA (1970)

40. Robertson, N., Seymour, P.D.: Graph minors. II. algorithmic aspects of tree-width. J. Algorithms **7**(3), 309–322 (1986)

41. Spira, P.: On time-hardware complexity of tradeoffs for boolean functions. In: Proceedings of the 4th Hawaii Symposium System Sciences, pp. 525–527. North Hollywood and Western Periodicals (1971)

42. Yao, A.C.-C.: Protocols for secure computations (extended abstract). In: 23rd Annual Symposium on Foundations of Computer Science, pp. 160–164. IEEE Computer Society Press, Chicago, Illinois, Nov. 3–5 (1982)
43. Yao, A.C.-C.: How to generate and exchange secrets (extended abstract). In: 27th Annual Symposium on Foundations of Computer Science, pp. 162–167. IEEE Computer Society Press, Toronto, Ontario, Canada, Oct. 27–29 (1986)

Oblivious Transfer from Trapdoor Permutations in Minimal Rounds

Arka Rai Choudhuri[1] , Michele Ciampi[2(✉)] , Vipul Goyal[3], Abhishek Jain[1], and Rafail Ostrovsky[4]

[1] Johns Hopkins University, Baltimore, USA
{achoud,abhishek}@cs.jhu.edu
[2] The University of Edinburgh, Edinburgh, UK
michele.ciampi@ed.ac.uk
[3] NTT Research, Carnegie Mellon University, Pittsburgh, USA
goyal@cs.cmu.edu
[4] University of California, Los Angeles, USA
rafail@cs.ucla.edu

Abstract. Oblivious transfer (OT) is a foundational primitive within cryptography owing to its connection with secure computation. One of the oldest constructions of oblivious transfer was from *certified* trapdoor permutations (TDPs). However several decades later, we do not know if a similar construction can be obtained from TDPs in general.

In this work, we study the problem of constructing round optimal oblivious transfer from trapdoor permutations. In particular, we obtain the following new results (in the plain model) relying on TDPs in a *black-box* manner:

– Three-round oblivious transfer protocol that guarantees indistinguishability-security against malicious senders (and semi-honest receivers).

– Four-round oblivious transfer protocol secure against malicious adversaries with black-box simulation-based security.

By combining our second result with an already known compiler we obtain the first round-optimal 2-party computation protocol that relies in a black-box way on TDPs.

A key technical tool underlying our results is a new primitive we call dual witness encryption (DWE) that may be of independent interest.

Keywords: Two-party computation · Trapdoor permutations · Oblivious transfer

1 Introduction

Oblivious transfer (OT) is one of the most recognizable protocols in cryptography. It is a protocol executed by two parties, designated as sender and receiver, with inputs (l_0, l_1) and b respectively. The goal of the protocol is for the receiver to learn l_b, while not learning anything about l_{1-b}. At the same time, the sender should be oblivious to the receiver's input b. The importance of OT is underlined

© International Association for Cryptologic Research 2021
K. Nissim and B. Waters (Eds.): TCC 2021, LNCS 13043, pp. 518–549, 2021.
https://doi.org/10.1007/978-3-030-90453-1_18

by its fundamental role in cryptography, as it is known to be both necessary and sufficient for secure multiparty computation (MPC) [31]. In fact, recent works [3,9] further strengthen this connection to devise round-preserving transformations from OT to MPC.

In this work, we revisit the well-studied problem of building *round-optimal* OT in the plain model that are secure against malicious adversaries, who may arbitrarily deviate from the protocol specification. We focus on the task of building such protocols from general assumptions, and in particular, *trapdoor permutations* (TDPs). Roughly speaking, TDPs are permutations that are easy to compute, but hard to invert unless one knows a "trapdoor" (in which case inversion becomes easy).

OT and TDPs are, in fact, historically linked—the first constructions of semi-honest[1] 1-out-of-2 OT protocols [13] were based on TDPs. Subsequent works devised compilation strategies to transform the protocol of [13] to the setting of malicious senders and receivers. In particular, [30] constructed a four-round OT protocol that makes non-black-box use of TDPs. More recently, [35] improved this result by only making *black-box* use of TDPs. Moreover, the round complexity of these protocols is *optimal* (w.r.t. black-box simulation) [30].

A significant disadvantage of these works (including [13]), however, is that when it comes to proving security against malicious adversaries, they require the TDPs to be *certifiable*. Namely, it must be possible to publicly recognize whether a given (possibly adversarially chosen) function is a permutation.

Investigating how to construct complex cryptographic protocols relying on trapdoor permutations is interesting from both the theoretical and the practical perspective.

Indeed, for this reason, the issue of certifiability of TDPs has garnered much interest in the context of the other popular application of TDPs, which is to build non-interactive zero-knowledge (NIZK) [1,6,14,18–21,23,29]. In a similar vein, in this work we ask whether it is possible to forego the reliance on certifiability in building round-optimal OT from TDPs:

Does there exist fully black-box round-optimal OT from trapdoor permutations?

Indeed, one simple way to relax the certifiability requirement is to let the party choosing the TDP proving in zero-knowledge that the TDP was sampled honestly. However this necessarily increases the number of rounds (or requires trusted assumptions). Such an approach has been used in [36], in which the authors show that one-way permutations (without trapdoors) are sufficient to construct OT if one of the two parties is all-powerful. Thus, the problem becomes interesting if one considers the round complexity of constructions.

On the use of Certifiability. To the best of our knowledge, we are not aware of any maliciously secure round-optimal OT protocol that uses the underlying trapdoor permutations even in a *non-black-box* way.

---

[1] A semi-honest adversary, unlike a malicious adversary, follows the protocol specification. However, it may still try to glean additional information from the execution of the protocol.

In both of the classical applications of TDPs, namely, NIZK and OT, the certifiability property is crucially used for security. In the case of NIZKs, it is used to guarantee soundness against malicious provers in the classical protocol of [14]. In the case of OT, it is used to guarantee security against malicious senders. In both of these applications, one of the parties (the prover, in the case of NIZKs, and the sender, in the case of OT) is required to sample a function f from a family of trapdoor permutations. This is done by sampling an index I via the index generation algorithm of the family of functions. If the party does not sample the index I honestly, the resultant function is no longer guaranteed to be a permutation. In such a scenario, in both of these applications, security completely breaks down (we will give an example hereafter in the paper). A cheating prover is able to break soundness, and a cheating sender is able to break receiver input privacy.

In the context of NIZKs, [1] proposed a technique to address this issue when the TDP family is *full domain*. Here, we say that a TDP family is full domain if the domain is $\{0,1\}^{p(n)}$ for some polynomial p, else we say that the domain is *partial*. Subsequent works [19–21, 23] showed that for the case of partial domain, it suffices for one to start with TDPs that are *doubly-enhanced*, i.e., TDPs that additionally have domain and range samplers with additional security properties (see Sect. 3.1). [6] was able to further relax the requirements for partial domain to only require TDPs that are *public-domain*, i.e. the domain is both efficiently recognizable, and almost uniformly sampleable. In [18] the authors propose a non-interactive proof to certify that the RSA public key specifies a permutation in the random-oracle (RO) model.

These solutions, however, are in the common random string (CRS) model (or in the RO model), and are *not* applicable to our plain model setting. The main technical focus of our work is to eliminate the use of certifiability in building OT, without relying on a CRS or on the RO, and requiring the least possible number of rounds. To achieve this goal, we rely on new notion of *dual witness encryption* (DWE).

1.1 Our Results

We resolve the aforementioned question in the affirmative, and provide details for our result below.

Dual Witness Encryption. As a stepping stone to our solution, we define the notion of dual witness encryption for the pair of disjoint languages (L_0, L_1) such that L_1 is in NP. Intuitively, the notion defines a public-key encryption scheme where the public key (the instance) can either come from L_0, L_1 or may even lie outside the union of these two sets. The scheme guarantees: (i) information theoretic security when encryption is performed using a public-key belonging to the set L_0; and (ii) efficient decryption when encrypted using a public-key belonging to the set L_1 if the decryptor is additionally in possession of a *witness* attesting to this fact.

For use in our OT protocols, we construct a dual witness encryption (DWE) scheme where the public keys will correspond to functions f. Specifically, we build a DWE scheme for (L_0, L_1) where (i) L_0 is the set functions for which a large fraction of points in the domain result in collisions (the reader can think of this as meaning that at least half the points in the domain result in collision on application of functions f in L_0); whereas (ii) L_1 is the set of TDPs output by an honest TDP generation algorithm Gen. While we discuss the details of the *encryption scheme* in the technical overview, for the purposes of this discussion it is helpful to think of an (overly) simplified version of a ciphertext in the encryption scheme to be $(f(k), k \oplus m)^2$ where k is a randomly sampled *key*, and m is the message to be encrypted. Intuitively, if the instance f used to compute an encryption is a function for which many points in the domain have the same image, then $f(k)$ (which is a part of the ciphertext) information theoretically hides the specific key k chosen for encryption, and thereby hides the message m. Instead, if the function f used for the decryption is a TDP, and the randomness used to generate such a function is known, then there exists an efficient procedure that inverts $f(k)$ and decrypts the message. We note that in this case there are instances that belong neither to L_0 nor to L_1 (e.g., the functions for which only a small fraction of points in the domain result in collisions). This is our main tool for tackling uncertifiability. As stated above, this is an oversimplification of our scheme, and we provide more details both for the construction of the tool, and how it is used, in the next section.

As an additional contribution, we show the existence of a dual witness encryption schemes for other languages. For instance the pair of languages (L_0, L_1), where L_0 represents the language of Diffie-Hellman (DH) tuples, and L_1 represents the language of non-DH tuples. In this case, when an encryption is computed using a DH tuple, the encrypted message is information theoretically hidden. In any other case, when the encryption is computed using a tuple that is not DH, it is possible to efficiently decrypt the message. Moreover, the decryption is efficient if the exponents of the non-DH-tuple are known by the decryptor. We also argue that it is possible to extend the above construction to the language of non-Quadratic Residuosity tuples [24][3].

Comparison with Similar Notions. Dual witness encryption is similar to witness encryption with some important differences: First, we require semantic security to hold even against unbounded adversaries when the instance used for the encryption belongs to L_0. Second, unlike witness encryption, we do not define completeness or hiding for instances that are outside L_0 and L_1.

The notion of *instance-dependent commitment (ID commitment)* [7] enables a committer to commit to a message with respect to an NP language L. When the statement used to compute the commitment is not in L, then the commitment is statistically hiding, in any other case the commitment is statistically

---

[2] Note that this is *not* an accurate description of the encryption scheme, but is helpful to provide an intuition.

[3] We note that in this example $L_0 \cup L_1 = \{0, 1\}^\star$, but this is not always the case, as we show hereafter.

binding. The notion of *extractable ID commitment*, in addition, admits an efficient extraction procedure that on input a commitment computed with respect to an instance in L, outputs the committed message. In [17] the authors show how to construct such an extractable ID commitment scheme for all the languages that admit hash proof systems (e.g., QNR, QR, DDH, DCR). It is easy to see that an extractable ID commitment for the language L is a DWE for the languages (L_0, L_1) with $L_0 = \{0,1\}^\star - L$ and $L_1 = L$. Moreover, any DWE such that $L_0 \cup L_1 = \{0,1\}^\star$ is an extractable ID commitment for the language L_1. The main difference between DWEs and extractable ID commitments is that the extractable ID commitments are defined with respect to one NP-language, whereas our notion provides different guarantees depending on whether the statement is in L_0, L_1 or in neither of the two languages.

Round Optimal Oblivious Transfer. Using Dual Witness Encryption (DWE), we obtain the following results.

Theorem 1 (informal). *Assuming full domain trapdoor permutations, we construct a fully black-box three-round oblivious transfer protocol that is secure against semi-honest receivers and malicious senders.*

Theorem 2 (informal). *Assuming full domain trapdoor permutations, we construct a fully black-box four-round fully simulatable oblivious transfer protocol.*

Round Optimal Two-Party Computation. An immediate corollary from the Theorem 1, in conjunction with the work of [28] building a non-interactive secure two-party protocol in the OT-hybrid model is the following.

Corollary 1. *Assuming full domain trapdoor permutations, there exists a fully black-box round optimal secure two-party computation protocol.*

Functions with Partial Domain. To the best of our knowledge, to extend the results of previous works [30,35] in the case of functions with partial domain requires, in addition to the certifiability property, (i) the existence of a sampler which uniformly samples elements from the domain/range; and (ii) the existence of an efficient algorithm that checks whether a given element belongs inside or outside the domain of the function. These properties are called respectively *efficiently sampleable domain/range* and *efficiently recognizable domain*. We show how to extend our theorems and corollary to the case of functions with partial domain by removing the requirement on the function to be certifiable, while maintaining the same requirements of efficiently sampleable domain/range and efficiently recognizable domain.

2 Technical Overview

To illustrate the main ideas underlying this work, it will suffice to assume full domain TDPs, and the extension to partial domains are deferred to the technical sections.

Background: 3-Round Semi-Honest OT. Before we describe the main ideas in our construction, let us recall the basic three-round construction based on enhanced trapdoor permutations (TDPs) in the semi-honest setting (EGL) [13,30].

Let $l_0, l_1 \in \{0, 1\}$ be the input of the sender S and b be the input bit of the receiver R, the construction is presented in Fig. 1.

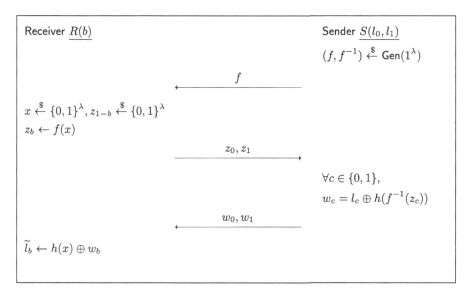

Fig. 1. The EGL OT protocol [13]. Security holds against semi-honest receivers and malicious senders

Here $h(\cdot)$ is a hardcore bit of f. If the parties follow the protocol (i.e. in the semi-honest setting) then S cannot learn the receiver's input (the bit b) as both z_0 and z_1 are random strings. Also, due to the one-way property of f and the security of the hard-core predicate, R cannot distinguish w_{1-b} from random as long as z_{1-b} is randomly chosen.

Prior works [30] ([35] respectively) devised non-black-box (black-box respectively) approaches to deal with both malicious senders and receivers. When dealing with malicious senders, they still require certifiable TDPs. Without certifiability, challenges arise, which are highlighted below.

Main Challenge: Necessity of Certification. In the above described semi-honest protocol, a malicious sender is free to deviate from the protocol. If the malicious sender sends a function f that is not a permutation, by simply looking at values z_0 and z_1, it could decide which one of the values is randomly sampled from the domain of the function, and which one is computed by evaluating f on a random point. Specifically, $\{x \xleftarrow{\$} \{0,1\}^\lambda : x\}$ and $\{x \xleftarrow{\$} \{0,1\}^\lambda : f(x)\}$ are distinguishable to the sender for such an f, thereby leaking the receiver's input. To see why this is true, let us consider an extreme case in which a malicious sender picks a function f in which half of the points in the domain of f all have the same image y. Such a malicious sender, upon receiving the values z_0, z_1, checks if there exists $d \in \{0,1\}$ such that $y = z_d$. If this is the case, then the malicious sender outputs d, otherwise it outputs a random bit. It is easy to see that such a malicious sender guesses the input of the receiver with the probability negligibly close to $1/2 + 1/4$. The natural approach to dealing with a malicious adversary is to force an adversarial party to prove honest behavior using a zero-knowledge proof. In fact, in the NIZK constructions based on certifiable TDPs, removing certification is non-trivial since it has direct bearing on the soundness. A cheating prover that picks a function f that is not a permutation can break the soundness of the NIZK. In this context, [1] proposed the first approach to avoiding certifiability. Their solution proposes a special purpose NIZK to prove that f is a trapdoor permutation over the full domain. Thus the prover, when sending over f also sends a special purpose proof that f is indeed a trapdoor permutation over the full domain. As mentioned earlier, these results were further extended to the partial domain setting by [6,23] for a more restricted class of TDPs. Unfortunately, all the above solutions are in the common random string (CRS) model, and therefore not applicable in our setting. Following the above line of work, the natural idea could be to devise a zero-knowledge proof in the plain model whereby the sender proves that the function f is indeed a trapdoor permutation. However, as we discuss below, this runs into fundamental barriers. The main challenge in requiring the sender to send a zero-knowledge proof to the receiver, is the limitation on the number of rounds. Even in the four-round setting, the receiver sends its last message in the third round, and thereby must know by the end of the second round if f sent by the sender is a permutation. This would thereby require the sender to complete its zero-knowledge proof by the send round, but providing such a zero-knowledge proof in two rounds is impossible [22]. Another naïve solution to extend the techniques of [1] in the plain model, would be to run a *challenge-response* protocol. In this, the party that wants to check if a function f is a permutation (the receiver R in this case), upon receiving the function f from the party that wants to certify that f is a permutation (the sender S in this case), samples random values from the domain, evaluates them, and sends them to S. S then inverts the received values and sends them back to R. R now can check if the received values correspond to the values he sampled from the domain of the function. It is easy to see that if the function is not a permutation, then (with some probability) one of the evaluated points R sends to S has a multiple pre-images, and S has no way to determine which pre-image R picked, resulting in R rejecting the function. The problem with this approach is that it requires at least three rounds of communication. And this is clearly unacceptable if we want to construct an OT protocol that overall consists of three (or even four) rounds.

Dual Witness Encryption (DWE). As alluded to in our result section, we will rely on a Dual Witness Encryption scheme for the languages (L_0, L_1), where L_1 is an NP language. A Dual Witness Encryption is described by an encryption algorithm and a decryption algorithm. The encryption algorithm takes as input an instance (either in L_0 or in L_1) and a message, and outputs a ciphertext ct. The decryption algorithm takes as input a ciphertext, an instance $x \in L_1$ and a witness for x, and returns a string. A DWE enjoys the following two properties:

Completeness: If the cipthertext ct is computed using an instance $x \in L_1$, then the decryption algorithm, on input x and a witness for x, efficiently outputs the plaintext of ct.

Hiding: If the cipthertext ct is computed using an instance $x \in L_0$, then ct hides the plaintext in an information-theoretic sense.

Our Main Idea in a Nutshell. We now show how to use our techniques to transform the EGL protocol of Fig. 1 into a protocol that protects the input of the receiver against malicious senders relying on TDPs only. An honest receiver wants to prevent a cheating sender from being able to view z_0 and z_1 if the sender has not picked f honestly. To facilitate this intuition, the receiver encrypts, using the dual witness encryption using f as the instance, its messages (z_0 and z_1), and sends over the corresponding ciphertext to the sender. On the one hand, if the sender has indeed picked a function by running the generation algorithm Gen, then it can decrypt and obtain z_0 and z_1, on the other hand if the selected function has a lot of collisions, then the ciphertext will hide z_0 and z_1. But this only gives us a weak form of security against malicious senders since the f picked might not have a lot of collisions. The security is then amplified using a weak notion of *OT combiners*. More precisely, we use a $(1, k)$-combiner that takes as input k OT instantiations and outputs a secure OT against malicious senders as long as there is at least one OT that is secure against malicious sender. We note that for simulation based security, we will have to do some further work and add an additional round. This construction is already sufficient to obtain a 3-round OT protocol that retains its security against malicious senders and semi-honest receivers[4] relying on uncertified TDPs.

Constructing a DWE Scheme for TDPs. We start with the construction of the main tool used in our work: a DWE that encrypts with respect to a function f. For simplicity, we will limit our discussion to a bit encryption scheme, with a natural extension to encryption of bit strings. The rough idea to encrypt a bit m, is to sample an element x from the domain, compute $y \leftarrow f(x)$, and generate the ciphertext to be $(y, x_j \oplus m, j)$, where x_j is the j-th bit of x for a randomly sampled j. On the one hand, if f was indeed a permutation, generated alongside the corresponding trapdoor f^{-1} (that can be obtained from the randomness used to ran the generation algorithm), one can decrypt the ciphertext. On the other hand, if f is not a permutation, then with some probability y has a collision, and thereby there exists at least another $x' \neq x$ such that $f(x') = f(x) = y$. Hence, with probability $1/n$ x and x' differ at the j-th position (where n is the size of x), thereby hiding m since the decryptor has no way to tell whether x or x' was used

---

[4] We provide privacy for the input of the receiver in the sense that a malicious sender cannot distinguishes between when the receiver is using the input 0 and when he is using the input 1.

in the encryption. Of course, this only achieves a weak notion of security, that needs to be amplified. In order to amplify the security, we want to increase the likelihood of sampling an x such that $f(x)$ has a collision. We take the natural approach and additively secret share m as $m \leftarrow m_1 \oplus \cdots \oplus m_q$, for an appropriate parameter q, and repeat the above strategy of encryption, with fresh randomness for each m_i separately. Now, when f is not a permutation, as long as at least one of the m_i remains hidden, m remains information theoretically hidden. In the technical section, we elaborate on this idea, and discuss the appropriate parameters required to guarantee security.

Towards a Simulation-Based Secure Construction. To obtain a complete solution (i.e., a protocol that is simulation based secure against malicious senders and receivers), we integrate the above idea in the [35] construction. However, doing so creates further challenges. The remainder of the section is dedicated to our solution, and how we tackle the challenges that arise.

Let us now look at our solution is more detail.

The ORS [35] Methodology. The starting point for our protocol is the black-box OT protocol presented in [35]. Their protocol is constructed in two steps. In the first step, they construct a black-box OT protocol that is one-sided simulatable, i.e. the protocol is fully simultable against a malicious receiver, but only satisfies input indistinguishability against a malicious sender. In the second step, they then provide a general transformation that allows one to go from *one sided simulatable* OT to *fully simulatable* OT in a black-box manner. Since we can directly use their transformation in the second step, we limit our discussion to the construction of a *one sided simulatable* OT protocol. Looking back at our description of the semi-honest three-round oblivious transfer protocol, if we are to consider a fully malicious receiver $R^\star$ then this protocol is already no longer secure. Indeed $R^\star$ could just compute $z_{1-b} = f(y)$ picking a random $y \xleftarrow{\$} \{0,1\}^\lambda$. In this way $R^\star$ can retrieve both the inputs of the sender l_0 and l_1. In [30] the authors solve this problem by having the parties engage in a coin-flipping protocol such that the receiver is forced to set at least one of z_0 and z_1 to a random string. This is done by forcing the receiver to commit to two strings (r_0, r_1) in the first round (for the coin-flipping) and providing a witness-indistinguishable proof of knowledge (WIPoK) that either $z_0 = r_0 \oplus r_0'$ or $z_1 = r_1 \oplus r_1'$ where r_0' and r_1' are random strings sent by the sender in the second round. The resulting protocol, as observed in [35], leaks no information to S about R's input. Moreover, the soundness of the WIPoK forces a malicious $R^\star$ to behave honestly, and the PoK allows to extract the input from the adversary in the simulation. Therefore, the protocol constructed in [30] is one-sided simulatable. The main drawback in the above approach, addressed in [35], is that the use of a WI scheme requires using the commitment scheme in a non-black-box manner. Instead, in [35] the authors propose an approach that makes only black-box use of the underlying primitives. The main insight in [35] was to recast the problem in terms of equivocal and binding commitments, and having the output of the coin-flipping to be a pair of strings (z_0, z_1).

1. Receiver R, on secret input b, chooses random strings r_0 and r_1. R then sends across commitments $\mathsf{com}_0, \mathsf{com}_1$ such that com_{1-b} is a commitment to r_{1-b} while com_b is an equivocal commitment. R now proves that one of the commitments is binding.

2. The sender S then samples a trapdoor permutation from the family $f, f^{-1} \leftarrow \mathsf{Gen}(1^\lambda)$, and sends f to R. S also additionally samples a random string r, and sends it over to R.

3. R will now choose its decommitments to send to S. For com_{1-b} it will decommit to r_{1-b}, but for com_b, R does the following. R sample $x \xleftarrow{\$} \{0,1\}^\lambda$ and computes $z_b \leftarrow f(x)$, and sets $r_b \leftarrow z_b \oplus r$. R now decommits com_b to r_b, and both decommitments are sent to S.

4. S on receiving the decommitments, checks if they are valid before proceeding. It then sets $z_a \leftarrow r_a \oplus r$ for $a \in \{0,1\}$, and sends (w_0, w_1) to the receiver where $w_a \leftarrow \ell_a \oplus h(f^{-1}(z_a))$.

Since one of the commitments are guaranteed to be binding from the soundness of the proof, the receiver can only equivocate one of the strings, and thereby knows the pre-image to only one of the strings. From the above description, the main technical contributions of [35] are to realize the above protocols in a black-box manner using the commit-and-prove protocol due to [32]. The above description is sufficient to discuss the main ideas and challenges underlying our work, for a more detailed discussion of [35] we refer the reader to the technical sections. Given the description of the above protocol, and equipped with the dual witness encryption, the natural approach is for the receiver to encrypt its decommitments sent in the third round using the function f sent by the sender. This seems to work as a valid defense against a malicious sender, but an unwanted consequence of this modification is that simulation now fails for a malicious receiver. Let us see why this is the case.

Defending Against a Malicious Receiver. Consider an execution of the simulator with a malicious receiver. At some point during the simulation, the simulator will receive the encrypted messages from the receiver, and must proceed with the simulation. But just from looking at the ciphertext, it does not know if the ciphertexts contain legitimate decommitments, or some arbitrary values. Why is this a problem? In the real execution of the OT protocol, an honest sender, having picked f to be a permutation, will decrypt the ciphertexts and abort if the ciphertexts do not decrypt to a legitimate decommitment. Therefore, in order to avoid a trivial distinguisher, the simulator must also perform this check. One natural way would be for the simulator to mimic the honest sender's behavior and decrypt the ciphertext, and then decide the appropriate action from the decrypted value. Unfortunately, this strategy does not work, and we illustrate why this would be a problem. In the above protocol, we said that the intuitive reason for the receiver not to learn l_{1-b} is that it does not know the pre-image of the random string, and thereby can do no better than guessing the hardcore predicate of the pre-image. To formalize this in the proof, we need to make a reduction to security of the hardcore bit of f. Such a reduction receives only the function f and but must be able to complete the interaction against the malicious receiver. And importantly, must do so without knowledge of the randomness ρ used to generate f. A consequence of this is that decrypting is no longer an option since the reduction does not have ρ. In essence, if we have to decrypt to check, then we are breaking the security of the hardcore predicate. One way to get around decrypting, is to have some sort of "public check" such as a witness indistinguishable proof of knowledge as done in [30]. But the trivial application of this approach results in a non-black-box use of the underlying primitives, which we cannot afford to do. And indeed, it is unclear how one would prove honest behavior in such a scenario in a black-box manner. Taking a step back, we are seemingly deriving two distinct security properties from the function f: (i) for the security of the hardcore predicate against a malicious receiver; and (ii) hiding of the DWE scheme if f is not a permutation. The issue then is that when we want to rely on the security of the hardcore predicate, we do not care for the ciphertext to be hiding, since we are guaranteed that the function f used in the reduction, is a permutation. This seems to indicate that, while the current construction ties both these security properties, it does not necessarily have to be the case. Our approach is to decouple the above properties in a surprisingly simple manner. We use now two functions, an inner f_{OT} for the OT (and security of the hardcore predicate), and an outer f_{dWE} for the DWE scheme. The sender now samples the two functions along with the corresponding trapdoors. As before, the functions are sent to the receiver in the second round. The receiver then uses f_{OT} to compute z_b and uses f_{dWE} to encrypt the decommitment. This solves the issue indicated above since the reduction can decrypt without breaking the security of the hardcore predicate. This means that we can now reduce the security of the scheme to the security of the function f_{OT}. But now, a malicious sender could choose f_{dWE} to be a permutation, while choosing f_{OT} maliciously. We seem to have lost the advantage of using the DWE scheme. Our final solution is to stick to the idea of using two functions. But instead of fixing the roles of the two functions, allow the receiver to determine the roles of the corresponding function. As mentioned before, this provides only a weak guarantee and is amplified through the use of OT combiners. While we have described the main ideas underlying the construction, implementing these ideas involve further work, and we refer the reader to the relevant technical sections for the details.

2.1   Related Work

Oblivious Transfer. As stated earlier, oblivious transfer (OT) plays a fundamental role in cryptography and has a large body of work starting with [13]. We restrict ourselves to relevant works focusing on the round optimality of OT. In the random oracle model, [34] constructs a two-round OT protocol with indistinguishability based security against malicious receivers, but simulation security against malicious senders. In the CRS model, [37] constructs a fully maliciously secure two-round protocol. Moving to the relevant setting of the plain model, [30] showed that four rounds are necessary for a fully maliciously secure OT protocol with black-box simulation, and further proved that this was tight by constructing a four round OT protocol. The subsequent work [35] improved this construction by making only black-box use of the underlying primitives. In [26] the authors propose a weaker notion of trapdoor permutations whose permutation domains are polynomially dense (i.e., contain polynomial fractions of all strings of a particular length), and shows that these are sufficient to obtain semi-honest OT. Unfortunately, it does not seem that the construction of [26] would work against malicious senders, as the security of the protocol relies on the trapdoor function having a specific structure (i.e., being polynomially dense) that needs to be certifiable.

Round-Complexity of 2PC. Studying the round complexity for secure computation has been the focus of many works in the past years. Whereas for unconditional security it is inherent to have protocol that are non-constant round [2,8,12], for the computational case it was showed that three rounds are sufficient to achieve security against semi-honest adversaries [40,41], and subsequently [31,33] showed constant round protocols for the case of malicious adversaries. In [30] the authors show that five rounds are necessary and sufficient to compute any two-party functionality where both parties can get the output (with black-box simulation)[5]. This result was later improved in [35] by showing how to obtain a 5-round protocol with black-box use of the underlying certifiable enhanced trapdoor permutations. In [16] the authors consider the case where the parties have a simultaneous message exchange channel[6] available and show that four rounds are necessary and sufficient to do secure computation assuming 3-robust non-malleable commitments. A followup work [10] showed how to obtain a four-round secure protocol when a simultaneous message exchange channel is available under the assumption of enhanced certifiable trapdoor permutations. We remark that in this paper we do not assume simultaneous message exchange channels.

Certifying Trapdoor Permutations. We have already mentioned some relevant works in this area and we now extend our discussion. [23,39] discuss the security of the 1-out-of-k oblivious transfer protocol [13] which is based on trapdoor permutations, noting that its security is compromised in the case of partial-domain trapdoor functions (when $k \geq 3$). [23,39] then show how doubly enhanced trapdoor functions can be used to overcome this issue. Clearly, the problem of certifying trapdoor permutations does not arise when only semi-honest parties are considered (like in the case of semi-honest OT), but it is fundamental in the case of malicious adversary. This problem, for the case of secure computation, has been circumvented in [10,16,30,35] by simply using certifiable trapdoor permutations. That is, by using trapdoor permutations equipped with a verification algorithm that can be used to check if a function is a permutation or not. The problem of getting rid of the certifiability property has been studied mostly for the case of NIZK in the shared random string model [1]. Recently [6] has studied

---

[5] In this work we only refer to black-box simulation.
[6] In this model everyone can send messages at the same time.

additional certifiable properties that allows recognizing elements in the domain, as well as uniformly sample from it even for illegitimate functions, and show that some of these properties are necessary to apply the results of [1] to obtain a secure NIZK even for maliciously sampled trapdoor functions.

2.2 Organization of the Paper

In the next section we provide the fundamental background required to read our paper. We dedicate Sect. 4 to defining the notion of dual witness encryption, providing a few examples for the languages of DH tuples and QR tuples. In Sect. 5 we show how to instantiate a DWE for the language of non-TDPs. We devote Sect. 6 and 7 to our 4-round OT protocol secure against malicious adversaries, and Sect. 8 to our round-optimal 2-PC protocol. For the formal construction and proofs of our 3-round OT protocol we refer the reader to the full version.

3   Background

Notation. We denote the security parameter by λ and use "$||$" as concatenation operator (i.e., if a and b are two strings then by $a||b$ we denote the concatenation of a and b). For a finite set Q, $x \xleftarrow{\$} Q$ denotes a sampling of x from Q with uniform distribution. We use "$=$" to check equality of two different elements (i.e. $a = b$ then...), "$\leftarrow$" as the assigning operator (e.g. to assign to a the value of b we write $a \leftarrow$ b). and $:=$ to define two elements as equal. We use the abbreviation PPT that stands for probabilistic polynomial time. We use $\mathsf{poly}(\cdot)$ to indicate a generic polynomial function. A *polynomial-time relation* $\mathcal{R}$ (or *polynomial relation*, in short) is a subset of $\{0,1\}^* \times \{0,1\}^*$ such that membership of (x, w) in $\mathcal{R}$ can be decided in time polynomial in $|x|$. For $(x, w) \in \mathcal{R}$, we call x the *instance* and w a *witness* for x. For a polynomial-time relation $\mathcal{R}$, we define the NP-language $L_{\mathcal{R}}$ as $L_{\mathcal{R}} = \{x | \exists w : (x, w) \in \mathcal{R}\}$. Analogously, unless otherwise specified, for an NP-language L we denote by $\mathcal{R}_{\mathsf{L}}$ the corresponding polynomial-time relation (that is, $\mathcal{R}_{\mathsf{L}}$ is such that $L = L_{\mathcal{R}_{\mathsf{L}}}$).

When it is necessary to refer to the randomness r used by and algorithm A we use the following notation: $A(\cdot; r)$. We assume familiarity with the notion of computational and statistical indistinguishability, sigma-protocols and with the DDH assumption. We refer to the full version for the formal definitions.

3.1   Injective TDFs and TDPs

In this section we define the notion of trapdoor function following mostly the notation proposed in [6].

Definition 1 (Trapdoor function). *A family of one-way trapdoor functions, or TDFs, is a collection of finite functions, denoted $f_\alpha : \{D_\alpha \to R_\alpha\}$, accompanied by PPT algorithms Gen, S_D (domain sampler), S_R (range sampler) and two (deterministic) polynomial time algorithms Eval (forward evaluator) and Inv (backward evaluator) such that the following conditions hold.*

1. *On input 1^λ, the algorithm* Gen *selects a random index α of a function f_α, along with a corresponding trapdoor* td.
2. *On input α, algorithm S_D samples an element from domain D_α.*
3. *On input α, algorithm S_R samples an image from the range R_α.*
4. *On input α and any $x \in D_\alpha$, $y \leftarrow$ Eval(α, x) with $y = f_\alpha(x)$.*
5. *On input* td *and any $y \in R_\alpha$,* Inv$($td$, y)$ *outputs x such that* Eval$(\alpha, x) = y$.

The standard hardness condition refers to the difficulty of inverting f_α on a random image, sampled by S_R or by evaluating Eval *on a random pre-image sampled by S_D, when given only the image and the index α but not the trapdoor* td. *That is, let $I_0(1^\lambda)$ denote the first element in the output of* Gen(1^λ) *(i.e., the index); then, for every polynomial-time algorithm $\mathcal{A}$, it holds that:*

$$\Pr[(\alpha \xleftarrow{\$} I_0(1^\lambda); x \xleftarrow{\$} S_D(\alpha); y \leftarrow \textsf{Eval}(\alpha, x), x' \xleftarrow{\$} \mathcal{A}(\alpha, y) : \textsf{Eval}(\alpha, x') = y] \leq \nu(\lambda). \quad (1)$$

Or, when sampling an image directly using the range sampler:

$$\Pr[(\alpha \xleftarrow{\$} I_0(1^\lambda); y \xleftarrow{\$} S_R(\alpha); x' \xleftarrow{\$} \mathcal{A}(\alpha, y) : \textsf{Eval}(\alpha, x') = y] \leq \nu(\lambda). \quad (2)$$

Additionally, it is required that, for any $\alpha \xleftarrow{\$} I_0(1^\lambda)$, the distribution sampled by S_R should be close the distribution sampled by Eval$(S_D(\alpha))$. *In this context we require the two distributions be computationally indistinguishable. We note that this requirement implies that the two hardness requirements given in Eqs. 1 and 2 are equivalent. The issue of closeness of the sampling distributions is discussed further at the end of this section. If f_α is injective for all $\alpha \xleftarrow{\$} I_0(1^\lambda)$, we say that our collection describes an* injective trapdoor function family, *or iTDFs (in which case* Inv$($td$, \cdot)$ *inverts any images to its sole pre-image). If additionally D_α and R_α coincide than for any $\alpha \xleftarrow{\$} I_0(1^\lambda)$, the resulting primitive is a trapdoor permutation. If for any $\alpha \xleftarrow{\$} I(1^\lambda)$, $S_D = \{0,1\}^{\textsf{poly}(\lambda)}$, that is, every poly-bit string describes a valid domain element, we say the function is* full domain. *Otherwise we say the domain is* partial.

Definition 2 (Hard-Core Predicate). *h is a* hard-core predicate *for f_α if its value is hard to predict for a random domain element x, given only α and $f_\alpha(x)$. That is, if for any* PPT *adversary $\mathcal{A}$ there exists a negligible function ν such that*

$$\Pr[(\alpha \xleftarrow{\$} I_0(1^\lambda); x \xleftarrow{\$} S_D(\alpha); y \xleftarrow{\$} \textsf{Eval}(\alpha, x), h(x) \leftarrow \mathcal{A}(\alpha, y)] \leq 1/2 + \nu(\lambda).$$

Enhancements. Goldreich [19] suggested the notion of enhanced TDPs, which can be used for cases where sampling is required to be available in a way that does not expose the pre-image. We recall the notion of *enhanced injective TDF* proposed in [6] that extends the definition proposed by Goldreich to the case of injective TDF (where the domain and range are not necessarily equal).

Definition 3 (Enhanced injective TDF [19]**).** *Let* $\{f_\alpha : D_\alpha \to R_\alpha\}$ *be a collection of injective TDFs, and let* S_D *be the domain sampler associated with it. We say that the collection is* enhanced *if there exists a range sampler* S_R *that returns a random sample out of* R_α*, and such that, for every polynomial-time algorithm* $\mathcal{A}$*, it holds that*

$$\text{Prob}\left[(\alpha \overset{\$}{\leftarrow} I_0(1^\lambda); y \overset{\$}{\leftarrow} S_R(\alpha; r); x' \overset{\$}{\leftarrow} \mathcal{A}(\alpha, r) : \text{Eval}(\alpha, x') = y \right] \leq \nu(\lambda).$$

Definition 4 (Enhanced Hard-Core Predicate [21]**).** *Let* $\{f_\alpha : D_\alpha \to R_\alpha\}$ *be an enhanced collection of injective TDFs with domain sampler* S_D *and range sampler* S_R*. We say that the predicate* h *is an* enhanced hard-core predicate *of* f_α *if it is computable in* PPT *time and for any* PPT *adversary* $\mathcal{A}$ *there exists a negligible function* ν *such that*

$$\Pr[(\alpha, \text{td}) \overset{\$}{\leftarrow} \text{Gen}(1^\lambda); r \overset{\$}{\leftarrow} \{0,1\}^\lambda; y \leftarrow S_R(\alpha; r); x \leftarrow \text{Inv}(\text{td}, y); \mathcal{A}(\alpha, r)$$
$$= h(\alpha, x)] \qquad \leq 1/2 + \nu(\lambda)$$

or equivalently, if the following two distribution ensembles are computationally indistinguishable:

$$\{(\alpha, r, h(\alpha, \text{Inv}(\text{td}, S_R(\alpha, rw\alpha, \text{td})) \overset{\$}{\leftarrow} \text{Gen}(1^\lambda), r \overset{\$}{\leftarrow} \{0,1\}^\star\}$$

$$\{(\alpha, r, u) : \alpha \overset{\$}{\leftarrow} I_0(1^\lambda), r \overset{\$}{\leftarrow} \{0,1\}^\star, u \overset{\$}{\leftarrow} \{0,1\}\}$$

Additional Properties. We define multiple notions of certifiability for trap-door functions, where each requires the existence of a general prover and verifier protocol for the function family. Let $f_\alpha : \{D_\alpha \to D_\alpha\}$ be a trapdoor permutation family, given by (Gen, S, Eval, Inv) (where $S = S_R = S_D$), we now define the following properties.

Efficiently recognizable domain: that is, there exists a polynomial-time algorithm R_D which, for any index α and any string $x \in \{0,1\}^*$, accepts on (α, x) if and only if $x \in D_\alpha$. In other words, D_α is defined as the set of all strings x such that $R_D(\alpha, x)$ accepts.
Efficiently sampleable domain: that is, there exists a PPT algorithm S_{DR} that on input α outputs a pair of (x, r) such that $\text{Eval}(\alpha, x) = S(\alpha; r)$ where x is sampled uniformly in D_α.
Efficiently sampleable range: that is, for any index α and $r \overset{\$}{\leftarrow} \{0,1\}^\lambda$, $S(\alpha; r)$ samples uniformly in D_α.

We stress that these properties should hold with respect to any α, including ones that were not generated by running $\text{Gen}(1^\lambda)$. We also note that despite the similarities between the notions of doubly enhancement and efficiently sampleable domain, these two are incomparable. The notion of efficiently sampleable domain just requires the existence of a sampling algorithm that samples uniformly in D_α even for a maliciously chosen α, and it puts *no requirements* of one-wayness. Note that any trapdoor permutation family with full domain trivially enjoys all the properties listed above (one example is given by the candidate trapdoor permutation proposed in [38]). We show how to obtain a secure 2-party computation that relies on injective enhanced trapdoor permutations that have efficiently sampleable range and domain in a black-box way (note that we put no requirements on the certifiability of the injectivity). We finally recall that previous works required the existence of the same samplers even in the case of certifiable TDPs.

3.2 Commit-and-Open Protocols

In [15] the authors provide the definition of 3-round *commit-and-open* protocols. In this the prover (committer) has two inputs $m_0, m_1 \in \mathcal{M}$ and a bit $b \in \{0, 1\}$ (we denote with $\mathcal{M}$ the message space of the commitment scheme). Informally, the message m_b is fixed in the first round of the protocol, and the message m_{1-b} can be decided in the last round where the messages (m_0, m_1) are revealed to the verifier (receiver). More formally, a commit-and-open protocol is a tuple of PPT algorithms $\Pi_{\mathsf{c\&o}} := (\mathsf{P} := (\mathsf{P}_0, \mathsf{P}_1), \mathsf{V} := (\mathsf{V}_0, \mathsf{V}_1))$ specified as follows. The algorithm P_0 takes as input m_b and outputs a string $\gamma \in \{0, 1\}^\star$ and auxiliary state information $\alpha \in \{0, 1\}^\star$. The algorithm V_0 outputs a random string $\beta \xleftarrow{\$} \mathcal{B}$ (where $\mathcal{B}$ represents the message space of the valid second rounds for $\Pi_{\mathsf{c\&o}}$). The algorithm P_1 takes as input $(\alpha, \beta, \gamma, m_{1-d})$ and outputs a string $\delta \in \{0, 1\}^\star$. The deterministic algorithm V_1 takes a transcript $(\gamma, \beta, (\delta, m_0, m_1))$ and outputs a bit. Following [15], we denote with $< \mathsf{P}(m_0, m_1, b), \mathsf{V}(1^\lambda) >$ an execution of P where P uses (m_0, m_1, b) as input, and denote with $T := (\gamma, \beta, (\delta, m_0, m_1))$ the transcript obtained in this execution. We say that P satisfies completeness if honestly generated transcripts are always accepting (i.e., V_1 outputs 1).

Definition 5 (Secure commit-and-open protocol [15]). *We say that a 3-round protocol $\Pi_{\mathsf{c\&o}}$ is secure if it enjoys completeness and satisfies the following properties.*

Existence of Committing Branch: *for every* PPT *malicious prover* $\mathsf{P}^\star := (\mathsf{P}_0^\star, \mathsf{P}_1^\star)$ *there exists a negligible function ν such that*

$$\Pr[\mathsf{V}_1(T) = 1 \text{ and } \mathsf{V}_1(T') = 1 \text{ and } m_0 \neq m_0' \text{ and } m_1 \neq m_1' : (\gamma, \alpha) \xleftarrow{\$} \mathsf{P}_0^\star,$$
$$\beta, \beta' \xleftarrow{\$} \mathsf{V}_0, (\delta, m_0, m_1) \xleftarrow{\$} \mathsf{P}_1^\star(\alpha, \beta), (\delta', m_0', m_1') \xleftarrow{\$} \mathsf{P}_1^\star(\alpha, \beta')] \leq \nu(\lambda)$$

where $T := (\gamma, \beta, (\delta, m_0, m_1))$ and $T' := (\gamma, \beta', (\delta', m_0', m_1'))$, and where the probability is taken over the random coin tosses of P and V.

Committing Branch Indistinguishability: *for all* PPT *malicious verifier* $\mathsf{V}^\star$, *and for all messages $m_0, m_1 \in \mathcal{M}$, we have that the following are indistinguishable*

$$\{T : T \xleftarrow{\$} < P(m_0, m_1, 0), \mathsf{V}^\star(1^\lambda) > \}_{\lambda \in \mathbb{N}}$$

$$\{T : T \xleftarrow{\$} < P(m_0, m_1, 1), \mathsf{V}^\star(1^\lambda) > \}_{\lambda \in \mathbb{N}}$$

The authors of [15] show that one of the protocols proposed in [35] that relies on statistically binding and computationally hiding commitment (and it is black-box in the use of the underlying primitives) satisfies the above definition. Since statistically binding and computationally hiding commitments can be constructed using one-to-one one way-functions in a black-box manner then there exists a secure commit-and-open protocol that uses the underlying one-way function is a black-box way. We refer to [15] for more discussion on the notion of commit-and-open and for its black-box instantiation from one-to-one one-way-functions.

3.3   Oblivious Transfer and 2-PC

Here we follow [35]. Oblivious Transfer (OT) is a two-party functionality $F_{\mathcal{OT}}$, in which a sender S holds a pair of strings (l_0, l_1), and a receiver R holds a bit b, and wants to obtain the string l_b. The security requirement for the $F_{\mathcal{OT}}$ functionality is that any malicious receiver does not learn anything about the string l_{1-b} and any malicious sender does not learn which string has been transferred. This security requirement is formalized via the ideal/real world paradigm. In the ideal world, the functionality is implemented by a trusted party that takes the inputs from S and R and provides the output to R and is therefore secure by definition. A real world protocol Π securely realizes the ideal $F_{\mathcal{OT}}$ functionalities, if the following two conditions hold. (a) Security against a malicious receiver: the output of any malicious receiver $R^\star$ running one execution of Π with an honest sender S can be simulated by a PPT simulator Sim that has only access to the ideal world functionality $F_{\mathcal{OT}}$ and oracle access to $R^\star$. (b) Security against a malicious sender. The joint view of the output of any malicious sender $S^\star$ running one execution of Π with R and the output of R can be simulated by a PPT simulator Sim that has only access to the ideal world functionality $F_{\mathcal{OT}}$ and oracle access to $S^\star$. We also consider the weaker definition of OT introduced in [35] which is referred as *one-sided simulatable OT*. In this we do not demand the existence of a simulator against a malicious sender, but we only require that a malicious sender cannot distinguish whether the honest receiver is playing with bit 0 or 1. That is, we require that for any PPT malicious sender $S^\star$ the view of $S^\star$ executing Π with the receiver R playing with bit 0 is computationally indistinguishable from the view of $S^\star$ where R is playing with the bit 1. Finally, we consider the $F_{\mathcal{OT}}^m$ functionality where the sender S and the receiver R run m executions of OT in parallel.

Definition 6 ([35]).   *Let $F_{\mathcal{OT}}$ be the Oblivious Transfer functionality as described previously. We say that a protocol Π securely computes $F_{\mathcal{OT}}$ with one-sided simulation if the following holds:*

1. *For every non-uniform* PPT *adversary* $R^\star$ *controlling the receiver in the real model, there exists a non-uniform* PPT *adversary* Sim *for the ideal model such that:* $\{\mathsf{REAL}_{\Pi, R^\star(z)}(1^\lambda)\}_{z \in \{0,1\}^\lambda} \approx \mathsf{IDEAL}_{F_{\mathcal{OT}}, \mathsf{Sim}(z)}(1^\lambda)\}_{z \in \{0,1\}^\lambda},$
where $\mathsf{REAL}_{\Pi, R^\star(z)}(1^\lambda)$ *denotes the distribution of the output of the adversary* $R^\star$ *(controlling the receiver) after a real execution of protocol* Π, *where the sender* S *has inputs* l_0, l_1 *and the receiver has input* b. $\mathsf{IDEAL}_{f, \mathsf{Sim}(z)}(1^\lambda)$ *denotes the analogous distribution in an ideal execution with a trusted party that computes* $F_{\mathcal{OT}}$ *for the parties and hands the output to the receiver.*
2. *For every non-uniform* PPT *adversary* $S^\star$ *controlling the sender it holds that:*
$\{\mathsf{View}_{\Pi, S^\star(z)}^R(l_0, l_1, 0)\}_{z \in \{0,1\}^\star} \approx \{\mathsf{View}_{\Pi, S^\star(z)}^R(l_0, l_1, 1)\}_{z \in \{0,1\}^\star}$
where $\mathsf{View}_{\Pi, S^\star(z)}^R$ *denotes the view of adversary* $S^\star$ *after a real execution of protocol* Π *with the honest receiver* R.

Definition 7 ([35]). *A protocol* Π *securely realizes* $F_{\mathcal{OT}}$ *with fully simulatability if* Π *is one-sided simulatable and additionally for every non-uniform* PPT *adversary* $S^\star$ *controlling the sender in the real model, there exists a non-uniform* PPT *adversary* Sim *for the ideal world such that*

$$\{\mathsf{REAL}_{\Pi, S^\star(z)}(1^\lambda, b)\}_{z \in \{0,1\}^\lambda} \approx \mathsf{IDEAL}_{F_{\mathcal{OT}}, \mathsf{Sim}(z)}(1^\lambda, b)\}_{z \in \{0,1\}^\lambda}$$

where $\mathsf{REAL}_{\Pi, S^\star(z)}(1^\lambda, b)$ *denotes the distribution of the output of the adversary* $S^\star$ *(controlling the sender) and the output of the honest receiver, after a real execution of protocol* Π, *where the receiver has input* b. $\mathsf{IDEAL}_{F_{\mathcal{OT}}, \mathsf{Sim}(z)}(1^\lambda, b)$ *denotes the analogous distribution but in an ideal execution with a trusted party that computes* $F_{\mathcal{OT}}$ *for the parties and hands the output to the honest receiver.*

In this work we also consider the notion of parallel OT, which is the same as the previous definition, except that the sender has multiple pairs of inputs and the receiver has multiple bits.

Secure Two-Party Computation [35]. Let $F(x_1, x_2)$ be a two-party functionality run between parties P_1 holding input x_1 and P_2 holding input x_2. In the ideal world, P_i with $(i \in \{1, 2\})$ sends its input x_i to the F and obtains only $y = F(x_1, x_2)$. We say that a protocol Π securely realizes F if the view of any malicious $P_i^\star$ executing Π with an honest P_j with $i \neq j$ combined with the output of P_j (if any) can be simulated by a PPT simulator that has only access to F and has oracle access to $P_i^\star$.

4   Dual Witness Encryption (DWE)

A Dual Witness Encryption scheme for the languages L_0, L_1 with $L_0, L_1 \subseteq \{0,1\}^\star$ is equipped with two PPT algorithms: Enc and Dec. Enc takes as input $x \in \{0,1\}^\lambda$, a message $m \in \{0,1\}^\lambda$ and outputs $ct \in \{0,1\}^{\mathsf{poly}(\lambda)}$. Dec takes as input $x \in \{0,1\}^\lambda, w \in \{0,1\}^\lambda, ct \in \{0,1\}^{\mathsf{poly}(\lambda)}$ and outputs a message $m \in \{0,1\}^\lambda \cup \{\bot\}$.

Definition 8. *A Dual Witness Encryption scheme* PK-IBS $=$ (Gen, Enc, Dec) *for the languages* (L_0, L_1) *is secure if it enjoys the following properties.*

Completeness: $\Pr[m \leftarrow \mathsf{Dec}(x, w, \mathsf{Enc}(x, m)) = 1 : (x, w) \in \mathcal{R}_{L_1}] \geq 1 - \nu(\lambda)$.
Hiding: *For any adversary* $\mathcal{A}$ *and for any* $x \in L_0$ *the following holds:*
$$\Pr[b \xleftarrow{\$} \{0, 1\}; (m_0, m_1) \leftarrow \mathcal{A}(x) \wedge b \leftarrow \mathcal{A}(\mathsf{aux}, \mathsf{Enc}(x, m_b))] < \nu(\lambda)$$

4.1 DWE for the Languages of DH and QR Tuples

In this section we show how to construct a DWE for the languages of DH and QR tuples. We do not need these constructions to build our OT and 2PC protocols, we only want to show that our primitive can be instantiated also with respect to other languages. The two constructions rely on similar ideas, hence, we provide the details only for the construction for DH tuples. Our constructions are based on the sigma-protocol for the language of the DH and QR tuples and on some observations made in [5,11] on these sigma protocols. Following [11], we recall the well-known Sigma protocol $\Sigma_{DH} = (\mathcal{P}, \mathcal{V})$ for the language $L_0 := \{(g, h, U, V) : \exists \alpha \text{ s.t. } U = g^\alpha \text{ and } V = h^\alpha\}$. On common input $T = (g, h, U, V)$, and honest prover's private input α such that $U = g^\alpha$ and $V = h^\alpha$, the following steps are executed. We denote the size of the group $\mathcal{G}$ by q.

- $\mathcal{P}$ picks $r \in \mathbb{Z}_q$ at random and computes and sends $A := g^r$, $B := h^r$ to $\mathcal{V}$;
- $\mathcal{V}$ chooses a random challenge $c \in \{0, 1\}$ and sends it to $\mathcal{P}$;
- $\mathcal{P}$ computes and sends $z = r + \alpha \cdot c$ to $\mathcal{V}$;
- $\mathcal{V}$ accepts if and only if $g^z = A \cdot U^c$ and $h^z = B \cdot V^c$.

In [11] the authors observe that the above protocol has the following interesting property. There exists a PPT algorithm ChallExt that on input a first round $a = (A, B)$ of Σ_{DH}, a non-DH tuple T and γ such that $h = g^\gamma$, outputs the only valid second round $c \in \{0, 1\}$ (if any exists) such that there is some z that would make the verifier to (mistakenly) accept the transcript (a, c, z) with respect to the instance T. The algorithm ChallExt works as follows. Let $T = (g, h, X, W)$ be a non-DH tuple such that $X = g^\alpha$, $W = h^\beta$, $\alpha \neq \beta$ and $h = g^\gamma$. Upon input $(T = (g, h, X, W), a, \gamma)$, algorithm ChallExt parses a as (A, B), and if $A^\gamma = B$ then it outputs 0, else it outputs 1. Note that when the first round of Σ_{DH} corresponds to a DH tuple, $(i.e., A^\gamma = B)$ and T is not a DH tuple, then the only c that would make true the conditions $g^z = A \cdot U^c$ and $h^z = B \cdot V^c$ is $c = 0$. Instead, if (g, h, A, B) does not represent a DH tuple $(i.e., A^\gamma \neq B)$ then there exists z such that $g^z = A \cdot U^c$ and $h^z = B \cdot V^c$ if and only if $c = 1$. In what follows, we make use of this special property of Σ_{DH}, and we refer to ChallExt as the *bad-challenge extractor*. The same holds true for the classical Sigma protocol for QR [25] (along the lines of the full version of [5, Sec. 6.2]). The above observation, together with the fact that Σ_{DH} is SHVZK immediately yields to a DWE for the languages (L_0, L_1) where $L_1 = \{0, 1\}^\star - L_0$, and where the NP-relation associated to L_1 is $\mathcal{R}_{L_1} := \{(g, h, X, W), \gamma : h = g^\gamma \text{ and } W \neq X^\gamma\}$.

In more detail, the encryption algorithm works by running the SHVZK simulator for Σ_{DH} on input $T \in L_0 \cup L_1$ and the message to be encrypted $m \in \{0, 1\}$.

The output of the SHVZK algorithm corresponds to $(A := g^{z-\alpha m}, B := h^{z-\beta m}, z)$. The output of our encryption algorithm then corresponds to (A, B).

If $T \in L_1$ (i.e., it is a non-DH tuple), then we can run the bad-challenge extractor ChallExt to reconstruct m in polynomial-time (note that the tuple (g, h, A, B) is DH only if $m = 0$). In the case when T is a DH tuple, then, by the completeness and the SHVZK properties of Σ_{DH}, (A, B) encodes no information on the message m. Indeed, it is alway possible to find a valid z that makes the transcript $(A, B), m, z$ accepting for any $m \in \{0, 1\}$. For sake of completeness we now provide the formal description of our protocol, that we denote with $(\mathsf{Enc}^{\mathsf{NDH}}, \mathsf{Dec}^{\mathsf{NDH}})$.

- Let $m \in \{0, 1\}$ be the message to be encrypted. The encryption algorithm $\mathsf{Enc}^{\mathsf{NDH}}$ takes as input the tuple $T = (g, h, X, W)$ and the message $m \in \{0, 1\}$ and does the following steps.
  1. Sample $z \in \mathbb{Z}_q$ and compute $A \leftarrow \frac{g^z}{X^m}, B \leftarrow \frac{h^z}{W^m}$
  2. Output A, B.
- The algorithm $\mathsf{Dec}^{\mathsf{NDH}}$ takes as input $T \in L_1$, the ciphertext (A, B) and the witness γ such that $(T, \gamma) \in \mathcal{R}_{L_1}$, and outputs $\mathsf{ChallExt}(T, A, B, \gamma)$.

Theorem 3. $(\mathsf{Enc}^{\mathsf{NDH}}, \mathsf{Dec}^{\mathsf{NDH}})$ *is a secure black-box DWE scheme with message space $\{0, 1\}$ for the languages (L_0, L_1) defined above, where the relation associated to L_1 is $\mathcal{R}_{L_1}$.*

DWE for All NP Languages. If we do not care about the decryption algorithm being efficient (PPT), then the above approach can be extended to any NP language L that admits a sigma-protocol Σ. Indeed, if the instance used during the encryption is $x \notin L$, then the special soundness of Σ guarantees that for any first round of Σ there exists at most one challenge that would make the verifier to accept. This means that the first output of the SHVZK simulator of Σ on input x and the message $m \in \{0, 1\}$ encodes m. Hence, an unbounded decryptor can easily compute it. On the other hand, when $x \in L$, then the first round of Σ (hence, the first output of the SHVZK simulator) information theoretically hides the message m (due to the completeness and the SHVZK properties of Σ).

5   Black-Box DWE for Trapdoor Permutations

A function $f_\alpha : D_\alpha \rightarrow D_\alpha$ is an ϵ-permutation if at most an ϵ fraction of the points in D_α have more than one pre-image (under f_α). More formally, we have the following.

Definition 9. *Let $f_\alpha : \{D_\alpha \rightarrow D_\alpha\}$. The collision set of f_α, denoted with $C(f_\alpha)$, is $\{x_1 \in D_\alpha : \exists x_2 \in D_\alpha \text{ s.t. } x_1 \neq x_2 \text{ and } \mathsf{Eval}(\alpha, x_1) = \mathsf{Eval}(\alpha, x_2)\}$. Let $\epsilon \in [0, 1]$, we call f_α an ϵ-permutation if $|C(f_\alpha)| \leq \epsilon |D_\alpha|$.*

We say that f_α is an *almost* permutation if it is an $\epsilon(n)$-permutation where ϵ is a negligible function and $n = |D_\alpha|$. Let $f_\alpha : \{D_\alpha \to D_\alpha\}$ be a collection of trapdoor permutations with efficiently sampleable range and domain accompanied by the algorithms (Gen, S, Eval, Inv). We then define L as the language of trapdoor functions with efficiently sampleable range and domain that have a collision set greater (or equal) than half of the entire domain. More formally, $L_0 = \{\alpha : |C(f_\alpha)| \geq 2^{-1}|D_\alpha|\}$. We also define L_1 as the set trapdoor function in the range of the generation algorithm Gen (i.e., $L_1 = \{\alpha : (\alpha, \mathsf{td}) \leftarrow \mathsf{Gen}(1^\lambda; r), r \in \{0,1\}^\lambda\}$) We provide a DWE scheme for the languages (L_0, L_1). Informally, this encryption scheme maintains the hiding of the encrypted message if the collision set of f_α is sufficiently large (i.e., f_α is *a lot* non-injective). Instead, if the function is generated using $\mathsf{Gen}(1^\lambda)$, then any message can be decrypted using the corresponding trapdoor (which is also an output of Gen and thus can be obtained from the randomness r, which represents the witness).

5.1   Our Constructions

We start by constructing a dual witness encryption scheme $(\mathsf{Enc}_1^\mathsf{f}, \mathsf{Dec}_1^\mathsf{f})$ for one-bit messages for the language (L_0, L_1) described above. Let f_α be a trapdoor permutation with efficiently sampleable range accompanied by the algorithms (Gen, S, Eval, Inv) with domain (and range) of size 2^λ.

- Let $m \in \{0, 1\}$ be the message to be encrypted, $\alpha \in L_1$, and $n := 2\lambda^2$. The encryption algorithm $\mathsf{Enc}_1^\mathsf{f}$ takes as input (α, m) and does the following steps.
  1. Compute a random secret sharing of m such that $m = m_1 \oplus \cdots \oplus m_n$.
  2. For $i \leftarrow 1, \ldots, n$ pick $x_i \xleftarrow{\$} S(\alpha)$ and compute $y_i \leftarrow f_\alpha(x_i)$.[7]
  3. For $i \leftarrow 1, \ldots, n$ parse x_i as $x_i^1 || \ldots || x_i^\lambda$, pick $j_i \xleftarrow{\$} \{1, \ldots, \lambda\}$ and compute $c_i \leftarrow m_i \oplus x_i^{j_i}$.
  4. Output $ct \leftarrow (j_i, y_i, c_i)_{i \in [n]}$.
- The algorithm $\mathsf{Dec}_1^\mathsf{f}$ takes as input α, r and a ciphertext ct_i, and executes the following steps.
  1. Compute $(\alpha, \mathsf{td}) \leftarrow \mathsf{Gen}(1^\lambda; r)$.
  2. Parse ct as $(j_i, y_i, c_i)_{i \in [n]}$.
  3. For $i = 1, \ldots, n$ compute $x_i \leftarrow \mathsf{Inv}(\alpha, \mathsf{td}, y_i)$, parse x_i as $x_i^1 || \ldots || x_i^n$ and compute $m_i \leftarrow c_i \oplus x_i^{j_i}$.
  4. Compute and output $m \leftarrow m_1 \oplus \cdots \oplus m_n$.

Theorem 4. $(\mathsf{Enc}_1^\mathsf{f}, \mathsf{Dec}_1^\mathsf{f})$ *is a secure black-box DWE scheme for the languages* (L_0, L_1) *with message space* $\{0, 1\}$.

We refer to the full version for the formal proof of the theorem. We note that to obtain a DWE secure scheme $(\mathsf{Enc}^\mathsf{f}, \mathsf{Dec}^\mathsf{f})$ for messages of length $\kappa \in \mathbb{N}$ we can just run κ parallel executions of $(\mathsf{Enc}_1^\mathsf{f}, \mathsf{Dec}_1^\mathsf{f})$.

---

[7] To not overburden the notation we use f_α instead of $\mathsf{Eval}(\alpha, \cdot)$ as the evaluation algorithm hereafter in the paper.

DWE for *or* Statements. For our OT constructions we use as a main tool a DWE for the languages (L_0^{2f}, L_1^{2f}) where $L_0^{2f} := \{\alpha_0, \alpha_1 : |C(f_{\alpha_0})| \geq 2^{-1}|D_{\alpha_0}|$ or $|C(f_{\alpha_1})| \geq 2^{-1}|D_{\alpha_1}|\}$ and $L_1^{2f} = \{\alpha_0, \alpha_1 : (\alpha_0, \mathsf{td}_0) \leftarrow \mathsf{Gen}(1^\lambda; r_0)$ and $(\alpha_1, \mathsf{td}_1) \leftarrow \mathsf{Gen}(1^\lambda; r_1), r_0, r_1 \in \{0,1\}^\lambda\}$. (we recall that we denote with $C(f_\alpha)$ the collision set of the function indexed by α). Informally, we require the semantic security of the encryption scheme to hold if *at least one* of the functions used as a part of the public-key has a collision set of subexponential size. Our scheme $(\mathsf{Enc}^{2f}, \mathsf{Dec}^{2f})$ works as follows.

- The encryption algorithm Enc^{2f} on input $x := (\alpha_0, \alpha_1)$ and the message to be encrypted $m \in \{0,1\}^\kappa$ does the following steps.
  1. Run Enc^f on input α_0 and m thus obtaining ct_0.
  2. Run Enc^f on input α_1 and ct thus obtaining ct_1 and output ct_1
- The decryption algorithm Dec^{2f} on input $x := (\alpha_0, \alpha_1)$, the witness $w := (r_0, r_1)$ and the ciphertext ct_1, executes the following steps.
  1. Compute $(\alpha_0, \mathsf{td}_0) \leftarrow \mathsf{Gen}(1^\lambda; r_0)$ and $(\alpha_1, \mathsf{td}_1) \leftarrow \mathsf{Gen}(1^\lambda; r_1)$.
  2. Run Dec^f on input α_1, r_1, ct_1 and td_1 thus obtaining ct_0.
  3. Run Dec^f on input α_0, r_0 ct_0 and td_0 thus obtaining m and output m.

Theorem 5. $(\mathsf{Enc}^{2f}, \mathsf{Dec}^{2f})$ *is a black-box DWE scheme for the languages* (L_0^{2f}, L_1^{2f}) *with message space* $\{0,1\}^\kappa$.

The proof in this case follow via standard hybrid arguments.

6 *Almost Secure* OT Protocol

In this section we show how to obtain a protocol $\Pi_{\mathcal{OT}} = (S_{\mathcal{OT}}, R_{\mathcal{OT}})$ that securely realizes $F_{\mathcal{OT}}$ with one-sided simulation against any *weak* adversarial sender $S_{\mathcal{OT}}^\star$. Informally, we show that if the malicious sender $S_{\mathcal{OT}}^\star$ samples the trapdoor permutations used in the protocol in some particular ways then $\Pi_{\mathcal{OT}}$ is secure, otherwise we give no security guarantees. At a very high level our protocol works like the four-round one-side simulatable OT protocol proposed in [35]. As highlighted in the Introduction, in the ORS protocol the sender sends a trapdoor permutation f in the second round which is used by the receiver to compute the third round. In case that f is non-injective then a malicious sender, by just inspecting the third round sent by the receiver, could extract the receiver's input. In our protocol we try to avoid this attack by modifying the ORS protocol in two aspects: 1) the sender sends two trapdoor functions[8] in the first round and 2) the receiver samples a random bit to decide which function to use to run ORS and which function to use to run DWE scheme Π. Π is a DWE scheme that guarantees security if the trapdoor function used for the encryption has a lot of collisions, and it is used by the receiver to encrypt the third round of ORS. Unfortunately we cannot prove that this OT protocol is (in general) secure, but we can prove that it is secure if one of the following cases occurs.

---

[8] We need to send two pairs of functions, but for now we omit this since it is a technical detail that will be helpful in the security proof.

1. The malicious sender uses functions that are almost permutation. This comes with no surprise since in this case an execution of $\Pi_{\mathcal{OT}}$ looks like an execution of the ORS protocol.
2. The malicious sender uses functions that have a lot of collisions (exponentially many). In this case the security of the DWE scheme kicks in protecting all the information that are related to the ORS protocol that depends on the TDPs (i.e., the information that could leak the receiver's bit when the functions sampled by the sender are non-injective).

Despite this limitation, in Sect. 7 we show that the security enjoyed by $\Pi_{\mathcal{OT}}$ is (surprisingly) enough to obtain a secure OT protocol. We now provide a more detailed description of $\Pi_{\mathcal{OT}}$ and prove formally its *weak* security in the case of malicious sender. Moreover, we show that $\Pi_{\mathcal{OT}}$ is secure against any PPT adversarial receiver under the standard simulation base security notion.

To construct $\Pi_{\mathcal{OT}}$ we make use of the following tools.

1. A commit-and-open protocol $\Pi_{\mathsf{c\&o}} := (\mathsf{P}_0, \mathsf{P}_1, \mathsf{V}_0, \mathsf{V}_1)$.
2. An enhanced trapdoor permutation with efficiently sampleable range and domain $\mathcal{F} := (\mathsf{Gen}, S, S_{DR}, f, f^{-1})$[9] with hard-core predicate h and domain (and range) of size 2^λ.
3. The DWE scheme $(\mathsf{Enc}^{2\mathsf{f}}, \mathsf{Dec}^{2\mathsf{f}})$ for the languages $(L_0^{2\mathsf{f}}, L_1^{2\mathsf{f}})$ described in Sect. 5.

We now give an informal description of our protocol and refer to Fig. 2 for the formal description.

Let $b \in \{0,1\}$ be the input of $R_{\mathcal{OT}}$ and $l_0, l_1 \in \{0,1\}$ be the input of $S_{\mathcal{OT}}$.

In the **first round** $R_{\mathcal{OT}}$ runs P_0 on input a string $r_{1-b} \xleftarrow{\$} \{0,1\}^\lambda$ thus obtaining the first round of the commit-and-open protocol $\Pi_{\mathsf{c\&o}}$.

In the **second round** $S_{\mathcal{OT}}$ picks a pair of random strings and samples four trapdoor permutations. That is, $S_{\mathcal{OT}}$ picks $R_0 \xleftarrow{\$} \{0,1\}^\lambda$, $R_1 \xleftarrow{\$} \{0,1\}^\lambda$, and for all $i,j \in \{0,1\}$ samples $\rho_{i,j} \xleftarrow{\$} \{0,1\}^\lambda$, computes $(f_{i,j}, f_{i,j}^{-1}) \xleftarrow{\$} \mathsf{Gen}(1^\lambda, \rho_{i,j})$. Then $S_{\mathcal{OT}}$ runs V_0 thus obtaining γ and sends $\{f_{i,j}\}_{i,j \in \{0,1\}}, \beta, R_0, R_1$ to $R_{\mathcal{OT}}$.

In the **third round** $R_{\mathcal{OT}}$ chooses a bit d and computes $(z', r') \xleftarrow{\$} S_{DR}(f_{\mathsf{d},b})$ and $r_b \leftarrow r' \oplus R_b$. Then $R_{\mathcal{OT}}$ computes the third round δ of $\Pi_{\mathsf{c\&o}}$ to open the commitment to the messages r_{1-b} (that is fixed in the first round) and r_b by running P_1 on input α, β, γ and r_b. In the end, $R_{\mathcal{OT}}$ encrypts the opening of $\Pi_{\mathsf{c\&o}}$ using the DWE scheme on input $(f_{1-\mathsf{d},0}, f_{1-\mathsf{d},1})$ and the message $\delta||r_0||r_1$ thus obtaining c and sends (c, d) to $S_{\mathcal{OT}}$.

In the **fourth round** $S_{\mathcal{OT}}$ decrypts c using the witness $\rho_{1-\mathsf{d},0}$ and $\rho_{1-\mathsf{d},1}$, thus obtaining the opening information of $\Pi_{\mathsf{c\&o}}$ represented by δ, r_0 and r_1. Then $S_{\mathcal{OT}}$ checks if (δ, r_0, r_1) represents a valid opening for $\Pi_{\mathsf{c\&o}}$ by running

---

[9] For convenience, we drop $(\mathsf{Eval}(\alpha, \cdot), \mathsf{Inv}(\alpha, \cdot))$ from the notation, and write $f(\cdot)$, $f^{-1}(\cdot)$ to denote algorithms $\mathsf{Eval}(f_\alpha, \cdot)$, $\mathsf{Inv}(f_\alpha, \mathsf{td}, \cdot)$ respectively, when f_α and td are clear from the context. We also use the function f_α instead of the index α as input of the algorithm S and S_{DR}.

V_1. If it is not, then $S_{\mathcal{O}T}$ stops and outputs $\bot$, otherwise she computes $\omega_0 \leftarrow f_{d,0}^{-1}(S(f_{d,0}, r_0 \oplus R_0))$ and $\omega_1 \leftarrow f_{d,1}^{-1}(S(f_{d,1}, r_1 \oplus R_1))$. Then for $j = 0, 1$, $S_{\mathcal{O}T}$ encrypts the input l_j via one-time pad using as a key the output of the hard-core predicate of $f_{d,j}$ on input ω_j thus obtaining W_j. $S_{\mathcal{O}T}$ then sends (W_0, W_1) to $R_{\mathcal{O}T}$ and stops.

In the **output phase**, $R_{\mathcal{O}T}$ computes and outputs $l_b = W_b^1 \oplus h(f_{d,b}, z_1')$.

In Fig. 2 we propose a formal description of the protocol.

Theorem 6. *If $\mathcal{F}$ is family of enhanced trapdoor permutations then for every non-uniform* PPT *adversary $R^\star$ controlling the receiver in the real model, there exists a non-uniform* PPT *adversary* Sim *for the ideal model such that* $\{\mathsf{REAL}_{\Pi_{\mathcal{O}T}, R_{\mathcal{O}T}^\star(z)}(1^\lambda)\}_{z \in \{0,1\}^\lambda} \approx \mathsf{IDEAL}_{F_{\mathcal{O}T}, \mathsf{Sim}(z)}(1^\lambda)\}_{z \in \{0,1\}^\lambda}.$[10]

We refer to the full version for the formal proof of the theorem.

Theorem 7. *For every non-uniform* PPT *adversary $S_{\mathcal{O}T}^\star$ controlling the sender, if one of the following holds with overwhelming probability*

1. $f_{0,0}$ *and* $f_{0,1}$ *and* $f_{1,0}$ *and* $f_{1,1}$ *are almost permutations or*
2. $(f_{0,0}, f_{0,1}) \in L_0^{2f}$ *and* $(f_{1,0}, f_{1,1}) \in L_0^{2f}$.

then $\{\mathsf{View}_{\Pi_{\mathcal{O}T}, S_{\mathcal{O}T}^\star(z)}^{R_{\mathcal{O}T}}(l_0, l_1, 0)\}_{z \in \{0,1\}^\star} \approx \{\mathsf{View}_{\Pi_{\mathcal{O}T}, S_{\mathcal{O}T}^\star(z)}^{R_{\mathcal{O}T}}(l_0, l_1, 1)\}_{z \in \{0,1\}^\star}$

We refer the reader to the full version for the formal proof of the theorem. In the full version we also prove the following lemma that will be helpful hereafter. Before stating the lemma, we introduce some additional notations. We say that a value $y \in Y$ is *good* if there exists and is unique a value x such that $f_\alpha(x) = y$. We now denote with $\mathsf{E_g}^i$ the event in which a randomly sampled element from the range of f_i is *good* and prove this additional lemma.

Lemma 1. *For every non-uniform* PPT *adversary $S_{\mathcal{O}T}^\star$ controlling the sender, if one of the following holds with overwhelming probability*

1. $\mathrm{Prob}\left[\mathsf{E_g}^{i,j}\right] \geq 1 - \nu(\lambda) \; \forall i, j \in \{0, 1\}$ *or*
2. $\mathrm{Prob}\left[\mathsf{E_g}^{0,0}\right] < 2^{-1}$ *or* $\mathrm{Prob}\left[\mathsf{E_g}^{0,1}\right] < 2^{-1}$ *and* $\mathrm{Prob}\left[\mathsf{E_g}^{1,0}\right] < 2^{-1}$ *or* $\mathrm{Prob}\left[\mathsf{E_g}^{1,1}\right] < 2^{-1}$

then $\{\mathsf{View}_{\Pi_{\mathcal{O}T}, S_{\mathcal{O}T}^\star(z)}^{R_{\mathcal{O}T}}(l_0, l_1, 0)\}_{z \in \{0,1\}^\star} \approx \{\mathsf{View}_{\Pi_{\mathcal{O}T}, S_{\mathcal{O}T}^\star(z)}^{R_{\mathcal{O}T}}(l_0, l_1, 1)\}_{z \in \{0,1\}^\star}$

7   Secure OT from Almost Secure OT

In Theorem 7 we have showed that $\Pi_{\mathcal{O}T} = (S_{\mathcal{O}T}, R_{\mathcal{O}T})$ guarantees that the input of the receiver is protected only in the case that at least one of the following properties holds:

1. $f_{0,0}$ and $f_{0,1}$ and $f_{1,0}$ and $f_{1,1}$ are almost permutations or

---

[10] We refer to Sect. 3.3 for a formal definition of $\mathsf{REAL}_{\Pi_{\mathcal{O}T}, R_{\mathcal{O}T}^\star(z)}$ and $\mathsf{IDEAL}_{F_{\mathcal{O}T}, \mathsf{Sim}(z)}$.

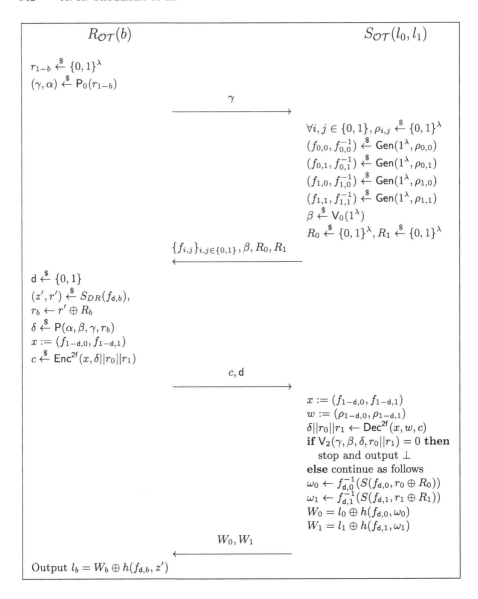

Fig. 2. Description of $\Pi_{\mathcal{OT}}$.

2. $(f_{0,0}, f_{0,1}) \in L_0^{2f}$ and $(f_{1,0}, f_{1,1}) \in L_0^{2f}$.

Moreover, Theorem 6 guarantees $\Pi_{\mathcal{OT}}$ is secure against malicious receivers. In this section we show that the above property is sufficient to obtain a one-sided simulatable OT by means of a compiler that takes as input $\Pi_{\mathcal{OT}}$ and outputs a one-sided simulatable OT. Our compiler is inspired by the work of [27]. In this the authors show how to combine k OTs (that we call OT candidates) to obtain an OT protocol that is secure against malicious sender even if $k - 1$ of the OT candidates are insecure against malicious senders[11]. At a very high level the construction proposed in [27] works as follows. First Harnik et al. show a construction that works for $k = 2$ and then propose a generic compiler that transforms $(1, 2)$-combiner into a $(1, k)$-combiner. The $(1, 2)$-combiner works as follows. Consider two OT candidates $\Pi^0_{\mathcal{OT}}$ and $\Pi^1_{\mathcal{OT}}$. Let b be the input of the receiver and (l_0, l_1) be the input of the sender.

1. The sender chooses a random bit r
2. The receiver chooses random bits b_0, b_1 such that $b = b_0 \oplus b_1$.
3. The parties run $\Pi^0_{\mathcal{OT}}$ where the receiver uses b_0 as input and the sender uses the pair $(r, r \oplus l_0 \oplus l_1)$. The parties also run $\Pi^1_{\mathcal{OT}}$ where the receiver uses b_1 as input and sender uses $(r \oplus l_0, r \oplus l_1)$
4. The receiver output corresponds to the XOR of his outputs in both executions.

To extend the above construction to the case where $k > 2$, Harnik et al. consider k OT candidates and organize them as leaves of a binary tree, and applies the construction proposed above to every internal node (in a bottom up fashion). Now, by the properties of the combiner, for every node that securely implements OT, its ancestor must also securely implement OT. The output of the whole tree must therefore also securely implement OT since the root is an ancestor to all leaves. If the running time of the above $(1, 2)$-combiner for malicious sender is m times that of its candidates, then the running time of the whole construction is $m^{\Omega(\log k)}$. Thus, in order for the running time to be polynomial, m must be a constant (which it is actually the case if we use the $(1, 2)$-combiner showed in this section). We now denote with $\Pi_{\overline{\mathcal{OT}}} = (S_{\overline{\mathcal{OT}}}, R_{\overline{\mathcal{OT}}})$ the protocol obtained by combining $4\lambda^2$ parallel executions of $\Pi_{\mathcal{OT}}$ as described above, we prove that $\Pi_{\overline{\mathcal{OT}}}$ is secure with one-sided simulation accordingly to Definition 6.

In our formal description we assume, without loss of generality, that the sender's (receiver's) algorithm of $\Pi_{\mathcal{OT}}$ to compute its first message takes as input the security parameter, the input and a message (if any), and returns an auxiliary input and the first message to be sent. To compute the message for the round i, the sender's (receiver's) algorithm takes as input the auxiliary input and all the messages that have been send and received up to that round, and returns the message to be send. We propose a formal description of $\Pi_{\overline{\mathcal{OT}}}$ in Fig. 3. To prove that $\Pi_{\overline{\mathcal{OT}}}$ is secure we cannot just rely on the security of the combiner since a malicious sender could sample the trapdoor functions in such a way that the security of all the OT executions is compromised. We show that this can happen only with negligible probability. We denote with $\Pi^i_{\mathcal{OT}}$ the i-th execution of $\Pi_{\mathcal{OT}}$ in a run of $\Pi_{\overline{\mathcal{OT}}}$. To denote the messages of $\Pi^i_{\mathcal{OT}}$ we extend the notation used in the description of $\Pi_{\mathcal{OT}}$ by writing m^i (or m_i) if m is a

---

[11] To prove our theorem we do not need a fully secure combiner. That is, we only need a combiner that guarantees security in the case that one execution of $\Pi_{\mathcal{OT}}$ is secure against malicious senders and all the executions of $\Pi_{\mathcal{OT}}$ are secure against malicious receivers.

Common input: Security parameters: $\lambda := 2^\kappa$ for some $k \in \mathbb{N}$, $n := 4\lambda^2$

Input to $R_{\overline{OT}}$: $b \in \{0,1\}$. **Input to $S_{\overline{OT}}$:** $l_0 \in \{0,1\}, l_1 \in \{0,1\}$.

   $R_{\overline{OT}} \to S_{\overline{OT}}$

    1. Run GB on input $(b, 1, \log(n))$ thus obtaining $b^1, \ldots, b^n$.

    2. For $i = 1, \ldots, n$ run R_{OT} on input 1^λ and b^i thus obtaining $(\mathsf{aux}_r^i, \mathsf{ot}_1^i)$.

    3. Send $\mathsf{ot}_1^1, \ldots, \mathsf{ot}_1^n$ to $S_{\overline{OT}}$

   $S_{\overline{OT}} \to R_{\overline{OT}}$

    1. Run GL on input $(l_0, l_1, i, \log(n))$ thus obtaining $(l_0^1, l_1^1), \ldots, (l_0^n, l_1^n)$.

    2. For $i = 1, \ldots, n$ run S_{OT} on input 1^λ, ot_1^i, $(\mathsf{aux}_s^i, l_0^i, l_1^i)$ thus obtaining ot_2^i.

    3. Send $\mathsf{ot}_2^1, \ldots, \mathsf{ot}_2^n$ to $R_{\overline{OT}}$.

   $R_{\overline{OT}} \to S_{\overline{OT}}$

    1. For $i = 1, \ldots, n$ run R_{OT} on input $(\mathsf{ot}_1^i, \mathsf{ot}_2^i, \mathsf{aux}_r^i)$ thus obtaining ot_3^i.

    2. Send $\mathsf{ot}_3^1, \ldots, \mathsf{ot}_3^n$ to $S_{\overline{OT}}$

   $S_{\overline{OT}} \to R_{\overline{OT}}$

    1. For $i = 1, \ldots, n$ run Π_{OT} on input $(\mathsf{ot}_1^i, \mathsf{ot}_2^i, \mathsf{ot}_3^i, \mathsf{aux}_s^i)$ thus obtaining ot_4^i.

    2. Send $\mathsf{ot}_4^1, \ldots, \mathsf{ot}_4^n$ to $R_{\overline{OT}}$.

Output Phase of $R_{\overline{OT}}$

   1. For $i = 1, \ldots, n$ run R_{OT} on input $(\mathsf{ot}_1^i, \mathsf{ot}_2^i, \mathsf{ot}_3^i, \mathsf{ot}_4^i)$ and aux_r^i thus obtaining $l_{b^i}^i$.

   2. Output $l_{b^1}^1 \oplus \cdots \oplus l_{b^n}^n$

$\mathsf{GB}(b, i, n)$

   Pick $r \xleftarrow{\$} \{0,1\}$, compute $b_0 \leftarrow b \oplus r$ and set $b_1 \leftarrow r$.

   If $i = n$ **then** return (b_0, b_1) **else** return $\mathsf{GB}(b_0, i+1, n), \mathsf{GB}(b_1, i+1, n)$.

$\mathsf{GL}((l_0, l_1), i, n)$

   Pick $r \xleftarrow{\$} \{0,1\}$, compute $l_{0,0} \leftarrow r$, $l_{0,1} \leftarrow r \oplus l_0 \oplus l_1$, $l_{1,0} \leftarrow r \oplus l_0$, $l_{1,1} \leftarrow r \oplus l_1$.

   If $i = n$ **then** return $(l_{0,0}, l_{0,1}), (l_{1,0}, l_{1,1})$

   else return $\mathsf{GL}((l_{0,0}, l_{0,1}), i+1, n), \mathsf{GL}((l_{1,0}, l_{1,1}), i+1, n)$.

Fig. 3. Formal description of $\Pi_{\overline{OT}}$

symbol used in the description of Π_{OT} (e.g., in the second round of Π_{OT}^i the sender sends $f_{0,0}^i, \ldots f_{1,1}^i, \beta^i, R_0^i, R_1^i$). At a high level the proof works in this way. If by contradiction all the OT executions are insecure this implies that in any of the OT executions the malicious sender sends the TDPs $(f_{0,0}^i, f_{0,1}^i, f_{1,0}^i, f_{1,1}^i)$ such that for all $p_i \in \{0,1\}$

1. if the instance $(f_{p_i,0}^i, f_{p_i,1}^i)$ is used to run the DWE scheme then hiding of the DWE would not hold and

2. if $(f^i_{1-p_i,0}, f^i_{1-p_i,1})$ are used to run the remaining computation of $\Pi^i_{\mathcal{OT}}$ then $\Pi^i_{\mathcal{OT}}$ would be insecure (i.e., $(f^i_{1-p_i,0}, f^i_{1-p_i,1})$ might not be injective).

This means that any OT executions $\Pi^i_{\mathcal{OT}}$ has a pair of TDPs $(f^i_{\mathsf{d}',0}, f^i_{\mathsf{d}',1})$ with $\mathsf{d}' \in \{0,1\}$ that are not injective and that have a collision set smaller than $2^{-1}|D_\alpha|$. However, we note that if $\mathsf{d}_i = \mathsf{d}'_i$ in a sufficiently large number of executions then we have that the there is an execution j where $r^j_0 \oplus R^j_0$ and $r^j_1 \oplus R^j_1$ are such that $y^j_0 \leftarrow S(f^j_{d_j,0}, r^j_0 \oplus R^j_0)$ and $y^j_1 \leftarrow S(f^j_{d_j,1}, r^j_1 \oplus R^j_1)$ have exactly one pre-image each with overwhelming probability. This would allow us to apply the Lemma 1 and state that $\Pi^i_{\mathcal{OT}}$ is secure. Then we can simply rely on the security of the combiner to claim that $\Pi_{\overline{\mathcal{OT}}}$ is secure. To argue that such a value j exists we use the fact that the receiver picks d_i randomly in $\{0,1\}$ for all $i \in \{1, \ldots, 4\lambda^2\}$.

Theorem 8. *If enhanced permutations with efficiently sampleable range and domain exist, then $\Pi_{\overline{\mathcal{OT}}}$ securely realizes the oblivious transfer functionality $F_{\mathcal{OT}}$ with one-sided simulation with black-box use of the underlying primitive.*

We refer to the full version for the proof of the theorem. The protocol $\Pi_{\overline{\mathcal{OT}}}$ described in this section restricts the sender to use two bits as input (bit-OT). In some applications (as the one that we are going to consider in this work) it is crucial that the sender input is represented by strings $l_0 \in \{0,1\}^\kappa, l_1 \in \{0,1\}^\kappa$ with $\kappa \in \mathbb{N}$ (string-OT). The work of Brassard et al. [4] proposes a way to construct an information theoretically secure string OT protocol from an information theoretically secure bit OT protocol. The idea proposed in [4] is to use run κ bit-OT executions in such a way that regardless of the choices of the input bits of malicious receivers in these executions, he can only obtain one of the two inputs. We show how to use the technique proposed in [4] to transform our bit-OT protocol $\Pi_{\overline{\mathcal{OT}}}$ into a string-OT protocol $\Pi^\kappa_{\overline{\mathcal{OT}}} := (S^\kappa_{\overline{\mathcal{OT}}}, R^\kappa_{\overline{\mathcal{OT}}})$. We refer the reader to the full version for the formal description of the protocol and its proof. We note that $\Pi^\kappa_{\overline{\mathcal{OT}}}$ can be easily run in parallel polynomial many times.

8 Black-Box Round Optimal 2PC

In [35, Sec. 3.2] the authors show how to obtain a fully simulatable OT protocol using in a black-box way: (parallel) one-sided simulatable OTs and one-to-one one-way functions. Using this result we can state the following theorem.

Theorem 9. *If enhanced trapdoor permutations with efficiently sampleable range and domain exist, then there exists a 4-round protocol $\mathcal{OT}$ that securely realizes the oblivious transfer functionality $F^m_{\mathcal{OT}}$ with black-box use of the underlying primitive.*

An immediate corollary from the above result, in conjunction with the work of [28] building a non-interactive secure two-party protocol in the OT-hybrid model is the following.

Corollary 2. *If enhanced trapdoor permutations with efficiently sampleable range/domain and one-to-one OWFs exist, then there exists a round optimal protocol that securely realizes any 2-party functionality with BB use of the primitives.*

Acknowledgments. Arka Rai Choudhuri is supported by NSF CNS-1814919, NSF CAREER 1942789, Johns Hopkins University Catalyst award, NSF CNS-1908181, Office of Naval Research N00014-19-1-2294.

Michele Ciampi has done part of this work while consulting for Stealth Software Technologies, Inc.

Vipul Goyal is supported in part by the NSF award 1916939, DARPA SIEVE program, a gift from Ripple, a DoE NETL award, a JP Morgan Faculty Fellowship, a PNC center for financial services innovation award, and a Cylab seed funding award.

Abhishek Jain is supported in part by an NSF CNS grant 1814919, NSF CAREER award 1942789, Johns Hopkins University Catalyst award and Office of Naval Research grant N00014-19-1-2294.

Rafail Ostrovsky is supported in part by DARPA under Cooperative Agreement HR0011-20-2-0025, NSF grant CNS-2001096, US-Israel BSF grant 2015782, Google Faculty Award, JP Morgan Faculty Award, IBM Faculty Research Award, Xerox Faculty Research Award, OKAWA Foundation Research Award, B. John Garrick Foundation Award, Teradata Research Award, Lockheed-Martin Research Award and Sunday Group. The views and conclusions contained herein are those of the authors and should not be interpreted as necessarily representing the official policies, either expressed or implied, of DARPA, the Department of Defense, or the U.S. Government. The U.S. Government is authorized to reproduce and distribute reprints for governmental purposes not withstanding any copyright annotation therein.

References

1. Bellare, M., Yung, M.: Certifying cryptographic tools: the case of trapdoor permutations. In: Brickell, E.F. (ed.) CRYPTO 1992. LNCS, vol. 740, pp. 442–460. Springer, Heidelberg (1993). https://doi.org/10.1007/3-540-48071-4_31
2. Ben-Or, M., Goldwasser, S., Wigderson, A.: Completeness theorems for non-cryptographic fault-tolerant distributed computation (extended abstract). In: 20th ACM STOC, pp. 1–10. ACM Press, May 1988. https://doi.org/10.1145/62212.62213
3. Benhamouda, F., Lin, H.: k-round multiparty computation from k-round oblivious transfer via garbled interactive circuits. In: Nielsen, J.B., Rijmen, V. (eds.) EUROCRYPT 2018, Part II. LNCS, vol. 10821, pp. 500–532. Springer, Cham (2018). https://doi.org/10.1007/978-3-319-78375-8_17
4. Brassard, G., Crépeau, C., Santha, M.: Oblivious transfers and intersecting codes. IEEE Trans. Inf. Theory **42**(6), 1769–1780 (1996). https://doi.org/10.1109/18.556673
5. Canetti, R., et al.: Fiat-Shamir: from practice to theory. In: Charikar, M., Cohen, E. (eds.) 51st ACM STOC, pp. 1082–1090. ACM Press, June 2019. https://doi.org/10.1145/3313276.3316380

6. Canetti, R., Lichtenberg, A.: Certifying trapdoor permutations, revisited. In: Beimel, A., Dziembowski, S. (eds.) TCC 2018, Part I. LNCS, vol. 11239, pp. 476–506. Springer, Cham (2018). https://doi.org/10.1007/978-3-030-03807-6_18

7. Chailloux, A., Ciocan, D.F., Kerenidis, I., Vadhan, S.: Interactive and noninteractive zero knowledge are equivalent in the help model. In: Canetti, R. (ed.) TCC 2008. LNCS, vol. 4948, pp. 501–534. Springer, Heidelberg (2008). https://doi.org/10.1007/978-3-540-78524-8_28

8. Chaum, D., Crépeau, C., Damgård, I.: Multiparty unconditionally secure protocols (extended abstract). In: 20th ACM STOC, pp. 11–19. ACM Press, May 1988. https://doi.org/10.1145/62212.62214

9. Rai Choudhuri, A., Ciampi, M., Goyal, V., Jain, A., Ostrovsky, R.: Round optimal secure multiparty computation from minimal assumptions. In: Pass, R., Pietrzak, K. (eds.) TCC 2020, Part II. LNCS, vol. 12551, pp. 291–319. Springer, Cham (2020). https://doi.org/10.1007/978-3-030-64378-2_11

10. Ciampi, M., Ostrovsky, R., Siniscalchi, L., Visconti, I.: Round-optimal secure two-party computation from trapdoor permutations. In: Kalai, Y., Reyzin, L. (eds.) TCC 2017, Part I. LNCS, vol. 10677, pp. 678–710. Springer, Cham (2017). https://doi.org/10.1007/978-3-319-70500-2_23

11. Ciampi, M., Parisella, R., Venturi, D.: On adaptive security of delayed-input sigma protocols and Fiat-Shamir NIZKs. In: Galdi, C., Kolesnikov, V. (eds.) SCN 2020. LNCS, vol. 12238, pp. 670–690. Springer, Cham (2020). https://doi.org/10.1007/978-3-030-57990-6_33

12. Damgård, I., Nielsen, J.B., Polychroniadou, A., Raskin, M.: On the communication required for unconditionally secure multiplication. In: Robshaw, M., Katz, J. (eds.) CRYPTO 2016, Part II. LNCS, vol. 9815, pp. 459–488. Springer, Heidelberg (2016). https://doi.org/10.1007/978-3-662-53008-5_16

13. Even, S., Goldreich, O., Lempel, A.: A randomized protocol for signing contracts. In: Chaum, D., Rivest, R.L., Sherman, A.T. (eds.) CRYPTO 1982, pp. 205–210. Plenum Press, New York (1982)

14. Feige, U., Lapidot, D., Shamir, A.: Multiple non-interactive zero knowledge proofs based on a single random string (extended abstract). In: 31st FOCS. pp. 308–317. IEEE Computer Society Press, October 1990. https://doi.org/10.1109/FSCS.1990.89549

15. Friolo, D., Masny, D., Venturi, D.: A black-box construction of fully-simulatable, round-optimal oblivious transfer from strongly uniform key agreement. In: Hofheinz, D., Rosen, A. (eds.) TCC 2019. LNCS, vol. 11891, pp. 111–130. Springer, Cham (2019). https://doi.org/10.1007/978-3-030-36030-6_5 https://eprint.iacr.org/2018/473

16. Garg, S., Mukherjee, P., Pandey, O., Polychroniadou, A.: The exact round complexity of secure computation. In: Fischlin, M., Coron, J.-S. (eds.) EUROCRYPT 2016, Part II. LNCS, vol. 9666, pp. 448–476. Springer, Heidelberg (2016). https://doi.org/10.1007/978-3-662-49896-5_16

17. Garg, S., Ostrovsky, R., Visconti, I., Wadia, A.: Resettable statistical zero knowledge. In: Cramer, R. (ed.) TCC 2012. LNCS, vol. 7194, pp. 494–511. Springer, Heidelberg (2012). https://doi.org/10.1007/978-3-642-28914-9_28

18. Goldberg, S., Reyzin, L., Sagga, O., Baldimtsi, F.: Efficient noninteractive certification of RSA moduli and beyond. In: Galbraith, S.D., Moriai, S. (eds.) ASIACRYPT 2019, Part III. LNCS, vol. 11923, pp. 700–727. Springer, Cham (2019). https://doi.org/10.1007/978-3-030-34618-8_24

19. Goldreich, O.: Foundations of Cryptography: Basic Applications, vol. 2. Cambridge University Press, Cambridge (2004)

20. Goldreich, O.: Computational complexity: a conceptual perspective. SIGACT News **39**(3), 35–39 (2008). https://doi.org/10.1145/1412700.1412710

21. Goldreich, O.: Basing non-interactive zero-knowledge on (enhanced) trapdoor permutations: the state of the art (2011)

22. Goldreich, O., Oren, Y.: Definitions and properties of zero-knowledge proof systems. J. Cryptol. **7**(1), 1–32 (1994). https://doi.org/10.1007/BF00195207

23. Goldreich, O., Rothblum, R.D.: Enhancements of trapdoor permutations. J. Cryptol. **26**(3), 484–512 (2013). https://doi.org/10.1007/s00145-012-9131-8

24. Goldwasser, S., Micali, S., Rackoff, C.: The knowledge complexity of interactive proof-systems (extended abstract). In: 17th ACM STOC, pp. 291–304. ACM Press, May 1985. https://doi.org/10.1145/22145.22178

25. Goldwasser, S., Micali, S., Rackoff, C.: The knowledge complexity of interactive proof systems. SIAM J. Comput. **18**(1), 186–208 (1989). https://doi.org/10.1137/0218012

26. Haitner, I.: Implementing oblivious transfer using collection of dense trapdoor permutations. In: Naor, M. (ed.) TCC 2004. LNCS, vol. 2951, pp. 394–409. Springer, Heidelberg (2004). https://doi.org/10.1007/978-3-540-24638-1_22

27. Harnik, D., Kilian, J., Naor, M., Reingold, O., Rosen, A.: On robust combiners for oblivious transfer and other primitives. In: Cramer, R. (ed.) EUROCRYPT 2005. LNCS, vol. 3494, pp. 96–113. Springer, Heidelberg (2005). https://doi.org/10.1007/11426639_6

28. Ishai, Y., Kushilevitz, E., Ostrovsky, R., Prabhakaran, M., Sahai, A.: Efficient non-interactive secure computation. In: Paterson, K.G. (ed.) EUROCRYPT 2011. LNCS, vol. 6632, pp. 406–425. Springer, Heidelberg (2011). https://doi.org/10.1007/978-3-642-20465-4_23

29. Kakvi, S.A., Kiltz, E., May, A.: Certifying RSA. In: Wang, X., Sako, K. (eds.) ASIACRYPT 2012. LNCS, vol. 7658, pp. 404–414. Springer, Heidelberg (2012). https://doi.org/10.1007/978-3-642-34961-4_25

30. Katz, J., Ostrovsky, R.: Round-optimal secure two-party computation. In: Franklin, M. (ed.) CRYPTO 2004. LNCS, vol. 3152, pp. 335–354. Springer, Heidelberg (2004). https://doi.org/10.1007/978-3-540-28628-8_21

31. Kilian, J.: Founding cryptography on oblivious transfer. In: 20th ACM STOC, pp. 20–31. ACM Press, May 1988. https://doi.org/10.1145/62212.62215

32. Kilian, J.: A note on efficient zero-knowledge proofs and arguments (extended abstract). In: 24th ACM STOC, pp. 723–732. ACM Press, May 1992. https://doi.org/10.1145/129712.129782

33. Lindell, Y.: Parallel coin-tossing and constant-round secure two-party computation. In: Kilian, J. (ed.) CRYPTO 2001. LNCS, vol. 2139, pp. 171–189. Springer, Heidelberg (2001). https://doi.org/10.1007/3-540-44647-8_10

34. Naor, M., Pinkas, B.: Efficient oblivious transfer protocols. In: Kosaraju, S.R. (ed.) 12th SODA, pp. 448–457. ACM-SIAM, January 2001

35. Ostrovsky, R., Richelson, S., Scafuro, A.: Round-optimal black-box two-party computation. In: Gennaro, R., Robshaw, M. (eds.) CRYPTO 2015, Part II. LNCS, vol. 9216, pp. 339–358. Springer, Heidelberg (2015). https://doi.org/10.1007/978-3-662-48000-7_17

36. Ostrovsky, R., Venkatesan, R., Yung, M.: Fair games against an all-powerful adversary. In: Cai, J. (ed.) Advances in Computational Complexity Theory, Proceedings of a DIMACS Workshop, New Jersey, USA, 3–7 December 1990. DIMACS Series in Discrete Mathematics and Theoretical Computer Science, vol. 13, pp. 155–169. DIMACS/AMS (1990). https://doi.org/10.1090/dimacs/013/09

37. Peikert, C., Vaikuntanathan, V., Waters, B.: A framework for efficient and composable oblivious transfer. In: Wagner, D. (ed.) CRYPTO 2008. LNCS, vol. 5157, pp. 554–571. Springer, Heidelberg (2008). https://doi.org/10.1007/978-3-540-85174-5_31

38. Rabin, M.O.: Digital signatures and public key functions as intractable as factorization. Technical report MIT/LCS/TR-212, Massachusetts Institute of Technology, January 1979

39. Rothblum, R.: A taxonomy of enhanced trapdoor permutations. Electron. Colloq. Comput. Complex. (ECCC) **17**, 145 (2010). http://eccc.hpi-web.de/report/2010/145

40. Yao, A.C.C.: Protocols for secure computations (extended abstract). In: 23rd FOCS, pp. 160–164. IEEE Computer Society Press, November 1982. https://doi.org/10.1109/SFCS.1982.38

41. Yao, A.C.C.: How to generate and exchange secrets (extended abstract). In: 27th FOCS, pp. 162–167. IEEE Computer Society Press, October 1986. https://doi.org/10.1109/SFCS.1986.25

The Cost of Adaptivity in Security Games on Graphs

Chethan Kamath[1], Karen Klein[2(✉)], Krzysztof Pietrzak[3], and Michael Walter[4]

[1] Tel Aviv University, Tel Aviv-Yafo, Israel
[2] ETH Zurich, Zürich, Switzerland
[3] IST Austria, Klosterneuburg, Austria
pietrzak@ist.ac.at
[4] Zama, Paris, France
michael.walter@zama.ai

Abstract. The security of cryptographic primitives and protocols against adversaries that are allowed to make adaptive choices (e.g., which parties to corrupt or which queries to make) is notoriously difficult to establish. A broad theoretical framework was introduced by Jafargholi et al. [Crypto'17] for this purpose. In this paper we initiate the study of lower bounds on loss in adaptive security for certain cryptographic protocols considered in the framework. We prove lower bounds that almost match the upper bounds (proven using the framework) for proxy re-encryption, prefix-constrained PRFs and generalized selective decryption, a security game that captures the security of certain group messaging and broadcast encryption schemes. Those primitives have in common that their security game involves an underlying graph that can be adaptively built by the adversary.

Some of our lower bounds only apply to a restricted class of black-box reductions which we term "oblivious" (the existing upper bounds are of this restricted type), some apply to the broader but still restricted class of non-rewinding reductions, while our lower bound for proxy re-encryption applies to all black-box reductions. The fact that some of our lower bounds seem to crucially rely on obliviousness or at least a non-rewinding reduction hints to the exciting possibility that the existing upper bounds can be improved by using more sophisticated reductions. Our main conceptual contribution is a two-player multi-stage game called the Builder-Pebbler Game. We can translate bounds on the winning

C. Kamath—Supported by Azrieli International Postdoctoral Fellowship. Most of the work was done while the author was at Northeastern University and Charles University, funded by the IARPA grant IARPA/2019-19-020700009 and project PRIMUS/17/SCI/9, respectively.

K. Klein—Supported in part by ERC CoG grant 724307. Most of the work was done while the author was at IST Austria funded by the European Research Council (ERC) under the European Union's Horizon 2020 research and innovation programme (682815 - TOCNeT).

K. Pietrzak—Funded by the European Research Council (ERC) under the European Union's Horizon 2020 research and innovation programme (682815 - TOCNeT).

K. Nissim and B. Waters (Eds.): TCC 2021, LNCS 13043, pp. 550–581, 2021.
https://doi.org/10.1007/978-3-030-90453-1_19

probabilities for various instantiations of this game into cryptographic lower bounds for the above-mentioned primitives using oracle separation techniques.

1 Introduction

Consider the following game played between a challenger C and an adversary A using a symmetric-key encryption (SKE) scheme $(\mathsf{Enc}, \mathsf{Dec})$. The challenger first samples, independently and uniformly at random, N keys $\mathsf{k}_1, \ldots, \mathsf{k}_N$. These correspond to users $U_1, \ldots, U_N$ respectively. The adversary A is now allowed to *adaptively* make two types of queries:

1. Ask for an encryption of k_j under the key k_i to obtain $\mathsf{Enc}(\mathsf{k}_i, \mathsf{k}_j)$, or
2. Corrupt a user U_i to obtain the key k_i.

At the end of the game, A challenges C on a user U_{i^*} and is given either the real key k_{i^*} or an independent, random key r. A wins this "real or random game" if it correctly guesses which of the two it got. If no efficient A can win with probability higher than $1/2 + \epsilon$ we say the protocol is 2ϵ secure.

The above game can be thought of as the adversary A adaptively building a "key-graph" $G = (\mathcal{V}, \mathcal{E})$, where the vertices $\mathcal{V} = \{1, \ldots, N\}$ correspond to the users and their keys, whereas the (directed) edges $\mathcal{E}$ correspond to the encryption queries that A makes: a directed edge (i, j) is added to $\mathcal{E}$ if A requests the encryption of k_j under the key k_i. Note that for i^* to be a non-trivial challenge, i^* must be a sink and must *not* be reachable (in the graph-theoretic sense) from any of the corrupted vertices—otherwise, A can simply decrypt the ciphertexts along the path from any corrupted node to the challenge to learn k_{i^*}.

The above game is called *generalised selective decryption* (GSD) and it captures the security of protocols for multicast encryption [43] and continuous group key agreements (CGKA) [1,2]. We will use GSD in this introduction as the running example to convey our ideas. The main question regarding GSD is whether the security of this game (given that the key-graph is *acyclic*) can be based on the IND-CPA security of the underlying SKE.[1] For this we need to prove a computational soundness (i.e., security) theorem of the form: if the SKE is ϵ-secure then the GSD game is ϵ'-secure for some ϵ' that depends on ϵ. Ideally, the loss of security should be kept to a polynomial, i.e., $\epsilon' = \epsilon \cdot \mathbf{poly}(N)$. Otherwise, this requires to either set the security parameter of the underlying SKE very large if one wants to maintain provable security guarantees, which will lead to inefficiency. Or the provided security is only heuristic, leaving the possibility of an attack against GSD which does not break the underlying SKE.

---

[1] In case the key-graph contains cycles, one must additionally assume that the SKE is key-dependent message (KDM) secure [7]. Such problems are of a different flavour and we don't deal with them. As mentioned before, the GSD game is typically used to capture the security of protocols where the acyclicity is enforced by the protocol rules.

The simpler task of proving a soundness theorem in case the adversary is *selective*, in the sense that it commits to its queries (and thus the key-graph G) at the beginning of the GSD game, is relatively straightforward to achieve. If the graph is known ahead of time, it is easy to construct a series of $O(N^2)$ hybrids, each of which can be shown indistinguishable under the security of the SKE (see, e.g., [31]). The study of adaptive security of GSD, where the key-graph is unknown at the beginning of the game and is only gradually revealed during the query phase, was initiated in [43] and remains notoriously hard. In particular, non-trivial results are only known in settings, where the adversary is restricted to query (subgraphs of) specific key-graphs (which needs to be enforced by the higher level protocol). The state of the art is represented by the general Piecewise-Guessing framework [31,38].

1.1   Our Results

The Piecewise-Guessing Framework has been successfully used to give improved security guarantees against adaptive attacks for various applications [1,2,20, 35,38], but there still are significant gaps to knows attacks. In this paper we approach this question from the other "lower bounds" direction, and for several applications show that this will not be possible, at least not when using existing techniques. In particular, (in the full version [33] of this paper) we show that there do not exist efficient non-rewinding black-box reductions – henceforth called "straight-line" reductions for brevity – that prove security of

- certain forms of restricted GSD (including its public key variant) based on the IND-CPA security of the underlying SKE (see Sect. 6),
- popular protocols for CGKA based on the IND-CPA security of the underlying public-key encryption (PKE) (see full version [33, Section 7]),
- the GGM construction for prefix-constrained PRFs based on the pseudorandomness of the underlying PRG (see Sect. 7)
- proxy re-encryption[2] (PRE) schemes [8] based on the IND-CPA security of the PKE and N-weak key privacy (see full version [33, Section 9])

with only polynomial loss in advantage. For PRE we can even rule out general (i.e., rewinding) black-box reductions. For the theorem statements of the latter three results, we refer to the corresponding sections, but we will discuss GSD in a little more detail, so we provide an informal statement here.

Theorem 1 (Informally Stated, Corollary 1). *Any straight-line reduction proving security of unrestricted adaptive GSD based on the IND-CPA security of the underlying SKE scheme loses at least a factor that is* super-polynomial $(N^{\Omega(\log N)})$ *in the number of users N.*

---

[2] A proxy re-encryption scheme is a public-key encryption scheme that allows the holder of a key pk to derive a re-encryption key for any other key pk'. This re-encryption key lets anyone transform ciphertexts under pk into ciphertexts under pk' without having to know the underlying message.

Table 1. Summary of lower bounds on the loss in security established in our work. $N = 2^n$ denotes the size of the graph. Therefore, in the case of GGM constrained PRF, n denotes the length of the input string. For TreeKEM, M denotes the number of users and Q refers to the number of queries allowed to the adversary.

Application	Underlying graph	Lower bound	Reduction	Upper bound
GSD	Path P_N	$N^{\Omega \log(N)}$	Oblivious	$N^{O \log(N)}$ [19]
	Rooted binary in-tree B_n	$N^{\Omega \log(N)}$	Oblivious	$N^{O \log(N)}$ [43]
	Tree[a]	$N^{\Omega \log(N)}$	Straight-line	$N^{O \log(N)}$ [19]
	Arbitrary DAG	$2^{\Omega \sqrt{N}}$	Oblivious	$N^{O N / \log(N)}$ [31]
PRE	Path P_N	$N^{\Omega \log(N)}$	Oblivious	$N^{O \log(N)}$ [20]
	Binary Tree B_n	$N^{\Omega \log(N)}$	Oblivious	$N^{O \log(N)}$ [20]
	Arbitrary DAG	$2^{\Omega N}$	Arbitrary	$N^{O N / \log(N)}$ [20]
GGM CPRF	Tree	$n^{\Omega \log(n)}$	Straight-line	$n^{O \log(n)}$ [21]
TreeKEM	Regular Tree	$M^{\Omega \log(\log(M))}$	Straight-line	$Q^{O \log(M)}$ [1]

[a]Recall that a tree does not necessarily have to be rooted, so this includes any DAG such that the corresponding undirected graph does not contain any cycles.

For the proof we rely heavily on the adversary's freedom to query arbitrary directed acyclic graphs (DAG). (Actually, the graphs have some structure and so certain conditions may be imposed on it but these restrictions are very weak.) In many applications however, the adversary is much more restricted in terms of the graphs it can query, e.g. in protocols for multicast encryption like logical key hierarchies (LKH) [13,51,52], and hence our bound does not apply. However, for a certain sub-class of straight-line reductions, which we term "oblivious" (see discussion below), we obtain results for such applications. These results show that the upper bounds for GSD given in [31], which are oblivious, are essentially tight and can only be improved by exploiting new non-oblivious techniques (and similarly for the bounds for PRE given in [20]), as stated informally below.

Theorem 2 (Informally Stated, Corollaries 2 to 4 in Full Version [33]). *Any oblivious reduction proving security of adaptive GSD restricted to* paths *or binary trees based on the IND-CPA security of the underlying SKE scheme loses a factor that is* super-polynomial *($N^{\Omega(\log N)}$) in the number of users N; for unrestricted GSD the loss is* sub-exponential *($2^{\Omega(\sqrt{N})}$).*

Our results for PRE have a similar flavor, but are even stronger, since in this case the reduction is naturally more restricted. A summary of the results can be found in Table 1.

The common thread to the applications we consider is that their security game can be abstracted out by a two-player multi-stage game which we call the "Builder-Pebbler Game". We are unable to establish lower bounds for other applications of the Piecewise-Guessing Framework (e.g., computational secret sharing or garbling circuits) as their security model is not quite captured by the Builder-Pebbler Game. The high level reason for this is that the graphs (e.g., the circuit to be garbled or the access structure) in these applications is fixed ahead of the time and the adaptivity comes from other sources (e.g., choice of garbling input or targeted user). Therefore we would require other combinatorial abstractions to establish lower bounds for them. In fact, building on the high level ideas introduced in this work, [34] showed lower bounds for adaptive security of Yao's garbling (see Sect. 1.2.2 for a comparison). We defer the discussion on the Builder-Pebbler Game to the next section (Sect. 2.2) and explain informally what we mean by oblivious reductions next, mostly from the perspective of GSD. We will then argue that this comprises a natural class of reductions.

Oblivious Reductions. Oblivious reductions are a certain class of black-box reductions and our definition is motivated by the reductions in [31]. On a high level, the behaviour of an oblivious reduction is "independent" of the adversary's behaviour throughout the simulation of the security game. To see what we mean by this, let's return to the example of GSD. A reduction (simulating some consecutive hybrids) can decide to answer an encryption query issued by the adversary either with a consistent or an inconsistent ciphertext (let's ignore the challenge ciphertext for the moment). In particular, it has total control over the number of inconsistencies in the final simulation (assuming it knows the number of queries the adversary will make). However, as the key-graph is only gradually revealed to the reduction, it doesn't know where the edge (representing the encryption query) will end up within the key-graph. We call a GSD reduction *oblivious* if it does not make use of the partial graph structure it learns during the game but rather sticks to some strategy that is independent of the history of the adversary's queries. There are several ways one could formalise this: for example, one could require the reduction as initially "committing" to which queries it will answer inconsistently. However, this does not mean that for all queries it has to commit to its decision, but rather commit to some minimal description of the edges it intends to respond inconsistently to. In order to capture as many reductions as possible (while still being able to prove lower bounds), we ended up defining them as reductions which commit to a minimal set of nodes which *covers* all inconsistent edges, i.e., a minimal *vertex cover*.[3] For example in the case of graphs of high indegree, clearly, guessing the set of sinks of inconsistent edges gives a much more succinct representation. A formal definition of an oblivious GSD reduction is given in the full version [33, Definition 21]; the corresponding definition for PREs is given in the full version [33, Definition 34].

Why Oblivious Reductions? We note that oblivious reductions are a quite natural notion, since they can easily be defined uniformly for all adversaries. Not surprisingly, they encompass some of the key reductions in the literature. Beside the reductions proposed and analysed in [31] (and its follow-up works), partitioning-based reductions, which have been successfully employed in a plethora of works [15], also roughly behave in an oblivious manner.[4] Moreover,

---

[3] Technically, we do not require *minimal* vertex cover, but a weaker notion which we call "non-trivial" vertex cover (see Definition 2).

[4] On every signature query issued by the adversary, the reduction in [15] tosses a (biased) random coin (*independent* of the history of the simulation) and depending on its outcome decides whether or not to embed the (RSA) challenge in the signature. The simulation is identical if these coin-tosses are all carried out together at the beginning of the game.

oblivious reductions encompass the currently-known techniques for establishing upper bounds for primitives with dynamic graph-based security games, like GSD, PRE, CPRFs etc.. Therefore, our results imply that in order to obtain better upper bounds on the loss function Λ even in the more restricted settings, one needs to deviate significantly from the current proof techniques (i.e., non-oblivious or rewinding reductions for GSD and restricted PRE). Accordingly, our results on oblivious reductions should not be viewed as separations, but rather as a guide towards new avenues to finding better reductions by ruling out a large class of reductions – such possibilities are discussed in the full version [33, Section 10].

1.2   Related Work

1.2.1   Adaptive Security

The security of multi-party computation in the context of adaptive corruption has been well studied. It is known that a protocol that is proven secure against static (i.e., non-adaptive) adversaries may turn out insecure once the adversary is allowed adaptive corruption [12]. On the other hand, in the (programmable) random oracle model it *is* possible to compile a selective protocol into an adaptively-secure one through non-committing encryption [41].

The notion of generalised selective decryption (GSD) was introduced by Panjwani [43] to study adaptive corruption in restricted settings. His motivation was to better understand the problem of selective decommitment [16] (which is also known as selective opening in some works [5]) and the closely-related problem of selective decryption. The problem was further studied by Fuchsbauer et al. [19] who gave a quasi-polynomial reduction when the GSD game is restricted to trees.

In parallel, the study of adaptive security in the setting of circuit garbling was undertaken in the works of Bellare et al. [4], Hemenway et al. [29] and Jafargholi and Wichs [32]. The latter two works are especially relevant since they established a relationship between adaptive security and graph pebbling. It is also worth noting that the study of adaptive security of garbled RAM was carried out in [22,23].

The above two series of works culminated in the Piecewise-Guessing Framework of Jafargholi et al. [31] who managed to abstract out the ideas therein and give even more fine-grained reductions. In addition to capturing the results from [19,21,32], they applied the framework to obtain new results for adaptive secret sharing. The framework was further applied to argue adaptive security for attribute-based encryption schemes [38], proxy re-encryption schemes [20], continuous group key-agreement [1,2] and non-interactive zero-knowledge [35].

1.2.2   Limitations of Reductions

The study of limitations of reductions (see Footnote 8) was initiated in the seminal work of Impagliazzo and Rudich [30]. They used *oracle separations* to rule out fully black-box reduction of key agreement to symmetric-key primitives.

This approach turned out quite useful and has been further exploited to rule out fully black-box reduction of a variety of cryptographic primitives from one another (e.g., [48,50]). A fine-grained study of the notion of reductions and separations was later carried out by Reingold et al. [47].

In addition to ruling out reductions, the more fine-grained question of efficiency of reduction of one primitive to another has also been studied [24,25,37]. This has been applied to the case of adaptive security as well. Perhaps the works most relevant to ours is that of Lewko and Waters [40], who showed that the security of adaptively-secure hierarchical identity-based encryption must degrade exponentially in the depth, and Fuchsbauer et al. [21], who showed that certain types of constrained PRFs must incur an exponential loss (in the size of the input) in adaptive security. Note that this class of constrained PRFs does not include the prefix-constrained PRF construction we consider in this work. Both aforementioned works employ the more recent meta-reduction technique [9,26,45], which is of different flavour from oracle separations.

Comparison with [34]. Building on the high level ideas in this paper, [34] showed lower bounds on the adaptive security of Yao's garbling scheme. As pointed out in the introduction, the graph (i.e., the circuit) in Yao's garbling scheme is fixed ahead of time and the adaptivity comes from the choice of (garbling) input. (The difficulty of the reduction comes from having to guess the bits running over a subset of wires during evaluation of the circuit.) Therefore they had to rely on a different combinatorial abstraction from Builder-Pebbler Game (viz., a black-gray pebble game on the circuit) to establish their lower bound. However, since the security game for Yao's garbling consists of just two rounds, [34] did not encounter some of the difficulties (to do with the multiple rounds of interaction) we do and therefore were able to rule out arbitrary black-box reductions. While both [34] and this work model choices made by a reduction by putting pebbles on a graph structure, the analogy basically ends there. None of the main ideas from [34] seem applicable in this setting and vice versa.

1.2.3   Graph Pebbling

The notion of graph pebbling, first introduced in the 70's to study programming languages, turned out quite useful in computational complexity theory to study the relationship between space and time; in recent years, pebbling has found applications in cryptography as well [3,17,18]. The notion of node pebbling first appeared (albeit implicitly) in [46], whereas the notion of *reversible* node pebbling was introduced by Bennett to study reversible computation [6]. The notion of edge pebbling used in this work is defined in [31]. The lower bound on the reversible node pebbling complexity of paths was established by Chung et al. [14] and an alternative proof can be found in [39]. As for the lower bound on the node pebbling complexity for binary trees, a proof can be found in [49]. We refer the reader to the textbook by Savage [49] or the excellent survey by Nordström [42] for more details on pebbling.

2   Technical Overview

On a high level, our approach can be divided into two steps. In the first step (Sect. 2.2), which is purely combinatorial, we analyse a two-player multi-stage game which we call the Builder-Pebbler Game. In particular, we exploit ideas from pebbling lower bounds to establish upper bounds for the success probability of the Pebbler (who is one of two players). These upper bounds are then, in the second step (Sect. 2.3), translated to lower bounds on the loss in security of concrete cryptographic protocols using oracle separation techniques to yield the results stated in Sect. 1.1. Before explaining the two steps, we provide a summary of the overall approach so that the two steps, especially the motivation behind some of the underlying definitions, can be better appreciated.

2.1   Our Approach

Our goal is to design adversaries that break the GSD game but where any reduction (in a specified class) to the security of the underlying SKE scheme loses a significant (super-polynomial) factor in the advantage. Since we are aiming to rule out black-box reductions, we have the luxury of constructing inefficient adversaries and SKE schemes. The output of our adversaries will solely depend on the distribution of inconsistent edges in the final key-graph, which we will denote as *pebbles* in the following. Clearly, in order to win the GSD game, our adversaries need to output 0 if the final key-graph is entirely consistent (i.e., contains no pebbles), and 1 if the final key-graph is entirely consistent except for the edges incident on the challenge key. Otherwise, we have complete freedom in assigning output probabilities of 0 and 1 to the remaining pebbling configurations of the final key-graph.

   As we prove formally in Sect. 6, any reduction attempting to take advantage of our adversaries must send its IND-CPA challenge as a response to a query and exploit the fact that the real and the random challenge will lead to different pebbling configurations of the key-graph. Its hope is that the output distribution of the adversary differs significantly between the two configurations. Note however, that when embedding the challenge in some edge (i, j) of the key-graph, all edges incident to i will, with overwhelming probability, be inconsistent independently of the challenge ciphertext, since the reduction does not know the challenge secret key and thus is unlikely to be able to send consistent responses to queries incident to i. In other words, the challenge can only be embedded into an edge where the edges incident to the source are all pebbled. This naturally leads to studying configurations that are related by valid moves in the *reversible edge-pebbling* game: a pebble on an edge may only be added or removed if all edges incident to the source are pebbled.

   We may now define the configuration graph of our key-graph G: The vertices of the configuration graph $\mathcal{P}^G$, as the name suggests, consist of all possible pebbling configurations of G. Therefore it is the power set of the edges of $G = (\mathcal{V}, \mathcal{E})$. An edge is present from a vertex $\mathcal{P}_i$ to another vertex $\mathcal{P}_j$ if $\mathcal{P}_j$ can be obtained from $\mathcal{P}_i$ using a valid pebbling move. The edges represent pairs of configurations, where the reduction may embed its IND-CPA challenge, in other words, a hybrid (from the reduction's point of view). Since we consider reversible pebbling games, the edges in our configuration graphs are undirected. Therefore one can think of $\mathcal{P}^G$ as a subgraph of the Boolean hypercube on $2^{|\mathcal{E}|}$ vertices. Assuming that G has a single sink vertex T, $\mathcal{P}^G$ has two special vertices denoted $\mathcal{P}_{\text{start}} = \emptyset$ and $\mathcal{P}_{\text{target}}$ which consist of the pebbling configuration where all incoming edges to T carry a pebble. The configuration graph for C_4, the path of length 4, is given in Fig 1. A path from $\mathcal{P}_{\text{start}}$ to $\mathcal{P}_{\text{target}}$ corresponds to a pebbling sequence in the reversible edge-pebbling game. Any such path can be used for a hybrid argument to prove upper bounds for the loss in security, which is what prior works did [31,43]. In this work we are interested in ruling out the possibility of using any of the paths (or multiple at once) to improve on these results.

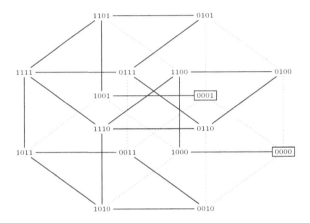

Fig. 1. Configuration graph for paths of length four, $C_4 = ([5], \{(1,2),(2,3),(3,4),(4,5)\})$. It is a subgraph of the Boolean hypercube of dimension four (the missing edges are dotted). The labels of the vertices encode the pebbling status of the corresponding edge and therefore represents a pebbling configuration: e.g., the vertex labelled 0000 is completely unpebbled (configuration $\mathcal{P} = \emptyset$) whereas the vertex labelled 1000 has a pebble only on the first edge $(1,2)$ (configuration $\mathcal{P} = \{(1,2)\}$). An edge exists between a configuration $\mathcal{P}_i$ and $\mathcal{P}_j$ if $\mathcal{P}_j$ can be obtained from $\mathcal{P}_i$ via *one* valid pebbling move. The special vertices for $\mathcal{P}^{C_4}$ are $\mathcal{P}_{\text{start}} = 0000$ and $\mathcal{P}_{\text{target}} = 0001$ (both boxed). A cut for this configuration graph consists of the set of (red) vertices that lie on the 'bottom' half of the graph: $\{0000, 0010, 1010, 1011, 0011, 1000, 0110, 1110\}$. The set of edges from the top half to the bottom half form cut set: $\{(1111, 1110), (1111, 1011), (1100, 1110), (1100, 1000), (0111, 0110), (0100, 0110)\}$. (Color figure online)

Pebbling Lower Bounds: Barriers to Better Cryptographic Upper Bounds. In our approach, we will show that in *any* sequence of hybrids there exist "bottleneck" configurations related to pebbling lower bounds. These bottleneck configurations define a cut for the configuration graph $\mathcal{P}^G$. Looking ahead, our adversaries will concentrate all their advantage on these cuts and we will show that it is hard for any reduction to guess the pebbled edges of the corresponding pebbling configurations.

From Pebbling Lower Bounds to Cryptographic Lower Bounds via Builder-Pebbler Game. The immediate idea would be to translate pebbling lower bounds directly to cryptographic lower bounds. But pebbling lower bounds apply to fixed graphs. Therefore we are missing a component that captures the dynamic nature of the security games, like that of GSD, which involves (the adversary) choosing a graph G randomly from a class of graphs $\mathcal{G}$. To remedy this, we introduce a two-player multi-stage game that we call the Builder-Pebbler Game and then show that pebbling lower bounds can be used to upper bound the probability of success of the Pebbler (Step I: Sect. 2.2), one of the players. Then we will use oracle separation techniques to translate these upper bounds into cryptographic lower bounds (Step II: Sect. 2.3).

2.2   Step I: Combinatorial Upper Bounds

We start off with an informal description of the Builder-Pebbler Game, a two-player game that will abstract out the combinatorial aspect of establishing lower bounds for cryptographic protocols that are modelled by multi-user games where the adversary adaptively builds a graph structure among the set of users, as in GSD (formal definition in Sect. 4). The game is played between a Pebbler and a Builder, and intuitively, Pebblers play the role of reduction algorithms whereas Builders correspond to adversaries in security games.

Builder-Pebbler Game. For a parameter $N \in \mathbb{N}$, the Builder-Pebbler Game is played between a Builder and a Pebbler in rounds. The game starts with an empty DAG $G = (\mathcal{V} = [1, N], \mathcal{E} = \emptyset)$ and an empty pebbling configuration $\mathcal{P}$, and in each round the following happens: the Builder first picks an edge $e \in [1, N]^2 \setminus \mathcal{E}$ and adds it to the DAG and the Pebbler then decides whether or not to place a pebble on e. This way the Builder and the Pebbler will construct a graph G and a pebbling configuration $\mathcal{P}$ on this graph. The Builder can stop the game at any point by choosing a sink in G as the challenge. This results in a *challenge* DAG $G^* = (\mathcal{V}^*, \mathcal{E}^*)$, the subgraph of G that is induced by all nodes from which the challenge is reachable. The Pebbler wins if it ends up with a pebbling configuration $\mathcal{P}$ that is in a designated subset of all configurations. This winning set is determined by the graph G. Otherwise, the Builder is declared the winner. In case the strategies are randomised, we call the probability with which the Builder (resp., the Pebbler) wins the game as *Builder's (resp., Pebbler's) advantage*, and denote it by $\beta = \beta(N)$ (resp., $\pi = \pi(N)$). We also consider restricted games where the Builder is restricted to query graphs G that are subgraphs of some family of graphs $\mathcal{G}$. In summary, one can think of the game as the Builder building a graph and the Pebbler placing pebbles on this graph with the aim of getting into a winning configuration and the Builder preventing this from happening.[5]

Defining Winning Configurations via Cuts of the Configuration Graph. Although the Builder-Pebbler Game is meaningful for any notion of winning configuration, we are interested in a particular definition that is essential in establishing our cryptographic lower bounds: we will set the winning configurations as the ones that belong to bottleneck configurations in the configuration graph of G. The goal is to prove that it will be difficult for Pebblers to get into such configurations. In some cases we can do so directly, but in others the Pebbler may be able to achieve this by "flooding" the graph with many pebbles. Our solution is to "artificially" restrict the Pebbler to placing very few pebbles by requiring it to leave the part of the query graph that is not in the challenge graph entirely unpebbled, i.e., if at the end of the game there is a pebble on an edge that is not rooted in the challenge graph, the Pebbler loses. Note that this does not trivialize our task of finding a suitable Builder, because for our application to cryptographic lower bounds to work, the Builder's querying strategy (including the challenge) needs to be independent of the pebbles placed by the Pebbler. (We call such Builders also *oblivious*, see below.) Of course, care must be taken that this behaviour cannot be exploited by the reduction. Intuitively, the reason this works is that in all our applications, if the reduction were to embed the challenge outside of the challenge graph, our adversaries will almost always interpret it to be a pebble, no matter if the challenge was real or random.

Combinatorial Upper Bounds in the Builder-Pebbler Game. We bound the advantage of Pebblers from above against Builders with varying degree of freedom, i.e., Builders that are restricted to querying certain classes of graphs. The upper bounds in Theorems 3 to 5 are (almost) tight since a random Pebbler yields (almost) matching lower bounds.

Theorem 3 (Informally Stated, Theorems 6 and 8 in Full Version [33]). *Any oblivious[6] Pebbler in the Builder-Pebbler Game restricted to* paths or binary trees *has advantage at most inverse* quasi-polynomial $(N^{-\Omega(\log N)})$ *in N, the size of the graph.*

---

[5] This is reminiscent of Maker-Breaker games [28], a class of positional games (which includes Shannon Switching Game, Tic-Tac-Toe and Hex) which are played between a Maker, who is trying to end up with a (winning) position and a Breaker, whose goal is to prevent the Maker from getting into such (winning) positions. One fundamental difference between Maker-Breaker Games and the Builder-Pebbler Game is that in Maker-Breaker games one usually considers optimal (deterministic) strategies, whereas we consider randomised strategies for the Builder-Pebbler Game. (Another way of looking at this is that our "board" is dynamic.) Another difference is the asymmetry in the nature of moves.

[6] The notion of obliviousness for Pebblers is naturally derived from the one for reductions, see discussion above and Definition 9.

Theorem 4 (Informally Stated, Theorem 9 in Full Version [33]). *Any oblivious Pebbler in the unrestricted Builder-Pebbler Game has advantage at most inverse sub-exponential ($2^{-\Omega(\sqrt{N})}$) in N, the size of the graph.*

Theorem 5 (Informally Stated, Theorem 6). *Any Pebbler in the Builder-Pebbler Game restricted to* trees *has advantage at most inverse quasi-polynomial ($N^{-\Omega(\log N)}$) in N, the size of the graph.*

Remark 1 (On Builder Obliviousness). It is worth mentioning that all our Builder strategies are also *oblivious*, where oblivious is defined different for Builders than for Pebblers: it means that the query strategy is independent of the Pebbler's responses (see Sect. 4.1).[7] The reason we restrict ourselves to such Builders is mostly for our convenience: looking ahead, it means that we can ensure that the reductions in our cryptographic applications cannot exploit the querying behaviour of the adversary to gain a larger advantage, rather they must rely solely on the final output bit.

2.3 Step II: From Combinatorial Upper Bounds to Cryptographic Lower Bounds

For translating upper bounds established in Step I into loss in security of concrete cryptographic protocols, we adapt ideas from oracle separations.

Ruling out Tight Black-Box Reductions. Oracle separations are used to rule out the reduction[8] of a primitive Q (e.g., PKE) to another primitive P (e.g., SKE). Our case is slightly different since it involves a primitive P (e.g., SKE) that is used in a graph-based "multi-instance" setting Q^P (e.g., GSD with SKE). In this setting, we are interested in the more fine-grained question of bounding Λ, the loss in security incurred by any efficient black-box reduction R that breaks P when given black-box access to an adversary that breaks Q^P (i.e., from P to Q^P). This means we must show that for *every* R, there exists

- an instance P (not necessarily efficiently-implementable) of P and
- an adversary A_Q (not necessarily efficient) that breaks Q^P

---

[7] One could think of the Builder playing the role of "nature" (who also adopts a strategy that is oblivious of the opposing player) in Papadimitrou's *Games Against Nature* [44].

[8] The usage of the word 'reduction' here and in Sect. 1.2.2 is in a constructive sense [47]: a primitive Q is reduced to another primitive P if (i) there is an efficient *construction* C that takes an implementation P of P and gives an implementation Q of Q and (ii) there is an efficient *security reduction* R which takes an adversary A_Q that breaks Q and constructs an adversary A_P that breaks P. For example, the most common type of reduction used in cryptography is a *fully* black-box reduction where both R and C are black-box in that they only have black-box access to P and A_Q, respectively. In the rest of the paper, 'reduction' is used to refer to a security reduction as in (ii).

such that the loss in security incurred by R in breaking P is at least Λ.[9] To this end, we establish a tight *coupling* between the security game for Q^P and the Builder-Pebbler Game (e.g., Lemma 2). If Q^P involves a graph family $\mathcal{G}$ then the Builder-Pebbler Game will be played on $\mathcal{G}$ (or sometimes another family related to $\mathcal{G}$) and the winning condition is determined by the cut for $\mathcal{G}$. The coupling is established using a Builder strategy B and a related adversary A_Q such that

- every reduction R can be translated to a Pebbler strategy P against B on $\mathcal{G}$, and
- if R has a security loss of at most Λ then B's advantage against P is at least $1/\Lambda$ (up to negligible additive factors).

If $\mathcal{G}$ is a class for which we derived an upper bound of π for Pebbler strategies (in Step I) then any reduction R such that $1/\Lambda > \pi$ cannot exist. Put differently, an upper bound on the success probability of the Pebbler in the Builder-Pebbler Game translates to a lower bound on the loss in security for the reduction R. In the remainder of the section, we explain how the coupling works in a bit more detail using GSD on binary trees as the running example. To keep the exposition simple, we will brush a lot of issues (e.g., dealing with 'flooding' reductions) under the rug and refer the readers to Sect. 6 for a more formal treatment.

Example: GSD on Binary Trees. Let's consider the case where P is SKE and Q^P is the GSD game played on $\mathcal{G} = \mathcal{B}_n$, the class of binary trees of depth n. Intuitively, the GSD adversary A_Q "simulates" the oblivious Builder B used to derive Theorem 3. That is, it

1. chooses a binary tree $B_n \in \mathcal{B}_n$ uniformly at random,
2. queries, in a random order, each edge $(u, v) \in E(B_n)$ to obtain the corresponding ciphertext $\mathsf{Enc}(\mathbf{k}_u, \mathbf{k}_v)$ from the reduction R and
3. challenges the sole sink T at the end of the game.

For it to be a valid adversary, A_Q must distinguish the extreme games, i.e., the real game where all the ciphertexts are real and the random game where the ciphertexts incoming to T are both random. To this end, it looks at the ciphertexts it obtained and extracts a pebbling configuration $\mathcal{P}$ from it (as described in Sect. 2.1). Note that the extreme hybrids corresponds to $\mathcal{P}_{\text{start}} = \emptyset$ (real) and $\mathcal{P}_{\text{target}}$ such that both the edges incoming to T carry a pebble (random). A_Q distinguishes these by concentrating all its advantage in the cut in the configuration graph of B_n defined in Sect. 2.1: i.e., it outputs 0 if $\mathcal{P}$ is on one side of the cut and 1 otherwise. To help A_Q faithfully distinguish real ciphertexts from random ones so that it can infer the exact pebbling configuration $\mathcal{P}$, we fix P to be an ideal implementation $(\mathsf{Enc}, \mathsf{Dec})$ of SKE:

---

[9] This is obtained by simply negating the definition of a black-box reduction: *there exists an efficient reduction R such that for every (not necessarily efficient) implementation P of P and for every (not necessarily efficient) adversary A_Q that breaks Q^P the loss in security is at most Λ.*

- Enc is a random expanding function that implements encryption and
- Dec is the decryption function defined to be "consistent" with Enc.[10]

Since Enc is injective with overwhelming probability, given a ciphertext A_Q can brute force Enc to determine (exactly) whether or not the ciphertext corresponding to an edge is real. By carrying this out for all the edges, it can extract a *unique* pebbling configuration corresponding to R's simulation. Since A_Q concentrates its advantage in the cut, for R to have any chance of winning, its own challenge c^* must be 'embedded at the cut' so that – depending on whether or not c^* is real – $\mathcal{P}$ switches from one side of the cut to the other. Since this is the *only* way R can exploit A_Q, we may infer that a reduction with loss in security at most Λ ends up in the cut with probability at least $1/\Lambda$. However, thanks to the fidelity of the extraction, this also means that the natural Pebbler strategy P that underlies R, which simply places a pebble whenever R fakes, wins against B in the Builder-Pebbler Game on $\mathcal{B}_n$ with an advantage at least $\pi = 1/\Lambda$ (formally, Lemma 1). If particular, if Λ is significantly less than quasi-polynomial in $N = 2^n$, it would imply the existence of a Pebbler that is successful with a probability greater than inverse quasi-polynomial, a contradiction to Theorem 3. Since Theorem 3 only holds for oblivious Pebblers, the bound on Λ only holds for oblivious GSD reductions.

3   Preliminaries

We use the notation $[N] = \{1, \ldots, N\}$ and $[N]_0 = \{0\} \cup [N]$. For a string $x = x_0, \ldots, x_{n-1} \in \{0,1\}^n$, for $0 \le a \le b < n$, we use $x[a, b]$ to denote the substring $x_a, \ldots, x_b$.

3.1   Graph Theory

Let $N \in \mathbb{N}$ and $G = (\mathcal{V}, \mathcal{E})$ define a directed acyclic graph (DAG) with vertex set $\mathcal{V} = [N]$, edge set $\mathcal{E} \subset [N] \times [N]$, and a set of sinks $\mathcal{T}$. For a subset $\mathcal{S} \subseteq [N]$ of nodes, let $in(\mathcal{S})$ denote the set of ingoing edges and $parents(\mathcal{S})$ denote the set of parent nodes of nodes in $\mathcal{S}$. For a set of n edges $\mathcal{P} = \{(v_i, w_i)\}_{i=1}^n$, let $\mathcal{V}(\mathcal{P}) := \bigcup_{i=1}^n \{v_i, w_i\}$ denote the set of nodes that have an incident edge in $\mathcal{P}$. The edge set $\mathcal{P}$ is called *disjoint*, if they do not share a node, i.e. if $|\mathcal{V}(\mathcal{P})| = |\bigcup_{i=1}^n \{v_i, w_i\}| = 2n$. We denote by $E(G)$ (resp., $V(G)$) the edges $\mathcal{E}$ (resp., vertices $\mathcal{V}$) of G. By $\mathcal{B}_n$, we denote a binary tree of depth n – the binary tree is *perfect* if it has all $2^{n+1} - 1$ vertices. We assume the standard indexing of the vertices in $\mathcal{B}_n$ by associating them with binary strings in $\{0,1\}^{\le n}$ determined by their position in the tree: i.e., the root has index ε and the left (resp., right) child of a vertex with index i is $i\|0$ (resp., $i\|1$).

---

[10] Since most of our ideal functionalities are implemented using random oracles, it is possible using standard tricks [30] to switch the order of the quantifiers and establish the stronger statement that there exists a *single* oracle P and adversary A_Q which work *for all* reductions.

Definition 1 (cuts, cut-sets, frontiers). *Let* $G = (\mathcal{V}, \mathcal{E})$ *be an undirected graph. A cut* $\mathcal{S}$ *of* G *is a subset of the nodes* $\mathcal{V}$. *For two nodes* $v_1, v_2 \in \mathcal{V}$ *an s-t-cut that separates* v_1 *and* v_2 *is a cut* $\mathcal{S}$ *such that* $v_1 \in \mathcal{S}$ *and* $v_2 \notin \mathcal{S}$. *The* cut-set *of a cut* $\mathcal{S}$ *is the set of edges with one endpoint in* $\mathcal{S}$ *and the other outside of* $\mathcal{S}$. *We call the* frontier *of a cut* $\mathcal{S}$ *the set of all nodes in* $\mathcal{S}$ *that have an incident edge in the cut-set of* $\mathcal{S}$.

Definition 2 (Vertex Covers). *Let* $G = (\mathcal{V}, \mathcal{E})$ *be a directed or undirected graph and* $\mathcal{P} \subseteq \mathcal{E}$ *be a subset of edges. A* vertex cover *of* $\mathcal{P}$ *is a subset* $\mathcal{S}$ *of* $[N]$ *such that for each edge* $(i, j) \in \mathcal{P}$ *either the source* i *or the sink* j *lies in* $\mathcal{S}$. *We define a* non-trivial vertex cover *to be a vertex cover* $\mathcal{S}$ *such that* $\mathcal{S} \subseteq \mathcal{V}(\mathcal{P})$. *We denote the size of a minimal vertex cover of* $\mathcal{P}$ *by*

$$\mathsf{VC}(\mathcal{P}) := \min\{|\mathcal{S}| : \mathcal{S} \subseteq [N] \ covers \ \mathcal{P}\}.$$

3.2 Graph Pebbling

A *pebbling configuration* on the graph $\mathcal{G}$ is a set $\mathcal{P} \subseteq \mathcal{E}$ defining the subset of pebbled edges. Let $|\mathcal{P}|$ denote the number of pebbles in the configuration and $\mathcal{V}(\mathcal{P})$ the set of nodes involved in the pebbling. We define the *complexity* of a pebbling configuration $\mathcal{P}$ as the size of a minimal vertex cover of $\mathcal{P}$. For a pebbling sequence $\boldsymbol{P} = (\mathcal{P}_0, \ldots, \mathcal{P}_\ell)$, we define $\mathsf{VC}(\boldsymbol{P}) := \max_{i \in [L]_0} \mathsf{VC}(\mathcal{P}_i)$.

Let $\mathcal{P}_{\mathrm{start}}$ denote the unique configuration with $|\mathcal{P}_{\mathrm{start}}| = \mathsf{VC}(\mathcal{P}_{\mathrm{start}}) = 0$, i.e., $\mathcal{P}_{\mathrm{start}} = \emptyset$, and $\mathcal{P}_{\mathrm{target}} = \mathrm{in}(T) = \{(i, T) \in \mathcal{E}\}$ denote the configuration where only all the edges incident on some sink $T \in \mathcal{T}$ are pebbled. We will consider sequences of pebbling configurations $\boldsymbol{P} = (\mathcal{P}_{\mathrm{start}}, \ldots, \mathcal{P}_{\mathrm{target}})$ where subsequent configurations have to follow certain pebbling rules.

Reversible Pebbling. We consider the pebbling game from [31].

Definition 3 (Edge-Pebbling). *An edge pebbling of a DAG* $G = (\mathcal{V}, \mathcal{E})$ *with unique sink* T *is a pebbling sequence* $\boldsymbol{P} = (\mathcal{P}_0, \ldots, \mathcal{P}_\ell)$ *with* $\mathcal{P}_0 = \mathcal{P}_{\mathrm{start}}$ *and* $\mathcal{P}_\ell = \mathcal{P}_{\mathrm{target}}$, *such that for all* $i \in [\ell]$ *there is a unique* $(u, v) \in \mathcal{E}$ *such that:*

- $\mathcal{P}_i = \mathcal{P}_{i-1} \cup \{(u, v)\}$ *or* $\mathcal{P}_i = \mathcal{P}_{i-1} \setminus \{(u, v)\}$,
- $\mathrm{in}(u) \subseteq \mathcal{P}_{i-1}$.

Definition 4 (Configuration Graph). *Let* $G = (\mathcal{V}, \mathcal{E})$ *be some graph. We define the associated* configuration graph $\mathcal{P}^G$ *as the graph that has as its vertex set all* $2^{|\mathcal{E}|}$ *possible pebbling configurations of* G. *The edge set will contain an edge between two vertices, if the transisition between the two vertices is an allowed pebbling move according to the pebbling game rules.*

Note that the configuration graph depends on the pebbling game. If we consider reversible pebbling as in Definition 3, the configuration graph is undirected.

4 The Builder-Pebbler Game

In this work, we consider security games for multi-user schemes where an adversary can adaptively do the following actions:

- query for information between pairs of users,
- corrupt users and gain secret information associated to these users,
- issue a distinguishing challenge query associated to a target user of its choice,
- guess a bit $b \in \{0, 1\}$.

We consider such games as games on graphs, where users represent the nodes of the graph and edges are defined by the adversary's pairwise queries. If the pairwise information depends asymmetrically on the two users, then this is represented by the direction of the corresponding edge and after the game one can extract a directed graph structure from the transcript of the game. Here, we only consider the case of directed *acyclic* graphs, i.e., where the adversary is forbidden to query cycles. Furthermore, to avoid trivial winning strategies, the adversary must not query a challenge on a node which is reachable from a corrupt node.

To prove a scheme secure under such an adaptive game based on standard assumptions (e.g., the security of some involved primitive), a common approach is to construct a reduction that has black-box access to an adversary against the scheme and tries to use the advantage of this adversary to break the basic assumption. To this aim, the reduction has to simulate the game to the adversary and at the same time embed some challenge c on the basic assumption into its answers so that the adversary's output varies depending on this embedded challenge. Hence, the reduction might not answer all queries correctly but rather "fakes" some of the edges; such wrong answers will be represented as *pebbled* edges in the graph. However, if the reduction answers all queries connected to the challenge node independent of the challenge user's secrets, then the edge queries do not help the adversary to distinguish its challenge and its advantage in this game can be at most the advantage it has in an alternative security game where no edge queries are possible. Indistinguishability in such a weaker scenario usually follows trivially by some basic assumption.

Thus, we are interested in games that can be abstracted by the following two-player game.

Definition 5 (N- and $(N, \mathcal{G})$-Builder-Pebbler Game). *For a parameter $N \in \mathbb{N}$, the N-Builder-Pebbler Game is played between two players, called Builder and Pebbler, in at most $N \cdot (N - 1)/2$ rounds. The game starts with an empty DAG $G = ([1, N], \mathcal{E} = \emptyset)$ and an empty set $\mathcal{P} = \emptyset$. In each round:*

1. *the Builder first picks an edge $e \in [1, N]^2 \setminus \mathcal{E}$ and adds it to G (i.e., $\mathcal{E} := \mathcal{E} \cup \{e\}$); the Builder is restricted to only query edges that do not form cycles; and*
2. *the Pebbler then either places a pebble on e (i.e., $\mathcal{P} := \mathcal{P} \cup \{e\}$) or not (i.e., $\mathcal{P}$ remains the same).*

The Builder can stop the game at any point by choosing a sink in G as the challenge. This results in a challenge DAG $G^* = (\mathcal{V}^*, \mathcal{E}^*)$, the subgraph of G that is induced by all nodes from which the challenge is reachable.

In an $(N, \mathcal{G})$-Builder-Pebbler Game, the Builder is restricted to building graphs (isomorphic to subgraphs of) $G \in \mathcal{G}$ for a class of graphs $\mathcal{G}$.

Definition 6 (Winning Condition and Advantage for $(N, \mathcal{G})$-Builder-Pebbler Game). *Consider an $(N, \mathcal{G})$-Builder-Pebbler Game and let $G = (\mathcal{V}, \mathcal{E})$, $G^* = (\mathcal{V}^*, \mathcal{E}^*)$ and $\mathcal{P}$ be as in Definition 5. We model the winning condition for the game through a function X that maps a graph to a collection of subsets of its own edges. We say that the Pebbler wins the $(N, \mathcal{G})$-Builder-Pebbler Game under winning condition X if the following two conditions are satisfied:*

1. *only edges rooted in $\mathcal{V}^*$ are pebbled, i.e. $\mathcal{P} \subseteq \{(u, v) \in \mathcal{E} \mid u \in \mathcal{V}^*\}$*
2. *the pebbling induced on G^* satisfies the winning condition, i.e., $\mathcal{P}|_{G^*} \in X(G^*)$.*

Otherwise, the Builder is declared the winner. In case the strategies are randomised, we call the probability (over the randomness of the strategies) with which the Builder (resp., Pebbler) wins the game the Builder's (resp., Pebbler's) advantage, and denote it by $\beta = \beta(N)$ (resp., $\pi = \pi(N)$). Since there are no draws, we have $\beta + \pi = 1$.

Remark 2. The corresponding definitions for the N-Builder-Pebbler Game can be obtained by simply ignoring the restriction to $\mathcal{G}$.

In our setting we will be interested in functions X that output sets of vertices that represent the frontier of a cut in the configuration graph of the input.

Definition 7 (Cut Function). *For a family $\mathcal{G} = (\mathcal{V}, \mathcal{E})$ of graphs, a function $X : \mathcal{G} \mapsto 2^{\mathcal{E}}$ is called a* cut function *if $X(G)$ is the frontier of an s-t-cut of the configuration graph $\mathcal{P}^G$ that separates $\mathcal{P}_{\text{start}}$ from $\mathcal{P}_{\text{target}}$ for any input $G \in \mathcal{G}$. For a cut function X defined on $\mathcal{G}$ and $G \notin \mathcal{G}$, we set $X(G) = \emptyset$.*

4.1 Player Strategies

Builder Strategies. As motivated in Remark 1, we will be dealing in this paper mostly with a class of Builders who play *independently* of the Pebbler's strategy.[11]

Definition 8 (Oblivious Builders). *We say that a Builder's strategy in the $(N, \mathcal{G})$-Builder-Pebbler Game is* oblivious *if its choice of graph $G \in \mathcal{G}$ and order of edge queries are independent of (i.e., oblivious to) the Pebbler's strategy.*

This restriction on the Builder serves two main purposes.

---

[11] The exact definition of the strategy will depend on the graph and the application.

1. Firstly, it ensures that the Builder-Pebbler Game is not trivial for the cut functions we are interested in: otherwise, it is easy to come up with Builder strategies in which any Pebbler has advantage 0.
2. Moreover, non-oblivious Builder strategies are less interesting in our setting since they could potentially allow reductions to exploit the query behaviour of the adversary built on top of a non-oblivious Builder to gain advantage in the security game.

Pebbler Strategies. Ideally, we would like to establish lower bounds that hold against all Pebblers. Since this is not always possible, we consider Builder-Pebbler Games where the Pebbler strategy is restricted to *oblivious* strategies.

Definition 9 (Oblivious Pebbler). *We say that a Pebbler's strategy is oblivious if it fixes a subset of vertices $S \subseteq [1, N]$ at the beginning of the game, and at the end of the game S is always a non-trivial vertex cover of the pebbling $\mathcal{P}$.*

Note that the notion of obliviousness differs from that in Definition 8. Definition 9 is motivated by oblivious reductions used in [31] (see Sect. 1.1) and the goal is to capture *prior knowledge* that a Pebbler may have about the graph structure that a Builder builds during the query phase. This is captured in Definition 9 by requiring the Pebbler to commit to a non-trivial vertex cover of the pebbling configuration. This allows compressing of pebbling configurations based on the graph structure: e.g., if the Pebbler knows that the graph contains nodes with high degree and it aims to pebble all (or some) of the incident edges of such a node, it may guess this node ahead of time and then adjust its query responses assuming the guess is correct. In the known upper bounds for the applications we consider, this is used to compress the amount of information that needs to be guessed ahead of time. The fact that the vertex cover is required to be non-trivial ensures that this restriction is also non-trivial: otherwise, the Pebbler may simply output the entire set $[1, N]$. On the other hand, using a minimal vertex cover seems too strong, since we do not actually require it to prove our bounds.

Remark 3. Note that restricting the Builder strategy does not weaken our results: we are constructing lower bounds for reductions and an oblivious Builder gives rise to oblivious adversaries. In contrast restricting to oblivious does weaken the result. However, looking ahead, these restrictions allow us to prove much stronger bounds compared to an unrestricted Pebbler.

5 Combinatorial Upper Bounds

In this section we show upper bounds for Pebblers in the Builder-Pebbler Game by constructing Builders (potentially in a restricted Builder-Pebbler Game) and then showing that no Pebbler can have a good advantage against such a Builder. In the following, we show a bound that holds for arbitrary Pebblers. In the full version of this paper, we also provide bounds for oblivious Pebblers [33, Section 5.1] and so-called *node Pebblers* [33, Section 5.2], i.e. Pebblers that may only pebble all or none of the edges incident on any node.

5.1   Unrestricted Pebblers

In this section we prove a first combinatorial upper bound for unrestricted – i.e., non-oblivious – Pebblers in the Builder-Pebbler Game. While our upper bound on the advantage of unrestricted Pebblers is significantly weaker than the result for oblivious Pebblers in the full version of this paper [33, Section 5.1], it is still non-trivial.

Generalized Pebbling Characteristics of Paths. Let $k \in [N]$ be arbitrary. We prove that any pebbling sequence on a path of length N must contain a pebbling configuration such that $\lfloor \log(\lceil N/k \rceil) \rfloor + 1$ of the $\lceil N/k \rceil$ subpaths of length $\leq k$ contain at least one pebble respectively. For $k = 1$ this result is well-known, for a proof we refer to the full version [33, Section 5.1.1]. Assume, for contradiction, that there exists a $k > 1$ and a valid pebbling strategy $\mathcal{P}$ for paths of length N such that the claim was false. Then this strategy implies a pebbling strategy $\mathcal{P}'$ of complexity less than $\lfloor \log(\lceil N/k \rceil) \rfloor + 1$ for paths of length $\lceil N/k \rceil$ as follows: For each pebbling configuration $\mathcal{P}$ in $\mathcal{P}$, define $\mathcal{P}'$ in $\mathcal{P}'$ to contain a pebble on the ith edge if the ith subpath of $\mathcal{P}$ contains a pebble. Cancelling redundant steps in $\mathcal{P}'$, i.e., configurations that equal the preceding configuration in the sequence, implies a valid pebbling sequence of complexity less than $\lfloor \log(\lceil N/k \rceil) \rfloor + 1$ for paths of length $\lceil N/k \rceil$ – a contradiction.

We will use the following definition of k-cuts for paths matching this generalized pebbling lower bound.

Definition 10 (k-good pebbling configurations, k-cuts and k-cut function for paths). *For $k \in \mathbb{N}$ we call a pebbling configuration $\mathcal{P}$ for a path $C = C_N$ on N nodes k-good if $\lfloor \log(\lceil N/k \rceil - 1) \rfloor$ of the $\lceil N/k \rceil - 1$ non-source subpaths of C of length $(\leq)k$ contain at least one pebble respectively[12], and there exists a valid pebbling sequence $\mathcal{P} = (\mathcal{P}_{\text{start}}, \ldots, \mathcal{P})$ such that in all configurations in $\mathcal{P}$ at most $\lfloor \log(\lceil N/k \rceil - 1) \rfloor$ of the subpaths simultaneously carry a pebble. We define a k-cut set $\mathcal{X}$ in the configuration graph $\mathcal{P}^C$ as the set of all edges consisting of a k-good pebbling configuration and a configuration which can be obtained from this good configuration by adding one pebble (following the pebbling rules) in a previously unpebbled subpath. The k-cut function $X_{C,k}$ is defined as in Definition 7 as the frontier of this cut.*

The Upper Bound. The Builder strategy is to query a (polynomial-sized) subgraph of an exponential-sized tree of *outdegree* $\delta_{out} \geq 2$, so that in order to pebble any edge in the final challenge path the Pebbler has to guess one out of many source nodes at the same depth in the tree.

Theorem 6 (Combinatorial Upper Bound for Unrestricted Pebblers). *Let $\mathcal{G}$ be the family of directed trees on $N = 2^n$ nodes (with $n \in \mathbb{N}$). Then there exists a Builder strategy querying a challenge path $G^* \in \mathcal{C}_{\sqrt{N}}$, such that the advantage of any Pebbler against this Builder in the $(N, \mathcal{G})$-Builder-Pebbler Game with the winning condition $X_{C_{\sqrt{N}},1}$ defined as in Definition 10 is at most*

---

[12] For technical reasons, we exclude the first subpath of length k in C.

$$\pi \leq 1/N^{\log(N)/8}.$$

Let $\mathcal{G}_2 \subset \mathcal{G}$ be the subset of graphs in $\mathcal{G}$ of bounded outdegree $\delta_{out} = 2$. Then there exists a Builder strategy querying a challenge path $G^* \in \mathcal{C}_{\sqrt{N}}$, such that the advantage of any Pebbler against Builder in the $(N, \mathcal{G}_2)$-Builder-Pebbler Game with the winning condition $X_{\mathcal{C}_{\sqrt{N}}, k}$ for $k = \log(N)/4$ defined as in Definition 10 is at most

$$\pi \leq 1/N^{\log(N)/8 - \log(\log(N))/4}.$$

Proof. We define a Builder strategy B for graph family $\mathcal{G}_{\delta_{out}}$ of outdegree bounded by δ_{out} as follows: First, B chooses a source node in $[N]$ uniformly at random. It then proceeds in $D = N/\delta_{out}^{2k}$ rounds (where k is the 'overlap parameter' and will be specified later), increasing the current graph's depth by 1 in each round. In each round $R \leq 2k$ and each round $R \not\equiv 1 \mod k$, for all sinks at depth $R - 1$ in the current graph B queries δ_{out} outgoing edges respectively. Note, after the first $2k$ rounds, B's queries form a δ_{out}-regular tree directed from root to leaves, with δ_{out}^{2k} sinks at depth $2k$. For all rounds such that $R > 2k$ and $R \equiv 1 \mod k$, the Builder B first chooses an integer $i \in [\delta_{out}^k]$ and then only queries edges outgoing from the ith batch of δ_{out}^k sinks at depth $R - 1$. Finally, B chooses the target node uniformly at random from the δ_{out}^{2k} sinks at depth $D = N/\delta_{out}^{2k}$.

First note that B's queries involve less than $D \cdot \delta_{out}^{2k} = N$ nodes and the challenge graph forms a path of length D. To win the game, the Pebbler needs to place at least one pebble on $\lfloor \log(\lceil D/k \rceil - 1) \rfloor$ of the disjoint subpaths of length k in the challenge path respectively. But whenever it wants to place a pebble in a subpath starting from depth $i \cdot k$ with $i \geq 1$, the Pebbler has to at least guess which of the δ_{out}^k sources of edges at depth $i \cdot k$ will end up in the challenge graph. Since this choice is made uniformly at random by the Builder B only after all queries at depth $(i + 1) \cdot k$ were made, the advantage of the Pebbler to correctly pebble an edge in the subpath sourced at depth $i \cdot k$ is at most $1/\delta_{out}^k$. Since this bound holds also conditioned on the event that previous guesses were done correctly, and to win the game, the Pebbler has to pebble $\lfloor \log(\lceil D/k \rceil - 1) \rfloor$ subpaths of the challenge path, we obtain

$$\pi \leq 1/\delta_{out}^{k \cdot \lfloor \log(\lceil D/k \rceil - 1) \rfloor}. \tag{1}$$

Now, for the graph family $\mathcal{G}$ of unbounded outdegree, we set $\delta_{out} = N^{1/4}$ and $k = 1$ to obtain $D = \sqrt{N}$ and hence $\pi \leq 1/N^{1/4 \log(\sqrt{N})} = 1/N^{\log(N)/8}$. For $\delta_{out} = 2$, on the other hand, we set $k = \log(N)/4$ to obtain $D = \sqrt{N}$ and $\pi \leq 1/N^{1/4(\log(\sqrt{N}) - \log(\log(N)/4))} = 1/N^{\log(N)/8 - \log\log(N)/4}$. □

6 Cryptographic Lower Bound I: Generalised Selective Decryption

The generalized selective decryption game (GSD) was informally introduced in Sect. 1; we refer to the full version [33, Section 6.1] for a formal definition. In the following we interpret the combinatorial upper bound from Sect. 5.1 for GSD. In the full version, we establish analogous lower bounds for *public-key* GSD, where PKE is used instead of SKE as the underlying primitive; these can be used as a basis for the lower bound on the continuous group key agreement protocol TreeKEM [33, Section 5.1].

6.1 Lower Bounds for GSD

In many applications one considers games where the adversary's queries are restricted to certain graph structures, e.g., paths, "in-trees" (i.e. rooted trees directed from the leaves to the root), or low-depth graphs. These restrictions depend on the protocol under consideration and often allow to construct stronger reductions.

Interesting upper bounds are known for specific settings for (oblivious) black-box reductions R proving adaptive GSD security based on IND-CPA security (short, GSD reductions). Our results now allow us to prove lower bounds on Λ for GSD with various restrictions (which cover similar settings as known upper bounds). Note that our lower bounds are stronger and more widely applicable the more restrictions they can handle.

Definition 11 (Black-Box and Straight-Line GSD Reduction). R *is a black-box GSD reduction if for every SKE* SKE = (Enc, Dec) *and every adversary* A *that wins the GSD game played on* SKE, R *breaks* SKE. *Moreover, if* A *is an* (ϵ, t) *GSD adversary and* R (ϵ', t')-*breaks* SKE *(where* ϵ' *and* t' *are functions of* ϵ *and* t*) then the loss in security is defined to be* $(t'\epsilon)/(t\epsilon')$. *A black-box GSD reduction* R *is* straight-line *if it, additionally, does not rewind* A.

The following definition mirrors the obliviousness of Pebblers in the context of the Builder-Pebbler Game (cf. Definition 9).

Definition 12 (Oblivious GSD Reduction). *A straight-line GSD reduction* R *(Definition 11) is* oblivious *if it commits to a non-trivial vertex cover of all inconsistent edges at the beginning of the game.*

In all our bounds we require the reduction to assign keys to nodes at the beginning of the game.

Definition 13 (Key-Committing GSD Reduction). *A black-box GSD reduction* R *is* key-commiting *if it commits to an assignment of keys to all nodes at the beginning of the game.*

This is due to the fact that Pebblers in the Builder-Pebbler Game commit to whether an edge is pebbled or not as soon as they respond to the query. Without this requirement, this is not true for reductions in the GSD game, since they could potentially respond to a query and decide later if that edge is consistent or inconsistent by choosing the key for the target accordingly (as long as this node does not have an outgoing edge). However, this requirement should not be seen as a very limiting restriction, but we introduce it for ease of exposition, since there are several "work arounds" to this issue. 1) One could use an adversary that "fingerprints" the keys by querying the encryption of some message under each key before starting the rest of the query phase. This would entail adding the corresponding oracle to the GSD game, which seems reasonable in many (but not all) applications, since the keys are often not created for their own sake, but to encrypt messages. 2) In case the adversary is not too restricted (which is application dependent), there is a generic fix where the adversary abuses the `encrypt` oracle to achieve this fingerprinting by introducing a new node and querying the edges from every other node to this new node. This introduces only a slight loss in the number N of nodes.

Both of these approaches work, but would make the proof more complicated: recall that the challenge node must be a sink, so neither of the two fixes can be applied to it. We can still fix all other nodes (which is sufficient), thereby giving away the challenge node right at the start of the game. But this can only increase the reduction's advantage by a factor N, since it could also simply guess the challenge node. Since we are only interested in super-polynomial losses in this work, this would not affect the results. But for the sake of clarity we refrain from applying this workaround and simply keep this mild condition on the GSD reductions. In the full version [33], we see that some protocols are based on a public key version of GSD rather than the secret key version we consider here. In such cases the public keys are known to the adversary and commit the reduction to the corresponding secret keys and thus no assumption or extra fix are required.

We now give a general lemma that allows to turn lower bounds for the Builder-Pebbler Game into lower bounds for the GSD game.

Lemma 1 (Coupling Lemma for GSD). *Let $\mathcal{G}$ be a family of DAGs and X a cut function. Let B be an oblivious Builder in the $(N, \mathcal{G})$-Builder-Pebbler Game with winning condition X. Then there exists*

1. *an ideal SKE scheme $\Pi = (\mathsf{Enc}, \mathsf{Dec})$*
2. *a GSD adversary A in* **PSPACE**

such that for any key-committing straight-line reduction R there exists a Pebbler P such that the advantage $1/\Lambda$ of R is at most the advantage π of P against B (up to an additive term $\mathbf{poly}(N)/2^{\Omega(N)}$). Moreover, if R is oblivious then so is P.

Proof. We first construct $\Pi = (\mathsf{Enc}, \mathsf{Dec})$: We will pick Enc to be a random expanding function (which is injective with overwhelming probability). More precisely, assuming (for simplicity) the key k, the message m and the randomness r are all λ-bit long, $\mathsf{Enc}(k, m; r)$ maps to a random ciphertext of length, say, 6λ with $\lambda = \Theta(N)$. Dec is simulated accordingly to be always consistent with Enc.

We now define a map ϕ from GSD adversaries and reductions to Builder-Pebbler GameBuilders and Pebblers:

- The number N of nodes in the Builder-Pebbler Game corresponds to the number N of keys in the GSD game.
- An encryption query $(\mathsf{encrypt}, v_i, v_j)$ maps to an edge query (i, j) in the Builder-Pebbler Game.
- A response to a query $(\mathsf{encrypt}, v_i, v_j)$ is mapped to "no pebble" if it consists of a valid encryption of k_j under the key k_i, and to "pebble" otherwise. (Note that this is always well-defined for key-committing GSD reductions.)
- A corruption query $(\mathsf{corrupt}, v_i)$ is ignored in the Builder-Pebbler Game.
- The challenge query $(\mathsf{challenge}, v_t)$ is mapped to the challenge node t.

Let $\mathsf{A} \in \mathbf{PSPACE}$ be the following preimage of B under ϕ: A performs the same encryption queries as B and selects its GSD challenge node as the challenge node chosen by B. It then corrupts all nodes not in the challenge graph G^t. If there is an inconsistency (i.e. a pebble) in $G \setminus G^t$, A aborts and outputs 0. Finally, it uses its computational power to decrypt all the received ciphertexts and determines the resulting pebbling configuration $\mathcal{P}$ on G^t. If $\mathcal{P}$ is in the cut defined by the frontier $X(G^t)$, A outputs 0, otherwise it outputs 1. Clearly, A wins the GSD game against Π with probability 1. We will now show that the advantage of R in using the GSD-adversary A to break the IND-CPA security of Π is at most the advantage of $\mathsf{P} = \phi(\mathsf{R})$ against B (up to a negligible additive term).

Note that since Enc is a random function, the GSD game is entirely independent of the challenge bit b until the tuple $(\mathbf{k}, m_b, r)$ such that $c^* = \mathsf{Enc}(\mathbf{k}, m_b; r)$ (where c^* is the challenge ciphertext) is queried to Enc. Since R is PPT, the probability of R doing this is at most $\mathbf{poly}(N)/2^{\Omega(N)}$. Accordingly, to gain a larger advantage, R must send c^* to A as response to some edge query. Since $\mathsf{B} = \phi(\mathsf{A})$ is oblivious, the behaviour of A does not depend on c^* (and thus not on b) during the entire query phase. This means that the statistical distance of A induced by $b = 0$ and $b = 1$ is

$$\sum_{(\mathcal{P}_i, \mathcal{P}_j) \in \mathcal{P}^{G^t}} p_{i,j} |\Pr[\mathsf{A}(\mathcal{P}_i) \to 1] - \Pr[\mathsf{A}(\mathcal{P}_j) \to 1]|$$

where $p_{i,j}$ is the probability that the query phase results in the configuration $\mathcal{P}_i$ or $\mathcal{P}_j$ depending on c^*. More formally, for an edge $(\mathcal{P}_i, \mathcal{P}_j)$ in the configuration graph $\mathcal{P}^{G^t}$, let $\mathcal{P}_{ij}^c$ be the "configuration" that is equal to $\mathcal{P}_i$ if c^* represents a consistent encryption edge (i.e. is not a pebble) and equal to $\mathcal{P}_j$ if c is inconsistent (i.e. a pebble). Then we define $p_{i,j}$ as the probability of the query phase resulting in $\mathcal{P}_{ij}^c$. Clearly, we have $|\Pr[\mathsf{A}(\mathcal{P}_1) \to 1] - \Pr[\mathsf{A}(\mathcal{P}_2) \to 1]| = 0$ for any edge $(\mathcal{P}_1, \mathcal{P}_2)$ where $\mathcal{P}_1 \notin X(G^t)$ and 1 otherwise. The statistical distance of A induced by b is thus bounded by the probability of the querying phase ending up in a configuration in $X(G^t)$ (if c^* is considered not a pebble for this argument).

This is exactly the advantage of Pebbler $\mathsf{P} = \phi(\mathsf{R})$ in the Builder-Pebbler Game against B. By data processing inequality, this also means that the advantage of R is bounded from above by the same quantity.

For the final statement of the lemma, note that ϕ maps oblivious GSD reductions to oblivious Pebblers. □

The following lower bound on GSD now easily follows from Lemma 1 and Theorem 6; for stronger lower bounds for oblivious reductions we refer to the full version [33, Corollaries 2 to 4].

Corollary 1 (Lower bound for GSD on Trees, Straight-Line Reductions). *Let N be the number of users in the GSD game. Any* key-committing straight-line *reduction proving adaptive GSD-security restricted to* trees *based on the IND-CPA security of the underlying encryption scheme loses at least a factor*

$$\Lambda \geq N^{\log(N)/8}.$$

Even if the adversary is restricted to querying graphs with outdegree 2, the reduction loses at least a factor

$$\Lambda \geq N^{\log(N)/8 - \log(\log(N))/4}.$$

7 Cryptographic Lower Bound II: Constrained PRF

In this section we use our combinatorial results for the Builder-Pebbler Game to prove that the constrained pseudorandom function (CPRF) [10,11,36] based on the GGM PRF [27] cannot be proven adaptively-secure based on the security of the underlying pseudorandom generator (PRG) using a *straight-line* reduction. Our lower bound almost matches the best-known upper bound by Fuchsbauer et al. [21].

7.1 Definition, Construction and Security Assumption

The following definitions are essentially taken from [31].

Definition 14 (GGM PRF). *Given a* $\mathsf{PRG} : \{0,1\}^\lambda \to \{0,1\}^{2\lambda}$, *the PRF* $\mathsf{F}_{GGM} : \{0,1\}^\lambda \times \{0,1\}^* \to \{0,1\}^\lambda$ *is defined as*

$$\mathsf{F}_{GGM}(k, x) = k_x \text{ where } k_\emptyset = k \text{ and } \forall z \in \{0,1\}^* : k_{z\|0}\|k_{z\|1} = \mathsf{PRG}(k_z).$$

A graphical representation of the GGM construction is depicted in Fig. 2.

Next, we give the definitions for CPRFs that are tailored to prefix-constrained PRFs.

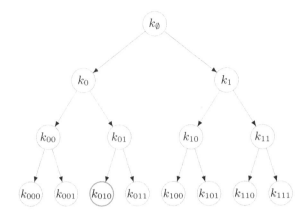

Fig. 2. Illustration of the GGM PRF. Every left child $k_{x\|0}$ of a node k_x is defined as the first half of $\mathsf{PRG}(k_x)$, the right child $k_{x\|1}$ as the second half. The thick node (shaded in green) corresponds to $\mathsf{F}_{GGM}(k_\emptyset, 010)$. (Color figure online)

Definition 15 (Prefix-constrained PRF). *For $n \in \mathbb{N}$, a function $\mathsf{F} : \mathcal{K} \times \{0,1\}^n \to \mathcal{Y}$ is a prefix-constrained PRF if there are algorithms $\mathsf{F.Constrain} : \mathcal{K} \times \{0,1\}^{\leq n} \to \mathcal{K}_{pre}$ and $\mathsf{F.Eval} : \mathcal{K}_{pre} \times \{0,1\}^n \to \mathcal{Y}$ which for all $k \in \mathcal{K}$, $x \in \{0,1\}^{\leq n}$ and $k_x \leftarrow \mathsf{F.Constrain}(k, x)$ satisfy*

$$\mathsf{F.Eval}(k_x, x') = \begin{cases} \mathsf{F}(k, x') & \text{if } x \text{ is a prefix of } x' \\ \bot & \text{otherwise.} \end{cases}$$

That is, $\mathsf{F.Constrain}(k, x)$ outputs a key k_x that allows evaluation of $\mathsf{F}(k, \cdot)$ on all inputs that have x as a prefix. We can derive a prefix-constrained PRF from the GGM construction by setting $\mathcal{K} = \{0,1\}^\lambda$, $\mathcal{Y} = \{0,1\}^\lambda$, and for a random $k \leftarrow \mathcal{K}$ and $x \in \{0,1\}^l$ with $l \leq n$ defining $\mathsf{F}_{GGM}.\mathsf{Constrain}(k, x) = (k_x^1, k_x^2) := (x, \mathsf{F}_{GGM}(k, x))$ and

$$\mathsf{F}_{GGM}.\mathsf{Eval}(k_x, x') := \begin{cases} \mathsf{F}_{GGM}(k_x^2, z) & \text{if } x' = x\|z \text{ for some } z \in \{0,1\}^{n-l} \\ \bot & \text{otherwise.} \end{cases}$$

The security for prefix-constrained PRFs is argued using the following game.

Definition 16. *The game is played between a challenger G (which is either G_L or G_R) and an adversary A using F. The challenger G picks a random key $k \leftarrow \mathcal{K}$, and initialises a set $\mathcal{X} = \emptyset$. A can make at most $q = q(n)$ queries, which is either:*

- *Constrain queries, $(\textbf{constrain}, x)$: G returns $\mathsf{F.Constrain}(k, x)$, and adds x to $\mathcal{X}$.*
- *One challenge query $(\textbf{challenge}, x^*)$: Here the answer differs between G_L and G_R: G_L answers with $\mathsf{F.Eval}(k, x^*)$ (real output), whereas G_R answers with random $r \leftarrow \mathcal{Y}$ (fake, random output) – for the task to be non-trivial, no element in $\mathcal{X}$ must be a prefix of x^*. G adds x^* to $\mathcal{X}$.*

Definition 17. *A prefix-constrained PRF* F *is* (s, ε, q)-*adaptive-secure if* G_L *and* G_R *are* (s, ε)-*indistinguishable.*

7.2 Lower Bound for the GGM CPRF

To prove a lower bound for GGM, we use the combinatorial upper bound from Sect. 5.1 for non-oblivious Pebblers, restricted to the class of graphs with outdegree 2. The main challenge here is that – in contrast to our Builder from Sect. 5.1 – the constrain queries of an adversary in the security game for prefix-constrained PRFs correspond to paths in an exponentially large binary tree (see Fig. 3). But it's not only that the adversary has to follow a certain query pattern, but more importantly for each query (which corresponds to a path of up to n edges) it only receives a single evaluation (and this evaluation allows A to efficiently compute any evaluations for the entire subtree below it). While A might be able to use its unrestricted computational power to distinguish whether the answer to its query lies in the image of the PRG (for an appropriately chosen PRG), it is impossible to extract a pebbling configuration on the entire path given just the single evaluation. This is why we follow a different approach and instead of choosing a PRG with sparse output range construct a PRG from two random permutations, which allows A to invert the function and compare whether two queries were computed from the same seed. Similar to the Builder strategy in Sect. 5.1, our adversary A makes bunches of queries forming complete binary subtrees, threaded along the challenge path. However, these queries are now paths of length n such that their *prefixes* cover the binary subtrees, respectively. Accordingly, we then map these bunches of queries to a pebbling strategy on the corresponding binary subtrees, instead of mapping single edges to a pebble or no pebble, as we did in previous applications. Fortunately, the combinatorial bound from Sect. 5.1 still holds for Builders revealing such bunches of queries at once.

Lemma 2 (Coupling Lemma for GGM CPRF). *Let* $\mathcal{G}$ *be the family of trees of depth* D, *size* $N = \mathbf{poly}(D)$, *indegree 1, outdegree 2 and a single source; i.e.* $\mathcal{G}$ *denotes the set of* $\mathbf{poly}(D)$-*sized subtrees of the binary tree of depth* D *which include the root, where edges are directed from the root to the leaves. Furthermore, let* B *and* $X_{\mathcal{C}_D,k}$ *for* $k = \log(D)/2$ *be the Builder and the cut from Theorem 6. Then there exists*

1. an information-theoretically secure length-doubling PRG scheme PRG
2. a CPRF adversary A *in* **PSPACE**

such that for any straight-line *reduction* R *that proves CPRF security of the GGM construction for input length* $D + 1$ *based on the security of the underlying PRG scheme there exists a Pebbler* P *such that the advantage* $1/\Lambda$ *of* R *is at most the advantage of* P *against* B *(up to a negligible additive term* $\mathbf{poly}(D)/2^{\Omega(D)}$*).*

To prove this lemma, we will use the following construction of an information-theoretically secure PRG scheme.

Lemma 3. *Let* $\pi_0, \pi_1 : \{0,1\}^\lambda \to \{0,1\}^\lambda$ *be two random permutations. Then* $\mathsf{PRG} : \{0,1\}^\lambda \to \{0,1\}^{2\lambda}$ *defined by* $\mathsf{PRG}(x) := (\pi_0(x), \pi_1(x))$ *is a* $\mathbf{poly}(\lambda)/2^{\lambda/2}$- *secure length-doubling PRG.*

Proof. Since random permutations are indistinguishable from random functions using only polynomially many queries, we may consider the PRG as a concatenation of two $\mathbf{poly}(\lambda)/2^{\lambda/2}$-secure PRFs by a hybrid argument. Again by hybrid argument, the concatenation of two secure PRFs yields a PRF from $\{0,1\}^\lambda$ to $\{0,1\}^{2\lambda}$. The lemma follows, since length extending PRFs are PRGs.

Having a construction of a PRG in place, we are now ready to prove Lemma 2.

Proof (Proof of Lemma 2). We pick the PRG from Lemma 3 for $\lambda = \Theta(D)$.

Analogously to the proof of Lemma 1 we define a map ϕ between the CPRF game and the Builder-Pebbler Game:

- For a constrain query by adversary A, $(\mathtt{constrain}, x)$, we make a case distinction on the length l of x:
  - if $l = D + 1$, the Builder B extends the current tree in the natural way, ignoring k-sized blocks of trailing zeros in x and adding random nodes as needed. More formally, write $x = x^1 || x^2 || x^3 \in \{0,1\}^{l_1} \times \{0,1\}^{l_2} \times \{0\}^{l_3} \times \{0,1\}$ with $l_1, l_2, l_3 \geq 0$ and $k | l_3$, where x^1 is the longest prefix of x that has been queried so far. For each prefix x' of x with length between $l_1 + 1$ and $l_1 + l_2$, B chooses a uniformly random node (that is not associated to any prefix yet) and associates it to x'. Writing $x^2 = (x_1^2, x_2^2, \dots)$, it then queries the edges between the nodes associated with x^1 and $x^1 || x_1^2$, between $x^1 || x_1^2$ and $x^1 || x_1^2 || x_2^2$, etc.
  - if $l \leq D$, B ignores the query.
- For the challenge query $(\mathtt{challenge}, x^*)$, proceed as for constrain queries to extend the tree. Choose the node associated to x^* as the challenge T.
- Pebbles are determined in the following way. Recall that the Builder from Theorem 6 always extends the tree in chunks of entire subtrees (and the queries comprising such a chunk can be sent at the same time). So we may restrict the definition of ϕ to preimages of such Builders. To determine which edges in such a subtree are pebbled, consider the responses y_i corresponding to the queries x_i in such a chunk. For each y_i invert π_0 repeatedly to obtain the seed associated to the i-th leaf in the subtree. Then for every node, bottom-up, if
  - the children are associated with seeds s_0, s_1, resp., check if $\pi_0^{-1}(s_0) = \pi_1^{-1}(s_1)$. If this is true, associate the node with this computed seed. Otherwise, consider both outgoing edges from this node as pebbled and set the seed of this node to $\bot$.
  - only the left (right) child is associated with a seed s, set the seed of this node to $\pi_0^{-1}(s)$ $(\pi_1^{-1}(s)$, resp.$)$.
  - neither of the children is associated with a seed, set the seed of the current node to $\bot$.

For the root of the subtree, which already has a seed s (or $\perp$) associated to it, check if s is consistent with its children; if not, update to $\perp$ and pebble both outgoing edges.

Let A be the preimage under ϕ of B from Theorem 6 as follows: A first queries CPRF evaluations for $\{0,1\}^{2k}||0^{D-2k+1}$ in reverse order (i.e. starting from $1^{2k}||0^{D-2k+1})^{13}$ – this is in analogy to the first $2k$ rounds of B (see Fig. 3). Then it proceeds in $[D/k-2]$ rounds, where in round $j \in [D/k-2]$ it first samples $x_j^* \in \{0,1\}^k$ and then makes 2^{2k} queries $x_1^*||\ldots||x_j^*||\{0,1\}^{2k}||0^{D-(j+2)k+1}$ in reverse order, starting with $x_1^*||\ldots||x_j^*||1^{2k}||0^{D-(j+2)k+1}$. Next, A samples a challenge $x^* = (x_1^*,\ldots,x_D^*,1)$ in $x_1^*||\ldots||x_{D/k-2}^*||\{0,1\}^{2k}||1$ uniformly at random. Furthermore, it makes constrain queries for all prefixes $(x_1^*,\ldots,x_{j-1}^*,\bar{x}_j)$ for $j \in [D]$. If the answers to the prefixes are not consistent with the previous CPRF queries, then A aborts and outputs 0. Otherwise, A uses its unrestricted computational power to compute the mapping ϕ from the reduction's answers to its queries to a pebbling configuration on the subtree. Note that due to the previous check, there must not be any pebbles on edges rooted at nodes outside the challenge path. A now considers the pebbling configuration induced on the challenge path. If this pebbling configuration lies in the cut defined by $X_{\mathcal{C}_D,k}$, the adversary A outputs 0, otherwise 1.

Clearly, A wins the CPRF game with probability 1. Now, let R be an arbitrary straight-line reduction. First, note that the probability that R queries PRG on the challenge seed is negligibly small $(\mathbf{poly}(D)/2^{\Omega(D)})$. Assuming this does not happen, R can only gain a bigger advantage if it embeds its PRG challenge when interacting with A and manages to hit a pebbling configuration in the cut, i.e. such that depending on the challenge being real or random the pebbling configuration which A extracts lies either in the cut set or not. Note that choosing a value in the tree at random instead of applying PRG to the correct output is equivalent (w.r.t. A's behavior) to responding to the respective queries inconsistently and will thus yield a pebble with overwhelming probability. Furthermore, the consistency check after the constrain queries ensures that R may only place pebbles on edges rooted in the challenge graph and can only embed its challenge in the challenge graph. Similar to the proof in Lemma 1, one can see that R maps (under ϕ) to a Pebbler in the Builder-Pebbler Game which has at least the same advantage of achieving such a configuration.

$\square$

Using the above lemma, the following corollary now easily follows from Theorem 6.

---

[13] This is for technical reasons: We defined the mapping ϕ to ignore k-blocks of trailing zeros in order to associate queries $x||0^{D-2k+1}$ to (non-disjoint) paths of length $2k$. To this aim ϕ prolongs the longest already existing subpath associated to some prefix x' of x. If A now starts querying the string 0^{D+1}, this query would simply be ignored. On the other hand, if there was a preceding query $0^{2k-1}||1||0^{D-2k+1}$, then the query 0^{D+1} is mapped to an edge extending the path associated with the prefix 0^{2k-1}.

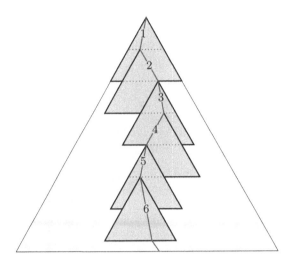

Fig. 3. A schematic diagram showing the adversarial query strategy for GGM CPRF in Lemma 2. The outer (gray) triangle represents the perfect binary tree of depth $D = 7k + 1$ representing the GGM PRF. The internal (blue) triangles represent perfect binary trees of depth $2k$ with the j-th triangle representing the 2^{2k} queries $x_1^*||\ldots||x_j^*||\{0,1\}^{2k}||0^{D-(j+2)k+1}$. The challenge x^* is highlighted (in red) with the label j indicating the string x_j^*. (Color figure online)

Corollary 2 (Lower Bound for GGM). *Let n be the input length of the GGM CPRF scheme. Then any straight-line reduction proving cPRF security of the GGM construction based on the security of the underlying PRG scheme loses at least a factor $\Lambda \geq n^{(\log(n)-\log\log(n))/2}$.*

References

1. Alwen, J., et al.: Keep the dirt: tainted TreeKEM, adaptively and actively secure continuous group key agreement. Cryptology ePrint Archive, Report 2019/1489 (2019). https://eprint.iacr.org/2019/1489
2. Alwen, J., Coretti, S., Dodis, Y., Tselekounis, Y.: Security analysis and improvements for the IETF MLS standard for group messaging. In: Micciancio, D., Ristenpart, T. (eds.) CRYPTO 2020, Part I. LNCS, vol. 12170, pp. 248–277. Springer, Cham (2020). https://doi.org/10.1007/978-3-030-56784-2_9
3. Alwen, J., Serbinenko, V.: High parallel complexity graphs and memory-hard functions. In: Servedio, R.A., Rubinfeld, R. (eds.) 47th ACM STOC, pp. 595–603. ACM Press, June 2015
4. Bellare, M., Hoang, V.T., Rogaway, P.: Adaptively secure garbling with applications to one-time programs and secure outsourcing. In: Wang, X., Sako, K. (eds.) ASIACRYPT 2012. LNCS, vol. 7658, pp. 134–153. Springer, Heidelberg (2012). https://doi.org/10.1007/978-3-642-34961-4_10
5. Bellare, M., Hofheinz, D., Yilek, S.: Possibility and impossibility results for encryption and commitment secure under selective opening. In: Joux, A. (ed.) EURO-

CRYPT 2009. LNCS, vol. 5479, pp. 1–35. Springer, Heidelberg (2009). https://doi.org/10.1007/978-3-642-01001-9_1

6. Bennett, C.H.: Time/space trade-offs for reversible computation. SIAM J. Comput. **18**(4), 766–776 (1989)

7. Black, J., Rogaway, P., Shrimpton, T.: Encryption-scheme security in the presence of key-dependent messages. In: Nyberg, K., Heys, H. (eds.) SAC 2002. LNCS, vol. 2595, pp. 62–75. Springer, Heidelberg (2003). https://doi.org/10.1007/3-540-36492-7_6

8. Blaze, M., Bleumer, G., Strauss, M.: Divertible protocols and atomic proxy cryptography. In: Nyberg, K. (ed.) EUROCRYPT 1998. LNCS, vol. 1403, pp. 127–144. Springer, Heidelberg (1998). https://doi.org/10.1007/BFb0054122

9. Boneh, D., Venkatesan, R.: Breaking RSA may not be equivalent to factoring. In: Nyberg, K. (ed.) EUROCRYPT 1998. LNCS, vol. 1403, pp. 59–71. Springer, Heidelberg (1998). https://doi.org/10.1007/BFb0054117

10. Boneh, D., Waters, B.: Constrained pseudorandom functions and their applications. In: Sako, K., Sarkar, P. (eds.) ASIACRYPT 2013, Part II. LNCS, vol. 8270, pp. 280–300. Springer, Heidelberg (2013). https://doi.org/10.1007/978-3-642-42045-0_15

11. Boyle, E., Goldwasser, S., Ivan, I.: Functional signatures and pseudorandom functions. In: Krawczyk, H. (ed.) PKC 2014. LNCS, vol. 8383, pp. 501–519. Springer, Heidelberg (2014). https://doi.org/10.1007/978-3-642-54631-0_29

12. Canetti, R., Feige, U., Goldreich, O., Naor, M.: Adaptively secure multi-party computation. In: 28th ACM STOC, pp. 639–648. ACM Press, May 1996

13. Canetti, R., Garay, J.A., Itkis, G., Micciancio, D., Naor, M., Pinkas, B.: Multicast security: a taxonomy and some efficient constructions. In: IEEE INFOCOM 1999, New York, NY, USA, pp. 708–716, 21–25 March 1999

14. Chung, F., Diaconis, P., Graham, R.: Combinatorics for the east model. Adv. Appl. Math. **27**(1), 192–206 (2001)

15. Coron, J.-S.: On the exact security of full domain hash. In: Bellare, M. (ed.) CRYPTO 2000. LNCS, vol. 1880, pp. 229–235. Springer, Heidelberg (2000). https://doi.org/10.1007/3-540-44598-6_14

16. Dwork, C., Naor, M., Reingold, O., Stockmeyer, L.J.: Magic functions. In: 40th FOCS, pp. 523–534. IEEE Computer Society Press, October 1999

17. Dwork, C., Naor, M., Wee, H.: Pebbling and proofs of work. In: Shoup, V. (ed.) CRYPTO 2005. LNCS, vol. 3621, pp. 37–54. Springer, Heidelberg (2005). https://doi.org/10.1007/11535218_3

18. Dziembowski, S., Kazana, T., Wichs, D.: One-time computable self-erasing functions. In: Ishai, Y. (ed.) TCC 2011. LNCS, vol. 6597, pp. 125–143. Springer, Heidelberg (2011). https://doi.org/10.1007/978-3-642-19571-6_9

19. Fuchsbauer, G., Jafargholi, Z., Pietrzak, K.: A quasipolynomial reduction for generalized selective decryption on trees. In: Gennaro, R., Robshaw, M. (eds.) CRYPTO 2015, Part I. LNCS, vol. 9215, pp. 601–620. Springer, Heidelberg (2015). https://doi.org/10.1007/978-3-662-47989-6_29

20. Fuchsbauer, G., Kamath, C., Klein, K., Pietrzak, K.: Adaptively secure proxy re-encryption. In: Lin, D., Sako, K. (eds.) PKC 2019, , Part II. LNCS, vol. 11443, pp. 317–346. Springer, Cham (2019). https://doi.org/10.1007/978-3-030-17259-6_11

21. Fuchsbauer, G., Konstantinov, M., Pietrzak, K., Rao, V.: Adaptive security of constrained PRFs. In: Sarkar, P., Iwata, T. (eds.) ASIACRYPT 2014, Part II. LNCS, vol. 8874, pp. 82–101. Springer, Heidelberg (2014). https://doi.org/10.1007/978-3-662-45608-8_5

22. Garg, S., Ostrovsky, R., Srinivasan, A.: Adaptive garbled RAM from laconic oblivious transfer. In: Shacham, H., Boldyreva, A. (eds.) CRYPTO 2018, Part III. LNCS, vol. 10993, pp. 515–544. Springer, Cham (2018). https://doi.org/10.1007/978-3-319-96878-0_18

23. Garg, S., Srinivasan, A.: Adaptively secure garbling with near optimal online complexity. In: Nielsen, J.B., Rijmen, V. (eds.) EUROCRYPT 2018, Part II. LNCS, vol. 10821, pp. 535–565. Springer, Cham (2018). https://doi.org/10.1007/978-3-319-78375-8_18

24. Gennaro, R., Gertner, Y., Katz, J., Trevisan, L.: Bounds on the efficiency of generic cryptographic constructions. SIAM J. Comput. $35(1)$, 217–246 (2005)

25. Gennaro, R., Trevisan, L.: Lower bounds on the efficiency of generic cryptographic constructions. In: 41st FOCS, pp. 305–313. IEEE Computer Society Press, November 2000

26. Gentry, C., Wichs, D.: Separating succinct non-interactive arguments from all falsifiable assumptions. In: Fortnow, L., Vadhan, S.P. (eds.) 43rd ACM STOC, pp. 99–108. ACM Press, June 2011

27. Goldreich, O., Goldwasser, S., Micali, S.: On the cryptographic applications of random functions (extended abstract). In: Blakley, G.R., Chaum, D. (eds.) CRYPTO 1984. LNCS, vol. 196, pp. 276–288. Springer, Heidelberg (1985). https://doi.org/10.1007/3-540-39568-7_22

28. Hefetz, D., Krivelevich, M., Stojakovic, M., Szabó, T.: Positional Games. Birkhäuser Basel (2014)

29. Hemenway, B., Jafargholi, Z., Ostrovsky, R., Scafuro, A., Wichs, D.: Adaptively secure garbled circuits from one-way functions. In: Robshaw, M., Katz, J. (eds.) CRYPTO 2016, Part III. LNCS, vol. 9816, pp. 149–178. Springer, Heidelberg (2016). https://doi.org/10.1007/978-3-662-53015-3_6

30. Impagliazzo, R., Rudich, S.: Limits on the provable consequences of one-way permutations. In: 21st ACM STOC, pp. 44–61. ACM Press, May 1989

31. Jafargholi, Z., Kamath, C., Klein, K., Komargodski, I., Pietrzak, K., Wichs, D.: Be adaptive, avoid overcommitting. In: Katz, J., Shacham, H. (eds.) CRYPTO 2017, Part I. LNCS, vol. 10401, pp. 133–163. Springer, Cham (2017). https://doi.org/10.1007/978-3-319-63688-7_5

32. Jafargholi, Z., Wichs, D.: Adaptive security of Yao's garbled circuits. In: Hirt, M., Smith, A. (eds.) TCC 2016, Part I. LNCS, vol. 9985, pp. 433–458. Springer, Heidelberg (2016). https://doi.org/10.1007/978-3-662-53641-4_17

33. Kamath, C., Klein, K., Pietrzak, K., Walter, M.: The cost of adaptivity in security games on graphs. Cryptology ePrint Archive, Report 2021/059 (2021). https://eprint.iacr.org/2021/059

34. Kamath, C., Klein, K., Pietrzak, K., Wichs, D.: Limits on the adaptive security of Yao's garbling. In: Malkin, T., Peikert, C. (eds.) CRYPTO 2021, Part II. LNCS, vol. 12826, pp. 486–515. Springer, Cham (2021). https://doi.org/10.1007/978-3-030-84245-1_17

35. Katsumata, S., Nishimaki, R., Yamada, S., Yamakawa, T.: Compact NIZKs from standard assumptions on bilinear maps. In: Canteaut, A., Ishai, Y. (eds.) EUROCRYPT 2020, Part III. LNCS, vol. 12107, pp. 379–409. Springer, Cham (2020). https://doi.org/10.1007/978-3-030-45727-3_13

36. Kiayias, A., Papadopoulos, S., Triandopoulos, N., Zacharias, T.: Delegatable pseudorandom functions and applications. In: Sadeghi, A.-R., Gligor, V.D., Yung, M. (eds.) ACM CCS 2013, pp. 669–684. ACM Press, November 2013

37. Kim, J.H., Simon, D.R., Tetali, P.: Limits on the efficiency of one-way permutation-based hash functions. In: 40th FOCS, pp. 535–542. IEEE Computer Society Press, October 1999

38. Kowalczyk, L., Wee, H.: Compact adaptively secure ABE for NC^1 from k-Lin. In: Ishai, Y., Rijmen, V. (eds.) EUROCRYPT 2019, Part I. LNCS, vol. 11476, pp. 3–33. Springer, Cham (2019). https://doi.org/10.1007/978-3-030-17653-2_1

39. Král'ovič, R.: Time and space complexity of reversible pebbling. In: Pacholski, L., Ružička, P. (eds.) SOFSEM 2001. LNCS, vol. 2234, pp. 292–303. Springer, Heidelberg (2001). https://doi.org/10.1007/3-540-45627-9_26

40. Lewko, A., Waters, B.: Why proving HIBE systems secure is difficult. In: Nguyen, P.Q., Oswald, E. (eds.) EUROCRYPT 2014. LNCS, vol. 8441, pp. 58–76. Springer, Heidelberg (2014). https://doi.org/10.1007/978-3-642-55220-5_4

41. Nielsen, J.B.: Separating random oracle proofs from complexity theoretic proofs: the non-committing encryption case. In: Yung, M. (ed.) CRYPTO 2002. LNCS, vol. 2442, pp. 111–126. Springer, Heidelberg (2002). https://doi.org/10.1007/3-540-45708-9_8

42. Nordström, J.: New wine into old wineskins: a survey of somepebbling classics with supplemental results (2015)

43. Panjwani, S.: Tackling adaptive corruptions in multicast encryption protocols. In: Vadhan, S.P. (ed.) TCC 2007. LNCS, vol. 4392, pp. 21–40. Springer, Heidelberg (2007). https://doi.org/10.1007/978-3-540-70936-7_2

44. Papadimitriou, C.H.: Games against nature. J. Comput. Syst. Sci. **31**(2), 288–301 (1985)

45. Pass, R.: Unprovable security of perfect NIZK and non-interactive non-malleable commitments. In: Sahai, A. (ed.) TCC 2013. LNCS, vol. 7785, pp. 334–354. Springer, Heidelberg (2013). https://doi.org/10.1007/978-3-642-36594-2_19

46. Paterson, M.S., Hewitt, C.E.: Comparative schematology. In: Record of the Project MAC Conference on Concurrent Systems and Parallel Computation, pp. 119–127. ACM, New York, NY, USA (1970)

47. Reingold, O., Trevisan, L., Vadhan, S.: Notions of reducibility between cryptographic primitives. In: Naor, M. (ed.) TCC 2004. LNCS, vol. 2951, pp. 1–20. Springer, Heidelberg (2004). https://doi.org/10.1007/978-3-540-24638-1_1

48. Rudich, S.: Limits on the provable consequences of one-way functions. Ph.D. thesis, EECS Department, University of California, Berkeley, December 1988

49. Savage, J.E.: Models of Computation - Exploring the Power of Computing. Addison-Wesley, Boston (1998)

50. Simon, D.R.: Finding collisions on a one-way street: can secure hash functions be based on general assumptions? In: Nyberg, K. (ed.) EUROCRYPT 1998. LNCS, vol. 1403, pp. 334–345. Springer, Heidelberg (1998). https://doi.org/10.1007/BFb0054137

51. Wallner, D.M., Harder, E.J., Agee, R.C.: Key management for multicast: issues and architectures. Internet Draft, September 1998. http://www.ietf.org/ID.html

52. Wong, C.K., Gouda, M.G., Lam, S.S.: Secure group communications using key graphs. IEEE/ACM Trans. Netw. **8**(1), 16–30 (2000)

Concurrent Composition of Differential Privacy

Salil Vadhan[1,2] and Tianhao Wang[1,2(✉)]

[1] Harvard University, Cambridge, USA
salil_vadhan@harvard.edu
[2] Princeton University, Princeton, USA
tianhaowang@princeton.edu

Abstract. We initiate a study of the composition properties of *interactive* differentially private mechanisms. An interactive differentially private mechanism is an algorithm that allows an analyst to adaptively ask queries about a sensitive dataset, with the property that an adversarial analyst's view of the interaction is approximately the same regardless of whether or not any individual's data is in the dataset. Previous studies of composition of differential privacy have focused on non-interactive algorithms, but interactive mechanisms are needed to capture many of the intended applications of differential privacy and a number of the important differentially private primitives.

We focus on *concurrent composition*, where an adversary can arbitrarily interleave its queries to several differentially private mechanisms, which may be feasible when differentially private query systems are deployed in practice. We prove that when the interactive mechanisms being composed are *pure* differentially private, their concurrent composition achieves privacy parameters (with respect to pure or approximate differential privacy) that match the (optimal) composition theorem for noninteractive differential privacy. We also prove a composition theorem for interactive mechanisms that satisfy approximate differential privacy. That bound is weaker than even the basic (suboptimal) composition theorem for noninteractive differential privacy, and we leave closing the gap as a direction for future research, along with understanding concurrent composition for other variants of differential privacy.

Keywords: Interactive differential privacy · Concurrent composition theorem

1 Introduction

1.1 Differential Privacy

Differential privacy is a framework for protecting privacy when performing statistical releases on a dataset with sensitive information about individuals. (See the

---

S. Vadhan—Supported by NSF grant CNS-1565387, a grant from the Sloan Foundation, and a Simons Investigator Award.
T. Wang—Work done while at Harvard University.

K. Nissim and B. Waters (Eds.): TCC 2021, LNCS 13043, pp. 582–604, 2021.
https://doi.org/10.1007/978-3-030-90453-1_20

surveys [10,23].) Specifically, for a differentially private mechanism, the probability distribution of the mechanism's outputs of a dataset should be nearly identical to the distribution of its outputs on the same dataset with any single individual's data replaced. To formalize this, we call two datasets x, x', each multisets over a data universe $\mathcal{X}$, *adjacent* if one can be obtained from the other by adding or removing a single element of $\mathcal{X}$.

Definition 1.1 (Differential Privacy [8]). *For $\varepsilon, \delta \geq 0$, a randomized algorithm $\mathcal{M} : \mathrm{MultiSets}(\mathcal{X}) \to \mathcal{Y}$ is (ε, δ)-differentially private if for every pair of adjacent datasets $x, x' \in \mathrm{MultiSets}(\mathcal{X})$, we have:*

$$\forall T \subseteq \mathcal{Y} \ \Pr[\mathcal{M}(x) \in T] \leq e^{\varepsilon} \cdot \Pr[\mathcal{M}(x') \in T] + \delta \tag{1}$$

where the randomness is over the coin flips of the algorithm $\mathcal{M}$.

In the practice of differential privacy, we generally view ε as "privacy-loss budget" that is small but non-negligible (e.g. $\varepsilon = 0.1$), and we view δ as cryptographically negligible (e.g. $\delta = 2^{-60}$). We refer to the case where $\delta = 0$ as *pure differential privacy*, and the case where $\delta > 0$ as *approximate differential privacy*.

1.2 Composition of Differential Privacy

A crucial property of differential privacy is its behavior under composition. If we run multiple distinct differentially private algorithms on the same dataset, the resulting composed algorithm is also differentially private, with some degradation in the privacy parameters (ε, δ). This property is especially important and useful since in practice we rarely want to release only a single statistic about a dataset. Releasing many statistics may require running multiple differentially private algorithms on the same database. Composition is also a very useful tool in algorithm design. In many cases, new differentially private algorithms are created by combining several simpler algorithms. The composition theorems help us analyze the privacy properties of algorithms designed in this way.

Formally, let $\mathcal{M}_0, \mathcal{M}_1, \ldots, \mathcal{M}_{k-1}$ be differentially private mechanisms, we define the composition of these mechanisms by independently executing them. Specifically, we define $\mathcal{M} = \mathrm{Comp}(\mathcal{M}_0, \mathcal{M}_1, \ldots, \mathcal{M}_{k-1})$ as follows:

$$\mathcal{M}(x) = (\mathcal{M}_0(x), \ldots, \mathcal{M}_{k-1}(x))$$

where each $\mathcal{M}_i$ is run with independent coin tosses. For example, this is how we might obtain a mechanism answering a k-tuple of queries.

A handful of composition theorems already exist in the literature. The Basic Composition Theorem says that the privacy degrades at most linearly with the number of mechanisms executed.

Theorem 1.2 (Basic Composition [7]). *For every $\varepsilon \geq 0$, $\delta \in [0, 1]$, if $\mathcal{M}_0, \ldots, \mathcal{M}_{k-1}$ are each (ε, δ)-differentially private mechanisms, then their composition $\mathrm{Comp}(\mathcal{M}_0, \ldots, \mathcal{M}_{k-1})$ is $(k\varepsilon, k\delta)$-differentially private.*

Theorem 1.2 shows the global privacy degradation is linear in the number of mechanisms in the composition. However, if we are willing to tolerate an increase in the δ term, the privacy parameter ε only needs to degrade proportionally to $\sqrt{k}$:

Theorem 1.3 (Advanced Composition [12]). *For all $\varepsilon \geq 0$, $\delta \in [0,1]$, if $\mathcal{M}_0, \ldots, \mathcal{M}_{k-1}$ are each (ε, δ)-differentially private mechanisms and $k < 1/\varepsilon^2$, then for all $\delta' \in (0, 1/2)$, the composition $(\mathcal{M}_0, \ldots, \mathcal{M}_{k-1})$ is $\left(O\left(\sqrt{k \log(1/\delta')} \right) \cdot \varepsilon, k\delta + \delta' \right)$-differentially private.*

Theorem 1.3 is an improvement if $\delta' = 2^{-o(k)}$. However, despite giving an asymptotically correct upper bound for the global privacy parameter, Theorem 1.3 is not exact. Kairouz, Oh, and Viswanath [18] shows how to compute the optimal bound for composing k mechanisms where all of them are (ε, δ)-differentially private. Murtagh and Vadhan [21] further extends the optimal composition for the more general case where the privacy parameters may differ for each algorithm in the composition:

Theorem 1.4 (Optimal Composition [18,21]). *If $\mathcal{M}_0, \ldots, \mathcal{M}_{k-1}$ are each $(\varepsilon_i, \delta_i)$-differentially private, then given any $\delta_g > 0$, $\mathrm{Comp}(\mathcal{M}_0, \ldots, \mathcal{M}_{k-1})$ is $(\varepsilon_g, \delta_g)$-differentially private for the least value of $\varepsilon_g \geq 0$ such that*

$$\frac{1}{\prod_{i=0}^{k-1} (1 + e^{\varepsilon_i})} \sum_{S \subseteq \{0, \ldots, k-1\}} \max \left\{ e^{\sum_{i \in S} \varepsilon_i} - e^{\varepsilon_g} \cdot e^{\sum_{i \notin S} \varepsilon_i}, 0 \right\} \leq 1 - \frac{1 - \delta_g}{\prod_{i=0}^{k-1} (1 - \delta_i)}$$

A special case when all $\mathcal{M}_0, \ldots, \mathcal{M}_{k-1}$ are (ε, δ)-differentially private, then privacy parameter is upper bounded by the least value of $\varepsilon_g \geq 0$ such that

$$\frac{1}{(1 + e^{\varepsilon})^k} \sum_{i=0}^{k} \binom{k}{i} \max \left\{ e^{i\varepsilon} - e^{\varepsilon_g} \cdot e^{(k-i)\varepsilon}, 0 \right\} \leq 1 - \frac{1 - \delta_g}{(1 - \delta)^k}$$

1.3   Interactive Differential Privacy

The standard treatment of differential privacy, as captured by Definition 1.1, refers to a *noninteractive* algorithm $\mathcal{M}$ that takes a dataset x as input and produces a statistical release $\mathcal{M}(x)$, or a batch by taking $\mathcal{M} = \mathrm{Comp}(\mathcal{M}_0, \ldots, \mathcal{M}_{k-1})$. However, in many of the motivating applications of differential privacy, we don't want to perform all of our releases in one shot, but rather allow analysts to make adaptive queries to a dataset. Thus, we should view the mechanism $\mathcal{M}$ as a party in a two-party protocol, interacting with a (possibly adversarial) analyst.

To formalize the concept of interactive DP, we recall one of the standard formalizations of an interactive protocol between two parties A and B. We do this by viewing each party as a function, taking its private input, all messages it has received, and the party's random coins, to the party's next message to be sent out.

Definition 1.5 (Interactive protocols). *An* interactive protocol (A, B) *is any pair of functions. The interaction between A with input x_A and B with input x_B is the following random process (denoted $(A(x_A), B(x_B))$):*

1. *Uniformly choose random coins r_A and r_B (binary strings) for A and B, respectively.*
2. *Repeat the following for $i = 0, 1, \ldots$:*
   (a) *If i is even, let $m_i = A(x_A, m_1, m_3, \ldots, m_{i-1}; r_A)$.*
   (b) *If i is odd, let $m_i = B(x_B, m_0, m_2, \ldots, m_{i-1}; r_B)$.*
   (c) *If $m_{i-1} = \mathtt{halt}$, then exit loop.*

We further define the view of a party in an interactive protocol to capture everything the party "sees" during the execution:

Definition 1.6 (View of a party in an interactive protocol). *Let (A, B) be an interactive protocol. Let r_A and r_B be the random coins for A and B, respectively. A's view of $(A(x_A; r_A), B(x_B; r_B))$ is the tuple $\mathtt{View}_A \langle A(x_A; r_A), B(x_B; r_B) \rangle = (r_A, x_A, m_1, m_3, \ldots)$ consisting of all the messages received by A in the execution of the protocol together with the private input x_A and random coins r_A. If we drop the random coins r_A and/or r_B, $\mathtt{View}_A \langle A(x_A), B(x_B) \rangle$ becomes a random variable. B's view of $(A(x_A), B(x_B))$ is defined symmetrically.*

In our case, A is the adversary and B is the mechanism whose input is usually a database x. Since A does not have an input in our case, we will denote the interactive protocol as $(A, B(x))$ for the ease of notation. Since we will only be interested in A's view and A does not have an input, we will drop the subscript and write A's view as $\mathtt{View}\langle A, B(x) \rangle$.

Now we are ready to define the interactive differential privacy as a type of interactive protocol between an adversary (without any computational limitations) and an interactive mechanism of special properties.

Definition 1.7 (Interactive Differential Privacy). *A randomized algorithm $\mathcal{M}$ is an (ε, δ)-differentially private interactive mechanism if for every pair of adjacent datasets $x, x' \in \mathrm{MultiSets}(\mathcal{X})$, for every adversary algorithm $\mathcal{A}$ we have:*

$$\forall T \subseteq \mathrm{Range}\left(\mathtt{View}\langle \mathcal{A}, \mathcal{M}(\cdot) \rangle\right),$$
$$\Pr\left[\mathtt{View}\langle \mathcal{A}, \mathcal{M}(x) \rangle \in T\right] \leq e^{\varepsilon} \Pr\left[\mathtt{View}\langle \mathcal{A}, \mathcal{M}(x') \rangle \in T\right] + \delta \tag{2}$$

where the randomness is over the coin flips of both the algorithm $\mathcal{M}$ and the adversary $\mathcal{A}$.

In addition to being the "right" modelling for many applications of differential privacy, interactive differential privacy also captures the full power of fundamental DP mechanisms such as the Sparse Vector Technique [9,22] and Private Multiplicative Weights [17], which are in turn useful in the design of other DP algorithms (which can use these mechanisms as subroutines and issue adaptive queries to them). Interactive DP was also chosen as the basic abstraction in the programming framework for the new open-source software project OpenDP [14], which was our motivation for this research.

Despite being such a natural and useful notion, interactive DP has not been systematically studied in its own right. It has been implicitly studied in the context of distributed forms of DP, starting with [1], where the sensitive dataset is split amongst several parties, who execute a multiparty protocol to estimate a joint function of their data, while each party ensures that their portion of the dataset has the protections of DP against the other parties. Indeed, in an m-party protocol, requiring DP against malicious coalitions of size $m - 1$ is equivalent to requiring that each party's strategy is an interactive DP mechanism in the sense of Definition 1.7. An extreme case of this is the *local model* of DP, where each party holds a single data item in $\mathcal{X}$ representing data about themselves [19]. There been extensive research about the power of interactivity in local DP; see [5] and the references therein. In contrast to these distributed models, in Definition 1.7 we are concerned with the *centralized DP* scenario where only one party ($\mathcal{M}$) holds sensitive data, and how an adversarial data analyst ($\mathcal{A}$) may exploit adaptive queries to extract information about the data subjects.

Some of the aforementioned composition theorems for noninteractive DP, such as in [12,21], are framed in terms of an adaptive "composition game" where an adversary can adaptively select the mechanisms $\mathcal{M}_0, \ldots, \mathcal{M}_{k-1}$, and thus the resulting composition $\mathrm{Comp}(\mathcal{M}_0, \ldots, \mathcal{M}_{k-1})$ can be viewed as an interactive mechanism, but the results are not framed in terms of a general definition of Interactive DP. In particular, the mechanisms $\mathcal{M}_i$ being composed are restricted to be noninteractive in the statements and proofs of these theorems.

1.4   Our Contributions

In this paper, we initiate a study of the composition of interactive DP mechanisms. Like in the context of cryptographic protocols, there are several different forms of composition we can consider. The simplest is *sequential composition*, where all of the queries to $\mathcal{M}_{i-1}$ must be completed before any queries are issued to $\mathcal{M}_i$. It is straightforward to extend the proofs of the noninteractive DP composition theorems to handle sequential composition of interactive DP mechanisms; in particular the Optimal Composition Theorem (Theorem 1.4) extends to this case. (Details omitted.)

Thus, we turn to *concurrent composition*, where an adversary can arbitrarily interleave its queries to the k mechanisms. Although the mechanisms use independent randomness, the adversary may create correlations between the executions by coordinating its actions; in particular, its queries in one execution may also depend on messages it received in other executions. Concurrent composability is important for the deployment of interactive DP in practice, as one or more organizations may set up multiple DP query systems on datasets that refer to some of the same individuals, and we would not want the privacy of those individuals to be violated by an adversary that can concurrently access those systems. Concurrent composability may also be useful in the design of DP algorithms; for example, one might design a DP machine learning algorithm that uses adaptive and interleaved queries to two instantiations of an interactive DP mechanism like the Sparse Vector Technique [9,22].

Although the concurrent composition for the case of differential privacy has not been explored before, it has been studied extensively for many primitives in cryptography, and it is often much more subtle than the sequential composition. (See the surveys [4,15].)

For example, standard zero-knowledge protocols are no longer zero-knowledge when a single prover is involved in multiple, simultaneous zero-knowledge proofs with one or multiple verifiers [13,16].

We use $\mathrm{ConComp}(\mathcal{M}_0, \ldots, \mathcal{M}_{k-1})$ to denote the concurrent composition of interactive mechanisms $\mathcal{M}_0, \ldots, \mathcal{M}_{k-1}$. (See Sect. 2 for a formal definition.)

Our first result is roughly an analogue of the Basic Composition Theorem.

Theorem 1.8. *If interactive mechanisms* $\mathcal{M}_0, \ldots, \mathcal{M}_{k-1}$ *are each* (ε, δ)-*differentially private, then their concurrent composition* $\mathrm{ConComp}(\mathcal{M}_0, \ldots, \mathcal{M}_{k-1})$ *is* $\left(k \cdot \varepsilon, \frac{e^{k\varepsilon}-1}{e^{\varepsilon}-1} \cdot \delta\right)$-*differentially private.*

More generally, if interactive mechanism $\mathcal{M}_i$ *is* $(\varepsilon_i, \delta_i)$-*differentially private for* $i = 0, \ldots, k-1$, *then the concurrent composition* $\mathrm{ConComp}(\mathcal{M}_0, \ldots, \mathcal{M}_{k-1})$ *is* $(\varepsilon_g, \delta_g)$-*differentially private, where*

$$\varepsilon_g = \sum_{i=0}^{k-1} \varepsilon_i, \ and$$

$$\delta_g = \sum_{i=0}^{k-1} e^{\sum_{j=0}^{i-1} \varepsilon_j} \cdot \delta_i \leq e^{\varepsilon_g} \cdot \sum_{i=0}^{k-1} \delta_i.$$

Just like in the Basic Composition Theorem for noninteractive DP (Theorem 1.2), the privacy-loss parameters ε_i just sum up. However, the bound on δ_g is worse by a factor of at most e^{ε_g}. In the typical setting where we want to enforce a global privacy loss of $\varepsilon_g = O(1)$, this is only a constant-factor loss compared to the Basic Composition Theorem, but that constant can be important in practice. Note that expression for δ_g depends on the ordering of the k mechanisms $\mathcal{M}_0, \ldots, \mathcal{M}_{k-1}$, so one can optimize it further by taking a permutation of the mechanisms that minimizes δ_g.

The proof of Theorem 1.8 is by a standard hybrid argument. We compare the distributions of $H_0 = \mathtt{View}\langle \mathcal{A}, \mathrm{ConComp}(\mathcal{M}_0(x), \mathcal{M}_1(x), \ldots, \mathcal{M}_{k-1}(x))\rangle$ and $H_k = \mathtt{View}\langle \mathcal{A}, \mathrm{ConComp}(\mathcal{M}_0(x'), \mathcal{M}_1(x'), \ldots, \mathcal{M}_{k-1}(x'))\rangle$ on adjacent datasets x, x' by changing x to x' for one mechanism at a time, so that H_{i-1} and H_i differ only on the input to $\mathcal{M}_{i-1}$. To relate H_{i-1} and H_i we consider an adversary strategy $\mathcal{A}_i$ that emulates $\mathcal{A}$'s interaction with $\mathcal{M}_{i-1}$, while internally simulating all of the other $\mathcal{M}_j$'s. Applying a "triangle inequality" to the distance notion given in Requirement (2) yields the result. This proof is very similar to the proof of the "group privacy" property of (noninteractive) differential privacy, where (ε, δ)-DP for datasets that differ on one record implies $\left(k \cdot \varepsilon, \frac{e^{k\varepsilon}-1}{e^{\varepsilon}-1} \cdot \delta\right)$ for datasets that differ on k records.

Next we show that the Advanced and Optimal Composition Theorems (Theorems 1.3 and 1.4) for noninteractive DP extend to interactive DP, provided that the mechanisms $\mathcal{M}_i$ being composed satisfy pure DP (i.e. $\delta_i = 0$). Note that the final composed mechanism $\mathrm{ConComp}(\mathcal{M}_0, \ldots, \mathcal{M}_{k-1})$ can be approximate DP, by taking $\delta_g = \delta' > 0$, and thereby allowing for a privacy loss ε_g that grows linearly in $\sqrt{k}$ rather than k.

We do this by extending the main proof technique of [18,21] to interactive DP mechanisms. Specifically, we reduce the analysis of interactive $(\varepsilon, 0)$-DP mechanisms to that of analyzing the following simple "randomized response" mechanism:

Definition 1.9 ([8,25]). *For $\varepsilon > 0$, define a randomized noninteractive algorithm* $\mathrm{RR}_\varepsilon : \{0,1\} \to \{0,1\}$ *as follows:*

$$\mathrm{RR}_\varepsilon(b) = \begin{cases} b & w.p. \ \frac{e^\varepsilon}{1+e^\varepsilon} \\ \neg b & w.p. \ \frac{1}{1+e^\varepsilon}. \end{cases}$$

Note that RR_ε is a noninteractive $(\varepsilon, 0)$-DP mechanism. We show that every interactive $(\varepsilon, 0)$-DP mechanism can be, in some sense, simulated from RR_ε:

Theorem 1.10. *Suppose that $\mathcal{M}$ is an interactive $(\varepsilon, 0)$-differentially private mechanism. Then for every pair of adjacent datasets x_0, x_1 there exists an interactive mechanism T s.t. for every adversary $\mathcal{A}$ and every $b \in \{0,1\}$ we have*

$$\mathit{View}(\mathcal{A}, \mathcal{M}(x_b)) \equiv \mathit{View}(\mathcal{A}, T(\mathrm{RR}_\varepsilon(b)))$$

Here T is an interactive mechanism that depends on $\mathcal{M}$ as well as a fixed pair of adjacent datasets x_0 and x_1. It receives a single bit as an output of $\mathrm{RR}_\varepsilon(b)$, and then interacts with the adversary $\mathcal{A}$ just like $\mathcal{M}$ would. Kairouz, Oh, and Viswanath [18] proved Theorem 1.10 result for the case that $\mathcal{M}$ and T are noninteractive. The interactive case is more involved because we need a single T that works for all adversary strategies $\mathcal{A}$. (If we allow T to depend on the adversary strategy $\mathcal{A}$, then the result would readily follow from that of [18], but this would not suffice for our application to concurrent composition.)

Given the Theorem 1.10, to analyze $\mathrm{ConComp}(\mathcal{M}_0(x_b), \ldots, \mathcal{M}_{k-1}(x_b))$ on $b = 0$ vs. $b = 1$, it suffices to analyze $\mathrm{ConComp}(T_0(\mathrm{RR}_{\varepsilon_0}(b)), \ldots, T_{k-1}$ $(\mathrm{RR}_{\varepsilon_{k-1}}(b)))$. An adversary's view interacting with the latter concurrent composition can be simulated entirely from the output of $\mathrm{Comp}(\mathrm{RR}_{\varepsilon_0}(b), \ldots, \mathrm{RR}_{\varepsilon_{k-1}}(b))$, which is the composition of entirely noninteractive mechanisms. Thus, we conclude:

Corollary 1.11. *The Advanced and Optimal Composition Theorems (Theorems 1.3 and 1.4) extend to the concurrent composition of $(\varepsilon_i, \delta_i)$-interactive DP mechanisms $\mathcal{M}_i$ provided that $\delta_0 = \delta_1 = \cdots = \delta_{k-1} = 0$.*

We leave the question of whether or not the Advanced and/or Optimal Composition Theorems extend to the concurrent composition of approximate DP mechanisms (with $\delta_i > 0$) for future work. The Optimal Composition Theorem for noninteractive approximate DP (Theorem 1.4) is also proven by showing that any noninteractive (ε, δ)-DP mechanism can be simulated by an approximate-DP generalization of randomized response, $\mathrm{RR}_{(\varepsilon,\delta)}$, analogously to Theorem 1.10. Based on computer experiments described in Sect. 6, we conjecture that such a simulation also exists for every approximate DP interactive mechanism, and the Optimal Composition Theorem should extend at least to 2-round interactive mechanisms in which all messages are 1 bit long.

Another interesting question for future work is analyzing concurrent composition for variants of differential privacy, such as Concentrated DP [2,3,11], Rényi DP [20], and Gaussian DP [6]. Some of these notions require bounds on Rényi divergences, e.g. that

$$D_\alpha(\texttt{View}\langle \mathcal{A}, \mathcal{M}(x)\rangle \| \texttt{View}\langle \mathcal{A}, \mathcal{M}(x')\rangle) \le \rho,$$

for adjacent datasets x, x' and certain pairs (α, ρ). Here sequential composition can be argued using a chain rule for Rényi divergence:

$$D_\alpha((Y, Z)\|(Y', Z')) \le D_\alpha(Y\|Y') + \sup_y D_\alpha(Z|_{Y=y} \| Z'|_{Y'=y}). \qquad (3)$$

Taking Y to be the view of the analyst interacting with $\mathcal{M}_0(x)$, Z to be the view of the analyst in a subsequent interaction with $\mathcal{M}_1(x)$, and Y' and Z' to be analogously defined with respect to an adjacent dataset x', we obtain the usual composition bound of $\rho_0 + \rho_1$ on the overall Rényi divergence of order α, where ρ_0 and ρ_1 are the privacy-loss parameters of the individual mechanisms. However, this argument fails for concurrent DP, since we can no longer assert the privacy properties of $\mathcal{M}_1$ conditioned on any possible value y of the adversary's view of the interaction with $\mathcal{M}_0$. Unfortunately, the Chain Rule (3) does not hold if we replace the supremum with an expectation, so a new proof strategy is needed (if the composition theorem remains true).

2   Definitions and Basic Properties

The formal definition of the concurrent composition of interactive protocols is provided here.

Definition 2.1 (Concurrent Composition of Interactive Protocols). *Let $\mathcal{M}_0, \ldots, \mathcal{M}_{k-1}$ be interactive mechanisms. We say $\mathcal{M} = \mathrm{ConComp}(\mathcal{M}_0, \ldots, \mathcal{M}_{k-1})$ is the concurrent composition of mechanisms $\mathcal{M}_0, \ldots, \mathcal{M}_{k-1}$ if $\mathcal{M}$ runs as follows:*

1. *Random coin tosses for $\mathcal{M}$ consist of $r = (r_0, \ldots, r_{k-1})$ where r_j are random coin tosses for $\mathcal{M}_j$.*
2. *Inputs for $\mathcal{M}$ consists of $x = (x_0, \ldots, x_{k-1})$ where x_j is private input for $\mathcal{M}_j$.*

3. $\mathcal{M}(x, m_0, \ldots, m_{i-1}; r)$ *is defined as follows:*

    (a) *Parse m_{i-1} as (q, j) where q is a query and $j \in [k]$. If m_{i-1} cannot be parsed correctly, output* `halt`.

    (b) *Extract history $(m_0^j, \ldots, m_{t-1}^j)$ from $(m_0, \ldots, m_{i-1})$ where m_i^j are all of the queries to mechanism $\mathcal{M}_j$.*

    (c) *Output $\mathcal{M}_j(x_j, m_0^j, \ldots, m_{t-1}^j; r_j)$.*

We are mainly interested in the case where all mechanisms operate on the same dataset, i.e., the private input for each $\mathcal{M}_i$ are all the same.

We show that to prove an interactive DP mechanism is (ε, δ)-differentially private, it suffices to consider all deterministic adversaries.

Lemma 2.2. *An interactive mechanism $\mathcal{M}$ is (ε, δ)-differentially private if and only if for every pair of adjacent datasets x, x', for every deterministic adversary algorithm $\mathcal{A}$, for every possible output set $T \subseteq \mathrm{Range}\left(\mathit{View}\langle \mathcal{A}, \mathcal{M}(\cdot)\rangle\right)$ we have*

$$\Pr\left[\mathit{View}\langle \mathcal{A}, \mathcal{M}(x)\rangle \in T\right] \le e^{\varepsilon} \Pr\left[\mathit{View}\langle \mathcal{A}, \mathcal{M}(x')\rangle \in T\right] + \delta \tag{4}$$

Proof. The necessity is immediately implied by the definition of interactive differential privacy. We prove the direction of sufficiency here. Assume that mechanism $\mathcal{M}$ satisfies (4) for every deterministic adversary. Suppose, for contradiction, that there exists a randomized adversary $\mathcal{A}$ and some output set T s.t.

$$\Pr\left[\mathtt{View}\langle \mathcal{A}, \mathcal{M}(x)\rangle \in T\right] > e^{\varepsilon} \Pr\left[\mathtt{View}\langle \mathcal{A}, \mathcal{M}(x')\rangle \in T\right] + \delta \tag{5}$$

Since the random coins of $\mathcal{A}$ and $\mathcal{M}$ are independently chosen, we have

$$\Pr\left[\mathtt{View}\langle \mathcal{A}, \mathcal{M}(x)\rangle \in T\right] = \mathbb{E}_{r_A}\left[\Pr_{r_{\mathcal{M}}}\left[\mathtt{View}\langle \mathcal{A}(r_A), \mathcal{M}(x; r_{\mathcal{M}})\rangle \in T\right]\right].$$

Therefore, there must exists at least one fixed r_A s.t.

$$\Pr\left[\mathtt{View}\langle \mathcal{A}(r_A), \mathcal{M}(x)\rangle \in T\right] > e^{\varepsilon} \Pr\left[\mathtt{View}\langle \mathcal{A}(r_A), \mathcal{M}(x')\rangle \in T\right] + \delta$$

otherwise 5 is impossible. Therefore, we can define a deterministic adversary $\mathcal{A}_{r_A} = \mathcal{A}(r_A)$. For set $T_{r_A} = \{(m_1, m_3, \ldots) : (r_A, m_1, m_3, \ldots) \in T\}$, since we have

$$\Pr\left[\mathtt{View}\langle \mathcal{A}(r_A), \mathcal{M}(x)\rangle \in T\right] = \Pr\left[\mathtt{View}\langle \mathcal{A}_{r_A}, \mathcal{M}(x)\rangle \in T_{r_A}\right]$$

we know that $\mathcal{A}_{r_A}$ is a counter example for our assumption, which leads to the conclusion. $\quad\square$

For the convenience of the proof, we introduce a variant of concurrent composition of interactive protocols, which only accept queries in the exact order of $\mathcal{M}_0, \ldots, \mathcal{M}_{k-1}$.

Definition 2.3 (Ordered Concurrent Composition of Interactive Protocols). *Let $\mathcal{M}_0, \ldots, \mathcal{M}_{k-1}$ be interactive mechanisms. We say $\mathcal{M} = \mathrm{ConComp}_{order}(\mathcal{M}_0, \ldots, \mathcal{M}_{k-1})$ is the ordered concurrent composition of mechanisms $\mathcal{M}_0, \ldots, \mathcal{M}_{k-1}$ if $\mathcal{M}(x)$ runs as follows:*

1. *Random coin tosses and inputs for* $\mathcal{M}$ *are the same as* ConComp$(\mathcal{M}_0, \ldots, \mathcal{M}_{k-1})$.
2. $\mathcal{M}(x, m_0, \ldots, m_{i-1}; r)$ *is defined as follows:*
   (a) *Let* $j = i \bmod k$, $t = \lfloor i/k \rfloor$.
   (b) *Output* $\mathcal{M}_j(x, m_j, m_{j+k}, \ldots, m_{j+t \cdot k}; r_j)$.

We also introduce a special kind of interactive mechanism, which ignores all query strings begin with 0.

Definition 2.4 (Null-query Extension). *Given an interactive mechanism* $\mathcal{M}$, *define its* null-query extension $\mathcal{M}^\emptyset$ *defined as follows: For any input message sequence* m, $\mathcal{M}^\emptyset(x, m; r) = \mathcal{M}(x, m'; r)$ *where* $m' = (m'_1, \ldots, m'_k)$ *such that* $(1m'_1, \ldots, 1m'_k)$ *is the subsequence of* m *consisting of all strings that begin with bit 1. That is, all messages that begin with 0 are "null queries" that are ignored. By convention,* $\mathcal{M}(x, \lambda; r) = \bot$ *where* λ *is an empty tuple.*

Now we show that in order to prove ConComp$(\mathcal{M}_0, \ldots, \mathcal{M}_{k-1})$ is (ε, δ)-differentially private, it suffices to prove a corresponding ordered concurrent composition is also (ε, δ)-differentially private. We use $X \equiv Y$ to denote that two random variables X and Y have the same distribution.

Lemma 2.5. ConComp$(\mathcal{M}_0, \ldots, \mathcal{M}_{k-1})$ *is an* (ε, δ)-*differentially private interactive mechanism if the ordered concurrent composition of the null-query extensions of* $\mathcal{M}_0, \ldots, \mathcal{M}_{k-1}$, *i.e.,*
ConComp$_{order}(\mathcal{M}_1^\emptyset, \ldots, \mathcal{M}_k^\emptyset)$, *is an* (ε, δ)-*differentially private interactive mechanism.*

Proof. Suppose ConComp$_{order}(\mathcal{M}_0^\emptyset, \ldots, \mathcal{M}_{k-1}^\emptyset)$ is (ε, δ)-differentially private. For every adversary $\mathcal{A}$ interacting with ConComp$(\mathcal{M}_0, \ldots, \mathcal{M}_{k-1})$, we construct another adversary $\mathcal{A}'$ interacting with ConComp$_{order}(\mathcal{M}_0^\emptyset, \ldots, \mathcal{M}_{k-1}^\emptyset)$ as follows: given any settings of coin tosses r, and any history $(q_0, a_0, \ldots, q_{i-1}, a_{i-1})$ between $\mathcal{A}$ and ConComp$(\mathcal{M}_0, \ldots, \mathcal{M}_{k-1})$,

1. Let $q_i = \mathcal{A}(a_0, \ldots, a_{i-1}; r)$.
2. Parse q_{i-1} as (q_{i-1}^*, s) where q_{i-1}^* is a query and $s \in \{0, \ldots, k-1\}$ the index of target mechanism. Parse q_i as (q_i^*, t) in a similar way.
3. Send the null query 0 to $\mathcal{M}_{(s+1) \bmod k}^\emptyset, \ldots, \mathcal{M}_{(t-1) \bmod k}^\emptyset$ in order.
4. Send $1q_i^*$ to $\mathcal{M}_t^\emptyset$.

Write $\mathcal{M} = $ ConComp$(\mathcal{M}_0, \ldots, \mathcal{M}_{k-1})$, and $\mathcal{M}' = $ ConComp$_{order}(\mathcal{M}_0^\emptyset, \ldots, \mathcal{M}_{k-1}^\emptyset)$. For every query sequence q from $\mathcal{A}$, we have $\mathcal{M}(x, q; r) = \mathcal{M}'(x, q'; r)$ where q' is the sequence of queries that $\mathcal{A}'$ asks based on q (with '1' in front of every query in q and additional 0s). Therefore, for every $\mathcal{A}$ interact with $\mathcal{M}$, and for every dataset x we have

$$\text{View}\langle \mathcal{A}, \mathcal{M}(x) \rangle \equiv \text{Post}(\text{View}\langle \mathcal{A}', \mathcal{M}'(x) \rangle)$$

where Post refers to remove all repeated answers due to the null queries. This immediately leads to

$$\begin{aligned}
&\Pr[\texttt{View}\langle \mathcal{A}, \mathcal{M}(x)\rangle \in T] \\
&= \Pr[\texttt{Post}(\texttt{View}\langle \mathcal{A}', \mathcal{M}'(x)\rangle) \in T] \\
&\leq e^{\varepsilon} \Pr[\texttt{Post}(\texttt{View}\langle \mathcal{A}', \mathcal{M}'(x')\rangle) \in T] + \delta \\
&= e^{\varepsilon} \Pr[\texttt{View}\langle \mathcal{A}, \mathcal{M}(x')\rangle \in T] + \delta
\end{aligned}$$

Therefore, $\mathcal{M}$ is also (ε, δ)-DP.

Given Lemma 2.5, for all of the concurrent compositions we considered in this paper, we assume that the concurrent compositions are ordered. For example, if an adversary $\mathcal{A}$ is concurrently interacting with two mechanisms $\text{ConComp}(\mathcal{M}_0, \mathcal{M}_1)$, we assumes that the queries are alternates between $\mathcal{M}_0$ and $\mathcal{M}_1$.

3   Concurrent Composition for Pure Interactive Differential Privacy

In this section, we show that for pure differential privacy, the privacy bound for concurrent composition is the same as for sequential or noninteractive composition. The proof idea is that in an interactive protocol where the adversary is concurrently interacting with multiple mechanisms, its interaction with one particular mechanism could be viewed as the combination of the adversary and the remaining mechanisms interacting with that mechanism, and the differential privacy guarantee still holds for the "combined adversary".

A useful notation for thinking about differential privacy and simplify presentations is defined below.

Definition 3.1. *Two random variables Y and Z taking values in the same output space $\mathcal{Y}$ is (ε, δ)-indistinguishable if for every event $T \subseteq \mathcal{Y}$, we have:*

$$\Pr[Y \in T] \leq e^{\varepsilon} \Pr[Z \in T] + \delta$$

$$\Pr[Z \in T] \leq e^{\varepsilon} \Pr[Y \in T] + \delta$$

which is denoted as $Y \overset{(\varepsilon,\delta)}{\approx} Z$.

Notice that an algorithm $\mathcal{M}$ is (ε, δ) differentially private if and only if for all pairs of adjacent datasets x, x', we have $\mathcal{M}(x) \overset{(\varepsilon,\delta)}{\approx} \mathcal{M}(x')$.

Lemma 3.2 ([23]). *For random variables X, Y, Z, if $X \overset{(\varepsilon_1,0)}{\approx} Y$, $Y \overset{(\varepsilon_2,0)}{\approx} Z$, then $X \overset{(\varepsilon_1+\varepsilon_2,0)}{\approx} Z$.*

Theorem 3.3 (Basic Composition of Pure Interactive Differential Privacy). *If interactive mechanisms $\mathcal{M}_0, \ldots, \mathcal{M}_{k-1}$ are each $(\varepsilon_i, 0)$-differentially private, then their concurrent composition $\mathrm{ConComp}(\mathcal{M}_0, \ldots, \mathcal{M}_{k-1})$ is $\left(\sum_{i=0}^{k-1} \varepsilon_i, 0\right)$-interactive differentially private.*

Proof. We first consider the simplest case that $\mathcal{A}$ concurrently interact with 2 mechanisms $\mathcal{M}, \tilde{\mathcal{M}}$, and then extend the result to general amount of mechanisms. Suppose $\mathcal{M}$ and $\tilde{\mathcal{M}}$ are each $(\varepsilon, 0)$ and $(\tilde{\varepsilon}, 0)$-differentially private interactive mechanisms. Denote the messages received by $\mathcal{A}$ from $\mathcal{M}$ as $(a_0, a_1, \ldots,)$, and the messages received by $\mathcal{A}$ from $\tilde{\mathcal{M}}$ as $(\tilde{a}_0, \tilde{a}_1, \ldots,)$. Due to Lemma 2.5, we can WLOG assume $\mathcal{A}$ alternates messages between $\mathcal{M}$ and $\tilde{\mathcal{M}}$, i.e., the sequence of messages $\mathcal{A}$ received is $(a_0, \tilde{a}_0, a_1, \tilde{a}_1, \ldots,)$. We use $r_{\mathcal{A}}$, $r_{\mathcal{M}}, r_{\tilde{\mathcal{M}}}$ to denote the random coin tosses for $\mathcal{A}$, $\mathcal{M}$, and $\tilde{\mathcal{M}}$, respectively. We can view $\mathcal{A}$ and $\tilde{\mathcal{M}}(x)$ as a single adversary $\mathcal{A}^*_{\tilde{\mathcal{M}}}(x)$ interacting with $\mathcal{M}(x)$ defined as follows:

1. Random coin tosses for $\mathcal{A}^*_{\tilde{\mathcal{M}}}(x)$ consist of $r = (r_{\mathcal{A}}, r_{\tilde{\mathcal{M}}})$.
2. $\mathcal{A}^*_{\tilde{\mathcal{M}}}(x)(a_0, a_1, \ldots, a_{i-1}; r)$ is computed as follows:
   (a) $\tilde{q}_{i-1} = \mathcal{A}(a_0, \tilde{a}_0, a_1, \tilde{a}_1, \ldots, a_{i-1}; r_{\mathcal{A}})$.
   (b) $\tilde{a}_{i-1} = \tilde{\mathcal{M}}(x, \tilde{q}_0, \tilde{q}_1, \ldots, \tilde{q}_{i-1}; r_{\tilde{\mathcal{M}}})$.
   (c) $q_i = \mathcal{A}(a_0, \tilde{a}_0, \ldots, a_{i-1}, \tilde{a}_{i-1}; r_{\mathcal{A}})$.
   (d) Output q_i.

We can see that $\mathcal{A}^*_{\tilde{\mathcal{M}}}(x)$ is a well-defined strategy throughout the entire interactive protocol with $\mathcal{M}$, where the randomness of $\mathcal{A}^*_{\tilde{\mathcal{M}}}(x)$ is fixed as $(r_{\mathcal{A}}, r_{\tilde{\mathcal{M}}})$. Given a transcript of $\mathcal{A}^*_{\tilde{\mathcal{M}}}(x)$'s view $(r_{\mathcal{A}}, r_{\tilde{\mathcal{M}}}, x, a_0, a_1, \ldots,)$, we can recover the corresponding transcript of $\mathrm{View}\langle \mathcal{A}, \mathrm{ConComp}(\mathcal{M}(x), \tilde{\mathcal{M}}(x)) \rangle$ through the following post-processing algorithm Post, which is defined as follows:
$\mathrm{Post}\,(r_{\mathcal{A}}, r_{\tilde{\mathcal{M}}}, a_0, a_1, \ldots, a_{T-1})$:

1. For $i = 1 \ldots T - 1$, compute
   (a) $\tilde{q}_{i-1} = \mathcal{A}(a_0, \tilde{a}_0, \ldots, a_{i-1}; r_{\mathcal{A}})$
   (b) $\tilde{a}_{i-1} = \tilde{\mathcal{M}}(x, \tilde{q}_1, \tilde{q}_2, \ldots, \tilde{q}_{i-1}; r_{\tilde{\mathcal{M}}})$
2. Output $(r_{\mathcal{A}}, a_0, \tilde{a}_0, \ldots, a_{T-1}, \tilde{a}_{T-1})$.

Observe that for every $(x, r_{\mathcal{A}}, r_{\mathcal{M}}, r_{\tilde{\mathcal{M}}})$,

$$\mathrm{Post}\,\big(\mathrm{View}\langle \mathcal{A}^*_{\tilde{\mathcal{M}}}(x; r_{\mathcal{A}}, r_{\tilde{\mathcal{M}}}), \mathcal{M}(x; r_{\mathcal{M}}) \rangle\big)$$
$$= \mathrm{View}\langle \mathcal{A}(r_{\mathcal{A}}), \mathrm{ConComp}(\mathcal{M}(x; r_{\mathcal{M}}), \tilde{\mathcal{M}}(x; r_{\tilde{\mathcal{M}}})) \rangle$$

Therefore we have

$$\Pr\left[\mathrm{View}\langle \mathcal{A}, \mathrm{ConComp}(\mathcal{M}(x), \tilde{\mathcal{M}}(x)) \rangle \in T \right]$$
$$\equiv \Pr\left[\mathrm{Post}\,\big(\mathrm{View}\langle \mathcal{A}^*_{\tilde{\mathcal{M}}}(x), \mathcal{M}(x) \rangle\big) \in T \right]$$

for every $T \subseteq \mathrm{Range}(\mathrm{View}\langle \mathcal{A}, \mathrm{ConComp}(\mathcal{M}(x), \tilde{\mathcal{M}}(x)) \rangle)$.

Since $\mathcal{M}$ is ε-differentially private, we know that

$$\text{View}\langle \mathcal{A}^*_{\tilde{\mathcal{M}}}(x), \mathcal{M}(x)\rangle \stackrel{(\varepsilon,0)}{\approx} \text{View}\langle \mathcal{A}^*_{\tilde{\mathcal{M}}}(x), \mathcal{M}(x')\rangle$$

which leads to

$$\begin{aligned}
&\text{View}\langle \mathcal{A}, \text{ConComp}(\mathcal{M}(x), \tilde{\mathcal{M}}(x))\rangle \\
&\equiv \text{Post}\left(\text{View}\langle \mathcal{A}^*_{\tilde{\mathcal{M}}}(x), \mathcal{M}(x)\rangle\right) \\
&\stackrel{(\varepsilon,0)}{\approx} \text{Post}\left(\text{View}\langle \mathcal{A}^*_{\tilde{\mathcal{M}}}(x), \mathcal{M}(x')\rangle\right) \\
&\equiv \text{View}\langle \mathcal{A}, \text{ConComp}(\mathcal{M}(x'), \tilde{\mathcal{M}}(x))\rangle
\end{aligned}$$

Symmetrically, we can obtain

$$\begin{aligned}
&\text{View}\langle \mathcal{A}, \text{ConComp}(\mathcal{M}(x'), \tilde{\mathcal{M}}(x))\rangle \\
&\stackrel{(\tilde{\varepsilon},0)}{\approx} \text{View}\langle \mathcal{A}, \text{ConComp}(\mathcal{M}(x'), \tilde{\mathcal{M}}(x'))\rangle
\end{aligned}$$

Therefore, we have

$$\begin{aligned}
&\text{View}\langle \mathcal{A}, \text{ConComp}(\mathcal{M}(x), \tilde{\mathcal{M}}(x))\rangle \\
&\stackrel{(\varepsilon+\tilde{\varepsilon},0)}{\approx} \text{View}\langle \mathcal{A}, \text{ConComp}(\mathcal{M}(x'), \tilde{\mathcal{M}}(x'))\rangle
\end{aligned}$$

The result can be easily extended to the case when more than 2 mechanisms are concurrently composed by induction. Therefore for every $\varepsilon_i \geq 0$, if interactive mechanism $\mathcal{M}_i$ is $(\varepsilon_i, 0)$-differentially private for $i = 0, \ldots, k-1$, then the concurrent composition $\text{ConComp}(\mathcal{M}_0, \ldots, \mathcal{M}_{k-1})$ is $\left(\sum_{i=0}^{k-1} \varepsilon_i, 0\right)$-differentially private.

This result tells us that even under concurrent composition, the privacy parameters of the resulting composed mechanisms are the "sum up" of the individual algorithms for the case pure differential privacy.

4   Concurrent Composition for Approximate Interactive Differential Privacy

In this section, we explore the privacy guarantee for the concurrent composition of interactive differential privacy when $\delta > 0$. We show a privacy guarantee of concurrent composition in a similar logic flow as in Theorem 3.3, but in approximate differential privacy. As argued in the proof of Theorem 3.3, when the adversary is interacting with two mechanisms, we can view $\mathcal{A}$ and one of the mechanisms as a single adversary interacting with another mechanism, and the view of the combined adversary still enjoy the differential privacy guarantee. Therefore, if both interactive mechanisms $\mathcal{M}$ and $\tilde{\mathcal{M}}$ are (ε, δ)-differentially private, then for all $S \subseteq \mathrm{Range}(\mathtt{View}\langle \mathcal{A}, \mathrm{ConComp}(\mathcal{M}(x), \tilde{\mathcal{M}}(x)) \rangle)$, we know that

$$\Pr \left[\mathtt{View}\langle \mathcal{A}, \mathrm{ConComp}(\mathcal{M}(x), \tilde{\mathcal{M}}(x)) \rangle \in S \right]$$
$$\leq e^{\varepsilon} \Pr \left[\mathtt{View}\langle \mathcal{A}, \mathrm{ConComp}(\mathcal{M}(x'), \tilde{\mathcal{M}}(x)) \rangle \in S \right] + \delta$$

and

$$\Pr \left[\mathtt{View}\langle \mathcal{A}, \mathrm{ConComp}(\mathcal{M}(x'), \tilde{\mathcal{M}}(x)) \rangle \in S \right]$$
$$\leq e^{\varepsilon} \Pr \left[\mathtt{View}\langle \mathcal{A}, \mathrm{ConComp}(\mathcal{M}(x'), \tilde{\mathcal{M}}(x')) \rangle \in S \right] + \delta$$

and therefore we know that

$$\Pr \left[\mathtt{View}\langle \mathcal{A}, \mathrm{ConComp}(\mathcal{M}(x), \tilde{\mathcal{M}}(x)) \rangle \in S \right]$$
$$\leq e^{\varepsilon} \Pr \left[\mathtt{View}\langle \mathcal{A}, \mathrm{ConComp}(\mathcal{M}(x'), \tilde{\mathcal{M}}(x)) \rangle \in S \right] + \delta$$
$$\leq e^{\varepsilon} (e^{\varepsilon} \Pr \left[\mathtt{View}\langle \mathcal{A}, \mathrm{ConComp}(\mathcal{M}(x'), \tilde{\mathcal{M}}(x')) \rangle \in S \right] + \delta) + \delta$$
$$\leq e^{2\varepsilon} \Pr \left[\mathtt{View}\langle \mathcal{A}, \mathrm{ConComp}(\mathcal{M}(x'), \tilde{\mathcal{M}}(x')) \rangle \in S \right] + (1 + e^{\varepsilon})\delta$$

A more general concurrent composition bound is stated and derived as follows:

Theorem 4.1 (Theorem 1.8 restated). *Let* $\sigma : \{0, 1, \ldots, n - 1\} \to \{0, 1, \ldots, n - 1\}$ *be any permutation of* $0, \ldots, n - 1$. *If interactive mechanisms* $\mathcal{M}_0, \ldots, \mathcal{M}_{k-1}$ *are each* $(\varepsilon_i, \delta_i)$-*differentially private, then their concurrent composition* $\mathrm{ConComp}(\mathcal{M}_0, \ldots, \mathcal{M}_{k-1})$ *is* $\left(\sum_{i=0}^{k-1} \varepsilon_i, \delta_g \right)$-*differentially private, where*

$$\delta_g = \min_{\sigma} \left(\delta_{\sigma(0)} + \sum_{i=1}^{k-1} e^{\sum_{j=0}^{i-1} \varepsilon_{\sigma(j)}} \delta_{\sigma(i)} \right)$$

For mathematical convenience, we use an upper bound for δ_g *in practice and* $\mathrm{ConComp}(\mathcal{M}_0, \ldots, \mathcal{M}_{k-1})$ *is* $\left(\sum_{i=0}^{k-1} \varepsilon_i, k e^{\sum_{i=0}^{k-1} \varepsilon_i} \max_i(\delta_i) \right)$-*differentially private.*

Proof. We use a hybrid argument. For each $0 \leq i \leq k - 1$, since $\mathcal{M}_i$ is $(\varepsilon_i, \delta_i)$ differentially private, we know that

$$\Pr \left[\mathtt{View}\langle \mathcal{A}, \mathrm{ConComp}(\mathcal{M}_0(x'), \ldots, \mathcal{M}_{i-1}(x'), \mathcal{M}_i(x), \ldots, \mathcal{M}_{k-1}(x)) \rangle \in S \right]$$
$$\leq e^{\varepsilon_i} \Pr \left[\mathtt{View}\langle \mathcal{A}, \mathrm{ConComp}(\mathcal{M}_0(x'), \ldots, \mathcal{M}_{i-1}(x'), \mathcal{M}_i(x'), \ldots, \mathcal{M}_{k-1}(x)) \rangle \in S \right] + \delta_i$$

by viewing $\mathcal{A}$ and $\mathcal{M}_0, \ldots, \mathcal{M}_{i-1}, \mathcal{M}_{i+1}, \mathcal{M}_{k-1}$ as a combined adversary and follow a similar argument as in the proof of Theorem 1.8.

Therefore,

$$\Pr\left[\mathtt{View}\langle\mathcal{A}, \mathrm{ConComp}(\mathcal{M}_0(x), \mathcal{M}_1(x), \dots, \mathcal{M}_{k-1}(x))\rangle \in S\right]$$
$$\leq e^{\varepsilon_0}\Pr\left[\mathtt{View}\langle\mathcal{A}, \mathrm{ConComp}(\mathcal{M}_0(x'), \mathcal{M}_1(x), \dots, \mathcal{M}_{k-1}(x))\rangle \in S\right] + \delta_0$$
$$\leq e^{\varepsilon_0}(e^{\varepsilon_1}\Pr\left[\mathtt{View}\langle\mathcal{A}, \mathrm{ConComp}(\mathcal{M}_0(x'), \mathcal{M}_1(x'), \dots, \mathcal{M}_{k-1}(x))\rangle \in S\right] + \delta_1) + \delta_0$$
$$\leq \dots$$
$$\leq e^{\sum_{i=0}^{k-1}\varepsilon_i}\Pr\left[\mathtt{View}\langle\mathcal{A}, \mathrm{ConComp}(\mathcal{M}_0(x'), \mathcal{M}_1(x'), \dots, \mathcal{M}_{k-1}(x'))\rangle \in S\right]$$
$$+ (\delta_0 + e^{\varepsilon_0}\delta_1 + e^{\varepsilon_0+\varepsilon_1}\delta_2 + \dots + e^{\sum_{i=0}^{k-2}\varepsilon_i}\delta_{k-1})$$

We can see that the δ term of $\mathrm{ConComp}(\mathcal{M}_0, \dots, \mathcal{M}_{k-1})$ depends on different permutations of $(\mathcal{M}_0, \dots, \mathcal{M}_{k-1})$, and the tightest possible bound for the δ term is

$$\min_\sigma \left(\delta_{\sigma(0)} + \sum_{i=1}^{k-1} e^{\sum_{j=0}^{i-1}\varepsilon_{\sigma(j)}}\delta_{\sigma(i)}\right)$$

We also note that $\delta_0 + e^{\varepsilon_0}\delta_1 + e^{\varepsilon_0+\varepsilon_1}\delta_2 + \dots + e^{\sum_{i=0}^{k-2}\varepsilon_i}\delta_{k-1} \leq k e^{\sum_{i=0}^{k-1}\varepsilon_i}\max_i(\delta_i)$, which is more easier to work with in practice.

Notice that if the privacy parameters are homogeneous, i.e. every interactive mechanism is (ε, δ) differentially private, then this bound reduce to the bound of group privacy for (ε, δ)-differential privacy.

5 Characterization of ConComp for Pure Interactive Differential Privacy

[18] shows that to analyze the composition of arbitrary noninteractive $(\varepsilon_i, \delta_i)$-DP algorithms, it suffices to analyze the composition of the following simple variant of randomized response.

Definition 5.1 ([18]). *Define a randomized noninteractive algorithm* $\mathrm{RR}_{(\varepsilon,\delta)}$: $\{0,1\} \to \{0,1, \text{`Iam0'}, \text{`Iam1'}\}$ *as follows:*

$$\Pr\left[\mathrm{RR}_{(\varepsilon,\delta)}(0) = \text{`Iam0'}\right] = \delta \qquad \Pr\left[\mathrm{RR}_{(\varepsilon,\delta)}(1) = \text{`Iam0'}\right] = 0$$
$$\Pr\left[\mathrm{RR}_{(\varepsilon,\delta)}(0) = 0\right] = (1-\delta)\cdot\frac{e^\varepsilon}{1+e^\varepsilon} \quad \Pr\left[\mathrm{RR}_{(\varepsilon,\delta)}(1) = 0\right] = (1-\delta)\cdot\frac{1}{1+e^\varepsilon}$$
$$\Pr\left[\mathrm{RR}_{(\varepsilon,\delta)}(0) = 1\right] = (1-\delta)\cdot\frac{1}{1+e^\varepsilon} \quad \Pr\left[\mathrm{RR}_{(\varepsilon,\delta)}(1) = 1\right] = (1-\delta)\cdot\frac{e^\varepsilon}{1+e^\varepsilon}$$
$$\Pr\left[\mathrm{RR}_{(\varepsilon,\delta)}(0) = \text{`Iam1'}\right] = 0 \qquad \Pr\left[\mathrm{RR}_{(\varepsilon,\delta)}(1) = \text{`Iam1'}\right] = \delta$$

Note that $\mathrm{RR}_{(\varepsilon,\delta)}$ is a noninteractive (ε, δ)-differentially private mechanism. [18] and [21] showed that $\mathrm{RR}_{(\varepsilon,\delta)}$ can be used to simulate the output of every (noninteractive) (ε, δ)-DP algorithm on adjacent databases. RR refers to "randomized response", as this mechanism is a generalization of the classic randomized response to $\delta > 0$ and $\varepsilon \neq \ln 2$ [25].

Theorem 5.2 ([18]). *Suppose that* $\mathcal{M}$ *is* (ε, δ)-*differentially private. Then for every pair of adjacent datasets* x_0, x_1 *there exists a randomized algorithm* T *s.t.* $T(\mathrm{RR}(b))$ *is identically distributed to* $\mathcal{M}(x_b)$ *for both* $b = 0$ *and* $b = 1$.

This theorem is useful due to one of the central properties of differential privacy is that it is preserved under "post-processing" [8,10], which is formulated as follows:

Lemma 5.3 (Post-processing). *If a randomized algorithm $\mathcal{M} : \mathcal{X} \to \mathcal{Y}$ is (ε, δ)-differentially private, and $\mathcal{F} : \mathcal{Y} \to \mathcal{Z}$ is any randomized function, then $\mathcal{F} \circ \mathcal{M} : \mathcal{X} \to \mathcal{Z}$ is also (ε, δ)-differentially private.*

In noninteractive setting, Theorem 5.2 can be used to prove the optimal composition theorem [18,21] since to analyze the composition of arbitrary $(\varepsilon_i, \delta_i)$-DP algorithms, it suffices to analyze the composition of $\mathrm{RR}_{(\varepsilon_i, \delta_i)}$ algorithms.

If we are able to prove a similar result that arbitrary interactive differential private mechanisms can also be simulated by the post-processing of randomized response where the interactive post-processing algorithm does not depend on the adversary, then we will be able to extend all results of composition theorem for noninteractive mechanisms to interactive mechanisms. In this paper, we consider the case of pure differential privacy.

Theorem 5.4 (Theorem 1.10 restated). *Suppose that $\mathcal{M}$ is an interactive $(\varepsilon, 0)$-differentially private mechanism. Then for every pair of adjacent datasets x_0, x_1 there exists an interactive mechanism T s.t. for every adversary $\mathcal{A}$ and every $b \in \{0, 1\}$ we have*

$$\mathit{View}(\mathcal{A}, \mathcal{M}(x_b)) \equiv \mathit{View}(\mathcal{A}, T(\mathrm{RR}_{(\varepsilon, 0)}(b)))$$

Proof. For arbitrary sequence of queries $\boldsymbol{q}^{(t)} = (q_0, \dots, q_{t-1})$ from $\mathcal{A}$, we denote by $\vec{\mathcal{M}}(x, \boldsymbol{q}^{(t)}) = (\mathcal{M}(x, \boldsymbol{q}^{(1)}), \mathcal{M}(x, \boldsymbol{q}^{(2)}), \dots, \mathcal{M}(x, \boldsymbol{q}^{(t)}))$ the random variable consisting of the first t responses from mechanism $\mathcal{M}$. We construct the interactive mechanism T receiving queries $\boldsymbol{q}^{(t)}$ as follows:

1. If $t = 0$, we have

$$\Pr\left[T(0, q_0) = a_0\right] = \frac{e^\varepsilon \Pr[\mathcal{M}(x_0, q_0) = a_0] - \Pr[\mathcal{M}(x_1, q_0) = a_0]}{e^\varepsilon - 1} \quad (6)$$

$$\Pr\left[T(1, q_0) = a_0\right] = \frac{e^\varepsilon \Pr[\mathcal{M}(x_1, q_0) = a_0] - \Pr[\mathcal{M}(x_0, q_0) = a_0]}{e^\varepsilon - 1} \quad (7)$$

2. If $t > 0$, given earlier responses $(a_0, \dots, a_{t-2})$, we define

$$\Pr\left[T(0, \boldsymbol{q}^{(t)}) = a_{t-1} | a_0, \dots, a_{t-2}\right]$$

$$= \frac{e^\varepsilon \Pr\left[\vec{\mathcal{M}}(x_0, \boldsymbol{q}^{(t)}) = (a_0, \dots, a_{t-1})\right] - \Pr\left[\vec{\mathcal{M}}(x_1, \boldsymbol{q}^{(t)}) = (a_0, \dots, a_{t-1})\right]}{(e^\varepsilon - 1) \Pr\left[\vec{T}(0, \boldsymbol{q}^{(t-1)}) = (a_0, \dots, a_{t-2})\right]}$$

$$\quad (8)$$

$$\Pr\left[T(1, \boldsymbol{q}^{(t)}) = a_{t-1} | a_0, \dots, a_{t-2}\right]$$

$$= \frac{e^\varepsilon \Pr\left[\vec{\mathcal{M}}(x_1, \boldsymbol{q}^{(t)}) = (a_0, \dots, a_{t-1})\right] - \Pr\left[\vec{\mathcal{M}}(x_0, \boldsymbol{q}^{(t)}) = (a_0, \dots, a_{t-1})\right]}{(e^\varepsilon - 1) \Pr\left[\vec{T}(1, \boldsymbol{q}^{(t-1)}) = (a_0, \dots, a_{t-2})\right]}$$

$$\quad (9)$$

Therefore, the distribution of $\vec{T}$ is

$$\Pr\left[\vec{T}(0, \boldsymbol{q}^{(t)}) = (a_0, \ldots, a_{t-1})\right]$$

$$= \frac{e^{\varepsilon} \Pr\left[\vec{\mathcal{M}}(x_0, \boldsymbol{q}^{(t)}) = (a_0, \ldots, a_{t-1})\right] - \Pr\left[\vec{\mathcal{M}}(x_1, \boldsymbol{q}^{(t)}) = (a_0, \ldots, a_{t-1})\right]}{e^{\varepsilon} - 1}$$

$$\Pr\left[\vec{T}(1, \boldsymbol{q}^{(t)}) = (a_0, \ldots, a_{t-1})\right]$$

$$= \frac{e^{\varepsilon} \Pr\left[\vec{\mathcal{M}}(x_1, \boldsymbol{q}^{(t)}) = (a_0, \ldots, a_{t-1})\right] - \Pr\left[\vec{\mathcal{M}}(x_0, \boldsymbol{q}^{(t)}) = (a_0, \ldots, a_{t-1})\right]}{e^{\varepsilon} - 1}$$

We can easily verify that all of the above are valid probability distributions. For example,

$$\sum_{a_{t-1}} \Pr\left[T(0, \boldsymbol{q}^{(t)}) = a_{t-1} | a_0, \ldots, a_{t-2}\right]$$

$$= \frac{e^{\varepsilon} \sum_{a_{t-1}} \Pr\left[\vec{\mathcal{M}}(x_0, \boldsymbol{q}^{(t)}) = (a_0, \ldots, a_{t-1})\right] - \sum_{a_{t-1}} \Pr\left[\vec{\mathcal{M}}(x_1, \boldsymbol{q}^{(t)}) = (a_0, \ldots, a_{t-1})\right]}{(e^{\varepsilon} - 1) \Pr\left[\vec{T}(0, \boldsymbol{q}^{(t-1)}) = (a_0, \ldots, a_{t-2})\right]}$$

$$= \frac{e^{\varepsilon} \Pr\left[\vec{\mathcal{M}}(x_0, \boldsymbol{q}^{(t)}) = (a_0, \ldots, a_{t-2})\right] - \Pr\left[\vec{\mathcal{M}}(x_1, \boldsymbol{q}^{(t)}) = (a_0, \ldots, a_{t-2})\right]}{(e^{\varepsilon} - 1) \Pr\left[\vec{T}(0, \boldsymbol{q}^{(t-1)}) = (a_0, \ldots, a_{t-2})\right]}$$

$$= 1$$

and for every possible a_{t-1}, the probability density is never negative since

$$\Pr\left[\vec{\mathcal{M}}(x_0, \boldsymbol{q}^{(t)}) = (a_0, \ldots, a_{t-1})\right] \leq e^{\varepsilon} \Pr\left[\vec{\mathcal{M}}(x_1, \boldsymbol{q}^{(t)}) = (a_0, \ldots, a_{t-1})\right]$$

as $\mathcal{M}$ is $(\varepsilon, 0)$-DP.

We now show

$$\texttt{View}(\mathcal{A}, \mathcal{M}(x_b)) \equiv \texttt{View}(\mathcal{A}, T(\mathrm{RR}_{(\varepsilon,0)}(b)))$$

for the case of $b = 0$.

Fix any possible view $(r, a_0, \ldots, a_{t-1})$, we can derive the queries $\boldsymbol{q}^{(t)} = (q_0, \ldots, q_{t-1})$ from $\mathcal{A}$, where $q_i = \mathcal{A}(a_0, \ldots, a_{i-1}; r)$. Denote R as the random variable of the randomness of $\mathcal{A}$.

$$\Pr\left[\texttt{View}(\mathcal{A}, T(\text{RR}_{(\varepsilon,0)}(0))) = (r, a_0, \dots, a_{t-1})\right]$$
$$= \Pr\left[\text{RR}_{(\varepsilon,0)}(0) = 0\right]\Pr\left[\texttt{View}(\mathcal{A}, T(0)) = (r, a_0, \dots, a_{t-1})\right]$$
$$\quad + \Pr\left[\text{RR}_{(\varepsilon,0)}(1) = 0\right]\Pr\left[\texttt{View}(\mathcal{A}, T(1)) = (r, a_0, \dots, a_{t-1})\right]$$
$$= \frac{e^{\varepsilon}}{1 + e^{\varepsilon}}\Pr\left[\texttt{View}(\mathcal{A}, T(0)) = (r, a_0, \dots, a_{t-1})\right]$$
$$\quad + \frac{1}{1 + e^{\varepsilon}}\Pr\left[\texttt{View}(\mathcal{A}, T(1)) = (r, a_0, \dots, a_{t-1})\right]$$
$$= \frac{e^{\varepsilon}}{1 + e^{\varepsilon}}\Pr\left[R = r\right]\Pr\left[\vec{T}(0, \boldsymbol{q}_r^{(t)}) = (a_0, \dots, a_{t-1})|R = r\right]$$
$$\quad + \frac{1}{1 + e^{\varepsilon}}\Pr\left[R = r\right]\Pr\left[\vec{T}(1, \boldsymbol{q}_r^{(t)}) = (a_0, \dots, a_{t-1})|R = r\right]$$
$$= \Pr\left[R = r\right]\Pr\left[\vec{\mathcal{M}}(x_0, \boldsymbol{q}_r^{(t)}) = (a_0, \dots, a_{t-1})|R = r\right]$$
$$= \Pr\left[\texttt{View}(\mathcal{A}, \mathcal{M}(x_0)) = (r, a_0, \dots, a_{t-1})\right]$$

The case of $b = 1$ could be similarly proved. Therefore, we proved the existence of such an interactive mechanism T for any $(\varepsilon, 0)$ interactive DP mechanisms.

The above theorem suggests that the noninteractive $\text{RR}_{(\varepsilon,0)}$ can simulate any $(\varepsilon, 0)$ interactive DP algorithm. Since it is known that post-processing preserves differential privacy (Lemma 5.3), it follows that to analyze the concurrent composition of arbitrary $(\varepsilon_i, 0)$ interactive differentially private algorithms, it suffices to analyze the composition of randomized response $\text{RR}_{(\varepsilon_i,0)}$. For an interactive mechanism $\mathcal{M}$, we define $\text{PrivLoss}(\mathcal{M}, \delta) = \inf\{\varepsilon \geq 0 : \mathcal{M}\text{is }(\varepsilon, \delta)\text{ -DP}\}$, thus given a target security parameter δ_g, the privacy loss of the concurrent composition of mechanisms $\mathcal{M}_0, \dots, \mathcal{M}_{k-1}$ is denoted as $\text{PrivLoss}(\text{ConComp}(\mathcal{M}_0, \dots, \mathcal{M}_{k-1}), \delta_g)$. When the mechanisms $\mathcal{M}_i$ are noninteractive (like $\text{RR}_{(\varepsilon,\delta)}$) we write Comp rather than ConComp.

Lemma 5.5. *Suppose there are interactive mechanisms $\mathcal{M}_0, \dots, \mathcal{M}_{k-1}$ where for each $0 \leq i \leq k - 1$, $\mathcal{M}_i$ is $(\varepsilon_i, 0)$-differentially private. For any values of $\varepsilon_0, \dots, \varepsilon_{k-1} \geq 0$, $\delta_g \in [0, 1)$, we have*

$$\text{PrivLoss}(\text{ConComp}(\mathcal{M}_0, \dots, \mathcal{M}_{k-1}), \delta_g)$$
$$= \text{PrivLoss}\left(\text{Comp}(\text{RR}_{(\varepsilon_0,0)}, \dots, \text{RR}_{(\varepsilon_{k-1},0)}), \delta_g\right)$$

Proof. We want to show that

$$\inf\{\varepsilon_g \geq 0 : \text{ConComp}(\mathcal{M}_0, \dots, \mathcal{M}_{k-1}) \text{ is } (\varepsilon_g, \delta_g) - \text{DP}\}$$
$$= \inf\{\varepsilon_g \geq 0 : \text{Comp}\left(\text{RR}_{(\varepsilon_0,0)}, \dots, \text{RR}_{(\varepsilon_{k-1},0)}\right) \text{ is } (\varepsilon_g, \delta_g) - \text{DP}\}$$

Since the noninteractive $\text{RR}_{(\varepsilon_0,0)}, \dots, \text{RR}_{(\varepsilon_{k-1},0)}$ can be viewed as a special case of interactive DP mechanisms, we have

$$\inf\{\varepsilon_g \geq 0 : \text{ConComp}(\mathcal{M}_0, \dots, \mathcal{M}_{k-1}) \text{ is } (\varepsilon_g, \delta_g) - \text{DP}\}$$
$$\geq \inf\{\varepsilon_g \geq 0 : \text{Comp}\left(\text{RR}_{(\varepsilon_0,0)}, \dots, \text{RR}_{(\varepsilon_{k-1},0)}\right) \text{ is } (\varepsilon_g, \delta_g) - \text{DP}\}$$

For the other direction, suppose $\mathrm{Comp}\left(\mathrm{RR}_{(\varepsilon_0,0)},\ldots,\mathrm{RR}_{(\varepsilon_{k-1},0)}\right)$ is $(\varepsilon_g^*,\delta_g)$-DP. By post-processing inequality, we know any for any tuple of post-processing interactive mechanisms $T_0,\ldots,T_{k-1}$, $\mathrm{ConComp}\big(T_0\big(\mathrm{RR}_{(\varepsilon_0,0)}\big),\ldots,T_{k-1}$ $\big(\mathrm{RR}_{(\varepsilon_{k-1},0)}\big)\big)$ is also $(\varepsilon_g^*,\delta_g)$-DP. We know from Theorem 1.10 that for every pair of adjacent datasets x_0,x_1, there must exist interactive mechanisms $T_0,\ldots,T_{k-1}$ such that for every adversary $\mathcal{A}$, $\mathtt{View}\langle\mathcal{A},\mathcal{M}_i(x_b)\rangle$ is identically distributed as $\mathtt{View}\langle\mathcal{A},T_i(\mathrm{RR}_{(\varepsilon,0)}(b))\rangle$ for all $i = 0,\ldots,k-1$. Therefore, we know that $\mathrm{ConComp}(\mathcal{M}_0,\ldots,\mathcal{M}_{k-1})$ is also $(\varepsilon_g^*,\delta_g)$-DP. Taking the infimum over ε_g^* will then complete the proof.

We note that $\mathrm{RR}_{(\varepsilon_0,0)},\ldots,\mathrm{RR}_{(\varepsilon_{k-1},0)}$ are noninteractive mechanisms, therefore we can use any composition theorems for noninteractive DP mechanisms to bound the privacy parameter of their composition. The tightest composition theorem for noninteractive DP is derived in [21].

Theorem 5.6 (Optimal Composition Theorem for noninteractive DP).
If $\mathcal{M}_0,\ldots,\mathcal{M}_{k-1}$ are each (ε_i,δ_i)-differentially private, then given the target security parameter δ_g, the privacy parameter of concurrent composition $\mathrm{ConComp}(\mathcal{M}_0,\ldots,\mathcal{M}_{k-1})$ is upper bounded by the least value of $\varepsilon_g \geq 0$ such that

$$\frac{1}{\prod_{i=0}^{k-1}(1+\mathrm{e}^{\varepsilon_i})}\sum_{S\subseteq\{0,\ldots,k-1\}}\max\left\{\mathrm{e}^{\sum_{i\in S}\varepsilon_i}-\mathrm{e}^{\varepsilon_g}\cdot\mathrm{e}^{\sum_{i\notin S}\varepsilon_i},0\right\}\leq 1-\frac{1-\delta_g}{\prod_{i=0}^{k-1}(1-\delta_i)}$$

Therefore, we are ready to bound the concurrent composition for an arbitrary set of interactive differentially private algorithms by simply plugging parameters to the optimal composition bound for noninteractive DP mechanisms in [21].

Theorem 5.7 (Corollary 1.11 Restated). *If $\mathcal{M}_0,\ldots,\mathcal{M}_{k-1}$ are each $(\varepsilon_i,0)$-differentially private, then given the target security parameter δ_g, the privacy parameter of concurrent composition $\mathrm{ConComp}(\mathcal{M}_0,\ldots,\mathcal{M}_{k-1})$ is upper bounded by the least value of $\varepsilon_g \geq 0$ such that*

$$\frac{1}{\prod_{i=0}^{k-1}(1+\mathrm{e}^{\varepsilon_i})}\sum_{S\subseteq\{0,\ldots,k-1\}}\max\left\{\mathrm{e}^{\sum_{i\in S}\varepsilon_i}-\mathrm{e}^{\varepsilon_g}\cdot\mathrm{e}^{\sum_{i\notin S}\varepsilon_i},0\right\}\leq\delta_g$$

A special case when all $\mathcal{M}_0,\ldots,\mathcal{M}_{k-1}$ are $(\varepsilon,0)$-differentially private, then privacy parameter is upper bounded by the least value of $\varepsilon_g \geq 0$ such that

$$\frac{1}{(1+\mathrm{e}^{\varepsilon})^k}\sum_{i=0}^{k}\binom{k}{i}\max\left\{\mathrm{e}^{i\varepsilon}-\mathrm{e}^{\varepsilon_g}\cdot\mathrm{e}^{(k-i)\varepsilon},0\right\}\leq\delta_g$$

6 Experimental Results

In this section, we present empirical evidence for our conjecture that the Optimal Composition Theorems can be extended to the concurrent composition of approximate DP mechanisms. Specifically, we experimentally evaluate the conjecture for 3-message interactive mechanisms with 1-bit messages, as illustrated in Fig. 1. The input for the mechanism is a bit $x \in \{0, 1\}$ (corresponding to fixing two adjacent datasets). In the first round, the mechanism outputs a bit a_0 regardless of the query, so we omit q_0 and directly writing the probability of outputting a_0 as $\Pr[\mathcal{M}(x) = a_0]$. In the second round, the mechanism receives a query bit $\mathcal{A}(a_0)$ from the adversary, and output another bit a_1. Each such mechanism $\mathcal{M}_{\boldsymbol{p}}$ is defined by 10 parameters $\boldsymbol{p} = (p_0, p_{00}, p_{01}, p_{10}, p_{11}, p'_0, p'_{00}, p'_{01}, p'_{10}, p'_{11})$, where $p_0 = \Pr[\mathcal{M}_{\boldsymbol{p}}(0) = 0]$, $p'_0 = \Pr[\mathcal{M}_{\boldsymbol{p}}(1) = 0]$, $p_{ij} = \Pr[\mathcal{M}_{\boldsymbol{p}}(0, j) = (i, 0)]$, $p'_{ij} = \Pr[\mathcal{M}_{\boldsymbol{p}}(1, j) = (i, 0)]$. We note that the concurrent composition of two copies of such a mechanism already has a nontrivial interleaving, as shown in Fig. 2.

We experimentally test whether instantiations of this 2-round interactive mechanism that are (ε, δ)-DP can be simulated as the interactive post-processing of randomized response $\mathrm{RR}_{(\varepsilon, \delta)}$. Specifically, we sample over 10,000 choices of the parameter vector $\boldsymbol{p}$ defining the mechanism $\mathcal{M}_{\boldsymbol{p}}$. For each one, we pre-define a value for δ and compute $\varepsilon = \mathrm{PrivLoss}(\mathcal{M}_{\boldsymbol{p}}, \delta)$ through enumerating over all possible adversaries.

Next, we used linear programming to see if there exists an interactive post-processing mechanism $\vec{T}$ which takes an output from $\mathrm{RR}_{(\varepsilon, \delta)}$, and sets it to have the exact same output distribution as the original 2-round for every possible query $q = (q_1)$ and output sequence (a_0, a_1):

$$\Pr\left[\vec{\mathcal{M}}(0, q) = (a_0, a_1)\right] = \delta \cdot \Pr\left[\vec{T}(\text{'Iam0'}, q) = (a_0, a_1)\right]$$
$$+ (1 - \delta) \cdot \frac{e^\varepsilon}{e^\varepsilon + 1} \Pr\left[\vec{T}(0, q) = (a_0, a_1)\right] + (1 - \delta) \cdot \frac{1}{e^\varepsilon + 1} \Pr\left[\vec{T}(1, q) = (a_0, a_1)\right]$$

$$\Pr\left[\vec{\mathcal{M}}(1, q) = (a_0, a_1)\right] = (1 - \delta) \cdot \frac{1}{e^\varepsilon + 1} \Pr\left[\vec{T}(0, q) = (a_0, a_1)\right]$$
$$+ (1 - \delta) \cdot \frac{e^\varepsilon}{e^\varepsilon + 1} \Pr\left[\vec{T}(1, q) = (a_0, a_1)\right] + \delta \cdot \Pr\left[\vec{T}(\text{'Iam1'}, q) = (a_0, a_1)\right]$$

Each $\Pr\left[\vec{T}(c, q) = (a_0, a_1)\right]$ is an unknown parameter here, where $c \in \{0, 1, \text{'Iam0'}, \text{'Iam1'}\}$. We also enforce them formulating valid distributions:

$$\forall c, q, a_0, a_1, \Pr\left[\vec{T}(c, q) = (a_0, a_1)\right] \geq 0$$

$$\forall c, \mathcal{A}, \sum_{a_0, a_1} \Pr\left[\vec{T}(c, \mathcal{A}(a_0)) = (a_0, a_1)\right] = 1$$

Besides, to construct a valid two-round mechanism, the probability of outputting a_0 in the first round should not depend on the future query q_1:

$$\forall c, a_0, \sum_{a_1} \Pr\left[\vec{T}(c, 0) = (a_0, a_1)\right] = \sum_{a_1} \Pr\left[\vec{T}(c, 1) = (a_0, a_1)\right]$$

We use the linear programming solver from SciPy [24] for solving the linear equation systems.

In all of our trials, we find a feasible $\vec{T}$, concluding that each of the mechanisms $\mathcal{M}_p$ can be simulated by the post-processing of randomized response of the same (ε, δ) parameters.

Based on the above findings, we conjecture that the concurrent composition of interactive DP mechanisms may still have the same bound as the composition for noninteractive DP mechanisms. Besides, we might be able to prove it through a similar construction of interactive post-processing mechanisms as we did in Theorem 1.10. This means that every interactive DP mechanisms can be reduced to noninteractive randomized response. We leave the resolution of these conjectures for future work.

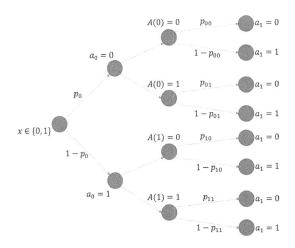

Fig. 1. 2-round mechanism we use in the experiment.

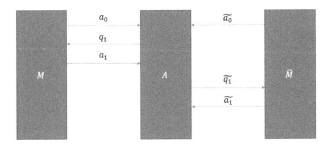

Fig. 2. Concurrent Composition of 2-round Mechanisms

Acknowledgements. We sincerely thank Boaz Barak, Cynthia Dwork, Marco Gaboardi, Michael Hay, Weiwei Pan, and Andy Vyrros for helpful comments and discussions.

References

1. Beimel, A., Nissim, K., Omri, E.: Distributed private data analysis: simultaneously solving how and what. In: Wagner, D. (ed.) CRYPTO 2008. LNCS, vol. 5157, pp. 451–468. Springer, Heidelberg (2008). https://doi.org/10.1007/978-3-540-85174-5_25
2. Bun, M., Dwork, C., Rothblum, G.N., Steinke, T.: Composable and versatile privacy via truncated CDP. In: Proceedings of the 50th Annual ACM SIGACT Symposium on Theory of Computing, pp. 74–86 (2018)
3. Bun, M., Steinke, T.: Concentrated differential privacy: simplifications, extensions, and lower bounds. In: Hirt, M., Smith, A. (eds.) TCC 2016. LNCS, vol. 9985, pp. 635–658. Springer, Heidelberg (2016). https://doi.org/10.1007/978-3-662-53641-4_24
4. Canetti, R., Feige, U., Goldreich, O., Naor, M.: Adaptively secure multi-party computation. In: Proceedings of the Twenty-Eighth Annual ACM Symposium on Theory of Computing, pp. 639–648 (1996)
5. Chen, L., Ghazi, B., Kumar, R., Manurangsi, P.: On distributed differential privacy and counting distinct elements. arXiv preprint arXiv:2009.09604 (2020)
6. Dong, J., Roth, A., Su, W.J.: Gaussian differential privacy. arXiv preprint arXiv:1905.02383 (2019)
7. Dwork, C., Kenthapadi, K., McSherry, F., Mironov, I., Naor, M.: Our data, ourselves: privacy via distributed noise generation. In: Vaudenay, S. (ed.) EUROCRYPT 2006. LNCS, vol. 4004, pp. 486–503. Springer, Heidelberg (2006). https://doi.org/10.1007/11761679_29
8. Dwork, C., McSherry, F., Nissim, K., Smith, A.: Calibrating noise to sensitivity in private data analysis. In: Halevi, S., Rabin, T. (eds.) TCC 2006. LNCS, vol. 3876, pp. 265–284. Springer, Heidelberg (2006). https://doi.org/10.1007/11681878_14
9. Dwork, C., Naor, M., Reingold, O., Rothblum, G.N., Vadhan, S.: On the complexity of differentially private data release: efficient algorithms and hardness results. In: Proceedings of the Forty-First Annual ACM Symposium on Theory of Computing, pp. 381–390 (2009)
10. Dwork, C., Roth, A., et al.: The algorithmic foundations of differential privacy. Found. Trends Theor. Comput. Sci. **9**(3–4), 211–407 (2014)
11. Dwork, C., Rothblum, G.N.: Concentrated differential privacy. arXiv preprint arXiv:1603.01887 (2016)
12. Dwork, C., Rothblum, G.N., Vadhan, S.: Boosting and differential privacy. In: 2010 IEEE 51st Annual Symposium on Foundations of Computer Science, pp. 51–60. IEEE (2010)
13. Feige, U., Shamir, A.: Zero knowledge proofs of knowledge in two rounds. In: Brassard, G. (ed.) CRYPTO 1989. LNCS, vol. 435, pp. 526–544. Springer, New York (1990). https://doi.org/10.1007/0-387-34805-0_46
14. Gaboardi, M., Hay, M., Vadhan, S.: A programming framework for OpenDP (2020)
15. Goldreich, O.: Providing Sound Foundations for Cryptography: On the Work of Shafi Goldwasser and Silvio Micali. Morgan & Claypool (2019)
16. Goldreich, O., Krawczyk, H.: On the composition of zero-knowledge proof systems. SIAM J. Comput. **25**(1), 169–192 (1996)

17. Hardt, M., Rothblum, G.N.: A multiplicative weights mechanism for privacy-preserving data analysis. In: 2010 IEEE 51st Annual Symposium on Foundations of Computer Science, pp. 61–70. IEEE (2010)
18. Kairouz, P., Oh, S., Viswanath, P.: The composition theorem for differential privacy. In: International Conference on Machine Learning, pp. 1376–1385. PMLR (2015)
19. Kasiviswanathan, S.P., Lee, H.K., Nissim, K., Raskhodnikova, S., Smith, A.: What can we learn privately? SIAM J. Comput. **40**(3), 793–826 (2011)
20. Mironov, I.: Rényi differential privacy. In: 2017 IEEE 30th Computer Security Foundations Symposium (CSF), pp. 263–275. IEEE (2017)
21. Murtagh, J., Vadhan, S.: The complexity of computing the optimal composition of differential privacy. In: Theory of Computing, pp. 157–175. Theory of Computing (2016)
22. Roth, A., Roughgarden, T.: Interactive privacy via the median mechanism. In: Proceedings of the Forty-Second ACM Symposium on Theory of Computing, pp. 765–774 (2010)
23. Vadhan, S.: The complexity of differential privacy. In: Lindell, Y. (ed.) Tutorials on the Foundations of Cryptography. ISC, pp. 347–450. Springer, Cham (2017). https://doi.org/10.1007/978-3-319-57048-8_7
24. Virtanen, P., et al.: SciPy 1.0: fundamental algorithms for scientific computing in python. Nat. Methods **17**(3), 261–272 (2020)
25. Warner, S.L.: Randomized response: a survey technique for eliminating evasive answer bias. J. Am. Stat. Assoc. **60**(309), 63–69 (1965)

Direct Product Hardness Amplification

David Lanzenberger$^{(\boxtimes)}$ and Ueli Maurer

Department of Computer Science, ETH Zurich, 8092 Zurich, Switzerland
{landavid,maurer}@inf.ethz.ch

Abstract. We revisit one of the most fundamental hardness amplification constructions, originally proposed by Yao (FOCS 1982). We present a hardness amplification theorem for the direct product of certain games that is simpler, more general, and stronger than previously known hardness amplification theorems of the same kind. Our focus is two-fold. First, we aim to provide close-to-optimal concrete bounds, as opposed to asymptotic ones. Second, in the spirit of abstraction and reusability, our goal is to capture the essence of direct product hardness amplification as generally as possible. Furthermore, we demonstrate how our amplification theorem can be applied to obtain hardness amplification results for non-trivial interactive cryptographic games such as MAC forgery or signature forgery games.

1 Introduction

1.1 Security Amplification

Security amplification is a central theme of cryptography. Turning weak objects into strong objects is useful as it allows to weaken the required assumptions.

Almost all cryptographic constructions rely on the hardness of a certain problem, often modeled as games. As such, hardness amplification is of fundamental importance. Direct product theorems are one of the most natural and intuitive ways to amplify hardness: If a game can be won with probability at most δ, one would expect that n parallel instances of the game can be won with probability at most δ^n. While intuitive and usually trivial in an information-theoretic setting, these results are often surprisingly difficult to establish in a typical computational setting.

The main challenge of computational direct product hardness amplification statements is that they are essentially always based on a reduction, trying to turn *any* winner (or solver) for the direct product with some small winning probability into a winner for a single instance with much larger winning probability. Even though the instances of the direct product are all independent, a winner is not restricted to solving these instances independently. The main difficulty is usually to work around such potential dependencies.

K. Nissim and B. Waters (Eds.): TCC 2021, LNCS 13043, pp. 605–625, 2021.
https://doi.org/10.1007/978-3-030-90453-1_21

1.2   Hardness of the Direct Product of Two Games

Consider two probabilistic games G and H, i.e., probability distributions over deterministic instances of games from sets $\mathcal{G}$ and $\mathcal{H}$, respectively. Let $[G, H]^{\wedge}$ denote the independent parallel composition of the two games that is won exactly if *both* G and H are won. Consider a winner (or player) W winning the two games $[G, H]^{\wedge}$ in parallel with probability δ.

Intuitively, we would like to argue that if W wins $[G, H]^{\wedge}$ with probability δ, then we can (by a simple reduction) use W to win at least one of the games G or H with much higher probability, say, $\sqrt{\delta}$. Note that this is trivially possible if W played both games G and H completely independently.

If W was known to play deterministically[1], certain instances $\mathcal{S} \subseteq \mathcal{G} \times \mathcal{H}$ are (always) solved successfully, while none of the other instances $\overline{\mathcal{S}}$ are ever solved. How does the set $\mathcal{S}$ look like? Suppose that $\mathcal{S} = \mathcal{S}_{\mathcal{G}} \times \mathcal{S}_{\mathcal{H}}$ for some $\mathcal{S}_{\mathcal{G}} \subseteq \mathcal{G}$ and $\mathcal{S}_{\mathcal{H}} \subseteq \mathcal{H}$. This would, for example, be the case if W solved both given instances independently. Visually, this means that $\mathcal{S}$ forms a rectangle as depicted in Fig. 1.

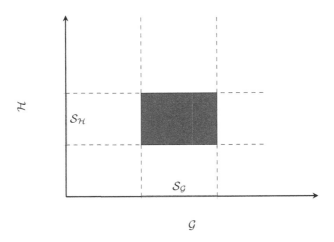

Fig. 1. The considered winner W is deterministic and wins exactly the instances $\mathcal{S}_{\mathcal{G}} \times \mathcal{S}_{\mathcal{H}}$ (marked in green) of the game $[G, H]^{\wedge}$.

If we want to use W to win, say, the game G, we need to simulate an instance of H towards W. In general, the only easy way to do this is simply by sampling an independent instance from the distribution of H, resulting in a winner we denote by $W_{(\cdot, H)}$. However, it is easy to see (in our example) that it is necessary that we hit into the set $\mathcal{S}_{\mathcal{H}}$ in order to win G. This means that the winner $W_{(\cdot, H)}$ for G might have the exact same winning probability that W has for $[G, H]^{\wedge}$.

For many types of games[2] such as one-way function inversion or collision-finding for hash functions, we can overcome this problem by repeating the given

---

[1] Of course, this is not without loss of generality.

[2] Such games are called *clonable* in [9].

winner, such that we are overall successful if only a single one of our attempts has been successful. It is important to note that this property for itself does *not* allow to amplify the winning probability of *any* winner. In particular, if the winning probability on any instance is always either 0 or 1 (i.e., never in-between), no amplification is achieved. However, one can argue that in the given scenario, at least one of $W_{(\cdot, H)}$ or $W_{(G, \cdot)}$ must be amplifiable to a certain degree. A typical analysis such as in [5,9] would achieve this as follows.

1. First, it is argued that if W wins $[G, H]^\wedge$ with probability δ, the following statement is true[3] for any $\epsilon > 0$:

   With probability at least $\sqrt{\delta - 2\epsilon}$ over G, the winner $W_{(\cdot, H)}$ wins the sampled instance of G with probability at least ϵ, or otherwise the analogue is true for $W_{(G, \cdot)}$ on H.

2. Second, it is argued that repeating $W_{(\cdot, H)}$ for some q number of times, we obtain a winning probability of at least

$$\sqrt{\delta - 2\epsilon} \cdot (1 - (1 - \epsilon)^q),$$

approaching $\sqrt{\delta}$ as desired.

For example, to amplify a winning probability of $\delta = 0.01$ to close to $\sqrt{\delta} = 0.1$, say to 0.099, we need about $q \approx 76'600$ repetitions (with the optimal choice of $\epsilon \approx 8.65 \cdot 10^{-5}$). Even for a much less ambitious amplification to 0.09 only, we need $q = 4'981$ repetitions (choosing $\epsilon \approx 7.56 \cdot 10^{-4}$).

In the above two-step analysis, it seems that both steps are (essentially) optimal. Yet, their composition is, at least in certain regimes, quite far from optimal. We present a *combined* analysis that takes into account how the winning set $\mathcal{S}$ behaves under the amplification, proving the very same reduction to be more efficient. In the above example, the desired amplification is achieved with only $q = 90$ and $q = 45$ repetitions, respectively (instead of $q \approx 76'600$ and $q = 4'981$).

It is easy to verify that if the winning set $\mathcal{S}$ was a perfect square (similar to the rectangle in Fig. 1), we would need $q = 44$ and $q = 22$ repetitions. A consequence of our results is that a rectangle as in Fig. 1, even though it may seem to be a naively optimistic perspective, is actually close to the *worst* that can happen for the amplification.

1.3   Contributions and Outline

We briefly state our main contributions in a simplified manner. In Sect. 3, we present amplification theorems at the level of probability theory. We start by showing a basic amplification theorem (Theorem 2) that yields an amplification similar to the known results [2,5,9]. Then, we show an improved analysis of the same type of statement, obtaining stronger amplification (Theorem 4).

---

[3] See our proof of Theorem 1.

In Sect. 4, we discuss that the proved amplification result is close to optimal, though still not perfect. We state a conjecture for a perfectly optimal amplification bound.

Finally, in Sect. 5, we demonstrate how the presented type of amplification theorem can be applied to non-trivial interactive games. We prove hardness amplification results for a general type of game (which includes the MAC forgery and the signature forgery game, and the simpler one-way function inversion as well as the hash function collision finding game), and give a comparison to related results of [3].

1.4   Related Work

There exists a vast amount of literature on hardness amplification. We just mention some of them. Yao [10] originally proposed the direct product construction for one-way functions. Goldreich [5] showed an asymptotic hardness amplification result, stating that the direct product of weak one-way functions is a strong one-way function. Canetti et al. [2] studied the amplification of hash function collision resistance. They analyze a direct product construction similar to [5], mainly to provide a baseline to compare against other constructions. [9] introduced the notion of clonable games, and proved a bound similar to [5] but for concrete parameters (non-asymptotic).

A related line of research [1,3,6–8] studies hardness amplification via the direct product for games that are weakly-verifiable, i.e., where a solver may not be able to verify itself (efficiently) whether a given answer is correct. Some of these results are based on (a variant of) the XOR-Lemma.

In [4], it is shown that direct product hardness amplification "beyond negligible" is in general impossible (under certain plausible assumptions), meaning that for any negligible function $\epsilon(n)$, there exist cryptographic games such that their direct product can always be won with probability $\epsilon(n)$, no matter how many copies one takes.

2   Preliminaries

Notation. For $n \in \mathbb{N}$, we let $[n]$ denote the set $\{1, \ldots, n\}$ with the convention $[0] = \emptyset$. The set of sequences (or strings) of length n over the alphabet $\mathcal{A}$ is denoted by $\mathcal{A}^n$. An element of $\mathcal{A}^n$ is denoted by $a^n = (a_1, \ldots, a_n)$ for $a_i \in \mathcal{A}$.

In this paper, we assume all probability distributions to be over a finite set (or at least to have finite support). We let $\mathsf{supp}(X)$ denote the *support* of a probability distribution X. Moreover, for two probability distributions X and Y, we let XY denote the independent joint distribution of X and Y. For example, we have $\mathbb{E}_{XY}[f(X,Y)] = \sum_{x \in \mathcal{X}} \sum_{y \in \mathcal{Y}} \Pr^X(X = x) \cdot \Pr^Y(Y = y) \cdot f(x,y)$.

We will need the following lemma.

Lemma 1. *For some $\gamma \in \mathbb{R}_+$, let $\psi : [0, \gamma] \to \mathbb{R}_+$ be a concave function. Then, we have for any $0 \leq a \leq b \leq \gamma$*

$$a\psi(b) \leq b\psi(a).$$

Proof. Assume without loss of generality $b \neq 0$ (since otherwise $a = 0$, so the inequality holds trivially). We have

$$a\psi(b) = b \cdot \frac{a}{b} \cdot \psi(b)$$
$$\leq b \cdot \left(\frac{a}{b}\psi(b) + \left(1 - \frac{a}{b}\right)\psi(0) \right)$$
$$\leq b \cdot \psi \left(\frac{a}{b} \cdot b + \left(1 - \frac{a}{b}\right) \cdot 0 \right)$$
$$= b\psi(a).$$

In the third step, we have used that ψ is concave. $\square$

3   The Amplification Theorem

3.1   The Setting

In order to justify the type of amplification theorems we will prove (and in order to provide some intuition), we briefly explain the typical way they can be used.

  We assume two finite sets $\mathcal{G}$ and $\mathcal{H}$, representing the deterministic instances of games[4]. Since the actual games are probabilistic, they are (not necessarily uniform) probability distributions G and H over the sets $\mathcal{G}$ and $\mathcal{H}$. Wherever a joint distribution of G and H is needed, we mean the *independent* joint distribution (i.e., the product distribution).

  We further consider a winner W for the product game $[G, H]^\wedge$, and let the function $\mu : \mathcal{G} \times \mathcal{H} \to [0, 1]$ denote the winning probability of W. This means that for each pair of instances $(g, h) \in \mathcal{G} \times \mathcal{H}$, the probability that W wins *both* g and h is $\mu(g, h)$. Hence, the probability that W wins the game $[G, H]^\wedge$ is the expected value

$$\mathbb{E}_{GH}[\mu(G, H)].$$

In order to use W as a winner for G, we simulate (or absorb) an instance of H towards W to obtain a winner $W_{(\cdot, H)}$. On a sampled instance $g \in \mathsf{supp}(G)$ we want to win, we then apply an *amplification* to our winner $W_{(\cdot, H)}$, such that if its original success probability is[5] ϵ on this fixed instance g, we obtain an amplified

---

[4] For the amplification theorem itself, it will not be important what exact (type of) object the games (i.e., the elements of $\mathcal{G}$ and $\mathcal{H}$) are. For example, they may be Turing machines (of a certain kind).

[5] Of course, this probability will depend on the sampled instance $g \in \mathsf{supp}(G)$, so we will not actually know the value of ϵ in general.

success probability of $\psi(\epsilon)$ (for some amplification function $\psi : [0,1] \to [0,1]$). This means that our winning probability on G is (at least) the nested expectation

$$\mathbb{E}_G[\psi(\mathbb{E}_H[\mu(G,H)])].$$

In the most straightforward applications, the amplification is achieved by repeating the winner q times independently, such that we are successful exactly if one repetition has been successful, resulting in the amplification function $\psi(x) = 1 - (1-x)^q$. This works for example for one-way function inversion [5] or for hash function collision finding [2], where the winner needs to provide a solution (such as a pre-image of a given value) and we can efficiently verify whether an obtained solution is correct or not.

Loosely speaking, the amplification statements we will prove are of the following type:

If $\mathbb{E}_G[\psi(\mathbb{E}_H[\mu(G,H)])]$ and $\mathbb{E}_H[\psi(\mathbb{E}_G[\mu(G,H)])]$ are both "somewhat small", then $\mathbb{E}_{GH}[\mu(G,H)]$ must be "much smaller".

Turned around this means that

If $\mathbb{E}_{GH}[\mu(G,H)]$ is at least "somewhat large", then at least one of $\mathbb{E}_G[\psi(\mathbb{E}_H[\mu(G,H)])]$ or $\mathbb{E}_H[\psi(\mathbb{E}_G[\mu(G,H)])]$ is "much larger".

3.2   Amplification for Monotonic ψ

We first present a basic amplification theorem that works whenever the amplification function ψ is monotonically increasing. Technically, the proof is a simplified version of the main idea in the amplification theorems of [5,9].

Theorem 1. *Let* $\mu : \mathcal{X} \times \mathcal{Y} \to [0,1]$ *be any function, and let* X *and* Y *be probability distributions over* $\mathcal{X}$ *and* $\mathcal{Y}$, *respectively. Moreover, let* ψ *and* ψ' *be monotonically increasing on* $[0,1]$, *and assume that*

$$\mathbb{E}_X[\psi(\mathbb{E}_Y[\mu(X,Y)])] \leq \epsilon\psi(\delta) \quad and \quad \mathbb{E}_Y[\psi'(\mathbb{E}_X[\mu(X,Y)])] \leq \epsilon'\psi'(\delta')$$

for some $\epsilon,\delta,\epsilon',\delta' \in [0,1]$. *Then we have*

$$\mathbb{E}_{XY}[\mu(X,Y)] \leq \epsilon\epsilon' + \delta + \delta'.$$

Proof. We first define the two sets

$$\mathcal{X}_{\geq\delta} := \{x \in \mathcal{X} \mid \mathbb{E}_Y[\mu(x,Y)] \geq \delta\} \text{ and } \mathcal{Y}_{\geq\delta'} := \{y \in \mathcal{Y} \mid \mathbb{E}_X[\mu(X,y)] \geq \delta'\}.$$

The assumption implies that

$$\mathrm{Pr}^X(X \in \mathcal{X}_{\geq\delta}) \leq \epsilon \quad and \quad \mathrm{Pr}^Y(Y \in \mathcal{Y}_{\geq\delta'}) \leq \epsilon'.$$

Now, observe that

$$
\begin{aligned}
\mathbb{E}_{XY}&[\mu(X,Y)] \\
&\leq \mathrm{Pr}^{XY}((X,Y) \in \mathcal{X}_{\geq\delta} \times \mathcal{Y}_{\geq\delta'}) \cdot \mathbb{E}_{XY}[\mu(X,Y) \mid (X,Y) \in \mathcal{X}_{\geq\delta} \times \mathcal{Y}_{\geq\delta'}] \\
&\quad + \mathrm{Pr}^{X}(X \notin \mathcal{X}_{\geq\delta}) \cdot \mathbb{E}_X[\mathbb{E}_Y[\mu(X,Y)] \mid X \notin \mathcal{X}_{\geq\delta}] \\
&\quad + \mathrm{Pr}^{Y}(Y \notin \mathcal{Y}_{\geq\delta'}) \cdot \mathbb{E}_Y[\mathbb{E}_X[\mu(X,Y)] \mid Y \notin \mathcal{Y}_{\geq\delta'}] \\
&\leq \mathrm{Pr}^{X}(X \in \mathcal{X}_{\geq\delta}) \cdot \mathrm{Pr}^{Y}(Y \in \mathcal{Y}_{\geq\delta'}) \\
&\quad + \mathbb{E}_X[\mathbb{E}_Y[\mu(X,Y)] \mid X \notin \mathcal{X}_{\geq\delta}] + \mathbb{E}_Y[\mathbb{E}_X[\mu(X,Y)] \mid Y \notin \mathcal{Y}_{\geq\delta'}] \\
&\leq \epsilon\epsilon' + \delta + \delta'.
\end{aligned}
$$

This concludes the proof.   □

A generalized n-fold version of Theorem 1 is as follows.

Theorem 2. *Let $\mu : \mathcal{X}^n \to [0,1]$ be any function, and let $\{X_i\}_{i\in[n]}$ be probability distributions over $\mathcal{X}$. Moreover, let $\{\psi_i\}_{i\in[n]}$ be a family of monotonically increasing functions on $[0,1]$, and assume that for all $i \in [n]$ we have*

$$
\mathbb{E}_{X_i}[\psi_i(\mathbb{E}_{X_1,\ldots,X_{i-1},X_{i+1},\ldots,X_n}[\mu(X_1,\ldots,X_n)])] \leq \epsilon_i \cdot \psi_i(\delta_i)
$$

for some $\epsilon_i, \delta_i \in [0,1]$. Then we have

$$
\mathbb{E}_{X_1\ldots X_n}[\mu(X_1,\ldots,X_n)] \leq \prod_{i\in[n]} \epsilon_i + \sum_{i\in[n]} \delta_i.
$$

As mentioned in the introduction, the typical amplification function is of the form $\psi(x) = 1 - (1-x)^q$ for some $q \in \mathbb{N}$. This motivates the following corollary that is proved in Appendix A.

Corollary 1. *For arbitrary $\epsilon \in (0,1)$ and $\delta_i \in (0,1)$, let $\psi(x) = 1 - (1-x)^q$ for q such that*

$$
q \geq n \cdot \nu_{n,\epsilon} \cdot \prod_{i\in[n]} \delta_i^{-1},
$$

*where $\nu_{n,\epsilon} := \inf_{c\in(0,1)} \frac{-\ln(1-(1-\epsilon)^{1-c})}{1-(1-\epsilon)^{cn}} \in \left[\frac{\ln(1/\epsilon)}{1-(1-\epsilon)^n}, \frac{\ln(2/\epsilon)}{1-(1-\epsilon/2)^n} \right]$.
Assume that for all $i \in [n]$*

$$
\mathbb{E}_{X_i}[\psi(\mathbb{E}_{X_1,\ldots,X_{i-1},X_{i+1},\ldots,X_n}[\mu(X_1,\ldots,X_n)])] \leq (1-\epsilon)\delta_i.
$$

Then, we have

$$
\mathbb{E}_{X_1\ldots X_n}[\mu(X_1,\ldots,X_n)] \leq \prod_{i\in[n]} \delta_i.
$$

3.3 Amplification for Monotonic and Concave ψ

As mentioned in Sect. 3.1, the standard amplification function for such theorems is $\psi(x) = 1 - (1-x)^q$, which is concave. In the following, we exploit the concavity of ψ to obtain a stronger amplification.

Theorem 3. *Let $\mu : \mathcal{X} \times \mathcal{Y} \to [0,1]$ be any function, and let X and Y be probability distributions over $\mathcal{X}$ and $\mathcal{Y}$, respectively. Moreover, let ψ and ψ' be monotonically increasing and concave on $[0,1]$, and assume that*

$$\mathbb{E}_X[\psi(\mathbb{E}_Y[\mu(X,Y)])] \leq \epsilon\psi(\delta) \quad and \quad \mathbb{E}_Y[\psi'(\mathbb{E}_X[\mu(X,Y)])] \leq \epsilon'\psi'(\delta')$$

for some $\epsilon, \delta, \epsilon', \delta' \in [0,1]$. Then we have

$$\mathbb{E}_{XY}[\mu(X,Y)] \leq \max(\epsilon\epsilon', \epsilon\delta + \epsilon'\delta').$$

Before proving the theorem, we remark that at first glance, one might expect the proof to rely on Jensen's inequality. For concave ψ, Jensen's inequality would give us

$$\mathbb{E}_X[\psi(\mathbb{E}_Y[\mu(X,Y)])] \leq \psi(\mathbb{E}_{XY}[\mu(X,Y)])$$
$$\Longleftrightarrow \quad \psi^{-1}(\mathbb{E}_X[\psi(\mathbb{E}_Y[\mu(X,Y)])]) \leq \mathbb{E}_{XY}[\mu(X,Y)].$$

However, our goal is to *upper* bound $\mathbb{E}_{XY}[\mu(X,Y)]$. Observe that by considering one dimension only, say $\mathbb{E}_X[\psi(\mathbb{E}_Y[\mu(X,Y)])]$, no non-trivial bound on $\mathbb{E}_{XY}[\mu(X,Y)]$ can be obtained, as we might have

$$\mathbb{E}_{XY}[\mu(X,Y)] = \mathbb{E}_X[\psi(\mathbb{E}_Y[\mu(X,Y)])].$$

To consider *both* dimensions $\mathbb{E}_X[\psi(\mathbb{E}_Y[\mu(X,Y)])]$ and $\mathbb{E}_Y[\psi(\mathbb{E}_X[\mu(X,Y)])]$ is what will enable us to obtain a good upper bound on $\mathbb{E}_{XY}[\mu(X,Y)]$.

Proof (of Theorem 3). Just as in the proof of Theorem 1, we first define the two sets

$$\mathcal{X}_{\geq\delta} := \{x \in \mathcal{X} \mid \mathbb{E}_Y[\mu(x,Y)] \geq \delta\} \text{ and } \mathcal{Y}_{\geq\delta'} := \{y \in \mathcal{Y} \mid \mathbb{E}_X[\mu(X,y)] \geq \delta'\}.$$

We derive

$$\mathbb{E}_X[\psi(\mathbb{E}_Y[\mu(X,Y)]) \mid X \notin \mathcal{X}_{\geq\delta}] = \mathbb{E}_X\left[\frac{\delta}{\delta} \cdot \psi(\mathbb{E}_Y[\mu(X,Y)]) \mid X \notin \mathcal{X}_{\geq\delta}\right]$$
$$\geq \mathbb{E}_X\left[\frac{\psi(\delta)}{\delta} \cdot \mathbb{E}_Y[\mu(X,Y)] \mid X \notin \mathcal{X}_{\geq\delta}\right]$$
$$= \frac{\psi(\delta)}{\delta} \mathbb{E}_X[\mathbb{E}_Y[\mu(X,Y)] \mid X \notin \mathcal{X}_{\geq\delta}].$$

The second step is due to Lemma 1. This implies that

$$\mathbb{E}_X[\psi(\mathbb{E}_Y[\mu(X,Y)])] = \Pr^X(X \in \mathcal{X}_{\geq\delta}) \cdot \mathbb{E}_X[\psi(\mathbb{E}_Y[\mu(X,Y)]) \mid X \in \mathcal{X}_{\geq\delta}]$$
$$+ \Pr^X(X \notin \mathcal{X}_{\geq\delta}) \cdot \mathbb{E}_X[\psi(\mathbb{E}_Y[\mu(X,Y)]) \mid X \notin \mathcal{X}_{\geq\delta}]$$
$$\geq \Pr^X(X \in \mathcal{X}_{\geq\delta}) \cdot \psi(\delta)$$
$$+ \Pr^X(X \notin \mathcal{X}_{\geq\delta}) \cdot \frac{\psi(\delta)}{\delta} \mathbb{E}_X[\mathbb{E}_Y[\mu(X,Y)] \mid X \notin \mathcal{X}_{\geq\delta}].$$

Since we have $\epsilon\psi(\delta) \geq \mathbb{E}_X[\psi(\mathbb{E}_Y[\mu(X,Y)])]$ by assumption, we obtain

$$\mathrm{Pr}^X(X \notin \mathcal{X}_{\geq\delta}) \cdot \mathbb{E}_X[\mathbb{E}_Y[\mu(X,Y)] \mid X \notin \mathcal{X}_{\geq\delta}] \leq \delta \cdot (\epsilon - \mathrm{Pr}^X(X \in \mathcal{X}_{\geq\delta})).$$

Analogously, we obtain

$$\mathrm{Pr}^Y(Y \notin \mathcal{Y}_{\geq\delta'}) \cdot \mathbb{E}_Y[\mathbb{E}_X[\mu(X,Y)] \mid Y \notin \mathcal{Y}_{\geq\delta'}] \leq \delta' \cdot (\epsilon' - \mathrm{Pr}^Y(Y \in \mathcal{Y}_{\geq\delta'})).$$

Now, observe that

$$
\begin{aligned}
\mathbb{E}_{XY}&[\mu(X,Y)] \\
&\leq \mathrm{Pr}^{XY}((X,Y) \in \mathcal{X}_{\geq\delta} \times \mathcal{Y}_{\geq\delta'}) \cdot \mathbb{E}_{XY}[\mu(X,Y) \mid (X,Y) \in \mathcal{X}_{\geq\delta} \times \mathcal{Y}_{\geq\delta'}] \\
&\quad + \mathrm{Pr}^X(X \notin \mathcal{X}_{\geq\delta}) \cdot \mathbb{E}_X[\mathbb{E}_Y[\mu(X,Y)] \mid X \notin \mathcal{X}_{\geq\delta}] \\
&\quad + \mathrm{Pr}^Y(Y \notin \mathcal{Y}_{\geq\delta'}) \cdot \mathbb{E}_Y[\mathbb{E}_X[\mu(X,Y)] \mid Y \notin \mathcal{Y}_{\geq\delta'}] \\
&\leq \mathrm{Pr}^X(X \in \mathcal{X}_{\geq\delta}) \cdot \mathrm{Pr}^Y(Y \in \mathcal{Y}_{\geq\delta'}) \\
&\quad + \delta \cdot (\epsilon - \mathrm{Pr}^X(X \in \mathcal{X}_{\geq\delta})) + \delta' \cdot (\epsilon' - \mathrm{Pr}^Y(Y \in \mathcal{Y}_{\geq\delta'})).
\end{aligned}
$$

By assumption we must have $\mathrm{Pr}^X(X \in \mathcal{X}_{\geq\delta}) \leq \epsilon$ and $\mathrm{Pr}^Y(Y \in \mathcal{Y}_{\geq\delta'}) \leq \epsilon'$, so let $\mathrm{Pr}^X(X \in \mathcal{X}_{\geq\delta}) = \gamma\epsilon$ and $\mathrm{Pr}^Y(Y \in \mathcal{Y}_{\geq\delta'}) = \omega\epsilon'$ for $\gamma, \omega \in [0,1]$. Then we get

$$
\begin{aligned}
\mathbb{E}_{XY}[\mu(X,Y)] &\leq \gamma\omega\epsilon\epsilon' + \epsilon\delta(1-\gamma) + \epsilon'\delta'(1-\omega) \\
&\leq \gamma\omega\epsilon\epsilon' + \epsilon\delta(1-\gamma\omega) + \epsilon'\delta'(1-\gamma\omega) \\
&= \gamma\omega\epsilon\epsilon' + (1-\gamma\omega)(\epsilon\delta + \epsilon'\delta') \\
&\leq \max(\epsilon\epsilon', \epsilon\delta + \epsilon'\delta').
\end{aligned}
$$

$\square$

In the symmetric case, the optimal choice is $\epsilon = \epsilon' = 2\delta = 2\delta'$. This gives the following bound.

Corollary 2. *For any $\mu : \mathcal{X} \times \mathcal{Y} \to [0,1]$ and any monotonically increasing and concave function $\psi : [0,1] \to [0,1]$, let $\xi(x) := x \cdot \psi(x)$. We have*

$$\mathbb{E}_{XY}[\mu(X,Y)] \leq 4 \cdot \xi^{-1}\left(\frac{\max(\mathbb{E}_X[\psi(\mathbb{E}_Y[\mu(X,Y)])], \mathbb{E}_Y[\psi(\mathbb{E}_X[\mu(X,Y)])])}{2}\right)^2.$$

Equivalently,

$$\max(\mathbb{E}_X[\psi(\mathbb{E}_Y[\mu(X,Y)])], \mathbb{E}_Y[\psi(\mathbb{E}_X[\mu(X,Y)])]) \geq 2\xi(\sqrt{\mathbb{E}_{XY}[\mu(X,Y)]}/2).$$

A generalized n-fold version of Theorem 3 is as follows.

Theorem 4. *Let $\mu : \mathcal{X}^n \to [0,1]$ be any function, and let $\{X_i\}_{i\in[n]}$ be probability distributions over $\mathcal{X}$. Moreover, let $\{\psi_i\}_{i\in[n]}$ be a family of monotonically increasing and concave functions on $[0,1]$, and assume that for all $i \in [n]$ we have*

$$\mathbb{E}_{X_i}[\psi_i(\mathbb{E}_{X_1,\ldots,X_{i-1},X_{i+1},\ldots,X_n}[\mu(X_1,\ldots,X_n)])] \leq \epsilon_i \cdot \psi_i(\delta_i)$$

for some $\epsilon_i, \delta_i \in [0,1]$. Then we have

$$\mathbb{E}_{X_1\ldots X_n}[\mu(X_1,\ldots,X_n)] \leq \max\left(\prod_{i\in[n]} \epsilon_i, \sum_{i\in[n]} \epsilon_i\delta_i\right).$$

The following corollary is proved in Appendix A.

Corollary 3. *For any $i \in [n]$, let $\ell_i \geq 1$, $\epsilon_i \in (0,1)$, $\delta_i \in (0,1)$, and*

$$q_i \geq n \cdot \ell_i \cdot \ln(1/\epsilon_i) \cdot \prod_{j\in[n],j\neq i} \delta_j^{-1}$$

be arbitrary, and assume that for $\psi_i(x) = 1 - (1 - x/\ell_i)^{q_i}$ we have

$$\mathbb{E}_{X_i}[\psi_i(\mathbb{E}_{X_1,\ldots,X_{i-1},X_{i+1},\ldots,X_n}[\mu(X_1,\ldots,X_n)])] \leq (1 - \epsilon_i)\delta_i.$$

Then,

$$\mathbb{E}_{X_1\ldots X_n}[\mu(X_1,\ldots,X_n)] \leq \prod_{i\in[n]} \delta_i.$$

Note that Corollary 3 is a strictly stronger version of Corollary 1, where (assuming all ϵ_i are equal to ϵ, and $\ell_i = 1$) we needed

$$q \geq n \cdot \nu_{n,\epsilon} \cdot \prod_{i\in[n]} \delta_i^{-1}.$$

The improvements of the new bound are two-fold:

1. First, the weaker version has a factor of (at least)

$$\nu_{n,\epsilon} \geq \frac{\ln(1/\epsilon)}{1 - (1 - \epsilon)^n} \geq \frac{\ln(1/\epsilon)}{n\epsilon} \quad \text{instead of just} \quad \ln(1/\epsilon).$$

For fixed n, this means that q is proportional to $(1/\epsilon)\ln(1/\epsilon)$ instead of just $\ln(1/\epsilon)$. It is easy to see that, at least in certain regimes, the value $\nu_{n,\epsilon}$ is significantly larger than $\ln(1/\epsilon)$. For example, for $n = 2$ and $\epsilon = 0.001$ we have $\nu_{n,\epsilon} \approx 5118.5$, and $\ln(1/\epsilon) \approx 6.9$.

Moreover, this means that how close one can efficiently amplify δ^n to δ does not depend any more on n.

2. Second, the weaker version has a factor of

$$\prod_{j\in[n]} \delta_j^{-1} \quad \text{instead of just} \quad \prod_{j\in[n], j\neq i} \delta_j^{-1}.$$

Technically, the difference may seem to be small (in particular for large n and all δ_j close to 1). Conceptually, however, the new term is exactly what one would naturally expect, and the best one can hope for in an amplification theorem of a very general type: If we want to boost the winning probability of a winner W from δ^n to δ by running W q times with a success probability of at most δ^n in each run, we need $q \cdot \delta^n \geq \delta \iff q \geq (1/\delta)^{n-1}$. Put differently: When amplifying the hardness from δ to δ^n, the cost of the reduction is inversely proportional to the hardness *increase* (which is unavoidable), as opposed to the *target* hardness δ^n.

4 The Square Is Not (Always) Optimal

How tight are the bounds shown in the previous section, in particular those for concave amplification function (Theorem 3 and Theorem 4)? It is easy to see that the rectangle (or, in the symmetric case, the square) is optimal within a factor of at most 2 (see the discussion in Sect. 1.2).

Corollary 4. *Let $\mu : \mathcal{X} \times \mathcal{Y} \to [0,1]$ be any function, let ψ and ψ' be monotonically increasing and concave on $[0,1]$, and assume that*

$$\mathbb{E}_X[\psi(\mathbb{E}_Y)] \leq \epsilon\psi(\epsilon') \quad and \quad \mathbb{E}_Y[\psi'(\mathbb{E}_X)] \leq \epsilon'\psi'(\epsilon).$$

Then we have

$$\mathbb{E}_{XY}[\mu(X,Y)] \leq 2\epsilon\epsilon'.$$

More generally, an n-dimensional orthotope (or hyperrectangle) is optimal within a factor of at most n.

One might conjecture that the rectangle is always optimal, i.e., that the factor of 2 in the above corollary can be removed. In the following, we show that this is not true.

Proposition 1. *There exist $\mu : \mathcal{X} \times \mathcal{Y} \to [0,1]$, monotonically increasing and concave functions ψ and ψ' on $[0,1]$, as well as distributions X and Y over $\mathcal{X}$ and $\mathcal{Y}$, and $\epsilon, \epsilon' \in [0,1]$, such that*

$$\mathbb{E}_X[\psi(\mathbb{E}_Y[\mu(X,Y)])] \leq \epsilon \cdot \psi(\epsilon') \text{ and } \mathbb{E}_Y[\psi'(\mathbb{E}_X[\mu(X,Y)])] \leq \epsilon' \cdot \psi'(\epsilon),$$

but

$$\mathbb{E}_{XY}[\mu(X,Y)] > \epsilon\epsilon'.$$

Proof. Consider the following function $\mu : \{x_1, x_2\} \times \{y_1, y_2\} \to [0,1]$:

$$\begin{array}{c|cc}
y_2 & 1 & 0 \\
y_1 & 1 & 1 \\
\hline
 & x_1 & x_2
\end{array}$$

Moreover, let $\Pr^X(x_1) = \Pr^Y(y_1) = \frac{1}{4}$, and $\psi(x) = \psi'(x) = 1 - (1-x)^2$. For $\epsilon = \epsilon' = 0.65582$ we have

$$\mathbb{E}_X[\psi(\mathbb{E}_Y[\mu(X,Y)])] = \mathbb{E}_Y[\psi'(\mathbb{E}_X[\mu(X,Y)])] = \frac{37}{64} \le \epsilon' \cdot \psi'(\epsilon) = \epsilon \cdot \psi(\epsilon').$$

However,

$$\mathbb{E}_{XY}[\mu(X,Y)] = \frac{7}{16} = .4375 > \epsilon\epsilon' = \epsilon^2 \approx .431.$$

$\square$

The choice of μ in the above example seems to works for any function of the form $\psi(x) = 1 - (1-x)^q$, though for larger q we need $\Pr^X(x_1)$ and $\Pr^Y(y_1)$ to be closer to 0.

Even though the square is not optimal in general, we believe that whenever it is not optimal, the "opposite square" is optimal. By "opposite square" we mean that there is a square $\mathcal{S} = \mathcal{X}' \times \mathcal{Y}' \subseteq \mathcal{X} \times \mathcal{Y}$ such that $\mu(x,y) = 0$ if $(x,y) \in \mathcal{S}$ and $\mu(x,y) = 1$ otherwise. Loosely speaking, this means that the worst that can happen in terms of amplification is that either the *success* probability of a winner is maximally concentrated (into a square), or the *failure* probability is maximally concentrated. The following makes this mathematically rigorous.

Conjecture 1. Let $\mu : \mathcal{X} \times \mathcal{Y} \to [0,1]$ be any function, and X and Y arbitrary distributions over $\mathcal{X}$ and $\mathcal{Y}$, respectively. Moreover, let $\psi(x) = 1 - (1-x)^q$ for some $q \in \mathbb{N}$, and assume that

$$\max(\mathbb{E}_X(\psi(\mathbb{E}_Y[\mu(X,Y)])), \mathbb{E}_Y(\psi(\mathbb{E}_X[\mu(X,Y)]))) \le \epsilon\psi(\epsilon)$$

for some $\epsilon \in [0,1]$. Let $\delta \in [0,1]$ be the (unique) value such that

$$\epsilon\psi(\epsilon) = (1-\delta) + \delta\psi(1-\delta).$$

Then, we have

$$\mathbb{E}_{XY}[\mu(X,Y)] \le \max(\epsilon^2, 1 - \delta^2).$$

The above conjecture is stated for the two-dimensional symmetric case and only for the function $\psi(x) = 1 - (1-x)^q$, but we conjecture natural generalizations to be true as well.

5 Applying the Amplification Theorem

As mentioned in the introduction, it is easy to obtain concrete hardness amplification results for certain games such as one-way function inversion or hash collision finding. Known asymptotic results such as "weak one-way functions imply strong one-way functions" are straightforward to derive from Corollary 3 (with a more efficient reduction). Such games have been called *clonable* in [9].

In the following, we demonstrate how the presented amplification theorems can be applied to more involved games that are not clonable, such as MAC forgery or signature forgery games.

We first give a redefinition (with some minor changes) of the type of game that has been introduced as "Dynamic Weakly Verifiable Puzzle" (or DWVP) in [3]. A DWVP is an abstraction that captures certain cryptographic games such as the MAC forgery game or the signature forgery game (but includes the simpler one-way function inversion game as well as the hash function collision finding game).

Definition 1. *A deterministic DWVP is characterized by a function $h : \mathcal{M} \to \mathcal{H}$ and a relation $\sigma \subseteq \mathcal{M} \times \mathcal{S}$. The game supports the following query types:*

- HINT-*query: A query of the form $m \in \mathcal{M}$ that is answered with $h(m)$.*
- VERIFICATION-*query: A query of the form $(m', s) \in \mathcal{M} \times \mathcal{S}$. This query is always answered with a fixed symbol (say, $\perp$).*

The game is won when a VERIFICATION-*query (m', s) is made such that*

$$(m', s) \in \sigma \text{ and } m' \text{ was not asked before as } \mathsf{HINT}\text{-}query.$$

Moreover, the game may support arbitrary additional query types.

Definition 2. *A probabilistic DWVP is a probability distribution over (compatible) deterministic DWVPs.*

For the MAC forgery game, for example, the HINT-queries would enable the winner to ask for tags of chosen messages, and the VERIFICATION-queries would correspond to forgery attempts ($\mathcal{H} = \mathcal{S}$ would correspond to the set of tags).

For certain games, an additional query type may be used to inform the winner about the instance to be solved (in a way that does not count as a hint). For example, a signature forgery game may use this to output the generated public key. Or, a one-way function inversion game would use this to output the function image y that is supposed to be inverted.

Now, we define the direct product of DVWPs. In contrast to [3], we give a more general definition, taking the direct product of arbitrary (potentially different) DVWPs, and define the direct product in a way such that the resulting game is not necessarily a DVWP anymore.

Definition 3. *The* direct product *of deterministic DWVPs* $\{g_i\}_{i \in [n]}$, *denoted by*

$$[g_1, \ldots, g_n]^\wedge,$$

is the game which answers queries of the form (i, q), *where* $i \in [n]$ *and* q *is a query for the subgame* g_i. *It is won exactly when* all *subgames* g_i *are won.*

The direct product $[G_1, \ldots, G_n]^\wedge$ *of probabilistic DWVPs is defined by lifting the deterministic definition via the independent joint distribution.*

Notation 1. Analogous to the above games, we model (compatible) *winners* (or solvers) as probability distributions over deterministic winners.

We assume a predicate ω that describes whether a deterministic winner w wins a game g or not, i.e., $\omega(g, w) = 1$ if w wins g (and $\omega(g, w) = 0$ otherwise). For a given probabilistic winner W for a game G, we let

$$\omega(G, W) = \mathbb{E}_{GW}[\omega(G, W)] \in [0, 1]$$

denote the winning (or success) probability of W playing G.

In the following, we present a direct product hardness amplification theorem for arbitrary DWVPs.

Theorem 5. *Let* $\{G_i\}_{i \in [n]}$ *be a family of probabilistic DWVPs. Let* W *be a winner for the direct product* $[G_1 \ldots G_n]^\wedge$, *and asking up to* h_i HINT-*queries to* G_i.

For any $\{\delta_j\}_{j \in [n]}$ *and* $\{\epsilon_j\}_{j \in [n]}$ *with* $\delta_j, \epsilon_j \in (0, 1]$, *there are uniform reductions* $\{\rho_i\}_{i \in [n]}$ *and non-uniform reductions* $\{\rho'_i\}_{i \in [n]}$, *such that if* W *has a winning probability of*

$$\prod_{j \in [n]} \delta_j,$$

then,

(i) For some $i \in [n]$, *the winner* $\rho_i(W)$ *for* G_i *has winning probability at least*

$$\omega(G_i, \rho_i(W)) \geq \frac{(1 - \epsilon_i)\delta_i}{e(h_i + 1)},$$

where ρ_i *runs the winner* W *for the direct product* $\lceil q_i \rceil$ *times for*

$$q_i = n \cdot \ln(1/\epsilon_i) \cdot \prod_{j \in [n], j \neq i} \delta_j^{-1}.$$

(ii) For some $i \in [n]$, *the winner* $\rho'_i(W)$ *for* G_i *has winning probability at least*

$$\omega(G_i, \rho'_i(W)) \geq (1 - \epsilon_i)\delta_i,$$

where ρ'_i *runs the winner* W *for the direct product* $\lceil q'_i \rceil$ *times for*

$$q'_i = n \cdot e(h_i + 1) \cdot \ln(1/\epsilon_i) \cdot \prod_{j \in [n], j \neq i} \delta_j^{-1}.$$

We provide some intuition before proving the theorem. We would like to amplify the winning probability of W by repeating it multiple times. The problem is that this might not increase our winning probability, since it can happen that W makes a successful VERIFICATION-query on a message which was asked as a HINT-query in an earlier repetition. To overcome this problem, the natural idea, originating in [3], is to disallow certain messages to be asked as HINT-query. We show two possibilities of achieving this: In the first version, we simply pick messages randomly (ad-hoc) to disallow as HINT-query. This enables a uniform and efficient reduction, but comes at the cost of introducing a loss factor of $(h_i + 1)$ in the obtained winning probability. This is why we present a second version, in which we provide the reduction with some non-uniform advice (that depends on the winner W). The advice essentially describes a fixed set of messages that are supposed to be disallowed as HINT-query, such that the loss in winning probability of the first (uniform) version can be overcome just by repeating more often (by a factor of $(h_i + 1)$). Our non-uniform version can be made uniform in a similar way as in [3], at the cost of introducing a similarly expensive precomputation.

We stress that the following proof is almost entirely concerned with analyzing the loss when certain messages are disallowed as HINT-queries, whereas the actual direct product amplification simply follows from Corollary 3.

Proof (of Theorem 5). The main idea, originating in [3], is to prevent certain messages to be asked as HINT-query. This is why we introduce a filter system F, acting as a proxy between a winner W and a game G_i that does the following:

1. First, for each[6] message $m \in \mathcal{M}$, F decides independently with probability $1/(h_i + 1)$ that m is disallowed to ask as a HINT-query.
2. Then, all queries from the connected winner are proxied and the response is forwarded back, unless a HINT-query m is asked for a disallowed message m, in which case F just returns an error symbol, say $\perp$, as response.

For any filter $f \in \mathsf{supp}(F)$ and any winner W_i for an instance $g \in \mathsf{supp}(G_i)$, we let

$$\hat{\omega}(g, W_i, f)$$

denote the f-restricted winning probability of W_i playing g through the filter f, where only VERIFICATION-queries that are *disallowed* as HINT-queries by the filter f are taken into account[7]. This gives us the following useful property: When

---

[6] Of course, this is most efficiently done by sampling lazily as we go, only for the messages that actually appear.

[7] Note that W_i's *actual* winning probability through the filter may be larger than $\hat{\omega}(g, W_i, f)$, since we allow to ask VERIFICATION-queries that are allowed as HINT-queries as well. We do not want to disallow those with the filter, since it may happen that W_i first asks some VERIFICATION-queries that are allowed as HINT-queries and then still makes a successful VERIFICATION-query that is disallowed as HINT-query.

a winner W_i for G_i is run q times independently through any fixed (deterministic) filter $f \in \mathsf{supp}(F)$, the obtained success probability is at least

$$1 - (1 - \hat{\omega}(G_i, W_i, f))^q.$$

Observe that for any deterministic instance g, we have

$$\omega(g, W_i) \le (e \cdot (h_i + 1)) \cdot \hat{\omega}(g, W_i, F).$$

This is because if we have h_i (distinct) hint queries $M_1, \ldots, M_{h_i}$ and the first successful attack query is M_{h_i+1}, the probability that the attack is also successful through the filter F *and* M_{h_i+1} is disallowed as a HINT-query is at least

$$\left(1 - \frac{1}{h_i + 1}\right)^{h_i} \cdot \frac{1}{h_i + 1} \ge \frac{1}{e \cdot (h_i + 1)}.$$

In the following, let $W_{i\sim}$ denote the winner for G_i that is obtained from W by simulating independent instances of $(G_1, \ldots, G_{i-1}, G_{i+1}, \ldots, G_n)$ towards W.

For claim (i), consider the following reduction: ρ_i maps a winner W for the game $[G_1 \ldots G_n]^\wedge$ to a winner W_i for G_i which simply runs $W_{i\sim}$ q_i times independently through the filter F (without resetting the filter). Let $\chi_i(x) := 1 - (1 - x)^{q_i}$. For any $g \in \mathsf{supp}(G_i)$ we have

$$
\begin{aligned}
\frac{\chi_i(\omega([G_1 \ldots G_{(i-1)} \; g \; G_{(i+1)} \ldots G_n]^\wedge, W))}{e \cdot (h_i + 1)}
&\le \frac{\chi_i(\omega(g, W_{i\sim}))}{e \cdot (h_i + 1)} \\
&\le \frac{\chi_i(\omega(g, W_{i\sim}))}{\omega(g, W_{i\sim})} \cdot \hat{\omega}(g, W_{i\sim}, F) \\
&= \frac{\chi_i(\omega(g, W_{i\sim}))}{\omega(g, W_{i\sim})} \cdot \mathbb{E}_F\left[\hat{\omega}(g, W_{i\sim}, F)\right] \\
&= \mathbb{E}_F\left[\frac{\hat{\omega}(g, W_{i\sim}, F)}{\omega(g, W_{i\sim})} \chi_i(\omega(g, W_{i\sim}))\right] \\
&\le \mathbb{E}_F\left[\frac{\omega(g, W_{i\sim})}{\omega(g, W_{i\sim})} \chi_i(\hat{\omega}(g, W_{i\sim}, F))\right] \\
&= \mathbb{E}_F[\chi_i(\hat{\omega}(g, W_{i\sim}, F))] \\
&\le \omega(g, \rho_i(W)).
\end{aligned}
$$

In the first step, we have used that χ_i is monotonically increasing and that

$$\omega([G_1 \ldots G_{(i-1)} \; g \; G_{(i+1)} \ldots G_n]^\wedge, W) \le \omega(g, W_{i\sim}).$$

The second step is due to the inequality $\omega(g, W_{i\sim}) \le (e \cdot (h_i + 1)) \cdot \hat{\omega}(g, W_{i\sim}, F)$. The fifth step is due to χ_i being concave, Lemma 1, and the above inequality $\hat{\omega}(g, W_{i\sim}, f) \le \omega(g, W_{i\sim})$ for *any* $f \in \mathsf{supp}(F)$. Since the shown inequality holds for any $g \in \mathsf{supp}(G_i)$, it also holds in expectation:

$$
\begin{aligned}
e(h_i + 1) \cdot \omega(G_i, \rho_i(W)) &= e(h_i + 1) \cdot \mathbb{E}_{G_i}[\omega(G_i, \rho_i(W))] \\
&\ge \mathbb{E}_{G_i}[\chi_i(\omega([G_1 \ldots G_{(i-1)} \; G_i \; G_{(i+1)} \ldots G_n]^\wedge, W))].
\end{aligned}
$$

By Corollary 3 we must have

$$\mathbb{E}_{G_i}[\chi_i(\omega([G_1 \ldots G_{(i-1)} \;\; G_i \;\; G_{(i+1)} \ldots G_n]^\wedge, W))] \geq (1 - \epsilon_i)\delta_i$$

for some $i \in [n]$, implying the first claim.

Now, we consider claim (ii). Recall that we have

$$\omega(g, W_{i\sim}) \leq (e \cdot (h_i + 1)) \cdot \hat{\omega}(g, W_{i\sim}, F)$$

for any $g \in \mathsf{supp}(G_i)$, so the same is true in expectation:

$$\omega(G_i, W_{i\sim}) \leq (e \cdot (h_i + 1)) \cdot \hat{\omega}(G_i, W_{i\sim}, F) = (e \cdot (h_i + 1)) \cdot \mathbb{E}_F[\hat{\omega}(G_i, W_{i\sim}, F)].$$

Thus, there exists $f' \in \mathsf{supp}(F)$ such that

$$\omega(G_i, W_{i\sim}) \leq (e \cdot (h_i + 1)) \cdot \hat{\omega}(G_i, W_{i\sim}, f').$$

Now, let the reduction ρ'_i map a winner W for $[G_1 \ldots G_{(i-1)} \;\; G_i \;\; G_{(i+1)} \ldots G_n]^\wedge$ to the winner W'_i that simply runs $W_{i\sim}$ q'_i times independently through the filter[8] f'. Note that since we only use that the events $\mathcal{E}_i$ of message m_i being disallowed as a HINT-query are (h_i+1)-wise independent, an appropriate f' with short description always exists (one can take, for example, a $(h_i + 1)$-universal hash function).

For $\chi_i(x) = 1 - (1 - x)^{q_i}$ we have

$$\mathbb{E}_{G_i}\left[\chi_i\left(\frac{\omega([G_1 \ldots G_{(i-1)} \;\; G_i \;\; G_{(i+1)} \ldots G_n]^\wedge, W)}{e \cdot (h_i + 1)}\right)\right] \leq \mathbb{E}_{G_i}\left[\chi_i\left(\frac{\omega(G_i, W_{i\sim})}{e \cdot (h_i + 1)}\right)\right]$$

$$\leq \chi_i\left(\frac{\mathbb{E}_{G_i}[\omega(G_i, W_{i\sim})]}{e \cdot (h_i + 1)}\right)$$

$$= \chi_i\left(\frac{\omega(G_i, W_{i\sim})}{e \cdot (h_i + 1)}\right)$$

$$\leq \chi_i(\hat{\omega}(G_i, W_{i\sim}, f'))$$

$$\leq \omega(G_i, \rho'_i(W)).$$

The second step is due to Jensen's inequality (χ_i is concave). By instantiating Corollary 3 with $\ell_i = e(h_i + 1)$ we obtain

$$\mathbb{E}_{G_i}\left[\chi_i\left(\frac{\omega([G_1 \ldots G_{(i-1)} \;\; G_i \;\; G_{(i+1)} \ldots G_n]^\wedge, W)}{e \cdot (h_i + 1)}\right)\right] \geq (1 - \epsilon_i)\delta_i$$

for some $i \in [n]$, implying the second claim. $\square$

---

[8] If the filter answers a HINT-query with $\perp$, the current repetition can be aborted.

We point out some differences between our non-uniform amplification statement from Theorem 5 and the non-uniform DWVP amplification Theorem 4 of [3].

- The reduction in [3] guarantees that only a *single* VERIFICATION-query is asked. This makes their analysis very complicated, and comes at the cost of an increased number of asked HINT-queries (by an additional factor of h compared to our bounds, where h is the total number of HINT-queries asked by the considered winner W). We describe a reduction that executes the winner multiple times and submits *all* VERIFICATION-queries.

  It is important to note that it depends on the concrete game whether the number of VERIFICATION-queries asked is important or not. For example, in the case of the signature forgery game, it is trivial to reduce the number of submitted VERIFICATION-queries to one, since one can efficiently check whether a forgery attempt will be accepted or not. The same is true for any game where one can verify a VERIFICATION-query efficiently before submitting it.

  For the MAC forgery game it will in general not be possible to verify a forgery attempt efficiently. However, it is still meaningful (and quite natural) to consider the case where the adversary is allowed to make multiple forgery attempts. Note, however, that our amplification statement is not applicable for games that allow only very few (or even just one) VERIFICATION-queries. This may be the case, for example, if the goal of the game is to guess a value from a small set (say, a bit).

- The statement in [3] is a Chernoff-type amplification result that covers the threshold case, i.e., it is in the more general setting where a winner does not solve *all* n independent instances, but only a fraction of them. It seems though that for MAC forgery and signature forgery games, the basic non-threshold case (which we cover) is of most interest.

- Our Theorem 5 provides concrete (non-asymptotic) bounds with very small constant factors. In contrast, the statements of [3] hide large constants in asymptotic bounds. Moreover, we have a loss of a factor $(h_i + 1)$, that is independent of the number of VERIFICATION-query asked, whereas the loss in [3] is $\mathcal{O}(h + v)$, where h and v are the total number of HINT- and VERIFICATION-queries asked.

- We consider the direct product of n arbitrary DWVPs, i.e., the individual games are not required to be the same. In contrast, [3] studies the case where all n games are equal, and uses a restricted direct product definition that requires to ask the same query m to all instances in parallel.

  Note that because our games $\{G_i\}_{i \in [n]}$ may be all different, we obtain an amplifying reduction for *some* G_i. If the games $\{G_i\}_{i \in [n]}$ are all the same, and one is aiming for a uniform reduction, it is a standard technique to embed the given instance g at a uniform random position $I \in [n]$. It may seem that one would lose a factor of n in winning probability when this is done. However, we note that by the AM–GM inequality, the conclusion of Corollary 3 can be extended to

$$\mathbb{E}_{X_1 \dots X_n}[\mu(X_1, \dots, X_n)] \leq \prod_{i \in [n]} \delta_i \leq \left(\sum_{i \in [n]} \frac{\delta_i}{n} \right)^n.$$

This prevents losing a factor of n when embedding the given instance at a uniform position.

6 Conclusions and Open Problems

We presented an abstract direct product hardness amplification theorem at the level of probability theory. Our hope is that phrasing it at this level enables reusability and leads to a more modular analysis of hardness amplification statements, similar as in our proof of hardness amplification for DVWPs (Theorem 5). The theorem assumes an arbitrary concave amplification function ψ, simply because the proof does not require further assumptions. This leads to the question of whether natural examples of games with corresponding reductions exist, where the function ψ is something totally different than $1 - (1 - x)^q$ or $1 - (1 - x/\ell)^q$.

Moreover, the shown bounds are close to optimal, but still not perfectly tight. We phrased a conjecture for a perfectly tight bound, which states that the worst case in terms of amplification is that either the *success* probability or the *failure* probability of the considered winner is maximally concentrated. Independently of this conjecture, it seems that the factor of n in the number of repetitions q (see Corollary 3) can be significantly reduced.

Finally, we leave it for future work to generalize the amplification statements beyond the "product" setting, for example to the "threshold" setting.

Appendix

A   Proofs

Proof (of Corollary 1). Let $c \in (0, 1)$ be arbitrary. Moreover, we let $a_i = (1-\epsilon)^c \delta_i$ and $b_i = -\ln(1 - (1 - \epsilon)^{1-c})/q$.

$$\begin{aligned}
a_i \cdot \psi(b_i) &= (1 - \epsilon)^c \delta_i \cdot \psi_i(-\ln(1 - (1 - \epsilon)^{1-c})/q) \\
&= (1 - \epsilon)^c \delta_i \cdot (1 - (1 - (-\ln(1 - (1 - \epsilon)^{1-c})/q)^q)) \\
&\geq (1 - \epsilon)^c \delta_i \cdot (1 - (\exp(\ln(1 - (1 - \epsilon)^{1-c})/q)^q)) \\
&= (1 - \epsilon)^c \delta_i \cdot (1 - \epsilon)^{1-c} \\
&= (1 - \epsilon)\delta_i.
\end{aligned}$$

From Theorem 2 we obtain

$$\mathbb{E}_{X_1 \ldots X_n}[\mu(X_1, \ldots, X_n)] \leq \prod_{i \in [n]} a_i + \sum_{i \in [n]} b_i$$

$$= (1 - \epsilon)^{cn} \prod_{i \in [n]} \delta_i + \sum_{i \in [n]} b_i$$

$$= (1 - \epsilon)^{cn} \prod_{i \in [n]} \delta_i + n \cdot -\ln(1 - (1 - \epsilon)^{1-c})/q$$

$$\leq (1 - \epsilon)^{cn} \prod_{i \in [n]} \delta_i + n \cdot \frac{-\ln(1 - (1 - \epsilon)^{1-c})}{n \cdot \nu_{n,\epsilon} \cdot \prod_{i \in [n]} \delta_i^{-1}}$$

$$\leq (1 - \epsilon)^{cn} \prod_{i \in [n]} \delta_i + (1 - (1 - \epsilon)^{cn}) \cdot \prod_{i \in [n]} \delta_i$$

$$= \prod_{i \in [n]} \delta_i.$$

Finally, we show that

$$\nu_{n,\epsilon} \in \left[\frac{\ln(1/\epsilon)}{1 - (1 - \epsilon)^n}, \frac{\ln(2/\epsilon)}{1 - (1 - \epsilon/2)^n} \right].$$

First, observe that

$$\nu_{n,\epsilon} = \inf_{c \in (0,1)} \frac{-\ln(1 - (1 - \epsilon)^{1-c})}{1 - (1 - \epsilon)^{nc}} \geq \frac{\inf_{c \in (0,1)} -\ln(1 - (1 - \epsilon)^{1-c})}{\sup_{c \in (0,1)} 1 - (1 - \epsilon)^{nc}}$$

$$= \frac{\ln(1/\epsilon)}{1 - (1 - \epsilon)^n}.$$

The upper bound is shown as follows.

$$\nu_{n,\epsilon} = \inf_{c \in (0,1)} \frac{-\ln(1 - (1 - \epsilon)^{1-c})}{1 - (1 - \epsilon)^{nc}} \leq \inf_{c \in (0,1)} \frac{-\ln(1 - (1 - (1 - c)\epsilon))}{1 - (1 - c \cdot \epsilon)^n}$$

$$= \inf_{c \in (0,1)} \frac{-\ln((1 - c)\epsilon)}{1 - (1 - c \cdot \epsilon)^n}$$

$$\leq \frac{\ln(2/\epsilon)}{1 - (1 - \epsilon/2)^n}.$$

This concludes the proof. □

Proof (of Corollary 3). Observe that for any $i \in [n]$ we have

$$\delta_i \cdot \psi_i(\ell_i \ln(1/\epsilon_i)/q_i) = \delta_i \cdot (1 - (1 - \ln(1/\epsilon_i)/q_i)^{q_i})$$

$$\geq \delta_i \cdot (1 - (e^{-\ln(1/\epsilon_i)/q_i})^{q_i})$$

$$= (1 - \epsilon_i)\delta_i.$$

Thus, we have by Theorem 4

$$\mathbb{E}_{X_1 \dots X_n}[\mu(X_1, \dots, X_n)] \leq \max \left(\prod_{i \in [n]} \delta_i, \sum_{i \in [n]} \delta_i \ell_i \ln(1/\epsilon_i)/q_i \right)$$

$$\leq \max \left(\prod_{i \in [n]} \delta_i, \prod_{i \in [n]} \delta_i \right)$$

$$= \prod_{i \in [n]} \delta_i.$$

This concludes the proof.   □

References

1. Canetti, R., Halevi, S., Steiner, M.: Hardness amplification of weakly verifiable puzzles. In: Kilian, J. (ed.) TCC 2005. LNCS, vol. 3378, pp. 17–33. Springer, Heidelberg (2005). https://doi.org/10.1007/978-3-540-30576-7_2
2. Canetti, R., Rivest, R., Sudan, M., Trevisan, L., Vadhan, S., Wee, H.: Amplifying collision resistance: a complexity-theoretic treatment. In: Menezes, A. (ed.) CRYPTO 2007. LNCS, vol. 4622, pp. 264–283. Springer, Heidelberg (2007). https://doi.org/10.1007/978-3-540-74143-5_15
3. Dodis, Y., Impagliazzo, R., Jaiswal, R., Kabanets, V.: Security amplification for interactive cryptographic primitives. In: Reingold, O. (ed.) Theory of Cryptography, pp. 128–145. Springer, Heidelberg (2009)
4. Dodis, Y., Jain, A., Moran, T., Wichs, D.: Counterexamples to hardness amplification beyond negligible. In: Cramer, R. (ed.) TCC 2012. LNCS, vol. 7194, pp. 476–493. Springer, Heidelberg (2012). https://doi.org/10.1007/978-3-642-28914-9_27
5. Goldreich, O.: Foundations of Cryptography, vol. 1. Cambridge University Press, Cambridge (2001). https://doi.org/10.1017/CBO9780511546891
6. Holenstein, T., Schoenebeck, G.: General hardness amplification of predicates and puzzles. In: Ishai, Y. (ed.) Theory of Cryptography. pp. 19–36. Springer Berlin Heidelberg, Berlin, Heidelberg (2011)
7. Impagliazzo, R., Jaiswal, R., Kabanets, V.: Chernoff-type direct product theorems. J. Cryptol. **22**(1), 75–92 (2008). https://doi.org/10.1007/s00145-008-9029-7
8. Jutla, C.S.: Almost optimal bounds for direct product threshold theorem. In: Micciancio, D. (ed.) Theory of Cryptography, pp. 37–51. Springer, Heidelberg (2010)
9. Maurer, U.: An information-theoretic approach to hardness amplification. In: 2017 IEEE International Symposium on Information Theory (ISIT), June 2017
10. Yao, A.C.: Theory and application of trapdoor functions. In: 23rd Annual Symposium on Foundations of Computer Science (SFCS 1982), pp. 80–91 (1982). https://doi.org/10.1109/SFCS.1982.45

On the (Ir)Replaceability of Global Setups, or How (Not) to Use a Global Ledger

Christian Badertscher[1]($^{(\boxtimes)}$)(iD), Julia Hesse[2], and Vassilis Zikas[3]

[1] IOHK, Zurich, Switzerland
christian.badertscher@iohk.io
[2] IBM Research Europe, Zurich, Switzerland
jhs@zurich.ibm.com
[3] Purdue University, West Lafayette, USA
vzikas@cs.purdue.edu

Abstract. In universally composable (UC) security, a global setup is intended to capture the ideal behavior of a primitive which is accessible by multiple protocols, allowing them to share state. A representative example is the Bitcoin ledger. Indeed, since Bitcoin—and more generally blockchain ledgers—are known to be useful in various scenarios, it has become increasingly popular to capture such ledgers as global setup. Intuitively, one would expect UC to allow us to make security statements about protocols that use such a global setup, e.g., a global ledger, which can then be automatically translated into the setting where the setup is replaced by a protocol implementing it, such as Bitcoin.

We show that the above reasoning is flawed and such a generic security-preserving replacement can only work under very (often unrealistic) strong conditions on the global setup and the security statement. For example, the UC security of Bitcoin for realizing a ledger proved by Badertscher *et al.* [CRYPTO'17] is *not* sufficient per se to allow us to replace the ledger by Bitcoin when used as a global setup. In particular, we cannot expect that all security statements in the global ledger-hybrid world would be preserved when using Bitcoin as a ledger.

On the positive side, we provide characterizations of security statements for protocols that make use of global setups, for which the replacement is sound. Our results can be seen as a first guide on how to navigate the very tricky question of what constitutes a "good" global setup and how to use it in order to keep the modular protocol-design approach intact.

1 Introduction

Universally Composable (UC) security [Can01] ensures strong composability guarantees: Informally, a UC secure protocol remains secure no matter what

---

C. Badertscher—Work done in part while the author was visiting the *Simons Institute for the Theory of Computing*, UC Berkeley.

V. Zikas—Work done in part while the author was at the University of Edinburgh and at the *Simons Institute for the Theory of Computing*, UC Berkeley. Research supported in part by Sunday Group and by the NSF grant no. 2055599.

K. Nissim and B. Waters (Eds.): TCC 2021, LNCS 13043, pp. 626–657, 2021.
https://doi.org/10.1007/978-3-030-90453-1_22

environment it is placed in, i.e., no matter what other protocols might be executed alongside. This powerful security definition enables a constructive approach to protocols, where protocols can be designed and proved secure assuming access to idealized primitives/functionalities, and instantiating the idealized functionalities with UC-secure protocols does not affect the proven guarantees.

Canetti and Rabin [CR03] pointed out a limitation of the standard universal composition theorem. In a nutshell, the issue is as follows: Assume that a protocol π securely realizes a functionality $\mathcal{F}$ in the public-key infrastructure (PKI) model. The UC composition theorem ensures that $\mathcal{F}$ can be replaced by π (and its PKI) in *any* context. However, if a context protocol makes calls to two independent instances of $\mathcal{F}$, then any replacing instance of π needs to come with its own independent (local to π) PKI; in other words, the two replaced instances of π cannot share the same PKI[1]. This is a clear mismatch with reality, where we would not create a different PKI for each protocol (instance), but rather people would have one public-key/private-key pair which they would use in multiple – and beyond this example, even different – protocols.

The first attempt to augment composable frameworks to realistically capture shared setups was the JUC (Universal Composition with Joint State, [CR03]) model. However, JUC is limited to settings where we know in advance (the number and even the session identifiers of) the protocols that will be using a shared setup. Lifting this restriction, *UC with global setups* was proposed by Canetti et al. [CDPW07], often referred to as the *GUC* framework. Intuitively, a global setup can be accessed by arbitrary (unknown) protocols, and due to those protocols the setup may be in any possible state at the point it gets accessed by another protocol. Subsequently, a recent work [BCH+20] casts the notion of global setups within the plain UC framework, eliminating the need for a new model and thus enabling re-use of the vast literature about UC-secure protocols. Both models come with a composition theorem that allows secure replacement of protocols *in the presence* of a global setup.

REPLACING GLOBAL SETUPS. In all the above models, the global setup is treated as a functionality with fixed code that will eventually be implemented by a trusted authority. In this paper, we investigate whether we can change this code without affecting security of the context. More detailed, we analyze whether we can *replace a global setup* with a (globally accessible) protocol that UC-emulates the setup, and to which extent such a replacement preserves security statements of protocols jointly using the global setup[2]. At first sight, it might be surprising that none of the existing composition theorems solve this question. Intuitively, as we depict a bit more formally in Fig. 1, composition theorems allow us to

---

[1] The statement applies also to any non-trivial type of hybrid functionalities whose use might correlate the views of the protocols calling them, e.g., the common reference string (CRS).

[2] The terms *setup* and *subroutine* are synonyms in the context of UC and refer to a protocol instance that is called by another protocol. Subroutines can be any type of protocol: interactive such as Bitcoin, or trusted parties ("ideal functionalities") such as the ideal ledger.

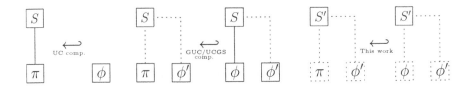

Fig. 1. Applying composition theorems in the UC literature. Here, $X \hookleftarrow Y$ denotes that X can replace Y in arbitrary contexts. π, ϕ, ϕ' denote protocols potentially calling setup S. Assume π UC-emulates ϕ (with access to S) and that S' UC-emulates S. **UC composition (left):** If S is only called by π, then π^S can replace ϕ in arbitrary contexts. **GUC/UCGS composition (middle):** π^S can replace ϕ^S even if the setup S is called by other protocols, too, and hence is *global.* **This work (right):** $\pi^{S'}$ can replace $\phi^{S'}$ (under certain conditions), i.e., replacing ϕ by π works, even when the global setup S (that both protocols call) is replaced by its realization S'.

argue when we can replace some protocol ϕ by its UC-realization π. If π calls a local setup S, then in any context any call to ϕ can be replaced by a call to π^S by the UC composition theorem. However, the UC composition theorem cannot argue about ϕ and π anymore if any of these protocols call a setup that is not local to them, i.e., that is also called by other protocols and hence *global.*

But why is considering global setups interesting? Indeed, until recently, global setups such as an ideal PKI were intended to be replaced by trusted authorities implementing the exact same functionality as the global PKI [CSV16]. But with the rise of blockchain technology, more and more interactive protocols are proposed to securely implement a global PKI [BdM93, RY16, MR17, GKLP18, KKM19, PSKR20], a global clock [BGK+21] or a global ledger [BMTZ17]. Suddenly, the above question of global setup replacement becomes highly relevant! Does a protocol's claimed security in the presence of an ideal global PKI such as, e.g., [CSV16, PS18, DPS19] still hold when the protocol is deployed with an interactive PKI protocol instead? Does a security analysis carried out w.r.t an ideal global ledger functionality [KZZ16, CGL+17, DFH18, DEFM19, DEF+19, EMM19, CGJ19, ACKZ20, KL20] remain valid when the global ledger is replaced by, e.g., the Bitcoin blockchain? The same question can be asked for protocols using a global clock [KZZ16, BGK+18, DFH18, DEF+19] or a global CRS [CKWZ13]. Our findings towards answering such questions are manifold. On the positive side, we give several simple conditions on the global setup, or both the global setup and the security statement, under which global replacement preserves a security statement. On the negative side, our results indicate that global setups need to be designed with care in order to not render the setup "irreplaceable". Unless such irreplaceable setups are hard-coded as trusted third parties, security results stated with respect to them are mainly of theoretical interest.

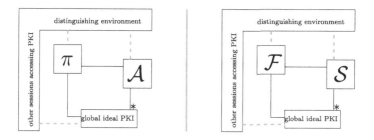

Fig. 2. Topology of a security statement with a global setup.

Technical Challenges of Global Replacement. Let us first explain the general topology of a security statement in the presence of a global setup in its most common schenario. In Fig. 2, protocol π securely realizes functionality $\mathcal{F}$ in the presence of a global ideal PKI functionality. Being globally accessible by protocols that are part of the distinguishing environment, the global PKI exists in *both* the real execution with π and the ideal execution with $\mathcal{F}$. The adversarial interface at the global PKI is marked with $*$ in Fig. 2, and it might allow the adversary to, e.g., read public keys of others and register his own keys.

To understand why the global PKI in the above illustration might not be replaceable by some protocol Φ_{PKI} that securely realized an ideal PKI, we need to review what "realization" (or UC-emulation, as it is often called) means here. Φ_{PKI} UC-realizes an ideal PKI if it is *at least as strong* as the ideal PKI. Hence, intuitively, UC realization draws the "upper bound" of the attack surface against Φ_{PKI} in the following sense: protocol Φ_{PKI} does not admit more attacks than the ideal PKI. We use the notion of an "attack" to describe something that the adversary can achieve via the adversarial interface. However, UC realization does not imply a lower bound on attacks: Φ_{PKI} can have arbitrarily strong guarantees, thereby preventing several attacks that the ideal PKI admits[3]. And this lack of a lower bound causes trouble in replacing a global protocol with its realization: under replacement, the adversarial interface $*$ becomes restricted in an arbitrary way, causing failure in the simulation carried out by $\mathcal{S}$. If there is no way to rescue the simulation (i.e., to work with the restricted interface), the security statement witnessed by $\mathcal{S}$ is void and π does indeed not emulate $\mathcal{F}$ anymore in the presence of the interactive PKI protocol Φ_{PKI}.

With the above explanation, it should become clear that an extensive adversarial interface at the global setup hinders its replacement. For example, the ideal PKI might allow the adversary to register an unlimited amount of (fresh)

---

[3] As an example, it is possible that a PKI protocol that disallows registration of duplicate or non-wellformed public keys UC-emulates an ideal PKI that allows the adversary to register arbitrary public keys. Intuitively, the larger the gap in the guarantees, the easier is the UC realization to prove.

public keys without delays, while a blockchain-based PKI protocol might protect against such "flooding" of the PKI simply because transaction throughput is limited. A security statement in the presence of a global PKI with a simulation that exploits the public key flooding of the global PKI thus fails under replacement. Along these lines we can further give examples of ideal ledgers from the literature that require care when cast as global ledgers. For example, consider an ideal transaction ledger that allows the adversary to arbitrarily reorder transactions [BMTZ17]. A blockchain-based protocol realizing this ledger, however, might enforce a transaction order that is partially determined by honest miners. Thus, simulators exploiting adversarial reordering would not work with access to the blockchain-based protocol instead of the ideal transaction ledger. Another example is a global account ledger that allows the adversary to transfer arbitrary amounts of his own money (i.e., money owned by corrupted parties) with arbitrary delays [DEFM19]. Any security statement exploiting this weakness of the ledger in its simulation is not preserved when, instead of accessing the global account ledger, parties run a cryptocurrency protocol instead that, e.g., employs a monetary transaction limit or prevents large and sudden stake shift.[4]

WHEN REPLACEMENT VOIDS SECURITY I. One might be tempted to say that in the above examples, simulation can be adjusted to work with the stronger global protocol since, intuitively, the stronger global protocol also allows less attacks in the real world. However, this intuition can fail as we demonstrate now. We give a constructed but not overly artificial example of a global setup replacement that voids the underlying security statement, in the sense that there cannot exist any simulator witnessing the emulation statement. Consider the following "secure data distribution" protocol π_{secDD} run by some user U. The protocol needs access to a global repository $\mathcal{G}_{\mathsf{authBC}}$ where U can store data records: $\mathcal{G}_{\mathsf{authBC}}$ records (U, x) if user U provides input x and allows the adversary to read out any recorded pair from its storage. Such a repository could be realized by authenticated broadcast. Now, U first generates a key pair (pk, sk) and sends pk to the repository. It then takes an input message m and pushes an encryption $c := \mathrm{Enc}_{pk}(m)$ to $\mathcal{G}_{\mathsf{authBC}}$ and additionally sends c on a network to a list of receiving parties R_i. It also internally stores m and returns the activation to the caller.

The ideal functionality this simple protocol π_{secDD} realizes is an "encrypt-then-push" service that we call $\mathcal{F}_{\mathsf{enc+push}}$. $\mathcal{F}_{\mathsf{enc+push}}$ takes input m from U and asks the simulator for a public key pk (m is never leaked). Upon receiving pk, $\mathcal{F}_{\mathsf{enc+push}}$ encrypts m and provides the ciphertext as input to the repository in

---

[4] We note that our results, on the positive side, can be used to state the conditions such that a security proof is not jeopardized. For example, in the aforementioned work [DEFM19], this could be achieved by letting the protocol's security be oblivious of how exactly the base ledger settles an account balance, as long as it is eventually settled to the value the protocol (or the ideal functionality) demands. Intuitively, since this only depends on the black-box properties of persistence and liveness of the underlying ledger, such an approach would admit a replacement by known blockchain protocols.

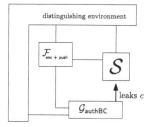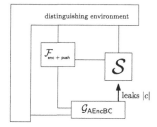

Fig. 3. When simulation fails under global replacement: simulator S works with cipher-text c (**left**), but might fail when only receiving ciphertext length $|c|$ (**right**) from the *stronger* global setup $\mathcal{G}_{\mathsf{AEncBC}}$ that replaces the weaker $\mathcal{G}_{\mathsf{authBC}}$.

the name of U. To prove that the protocol realizes $\mathcal{F}_{\mathsf{enc+push}}$ (under adaptive corruption of U), we come up with a proper simulator: the simulator simulates a public-private key pair (for U), provides $\mathcal{F}_{\mathsf{enc+push}}$ with the public key, and simply reads out the ciphertext that the functionality created (in the name of U) from $\mathcal{G}_{\mathsf{authBC}}$ to simulate the ciphertext on the network to be sent to the receivers. This is a perfect simulation of the real world. In case U is corrupted, the simulator provides the secret key to the adversary which is consistent with the encrypted input message m.

Now, assume we replace $\mathcal{G}_{\mathsf{authBC}}$ by a stronger version $\mathcal{G}_{\mathsf{AEncBC}}$ that works identically except that the adversary only receives the length $|x|$ when reading any of the user's records, which corresponds to encrypted broadcast to a list of receivers. Intuition says that working with a stronger repository, i.e., using encrypted and authenticated broadcast rather than authenticated only, cannot be of harm and improves security for everyone. But this change does not only make the above simulation strategy impossible; in fact, *no simulator* exists to prove the same statement, i.e., that π_{secDD} realizes $\mathcal{F}_{\mathsf{enc+push}}$ anymore. The simulator does not have access to the ciphertext anymore which is now kept secret by $\mathcal{G}_{\mathsf{AEncBC}}$, and hence must simulate a ciphertext without knowing the underlying message m. Figure 3 illustrates the issue. The simulation is trapped in the well-known commitment problem [Nie02][5]. We conclude that π_{secDD} as defined fails in realizing $\mathcal{F}_{\mathsf{enc+push}}$ when running with $\mathcal{G}_{\mathsf{AEncBC}}$ (which implies the weaker $\mathcal{G}_{\mathsf{encBC}}$). This means that we must change the protocol (e.g., use non-committing encryption) to again realize $\mathcal{F}_{\mathsf{enc+push}}$, or if we stick to protocol π_{secDD}, we must weaken the security guarantees of $\mathcal{F}_{\mathsf{enc+push}}$ (e.g., leak message m).

---

[5] In order to conclude the proof, the environment can perform a standard trick: after seeing the ciphertext on the network (either real or simulated), the distinguisher can afterwards instruct the (dummy) adversary to corrupt the user U to obtain the secret key and check that the ciphertext contains the right message. For ordinary encryption schemes, this test will always succeed in the real world, and with substantial probability fail in the ideal world [Nie02].

While this example is arguably constructed, the problem's core translates directly to more serious situations, such as protocols (e.g., state-channels) proven secure with respect to a global ledger abstraction that is instantiated with a concrete blockchain protocol that is typically stronger (i.e., offers less adversarial capabilities) than its abstraction.

We now sketch another technically easy example that shows that security statements can fail completely, once a global setup is replaced by another one that UC-emulates it. Again, we replace the global setup by a stronger variant to achieve the contradiction. The example also illustrates how security guarantees can be blurred when exploiting adversarial capabilities of the global setup, and it does not rely on adaptive corruptions in doing so.

WHEN REPLACEMENT VOIDS SECURITY II. Assume a simple protocol ϕ for some party P that works as follows: it expects as input transactions of a certain type. Before submitting them to a global transaction ledger, ϕ orders the transactions according to size and submits this list to the ledger. Assume that the ledger is a transaction ledger similar to the one in [BMTZ17] that allows the adversary to re-order transactions before a block is formed and added to the immutable ledger state.

The ideal functionality $\mathcal{F}_\phi$ that this protocol realizes can be the following: it takes as input the list of transactions provided by P, and orders them *differently*, say according to lexicographic order, and submits this list to the global transaction ledger. This is of course weird, but possible to simulate: to prove this construction, we observe that the simulator has the freedom to reorder freely (before the transactions are appended to the ledger state) and chooses the ordering that equals the one induced by the actions of the real-world adversary, which even yields a perfect simulation!

Now assume we use a stronger transaction ledger that does not allow to reorder the transaction list in the ledger and hence makes the adversarial capabilities less powerful. However, since no simulator can now change the order, the order of transactions in the transaction ledger directly signals to the environment, whether it interacts with the ideal world (lexicographic order) or the real world (size). Therefore, using a stronger ledger (which UC-realizes the weaker one) renders the construction invalid as no simulator does exist. The point here is that every simulator must crucially carry out a reordering attack and that there is no other strategy to rectify the ideal world if re-ordering is impossible. This shows how the usage of a global ideal ledger can create false impressions of obtained guarantees, since $\mathcal{F}_\phi$ is impossible to realize w.r.t any real transaction ledger protocol which disallows arbitrary reordering.

Our Results. We provide various conditions under which replacement of a global setup by a protocol realizing it does not affect the validity of the underlying security statement. Our results of Sect. 3 give a partial guide on how to navigate the very tricky question of what constitutes a "good" global setup. More concretely, we provide three theorems for soundly replacing global setups by their emulation in existing security statements. We note that only the first replacement strategy is conditioned on solely the global setup and its emulation, and is hence oblivious of the underlying security statement. Contrary, the latter replacement strategies require us to put conditions on the simulator of the underlying security statement.

REPLACEMENT WITH EQUIVALENT SETUP. A setup can be replaced with its realization if the realization is actually equivalent to the setup, including adversarial capabilities. The notion of equivalence of adversarial capabilities is formalized using the simulation argument: after replacing, there must be an efficient way to emulate all queries that were available before. This is formalized in Theorem 3 and recovers the, to our knowledge, only pre-existing result about global setup replacement in the literature [CSV16] (see related work below for details). However, replacement with equivalent protocols is only of limited interest in practise, and thus Theorem 3 merely constitutes a sanity check of our chosen methodology of considering global replacement using the UCGS terminology [BCH+20].

REPLACEMENTS FOR AGNOSTIC SIMULATIONS. We show that the replacement of a global setup $\mathcal{G}$ in a protocol π UC-realizing ϕ is sound if the simulator $\mathcal{S}$ witnessing this construction fulfills one of the following two conditions.

- $\mathcal{S}$ is *agnostic* of the adversarial capabilities of $\mathcal{G}$ and the only dependence is on exported capabilities that are available also to honest parties. This is formalized in Theorem 4.
- The interaction of $\mathcal{S}$ with the global setup can be characterized by a set I of adversarial queries that are *admissible*, a concrete technical condition that formalizes the idea that adversarial capabilities and their actions will be preserved once $\mathcal{G}$ is going to be replaced. This is formalized in Theorem 5. A generalization of the results to the case of several global subroutines is given in Sect. 4.

The first condition on the simulator is appealing as it is simple to check. As an example, [KZZ16] gives a security statement in the presence of a global ledger that allows reordering, but their simulation is agnostic of this particular adversarial capability. Similarly, the simulation of the lightning network in [KL20] works by only assuming that the simulator can access capabilities of honest parties to read the ledger state and submit transactions. We point out that since $\mathcal{F}$ can communicate with $\mathcal{G}$ naturally via an ordinary party identifier (see [BCH+20]) or in its own "name", the simulator $\mathcal{S}$ can indeed perform those tasks via $\mathcal{F}$ and hence use $\mathcal{G}$ just like an honest caller of the protocol (and importantly without making use of the adversarial interface of $\mathcal{G}$).[6]

The second condition brings more flexibility to protocol designers since $\mathcal{S}$ can use certain capabilities I at the adversarial interface. Formally, we introduce the concept of *filtering* adversarial queries Definition 8 that would hinder replacement,

---

[6] We note that prior works often leave it unspecified how exactly the simulator performs those tasks in the name of honest parties and how it will get the replies. The way we suggested, namely via $\mathcal{F}$, is actually the only admissible way without directly running into the replacement problem again.

leaving only a set I of adversarial queries which are fine to use relative to an implementation (or a set of implementations) that is going to replace the setup.

Our theorems further follow by applications of the UCGS and UC composition theorems at a level of abstraction which seems to share a lot of similarities with other frameworks and their composition theorems. For example, the exact corruption model is irrelevant, as long as the behavior of and upon corruption can be formulated via an "adversarial" interface, where the above conditions can be evaluated on (such as the backdoor tape in UC). Our results are formulated using terminology and composition theorem of [BCH+20], which equips the standard UC model with a definition for global subroutines and composition in the presence of such. In doing so, we refrain from introducing a new variant of UC in order to state our results. We further believe that our results are natural and can be adapted to other simulation-based frameworks than UC.

IMPLICATIONS ON THE GLOBAL RANDOM ORACLE MODEL. Often, a global setup is modeled as a pure setup assumption for proofs. The probably most prominent example is the global random oracle model (RO) [CJS14, BGK+18, CDG+18]. While our results are presented in a rather *constructive* way that help to evaluate protocol designers what impact their choice of global setup has as a building block to-be-replaced, our results are general and hence applicable to the global RO setting as well. For global random oracles, different versions of different (adversarial) strengths exist and the question about comparability and unification has been brought up by Camenisch et al. [CDG+18]. In fact, composing different constructions w.r.t different global random oracles is unfortunate, since the main reason to switch to global RO (vs. local RO) is that in practice, all random oracles are instantiated by a single hash function anyway. If composing constructions forces us to again have a couple of different global random oracles (which are supposedly replaced by a single hash function) we are back at square one. As we present in Sect. 3.4, our results provide a general framework to evaluate whether different RO assumptions can be unified across a set of constructions, which is very vital for the global RO model and nicely complements the study of [CDG+18] (in the sense outlined described in the related work section).

WHY REPLACING THE SETUP IN BOTH WORLDS? Looking back at Fig. 2 and the described issues of simulation failing under a replaced and restricted adversarial interface, one can ask the following question: why can't we replace the global PKI just in the real world, hence restricting only the real-world adversary? Indeed, we formally prove (using only standard UC composition) that we can just let π make subroutine calls to the replacement of global setup $\mathcal{G}$, and leave the ideal world to be $\mathcal{F}$ in combination with context $\mathcal{G}$. However, such replacement is not very useful: the different contexts allow to obscure the achieved level of security as formalized by $\mathcal{F}$. The high-level reason is that $\mathcal{F}$ is misleading in its role as idealization of π if we ignore the context. For example, $\mathcal{F}$ can offer much better security guarantees (for example, less powerful adversarial interface) *because of* the weak context that offers more influence to an adversary. In the sum, the real world is stronger and the ideal world is weaker (hence the statement must go through) but the exact idealization of π remains unclear because the context is not equal and cannot be "factored out". The second example above (the re-ordering example with a global ledger) is of this type.

WHY NOT SIMPLY USING A STRONGER IDEAL SETUP TO BEGIN WITH? To circumvent the replaceability issues that we deal with in this paper, we could simply prove our security statements with respect to a stronger global functionality that is very close or even UC-equivalent to the protocol. This way, we can likely argue that the simulator of our security statement works equally well with both setups, and we can allow for replacement of the global setup (cf. Theorem 3). What is the downside of this approach? The strengthened functionality no longer abstracts an "ideal service" to be used in a modular protocol analysis or design. For example, one could strengthen the ideal global ledger to exactly match the guarantees and adversarial interfaces of Bitcoin. But then the security analysis with respect to that ledger remains valid *only* when replacing it with Bitcoin, while an analysis with respect to an abstracted global ledger functionality can (if carried out as suggested in our paper) remain valid when replacing the global ledger with *any* blockchain that UC-realizes it. This idea of modular composition is at the core of universal composability frameworks and our paper shows how to preserve it for global functionalities.

CONCLUSION - WHAT IS A "GOOD" GLOBAL SETUP? Our results indicate that care has to be taken when global setups are used as building blocks intended to be replaced with interactive protocols. Since replacement requires conditions on both setup and security proof, "good" global setups cannot be identified as such by just looking at the setup. Of course, to be instantiable by another protocol at all, a "good" global ideal building block needs to be UC-realizable (in a non-trivial manner) in the first place. But it also matters that such a global building block is *used in a good way* in a security statement, meaning that the simulation does not overly exploit the adversarial interface, as otherwise it would be doomed to fail under replacement. We believe that our work provides good intuition and formal guidance on how to design *and use* global building blocks in modular protocol design.

Related Work. To our knowledge, there is very limited work on the replaceability of a global UC setup. In fact, the only work that has looked at the question in general is [CSV16]. However, the treatment there is in GUC which requires considerable effort to even define "global" protocols, and even then, the treatment inherits the inconsistencies of the GUC model. [CSV16] identifies emulation equivalence as a sufficient condition on the global setup and protocol replacing it, to allow a generic preservation of security properties. However, these conditions are too strict to be applied on more complicated primitives, such as blockchain ledgers, which have recently become a standard example of global subroutines. Nonetheless, we recover their result ("General Functionality Composition", Theorem 3.1 [CSV16]) in Theorem 4.

While our results are described using the recent UCGS modelling [BCH+20], they can easily be adapted to any framework which supports universal composition and global setups.

Finally, an investigation of replaceability targeted to special variants of global random oracles was recently made in [CDG+18]; in a nutshell, their approach is contrary to ours in the sense that their work investigates the replacement of a stronger by a weaker random oracle (i.e., one that gives the simulator more power). Such a replacement can only be sound for specific definitions of random oracles (ones that are defined to take away leverage from the real-world adversary, but not the simulator) and need to be accompanied by a protocol transformation. As we outline in Sect. 3.4, our most general theorem nicely complements their study on unifying different global RO assumptions.

Organization of this Paper. While our ideas are formulated in a generality such that they can be applied to several composable frameworks that support global setup [KMT20, MR11], when it comes to proofs, we must fix a particular model which we choose to be UC [Can20] and its treatment of global subroutines as recently established in [BCH+20]. We provide a brief introduction to UC and UCGS in Sect. 2, which should suffice to follow the ideas of our proofs. In Sect. 3 we provide global subroutine replacement theorems for protocols accessing only a single global setup. We generalize our concepts to many global subroutines in Sect. 4.

2   Preliminaries: Global Subroutines in UC

In this section we recap how to formalize global setups in the UC framework using the language of UCGS [BCH+20]. We first provide the minimal background on the UC model that is necessary to understand the concepts.

2.1   UC Basics

Formally, a protocol π is an algorithm for a distributed system and formalized as an interactive Turing machine. An ITM has several tapes, for example an identity tape (read-only), an activation tape, or input/output tapes to pass values to its program and return values back to the caller. A machine also has a backdoor tape where (especially in the case of ideal functionalities) interaction with an adversary is possible or corruption messages are handled. While an ITM is a static object, UC defines the notion of an ITM instance (denoted ITI), which is defined by the extended identity $\mathsf{eid} = (M, id)$, where M is the description of an ITM and $id = (\mathsf{sid}, \mathsf{pid})$ is a string consisting of a session identifier sid and a party identifier $\mathsf{pid} \in \mathcal{P}$. An instance, also called a session, of a protocol π (represented as an ITM M_π) with respect to a session number sid is defined as a set of ITIs $\{(M_\pi, id_{\mathsf{pid}})\}_{\mathsf{pid} \in \mathcal{P}}$ where $id_{\mathsf{pid}} = (\mathsf{sid}, \mathsf{pid})$.

The real process can now be defined by an environment $\mathcal{Z}$ (a special ITI) that spawns exactly one session of the protocol in the presence of an adversary $\mathcal{A}$ (also a special ITI), where $\mathcal{A}$ is allowed to interact with the ITIs via the *backdoor tape*, e.g., to corrupt them or to obtain information from the hybrid functionalities, e.g. authenticated channels, that the protocol is using. The adversary ITI can only communicate with the backdoor tapes of the protocol machines. An environment can be restricted by a so-called identity bound $\xi \in \Xi$ which formalizes which external parties the environment might claim when interacting as input provider to the protocol. The less restrictive the bound, the more general the composition guarantees are. The UC theorem is quantified by such a predicate.

The output of the execution is the bit output by $\mathcal{Z}$ and is denoted by $\mathrm{EXEC}_{\pi,\mathcal{A},\mathcal{Z}}(k,z,r)$ where k is the security parameter, $z \in \{0,1\}^*$ is the input to the environment, and randomness r for the entire experiment. Let $\mathrm{EXEC}_{\pi,\mathcal{A},\mathcal{Z}}(k,z)$ denote the random variable obtained by choosing the randomness r uniformly at random and evaluating $\mathrm{EXEC}_{\pi,\mathcal{A},\mathcal{Z}}(k,z,r)$. Let $\mathrm{EXEC}_{\pi,\mathcal{A},\mathcal{Z}}$ denote the ensemble $\{\mathrm{EXEC}_{\pi,\mathcal{A},\mathcal{Z}}(k,z)\}_{k\in\mathbb{N},z\in\{0,1\}^*}$.

Ideal-World Process. The ideal process is formulated with respect to an another protocol ϕ, which in its most familiar form is a protocol $\mathrm{IDEAL}_{\mathcal{F}}$ for an ITM $\mathcal{F}$ which is called an ideal functionality for which we describe the situation. In the ideal process, the environment $\mathcal{Z}$ interacts with $\mathcal{F}$, an ideal-world adversary (often called the simulator) $\mathcal{S}$ and a set of trivial, i.e., dummy ITMs representing the protocol machines of $\mathrm{IDEAL}_{\mathcal{F}}$ that forward to the functionality whatever is provided as inputs to them by the environment (and return back whatever received from the functionality). In the ideal world, the ideal-world adversary (aka the simulator) can decide to corrupt parties and can interact via the backdoor tape with the functionality. For example, via the backdoor tape, the functionality could for example leak certain values about the inputs, or allow certain influence on the system. We denote the output of this ideal-world process by $\mathrm{EXEC}_{\mathcal{F},\mathcal{A},\mathcal{Z}}(k,z,r)$ where the inputs are as in the real-world process. Let $\mathrm{EXEC}_{\mathcal{F},\mathcal{S},\mathcal{Z}}(k,z)$ denote the random variable obtained by choosing the randomness r uniformly at random and evaluating $\mathrm{EXEC}_{\mathcal{F},\mathcal{S},\mathcal{Z}}(k,z,r)$. Let $\mathrm{EXEC}_{\mathcal{F},\mathcal{S},\mathcal{Z}}$ denote the ensemble $\{\mathrm{EXEC}_{\mathcal{F},\mathcal{S},\mathcal{Z}}(k,z)\}_{k\in\mathbb{N},z\in\{0,1\}^*}$.

Secure Realization and Composition. In a nutshell, a protocol π ξ-UC-emulates (ideal) protocol ϕ if the "real-world" process (where π is executed) is indistinguishable from the ideal-world process (where ϕ is executed), i.e., if for any (efficient) adversary $\mathcal{A}$ there exists an (efficient) ideal-world adversary (the simulator) $\mathcal{S}$ such that for every (efficient) ξ-bounded environment $\mathcal{Z}$ it holds that $\mathrm{EXEC}_{\pi,\mathcal{A},\mathcal{Z}} \approx \mathrm{EXEC}_{\phi,\mathcal{S},\mathcal{Z}}$.

The emulation notion is composable, i.e., if π UC-emulates ϕ, then in a larger context protocol ρ, the subroutine ϕ can be safely replaced by π, denoted by $\rho^{\phi\to\pi}$. For this replacement to be well-defined, a few technical preconditions must be satisfied. First, the protocols must be compliant, which ensures that in case π and ϕ might both be subroutines in ρ they do not share the same session (ensuring that the replacement operator works as intended). Furthermore, compliance also makes sure that the protocol is invoked properly, i.e., with the correct identities specified in ξ. The definitions of these UC concepts relevant to our work are given in the full version [BHZ20]. The second major precondition is that protocols should be subroutine respecting, meaning that each session of π can run in parallel with other sessions of protocols without interfering with them (in order for the UC-emulation notion which considers a single challenge session to be a reasonable precondition for the composition theorem). The exact condition is as follows:

Definition 1 (Subroutine respecting [Can20]). *Protocol π is subroutine respecting if each session s of π, occurring within an execution of any protocol with any environment satisfies the following four requirements, in any execution of any protocol ρ with any adversary and environment (as per the definition of protocol execution; it is stressed that these requirements must be satisfied even when session s of π is a subroutine of ρ, and in particular when the execution involves ITIs which are not members of that extended session s):*

1. *The sub-parties of session s reject all inputs passed from an ITI which is not already a main party or subsidiary of session s (note that rejecting a message means that the recipient ITI returns to its state prior to receiving the message and ends the activation without sending any message; see [Can20, Section 3.1.2]).*
2. *The main parties and sub-parties of session s reject all incoming subroutine outputs passed from an ITI which is not already a main party or subsidiary of session s.*
3. *No sub-party of session s passes subroutine output to an existing ITI that is not already a main party or sub-party of session s.*
4. *No main party or sub-party of session s passes input to an existing ITI that is not already a main party or sub-party of session s.*

Theorem 1 (UC Theorem). *Let ρ, π, ϕ be protocols and let ξ be a predicate on extended identities, such that ρ is (π, ϕ, ξ)-compliant, both ϕ and π are subroutine exposing and subroutine respecting, and π UC-emulates ϕ with respect to ξ-identity-bounded environments. Then $\rho^{\phi \to \pi}$ UC-emulates protocol ρ.*

2.2   UC with Global Subroutines

A global subroutine can be imagined as a module that a protocol uses as a subroutine, but which might be available to more than this protocol only. While initial formalizations to capture when a module is available to everyone, i.e., to the environment, defined a UC-variant [CDPW07], it was recently shown that capturing this can be fully accommodated within UC [BCH+20]. In a nutshell, if π is proven to realize ϕ in the presence of a global subroutine γ, then the environment can access this subroutine in both, the ideal and the real world, which must be taken care of by the protocol. As a rule of thumb, proving that π realizes ϕ in the presence of global γ is harder than when γ is a local subroutine, i.e., not visible by the environment.

The framework presented in [BCH+20] defines a new UC-protocol $M[\pi, \gamma]$ that is an execution enclave of π and γ. $M[\pi, \gamma]$ provides the environment access to the main parties of π and γ in a way that does not change the behavior of the protocol or the set of machines. The clue is that $M[\pi, \gamma]$ itself is a normal UC protocol and the emulation is perfect under certain conditions on π and γ. We first state the definition from [BCH+20].

Definition 2 (UC emulation with global subroutines). *Let π, ϕ and γ be protocols. We say that π ξ-UC-emulates ϕ in the presence of γ if protocol $\mathsf{M}[\pi, \gamma]$ ξ-UC-emulates protocol $\mathsf{M}[\phi, \gamma]$.*

The first condition is the following and expresses the fact that γ might communicate with protocols outside of π's realm:

Definition 3 (γ-subroutine respecting). *A protocol π is called γ-subroutine respecting if the four conditions of Definition 1 required from any (sub-)party of some instance of π are relaxed as follows:*

- *the conditions do not apply to those sub-parties of instance s that also belong to some extended session s' of protocol γ;*
- *(sub-)parties of s may pass input to machines that belong to some extended session s' of protocol γ, even if those machines are not yet part of the extended instance of s.*

The second condition is a technical condition on the global subroutine which is called *regularity*. The condition says that (a) a shared subroutine does not spawn new ITIs by providing subroutine output to them, and (b) that the shared subroutine may not invoke the outside protocol as a subroutine. It is usually not a problem for global setups to satisfy this, since most of the time, we can model functionalities to be reactive and assume "signaling events" to happen out-of-band.

The formal definition is taken from [BCH+20].

Definition 4 (Regular setup). *Let ϕ, γ be protocols. We say that γ is a ϕ-regular setup if, in any execution, the main parties of an instance of γ do not invoke a new ITI of ϕ via a message destined for the subroutine output tape, and do not have an ITI with code ϕ as subsidiary.*

In [BCH+20, Proposition 3.5], the authors show that if the protocol π is γ-subroutine respecting, where γ itself is π-regular and subroutine respecting, then the interaction between π and the global subroutine γ is very structured without unexpected artifacts. We state the proposition here for completeness. Here, α is an arbitrary protocol and $\hat{\alpha}$ is a version of α that makes use of $\mathsf{M}[[]\pi, \gamma]$ instead of π and has an indistinguishable behavior. We refer to [BCH+20] and just state the proposition.

Proposition 1. *Let γ be subroutine respecting and π be γ-subroutine respecting. Then the protocol $\mathsf{M}[\pi, \gamma]$ is subroutine respecting. In addition, let γ be π-regular, and let α be a protocol that invokes at most one subroutine with code π. Denote by $\hat{\alpha}$ the transformed protocol described above. Then the transcript established by the set of virtual ITIs in an execution of some environment with $\hat{\alpha}$ is identical to the transcript established by the set of ITIs induced by the environment that has the same random tape but interacts with α.*

The UCGS theorem is then the composition theorem for protocols that are defined with respect to a global subroutine γ. Note that not γ is replaced, but ϕ by its implementation π.

Theorem 2 (Universal Composition with Global Subroutines – UCGS Theorem). *Let* ρ, ϕ, π, γ *be subroutine-exposing protocols, where* γ *is a* ϕ-*regular setup and subroutine respecting,* ϕ, π *are* γ-*subroutine respecting and* ρ *is* (π, ϕ, ξ)-*compliant and* $(\pi, \mathsf{M}[\mathsf{code}, \gamma], \xi)$-*compliant for* $\mathsf{code} \in \{\phi, \pi\}$. *Assume* π ξ-*UC-emulates* ϕ *in the presence of* γ, *then* $\rho^{\phi \to \pi}$ *UC-emulates* ρ.

3   Replacement Theorems for a Global Subroutine

In this section, we consider a setting where protocols access only one global subroutine, e.g., a global CRS, or a global ledger, but not both of them. That is, we only consider protocols whose shared setup is formulated as a single protocol. For this simplest global setting, we start by exploring which replacement of the global subroutine follows already from application of the UC composition theorem. Then, we recover the replacement theorem of [CSV16], which preserves security statements if the global subroutine is replaced by an equivalent protocol. And finally, we give conditions for security-preserving replacement of non-equivalent global subroutines.

3.1   Common Preconditions of Our Theorems

Throughout this section, we assume the following preconditions for our theorems. Recall that we are interested in replacing a global subroutine while preserving security statements made with respect to this subroutine. We assume the security statement to be the following: protocol π (potentially with access to further local hybrids $\mathcal{H}$) UC-emulates an ideal functionality $\mathcal{F}$ in the presence of global subroutine $\mathcal{G}$, with respect to dummy adversary $\mathcal{A}$. Simulator $\mathcal{S}_\mathcal{A}$ is a witness for this emulation. The statement is depicted below and referred to in the text as precondition (1).

(1)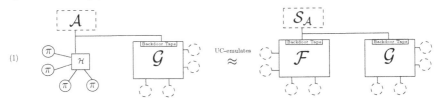

Second, since our aim is to investigate how UC emulation of global subroutines can be useful for context protocols, we assume that the global subroutine is emulated as follows: ψ UC-emulates $\mathcal{G}$, with respect to dummy adversary $\mathcal{D}$ (where ψ potentially makes use of other hybrids $\mathcal{H}'$). We call a simulator witnessing this statement $\mathcal{S}_\mathcal{D}$. We refer to this emulation as precondition (2).

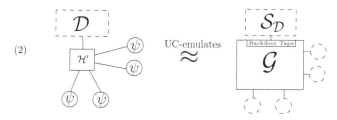

(2)

Given this notation, the core question of our work can be stated as follows: given preconditions (1) and (2), under which additional conditions does it hold that

$$\pi \text{ UC-emulates } \mathcal{F} \text{ in the presence of global } \psi?$$

Simplifying Notation. We note that, while our theorems hold for arbitrary UC protocols, to ease understanding, we formulate them with the special protocols $\text{IDEAL}_{\mathcal{F}}$ and $\text{IDEAL}_{\mathcal{G}}$. Intuitively, $\mathcal{F}$ is a "target" functionality that is to be realized and $\mathcal{G}$ a global ideal setup. To further simplify, we slightly abuse notation and write $\mathcal{G}$ instead of $\text{IDEAL}_{\mathcal{G}}$, e.g., we write "$\psi$ UC-emulates $\mathcal{G}$" instead of "ψ UC-emulates $\text{IDEAL}_{\mathcal{G}}$".

3.2   Warm-Up: Replacing Real-World Global Setups

Our first lemma states that under precondition (2) we can replace the shared subroutine by the construction that UC emulates it. Another way to view this is that "lifting" to global subroutines (w.r.t any application protocol π) preserves UC emulation. An important feature of this statement is that it follows from standard UC composition thanks to the embedding of global setups in standard UC. Throughout the section, we will maintain a running example to illustrate all our statements.

Running Example. Let $\mathcal{G} = \mathcal{G}_{\text{ledger}}$ be an ideal ledger and π a lottery protocol requiring a ledger. Further, let $\psi = \text{FunCoin}$ be a cryptocurrency implementing the ledger $\mathcal{G}_{\text{ledger}}$. By UC emulation, all manipulation and attacks allowed on FunCoin must also be allowed against $\mathcal{G}_{\text{ledger}}$. In particular, this holds for any manipulation or attack carried out while running a lottery.

Lemma 1. *Assume a protocol π makes subroutine calls to global subroutine $\mathcal{G}$ and that ψ is a protocol that UC-emulates $\mathcal{G}$. Then π invoking ψ instead of $\mathcal{G}$ UC-emulates protocol π.*

Proof. On a high level, the argument is as follows: if an environment could tell a run of π with ψ from a run of π with $\mathcal{G}$, then running π internally would already let the environment distinguish a run of ψ from a run of $\mathcal{G}$, violating the precondition of the lemma.

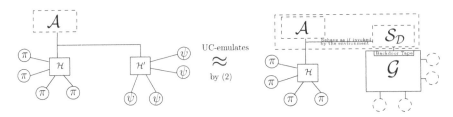

Since for the technical argument, we have to stick to a particular model, we have use the UC language in a more precise way: hence, we assume that π, ψ, $\mathcal{G}$ be protocols and let $\xi \in \Xi$ be a predicate on extended identities, such that π is $(\psi, \mathcal{G}, \xi)$-compliant, π, $\mathcal{G}$, ψ are subroutine exposing, $\mathcal{G}$ and ψ are subroutine respecting, and π is subroutine respecting except via calls to $\mathcal{G}$. We note that these technical conditions are as they appear in UC in order to guarantee that the UC-operator is well defined. To formalize emulation in the presence of a shared setup, we use the terminology of UCGS [BCH+20] (see Sect. 2.2 for a short recap), where global access to $\mathcal{G}$ is granted by an overlay $\mathsf{M}[\cdot, \mathcal{G}]$. In order for this overlay to be opaque to the execution of π with $\mathcal{G}$, we need to assume $\mathcal{G}$ to be π-regular (see Definition 4 and Proposition 1).

With this terminology, it remains to show that if ψ UC-emulates $\mathcal{G}$ with respect to ξ-identity-bounded environments, then $\mathsf{M}[\pi^{\mathcal{G} \to \psi}, \psi]$ UC-emulates protocol $\mathsf{M}[\pi, \mathcal{G}]$ (with respect to ξ-identity bounded environments). This follows from the UC composition theorem: First, observe that $\mathsf{M}[\pi, \mathcal{G}]$ is an ordinary UC-protocol, mimicking all effects that the global (and hence shared) subroutine might have with the environment. Similarly, $\mathsf{M}[\pi^{\mathcal{G} \to \psi}, \psi]$ is an ordinary UC-protocol where subroutine $\mathcal{G}$ is replaced by ψ. Note that, similar to the role of the control function in UC, the embedding $\mathsf{M}[\cdot]$ does not reveal the code of the main instances when interacting with the environment, and therefore we have that $\mathsf{M}[\pi, \mathcal{G}]^{\mathcal{G} \to \psi}$ and $\mathsf{M}[\pi^{\mathcal{G} \to \psi}, \psi]$ are equivalent protocols. Since ψ UC-emulates $\mathcal{G}$ w.r.t. all environments that are bounded by ξ, the UC composition theorem implies that $\mathsf{M}[\pi^{\mathcal{G} \to \psi}, \psi]$ UC-emulates $\mathsf{M}[\pi, \mathcal{G}]$. □

Lemma 1 will serve mainly as a tool in proving the upcoming theorems. Next, we can apply the UC composition theorem to our two preconditions. This yields the following theorem. It says that, in any UC emulation statement w.r.t a global setup, we can safely strengthen the *real-world* setup, while leaving the setup in the ideal world unchanged. The intuition behind it is illustrated with the following example.

Running Example. Back to our lottery. The lottery's provider wants to create trust in his product. He therefore proves that, when run with the global ideal ledger, the lottery protocol UC-emulates some ideal functionality $\mathcal{F}_{\mathsf{lottery}}$ which enforces a fair lottery. In his proof, both the lottery protocol and $\mathcal{F}_{\mathsf{lottery}}$ may exploit weaknesses of $\mathcal{G}_{\mathsf{ledger}}$. Since FunCoin is at least as secure as $\mathcal{G}_{\mathsf{ledger}}$, the provider can safely advertise that running the lottery with FunCoin is as secure as $\mathcal{F}_{\mathsf{lottery}}$ with $\mathcal{G}_{\mathsf{ledger}}$, since this replacement can only decrease the number of possible attacks on the global setup while running the lottery.

Lemma 2. *Assume a protocol π UC-emulates $\mathcal{F}$ in the presence of global subroutine $\mathcal{G}$ and that $\mathcal{G}$ is UC-emulated by ψ, then replacing π's subroutine $\mathcal{G}$ by ψ UC-emulates $\mathcal{F}$ that has access to global subroutine $\mathcal{G}$.*

Proof. We again need some technical conditions from standard UC and UCGS: Let π, $\mathcal{F}$, ψ, $\mathcal{G}$ be protocols and let ξ, $\xi' \in \Xi$ be predicates on extended identities, such that π is $(\psi, \mathcal{G}, \xi)$-compliant, π, $\mathcal{F}$, $\mathcal{G}$, ψ are subroutine exposing, $\mathcal{G}$ and ψ are subroutine respecting, π and $\mathcal{F}$ are subroutine respecting except via calls to $\mathcal{G}$ and $\mathcal{G}$ is π-regular. If ψ UC-emulates $\mathcal{G}$ with respect to ξ-identity-bounded environments, and if π UC-emulates $\mathcal{F}$ in the presence of $\mathcal{G}$ w.r.t. ξ'-identity-bounded environments, then what we have to prove is that $\mathsf{M}[\pi^{\mathcal{G}\to\psi}, \psi]$ UC-emulates protocol $\mathsf{M}[\mathcal{F}, \mathcal{G}]$ w.r.t. ξ'-identity-bounded environments. This however follows from standard composition: Recall that protocols $\mathsf{M}[\pi^{\mathcal{G}\to\psi}, \psi]$ and $\mathsf{M}[\pi, \mathcal{G}]$ from Lemma 1 are embeddings of protocols with global setup as normal UC protocols. Therefore, we can apply the UC composition theorem: $\mathsf{M}[\pi^{\mathcal{G}\to\psi}, \psi]$ UC-emulates $\mathsf{M}[\pi, \mathcal{G}]$, and by our assumption $\mathsf{M}[\pi, \mathcal{G}]$ UC-emulates $\mathsf{M}[\mathcal{F}, \mathcal{G}]$. $\quad\square$

The conclusion of this subsection is that under both conditions (1) and (2) it follows that both π and ψ running together are indistinguishable from the ideal world, where both components are idealized. This is often assurance enough that the protocol in combination with a particular implementation of the global setup achieves a good level of security. However, note that the security is stated in terms of abstractions of *both* real-world components. The overall guarantees are thus hard to tell, and false impressions of security might be created. Let us illustrate this issue with the following.

Running Example. Assume that the provider does not have a strong cryptographic background and that he actually struggled conducting the aforementioned proof. But suddenly, he realized that the proof is easy when he assumes that $\mathcal{G}_{\mathsf{ledger}}$, which is used by both the poker game and $\mathcal{F}_{\mathsf{lottery}}$, admits arbitrarily many adversarial ledger entries. He calls this new setup $\mathcal{G}_{\mathsf{weakLedger}}$ and is delighted when he finds out that it is still emulated by FunCoin (since UC emulation is transitive). He then happily applies Lemma 2 and rightfully advertises that his lottery (together with FunCoin) is as secure as $\mathcal{F}_{\mathsf{lottery}}$ (together with $\mathcal{G}_{\mathsf{weakLedger}}$).

With this example we see that Lemma 2 falls short in examining the security of the challenge protocol when proven w.r.t. an (even slight) abstraction of the setup and not its implementation. In the above example, $\mathcal{F}_{\mathsf{lottery}}$ might provide very strong fairness guarantees, that however can only be achieved with a simulation that crucially exploits introduction of adversarial entries into $\mathcal{G}_{\mathsf{weakLedger}}$. Thus, when looking only at $\mathcal{F}_{\mathsf{lottery}}$, false impressions of security guarantees are created. In particular, with the stronger global $\mathcal{G}_{\mathsf{ledger}}$ or the actual protocol FunCoin, which do not have this weakness, $\mathcal{F}_{\mathsf{lottery}}$ might not even be realizable by the lottery – to say the least, the existing simulation is likely to fall short in witnessing such an emulation statement.

To remedy the situation (and to blow our provider's cover), we need to understand the implications of replacing the global setup in the ideal world.

In particular, preventing a security proof from exploiting weaknesses in the abstraction of the setup seems to be crucial to arrive at a plausible and realistic level of security. In the remainder of this section, we ask under which conditions a security proof might be preserved when replacing the global setup in both worlds.

3.3   Full Replacement of the Global Subroutine

We now turn our attention to "full" replacement strategies, where the global subroutine is replaced by a protocol UC-emulating it in both the real and the ideal world. Of course, this is to be understood w.r.t an existing security statement, that is, our precondition (1). Let us emphasize again that we are only interested in replacement strategies that preserve the underlying security statement.

Equivalence Transformations of the Global Subroutine. Canetti et al. demonstrated, using the terminology of GUC, that replacing the global subroutine by an equivalent procedure preserves protocol emulation w.r.t the subroutine. The replacement theorem is proven in [CSV16], and we recover it here for completeness. Thanks to the embedding within plain UC that UCGS achieves, our proof is able to capture the arguments at a more abstract level, essentially reducing all steps to standard UC-emulation. Let us first illustrate how and why equivalence replacement works with the lottery.

Running Example. The provider keeps receiving calls from cryptographers who find it suspicious that his simulation exploits the weaknesses of $\mathcal{G}_{\mathsf{weakLedger}}$. Since FunCoin does not offer introduction of arbitrary adversarial blocks, the provider however cannot carry out his simulation with FunCoin. Searching the internet, the provider learns about a shady cryptocurrency called DarkCoin. Further investigating, the provider can prove that DarkCoin admits the exact same attacks as $\mathcal{G}_{\mathsf{weakLedger}}$, i.e., is UC-equivalent to $\mathcal{G}_{\mathsf{weakLedger}}$[7]. Thus, the provider can run his simulation with DarkCoin instead of $\mathcal{G}_{\mathsf{weakLedger}}$, since DarkCoin allows for all adversarial queries that are possible with $\mathcal{G}_{\mathsf{weakLedger}}$. Moreover, the provider can be assured that his simulation is still good for the now modified real world, since DarkCoin does not admit more attacks than $\mathcal{G}_{\mathsf{weakLedger}}$. Relieved, he announces that, when using the globally available DarkCoin, his lottery protocol emulates $\mathcal{F}_{\mathsf{lottery}}$.

Theorem 3 (Full Replacement via Equivalence Transformations). *Assume π UC-emulates $\mathcal{F}$ in the presence of a global subroutine $\mathcal{G}$. If ψ UC-emulates $\mathcal{G}$ and vice-versa, i.e., their adversarial interfaces are equivalent, then π, invoking ψ instead of $\mathcal{G}$, UC-emulates $\mathcal{F}$, invoking ψ instead of $\mathcal{G}$, and where ψ is the global subroutine.*

Proof. We again have to phrase our theorem in the language of UCGS: Let π, $\mathcal{F}$, ψ, $\mathcal{G}$ be protocols and let ξ, $\xi' \in \varXi$ be predicates on extended identities, such that π is $(\psi, \mathcal{G}, \xi)$-compliant, π, $\mathcal{F}$, $\mathcal{G}$, ψ are subroutine exposing, $\mathcal{G}$ and

---

[7] Formally, ψ and ψ' are UC-equivalent if ψ UC-emulates ψ' and ψ' UC-emulates ψ.

ψ are subroutine respecting, π and $\mathcal{F}$ are subroutine respecting except via calls to $\mathcal{G}$ and $\mathcal{G}$ is π-regular. If ψ UC-emulates $\mathcal{G}$ with respect to ξ-identity-bounded environments —and vice-versa— and if π UC-emulates $\mathcal{F}$ in the presence of $\mathcal{G}$ w.r.t. ξ'-identity-bounded environments, then $\mathsf{M}[\pi^{\mathcal{G} \to \psi}, \psi]$ UC-emulates protocol $\mathsf{M}[\mathcal{F}^{\mathcal{G} \to \psi}, \psi]$ w.r.t. ξ'-identity-bounded environments.

The sequence of steps needed in this proof are the following hybrid protocols.

- The real protocol $H_0 := \mathsf{M}[\pi^{\mathcal{G} \to \psi}, \psi]$.
- The first intermediate step $H_1 := \mathsf{M}[\pi, \mathcal{G}]$.
- The second intermediate step $H_2 := \mathsf{M}[\mathcal{F}, \mathcal{G}]$.
- The destination protocol $H_3 := \mathsf{M}[\mathcal{F}^{\mathcal{G} \to \psi}, \psi]$.

As in the proof of Lemma 1, H_0 is equivalent to $\mathsf{M}[\pi, \mathcal{G}]^{\mathcal{G} \to \psi}$ and hence $H_1 = H_0^{\psi \to \mathcal{G}}$. By standard composition, H_0 UC-emulates H_1 since the embedding is an normal UC-protocol and subroutine ψ UC-emulates $\mathcal{G}$. Next, the transition from H_1 to H_2 is trivial: H_1 UC-emulates H_2 by the theorem assumption. Finally, we go the "reverse" direction as in the argument of the first step thanks to the fact that we know that $\mathcal{G}$ UC-emulates ψ. More formally, we have $H_3 = \mathsf{M}[\mathcal{F}, \mathcal{G}]^{\mathcal{G} \to \psi}$ and again, H_3 is obtained by normal subroutine replacement within protocol H_2. Therefore, H_2 UC-emulates H_3 by the theorem assumption and we have that H_0 UC-emulates H_3 which concludes the proof.   □

To the best of our knowledge, Theorem 3 is the only composition theorem allowing for replacement of global subroutines with their UC emulation that already exists in the literature [CSV16]. It can be applied to soundly replace, e.g., a globally available ideal PKI with its implementation at a trusted PKI provider. However, it falls short in replacing global setups with protocols, which are likely to be stronger than their abstraction as a UC functionality. In the remainder of this section we discuss solutions for such replacements.

Global-Agnostic Simulations of the Challenge Protocol. The condition discussed in this section is useful for protocols designers to check whether their proof remains valid when a global subroutine is replaced, by means of checking the structure of the simulator. Intuitively, a sufficient condition is if the simulator can simulate without accessing the adversarial interface of the global setup. More generally speaking, for all UC-adversaries $\mathcal{A}$ the corresponding simulation strategy $\mathcal{S}_{\mathcal{A}}$ should only externally-write onto the backdoor tape of the global subroutine session(s) if the real-world adversary did so. An easy way to achieve this is to have the ideal functionality $\mathcal{F}$ communicate with the global setup $\mathcal{G}$ directly and if needed, provide the simulator (simulating the actions of π when having access to the backdoor tape of $\mathcal{F}$) with the necessary information. Intuitively, the reason this is sound is that the only way $\mathcal{F}$ can interact with the global setup just like an honest party would do (and in particular, not via the backdoor tape). Since replacing $\mathcal{F}$ by a protocol that implements it can never change the behavior for honest parties in a noticeable way (otherwise, it is obviously distinguishable) the replacement is unproblematic. We first formally capture what it means for a simulator to not use the adversarial interface of the global subroutine.

Definition 5 ($\mathcal{G}$-agnostic). *An adversary $\mathcal{S}$ interacting with subroutine $\mathcal{G}$ is $\mathcal{G}$-agnostic if the only external write requests (made by $\mathcal{S}$'s shell) destined for (the backdoor tape) of parties and subparties of any session of $\mathcal{G}$ are those instructed by the environment directly and any messages via the backdoor tapes of (sub-)parties of any session of $\mathcal{G}$ are delivered directly to the environment without activating the body of $\mathcal{S}$.*

Running Example. Recently, numbers of users participating in the provider's lottery dropped significantly. Being sure that this is because of his recent recommendation to use DarkCoin, the provider desperately hires a team of cryptographers. Examining the provider's simulation carried out with respect to $\mathcal{G}_{\text{weakLedger}}$, the team finds a better simulation strategy that only requires legitimate use of the ledger by sending transaction requests to it. The new simulator thus acts like an honest party using the ledger. In particular it does not exploit any of the adversarial interfaces of $\mathcal{G}_{\text{weakLedger}}$. Since FunCoin allows to submit transactions, replacing $\mathcal{G}_{\text{weakLedger}}$ by FunCoin in the proof does not hinder the new simulation. With FunCoin back in the picture, user statistics begin to slowly recover and the provider is delighted.

Theorem 4 (Full Replacement due to Agnostic Simulations I). *Assume π UC-emulates $\mathcal{F}$ in the presence of a global subroutine $\mathcal{G}$ such that the simulator $\mathcal{S}$ for this construction is $\mathcal{G}$-agnostic. Let further ψ UC-emulate $\mathcal{G}$. Then π, invoking ψ instead of $\mathcal{G}$, UC-emulates $\mathcal{F}$, invoking ψ instead of $\mathcal{G}$, and where ψ is the global subroutine.*

Proof. We first state the theorem in the language of UCGS as before. Let π, $\mathcal{F}$, ψ, $\mathcal{G}$ be protocols and let $\xi, \xi' \in \Xi$ be predicates on extended identities, such that π is $(\psi, \mathcal{G}, \xi)$-compliant, π, $\mathcal{F}$, $\mathcal{G}$, ψ are subroutine exposing, $\mathcal{G}$ and ψ are subroutine respecting, π and $\mathcal{F}$ are subroutine respecting except via calls to $\mathcal{G}$ and $\mathcal{G}$ is π-regular. Let ψ UC-emulate $\mathcal{G}$ with respect to ξ-identity-bounded environments and let π UC-emulate $\mathcal{F}$ in the presence of $\mathcal{G}$ w.r.t. ξ'-identity-bounded environments. Let $\mathcal{S}_A$ denote a simulator for the latter emulation that satisfies Definition 5. Then $\mathsf{M}[\pi^{\mathcal{G}\to\psi}, \psi]$ UC-emulates protocol $\mathsf{M}[\mathcal{F}^{\mathcal{G}\to\psi}, \psi]$ w.r.t. ξ'-identity-bounded environments.

The proof strategy is as follows:

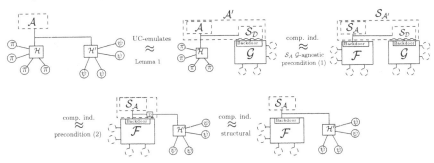

More formally, we make the following transitions, going from top left to bottom right in the picture.

$M[\pi^{\mathcal{G}\to\psi}, \psi]$ **UC-emulates** $M[\pi, \mathcal{G}]$. This directly follows from Lemma 1 and the precondition of ψ UC-emulating $\mathcal{G}$. Let $\mathcal{A}'$ denote the simulator of this emulation.

$\text{EXEC}_{\pi, \mathcal{A}', \mathcal{Z}} \approx \text{EXEC}_{\mathcal{F}, \mathcal{S}_{\mathcal{A}'}, \mathcal{Z}}$. We show how to simulate for the specific adversary $\mathcal{A}'$. $\mathcal{S}_{\mathcal{A}'}$ works as $\mathcal{S}_{\mathcal{A}}$, but lets the internally simulated $\mathcal{A}$ on π issue its external write requests to the global subroutine directly to $\mathcal{S}_{\mathcal{D}}$, which overall has the effect as if $\mathcal{A}$ and $\mathcal{S}_{\mathcal{D}}$ were combined when talking to the global subroutine. The simulator $\mathcal{S}_{\mathcal{A}}$ (simulating π while interacting with $\mathcal{F}$) performs a good simulation even against this combined attacker, because $\mathcal{S}_{\mathcal{A}}$ does not care about this interaction due to the agnostic property: $\mathcal{S}_{\mathcal{A}}$ does not issue any queries to $\mathcal{G}$ itself (that might get blocked or modified by $\mathcal{S}_{\mathcal{D}}$) and acts as a relay between $\mathcal{G}$ and $\mathcal{Z}$. Assume $\mathcal{Z}$ distinguishes both distributions. Then, $\mathcal{Z}$ running $\mathcal{S}_{\mathcal{D}}$ internally instead of sending requests to $\mathcal{S}_{\mathcal{D}}$ to the adversary is a successful distinguisher of $\pi, \mathcal{A}$ and $\mathcal{F}, \mathcal{S}_{\mathcal{A}}$, since due to $\mathcal{S}_{\mathcal{A}}$ being $\mathcal{G}$-agnostic, $\mathcal{Z}$ is oblivious of the order of $\mathcal{S}_{\mathcal{A}}$ and $\mathcal{S}_{\mathcal{D}}$ (and, naturally, of the order of $\mathcal{A}$ and $\mathcal{S}_{\mathcal{D}}$). Since such a $\mathcal{Z}$ would violate precondition (1), we conclude that both distributions are indistinguishable.

$\text{EXEC}_{\mathcal{F}, \mathcal{S}_{\mathcal{A}'}, \mathcal{Z}} \approx \text{EXEC}_{\mathcal{F}, \mathcal{S}', \mathcal{Z}}$, where $\mathcal{S}'$ denotes the simulator $\mathcal{S}_{\mathcal{A}}$ sending requests to ψ via dummy adversary $\mathcal{D}$. Recall that $\mathcal{S}_{\mathcal{A}'}$ combines $\mathcal{S}_{\mathcal{A}}$ and $\mathcal{S}_{\mathcal{D}}$. If both executions are distinguishable, an environment running $\mathcal{S}_{\mathcal{A}}$ and $\mathcal{F}$ could distinguish an execution of ψ and $\mathcal{D}$ from an execution of $\mathcal{S}_{\mathcal{D}}$ with $\mathcal{G}$, violating the precondition that ψ UC-emulates $\mathcal{G}$, i.e., precondition (2).

$\text{EXEC}_{\mathcal{F}, \mathcal{S}', \mathcal{Z}} \approx \text{EXEC}_{\mathcal{F}, \mathcal{S}_{\mathcal{A}}, \mathcal{Z}}$. Since the dummy adversary $\mathcal{D}$ is just a relay, we can safely remove it from the execution.

$\square$

General Condition for Global-Functionality Replacement. With the previous theorem, we showed that a global subroutine can be safely replaced by its emulation in all security statements which are proven via a simulator who does not access the global subroutine. This however not only means that the simulator cannot manipulate the state of the global setup, but is also completely oblivious of it. This is often too strong of a condition. For example, consider a simulator witnessing a protocol's security in the presence of a global CRS. Such a simulator should at least be allowed to *read* out the CRS, since, intuitively, the CRS is publicly available information. Similarly, a simulator in a global ledger world should at least be allowed to read the state of the ledger. And indeed, our next replacement theorem admits global replacements that do not interfere with such simulators, as long as the power of the simulator is reflected in the real world even with respect to the stronger emulation of the global subroutine.

To ease the technical presentation of the condition on the simulator, for the next theorem we restrict ourselves to the special case of functionalities as global subroutines. The treatment could be generalized to arbitrary global subroutines.

Let us start with introducing some technical tools which help us formalize interaction between adversaries and global functionalities.

Definition 6 (Ordered interaction). *Let I be a set of queries. An ideal functionality $\mathcal{G}$ is called I-ordered if G answers to inputs $x \in I$ on the backdoor tape with (x, y), and uses format $(\bot, \cdot)$ otherwise.*

The definition simply demands that ITM $\mathcal{G}$, in his answers to the adversary, repeats what query it responds to if the query belongs to some set I. Note that quite often in the literature, such an association is necessary but left implicit in the description, since it is obvious which query will result in which answer (by repeating the input and maintaining a clear order when answering adversarial requests). Next, we define some useful notation when running two programs in one machine. Essentially, we define a wrapper that routes incoming queries to the program which they are intended for.

Definition 7 (Parallel composition of adversaries). *Let $\mathcal{S}_1$ and $\mathcal{S}_2$ be two ITMs. Then $[\mathcal{S}_1, \mathcal{S}_2]$ denotes the adversary with the following shell: whenever activated with value (x, y) on the backdoor tape, it activates $\mathcal{S}_i$ if x was issued by $\mathcal{S}_i$ and in any other case activates $\mathcal{S}_2$ by default. Conversely, if activated with input (i, x) on the input tape (for any x), the shell activates $\mathcal{S}_i$ on input x.*

Definition 8 (Admissible backdoor-tape filter). *Let $\mathcal{S}_D$ be the simulator of condition (2), i.e., the construction of $\mathcal{G}$ from ψ. Let I be a subset of adversarial queries allowed by $\mathcal{G}$, and let $\mathcal{G}$ be I-ordered. Let further f_I denote a simple program which takes inputs $x \in I$ and writes them on the backdoor tape of $\mathcal{G}$, and if provided with input (x, y) on the backdoor tape, returns y to the caller that provided the corresponding input x (other values on the subroutine output tape are ignored by f). We say that f_I is an admissible backdoor-tape filter for $(\mathcal{S}_D, \psi, \mathcal{G})$ if there exists a simulator $[\mathcal{S}_{f_I}, \mathcal{D}]$ such that $\mathrm{EXEC}_{\mathcal{G}, [f_I, \mathcal{S}_D], \mathcal{Z}} \approx \mathrm{EXEC}_{\psi, [\mathcal{S}_{f_I}, \mathcal{D}], \mathcal{Z}}$. We omit $(\mathcal{S}_D, \psi, \mathcal{G})$ if it is clear from the context.*

Pictorially, f_I is an admissible filter if there is a simulator $\mathcal{S}_{f_I}$ such that:

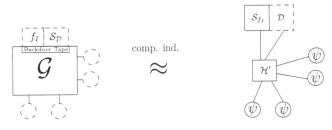

Note that a filter is nothing else than a program making the adversarial interface of $\mathcal{G}$ less powerful while not interfering with the assumed simulator.

Running Example. Let us assume that the ledger $\mathcal{G}_{\mathsf{weakLedger}}$ has adversarial interfaces $J := \{\mathtt{readState}, \mathtt{permute}, \mathtt{putEntry}\}$. DarkCoin UC-emulates $\mathcal{G}_{\mathsf{weakLedger}}$ with simulator $\mathcal{S}_D$ that, say, only uses interface $\mathtt{putEntry}$. Thus, $f_{\{\mathtt{readState}\}}$ is admissible for $(\mathcal{S}_\mathcal{D}, \text{DarkCoin}, \mathcal{G}_{\text{weakLedger}})$ since $\mathcal{S}_\mathcal{D}$ does not depend on how often $\mathcal{G}_{\text{weakLedger}}$ outputs the state. The simulator $\mathcal{S}_{f_{\{\text{readState}\}}}$ simply collects the state of the DarkCoin ledger from publicly available information. On the other hand, $f_{\{\text{permute}\}}$ (and $f_{\{\text{permute},\text{readState}\}}$) can only be admissible if $\mathcal{S}_\mathcal{D}$ performs a good simulation regardless of the order in which entries (including adversarial ones) appear on the ledger, and if there exists an attacker $\mathcal{S}_{f_{\{\text{permute}\}}}$ that can carry out a permuting attack against DarkCoin.

The next definition restricts the simulator's usage of the global functionality. Essentially, the simulator is not allowed to query the global $\mathcal{G}$ except for queries in some set I.

Definition 9 ($\mathcal{G} \setminus I$-agnostic). *Let $\mathcal{S}$ denote an adversary interacting with global subroutine $\mathcal{G}$ and let I denote a subset of the adversarial queries allowed by $\mathcal{G}$, and let $\mathcal{G}$ be I-ordered. $\mathcal{S}$ is called $\mathcal{G} \setminus I$-agnostic if the only external write requests (made by the simulator's shell) destined for $\mathcal{G}$ are either requests $x \in I$ or those instructed by the environment directly, and any messages via the backdoor tapes from the (sub-)parties of $\mathcal{G}$ are delivered directly to the environment without activating the body of $\mathcal{S}$, except when they are of the form $(x, \cdot)$ where the query $x \in I$ has been issued by the body of $\mathcal{S}$.*

We are now ready to state our most general replacement theorem for global subroutines for simulators that are global-agnostic except for queries in some set I that pass the backdoor-tape filter of the shared subroutine. Those queries can be asked by the simulator any time. The intuition is that, due to the admissible property, we know how to "attack" an instantiation of $\mathcal{G}$ to extract information from it that is indistinguishable from what the filtered adversarial interface of $\mathcal{G}$ offers.

Running Example. Bitcoin is known to UC-emulate a ledger functionality $\mathcal{G}_{\text{ledger}}$ [BMTZ17], which we assume to offer an adversarial interface readState[8]. Let $\mathcal{S}_\mathcal{D}$ denote the simulator of this emulation statement. Since any permissionless blockchain, and in particular Bitcoin, publicly encodes the ledger state, it holds that $f_{\{\text{readState}\}}$ is admissible for $(\mathcal{S}_\mathcal{D}, \text{Bitcoin}, \mathcal{G}_{\text{ledger}})$ (the simulator $\mathcal{S}_{f_{\{\text{readState}\}}}$ that witnesses admissibility is interacting with Bitcoin and obtains the state the same way an honest miner would do). Now if some blockchain application π proven w.r.t $\mathcal{G}_{\text{ledger}}$ comes with a simulation that only queries $\mathcal{G}_{\text{ledger}}$ with readState, the security statement remains valid when $\mathcal{G}_{\text{ledger}}$ is replaced with Bitcoin. That is, π is guaranteed to realize the *same* functionality, regardless of whether $\mathcal{G}_{\text{ledger}}$ or Bitcoin is used as global ledger.

Theorem 5 (Full Replacement due to Agnostic Simulations II). *Assume $\text{EXEC}_{\psi,\mathcal{D},\mathcal{Z}} \approx \text{EXEC}_{\mathcal{G},\mathcal{S}_D,\mathcal{Z}}$ and let I be a subset of adversarial queries allowed by $\mathcal{G}$ such that f_I is an admissible backdoor-tape filter for $(\mathcal{S}_\mathcal{D}, \psi, \mathcal{G})$.*

---

[8] In [BMTZ17], any party, including the adversary, can obtain the ledger state by sending $(\text{READ}, \text{sid})$ to $\mathcal{G}_{\text{ledger}}$.

Let further π UC-emulate $\mathcal{F}$ in the presence of the global subroutine $\mathcal{G}$ such that the simulator $\mathcal{S}_A$ for this precondition is $\mathcal{G} \setminus I$-agnostic. Then, π, invoking ψ instead of $\mathcal{G}$, UC-emulates $\mathcal{F}$, invoking ψ instead of $\mathcal{G}$, and where ψ is the global subroutine.

Proof. We first state the theorem in the language of UCGS as before. Let $\pi, \mathcal{F}, \psi,$ $\mathcal{G}$ be protocols and let $\xi, \xi' \in \Xi$ be predicates on extended identities, such that π is $(\psi, \mathcal{G}, \xi)$-compliant, $\pi, \mathcal{F}, \mathcal{G}, \psi$ are subroutine exposing, $\mathcal{G}$ and ψ are subroutine respecting, π and $\mathcal{F}$ are subroutine respecting except via calls to $\mathcal{G}$ and $\mathcal{G}$ is π-regular. Let ψ UC-emulate $\mathcal{G}$ with respect to ξ-identity-bounded environments. Let $\mathcal{S}_D$ denote the simulator of this condition, and be I a subset of adversarial queries allowed by $\mathcal{G}$ such that f_I is admissible for $(\mathcal{S}_D, \psi, \mathcal{G})$. Let further π UC-emulate $\mathcal{F}$ in the presence of $\mathcal{G}$ w.r.t. ξ'-identity-bounded environments. Let $\mathcal{S}_A$ denote a simulator for this emulation, and let $\mathcal{S}_A$ be $\mathcal{G} \setminus I$-agnostic. Then $\mathsf{M}[\pi^{\mathcal{G} \to \psi}, \psi]$ UC-emulates protocol $\mathsf{M}[\mathcal{F}^{\mathcal{G} \to \psi}, \psi]$ w.r.t. ξ'-identity-bounded environments.

The sequence of steps needed in this proof are the following.

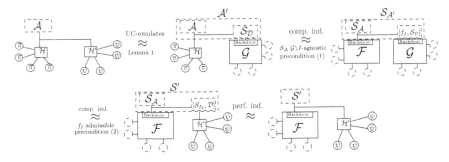

More formally, we make the following transitions, going from top left to bottom right in the picture.

$\mathsf{M}[\pi^{\mathcal{G} \to \psi}, \psi]$ **UC-emulates** $\mathsf{M}[\pi, \mathcal{G}]$. This directly follows from Lemma 1 and the precondition of ψ UC-emulating $\mathcal{G}$. Let $\mathcal{A}'$ denote the simulator of this emulation.

$\mathrm{EXEC}_{\pi, \mathcal{A}', \mathcal{Z}} \approx \mathrm{EXEC}_{\mathcal{F}, \mathcal{S}_{A'}, \mathcal{Z}}$. We show how to simulate for the specific adversary $\mathcal{A}'$. $\mathcal{S}_{A'}$ works as $\mathcal{S}_A$, but lets the internally simulated $\mathcal{A}$ on π issue its external write requests to the global subroutine directly to $[f_I, \mathcal{S}_D]$ (using the adressing mechanism described in Definition 7), which overall has the effect as if $\mathcal{A}$ and $[f_I, \mathcal{S}_D]$ were combined when talking to the global subroutine. We need to argue that the simulator $\mathcal{S}_A$ (simulating π while interacting with $\mathcal{F}$) still performs a good simulation even against this combined attacker. Due to $\mathcal{S}_A$ being $\mathcal{G} \setminus I$-agnostic, $\mathcal{S}_A$'s requests reach $\mathcal{G}$ unmodified since they pass f_I. Definition 9 further ensures that $\mathcal{S}_A$ acts as a dummy adversary regarding all requests between $\mathcal{Z}$ and $[f_I, \mathcal{S}_D]$. A distinguisher $\mathcal{Z}$ between both distributions can thus be turned into a distinguisher between executions $\pi, \mathcal{A}$ and $\mathcal{F}, \mathcal{S}_A$ which runs program $[f_i, \mathcal{S}_D]$ internally, violating precondition (1).

$\mathrm{EXEC}_{\mathcal{F},\mathcal{S}_{\mathcal{A}'},\mathcal{Z}} \approx \mathrm{EXEC}_{\mathcal{F},\mathcal{S}',\mathcal{Z}}$, where $\mathcal{S}'$ denotes the simulator $\mathcal{S}_{\mathcal{A}}$ sending requests to ψ via adversary $[\mathcal{S}_{f_I}, \mathcal{D}]$. Recall that $\mathcal{S}_{\mathcal{A}'}$ combines $\mathcal{S}_{\mathcal{A}}$ and $\mathcal{S}_{\mathcal{D}}$. If both executions are distinguishable, an environment running $\mathcal{S}_{\mathcal{A}}$ and $\mathcal{F}$ could distinguish an execution of ψ and $[\mathcal{S}_{f_I}, \mathcal{D}]$ from an execution of $[f_I, \mathcal{S}_{\mathcal{D}}]$ with $\mathcal{G}$, violating the precondition that f_I is an admissible backdoor-tape filter for $(\mathcal{S}_{\mathcal{D}}, \psi, \mathcal{G})$.

$\square$

3.4   Case Study: Comparable Constructions and Random Oracles

The benefit of composable security is that it enables a secure modular design of protocols. When one tries to achieve a new functionality, then one can rely on already realized functionalities as a setup, being assured that those can modularly be replaced by their already known implementations at any time. As we showed in this paper, this idea generally fails for global (hybrid) setups, but is partly restored by the above theorems by giving conditions on when such a replacement of a global setup is possible.

Still, the following mismatch might occur in such a modular protocol design which motivates another important aspect of Theorem 5. Assume two protocols are proven with respect to different global setups, π_1 realizes $\mathcal{F}_1$ in the GRO setting, and π_2, which makes (local) calls to $\mathcal{F}_1$ and realizes $\mathcal{F}_2$ w.r.t. a GRO that allows the adversary upon request to program random points of the function table and otherwise is identical to GRO. Therefore, obtaining a combined security claim w.r.t. a single RO assumption is in general not clear and might not be possible because they assume different global setups the realization of $\mathcal{F}_1$ w.r.t. the observable RO has never been formally realized. Applying the UCGS theorem is not possible and replacing, within π, the functionality $\mathcal{F}_1$ by π_1 can only be a heuristic in the best case. This situation is of course unfortunate. As pointed out in [CDG+18] obtaining a common RO for both constructions is very vital for the global RO model: the main reason to switch to global RO (vs. local RO) is that in practice, all random oracles are instantiated by a single hash function anyway. If composing constructions forces us to again have a couple of different global random oracles in the end (which we replace by a single hash function) we are back at square one.

Luckily, Theorem 5 gives us a tool to figure out whether π_2 actually achieves $\mathcal{F}_2$ in the presence of the plain GRO (which in turn would allow us to apply the UCGS composition theorem): For protocol π_2 UC-emulating $\mathcal{F}_2$ in the presence of a global RO that supports, say, adversarial queries I (e.g., including random-points programmability), it is therefore enough to specify the set $I' \subseteq I$ of filter requests for which the preconditions of Theorem 5 is satisfied. In this case, it follows that the very same construction can be proven with respect to any stronger version of the assumed GRO that blocks inputs from any subset of $I \setminus I'$ and hence preserving the queries that are necessary for this simulator. The reason is that the simulator in the UC-emulation proof of the construction π_2 is agnostic to what happens aside of its filter requests, and this includes the possibility that no request aside of its filter requests of queries in I' are made (and on the other hand, the protocol in the real world is not disturbed by the exact set of queries since it is proven w.r.t. the rpGRO).

The final conclusion is that incomparable constructions can become comparable by general security-preservation results, such as the one in Theorem 5: if I' does not contain the programmability request, then the two protocol π_1 and π_2 work for the same GRO as established by Theorem 5. Hence, for those two constructions, π_2 can replace hybrid $\mathcal{F}_1$ by π_1, which is then not a heuristic argument, but a sound composition step that is formally backed by the UCGS composition theorem.

We note that the study of [CDG+18] goes into the other direction by performing a transformation on π_1 in order to be secure w.r.t. some weaker oracle $\mathcal{G}_2$. Such transformations can only exist for specific choices of RO's (since generic composition results fail when using a weaker setup due to increased attack surface for the real attacker), and our results applied to global RO constructions gives a tool to go the other way in certain cases.

4   Generalization to Many Global Subroutines

We now consider protocols that use more than one global setup. Such a situation often appears in the literature, e.g., when a protocol makes use of a global ledger and a global clock, or a global PKI and a global random oracle. Formally, such a protocol is subroutine respecting except via calls to subroutines γ_i, $i \in [n]$. In this section, we show how to leverage the results from the previous section to replace one, or several, or all of the global subroutines γ_i. A bit more formally, we now assume precondition (1) be as follows:

(1) π UC-emulates $\mathcal{F}$ in the presence of global $\gamma_1, \ldots, \gamma_n$

Looking ahead, we will have to make some assumptions on the global subroutines $\gamma_1, \ldots, \gamma_n$ and the corresponding protocols $\psi_1, \ldots, \psi_n$ to realize them. Roughly speaking, ψ_n will not depend on any other global subroutine to realize γ_n, while ψ_{n-1} (and hence also γ_{n-1}) is allowed to depend γ_n but on no other global subroutine. We will be more formal about how to define "depend" in this context.

Before formalizing our results, let us describe the idea behind them. Essentially, we will interpret the setups $\gamma_1, \ldots, \gamma_n$ as a single global setup $\widehat{\gamma}$. $\widehat{\gamma}$ simply runs all γ_i internally and dispatches messages correspondingly. For this single global setup $\widehat{\gamma}$, we can interpret precondition (1) above as precondition (1) from the previous section with single setup $\widehat{\gamma}$, and apply the replacement theorems from the previous section. The only open question is: which protocol realizes the single global setup $\widehat{\gamma}$? Note that this emulation is needed to replace precondition (2) in Sect. 3.1. So let $\psi_1, \ldots, \psi_n$ denote the protocols we want to replace the global subroutines with, i.e., ψ_i UC-emulates γ_i for all i. We show that, under the condition that all setups form a hierarchy regarding who gives input to whom, $\widehat{\psi}$ UC-emulates $\widehat{\gamma}$.

We first state a general program structure:

Definition 10 (Merging subroutines.). *Let* $\widehat{\rho}_{\rho_1,\ldots,\rho_n} := [\rho_1,\ldots,\rho_n]$ *be a program that accepts inputs of the form* ($\mathsf{query}, \mathsf{sid}, i, x$) *and invokes subroutine* ρ_i *with input* x, *all with respect to the same session* sid.

In UC, we must ensure that this simple program structure can be made a compliant protocol (and subroutine exposing) as we are going to replace its subroutines later. For two protocols γ_i, ψ_i, the above program becomes (ψ_i, γ_i, ξ) compliant if it never relays inputs not satisfying the bound ξ by its caller. The remaining, more technical conditions for compliance can be trivially satisfied. In order not to overload notation, we assume such a predicate is known and enforced by $\widehat{\rho}_{\rho_1,\ldots,\rho_n}$. [9] We identify UC-realization with multiple setups with the single global subroutine case as follows:

Definition 11 (UC emulation with multiple global setups). *Let* π, ϕ *and* $\gamma_1,\ldots,\gamma_n$ *be protocols. We say that* π ξ-*UC-emulates* ϕ *in the presence of global subroutines* $\gamma_1,\ldots,\gamma_n$ *if protocols* π *and* ϕ *are formulated with respect to a global subroutine* $\widehat{\gamma}_{\gamma_1,\ldots,\gamma_n}$ *and* $\mathsf{M}[\pi,\widehat{\gamma}_{\gamma_1,\ldots,\gamma_n}]$ ξ-*UC-emulates protocol* $\mathsf{M}[\phi,\widehat{\gamma}_{\gamma_1,\ldots,\gamma_n}]$.

Note that the overlay we define is just a dispatching service. Hence, a protocol designer might still define π in the way of having π directly access each γ_i. This transition is straightforward. [10]

We hence obtained a reduction between the single global-subroutine world and the multiple global-subroutine world.

Remark 1. The following theorem makes the hierarchy idea formal that we discussed at the onset of this section. In order to express that γ_i does not depend on other subroutines γ_j, $j < i$ we use the concept of regularity to ensure that γ_i does only invoke global subroutines that presumably already have been replaced (by condition 1. below, only the γ_i's and no other protocol can be seen as global). This facilitates that for any subroutine γ_i we can make use of precondition 3. that ψ_i realizes γ_i in the presence of global subroutines γ_j, $j < i$, and be sure this is independent of what is yet to be replaced later. This gives a sound order of replacements.

Theorem 6 (Reduction Theorem). *Let* $\gamma_1,\ldots,\gamma_n$ *and* $\psi_1,\ldots,\psi_n$ *be protocols.* $\widehat{\psi}_{\psi_1,\ldots,\psi_n}$ *UC-emulates* $\widehat{\gamma}_{\gamma_1,\ldots,\gamma_n}$ *if for each protocol* $\rho_i \in \{\gamma_i, \psi_i\}$ *the following conditions hold:*

---

[9] The remaining conditions are technicalities such as setting the forced-write flag and not calling ψ_i and γ_i with the same session sid which obviously can be satisfied. For the UCGS theorem, this protocol is compliant if it additionally never invokes a model element, which is obvious.

[10] Whether the transition is also trivial is a different question. In frameworks that have a complex runtime structure, introducing such an intermediate dispatching machine might be costly and would require π to request more runtime-resources. In UC, this would cost k import more for π, where k denotes a security parameter.

1. ρ_i, when $i < n$, is subroutine respecting except for calls to $\gamma_{i+1}, \ldots, \gamma_n$. ρ_n is subroutine respecting. All ρ_i are subroutine exposing.
2. ρ_i, when $i > 1$, is γ_j-regular and ψ_j-regular for all $j \in \{1, \ldots, i-1\}$.
3. ψ_i ξ-UC-emulates γ_i, for $i < n$, in the presence of global subroutines $\gamma_{i+1}, \ldots, \gamma_n$. And ψ_n UC-emulates γ_n.

Proof. We again use the transitivity of indistinguishability of ensembles. The sequence of hybrid worlds that are needed to conclude are depicted below for the case of three global subroutines.

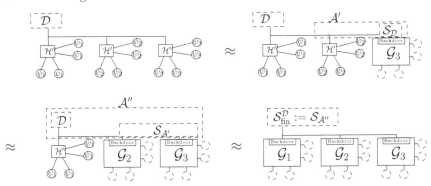

Each step is characterized by two elements: a single context protocol μ_i, and the number i which protocol is to be replaced. Let $\mu_i := [\psi_1, \ldots, \psi_i, \gamma_{i+1}, \ldots, \gamma_n]$, $i = 1, \ldots, n$ and $\mu_0 := \widehat{\gamma}_{\gamma_1, \ldots, \gamma_n}$. We start with $\mu_n := \widehat{\psi}_{\psi_1, \ldots, \psi_n}$.

Step 1: In the context protocol μ_{n-1} we perform the replacement $\mu_{n-1}^{\gamma_n \to \psi_n}$, resulting in μ_n. By the Theorem's precondition, we can invoke the UC composition theorem, since γ_n and ψ_n are subroutine respecting and subroutine exposing and μ_n is compliant. Therefore, the UC composition theorem implies $\text{EXEC}_{\mu_n, \mathcal{D}, \mathcal{Z}} \approx \text{EXEC}_{\mu_{n-1}, \mathcal{S}_n, \mathcal{Z}}$.

Step $2 \leq i \leq n$: starting with context protocol μ_{n-i} we replace $\mu_{n-i}^{\gamma_n \to \psi_n}$ which results in μ_{n-i+1}. For this step, we can invoke the UCGS theorem since the preconditions of the UCGS theorem are satisfied: γ_i resp. ψ_i can be treated as protocols that are subroutine respecting except with calls to $\gamma_{i+1}, \ldots, \gamma_n$ and hence Definition 11 applies. Furthermore, all protocols are subroutine exposing, and formally, the "global setup" of this construction, i.e., the subsystem consisting of $\gamma_{i+1}, \ldots, \gamma_n$, is γ_i- and ψ_i-regular as demanded by the precondition, i.e., they never send input to any of the subroutine prior to i that have not yet been replaced. Hence, the UCGS theorem yields that μ_{n-i} UC-emulates μ_{n-i+1} and in other words, $\text{EXEC}_{\mu_{n-i+1}, \mathcal{A}, \mathcal{Z}} \approx \text{EXEC}_{\mu_{n-i}, \mathcal{S}_{n-i+1}, \mathcal{Z}}$.

The final step follows by applying transitivity to obtain the final simulator $\mathcal{S}_{\text{fin}}$ for the overall construction. Since we started with the dummy real-world adversary for $\widehat{\psi}_{\psi_1, \ldots, \psi_n}$ this formally yields a simulator for the dummy adversary that proves $\text{EXEC}_{\widehat{\psi}, \mathcal{D}, \mathcal{Z}} \approx \text{EXEC}_{\widehat{\gamma}, \mathcal{S}_{\text{fin}}^{\mathcal{D}}, \mathcal{Z}}$. $\qquad\square$

We now set $\psi := \widehat{\psi}_{\psi_1,\dots,\psi_n}$, $\mathcal{G} := \widehat{\gamma}_{\gamma_1,\dots,\gamma_n}$ and $\mathcal{S}_\mathcal{D} := \mathcal{S}_{\text{fin}}^\mathcal{D}$ in precondition (2) in Sect. 3.1. This yields a precondition that lets us replace all global subroutines using the various replacement theorems from the previous section.

Remark 2. In some situations, we might want to replace only one global subroutine but not all of them. As an example, consider a protocol accessing a global PKI functionality γ_1, which in turn uses a global RO γ_2. In an instantiation, the global PKI is likely replaced by an interactive protocol ψ_1 (potentially involving a certificate authority, but still using the global RO). To ensure that the protocol's security proof remains valid under this replacement, we need to replace only γ_1 but not γ_2. However, due to the fact that every protocol trivially UC-emulates itself, we can apply Theorem 6 with $\psi_2 := \gamma_2$, which will leave the global RO as a proof element.

Acknowledgements. We would like to thank the anonymous reviewers for their thoughtful feedback on this work. In particular, the idea of describing the technical issue that arises with global replacement in terms of lack of lower bounds in UC statements is due to one anonymous EUROCRYPT 2021 reviewer, to which we are very thankful.

References

[ACKZ20] Abadi, A., Ciampi, M., Kiayias, A., Zikas, V.: Timed signatures and zero-knowledge proofs - timestamping in the blockchain era. In: ACNS (2020)

[BCH+20] Badertscher, C., Canetti, R., Hesse, J., Tackmann, B., Zikas, V.: Universal composition with global subroutines: capturing global setup within plain UC. In: Pass, R., Pietrzak, K. (eds.) TCC 2020. LNCS, vol. 12552, pp. 1–30. Springer, Cham (2020). https://doi.org/10.1007/978-3-030-64381-2_1

[BdM93] Benaloh, J., de Mare, M.: One-way accumulators: a decentralized alternative to digital signatures. In: Helleseth, T. (ed.) EUROCRYPT 1993. LNCS, vol. 765, pp. 274–285. Springer, Heidelberg (1994). https://doi.org/10.1007/3-540-48285-7_24

[BGK+18] Badertscher, C., Gaži, P., Kiayias, A., Russell, A., Zikas, V.: Ouroboros genesis: Composable proof-of-stake blockchains with dynamic availability. In: ACM SIGSAC Conference on Computer and Communications Security, CCS, pp. 913–930. ACM (2018)

[BGK+21] Badertscher, C., Gaži, P., Kiayias, A., Russell, A., Zikas, V.: Dynamic Ad Hoc clock synchronization. In: Canteaut, A., Standaert, F.-X. (eds.) EUROCRYPT 2021. LNCS, vol. 12698, pp. 399–428. Springer, Cham (2021). https://doi.org/10.1007/978-3-030-77883-5_14

[BHZ20] Badertscher, C., Hesse, J., Zikas, V.: On the (IR)replaceability of global setups, or how (not) to use a global ledger. Cryptology ePrint Archive, Report 2020/1489 (2020). https://ia.cr/2020/1489

[BMTZ17] Badertscher, C., Maurer, U., Tschudi, D., Zikas, V.: Bitcoin as a transaction ledger: a composable treatment. In: Katz, J., Shacham, H. (eds.) CRYPTO 2017. LNCS, vol. 10401, pp. 324–356. Springer, Cham (2017). https://doi.org/10.1007/978-3-319-63688-7_11

[Can01]   Canetti, R.: Universally composable security: a new paradigm for cryptographic protocols. In: IEEE Symposium on Foundations of Computer Science, FOCS 2001, pp. 136–145 (2001)

[Can20]   Canetti, R.: Universally composable security. J. ACM **67**(5) (2020)

[CDG+18] Camenisch, J., Drijvers, M., Gagliardoni, T., Lehmann, A., Neven, G.: The wonderful world of global random oracles. In: Nielsen, J.B., Rijmen, V. (eds.) EUROCRYPT 2018. LNCS, vol. 10820, pp. 280–312. Springer, Cham (2018). https://doi.org/10.1007/978-3-319-78381-9_11

[CDPW07] Canetti, R., Dodis, Y., Pass, R., Walfish, S.: Universally composable security with global setup. In: Vadhan, S.P. (ed.) TCC 2007. LNCS, vol. 4392, pp. 61–85. Springer, Heidelberg (2007). https://doi.org/10.1007/978-3-540-70936-7_4

[CGJ19]   Choudhuri, A.R., Goyal, V., Jain, A.: Founding secure computation on blockchains. In: Ishai, Y., Rijmen, V. (eds.) EUROCRYPT 2019. LNCS, vol. 11477, pp. 351–380. Springer, Cham (2019). https://doi.org/10.1007/978-3-030-17656-3_13

[CGL+17] Chiesa, A., Green, M., Liu, J., Miao, P., Miers, I., Mishra, P.: Decentralized anonymous micropayments. In: Coron, J.-S., Nielsen, J.B. (eds.) EUROCRYPT 2017. LNCS, vol. 10211, pp. 609–642. Springer, Cham (2017). https://doi.org/10.1007/978-3-319-56614-6_21

[CJS14]   Canetti, R., Jain, A., Scafuro, A.: Practical UC security with a global random oracle. In: ACM SIGSAC Conference on Computer and Communications Security, CCS (2014)

[CKWZ13] Choi, S.G., Katz, J., Wee, H., Zhou, H.-S.: Efficient, adaptively secure, and composable oblivious transfer with a single, global CRS. In: Kurosawa, K., Hanaoka, G. (eds.) PKC 2013. LNCS, vol. 7778, pp. 73–88. Springer, Heidelberg (2013). https://doi.org/10.1007/978-3-642-36362-7_6

[CR03]   Canetti, R., Rabin, T.: Universal composition with joint state. In: Boneh, D. (ed.) CRYPTO 2003. LNCS, vol. 2729, pp. 265–281. Springer, Heidelberg (2003). https://doi.org/10.1007/978-3-540-45146-4_16

[CSV16]   Canetti, R., Shahaf, D., Vald, M.: Universally composable authentication and key-exchange with global PKI. In: Cheng, C.-M., Chung, K.-M., Persiano, G., Yang, B.-Y. (eds.) PKC 2016. LNCS, vol. 9615, pp. 265–296. Springer, Heidelberg (2016). https://doi.org/10.1007/978-3-662-49387-8_11

[DEF+19] Dziembowski, S., Eckey, L., Faust, S., Hesse, J., Hostáková, K.: Multi-party virtual state channels. In: Ishai, Y., Rijmen, V. (eds.) EUROCRYPT 2019. LNCS, vol. 11476, pp. 625–656. Springer, Cham (2019). https://doi.org/10.1007/978-3-030-17653-2_21

[DEFM19] Dziembowski, S., Eckey, L., Faust, S., Malinowski, D.: Virtual payment hubs over cryptocurrencies. In: 2019 IEEE Symposium on Security and Privacy, SP (2019)

[DFH18]   Dziembowski, S., Faust, S., Hostáková, K.: General state channel networks. In: ACM SIGSAC Conference on Computer and Communications Security, CCS (2018)

[DPS19]   Daian, P., Pass, R., Shi, E.: Snow White: robustly reconfigurable consensus and applications to provably secure proof of stake. In: Goldberg, I., Moore, T. (eds.) FC 2019. LNCS, vol. 11598, pp. 23–41. Springer, Cham (2019). https://doi.org/10.1007/978-3-030-32101-7_2

[EMM19] Egger, C., Moreno-Sanchez, P., Maffei, M.: Atomic multi-channel updates with constant collateral in bitcoin-compatible payment-channel networks. In: ACM SIGSAC Conference on Computer and Communications Security, CCS (2019)

[GKLP18] Garay, J.A., Kiayias, A., Leonardos, N., Panagiotakos, G.: Bootstrapping the blockchain, with applications to consensus and fast PKI setup. In: Abdalla, M., Dahab, R. (eds.) PKC 2018. LNCS, vol. 10770, pp. 465–495. Springer, Cham (2018). https://doi.org/10.1007/978-3-319-76581-5_16

[KKM19] Kubilay, M.Y., Kiraz, M.S., Mantar, H.A.: Certledger: a new PKI model with certificate transparency based on blockchain. Comput. Secur. **85**, 333–352 (2019)

[KL20] Kiayias, A., Litos, O.S.T.: A composable security treatment of the lightning network. In 33rd IEEE Computer Security Foundations Symposium, CSF (2020)

[KMT20] Küsters, R., Tuengerthal, M., Rausch, D.: The IITM model: a simple and expressive model for universal composability. J. Cryptol. (2020)

[KZZ16] Kiayias, A., Zhou, H.-S., Zikas, V.: Fair and robust multi-party computation using a global transaction ledger. In: Fischlin, M., Coron, J.-S. (eds.) EUROCRYPT 2016. LNCS, vol. 9666, pp. 705–734. Springer, Heidelberg (2016). https://doi.org/10.1007/978-3-662-49896-5_25

[MR11] Maurer, U., Renner, R.: Abstract cryptography. In: Innovations in Computer Science (2011)

[MR17] Matsumoto, S., Reischuk, R.M.: IKP: turning a PKI around with decentralized automated incentives. In: 2017 IEEE Symposium on Security and Privacy, SP 2017, pp. 410–426. IEEE Computer Society (2017)

[Nie02] Nielsen, J.B.: Separating random oracle proofs from complexity theoretic proofs: the non-committing encryption case. In: CRYPTO (2002)

[PS18] Pass, R., Shi, E.: Thunderella: blockchains with optimistic instant confirmation. In: Nielsen, J.B., Rijmen, V. (eds.) EUROCRYPT 2018. LNCS, vol. 10821, pp. 3–33. Springer, Cham (2018). https://doi.org/10.1007/978-3-319-78375-8_1

[PSKR20] Patsonakis, C., Samari, K., Kiayias, A., Roussopoulos, M.: Implementing a smart contract PKI. IEEE Trans. Eng. Manage. 1–19 (2020)

[RY16] Reyzin, L., Yakoubov, S.: Efficient asynchronous accumulators for distributed PKI. In: Zikas, V., De Prisco, R. (eds.) SCN 2016. LNCS, vol. 9841, pp. 292–309. Springer, Cham (2016). https://doi.org/10.1007/978-3-319-44618-9_16

BKW Meets Fourier New Algorithms for LPN with Sparse Parities

Dana Dachman-Soled[1], Huijing Gong[2], Hunter Kippen[1],
and Aria Shahverdi[1(✉)]

[1] University of Maryland, College Park, USA
{danadach,hkippen,ariash}@umd.edu
[2] Intel Labs, Hillsboro, USA
huijing.gong@intel.com

Abstract. We consider the Learning Parity with Noise (LPN) problem with sparse secret, where the secret vector s of dimension n has Hamming weight at most k. We are interested in algorithms with asymptotic improvement in the *exponent* beyond the state of the art. Prior work in this setting presented algorithms with runtime $n^{c \cdot k}$ for constant $c < 1$, obtaining a constant factor improvement over brute force search, which runs in time $\binom{n}{k}$. We obtain the following results:

- We first consider the *constant* error rate setting, and in this case present a new algorithm that leverages a subroutine from the acclaimed BKW algorithm [Blum, Kalai, Wasserman, J. ACM '03] as well as techniques from Fourier analysis for p-biased distributions. Our algorithm achieves asymptotic improvement in the exponent compared to prior work, when the sparsity $k = k(n) = \frac{n}{\log^{1+1/c}(n)}$, where $c \in o(\log \log(n))$ and $c \in \omega(1)$. The runtime and sample complexity of this algorithm are approximately the same.
- We next consider the *low noise* setting, where the error is subconstant. We present a new algorithm in this setting that requires only a *polynomial* number of samples and achieves asymptotic improvement in the exponent compared to prior work, when the sparsity $k = \frac{1}{\eta} \cdot \frac{\log(n)}{\log(f(n))}$ and noise rate of $\eta \neq 1/2$ and $\eta^2 = \left(\frac{\log(n)}{n} \cdot f(n) \right)$, for $f(n) \in \omega(1) \cap n^{o(1)}$. To obtain the improvement in sample complexity, we create subsets of samples using the *design* of Nisan and Wigderson [J. Comput. Syst. Sci. '94], so that any two subsets have a small intersection, while the number of subsets is large. Each of these subsets is used to generate a single p-biased sample for the Fourier analysis step. We then show that this allows us to bound the covariance of pairs of samples, which is sufficient for the Fourier analysis.

D. Dachman-Soled—Supported in part by NSF grants #CNS-1933033, #CNS-1453045 (CAREER), and by financial assistance awards 70NANB15H328 and 70NANB19H126 from the U.S. Department of Commerce, National Institute of Standards and Technology.
H. Gong—Most of the work was done while the author was a student at the University of Maryland, College Park.
H. Kippen—Supported in part by the Clark Doctoral Fellowship from the Clark School of Engineering, University of Maryland, College Park.

© International Association for Cryptologic Research 2021
K. Nissim and B. Waters (Eds.): TCC 2021, LNCS 13043, pp. 658–688, 2021.
https://doi.org/10.1007/978-3-030-90453-1_23

– Finally, we show that our first algorithm extends to the setting where the noise rate is very high $1/2 - o(1)$, and in this case can be used as a subroutine to obtain new algorithms for learning DNFs and Juntas. Our algorithms achieve asymptotic improvement in the exponent for certain regimes. For DNFs of size s with approximation factor ϵ this regime is when $\log \frac{s}{\epsilon} \in \omega \left(\frac{c}{\log n \log \log c} \right)$, and $\log \frac{s}{\epsilon} \in n^{1-o(1)}$, for $c \in n^{1-o(1)}$. For Juntas of k the regime is when $k \in \omega \left(\frac{c}{\log n \log \log c} \right)$, and $k \in n^{1-o(1)}$, for $c \in n^{1-o(1)}$.

1   Introduction

The *(search) Learning Parity with Noise (LPN)* problem with dimension n and noise rate η, asks to recover the secret parity $\mathbf{s}$, given samples $(\mathbf{x}, \langle \mathbf{x}, \mathbf{s} \rangle \oplus e)$, where $\mathbf{x} \in \{0,1\}^n$ is chosen uniformly at random, $\mathbf{s} \in \{0,1\}^n$, error $e \in \{0,1\}$ is set to 1 with probability η and 0 with probability $1 - \eta$, and the dot product is taken modulo 2.

While solving a linear system of n equations over $\mathbb{F}_2$ to recover a secret of dimension n can be done in polynomial time via Gaussian elimination, even adding a small amount of noise e renders the above a seemingly hard learning problem, even given a large number of samples. Specifically, the search LPN problem, which typically assumes the noise rate is a small constant, is believed to be hard, with the asymptotically best algorithm (known as BKW) requiring runtime $2^{\Theta(n/\log(n))}$ and $2^{\Theta(n/\log(n))}$ number of samples to recover $\mathbf{s}$ of dimension n. Some evidence of its hardness comes from the fact that it provably cannot be learned efficiently in the so called *statistical query (SQ)* model under the uniform distribution [3,5].

Though originally arising in the fields of computational learning theory and coding theory, the LPN problem has found numerous applications in cryptography (see e.g. [4,13,17,18] for a partial list of applications) due to the fact that (1) there is a search-to-decision reduction, meaning that the decision version—which is more amenable to cryptographic applications and asks to distinguish $(\mathbf{x}, \langle \mathbf{x}, \mathbf{s} \rangle \oplus e)$ from $(\mathbf{x}, b)$, where b is random—is as hard as the search version (which asks to recover $\mathbf{s}$) and (2) the LPN problem is believed to be *quantum-hard*, as opposed to other standard cryptographic assumptions such as discrete log and factoring which are known to have polynomial time quantum algorithms [26].

Variants of the LPN problem have also been considered in the literature: Sparse LPN [6], where the $\mathbf{x}$ vectors in the LPN problem statement are sparse, LPN with structured noise, where the noise across multiple samples is guaranteed to satisfy some constraint [2], and Ring LPN [16]. While typically the error rate is assumed to be constant, LPN with low noise rate has also been considered with applications to cryptography [8]. Indeed, LPN with noise rate even as low as $\Omega(\log^2(n)/n)$ is considered a hard problem [8]. We further note that WLOG can assume that the secret is drawn from the same distribution as the noise, as there is a reduction from LPN with secret $\mathbf{s}$ to LPN with secret $\mathbf{e}$, where $\mathbf{e}$ is the error vector obtained after n samples are drawn [1].

In this work we consider LPN with sparse parities (i.e. the "sparsity" or Hamming weight k of the secret vector is significantly less than $\eta \cdot n$, where η is the error rate). We consider both the constant noise and the low noise setting (where the error rate is subconstant). Motivations for considering this variant of LPN include the fact that sparse secrets may be used in practical cryptosystems for efficiency purposes (as is the case for some fully homomorphic encryption implementations [9]), or some bits of the secret may be leaked via a side-channel attack. More generally, analyzing the security of LPN with sparse parities tests the robustness of the standard LPN assumption, since a lack of polynomial-time algorithms in the sparse parities setting (when k is super-constant) would then raise our confidence in the security of the standard setting. We also consider applications of our results to other learning problems, such as learning DNFs and Juntas. Prior work on LPN with sparse parities, has mainly considered obtaining algorithms with runtime $n^{c \cdot k}$ for constant $c < 1$ [14,27]. This beats the trivial brute force search with runtime $\binom{n}{k}$ in the regime where $k \ll n$. In this work, our focus is to achieve an algorithm which, for certain regimes of k, beats the prior best algorithms asymptotically *in the exponent*. Since our goal is to achieve asymptotic improvement in the exponent, we will compare our algorithm's runtime against brute force search and not the prior work of [14, 27], since the latter algorithms are equivalent to brute force search in terms of asymptotics in the exponent.

1.1   Our Results

We obtain new LPN algorithms for sparse parities that improve upon the state-of-the-art in certain regimes, which will be discussed below.

Our first result pertains to the constant noise setting, where the noise rate $\eta \in \Theta(1)$. In the theorem below, $p \in (0,1)$ is a free parameter that we set later to optimize our runtime.

Theorem 1.1. *For $\delta \in [0,1]$, $p \in (0,1)$, LPN for parities of sparsity k out of n variables and constant noise rate can be learned with total number of samples and total computation time of*

$$\mathsf{poly}\left(\frac{1}{(1-2\eta)^{\sqrt{np}} \cdot p^{2(k-1)}(1-p)^2} \cdot \ln(\frac{n}{\delta}) \cdot \left(2^{\frac{np}{\log(np)}} \cdot \log(np)\right)\right),$$

and success probability of $1 - \delta - \left(\frac{16}{(1-2\eta)^{\sqrt{8np}} \cdot p^{2(k-1)}(1-p)^2} \cdot \ln(\frac{2n}{\delta}) \cdot \exp(\frac{-pn}{8})\right)$.

By setting the parameter p appropriately, we obtain the following:

Corollary 1.2. *For sparisty $k = k(n) = \frac{n}{\log^{1+1/c}(n)}$, where $c \in o(\log\log(n))$ and $c \in \omega(1)$, the runtime of our new learning algorithm is contained in both $\log(n)^{o(k)}$ and $2^{o(n/\log(n))}$, and it succeeds with constant probability. For this range of k, Brute Force search requires runtime $\log(n)^{\Omega(k)}$ and BKW requires runtime of $2^{\Omega(n/\log(n))}$.*

Our second result pertains to the low noise setting, where the noise rate $\eta \in o(1)$. Again, $p \in (0,1)$ is a free parameter that we set later to optimize our runtime.

Theorem 1.3. *Assuming parameters are set such that*

$$\log \left(\frac{1}{(1-2\eta)^{2np+2}p^{2(k-1)}(1-p^2)} \right) \in o(1/\eta \cdot \log(np)),$$

and that $\delta \in [0,1]$, $p \in (0,1)$, LPN for parities of sparsity k out of n variables and noise rate $\eta \in o(1)$ can be learned using $(2np+1)^2 \cdot \log(n)$ number of samples, total computation time of $N := \mathsf{poly}\left(\frac{1}{(1-2\eta)^{2np+2}p^{2(k-1)}(1-p^2)} \right)$ and achieves success probability of

$$1 - \delta - \left(N \cdot \left(2 \cdot \exp(-p \cdot n/8) + \exp(-n/48) + 1/2^{np/4} \right) \right)$$

By setting the parameter p appropriately, we obtain the following:

Corollary 1.4. *For sparsity $k(n)$ such that $k = \frac{1}{\eta} \cdot \frac{\log(n)}{\log(f(n))}$, noise rate $\eta \neq 1/2$ such that $\eta^2 = \left(\frac{\log(n)}{n} \cdot f(n) \right)$, for $f(n) \in \omega(1) \cap n^{o(1)}$, the Learning Algorithm of Fig. 4 runs in time $O\left(\frac{1}{(1-2\eta)^{2np+2}p^{2k}} \cdot \log(n) \cdot (np)^3 \right) \in \left(\frac{n}{k} \right)^{o(k)}$ with constant probability. In this setting, the running time Brute Force is $\binom{n}{k} \geq \left(\frac{n}{k} \right)^k$ and the running time of Lucky Bruteforce is $e^{\eta n} \in \left(\frac{n}{k} \right)^{\omega(k)}$.*

Finally, applying known reductions to LPN [12] and solving LPN using our algorithm, we also obtain applications to learning other classes of functions such as DNF and juntas:

- Our algorithm can be applied to learn DNFs of size s and approximation factor ϵ, with asymptotic improvements over Verbeurgt's bound [28] of $O\left(n^{\log \frac{s}{\epsilon}}\right)$, and with negligible failure probability when $\log \frac{s}{\epsilon} \in \omega\left(\frac{c}{\log n \log \log c}\right)$, and $\log \frac{s}{\epsilon} \in n^{1-o(1)}$, where $c \in n^{1-o(1)}$.
- Our algorithm can be applied to learn Juntas of size k with a runtime of $n^{o(k)}$ and a negligible failure probability when $k \in \omega\left(\frac{c}{\log n \log \log c}\right)$, and $k \in n^{1-o(1)}$, where $c \in n^{1-o(1)}$.

1.2   Technical Overview

Fourier Analysis of Boolean Functions. Every Boolean function, $f : \{0,1\}^n \to \{0,1\}$—equivalently $f : \{-1,1\}^n \to \{-1,1\}$—can be represented as a linear combination $f(\mathbf{x}) = \sum_{S \subseteq [n]} \hat{f}(S) \cdot \chi_{S,p}(\mathbf{x})$, known as the Fourier representation of f. Typically, we consider the uniform distribution over examples $\mathbf{x}$, in which case $\chi_{S,p}(\mathbf{x})$ is defined as $\prod_{j \in S} \mathbf{x}[j]$ and $\hat{f}(S) = \mathbb{E}_{\mathbf{x} \sim \{-1,1\}^n} [f(\mathbf{x}) \cdot \chi_{S,p}(\mathbf{x})]$. However, for any product distribution $[p_1, \ldots, p_n]$, where $\mathbb{E}[\mathbf{x}[j]] = p_j$, we can also define

$\chi_{S,p}(\mathbf{x}) := \prod_{j \in S} \frac{\mathbf{x}[j]-p_j}{\sqrt{1-p_j^2}}$ and $\hat{f}(S) := \mathbb{E}_{\mathbf{x} \sim \mathcal{D}_p} [f(\mathbf{x}) \cdot \chi_{S,p}(\mathbf{x})]$, where $\mathcal{D}_p$ is a product distribution defined over $\{-1,1\}^n$ and is parameterized by its mean vector $[p_1, \ldots, p_n]$. Fourier analysis is a strong tool in computational learning theory for learning under the uniform distribution (and can be extended to product distributions as well). Specifically, the Low Degree Algorithm of [20] guarantees that if most of the Fourier weight of a Boolean function is concentrated on low degree parities (i.e. $\chi_{S,p}$ with small $|S|$), then an approximate version of the function can be reconstructed, *even in the presence of noise*. However, for learning large parities under the uniform distribution Fourier analysis is not useful since for a parity corresponding to secret $\mathbf{s}$ of Hamming weight k, all of the Fourier weight is on a single Fourier coefficient of degree k and searching for this Fourier coefficient would require a brute force search that enumerates over all possible parities of size at most k. If the distribution is p-biased instead of uniform, however, then the above is no longer the case. Specifically, if we consider a product distributions where the example $\mathbf{x}$ is no longer uniformly random, but each coordinate of $\mathbf{x}$ is set to 0 with probability $1/2+p/2$ and 1 with probability $1/2 - p/2$ (so the expectation $\mathbb{E}[x[j]] = p$ for each coordinate of $\mathbf{x}$), then the Fourier weight is now spread over all parities S such that $\forall j \in S, \mathbf{s}[j] = 1$. In particular, this means that by approximately computing the Fourier coefficient of all subsets consisting of a single element $S = \{\mathbf{s}[1]\}, \ldots, S = \{\mathbf{s}[n]\}$, we can distinguish the subsets of size 1 with non-zero versus zero Fourier weight and thus determine all i such that $\mathbf{s}[j] = 1$. We note that when the distribution is p-biased, the magnitude of the Fourier coefficients that we must approximate is of the order p^k, and we will therefore require $\mathsf{poly}((1/p)^k)$ samples to approximate the quantity (even without considering noise). We will see in the following that in order for our approach to improve upon known algorithms, we must consider *sparse parities* with $k \in o(n)$.

Attack Overview. Given the above discussion, the main idea of our attack is to convert samples drawn from the uniform distribution to samples drawn from a p-biased distribution and then use Fourier analysis techniques to learn the elements of the parity one by one.

In order for this approach to succeed, our algorithm first needs to generate a sufficient number of p-biased LPN samples, given uniformly random LPN samples. Specifically, the attacker has access to unbiased LPN oracle which outputs samples $\mathbf{x}_i$ and corresponding label b_i such that $b_i = \langle \mathbf{x}_i, \mathbf{s} \rangle + e_i$, noise e_i has rate η meaning that error e_i is 1 with probability η and 0 with probability $1 - \eta$. The attacker will generate new samples $\mathbf{x}_i'$, which are p-biased, and a corresponding label b_i', with a higher error rate η'. We then approximate the Fourier coefficient of coordinate j, constructed as above, by $\hat{b}_p(\{j\}) := \mathbb{E}_{\mathbf{x}' \sim \mathcal{D}_p}[b' \cdot \chi_{\{j\},p}(\mathbf{x}')]$. The main observation is that for the secret key coordinate j such that $\mathbf{s}[j] = 0$ we have $\hat{b}_p(\{j\}) = 0$ and for the coordinates j such that $\mathbf{s}[j] = 1$ we have $\hat{b}(\{j\}) = (1 - 2\eta') \cdot p^{k-1} \sqrt{1-p^2}$. The value of $\hat{b}_p(\{j\})$ is estimated by using a sample mean with a sufficient number of generated p-biased samples to approximate the expectation.

We present two algorithms for generating the p-biased samples, each algorithm is appropriate for a different scenario. Specifically, our first algorithm is appropriate for the standard case where the noise rate is constant, while our second algorithm is appropriate for the *low noise* case where the noise rate is sub-constant. After generating the p-biased samples, the Fourier estimation step is similar in both settings. We next elaborate on our algorithm for each of the two settings.

Constant Noise. In the case where the noise rate is constant, to generate the p-biased samples, we apply a variant of the BKW algorithm. The BKW algorithm gives an $2^{O(n/\log(n))}$-time algorithm for the LPN problem that also requires $2^{O(n/\log(n))}$ number of samples. An intermediate step of the BKW algorithm uses access to its LPN oracle to generates samples $(\mathbf{x}, \langle \mathbf{x}, \mathbf{s} \rangle \oplus e')$, where $\mathbf{x}$ is a vector that has all 0's except in a single position, and e' is an error term with higher noise rate than the original error. The key idea of our algorithm is that in order to create p-biased samples, we can choose a random set of coordinates, $R \subseteq [n]$, by including each $i \in [n]$ in the set R independently with probability p, and then run the subroutine of the BKW algorithm on the *smaller set* R, of expected size pn, in order to create a sample $\mathbf{x}$ that is set to 0 for all $i \in R$. Such a sample $\mathbf{x}$ is now distributed identically to a p-biased sample. The error rate increases, but since Fourier analysis is robust against noise, these p-biased samples can still be used to estimate the Fourier Coefficients corresponding to $S = \{\mathbf{s}[1]\}, \ldots, S = \{\mathbf{s}[n]\}$ to determine the secret $\mathbf{s}$. Crucially, our algorithm gains over simply running BKW on the entire instance because the set of coordinates we run BKW on is of size $O(pn)$ instead of size n. Thus, generating the biased samples runs in time $2^{O(pn/\log(pn))}$ instead of time $2^{O(n/\log(n))}$. When p is subconstant, we achieve an asymptotic gain in the exponent. In contrast, the Fourier estimation step runs in time $\mathsf{poly}((1/p)^k)$, so we must also set p large enough so that this step achieves asymptotic gain in the exponent beyond the brute force search time of $\binom{n}{k}$. We discuss at the end of the section the regime in which it is possible to set the parameter p so that our algorithm improves asymptotically in the exponent beyond the best known algorithms.

Low Noise. When the noise rate is sufficiently low, we can generate p-biased samples using a simpler approach. As before, we randomly select a set $R \subseteq [n]$, by including each $i \in [n]$ in the set R independently with probability p. Now, instead of running BKW on the coordinates in the set R, we simply choose $O(np)$ number samples (since R has expected size np) from the non-biased oracle and find a linear combination (guaranteed to exist) that sets all the coordinates in R to 0. Again, the noise increases in the generated sample. Nevertheless, we gain over the trivial approach (which instead of p-biasing the oracle simply creates linear combinations that have $\mathbf{x}$ set to all 0 except for in a single coordinate) because the linear combination we generate is over at most $O(np)$ versus $O(n)$

vectors, which in turn guarantees that the noise rate will be lower.[1] We gain from this technique by choosing p small enough to lower the noise rate but large enough to ensure that the $(1/p)^k$ necessary to estimate the Fourier coefficient still beats brute force search asymptotically in the exponent.

In the low noise case we further show that we can generate the large number of samples needed for the Fourier analysis using only a *polynomial size* set of examples from the original LPN oracle. In this case, the generated samples will not be i.i.d., but we will use a construction inspired by the *designs* of Nisan and Wigderson to generate an exponentially large set of samples, where each pair of samples from the generated set has low covariance.[2] See Sect. 4.1 for more details. This will be enough to then run the Fourier analysis, which requires that one can use random sampling to estimate the mean of a random variable. We can bound the deviation from the mean using Chebyshev's inequality since we guarantee that the covariance between any two distinct samples is small.

Parameters. We now discuss the regime of k and η in which we improve on prior algorithms, and how to set the parameter p to achieve the optimal run time. For the constant noise setting, with secret $\mathbf{s}$ with sparsity in the form $k = k(n) = \frac{n}{\log^{1+1/c}(n)}$, where $c \in o(\log\log(n))$ and $c \in \omega(1)$, we set $p = 1/\log^{1/(c)}(n)$ to obtain an algorithm that improves upon both Bruteforce and BKW asymptotically in the exponent. Recall that prior work on LPN with parities of sparsity k reduced the constant in the exponent beyond brute force, but did not achieve asymptotic improvement in the exponent. In our work we care about asymptotic improvement in the exponent and therefore do not compare against those algorithms. For the low noise setting we show that for sparsity $k = \frac{1}{\eta} \cdot \frac{\log(n)}{\log(f(n))}$ and the noise rate of $\eta \neq 1/2$ and $\eta^2 = \left(\frac{\log(n)}{n} \cdot f(n)\right)$, for $f(n) \in \omega(1) \cap n^{o(1)}$, by setting $p = \frac{1}{f(n)}$ and $\frac{1}{p} \in \left(\frac{n}{k}\right)^{o(1)}$, our algorithm improves upon both Bruteforce and "lucky Bruteforce"–i.e. an algorithm which gathers m samples until it has n noiseless samples with high confidence (where m depends on the noiserate) and then attempts Gaussian elimination with every possible subset of size n, giving runtime $\mathsf{poly}(\binom{m}{n})$–asymptotically in the exponent. To our knowledge, these are the best algorithms when considering asymptotics in the exponent.

Application to DNF and Juntas. In addition to parities, the reductions by Feldman et al. [12] provide a way to translate improvements in solving LPN to learning Juntas and DNFs. As such, we present a formulation of our constant noise algorithm that is parameterized according to these reductions, and provide parameter settings such that our algorithm, when applied to learning DNFs or

---

[1] We note that the above description is a bit inaccurate, since we must include an additional step to ensure that the added noise is independent of the set of samples. See discussion in Sect. 4.1, Fig. 3 and Lemma 4.1 for more details.

[2] It is also possible to use a random choice of subsets in place of this design. However, the deterministic procedure allows for bounding the covariance of the newly generated samples which is crucial in our analysis as seen later.

Juntas, yields asymptotic improvements in the exponent. For DNFs, we present an asymptotic result similar to that of [14] in that we improve on Verbeurgt's bound of $O(n^{\log \frac{s}{\epsilon}})$ for learning DNFs of size s with approximation factor ϵ for a different regime of $\frac{s}{\epsilon}$, where $\log \frac{s}{\epsilon} \in \omega\left(\frac{c}{\log n \log \log c}\right)$, and $\log \frac{s}{\epsilon} \in n^{1-o(1)}$, for $c \in n^{1-o(1)}$. Note that for Juntas, we present an algorithm that learns Juntas of k variables in $n^{o(k)}$ time for $k \in \omega\left(\frac{c}{\log n \log \log c}\right)$, and $k \in n^{1-o(1)}$, where $c \in n^{1-o(1)}$.

1.3 Related Work

LPN. Blum, Kalai and Wasserman [5] presented the first algorithm that improved upon the trivial $2^{\Omega(n)}$ time algorithm for LPN. They showed that LPN with constant error rate can be learned in slightly subexponential time $2^{O(n/\log n)}$ with the same amount of samples. To date, their algorithm remains the state-of-the-art in terms of asymptotics in the exponent in the constant error rate regime.

Lyubashevsky [22] extended the previous algorithm by Blum et al. [5] and reduced the overall sample complexity. Lyubashevsky developed an algorithm for creating a super-polynomial number of psuedorandom samples from a polynomial number of original samples. Thus, Lyubashevsky traded sample complexity for time complexity. More specifically, the algorithm solved LPN with constant error rate and parities of size n in time $2^{O(n/\log \log n)}$ using only $n^{1+\epsilon}$ samples.

In later work Bogos et al. [7] presented a unified framework for various improvements and optimizations of BKW. Specifically, they focused on tightening the analysis of several previous works [15,19] to give more accurate bounds for the time and sample complexity needed to solve the LPN problem. They improved the bounds of the variant of the BKW algorithm proposed by Leviel and Fouque [19] which is based on Walsh-Hadamard transform. Moreover, they analyzed the algorithm by Guo et al. [15] which used a "covering codes" technique to reduce the dimension of the problem. We note that the many of the improvements listed are heuristic in nature, while others provably improve the runtime. We also note that our usage of BKW in our algorithms is compatible with only some of these improvements. We only use the so-called "reduction" phase of the algorithm to generate our p-biased samples. Thus, improvements to this phase, such as covering codes, are applicable whereas others, such as the Walsh-Hadamard transform, are not.

LPN with Sparse Parities. Grigorescu et al. [14] showed an improvement of learning sparse parities with noise over brute force search, which has run time $\binom{n}{k}$. The algorithm ran in time $\mathsf{poly}\left(\log(\frac{1}{\delta}), \frac{1}{1-2\eta}\right) \cdot n^{\left(1+(2\eta)^2+o(1)\right)k/2}$ and had sample complexity of $\frac{k \log(n/\delta)\omega(1)}{(1-2\eta)^2}$ in the random noise setting under the uniform distribution, where η is the noise rate and δ is the confidence parameter.

Valiant [27] showed that the learning parity with noise problem can be solved in time $\approx n^{0.8k}\mathsf{poly}(\frac{1}{1-2\eta})$. He also showed that noisy k-juntas can be learned in time $n^{0.8k}\text{poly}\left(\frac{1}{1-2\eta}\right)$ and r-term DNF can be (ε, δ)-PAC learned in time poly $\left(\frac{1}{\delta}, \frac{r}{\varepsilon}\right) n^{0.8\log(\frac{r}{\varepsilon})}$, respectively. We note that the improvements of Grigorescu et al. [14] and Valiant [27] do not improve upon the runtime of brute force search of n^k in terms of asymptotics in the exponent.

Learning DNF and Juntas. Mossel et al. [24] showed the first learning algorithm which achieves a polynomial factor improvement over trivial brute force algorithm which runs time $O(n^k)$. It shows that k-juntas can be learned in absence of noise with confidence $1 - \delta$ from uniform random examples with run time of $\left(n^k\right)^{\frac{\omega}{\omega+1}} \cdot \text{poly}\left(2^k, n, \log(1/\delta)\right)$ where $\omega < 2.376$ is the matrix multiplication exponent.

Feldman et al. [11] presented a foundational work for learning both DNFs and Juntas. They developed an oracle transformation procedure that enabled reductions from learning DNFs and Juntas to that of LPN. In addition, Feldman et al. presented a learning algorithm for agnostically learning parities by showing a reduction from learning parities with adverserial noise to learning parities with random noise. With this reduction, they showed that the algorithm by Blum et al. [5] can learn parities with an adverserial noise rate of η in time $O(2^{\frac{n}{\log n}})$. In a follow up work [12], Feldman et al. refined their reductions and included the influence of sample complexity on the the runtime. These reductions have streamlined the process of improving algorithms for learning DNFs and Juntas, as improved algorithms for learning parities can be directly applied to both problems. Both the work of Grigorescu et al. [14], and Valiant [27] were examples of this.

One can also consider natural restrictions to the Junta problem. For monotone Juntas, Dachman-Soled et al. [10] found lower bounds for solving monotone Juntas in the statistical query model. Lipton et al. considered the problem of learning symmetric Juntas [21] and showed they can be learned in $n^{o(k)}$ time. Note here that the symmetry requirement is orthogonal to restrictions on the size of k.

2   Preliminaries

2.1   Notations

In this section we remind the reader some of the preliminary results used throughout the paper. We use := as deterministic assignment and $\leftarrow$ as uniformly randomized assignment. We also use bold lowercase, e.g. $\mathbf{x}$, to denote vectors and bold uppercase, e.g. $\mathbf{A}$, to denote matrix. The set $\{1, 2, \ldots, n\}$ is often denoted by $[n]$. The i-th coordinate of vector $\mathbf{x}$ is denoted by $\mathbf{x}[i]$. For the vector $\mathbf{x}$ of dimension n and a set R that is a subset of $[n]$, we denote $\mathbf{x}|_R$ to be the restriction of $\mathbf{x}$ to the coordinates in R, namely $\mathbf{x}|_R = \mathbf{x}[i_1]\|\mathbf{x}[i_2]\|\ldots\mathbf{x}[i_{|R|}], \forall i \in R\}$. The indices in $\mathbf{x}$ are from 1 to n. For simplicity, we reset the indices in $\mathbf{x}|_R$ and have the indices from 1 to $|R|$.

2.2   Fourier Analysis

The boolean Fourier transform is defined for boolean functions defined over the domain $\{-1, 1\}$. Throughout the rest of the paper, when we discuss boolean functions, we will use this representation. To map a boolean function from $\{0, 1\} \in \mathbb{F}_2$ to $\{-1, 1\}$, we set $-1 := 1_{\mathbb{F}_2}$ and $1 := 0_{\mathbb{F}_2}$. We now present some additional notation regarding the representation of the LPN problem in the $\{-1, 1\}$ domain.

Notation. Assuming the LPN secret $\mathbf{s}$ is represented in $\mathbb{F}_2^n$, the following represent the boolean inner product of input $\mathbf{x}$ with $\mathbf{s}$ in different notation.

$$f_{\mathbf{s}}(\mathbf{x}) := \langle \mathbf{x}, \mathbf{s} \rangle \in \mathbb{F}_2 \text{ for } \mathbf{x}, \mathbf{s} \in \mathbb{F}_2^n$$

$$f_{\mathbf{s}}(\mathbf{x}) = \prod_{i=1}^{n} \mathbf{x}[i]^{\mathbf{s}[i]} \in \{-1, 1\} \text{ for } \mathbf{x} \in \{-1, 1\}^n \text{ and } \mathbf{s} \in \mathbb{F}_2^n$$

hence to represent a sample $(\mathbf{x}, b)$ from LPN oracle $\mathcal{O}_{0,\eta}^{\mathsf{LPN}}(\mathbf{s})$ we have the following two notations

$$b = f_{\mathbf{s}}(\mathbf{x}) + e \text{ for } \mathbf{x}, \mathbf{s} \in \mathbb{F}_2^n \text{ and } e \in \mathbb{F}_2$$

$$b = f_{\mathbf{s}}(\mathbf{x}) \cdot e \text{ for } \mathbf{x} \in \{-1, 1\}^n, \mathbf{s} \in \mathbb{F}_2^n \text{ and } e \in \{-1, 1\}$$

Consider a vector $\mathbf{x} \in \{-1, 1\}^n$. We denote by $\mathcal{D}_p$ the product distribution over $\{-1, 1\}^n$, where each bit of the vector is independent and has mean p.

Definition 2.1 (Fourier Expansion). *For a product distribution $\mathcal{D}_p$ as above, every function $f : \{-1, 1\}^n \to \mathbb{R}$ can be uniquely expressed as the multilinear polynomial*

$$f(\mathbf{x}) = \sum_{S} \hat{f}_p(S) \chi_{S,p}(\mathbf{x}), \text{ where } \chi_{S,p}(\mathbf{x}) = \prod_{i \in S} \frac{\mathbf{x}[i] - p}{\sqrt{1 - p^2}}.$$

This expression is called the Fourier expansion of f with respect to $\mathcal{D}_p$, and the real numbers $\hat{f}(S)$ are called the Fourier coefficients of f on S.

The Fourier transform defines an inner product between two boolean functions f and g: $\langle f, g \rangle_p = \mathbb{E}_{\mathbf{x} \sim \mathcal{D}_p}[f(\mathbf{x}) \cdot g(\mathbf{x})]$. The Fourier coefficient for any $S \subset N$ over product distribution $\mathcal{D}_p$ is defined as follows:

$$\hat{f}_p(S) = \mathbb{E}_{\mathbf{x} \sim \mathcal{D}_p}[f(\mathbf{x}) \cdot \chi_S(\mathbf{x})].$$

Claim 2.2. Let $\mathbf{s}^p = (\mathbf{x}, b)$ be a p-biased sample and let $b = f_{\mathbf{s}}(\mathbf{x}) \cdot e$, where $e \in \{-1, 1\}$ is independent of $\mathbf{x}$ and $\mathbb{E}[e] = 1 - 2\eta'$. Define $\hat{b}_p(\{j\}) := \mathbb{E}_{\mathbf{x} \sim \mathcal{D}_p}[b \cdot \chi_{\{j\},p}(\mathbf{x})]$. If $\mathbf{s}^p.\mathbf{s}[j] = 0$, then $\hat{b}_p(\{j\}) = 0$. Whereas if $\mathbf{s}^p.\mathbf{s}[j] = 1$, then $\hat{b}_p(\{j\}) = (1 - 2\eta') \cdot p^{k-1} \sqrt{1 - p^2}$.

Proof. For the proof of the claim, refer to the full version of our paper available on ePrint.   □

3   Constant Noise Setting

In the constant noise setting, our algorithm consists of two steps. First, using a modification of the acclaimed BKW algorithm [5], we implement a p-biased LPN Oracle with noise rate η' and secret value $\mathbf{s}$ which is denoted by $\mathcal{O}^{\mathsf{LPN}}_{p,\eta'}(\mathbf{s})$ and is defined in Sect. A.2. We present this modification, entitled BKW$_\mathsf{R}$ (BKW restricted to set R), in Subsect. 3.1. In Subsect. 3.2 we present the integration of our p-biased oracle into the learning algorithm based on Fourier analysis. Finally, in Subsects. 3.3 and 3.4, we combine our analysis to present the regime in which we can set the free parameter p in order to improve on both BKW and brute force search asymptotically in the *exponent*.

3.1   BKW$_\mathsf{R}$

As a first step, we present our BKW$_\mathsf{R}$ algorithm in Fig. 1. The BKW$_\mathsf{R}$ algorithm is given access to an unbiased LPN Oracle $\mathcal{O}^{\mathsf{LPN}}_{0,\eta}(\mathbf{s})$ and its goal is to produce a sample that is p-biased. The presented algorithm works similarly to BKW by successively taking linear combinations of samples to produce a sample with all zero entries one 'block' at a time. The algorithm accomplishes this by maintaining successive tables such that samples in each table are combined to fill the next table. The number of tables is a parameter of the algorithm denoted $\mathfrak{a}$. The tables $T^{(1)}, \ldots, T^{(\mathfrak{a})}$ are each of size $2^{\mathfrak{b}}$, where $\mathfrak{b}$ is the size of each block, except the last table $T^{(\mathfrak{a})}$ which might have a smaller number of entries, specifically $2^{|R| \bmod \mathfrak{b}}$. Each table $T^{(j)}$ is indexed by the value of the coordinates in the j-th block of $\mathbf{x}|_R$, namely $\mathbf{x}|_R\left[(j-1) \cdot \mathfrak{b}, j \cdot \mathfrak{b} - 1\right]$. The element in row i of table j is denoted by $\left[T^{(j)}_i\right]$. Importantly, while the size of R may vary, $\mathfrak{a}$ remains constant each time the algorithm is called. This ensures that a constant number of samples are combined to produce the output. This decouples the noise present in the output from the size of R, ensuring that all generated samples are independent.

Construction of p-biased Oracle Given BKW$_\mathsf{R}$. The construction of the p-biased Oracle is quite simple. We sample an index set R where each index is selected independently with probability p. R is then passed as input to BKW$_\mathsf{R}$. By bounding the size of the set R, we can ensure that with overwhelming probability BKW$_\mathsf{R}$ outputs a p-biased sample in $2^{O(np/\log(np))}$ time. If the size of the set R exceeds this bound (captured by the event Event1 occurring), the runtime may be longer. Thus, when we invoke $\mathcal{O}^{\mathsf{LPN}}_{p,\eta'}(\mathbf{s})$ multiple times to generate a large number of p-biased samples for the Fourier analysis, we need to ensure that w.h.p. Event1 never occurs. We bound the probability of Event1 in Theorem 3.2.

Lemma 3.1.   *The samples $(\mathbf{x}', b')$ outputted by* BKW$_\mathsf{R}$ *Algorithm with access to* $\mathcal{O}^{\mathsf{LPN}}_{0,\eta}(\mathbf{s})$ *are independent and distributed identically to samples drawn from a p-biased LPN Oracle* $\mathcal{O}^{\mathsf{LPN}}_{p,\eta'}(\mathbf{s})$ *for $\eta' = \frac{1}{2} - \frac{1}{2}(1-2\eta)^{\sqrt{2np}}$.*

Proof. The proof can be found in Sect. A.4. $\square$

Algorithm 1: BKW$_R$

Result: Sample $(\mathbf{x}', b')$ such that the coordinates of $\mathbf{x}'$, which are defined by
    set R are set to 0.

if $|R| \geq 2np \vee |R| \leq pn/2$ **then**
  | Event1 occurs.
end

Set $\mathfrak{a} := \lceil \log(2np)/2 \rceil$ and $\mathfrak{b} := \lceil |R|/\mathfrak{a} \rceil$;

Set $T^{(1)}, \ldots, T^{(\mathfrak{a})}$ to empty tables;

while *True* **do**
  | Query a new sample from unbiased LPN Oracle $\mathcal{O}^{\mathsf{LPN}}_{0,\eta}(\mathbf{s})$;
  | $j := 1$;
  | **while** $j \leq \mathfrak{a}$ **do**
  | | **if** $\left[T^{(j)}_{\mathbf{x}|_R[(j-1)\cdot\mathfrak{b}, j\cdot\mathfrak{b}-1]} \right] = \emptyset$ **then**
  | | | $\left[T^{(j)}_{\mathbf{x}|_R[(j-1)\cdot\mathfrak{b}, j\cdot\mathfrak{b}-1]} \right] := (\mathbf{x}, b)$;
  | | | break;
  | | **end**
  | | **if** $\mathbf{x}|_R \left[(j-1) \cdot \mathfrak{b}, j \cdot \mathfrak{b} - 1 \right] \neq 0$ **then**
  | | | $(\mathbf{x}', b') := \left[T^{(j)}_{\mathbf{x}|_R[(j-1)\cdot\mathfrak{b}, j\cdot\mathfrak{b}-1]} \right]$;
  | | | $\mathbf{x}'' := \mathbf{x} + \mathbf{x}'$, $b'' := b + b'$;
  | | | $(\mathbf{x}, b) := (\mathbf{x}'', b'')$;
  | | **end**
  | | $j := j + 1$;
  | **end**
  | **if** $j = \mathfrak{a} + 1$ **then**
  | | break;
  | **end**
end

$(\mathbf{x}', b') := (\mathbf{x}, b)$;

return $(\mathbf{x}', b')$;

Fig. 1. BKW$_R$ "Zeroing" algorithm

Theorem 3.2. *Given access to LPN Oracle $\mathcal{O}^{\mathsf{LPN}}_{0,\eta}(\mathbf{s})$ which gives samples $\mathbf{s} = (\mathbf{x}, b)$, the oracle $\mathcal{O}^{\mathsf{LPN}}_{p,\eta'}(\mathbf{s})$ constructed from* BKW$_R$ *requires $O(2^{\frac{4np}{\log(2np)}} \cdot \log(2np))$ samples, and $O(2^{\frac{4np}{\log(2np)}} \cdot \log(2np))$ runtime with probability at least $1 - 2\exp(-p \cdot n/8)$.*

Proof. The proof can be found in Sect. A.5.   □

3.2 Learning Secret Coordinates

In this subsection we first present the Learning Algorithm in Fig. 2. The Algorithm starts by sampling num number of samples from a p-biased LPN Oracle $\mathcal{O}^{\mathsf{LPN}}_{p,\eta'}(\mathbf{s})$. As the samples are non-uniform, we can apply Fourier analysis technique described in Sect. 2.2.

The Learning Algorithm

The learning algorithm gets access to p-biased LPN Oracle $\mathcal{O}^{\mathsf{LPN}}_{p,\eta'}(\mathbf{s})$ which returns sample $s^p = (\mathbf{x}, b)$.

1. Initialize $\mathcal{S}, \mathcal{S}' := \emptyset$
2. For $i \in \mathsf{num}$:
   (a) Set $\mathbf{s}^p_i \leftarrow \mathcal{O}^{\mathsf{LPN}}_{p,\eta'}(\mathbf{s})$ to be the output sample from p-biased LPN Oracle.
   (b) Add $\mathbf{s}^p_i$ to the set $\mathcal{S}$.
3. Use the set $\mathcal{S}$ of num number of samples to estimate the Fourier coefficient of each coordinate of secret.
   - For each $j \in [n]$, approximate $\hat{b}_p(\{j\}) := \frac{1}{\mathsf{num}} \sum_{i=1}^{\mathsf{num}} b_i \cdot \chi_{\{j\},p}(\mathbf{x}_i)$, where each coordinate of $\mathbf{x}_i, b_i$ is switched to $\{-1,1\}$ from $\mathbb{F}_2$.
   - If $\hat{b}_p(\{j\}) > (1 - 2\eta')p^{k-1}\sqrt{1-p^2}/2$, add j to $\mathcal{S}'$.
4. Output $\mathbf{s}'$ such that $\mathbf{s}'[j] = 1$ for $j \in [n]$ if $j \in \mathcal{S}'$.

Fig. 2. LPN algorithm for constant noise

Lemma 3.3. *For $\delta \in [0,1]$, $p \in (0,1)$, the learning algorithm presented in Fig. 2 uses samples from Oracle $\mathcal{O}^{\mathsf{LPN}}_{p,\eta'}(\mathbf{s})$ to estimate the secret value $\mathbf{s}'$. The algorithm runs in time $\frac{8}{(1-2\eta')^2 \cdot p^{2(k-1)} \cdot (1-p)^2} \cdot \ln(2n/\delta)$, requires* $\mathsf{num} = \frac{8}{(1-2\eta')^2 \cdot p^{2(k-1)} \cdot (1-p)^2} \cdot \ln(2n/\delta)$ *number of samples and outputs the correct secret key, i.e. $\mathbf{s} = \mathbf{s}'$ with probability $1 - \delta$.*

Proof. The proof can be found in Sect. A.6. □

3.3 Combining the Results

Combining the results of Sects. 3.1 and 3.2 we obtain the following theorem:

Theorem 3.4. *For $\delta \in [0,1]$, $p \in (0,1)$, the Learning Parity with Noise algorithm presented in Fig. 2, learns parity with k out of n variables with the total number of samples and total computation time of*

$$\mathsf{poly}\left(\frac{1}{(1 - 2\eta)^{\sqrt{np}} \cdot p^{2(k-1)}(1-p)^2} \cdot \ln(\frac{n}{\delta}) \cdot 2^{\frac{np}{\log(np)}} \cdot \log(np)\right),$$

and achieves success probability of $1 - \delta - \left(\frac{16}{(1-2\eta)^{\sqrt{8np}} \cdot p^{2(k-1)}(1-p)^2} \cdot \ln(\frac{2n}{\delta}) \cdot \exp(\frac{-pn}{8})\right)$.

Proof. Using Lemma 3.3, we have that the number of p-biased samples required is $\mathsf{num} = \frac{8}{(1-2\eta')^2 \cdot p^{2(k-1)} \cdot (1-p)^2} \cdot \ln(2n/\delta)$ and using Lemma 3.1 we have that $\eta' = \frac{1}{2} - \frac{1}{2}(1 - 2\eta)^{\sqrt{2np}}$. From Theorem 3.2 we have that with probability $1 - 2\exp(-p \cdot n/8)$ each p-biased sample can be obtained by an invocation of the BKW$_R$ algorithm, which requires $O(2^{\frac{4np}{\log(2np)}} \cdot \log(2np))$ samples and $O(2^{\frac{4np}{\log(2np)}} \cdot \log(2np))$ runtime with probability $1 - 2\exp(-p \cdot n/8)$. Combining and taking a union bound, we have that the algorithm in Fig. 2 requires at most num ·

$O\left(2^{\frac{4np}{\log(2np)}} \cdot \log(2np)\right)$ samples and run time and succeeds with probability $1 - \delta - (2 \cdot \mathsf{num} \cdot \exp(-p \cdot n/8))$. $\qquad\square$

3.4 Parameter Settings

We consider the parameter setting for which our algorithm asymptotically outperforms the previous algorithms *in the exponent*. We consider two cases.

- The algorithm has to run faster than a brute force algorithm which tries all the $\binom{n}{k}$ combination to find the sparse secret. Note that the best algorithms for k-sparse LPN achieve only a constant factor improvement *in the exponent* beyond brute force search. Since we are concerned with asymptotic improvement in the exponent, these algorithms are equivalent to brute force search.
- The algorithm should run faster than the BKW algorithm for the length-n LPN problem, as BKW is the asymptotically best algorithm for length-n LPN.

Corollary 3.5. *For the sparsity $k = k(n) = \frac{n}{\log^{1+1/c}(n)}$, where $c \in o(\log\log(n))$ and $c \in \omega(1)$, the runtime of our learning algorithm in Fig. 2 is contained in both $\log(n)^{o(k)}$ and $2^{o(n/\log(n))}$, with constant failure probability. For this range of k, Brute Force search requires runtime $\log(n)^{\Omega(k)}$ and BKW requires runtime of $2^{\Omega(n/\log(n))}$.*

Proof. Setting $1/p = \log^{1/(c)}(n)$ and $k = \frac{n}{\log^{(c+1)/c}(n)}$ in Theorem 3.4, we find that our LPN Algorithm for constant noise rate presented in Fig. 2 succeeds with constant probability and has runtime

$$\left(\frac{1}{p}\right)^{2k} \cdot 2^{\frac{4np}{\log(2np)}} = \log(n)^{(1/c) \cdot \frac{n}{\log^{(c+1)/c}(n)}} \cdot 2^{\frac{4n/\log^{1/(c)}(n)}{\log(2n/\log^{1/(c)}(n))}} \in \log(n)^{O((1/c) \cdot k)}.$$

Note that if $c \in \omega(1)$, then our runtime is in $\log(n)^{o(k)}$. On the other hand, if $c \in o(\log\log(n))$ then our runtime

$$\log(n)^{O((1/c) \cdot k)} = 2^{O((\log\log(n)/c) \cdot k)} \in 2^{o(k)} \in 2^{o(n/\log(n))}.$$

and so asymptotically beats the above two algorithms *in the exponent* for any $c = c(n)$ that satisfies $c \in \omega(1)$ and $c \in o(\log\log(n))$. Plugging the above parameter into Theorem 3.4 yields probability of success of $1 - \delta - \mathsf{negl}(n) = 1 - \delta$. $\qquad\square$

4 Low Noise Setting

In this section we present an improved learning algorithm for the low noise setting. The algorithm will draw only a *polynomial number of samples* from the given LPN oracle, use them to construct a much larger set of p-biased samples that are not independent, but have certain desirable properties, and then present a learning algorithm that succeeds w.r.t. a set of p-biased samples satisfying these properties.

4.1   Sample Partition

In this section we present the SamP algorithm which draws a polynomial-sized set of samples from the original LPN oracle $\mathcal{O}_{\theta,\eta}^{\mathsf{LPN}}(\mathbf{s})$, and uses them to construct a far larger set of p-biased samples that are "close" to being pairwise independent. To achieve this, SamP constructs a large number of subsets of size $2np + 1$ from the polynomial-sized set of samples, such that each pair of distinct subsets has at most $t \ll 2np + 1$ number of samples in common Then, from each subset of size $2np + 1$, we construct a single p-biased sample $\mathbf{s}^p = (\mathbf{x}', b')$ as follows: First, a random subset $R \subseteq [n]$ of coordinates is chosen, by placing each index $i \in [n]$ in R with independent probability p. Note that with overwhelming probability, $|R| \leq 2np$. Thus, given our set of $2np + 1 \geq |R| + 1$ samples, we construct a matrix $\mathbf{M}$ that contains the samples as rows and we compute the left kernel of the matrix to find a vector $\mathbf{u}$ to zero out the coordinates of R – i.e. $(\mathbf{u} \cdot \mathbf{M})|_R = 0^{|R|}$ and the returned sample is $(\mathbf{x}', b') := \mathbf{u} \cdot \mathbf{M}$. This procedure is denoted by RLK (see Definition A.11 for more details). Note that the procedure always succeeds when the size of R is at most $2np + 1$.[3]

We show that the samples resulting from distinct subsets are "close" to independent, due to the small intersection of any pair of subsets. We next provide some additional details on the construction and guarantees on independence, before formally describing the algorithm and its properties.

Constructing the subsets with small pairwise intersection. Our algorithm given in Fig. 3 constructs the subsets using the *designs* of Nisan and Wigderson [25]: It first draws $(2np + 1)^2$ samples from the original LPN distribution and associates each sample with an ordered pair (x, y) for $x, y \in \mathbb{F}$, for the field $\mathbb{F}$ of size $2np+1$. There are $(2np+1)^t$ polynomials of degree $t-1$ in $\mathbb{F}$, and each subset is associated with a particular polynomial, i.e. the samples contained in a particular subset correspond to the $2np+1$ points that lie on the associated polynomial. Note that the maximum number of subsets that can be constructed is $(2np + 1)^t$ and that, furthermore, since any pair of distinct polynomials of degree $t - 1$ in $\mathbb{F}$ intersect in at most t points, any two subsets have at most t samples in common. Note that this construction allows at most $\mathsf{maxnum} := (2np + 1)^t$ number of p-biased samples to be generated. Looking ahead, in Sect. 4.2 we will present a learning algorithm that requires $O(\log(n))$ such independent sets of samples, each of size at most maxnum to learn the parity function.

---

[3] If the size of R is larger than this, a bad event Event1 occurs, and we must draw new independent samples from the oracle. We will later show that Event1 occurs with negligible probability.

Generating the p-biased samples

Obtain $(2np + 1)^2$ independent samples $\mathcal{S} = \{s_1, \ldots, s_{(2np+1)^2}\}$ from the unbiased LPN oracle $\mathcal{O}_{0,\eta}^{\mathsf{LPN}}(\mathbf{s})$. Run the following setup phase to create sets $\mathcal{O}_1, \mathcal{O}_2, \ldots, \mathcal{O}_{\mathsf{maxnum}}$ each of size $2np + 1$ such that for distinct i, j, $|\mathcal{O}_i \cap \mathcal{O}_j| \leq t$.

Setup Phase :

1. Consider a Finite Field $\mathbb{F}$ of size $2np+1$. Define a bijection π from $[(2np+1)^2]$ to pairs $(x, y) \in \mathbb{F} \times \mathbb{F}$.
2. Consider all polynomials of degree $t-1$ in the ring $\mathbb{F}[x]$. There are $\mathsf{maxnum} := (2np+1)^t$ such distinct polynomials $\mathsf{poly}_1, \ldots, \mathsf{poly}_{\mathsf{maxnum}}$.
3. For $j \in [\mathsf{maxnum}]$, $\mathcal{O}_j$ contains s_i if and only if $\pi(i) = (x, y)$ and $\mathsf{poly}_j(x) = y$.

Algorithm 2: SamP(j)

Result: p-biased sample $(\mathbf{x}', b')$.

To respond to the j-th query, **if** $j > \mathsf{maxnum}$ **then**
   | return $\perp$ and terminate.
end

Otherwise, sample a set R_j such that each $i \in [n]$ is selected independently into R_j with probability p;

if $|R_j| \geq 2np \vee |R_j| \leq pn/2$ **then**
   | Event1 occurs.;
   | Sample a fresh set of $|R_j| + 1$ samples from the LPN oracle and arrange them in rows of matrix $\mathbf{A}$ of size $(|R_j| + 1 \times n)$.;
   | Compute $(\mathbf{x}', \mathbf{u}) := \mathsf{RLK}(\mathbf{A}, R_j)$ such that $\mathbf{x}'|_{R_j} = 0^{|R_j|}$;   ▷ RLK is defined in Section A.3
   | Go To **L1**;
end

Select set $\mathcal{O}_j$ and arrange them in rows of matrix $\mathbf{A}$ of size $(2np + 1 \times n)$;

Compute $(\mathbf{x}', \mathbf{u}) := \mathsf{RLK}(\mathbf{A}, R_j)$ such that $\mathbf{x}'|_{R_j} = 0^{|R_j|}$;   ▷ RLK is defined in Section A.3

if $\mathbf{x}'|_{R_i} = 0^{|R_i|}$ *for some* $i \in [j-1]$ **then**
   | Event2 occurs;
   | Sample a fresh set of $2np + 1$ samples from the LPN oracle and arrange them in rows of matrix $\mathbf{A}$ of size $(2np + 1 \times n)$;
   | Compute $(\mathbf{x}', \mathbf{u}) := \mathsf{RLK}(\mathbf{A}, R_j)$ such that $\mathbf{x}'|_{R_j} = 0^{|R_j|}$;
end

L1 : $k := 1$;

$(\mathbf{x}', b') := \mathbf{u} \cdot \mathbf{A}$;

while $k < 2np + 1 - \mathsf{weight}(\mathbf{u})$ **do**
                        ▷ weight is defined in Section A.3
   | $b' := b' + \tilde{\mathcal{O}}_\eta$
end

return $(\mathbf{x}', b')$;

Fig. 3. SamP "Zeroing" algorithm

Near pairwise independence. We note that by construction, the Sample Partition Algorithm SamP presented in Fig. 3 constructs sets of size $(2np + 1)$ such the intersection of any two sets is at most t for $t \leq (np + 1)$. This will allow us to bound the covariance of the errors e'_i and e'_j obtained by taking linear combinations of elements in the sets $\mathcal{O}_i, \mathcal{O}_j$. Overall, the set of samples generated by SamP algorithm have certain properties enumerated in the following Lemma.

Lemma 4.1. *Consider an experiment in which the setup phase is run and two samples* $\mathsf{s}_i^p = (\mathbf{x}'_i, b'_i)$ *and* $\mathsf{s}_j^p = (\mathbf{x}'_j, b'_j)$ *are generated by running* SamP(i) *and* SamP(j) *for distinct* $i, j \leq$ maxnum *then the following hold:*

1. *Each individual sample* $(\mathbf{x}'_i, b'_i)$ *(resp.* $(\mathbf{x}'_j, b'_j)$*) outputted is distributed identically to a sample drawn from a p-biased LPN Oracle* $\mathcal{O}_{p,\eta'}^{\mathsf{LPN}}(\mathsf{s})$ *for* $\eta' = \frac{1}{2} - \frac{1}{2}(1 - 2\eta)^{2np+1}$.
2. $\mathbf{x}'_i$ *and* $\mathbf{x}'_j$ *are pairwise independent*
3. *Recall that* $b'_i = f_\mathsf{s}(\mathbf{x}'_i) + e'_i$ *and* $b'_j = f_\mathsf{s}(\mathbf{x}'_j) + e'_j$. *Then*

$$\mathrm{Cov}\left[e'_i, e'_j\right] \leq (1 - 2\eta)^{2(2np-t)+2} - (1 - 2\eta)^{4np+2}.$$

Proof. The proof can be found in Sect. A.7.   □

Finally, we analyze the runtime and sample complexity for each invocation of SamP.

Theorem 4.2. *Given access to LPN Oracle* $\mathcal{O}_{0,\eta}^{\mathsf{LPN}}(\mathsf{s})$ *which gives samples* $\mathsf{s} = (\mathbf{x}, b)$, *the* SamP *algorithm requires* $O\left((np)^2\right)$ *samples in total, and* poly(np) *runtime per invocation with probability at least* $1 - 2\exp(-p \cdot n/8) - (np)^t \cdot \exp(-n/48) - (np)^t \cdot 1/2^{np/4}$.

Proof. The proof can be found in Sect. A.8.   □

4.2   Learning Secret Coordinates

In this subsection we present our Learning Algorithm in Fig. 4. The input to the algorithm is $8\log(n)$ independently generated sets of p-biased samples with the properties given in Lemma 4.1. The algorithm uses the p-biased samples to estimate the values of the Fourier Coefficients of the target function.

Lemma 4.3. *For* $\delta \in [0, 1]$, $p \in (0, 1)$, *given as input* $8\log(n)$ *independent sets of samples* $\mathcal{S}_1, \mathcal{S}_2, \ldots, \mathcal{S}_{8\log(n)}$ *each of size* num $:= O\left(\frac{1}{(1-2\eta)^{2np+2}p^{2(k-1)}(1-p^2)}\right)$ *and each satisfying the properties given in Lemma 4.1 for some* $t \in \Theta(1/\eta)$, *the Learning Algorithm presented in Fig. 4 runs in time* poly$\left(\frac{1}{(1-2\eta)^{2np+2}p^{2(k-1)}(1-p^2)}\right)$ *and outputs the correct secret key, i.e.* $\mathsf{s} = \mathsf{s}'$ *with probability* $1 - \delta$.

Proof. The proof can be found in Sect. A.9.   □

The Learning Algorithm

The learning algorithm starts by having access to $8 \log(n)$ sets $\mathcal{S}_1, \mathcal{S}_2, \ldots, \mathcal{S}_{8 \log(n)}$ of randomly generated samples. Each set of samples is independent and satisfies the properties given in Lemma 4.1.

1. Initilizate set $\mathcal{S}' := \emptyset$.
2. For $j \in [n]$
    - count $:= 0$
    - $T := 8 \log(n)$
    - For $i' \in T$:
        (a) Use the set $\mathcal{S}_{i'}$ of num number of samples to approximate $\hat{b}_p(\{j\}) := \frac{1}{\text{num}} \sum_{i=1}^{\text{num}} b_i \cdot \chi_{\{j\},p}(\mathbf{x}_i)$, where each coordinate of $\mathbf{x}_i, b_i$ is switched to $\{-1, 1\}$ from $\mathbb{F}_2$.
        (b) If $\hat{b}_p(\{j\}) > (1 - 2\eta')p^{k-1}\sqrt{1 - p^2}/2$, count $:=$ count $+ 1$
    - if count $\geq T/2$
        • add j to $\mathcal{S}'$
3. Output $\mathbf{s}'$ such that $\mathbf{s}'[j] = 1$ for $j \in [n]$, if $j \in \mathcal{S}'$.

Fig. 4. Low-noise LPN algorithm

4.3 Combining the Results

Combining the results of Sects. 4.1 and 4.2 we obtain the following theorem:

Theorem 4.4. *Assuming parameters are set such that*

$$\log\left(\frac{1}{(1 - 2\eta)^{2np+2}p^{2(k-1)}(1 - p^2)}\right) \in o(1/\eta \cdot \log(np)), \qquad (4.1)$$

and with $\delta \in [0,1]$, $p \in (0,1)$, the Learning Parity from Noise Algorithm presented in Fig. 4, learns parity with k out of n variables and noise rate η using $(2np + 1)^2 \cdot \log(n)$ number of samples, total computation time of $N :=$ poly $\left(\frac{1}{(1-2\eta)^{2np+2}p^{2(k-1)}(1-p^2)}\right)$ *and achieves success probability of*

$$1 - \delta - \left(N \cdot \left(2 \cdot \exp(-p \cdot n/8) + \exp(-n/48) + 1/2^{np/4}\right)\right)$$

Proof. Using Lemma 4.3, we have that, for some $t \in \Theta(1/\eta)$, the number of p-biased samples with the following properties needed to succeed with probability $1 - \delta$ is poly $\left(\frac{1}{(1-2\eta)^{2np+2}p^{2(k-1)}(1-p^2)}\right)$. From Theorem 4.2, we have that as long as num = poly $\left(\frac{1}{(1-2\eta)^{2np+2}p^{2(k-1)}(1-p^2)}\right) \leq$ maxnum $= (2np + 1)^t$ we can generate the required samples using $(2np + 1)^2$ samples from the unbiased LPN oracle $\mathcal{O}_{\theta,\eta}^{\text{LPN}}(\mathbf{s})$, and with poly$(np)$ runtime per sample, with probability at least $1 - 2(np)^t \cdot \exp(-p \cdot n/8) - (np)^t \cdot \exp(-n/48) - (np)^t \cdot 1/2^{np/4}$. The fact that num and maxnum satisfy the above constraint is guaranteed by the assumption in the theorem on the setting of parameters and the fact that $t \in \Theta(1/\eta)$. Combining and taking a union bound, we have that the algorithm in Fig. 2 requires $(2np + 1)^2 \cdot 8 \log(n)$ samples, has run time $\text{poly}\left(\frac{1}{(1-2\eta)^{2np+2}p^{2(k-1)}(1-p^2)} \cdot \log(n)\right)$, and succeeds with probability $1 - \delta - \left(N \cdot \left(2 \cdot \exp(-p \cdot n/8) + \exp(-n/48) + 1/2^{np/4}\right)\right)$. $\qquad\square$

4.4   Parameter Settings

We consider the parameter setting for which our algorithm's runtime asymptotically outperforms the previous algorithms' runtime *in the exponent*. We consider two cases.

- The algorithm has to run faster than a brute force algorithm which tries all the $\binom{n}{k}$ combinations to find the sparse secret. Note that there are known algorithms that improve upon brute force search, but the improvement is a *constant factor in the exponent*. Since we are concerned with asymptotic improvement in the exponent, these algorithms are equivalent to brute force search.
- The algorithm should run faster than the algorithm which just gets lucky and gets n noiseless samples, we call this algorithm "Lucky Bruteforce". For this algorithm to succeed, it needs $\frac{n}{1-\eta}$ samples from LPN Oracle to ensures that there are approximately n noiseless samples. The next step is to just randomly select n out of these $\frac{n}{1-\eta}$ samples and try Gaussian elimination on them. The run time of such an algorithm for small η can be approximate by $e^{\eta n}$.

Corollary 4.5. *For sparsity $k(n)$ such that $k = \frac{1}{\eta} \cdot \frac{\log(n)}{\log(f(n))}$, noise rate $\eta \neq 1/2$ such that $\eta^2 = \left(\frac{\log(n)}{n} \cdot f(n)\right)$ for $f(n) \in \omega(1) \cap n^{o(1)}$, the Learning Algorithm of Fig. 4 runs in time $O\left(\frac{1}{(1-2\eta)^{2np+2}p^{2k}} \cdot \log(n) \cdot (np)^3\right) \in \left(\frac{n}{k}\right)^{o(k)}$ with constant probability. In this setting, the running time Brute Force is $\binom{n}{k} \geq \left(\frac{n}{k}\right)^k$ and the running time of Lucky Bruteforce is $e^{\eta n} \in \left(\frac{n}{k}\right)^{\omega(k)}$.*

Proof. For k, η defined as above, we choose the biased $p = \frac{1}{f(n)}$ and $\frac{1}{p} \in \left(\frac{n}{k}\right)^{o(1)}$, we have constraint (4.1) from Theorem 4.4 satisfied as follows:

$$\log\left(\frac{1}{(1-2\eta)^{2np+2}p^{2(k-1)}(1-p^2)}\right) \approx 4np\eta + 2k\log\left(\frac{1}{p}\right)$$
$$\in o(1/\eta \cdot \log(n)) \in o(1/\eta \cdot \log(np)),$$

the runtime of the Learning Algorithm of Fig. 4 is bounded by

$$\frac{1}{(1-2\eta)^{2np}p^{2k}} \cdot \log(n) \cdot O\left((np)^3\right) \approx e^{4np\eta} \cdot \left(\frac{1}{p}\right)^{2k} \cdot \log(n) \cdot O\left((np)^3\right)$$
$$\in e^{o(k)\cdot\log(n/k)} \cdot \left(\frac{n}{k}\right)^{o(k)} \cdot \log(n) \cdot o(n^3)$$
$$\in \left(\frac{n}{k}\right)^{o(k)},$$

which outperforms Brute Force and Lucky Bruteforce under the same parameter settings. Plugging the above parameters into Theorem 4.4 yields probability of success of $1 - \delta - \text{negl}(n)$.
□

5 Learning Other Classes of Functions

In the following we apply our LPN algorithms from Sect. 3 to learn other classes of functions. First, let us look at the reduction from learning DNFs to learning noisy parities.

Theorem 5.1 (Theorem 2 in [12]). *Let $\mathcal{A}$ be an algorithm that learns noisy parities of k variables on $\{0,1\}^n$ for every noise rate $\eta < 1/2$ in time $T(n,k,\frac{1}{1-2\eta})$ and using at most $S(n,k,\frac{1}{1-2\eta})$. Then there exists an algorithm that learns DNF expressions of size s in time $\tilde{O}\big(\frac{s^4}{\epsilon^2} \cdot T(n,\log B, B) \cdot S(n,\log B, B)^2\big)$, where $B = \tilde{O}(s/\epsilon)$.*

We are interested in determining the parameter range for which our algorithm yields an asymptotic improvement over the state of the art in the *exponent*. The work of Grigorescu [14] is the current state-of-the-art. They present an improvement of the bound from [28] of $2^{O(\log(n)\log \frac{s}{\epsilon})}$ for $\frac{s}{\epsilon} \in o\left(\frac{\log^{1/3} n}{\log\log n}\right)$. As we are similarly applying the reductions from Feldman, our algorithm yields a similar improvement on the bounds in [28] for a different range of $\frac{s}{\epsilon}$.

Note the reduction in Feldman [12] relates the ratio of the size of the DNF and its approximation factor to both the noise rate and sparsity of the parity function. Thus, the parameter range for which our algorithm is optimal will be expressed in terms of this ratio.

We begin by extending the runtime analysis of our algorithm from Sect. 3, which dealt with the constant noise setting, to the arbitrary noise $\eta < 1/2$.

Theorem 5.2. *The learning algorithm described in Fig. 2 has a runtime of*

$$T\left(n,k,\frac{1}{1-2\eta}\right) = \left(\frac{1}{1-2\eta}\right)^{2^{a+1}} \frac{8\ln(2n/\delta)}{p^{2(k-1)}(1-p)^2} O\left(\mathfrak{a}2^{\mathfrak{b}}\right)$$

and requires

$$S\left(n,k,\frac{1}{1-2\eta}\right) = \left(\frac{1}{1-2\eta}\right)^{2^{a+1}} \frac{8\ln(2n/\delta)}{p^{2(k-1)}(1-p)^2} O\left(\mathfrak{a}2^{\mathfrak{b}}\right)$$

LPN samples in the high noise setting, and achieves a success probability of

$$1 - \delta - \left(\frac{1}{1-2\eta}\right)^{2^{a+1}} \frac{16\ln(2n/\delta)}{p^{2(k-1)}(1-p)^2} e^{\frac{-np}{8}}$$

where $\mathfrak{a}\mathfrak{b} = np$.

Proof. The proof follows directly from Theorem 3.4. Instead of fixing a value for $\mathfrak{a}$ and $\mathfrak{b}$, we let them remain free parameters. As well, we no longer make assumptions on the noise rate η. Thus, we start with the runtime in terms of η'.

$$T(n,k,\eta') = \frac{8\ln(2n/\delta)}{(1-2\eta')^2 p^{2(k-1)}(1-p)^2} O\left(\mathfrak{a}2^{\mathfrak{b}}\right)$$

$$T(n,k,\eta) = \frac{8\ln(2n/\delta)}{(1-2\eta)^{2^{\mathfrak{a}+1}} p^{2(k-1)}(1-p)^2} O\left(\mathfrak{a}2^{\mathfrak{b}}\right)$$

$$T\left(n,k,\frac{1}{1-2\eta}\right) = \left(\frac{1}{1-2\eta}\right)^{2^{\mathfrak{a}+1}} \frac{8\ln(2n/\delta)}{p^{2(k-1)}(1-p)^2} O\left(\mathfrak{a}2^{\mathfrak{b}}\right)$$

The sample complexity of the algorithm is equal to its runtime complexity, and thus we need to just need to consider the success probability. In the high noise setting, the p-biased LPN oracle is called $\mathsf{num} = \left(\frac{1}{1-2\eta}\right)^{2^{\mathfrak{a}+1}} \frac{8\ln(2n/\delta)}{p^{2(k-1)}(1-p)^2}$ times, and the success probability calculation follows the same formula from Theorem 3.4. $\qquad\square$

As we are concerned with asymptotic improvement in the *exponent* of the runtime we will take the logarithm of the runtime and compare it to the state of the art for learning DNFs and Juntas.

Corollary 5.3. *The learning algorithm described in Fig. 2 learns DNFs of size s and approximation factor ϵ, with asymptotic improvements over Verbeurgt's bound [28] of $O\left(n^{\log\frac{s}{\epsilon}}\right)$, and with negligible failure probability when $\log\frac{s}{\epsilon} \in \omega\left(\frac{c}{\log n \log\log c}\right)$, and $\log\frac{s}{\epsilon} \in n^{1-o(1)}$, where $c \in n^{1-o(1)}$.*

Note here that the parameter regime in 5.3 requires setting the free parameters of the learning algorithm differently than in the constant noise setting. In order to minimize the runtime of the $\mathsf{BKW_R}$ step of the algorithm in the high noise setting, the value for $\mathfrak{a}$ must be changed from the description in Sect. 3. Thus we set $\mathfrak{a} = (1/2)\log\log(np)$. This change necessitates considerations for δ, the Fourier analysis confidence. This ensures that the failure probability of the full algorithm remains small, even after increasing the number of samples required. We set $\delta = 2^{-n}$. The free parameter p is set to $n^{-o(1)}$ to satisfy asymptotic requirements. These parameters are set similarly for Corollary 5.5.

Aside from DNFs we can also use our LPN algorithm to learn Juntas. By applying Feldman's reduction we are able to yield an algorithm that, for certain ranges for k, is able to improve on the $O(n^{0.7k})$ runtime cited in [27] asymptotically, not just by reducing the constant factor in the exponent.

Theorem 5.4. (Theorem 3 in [12]). *Let $\mathcal{A}$ be an algorithm that learns parities of k variables on $\{0,1\}^n$ for every noise rate $\eta < 1/2$ in time $T(n,k,\frac{1}{1-2\eta})$. Then there exists an algorithm that learns k-juntas in time $O\left(2^{2k}k \cdot T(n,k,2^{k-1})\right)$.*

Corollary 5.5. *The learning algorithm described in Fig. 2 learns Juntas of size k with a runtime of $n^{o(k)}$ and a negligible failure probability when $k \in \omega\left(\frac{c}{\log n \log \log c}\right)$, and $k \in n^{1-o(1)}$, where $c \in n^{1-o(1)}$.*

Acknowledgments. The authors would like to thank the anonymous reviewers of TCC 2021 for their insightful comments.

A   Appendix

A.1   Probability Bounds

The following inequality is used to bound the magnitude of an observed random variable with respect to the true expected value of that random variable. The Chernoff-Hoeffding bound extends the Chernoff bound to random variables with a bounded range. Another important fact is that Chernoff-Hoeffding bound assumes the random variables are independent whereas Chebyshev's bound applies to arbitrary random variables. The reader in encouraged to refer to [23] for more in depth reading.

Theorem A.1 (Multiplicative Chernoff Bounds). *Let $X_1, X_2, \ldots, X_n$ be n mutually independent random variables. Let $X = \sum_{i=1}^{n} X_i$ and $\mu = \mathbb{E}[X]$,*

$$\Pr[X \leq (1 - \beta)\mu] \leq \exp\left(\frac{-\beta^2 \mu}{2}\right) \text{ for all } 0 < \beta \leq 1$$

$$\Pr[X \geq (1 + \beta)\mu] \leq \exp\left(\frac{-\beta^2 \mu}{3}\right) \text{ for all } 0 < \beta \leq 1$$

Theorem A.2 (Chernoff-Hoeffding). *Consider a set of n independent random variables $X_1, X_2, \ldots, X_n$. If we know $a_i \leq X_i \leq b_i$, then let $\Delta_i = b_i - a_i$. Let $X = \sum_{i=1}^{n} X_i$. Then for any $\alpha \in (0, 1/2)$*

$$\Pr\left(\left|X - \mathbb{E}[X]\right| > \alpha\right) \leq 2\exp\left(\frac{-2\alpha^2}{\sum_{i=1}^{n} \Delta_i^2}\right).$$

Theorem A.3 (Chebyshev's). *Consider a set of n arbitrary random variable $X_1, X_2, \ldots, X_n$. Let $X = \sum_{i=1}^{n} X_i$. Then for any $\alpha > 0$,*

$$\Pr\left(\left|X - \mathbb{E}[X]\right| \geq \alpha\right) \leq \frac{\text{Var}[X]}{\alpha^2}.$$

The following lemma is being used to further simplify the Var[X] in Theorem A.3.

Lemma A.4. *Let $X_1, X_2, \ldots, X_n$ be n arbitrary random variables. Then*

$$\text{Var}\left[\sum_{i=1}^{n} X_i\right] = \sum_{i=1}^{n} \text{Var}[X_i] + 2\sum_{i=1}^{n}\sum_{j>i} \text{Cov}[X_i, X_j].$$

A.2   Learning Parities

In this subsection, we define three Oracles . The first is the *standard* LPN Oracle, that samples **x** uniformly. The second is the noise Oracle, which sets **x** to the zero vector. The purpose of this Oracle is to return additional noise sampled identically to the noise found in a normal LPN sample. The third Oracle is the p-biased LPN Oracle, which samples **x** according to a p-biased Bernoulli distribution.

Definition A.5 (Bernoulli Distribution). *Let $p \in [0,1]$. The discrete probability distribution of a random variable which takes the value 1 with probability η and the value 0 with probability $1 - \eta$ is called Bernoulli Distribution and it is denoted by Ber_η.*

Definition A.6 (LPN Oracle). *Let secret value $\mathbf{s} \leftarrow \mathbb{Z}_2^n$ and let $\eta < 1/2$ be a constant noise parameter. Let Ber_η be a Bernoulli distribution with parameter η. Define the following distribution $\mathcal{L}_{\mathbf{s},\eta}^{(1)}$ as follows*

$$\left\{ (\mathbf{x},b) \mid \mathbf{x} \leftarrow \mathbb{Z}_2^n, \ f_{\mathbf{s}}(\mathbf{x}) := \langle \mathbf{x}, \mathbf{s} \rangle, \ b = f_{\mathbf{s}}(\mathbf{x}) + e, \ e \leftarrow \mathsf{Ber}_\eta \right\} \in \mathbb{Z}_2^{n+1}$$

with the additions being done module 2. Upon calling the LPN Oracle $\mathcal{O}_{0,\eta}^{\mathsf{LPN}}(\mathbf{s})$, a new sample $\mathbf{s} = (\mathbf{x},b)$ from the distribution $\mathcal{L}_{\mathbf{s},\eta}^{(1)}$ is returned.

Definition A.7 (Noise Oracle). *Let secret value $\mathbf{s} \leftarrow \mathbb{Z}_2^n$ and let $\eta < 1/2$ be a constant noise parameter. Let Ber_η be a Bernoulli distribution with parameter η. Define the following distribution $\mathcal{L}_{\mathbf{s},\eta}^{(2)}$ as follows*

$$\left\{ (\mathbf{x},b) \mid \mathbf{x} := 0^n, \ f_{\mathbf{s}}(\mathbf{x}) := \langle \mathbf{x}, \mathbf{s} \rangle, \ b = f_{\mathbf{s}}(\mathbf{x}) + e, \ e \leftarrow \mathsf{Ber}_\eta \right\} \in \mathbb{Z}_2^{n+1}$$

with the additions being done module 2. Upon calling the Noise Oracle $\tilde{\mathcal{O}}_\eta$ a new sample $\mathbf{s} = (\mathbf{x},b)$ from the distribution $\mathcal{L}_{\mathbf{s},\eta}^{(2)}$ is returned.

Definition A.8 (p-biased LPN Oracle). *Let secret value $\mathbf{s} \leftarrow \mathbb{Z}_2^n$ and let $\eta < 1/2$ be a constant noise parameter. Let Ber_η be a Bernoulli distribution with parameter η and $\mathsf{Ber}_{(1-p)/2}^n$ be Bernoulli distribution with parameter $(1-p)/2$ over n coordinates. Define the following distribution $\mathcal{L}_{\mathbf{s},\eta,p}^{(3)}$ as follows*

$$\left\{ (\mathbf{x},b) \mid \mathbf{x} \leftarrow \mathsf{Ber}_{(1-p)/2}^n, \ f_{\mathbf{s}}(\mathbf{x}) := \langle \mathbf{x}, \mathbf{s} \rangle, \ b = f_{\mathbf{s}}(\mathbf{x}) + e, \ e \leftarrow \mathsf{Ber}_\eta \right\} \in \mathbb{Z}_2^{n+1}$$

with the additions being done modulo 2. Upon calling the p-biased LPN Oracle $\mathcal{O}_{p,\eta}^{\mathsf{LPN}}(\mathbf{s})$ a new sample $\mathbf{s}^p = (\mathbf{x},b)$ from the distribution $\mathcal{L}_{\mathbf{s},\eta,p}^{(3)}$ is returned.

As our algorithms require linear combinations of LPN samples, we present the following lemma that describes the noise growth associated with the linear combination.

Lemma A.9 (New Sample Error [5]). *Given a set of ℓ samples $(\mathbf{x}_1, b_1), \ldots, (\mathbf{x}_\ell, b_\ell)$ from an LPN Oracle $\mathcal{O}_{0,\eta}^{\mathsf{LPN}}(\mathbf{s})$ with secret $\mathbf{s}$, where the choice of samples may depend on the values of $\mathbf{x}_i$ but not on the values of b_i, then the new sample $\mathbf{s}_{\ell+1}$ can be formed as follows $\mathbf{s}_{\ell+1} = \sum_{i=1}^{\ell} \mathbf{s}_i$ which has the property that $b_{\ell+1}$ is independent of $\mathbf{x}_{\ell+1}$ and the probability that the label of the constructed sample is correct is as follows: $(1 - \eta') = \Pr[b' = \langle \mathbf{x}_{\ell+1}, s \rangle] = \frac{1}{2} + \frac{1}{2}(1 - 2\eta)^\ell$.*

For reference we additionally provide the runtime of the original BKW algorithm:

Theorem A.10 (BKW [5]). *The length-n parity problem, for noise rate η for any constant less than $1/2$, can be solved with number of samples and total computation time of $2^{O(n/\log n)}$.*

For sample i, the j-th coordinate of $\mathbf{x}$ is denoted by $\mathbf{s}_i.\mathbf{x}[j]$ and the j-th coordinate of $\mathbf{s}$ is denoted by $\mathbf{s}_i.\mathbf{s}[j]$. For simplicity, given two sample pairs $\mathbf{s}_1 = (\mathbf{x}_1, b_1)$ and $\mathbf{s}_2 = (\mathbf{x}_2, b_2)$ a new sample $\mathbf{s}_3 = \mathbf{s}_1 + \mathbf{s}_2$ can be formed by $\mathbf{s}_3 = (\mathbf{x}_1 + \mathbf{x}_2, b_1 + b_2)$ with the additions being done mod 2.

A.3   Miscellaneous

Definition A.11 (Restricted Left Kernel). *Given a matrix $\mathbf{A} \in \mathbb{Z}_2^{m \times n}$ for $m \leq n$ and set $R \subset [n]$ such that $|R| < m$, RLK first finds a vector $\mathbf{u} \in \mathbb{Z}_2^m$ such that $\mathbf{v} = \mathbf{u} \cdot \mathbf{A}$ and $\mathbf{v}|_R = 0^{|R|}$. The RLK algorithm returns $(\mathbf{v}, \mathbf{u}) := \mathsf{RLK}(\mathbf{A}, R)$.*

Note that the RLK algorithm mentioned above can be implemented by simply modifying matrix $\mathbf{A}$ and only takes the columns pointed by set R, i.e. restriction of $\mathbf{A}$ to only columns pointed by R. Let's denote the new matrix by $\mathbf{A}'$, find a vector in left kernel of $\mathbf{A}'$ and call it $\mathbf{u}$. Then $\mathbf{v}$ can simply be computed as $\mathbf{v} = \mathbf{u} \cdot \mathbf{A}$.

Definition A.12 (Hamming Weight). *Given a vector $\mathbf{u} \in \mathbb{Z}_2^m$, weight$(\mathbf{u})$ returns the number of 1's in vector $\mathbf{u}$, i.e. the Hamming weight of $\mathbf{u}$.*

A.4   Proof of Lemma 3.1

We first show that each coordinate of $\mathbf{x}'$ is set to 0 with independent probability $(1 + p)/2$. The probability that a coordinate j of $\mathbf{x}'$ in sample $\mathbf{s}^p$ is set to 0 after running $\mathsf{BKW_R}$ can be computed as follows:

$$\Pr[\mathbf{x}'[j] = 0] = \Pr[\mathbf{x}'[j] = 0 \mid j \in R] \cdot \Pr[j \in R] + \Pr[\mathbf{x}'[j] = 0 \mid j \notin R] \cdot \Pr[j \notin R]$$
$$= 1 \cdot p + 1/2 \cdot (1 - p) = (1 + p)/2$$

To show that the label b' is correct with probability η' and that the correctness of the label is independent of the instance $\mathbf{x}', \mathbf{s}$, note that $\mathbf{x}'$ is always constructed by XOR'ing a set of exactly 2^a number of samples and that the choice of the set of XOR'ed samples depends only on the random coins of the algorithm and on the $\mathbf{x}$ values, which are independent of the e value. Therefore, we can apply Lemma A.9 to conclude that the noise is independent and that b' is correct with probability $\eta' = \frac{1}{2} - \frac{1}{2}(1 - 2\eta)^{\sqrt{2np}}$.

A.5   Proof of Theorem 3.2

From the description of $\mathsf{BKW_R}$, it is clear to see that it takes $O(\mathfrak{a}2^{\mathfrak{b}})$ LPN samples and running time to generate a p-biased sample, where $\mathfrak{a} = \log(2np)/2, \mathfrak{b} = \lceil |R|/\mathfrak{a} \rceil$. Remember that the $\mathsf{BKW_R}$ algorithm will abort if $|R| \geq 2pn$ or $|R| \leq pn/2$, i.e. $\mathsf{Event1}$ occurs. By showing that $\mathsf{Event1}$ occurs with probability at most $2\exp(-p \cdot n/8)$, we obtain that $\mathsf{BKW_R}$ runs in time $O(2^{\frac{4np}{\log(2np)}} \cdot \log(2np))$ with probability at least $1 - 2\exp(-p \cdot n/8)$.

To bound the probability of $\mathsf{Event1}$ occurring, we notice that by multiplicative Chernoff bounds in Theorem A.1, we can bound the size of set R as follows:

$$\Pr[|R| \geq 2pn] \leq \exp(-p \cdot n/3)$$
$$\Pr[|R| \leq pn/2] \leq \exp(-p \cdot n/8)$$
$$\Pr[|R| \geq 2pn \vee |R| \leq pn/2] \leq \exp(-p \cdot n/3) + \exp(-p \cdot n/8) \leq 2\exp(-p \cdot n/8)$$
$$\Pr[pn/2 < |R| < 2pn] > 1 - 2\exp(-p \cdot n/8)$$

A.6   Proof of Lemma 3.3

Before proving Lemma 3.3, we present the following simple claims about the number of samples needed to estimate the Fourier Coefficient of a single index. Based on Claim 2.2, the magnitude of Fourier coefficient of the indexes with secret value of 0 is equal to 0, while for the secret coordinates 1 that is equal to $\varepsilon = (1 - 2\eta') \cdot p^{k-1}\sqrt{1 - p^2}$. In the Following Claim we compute how many samples are needed to estimate the magnitude of Fourier coefficient within distance of $\varepsilon/2$ of correct value. We will bound the failure probability with δ/n.

Claim A.13. For every $j \in [n]$, $\hat{b}_p(\{j\}) = \mathbb{E}[b \cdot \chi_{\{j\},p}(\mathbf{x})]$, where $(\mathbf{x}, b) \sim O^{\mathsf{LPN}}_{p,\eta'}(\mathbf{s})$, can be estimated within additive accuracy $\frac{\varepsilon}{2}$ and confidence $1 - \frac{\delta}{n}$ using $\frac{8}{\varepsilon^2} \cdot \frac{1+p}{1-p} \cdot \ln(2n/\delta)$ number of samples.

Proof. The estimate of $\hat{b}_p(\{j\})$ based on the m samples $\mathbf{s}_i^p = (\mathbf{x}_i, b_i)$ is.

$$\hat{b}_{\mathrm{estimate}}(\{j\}) = \frac{1}{m} \sum_{i=1}^{m} b_i \cdot \chi_{\{j\},p}(\mathbf{x}_i)$$

and notice that $\mathbb{E}\left[\hat{b}_{\mathrm{estimate}}(\{j\})\right] = \hat{b}_p(\{j\})$. Lets denote $X_i = \frac{1}{m} \cdot b_i \cdot \chi_{\{j\},p}(\mathbf{x}_i)$, then note that $|X_i| \leq (1/m)\sqrt{\frac{1+p}{1-p}}$. Finally by Chernoff-Hoeffding bound of Theorem A.2 we have the following.

$$\Pr\left[\left|\hat{b}_{\mathrm{estimate}}(\{j\}) - \hat{b}_p(\{j\})\right| \geq \varepsilon/2\right] \leq 2\exp\left(\frac{-m\varepsilon^2}{8} \cdot \frac{1-p}{1+p}\right)$$

Bounding the right hand side by δ/n and solving for m gives the desired value for number of samples.

Proof (Proof of Lemma 3.3). Invoking Claim 2.2, we have that for j such that $\mathsf{s}[j] = 1$ $\hat{b}_p(\{j\}) = (1 - 2\eta') \cdot p^{k-1}\sqrt{1 - p^2}$ while for j such that $\mathsf{s}[j] = 0$, $\hat{b}_p(\{j\}) = 0$. It is clear by inspection that Algorithm 2 succeeds when it correctly estimates the values of $\hat{b}_p(\{j\})$ to within additive $\varepsilon/2 := (1 - 2\eta') \cdot p^{k-1}\sqrt{1 - p^2}/2$ for all $j \in [n]$. By Claim A.13, $\frac{8}{\varepsilon^2} \cdot \frac{1+p}{1-p} \cdot \ln(2n/\delta)$ number of samples are sufficient to estimate a single coordinate within additive $\varepsilon/2$ of its correct value with confidence $1 - \frac{\delta}{n}$. By a union bound, the success probability of estimating all coordinates to within additive $\varepsilon/2$ is $1 - \delta$.   □

A.7   Proof of Lemma 4.1

The proof is similar to the proof of Lemma 3.1 and noticing that the SamP algorithm uses $2np + 1$ samples to generate a single p-biased sample. Two p-biased samples $\mathbf{x}'_i, \mathbf{x}'_j$, $j > i$ are pairwise independent, unless the same linear combination of samples in $\mathcal{S}$ was used to generate both of them. But in that case, during execution, the condition $\mathbf{x}'_j|_{R_i} = 0^{|R_i|}$ would evaluate to true, which means that Event2 occurred and so fresh samples (not from $\mathcal{S}$) would be used to generate $\mathbf{x}'_j$.

In the rest of the proof we switch to the ± 1 representation instead of the Boolean representation. The sample $\mathsf{s}^p_i = (\mathbf{x}'_i, b'_i)$ is obtained from the samples in set $\mathcal{O}_i$ alongside some extra error samples from Noise Oracle $\tilde{\mathcal{O}}_\eta$. In the following proof these are denoted by $e_1, e_2, \ldots, e_{2np+1}$. Moreover, notice that the sample $\mathsf{s}^p_j = (\mathbf{x}'_j, b'_j)$, obtained from set $\mathcal{O}_j$, has at most t elements in common with the sample obtained from the set $\mathcal{O}_i$. Hence we can represent the error in sample $\mathsf{s}^p_j = (\mathbf{x}'_j, b'_j)$ as $e_1, e_2, \ldots, e_t, e''_{t+1} \ldots e''_{2np+1}$. For the ease of notation we assumed that the t samples which are in common are at index 1 to t.

$$\begin{aligned} \mathrm{Cov}[e'_i, e'_j] &= \mathrm{Cov}[e_1 \cdot e_2 \ldots e_t \cdot e_{t+1} \ldots e_{2np+1} \ , \ e_1 \cdot e_2 \ldots e_t \cdot e''_{t+1} \ldots e''_{2np+1}] \\ &= \mathbb{E}[e_1^2 \cdot e_2^2 \ldots e_t^2 \cdot e_{t+1} \ldots e_{2np+1} \cdot e''_{t+1} \ldots e''_{2np+1}] \\ &\quad - \mathbb{E}[e_1 \cdot e_2 \ldots e_{2np+1}] \, \mathbb{E}[e_1 \cdot e_2 \ldots e_t \ldots e''_{t+1} \ldots e''_{2np+1}] \\ &= (1 - 2\eta)^{2(2np-t)+2} - (1 - 2\eta)^{4np+2} \end{aligned}$$

Where the last line follows from the independence of errors, $\mathbb{E}[e_i] = 1 - 2\eta$ and $\mathbb{E}[e_i^2] = 1$.

A.8   Proof of Theorem 4.2

Assuming Event1 and Event2 do not occur, the sample complexity and runtime can be verified by inspection and assuming RLK takes poly(np) time.

It remains to bound the probability of Event1 and Event2. We can upper bound the probability of Event1 by $2\exp(-p \cdot n/8)$, as in the proof of Theorem 3.2.

To upperbound the probability of Event2, we note that assuming Event1 does not occur, Event2 occurs only if one of the following two events occur:

– Event'1: For some distinct $i, j \in \mathsf{maxnum}$, $|R_i \cap R_j| \geq np/4$.

– Event$'$2: For some distinct $i, j \in$ maxnum, $|R_i \setminus R_j| \geq np/4$ and $\mathbf{x}'_j|_{R_i \setminus R_j} = 0^{|R_i \setminus R_j|}$.

Since for distinct i, j, each coordinate $\ell \in [n]$ is placed in *both* R_i and R_j with probability p^2, by a union bound over all pairs i, j and a standard Chernoff bound, Event$'$1 can be upperbounded by:

$$\mathsf{maxnum}^2 \cdot \exp(-n/48) = (np)^t \cdot \exp(-n/48).$$

Since for any $\mathbf{x}'_j$, the coordinates outside of R_j are uniformly random, Event$'$2 can be upperbounded by:

$$\mathsf{maxnum}^2 \cdot 1/2^{np/4} = (np)^t \cdot 1/2^{np/4}.$$

A.9   Proof of Lemma 4.3

Similar to Subsect. 3.2, before proving Lemma 4.3, we first present the following claim about the number of samples needed to estimate the Fourier Coefficient of a single index. The algorithm gets access to $8 \log(n)$ sets of p-biased samples. In the following claim we first prove how many samples are needed to be able to approximate the Fourier coefficient within additive distance of $\epsilon/2$ and later discuss how by repeating the approximation step, i.e. step 2b in Fig. 4, will reduce the error in approximation even further.

Claim A.14. *For $\delta \in [0, 1]$, $p \in (0, 1)$, given $8 \log(n)$ independent sets of samples $S_1, S_2, \ldots, S_{8 \log(n)}$ that each of size* num $:= O\left(\frac{1}{(1-2\eta)^{4np+2}p^{2(k-1)}(1-p^2)}\right)$ *and each satisfying the properties given in Lemma 4.1 for some $t \in \Theta(1/\eta)$, then for every $j \in [n]$, $\hat{b}_p(\{j\}) = \mathbb{E}[b \cdot \chi_{\{j\}, p}(\mathbf{x}))]$ can be estimated within additive accuracy $\frac{\epsilon}{2} = (1 - 2\eta')p^{k-1}\sqrt{1 - p^2}/2$ for $\eta' = \frac{1}{2} - \frac{1}{2}(1 - 2\eta)^{2np+1}$ with confidence $1 - \frac{\delta}{n}$.*

Proof. Let $X = \frac{1}{m}\sum_{i=1}^{m} b_i \cdot \chi_{S,p}(\mathbf{x}_i)$. Let f be a parity function. Assuming $S = \{k\}$, let $X_i = \frac{1}{m} \cdot b_i \cdot \chi_{\{k\}, p}(\mathbf{x}_i)$. First we compute $\mathrm{Cov}[X_i, X_j]$ for k such that $\mathbf{s}[k] = 1$

$$\mathrm{Cov}[X_i, X_j] = \mathrm{Cov}\left[\frac{1}{m} \cdot b'_i \cdot \chi_{\{k\}, p}(\mathbf{x}'_i), \; \frac{1}{m} \cdot b'_j \cdot \chi_{\{k\}, p}(\mathbf{x}'_j)\right]$$

$$\mathrm{Cov}[X_i, X_j] = \frac{1}{m^2} \cdot \mathrm{Cov}\left[b'_i \cdot \chi_{\{k\}, p}(\mathbf{x}'_i), \; b'_j \cdot \chi_{\{k\}, p}(\mathbf{x}'_j)\right]$$

$$= \frac{1}{m^2} \cdot \mathrm{Cov}\left[\left(\prod_{u:\mathbf{s}[u]=1} \mathbf{x}'_i[u]\right) \cdot e'_i \cdot \frac{\mathbf{x}'_i[k] - p}{\sqrt{1 - p^2}}, \; \left(\prod_{v:\mathbf{s}[v]=1} \mathbf{x}'_j[v]\right) \cdot e'_j \cdot \frac{\mathbf{x}'_j[k] - p}{\sqrt{1 - p^2}}\right] \tag{A.1}$$

$$= \frac{1}{m^2} \cdot \frac{1}{1 - p^2}\left(\mathrm{Cov}\left[\left(\prod_{u:\mathbf{s}[u]=1 \wedge u \neq k} \mathbf{x}'_i[u]\right) \cdot e'_i, \; \left(\prod_{v:\mathbf{s}[v]=1 \wedge v \neq k} \mathbf{x}'_j[v]\right) \cdot e'_j\right] - \right.$$

$$\left. \mathrm{Cov}\left[\left(\prod_{u:\mathbf{s}[u]=1 \wedge u \neq k} \mathbf{x}'_i[u]\right) \cdot e'_i, \; p \cdot \left(\prod_{v:\mathbf{s}[v]=1} \mathbf{x}'_j[v]\right) \cdot e'_j\right] - \right.$$

$$\text{Cov}\left[p\cdot\left(\prod_{u:s[u]=1}\mathbf{x}'_i[u]\right)\cdot e'_i\,,\,\left(\prod_{v:s[v]=1\wedge v\neq k}\mathbf{x}'_j[v]\right)\cdot e'_j\right]+$$

$$\text{Cov}\left[p\cdot\left(\prod_{u:s[u]=1}\mathbf{x}'_i[u]\right)\cdot e'_i\,,\,p\cdot\left(\prod_{v:s[v]=1}\mathbf{x}'_j[v]\right)\cdot e'_j\right]\right) \qquad (A.2)$$

$$=\frac{1}{m^2}\cdot\frac{1}{(1-p^2)}\left(p^{2(k-1)}\text{Cov}\,[e'_i,e'_j]-2p^{2k}\text{Cov}\,[e'_i,e'_j]+p^{2(k+1)}\text{Cov}\,[e'_i,e'_j]\right)$$
$$\qquad (A.3)$$

$$=m^{-2}p^{2(k-1)}(1-p^2)\text{Cov}\,[e'_i,e'_j]$$
$$=m^{-2}p^{2(k-1)}(1-p^2)\left[(1-2\eta)^{2(2np-t)+2}-(1-2\eta)^{4np+2}\right] \qquad (A.4)$$

where Eq. (A.1) follows from definition of Fourier Coefficients and noting that b'_i is multiplications of $\mathbf{x}_i$s and error term e_i, Eq. (A.2) follows from properties of Covariance, Eq. (A.3) follows from independence of $\mathbf{x}'_i$s and Eq. (A.4) follows from Lemma 4.1. We can also bound $\text{Var}[X_i]$ as follows

$$\text{Var}[X_i]=\text{Var}\left[\frac{1}{m}\cdot b'_i\cdot\chi_{\{k\},p}(\mathbf{x}'_i)\right]$$

$$=\frac{1}{m^2}\cdot\text{Var}\left[\left(\prod_{u:s[u]=1}\mathbf{x}'_i[u]\right)\cdot e'_i\cdot\frac{\mathbf{x}'_i[k]-p}{\sqrt{1-p^2}}\right]$$

$$=\frac{1}{m^2}\cdot\frac{1}{1-p^2}\left(\text{Var}\left[\left(\prod_{u:s[u]=1\wedge u\neq k}\mathbf{x}'_i[u]\right)\cdot e'_i\right]-p^2\cdot\text{Var}\left[\left(\prod_{v:s[v]=1}\mathbf{x}'_i[u]\right)\cdot e'_i\right]\right)$$

$$=\frac{1}{m^2}\cdot\frac{1}{1-p^2}\left(\mathbb{E}\left[\left(\prod_{u:s[u]=1\wedge u\neq k}\mathbf{x}'^2_i[u]\right)\cdot e'^2_i\right]-\mathbb{E}\left[\left(\prod_{u:s[u]=1\wedge u\neq k}\mathbf{x}'_i[u]\right)\cdot e'_i\right]^2-\right.$$

$$\left.p^2\cdot\mathbb{E}\left[\left(\prod_{u:s[u]=1}\mathbf{x}'^2_i[u]\right)\cdot e'^2_i\right]+p^2\cdot\mathbb{E}\left[\left(\prod_{u:s[u]=1}\mathbf{x}'_i[u]\right)\cdot e'_i\right]^2\right) \qquad (A.5)$$

$$=\frac{1}{m^2}\cdot\frac{1}{1-p^2}\left(1-p^{2(k-1)}(1-2\eta)^{2np}-p^2+p^{2(k+1)}(1-2\eta)^{2np}\right) \qquad (A.6)$$

$$=m^{-2}\left(1-p^{2(k-1)}(1+p^2)(1-2\eta)^{2np}\right)\leq m^{-2}$$

where Eq. (A.5) follows from properties of variance and Eq. (A.6) follows from independence of $\mathbf{x}'_i$s. Then we have the following bound from Chebyshev's bound of Theorem A.3

$$\Pr\left[|X-\mathbb{E}[X]|\geq\varepsilon/2\right]\leq\frac{\sum_{i=1}^m\text{Var}\,[X_i]+2\sum_{i=1}^m\sum_{j>i}\text{Cov}\,[X_i,X_j]}{\varepsilon^2/4}$$

$$\leq 4\cdot\frac{m^{-1}+p^{2(k-1)}(1-p^2)\left[(1-2\eta)^{2(2np-t)+2}-(1-2\eta)^{4np+2}\right]}{\varepsilon^2}$$

By substituting $\varepsilon=(1-2\eta')\cdot p^{k-1}\sqrt{1-p^2}$ for $\eta'=\frac{1}{2}-\frac{1}{2}(1-2\eta)^{2np+1}$, we can bound the right hand side by a constant less than $1/2$ by setting $t<-\frac{\ln(9/8-1/c)}{2\ln(1-2\eta)}$ and setting $m=c\cdot\frac{1}{(1-2\eta)^{4np+2}p^{2(k-1)}(1-p^2)}$, where $c>8$. We use random variable $Y_{i'}$ to represents whether the value of count in step i' is increased or not, specifically $Y_{i'} = 1$ represents the event that count is increased in step i'. Assume we repeat the protocol for T rounds in total. Let $Y = (1/T) \cdot \sum_{i'=1}^{T} Y_{i'}$. First, take the case that j such that $s[j] = 0$, we know that in each step of loop over i', $\Pr[Y_{i'} = 1] = 1/2 - \epsilon$. Note that the algorithm is run T times using independent sets $\mathcal{S}_{i'}$ each time and index j is only added if in the majority of the runs its estimated Fourier coefficient is more than $\varepsilon/2$. Using Chernoff bound, we can bound $\Pr[Y \geq T/2] \leq 1/n$.

$$\Pr[\text{index } j \text{ is added to set } \mathcal{S}'] = \Pr[\text{count} \geq T/2]$$

$$= \Pr[\frac{\sum_{i'=1}^{T} Y_{i'}}{T} \geq \frac{1}{2}]$$

$$\leq \Pr\left[|Y - E[Y]| > \varepsilon\right] \leq 2\exp(-2T\varepsilon^2)$$

We can bound the right hand side by $\frac{\delta}{n}$ for constant δ by setting $T = 8\log(n)$ and $\varepsilon = 1/4$. Similar argument applies to the case for j such that $s[j] = 1$. $\qquad\square$

Proof (Proof of Lemma 4.3). Invoking Claim 2.2, we have that for j such that $s[j] = 1$ $\hat{b}_p(\{j\}) = (1 - 2\eta') \cdot p^{k-1}\sqrt{1 - p^2}$ while for j such that $s[j] = 0$, $\hat{b}_p(\{j\}) = 0$. It is clear by inspection that Algorithm in Fig. 4 succeeds when it correctly estimates the values of $\hat{b}_p(\{j\})$ to within additive $\varepsilon/2 := (1 - 2\eta') \cdot p^{k-1}\sqrt{1 - p^2}/2$ for all $j \in [n]$. By Claim A.14, we need $8\log(n)$ sets such that each set has $O\left(\frac{1}{(1-2\eta)^{2np+2}p^{2(k-1)}(1-p^2)}\right)$ number of p-biased samples. So in total num $\cdot 8\log(n) = O\left(\frac{1}{(1-2\eta)^{2np+2}p^{2(k-1)}(1-p^2)} \cdot \log(n)\right)$ number of p-biased samples are sufficient to estimate a single coordinate within additive $\varepsilon/2$ of its correct value with confidence $1 - \frac{\delta}{n}$. By a union bound, the success probability of estimating all coordinates to within additive $\varepsilon/2$ is $1 - \delta$. $\qquad\square$

References

1. Applebaum, B., Cash, D., Peikert, C., Sahai, A.: Fast cryptographic primitives and circular-secure encryption based on hard learning problems. In: Halevi, S. (ed.) Advances in Cryptology - CRYPTO 2009. LNCS, vol. 5677, pp. 595–618. Springer, Heidelberg (2009). https://doi.org/10.1007/978-3-642-03356-8_35
2. Arora, S., Ge, R.: New algorithms for learning in presence of errors. In: Aceto, L., Henzinger, M., Sgall, J. (eds.) ICALP 2011: 38th International Colloquium on Automata, Languages and Programming, Part I. LNCS, vol. 6755, pp. 403–415. Springer, Heidelberg (2011). https://doi.org/10.1007/978-3-642-22006-7_34
3. Blum, A., Furst, M.L., Jackson, J.C., Kearns, M.J., Mansour, Y., Rudich, S.: Weakly learning DNF and characterizing statistical query learning using Fourier analysis. In: 26th Annual ACM Symposium on Theory of Computing, pp. 253–262. ACM Press, Montréal (1994). https://doi.org/10.1145/195058.195147
4. Blum, A., Furst, M.L., Kearns, M.J., Lipton, R.J.: Cryptographic primitives based on hard learning problems. In: Stinson, D.R. (ed.) Advances in Cryptology - CRYPTO 1993. LNCS, vol. 773, pp. 278–291. Springer, Heidelberg (1994). https://doi.org/10.1007/3-540-48329-2_24

5. Blum, A., Kalai, A., Wasserman, H.: Noise-tolerant learning, the parity problem, and the statistical query model. J. ACM **50**(4), 506–519 (2003)
6. Bogdanov, A., Sabin, M., Vasudevan, P.N.: XOR codes and sparse learning parity with noise. In: Proceedings of the Thirtieth Annual ACM-SIAM Symposium on Discrete Algorithms, SODA 2019, San Diego, California, USA, 6–9 January 2019, pp. 986–1004 (2019). https://doi.org/10.1137/1.9781611975482.61
7. Bogos, S., Tramer, F., Vaudenay, S.: On solving LPN using BKW and variants. Crypt. Commun. **8**(3), 331–369 (2016)
8. Brakerski, Z., Lombardi, A., Segev, G., Vaikuntanathan, V.: Anonymous IBE, leakage resilience and circular security from new assumptions. In: Nielsen, J.B., Rijmen, V. (eds.) Advances in Cryptology - EUROCRYPT 2018, Part I. LNCS, vol. 10820, pp. 535–564. Springer, Heidelberg (2018). https://doi.org/10.1007/978-3-319-78381-9_20
9. Cheon, J.H., Son, Y., Yhee, D.: Practical FHE parameters against lattice attacks. IACR Cryptology ePrint Archive 2021/39 (2021). https://eprint.iacr.org/2021/039
10. Dachman-Soled, D., Feldman, V., Tan, L.Y., Wan, A., Wimmer, K.: Approximate resilience, monotonicity, and the complexity of agnostic learning. In: Proceedings of the Twenty-Sixth Annual ACM-SIAM Symposium on Discrete Algorithms, pp. 498–511. SIAM (2014)
11. Feldman, V., Gopalan, P., Khot, S., Ponnuswami, A.K.: New results for learning noisy parities and halfspaces. In: 2006 47th Annual IEEE Symposium on Foundations of Computer Science (FOCS 2006), pp. 563–574 (2006). https://doi.org/10.1109/FOCS.2006.51
12. Feldman, V., Gopalan, P., Khot, S., Ponnuswami, A.K.: On agnostic learning of parities, monomials, and halfspaces. SIAM J. Comput. **39**(2), 606–645 (2009)
13. Gilbert, H., Robshaw, M.J.B., Seurin, Y.: How to encrypt with the LPN problem. In: Aceto, L., Damgård, I., Goldberg, L.A., Halldórsson, M.M., Ingólfsdóttir, A., Walukiewicz, I. (eds.) ICALP 2008, Part II. LNCS, vol. 5126, pp. 679–690. Springer, Heidelberg. https://doi.org/10.1007/978-3-540-70583-3_55
14. Grigorescu, E., Reyzin, L., Vempala, S.: On noise-tolerant learning of sparse parities and related problems. In: Kivinen, J., Szepesvári, C., Ukkonen, E., Zeugmann, T. (eds.) ALT 2011. LNCS, vol. 6925, pp. 413–424. Springer, Heidelberg (2011) https://doi.org/10.1007/978-3-642-24412-4_32
15. Guo, Q., Johansson, T., Löndahl, C.: Solving LPN using covering codes. In: Sarkar, P., Iwata, T. (eds.) ASIACRYPT 2014. LNCS, vol. 8873, pp. 1–20. Springer, Heidelberg (2014). https://doi.org/10.1007/978-3-662-45611-8_1
16. Heyse, S., Kiltz, E., Lyubashevsky, V., Paar, C., Pietrzak, K.: Lapin: an efficient authentication protocol based on ring-LPN. In: Canteaut, A. (ed.) FSE 2012, Revised Selected Papers, vol. 7549, pp. 346–365 (2012). https://doi.org/10.1007/978-3-642-34047-5_20
17. Hopper, N.J., Blum, M.: Secure human identification protocols. In: Boyd, C. (ed.) Advances in Cryptology - ASIACRYPT 2001. LNCS, vol. 2248, pp. 52–66. Springer, Heidelberg (2001). https://doi.org/10.1007/3-540-45682-1_4
18. Juels, A., Weis, S.A.: Authenticating pervasive devices with human protocols. In: Shoup, V. (ed.) Advances in Cryptology - CRYPTO 2005. LNCS, vol. 3621, pp. 293–308. Springer, Heidelberg (2005). https://doi.org/10.1007/11535218_18
19. Levieil, É., Fouque, P.A.: An improved LPN algorithm. In: De Prisco, R., Yung, M. (eds.) SCN 2006. LNCS, vol. 4116, pp. 348–359. Springer, Heidelberg. https://doi.org/10.1007/11832072_24 (2006)
20. Linial, N., Mansour, Y., Nisan, N.: Constant depth circuits, Fourier transform, and learnability. J. ACM **40**(3), 607–620 (1993)

21. Lipton, R.J., Markakis, E., Mehta, A., Vishnoi, N.K.: On the Fourier spectrum of symmetric Boolean functions with applications to learning symmetric juntas. In: 20th Annual IEEE Conference on Computational Complexity (CCC 2005), pp. 112–119. IEEE (2005)

22. Lyubashevsky, V.: The parity problem in the presence of noise, decoding random linear codes, and the subset sum problem. In: Chekuri, C., Jansen, K., Rolim, J.D.P., Trevisan, L. (eds.) Approximation, Randomization and Combinatorial Optimization. Algorithms and Techniques. APPROX 2005, RANDOM 2005. LNCS, vol. 3624, pp. 378–389. Springer, Heidelberg. https://doi.org/10.1007/11538462_32 (2005)

23. Mitzenmacher, M., Upfal, E.: Probability and Computing: Randomization and Probabilistic Techniques in Algorithms and Data Analysis. Cambridge University Press (2017)

24. Mossel, E., O'Donnell, R., Servedio, R.P.: Learning juntas. In: Proceedings of the Thirty-Fifth Annual ACM Symposium on Theory of Computing, pp. 206–212 (2003)

25. Nisan, N., Wigderson, A.: Hardness vs randomness. J. Comput. Syst. Sci. **49**(2), 149–167 (1994)

26. Shor, P.W.: Algorithms for quantum computation: discrete logarithms and factoring. In: 35th Annual Symposium on Foundations of Computer Science, pp. 124–134. IEEE Computer Society Press. https://doi.org/10.1109/SFCS.1994.365700

27. Valiant, G.: Finding correlations in subquadratic time, with applications to learning parities and juntas. In: 2012 IEEE 53rd Annual Symposium on Foundations of Computer Science, pp. 11–20. IEEE (2012)

28. Verbeurgt, K.: Learning DNF under the uniform distribution in quasi-polynomial time. In: Proceedings of the Third Annual Workshop on Computational Learning Theory, COLT 1990, pp. 314–326. Morgan Kaufmann Publishers Inc., San Francisco (1990)

Computational Robust (Fuzzy) Extractors for CRS-Dependent Sources with Minimal Min-entropy

Hanwen Feng[1] and Qiang Tang[2]([✉])

[1] Alibaba Group, Hangzhou, China
`fenghanwen.fhw@alibaba-inc.com`
[2] The University of Sydney, Sydney, Australia
`qiang.tang@sydney.edu.au`

Abstract. Robust (fuzzy) extractors are very useful for, e.g., authenticated key exchange from a shared weak secret and remote biometric authentication against active adversaries. They enable two parties to extract the same uniform randomness with a "helper" string. More importantly, they have an authentication mechanism built in that tampering of the "helper" string will be detected. Unfortunately, as shown by Dodis and Wichs, in the information-theoretic setting, a robust extractor for an (n, k)-source requires $k > n/2$, which is in sharp contrast with randomness extractors which only require $k = \omega(\log n)$. Existing works either rely on random oracles or introduce CRS and work only for CRS-independent sources (even in the computational setting).

In this work, we give a systematic study about robust (fuzzy) extractors for general CRS *dependent* sources. We show in the information-theoretic setting, the same entropy lower bound holds even in the CRS model; we then show we *can* have robust extractors in the computational setting for general CRS-dependent source that is only with minimal entropy. We further extend our construction to robust fuzzy extractors. Along the way, we propose a new primitive called κ-MAC, which is unforgeable with a weak key and hides all partial information about the key (both against auxiliary input); it may be of independent interests.

1 Introduction

Randomness extractors are well-studied tools that enable one to extract uniform randomness (usually with the help of a short random seed) from a weak random source with sufficient entropy. Robust (fuzzy) extractors, which are randomness extractors that can be against an active attacker, are very useful in the settings of authenticated key exchange (AKE) from shared weak secrets and remote biometric authentication. Sometimes, a one-message AKE protocol from weak secrets is directly known as a robust extractor (for close secrets, a robust fuzzy extractor) [4,7,9,10,19,22]. Informally, a robust extractor consists of a generation algorithm Gen producing a nearly-uniform string R along with a public helper string P (message sent in public) from a source W, and a reproduction

© International Association for Cryptologic Research 2021
K. Nissim and B. Waters (Eds.): TCC 2021, LNCS 13043, pp. 689–717, 2021.
https://doi.org/10.1007/978-3-030-90453-1_24

algorithm Rep recovering R from P and W. Besides the normal requirement as a randomness extractor that the extracted R should be uniform, the *robustness* ensures that any manipulation on P by active attackers will be detected. Furthermore, for composition with other applications that will use the extracted randomness, stronger robustness (called *post-application robustness*) is usually required, by allowing adversaries to have R directly, which ensures the security even after adversaries learning information about R from applications using R.

Robust extractors turn out to be expensive. It is known that information-theoretic robust extractors require the (min-)entropy k of the source $W \in \{0,1\}^n$ to be larger than $n/2$ [10,12], which is in contrast with regular randomness extractors that only require a minimal entropy $\omega(\log n)$ from the source. Naturally, leveraging a random oracle as a "super" randomness extractor could circumvent this entropy lower bound. Indeed, one can directly hash a source (with a minimal entropy like $\omega(\log n)$) for this purpose. Moreover, one can also transform a fuzzy extractor [3,11] into a robust fuzzy extractor [4]. However, it is always desirable to see whether we can remove this heuristic assumption [6], particularly in the setting of randomness extraction.

The other approach uses a common reference string (CRS), which could be generated by a trusted third party once and for all. It enables us to transform a strong extractor into a robust extractor by using the CRS as the seed. Clearly, this approach will not require more entropy from the source than the underlying extractor. It also can be extended to the fuzzy setting [7,19,20,22]. However, as the seed has to be independent of the source, this approach so far only works for CRS-independent sources.

In many cases, sources could be dependent on the CRS. For example, for sources generated from devices such as PUFs, adversaries might manufacture the devices after seeing the CRS and insert some CRS-dependent backdoor into the device to gain advantages. More seriously, for all sources, given a CRS-dependent leakage (which is possible as the leakage function is adversarially chosen after seeing the CRS), the distribution of the remained secret will be dependent on the CRS as well. We are interested in the following natural open question:

Can we have a robust (fuzzy) extractor that works for general CRS-dependent sources with minimal min-entropy ($\omega(\log n)$) without relying on an RO?[1]

Our Results. We systematically investigate this question, in both computational and information-theoretic settings, for both non-fuzzy and fuzzy cases. All related results are summarized in Table 1.

---

[1] For the non-fuzzy case, Dodis *et al.* [9] presented a partial solution in the computational setting. However, their construction only works for a very special source: the sample consists of (w, c) where c is a ciphertext that probabilistically encrypts 0s under w; they further require the source to have any linear fraction of min-entropy. In comparison, we are aiming for general sources that only have minimal super logarithmic entropy. For the fuzzy case, there is no feasibility result at all.

Table 1. Comparison between known robust (fuzzy) extractors. "Low Entropy-Rate?" asks whether the scheme works for (n, k)-sources with $k = \omega(\log n)$; "General Sources?" asks whether the scheme works for sources without other requirements beyond that on (n, k) (so CRS-independent ones are all not general). "Naive-RO" denotes the trivial construction that extracts randomness $H(w)$ using a random oracle H; "Naive-CRS" denotes a strong extractor using the CRS as the seed.

Fuzzy?	Schemes	Model	CRS-dependent?	IT/Computational?	Low Entropy Rate?	General Sources?
Non	Naive-RO	RO	–	Computational	√	√
	[10]	Plain	–	IT	×	√
	Naive-CRS	CRS	×	IT	√	×
	[9]	CRS	√	Computational	×	×
	Ours (Sect. 5)	CRS	√	Computational	√	√
Fuzzy	[4]	RO	–	Computational	√	√
	[10,16]	Plain	–	IT	×	√
	[7]	CRS	×	IT	√	×
	[19,20,22]	CRS	×	Computational	√	×
	Ours (Sect. 6)	CRS	√	Computational	√	√

Lower-Bound in the Information-Theoretic Setting. We first give a negative answer in the information-theoretic setting by proving that the lower bound for plain-model constructions [12] also holds in CRS-dependent constructions. Namely, if there is a CRS-model information-theoretically-secure (IT-secure) *pre-application* robust extractor working for every source $W \in \{0,1\}^n$ that has min-entropy greater than k even conditioned on the CRS (we refer such a source an (n, k)-source), it must be that $k > n/2$. This new lower bound justifies the necessity of the CRS-independent requirement in existing CRS-model IT-secure robust (fuzzy) extractors [7].

A Generic Construction of Computational CRS-Model Robust Extractors. We then consider circumventing our new lower bound in the computational setting. We present a generic construction of CRS-dependent *post-application* robust extractors and thus firmly confirm its existence. This construction is built upon a conventional randomness extractor and a novel message authentication code (MAC) termed by key-private auxiliary-input MAC (κ-MAC for short) for which we give efficient constructions from well-studied assumptions. Our construction works for any efficiently samplable sources that have sufficient min-entropy (conditional on CRS) just to admit a conventional randomness extractor.

An Extended Construction for Robust Fuzzy Extractors. We further extend our solution and construct a computational CRS-dependent robust *fuzzy* extractor by using a conventional randomness extractor, a secure sketch, and a stronger κ-MAC that can work in the fuzzy setting. Here, a q-secure sketch is a tool allowing one to convert a weak secret W' to a q-close one W with the help of a small amount of information about W, which is the core of many fuzzy extractors and has IT-secure instantiations.

For achieving error tolerance t, (namely, two close secrets W and W' whose distance is within t), our construction requires the source to support a $2t$-secure sketch[2]. This requirement indeed matches the requirement made by many existing CRS-model robust fuzzy extractors [19,20], while our construction is the first one working for CRS-dependent sources.

Our Techniques. We give a technical overview as follows.

Proving Lower-Bounds for CRS-Model IT-Secure Robust Extractor. Our main technique for the generalized lower bound is to show that a CRS-model IT-secure robust extractor implies a plain-model IT-secure "authentication scheme", which was the main tool for showing the lower bound of entropy rate [12].

Note that a CRS-model robust extractor for all (n, k)-sources trivially implies a CRS-model "authentication scheme" {Auth, Vrfy}: Auth runs the generation algorithm Gen and outputs the helper string P as an "authentication tag" ς; Vrfy runs Rep on input P and outputs 1 unless Rep fails. For any (n, k)-source W and any unbounded adversary $\mathcal{A}$, the scheme is correct and unforgeable w.r.t. a randomly sampled crs according to the CRS distribution CRS. To show a CRS-model "authentication scheme" gives a plain model one: we prove that there exist at least one concrete CRS string crs^* such that it will enable "correct" authentication *and* "unforgeability" for *all* CRS-dependent sources.

For unforgeability, assume that the advantage of any adversary forging a tag in the CRS-model scheme is bounded by δ. First, we show that, for each source W, any adversary $\mathcal{A}$, and any constants $c_0, c_1 \in (0, 1)$, there will be a good set $S_{W, \mathcal{A}}$ with weight at least c_0 (namely, $\Pr[\mathsf{CRS} \in S_{W, \mathcal{A}}] \geq c_0$) such that for every $\mathsf{crs} \in S_{W, \mathcal{A}}$, the advantage of $\mathcal{A}$ forging a valid tag for W is bounded by δ/c_0.

Note that the above discussions give a "locally good" set for each W, but we need a "globally good" set of CRSs for all sources and all adversaries. For any $\mathcal{A}$, we show that, $\widehat{S}_{\mathcal{A}}$, the intersection of $\{S_{W, \mathcal{A}}\}$ for all sources W, is with weight at least c_0; for every $\mathsf{crs} \in \widehat{S}_{\mathcal{A}}$, $\mathcal{A}$'s advantage is bounded by δ/c_0. We proceed with proof by contradiction: if not, its complement $\widehat{S}_{\mathcal{A}}^C$ will have the weight of at least $(1 - c_0)$. By definition, for every $\mathsf{crs}^{(i)} \in \widehat{S}_{\mathcal{A}}^C$, there is one source W (whose conditional distribution is $W_{\mathsf{crs}}^{(i)}$) s.t. $\mathcal{A}$ has advantage greater than δ/c_0. We can define a "new" (n, k)-source $W^* = \{W|_{\mathsf{crs}}\}$ where $W|_{\mathsf{crs}^{(i)}} = W_{\mathsf{crs}}^{(i)}$ if $\mathsf{crs}^i \in \widehat{S}_{\mathcal{A}}^C$ and uniform otherwise. For such W^* and $\mathcal{A}$, there is no good $S_{W^*, \mathcal{A}}$ with weight greater than c_0, which contradicts our previous argument. Finally, we can prove $\bigcap_{\mathcal{A}} \widehat{S}_{\mathcal{A}}$ is globally good, as otherwise, we can "construct" an adversary $\mathcal{A}^*$ contradicting the existence of $\widehat{S}_{\mathcal{A}^*}$.

By similar arguments, we can show there is a globally good CRS set $\widetilde{S}$ for correctness as well. Then by adequately choosing c_0 and c_1, the sum weight of $\widehat{S}$ and $\widetilde{S}$ can be greater than 1, thus there exists a crs^* which is globally good for both correctness and unforgeability. Hardcoded with this string crs^*, the CRS-model authentication scheme gives a plain-model authentication scheme.

---

[2] Note that secure sketches achieving t error tolerance are also subject to some entropy-rate lower-bounds [14]. However, for almost all error-rate t/n (except a small range), the bound is notably smaller than $1/2$.

Adding Post-application Robustness *to Randomness Extractor for "free".* We then turn to computational setting. In a conventional strong extractor Ext (which converts a weak secret w into a uniform r with the help of a uniform seed s), we may view the seed as the "helper string". To make it robust, we could let the "helper string" additionally include a MAC tag for the seed such that adversaries cannot malleate it without being detected. One might want to use r as the key, but the verifier will not have r until receiving s, which leads to circularity. We consider taking w as the MAC key directly.

We can see that a normal MAC will be insufficient. On the one hand, the secret w is non-uniform, especially when we consider post-application robustness, the randomness r and the seed s together give non-trivial information about w and will be leaked to adversaries. On the other hand, the authentication tag itself may contain information about w, which in turn affects the quality of randomness extraction.

We, therefore, introduce a new MAC called κ-MAC. Besides unforgeability, it satisfies *key privacy*, that is, adversaries cannot learn anything new about the key from an authentication tag. Thus, the authentication tag will not affect the randomness extraction (in the computational setting). Moreover, both unforgeability and key privacy should hold even when adversaries have arbitrary admissible auxiliary information about the secret, making this primitive co-exist with (r, s). We define κ-MAC in the CRS model and allow the distribution of secrets to be arbitrarily dependent on the CRS, as long as it is efficiently samplable and has sufficient min-entropy (conditioned on the CRS). We remark that a *one-time* κ-MAC suffices for constructing robust extractors.

κ-MAC from sLRH Relation. It is natural to view κ-MAC as a special leakage-resilient (more precisely, auxiliary-input secure) MAC; then upgrade it to add key privacy. The known approach to auxiliary-input MAC is using the auxiliary-input signature in the symmetric setting by taking both verification key vk and signing key sk as the MAC key k. But in κ-MAC, k is just a non-uniform string sampled from the source, which may not have a structure like (vk, sk); we have to deal with it carefully.

We revisit Katz-Vaikuntanathan signature [17] that is shown to be auxiliary-input secure [13]. On rough terms, they used a true-simulation-extractable NIZK (tSE-NIZK) [8] to prove the knowledge of a witness k^* w.r.t. a statement y (contained in the verification key), such that (k^*, y) satisfy a *leakage-resilient hard* (LRH) relation. In an LRH relation, for honest generated (y, k), and given y and leakage about k, it is infeasible to find a witness of y. If there is a successful forgery, we can extract k^* for y (by tSE-NIZK), which contradicts the LRH relation.

For our κ-MAC, we take the signing key sk as the authentication key k, but vk cannot be posted on a trusted bulletin board, as in signatures, or be in k as the source might not be structured. We address this challenge as follows. First, there is a part of vk (denoted by pp) that can be generated without k and reused across users, and we put it in the CRS. For the other part (denoted by yk), while adversaries can manipulate it, we strengthen the LRH relation to ensure this manipulation will not give advantages. Specifically, we define the strengthened LRH relation (sLRH relation): given honestly generated (pp, yk) along with leakage about k, adversaries cannot find a (yk', k') such that both (pp, yk', k') and (pp, yk', k) satisfy the sLRH relation. This strengthening is sufficient, since using tSE-NIZK to prove knowledge of k w.r.t. (pp, yk) and attaching yk (and the proof) to the authentication tag could give an auxiliary-input MAC from weak secrets. Here, the verifier algorithm checks whether (pp, yk', k) satisfies this relation and whether π is valid, and a forgery violates either the sLRH relation or tSE-NIZK.

For *key privacy*, we need yk to hide partial information about k, i.e., one can simulate the yk distribution without k. Accordingly, we formulate the privacy of generators for a sLRH relation. With a sLRH relation and its generator satisfying privacy (called a private generator), we have a κ-MAC construction in this way.

Constructing sLRH Relation from DPKE+NIZK. The privacy of generator indeed prevents adversaries from finding k from (pp, yk) and the leakage. If it further has a kind of "collision-resistance", namely, even when k is given, it is infeasible to find a distinct k' along with yk' such that both (pp, yk', k) and (pp, yk', k') belong to R_{LR}, R_{LR} with a private generator will be a sLRH relation. Specifically, consider an adversary that outputs (yk', k') and breaks the sLRH relation; if $k = k'$, it contradicts the privacy of generator; otherwise, it violates this "collision-resistance".

We use an auxiliary-input-secure deterministic encryption scheme to instantiate an NP relation R_{de} with a private generator. Specifically, $(pk, c, m) \in R_{de}$ iff $c = \mathsf{DEnc}(pk, m)$. From the security of DPKE, (pk, c) could hide partial information about m. For handling all hard-to-invert auxiliary information, the DPKE scheme from exponentially hard DDH assumption [24] will be the only choice.

Note that pk has to be a part of yk (not pp) since DPKE only works for message distributions independent of pk, and we need work for CRS-dependent sources. Now, the adversary can replace pk with a "bad" pk' such that $(pk', c' = \mathsf{DEnc}(pk', m))$ cannot uniquely determine the message m; so this relation (together with its private generator) is not a sLRH relation. To get around this obstacle, we let yk include a NIZK proof π (besides (pk, c)) demonstrating that pk defines an injection $\mathsf{DEnc}(pk, \cdot)$. Though NIZK needs a CRS as well, it is secure even when statements and witnesses are dependent on the CRS.

Extending to the Fuzzy Case. Finally, we extend our solutions to the fuzzy case. The starting point is using κ-MAC to authenticate the helper string of a fuzzy extractor. We take the standard secure-sketch-based fuzzy extractor as a building block, in which one can recover the secret w using his secret w' first.

The κ-MAC we just defined will be insufficient for the fuzzy case. Adversaries may manipulate the helper string, such that one recovers another secret w'' (which is t-close to w') that a forged tag can be verified under w''. We therefore need κ-MAC to satisfy *fuzzy unforgeability*, that is, given an authentication tag from w, adversaries cannot forge an authentication tag being accepted by any string close to w. Note that the distance between w'' and w is bounded by $2t$, the fuzzy unforgeability should prevent from a forgery w.r.t. any $2t$-close secret.

To construct a fuzzy unforgeable κ-MAC, we first introduce a fuzzy version of sLRH relation. More specifically, for a $2t$-fuzzy sLRH relation, it is infeasible to find (yk', k') to "frame" any secret k^* which is $2t$-close to k. It is easy to verify the according κ-MAC satisfies $2t$-fuzzy unforgeability.

Interestingly, we do not need other tools to construct a fuzzy sLRH relation. Our construction of sLRH relation is fuzzy already. Particularly, if a sLRH relation is "collision-resistant", the adversary can "frame" some k'' only when she exactly finds k''. It remains to argue that, given (pp, yk) from a private generator on input k and the leakage about k, can adversaries find a secret k'' that is $2t$-close to k?

This question seems straightforward at first glance but turns out to need some care. Note that the privacy of generator cannot ensure that (pp, yk) hides all partial information about k, as (pp, yk) itself must be non-trivial about k. A safe way to check whether a value can be recovered from (pp, yk) is to see whether this value is useful for distinguishing yk and $\widehat{yk}$; anything can be used to distinguish cannot be recovered. For small t (say, logarithmic in the security parameter), one knowing $k'' \in B_{2t}(k)$ can guess the original k with a nonnegligible probability, and then she can use k to distinguish. The situation gets complicated when t is large and $B_{2t}(k)$ has exponentially many points. In this case, one cannot naively guess k according to k''. We overcome this challenge by observing the task of recovering k from k'' can be done with the help of $2t$-secure sketch. More specifically, assume an adversary can recover k'' from (pp, yk). Then, the distinguisher specifies the leakage as a $2t$-secure sketch, invokes the adversary to have this $k'' \in B_{2t}(k)$, and converts k'' to k with the help of the secure sketch. Usually, auxiliary inputs are considered a "bad" object to be against, but our proof leverages the auxiliary input to get around barriers of security proof.

2   Preliminaries

Notations. All adversaries considered in this paper are non-uniform, and we model an adversary $\mathcal{A}$ by a family of circuits $\{A_\lambda\}_{n \in \mathbb{N}}$. For a set $\mathbb{X}$, $x \leftarrow_{\$} \mathbb{X}$ denotes sampling x from the uniform distribution over $\mathbb{X}$. For a distribution X, $x \leftarrow X$ denotes sampling x from X. Let (X, Y) be a joint distribution, $X|_y$ denotes the conditional distribution of X conditioned on $Y = y$.

Min-entropy. The min-entropy of a distribution W is defined by $\mathbf{H}_\infty(W) = -\min_{w \in \mathsf{Supp}(W)} \log \Pr[W = w]$. We say W has min-entropy of $\widehat{k}$ conditioned on Z, if $\mathbf{H}_\infty(W|_z) \geq \widehat{k}$ for every $z \in \mathsf{Supp}(Z)$.

Strong Extractor. Let n, k, ℓ be integer functions of the security parameter. An (n, k, ℓ) strong randomness extractor Ext is a deterministic algorithm, which on inputs $w \in \{0, 1\}^{n(\lambda)}$ along with a public seed i_{ext} (with length $si(\lambda)$) outputs another randomness $r \in \{0, 1\}^{\ell(\lambda)}$. Ext satisfies ϵ-privacy, if for any polynomial-time $\mathcal{A}$ and any (n, k)-sources $\mathcal{W}$, it holds that $\mathsf{Adv}^{\mathsf{ext}}_{\mathcal{W},\mathcal{A}}(\lambda) \leq \epsilon(\lambda)$, where $\mathsf{Adv}^{\mathsf{ext}}_{\mathcal{W},\mathcal{A}}(\lambda)$ is defined as

$$\left| \Pr \left[\begin{array}{l} w \leftarrow W_\lambda, i_{\mathsf{ext}} \leftarrow^{\$} \{0,1\}^{si(\lambda)} \\ r \leftarrow \mathsf{Ext}(i_{\mathsf{ext}}, w): \\ 1 \leftarrow \mathcal{A}(i_{\mathsf{ext}}, r) \end{array} \right] - \Pr \left[\begin{array}{l} w \leftarrow W_\lambda, i_{\mathsf{ext}} \leftarrow^{\$} \{0,1\}^{si(\lambda)} \\ r \leftarrow^{\$} \{0,1\}^{(\ell(\lambda))}: \\ 1 \leftarrow \mathcal{A}(i_{\mathsf{ext}}, r) \end{array} \right] \right|.$$

Metric Spaces. A metric space $\mathcal{M} = \{\mathcal{M}_\lambda\}_{\lambda \in \mathbb{N}}$ is a collection of sets with a distance function $\mathsf{dist} : \mathcal{M}_\lambda \times \mathcal{M}_\lambda \to [0, \infty)$. Throughout this paper we consider $\mathcal{M}_\lambda = \{0,1\}^{n(\lambda)}$ equipped with a distance function (e.g., Hamming distance).

Secure Sketch. Let $\mathcal{M}$ be a metric space. An $(\mathcal{M}, k, k', t)$-secure sketch scheme is a pair of PPT algorithms SS and Rec that satisfies correctness and security. For every $\lambda \in \mathbb{N}$, SS on input $w \in \mathcal{M}_\lambda$, outputs a sketch ss; Rec takes as inputs a sketch ss and $\widetilde{w} \in \mathcal{M}_\lambda$, and outputs w'.
Correctness. $\forall \widetilde{w} \in \mathcal{M}_\lambda$, if $\mathsf{dist}(w, \widetilde{w}) \leq t(\lambda)$, then $\mathsf{Rec}(\widetilde{w}, \mathsf{SS}(w)) = w$.
Security. For every λ, any distribution W over $\mathcal{M}_\lambda$ with min-entropy at least $k(\lambda)$, it holds that $H_\infty(W|\mathsf{SS}(W)) \geq k'(\lambda)$.
    We may abbreviate an $(\mathcal{M}, k, k', t)$-secure sketch by t-secure sketch without specifying other parameters.

NIZK. A non-interactive zero-knowledge proof system (NIZK) Π for an NP relation R can be described by the following three algorithms. $\mathsf{Setup}(1^\lambda)$ generates a CRS crs; $\mathsf{Prove}(\mathsf{crs}, x, \psi)$ takes as inputs a CRS crs, a statement x and a witness ψ, and outputs a proof π; $\mathsf{Verify}(\mathsf{crs}, x, \pi)$ checks the validity of π.
Π satisfies the *perfect completeness*, if for any $\lambda \in \mathbb{N}$ and for any $(x, \psi) \in R$,

$$\Pr[\mathsf{crs} \leftarrow \mathsf{Setup}(1^\lambda); \pi \leftarrow \mathsf{Prove}(\mathsf{crs}, x, \psi) : \mathsf{Verify}(\mathsf{crs}, x, \pi) = 1] = 1.$$

Π satisfies ϵ_{snd}-*adaptive soundness*, if for any polynomial-time adversary $\mathcal{A}$, it holds that $\mathsf{Adv}^{\mathsf{snd}}_{\mathcal{A}}(\lambda) \leq \epsilon_{\mathsf{snd}}(\lambda)$, where $\mathsf{Adv}^{\mathsf{snd}}_{\mathcal{A}}(\lambda)$ is defined as

$$\Pr[\mathsf{crs} \leftarrow \mathsf{Setup}(1^\lambda); (x, \pi) \leftarrow \mathcal{A}(\mathsf{crs}) : \mathsf{Verify}(\sigma, x, \pi) = 1 \wedge (\forall \psi, (x, \psi) \notin R)].$$

For zero-knowledgeness, we introduce the single theorem version, which suffices for our applications. Namely, we say Π satisfies ϵ_{zk}-ZK, if there exists a simulator $(\mathsf{SimSetup}, \mathsf{SimProve})$, such that for any polynomial-time $\mathcal{A} = (\mathcal{A}_1, \mathcal{A}_2)$, it holds that $\mathsf{Adv}^{\mathsf{zk}}_{\mathcal{A}}(\lambda) \leq \epsilon_{\mathsf{zk}}(\lambda)$, where $\mathsf{Adv}^{\mathsf{zk}}_{\mathcal{A}}(\lambda)$ is defined as

$$\left| \Pr \left[\begin{array}{l} \mathsf{crs} \leftarrow \mathsf{Setup}(1^\lambda) \\ (x, \psi, st) \leftarrow \mathcal{A}_1(\mathsf{crs}) \\ \pi \leftarrow \mathsf{Prove}(\mathsf{crs}, x, \psi): \\ 1 \leftarrow \mathcal{A}_2(st, \pi) \end{array} \right] - \Pr \left[\begin{array}{l} (\mathsf{crs}, \mathsf{tk}) \leftarrow \mathsf{SimSetup}(1^\lambda) \\ (x, \psi, st) \leftarrow \mathcal{A}_1(\mathsf{crs}) \\ \pi \leftarrow \mathsf{SimProve}(\mathsf{crs}, \mathsf{tk}, x): \\ 1 \leftarrow \mathcal{A}_2(st, \pi) \end{array} \right] \right|.$$

Furthermore, we will need a strengthened soundness termed by **true-simulation-extractability (tSE)** [8], which says that any efficient adversary

$\mathcal{A}$ cannot produce a valid proof π^* for x^* without knowing x^*'s witness, even $\mathcal{A}$ can see a simulated proof for a valid statement x. Note that a tSE-NIZK is implied by a simulation-extractable NIZK [18] which allows adversaries to see simulated proofs on arbitrary statements, including false statements. Moreover, tSE-NIZK may have more efficient constructions [8].

We now present the single-theorem version. We say Π satisfies $(\epsilon_{\mathsf{tse1}}, \epsilon_{\mathsf{tse2}})$-tSE, if there exists a simulation-knowledge extractor $(\mathsf{SESetup}, \mathsf{SimProve}, \mathsf{KExt})$, such that for any polynomial-time adversary $\mathcal{A}$ and $\mathcal{B} = (\mathcal{B}_1, \mathcal{B}_2)$, $\mathsf{Adv}_{\mathcal{A}}^{\mathsf{tse1}}(\lambda) \leq \epsilon_{\mathsf{tse1}}(\lambda)$, where $\mathsf{Adv}_{\mathcal{A}}^{\mathsf{tse1}}(\lambda)$ is defined as

$$\left| \Pr\left[\begin{array}{l} (\mathsf{crs}, \mathsf{tk}, \mathsf{ek}) \leftarrow \mathsf{SESetup}(1^\lambda) : \\ 1 \leftarrow \mathcal{A}(\mathsf{crs}, \mathsf{tk}) \end{array} \right] - \Pr\left[\begin{array}{l} (\mathsf{crs}, \mathsf{tk}) \leftarrow \mathsf{SimSetup}(1^\lambda) : \\ 1 \leftarrow \mathcal{A}(\mathsf{crs}, \mathsf{tk}) \end{array} \right] \right|,$$

and $\mathsf{Adv}_{\mathcal{A}}^{\mathsf{tse2}}(\lambda) \leq \epsilon_{\mathsf{tse2}}(\lambda)$, where $\mathsf{Adv}_{\mathcal{A}}^{\mathsf{tse2}}(\lambda)$ is defined as

$$\Pr\left[\begin{array}{l} (\mathsf{crs}, \mathsf{tk}, \mathsf{ek}) \leftarrow \mathsf{SESetup}(1^\lambda), (x, \psi, st) \leftarrow \mathcal{B}_1(\mathsf{crs}), \pi \leftarrow \mathsf{SimProve}(\mathsf{crs}, \\ \mathsf{tk}, x), (x^*, \pi^*) \leftarrow \mathcal{B}_2(st, \pi), w^* \leftarrow \mathsf{KExt}(\mathsf{crs}, \mathsf{tk}, x^*, \pi^*) : (x^*, w^*) \notin R \end{array} \right].$$

Deterministic Public-Key Encryption. A deterministic public-key encryption (DPKE) scheme Σ is defined by a triple of PPT algorithms $\{\mathsf{KeyGen}, \mathsf{Enc}, \mathsf{Dec}\}$ where Enc and Dec are deterministic.

A DPKE scheme Σ is $(n, \epsilon_{\mathsf{hv}}, \epsilon_{\mathsf{ind}})$-PRIV-IND-secure [5], if for any message source $\mathcal{W}$ defined over $\{\{0,1\}^{n(\lambda)}\}_{\lambda \in \mathbb{N}}$ and any function ensemble $\mathcal{F} = \{f_\lambda\}_{\lambda \in \mathbb{N}}$ such that $\mathcal{F}$ is ϵ_{hv}-hard-to-invert w.r.t. $\mathcal{W}$, for any polynomial-time adversary $\mathcal{A}$, it follows that $\mathsf{Adv}_{\mathcal{A}, \mathcal{W}, \mathcal{F}}^{\mathsf{ind}}(\lambda) \leq \epsilon_{\mathsf{ind}}(\lambda)$, where $\mathsf{Adv}_{\mathcal{A}, \mathcal{W}, \mathcal{F}}^{\mathsf{ind}}(\lambda)$ is defined as

$$\left| \Pr\left[\begin{array}{l} (pk, sk) \leftarrow \mathsf{KeyGen}(1^\lambda) \\ m \leftarrow W_\lambda, \\ c \leftarrow \mathsf{Enc}(pk, m) : \\ 1 \leftarrow \mathcal{A}(c, pk, f_\lambda(m)) \end{array} \right] - \Pr\left[\begin{array}{l} (pk, sk) \leftarrow \mathsf{KeyGen}(1^\lambda) \\ m \leftarrow W_\lambda, m' \leftarrow_\$ \{0,1\}^{n(\lambda)}, \\ c \leftarrow \mathsf{Enc}(pk, m') : \\ 1 \leftarrow \mathcal{A}(c, pk, f_\lambda(m)) \end{array} \right] \right|.$$

We assume w.l.o.g. that Σ has a key relation R_{pk} s.t. for every $(pk, sk) \in R_{pk}$, it follows that $\mathsf{Dec}(sk, \mathsf{Enc}(pk, m)) = m$ for any message m.

3   CRS-Model Robust Extractor: Definitions

In this section, we present both information-theoretic and computational definitions of robust extractors in the CRS model.

CRS-Dependent Sources. Being different from all previous CRS-model works of fuzzy extractors [7, 19–22] that require sources to be independent of the CRS, we consider all sources that could potentially depend on the CRS while having sufficient conditional min-entropy. Formally, We model a source $\mathcal{W}$ as an ensemble of distributions $\mathcal{W} = \{W_\lambda\}_{\lambda \in \mathbb{N}}$. Let $\mathsf{CRS} = \{\mathsf{CRS}_\lambda\}_{\lambda \in \mathbb{N}}$ be an ensemble of

CRS distributions, and we denote each W_λ by a collection $\{W_\lambda|_{crs}\}_{crs \in \mathsf{Supp}(\mathsf{CRS}_\lambda)}$. Here $W_\lambda|_{crs}$ is used to denote the conditional distribution of W_λ conditioned on that $\mathsf{CRS}_\lambda = crs$. For a distribution W_λ independent of CRS, it holds that $W_\lambda = W_\lambda|_{crs}$ for every crs. Moreover, any collection $\{W_{\lambda,crs}\}_{crs \in \mathsf{Supp}(\mathsf{CRS}_\lambda)}$ in turn defines a distribution W_λ for which $W_\lambda|_{crs} = W_{\lambda,crs}$.

Let n and k be integer functions of the security parameter. For a source $\mathcal{W}$ defined over $\{\{0,1\}^{n(\lambda)}\}_{\lambda \in \mathbb{N}}$, we call it an (n,k)-source (w.r.t. CRS), if for any λ, the distribution W_λ is an $(n(\lambda), k(\lambda))$-distribution (w.r.t. CRS_λ). Namely,

$$\mathbf{H}_\infty(W_\lambda) \geq k(\lambda) \text{ (or for any } crs \in \mathsf{Supp}(\mathsf{CRS}_\lambda), \mathbf{H}_\infty(W_\lambda|_{crs}) \geq k(\lambda).)$$

In the computational setting, we further require each W_λ to be efficiently samplable by a polynomial-bounded circuit.

Definition 1 (Efficiently-samplable source w.r.t. CRS). *For a distributions ensembles* $\mathsf{CRS} = \{\mathsf{CRS}_\lambda\}_{\lambda \in \mathbb{N}}$ *and* $\mathcal{W} = \{W_\lambda\}_{\lambda \in \mathbb{N}}$, *we call* W_λ *an efficiently-samplable distribution w.r.t.* CRS_λ, *if there is a circuit* G_λ *whose running time is polynomial in* λ, *such that for every* $crs \in \mathsf{Supp}(\mathsf{CRS}_\lambda)$, *it holds that*

$$G_\lambda(crs) = W_\lambda|_{crs}.$$

If for every $\lambda \in \mathbb{N}$, W_λ *is an efficiently-samplable distribution w.r.t.* CRS_λ, *we call* $\mathcal{W}$ *an efficiently-samplable source w.r.t.* CRS.

Remark 1. We consider efficiently samplable sources in the computational setting, as the dependence between a source being extracted and the CRS distribution is usually caused by an efficient adversary. A typical scenario could be that a non-uniform PPT adversary $\mathcal{A} = \{A_\lambda\}_{\lambda \in \mathbb{N}}$ "creates" a source after seeing the CRS. Therefore, we ask a *uniform* polynomial-bounded circuit G_λ (which can be considered as A_λ) for every $crs \in \mathsf{Supp}(\mathsf{CRS}_\lambda)$, rather than different polynomial-bounded circuits for different crs. Similar settings appeared in the recent works on two sources extractors [1,15].

Robust Extractor. A robust extractor rExt in the CRS-model is defined by a triplet of efficient algorithms $\{\mathsf{CRS}, \mathsf{Gen}, \mathsf{Rep}\}$. CRS is a sampler algorithm that specifies the CRS distribution. Gen takes as inputs a CRS and a weak secret w and outputs a randomness R along with a helper string P. Then, Rep can recover R from P using w. rExt requires *privacy* and *robustness*. The former says R is pseudorandom conditioned on P, and the latter captures the infeasibility of forging a different P that will not lead to the failure of Rep. Particularly, when $\mathcal{A}$ is given both R and P, the robustness is called *post-application* robustness; when only P is given, it is called *pre-application* robustness.

Formally, we define a robust extractor below.

Definition 2 (Robust extractor). *For integer functions* n, k, ℓ *of the security parameter, an* (n,k,ℓ)-*robust extractor* rExt *is defined by the following PPT algorithms.*

- $crs \leftarrow \mathsf{CRS}(1^\lambda)$. *On input the security parameter λ, it outputs a CRS crs, whose distribution is denoted by CRS_λ.*
- $(R, P) \leftarrow \mathsf{Gen}(crs, w)$. *On inputs crs and a string $w \in \{0,1\}^{n(\lambda)}$, it outputs a randomness $R \in \{0,1\}^{\ell(\lambda)}$ along with a helper string P.*
- $R \leftarrow \mathsf{Rep}(crs, w, P)$. *It recover the randomness R from P using w.*

Correctness: *For a function $\rho : \mathbb{N} \to [0,1]$, we say rExt satisfies ρ-correctness, if for any (n, k)-source $\mathcal{W}$, for every λ, it holds that*

$$\Pr\left[\begin{array}{l} crs \leftarrow \mathsf{CRS}_\lambda; w \leftarrow W_\lambda|_{crs}; \\ (R, P) \leftarrow \mathsf{Gen}(crs, w) : \mathsf{Rep}(crs, w, P) = R \end{array}\right] \geq \rho(\lambda).$$

Privacy: *For $\epsilon : \mathbb{N} \to (0, 1)$, rExt satisfies the ϵ-IT-privacy, if for any unbounded adversary $\mathcal{A}$ and any (n, k)-source $\mathcal{W}$, it holds that*

$$\mathsf{Adv}^{\mathrm{priv}}_{\mathcal{A},\mathcal{W}}(\lambda) := |\Pr[\mathsf{Exp}^{\mathrm{priv},0}_{\mathcal{A},\mathcal{W}}(\lambda) = 1] - \Pr[\mathsf{Exp}^{\mathrm{priv},1}_{\mathcal{A},\mathcal{W}}(\lambda) = 1]| \leq \epsilon(\lambda).$$

Robustness: *For $\delta : \mathbb{N} \to (0, 1)$, rExt satisfies the δ-IT-post-application-robustness (or pre-application robustness, without boxed items in the experiment $\mathsf{Exp}^{\mathrm{rob}}_{\mathcal{A},\mathcal{W}}$), if for any unbounded adversary $\mathcal{A}$, and any (n, k)-source $\mathcal{W}$, it holds that $\mathsf{Adv}^{\mathrm{rob}}_{\mathcal{A},\mathcal{W}}(\lambda) = \Pr[\mathsf{Exp}^{\mathrm{rob}}_{\mathcal{A},\mathcal{W}}(\lambda) = 1] \leq \delta(\lambda).$*

$\mathsf{Exp}^{\mathrm{priv},b}_{\mathcal{A},\mathcal{W}}(\lambda)$

$crs \leftarrow \mathsf{CRS}_\lambda; w \leftarrow W_\lambda|_{crs}; (R, P) \leftarrow \mathsf{Gen}(crs, w);$

$R_0 \leftarrow\!\!\$\ \{0,1\}^{\ell(\lambda)}; R_1 = R; b' \leftarrow \mathcal{A}(crs, P, R_b)$

return b'

$\mathsf{Exp}^{\mathrm{rob}}_{\mathcal{A},\mathcal{W}}(\lambda)$

$crs \leftarrow \mathsf{CRS}_\lambda; w \leftarrow W_\lambda|_{crs}$

$(R, P) \leftarrow \mathsf{Gen}(crs, w); P^* \leftarrow \mathcal{A}(crs, P\boxed{, R})$

if $P^* \neq P \wedge \mathsf{Rep}(crs, P^*, w) \neq\perp)$ **then return** 1

return 0

Computational definitions can be defined by only considering polynomial-time adversaries and efficiently-samplable sources. We directly call these computational versions ϵ-privacy and δ-post-application-robustness (by removing "IT").

Robust Fuzzy Extractor. When the generation algorithm Gen and the reproduction algorithm Rep could use different but close secrets $w, \widetilde{w}$, $\{\mathsf{CRS}, \mathsf{Gen}, \mathsf{Rep}\}$ defines a robust fuzzy extractor. More formally, we require that w and $\widetilde{w}$ are in a metric space $\mathcal{M}$ with a distance function dist. For an integer $\widehat{t}$, we say w is $\widehat{t}$-close to $\widetilde{w}$, if $\mathsf{dist}(w, \widetilde{w}) \leq \widehat{t}$. For $\mathcal{W} = \{W_\lambda\}_{\lambda \in \mathbb{N}}$ and $\widetilde{\mathcal{W}} = \{\widetilde{W_\lambda}\}_{\lambda \in \mathbb{N}}$ defined over $\mathcal{M}$, we say $(W, \widetilde{W})$ a t-pair for an integer function t, if for every $\lambda \in \mathbb{N}$ and $\mathsf{crs} \in \mathsf{Supp}(\mathsf{CRS}_\lambda)$, it holds that $\Pr[(w, \widetilde{w}) \leftarrow (W_\lambda|_{\mathsf{crs}}, \widetilde{W}_\lambda|_{\mathsf{crs}}) : \mathsf{dist}(w, \widetilde{w}) \leq t(\lambda)] = 1$. For simplicity, we assume $\mathcal{M}$ is $\{\{0, 1\}^{n(\lambda)}\}_{\lambda \in \mathbb{N}}$ equipped with a distance function dist (e.g., Hamming distance).

We call $\mathsf{rfExt} = \{\mathsf{CRS}, \mathsf{Gen}, \mathsf{Rep}\}$ an $(\mathcal{M}, k, \ell, t)$-robust fuzzy extractor, if it satisfies correctness, privacy, and robustness w.r.t. any t-pair of (n, k)-sources $(W, \widetilde{W})$. Formal definitions are given in the full paper.

4   A New Lower Bound for IT-Secure Robust Extractors

As briefly explained in the introduction, a plain-model IT-secure robust extractor for all (n, k)-sources exists only when $k > n/2$ [12]. This lower bound can be trivially circumvented by assuming a CRS and work only for the special sources that are *independent* of the CRS. We are interested in the case for general sources which may be CRS-dependent. This section gives a negative result that IT-secure robust extractors for all (n, k)-sources also require that $k > n/2$ in the CRS setting. The fuzzy case trivially inherits this generalized lower bound.

Previous Tool for the Plain Model Lower Bound. Dodis and Wichs's [12] lower-bound comes from a plain-model IT-secure authentication scheme (for an-$(\widehat{n}, \widehat{k})$-distribution W), which is trivially implied by an IT-secure robust extractor. Such an authentication scheme could be described by a pair of randomized functions $\{\mathsf{Auth}, \mathsf{Vrfy}\}$, formed by $\mathsf{Auth} : \{0, 1\}^{\widehat{n}} \to \{0, 1\}^{\widehat{s}}$, and $\mathsf{Vrfy} : \{0, 1\}^{\widehat{n}} \times \{0, 1\}^{\widehat{s}} \to \{0, 1\}$, where $\widehat{n}, \widehat{s}$ are integers. It satisfies (1) $\widehat{\rho}$-correctness: $\Pr[w \leftarrow W : \mathsf{Vrfy}(w, \mathsf{Auth}(w)) = 1] \geq \widehat{\rho}$; and (2) $\widehat{\delta}$-unforgeability: for any adversary $\mathcal{A}$, $\Pr[w \leftarrow W, \varsigma \leftarrow \mathsf{Auth}(w), \varsigma^* \leftarrow \mathcal{A}(\varsigma) : \mathsf{Vrfy}(w, \varsigma^*) = 1] \leq \widehat{\delta}$.

Lemma 1 ([12]). *If there exists an authentication scheme for all $(\widehat{n}, \widehat{k})$-distributions with $\widehat{\rho}$-correctness and $\widehat{\delta}$-unforgeability, and $\widehat{\delta} < \widehat{\rho}^2/4$, it follows that $\widehat{k} > \widehat{n}/2$.*

Generalizing the Lower-Bound. We present a new lower bound for the CRS-model in the following theorem; our main technical lemma is to show that a CRS-model authentication scheme could imply that in the plain model (Lemma 2).

Theorem 1. *Let $n, k, \ell : \mathbb{N} \to \mathbb{N}$ and $\rho, \delta : \mathbb{N} \to \{0, 1\}$ be functions of the security parameter. If there exists an (n, k, ℓ) IT-secure robust extractor with ρ-correctness and δ-pre-application-robustness, then for any $\lambda \in \mathbb{N}$ s.t. $\delta(\lambda) \leq \rho(\lambda)^2/4$, it follows that $k(\lambda) > n(\lambda)/2$.*

Proof. We first define a CRS-model authentication scheme, which consists $\{\mathsf{CAuth}, \mathsf{CVrfy}\}$ (randomized) along with a CRS distribution $\widehat{\mathsf{CRS}}$, satisfying the following, for any $(\widehat{n}, \widehat{k})$-source W:

- $\widehat{\rho}$-correctness: $\Pr[\mathsf{crs} \leftarrow \widehat{\mathsf{CRS}}, w \leftarrow W|_{\mathsf{crs}} : \mathsf{Vrfy}(\mathsf{crs}, w, \mathsf{Auth}(\mathsf{crs}, w)) = 1] \geq \widehat{\rho}$.

– $\widehat{\delta}$-unforgeability: for any adversary $\mathcal{A}$,

$$\Pr\left[\begin{array}{l} \mathtt{crs} \leftarrow \widehat{\mathsf{CRS}}, w \leftarrow W|_{\mathtt{crs}}, \varsigma \leftarrow \mathsf{Auth}(\mathtt{crs}, w), \\ \varsigma^* \leftarrow \mathcal{A}(\mathtt{crs}, \varsigma) : \mathsf{Vrfy}(\mathtt{crs}, w, \varsigma^*) = 1. \end{array}\right] \leq \widehat{\delta}.$$

It is easy to see that, if there is a CRS-model IT-secure (n, k, ℓ)-robust extractor $\{\mathsf{CRS}, \mathsf{Gen}, \mathsf{Rep}\}$ with ρ-correctness and δ-robustness, for each $\lambda \in \mathbb{N}$, we can construct $\{\mathsf{CAuth}, \mathsf{CVrfy}\}$ along with a CRS distribution $\widehat{\mathsf{CRS}} = \mathsf{CRS}_\lambda$ that satisfies $\widehat{\rho} = \rho(\lambda)$-correctness and $\widehat{\delta} = \delta(\lambda)$-unforgeability w.r.t. all $(n(\lambda), k(\lambda))$-distributions. More detailly,

– $\mathsf{CAuth}(\mathtt{crs}, w)$: Invoke $(R, P) \leftarrow \mathsf{Gen}(\mathtt{crs}, w)$, and return $\sigma = P$;
– $\mathsf{CVrfy}(\mathtt{crs}, w, \sigma)$: If $\mathsf{Rep}(\mathtt{crs}, w, \sigma) = \perp$, return 0; otherwise, return 1.

Next, we give our main technical lemma for the CRS-model authentication scheme, whose detailed proof is deferred later.

Lemma 2. *If there exists a CRS-model IT-secure authentication scheme $\{\mathsf{CAuth}, \mathsf{CVrfy}\}$ (along with a CRS distribution $\widehat{\mathsf{CRS}}$) for all $(\widehat{n}, \widehat{k})$- distributions with $\widehat{\rho}$-correctness and $\widehat{\delta}$-unforgeability, then for any $\widehat{c}_0, \widehat{c}_1 \in (0, 1)$ satisfying $(1 - \widehat{c}_1)\widehat{\rho} + \widehat{c}_0 > 1$, there exists a plain-model IT-secure authentication scheme $\{\mathsf{Auth}, \mathsf{Vrfy}\}$ for all $(\widehat{n}, \widehat{k})$-distributions with $\widehat{c}_1\widehat{\rho}$-correctness and $\widehat{\delta}/\widehat{c}_0$-unforgeability.*

By Lemma 1, if $\widehat{\delta}/\widehat{c}_0 < (\widehat{c}_1\widehat{\rho})^2/4$, $\{\mathsf{Auth}, \mathsf{Vrfy}\}$ established in Lemma 2 exists only when $\widehat{k} > \widehat{n}/2$. Putting requirements together, $\{\mathsf{CAuth}, \mathsf{CVrfy}\}$ with $\widehat{\rho}$-correctness and $\widehat{\delta}$-unforgeability could imply such $\{\mathsf{Auth}, \mathsf{Vrfy}\}$, if there exists $\widehat{c}_0, \widehat{c}_1 \in \{0, 1\}$, such that

$$\widehat{\delta} < \frac{\widehat{c}_0 \widehat{c}_1^2 \widehat{\rho}^2}{4}, \quad \text{and} \quad (1 - \widehat{c}_1)\widehat{\rho} + \widehat{c}_0 > 1. \tag{1}$$

It remains to show when such $(\widehat{c}_0, \widehat{c}_1)$ exist. Note for any $\widehat{\rho} \in (0, 1)$, there always exists $(\widehat{c}_0, \widehat{c}_1) \in (0, 1)^2$ satisfying $(1 - \widehat{c}_1)\widehat{\rho} + \widehat{c}_0 > 1$ (denote the solution space by $S_{\widehat{\rho}}$). Then, we can have $(\widehat{c}_0, \widehat{c}_1)$ satisfying Eq. 1 for $(\widehat{\rho}, \widehat{\delta})$, unless $\frac{4\widehat{\delta}}{\widehat{\rho}^2} \geq \widehat{c}_0 \widehat{c}_1^2$ for any $(\widehat{c}_0, \widehat{c}_1) \in S_{\widehat{\rho}}$.

By standard analysis, we have the following result: for any $\widehat{\rho}, \widehat{v} \in (0, 1)$, there always exists $(\widehat{c}_0, \widehat{c}_1) \in S_{\widehat{\rho}}$ such that $\widehat{c}_0 \widehat{c}_1^2 > \widehat{v}$. It follows that whenever $\widehat{\delta} < \widehat{\rho}^2/4$, such $(\widehat{c}_0, \widehat{c}_1)$ exist. Recall that for any λ s.t. $\delta(\lambda) < \rho(\lambda)^2/4$, the robust extractor could give such $\{\mathsf{CAuth}, \mathsf{CVrfy}\}$ for all $(n(\lambda), k(\lambda))$-distributions. It follows $k(\lambda) < n(\lambda)/2$ in this case. $\square$

Deferred Proof for Lemma 2. The over goal is to show there exists a "good" CRS $\mathtt{crs}^*$ in the support of $\widehat{\mathsf{CRS}}$, such that with $\mathtt{crs}^*$ hardcoded, $\{\mathsf{CAuth}(\mathtt{crs}^*, \cdot), \mathsf{CVrfy}(\mathtt{crs}^*, \cdot)\}$ is the plain-model authentication scheme. For both *correctness* and *unforgeability*, we will prove that there exist a sufficiently large "good" set of CRSs (S and $\tilde{\mathsf{S}}$) for each of them. Then by properly tuning parameters, we can see $\mathsf{S} \cap \tilde{\mathsf{S}} \neq \emptyset$, thus we can find a string $\mathtt{crs}^*$.

In the claim below, we show the existence of S (for *correctness*). We proceed in two steps. (i) For each source W and a randomly sampled crs, we have ρ-correctness; then, by simple probabilistic analysis, there must exist a large enough "good" set S_W that every element of it will enable "correctness" (with a smaller correctness parameter). (ii) To show $\bigcap_W \mathsf{S}_W$ is still with sufficient size, we can use proof by contradiction in a sense that if it does not hold, we can define a special source W^* whose "good" set S_{W^*} will be smaller than that established in the previous step.

Claim. For any constant $\widehat{c}_1 \in (0, 1)$, there exists a set $\mathsf{S} \in \mathsf{Supp}(\widehat{\mathsf{CRS}})$ such that $\Pr[\widehat{\mathsf{CRS}} \in \mathsf{S}] \geq (1 - \widehat{c}_1)\widehat{\rho}$, and for any $\mathtt{crs} \in \mathsf{S}$ and any $(\hat{n}, \hat{k})$-distribution W, it holds that

$$\Pr\left[w \leftarrow W|_{\mathtt{crs}}, \varsigma \leftarrow \mathsf{CAuth}(\mathtt{crs}, w) : \mathsf{CVrfy}(\mathtt{crs}, w, \varsigma) = 1\right] \geq \widehat{c}_1\widehat{\rho}.$$

Proof (of claim). For convenience, we define the "verified correctly" event w.r.t. W and $\mathtt{crs}$:

$$\mathsf{VC}_{W,\mathtt{crs}} := [w \leftarrow W|_{\mathtt{crs}}, \varsigma \leftarrow \mathsf{CAuth}(\mathtt{crs}, w) : \mathsf{CVrfy}(\mathtt{crs}, w, \varsigma) = 1].$$

Then define a "good" set S for an $(\hat{n}, \hat{k})$-distribution W. Namely,

$$\mathsf{S}_W := \{\mathtt{crs} \in \mathsf{Supp}(\mathsf{CRS}) : \Pr[\mathsf{VC}_{W,\mathtt{crs}}] \geq \widehat{c}_1\widehat{\rho}\}. \tag{2}$$

We now show

$$\Pr[\widehat{\mathsf{CRS}} \in \mathsf{S}_W] \geq (1 - \widehat{c}_1)\widehat{\rho} \tag{3}$$

for any $(\hat{n}, \hat{k})$-distribution W. If not, for some W, we have the following,

$$\Pr[\mathtt{crs} \leftarrow \widehat{\mathsf{CRS}} : \mathsf{VC}_{W,\mathtt{crs}}]$$
$$\leq \Pr[\mathsf{VC}_{W,\mathtt{crs}}|\mathtt{crs} \notin \mathsf{S}_W]\Pr[\widehat{\mathsf{CRS}} \notin \mathsf{S}_W] + \Pr[\widehat{\mathsf{CRS}} \in \mathsf{S}_W]$$
$$\leq \widehat{c}_1\widehat{\rho} + (1 - \widehat{c}_1)\widehat{\rho} = \widehat{\rho},$$

which contradicts the assumption that $\{\mathsf{CAuth}, \mathsf{CVrfy}\}$ along with $\widehat{\mathsf{CRS}}$ satisfies the $\widehat{\rho}$-correctness.

Note that S_W is a "locally good" set for W, and we need a "globally good" set S for all $(\hat{n}, \hat{k})$-distributions. By definition, S will be the intersection of all S_W, namely,

$$\mathsf{S} = \bigcap_{\forall (\hat{n},\hat{k})\text{-distribution } W} \mathsf{S}_W.$$

Our goal is to show $\Pr[\widehat{\mathsf{CRS}} \in \mathsf{S}] \geq (1 - \widehat{c}_1)\widehat{\rho}$. We proceed it by contradiction. Specifically, if not, the complement of S (denoted by S^C) will satisfy $\Pr[\widehat{\mathsf{CRS}} \in \mathsf{S}^C] > 1 - (1 - \widehat{c}_1)\widehat{\rho}$. By definition, for every $\mathtt{crs}_i \in \mathsf{S}^C$, there exists a $(\hat{n}, \hat{k})$-distribution W_i, such that

$$\Pr[\mathsf{VC}_{W_i,\mathsf{crs}_i}] < \widehat{c}_1\widehat{\rho}.$$

Next, we can define a distribution W^* for which the set S_{W^*} does not satisfy Eq. 3. Specifically, $W^* = \{W^*|_{\mathsf{crs}_i}\}_{\mathsf{crs}_i \in \mathsf{Supp}(\widehat{\mathsf{CRS}})}$, where

$$W^*|_{\mathsf{crs}_i} = \begin{cases} W_i|_{\mathsf{crs}_i}, & \text{if } \mathsf{crs}_i \in \mathsf{S}^C, \\ U_{\widehat{n}}, & \text{if } \mathsf{crs}_i \in \mathsf{S}. \end{cases} \tag{4}$$

Here $U_{\widehat{n}}$ denotes the uniform distribution over $\{0,1\}^{\widehat{n}}$. It is easy to verify W^* is an $(\widehat{n}, \widehat{k})$-distribution. However, from the definition of W^*, it follows that $\mathsf{S}_{W^*} \bigcap \mathsf{S}^C = \emptyset$, and thus $\Pr[\mathsf{CRS} \in \mathsf{S}_{W^*}] < (1 - \widehat{c}_1)\widehat{\rho}$, which contradicts the result Eq. 3. $\qquad\square$

For *unforgeability*, it follows similar idea. We have the following claim whose formal proof is given in the full paper.

Claim. For any constant $\widehat{c}_0 \in (0,1)$, there exists a set $\widetilde{\mathsf{S}} \in \mathsf{Supp}(\widehat{\mathsf{CRS}})$ such that $\Pr[\widehat{\mathsf{CRS}} \in \widetilde{\mathsf{S}}] \geq \widehat{c}_0$, and for any $\mathsf{crs} \in \widetilde{\mathsf{S}}$, any $(\widehat{n}, \widehat{k})$-distribution W, and any adversary $\mathcal{A}$, it holds that

$$\Pr\begin{bmatrix} w \leftarrow W|_{\mathsf{crs}}, \varsigma \leftarrow \mathsf{CAuth}(\mathsf{crs}, w), \\ \varsigma^* \leftarrow \mathcal{A}(\mathsf{crs}, \varsigma) : \mathsf{CVrfy}(\mathsf{crs}, w, \varsigma^*) = 1 \end{bmatrix} < \widehat{\delta}/\widehat{c}_0.$$

Finally, by the parameter condition in Eq. 1 that $(1-\widehat{c}_1)\widehat{\rho}+\widehat{c}_0 > 1$, it follows that $\mathsf{S} \cap \widetilde{\mathsf{S}} \neq \emptyset$. We pick one $\mathsf{crs}^* \in \mathsf{S} \cap \widetilde{\mathsf{S}}$, and define an ensemble of randomized function pairs $\{\mathsf{Auth} = \mathsf{CAuth}(\mathsf{crs}^*, \cdot), \mathsf{Vrfy} = \mathsf{CVrfy}(\mathsf{crs}^*, \cdot)\}$. It is easy to verify this $\{\mathsf{Auth}, \mathsf{Vrfy}\}$ satisfies $\widehat{c}_1\widehat{\rho}$-correctness and $\widehat{\delta}/\widehat{c}_0$ for all $(\widehat{n}, \widehat{k})$-distributions. $\qquad\square$

5   Computational Robust Extractors

In this section, we provide a generic framework in the CRS model that compiles any computational extractor into a robust one. Compared with previous works, our construction is the first that can work for any CRS *dependent* source with minimal entropy ($\omega(\log n)$ instead of $n/2$ as in the IT setting).

Intuitions. As briefly discussed in Introduction, a fairly intuitive idea is to add a MAC tag on the helper string. Namely, with a MAC $\{\mathsf{Tag}, \mathsf{Verify}\}$ (for simplicity here we omit the public parameters) and a strong extractor Ext, the generation procedure produces a helper string formed by $(s, \mathsf{Tag}(w, s))$ along with a randomness r, where s is the seed for Ext and r is the extracted randomness by Ext. The reproduce procedure first checks the validity of $\mathsf{Tag}(w, s)$, and reproduces $r = \mathsf{Ext}(s, w)$ if the tag is valid.

However, it is not hard to see the insufficiency of a normal MAC here. First, the secret w is non-uniform, and some information about w will be further leaked by (s, r) (for the strong post-application robustness), while a MAC usually requires a uniform key. Moreover, the tag $\mathsf{Tag}(w, s)$ may also leak partial information about w (e.g., some bits of it) and thus affect the quality of r. The above issues inspire us to consider a special MAC that can addresses the concerns above simultaneously. At a high level, (1) it should be secure w.r.t. auxiliary information about the *weak* secret w, as both the seed i_{ext} and the extracted string r generated from w are leaked to adversaries; (2) the tag of this MAC should also hide all partial information about w, such that given the tag the extracted string r remains pseudorandom. We call such a MAC κ-MAC (**Key-P**rivate **A**uxiliary-input Message Authentication). But, for constructing a robust extractor, we only need to ask the *one-time* security of κ-MAC.[3]

We formally define κ-MAC, present and analyze our framework of robust extractors from κ-MAC. Then, we show how to construct (one-time) κ-MAC from well-studied assumptions.

κ-MAC: Definitions. We define the syntax of κ-MAC in the CRS model.

Syntax. A κ-MAC scheme Σ consists of a triple of algorithms {Init, Tag, Verify}, with associated key space $\mathcal{K} = \{\mathcal{K}_\lambda\}_{\lambda \in \mathbb{N}}$, message space $\mathcal{M}es = \{\mathcal{M}es_\lambda\}_{\lambda \in \mathbb{N}}$, and tag space $\mathcal{T} = \{\mathcal{T}_\lambda\}_{\lambda \in \mathbb{N}}$.

- Init(1^λ). On input a security parameter 1^λ, it outputs a crs whose distribution is denoted by CRS_λ.
- Tag(crs, k, m). The authentication algorithm takes as inputs a CRS crs, a key $k \in \mathcal{K}_\lambda$, and a message $m \in \mathcal{M}es_\lambda$. It outputs a tag $\varsigma \in \mathcal{T}_\lambda$.
- Verify(crs, k, m, ς). The verification algorithm takes as inputs a CRS crs, a key k, a message m, and an authentication tag ς. It outputs either 1 accepting (m, ς) or 0 rejecting (m, ς).

The correctness states that for every crs $\leftarrow$ Init(1^λ), every secret $k \in \mathcal{K}_\lambda$, and every message $m \in \mathcal{M}es_\lambda$, we have $\Pr[\mathsf{Verify}(\mathbf{crs}, k, m, \mathsf{Tag}(\mathbf{crs}, k, m))] = 1$. A secure κ-MAC scheme should satisfy *unforgeability*, which is similar to regular MAC, and *key privacy*, which requires the tag to be simulatable without using the key. The main difference (with the conventional definitions) in the security notions is that they are all under auxiliary input. We first discuss the admissible auxiliary input and then present the formal definitions.

Admissible Auxiliary Inputs. Note that the auxiliary information cannot be arbitrary. (1) it must be hard-to-invert leakage, as defined by Dodis *et al.* [9]. Namely, the auxiliary input is a function $f(w)$ of the secret w, and we say f is hard-to-invert w.r.t. a distribution W, if it is infeasible to recover w from $f(w)$, for a random sample $w \leftarrow W$. (2) to avoid triviality, the auxiliary information should not contain a valid authentication tag. Note that the authentication algorithm is indeed "hard-to-invert", and thus we have to put other restrictions on the leakage function to exclude the trivial case. Similar issues arise in auxiliary-input secure digital signatures [13] that they require the admissible function f to be *exponentially* hard-to-invert. For our purpose, however, this treatment will put

---

[3] The RO-based MAC (where $\mathsf{Tag}(w, m) = H(w, m)$ for a random oracle H) employed in Boyen *et al.*'s robust (fuzzy) extractor [4] captures all above intuitions, and thus it can be considered as a κ-MAC in the random oracle model.

unnecessary restrictions on either the sources being extracted or the underlying extractor. Instead, we observe and leverage the following asymmetry: the authentication algorithm is only required to be hard-to-invert for a randomly chosen CRS; while the auxiliary-input function, particularly, the Gen of the underlying extractor, can be hard-to-invert for *every* CRS. By defining the hardness of inverting over every CRS, we can exclude the authentication algorithm from admissible auxiliary-input functions. By design, we can further ensure that any efficient algorithm that produces valid authentication tags may not be "hard-to-invert" for some CRSs. Considering all the above, we define admissible auxiliary inputs below.

Definition 3. *Let* $\mathsf{CRS} = \{\mathsf{CRS}_\lambda\}_{\lambda \in \mathbb{N}}$ *be an ensemble of CRS distributions and* $\mathcal{W}$ *be a source that may depend on* CRS. *We call an efficiently computable function ensemble* $\mathcal{F} = \{f_\lambda\}_{\lambda \in \mathbb{N}}$ ϵ-*hard-to-invert w.r.t.* $\mathcal{W}$ *and* CRS, *if for any polynomial-time* $\mathcal{A}$, *any* $\lambda \in \mathbb{N}$ *and any* $\mathit{crs} \in \mathsf{Supp}(\mathsf{CRS}_\lambda)$, *it holds that* $\Pr[k \leftarrow W_\lambda|_{\mathit{crs}} : \mathcal{A}(\mathit{crs}, f(\mathit{crs}, k)) = k] \leq \epsilon(\lambda)$.

One-Time Unforgeability. The unforgeability captures the infeasibility of forging an authentication tag being accepted by a secret key k drawn from a high-entropy source. Particularly, it considers a key from a non-uniform distribution and allows adversaries to obtain auxiliary information.

Definition 4 (One-time unforgeability). *Let* $\Sigma = \{\mathsf{Init}, \mathsf{Tag}, \mathsf{Verify}\}$ *be a* κ-*MAC scheme with the key space* $\{0,1\}^{n(\lambda)}$. *We say* Σ *satisfies* $(n, \epsilon_{\mathsf{unf}}, \epsilon_{\mathsf{hv}})$ *one-time unforgeability, if for any polynomial-time adversary* $\mathcal{A}$, *any efficiently-samplable source* $\mathcal{W}$ *(defined over* $\{\{0,1\}^{n(\lambda)}\}_{\lambda \in \mathbb{N}}$*) and any function ensemble* $\mathcal{F}$ *s.t.* $\mathcal{F}$ *is* ϵ_{hv} *hard-to-invert w.r.t.* $\mathcal{W}$ *and* CRS, *it holds that* $\mathsf{Adv}^{\mathsf{unf}}_{\mathcal{A},\mathcal{W},\mathcal{F}}(\lambda) = \Pr[\mathsf{Exp}^{\mathsf{unf}}_{\mathcal{A},\mathcal{W},\mathcal{F}}(\lambda) = 1] \leq \epsilon_{\mathsf{unf}}(\lambda)$. *The experiment* $\mathsf{Exp}^{\mathsf{unf}}_{\mathcal{A},\mathcal{W},\mathcal{F}}$ *is defined below.*

$$\boxed{\begin{array}{l} \mathsf{Exp}^{\mathsf{unf}}_{\mathcal{A},\mathcal{W},\mathcal{F}}(\lambda) \\ \hline \mathsf{crs} \leftarrow \mathsf{Init}(1^\lambda); k \leftarrow W_\lambda|_{\mathsf{crs}} \\ (m, st) \leftarrow \mathcal{A}(\mathsf{crs}, f_\lambda(\mathsf{crs}, k)); \varsigma \leftarrow \mathsf{Tag}(\mathsf{crs}, k, m) \\ (m^*, \varsigma^*) \leftarrow \mathcal{A}(\varsigma, st) \\ \mathbf{if}\ (m^*, \varsigma^*) \neq (m, \varsigma) \wedge \mathsf{Verify}(\mathsf{crs}, k, m^*, \varsigma^*) = 1\ \mathbf{then}\quad \mathbf{return}\ 1 \\ \mathbf{return}\ 0 \end{array}}$$

One-Time Key Privacy. This property seeks to capture that an adversary cannot learn anything new about the secret from an authentication tag.

We follow the simulation paradigm that was developed for defining non-interactive zero-knowledge [2]. Namely, with the help of some "trapdoor" information about the CRS, these tags can be simulated without the secret, and adversaries cannot distinguish simulated tags from real ones. The simulation procedure is done by the following pair: $\mathsf{SimInit}(1^\lambda)$ – the init simulation algorithm outputs a CRS crs along with its trapdoor τ. $\mathsf{SimTag}(\mathsf{crs}, \tau, m)$ – the tag simulation algorithm outputs a simulated tag ς for m. With the simulation algorithms, we can formally define this property.

Definition 5 (One-time key privacy). *Let* $\Sigma = \{\mathsf{Init}, \mathsf{Tag}, \mathsf{Verify}\}$ *be a* κ-*MAC scheme with the key space* $\{0,1\}^{n(\lambda)}$. *We say* Σ *satisfies* $(n, \epsilon_{\mathsf{kpriv}}, \epsilon_{\mathsf{hv}})$ *one-time key privacy, if there is a pair of PPT algorithms* $(\mathsf{SimInit}, \mathsf{SimTag})$, *and for any polynomial-time adversary* $\mathcal{A}$, *any efficiently-samplable source* $\mathcal{W}$ *(defined over* $\{\{0,1\}^{n(\lambda)}\}_{\lambda \in \mathbb{N}}$) *and any function ensemble* $\mathcal{F}$ *s.t.* $\mathcal{F}$ *is* ϵ_{hv} *hard-to-invert w.r.t.* $\mathcal{W}$ *and* CRS, *it holds that*

$$\mathsf{Adv}^{\mathsf{kpriv}}_{\mathcal{A}, \mathcal{W}, \mathcal{F}}(\lambda) = |\Pr[\mathsf{Exp}^{\mathsf{kpriv},0}_{\mathcal{A}, \mathcal{W}, \mathcal{F}}(\lambda) = 1] - \Pr[\mathsf{Exp}^{\mathsf{kpriv},1}_{\mathcal{A}, \mathcal{W}, \mathcal{F}}(\lambda) = 1]| \leq \epsilon_{\mathsf{unf}}(\lambda).$$

The experiments $\mathsf{Exp}^{\mathsf{kpriv},0}_{\mathcal{A}, \mathcal{W}, \mathcal{F}}$ *and* $\mathsf{Exp}^{\mathsf{kpriv},1}_{\mathcal{A}, \mathcal{W}, \mathcal{F}}$ *are defined below.*

$\mathsf{Exp}^{\mathsf{kpriv},0}_{\mathcal{A}, \mathcal{W}, \mathcal{F}}(\lambda)$	$\mathsf{Exp}^{\mathsf{kpriv},1}_{\mathcal{A}, \Sigma, \mathcal{W}, \mathcal{F}}(\lambda)$
$(\mathsf{crs}, \tau) \leftarrow \mathsf{SimInit}(1^\lambda); k \leftarrow W_\lambda\|_{\mathsf{crs}}$	$\mathsf{crs} \leftarrow \mathsf{Init}(1^\lambda); k \leftarrow W_\lambda\|_{\mathsf{crs}}$
$(m, st) \leftarrow \mathcal{A}(\mathsf{crs}, f_\lambda(\mathsf{crs}, k))$	$(m, st) \leftarrow \mathcal{A}(\mathsf{crs}, f_\lambda(\mathsf{crs}, k))$
$\varsigma \leftarrow \mathsf{SimTag}(\mathsf{crs}, \tau, m); b' \leftarrow \mathcal{A}(\varsigma, st)$	$\varsigma \leftarrow \mathsf{Tag}(\mathsf{crs}, k, m); b' \leftarrow \mathcal{A}(\varsigma, st)$
return b'	**return** b'

Making Any Computational Extractor Robust Without Requiring More Entropy. We then show how to compile a strong extractor into a robust extractor (for general CRS dependent sources) using one-time κ-MAC. Let Ext be a (n, k, ℓ) strong extractor (working on (n, k)-sources, and output ℓ bits) with the seed length $s\ell$, and let $\Sigma = \{\mathsf{Init}, \mathsf{Tag}, \mathsf{Verify}\}$ be a κ-MAC scheme with the key space $\mathcal{K} = \{\{0,1\}^{n(\lambda)}\}_{\lambda \in \mathbb{N}}$ and the message space $\mathcal{M}es$ that contains $\{\{0,1\}^{\ell(\lambda)+s\ell(\lambda)}\}_{\lambda \in \mathbb{N}}$. Then, we illustrate our robust extractor construction $\mathcal{E} = \{\mathsf{CRS}, \mathsf{Gen}, \mathsf{Rep}\}$ in Fig. 1.

$\mathsf{CRS}(1^\lambda)$	$\mathsf{Gen}(\mathsf{crs}, w)$	$\mathsf{Rep}(\mathsf{crs}, w, P)$
$\mathsf{crs} \leftarrow \mathsf{Init}(1^\lambda)$	$s \leftarrow^\$ \{0,1\}^{s\ell(\lambda)}, r \leftarrow \mathsf{Ext}(s, w)$	**if** $\mathsf{Verify}(\mathsf{crs}, w, s, \varsigma) = 1$
return crs	$\varsigma \leftarrow \mathsf{Tag}(\mathsf{crs}, w, s)$	**return** $R = \mathsf{Ext}(s, w)$
	return $R = r, P = (s, \varsigma)$	**return** $\perp$

Fig. 1. Robust extractor from randomness extractor + one time κ-MAC

Analysis. The correctness and security of our construction are fairly straightforward. We remark that we only require the source to have minimal min-entropy to enable a strong extractor. Formally, we have the following:

Theorem 2. *Let* Ext *be an* (n, k, ℓ)*-strong extractor with* ϵ_{ext}*-privacy,* Σ *be a* κ-*MAC with* $(n, \epsilon_{kpriv}, \epsilon_{hv})$ *one-time key privacy and* $(n, \epsilon_{unf}, \epsilon_{hv})$ *one-time robust-ness. If* $\epsilon_{hv} \geq \epsilon_{ext}$*, then for any* $\epsilon_{priv}, \delta_{rob}$*, satisfying* $\epsilon_{priv} \geq \epsilon_{ext} + 2\epsilon_{kpriv}$*, and* $\delta_{rob} >$ ϵ_{unf}*, the construction in Fig. 1 is an* (n, k, ℓ)*-robust extractor with* ϵ_{priv}*-privacy and* δ_{rob}*-post-application-robustness (defined in Sect. 4).*

We prove privacy and robustness in Lemmas 3 and 4, respectively.

Lemma 3. *Assume that* Ext *satisfies* ϵ_{ext}*-privacy, and* Σ *satisfies* $(n, \epsilon_{kpriv}, \epsilon_{hv})$ *one-time key privacy, where* $\epsilon_{hv} \geq \epsilon_{ext}$*. Then,* rExt *(in Fig. 3) satisfies* ϵ_{priv}*-privacy, for any* $\epsilon_{priv} > \epsilon_{ext} + 2\epsilon_{kpriv}$*.*

Proof. We prove this lemma by contradiction. Assume there is $\epsilon_0 > \epsilon_{ext} + 2\epsilon_{kpriv}$, and we have a polynomial-time adversary $\mathcal{B}$ who has an advantage greater than ϵ_0 w.r.t. some efficiently-samplable (n, k)-source $\mathcal{W}$. Then, we leverage $\mathcal{B}$ to construct a polynomial-time adversary $\mathcal{A}_{ext}$ for Ext, and two polynomial-time adversaries $\mathcal{A}_{mac,0}$ and $\mathcal{A}_{mac,1}$ for κ-MAC Σ, such that, for the source $\mathcal{W}$,

$$\mathsf{Adv}^{ext}_{\mathcal{A}_{ext}, \mathcal{W}}(\lambda) + \mathsf{Adv}^{kpriv}_{\mathcal{A}_{mac,0}, \mathcal{W}, \mathcal{F}}(\lambda) + \mathsf{Adv}^{kpriv}_{\mathcal{A}_{mac,1}, \mathcal{W}, \mathcal{F}}(\lambda) > \epsilon_0, \tag{5}$$

where $\mathcal{F}$ is a function ensemble implementing Ext. As $\epsilon_{hv} \geq \epsilon_{ext}$, such $\mathcal{F}$ is an admissible auxiliary inputs. Now, since we assume $\epsilon_0 > \epsilon_{ext} + 2\epsilon_{kpriv}$, it follows that either $\mathsf{Adv}^{ext}_{\mathcal{A}_{ext}, \mathcal{W}}(\lambda) > \epsilon_{ext}$, $\mathsf{Adv}^{kpriv}_{\mathcal{A}_{mac,0}, \mathcal{W}, \mathcal{F}}(\lambda) > \epsilon_{kpriv}$, or $\mathsf{Adv}^{kpriv}_{\mathcal{A}_{mac,1}, \mathcal{W}, \mathcal{F}}(\lambda) > \epsilon_{kpriv}$.

Now, we give the code of each adversary in Fig. 2.

Algorithm $\mathcal{A}_{ext}(i_{ext}, r)$	Algorithm $\mathcal{A}^{\mathcal{O}_\beta}_{mac,b}(\mathbf{crs}, (i_{ext}, r))$
$(\mathbf{crs}, \tau) \leftarrow \mathsf{SimInit}(1^\lambda)$	Query $\mathcal{O}_\beta$ with i_{ext}, and obtain ς
$\varsigma \leftarrow \mathsf{SimTag}(\mathbf{crs}, \tau, i_{ext})$	$R_0 \leftarrow\!\!{\$}\ \{0, 1\}^{\ell(\lambda)}, R_1 = r$
$b' \leftarrow \mathcal{B}(\mathbf{crs}, (i_{ext}, \varsigma), r)$	$\beta' \leftarrow \mathcal{B}(\mathbf{crs}, (i_{ext}, \varsigma), R_b)$
return b'	**return** β'

Fig. 2. Construction of $\mathcal{A}_{ext}$ and $\mathcal{A}_{am,b}$. In $\mathcal{A}_{ext}$, $(\mathsf{SimInit}, \mathsf{SimTag})$ is the simulator of κ-MAC. In $\mathcal{A}_{mac,b}$, r is the extracted randomness from w with the seed i_{ext}. $\mathcal{O}_\beta$ returns a real tag when $\beta = 1$ or returns a simulated tag when $\beta = 0$.

It is easy to see that $\mathcal{A}_{ext}$ and $\mathcal{A}_{am,b}$ are polynomial-time. Now, we argue advantages of each adversary.

Recall the privacy definition of a robust extractor (cf. Definition 2). The advantage of $\mathcal{B}$ against rExt's privacy w.r.t. $\mathcal{W}$ is defined by $\mathsf{Adv}^{priv}_{\mathcal{B}, \mathcal{W}}(\lambda) = |\Pr[\mathsf{Exp}^{priv,0}_{\mathcal{B}, W}(\lambda) = 1] - \Pr[\mathsf{Exp}^{priv,1}_{\mathcal{B}, W}(\lambda) = 1]|$. Let us assume that

$$p_0 = \Pr \left[\begin{array}{l} w \leftarrow W_\lambda, i_{ext} \leftarrow\!\!{\$}\ \{0, 1\}^{si(\lambda)} \\ r \leftarrow\!\!{\$}\ \{0, 1\}^{\ell(\lambda)} : 1 \leftarrow \mathcal{A}_{ext}(i_{ext}, r) \end{array} \right],$$

$$p_1 = \Pr\left[\begin{array}{l} w \leftarrow W_\lambda, i_{\text{ext}} \leftarrow\!\!\$ \{0,1\}^{si(\lambda)} \\ r \leftarrow \text{Ext}(i_{\text{ext}}, w) : 1 \leftarrow \mathcal{A}_{\text{ext}}(i_{\text{ext}}, r) \end{array}\right].$$

Then, by definition, the advantage of $\mathcal{A}_{\text{ext}}$ against Ext is $\text{Adv}^{\text{ext}}_{\mathcal{A}_{\text{ext}},\mathcal{W}}(\lambda) = |p_0 - p_1|$. For $b \in \{0,1\}$, we denote $\Pr[\text{Exp}^{\text{priv},b}_{\mathcal{B},\mathcal{W}}(\lambda) = 1] - p_b = \Delta_b$. By standard arguments, we have

$$\text{Adv}^{\text{priv}}_{\mathcal{B},\mathcal{W}}(\lambda) = \text{Adv}^{\text{ext}}_{\mathcal{A}_{\text{ext}},\mathcal{W}}(\lambda) + |\Delta_0| + |\Delta_1| \tag{6}$$

It is easy to verify that, at the point of $\mathcal{B}$'s view, the experiment $\text{Exp}^{\text{priv},b}_{\mathcal{B},\mathcal{W}}$ is identical to $\text{Exp}^{\text{kpriv},1}_{\mathcal{A}_{\text{mac},b},\mathcal{W},\mathcal{F}}$ (cf. Definition 5), and thus $\Pr[\text{Exp}^{\text{priv},b}_{\mathcal{B},\mathcal{W}}(\lambda) = 1] = \Pr[\text{Exp}^{\text{kpriv},1}_{\mathcal{A}_{\text{mac},b},\mathcal{W},\mathcal{F}}(\lambda) = 1]$. Similarly, we have $p_b = \Pr[\text{Exp}^{\text{kpriv},0}_{\mathcal{A}_{\text{mac},b},\mathcal{W},\mathcal{F}} = 1]$. Notice that $\text{Adv}^{\text{kpriv}}_{\mathcal{A}_{\text{mac},b},\mathcal{W},\mathcal{F}}(\lambda) = |\Pr[\text{Exp}^{\text{kpriv},0}_{\mathcal{A}_{\text{mac},b},\mathcal{W},\mathcal{F}}(\lambda) = 1] - \Pr[\text{Exp}^{\text{kpriv},1}_{\mathcal{A}_{\text{mac},b},\mathcal{W},\mathcal{F}}(\lambda) = 1]|$, we have $\text{Adv}^{\text{kpriv}}_{\mathcal{A}_{\text{mac},b},\mathcal{W},\mathcal{F}}(\lambda) = \Delta_b$, thus Eq. 6.   □

Lemma 4. *Assume that* Ext *satisfies* ϵ_{ext}-*privacy, and* Σ *satisfies* $(n, \epsilon_{\text{unf}}, \epsilon_{\text{hv}})$ *one-time unforgeability, where* $\epsilon_{\text{hv}} \geq \epsilon_{\text{ext}}$. *Then,* rExt *(in Fig. 3) satisfies* δ_{rob}-*post-application-robustness, for any* $\delta_{\text{rob}} \geq \epsilon_{\text{unf}}$.

Proof. We prove this lemma by contradiction. Assume there is $\delta_0 > \epsilon_{\text{unf}}$, and we have a polynomial-time adversary $\mathcal{B}$ who has an advantage greater than δ_0 w.r.t. some efficiently-samplable (n, k)-source $\mathcal{W}$. Then, we leverage $\mathcal{B}$ to construct a polynomial adversary $\mathcal{A}_{\text{mac}}$ against the unforgeability of κ-MAC Σ w.r.t. $\mathcal{W}$, with advantage $\text{Adv}^{\text{unf}}_{\mathcal{A}_{\text{mac}},\mathcal{W},\mathcal{F}}(\lambda) > \delta_0 > \epsilon_{\text{unf}}$. Here $\mathcal{F}$ is the function ensemble implementing Ext.

$\mathcal{A}_{\text{mac}}$ can be easily constructed. Given crs of Σ and (i_{ext}, r) which are the seed and the extracted randomness respectively from w (treated as auxiliary input), $\mathcal{A}_{\text{mac}}$ asks an authentication tag ς on i_{ext}, and invokes $\mathcal{B}$ by giving $(\text{crs}, (i_{\text{ext}}, \varsigma), r)$. When $\mathcal{B}$ breaks the robustness, *i.e.*, it outputs $P^* = (i^*_{\text{ext}}, \varsigma^*) \neq (i_{\text{ext}}, \varsigma)$ s.t. $\text{Verify}(\text{crs}, w, i^*_{\text{ext}}, \varsigma^*) = 1$, $\mathcal{A}_{\text{am}}$ can output $(i^*_{\text{ext}}, \varsigma^*)$ as a forgery. It is easy to see that $\mathcal{A}_{\text{am}}$ is polynomial-time.   □

Constructing One-Time κ-MAC. Now we discuss how to construct a κ-MAC. It is natural to view κ-MAC as a special leakage-resilient MAC, then upgrade it to add "key privacy". Given state of the art, the only known approach to MACs tolerating hard-to-invert leakage is using auxiliary-input secure signatures [13,23]. However, when considering weak keys and key privacy, it turns out to be more involved. We have to revisit the design framework of auxiliary-input secure signatures, adapt it to the symmetric setting, and address the subsequent challenges for realizing the new framework. To illustrate the challenges and ideas towards κ-MAC we first briefly recall Katz-Vaikuntanathan's leakage-resilient signature scheme [17] which was later shown by Faust *et al.* [13] to be secure against hard-to-invert leakage (with minor modifications). For the sake of clarification, we follow Dodis *et al.*'s [8] insightful abstraction, which bases KV signature upon the following building blocks.

– A leakage-resilient hard relation R_{LR} with its sampling algorithm $\mathsf{Gen}_{\mathsf{LR}}$. R is an NP relation, and $\mathsf{Gen}_{\mathsf{LR}}$ is a PPT algorithm which always outputs $(y, k) \in R_{\mathsf{LR}}$. We say R_{LR} is leakage-resilient, if for any efficient adversary $\mathcal{A}$ and any admissible leakage function f, we have

$$\Pr[(y, k) \leftarrow \mathsf{Gen}_{\mathsf{LR}}(1^\lambda), k^* \leftarrow \mathcal{A}(y, f(y, k)) : (y, k^*) \in R_{\mathsf{LR}}] \leq \mathsf{negl}(\lambda).$$

– A true-simulation-extractable NIZK (tSE-NIZK) [8] Π for the relation $\bar{R}_{\mathsf{LR}} :=$ $\{(y, k, m) : (y, k) \in R_{\mathsf{LR}}\}$. Π consists of a setup algorithm S_{zk}, a prover algorithm P_{zk}, and a verifier algorithm V_{zk}.

Informally, Katz-Vaikuntanathan signature proceeds as follows: To sign a message m, the signer with sk proves the knowledge of k for a statement $(y, k, m) \in \bar{R}_{\mathsf{LR}}$ and returns the proof π as the signature σ, where $(y, k) \in R_{\mathsf{LR}}$ is part of the verification key. Given that Π is a tSE-NIZK, a successful forgery will violate that R_{LR} is a leakage-resilient hard relation. Specifically, the zero-knowledge guarantees the signature will not leak new information about k, and the true-simulation-extractability ensures that an adversary who successfully generated a forgery must have k^* s.t. $(y, k^*) \in R_{\mathsf{LR}}$. It follows that this adversary could produce k^* only given the verification key y and the leakage $f(y, k)$, which contradicts our assumption that R_{LR} is leakage-resilient hard.

Towards κ-MAC. While we can trivially use a signature scheme as a MAC by taking both vk and sk as the authentication key, this approach will require the key to be uniform. However, κ-MAC needs to work for weak keys. The central question is how to safely generate and share (vk, sk) between the sender and the receiver (verifier), while they initially only have a weak key in common that relates to the CRS.

It is safe to treat the CRS of tSE-NIZK (contained in the verification key vk) as a part of CRS in our κ-MAC construction. We then deal with $(y, k) \in R_{\mathsf{LR}}$. A natural approach is to take the shared weak key as k and efficiently generate y according to k. However, while signatures can assume a bulletin board for posting verification keys, in κ-MAC, y has to be sent to the verifier via an unauthenticated channel (namely, being a part of the authentication tag). Consequently, adversaries might alter y to y', as the verifier will not notice this change if $(y', k) \in R_{\mathsf{LR}}$. To prevent those attacks, we take the following steps.

– Observe that there might be a part of y (denoted by pp) that could be generated without k and reused across statements. We let pp be a part of CRS such that adversaries cannot modify it.
– We strengthen the definition of leakage-resilient hard relation against adversaries who alter the other part of y (denoted by yk). Namely, given (pp, yk) and leakage about k, adversaries cannot generate (yk', k') s.t. $((\mathsf{pp}, yk'), k') \in R_{\mathsf{LR}}$ and $((\mathsf{pp}, yk'), k) \in R_{\mathsf{LR}}$. We call such a relation a strengthened leakage-resilient hard relation (sLRH relation).

Next, for *key privacy*, $\widetilde{yk}$ (as a statement) should be indistinguishable with another $\widetilde{yk}$ (simulated without k). Note that this requirement cannot be bypassed, even when yk is uniquely determined by (pp, k) and is not contained in the authentication tag explicitly, since a NIZK proof is not supposed to hide the statement being proved. We therefore require the generator of κ-MAC to be a private generator.

We formalize all notions and intuitions in the following definition.

Definition 6. *Let R_{LR} be an NP relation defined over $\{Y_\lambda \times \{0,1\}^{n(\lambda)}\}_{\lambda \in \mathbb{N}}$,*

- **Generator.** *A pair of PPT algorithms $(\mathsf{PGen}, \mathsf{SGen})$ is a generator of R_{LR}, if for every $\lambda \in \mathbb{N}$ and $k \in \{0,1\}^{n(\lambda)}$, it follows that*

$$\Pr[pp \leftarrow \mathsf{PGen}(1^\lambda), yk \leftarrow \mathsf{SGen}(pp, k) : ((pp, yk), k) \in R_{\mathsf{LR}}] = 1.$$

- **sLRH relation.** *R_{LR} along with $(\mathsf{PGen}, \mathsf{SGen})$ is an $(n, \epsilon_{\mathsf{lr}}, \epsilon_{\mathsf{hv}})$-sLRH relation, if for any efficiently-samplable source $\mathcal{W}$ (over $\{\{0,1\}^{n(\lambda)}\}_{\lambda \in \mathbb{N}}$ and dependent of PGen) and any function ensemble $\mathcal{F}$ s.t. $\mathcal{F}$ is ϵ_{hv} hard-to-invert w.r.t. $\mathcal{W}$ and PGen, for any P.P.T adversary $\mathcal{A}$, it holds that $\mathsf{Adv}^{\mathsf{slrh}}_{\mathcal{A}, \mathcal{W}, \mathcal{F}}(\lambda) \le \epsilon_{\mathsf{lr}}(\lambda)$ where $\mathsf{Adv}^{\mathsf{slrh}}_{\mathcal{A}, \mathcal{W}, \mathcal{F}}(\lambda)$ is defined as*

$$\Pr\left[\begin{array}{c} pp \leftarrow \mathsf{PGen}(1^\lambda), k \leftarrow \mathcal{W}_\lambda|_{pp}, yk \leftarrow \mathsf{SGen}(pp, k), \\ (yk', k') \leftarrow \mathcal{A}(pp, yk, f_\lambda(pp, k)) : (pp, yk', k'), (pp, yk', k) \in R_{\mathsf{LR}} \end{array} \right].$$

- **Private generator.** *$(\mathsf{PGen}, \mathsf{SGen})$ satisfies $(n, \epsilon_{\mathsf{pr}}, \epsilon_{\mathsf{hv}})$-privacy, if for $(\mathcal{A}, \mathcal{W}, \mathcal{F})$ above, $\mathsf{Adv}^{\mathsf{pr}}_{\mathcal{A}, \mathcal{W}, \mathcal{F}}(\lambda) \le \epsilon_{\mathsf{pr}}(\lambda)$, where $\mathsf{Adv}^{\mathsf{pr}}_{\mathcal{A}, \mathcal{W}, \mathcal{F}}(\lambda) =$*

$$\left| \Pr\left[\begin{array}{l} pp \leftarrow \mathsf{PGen}(1^\lambda) \\ k \leftarrow \mathcal{W}_\lambda|_{pp} \\ yk \leftarrow \mathsf{SGen}(pp, k) : \\ 1 = \mathcal{A}(pp, yk, f_\lambda(pp, k)) \end{array} \right] - \Pr\left[\begin{array}{l} pp \leftarrow \mathsf{PGen}(1^\lambda) \\ k \leftarrow \mathcal{W}_\lambda|_{pp}, k' \leftarrow_\$ \{0,1\}^{n(\lambda)} \\ yk \leftarrow \mathsf{SGen}(pp, k') : \\ 1 = \mathcal{A}(pp, yk, f_\lambda(pp, k)) \end{array} \right] \right|.$$

Remark 2. The auxiliary-input function f does not take as input yk, because yk is generated by the authentication algorithm, and the auxiliary input is supposed to be leaked before authenticating. The source $\mathcal{W}$ and the leakage are dependent on pp since it is a part of the CRS. Other parts of CRS are not considered explicitly since SGen does not use them.

The Final κ-MAC Construction. Using an sLRH relation R_{LR} along with its private generator $(\mathsf{PGen}, \mathsf{SGen})$ and a tSE-NIZK $\Pi = \{\mathsf{S_{zk}}, \mathsf{P_{zk}}, \mathsf{V_{zk}}\}$ for the relation $\bar{R}_{\mathsf{LR}} := \{(pp, yk, k, m) : ((pp, yk), k) \in R_{\mathsf{LR}}\}$, we construct an one-time κ-MAC scheme in Fig. 3.[4]

---

[4] The one-time κ-MAC is enough for our purpose; we may generalize our construction to get a full-fledged κ-MAC using multi-message secure DPKE [5], which will require concrete entropy bound on the source though.

$\mathsf{Init}(1^\lambda)$	$\mathsf{Tag}(\mathsf{crs}, k, m)$	$\mathsf{Verify}(\mathsf{crs}, k, m, \varsigma)$
$\mathsf{crs}_{\mathsf{zk}} \leftarrow \mathsf{S}_{\mathsf{zk}}(1^\lambda)$	$yk \leftarrow \mathsf{SGen}(\mathsf{pp}, k)$	**return** 1 iff
$\mathsf{pp} \leftarrow \mathsf{PGen}(1^\lambda)$	$\pi \leftarrow \mathsf{P}_{\mathsf{zk}}(\mathsf{crs}_{\mathsf{zk}},$	$(\mathsf{pp}, yk, k) \in R_{\mathsf{LR}}$ and
return	$(\mathsf{pp}, yk, m), k)$	$\mathsf{V}_{\mathsf{zk}}(\mathsf{crs}_{\mathsf{zk}}, (\mathsf{pp},$
$\quad \mathsf{crs} = (\mathsf{crs}_{\mathsf{zk}}, \mathsf{pp})$	**return** $\varsigma = (yk, \pi)$	$yk, m), \pi) = 1$

Fig. 3. One-time κ-MAC from tSE-NIZK + sLRH relation

Analysis. Correctness is easy to see. Regarding security: from the privacy of the generator SGen and the zero-knowledgeness of Π, efficient adversaries cannot learn new information about k from the tag (y, π), and the key privacy follows. The tSE-NIZK ensures an adversary who successfully forges an authentication tag can also output a pair $(y', k') \in R_{\mathsf{LR}}$ *s.t.* $(y', k) \in R_{\mathsf{LR}}$, which contradicts the sLRH relation, and thus the unforgeability follows. Formal analysis is presented in the full paper.

Theorem 3. *Let* $(\mathsf{PGen}, \mathsf{SGen})$ *be an* $(n, \epsilon_{\mathsf{pr}}, \epsilon_{\mathsf{hv}})$-*private generator for an NP relation* R_{LR}, *and* R_{LR} *along with* $(\mathsf{PGen}, \mathsf{SGen})$ *be an* $(n, \epsilon_{\mathsf{lr}}, \epsilon_{\mathsf{hv}})$-*sLRH relation. Let* $\Pi = \{\mathsf{S}_{\mathsf{zk}}, \mathsf{P}_{\mathsf{zk}}, \mathsf{V}_{\mathsf{zk}}\}$ *be a NIZK for the relation* $\bar{R}_{\mathsf{LR}}$ *satisfying* ϵ_{zk}-*ZK and* $(\epsilon_{\mathsf{tse1}}, \epsilon_{\mathsf{tse2}})$-*tSE. Then, the construction in Fig. 3 satisfies* $(n, \epsilon_{\mathsf{kpriv}}, \epsilon_{\mathsf{hv}})$ *one-time key privacy and* $(n, \epsilon_{\mathsf{unf}}, \epsilon_{\mathsf{hv}})$ *one-time unforgeability, for any* $\epsilon_{\mathsf{kpriv}} \geq \epsilon_{\mathsf{pr}} + \epsilon_{\mathsf{zk}}$, *and any* $\epsilon_{\mathsf{unf}} \geq \epsilon_{\mathsf{zk}} + \epsilon_{\mathsf{tse1}} + \epsilon_{\mathsf{tse2}} + \epsilon_{\mathsf{lr}}$.

As shown by Dodis *et al.* [8], a tSE-NIZK could be constructed using CPA-secure PKE and standard NIZK, or CCA-secure PKE and simulation-sound NIZK. Both approaches can be based on standard assumptions. However, while a leakage-resilient hard relation can be instantiated with a second-preimage-resistant hash function H, the statement $y = H(k)$ will leak some information about k. For key privacy, we need new constructions for strengthened LRH relations.

sLRH Relation from Deterministic PKE. Note that the privacy of generator is not an orthogonal property of sLRH relation; it indeed prevents adversaries from finding the exact k from (pp, yk) and the leakage. If it is further ensured that adversaries cannot find a distinct k' along with yk' such that both (pp, yk', k) and (pp, yk', k') belong to R_{LR}, R_{LR} with a private generator will be a sLRH relation. We therefore abstract a useful property of R_{LR} called "collision resistance" below.

Definition 7. R_{LR} *is* $(n, \epsilon_{\mathsf{cr}})$-*collision-resistant w.r.t.* PGen, *if for any polynomial-time* $\mathcal{A}$, *it holds that*

$$\Pr\left[\begin{array}{l} \boldsymbol{pp} \leftarrow \mathsf{PGen}(1^\lambda), (yk, k, k') \leftarrow \mathcal{A}(\boldsymbol{pp}) : \\ k \neq k' \wedge (\boldsymbol{pp}, yk, k) \in R_{\mathsf{LR}} \wedge (\boldsymbol{pp}, yk, k') \in R_{\mathsf{LR}} \end{array} \right] \leq \epsilon_{\mathsf{cr}}(\lambda).$$

As discussed before, a collision-resistant relation with a private generator will be a sLRH relation. (The formal proof is in the full paper.)

Lemma 5. *Let* $(\mathsf{PGen}, \mathsf{SGen})$ *be an* $(n, \epsilon_{\mathsf{pr}}, \epsilon_{\mathsf{hv}})$-*private generator for* R_{LR}. *If* R_{LR} *satisfies* $(n, \epsilon_{\mathsf{cr}})$-*collision-resistance w.r.t.* PGen, R_{LR} *with* $(\mathsf{PGen}, \mathsf{SGen})$ *is an* $(n, \epsilon_{\mathsf{lr}}, \epsilon_{\mathsf{hv}})$-*sLRH relation, for any* $\epsilon_{\mathsf{lr}} \geq \epsilon_{\mathsf{pr}} + \epsilon_{\mathsf{cr}}$.

We now construct a collision-resistant relation with a private generator. An auxiliary-input secure deterministic public-key encryption (DPKE) scheme is a natural tool for realizing an NP relation with a private generator. Since no randomness is used, it is easy to check whether a ciphertext c_{de} encrypts a message m_{de} under a public key pk_{de}. We can define an NP relation R_{de} such that $(pk_{\mathsf{de}}, c_{\mathsf{de}}, m_{\mathsf{de}}) \in R_{\mathsf{de}}$ iff $c_{\mathsf{de}} = \mathsf{E}_{\mathsf{de}}(pk_{\mathsf{de}}, m_{\mathsf{de}})$. From the auxiliary-input security of DPKE, the key generation algorithm and the encryption algorithm will give a private generator for R_{de}.

The relation R_{de} is almostly collision-resistant. Under a valid public key pk_{de} (namely, there is a secret key sk_{de} to decrypt all ciphertexts under pk_{de}), the (perfect) correctness of DPKE ensures that for any ciphertext c_{de} there is at most one message m_{de} such that $c_{\mathsf{de}} = \mathsf{E}_{\mathsf{de}}(pk_{\mathsf{de}}, m_{\mathsf{de}})$. While it seems straightforward to ensure the validity of pk_{de} by putting it into the CRS, however, it violates security. The problem inherits from that DPKE only applies to message distributions *independent* of public key, but our goal is to have a construction for CRS-*dependent* sources.

We enforce the validity of public key as follows: note that a valid pair $(pk_{\mathsf{de}}, sk_{\mathsf{de}})$ defines an NP relation R_{pk}, and pk_{de} can be ensured valid (with overwhelming probability) using a NIZK proof demonstrating the knowledge of sk_{de} s.t. $(pk_{\mathsf{de}}, sk_{\mathsf{de}}) \in R_{\mathsf{pk}}$ (the key relation). Now, pk_{de} (with its validity proof) can be outputted by SGen, and PGen is only used to establish a CRS of NIZK. Though CRS is still in need, adaptively secure NIZK does allow CRS-dependent statements. The relation R_{de} will be extended for verifying the proof. Formally, let $\varSigma_{\mathsf{de}} = \{\mathsf{K}_{\mathsf{de}}, \mathsf{E}_{\mathsf{de}}, \mathsf{D}_{\mathsf{de}}\}$ be an auxiliary-input secure DPKE scheme and the key relation R_{pk}, and $\varPi_{\mathsf{pk}} = \{\mathsf{S}_{\mathsf{pk}}, \mathsf{P}_{\mathsf{pk}}, \mathsf{V}_{\mathsf{pk}}\}$ be a NIZK for R_{pk}. We define an NP relation $R_{\mathsf{LR}}^{\mathsf{de}}$ and construct its generator $(\mathsf{PGen}_{\mathsf{de}}, \mathsf{SGen}_{\mathsf{de}})$ below.

- Let $\mathsf{pp} = \mathsf{crs}_{\mathsf{pk}}$, $yk = (c_{\mathsf{de}}, pk_{\mathsf{de}}, \pi_{\mathsf{de}})$ and $k = m_{\mathsf{de}}$. $(\mathsf{pp}, yk, k) \in R_{\mathsf{LR}}^{\mathsf{de}}$ iff $c_{\mathsf{de}} = \mathsf{E}_{\mathsf{de}}(pk_{\mathsf{de}}, m_{\mathsf{de}})$ and $\mathsf{V}_{\mathsf{pk}}(\mathsf{crs}_{\mathsf{pk}}, pk_{\mathsf{de}}, \pi_{\mathsf{de}}) = 1$.
- $\mathsf{PGen}_{\mathsf{de}}(1^\lambda)$. Invoke $\mathsf{crs}_{\mathsf{pk}} \leftarrow \mathsf{S}_{\mathsf{pk}}(1^\lambda)$, and return $\mathsf{pp} = \mathsf{crs}_{\mathsf{pk}}$.
- $\mathsf{SGen}_{\mathsf{de}}(\mathsf{pp}, k = m_{\mathsf{de}})$. Invoke $(pk_{\mathsf{de}}, sk_{\mathsf{de}}) \leftarrow \mathsf{K}_{\mathsf{de}}(1^\lambda)$, $\pi_{\mathsf{de}} \leftarrow \mathsf{P}_{\mathsf{pk}}(\mathsf{crs}_{\mathsf{pk}}, pk_{\mathsf{de}}, sk_{\mathsf{de}})$, and $c_{\mathsf{de}} \leftarrow \mathsf{E}_{\mathsf{de}}(pk_{\mathsf{de}}, m_{\mathsf{de}})$. Return $yk = (c_{\mathsf{de}}, pk_{\mathsf{de}}, \pi_{\mathsf{de}})$.

Summarizing above, we have the following result, whose formal analysis is in the full paper.

Lemma 6. *Let* $\varSigma_{\mathsf{de}}$ *be* $(n, \epsilon_{\mathsf{hv}}, \epsilon_{\mathsf{ind}})$-*PRIV-IND secure DPKE with message space* $\{\{0, 1\}^{n(\lambda)}\}_{\lambda \in \mathbb{N}}$, R_{pk} *be its key relation. Let* $\varPi_{\mathsf{pk}}$ *be a NIZK for* R_{pk} *with* ϵ_{zk}-*ZK and* ϵ_{snd}-*adaptive-soundness.* $(\mathsf{PGen}_{\mathsf{de}}, \mathsf{SGen}_{\mathsf{de}})$ *is a* $(n, \epsilon_{\mathsf{pr}}, \epsilon_{\mathsf{hv}})$-*private generator of* $R_{\mathsf{LR}}^{\mathsf{de}}$ *for any* $\epsilon_{\mathsf{pr}} \geq \epsilon_{\mathsf{ind}} + 2\epsilon_{\mathsf{zk}}$, *and* $R_{\mathsf{LR}}^{\mathsf{de}}$ *is* $(n, \epsilon_{\mathsf{cr}})$-*collision resistant w.r.t.* $\mathsf{PGen}_{\mathsf{de}}$, *for any* $\epsilon_{\mathsf{cr}} \geq \epsilon_{\mathsf{snd}}$.

Under the exponentially-hard DDH assumption [24], it is known to exist a DPKE which is perfectly correct and secure against any ϵ-hard-to-invert leakage (as long as ϵ is a negligible function and s is a polynomial). Following Theorem 3 and Lemma 6, we have a κ-MAC against any ϵ-hard-to-invert leakage and thus can compile any secure randomness extractor.

6 Extension to Robust Fuzzy Extractors

In this section, we construct robust fuzzy extractors.

Intuition. Similar to the non-fuzzy case, we use a κ-MAC scheme to authenticate the helper string of the underlying fuzzy extractor. However, correctness and security will not directly inherit from the non-fuzzy case. Correctness can be fixed easily. We can use secure sketches to construct the underlying fuzzy extractor; thus, one can recover the original secret w from the helper string using a close secret w'.

We now discuss the obstacles towards security. While the helper string has to contain a secure sketch, the adversary may manipulate the secure sketch such that secret w'' recovered from it is not identical to the original secret w, and she may forge an authentication tag being accepted by w'' to break the robustness. We can simply reject all w'' that are not t-close to w' (in this case w'' must be incorrect), and an allowed w'' will be $2t$-close to w. The challenge is to ensure that adversaries cannot forge an authentication tag being accepted by this $2t$-close secret. In the following, we introduce *fuzzy unforgeability* of κ-MAC and show that the construction in the last section already satisfies this property. Then, we construct a robust fuzzy extractor for CRS-dependent sources by using fuzzy-unforgeable κ-MAC.

κ-MAC with Fuzzy Unforgeability. A κ-MAC scheme $\Sigma = \{\mathsf{Init}, \mathsf{Tag}, \mathsf{Verify}\}$ satisfies q-fuzzy unforgeability, if given an authentication tag ς from k along with an auxiliary input about k, one cannot forge a new authentication tag being accepted by any secret k' which is q-close to k. The formal definition (presented in the full paper) is parameterized by $(n, q, \epsilon_{\mathsf{unf}})$ along with $\mathbb{W}$ and $\mathbb{F}$, where n is the length of the secret, ϵ_{unf} is the advantage of polynomial-time adversaries, $\mathbb{W}$ is the admissible family of sources, and $\mathbb{F}$ is the family of admissible leakage functions.

Construction from Fuzzy sLRH Relation. Recall our κ-MAC construction in Fig. 3. If an adversary who is given yk and leakage about k outputs a forgery being accepted by a secret k^*, then, by tSE-NIZK, the adversary is able to output (yk', k') such that both (pp, yk', k') and (pp, yk', k^*) belong to the relation R_{LR}. For one-time standard unforgeability, k and k^* are equal, and such an adversary contradicts the definition of sLRH relation. For one-time q-fuzzy unforgeability, k^* will just be q-close to w, and we therefore strengthen the sLRH relation into its fuzzy version accordingly. More precisely, we call an NP relation R_{LR} a q-fuzzy relation w.r.t. (PGen, SGen), if given (pp, yk) generated from k using the generator, one cannot find a new pair (yk', k') such that (pp, yk', k') and (pp, yk', k'')

belong to R_{LR} for some $k'' \in B_q(k)$. We show the κ-MAC construction in Fig. 3 will be a q-fuzzy unforgeable, if the underlying sLRH relation is a q-fuzzy sLRH relation. The formal definition of the relation and the proof will be deferred to the full paper.

Lemma 7. *Let R_{LR} along with $(\mathsf{PGen}, \mathsf{SGen})$ be an $(n, \epsilon_{\mathsf{lr}})$-$q$-fuzzy sLRH relation w.r.t. $\mathbb{W}$ and $\mathbb{F}$. Let $\Pi = \{\mathsf{S}_{\mathsf{zk}}, \mathsf{P}_{\mathsf{zk}}, \mathsf{V}_{\mathsf{zk}}\}$ be a NIZK for the relation $\bar{R}_{\mathsf{LR}}$ satisfying ϵ_{zk}-ZK and $(\epsilon_{\mathsf{tse1}}, \epsilon_{\mathsf{tse2}})$-tSE. Then, the construction in Fig. 3 satisfies $(n, q, \epsilon_{\mathsf{unf}})$ one-time fuzzy-unforgeability w.r.t. $\mathbb{W}$ and $\mathbb{F}$, for any $\epsilon_{\mathsf{unf}} > \epsilon_{\mathsf{zk}} + \epsilon_{\mathsf{tse1}} + \epsilon_{\mathsf{tse2}} + \epsilon_{\mathsf{lr}}$.*

Fuzzy sLRH Relation from Collision-Resistant Relation with Private Generator. For a "collision-resistant" sLRH relation, the adversary can "frame" some k'' only when she finds k''. If given (pp, yk) finding $k'' \in B_q^t$ is hard, then the relation will be a q-fuzzy sLRH relation. We argue when we can have the latter property from the privacy of the generator.

Note that the privacy of generator cannot ensure that (pp, yk) hides *all* partial information about k, as (pp, yk) itself must be non-trivial about k. Actually, the privacy ensures that adversaries cannot learn anything which is useful for deciding that yk is either generated by using the leaked key k or using an independent key. Then, for small q such that $B_q(k)$ only contains polynomial points, $k'' \in B_q(k)$ is surely hard-to-find from (pp, yk). However, for large q such that $B_q(k)$ could contain super-polynomial points, this argument does not apply.

We overcome this challenge by observing the task of recovering k from k'' can be done with the help of $2t$-secure sketch. More specifically, assume an adversary can recover k'' from (pp, yk). Then, the distinguisher specifies the leakage as a $2t$-secure sketch, invokes the adversary to have this $k'' \in B_{2t}(k)$, and converts k'' to k with the help of the secure sketch. We establish the following theorem, whose analysis is in the full paper.

Theorem 4. *Let $(\mathsf{PGen}, \mathsf{SGen})$ be a $(n, \epsilon_{\mathsf{pr}}, \epsilon_{\mathsf{hv}})$-private generator for an NP relation R_{LR}, and let R_{LR} be $(n, \epsilon_{\mathsf{cr}})$-collision-resistant w.r.t. PGen. Then R_{LR} along with $(\mathsf{PGen}, \mathsf{SGen})$ will be a $(n, q, \epsilon_{\mathsf{lr}})$-fuzzy sLRH relation, for any $\epsilon_{\mathsf{lr}} > \epsilon_{\mathsf{pr}} + \epsilon_{\mathsf{cr}}$, w.r.t. $\mathbb{W}$ and $\mathbb{F}$ which satisfy the following conditions. (1) There is a q-secure sketch $\{\mathsf{SS}, \mathsf{Rec}\}$ for each $\mathcal{W} \in \mathbb{W}$. (2)For each $f \in \mathbb{F}$, there is a one-way permutation g, and define $\widetilde{f} = (f, \mathsf{SS}, g)$. Then $\widetilde{f}$ is ϵ_{hv}-hard-to-invert w.r.t. every $\mathcal{W}$.*

Constructing Robust Fuzzy Extractors. For a robust fuzzy extractor with t-error tolerance, we use a $2t$-fuzzy unforgeable κ-MAC to authenticate the helper string of a fuzzy extractor with t-error tolerance. Note the helper string along with the extracted randomness forms the auxiliary input $f(w)$ of the κ-MAC, our $2t$-fuzzy unforgeable κ-MAC construction allows an auxiliary input function f when f together with a $2t$-secure sketch forms a hard-to-invert leakage. Therefore, although a t-secure sketch is sufficient for constructing a fuzzy extractor with t-error tolerance, we will use a $2t$-secure sketch instead, such that $f(w)$ along with a $2t$-secure sketch must be hard-to-invert.

Let $\{\mathsf{SS}, \mathsf{Rec}\}$ be a $2t$-secure sketch, $\Sigma = \{\mathsf{Init}, \mathsf{Tag}, \mathsf{Verify}\}$ be a κ-MAC with $2t$-fuzzy unforgeability, and Ext be a strong extractor. We present the detailed construction of robust fuzzy extractor in Fig. 4.

$\mathsf{CRS}(1^\lambda)$	$\mathsf{Gen}(\mathsf{crs}, w)$	$\mathsf{Rep}(\mathsf{crs}, w', P)$
$\mathsf{crs} \leftarrow \mathsf{Init}(1^\lambda)$	$\mathsf{ss} \leftarrow \mathsf{SS}(w)$	$w'' \leftarrow \mathsf{Rec}(\mathsf{ss}, w')$
return crs	$i \leftarrow\!\!\$\, \{0,1\}^s, r \leftarrow \mathsf{Ext}(w, i)$	**return** $R \leftarrow \mathsf{Ext}(w'', i)$, **if**
	$\varsigma \leftarrow \mathsf{Tag}(\mathsf{crs}, w, (\mathsf{ss}, i))$	$\mathrm{dist}(w'', w') \leq t$
	return $R = r, P = (\mathsf{ss}, i, \varsigma)$	$\mathsf{Verify}(\mathsf{crs}, w'', (\mathsf{ss}, i), \varsigma) = 1$
		return $\perp$

Fig. 4. Robust fuzzy extractor from randomness extractor + secure sketch + κ-MAC

Regarding security, we present the following theorem whose formal proof will be in the full paper.

Theorem 5. *Assume* $\{\mathsf{SS}, \mathsf{Rec}\}$ *is an* $(\mathcal{M}, k, k', 2t)$-*secure sketch scheme,* Ext *is an* (n, k', ℓ)-*strong extractor with* ϵ_{ext}-*privacy, and* Σ *is a* κ-*MAC with* $(n, 2t, \epsilon_{\mathsf{unf}})$-*fuzzy unforgeability w.r.t.* $\mathbb{W}$ *and* $\mathbb{F}$ *and* $(n, \epsilon_{\mathsf{kpriv}}, \epsilon_{\mathsf{hv}})$. *Then, if* $\mathbb{W}$ *is all* (n, k)-*sources,* $\mathbb{F}$ *contains function ensembles implementing* SS, *and* $\epsilon_{\mathsf{ext}} < \epsilon_{\mathsf{hv}}$, *the construction in Fig. 4 is an* $(\mathcal{M}, k, \ell, t)$-*robust fuzzy extractor with perfect correctness,* ϵ-*privacy and* δ-*robustness, for any* $\epsilon > \epsilon_{\mathsf{ext}} + 2\epsilon_{\mathsf{kpriv}}$ *and* $\delta > \epsilon_{\mathsf{unf}}$.

7   Conclusion and Open Problems

We give the first CRS-dependent (fuzzy) robust extractors with minimal min-entropy requirement (super-logarithmic) on the source, in the computational setting. They close the major gap left by the state-of-the-art robust extractors which require a linear fraction. Along the way, we formulate a new primitive κ-MAC.

We believe our new robust extractors (and our new tool of κ-MAC) could have broader applications. Also, converting other fuzzy extractors (not from secure sketch) into robust fuzzy extractors may be applicable to more general sources. We leave them all as interesting open problems.

Acknowledgement. Part of the work was done while both authors were at New Jersey Institute of Technology, and Qiang was then supported in part by NSF #1801492.

References

1. Aggarwal, D., Obremski, M., Ribeiro, J.L., Simkin, M., Siniscalchi, L.: Two-source non-malleable extractors and applications to privacy amplification with tamperable memory. IACR Cryptol. ePrint Arch. 2020, 1371 (2020)

2. Blum, M., Feldman, P., Micali, S.: Non-interactive zero-knowledge and its applications (extended abstract). In: STOC, pp. 103–112. ACM (1988)
3. Boyen, X.: Reusable cryptographic fuzzy extractors. In: ACM Conference on Computer and Communications Security, pp. 82–91. ACM (2004)
4. Boyen, X., Dodis, Y., Katz, J., Ostrovsky, R., Smith, A.: Secure remote authentication using biometric data. In: Cramer, R. (ed.) EUROCRYPT 2005. LNCS, vol. 3494, pp. 147–163. Springer, Heidelberg (2005). https://doi.org/10.1007/11426639_9
5. Brakerski, Z., Segev, G.: Better security for deterministic public-key encryption: the auxiliary-input setting. In: Rogaway, P. (ed.) CRYPTO 2011. LNCS, vol. 6841, pp. 543–560. Springer, Heidelberg (2011). https://doi.org/10.1007/978-3-642-22792-9_31
6. Canetti, R., Goldreich, O., Halevi, S.: The random oracle methodology, revisited (preliminary version). In: STOC, pp. 209–218. ACM (1998)
7. Cramer, R., Dodis, Y., Fehr, S., Padró, C., Wichs, D.: Detection of algebraic manipulation with applications to robust secret sharing and fuzzy extractors. In: Smart, N. (ed.) EUROCRYPT 2008. LNCS, vol. 4965, pp. 471–488. Springer, Heidelberg (2008). https://doi.org/10.1007/978-3-540-78967-3_27
8. Dodis, Y., Haralambiev, K., López-Alt, A., Wichs, D.: Efficient public-key cryptography in the presence of key leakage. In: Abe, M. (ed.) ASIACRYPT 2010. LNCS, vol. 6477, pp. 613–631. Springer, Heidelberg (2010). https://doi.org/10.1007/978-3-642-17373-8_35
9. Dodis, Y., Kalai, Y.T., Lovett, S.: On cryptography with auxiliary input. In: STOC, pp. 621–630. ACM (2009)
10. Dodis, Y., Katz, J., Reyzin, L., Smith, A.: Robust fuzzy extractors and authenticated key agreement from close secrets. In: Dwork, C. (ed.) CRYPTO 2006. LNCS, vol. 4117, pp. 232–250. Springer, Heidelberg (2006). https://doi.org/10.1007/11818175_14
11. Dodis, Y., Reyzin, L., Smith, A.: Fuzzy extractors: how to generate strong keys from biometrics and other noisy data. In: Cachin, C., Camenisch, J.L. (eds.) EUROCRYPT 2004. LNCS, vol. 3027, pp. 523–540. Springer, Heidelberg (2004). https://doi.org/10.1007/978-3-540-24676-3_31
12. Dodis, Y., Wichs, D.: Non-malleable extractors and symmetric key cryptography from weak secrets. In: STOC, pp. 601–610. ACM (2009)
13. Faust, S., Hazay, C., Nielsen, J.B., Nordholt, P.S., Zottarel, A.: Signature schemes secure against hard-to-invert leakage. In: Wang, X., Sako, K. (eds.) ASIACRYPT 2012. LNCS, vol. 7658, pp. 98–115. Springer, Heidelberg (2012). https://doi.org/10.1007/978-3-642-34961-4_8
14. Fuller, B., Reyzin, L., Smith, A.: When are fuzzy extractors possible? In: Cheon, J.H., Takagi, T. (eds.) ASIACRYPT 2016. LNCS, vol. 10031, pp. 277–306. Springer, Heidelberg (2016). https://doi.org/10.1007/978-3-662-53887-6_10
15. Garg, A., Kalai, Y.T., Khurana, D.: Low error efficient computational extractors in the CRS model. In: Canteaut, A., Ishai, Y. (eds.) EUROCRYPT 2020. LNCS, vol. 12105, pp. 373–402. Springer, Cham (2020). https://doi.org/10.1007/978-3-030-45721-1_14
16. Kanukurthi, B., Reyzin, L.: An improved robust fuzzy extractor. In: Ostrovsky, R., De Prisco, R., Visconti, I. (eds.) SCN 2008. LNCS, vol. 5229, pp. 156–171. Springer, Heidelberg (2008). https://doi.org/10.1007/978-3-540-85855-3_11
17. Katz, J., Vaikuntanathan, V.: Signature schemes with bounded leakage resilience. In: Matsui, M. (ed.) ASIACRYPT 2009. LNCS, vol. 5912, pp. 703–720. Springer, Heidelberg (2009). https://doi.org/10.1007/978-3-642-10366-7_41

18. De Santis, A., Di Crescenzo, G., Ostrovsky, R., Persiano, G., Sahai, A.: Robust non-interactive zero knowledge. In: Kilian, J. (ed.) CRYPTO 2001. LNCS, vol. 2139, pp. 566–598. Springer, Heidelberg (2001). https://doi.org/10.1007/3-540-44647-8_33

19. Wen, Y., Liu, S.: Robustly reusable fuzzy extractor from standard assumptions. In: Peyrin, T., Galbraith, S. (eds.) ASIACRYPT 2018. LNCS, vol. 11274, pp. 459–489. Springer, Cham (2018). https://doi.org/10.1007/978-3-030-03332-3_17

20. Wen, Y., Liu, S., Gu, D.: Generic constructions of robustly reusable fuzzy extractor. In: Lin, D., Sako, K. (eds.) PKC 2019. LNCS, vol. 11443, pp. 349–378. Springer, Cham (2019). https://doi.org/10.1007/978-3-030-17259-6_12

21. Wen, Y., Liu, S., Han, S.: Reusable fuzzy extractor from the decisional Diffie-Hellman assumption. Des. Codes Cryptogr. **86**(11), 2495–2512 (2018)

22. Wen, Y., Liu, S., Hu, Z., Han, S.: Computational robust fuzzy extractor. Comput. J. **61**(12), 1794–1805 (2018)

23. Yuen, T.H., Yiu, S.M., Hui, L.C.K.: Fully leakage-resilient signatures with auxiliary inputs. In: Susilo, W., Mu, Y., Seberry, J. (eds.) ACISP 2012. LNCS, vol. 7372, pp. 294–307. Springer, Heidelberg (2012). https://doi.org/10.1007/978-3-642-31448-3_22

24. Zhandry, M.: On ELFs, deterministic encryption, and correlated-input security. In: Ishai, Y., Rijmen, V. (eds.) EUROCRYPT 2019. LNCS, vol. 11478, pp. 3–32. Springer, Cham (2019). https://doi.org/10.1007/978-3-030-17659-4_1

Polynomial-Time Targeted Attacks on Coin Tossing for Any Number of Corruptions

Omid Etesami[1], Ji Gao[2(✉)], Saeed Mahloujifar[3], and Mohammad Mahmoody[2]

[1] School of Mathematics, IPM, P.O. Box 19395-5746, Tehran, Iran
[2] University of Virginia, Charlottesville, VA, USA
{jg6yd,mohammad}@virginia.edu
[3] Princeton University, Princeton, NJ, USA
sfar@princeton.edu

Abstract. Consider a coin tossing protocol in which n processors $P_1, \ldots, P_n$ agree on a random bit b in n rounds, where in round i P_i sends a single message w_i. Imagine a full-information adversary who prefers the output 1, and in every round i it knows all the finalized messages $w_1, \ldots, w_{i-1}$ so far as well as the prepared message w_i. A k-replacing attack will have a chance to replace the prepared w_i with its own choice $w_i' \neq w_i$ in up to k rounds. Taking majority protocol over uniformly random bits $w_i = b_i$ is robust in the following strong sense. Any k-replacing adversary can only increase the probability of outputting 1 by *at most* $O(k/\sqrt{n})$. In this work, we ask if the above simple protocol is tight.

For the same setting, but restricted to uniformly random bit messages, Lichtenstein, Linial, and Saks [Combinatorica'89] showed how to achieve bias $\Omega(k/\sqrt{n})$ for any $k \in [n]$. Kalai, Komargodski, and Raz [DISC'18, Combinatorica'21] gave an alternative *polynomial-time* attack when $k \geq \Theta(\sqrt{n})$. Etesami, Mahloujifar, and Mahmoody [ALT'19, SODA'20] extended the result of KKR18 to *arbitrary* long messages. It hence remained open to find *any* attacks of bias $\Omega(k/\sqrt{n})$ in the few-corruption regime $k = o(\sqrt{n})$ when the messages are of arbitrary length, and to find such *polynomial-time* (and perhaps tight) attacks when messages are uniformly random bits. In this work, we resolve both of these problems.

- For arbitrary length messages, we show that k-replacing polynomial-time attacks can indeed increase the probability of outputting 1 by $\Omega(k/\sqrt{n})$ for *any* k, which is optimal up to a constant factor. By plugging in our attack into the framework of Mahloujifar Mahmoody [TCC'17] we obtain similar data poisoning attacks against deterministic learners when adversary is limited to changing $k = o(\sqrt{n})$ of the n training examples.
- For uniformly random bits $b_1, \ldots, b_n$, we show that whenever $\Pr[b = 1] = \Pr[\sum b_i \geq t] = \beta_n^{(t)}$ for $t \in [n]$ is the probability of a Hamming ball, then online *polynomial-time* k-replacing attacks can increase $\Pr[b = 1]$ from $\beta_n^{(t)}$ to $\beta_n^{(t-k)}$, which is optimal due to the majority protocol. In comparison, the (information-theoretic) attack of LLS89 increased $\Pr[b = 1]$ to $\beta_{n-k}^{(t-k)}$, which is optimal for adaptive adversaries who *cannot* see the message before changing it. Thus, we obtain a computational variant of Harper's celebrated vertex isoperimetric inequality.

© International Association for Cryptologic Research 2021
K. Nissim and B. Waters (Eds.): TCC 2021, LNCS 13043, pp. 718–750, 2021.
https://doi.org/10.1007/978-3-030-90453-1_25

Keywords: Coin tossing protocols · Isoperimetric inequalities · Poisoning attacks

1   Introduction

Collective coin tossing [6] is a fundamental problem in cryptography in which a set of n parties aim to jointly produce a random bit b that remains (close to) random even if an adversary controls a subset of these parties. The simple majority protocol $\mathrm{maj}(b_1, \ldots, b_n)$, when n is odd and each bit b_i is broadcast by party P_i, is robust in the following strong sense: Any adversary who even gets to see *all* the messages and then replaces at most $k \in [n]$ of the them can only bias the output bit by at most by $O(k/\sqrt{n})$ [4]. In a nutshell, in this work we ask *how optimal is the majority protocol against such attacks?* We study this question from various angles as explained below.

Problem Setting. Suppose Π is an n-round coin-tossing protocol between n parties, where party P_i sends a single message w_i in round i that could depend on all the previous messages, and the final bit b is a deterministic function of all messages.[1] Now, suppose an adversary aims to increase the probability of $\Pr[b = 1]$. We call this a *targeted* attack, as adversary can choose the target direction of the bias.[2] We deal with *k-replacing* adversaries who can replace k of the messages as follows. Suppose messages $w_1, \ldots, w_{i-1}$ are already finalized and party P_i is about to send w_i in round i. The adversary will have a chance to replace w_i, based on the knowledge of w_i.[3] Equivalently, we will think of the protocol as a *random process* $(w_1, \ldots, w_n)$ with n steps, and a k-replacing adversary will be allowed to override the content of k of the steps, in which case the rest of the random process will depend on the new values. The goal of the adversary is to increase the probability of $\Pr[b = 1]$ for a Boolean function $f(w_1, \ldots, w_n) = b \in \{0, 1\}$. Informally speaking, we would like to know what are the most robust random processes in this setting.

Targeted Aspect. Studying targeted attacks is important due to several reasons. Firstly, targeted attacks allow modeling adversaries who have a particular output preferred in mind. For example, the coin tossing model's output might determine whether a contract would be signed or not. Then, a party who prefers signing the contract wants to increase the chance of outputting $b = 1$. Moreover, targeted attacks allow modeling attacks on specific "undesired" properties like $\mathcal{B}$ defined over random processes; namely, the adversary aims to increase the probability of B happening at the end. Below in the introduction we further discuss applications such as targeted poisoning attacks in adversarial machine learning and computational isoperimetry results. See the full version of this paper for formalization of these results.

Robustness of Threshold Functions. For a setting where w_i is a uniform random bit b_i, consider the threshold function f defined as $f(b_1, \ldots, b_n) = 1$ whenever $\sum b_i \geq t$ and let $\beta_n^{(t)} = \Pr[\sum b_i \geq t]$. Then we get a robust protocol in the following sense. Any k-replacing adversary will be limited to achieve $\Pr[b = 1] \leq \beta_n^{(t-k)}$, because all it can

---

[1] This is also called a *single-turn* protocol.

[2] In contrast, *untargeted* adversaries can bias the output towards *either* of 0 or 1.

[3] This is also called the *strongly adaptive* corruption model [13].

do is to replace k ones with zeros. In particular, it can be shown that for the majority function (for odd n) any k-replacing attack increase $\Pr[b = 1]$ by at most $O(k/\sqrt{n})$.

In this work, we study the optimality of the simple threshold/majority protocols and ask the following.

1. If $\Pr[b = 1] = 1/2$ holds originally, can k-replacing adversaries increase the probability of $\Pr[b = 1]$ by $\Omega(k/\sqrt{n})$ in *every* n-step random process with arbitrarily long messages?
2. For simpler models such as those with uniformly random bits, can we obtain *optimal* attacks that prove the threshold protocols to be the best possible for all $\Pr[b = 1] = \beta_n^{(t)}$?

We answer both questions above affirmatively. Notably, we even obtain *polynomial-time* attacks. Before describing our results in details, we briefly discuss what was known before our work.

Previous Work for Uniform Binary Messages. Lichtenstein, Linial, and Saks [24] showed that the threshold protocols are optimal when the messages are uniform random bits, but under a weaker attack model where the adversary is supposed to corrupt parties before seeing their message. In particular, they showed that if $\Pr[f(b_1, \ldots, b_n) = 1]$ without attack is the probability of the threshold function $\Pr[\sum b_i \geq t] = \beta_n^{(t)}$, then there is an *adaptive* attack with budget k that achieves $\Pr[f(b_1, \ldots, b_n) = 1] \geq \beta_{n-k}^{(t-k)}$. However, this attack was information theoretic and not polynomial time. It also remained open whether k-replacing attacks can improve upon the bound of [24] and potentially match the robustness of threshold functions. In other words, prior to our work, it was not known whether threshold functions are optimal against k-replacing attacks.

Previous Work on Arbitrary Length Messages. Kalai, Komargodski, and Raz [21] showed that in the "many-replacement" regime where $k = \Omega(\sqrt{n})$, a different attack in the binary setting of [24] can be achieved in polynomial time.[4] Building upon [21], Etesami, Mahloujifar and Mahmoody [12,27] showed how to extend this result to arbitrary message length and obtain (again targeted) attacks in polynomial time, but again only when $k \geq \Omega(\sqrt{n})$. (See Sect. 1.1 for more discussions on why those proofs lead to many replacements.) Finally, Khorasgani, Maji, Mukherjee, and Wang [22,23] showed how to get *non-targeted* attacks for large messages when $k = 1$.

Our Results. Previous works left open our two main questions. In this work, we resolve both of these questions and show that (1) when $\Pr[b = 1] = \Theta(1)$, then majority is optimal up to a constant factor against k-replacing adversaries for all adversary budget k (including the "few corruption regime"), and (2) when messages are uniformly random bits, for any initial probability of Hamming balls $\Pr[b = 1] = \Pr[\sum b_i \geq t]$, the corresponding threshold function is optimal, *even up to exact constants*.

---

[4] Interestingly, the main result of [21] focuses on *non-targeted* attacks and shows that the output of any single-turn protocol can be attacked (only information theoretically) by a (standard) adaptive *non-targeted* adversary replacing $k = \Omega(\sqrt{n})$ parties. The recent breakthrough of Haitner and Karidi-Heller [15] generalized the main result of [21] to any general, perhaps multi-turn, protocol. Our focus in this work, however, is on single-turn protocols.

Theorem 1 (Main result 1 – arbitrary messages). *Let Π be any single-turn polynomial-time coin-tossing protocol between n parties to obtain an output bit b in which, originally (before any attack) it holds that $\Pr[b = 1] = \mu$. For any $k = O(\sqrt{n})$, there is a k-replacing polynomial time attack that increases the probability of outputting $b = 1$ by a probability that can get arbitrarily close to:*

$$\left(1 - \left(1 - \frac{\mu}{\sqrt{n}}\right)^k\right) \cdot \left(1 - e^{-2} - \mu\right).$$

To prove Theorem 1, we use ideas from the attack of [27] (see Sect. 1.1). See Theorem 14 for a formalization of the information theoretic variant. For the polynomial-time variant of this theorem see the full version.

It can be shown that, as long as $k = O(\sqrt{n})$, the biasing bound of Theorem 1 is $\Omega(k \cdot \mu/\sqrt{n})$. Therefore, Theorem 1 resolves our first main question above; i.e., the majority protocol of [3] is optimal, up to a constant factor, for targeted attacks on any single-turn protocol when $\mu = \Theta(1)$.

Our next result solves the problem completely for protocols with uniform random bits, as long as the probability of outputting 1 is that of a threshold function.

Theorem 2 (Main result 2 – uniformly random bits). *Let Π be any single-turn polynomial-time coin-tossing protocol between n parties to obtain an output bit b in which the parties share uniformly random bits $b_1, \ldots, b_n$. Suppose originally (before any attack) it holds that $\Pr[b = 1] = \Pr[\sum b_i \geq t] = \beta_n^{(t)}$ for $t \in [n]$. Then, for any $k \in [n]$, there is a k-replacing attack that increases the probability of outputting $b = 1$ to $\beta_n^{(t-k)}$. Moreover, if it further holds that $\Pr[b = 1] \geq 1/\operatorname{poly}(n)$ is non-negligible, then there will be polynomial-time k-replacing attacks that can get arbitrarily close to the same bound of $\beta_n^{(t-k)}$.*

To prove Theorem 2, we also use ideas from the recent work of [23]. See Theorem 18 for a formal version of the information theoretic variant of Theorem 2. See the full version of the paper for how our specific information theoretic attack can be adapted minimally to run in polynomial time.

Note that Theorem 2 shows something perhaps surprising about the power of *online* attacks against coin tossing protocols. It shows that online attacks are *as powerful* as offline attacks, when we consider the most robust functions with $\Pr[b = 1] = \beta_n^{(t)}$ being that of a Hamming ball. In fact, we present such attacks that run in polynomial time, and this implies a new computational variant for the celebrated vertex isoperimetry inequality of Harper [19]. Indeed, the vertex isoperimetric inequality in the Boolean hypercube states that for any set $\mathcal{S} \subseteq \{0, 1\}^n$ of probability $\Pr[(b_1 \ldots, b_n) \in \mathcal{S}] = \beta_n^{(t)}$, the probability of the set of points (inside or outside $\mathcal{S}$) with a neighbor in $\mathcal{S}$ of distance at most k is at least $\beta_n^{(t-k)}$. Our Theorem 2 matches this bound exactly, and even shows how to *find* such close neighbors (in $\mathcal{S}$) in *polynomial time* and even in an *online manner* for at least $\beta_n^{(t-k)}$ fraction of $\{0, 1\}^n$.

Applications. We can directly apply the attacks of Theorems 1 and 2 to obtain the applications below (Table 1).

Table 1. Summary of related attacks on single-turn coin tossing protocols.

	Targeted	Poly-time	Corruption model	Budget k	Messages	Rounds
[24]	✓	–	Adaptive	Any	Uniform bits	Any
[21]	✓	✓	Adaptive	$\Omega(\sqrt{n})$	Uniform bits	Any
This work	✓	✓	Replacing	Any	Uniform bits	Any
[12,27]	✓	✓	Replacing	$\Omega(\sqrt{n})$	Arbitrary	Any
This work	✓	✓	Replacing	Any	Arbitrary	Any
[8]	–	–	Replacing	1	Arbitrary	Any
[13]	–	–	Replacing	$\Omega(\sqrt{n})$	Arbitrary	1
[31,35]	–	–	Replacing	Any	Arbitrary	1
[15,21]	–	–	Adaptive	$\Omega(\sqrt{n})$	Arbitrary	Any
[22]	–	–	Replacing	1	Arbitrary	Any
[23]	–	–	Adaptive	1	Arbitrary	Any

- **Targeted data poisoning on learners.** Theorem 1 can model any random process $(w_1, \ldots, w_m)$ that generates an object h that might or might not belong to an (undesirable) set $\mathcal{B}$ with some probability μ. In that case, we can define the output of the process to be $b = 1$ if $h \in \mathcal{B}$, and then an adversary can *increase* the probability of falling into S through a k-replacing attack. Now, suppose w_i is a batch of data provided by the iþ party, and let h be a model that is deterministically trained on the data set $w_1 \cup \cdots \cup w_n$. Suppose there is an specific (efficiently testable) property $\mathcal{B}$ defined over h that an adversary wants to increase its probability (e.g., h makes a specific decision on a particular test instance). Theorem 14 shows that the adversary can always increase the probability of $\mathcal{B}$ from μ to $\mu + \Omega(k/\sqrt{n})$ by changing only k of the training batches. Previously, Etesami, Mahloujifar, and Mahmoody [12,27] proved such results only for when $k \geq \Omega(\sqrt{n})$ and Diochnos, Mahloujifar, and Mahmoody [25,26,28] proved a weaker bound of $\mu + \Omega(k/n)$.

- **Computational isoperimetry in product spaces.** Let $\mathbf{w}_{\leq n} \equiv (\mathbf{w}_1 \times \cdots \times \mathbf{w}_n)$ be a product distribution of dimension n, and let HD be the Hamming distance $\text{HD}(w_{\leq n}, w'_{\leq n}) = |\{i \mid w_i \neq w'_i\}|$. Then, a basic question in functional analysis is how quickly noticeable events expand under Hamming distance. It is known, e.g., by results implicit in [1,32] and explicit in [31,35][5] that if a set S has measure μ, the k-expansion of it (i.e., the set of points with a neighbor in S of distance at most k) will have measure at least $\mu + \Omega(k \cdot \mu/\sqrt{n})$ for $k = O(\sqrt{n})$. The previous works of [12,27] introduced an *algorithmic* variant of the measure concentration phenomenon and showed how to obtain polynomial time algorithms that achieve the following. Given a random point $w_{\leq n} \in \mathbf{w}$, we can *find* a neighbor of distance at most k in S with probability $\mu + \Omega(k \cdot \mu/\sqrt{n})$.

---

[5] A weaker version for uniform bits is known as the blowing-up lemma [30].

Their result above only apply to the setting where $k \geq \Omega(\sqrt{n})$, and it remained open to obtain such computational concentration for any small $k = o(\sqrt{n})$. For such small k, the problem is more suitable to be called an *isoperimetric* problem, due to historic reasons. By applying our Theorem 1 we directly get computational concentration/isoperimetry results for any $k = o(\sqrt{n})$ in any product space. For the case of uniform random bits and probabilities corresponding to Hamming balls, our Theorem 2 shows how to obtain results that match the corresponding lower bound on the vertex isoperimetry [19], and we do so by using polynomial time algorithms. See the full version for the details of the polynomial time extension.

1.1 Technical Overview

Here, we describe the key ideas behind our main results of Theorems 1 and 2 at a high level. We prove Theorem 1 by giving a novel inductive analysis (over adversary's budget k) for a variant of the attack of [27]. Interestingly, even though the attack of [12] improves [27] for many-replacing regime, we are not able to build our few-replacing attacks on that of [12]! We also do a modification to the [27] (by *always* looking at a message before changing or not changing it) that allows us to significantly improve the exact bound. Our modification of the attack of [27] makes the attack's description simpler and allows for sharper analysis (even in the many-replacing regime of [27], but that is not our focus here). In fact, that change is crucial to obtain our Theorem 2 which gives an *optimal* bounds for uniform binary messages.

Our proof of Theorem 2 is inspired by the recent work of Khorasgani et al. [23] who studied 1-*replacing information-theoretic non-targeted* attacks, but we still use ideas from their work in our setting. In particular, we use a concave function as the lower bound of the success probability of our attack and use induction over the number of bits n. The exact attack and the details of our inductive proof, however, are quite different from the work of Khorasgani et al. [23].

Outline. We first describe our ideas for Theorem 1 and then will do so for Theorem 2. For Theorem 1, we will first sketch the proofs of [12,21,27][6] and explain why they require $k = \Omega(k)$ replacements to give a meaningful bound. Then, we explain our new ideas that allow bypassing the barrier of $k = \Omega(k)$.

In the following, we explain our new ideas behind the proof of Theorems 1 and 2.

Why the Attacks of [12,21,27] *Need* $k = \Omega(\sqrt{n})$ *Corruptions.* The targeted attacks of [12,21,27] have a similar core that make them rely on many $k = \Omega(\sqrt{n})$ number of corruptions to achieve bias towards 1. These attacks first show that certain specific attacks with *unlimited* budget can significantly bias the output of the function towards 1. Then, in the second step, they show that the number of corruptions of such ∞-replacing attacks will not be more than $O(\sqrt{n})$. To contrast our approach, the analysis of our attack for proving Theorem 1 starts from $k = 1$ and increases k, while those of [12,21,27] start from $k = \infty$ and show that it does not have to be more than $k = \Theta(\sqrt{n})$.

---

[6] In case [21], here we refer to their proof for the case of bitwise messages. Their attack for the long-message setting is (inherently) an non-targeted attack, and not a PPT one.

Notation. Let w_i be the i'th message sent by the i'th party, and let v_i be the possible modified version ($v_i \neq w_i$ if the adversary corrupts the $i\flat$ party and changes its message). We let $w_{\leq i} = (w_1, \ldots, w_i)$ and $v_{\leq i}$ is defined similarly. Let $f(v_1, \ldots, v_n) = b$ be the Boolean function that determines the final output bit b. Also $\mu = \Pr[b = 1]$ holds in the original (no-attack) protocol. (See Sect. 2 for all the definitions.)

The attacks of [12,21,27] all track the expected value $\bar{f}(v_{\leq i-1}) = \Pr[b = 1 \mid v_{\leq i-1}]$ of the final bit b conditioned on the current messages $v_{\leq i-1}$ (which forms a Doob martingale). Let w_i be the honestly prepared message of the i'th party that is about to be sent in round i. If the number of corruptions has not reached k yet, with the attack parameter $\lambda \in [0, 1]$, do as follows.

1. Even before looking at w_i, if there is *some* v_i that increases the expected value of b by λ (i.e., $\bar{f}(v_{\leq i}) > \bar{f}(v_{\leq i-1}) + \lambda$) then corrupt the i'th party and send v_i instead.
2. Otherwise, look at w_i. If, it is going to decrease the expected value of b by more than λ (i.e., $\bar{f}(v_{\leq i}, w_i) < \bar{f}(v_{\leq i-1}) - \lambda$), then again corrupt message w_i to v_i.
3. Otherwise, do not corrupt the i'th party, and let $v_i = w_i$ remain unchanged.

Analysis of [27]. The main ideas in the analysis of [27] are as follows.

1. Ignoring the number of corruptions, the ∞-replacing attack achieves expected value $1 - \mathrm{err}(\lambda, \mu, n)$, where $\mathrm{err}(\lambda, \mu, n) = e^{-\Omega(\mu^2/(n\lambda^2))}$ is an "Azuma error".
2. For every corruption, the expected value of the output jumps up by at least λ.

Relying on the above two keys, [27] proved that the total expected number of corruptions cannot be larger than $1/\lambda$, so by choosing $\lambda \approx \mu/\sqrt{n}$, they can achieve both (1) high expected value $1 - \mathrm{err}(\lambda, \mu, n)$ and (2) few corruptions $k \leq 1/\lambda \approx \sqrt{n}/\mu$.

A Candidate One-Replacing Targeted PPT Attack. We now propose our new one-replacing attack that we will analyze using new ideas. The first version of our attack follows that of [27] and immediately stops as soon as the first corruption happens. Note that, the analysis of [27] says nothing about the power of this 1-replacing attack, as this attack is cut prematurely.

Idea 1: we gain as soon as the corruption happens. Our first key idea is that, the additive attack of [27] (as opposed to the "multiplicative" attack of [12]) *always* gains by λ, whenever a corruption happens. So, to analyze our 1-replacing attacks, all we need is to lower bound the probability p_1 of one corruption.

Idea 2: 1-replacing is as good as ∞-replacing if no corruptions happens. As long as no corruption has happened, our one-replacing attacker is actually *identical* to an attack with no limit on the number of corruptions. Also, note that the probability of outputting 1 in the ∞-replacing attack of [27] is $1 - \mathrm{err}(\lambda, \mu, n)$. Therefore, we conclude that if we run the one-replacing attack, with probability $1 - \mathrm{err}(\lambda, \mu, n)$ we *either* output 1 (which is good enough) *or* do at least one corruption (which is also good for us!). Since the probability of outputting 1 *without* any attacks is exactly μ, we can now lower bound p_1 and conclude that

$$p_1 \geq 1 - \mathrm{err}(\lambda, \mu, n) - \mu.$$

Having the above bound on p_1, we lower bond output's expected value μ_1 under our 1-replacing attack is

$$\mu_1 \geq \mu + \lambda \cdot (1 - \mathrm{err}(\lambda, \mu, n) - \mu).$$

We can now choose $\lambda = \Theta(\mu/\sqrt{n})$ which leads to up bias $\Omega(\mu/\sqrt{n})$. This attack can be made polynomial time by approximating output's Doob martingale.

Induction on k to Obtain k -Replacing Targeted Attack. Having the 1-replacing attack above, it is now tempting to apply them recursively to get k-replacing attacks. Note that this is possible only because we have a *targeted* attack, and so we can recursively apply such attack k times, each of which is a one-replacing attack, and increase the expected value of the output bit gradually. This approach, however, remains polynomial time only for $k = O(1)$. Here, we take a different approach and directly analyze the k-replacing attack of [27] using induction on k.

The idea is to allow the ∞-replacing attack of [27] run for k corruptions in total rather than one, and then trying to analyze it by induction on k. Suppose p_k is the probability that the k-replacing attack reaches its k'th corruption. Also, let μ_i be the expected value of the output b under the i-replacing targeted attack. A key idea is that all we have to do is to lower bound the probability of the corruptions happening, and by linearity of expectation we will indeed gain by at least $\lambda \cdot k$ in expected value of the outcome. In fact, we go one step further and relate the gain in the k'th corruption directly to the gain already obtained through $k - 1$ corruptions. I.e., by linearity of expectation, we have:

$$\mu_k \geq \mu_{k-1} + \lambda \cdot p_k.$$

The intuition is that before reaching the k'th corruption, the two attack are the same, and once the k'th corruption happens, the k-replacing attack gets a jump of λ up compared to the $(k-1)$-replacing attack. Again, all we need is to lower bound p_k. To do so, we again use a generalization of the idea that we described for the case of one-replacing above. Namely, we note that as long as the k'th corruption does not happen in the k-replacing attack, it is again *indistinguishable* from the ∞-replacing attack of [27]. Also, the $(k-1)$-replacing attack reaches $b = 1$ with probability μ_{k-1} already. Using a union bound, we get:

$$p_k \geq 1 - \mathrm{err}(\lambda, \mu, n) - \mu_{k-1},$$

using which we can get that the expected value of b under the k-replacing attack is

$$\mu_k \geq \mu + \lambda \cdot (1 - \mathrm{err}(\lambda, \mu, n) - \mu_{k-1}).$$

Solving the recursive inequalities above, we lower bound μ_k as in Theorems 1 and 14.

We now describe some of the key ideas behind our proof of Theorem 2, which deals with uniform binary messages. In this section, we mainly focus on showing the core ideas that lead to the information theoretic optimal k-replacing attacks of Theorem 2, which deals with online attacks. In the full version of this paper we show how to use similar ideas (by approximating the Doob martingale of the final output bit) used for the polynomial-time attacks for Theorem 1 to also extend our information theoretic attacks for Theorem 2 to polynomial time variants.

Notation. First, we define the key notations that are needed for our overview of the ideas behind the proof of our Theorem 2. Here, all the original messages are *independent and uniform* random bits, which we denote with $(u_1, \ldots, u_n)$. Also, we let $\mathcal{S}$ be the set of input sequences that lead to output 1, namely $\mathcal{S} = \{x \mid f(x) = 1\}$. We know that $\Pr[(u_1, \ldots, u_n) \in \mathcal{S}] = \Pr[\sum u_i \geq t] = \beta_n^{(t)}$ is that of a Hamming ball. The goal of the adversary is to maximize the probability of falling into $\mathcal{S}$ through k-replacements in an online way. We now define the "online expansion" under optimal online k-replacing attacks, both as a function of sets, or as a function of set probabilities. (See Definition 17 for more details.) Let A be an online k-replacing adversary over the uniform distribution over $\{0,1\}^n$. Let $\mathsf{OnExp}^{(A)}(\mathcal{S})$ be the probability that A can map a random input to $\mathcal{S}$ through its online k-replacing attack. Let $\mathsf{OnExp}^{(k)}(\mathcal{S})$ be the maximum over $\mathsf{OnExp}^{(A)}(\mathcal{S})$ among all k-replacing attacks, and let the following be the minimum of $\mathsf{OnExp}^{(k)}(\mathcal{S})$ among all sets of measure μ.

$$\mathsf{OnExp}_n^{(k)}(\mu) = \inf_{\mathcal{S}, \Pr[\mathcal{S}] \geq \mu} \mathsf{OnExp}^{(k)}(\mathcal{S}).$$

Our key idea is to show that the following piecewise-linear function is a *lower bound* on the power of k-replacing attacks. We prove this by induction on n. In comparison, [23] also used similar piecewise-linear functions, but their goal was to obtain *1-corrupting information theoretic non-targeted* attacks. It is possible that using similar techniques, one can make the attack of [23] also polynomial time, but the key differences are due to the fact that [23] aims for a non-targeted attack, and hence it ends up with a completely different recursive relation and induction on n.

Definition 3 (The piecewise-linear lower bound – informal). For any non-negative integers k, n, the function $\ell_n^{(k)} : [0, 1] \to [0, 1]$ is defined as follows.

- If $\mu = \beta_n^{(t)}$ for any $t \in [n]$, it holds that $\ell_n^{(k)}\left(\beta_n^{(t)}\right) = \beta_n^{(t-k)}$. Namely, when the input probability is that of an exact Hamming balls, $\ell_n^{(k)}$ returns their probability after expanding them to include anything within their k Hamming distance (which is also a Hamming ball).
- Connect all the $n + 2$ points above to obtain a piecewise-linear function $\ell_n^{(k)}$.

See Definition 24 for a formal definition of the function above.

Recursive Relation for $\mathsf{OnExp}_n^{(k)}(\mu)$. We then use a recursive relation that can be used to exactly compute $\mathsf{OnExp}_n^{(k)}(\mu)$ for all k, n, μ (see Definition 20). The idea of the recursive relation is to model adversary's decision based on optimal decisions. In fact, if an adversary is given a bit $u_i = 0$, and it holds that $\Pr[(0, u_2, \ldots, u_n) \in \mathcal{S}] = \mu_0, \Pr[(1, u_2, \ldots, u_n) \in \mathcal{S}] = \mu_1$. Then, an optimal online adversary shall decide between changing it to 1 or not, and if it knows the optimal solutions for $\mathsf{OnExp}_{n-1}^{(k)}(\mu_0)$ (reflecting the "no change" decision) and $\mathsf{OnExp}_{n-1}^{(k-1)}$ (reflecting the "change" decision) it can make the optimal decision.

Using Lower Bounds Lead to Lower Bounds. We prove by induction on n, that if one uses *lower bounds* (e.g., $\ell_{n-1}^{(k)}$ and $\ell_{n-1}^{(k-1)}$) instead of $\mathsf{OnExp}_{n-1}^{(k)}(\mu_0)$ and

$\mathsf{OnExp}_{n-1}^{(k-1)}(\mu_1)$ in the recursive relation that computes $\mathsf{OnExp}_n^{(k)}$, then one obtains a lower bound on $\mathsf{OnExp}_n^{(k)}(\mu)$. This part of the proof follows from the monotonicity of the recursive relation for $\mathsf{OnExp}_n^{(k)}$.

Function $\mathsf{OnExp}_n^{(k)}(\mu)$ *Remains a Lower Bound for* $\ell_n^{(k)}$. We also show that when we apply the recursive relation over $\ell_{n-1}^{(k)}$ and $\ell_{n-1}^{(k-1)}$, the result will be an *upper bound* on $\ell_n^{(k)}$. This, together with the step above implies that $\ell_n^{(k)}$ remains a lower bound $\ell_n^{(k)}$. This is the most technical step of the proof that goes through a careful case study and heavily relies on the concavity and monotonicity of $\ell_n^{(k)}$.

Making the Attack Polynomial Time. In the actual polynomial time attack, the adversary approximates μ, and it uses $\ell_n^{(k)}$ (which is efficiently computable) instead of $\mathsf{OnExp}_n^{(k)}(\mu)$ in the recursive relation and decides to change or not change the bits. See the full version of the paper for the details of making the attack polynomial time.

1.2 Further Related Work

Many of the related works were already discussed in previous sections. In this section, we discuss other works related to ours, mostly in the context of coin tossing protocols.

Adaptive Corruption. As explained above, our results are proved in the *strong* adaptive corruption model. However, many works study the power of standard adaptive corruption in coin tossing protocols. The main result in [21] indeed proves the existence of such attacks that achieve *non-targeted* biasing that controls the output fully when the number of corruptions is $k \geq \sqrt{n}$. Haitner and Karidi-Heller [15] further generalized this result to multi-turn protocols, resolving a long-standing open problem of Ben-Or and Linial [4]. Dodis [11] previously proved that certain black-box methods cannot break this conjecture. The recent work of Khorasgani, Maji, and Wang [22,23] showed that for the case of 1 replacing, (computationally unbounded) adaptive adversaries can achieve *non-targeted* bias $\Omega(1/\sqrt{n})$ in single-turn protocols.

Static Corruption. A static adversary chooses the corrupted parties independently of the execution of the protocol, and hence can fix the corrupted set ahead of the execution. The previously mentioned works of [3,5,25,26,28] all fall into this framework and prove that corrupting k parties can lead to bias $\Omega(\mu k/n)$ statically. These results hold even if the statically corrupted set is chosen *at random*. For single-round protocols in which each party sends a single bit, Kahn, Kalai and Linial [20] showed that any protocol is susceptible to $\Omega(n/\log n)$ corruptions. A long line of exciting works (see [34]) showed how to achieve robustness to $(1 - \delta) \cdot n$ static corruption for any $\delta < 1$.

Fair Coin Tossing. Another line of work in coin tossing protocols aims to study the power of *fair* protocols in which the parties *need* to output a bit even if the other party is caught cheating (e.g., by aborting in the middle of the protocol). The work of Cleve [7] showed that in any such protocol with r rounds between two parties, there is a PPT attacker that biases the output of the other party by at least $\Omega(1/r)$. The work of Moran, Naor, and Segev [33] showed how to *match* this bound assuming oblivious transfer, leading to an "optimally fair" protocol. A sequence of works [9,10,16,17] showed barriers for doing so from one-way functions, and finally, the beautiful work of Maji and Wang [29] completely resolved this question for black-box constructions. For works on fair coin tossing in the multiparty settings see [2,18].

2   Preliminaries

General Notation. We use calligraphic letters (e.g., $\mathcal{X}$) for sets. All distributions and random variables in this work are discrete. We use bold letters (e.g., $\mathbf{w}$) to denote random variables that return a sample from a corresponding discrete distribution. By $w \leftarrow \mathbf{w}$ we denote sampling w from the random variable $\mathbf{w}$. By $\mathrm{Supp}(\mathbf{w})$ we denote the support set of $\mathbf{w}$. For an event $\mathcal{S} \subseteq \mathrm{Supp}(\mathbf{w})$, the probability function of $\mathbf{w}$ for $\mathcal{S}$ is denoted as $\Pr[\mathbf{w} \in \mathcal{S}] = \Pr_{w \leftarrow \mathbf{w}}[w \in \mathcal{S}]$ or simply as $\Pr[\mathcal{S}]$ when $\mathbf{w}$ is clear from the context. By $\mathbf{u} \equiv \mathbf{v}$ we denote that the random variables $\mathbf{u}$ and $\mathbf{v}$ have the same distributions. Unless stated otherwise, we denote vectors by using a bar over a variable. By $(\mathbf{w}_1, \mathbf{w}_2, \ldots, \mathbf{w}_n)$ we refer to a sequence of n *jointly sampled* random variables. For a vector $(w_1 \ldots w_n)$, we use $w_{\leq i}$ to denote the prefix $(w_1, \ldots, w_i)$, and we use the same notation $\mathbf{w}_{\leq i}$ for jointly distributed random variables. For vector $x = u_{\leq i-1}$ and $y = u_i$, by, by xy we denote the vector $u_{\leq i-1}$ that appends u_i as the last coordinate of x. For a jointly distributed random variables $(\mathbf{u}, \mathbf{v})$, by $(\mathbf{u} \mid \mathbf{v} = v)$ or we denote the random variable $\mathbf{u}$ conditioned on $\mathbf{v} = v$. When it is clear from the context, we simply write $(\mathbf{u} \mid v)$ or $\mathbf{u}[v]$ instead. By $\mathbf{u} \times \mathbf{v}$ we refer to the product distribution in which $\mathbf{u}$ and $\mathbf{v}$ are sampled independently. $\mathrm{HD}(u_{\leq n}, v_{\leq n}) = |\{i \mid u_i \neq v_i\}|$ denotes the Hamming distance for vectors of n coordinates.

Random Processes. Let $\mathbf{w}_{\leq n} \equiv (\mathbf{w}_1, \ldots, \mathbf{w}_n)$ be a sequence of jointly distributed random variables. We can interpret the distribution of $\mathbf{w}_{\leq i}$ as a random process in which the iþ block w_i is sampled from the marginal distribution $(\mathbf{w}_i \mid w_{\leq i-1}) \equiv (\mathbf{w}_i \mid \mathbf{w}_{\leq i-1} = w_{\leq i-1}) \equiv \mathbf{w}_i[w_{\leq i-1}]$. We also use $\mathbf{w}_{\leq n}[\cdot]$ to denote an oracle sampling algorithm that given $w_{\leq i}$ returns a sample from $\mathbf{w}_{\leq n}[w_{\leq i}]$.

Attack Model. Our adversaries *replace* a message/block in a random process. Namely, they observe the blocks one by one and sometimes intervene to replace them with a new value. (The new values will subsequently change the way the random process will proceed.) Hence, we refer to them as *replacing* adversaries. Such adversaries are equivalent to *strongly adaptive corrupting* adversaries as defined in [13].

Definition 4 (Online replacing attacks on random processes). Let $\mathbf{w}_{\leq n} \equiv (\mathbf{w}_1, \ldots, \mathbf{w}_n)$ be a random process. Suppose $\mathsf{A}(x, \sigma) \to (x', \sigma')$ is a (potentially randomized) algorithm with the following syntax. It takes as input some (randomness,) x and σ, where σ is interpreted as a "state", and it outputs (x', σ'). We call such algorithm an *online replacing adversary* and define the following properties for it. We define the following notions for $\mathbf{w}_{\leq n}$.

- **The generated and output random processes under replacing attacks.** Suppose A is an replacing algorithm. We now define two random processes that result from running the replacing adversary A to influence the original random process $\mathbf{w}_{\leq n}$. For

$i = 1, 2, \ldots, n$, we first sample $u_i \leftarrow (\mathbf{w}_i \mid \mathbf{w}_{\leq i-1} = v_{\leq i-1})$, and then we obtain $(v_i, \sigma_i) \leftarrow \mathsf{A}(u_i, \sigma_{i-1})$. If at any point during this process $\Pr[\mathbf{w}_{\leq i} = v_{\leq i}] = 0$, we will output $u_{i+1} = \cdots = u_n = v_{i+1} = \cdots = v_n = \bot$. We call $(\mathbf{u}_{\leq n}, \mathbf{v}_{\leq n})$ the *jointly generated* random processes under the attack. We also refer to $u_{\leq n}$ as the *original values* and $v_{\leq n}$ as the *output* of the random process under the attack A.

- **Online replacing.** We call A a *valid* (online replacing) attack on $\mathbf{w}_{\leq n}$, if with probability 1 over the generation of $u_{\leq n}, v_{\leq n}$, it holds that none of the coordinates are $\bot$ (i.e., $\Pr[\mathbf{w}_{\leq i} = v_{\leq i}] \neq 0$.) In this work we always work with valid online replacing attacks, even if they are not called valid.

- **Budget of replacing attacks.** Replacing adversary A has *budget* k, if

$$\Pr[\mathrm{HD}(\mathbf{u}_{\leq n}, \mathbf{v}_{\leq n}) \leq k] = 1,$$

where $(\mathbf{u}_{\leq n}, \mathbf{v}_{\leq n})$ are the jointly generated random processes that are also jointly distributed.

- **Algorithmic efficiency of attacks.** If $\mathbf{w}_{\leq n}$ is indexed by n as a member of a *family* of joint distributions defined for all $n \in \mathbb{N}$, then we call an online or offline replacing algorithm *efficient*, if its running time is at most $\mathrm{poly}(N)$ where N is the total bit-length representation of any $w_{\leq n} \in \mathrm{Supp}(\mathbf{w}_{\leq n})$. We would also consider efficiency where the replacing algorithm uses an oracle. In particular, we say an attack $\mathsf{A}^{\mathbf{w}_{\leq n}[\cdot]}$ with oracle access to sampler $\mathbf{w}_{\leq n}[\cdot]$ is efficient if it runs in time $\mathrm{poly}(N)$.

We now recall the so-called Doob martingale of a (Boolean-output) random process.

Definition 5 (Doob martingale, partial averages, and their approximate variant). For random process $\mathbf{w}_{\leq n} \equiv (\mathbf{w}_1, \ldots, \mathbf{w}_n)$, let $f \colon \mathrm{Supp}(\mathbf{w}_{\leq n}) \mapsto \mathbb{R}$, $i \in [n]$, and $w_{\leq i} \in \mathrm{Supp}(\mathbf{w}_{\leq i})$. Then we use the notation $\bar{f}(w_{\leq i}) = \mathop{\mathbb{E}}\limits_{w_{\leq n} \leftarrow (\mathbf{w}_{\leq n} \mid w_{\leq i})} [f(w_{\leq n})]$ to define the expected value of f for a sample from $\mathbf{w}_{\leq n}$ conditioned on the prefix $w_{\leq i}$ and refer to it as a *partial-average* of f. In particular, using notation $w_{\leq 0} = \varnothing$, we have $\bar{f}(\varnothing) = \mathbb{E}[f(\mathbf{w}_{\leq n})]$. The random process $(\bar{f}(\mathbf{w}_{\leq 1}), \ldots, \bar{f}(\mathbf{w}_{\leq n}))$ is called the Doob martingale of the function f over the random process $\mathbf{w}_{\leq n}$. For the same $\mathbf{w}_{\leq n}$ and $\bar{f}(\cdot)$, we call $\tilde{f}(\cdot)$ an (additive) ε-approximation of $\bar{f}(\cdot)$, if for all $w_{\leq i} \in \mathrm{Supp}(\mathbf{w}_{\leq i})$, it holds that $\tilde{f}(w_{\leq i}) \in \bar{f}(w_{\leq i}) \pm \varepsilon$.

If one is given oracle access to ℓ samples from $(\mathbf{w}_i \mid w_{\leq i})$, then by averaging them, one can obtain (due to the Hoeffding inequality) an ε-approximation of $\tilde{f}(w_{\leq i})$ for with probability $1 - \exp(-\ell/\varepsilon^2)$.

2.1 Useful Facts

We use the following variant of the Azuma inequality which is proved in [14].

Lemma 6 (Azuma's inequality for dynamic interval lengths (Theorem 2.5 in [14])). *Let* $\mathbf{t}_{\leq n} \equiv (\mathbf{t}_1, \ldots, \mathbf{t}_n)$ *be a sequence of* n *jointly distributed random variables such that for all* $i \in [n]$, *and for all* $t_{\leq i-1} \leftarrow \mathbf{t}_{\leq i-1}$, *we have*

$$\exists t^*, \quad \Pr_{t_i \leftarrow \mathbf{t}_i \mid t_{\leq i-1}} [t^* + \eta_i \geq t_i \geq t^* - \eta_i] = 0$$

and $\mathbb{E}[\mathbf{t}_i \mid t_{\leq i-1}] \geq 1$. *Then, we have*

$$\Pr\left[\sum_{i=1}^{n} \mathbf{t}_i \leq -s\right] \leq e^{\frac{-s^2}{2\sum_{i=1}^{n} \eta_i^2}}$$

Lemma 7 (Azuma's inequality for dynamic interval lengths under approximate conditions). *Let* $\mathbf{t}_{\leq n} \equiv (\mathbf{t}_1, \ldots, \mathbf{t}_n)$ *be a sequence of n jointly distributed random variables such that for all $i \in [n]$, and for all $t_{\leq i-1} \leftarrow \mathbf{t}_{\leq i-1}$, we have*

$$\exists t^*, \quad \Pr_{t_i \leftarrow \mathbf{t}_i \mid t_{\leq i-1}}[|t_i| \geq 1] = 0$$

$$\exists t^*, \quad \Pr_{t_i \leftarrow \mathbf{t}_i \mid t_{\leq i-1}}[t^* + \eta_i \geq t_i \geq t^* - \eta_i] \geq 1 - \gamma$$

and $\mathbb{E}[\mathbf{t}_i \mid t_{\leq i-1}] \geq -\gamma$. *Then, we have*

$$\Pr\left[\sum_{i=1}^{n} \mathbf{t}_i \leq -s\right] \leq e^{\frac{-(s-2n\gamma)^2}{2\sum_{i=1}^{n} \eta_i^2}} + n \cdot \gamma$$

Proof. If we let $\gamma = 0$, Lemma 7 becomes equivalent to Lemma 6. Here we sketch why Lemma 7 can also be reduced to the case that $\gamma = 0$ (i.e., Azuma inequality). We build a sequence t_i' from $\mathbf{t}_i$ as follows: Sample $t_i \leftarrow \mathbf{t}_i \mid t_{\leq i-1}$, if $|t_i - t^*| \leq \eta_i$, output $t_i' = t_i + 2\gamma$ otherwise output $t^* + 2\gamma$. We have $\mathbb{E}[t_i' \mid t'_{\leq i-1}] \geq 0$ and $\Pr[|t_i' - t^* - 2\gamma| > \tau_i] = 0$. Now we can use Lemma 7 for the basic case of $\gamma = 0$ for the sequence $\mathbf{t}_i'$ and use it to get a looser bound for sequence $\mathbf{t}_i$, using the fact that $\exists i \in [n], |t_i - t^*| \geq \eta_i$ happens with probability at most $n \cdot \gamma$.   □

Lemma 8 (Composition of concave functions). *Suppose ℓ_1 and ℓ_2 are two non-decreasing concave functions. Then $\ell_1(\ell_2)$ is also non-decreasing and concave.*

3   Attacking Protocols with Any Message Length

In this section, we design and analyze our k-replacing up-biasing attack on random processes with arbitrary alphabet size. We first describe our attack in an idealized model in which the partial-average oracle $\bar{f}(\cdot)$ and "maximum child" of a prefix of the process are available for free. In the full version of this paper, we show that our attack can be made polynomial-time using an approximation of the partial-average oracle that can be obtained in polynomial time.

Construction 9 (k-replacing attack using exact oracles). This attack uses the exact partial-average oracle $\bar{f}(\cdot)$ and another oracle that returns "the best choice" for the next block (see u_{i+1}^* defined below). The attack is also parameterized by a vector $\lambda_{\leq k} = (\lambda_1, \ldots, \lambda_k) \in [0,1]^k$ for some integer $k \leq n$ which is adversary's budget. The attack will keep state $\sigma_i = (u_{\leq i}, v_{\leq i})$ where $u_{\leq i}$ are the original values and $v_{\leq i}$ are the output values under attack.[7] Having state $(u_{\leq i}, v_{\leq i})$ and for given u_{i+1} the algorithm A will

---

[7] Attack would need $v_{\leq i}$ and the "used part of the budget" $\mathrm{HD}(u_{\leq i}, v_{\leq i})$. Both of these can be obtained from $\sigma_i = (u_{\leq i}, v_{\leq i})$.

decide on whether to keep or replace u_{i+1}, using $u_{i+1}^* = \text{argmax}_{u'_{i+1}} \bar{f}(v_{\leq i}, u'_{i+1})$, $\bar{f}^* = \bar{f}(v_{\leq i}, u_{i+1}^*)$, and $d = \text{HD}(u_{\leq i}, v_{\leq i})$ as follows.

- (Case 0) If $d \geq k$, do not change u_{i+1} and output $v_{i+1} = u_{i+1}$.
- (Case 1) if Case 0 does not happen and $\bar{f}(v_{\leq i}, u_{i+1}) < \bar{f}^* - \lambda_{d+1}$, then $A[\lambda_{\leq k}](u_{i+1})$ will return the output $v_{i+1} = u_{i+1}^*$ which is different from u_{i+1}.
- (Case 2) If Cases 0, 1 do not happen, do not change u_{i+1} and output $v_{i+1} = u_{i+1}$.

In all the cases above, A will also update the state as $\sigma_{i+1} = (u_{\leq i+1}, v_{\leq i+1})$.

Notation. Suppose we run the attack $A[\lambda_{\leq k}]$ on random process $\mathbf{w}_{\leq n}$ through the process described in Definition 4. (In particular, u_{i+1} will be sampled from $(\mathbf{w}_{i+1} \mid \mathbf{w}_{\leq i} = v_{\leq i})$.) We use $(\mathbf{u}_{\leq n}^{(k)}, \mathbf{v}_{\leq n}^{(k)})$ to denote the jointly generated random processes under the attack $A[\lambda_{\leq k}]$. (This notation allows us to distinguish between the generated random processes under attacks with different budget.) We sometimes use $(\mathbf{u}_{\leq n}^{(\infty)}, \mathbf{v}_{\leq n}^{(\infty)})$ to denote $(\mathbf{u}_{\leq n}^{(n)}, \mathbf{v}_{\leq n}^{(n)})$ as they are the same distributions. Also, let

$$\mu_k = \mathop{\mathbb{E}}_{(u_{\leq n}, v_{\leq n}) \leftarrow (\mathbf{u}_{\leq n}^{(k)}, \mathbf{v}_{\leq n}^{(k)})} [f(v_{\leq n})]$$

denotes the expected value of f over the sequence that is the output of k-replacing attack of Construction 9. For $k = 0$ we have and $\mu_0 = \mu = \mathbb{E}[f(\mathbf{w}_{\leq n})]$.

Lemma 10 below shows that the increase in μ_k compared with μ_{k-1} can be related to the "threshold parameter" λ_k and the probability that an attack with *unlimited* (or equivalently just n) budget with threshold parameters $\lambda_1, \ldots, \lambda_k, \lambda'_{k+1}, \ldots, \lambda'_n$ makes at least k replacements.

Lemma 10. *We have*

$$\mu_k \geq \mu_{k-1} + \lambda_k \cdot \mathop{\text{Pr}}_{(u_{\leq n}, v_{\leq n}) \leftarrow (\mathbf{u}_{\leq n}^{(\infty)}, \mathbf{v}_{\leq n}^{(\infty)})} [\text{HD}(u_{\leq n}, v_{\leq n}) \geq k].$$

Proof. For any $j \in \{0, 1, 2\}$, let C_j^k be the Boolean random variable over (u_{i+1}, σ_i) that determines which case of the attack A with budget k happens on prefix $(v_{\leq i}, u_{i+1})$ where $v_{\leq i}$ is the finalized output prefix, $u_{\leq i}$ is the original prefix and u_{i+1} is the original sampled block at round $i+1$. For all $(v_{\leq i}, u_{\leq i}, u_{i+1})$ we have $\sum_{j=0}^2 C_j^k(u_{i+1}, \sigma_i) = 1$ because the cases complement each other.

In the rest of the proof, whenever $u_{\leq i}$ and $v_{\leq i}$ are clear from the context, we will use $C_j^k(u_{i+1})$ instead of $C_j^k(u_{i+1}, \sigma_i)$. In the following, when the threshold parameters $\lambda_1, \ldots, \lambda_k$ are clear from the context, we will use A instead of $A[\lambda_{\leq k}]$.

For all $u_{\leq i}, v_{\leq i} \in \text{Supp}(\mathbf{u}_{\leq i}, \mathbf{v}_{\leq i})$ we have the following qualities for different cases of the attack.

- Case 0:

$$\mathop{\mathbb{E}}_{(u_{i+1}, v_{i+1}) \leftarrow (\mathbf{u}_{i+1}^k, \mathbf{v}_{i+1}^k)[u_{\leq i}, v_{\leq i}]} \left[\left(\bar{f}(v_{\leq i}, v_{i+1}) - \bar{f}(v_{\leq i}, u_{i+1}) \right) \cdot C_0^k(u_{i+1}) \right] = 0.$$

$$(1)$$

- Case 1:

$$C_1^k(u_{i+1}) = (C_1^\infty(u_{i+1}) \wedge \mathrm{HD}(u_{\leq i}, v_{\leq i}) < k). \tag{2}$$

This is because as long as the number of replacements is fewer than k, Case 1 of the attack with budget k would go through whenever A with budget of n does so.
- Case 2:

$$\mathop{\mathbb{E}}_{(u_{i+1}, v_{i+1}) \leftarrow (\mathbf{u}_{i+1}^k, \mathbf{v}_{i+1}^k)[u_{\leq i}, v_{\leq i}]} \left[\left(\bar{f}(v_{\leq i}, v_{i+1}) - \bar{f}(v_{\leq i}, u_{i+1}) \right) \cdot C_2^k(u_{i+1}) \right] = 0. \tag{3}$$

This is correct because either $C_2^k(v_{\leq i}, u_{i+1}) = 0$ or $u_{i+1} = v_{i+1}$.

We define a notation $g(v_{\leq i+1}, u_{\leq i+1}) = \bar{f}(v_{\leq i+1}) - \bar{f}(v_{\leq i}, u_{i+1})$. In the following We use the shorten forms of $\mathbb{E}_{(\mathbf{u}_{\leq i}, \mathbf{v}_{\leq i})}$ and $\mathbb{E}_{(\mathbf{u}_{\leq n}, \mathbf{v}_{\leq n})[u_{\leq i}, v_{\leq i}]}$ to refer to $\mathbb{E}_{(u_{\leq i}, v_{\leq i}) \leftarrow (\mathbf{u}_{\leq i}, \mathbf{v}_{\leq i})}$ and $\mathbb{E}_{(u, v) \leftarrow (\mathbf{u}_{\leq n}, \mathbf{v}_{\leq n})[u_{\leq i}, v_{\leq i}]}$. We have

$$\mathop{\mathbb{E}}_{(\mathbf{u}_{\leq n}^{(k)}, \mathbf{v}_{\leq n}^{(k)})} [f(v_{\leq n})] - \mu = \mathop{\mathbb{E}}_{(\mathbf{u}_{\leq n}^{(k)}, \mathbf{v}_{\leq n}^{(k)})} \left[\sum_{i=0}^{n-1} (\bar{f}(v_{\leq i+1}) - \bar{f}(v_{\leq i})) \right]$$

$$= \mathop{\mathbb{E}}_{(\mathbf{u}_{\leq n}^{(k)}, \mathbf{v}_{\leq n}^{(k)})} \left[\sum_{i=0}^{n-1} (\bar{f}(v_{\leq i+1}) - \bar{f}(v_{\leq i}, u_{i+1})) \right] \quad \text{(by the definition of } \bar{f}) \tag{4}$$

$$= \sum_{i=0}^{n-1} \mathop{\mathbb{E}}_{(\mathbf{u}_{\leq i}^k, \mathbf{v}_{\leq i}^k)} \mathop{\mathbb{E}}_{(\mathbf{u}_{\leq n}^{(k)}, \mathbf{v}_{\leq n}^{(k)})[u_{\leq i}, v_{\leq i}]} \left[g(v_{\leq i+1}, u_{\leq i+1}) \cdot \left(\sum_{j=0}^{2} C_j^k(u_{i+1}) \right) \right]$$

$$= \sum_{i=0}^{n-1} \mathop{\mathbb{E}}_{(\mathbf{u}_{\leq i}^k, \mathbf{v}_{\leq i}^k)} \mathop{\mathbb{E}}_{(\mathbf{u}_{\leq n}^{(k)}, \mathbf{v}_{\leq n}^{(k)})[u_{\leq i}, v_{\leq i}]} \left[g(v_{\leq i+1}, u_{\leq i+1}) \cdot C_1^k(u_{i+1}) \right] \quad \text{(by (3) and (1))} \tag{5}$$

$$= \sum_{i=0}^{n-1} \mathop{\mathbb{E}}_{(\mathbf{u}_{\leq i}^k, \mathbf{v}_{\leq i}^k)} \mathop{\mathbb{E}}_{(\mathbf{u}_{\leq n}^{(k)}, \mathbf{v}_{\leq n}^{(k)})[u_{\leq i}, v_{\leq i}]} \left[g(v_{\leq i+1}, u_{\leq i+1}) \cdot (C_1^{(\infty)}(u_{i+1}) \wedge (\mathrm{HD}(u_{\leq i}, v_{\leq i}) < k) \right]$$

$$= \sum_{i=0}^{n-1} \mathop{\mathbb{E}}_{(\mathbf{u}_{\leq i}^\infty, \mathbf{v}_{\leq i}^\infty)} \mathop{\mathbb{E}}_{(\mathbf{u}_{\leq n}^{(k)}, \mathbf{v}_{\leq n}^{(k)})[u_{\leq i}, v_{\leq i}]} \left[g(v_{\leq i+1}, u_{\leq i+1}) \cdot (C_1^\infty(u_{i+1}) \wedge (\mathrm{HD}(u_{\leq i}, v_{\leq i}) < k)) \right]. \tag{6}$$

The last equality above holds, because for all $u_{\leq i}, v_{\leq i}$ where $\mathrm{HD}(u_{\leq i}, v_{\leq i}) < k$,

$$\Pr[(\mathbf{u}_{\leq i}^k, \mathbf{v}_{\leq i}^k) = (u_{\leq i}, v_{\leq i})] = \Pr[(\mathbf{u}_{\leq i}^{(\infty)}, \mathbf{v}_{\leq i}^{(\infty)}) = (u_{\leq i}, v_{\leq i})].$$

The reason for this is that as long as we have not used the full budget k, the k-replacing attack will behave as if its budget is infinite.

Similarly, for the adversary A with budget $k - 1$ we have

$$\mathop{\mathbb{E}}_{(\mathbf{u}_{\leq n}^{(k-1)}, \mathbf{v}_{\leq n}^{(k-1)})} [f(v_{\leq n})] - \mu = \sum_{i=0}^{n-1} \mathop{\mathbb{E}}_{(\mathbf{u}_{\leq i}^{(\infty)}, \mathbf{v}_{\leq i}^{(\infty)})_{\leq i}} \mathop{\mathbb{E}}_{(\mathbf{u}_{\leq n}^{(k-1)}, \mathbf{v}_{\leq n}^{(k-1)})[u_{\leq i}, v_{\leq i}]} \left[\eta(u_{\leq i+1}, v_{\leq i+1}) \right]. \tag{7}$$

where $\eta(u_{\leq i+1}, v_{\leq i+1}) = g(v_{\leq i+1}, u_{\leq i+1}) \cdot \left(C_1^\infty(u_{i+1}) \wedge (\mathrm{HD}(u_{\leq i}, v_{\leq i}) < k - 1)\right)$.
Therefore, by combining Eqs. (6) and (7) we have

$$
\begin{aligned}
&\mathop{\mathbb{E}}_{(\mathbf{u}_{\leq n}^{(k)}, \mathbf{v}_{\leq n}^{(k)})}[f(v_{\leq n})] - \mathop{\mathbb{E}}_{(u_{\leq n}, v_{\leq n}) \leftarrow (\mathbf{u}_{\leq n}^{(k-1)}, \mathbf{v}_{\leq n}^{(k-1)})}[f(v_{\leq n})] \\
&= \sum_{i=0}^{n-1} \mathop{\mathbb{E}}_{(\mathbf{u}_{\leq i}^{(\infty)}, \mathbf{v}_{\leq i}^{(\infty)})} \mathop{\mathbb{E}}_{(\mathbf{u}_{\leq n}^{(k)}, \mathbf{v}_{\leq n}^{(k)})[u_{\leq i}, v_{\leq i}]} \left[g(v_{\leq i+1}, u_{\leq i+1}) \cdot C_1^\infty(u_{i+1}) \cdot (\mathrm{HD}(u_{\leq i}, v_{\leq i}) = k - 1) \right] \\
&\geq \sum_{i=0}^{n-1} \mathop{\mathbb{E}}_{(\mathbf{u}_{\leq i}^{(\infty)}, \mathbf{v}_{\leq i}^{(\infty)})} \left[\lambda_k \cdot \mathop{\mathbb{E}}_{(\mathbf{u}_{\leq n}^{(k)}, \mathbf{v}_{\leq n}^{(k)})[u_{\leq i}, v_{\leq i}]} \left[C_1^\infty(u_{i+1}) \cdot (\mathrm{HD}(u_{\leq i}, v_{\leq i}) = k - 1) \right] \right] \\
&= \lambda_k \cdot \mathop{\Pr}_{(\mathbf{u}_{\leq n}^{(\infty)}, \mathbf{v}_{\leq n}^{(\infty)})} [\mathrm{HD}(u_{\leq n}, v_{\leq n}) \geq k].
\end{aligned}
$$

The last equality above holds because whenever $C_1^{(\infty)}$ holds, we know that A will replace u_{i+1} with $v_{i+1} \neq u_{i+1}$ and this makes the hamming distance of $u_{\leq i+1}$ from $v_{\leq i+1}$ equal to k. $\qquad\square$

Now we prove the following lemma about the power of attacks with infinite budget. The work of [27] also prove a similar bound (see Claim 19 in [27]) for their attack but our attack achieves a better bound because of the fact that our attack has only one step in which the replacement might happen which allows us to make a better use of Azuma's inequality with dynamic interval (See Lemma 6).

Lemma 11. *If* $\mu_\infty = \mathbb{E}_{(u_{\leq n}, v_{\leq n}) \leftarrow (\mathbf{u}_{\leq n}^{(\infty)}, \mathbf{v}_{\leq n}^{(\infty)})}[f(v_{\leq n})]$ *and* $\lambda = \max_{i \in [n]} \lambda_i$, *then*

$$
\mu_\infty \geq 1 - e^{-\frac{2\mu^2}{n\lambda^2}}.
$$

Proof. We define a sequence of random variables $\mathbf{t}_{\leq n} = (\mathbf{t}_1, \ldots, \mathbf{t}_n)$, where $t_{i+1} = \bar{f}(v_{\leq i+1}) - \bar{f}(v_{\leq i})$ is a random variable that is dependent on $v_{\leq i+1}$. Then we have

$$
\begin{aligned}
&\mathop{\mathbb{E}}_{(\mathbf{u}_{\leq n}^{(\infty)}, \mathbf{v}_{\leq n}^{(\infty)})[u_{\leq i}, v_{\leq i}]} [\bar{f}(v_{\leq i+1}) - \bar{f}(v_{\leq i})] \\
&\geq \mathop{\mathbb{E}}_{(\mathbf{u}_{\leq n}^{(\infty)}, \mathbf{v}_{\leq n}^{(\infty)})[u_{\leq i}, v_{\leq i}]} [\bar{f}(v_{\leq i}, u_{i+1}) - \bar{f}(v_{\leq i})] = 0.
\end{aligned}
$$

Therefore, $\mathbf{t}_{\leq n}$ defines a sub-martingale. Furthermore, we have

$$
\bar{f}^* \geq \bar{f}(v_{\leq i+1}) \geq \bar{f}^* - \lambda.
$$

Therefore, t_i always falls in an interval of size λ. Hence, applying the right variant of Azuma's Inequality (as stated in Lemma 6) over $\mathbf{t}_{\leq n}$, we have

$$
\mathop{\Pr}_{(\mathbf{u}_{\leq n}^{(\infty)}, \mathbf{v}_{\leq n}^{(\infty)})} [f(v_{\leq n}) = 0] = \mathop{\Pr}_{(\mathbf{u}_{\leq n}^{(\infty)}, \mathbf{v}_{\leq n}^{(\infty)})} \left[\sum_{i=1}^{n} t_i \leq -\mu \right] \leq e^{-\frac{2\mu^2}{n\lambda^2}}. \tag{8}
$$

Now, leveraging the fact that f outputs in $\{0, 1\}$ and relying on Inequality (8), we have

$$\Pr_{(\mathbf{u}_{\leq n}^{(\infty)}, \mathbf{v}_{\leq n}^{(\infty)})} [f(v_{\leq n}) = 1] = 1 - \Pr_{(\mathbf{u}_{\leq n}^{(\infty)}, \mathbf{v}_{\leq n}^{(\infty)})} [f(v_{\leq n}) - \mu \leq -\mu] \geq 1 - e^{-\frac{2\mu^2}{n\lambda^2}}.$$

$\square$

Lemma 12. *If* $\lambda = \max_{i \in [k]} \lambda_i$, *then*

$$\Pr_{(\mathbf{u}_{\leq n}^{(\infty)}, \mathbf{v}_{\leq n}^{(\infty)})} [\mathrm{HD}(u_{\leq n}, v_{\leq n}) \geq k] \geq 1 - e^{-\frac{2\mu^2}{n\lambda^2}} - \mu_{k-1}.$$

Proof. First we have

$$\Pr_{(\mathbf{u}_{\leq n}^{(\infty)}, \mathbf{v}_{\leq n}^{(\infty)})} [(f(v_{\leq n}) = 1 \wedge \mathrm{HD}(u_{\leq n}, v_{\leq n}) < k) \vee (\mathrm{HD}(u_{\leq n}, v_{\leq n}) \geq k)]$$

$$= \Pr_{(\mathbf{u}_{\leq n}^{(\infty)}, \mathbf{v}_{\leq n}^{(\infty)})} [f(v_{\leq n}) = 1 \vee \mathrm{HD}(u_{\leq n}, v_{\leq n}) \geq k]$$

$$\geq \Pr_{(\mathbf{u}_{\leq n}^{(\infty)}, \mathbf{v}_{\leq n}^{(\infty)})} [f(v_{\leq n}) = 1]$$

$$= \mu_\infty \geq 1 - e^{-\frac{2\mu^2}{n\lambda^2}} \text{ (by Lemma 11).} \tag{9}$$

On the other hand, by a union bound we have

$$\Pr_{(\mathbf{u}_{\leq n}^{(\infty)}, \mathbf{v}_{\leq n}^{(\infty)})} [(f(v_{\leq n}) = 1 \wedge \mathrm{HD}(u_{\leq n}, v_{\leq n}) < k) \vee (\mathrm{HD}(u_{\leq n}, v_{\leq n}) \geq k)]$$

$$\leq \Pr_{(\mathbf{u}_{\leq n}^{(\infty)}, \mathbf{v}_{\leq n}^{(\infty)})} [f(v_{\leq n}) = 1 \wedge \mathrm{HD}(u_{\leq n}, v_{\leq n}) < k] + \Pr_{(\mathbf{u}_{\leq n}^{(\infty)}, \mathbf{v}_{\leq n}^{(\infty)})} [\mathrm{HD}(u_{\leq n}, v_{\leq n}) \geq k]. \tag{10}$$

The generated process under $k - 1$ replacing attack is same as n-replacing attack as long as the number of replacements is less than k. Therefore, it holds that

$$\Pr_{(\mathbf{u}_{\leq n}^{(\infty)}, \mathbf{v}_{\leq n}^{(\infty)})} [(f(v_{\leq n}) = 1 \wedge \mathrm{HD}(u_{\leq n}, v_{\leq n}) < k)] \leq \Pr_{(\mathbf{u}_{\leq n}^{(k-1)}, \mathbf{v}_{\leq n}^{(k-1)})} [f(v_{\leq n}) = 1] = \mu_{k-1}. \tag{11}$$

Now, combining Inequalities (9), (10) and (11) we get

$$\Pr_{(\mathbf{u}_{\leq n}^{(\infty)}, \mathbf{v}_{\leq n}^{(\infty)})} [\mathrm{HD}(u_{\leq n}, v_{\leq n}) \geq k] \geq 1 - e^{-\frac{2\mu^2}{n\lambda^2}} - \mu_{k-1}.$$

$\square$

Corollary 13. *If* $\lambda = \max_{i \in [k]} \lambda_i$, *then we have*

$$\mu_k \geq \mu_{k-1} + \lambda_k \cdot \left(1 - e^{\frac{-2\mu^2}{n \cdot \lambda^2}} - \mu_{k-1}\right).$$

Proof. Combining Lemmas 12 and 10 we have

$$\mu_k \geq \mu_{k-1} + \lambda_k \cdot \Pr_{(\mathbf{u}_{\leq n}^{(\infty)}, \mathbf{v}_{\leq n}^{(\infty)})} [\mathrm{HD}(u_{\leq n}, v_{\leq n}) \geq k] \text{ (by Lemma 10)}$$

$$\geq \mu_{k-1} + \lambda_k \cdot \left(1 - e^{\frac{-2\mu^2}{n \cdot \lambda^2}} - \mu_{k-1}\right) \text{ (by Lemma 12).}$$

$\square$

Theorem 14. *If $\lambda = \max_{i \in [k]} \lambda_i$, then we have*

$$\mu_k \geq \mu + \left(1 - \prod_{i=1}^{k}(1 - \lambda_i)\right) \cdot \left(1 - e^{\frac{-2\mu^2}{n \cdot \lambda^2}} - \mu\right).$$

In particular, by setting all $\lambda_i = \frac{\mu}{\sqrt{n}}$ we get

$$\mu_k \geq \mu + \left(1 - \left(1 - \frac{\mu}{\sqrt{n}}\right)^k\right) \cdot \left(1 - e^{-2} - \mu\right).$$

Note that the choice of $\lambda_i = u/\sqrt{n}$ above is not optimal. The optimal choice does not have a compact closed form and is actually by setting different λ_i's for different remaining budgets.

Proof. We prove this by induction on k. The case of $k = 1$ directly follows from Corollary 13. For $k > 1$, by Corollary 13 we have

$$\mu_k \geq \mu_{k-1} + \lambda_k \cdot \left(1 - e^{\frac{-2\mu^2}{n \cdot \lambda^2}} - \mu_{k-1}\right),$$

which implies that

$$\mu_k \geq (1 - \lambda_k) \cdot \mu_{k-1} + \lambda_k \cdot \left(1 - e^{\frac{-2\mu^2}{n \cdot \lambda^2}}\right).$$

Now we can use the induction's hypothesis and replace μ_{k-1} with $\mu + \left(1 - \prod_{i=1}^{k-1}(1 - \lambda_i)\right) \cdot \left(1 - e^{-2\mu^2/(n \cdot \lambda^2)} - \mu\right)$ which implies that

$$\mu_k \geq \mu + \left(1 - \prod_{i=1}^{k}(1 - \lambda_i)\right) \cdot \left(1 - e^{\frac{-2\mu^2}{n \cdot \lambda^2}} - \mu\right),$$

and that proves the claim. $\square$

4   Optimal Attacks for Uniform Binary Messages

In this section, we focus on the setting in which n parties each send a uniform random bit and then a final bit is chosen based on the published messages. We will show how to obtain *optimal* online k-replacing attacks that *match* the power of *offline* attacks.

Notation. $\mathbf{u}_{\leq n} \equiv (\mathbf{u}_1 \times \cdots \times \mathbf{u}_n)$ denotes the uniform random variable over $\{0,1\}^n$, where each $\mathbf{u}_i$ is a uniform and independent random bit. In this section, for simplicity we use notation $\mathbf{U}_n$ for this distribution. We will study k-replacing attacks on $\mathbf{U}_n$.[8] $\mathrm{HW}(x) = \mathrm{HD}(x, 0^n)$ denotes Hamming weight of $x \in \{0,1\}^n$. We let $[n] = \{1, \ldots, n\}$, $\langle n] = \{0, \ldots, n\}$ and $\langle n \rangle = \{0, \ldots, n+1\}$. For $t \in \langle n]$, we define the threshold function $\tau_t \colon \{0,1\}^n \to \{0,1\}$ as $\tau_t(x) = 1$ iff $\mathrm{HW}(x) \geq t$. (τ_0 is the constant function 1 function and τ_{n+1} is the constant 0 function.) We let $\beta_n^{(t)} = 2^{-n} \cdot \sum_{i=t}^n \binom{n}{i}$ be the probability of the Hamming ball defined by τ_t, and when n is clear from the context we write it as $\beta^{(t)}$. We also let $s_n^{(t)} = 2^n \cdot \beta_n^{(t)}$ be the size of the same Hamming ball. For set $\mathcal{S} \subset \mathbb{R}, r \in \mathbb{R}$, we use the notation $r\mathcal{S} = \{rx \mid x \in \mathcal{S}\}$, e.g., $r\langle n] = \{0, r, 2r, \ldots, nr\}$. We let $\binom{n}{k} = 0$ if $k < 0$ or $k > n$. For a set $\mathcal{S} \subseteq \{0,1\}^n$ and $r \in \{0,1\}^d$ for $d \in [n]$, we let

$$\mathcal{S}[r] = \left\{ x' \mid x \in \mathcal{S} \land \exists x' \in \{0,1\}^{n-d} \text{ such that } x = (r, x') \right\}$$

be the set of suffixes of strings in $\mathcal{S}$ of length $n - d$ with r as their prefix.

We first define the isoperimetry function that capture the power of "offline" attacks.

Definition 15 (The offline expansion and isoperimetry functions). For $k \in [n], \mathcal{S} \subseteq \{0,1\}^n$, the offline k-expansion (probability) of $\mathcal{S}$ is the probability of all points within Hamming distance k of $\mathcal{S}$

$$\mathsf{OffExp}^{(k)}(\mathcal{S}) = \frac{|\{y \in \{0,1\}^n \mid \exists x \in \mathcal{S}, \mathrm{HD}(x,y) \leq k\}|}{2^n}.$$

For a given probability μ, the k-expansion of μ is equal to:

$$\mathsf{OffExp}^{(k)}(\mu) = \inf_{\mathcal{S}, \Pr[\mathcal{S}] \geq \mu} \mathsf{OffExp}^{(k)}(\mathcal{S}).$$

Finally, for a set $\mathcal{S}$ and probability μ, we define the (offline) k-isoperimetry function

$$\mathsf{OffIso}^{(k)}(\mathcal{S}) = \mathsf{OffExp}^{(k)}(\mathcal{S}) - \Pr[\mathcal{S}], \quad \mathsf{OffIso}_n^{(k)}(\mu) = \mathsf{OffExp}_n^{(k)}(\mu) - \mu.$$

Note that whenever the input is a set $\mathcal{S} \subseteq \{0,1\}^n$, it already determines n on its own, and hence we do not need to state it explicitly, but when the input is $\mu \in \mathbb{R}$, we explicitly state n as the index of the function.

Theorem 16 (Implied by the vertex isoperimetric inequality in Boolean hypercube [19]). *For any* $t \in \langle n]$, *it holds that* $\mathsf{OffExp}^{(k)}(\beta^{(t)}) = \beta^{(t-k)}$.

Online Attacks vs. Offline Attacks. Suppose an adversary wants to increase the probability of falling into a set $\mathcal{S}$ in an "offline" attack, in which the adversary gets a point $x \leftarrow \mathbf{U}_n$ and then can replace k of the bits of x. It is easy to see that the adversary can

---

[8] In Sects. 2 and 3, we called the original random process $\mathbf{w}_{\leq n}$ and $\mathbf{U}_n$ was one of the generated random processes (modeling the original samples). However, since we are starting from a *product* distribution, it would hold that $\mathbf{U}_n \equiv \mathbf{w}_{\leq n}$, and thus we simply call the original distribution $\mathbf{u}$.

increase the probability of falling into $\mathcal{S}$ exactly by $\mathsf{OffIso}^{(k)}(\mathcal{S})$. Accordingly, we can define the *online* variant of such attacks as defined in Sect. 4. In such online attacks, the adversary gets to see the independent and uniformly sampled random bits $(\mathbf{u}_1, \ldots, \mathbf{u}_n)$ one by one, and after seeing $u_i \leftarrow \mathbf{u}_i$, it can decide to keep or change it.

Definition 17 (The online expansion OnExp and isoperimetry OnIso functions). Let A be an online adversary of budget k over the uniform distribution $\mathbf{U}_n$ over $\{0, 1\}^n$. Let $\mathbf{v}_{\leq n}$ be the generated output random process (distributed over $\{0, 1\}^n$) under attack A (as defined in Definition 4). We define $\mathsf{OnExp}^{(A)}(\mathcal{S}) = \Pr[\mathbf{v}_{\leq n} \in \mathcal{S}]$. Let $\mathcal{A}_k$ be the set of *all* k-replacing attacks on $\mathbf{U}_n$. We define $\mathsf{OnExp}^{(k)}(\mathcal{S})$ as the maximum probability of points in $\{0, 1\}^n$ that any online adversary can map to $\mathcal{S}$ by up to k changes to a stream of n uniformly random bits. Namely,

$$\mathsf{OnExp}^{(k)}(\mathcal{S}) = \max_{A \in \mathcal{A}_k} \mathsf{OnExp}^{(A)}(\mathcal{S}).$$

Also, for any $\mu \in [0, 1]$, we define

$$\mathsf{OnExp}_n^{(k)}(\mu) = \inf_{\mathcal{S}, \Pr[\mathcal{S}] \geq \mu} \mathsf{OnExp}^{(k)}(\mathcal{S})$$

as the minimum $\mathsf{OnExp}^{(k)}(\mathcal{S})$ among all sets of probability at least μ. Finally, for any set $\mathcal{S}$ and probability μ, we define the *online k-isoperimetry* functions as follows

$$\mathsf{OnIso}^{(k)}(\mathcal{S}) = \mathsf{OnExp}^{(k)}(\mathcal{S}) - \Pr[\mathcal{S}], \quad \mathsf{OnIso}_n^{(k)}(\mu) = \mathsf{OnExp}_n^{(k)}(\mu) - \mu$$

as the *growth* in probability of falling into sets (of probability μ) under optimal online k-replacing attacks.

Since offline adversaries know as much as online adversaries when making decision to change or not, it always holds that $\mathsf{OffIso}(\mathcal{S}) \geq \mathsf{OnIso}(\mathcal{S})$, and hence $\mathsf{OffIso}_n^{(k)}(\mu) \geq \mathsf{OnIso}_n(\mu)$ for all n, $\mathcal{S} \subseteq \{0, 1\}^n$, and $\mu \in [0, 1]$. The surprising phenomenon stated in the next theorem is that when μ is the probability of a Hamming ball, online and offline attacks have the *same exact* power as a function of the measure μ, and consequently the online and offline k-isoperimetry functions would be equal.

Theorem 18 (Power of online vs. offline attacks for the uniform distribution over $\{0, 1\}^n$). *For all $n \in \mathbb{N}, t \in [n], k \leq t$, if $\beta^{(t)} = \Pr[\mathsf{HW}(\mathbf{U}_n) \geq t]$ be the probability of a Hamming ball. Then it holds that*

$$\mathsf{OnExp}_n^{(k)}(\beta^{(t)}) = \mathsf{OffExp}_n^{(k)}(\beta^{(t)}) = \beta^{(t-k)}.$$

In words, if $\mu = \beta^{(t)}$, then the power of online k-replacing adversaries to increase the probability of falling into a set $\mathcal{S}$, in the minimum over all sets of probability at least $\beta^{(t)}$, is equal to that of offline attacks.

Reaching a Target Probability. Suppose $\Pr[\mathcal{S}] = \mu$, and suppose we want to increase the probability of falling into $\mathcal{S}$ to $\mu' > \mu$. How much budget an adversary needs? Theorem 18 shows that as long as μ is the probability of a Hamming ball (i.e., $\mu = \beta^{(t)}$), then in the worst case (among all possible sets S of probability μ) the power of online and offline attacks are *exactly the same*. Therefore, this brings up the natural question of what happens in general, when μ is *not* exactly the probability of a Hamming ball. As stated in Corollary 19 below, Theorem 18 already shows that the power of offline and online attacks is different by at most one. In fact, as we will see later, these quantities are not equal in general. In particular, Fig. 1 compares $\mathsf{OnIso}_n(\mu)$ and $\mathsf{OffIso}_n^{(k)}(\mu)$ for all μ when $n = 10$ (and $k = 1$).

Corollary 19 (Budget of online vs. offline attacks to reach a target probability). *For* $0 < \mu < \mu' \le 1$, *let*

$$\mathsf{OfBud}_n(\mu \to \mu') = \min_{k \in [n]} [\mathsf{OffExp}_n^{(k)}(\mu) \ge \mu']$$

be the minimum budget k that an offline adversary needs to increase the probability of falling into any set S of probability at least μ to μ'. Let

$$\mathsf{OnBud}_n(\mu \to \mu') = \min_{k \in [n]} [\mathsf{OnExp}_n^{(k)}(\mu) \ge \mu']$$

be the similar quantity for online attacks. Then, it always holds that

$$\mathsf{OfBud}_n(\mu \to \mu') \le \mathsf{OnBud}_n(\mu \to \mu') \le \mathsf{OfBud}_n(\mu \to \mu') + 1$$

and $\mathsf{OfBud}_n(\beta^{(t)} \to \mu') = \mathsf{OnBud}_n(\beta^{(t)} \to \mu')$ *for all* $t \in [n+1]$.

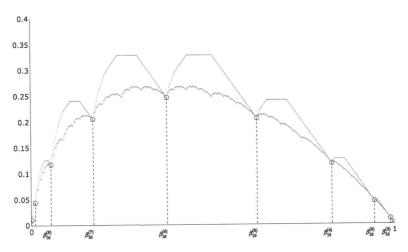

Fig. 1. Comparing the online isoperimetric function OnIso (blue) versus the offline isoperimetric function OffIso (red) for $n = 10$. (Color figure online)

We first prove Corollary 19 using Theorem 18 and then will prove Theorem 18.

Proof of Corollary 19. Let $k = \mathsf{OfBud}_n(\mu \to \mu')$, we have $\mathsf{OffExp}_n^{(k)}(\mu) \geq \mu'$ and $\mathsf{OffExp}_n^{(k-1)}(\mu) < \mu'$. Let $t \in \langle n \rangle$ be the minimum such t that $\beta^{(t)} \geq \mu$, and so we have $\beta^{(t+1)} \leq \mu \leq \beta^{(t)}$. By the monotonicity of $\mathsf{OnExp}_n^{(k)}$ function, we have

$$\mathsf{OnExp}_n^{(k+1)}(\beta^{(t+1)}) \leq \mathsf{OnExp}_n^{(k+1)}(\mu). \tag{12}$$

By Theorem 18 it holds that $\mathsf{OnExp}_n^{(k+1)}(\beta^{(t+1)}) = \mathsf{OffExp}_n^{(k+1)}(\beta^{(t+1)})$. Now, because $\beta^{(t+1)} \leq \mu \leq \beta^{(t)}$, by the monotonicity of $\mathsf{OffExp}_n^{(k)}(\mu)$ we have

$$\mathsf{OffExp}_n^{(k)}(\mu) \leq \mathsf{OffExp}_n^{(k)}(\beta^{(t)}) = \mathsf{OffExp}_n^{(k+1)}(\beta^{(t+1)}) = \mathsf{OnExp}_n^{(k+1)}(\beta^{(t+1)}). \tag{13}$$

Combining (12) and (13), we have

$$\mathsf{OffExp}_n^{(k)}(\mu) \leq \mathsf{OnExp}_n^{(k+1)}(\beta^{(t+1)}) \leq \mathsf{OnExp}_n^{(k+1)}(\mu).$$

Therefore we have,

$$\begin{aligned}
\mathsf{OfBud}_n(\mu \to \mu') + 1 &= \min_{k \in [n]}[\mathsf{OffExp}_n^{(k)}(\mu) \geq \mu'] + 1 \\
&\geq \min_{k \in [n]}[\mathsf{OnExp}_n^{(k+1)}(\mu) \geq \mu'] + 1 \\
&= \min_{k+1 \in [n]}[\mathsf{OnExp}_n^{(k+1)}(\mu) \geq \mu'] \\
&= \mathsf{OnBud}_n(\mu \to \mu').
\end{aligned}$$

The inequality holds because let $k' = \min_{k \in [n]}[\mathsf{OffExp}_n^{(k)}(\mu) \geq \mu']$, we have $\mathsf{OnExp}_n^{(k'+1)}(\mu) \geq \mu'$, and therefore $\min_{k \in [n]}[\mathsf{OnExp}_n^{(k+1)}(\mu) \geq \mu'] \leq k'$. Since we also have $\mathsf{OffExp}_n^{(k)}(\mu) \geq \mathsf{OnExp}_n^{(k)}(\mu)$ for any μ, $\mathsf{OfBud}_n(\mu \to \mu') \leq \mathsf{OnBud}_n(\mu \to \mu') \leq \mathsf{OfBud}_n(\mu \to \mu') + 1$.

Finally, because $\mathsf{OffExp}_n^{(k)}(\beta^{(t)}) \geq \mathsf{OnExp}_n^{(k)}(\beta^{(t)})$ holds for any k and t, we have $\mathsf{OfBud}_n(\beta^{(t)} \to \mu') = \mathsf{OnBud}_n(\beta^{(t)} \to \mu')$ for all $t \in [n + 1]$.

In the rest of this section, we prove Theorem 18.

Proof of Theorem 18. In order to prove Theorem 18, we start by deriving a recursive relation for $\mathsf{OnExp}_n^{(k)}(\cdot)$. Before doing so, we define some mathematical notation.

Definition 20 (Definitions related to the recursive relation of online expansion). For $s \in \langle 2^n \rangle$, let

$$\mathcal{D}iv_{n-1}(s) = \left\{(s_0, s_1) \mid s_0, s_1 \in \langle 2^{n-1}], 0 \leq s_0 \leq s_1 \leq 2^{n-1}, s = s_0 + s_1\right\}$$

be the set of ways in which a "set size" $s \in \langle 2^{n-1}]$ can be divided into two sizes. For $(s_0, s_1) \in \mathcal{D}iv_{n-1}(s)$ and a *fixed* pair of integers n, k let $\mathsf{Rec}_n^{(k)}(\cdot, \cdot)$ be defined as

$$\mathsf{Rec}_n^{(k)}(s_0, s_1) = \frac{\mathsf{Rec}_{n-1}^{(k)}\left(\frac{s_1}{2^{n-1}}\right) + \max\left\{\mathsf{Rec}_{n-1}^{(k)}\left(\frac{s_0}{2^{n-1}}\right), \mathsf{Rec}_{n-1}^{(k-1)}\left(\frac{s_1}{2^{n-1}}\right)\right\}}{2} \tag{14}$$

based on functions $\mathrm{Rec}_{n-1}^{(k)}, \mathrm{Rec}_{n-1}^{(k-1)}$ to be specified later. Finally, for $\mu \in 2^{-n}\langle 2^n]$ let

$$\mathrm{Rec}_n^{(k)}(\mu) = \inf_{(s_0,s_1) \in \mathcal{D}iv_n(2^n \cdot \mu)} \mathrm{Rec}_n^{(k)}(s_0, s_1). \tag{15}$$

Transformation $\mathrm{Rec}_n^{(k)}[p, q]$. For functions p, q defined on input space $2^{-n}\langle 2^n]$. Suppose we use p instead of $\mathrm{Rec}_{n-1}^{(k)}$ and q instead of $\mathrm{Rec}_{n-1}^{(k-1)}$ in Eq. (14). Then by $\mathrm{Rec}_n^{(k)}[p, q](\cdot, \cdot)$ (resp. $\mathrm{Rec}_n^{(k)}[p, q](\cdot)$) we denote the function that one obtains in Eq. (14) (resp. Eq. (15)).

Interpretation. $\mathrm{Rec}_n^{(k)}(s_0, s_1)$ represents the optimal choice that a tampering adversary can make to increase the probability of falling into a set of size s, when $\mathcal{S}[0] = \mathcal{S}_0, \mathcal{S}[1] = \mathcal{S}_1$ are adversarially chosen based on their sizes s_0, s_1 where $s_0 \leq s_1$, and when the optimal online expansions for s_0, s_1 can be applied by (appropriate use of) functions $\mathrm{Rec}_{n-1}^{(k)}, \mathrm{Rec}_{n-1}^{(k-1)}$.

Notation. Let f, g be defined over the same input domain $\mathcal{D}$. We say $f \leq g$, if $\forall \mu \in \mathcal{D}, f(\mu) \leq g(\mu)$.

We now show that the transformation of Definition 20 has some desired properties.

Claim 21 (Transformation of Definition 20 is monotone). *Let* $\mathsf{u}_{n-1}^{(k)} \leq \mathsf{v}_{n-1}^{(k)}$ *and* $\mathsf{u}_{n-1}^{(k-1)} \leq \mathsf{v}_{n-1}^{(k-1)}$, *and let*

$$\mathsf{u}_n^{(k)} = \mathrm{Rec}_n^{(k)}[\mathsf{u}_{n-1}^{(k)}, \mathsf{u}_{n-1}^{(k-1)}], \quad \mathsf{v}_n^{(k)} = \mathrm{Rec}_n^{(k)}[\mathsf{v}_{n-1}^{(k)}, \mathsf{v}_{n-1}^{(k-1)}]$$

as defined in Definition 20. Then, it holds that $\mathsf{u}_n^{(k)} \leq \mathsf{v}_n^{(k)}$.

Proof. We first show that for any $s_0, s_1 \in \mathcal{D}iv_n(2^n \cdot \mu)$, we have $\mathsf{u}_n^{(k)}(s_0, s_1) \leq \mathsf{v}_n^{(k)}(s_0, s_1)$. Because $\mathsf{u}_{n-1}^{(k)} \leq \mathsf{v}_{n-1}^{(k)}$ and $\mathsf{u}_{n-1}^{(k-1)} \leq \mathsf{v}_{n-1}^{(k-1)}$, we have $\mathsf{u}_{n-1}^{(k)}(s_1/2^{n-1}) \leq \mathsf{v}_{n-1}^{(k)}(s_1/2^{n-1})$ and

$$\max\{\mathsf{u}_{n-1}^{(k)}(s_0/2^{n-1}), \mathsf{u}_{n-1}^{(k)}(s_1/2^{n-1})\} \leq \max\{\mathsf{v}_{n-1}^{(k)}(s_0/2^{n-1}), \mathsf{v}_{n-1}^{(k)}(s_1/2^{n-1})\}.$$

Therefore, $\mathsf{u}_n^{(k)}(s_0, s_1) \leq \mathsf{v}_n^{(k)}(s_0, s_1)$ holds for any s_0, s_1.

From Eq. (15), let $(s_0', s_1') = \arg\inf_{(s_0,s_1) \in \mathcal{D}iv_n(2^n \cdot \mu)} \mathsf{v}_n^{(k)}(s_0, s_1)$ be the partition where $\mathsf{v}_n^{(k)}(\mu)$ achieves its minimum. Then we have $\mathsf{u}_n^{(k)}(\mu) \leq \mathsf{u}_n^{(k)}(s_0', s_1') \leq \mathsf{v}_n^{(k)}(s_0', s_1') = \mathsf{v}_n^{(k)}(\mu)$. $\square$

Claim 22 (Recursive relation for online expansion). *One can recursively compute* $\mathrm{OnExp}_n^{(k)}(\mu)$ *for all* $\mu \in 2^{-n}\langle 2^n]$ *as follows.*

- *If* $k = 0$ *and* $n \geq 0$, *then* $\mathrm{OnExp}_n^{(0)}(\mu) = \mu$.
- *If* $k \geq 1$ *and* $k \geq n$, *then:* $\mathrm{OnExp}_n^{(k)}(0) = 0$ *and* $\mathrm{OnExp}_n^{(k)}(\mu) = 1$ *for* $\mu > 0$.
- *If* $k \geq 1$ *and* $k < n$, *then* $\mathrm{OnExp}_n^{(k)} = \mathrm{Rec}_n^{(k)}[\mathrm{OnExp}_{n-1}^{(k)}, \mathrm{OnExp}_{n-1}^{(k-1)}]$ *as in Definition 20.*

Proof Sketch. The extremal cases of the recursive relation stated in the first two bullets hold trivially. Below we argue why the inductive step as stated in the third bullet holds as well.

Suppose by fixing the first bit to b we get a subset of size s_b, and $s_0 \leq s_1$, and suppose in both cases the residual subsets $S[0], S[1]$ are chosen in the "worst" case (against the adversary) based on their sizes s_0, s_1, minimizing the success probability of an online adversary. Since $\mathsf{OnExp}(\cdot)$ is a monotone function, then when the first bit is selected to be 1, the adversary has no motivation to replace it with 0. When the first bit is selected to be 0, the adversary has choose between maximum of the expansions that arise from changing or not changing the bit to 1. Once we consider all ways that s can be split into $s = s_0 + s_1$, this leads to the definition of the recursion of Eq. (15) and the transformation of Definition 20.

Claim 23 *Suppose* $p \leq \mathsf{OnExp}_{n-1}^{(k)}, q \leq \mathsf{OnExp}_{n-1}^{(k-1)}$ *for functions* p, q. *Then, it holds that* $\mathsf{Rec}_n^{(k)}[p, q] \leq \mathsf{OnExp}_n^{(k)}$ *(see Definition 20).*

Proof. The proof directly follows from Claims 22 and 21.   □

We now define a piecewise-linear function $\ell_n^{(k)}$ to later prove to be a lower bound for $\mathsf{OnExp}_n^{(k)}$.

Definition 24 (The piecewise-linear (lower bound) function). For any non-negative integers k, n, the function $\ell_n^{(k)} : [0, 1] \to [0, 1]$ is defined as follows.

- If $\mu = \beta_n^{(t)}$ for any $t \in \langle n \rangle$, it holds that $\ell_n^{(k)}\left(\beta_n^{(t)}\right) = \mathsf{OffExp}_n^{(k)}\left(\beta_n^{(t)}\right)$. Namely, $\ell_n^{(k)}\left(\beta_n^{(n+1)}\right) = \mathsf{OffExp}_n^{(k)}(0) = 0$, and for any $t \in \langle n \rangle$, $\ell_n^{(k)}\left(\beta_n^{(t)}\right) = \beta_n^{(t-k)} = \Pr\left[\mathsf{HW}(\mathbf{U}_n) \geq t - k\right]$.
- If $\mu = \alpha\beta_n^{(t)} + (1 - \alpha)\beta_n^{(t-1)}$ for $0 < \alpha < 1$ and any $t \in \langle n \rangle$, then $\ell_n^{(k)}(\mu) = \alpha \cdot \ell_n^{(k)}\left(\beta_n^{(t)}\right) + (1 - \alpha) \cdot \ell_n^{(k)}\left(\beta_n^{(t-1)}\right)$.

Proposition 25 (Composition of the lower bound function). *For any* $k_1, k_2, n \geq 0$ *and* $\mu \in [2^{-n}, 1]$, *it hold that* $\ell_n^{(k_1+k_2)}(\mu) = \ell_n^{(k_1)}\left(\ell_n^{(k_2)}(\mu)\right)$.

Proof. Consider every case,

- If $\mu = \beta_n^{(t)}$. By Definition 24 we have $\ell_n^{(k_1)}\left(\ell_n^{(k_2)}(\mu)\right) = \ell_n^{(k_1)}\left(\mathsf{OffExp}_n^{(k_2)}\left(\beta_n^{(t)}\right)\right)$. As $\mu \in [2^{-n}, 1]$, we have $t \leq n$. Therefore, $\mathsf{OffExp}_n^{(k_2)}\left(\beta_n^{(t)}\right) = \beta_n^{(t-k_2)}$. Therefore, we have

$$\ell_n^{(k_1)}\left(\ell_n^{(k_2)}\left(\beta_n^{(t)}\right)\right) = \ell_n^{(k_1)}\left(\beta_n^{(t-k_2)}\right) = \beta_n^{(t-(k_2+k_1))} = \ell_n^{(k_1+k_2)}\left(\beta_n^{(t)}\right).$$

- If $\mu = \alpha\beta_n^{(t)} + (1 - \alpha)\beta_n^{(t-1)}$ for $0 < \alpha < 1$, In this case, by Definition 24 we have $\ell_n^{(k_2)}(\mu) = \alpha \cdot \ell_n^{(k_2)}\left(\beta_n^{(t)}\right) + (1 - \alpha) \cdot \ell_n^{(k_2)}\left(\beta_n^{(t-1)}\right)$. As $\mu \in [2^{-n}, 1]$, we have

$t \leq n$. Therefore, we have $\ell_n^{(k_2)}(\mu) = \alpha \cdot \beta_n^{(t-k_2)} + (1-\alpha) \cdot \beta_n^{(t-1-k_2)}$. We then have

$$
\begin{aligned}
\ell_n^{(k_1)}\left(\ell_n^{(k_2)}(\mu)\right) &= \ell_n^{(k_1)}\left(\alpha \cdot \beta_n^{(t-k_2)} + (1-\alpha) \cdot \beta_n^{(t-1-k_2)}\right) \\
&= \alpha \cdot \beta_n^{(t-k_2-k_1)} + (1-\alpha) \cdot \beta_n^{(t-1-k_2-k_1)} \\
&= \ell_n^{(k_1+k_2)}(\mu).
\end{aligned}
$$

$\square$

Lemma 26. $\ell_n^{(k)}$ *is concave for all* $n, k \geq 0$.

Proof. $\ell_n^{(0)}$ is linear, and hence concave, so suppose $k \geq 1$. Let fix n, and define $\hat{\ell}(\mu) = \ell_n^{(1)}(\mu) - \mu$ for $\mu \in [0, 1]$. To prove that $\ell_n^{(k)}(\mu)$ is concave over $[2^{-n}, 1]$, it is sufficient to show that $\hat{\ell}(\mu)$ is concave over $[2^{-n}, 1]$, because:

1. If $\hat{\ell}(\mu)$ is concave, then $\hat{\ell}(\mu) + \mu = \ell_n^{(1)}(\mu)$ is concave as well.
2. If $\ell_n^{(1)}(\mu)$ is concave, since it is non-decreasing, by repeated applications of Lemma 8 and Proposition 25, it follows that $\ell_n^{(k)}$ is also concave for all $k \geq 1$ as well, when we limit the inputs to $\mu \geq 2^{-n}$.

Therefore, in the following, we only aim to prove that (1) $\hat{\ell}(\mu)$ is concave over $[2^{-n}, 1]$, and (2) the left and right derivatives of $\hat{\ell}(\mu)$ over $\mu = 2^{-n}$ do not violate its concavity.

In the following, we will fix n and $k = 1$. Because n, k are both fixed, in the rest of the proof of Lemma 26 we do not represent them explicitly as indexes anymore.

It holds that $\hat{\ell}(\beta^{(t)}) = \mathsf{Offlso}(\beta^{(t)})$ for all $t \in \langle n \rangle$. Also, for $\mu \in (\beta^{(t)}, \beta^{(t-1)})$ (recall that $\beta^{(t)} < \beta^{(t-1)}$) where $\mu = \alpha \beta^{(t)} + (1-\alpha)\beta^{(t-1)}$, we have

$$
\begin{aligned}
\hat{\ell}(\mu) &= \alpha \ell(\beta^{(t)}) + (1-\alpha)\ell(\beta^{(t-1)}) - \alpha \beta^{(t)} - (1-\alpha)\beta^{(t-1)} \\
&= \alpha \mathsf{Offlso}(\beta^{(t)}) + (1-\alpha)\mathsf{Offlso}(\beta^{(t-1)}).
\end{aligned}
$$

Since the curve $\hat{\ell}$ is linear over every interval $\mu \in [\beta^{(t)}, \beta^{(t-1)}]$ for all $t \in [n+1]$, to prove its concavity, we only have to compare its left and right derivatives at every $\beta^{(t)}, t \in [n]$, where it holds that $\hat{\ell}(\beta^{(t)}) = \mathsf{Offlso}(\beta^{(t)})$. Hence, for all $t \in [n]$, we need to prove the following.

$$
\frac{\mathsf{Offlso}(\beta^{(t)}) - \mathsf{Offlso}(\beta^{(t+1)})}{\beta^{(t)} - \beta^{(t+1)}} \geq \frac{\mathsf{Offlso}(\beta^{(t-1)}) - \mathsf{Offlso}(\beta^{(t)})}{\beta^{(t-1)} - \beta^{(t)}} \tag{16}
$$

Note that by letting $t = n$ in Inequality (16), we have $\hat{\ell}$ is still concave for point 2^{-n}. We first verify Inequality (16) for extreme cases of $t = 1, n$. If $t = 1$, then Inequality (16) holds because

$$
\frac{1-n}{n} = \frac{\mathsf{Offlso}(\beta^{(t)}) - \mathsf{Offlso}(\beta^{(t+1)})}{\beta^{(t)} - \beta^{(t+1)}} \geq \frac{\mathsf{Offlso}(\beta^{(t-1)}) - \mathsf{Offlso}(\beta^{(t)})}{\beta^{(t-1)} - \beta^{(t)}} = \frac{0-1}{1}.
$$

If $t = n$, a generalization of Inequality 16 for any k holds because

$$
\frac{\sum_{i=0}^{k}\binom{n}{i} - 0}{1 - 0} = \frac{\ell^{(k)}(\beta^{(t)}) - \ell^{(k)}(\beta^{(t+1)})}{\beta^{(t)} - \beta^{(t+1)}} \geq \frac{\ell^{(k)}(\beta^{(t-1)}) - \ell^{(k)}(\beta^{(t)})}{\beta^{(t-1)} - \beta^{(t)}} = \frac{\binom{n}{k+1}}{n},
$$

which in turn is correct because $\sum_{i=0}^{k} \binom{n}{i} > \binom{n}{k} \geq \binom{n}{k+1}/n$.

For the intermediate cases, for all $t \in \{n-1, \ldots, 2\}$, we have to prove:

$$\frac{\binom{n}{t-k} - \binom{n}{t}}{\binom{n}{t}} = \frac{\mathsf{Offlso}(\beta^{(t)}) - \mathsf{Offlso}(\beta^{(t+1)})}{\beta^{(t)} - \beta^{(t+1)}}$$

$$\geq \frac{\mathsf{Offlso}(\beta^{(t-1)}) - \mathsf{Offlso}(\beta^{(t)})}{\beta^{(t-1)} - \beta^{(t)}} = \frac{\binom{n}{t-2} - \binom{n}{t-1}}{\binom{n}{t-1}}$$

which is equivalent to proving the following true statement

$$\frac{t}{n-t+1} = \frac{t!(n-t)!}{(t-1)!(n-t+1)!} = \frac{\binom{n}{t-1}}{\binom{n}{t}} \geq \frac{\binom{n}{t-2}}{\binom{n}{t-1}}$$

$$= \frac{(t-1)!(n-t+1)!}{(t-2)!(n-t+2)!} = \frac{t-1}{n-t+2}.$$

$\square$

The main step of the proof of Theorem 18 is to show the following claim.

Claim 27. *It holds that* $\ell_n^{(k)} \leq \mathsf{Rec}_n^{(k)} \left[\ell_{n-1}^{(k)}, \ell_{n-1}^{(k-1)} \right]$.

Proof. In the following, for simplicity we let $\mathsf{Rec} = \mathsf{Rec}_n^{(k)} \left[\ell_{n-1}^{(k)}, \ell_{n-1}^{(k-1)} \right]$.

Case of Exact Hamming Ball Probabilities. We first prove

$$\forall t \in \langle n \rangle, \ \ell_n^{(k)}(\beta^{(t)}) \leq \mathsf{Rec}(\beta^{(t)}) \tag{17}$$

and then will extend the proof of this inequality to an arbitrary $\mu \in 2^{-n}\langle 2^n \rangle$. We only need to prove Inequality 17 for $t \in [n]$, because $\beta_n^{(n+1)} = 0, \beta^{(0)} = 1$, and so

$$\ell_n^{(k)}(0) = \mathsf{Rec}(0) = 0, \quad \ell_n^{(k)}(1) = \mathsf{Rec}(1) = 1.$$

Recall that $\ell_n^{(k)} \left(\beta_n^{(t)} \right) = \mathsf{OffExp}_n^{(k)} \left(\beta_n^{(t)} \right) = \beta_n^{(t-k)}$. Hence, for $s = s_n^{(t)} = \beta^{(t)} \cdot 2^n$ where $t \in [n]$, our goal is to prove the following

$$\beta_n^{(t-k)} \leq \inf_{(s_0, s_1) \in \mathcal{D}iv_n(s)} \mathsf{Rec}(s_0, s_1). \tag{18}$$

Case Studies. Note that $\beta_n^{(t)} 2^n = s_n^{(t)} = s_{n-1}^{(t)} + s_{n-1}^{(t-1)}$ because of the Pascal equality. Also by the definition of $\mathcal{D}iv_n$, we have $s_0 \leq s_1$ and $s_0 + s_1 = s_n^{(t)}$ for any choice of $(s_0, s_1) \in \mathcal{D}iv_n(s)$ in the right hand side of Eq. 18. Then, one of the following three cases must hold: (1) $s_0 = s_{n-1}^{(t)}$, (2) $s_0 < s_{n-1}^{(t)}$, or (3) $s_0 > s_{n-1}^{(t)}$. Hence, we divide our analysis to the same three cases, and then prove that $\beta_n^{(t-k)} \leq \mathsf{Rec}(s_0, s_1)$ holds in all of them. We will also use the Pascal equality in the form of $\beta_n^{(t-k)} = (\beta_{n-1}^{(t-k-1)} + \beta_{n-1}^{(t-k)})/2$.

1. $s_{n-1}^{(t)} = s_0 < s_1 = s_{n-1}^{(t-1)}$. In this case, we have

$$\ell_{n-1}^{(k)}\left(\frac{s_0}{2^{n-1}}\right) = \ell_{n-1}^{(k-1)}\left(\frac{s_1}{2^{n-1}}\right) = \beta_{n-1}^{(t-k)}$$

which, informally speaking means that, it does not matter if the adversary intervenes to change 0 to 1 when the first bit is fixed to 0. Formally, we have

$$\mathsf{Rec}(s_0, s_1) = \mathsf{Rec}(s_{n-1}^{(t)}, s_{n-1}^{(t-1)})$$
$$= \frac{\ell_{n-1}^{(k)}\left(\frac{s_1}{2^{n-1}}\right) + \max\left\{\ell_{n-1}^{(k)}\left(\frac{s_0}{2^{n-1}}\right), \ell_{n-1}^{(k-1)}\left(\frac{s_1}{2^{n-1}}\right)\right\}}{2}$$
$$= \frac{\beta_{n-1}^{(t-k-1)} + \beta_{n-1}^{(t-k)}}{2} = \beta_n^{(t-k)}.$$

2. $s_{n-1}^{(t)} < s_0 \leq s_1 < s_{n-1}^{(t-1)}$. Informally speaking, in this case the adversary does not change the bit and we use the piece-wise linearity of the ℓ function on $[\beta_{n-1}^{(t)}, \beta_{n-1}^{(t-1)}]$. More formally,

$$\mathsf{Rec}(s_0, s_1) = \frac{\ell_{n-1}^{(k)}\left(\frac{s_1}{2^{n-1}}\right) + \max\left\{\ell_{n-1}^{(k)}\left(\frac{s_0}{2^{n-1}}\right), \ell_{n-1}^{(k-1)}\left(\frac{s_1}{2^{n-1}}\right)\right\}}{2}$$
$$\geq \frac{\ell_{n-1}^{(k)}\left(\frac{s_1}{2^{n-1}}\right) + \ell_{n-1}^{(k)}\left(\frac{s_0}{2^{n-1}}\right)}{2}$$
$$= \frac{\ell_{n-1}^{(k)}\left(\frac{s_{n-1}^{(t-1)}}{2^{n-1}}\right) + \ell_{n-1}^{(k)}\left(\frac{s_{n-1}^{(t)}}{2^{n-1}}\right)}{2} \quad \text{(by piece-wise linearity of } \ell_{n-1}^{(k)})$$
$$= \mathsf{Rec}\left(s_{n-1}^{(t)}, s_{n-1}^{(t-1)}\right) = \beta_n^{(t-k)}.$$

3. $s_0 < s_{n-1}^{(t)} < s_{n-1}^{(t-1)} < s_1$. Informally speaking, in this case the adversary does change the bit 0 into 1, and we also use the fact that $\ell_{n-1}^{(k)}$ is monotone. More formally,

$$\mathsf{Rec}(s_0, s_1) = \frac{\ell_{n-1}^{(k)}\left(\frac{s_1}{2^{n-1}}\right) + \max\left\{\ell_{n-1}^{(k)}\left(\frac{s_0}{2^{n-1}}\right), \ell_{n-1}^{(k-1)}\left(\frac{s_1}{2^{n-1}}\right)\right\}}{2}$$
$$\geq \frac{\ell_{n-1}^{(k)}\left(\frac{s_1}{2^{n-1}}\right) + \ell_{n-1}^{(k-1)}\left(\frac{s_1}{2^{n-1}}\right)}{2}$$
$$\geq \frac{\ell_{n-1}^{(k)}\left(\frac{s_{n-1}^{(t-1)}}{2^{n-1}}\right) + \ell_{n-1}^{(k-1)}\left(\frac{s_{n-1}^{(t-1)}}{2^{n-1}}\right)}{2} \quad \text{(by monotonicity of } \ell_{n-1}^{(k)})$$
$$= \mathsf{Rec}\left(s_{n-1}^{(t)}, s_{n-1}^{(t-1)}\right) = \beta_n^{(t-k)}.$$

Case of Other Probabilities. Here we no longer assume that $\mu = \beta^{(t)}$ for some $t \in [n]$, and assume $\mu = \alpha\beta_n^{(t)} + (1-\alpha)\beta_n^{(t-1)}$ for some $t \in [n+1]$ and $0 < \alpha < 1$. Recall that

$\beta^{(t)}2^n = s_n^{(t)} = s_{n-1}^{(t)} + s_{n-1}^{(t-1)}$ and $\beta^{(t-1)}2^n = s_n^{(t-1)} = s_{n-1}^{(t-1)} + s_{n-1}^{(t-2)}$. We define

$$s_0' = \alpha \cdot s_{n-1}^{(t)} + (1-\alpha) \cdot s_{n-1}^{(t-1)}, \quad s_1' = \alpha \cdot s_{n-1}^{(t-1)} + (1-\alpha) \cdot s_{n-1}^{(t-2)}.$$

By the definition of μ, it holds that $\mu \cdot 2^n = s = s_0' + s_1'$ because

$$s_0' + s_1' = \alpha \cdot \left(s_{n-1}^{(t)} + s_{n-1}^{(t-1)}\right) + (1-\alpha) \cdot \left(s_{n-1}^{(t-1)} + s_{n-1}^{(t-2)}\right) = \alpha \cdot s_n^{(t)} + (1-\alpha) \cdot s_n^{(t-1)} = s.$$

In general, s_0', s_1' are not integers, but intuitively, $s_0' + s_1'$ gives the critical way of splitting s into two numbers at which the replacing and no-replacing strategies give the same bound and we can do the case studies. (In particular s_0', s_1' take the role of $s_{n-1}^{(t)}, s_{n-1}^{(t-1)}$ when we previously assumed that $\mu = \beta^{(t)}$.)

Useful Observations. By the piecewise linearity of $\ell_{n-1}^{(k)}, \ell_{n-1}^{(k-1)}$ we have

$$\ell_{n-1}^{(k)}\left(\frac{s_0'}{2^{n-1}}\right) = \alpha\ell_{n-1}^{(k)}\left(\frac{s_{n-1}^{(t)}}{2^{n-1}}\right) + (1-\alpha)\ell_{n-1}^{(k)}\left(\frac{s_{n-1}^{(t-1)}}{2^{n-1}}\right),$$

$$\ell_{n-1}^{(k)}\left(\frac{s_1'}{2^{n-1}}\right) = \alpha\ell_{n-1}^{(k)}\left(\frac{s_{n-1}^{(t-1)}}{2^{n-1}}\right) + (1-\alpha)\ell_{n-1}^{(k)}\left(\frac{s_{n-1}^{(t-2)}}{2^{n-1}}\right),$$

$$\ell_{n-1}^{(k-1)}\left(\frac{s_1'}{2^{n-1}}\right) = \alpha\ell_{n-1}^{(k-1)}\left(\frac{s_{n-1}^{(t-1)}}{2^{n-1}}\right) + (1-\alpha)\ell_{n-1}^{(k-1)}\left(\frac{s_{n-1}^{(t-2)}}{2^{n-1}}\right),$$

$$\ell_{n-1}^{(k)}\left(\frac{s_{n-1}^{(t)}}{2^{n-1}}\right) = \beta_{n-1}^{(t-k)} = \ell_{n-1}^{(k-1)}\left(\frac{s_{n-1}^{(t-1)}}{2^{n-1}}\right),$$

$$\text{and} \quad \ell_{n-1}^{(k)}\left(\frac{s_{n-1}^{(t-1)}}{2^{n-1}}\right) = \beta_{n-1}^{(t-k-1)} = \ell_{n-1}^{(k-1)}\left(\frac{s_{n-1}^{(t-2)}}{2^{n-1}}\right).$$

Therefore, we get the following.

$$\ell_{n-1}^{(k)}\left(\frac{s_0'}{2^{n-1}}\right) = \ell_{n-1}^{(k-1)}\left(\frac{s_1'}{2^{n-1}}\right) = \alpha\beta_{n-1}^{(t-k)} + (1-\alpha)\beta_{n-1}^{(t-k-1)}, \tag{19}$$

$$\ell_{n-1}^{(k)}\left(\frac{s_1'}{2^{n-1}}\right) = \alpha\beta_{n-1}^{(t-k-1)} + (1-\alpha)\beta_{n-1}^{(t-k-2)}. \tag{20}$$

Case Studies. We now again partition into three different categories and separately prove that $\ell_n^{(k)}(\mu) \leq \mathsf{Rec}(s_0, s_1)$ holds for each category.

1. $s_0' = s_0 < s_1 = s_1'$. In this case, using Eqs. (19) and (20) we get

$$\mathsf{Rec}(s_0', s_1')$$

$$= \frac{\ell_{n-1}^{(k)}\left(\frac{s_1'}{2^{n-1}}\right)}{2} + \frac{\max\left\{\ell_{n-1}^{(k)}\left(\frac{s_0'}{2^{n-1}}\right), \ell_{n-1}^{(k-1)}\left(\frac{s_1'}{2^{n-1}}\right)\right\}}{2}$$

$$= \frac{\alpha \cdot \beta_{n-1}^{(t-k-1)} + (1-\alpha) \cdot \beta_{n-1}^{(t-k-2)}}{2} + \frac{\alpha \cdot \beta_{n-1}^{(t-k)} + (1-\alpha) \cdot \beta_{n-1}^{(t-k-1)}}{2}$$

$$= \alpha \cdot \beta_n^{(t-k)} + (1-\alpha) \cdot \beta_n^{(t-k-1)}$$

$$= \alpha \cdot \ell_n^{(k)}(\beta^{(t)}) + (1-\alpha) \cdot \ell_n^{(k)}(\beta^{(t-1)}) = \ell_n^{(k)}(\mu).$$

2. $s_0' < s_0 \leq s_1 < s_1'$. Informally speaking, in this case the adversary does not tamper and leave the bit 0 unchanged. We will use the fact that $\ell_{n-1}^{(k)}$ is *concave*, which was proved in Lemma 26. Note that in the corresponding Case 2 when the probability μ was that of an exact ball ($\mu = \beta_n^{(t)}$) we could have also used the fact that $\ell_{n-1}^{(k)}$ is concave, but in that case we only used the concavity over a linear part of $\ell_{n-1}^{(k)}$. However, in our current case, we could no longer only rely on the piecewise linearity of $\ell_{n-1}^{(k)}$ and we would use its concavity. More formally,

$$\mathsf{Rec}(s_0, s_1) = \frac{\ell_{n-1}^{(k)}\left(\frac{s_1}{2^{n-1}}\right) + \max\left\{\ell_{n-1}^{(k)}\left(\frac{s_0}{2^{n-1}}\right), \ell_{n-1}^{(k-1)}\left(\frac{s_1}{2^{n-1}}\right)\right\}}{2}$$

$$\geq \frac{\ell_{n-1}^{(k)}\left(\frac{s_1}{2^{n-1}}\right) + \ell_{n-1}^{(k)}\left(\frac{s_0}{2^{n-1}}\right)}{2}$$

$$\geq \frac{\ell_{n-1}^{(k)}\left(\frac{s_1'}{2^{n-1}}\right) + \ell_{n-1}^{(k)}\left(\frac{s_0'}{2^{n-1}}\right)}{2} \quad \text{(by \textbf{concavity} of } \ell_{n-1}^{(k)})$$

$$= \mathsf{Rec}(s_0', s_1') = \ell_n^{(k)}(\mu).$$

3. $s_0 < s_0' < s_1' < s_1$. Informally speaking, in this case the adversary does change the bit 0 into 1, and we rely on the monotonicity of $\ell_{n-1}^{(k)}$. More formally,

$$\mathsf{Rec}(s_0, s_1) = \frac{\ell_{n-1}^{(k)}\left(\frac{s_1}{2^{n-1}}\right) + \max\left\{\ell_{n-1}^{(k)}\left(\frac{s_0}{2^{n-1}}\right), \ell_{n-1}^{(k-1)}\left(\frac{s_1}{2^{n-1}}\right)\right\}}{2}$$

$$\geq \frac{\ell_{n-1}^{(k)}\left(\frac{s_1}{2^{n-1}}\right) + \ell_{n-1}^{(k-1)}\left(\frac{s_1}{2^{n-1}}\right)}{2}$$

$$\geq \frac{\ell_{n-1}^{(k)}\left(\frac{s_1'}{2^{n-1}}\right) + \ell_{n-1}^{(k-1)}\left(\frac{s_1'}{2^{n-1}}\right)}{2} \quad \text{(by monotonicity of } \ell_{n-1}^{(k)})$$

$$= \mathsf{Rec}(s_0', s_1') = \ell_n^{(k)}(\mu).$$

$\square$

Claim 28. $\ell_n^{(k)} \leq \mathsf{OnExp}_n^{(k)}$.

Proof. The proof is by induction on n. The claim hold for $n = 0$. Using Claims 23 and 27 and induction we get:

$$\mathsf{OnExp}_n^{(k)} \geq \mathsf{Rec}_n^{(k)} \left[\ell_{n-1}^{(k)}, \ell_{n-1}^{(k-1)} \right] \geq \ell_n^{(k)}.$$

$\square$

Now we can finish the proof of Theorem 18. If $\mu = \beta_n^{(t)}$ for some $t \in \langle n \rangle$, it then always holds that $\ell_n^{(k)}(\mu) \geq \mathsf{OnExp}_n^{(k)}(\mu)$ simply because $\ell_n^{(k)}(\mu)$ describes how much one particular protocol (i.e., τ_t) can bound adversary's power, while $\mathsf{OnExp}_n^{(k)}(\mu)$ is equal to the *minimum* of the same quantity among all protocols. Therefore, by Claim 28, $\mathsf{OnExp}_n^{(k)}\left(\beta_n^{(t)}\right) = \ell_n^{(k)}\left(\beta_n^{(t)}\right) = \beta_n^{(t-k)}$. $\square$

Relaxing the Last Message to Non-binary. Here we discuss an extension to Theorem 18 that follows essentially from the same proof. Theorem 18 shows that online attacks are as powerful as offline attacks when we focus on protocols with uniform binary messages. Now, suppose we allow the last message of the protocol to be an arbitrary long message, while every other message is supposed to be a uniform bit. We refer to such protocols as *binary-except-last-message* (BELM) protocols. Note that BELM protocols constitute a *larger* set of protocols, and hence they potentially could include more robust protocols that further limits the power of (offline or online) attacks. We observe that, essentially the same proof as that of Theorem 18 shows that we can strengthen Theorem 18 as follows.

Theorem 29 (Informally stated: extending Theorem 18 to BELM protocols). *Suppose a random process $\mathbf{w}_{\leq n} = (\mathbf{w}_1, \dots, \mathbf{w}_n)$ has the property that all the first $n - 1$ blocks are independent and uniform random bits, and suppose f is a Boolean function defined over this random process. Suppose $\Pr[f(\mathbf{w}_{\leq n}) = 1] = \beta_n^{(t)}$ for some $t \in [n]$. Then, there is an online k-replacing adversary over $\mathbf{u}_{\leq n}$ that generates joint random process $(\mathbf{u}_{\leq n}, \mathbf{v}_{\leq n})$ with $\mathbf{v}_{\leq n}$ being the output process, such that $\Pr[f(\mathbf{w}_{\leq n}) = 1] \geq \beta_n^{(t-k)}$. Note that this is optimal in a strong sense: there is a fully binary protocol (i.e., the threshold function τ_t) for which even offline k-replacing adversaries are limited to achieve offline expansion at most $\beta_n^{(t-k)}$.*

Proof Sketch. The proof of the above improved variant of Theorem 18 relies on two observations. One of them is the basis of the induction, when $n = 1$, and the other one is the improved induction step which follows from the improve variant of Claim 27 as explained below.

Relaxing Transformation of Definition 20. Claim 27 was the heart of the proof of Theorem 18. In this claim, we deal with the recursion of Eq. (15) which is defined by splitting integer s into smaller integers, computing some recursive expansions and taking the minimum. It is easy to see that Claim 27 holds even if we relax the way we split s into smaller quantities and pick such pairs as *real* values

$$\widetilde{Div}_{n-1}(s) = \left\{ (s_0, s_1) \mid s_0, s_1 \in \mathbb{R}, 0 \leq s_0 \leq s_1 \leq 2^{n-1}, s = s_0 + s_1 \right\}.$$

In particular, let $\widetilde{\mathsf{Rec}}_n^{[k]}$ be the similar transformation using this relaxed variant $\widetilde{\mathcal{D}iv}_{n-1}(s)$ instead. First, note that by this relaxation instead, we might end up getting *smaller* expansions; namely, $\widetilde{\mathsf{Rec}}_n^{(k)} \leq \mathsf{Rec}_n^{(k)}$. Yet, the same proof shows that Claim 27 holds even if we use $\widetilde{\mathsf{Rec}}_n^{(k)}$ instead of $\mathsf{Rec}_n^{(k)}$. Moreover, in (both variants of) Case 1, it is now always possible to achieve the equality using some pair in $\widetilde{\mathcal{D}iv}_{n-1}(s)$. Therefore, this time we obtain a slightly stronger statement than that of Claim 27 for BELM protocols as follows.

Claim 30 (Variant of Claim 27 for BELM protocols). $\ell_n^{(k)} = \widetilde{\mathsf{Rec}}_n^{(k)}[\ell_{n-1}^{(k)}, \ell_{n-1}^{(k-1)}]$.

The proof of the claim above is identical to that of Claim 27. □

References

1. Amir, D., Milman, V.: Unconditional and symmetric sets in n-dimensional normed spaces. Israel J. Math. **37**(1–2), 3–20 (1980)
2. Beimel, A., Haitner, I., Makriyannis, N., Omri, E.: Tighter bounds on multi-party coin flipping via augmented weak martingales and differentially private sampling. In: 2018 IEEE 59th Annual Symposium on Foundations of Computer Science (FOCS), pp. 838–849. IEEE (2018)
3. Ben-Or, M., Linial, N.: Collective coin flipping. Adv. Comput. Res. **5**, 91–115 (1989)
4. Ben-Or, M., Linial, N.: Collective coin flipping. Adv. Comput. Res. **5**, 91–115 (1990)
5. Bentov, I., Gabizon, A., Zuckerman, D.: Bitcoin beacon. arXiv preprint arXiv:1605.04559 (2016)
6. Blum, M.: How to exchange (secret) keys. ACM Trans. Comput. Syst. **1**, 175–193 (1984)
7. Cleve, R.: Limits on the security of coin flips when half the processors are faulty. In: Proceedings of the Eighteenth Annual ACM Symposium on Theory of Computing, pp. 364–369. ACM (1986)
8. Cleve, R., Impagliazzo, R.: Martingales, collective coin flipping and discrete control processes. Manuscript (1993)
9. Dachman-Soled, D., Lindell, Y., Mahmoody, M., Malkin, T.: On the black-box complexity of optimally-fair coin tossing. In: Ishai, Y. (ed.) TCC 2011. LNCS, vol. 6597, pp. 450–467. Springer, Heidelberg (2011). https://doi.org/10.1007/978-3-642-19571-6_27
10. Dachman-Soled, D., Mahmoody, M., Malkin, T.: Can optimally-fair coin tossing be based on one-way functions? In: Lindell, Y. (ed.) TCC 2014. LNCS, vol. 8349, pp. 217–239. Springer, Heidelberg (2014). https://doi.org/10.1007/978-3-642-54242-8_10
11. Dodis, Y.: New imperfect random source with applications to coin-flipping. In: Orejas, F., Spirakis, P.G., van Leeuwen, J. (eds.) ICALP 2001. LNCS, vol. 2076, pp. 297–309. Springer, Heidelberg (2001). https://doi.org/10.1007/3-540-48224-5_25
12. Etesami, O., Mahloujifar, S., Mahmoody, M.: Computational concentration of measure: optimal bounds, reductions, and more. In: Proceedings of the Fourteenth Annual ACM-SIAM Symposium on Discrete Algorithms, pp. 345–363. SIAM (2020)
13. Goldwasser, S., Kalai, Y.T., Park, S.: Adaptively secure coin-flipping, revisited. In: Halldórsson, M.M., Iwama, K., Kobayashi, N., Speckmann, B. (eds.) ICALP 2015. LNCS, vol. 9135, pp. 663–674. Springer, Heidelberg (2015). https://doi.org/10.1007/978-3-662-47666-6_53

14. Habib, M., McDiarmid, C., Ramirez-Alfonsin, J., Reed, B.: Probabilistic Methods for Algorithmic Discrete Mathematics, vol. 16. Springer, Heidelberg (2013)
15. Haitner, I., Karidi-Heller, Y.: A tight lower bound on adaptively secure full-information coin flip. In: IEEE 61st Annual Symposium on Foundations of Computer Science (FOCS) (2020)
16. Haitner, I., Makriyannis, N., Omri, E.: On the complexity of fair coin flipping. In: Beimel, A., Dziembowski, S. (eds.) TCC 2018. LNCS, vol. 11239, pp. 539–562. Springer, Cham (2018). https://doi.org/10.1007/978-3-030-03807-6_20
17. Haitner, I., Nissim, K., Omri, E., Shaltiel, R., Silbak, J.: Computational two-party correlation: a dichotomy for key-agreement protocols. In: 2018 IEEE 59th Annual Symposium on Foundations of Computer Science (FOCS), pp. 136–147. IEEE (2018)
18. Haitner, I., Tsfadia, E.: An almost-optimally fair three-party coin-flipping protocol. SIAM J. Comput. **46**(2), 479–542 (2017)
19. Harper, L.H.: Optimal numberings and isoperimetric problems on graphs. J. Comb. Theory **1**(3), 385–393 (1966)
20. Kahn, J.: The influence of variables on Boolean functions. In: Proceedings of the 29th Annual IEEE Symposium on Foundations of Computer Science (1988)
21. Kalai, Y.T., Komargodski, I., Raz, R.: A lower bound for adaptively-secure collective coin-flipping protocols. In: 32nd International Symposium on Distributed Computing (2018)
22. Khorasgani, H.A., Maji, H.K., Mukherjee, T.: Estimating gaps in martingales and applications to coin-tossing: constructions and hardness. In: Hofheinz, D., Rosen, A. (eds.) TCC 2019. LNCS, vol. 11892, pp. 333–355. Springer, Cham (2019). https://doi.org/10.1007/978-3-030-36033-7_13
23. Khorasgani, H.A., Maji, H.K., Wang, M.: Optimally-secure coin-tossing against a byzantine adversary. Cryptology ePrint Archive, Report 2020/519 (2020). https://eprint.iacr.org/2020/519
24. Lichtenstein, D., Linial, N., Saks, M.: Some extremal problems arising from discrete control processes. Combinatorica **9**(3), 269–287 (1989)
25. Mahloujifar, S., Diochnos, D.I., Mahmoody, M.: Learning under p-tampering attacks. In: ALT, pp. 572–596 (2018)
26. Mahloujifar, S., Mahmoody, M.: Blockwise p-tampering attacks on cryptographic primitives, extractors, and learners. In: Kalai, Y., Reyzin, L. (eds.) TCC 2017. LNCS, vol. 10678, pp. 245–279. Springer, Cham (2017). https://doi.org/10.1007/978-3-319-70503-3_8
27. Mahloujifar, S., Mahmoody, M.: Can adversarially robust learning leverage computational hardness? In: Garivier, A., Kale, S. (eds.) Proceedings of the 30th International Conference on Algorithmic Learning Theory. Proceedings of Machine Learning Research, vol. 98, pp. 581–609. PMLR, Chicago, Illinois (2019). http://proceedings.mlr.press/v98/mahloujifar19a.html
28. Mahloujifar, S., Mahmoody, M., Mohammed, A.: Universal multi-party poisoning attacks. In: Proceedings of the 36th International Conference on Machine Learning, vol. 97, pp. 4274–4283 (2019)
29. Maji, H.K., Wang, M.: Black-box use of one-way functions is useless for optimal fair coin-tossing. In: Micciancio, D., Ristenpart, T. (eds.) CRYPTO 2020. LNCS, vol. 12171, pp. 593–617. Springer, Cham (2020). https://doi.org/10.1007/978-3-030-56880-1_21
30. Margulis, G.A.: Probabilistic characteristics of graphs with large connectivity. Problemy peredachi informatsii **10**(2), 101–108 (1974)
31. McDiarmid, C.: On the method of bounded differences. Surv. Comb. **141**(1), 148–188 (1989)
32. Milman, V.D., Schechtman, G.: Asymptotic Theory of Finite Dimensional Normed Spaces, vol. 1200. Springer, Heidelberg (1986). https://doi.org/10.1007/978-3-540-38822-7
33. Moran, T., Naor, M., Segev, G.: An optimally fair coin toss. In: Reingold, O. (ed.) TCC 2009. LNCS, vol. 5444, pp. 1–18. Springer, Heidelberg (2009). https://doi.org/10.1007/978-3-642-00457-5_1

34. Russell, A., Saks, M., Zuckerman, D.: Lower bounds for leader election and collective coin-flipping in the perfect information model. SIAM J. Comput. **31**(6), 1645–1662 (2002)
35. Talagrand, M.: Concentration of measure and isoperimetric inequalities in product spaces. Publications Mathématiques de l'Institut des Hautes Etudes Scientifiques **81**(1), 73–205 (1995)

Author Index